FOUNDATIONS OF EDUCATION
Second Edition

Volume II
Instructional Strategies for Teaching Children and Youths with Visual Impairments

Alan J. Koenig
M. Cay Holbrook
Editors

AFB
PRESS

Printed in the United States of America
2009 reprinting

Library of Congress Cataloging-in-Publication Data

Foundations of education / M. Cay Holbrook and Alan J. Koenig, editors.
    p. cm.
    Vol. 2: Alan J. Koenig and M. Cay Holbrook, editors.
    Vol. 2: 2nd ed.
    Includes bibliographical references and index.
    Contents: v. 1. History and theory of teaching children and youths with visual
impairments—v. 2. Instructional strategies for teaching children and youths with visual impairments.
    ISBN 978-0-89128-340-9 (v. 1 : alk. paper)—ISBN 978-0-89128-339-3 (v. 2 : alk. paper)
    1. Visually handicapped—Education.   2. Visually handicapped children—Education.   I.
Holbrook, M. Cay, 1955–   II. Koenig, Alan J., 1954–

HV1626 .F65 2000
371.91′1—dc21

    00-040575

Photo credits: Chapters 12 and 18, Carol Farrenkopf and Duncan McGregor; Chapter 15, Nora Griffin-Shirley.

The American Foundation for the Blind—the organization to which Helen Keller devoted more than 40 years of her life—is a national nonprofit whose mission is to eliminate the inequities faced by the ten million Americans who are blind or visually impaired. Headquartered in New York City, AFB maintains offices in Atlanta, Chicago, Dallas, and San Francisco, and a governmental relations office in Washington, DC.

*This book is dedicated to the memory of
Dr. Virginia Murray Sowell. She taught us to hold high
expectations, to admire quality teaching, and to
respect professionalism. Through her daily life,
she modeled for us the importance of being kind
and gracious to others.*

C O N T E N T S

CHAPTER REVIEWERS

Lou Alonso
Michigan State University, East Lansing

Natalie Barraga
University of Texas at Austin

Virginia E. Bishop
University of Texas at Austin, Texas Tech
   University, and Stephen F. Austin University

Bob Brasher
American Printing House for the Blind

Frances Mary D'Andrea
American Foundation for the Blind

Jamie Dote-Kwan
California State University, Los Angeles

William Evans
Springfield High School, Illinois

Diane Fazzi
California State University, Los Angeles

Amanda Hall-Lueck
San Francisco State University

Rebecca Heck
Indiana School for the Blind

Laurel Hudson
Perkins School for the Blind

Kathleen M. Huebner
Pennsylvania College of Optometry

Bernadette Kappen
Overbrook School for the Blind

Sandra Lewis
Florida State University, Tallahassee

Susan A. Osterhaus
Texas School for the Blind and Visually Impaired

Ike Presley
American Foundation for the Blind

Mary Jean Sanspree
Liz Moore Low Vision Center

Charlotte Schrock
Indiana School for the Blind

Mary Ann Siller
American Foundation for the Blind

Frank Simpson
Child Development Center, Lighthouse
   International

Louis Tutt
Maryland School for the Blind

Diane Wormsley
Pennsylvania College of Optometry

F O R E W O R D

At the invitation of the American Foundation for the Blind, it was my privilege to serve as reviewer and critic for the first draft of the revision of both volumes of *Foundations of Education*. It was both a daunting and satisfying assignment, satisfying in that my expectations for focus, quality, depth, and presentation were satisfied. Whereas Volume I wisely offers a scholarly information base of history, theory, and principles, Volume II provides a clear guide to essential, important, and practical "instructional strategies and practices" for promoting effective student learning by clarifying the role of each educational participant, including the student.

What stamps Volume II for me is the candor, openness, and responsiveness of the editors and writers to the inherent pressures and responsibilities associated with being a teacher, parent, or other educational team member for students who are visually impaired or blind, including students with additional impairments. I hope that general education teachers and parents are among the frequent readers of this text so they may come to appreciate the important roles they play in reaching a mutual goal of equity and success in education for their students. Surely the intended audience of teachers, other team members, and researchers will rate highly the notable effort of the authors to offer remarkably detailed content within the continuum of the unique "core curriculum" for students with blindness or visual impairment. Readers can rest assured that the discussed teaching practices are valid, based on the demon-

strated knowledge base of reliable, experienced educators and researchers.

If you are looking for new information on teaching or raising a child who is visually impaired or blind, *Foundations of Education: Instructional Strategies for Teaching Children and Youths with Visual Impairments* can help. Indeed, it is at once a medium of ideas, a practical textbook, and a useful reference. Importantly, the fundamental philosophy that guides this text is this: Children and youths with visual impairment or blindness, including those with additional impairment, are expected to be learners. Wisely, the authors emphasize the ability of students. They recognize that each motivated child and youth can be expected to advance when provided an appropriate educational program and placement, and taught by conscientious, well-prepared, coordinated team members, including his or her parents. To this end, you will find suggestions to enable each team member to make meaningful contributions to an individual child's progress.

As a text, *Instructional Strategies* adds significantly to our understanding of how teachers and preservice interns of students who are blind or visually impaired may collaborate effectively with orientation and mobility instructors, parents, general and special education teachers, and other team members, to secure expected individualized educational program outcomes for their students. It provides the reader with validated techniques, practices, suggestions, and ideas for support related to the use of accommodative technology, adaptive materials, communication, collaboration, advocacy, and student evaluation for each teacher, intern, paraeducator, therapist, parent, administrator, building principal, custodian, and other team members. Each team member can use these ideas to collaborate more effectively in developing an individualized program of appropriate annual long-term goals and short-term objectives to ensure that each student will reach the expected outcomes of education at transition from school.

Readers of this volume will come to appreciate the totality of its content, matching as it does the widest possible range of student learning needs with curricula, materials, and strategies for planning and teaching children from infancy through school-leaving age. Helpful vignettes are thoughtfully included for emphasis and clarification, as are charts and lists to help ease uncertainties and record-keeping responsibilities. In practical terms, the authors address the instructional needs of a diverse population of children to reflect their range of age, abilities, interests, and needs, matched with the preferences of their parents. Moreover, the authors recognize that you as readers and learners are also diverse, coming as you do from varied specializations such as general education, special education, orientation and mobility, administration or other preparation; and as parents or university interns preparing to teach students with a visual impairment or blindness. Useful references will assist and sustain you in your role as effective leader and team member.

The authors and editors of *Instructional Strategies* present a much anticipated and needed update of the original *Foundations of Education*, published more than a decade ago under the able leadership of Geraldine Scholl, my teacher and mentor. Not to be overlooked is the progress achieved during this relatively short period of time, progress that surely reflects well on this generation of authors and the tireless efforts of countless conscientious professionals, parents, and students themselves. This book is a unique and valuable contribution to the literature of our field.

Congratulations and thanks to editors Cay Holbrook and Alan Koenig; to each author; and to Natalie Hilzen of AFB Press at the American Foundation for the Blind for her considerable support. Their combined efforts have resulted in a scholarly, readable, and usable text. Readers will do well to take time to check out the useful references and engage in conversations with professors, supervising teachers, and peers to promote greater understanding and in-depth knowledge. I foresee team members using this text as a sound blueprint for coming together to secure personal and student success.

I will close with a challenge to you the reader as a current or future special or general education teacher, parent, or other team member for children with visual impairment or blindness: Upon completion of your readings, discussions, reflections, and research, and using a hypothetical or known situation, devise a plan for how you and a specified team might meet the daily objectives of a large caseload of diverse students, objectives that seem to require more time than is available for teaching the "core curriculum" to each of the students. Discuss your plan with your team, and think about presenting it at a local, state, regional, or national conference for further discussion and consideration. Given the current shortage of qualified teachers and orientation and mobility instructors, together with local district budget constraints, grave needs with respect to caseloads beg to be addressed. Success or failure in resolving the dilemma of large caseload numbers—and student progress—rests with you and your colleagues.

But now it is time for you to read and learn to use the powerful ideas you will find in the following pages!

Lou Alonso
Professor Emeritus
Department of Counseling, Educational
Psychology and Special Education
Former Coordinator, Teacher Education
in Visual Impairment and Blindness,
Orientation and Mobility, and
Deafblindness
Michigan State University
East Lansing, Michigan

ACKNOWLEDGMENTS

A book of this magnitude could not be written, or written as well, without the help and cooperation of many people. To all those who assisted in any way in preparing this book, you have our genuine respect and profound appreciation. Your valuable contributions far exceed the recognition that you will receive by simple mention in these acknowledgments, but we doubt that bringing recognition to yourself was ever your intention in the first place. We must acknowledge that our human imperfections undoubtedly will cause us to miss some individuals. Please know that we appreciate your contributions as much as those mentioned next.

First and foremost, we extend our sincere appreciation to Dr. Geraldine Scholl. Her edited textbook, *Foundations of Education for Blind and Visually Handicapped Children and Youth,* represented a milestone in professional writing in our field. We have marveled many times at the professional and personal commitment Dr. Scholl made to the publication of *Foundations.* She provided wise and seasoned guidance and support throughout the preparation of this book and its companion volume.

We also wish to recognize the outstanding contributions made to this book by each of the contributing authors: Virginia E. Bishop, Anne L. Corn, Jo Ellen Croft, Linda B. DePriest, Jane N. Erin, Carol Farrenkopf, Nora Griffin-Shirley, Toni Heinze, Gaylen Kapperman, Pat Kelley, Christine Kline, Carol A. Layton, Duncan McGregor, Donna McNear, Ike Presley, Rachel Rickard, Margaret C. Robinson, David B. Ross, Sharon Zell Sacks, Rosanne K. Silberman, Pat Smith, Jodi Sticken, Irene L. Topor, Sharon Trusty, and Karen E. Wolffe. As a group, these professionals represent a wealth of knowledge, skill, and experience that is truly extraordinary. They responded to deadlines, requests for revisions and additional information, and other matters with efficiency and kindness. We could not have edited this book without their contributions and cooperation.

We also wish to recognize persons who contributed sidebars and other information to the book. M. Beth Langley gave freely of her time and energy to develop a series of sidebars on teaching students with additional disabilities that are presented throughout the second part of this book. Also, Margaret C. Robinson creatively crafted most of the vignettes that introduce the chapters and skillfully prepared or finalized the resource sidebars throughout the text.

A true debt of gratitude is extended to the cadre of professionals who served as field reviewers for the chapters of this book. We especially want to thank Lou Alonso, who, in her "retirement," reviewed all 21 chapters of this book and 10 chapters of its companion volume. Lou's commitment to the field and to scholarly writing is truly remarkable. The quality of this book was greatly enhanced through the efforts of Lou and the other field reviewers.

The editors and staff at AFB Press also deserve much recognition for the quality of this book. Natalie Hilzen worked with us throughout the entire project, from the original idea to publication, and her thoughtful guidance and gentle prodding were much appreciated. Others at AFB Press—Ellen Bilofsky, Carol Boston, Beatrice Jacinto—and their colleague Barbara Chernow—were also crucial to the completion of a manuscript of high quality. Our appreciation for AFB Press and the vital role that it plays in publishing key books and resources in our field was greatly enhanced throughout the course of this project.

Finally, we would like to thank the people in our lives who helped us maintain a steady course, but who were not directly involved in the manuscript. We wish to recognize and extend sincere appreciation to our mentors—Dr. Evelyn Rex, Dr. Samuel Ashcroft, Dr. Gideon Jones, Marie Kovesci, and Pat Carpenter—who nurtured us to become the professionals we are today. We also extend thanks to our families and friends, who encouraged and supported us, and to our cats—Paws, Claws, and Ponyo—who comforted and sustained us without casting any judgments.

Alan J. Koenig
Texas Tech University
Lubbock

M. Cay Holbrook
University of British Columbia
Vancouver

INTRODUCTION

The job of a teacher of students with visual impairments is both rewarding and challenging. The rewards come from working closely with individual students or small groups of students who are blind or visually impaired, providing instruction in unique skills, and watching them grow with increasing independence and self-actualization to young adulthood. Given this individualized approach, teachers of students with visual impairments have many opportunities for working closely with parents, general education teachers, and administrators. Teachers in this field often have more autonomy than do professionals in other jobs, and their work may vary greatly from day to day. Furthermore, there is a close camaraderie that exists among teachers and other specialists who work with students who are blind or visually impaired. Those entering the field are often surprised that they can contact the most noted authorities and receive personal advice and guidance.

Although there are many unique rewards for teachers of students with visual impairments, there are also significant challenges. Given the low-incidence nature of this population of students, it is highly likely that supervisors and administrators will have little or no knowledge of or special preparation in the area of blindness and visual impairment. If this is the case, they may not be prepared to plan and administer programs for students who are visually impaired. As a result,

caseloads assigned to teachers in day school programs often exceed reasonable numbers. Circumstances such as these can place teachers in the uncomfortable position of addressing some, but not all, student needs, or addressing needs in a superficial manner. In addition, students with visual impairments vary greatly in their individual characteristics, both in the extent of visual impairment and in the presence additional disabilities. Teachers are expected to carry out a variety of specialized assessments, as well as to teach the many unique skills that students with visual impairments need to be independent. Teachers of visually impaired students are expected to know how to provide support to a high school student who is blind in a trigonometry class, while at the same time know how to teach a toddler with severe disabilities to feed himself or herself.

Accomplished teachers of students with visual impairments balance the challenges of the profession with the overarching rewards that are interwoven throughout. For new professionals entering the field, the daily complexities of the job may at first seem to be insurmountable. New teachers should remember, however, that other professionals are always willing to provide assistance, advice, and support. Also, an ever-expanding wealth of materials and resources are available to assist the beginning teacher of students who are visually impaired. The book you are now reading represents part of that wealth of materials.

Foundations of Education: Instructional Strategies for Teaching Children and Youths with Visual Impairments presents information and strategies for assessing, planning programs for, and teaching students who are blind or visually impaired. It is intended to be a basic methods textbook in visual impairment and, as such, is written to address the needs of university students in undergraduate and graduate preservice programs. Practicing teachers of students with visual impairments will also find this book useful, as it presents updated and new strategies for teaching their students. Parents, administrators, orientation and mobility specialists, general classroom teachers, and eye care specialists will also find the information to be helpful and, along with a wider audience, may use this book as an important desk reference.

While some beginning and practicing teachers in the field may look for a "cookbook" to help them address all of the complex needs of their students, this book is not such a resource. Although cookbooks are effective resources for preparing meals, they rarely, if ever, address the real-life issues and strategies needed to meet the complicated needs of students with visual impairments. *Instructional Strategies* presents essential background information and theory, with a focus on strategies that will be useful to teachers. However, these strategies must be tailored, modified, and expanded to meet the individual needs of each student. To accomplish this, teachers should observe the behavior of their students carefully, use principles of diagnostic teaching skillfully, and make changes on an ongoing basis to address their students' changing needs. The information in this book should be considered a springboard for the creative and reflective teacher to begin planning appropriate strategies, knowing that other resources, ongoing professional development, and a solid dose of common sense will be needed to refine effective teaching techniques.

Instructional Strategies for Teaching Children and Youths with Visual Impairments is divided into two sections. The first section focuses on the topics of teaming, assessment, and basic instructional strategies. The book begins with a chapter on fundamental principles and strategies for working as an effective team member, the basis for all work of teachers of students with visual impairments. Then three chapters present assessment strategies for students who are blind or visually impaired. A key role of the teacher is to provide information to diagnosticians and school psychologists on effective assessment techniques, as well as to carry out portions of the assessment related to unique skills. This section concludes with two chapters on basic instructional strategies. The first relates to principles for making appropriate modifications in instruction, whereas the second relates to strategies for designing instruction in the areas of unique skills, called the expanded core curriculum, needed by students with visual impairments.

The second section focuses on specific instructional strategies in various areas or for specific groups of students. This section begins with a comprehensive chapter on addressing the needs of infants, toddlers, and preschoolers with visual impairments. The next five chapters focus on academic subject matter areas—literacy skills, social studies and science, mathematics, fine arts, and physical education and health—with special emphasis given to teaching the unique skills in each of these areas. The next seven chapters focus on specific components of the expanded core curriculum for students with visual impairments. These include the areas of visual efficiency, assistive technology, orientation and mobility, independent living skills, social skills, recreation and leisure skills, and career education. The success of students with visual impairments is influenced heavily by mastery of skills in these disability-specific areas and, therefore, a substantial portion of the book is devoted to these essential topics.

A chapter is then presented on general strategies for teaching students with additional disabilities, although the beginning teacher will need further information and strategies to work effectively with this population. Additional readings are offered for this purpose, as well as additional strategies on this topic in Chapters 7–19. The book ends with a chapter devoted to providing information on blindness and visual impairment to parents and the general public, a unique role of teachers of students with visual impairments.

A key component of success for a teacher of students with visual impairments is a commitment to lifelong learning and continued professional development. New strategies, materials, resources, and technologies are being developed at a rapid pace, and the successful teacher must take steps to gain new information on an ongoing basis. *Instructional Strategies for Teaching Children and Youths with Visual Impairments* presents a wealth of information from highly skilled professionals in the field and represents a foundation on which further knowledge and skills may be built.

THE CONTRIBUTORS

Alan J. Koenig, Ed.D., is Professor and Associate Dean of Graduate Education in the College of Education at Texas Tech University in Lubbock. He received his doctoral degree from Vanderbilt University in 1987 and has been preparing teachers of students with visual impairments since that time. Previously, he taught children with visual impairments and served as a state consultant in visual impairment for the state of Iowa. Dr. Koenig is actively involved in professional organizations and has served as the president of the Division on Visual Impairments of the Council for Exceptional Children. He is a leading researcher in the education of students who are blind or visually impaired whose work includes examining the development of literacy skills for visually impaired students.

M. Cay Holbrook, Ph.D., is Associate Professor in the Faculty of Education at the University of British Columbia in Vancouver, BC, Canada. She received her doctoral degree from Florida State University in 1986 and has prepared teachers of students with visual impairments at Johns Hopkins University and the University of Arkansas at Little Rock. Dr. Holbrook taught children with visual impairments in public school programs in South Carolina, Georgia, and Florida and has been actively involved in the Association for Education and Rehabilitation of the Blind and Visually Impaired and the Council for Exceptional Children. She has written and presented numerous workshops to teachers and parents relating to the education of children with visual impairments.

Lou Alonso is Professor Emeritus, Department of Counseling, Educational Psychology and Special Education at Michigan State University in East Lansing.

Virginia E. Bishop, Ph.D., is Adjunct Professor at the University of Texas at Austin, Texas Tech University in Lubbock, and Stephen F. Austin University in Nacogdoches.

Anne L. Corn, Ed.D., is Professor of Special Education, Ophthalmology, and Visual Sciences at Vanderbilt University in Nashville, Tennessee.

Jo Ellen Croft is an itinerant vision teacher and orientation and mobility specialist with the Pulaski County Special School District and Adjunct Professor at the University of Arkansas at Little Rock.

Linda B. DePriest, Ed.D., is Special Education Consultant in the Metro Nashville Public Schools and Adjunct Professor in the Program for Visual Disabilities at Vanderbilt University in Nashville, Tennessee.

Jane N. Erin, Ph.D., is Associate Professor in the Department of Special Education and Rehabilitation at the University of Arizona in Tucson and Editor-in-Chief of the *Journal of Visual Impairment & Blindness.*

Carol Farrenkopf, Ed.D., is an itinerant teacher of students who are visually impaired for the Toronto District School Board and Instructor, Teacher Preparation Program, College of Education, at the University of Western Ontario in Canada.

Nora Griffin-Shirley, Ph.D., is Co-Director of the Virginia Murray Sowell Center for Research and Education in Visual Impairment and Program Coordinator of the Special Education and Orientation and Mobility Program at Texas Tech University in Lubbock.

Toni Heinze, Ed.D., is Associate Professor in the Teacher Education Department at Northern Illinois University in Dekalb.

Gaylen Kapperman, Ed.D., is Professor and Coordinator, Programs in Vision, Department of Teacher Education, at Northern Illinois University in Dekalb.

Pat Kelley, Ed.D., is Research Associate Professor at Texas Tech University in Lubbock.

Tracy Jo Kiel is a college freshman majoring in music at Concordia College in Moorhead, Minnesota. At the time of writing, she was a high school senior at the Milaca High School in Milaca, Minnesota.

Christine Kline is an orientation and mobility specialist and teacher of visually impaired students in Fayetteville, Arkansas.

M. Beth Langley is Educational Diagnostician, Prekindergarten Handicapped Assessment Team, at the Pinellas County Schools in St. Petersburg, Florida.

Carol A. Layton, Ed.D., is Assistant Professor at Texas Tech University in Lubbock, Texas.

Duncan McGregor, Ed.D., is a vision resource teacher and orientation and mobility specialist

with the York Region District School Board in Aurora, Ontario, in Canada.

Donna McNear is a teacher of students who are blind and visually impaired at the Rum River Special Education Cooperative and a certified orientation and mobility specialist in Cambridge, Minnesota.

Ike Presley is National Program Associate for Literacy at the American Foundation for the Blind in Atlanta, Georgia.

Rachel Rickard is an orientation and mobility specialist in the Region III Education Service Center in Victoria, Texas.

Margaret C. Robinson is a research assistant and doctoral student at Texas Tech University in Lubbock.

David B. Ross, Ed.D., is Professor, Program on Visual Impairment, at Kutztown University in Pennsylvania.

Sharon Zell Sacks, Ph.D., is Assistant Superintendent of the California School for the Blind in Fremont.

Rosanne K. Silberman, Ed.D., is Professor of Special Education and Coordinator, Graduate Teacher Preparation Programs in Blindness and Visual Impairment and Severe Disabilities Including Deafblindness, at Hunter College of the City University of New York.

Leon J. Sieve is Director of Bands and Head of the Music Department at Milaca High School in Milaca, Minnesota.

Pat Smith, Ph.D., is Chairperson of the Department of Counseling, Adult and Rehabilitation Education and Coordinator of the Rehabilitation Teaching for the Blind Program at the University of Arkansas at Little Rock.

Jodi Sticken is Instructor and Clinical Supervisor, Programs in Vision, at Northern Illinois University in Dekalb; Research Associate, Research and Development Institute in Sycamore, Illinois; and Consultant, Autism Program, Chicago Public Schools in Illinois.

Irene L. Topor, Ph.D., is Low Vision Specialist at the Arizona State Schools for the Deaf and Blind in Tucson, Arizona, and Adjunct Associate Professor at the University of Arizona in Tucson.

Sharon Trusty is Education Specialist, Region XVII Education Service Center and a certified orientation and mobility specialist in Lubbock, Texas; and Assistive Technology Provider at RESNA.

Karen E. Wolffe, Ph.D., is a career counselor and private consultant in Austin, Texas, and National Program Associate, American Foundation for the Blind.

PART ONE

Ensuring High-Quality Instruction

CHAPTER 1

Creating and Nurturing Effective Educational Teams

Irene L. Topor, M. Cay Holbrook, and Alan J. Koenig

KEY POINTS

◆ Students with visual impairments have complex learning needs.

◆ Meeting the needs of students with visual impairments necessitates a team of individuals working together to design and implement each student's Individualized Education Program (IEP).

◆ The teacher of students with visual impairments is an integral member of the educational team and often serves as a leader in guiding the team.

◆ Parents or caregivers are essential members of the educational team.

◆ Serving as an effective team member often necessitates gaining new knowledge from others and releasing responsibility to other members.

◆ Effective and ongoing communication is one key to effective collaboration among team members.

VIGNETTE

A month after their initial meeting, Doug's educational team met again. Although Doug's mother was not present at the second meeting, Doug's general education teacher, Ms. Krause, had the notebook that 9-year-old Doug carried between school and home, in which his mother and his teacher asked and answered questions and shared information. According to his mother, Doug liked his new school but complained that the other students worked too fast. Ms. Krause confirmed that Doug was often behind; he was slow to find the right book, to finish reading, and to solve math problems. Ms. Valencia, the teacher of students with visual impairments, noted these issues in her planner and suggested that the group discuss them one at a time.

Ms. Boyer, the classroom paraeducator, volunteered that Doug was slow to find his books because his desk was a mess. "Papers are spilling out all over the floor. Am I supposed to clean them up for him?" she asked.

Ms. Valencia and Mr. Morgan, the orientation and mobility (O&M) instructor, immediately agreed that this was not Ms. Boyer's job. "However," said Mr. Morgan, "you could play a *big* role by reinforcing the organizational skills that Ms. Valencia and I have begun to teach Doug. We've made sure he has plenty of storage space right beside his desk, but he doesn't yet think about putting things back in their places when he's through with them. I have a checklist in my office that could help you guide him in practicing these skills. I'll bring it to you. Organizational skills are really important for a student who is blind."

Ms. Krause laughed. "He's not my only disorganized student. I'll start reminding the whole class to clean up a bit, and I'll watch to be sure Doug knows I mean him, too."

"Now, about Doug's slow reading . . ." began Ms. Valencia. "I've finished my assessment of his reading skills, and Doug knows the braille code well. However, his speed while reading is only 50 words a minute. It isn't unusual for a braille reader to reach this rate and 'level off,' but a reading speed this slow interferes with both comprehension and reading pleasure—not to mention completing assignments on time. We certainly don't want Doug to remain at that rate! Doug tells me he doesn't like to read and never reads outside class. I wonder if one approach to help him pick up his reading speed may be simply to promote outside reading."

Ms. Krause commented, "I've seen it work with other reluctant readers. Sometimes children just haven't found the right books to interest them."

"Well, I have some sources of braille books for children," said Ms. Valencia, "and if we look through my catalogs, maybe you can identify some that may be just right for Doug."

"Good idea," said Ms. Krause. "Maybe I can find books that match some selections in our class library. Then when Doug reads one of them, I can find another child who really enjoyed that book to discuss it with him. You know, a really enthusiastic reader. . . ."

"And as for math," Ms. Valencia continued, "I'd like to begin teaching Doug to use an abacus. He knows the steps in computation on the braillewriter, but now that he's in the fourth grade, some of the problems are getting pretty big! I think he would be faster on the abacus, and besides, he can use the abacus on the standardized state tests in the spring."

"Would he be allowed to do that?" asked Ms. Krause. "Students aren't allowed to use calculators on the state test."

"An abacus isn't a calculator," Ms. Valencia explained. "It's similar to a pencil and paper because it's a means of keeping track of the intermediate steps as a problem is calculated. Yes, an abacus is allowed on the tests in our state, although a calculator isn't."

Mr. Robles, the adaptive physical education teacher, spoke up for the first time. His role was to assure that Doug develops stamina, balance, and gross motor skills similar to those of his peers. "I'd like to report that Doug is doing really well on the playground. When Mr. Morgan offered to teach me how to orient a blind child to the playground, well, I just wasn't sure I could do it. But now Doug can find the playground equipment easily, and I've noticed that he seems a lot more comfortable outdoors in general."

"There is one problem on the playground, though," Mr. Robles continued. "If Doug puts his cane down by the swings or at the bottom of the slide, other children sometimes pick it up and play with it. They don't always put it back where Doug left it!"

"Why don't we say something at the next faculty meeting?" suggested Ms. Krause. "We could ask all the teachers to tell their students what a problem this can be for Doug."

"That should help," agreed Mr. Robles. "What about you, Mr. Morgan? How's he doing in O&M?"

"Doug can independently travel along all the routes that are part of his daily routine, such as going from his classroom to the gym and back and from his classroom to the lunchroom and back," Mr. Morgan responded. "But when I asked him to walk from the gym to the lunchroom, he went all the way to his classroom first, instead of taking the path that goes straight from the gym to the lunchroom. In other words, he doesn't yet understand the relationships between one part of the campus and another well enough to create new routes between familiar places. We're working on it. Part of this task is learning cardinal directions. Ms. Krause, you could help Doug with this problem."

Ms. Krause looked surprised. "I don't know north from south!" she said. "How can I help Doug with it?"

Mr. Morgan laughed. "Suppose Doug and I put North, South, East, and West signs on your classroom walls. Could you use them to refer to directions in the room? You know, by saying things like, 'Put the books on the shelves on the west wall'?"

"Okay," said Ms. Krause, "I can do that. And I can find ways to include cardinal directions in our social studies lessons more often."

Ms. Valencia looked around the table. "Is there anything else? I think we've done really well for one month! Shall we meet again on the first Tuesday of next month at the same time? I'd like to hear if Doug found the right book and is reading any faster and whether he has *willingly* read a book outside class. What do you think about inviting Doug to our next meeting so we can hear how *he* thinks things are going?"

The team agreed that this would be a good idea, and, with some feelings of accomplishment, each member moved on to his or her next task.

INTRODUCTION

Teachers of students with visual impairments have a complex, challenging, and gratifying role to play in the education of students who are blind or visually impaired. These specialists work in a variety of settings and with students who have different needs. They may work with infants and toddlers, with teenagers who had become accomplished students using print before they lost their vision, or with children with other physical and sensory disabilities in addition to visual impairments. The role is broad because these specialists are responsible for teaching skills that are unique to learning how to live with a visual impairment—including everyday life skills—and also for helping students succeed in every area of their regular school subjects. Because teachers of students who are visually impaired have specialized knowledge, they are also involved in assessing the capabilities and progress of their students in many areas and serve as consultants to other teachers and professionals who work with their students. Because of the complexity of the needs of the students with whom they work and the importance of their role in the education and lives of these students, much has been written about teachers of students with visual impairments. Appendixes A–F at the end of this book contain discussions of the needs of students and the role of teachers vital to the understanding of educational programming for students with visual impairments.

This volume on instructional strategies begins with the educational team because of the centrality of the team, under current law, in assessing, planning, and implementing a student's education (see Sidebar 1.1). In addition, teachers of students with visual impairments must be closely involved with others to provide a comprehensive, effective educational program for their students. Working in collaborative teams is essential in situations in which students with visual impairments have contact with a variety of educators, most of whom are not specialists in visual impairment. Working in collaborative teams is perhaps most significant in inclusive settings, that is, settings in which students are enrolled in neighborhood schools and receive their primary instruction in general education classrooms. Educational teams are also important in residential schools for students who are blind or visually impaired, although in these schools, the majority of professionals have been trained in and are knowledgeable about visual impairments, so the dynamics of the teams may be somewhat different. Finally, educational teams are critical for meeting the needs of students who are enrolled in educational programs in self-contained settings. These students may have a majority of their educational needs provided by special education teachers in collaboration with a teacher of students with visual impairments.

Selecting a team and organizing the team to interact and function effectively when planning an educational program is a comprehensive way to deliver services to students with visual impairments, including those with additional disabilities. Collaboration, one way for a group of people to work together, is the process by which all members of the team serving a student with a visual impairment interact with and are supportive of one another to provide the highest-quality assessment, curriculum, and instruction to meet the student's diverse needs (Pugach & Johnson, 1995). Each team member is committed to the educational goals for the student and interactions among the team members facilitate progress in achieving these goals.

One cannot assume that a team of profession-

SIDEBAR 1.1

IDEA, the Educational Team, and the Role of the Teacher of Students with Visual Impairments

In many ways, the role of the teacher of students with visual impairments is shaped by federal legislation governing the education of children with disabilities. This law is the Individuals with Disabilities Education Act, or IDEA (P.L. 105-17).

IDEA grants specific rights to children with disabilities and their families and mandates specific procedures. The most basic right is to a fair and appropriate education in the least-restrictive environment that is appropriate for a child. Thus, children must be assessed to determine their needs and capabilities. Children also have a right to the supports and services necessary to obtain an education in the least-restrictive environment. Parents have the right to be involved in planning and implementing their children's education and necessary services, as well as due process rights regarding oversight and appeal.

Assessing a child and planning for his or her education are done by a team of professionals from various disciplines, who are charged with preparing a written document, known as the Individualized Education Program (IEP) or for children under age 3, an Individualized Family Service Plan (IFSP). The team must include the parents or other caretakers. Thus, the educational team becomes a central force in the education of a child with disabilities and his or her family. And for a child who is visually impaired or has additional disabilities that include visual impairment, the teacher of children with visual impairments is a key member of the educational team.

---

als is working collaboratively just because all are assigned to offer services to the same student. Thousand and Villa (1992, p. 76) defined collaborative teams as those whose efforts are characterized by the following:

♦ Coordination of their work to achieve at least one common agreed-upon goal (Appleby & Winder, 1977);

♦ A belief system that all members of the team have unique and needed expertise (Vandercook & York, 1990);

♦ Demonstration of parity—the equal valuation of each member's input by alternately engaging in the dual role of teacher and learner, expert and recipient, consultant and consultee (Friend & Cook, 1992; Villa, Thousand, Paolucci-Whitcomb, & Nevin, 1990);

♦ Use of a distributed function theory of leadership in which the task and relationship functions of the traditional lone learner are distributed among all members of the group (Johnson & Johnson, 1987a, 1987b); and

♦ Use of a collaborative teaming process that involves face-to-face interaction; positive interdependence; the performance, monitoring, and processing of interpersonal skills; and individual accountability (Thousand & Villa, 1992).

This chapter describes the role of the teacher of students with visual impairments in the consultative process. In addition, it discusses the principles of collaborative consultation and the characteristics of team members who are successful within a collaborative model. Finally, it offers suggestions for how teachers can be most effective as collaborative consultants when conducting assessments and providing instruction.

ROLE OF THE TEACHER OF STUDENTS WITH VISUAL IMPAIRMENTS

The teacher of students with visual impairments plays a critical role in establishing and maintaining effective teams. Although all members of the educational team are equally important in planning and implementing the student's educational program, the specialist in visual impairment often takes the lead in coordinating the team's efforts for several reasons:

◆ The teacher of students with visual impairments generally has more experience than the other team members in developing educational plans for students with visual impairments;

◆ Other members of the team may feel less knowledgeable and therefore less willing to initiate team efforts; and

◆ The teacher of students with visual impairments may have more opportunities to interact regularly with all members of the educational team, and other team members may not have ongoing contact with each other.

Therefore, the role of the teacher of students with visual impairments in building collaborative teams is to do the following:

◆ Ensure that the team includes the student's parents or other caregivers and the range of professionals who are needed to address the student's needs (see Sidebar 1.2);

◆ Nurture a spirit of cooperation and shared decision making among team members to meet the needs of each student most effectively;

◆ Serve as team member or team leader, depending on which role is decided among all members of the student's educational team;

◆ Contribute information and insights to other team members on the unique needs of students with visual impairments and on appropriate ways to address the students' needs in assessment and instructional activities;

◆ Assist other team members in feeling confident in their knowledge and abilities to contribute to the educational team and therefore to the total educational program for the student; and

◆ Facilitate communication and collaboration among team members to plan and implement an effective educational program.

HOW TEAMS WORK

Types of Educational Teams

Three types of teams are typically used in educational settings: multidisciplinary, interdisciplinary, and transdisciplinary. Campbell (1987) described these models as follows:

Multidisciplinary teams include persons from a number of disciplines, each of whom conducts his or her own assessment and provides instruction or other services in isolation from others on the team.

Interdisciplinary teams include persons from a number of disciplines who share the findings of their assessments and plan the student's educational program together, but each team member implements his or her own intervention program.

Transdisciplinary teams decide on a "primary programmer" who is responsible for implementing the intervention programs in collaboration with the teachers or specialists who conducted various assessments and designed intervention programs.

Table 1.1 compares these three team models.

Educational teams generally adopt a team model that best meets the needs of a particular

Other Specialists Who May Work with Students Who Have Visual Impairments

Along with the teacher of students with visual impairments, the general education teacher, and the student's parents, the following professionals are frequently members of a student's educational team.

ORIENTATION AND MOBILITY SPECIALIST

A professional who specializes in teaching safe travel skills to students who are blind or visually impaired, including sighted guide technique, or use of a cane, dog guide, or sophisticated electronic travel devices.

ADAPTIVE PHYSICAL EDUCATION TEACHER

A physical education teacher who has special training to work with students who need individualized instruction to improve motor skill development, including increased stamina and balance.

SPEECH AND LANGUAGE THERAPIST

A professional trained to evaluate students' ability to understand what another person is conveying to them (receptive communication skills) and to express what they want (expressive communication skills). This individual may provide individualized intervention to students to improve communication skills, give suggestions to other professionals about ways to improve a student's communication skills throughout a typical day, and/or work with small groups of students to improve communication strategies.

OCCUPATIONAL THERAPIST

A professional who is concerned with maximizing an individual's potential for age appropriate functional behaviors through the use of purposeful activities. Occupational therapists may work with a student who is blind or visually impaired because a visual impairment may affect an array of daily life activities, from learning an activity through observation through visually directed hand use. Occupational therapy is warranted for a child if there are functional or performance deficits in the ability to optimally perform daily life tasks.

LOW VISION SPECIALIST

A professional who specializes in identifying the vision capabilities of an individual with low vision through assessment of functional vision or of the environment and through preassessment of optical and nonoptical devices. The low vision specialist develops programs to teach a student efficient use of vision within the student's current educational program. After a clinical low vision evaluation is conducted by a specially trained low vision clinician, the low vision specialist will teach use of prescribed optical devices within tasks and environments where they are needed to maximize use of vision and independently perform a task.

PARAEDUCATOR

An individual who works under the direction of the teacher of students who have visual impairments. Paraeducator activities may include preparing materials such as braille, tactile graphics, and enlarged print. Paraeducators may perform general school duties, reinforce children's orientation and mobility skills during travel, perform self-care routines for students who need assistance, provide feedback about visual activities, and reinforce the use of optical devices.

CASE MANAGER

An individual designated by a team to take primary responsibility for compiling medical, educational, and other information relevant to educational program planning for a student. This individual can assist with a variety of matters, including scheduling meetings and serving as a liaison between team members when issues concerning the student arise throughout the school year.

Table 1.1. Comparison of Three Team Models

Function	Multidisciplinary	Interdisciplinary	Transdisciplinary
Evaluation	All the team members do separate evaluations and prepare their own reports.	All the team members do separate evaluations. Team members have some informal discussions with the other team members before evaluations. All team members prepare separate reports.	The team members do a joint evaluation. Preliminary discussions among the team members are essential.
Planning	All the team members present their reports and plan their own services.	Although separate reports are presented, much discussion occurs across disciplines. Services are interrelated.	The team members develop a joint service plan, implemented by a primary service provider.
Programming	All the team members deliver their own services and chart the student's progress in their own areas of expertise.	All the team members deliver their own services but utilize suggestions from other team members. All the team members chart the student's progress in their own area of expertise.	The primary service provider delivers services and charts the student's progress.
Role of the parent	Largely a contributor. Occasionally an implementer.	A contributor and an implementer.	May be the primary service provider and is often a strong component of the team.
Role of the specialist in visual impairment	A member of the team and a provider of direct services.	A member of the team but may share roles with other members.	A contributing member of the team but rarely a direct service provider.

Characteristics	Multidisciplinary	Interdisciplinary	Transdisciplinary
Advantages	The student receives in-depth evaluations and programming from a number of disciplines.	The team members learn from each other. Programming is usually better coordinated. The parent is more likely to be included at the programming level.	The team is a unified force and shares both responsibility and expertise. The parent is fully involved.
Disadvantages	Segmented evaluation and programming. The parent is often on the sidelines.	Still some separation of disciplines.	Success depends on the team members' personalities and level of commitment and on the ability/receptivity of the primary service provider.

Source: Adapted from V. E. Bishop, *Teaching Visually Impaired Children,* 2nd ed. (Springfield, IL.: Charles C Thomas, 1996), p. 167.

student. Today, many professionals believe that the traditional multidisciplinary team is inadequate for meeting the needs of students with visual impairments, since much of the work of the team members is conducted in isolation from each other. The interdisciplinary team reduces or eliminates this isolation by ensuring that the team members discuss the results of assessments and plan programs together; then when each team member carries out his or her instruction, it is influenced by the collective thinking of all the members. The transdisciplinary team takes the ultimate step in teaming by giving one person the responsibility to carry out the student's instructional program, guided by the findings of assessments and collaboration with other team members. Because of the focus on sharing information and expertise, the interdisciplinary and transdisciplinary team approaches are perhaps the most beneficial to use with students who are blind or visually impaired.

Collaborative Consultation

The sharing or transferring of information and skills across traditional disciplinary boundaries is characteristic of collaborative consultation. Team members could include any of the following in addition to the student:

Immediate and extended family members

Teacher of students with visual impairments

General education and/or special education classroom teacher

Orientation and mobility (O&M) specialist

Eye care specialist

General or adaptive physical education specialist

School nurse

Audiologist

Psychologist

Speech and language specialist

Occupational therapist

Physical therapist

Specialist in deaf-blindness

Teacher of students with hearing impairments

Nutritionist

Neurologist

Low vision specialist

Paraeducator

Braille transcriber

School principal or other school administrators

Case manager

Computer technology specialist

Rehabilitation teacher or rehabilitation counselor

Other medical professionals (such as the child's pediatrician)

The needs of the student will determine the composition of the team and the role of each member. Effective collaborative consultation means that all team members work together toward mutually agreed-upon goals. The role of team members may change, as is discussed later in this chapter.

ROLES OF TEAM MEMBERS

Four Basic Roles

When interacting with colleagues, professionals draw on and shift among four basic roles, all of which represent dimensions of collaboration. The purpose of all these aspects of collaboration is to improve the practice of teaching so that a diverse range of students can be provided with high-quality educational services. The four roles that form the underlying framework of collaboration are the *supportive* role, the *facilitative* role, the *informative* role, and the *prescriptive* role (Pugach & Johnson, 1995).

The Supportive Role. This role represents the basic level of caring between individuals during times of need or when they are trying out new methods of instruction. Teachers of students with visual impairments often work in teams with other professionals who have no expertise or experience teaching students who are blind or visually impaired. Therefore, an important role for them is to offer reinforcement and support to these other professionals. The following are suggestions for doing so:

♦ Keep in close contact with the other team members by telephone, E-mail, or brief meetings, especially when they are trying new strategies with the student, to check on progress, and to offer help during critical times.

♦ Follow through on feedback and suggestions and ask questions about the success of a team member's efforts. It may be helpful to make a note in a day planner as a reminder to follow up on a conversation after a week or two has passed.

♦ Provide specific feedback. Reinforcement and support are much more effective when paired with specific examples. A teacher of students with visual impairments who makes general comments, like "I think things are going well for Jim in your classroom," can increase the impact of the feedback by adding examples of *how* things are going well, such as "I think things are going well for Jim in your classroom. When I was there yesterday, I noticed that he was using his monocular and that you had set up special seating and lighting that he can adjust himself."

♦ Follow up verbal feedback with a written note every once in a while. Written messages will document your suggestions and feedback in a concrete way. The team member can then refer back to these notes if needed.

The Facilitative Role. The role of facilitator involves helping other team members develop the capacity to solve problems, engage in tasks, or deal independently with challenges and hence to enhance their own skills and knowledge to a greater extent than before. It may include demonstrating a specific method, coaching, or giving feedback to a member after he or she has attempted to implement a new method. Teachers who want assistance with a classroom-based problem work with colleagues who help them use all the information and expertise they have to develop and implement practical, creative solutions. The following suggestions may be helpful in performing this role with other team members, including the student and his or her parents:

♦ Become as familiar as possible with the student's classroom and home environments so that realistic goals and expectations can be set. Spend some time observing the student in a variety of settings to see how the student acts without intervention and talk informally with his or her parents and teachers to gain their perspectives on the student's strengths and needs.

♦ Use the experience and knowledge of each member of the team to reach creative solutions to difficult problems. For example, a general education teacher often has extensive experience planning and conducting various types of field trips. Using the teacher's knowledge of past visits to a zoo or a museum can be helpful in identifying areas of special concern for a student who is blind or visually impaired and planning adaptations before a trip.

♦ Tap into the specialized knowledge of each team member by asking questions during team meetings that are designed to gather information from everyone. For example, the parents may be asked "In your experience at home, how much time does it take Tommy to tie his shoes? Is there anything that helps him tie his shoes more quickly?"

The Informative Role. The goal of the informative role is to provide direct assistance to one's colleagues so they are better equipped to deal with problems on an ongoing basis. For example, one can share one's knowledge of appropriate resources or describe what has worked in one's own experiences. Here are some specific suggestions:

◆ Put team members in touch with other professionals or parents who may be able to assist them. One way to do so is to invite parents or teachers to attend meetings of local, regional, or national support groups to link them with others who have similar questions, concerns, and ideas.

◆ Teach a short- or long-term braille class for parents and other team members. Learning the braille alphabet or even more of the braille code helps them communicate with the student and demystifies braille.

◆ Keep a professional library, including copies of professional journals and newsletters, and a resource file with materials that can be shared with the other team members.

◆ Invite other team members to attend special seminars and conferences (for example, state, regional, or national conferences of the Association for Education and Rehabilitation of the Blind and Visually Impaired) that would offer information about providing service to students with visual impairments.

◆ Give team members addresses of pertinent Web sites on the Internet. Useful, current information can be found through these resources.

The Prescriptive Role. In this role, one team member prescribes a specific path of action for others to follow. For example, the teacher of students with visual impairments may suggest that all the other members follow specific procedures for reinforcing a student's use of eye contact. Unlike the other roles described here, which encourage the other team members to take responsibility for the changes and methods they are trying to implement, this one is used when other team

members request direct assistance or want specific help trying a new technique with a student. When working within the prescriptive role, it is helpful to do the following:

◆ Make sure that the suggestions are clear and concise. Provide specific written instructions or key points so that the other team members can refer to them later.

◆ Follow up suggestions with questions about how various techniques are working. If a particular technique is not working appropriately, suggest changes that may make it easier to use or another technique that may be more effective.

◆ Link suggestions and a plan of action to the goals that the team agreed upon. Make sure that the parents, other professionals, and administrators understand how the plan will result in the achievement of short- or long-term goals.

Successful collaboration among members of the educational team includes all four roles. In practice, teachers of students with visual impairments shift among these roles, depending on the skills of the other team members. Building team relationships means that all the members need to engage in continuous collaboration for a variety of purposes related to each goal for a student. Not everyone takes part in all forms of collaboration all the time, but each of the four roles is essential if collaboration is to work.

Alleviation of Role Conflict

Role conflict arises when team members have incompatible expectations about their roles on the team. For example, the teacher of students with visual impairments should carefully define his or her role in order to avoid misunderstandings by others on the team. Some may view the teacher of students with visual impairments as an expert and feel that all educational and instructional decisions should be made and implemented by this specially trained professional. Others may see the teacher of students with visual impairments as a storekeeper of materials; the person who provides bold lined paper, enlarges copies, and provides felt-tip pens to the students. Once the teacher of students with visual impairments has clearly defined his or her role as contributing information as well as assisting other team members to feel confident in their knowledge and abilities to contribute to the educational team, the incompatible expectations by others on the team should decrease.

Wood (1998) found that professionals who served students with severe disabilities in inclusive settings established role boundaries that were commensurate with the jobs that they were hired to do and found it difficult to vary their roles according to the decisions of the educational team and the needs of the students in specific situations that arose. As the school year progressed and they had more experience working on an educational team, their perceptions of their roles became less rigid, and they became more cooperative. Collaborative work among the team members helped them meet the challenge of changing from their conventional roles to roles that better met the needs of the students with whom they were working. Limited time to consult with other team members, funding issues, and large caseloads of students were other obstacles to effective collaboration among the team members. In-service workshops on the kinds of roles played by team members are also helpful in alleviating role conflict. Suggestions for conducting in-service presentations to teachers and others are presented in Chapter 21 of this volume. The most important factor in overcoming role conflict and uncertainty about roles is effective communication, discussed next.

Effective Communication

Professionals and parents may not be able to dismiss their feelings of role ambiguity or discomfort when they are uncertain about their purpose and role on an educational team. However, when strategies are used to promote effective, clear communication among team members, the messages that are sent help clarify the members' roles and support the importance of everyone's participation on the team. Pugach and Johnson (1995) suggested some skills that enhance communication:

◆ Start with general questions and statements. For example, ask broad questions such as "How are things going?" to begin a conversation and gain a general idea of how the other team members are faring.

◆ Offer support to team members and follow through on commitments with realistic time frames and reactions.

◆ Use reflection to restate key phases of another team member's statement, so the other person can hear what was understood as the main point. Reflection, combined with stating the implied message (one's understanding of the message), gives the team member a chance to refine and develop his or her thoughts.

◆ Seek clarification of statements that are not understood.

◆ Remain silent at intervals to maintain a natural interaction style, especially if someone on the team is timid about entering the conversation.

◆ Summarize the information learned from an interaction, especially regarding activities to be accomplished by the other team members.

There are also behaviors that serve as barriers to effective communication. These barriers include the following:

◆ Giving advice that creates dependence. For example, a specialist who says, "When Juan's monocular gets dirty, be sure to let me know so I can clean it" is fostering dependence. Teaching team members, including Juan and his parents, the steps in cleaning the lenses of the monocular fosters independence.

◆ Giving false reassurances that minimize the importance of a problem. Saying "Don't worry that Jennifer won't be able to get her driver's permit along with her classmates" minimizes the real difficulties that will arise during that critical time.

◆ Asking unfocused questions that stifle the development of a train of thought. Be sensitive to the conversations that occur during a meeting and avoid changing the subject or diverting team members' thoughts, even when the discussion is heated or otherwise uncomfortable. For example, parents who complain that their child's braille textbook is two months late need not only to express their frustration, but, through discussion, to come up with possible alternative short-term solutions while waiting for the textbook to arrive.

◆ Wandering thoughts and changing topics that shift attention away from the topic being discussed. Even though the team may have several items on the agenda of a meeting, it is important to allow enough time to finish one discussion before another is begun. If the agenda is long and all the topics are not covered, a second meeting may be necessary to discuss the remaining topics.

◆ Interrupting a team member. It may be difficult to avoid interrupting a speaker, since each team member may have important issues or comments to contribute to the discussion. However, team members who are interrupted while expressing their views may begin to believe that their opinions are not important. It may be helpful to begin team meetings with a list of ground rules, such as suggesting that the team members avoid interrupting each other.

◆ Using clichés that trivialize the importance of the communication. When discussing a potentially troublesome problem with a student, team members should avoid statements like "Been there, done that" or "Sticks and stones. . . ." Listening respectfully to the communication of other team members encourages creative and sensitive problem solving.

◆ Responding to team members by minimizing their feelings. Some people seem to believe that minimizing a person's feelings will help the person see that his or her problem is not as big or as overwhelming as the person thinks it is. In fact, minimizing someone's feelings actually may make a person feel that he or she is incompetent and not intelligent. It may also make a person hostile and resentful. Consequently, the person may withdraw from team discussions. Saying to a parent "dealing with your daughter's fear of not going to the prom isn't so bad; after all, she got an A on her last English exam" will discourage the parent from expressing these concerns in the future.

◆ Jumping to a quick conclusion without considering all possible solutions to a problem. This is an area that may be especially difficult for experienced educators, since they may try to impose solutions that helped in earlier situations. All possible solutions and team members' suggestions should be considered equally when the team searches for answers to difficult issues.

Teachers of students with visual impairments have unique issues related to communication. Many serve students in itinerant settings and thus are not always in the same location as the other team members. Itinerant teachers often complain that they do not have time to chat casually with colleagues. They also find that it is sometimes difficult to communicate with others who have negative or uninformed attitudes toward visual impairments. The following suggestions may help itinerant teachers communicate with other team members:

◆ Set up a mailbox in the school or classroom so that the general education teacher can jot quick notes about their concerns. Be sure to follow up quickly on the teacher's notes.

◆ Invest in a cellular phone. A cell phone not only allows for a teacher to call for help with car problems while traveling from one school to another, it also facilitates the teacher's communication with school personnel and students' families.

◆ Find out if team members prefer casual contact or formal appointments and be sensitive to their wishes.

◆ Develop standard forms for regular communication between team members. A set of forms to establish communication and document team activitites is provided in Figures 1.1 through 1.4. Figure 1.1 can be distributed to all team members so that they have contact information to communicate in between meetings as frequently as is necessary with individual team members. Distribution of such forms to parents is very helpful, especially when they are unable to attend meetings. They are also very useful in developing a student's Individualized Education Program (IEP). Blank forms can also be provided for the team to use with individual students. Olmstead (1991) provided other helpful forms but those in this chapter are shown here in regard to Doug, the student who is mentioned at the beginning of this chapter. In this example, Ms. Valencia took responsibility for filling out the assessment form (Figure 1.2) and called a team meeting to discuss the results of the assessment. This initial report of assessment served as a catalyst to discuss other educational programming concerns, and these are documented on the notes of the team

meeting (Figure 1.3). After a designated period of time (in this case, one month), the team met again to discuss what had happened with Doug's educational program, and these results were documented on the results of activities form (Figure 1.4).

◆ Exchange E-mail addresses. If possible, set up Internet connections (list-serves, bulletin boards, or chat rooms) for the team members.

Role Transitions

The collaborative consultation process specific to working with students with visual impairments involves a variety of transitions among the team members' roles. These role transitions may occur in six ways: role extension, role enrichment, role expansion, role exchange, role release, and role support (Garland, McGonigel, Frank, & Buck, 1989). Role transitions may lead to ambiguity among team members about each other's roles because the roles are constantly changing in consideration of the student's progress. The following section discusses the six ways in which team members' roles may change as they work with a student who is visually impaired.

Role Extension. With role extension, a team member acts to gain greater expertise in his or her discipline, that is, to increase his or her knowledge and skills. Actions may include staying current with professional literature, attending conferences, and engaging in other forms of staff development. For example, a teacher of students with visual impairments may attend a workshop on how a student's visual field may influence the selection of an augmentative or alternative communication system.

Teachers of students with visual impairments face unique challenges in extending their roles, since there are sometimes few local opportunities for enhanced professional development. To continue to develop professional skills and knowledge, they may do the following:

Date <u>Febuary 21, 2000</u>

Child's Name <u>Doug Sanchez</u>

Date of Birth <u>October 13, 1991</u>

Parent's Name <u>Marsha Sanchez</u>

Team Member's Name	Discipline
D. Krause	4th grade teacher

Location/ Address	Hollinger Elementary 2336 Altura Heights Dr. Boemer, Californa 94559	

Business Phone	Home Phone
(707) 555-1985	(707) 555-2324

Fax	E-mail
(707) 555-1900	Krause@rocketmail.com

Team Member's Name	Discipline
V. Valencia	Teacher of visually impaired students

Location/ Address	Scholastic Unified School District Rodale Elementary Boemer, California 94559	

Business Phone	Home Phone
(707) 256-1945	(707) 259-0608

Fax	E-mail
(707) 256-1940	val@schol.org

Team Member's Name	Discipline
Randy Boyer	Paraeducator

Location/ Address	Hollinger Elementary—see D. Krause information	

Business Phone	Home Phone
See D. Krause information	None given

Fax	E-mail
See D. Krause information	rboyer@aol.com

Figure 1.1. Sample Team Members' Contact Information Form

Date _January 21, 2000_

Child's Name _Doug Sanchez_

Date of Birth _10/13/91_

Parent's Name _Marsha Sanchez_

Name of Assessment	Assessor
Braille reading efficiency	_Valencia_

Results

Doug states he doesn't like to read.

Johns Reading Inventory:
Independent Reading Level: 4th grade
  Reading rates (100 words)
    Oral reading: 50 words/minute
    Silent reading: 73 words/minute
 Long-term reading (250 words)
  Alternate 2 minutes oral; 5 minutes silent (20 minutes)
    Expository: 41 words minute—average oral rate
    Narrative: 52 words minute—average oral rate
Comprehension: 99–100% short passages; 90% long passages

Actions

Doug knows braille code; reading speed needs improvement.

Meet with team to discuss characteristics of braille readers.

Offer suggestions about encouraging Doug to read outside of class.

Ask Ms. Krause for her input about how to improve Doug's motivation to read.

Share discussion with Marsha, Doug's mother, and ask for input about improving Doug's motivation to read.

Figure 1.2. Sample Assessment Information Form

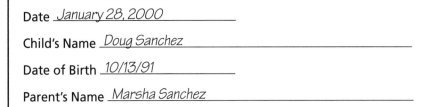

Date _January 28, 2000_

Child's Name _Doug Sanchez_

Date of Birth _10/13/91_

Parent's Name _Marsha Sanchez_

List of Attendees:

Ms. Krause, 4th grade teacher, Ms. Valencia, teacher of students with visual impairments, Mr. Boyer, paraeducator, Mr. Robles, adaptive physical education teacher, Mr. Morgan, O&M instructor

---

What was discussed:

Doug's reading rate and motivation to read

Doug's organizational skills

Doug's ability to complete assignments on time

Abacus instruction

O&M—use of cane on the playground; children removing Doug's cane from its original location; creating new routes between familiar places

---

Decisions and actions to be taken:

Ms. Valencia will work with Ms. Krause to encourage Doug to read books outside of class time.

Ms. Valencia will begin teaching Doug abacus skills.

Ms. Krause and Mr. Morgan will reinforce Doug's knowledge of cardinal directions so that he can create routes between familiar places on the school campus.

Ms. Krause will talk to school staff about the importance of other children leaving Doug's cane in the place where he leaves it on the playground.

Schedule another meeting in one month and invite Doug.

Talk to Marsha, Doug's mother, and ask if she has additional concerns or questions about Doug's school program.

Figure 1.3. Sample Notes on the Team Meeting

Date _February 5, 2000_

Child's Name _Doug Sanchez_

Date of Birth _10/13/91_

Parent's Name _Marsha Sanchez_

List of goals or activities:

Doug will plan a new, shorter route from the gym to the lunchroom.

Doug will select one book outside of class to read for pleasure and provides an oral summary of its contents.

Doug will compute simple one-digit addition and subtraction problems on the abacus.

Doug will develop a system to organize his classroom assignments.

Results and outcomes:

Doug successfully planned a new route from the gym to the lunchroom because of the encouragement and reinforcement he received from Ms. Krause, Mr. Morgan, Ms. Valencia, Mr. Robles, and Mr. Boyer.

Doug recently selected a book that he wants to read for pleasure but he hasn't completed it.

Doug is quickly learning to compute on the abacus and has mastered single-digit addition and subtraction problems.

Doug is using the storage space beside his desk to put books and assignments back in their original places.

Figure 1.4. Sample Results of Activities Form

◆ Attend regional or international conferences on the needs of students who are visually impaired,

◆ Subscribe to professional list-serves on the Internet to interact with colleagues in various locations and use the Internet for research,

◆ Subscribe to professional journals and read professional books to keep up to date on research related to the education of students who are visually impaired, and

◆ Work toward an advanced degree in special education with an emphasis on the education of students with visual impairments or take courses in specific areas of interest.

Role Enrichment. Team members develop a general awareness of the terminology and basic practices of other disciplines. For example, a communication specialist may describe to another team member the differences between touch cues and object cues in receptive communication intervention for a student with a visual impairment and additional disabilities (see Chapter 20). Teachers of students with visual impairments have two roles to play with regard to role enrichment: They need to enrich their own roles by learning about other disciplines and provide the information about visual impairments needed to enrich the roles of the other team members. Some suggestions for role enrichment are these:

◆ Attend periodic local or regional conferences that focus on other professional areas;

◆ Listen carefully as other team members share professional information related to their areas of expertise; and

◆ Share basic information and materials on visual impairment, such as *When You Have a Visually Handicapped Child in Your Classroom: Suggestions for Teachers* (Torres & Corn, 1990), with other team members.

Role Expansion. When a team member acquires sufficient information from other disciplines, he

or she can make knowledgeable observations and recommendations outside his or her own discipline. For example, a teacher who is trained to work with students with severe cognitive impairments observes that a student benefits from using a vertical slant board on his tray to increase his ability to discriminate the pictures or objects in his schedule book, so the teacher explores the issue further to determine if combining the slant board with a change in illumination would be even more helpful.

Role Exchange. When a team member implements the knowledge and skills of other disciplines under the supervision of relevant team members, roles have been exchanged. For example, when a parent demonstrates to the teacher of students with visual impairments that her son is more motivated to find food items independently when the food is placed on a blue background instead of a white background, the parent has temporarily assumed the role of the teacher.

Role Release. In some situations, it is appropriate for members of the educational team to pull back from specialized instruction (role release) when other members of the educational team become knowledgeable and skilled. For example, after a teacher of students with visual impairments has taught a general education teacher how to use sighted guide techniques during classroom activities and feels assured that the general education teacher feels comfortable with this procedure, the specialist may release his or her role in this regard. Then the general education teacher assumes the responsibility for overseeing the general education students' appropriate use of sighted guide techniques with the student who is visually impaired in the classroom.

Caution must be exercised, however, to make sure that role release is used appropriately. It is not appropriate for role release to be used to minimize the amount of time that a student receives specialized instruction from a qualified teacher. For example, it is not appropriate for paraeducators to teach braille reading and writing skills just because they know the braille code. In this situation, role release may be confined to the paraeducators' production of educational materials in braille and the practice of skills taught by a qualified teacher of students with visual impairments. To use role release effectively, team members need to do the following:

◆ Keep the best interests of the student at the forefront; never sacrifice the student's needs for the principle of role release.

◆ Encourage parents and other team members to use skills related to visual impairment throughout the year, taking small steps first.

◆ Keep in close contact with team members to answer their questions or concerns about their new responsibilities.

Role Support. With role support, team members formally and informally encourage each other. For example, the O&M specialist assists the other team members when the student travels on established routes from the classroom to other areas of the school campus or the community. To provide appropriate role support, team members need to do these things:

◆ Communicate regularly about issues related to the other team members' participation with the student who is visually impaired.

◆ Remember that full participation is an ongoing process that requires a great commitment of time from all the team members; changes do not happen overnight.

◆ Continue to provide information and support to the other team members as their knowledge and skills increase. For example, putting a current article about an area of educational concern from a professional newsletter in a general education teacher's school mailbox can encourage the teacher to learn more about the subject and helps keep the lines of communication among the team members open.

STRATEGIES FOR SUPPORTING THE TEAM

Team members can use these specific strategies that support the collaborative team approach:

◆ Define the special language of each discipline. For example, a physical therapist may define *hypotonic* for the other team members and discuss its implications.

◆ Agree on methods of verbal and written communication.

◆ Attend regularly scheduled meetings. When regular attendance is not possible, the team decides on other ways to keep communication consistent.

◆ Keep a log of activities in the student's school and ask all the professionals who work with the student to record their interactions with the student and other adults. Figures 1.1, 1.2, 1.3, and 1.4 (presented previously) are examples of forms that may be used to keep records of activities and other data, such as team members' contact information, the results of assessments, notes on team meetings, and the results of activities.

◆ Agree that questions posed by team members will be answered in a consistent method.

◆ Establish other means of quick communication. For example, team members can exchange E-mail addresses and create address lists to automate the process of E-mailing each other about student concerns and issues. Fax numbers can also be exchanged.

Smith and Levack (1996) suggested these additional activities for expanding the role of team members:

◆ Use regularly scheduled observations of activities in which strategies have been role released to others.

♦ Review videotapes of activities when observations cannot be conducted in person.

♦ Keep a school-home notebook so that parents can ask questions and share information about the student's activities at home.

Even with the best intentions and all the strategies suggested here, team members sometimes have difficulty interacting with each other. In these situations, a teacher of students with visual impairments can use the following strategies to help get the team effort back on track:

♦ Make sure that team members have enough time to talk to each other. Rushed conversations can lead to misunderstandings.

♦ Bring in an outside mediator during discussions. Sometimes a person with a fresh perspective can help team members communicate more effectively.

♦ Ask team members to write out their concerns before a meeting. Written notes help focus discussions.

♦ Refocus the team on the needs of the student.

BUILDING TEAMWORK

Partnerships and teamwork among professionals who work with students with visual impairments are recognized as indicators of best practice in providing services to students with disabilities (Rainforth, York, & Macdonald, 1992). The student with a visual impairment will benefit educationally from a team of professionals from different disciplines who know how to move in and out of their roles on the team smoothly without feeling ambiguous about the role transitions. For example, the teacher of students with visual impairments is qualified to conduct specialized assessments and instruction in the areas of sensory and adaptive skill functioning and material and environmental adaptations. His or her ability to help

other team members make use of the resulting information through effective communication and the collaborative-consultative techniques desribed in this chapter—such as role extension, enrichment, expansion, exchange, release, and support—will benefit the student.

The following list of special considerations is important for building teamwork among professionals who are working with students with visual impairments:

♦ Provide accessible materials for all team members and attend to the need for such accommodations as braille copies, assistive technology, optical devices, and tactile graphics. Records of team proceedings and student notes can be provided in a variety of formats depending on team member needs and on the activities to be accomplished.

♦ Communicate with eye care specialists. Team members need information about the student's eye health status prior to developing an educational program. If the eye condition is deteriorating, team members must know the status of the condition to determine how it may affect the student's educational program. Feedback to the low vision clinician about a prescribed device is recommended to decide how effectively the device is being used and what if any changes are needed.

♦ Select learning and literacy media for the student. All team members, including parents, can contribute to this process. This assessment is critical to planning the student's educational program and guides the team in making deliberate and informed decisions for instructional materials and media (see Chapter 4 for additional information).

♦ Determine the level of influence of visual or other disabilities on the student's learning. Team members need to discuss the results of their assessments and determine if the visual impairment is affecting the student's ability to learn or if a delay in learning is primarily due to a motor, cognitive, or other learning disability. In the case of the latter, other professionals will play a major role in developing a student's educational program.

◆ Engage in frequent communication among all teachers, parents, dormitory staff (in specialized schools), paraeducators, and related service specialists. Such communication will assure consistent instruction and prevent misunderstandings.

◆ Decide how the core (e.g., mathematics, social studies) and expanded core curricula (e.g., adaptive living skills; visual efficiency training; career and transition education; social, recreation, and leisure O&M skills; and use of assistive technology) will be taught to the student (see Chapter 6 for additional information).

SUMMARY

Developing a successful team is both challenging and rewarding. Parents, educators, and related service personnel do not singularly possess all the information and skills necessary to meet the varied needs of students with visual impairments. The collective contributions of parents and other team members from a range of disciplines are an important aspect of ensuring that all students achieve their maximum potential.

The remainder of this volume presents strategies for conducting meaningful assessments and for implementing effective educational programs for students with visual impairments. Although much of the information in the chapters focuses on the teacher of students with visual impairments, all educational programs should be implemented through collaborative teaming.

ACTIVITIES

1. Compile a resource notebook or file containing useful information to share with parents, general education teachers, and other professionals.

2. Consider carefully the four types of roles that team members play (the supportive role, the facilitative role, the informative role, and the prescriptive role). Describe two examples of ways that teachers of students with visual impairments could function in each role.

3. Review the list of skills that enhance communication and behaviors that inhibit communication. Keep a journal for two weeks, making note of daily examples of enhancing or inhibiting behaviors and the impact of these behaviors on communication.

4. Make a list of appropriate ways to increase your knowledge or expertise. Pick one role-extension activity and do it. This activity could involve joining a professional organization, attending a professional conference, reading and reviewing an article in a professional journal, among other activities.

5. Interview an experienced teacher of students with visual impairments. Ask the teacher to share strategies that have been helpful in maintaining effective communication with other team members. Also ask the teacher for two or more situations in which communication was difficult and the solutions that were used to improve team interactions. Share this information with your classmates.

REFERENCES

Appleby, D. G., & Winder, A. E. (1977). An evolving definition of collaboration and some implications for the world of work. *Journal of Applied Behavioral Service, 13,* 279–291.

Campbell, P. H. (1987). The integrated programming team: An approach for coordinating professionals of various disciplines in programs for students with severe and multiple disabilities. *Journal of the Association for Persons with Severe Handicaps, 12,* 107–116.

Ferrell, K. A. (1985). *Reach out and teach.* New York: American Foundation for the Blind.

Friend, M., & Cook, L. (1992). *Interactions. Collaboration skills for school professionals.* New York: Longman.

Garland, C., McGonigel, M., Frank, A., & Buck, D. (1989). *The transdisciplinary model of service delivery.* Lightfoot, VA: Child Development Resource.

Hazekamp, J., & Huebner, K. M. (Eds.). (1989). *Program planning and evaluation for blind and visually impaired students: National guidelines for educational excellence.* New York: American Foundation for the Blind.

Hudson, L. J. (1997). *Classroom collaboration.* Watertown, MA: Perkins School for the Blind.

Johnson, D. W., & Johnson R. T. (1987a). *Joining together: Group theory and skills* (2nd ed.). Englewood Cliffs, NJ: Prentice Hall.

Johnson, D. W., & Johnson, R. T. (1987b). *Learning together and alone: Cooperation, competition, and individualization* (2nd ed). Englewood Cliffs. NJ: Prentice Hall.

Miller, C., & Levack, N. (1997). *A paraprofessional's handbook for working with students who are visually impaiered.* Austin: Texas School for the Blind and Visually Impaired.

Olmstead, J. E. (1991). *Itinerant teaching: Tricks of the trade for teachers of blind and visually impaired students.* New York: American Foundation for the Blind.

Pugach, M. C., & Johnson, L. J. (1995). *Collaborative practitioners, collaborative schools.* Denver, CO: Love.

Pugh, G., & Erin, J. N. (Eds.). (1999). *Blind and visually impaired students: Educational service guidelines.* Watertown, MA: Perkins School for the Blind.

Rainforth, B., York, J., & Macdonald, C. (1992). *Collaborative teams for students with severe disabilities: Integrating therapy and educational services.* Baltimore, MD: Paul H. Brookes.

Smith, M., & Levack, N. (1996). *Teaching students with visual and multiple impairments: A resource guide.* Austin: Texas School for the Blind and Visually Impaired.

Thousand, J. S., & Villa, R. A. (1992). Collaborative teams: A powerful tool in school restructuring. In R. A. Villa, J. S. Thousand, W. Stainback, & S. Stainback (Eds.), *Restructure for caring and effective education: An administrative guide to creating heterogeneous schools* (pp. 73–108). Baltimore, MD: Paul H. Brookes.

Torres, I., & Corn, A. L. (1990). *When you have a visually handicapped child in your classroom: Suggestions for teachers.* New York: American Foundation for the Blind.

Vandercook, T., & York, J. (1990). A team approach to program development and support. In W. Stainback, & S. Stainback (Eds.), *Support networks for inclusive schooling: Interdependent integrated education* (pp. 95–122). Baltimore, MD: Paul H. Brookes.

Villa, R. A., Thousand, J., Paolucci-Whitcomb, P., & Nevin, A. (1990). In search of a new paradigm for collaborative consultation. *Journal of Educational and Psychological Consultation, 1,* 23–40.

Wood, M. (1998). Whose job is it anyway? Educational roles in inclusion. *Exceptional Children, 64,* 181–195.

R E S O U R C E S

Suggested Resources for Creating and Nurturing Effective Educational Teams

Resource	Type	Source	Description
Blind and Visually Impaired Students: Educational Service Guidelines (Pugh & Erin, 1999)	Book	Perkins School for the Blind Watertown (through the National Association of Special Education Directors)	Policy statement of best practices compiled by groups of professionals in the field of visual impairment. Manual for sharing with administrators in public schools who may be unaware of the needs of students who are blind or visually impaired.
Classroom Collaboration (Hudson, 1997)	Book	Perkins School for the Blind	Practical strategies for including students with visual impairments in general education classrooms using collaborative consultation.
Itinerant Teaching: Tricks of the Trade for Teachers of Blind and Visually Impaired Students (Olmstead, 1991)	Book	American Foundation for the Blind	Practical suggestions for the teacher of students with visual impairments, including "Relationships and responsibilities in schools" and "Your rights in schools."
Paraprofessional's Handbook for Working with Students Who Are Visually Impaired (Miller & Levack, 1997)	Book	Texas School for the Blind and Visually Impaired	Basic information for paraeducators who work with students with visual impairments Addresses their role in social skills, daily living skills, orientation and mobility skills, technology, adaptation of materials, and working with students with multiple impairments.

(continued on next page)

Suggested Resources (*Continued*)

Resource	Type	Source	Description
Program Planning and Evaluation for Blind and Visually Impaired Students: National Guidelines for Educational Excellence (Hazekamp & Huebner, 1989)	Book	American Foundation for the Blind	Guidelines that are designed as a tool to help those involved in planning and providing services to students with visual impairments to develop more effective programs. Among other topics, it addresses planning and providing instruction and services and organizing and supporting instruction and services.
Reach Out and Teach (Ferrell, 1985)	Book	American Foundation for the Blind	A two-part guide for preparing parents to teach infants and preschoolers with visual impairments, with an emphasis on collaboration between parents and professionals.
When You Have a Visually Handicapped Child in Your Classroom: Suggestions for Teachers (Torres & Corn, 1990)	Booklet	American Foundation for the Blind	A practical, easy-to-read booklet describing methods for including students who are visually impaired in general education classrooms. A useful resource to be shared with general education teachers in inclusive settings.

Contact information for each of the resources listed will be found in the Sources of Products, Materials, Equipment, and Services section at the back of this book.

CHAPTER 2

Comprehensive Assessment

Toni Heinze

KEY POINTS

- The assessment of students with visual impairments is a complex task that requires careful planning and consideration by members of the students' educational teams.

- Teachers of students with visual impairments help to select assessment instruments for various areas, depending on the purposes of the assessments and the needs of the students.

- Teachers of students with visual impairments conduct assessments in areas that are specifically related to students' visual impairments and assist other members of educational teams to adapt, conduct, and interpret their assessments of the students to ensure that the students receive meaningful and valid assessments.

- Most formal assessments are not standardized on a population that includes students with visual impairments, so the interpretation of results from formal assessments must be considered carefully.

- Using tests that present tasks without requiring major modification of format, presentation, content, or time can help the educational team gather information without penalizing the student's performance because of his or her visual impairment;

when such modifications are necessary, interpretation must carefully consider selection and their impact on results.

VIGNETTE

Ms. Lake, Matt's teacher of students with visual impairments, and Mr. Jensen, Matt's fifth grade teacher, looked at the papers on the table in front of them. The reports included the results of a statewide assessment and a diagnostic test called the KeyMath, along with an updated functional vision assessment and a learning media assessment. "I'm surprised at the results of the math section of the statewide assessment," Mr. Jensen noted. "Matt generally does well in math, but this test shows a grade level of 4.5. I would have expected it to be closer to grade level."

"Several things could have affected that score, and we'll need to interpret it very cautiously," Ms. Lake responded. She knew that the test had not included students with visual impairments in its standardization procedures, and that several modifications had been necessary. Based on the results of Matt's recently updated functional vision assessment, the print, pictures, symbols, and numbers on the statewide test had been enlarged, and Matt had used his magnifier as needed. He had also used his adjustable reading stand and lamp. In addition, Matt had been given extra time for the test. Since the testing had taken place over several days, however, he had been showing some fatigue by the time he got to the math section.

More recently, Ms. Lake had given Matt the Key-Math test, since the functional vision assessment had indicated that its visual presentation and many oral problems would be appropriate for him; the computation problems had been enlarged for him. Even though Matt had scored at grade level on the Key-Math, Ms. Lake pointed out that it was still relevant to his assessment for her and Mr. Jensen to determine the type and cause of Matt's difficulties. On the Key-Math, Ms. Lake observed, Matt had difficulty with confusing symbols on some computation problems and with measurement and money combinations. "This may reflect Matt's difficulty with small detail, like the math symbols," she suggested, "even though he did use his magnifier and the problems were enlarged. His limited real experience using money may also be a factor. He rarely does any shopping on his own. Matt also likes to work fast, and sometimes he skips over symbols too quickly."

Mr. Jensen looked over the reading and language arts section on the statewide test. "Matt did fine, right at grade level, on comprehension. But he seemed to make a variety of errors in using word analysis skills." "Yes," Ms. Lake added, "and he also had some difficulty picking up differences in similar punctuation marks. Calling his attention to these and encouraging the use of his magnifier should help Matt with these and with the math symbols." "That seems in agreement with the curriculum-based assessments we've been using," observed Mr. Jensen, "While the statewide test gave us some information about Matt's general grade level in this area, and a little data on problem areas, it also raised several questions about Matt's specific reading and language arts performance. I'd like us to do an informal reading inventory with Matt to get a closer look at some of these areas. We could work together to make sure it was in a good format for Matt." "That sounds great," agreed Ms. Lake, "In fact, the Johns Informal Reading Inventory is available in large print; that along with his reading stand, lamp, and low vision device should work well for Matt."

Ms. Lake continued, "While Matt's functional vision assessment and learning media assessment did not indicate a need for change in his learning or reading media, I am concerned that he is still missing several details, and his math and reading assignments will be getting more involved and the print smaller in size, so his parents and I have discussed having a clinical low vision evaluation done to see what additional low vision aids might be helpful to him." "Our working together is really important," observed Mr. Jensen, "There's sure a lot more to assessment than looking at the overall score from one test!"

INTRODUCTION

All students enrolled in education programs undergo regular assessments of their progress. In some cases, they are given state-mandated tests that provide information about how they are progressing in all subject areas compared to their classmates and other students of the same age. Students with visual impairments have unique challenges in relation to formal academic assessments. First, tests that address the assessment questions and the students' needs must be selected. Second, the students must be provided with appropriate modifications of the assessment materials, such as braille or large-print copies of tests or a series of tactile graphics for material included in the tests. Third, educators must ensure that the students have time to complete the assessments. Fourth, the interpretation of the results must take into consideration the students' need for and provision of modified materials and time allotments. Since many tests that are used in schools are not standardized on a population of students with visual impairments, the interpretation of test data is crucial. All these important issues must be examined by the students' educational team during the assessment process.

This chapter begins with a discussion of the role of the teacher of students with visual impairments in the assessment process. It then presents the various reasons for conducting assessments, followed by a discussion of the sequence of the assessment process, types of assessments, and modifications of formal assessments for use with students who are visually impaired. The chapter concludes with a look at the various areas that require assessment and some examples of assessments that are used with students who have visual impairments.

ROLE OF THE TEACHER OF STUDENTS WITH VISUAL IMPAIRMENTS

The teacher of students with visual impairments has a multifaceted role in the assessment process. First, he or she is the primary evaluator of all the skills that are specifically related to the student's visual impairment. These areas include, but are not limited to, the functional vision assessment (the evaluation of the student's use of remaining vision); the learning media assessment (the determination of the most appropriate learning and literacy media); braille reading and writing; the student's potential for using assistive technology; and the use of other aids, such as the abacus and tactile displays. In these cases, the teacher of students with visual impairments conducts special assessments, makes adaptations, interprets results, and shares information with the other members of the educational team to determine the student's eligibility for special services, establish goals for teaching, or monitor the student's progress. Chapter 4 contains more information about these specialized assessments.

The teacher of students with visual impairments also plays an important collaborative role with other members of the student's assessment team. In general, he or she shares information with colleagues about the impact of the visual impairment on learning and assessment, assists with the selection of appropriate assessment tools, makes necessary adaptations to assessment tools to make them accessible to students with visual impairments, and assists with the interpretation of the results of the assessment and their implications. For example, the teacher of students with visual impairments may collaborate with various team members as follows:

◆ Classroom teachers: determining the accessibility of and making adaptations to curriculum-based and other classroom assessment activities.

◆ School psychologists: assisting with the selection of appropriate assessment tools on the basis of visual characteristics and with the adaptations that may be necessary and sharing information about the impact of the student's ocular condition, experiential background, and concept development.

◆ Speech and language therapists: providing information on the impact of visual impairment on concept and language development, determining the appropriate use of pictures, helping to design communication boards, assisting with selections and adaptations of other assistive technology devices, and helping to select assessment tools.

◆ Physical therapists: providing information about the impact of a visual impairment on motor development and assisting with the selection of objects and environments that motivate and facilitate the development of movement skills.

PURPOSE OF ASSESSMENT

"Assessment is the process of collecting data for the purpose of making appropriate decisions about students" (Salvia & Ysseldyke, 1995, p. 5). Specifically, information collected during assessments is used in making decisions related to screening, eligibility, development of Individualized Education Programs (IEPs), placement, monitoring students' progress, and general program accountability. These decisions ultimately should make a positive difference in students' educational experiences and opportunities and in the quality of their lives; otherwise, the assessment process has no real value.

Tests used in the assessment process can be formal or informal and norm referenced or criterion referenced, as explained in the next section. They can involve the performance of tasks, systematic observation, and/or a collection of a student's work over time. Just as the specific purposes of assessment can vary, so can the purposes of specific assessment tools. For example, one test may compare one student to other students of a similar age or grade in academic subjects, while another may identify the steps of a skill that the student has mastered versus those that he or she has not.

An appropriate match must be made between the purpose of conducting the assessment and the tools used to gather the information. To determine the appropriate selection, use, and interpretation of formal or informal tests and procedures, the teacher or evaluator must understand several major characteristics of these assessment tools.

IDEA GUIDELINES AND IMPLICATIONS

The 1997 amendments to the Individuals with Disabilities Education Act (IDEA), or P.L. 105–17, include several references to assessment, with respect to screening, initial evaluation of eligibility for special services, and data collection for the development of IEPs, placement in appropriate programs, and for monitoring students' progress. Several major guidelines in IDEA that relate to the assessment of students with visual impairments are these:

♦ A variety of assessment tools must be used. Tools for assessing a student's performance may not be limited to formal, standardized tests.

♦ The tests that are used must be technically sound and valid for the specific purposes for which they are used.

♦ Both the parents and a team of qualified professionals must participate in determining the student's eligibility for special services.

♦ Students must participate in state and local assessments with accommodations when necessary. If it is not possible to provide these accommodations, the state must de-

velop alternate assessments. (States must report the performance of students with disabilities on required assessments or the student's performance on alternate assessments if these assessments are determined to be necessary.)

♦ An IEP must include a statement of any individual modifications used in the administration of district-wide assessments of a student's achievement that are needed for the student to participate in such assessment. If the IEP team determines that the student will not participate in a particular state- or district-wide assessment of achievement, it must provide a statement of why that assessment is not appropriate for the student and how the student will be assessed (Maloney, 1997).

♦ In addition to a special education teacher, the IEP team must include an individual who can interpret the instructional implications of the results of the evaluation.

♦ Every three years, the IEP team must review the evaluation data on a student and, on the basis of these data and input from the parents, identify what additional information, if any, is needed (NICHCY, 1997).

♦ The state must establish goals for the performance of students with disabilities and develop indicators to judge the students' progress.

♦ After evaluating the reading and writing skills, needs, and media, as well as future needs for braille of a student who is visually impaired, the IEP team will determine if braille instruction is appropriate (NICHCY, 1997).

These requirements of IDEA have both direct and indirect implications for teachers of students with visual impairments. They will be directly involved in assessments of functional vision, communication skills (including learning and literacy media), concept development and academic skills, independent living skills, and the need for assistive technology and environmental modifications for developing IEPs, determining teaching approaches, and monitoring progress. They will be indirectly involved when collaborating with general and special education teachers, orientation and mobility (O&M) specialists, therapists, psychologists, psychometrists, and screeners to select appropriate tools and modifications.

In this chapter, the term "evaluator" will refer to the individual responsible for the assessment being discussed; in most cases this will be the teacher of students with visual impairments, but in some cases, it may be a psychologist, O&M specialist, therapist, or classroom teacher. The term "screeners" refers to those who perform preliminary testing to determine the need for further examination.

PROCESS AND SEQUENCE OF ASSESSMENT

There are eight steps in the process of assessing students with visual impairments:

1. Identify the reason for the assessment,
2. Gather background information,
3. Observe the student,
4. Develop an assessment plan,
5. Conduct the assessment,
6. Integrate and interpret information,
7. Make recommendations for intervention, and
8. Monitor the student's progress.

The manner in which the individual steps are approached depends primarily on the purpose or purposes of an assessment. For example, if the purpose is to make an initial determination of a student's eligibility for services, the design of a program, or a major change in services, then a comprehensive assessment would require evaluating all skills and abilities that are pertinent to the student's education. If the evaluation is intended to update information on a specific skill, however, then that area should be the focus, rather than testing other areas unnecessarily (Hall, Scholl, &

Swallow, 1986). The steps in the assessment process are discussed in the following sections.

Identify the Reason for the Assessment

The first step in an assessment of a student is to identify the specific reason for or purpose of the assessment. To do so, members of the student's educational team meet to discuss the reason for conducting the assessment. They must agree on the scope and purpose of the assessment, so the appropriate assessment approach and tools can be identified and an assessment plan can be developed.

If the reason for the evaluation is to determine eligibility for services, the team typically begins with the results of an ocular report, followed by a functional vision assessment, a learning media assessment (these assessments are discussed in Chapter 4), and an educational team case study. Once eligibility is determined, considerable information is necessary to develop the student's IEP and to determine the type and number of services to be provided, the appropriate placement option, and a plan for ongoing monitoring of the student's progress. Furthermore, at any time during the student's program, the student can be referred for evaluations of a variety of specific skill areas, depending on additional questions or concerns identified by the team members, including the parents, such as whether there are additional learning problems that are affecting the child's progress or whether a change in vision necessitates a change in reading media or assistive technology. In these cases, the more specifically the question or concern can be articulated, the more efficient the type and degree of assessment is likely to be (Hall et al., 1986).

Gather Background Information

Usually, some relevant information about the student is available to the evaluator, and this information can be helpful in determining what assessments should be conducted. For example, current ocular and medical reports can provide information about the student's eye condition and its stability; additional disabilities that may be present; and medications, therapies, and positioning that are relevant. A current functional vision evaluation or clinical low vision evaluation can provide important information for determining goals and objectives, and which tools and approaches would be most appropriate for any additional testing that is deemed necessary.

Another source of valuable background information is interviews with parents, general and special education teachers, various therapists (including the occupational therapist and the physical therapist) and other professionals. These interviews can provide insights that may not be otherwise available to the evaluator. Interviews can also raise pertinent questions that should be addressed in the assessment.

Observe the Student

Observations of the student in his or her classroom, home, and other relevant settings is an extremely important technique for gathering information. Such observations should be structured to address issues that may have already been identified or that may be relevant to the purpose of the evaluation and should be flexible enough to gather unexpected information. (See Chapter 3 for more information on conducting observations.)

With regard to a student's functional vision, for example, observation could provide initial information about the impact of environmental variables and the student's ability to handle a variety of materials and tasks he or she is confronted with daily. A carefully thought-out observation also provides information about the student's social interactions and independent living skills, as well as about the student's performance in relevant natural settings. In addition, the observation provides valuable assistance in planning further assessment, identifying specific areas to be assessed, and selecting appropriate tools and approaches. Not only is observation an essential early step in the assessment process, it is also a critical source of information during the administration of formal tests. In addition to specific item responses and scores when appropriate, the evaluator can gain valuable information by observing the student's problem-solving approaches, attention span, and handling of frustration and other behaviors that have an impact on the student's performance on tests and implications for the student's general performance.

Develop an Assessment Plan

On the basis of the background information that was gathered, and guided by the reasons for the assessment, the assessment team develops an assessment plan. During this team process, the teacher of students with visual impairments collaborates with other team members, especially the school psychologist or educational diagnostician, but also the parents, general and special education teachers, and various therapists, to determine appropriate assessment tools and strategies to use to gather needed information. Another key part of the planning process is modifying any tests or procedures that will be used in the assessment.

Again, the reasons for the assessment determine the approach that is taken. If an initial IEP must be developed and placement decisions must be made, a comprehensive assessment and team approach are necessary to identify appropriate goals and service options. A comprehensive assessment involves examining multiple areas as appropriate, such as functional vision, learning media, cognitive ability, language and academic achievement, orientation and mobility (O&M), and independent living skills, and using multiple assessment tools and multiple sources of information. Each member of the educational team conducts an assessment in his or her particular area of expertise, shares information about the results, and contributes to the interpretation of these results and their implications for services and programming.

Especially in the case of a comprehensive evaluation, conducting the functional vision assessment and learning media assessment early enables the evaluators to identify goals in these areas, determine additional specific areas that need to be assessed, and make appropriate environmental and testing modifications (see Chapter 4). For example, the functional vision assessment identifies the student's needs with regard to lighting and print size, ability to use pictures and print in testing situations, and types of devices required for accessibility to printed information. It also identifies skill areas that warrant specific training, such as visual motor skills for daily living or writing tasks, or the use of specific low vision devices or eccentric viewing techniques.

The learning media assessment identifies the student's best learning and response channels and needs for reading media—that is, whether visual or tactile assessment approaches, braille or print materials, pictures, tactile graphics or manipulatives are necessary for appropriate testing. In addition, these assessments help the evaluator identify the skills that must be further assessed, such as specific reading and listening skills, and the student's efficiency with assistive technology. In this respect, conducting these specialized assessments assists in the planning process. This information can then be shared with team members, and the additional areas of assessment can be addressed. If the purpose of the assessment is to monitor progress or changes in a particular area, then tasks and tools specific to that area are needed; such specific assessments are usually carried out by the teachers of students with visual impairments, the O&M specialists, or the classroom teacher.

As discussed later in this chapter, the evaluator must be especially cautious when using formal tests, particularly norm-referenced tests. Few such tests are available whose design or standardization has involved students with visual impairments (Bradley-Johnson, 1994; Hall et al., 1986). The teacher of students with visual impairments may need to collaborate with the school psychologist, the physical therapist, the low vision clinician, the O&M specialist, and others to help select the most appropriate tools, to present assessment tasks appropriately, to elicit the most accurate information from students, and to interpret the information that is gathered.

IDEA requires that tests must be valid for their intended purpose. The selection of technically adequate tests and the careful consideration of the impact of various modifications on reliability and validity will help to ensure that the assessment of the student with visual impairments is appropriate. This is most likely to be successful when team members work together.

Another approach that is both logical and mandated by IDEA is the use of information gathered by way of a variety of tools and techniques. Such an approach increases the likelihood that the team will identify a broader and more representative sample of the student's abilities and that its decisions will not be made on the basis of limited and possibly inaccurate information.

Conduct the Assessment

With appropriate and thorough planning, the actual assessment should proceed smoothly. As was mentioned earlier, the purpose of the assessment determines its type and breadth and the team members who are to be involved. In some cases, the teacher of students with visual impairments may be the primary evaluator, such as for the functional vision assessment and the learning media assessment (though parts of these assessments are likely to involve general education and special education teachers, parents, various therapists, or the assistive technology specialist), or for assessments of specific skills like braille reading and writing, using an abacus, or using low vision devices and assistive technology related to the visual impairment.

When conducting a comprehensive evaluation or reevaluating several areas for an annual review, the teacher of students with visual impairments collaborates with other team members with expertise in specific areas. For example, the specialist works with a psychologist to evaluate the student's cognitive ability and possible specific learning difficulties; the general education teacher, to evaluate the student's general academic skills using formal or curriculum-based measures; physical and/or occupational therapists, to evaluate the student's motor skills and positions that may be necessary for optimum functioning; parents, to evaluate the student's independent living skills and functional vision; the O&M specialist, to assess the student's orientation skills and safe and efficient movement skills around the school. The specialist's collaborative role also includes ensuring that the necessary environmental modifications (including lighting, writing materials, adapted displays, and low vision devices) are available for the student. If tactile graphics, braille materials, or other specialized materials or equipment are needed, the teacher of students with visual impairments may conduct formal and informal academic assessments in collaboration with the general education teacher. (See Chapter 5 for a detailed discussion of the adaptation and modification of instructional materials.) In addition to actually conducting specific assessments, the specialist needs to be involved throughout the direct assessment to answer questions from the other team members, provide insights into observed behaviors, or suggest further modifications. He or she can also provide insights into the student's behavior or performance (such as the student's limited experience with certain types of situations or difficulties with cause and effect or part-whole concepts).

Although the assessment plan should guide the process, it should be flexible enough to be modified if necessary. If the team members find, during the course of the assessment, that additional information is required, they should be able to include appropriate tests or techniques to gather this information.

There are several techniques that evaluators can use to facilitate the likelihood that the student will have an optimum testing experience. Such an experience is one that is as fair and informative as possible without causing the student undue stress. Some general guidelines include these:

◆ Become familiar with the assessment procedures and materials to be used.

◆ Ensure that appropriate environmental and procedural modifications (such as appropriate lighting and furniture, the lack of visual or auditory distractions, and postural supports for students with motor impairments) are provided.

◆ Confirm beforehand the student's ability to use any modifications of materials or equipment (such as the Nemeth Code and tactile displays) that seem to be appropriate.

◆ Establish rapport with the student before the assessment if the student is unfamiliar with the evaluator; this can be done during an earlier observation, by having the student give the evaluator a brief tour of a familiar area of the school, or through another such activity.

◆ Give the student an initial orientation to the testing area. This orientation provides a further opportunity to establish rapport.

◆ Give the student appropriate information about the assessment and its purpose.

◆ Allow the student to become familiar with the materials to be used and the field (work area in which test materials may be placed) for which he or she is responsible. Work trays or mats may help to define this field for the student, thereby facilitating efficient searching, checking, or arranging of materials as needed.

◆ Encourage the student without suggesting answers or being too specific about the correctness of his or her answers.

◆ Avoid physical intrusion by first asking permission or announcing ahead of time your intent to physically interact with the student (by saying, for example, "May I take your hand?" or "Let me take your hand"). Such physical contact may be necessary to demonstrate tasks, orient to the work field, and so on. Asking permission prior to physical contact is important for all students.

◆ Avoid timed tests unless timed proficiency is relevant to the purpose of the assessment.

◆ Be alert to the student's fatigue and the possible need to conduct the assessment process over multiple sessions.

Integrate and Interpret Information

When forming conclusions from information gathered during the assessment, the evaluator must keep several points in mind. First, interpretations must take into account factors related to the student's visual impairment, including the amount of vision, age at onset, implications for a learning approach, and background experiences. Any modifications that were made to the testing procedure and interpretive cautions or limitations of the assessment tools, especially as a result of modifications or a limited norming sample, must also be reported.

Second, when the student's performance is described, specific examples should be presented and applications to functional situations should be included when possible. If a comprehensive evaluation was conducted, the team members need to review all the assessment results and discuss and decide on possible intervention strategies. The teacher of students with visual impairments shares his or her expertise regarding special assessments that he or she has carried out, the impact of the student's visual impairment on learning and performance, and necessary modifications that were made to the assessment process.

Make Recommendations for Intervention

Recommendations made by the assessment team may be related to the type and number of services, the development of goals and objectives for the student's IEP, and the determination of the student's placement. They may also involve the determination of the student's learning and literacy media and any special environmental modifications or special equipment and aids that are deemed appropriate. The recommendations should be written with sufficient detail so that parents and other members of the educational team can use the information to make appropriate changes in the student's educational program.

Monitor the Student's Progress

Ongoing assessment documents the student's progress in achieving the goals and objectives of the IEP, the continued appropriateness of the student's program and services, and identifies when modifications of the student's program may be necessary. This ongoing assessment may involve formal tools, but is more likely to involve such informal tools as criterion-referenced tests, checklists for specific skills, curriculum-based measures, and the student and teacher evaluation components of a prescriptive teaching approach. (See Chapter 3 for more information on informal assessment techniques.)

TYPES OF ASSESSMENTS

Assessment tools and approaches have many different characteristics, some of which have important implications for their use with students with visual impairments. A description of several major types of assessment instruments follows.

Formal and Informal Tests

Formal tests are those that require careful adherence to directions for their administration and scoring. They provide a numerical or quantitative score that is often compared to the scores of a particular group and they may have time limits (Hall et al., 1986). These tests typically include norm-referenced and standardized tests (described later in this section). The appropriateness and usefulness of such tests is dependent on the similarity of the student to the standardization sample, the adaptations that may have been made (time limits, partial administration, and the use of different materials), and the skill of the evaluator.

Few formal instruments are designed specifically for students with visual impairments or can be used with this population without modifications in their administration and interpretation. However, formal tests can be used appropriately if the following guidelines are adhered to:

- Comparisons are made for appropriate purposes (for example, a performance range is needed to determine a student's placement at a particular grade level);

- Necessary modifications do not significantly change the content of the test; and

- Interpretation is cautious, relying on an analysis of the student's performance, rather than only examining the test scores.

Information gained from such tests could then have practical diagnostic value by identifying areas for which additional probes are needed.

However, since most formal tests have not included students with visual impairments in their standardization populations and many such tests require considerable modifications for use with these students, the appropriate use of such tests can be significantly jeopardized. Furthermore, the types of comparisons made, whether valid or invalid, may have limited value for a student with visual impairments and his or her educational program. The evaluator must weigh the advantages and disadvantages carefully when considering the use of formal tests.

Informal tests, on the other hand, often provide much more practical information that can be applied to develop instructional goals and objectives and to monitor the student's progress in achieving them. Informal tests and assessment tools allow for more flexibility regarding the manner in which they are administered. No time limits are required, although proficiency in completing a task or skill may be a factor. These tests and tools include many criterion-referenced tests, portfolio collections, observation techniques, and checklists (as discussed in Chapter 3). Their results are described in a qualitative, rather than a quantitative, manner. The validity and reliability of such tools—that is, the extent to which a test consistently measures what it is supposed to measure—depend, to a great extent, on the skill of the evaluator (Hall et al., 1986). These factors are explained in detail later.

Verbal and Performance Tests

Verbal tests rely on verbal presentations of questions, problems, or directions and require verbal responses from the student. The following are examples of verbal items:

- "Repeat after me . . . ,"
- "Tell me what you would do if . . . ,"
- "What does ＿＿ mean?"

Tests that are completely verbal can inaccurately depict the abilities of students with visual impairments because the students may not have the necessary language to respond to the test items or may use language for which they do not really have a conceptual understanding.

Performance tests are those in which students actually carry out activities to demonstrate their ability, and directions are often modeled for the students. Copying, arranging pictures in a particular order, and identifying specific characteristics of pictures or objects are examples of performance items. Since many performance items are presented visually, they are often omitted or modified for students with visual impairments. In such cases, the validity may be seriously jeopardized because only part of the test is given, and the evaluator must exercise caution in interpreting the student's overall abilities.

Aside from the problems associated with visually oriented performance items on formal tests, performance tasks are an appropriate type of assessment for students with visual impairments. They provide the most accurate way for students to demonstrate their real understanding of many concepts or skills that could not otherwise be evaluated. For example, a student can read about a concept or listen to a description of it and repeat that information in a verbal test, but with limited or no access to pictures, demonstrations, incidental observation, or personal experience, the student may have no real understanding of the concept. Many concepts and skills related to science, O&M, daily living skills, and other areas require the assessment of performance tasks.

Group and Individual Tests

Group tests are designed to be administered to more than one individual at a time. Although they may also be administered individually and such a practice is likely to provide more discrete qualitative information, the reliability can be affected because the tests were designed to be administered in a group setting.

Individual tests are administered on a one-to-one basis, which allows for more careful attention to an individual student's performance and behavior. Generally, individual assessment approaches are more appropriate for students with visual impairments, since they allow the examiner to observe the student's behavior, consider factors that may be influencing the student's performance, and identify areas for follow-up assessment or diagnostic teaching.

Standardized and Nonstandardized Tests

Standardized tests are formal instruments that have been standardized with regard to the manner in which they are administered and the population to which they relate. First, the administration procedures of standardized tests must be carried out consistently according to specific guidelines. Second, standardized instruments have been administered to large groups of individuals with similar backgrounds and demographic characteristics, and norms are then determined on the basis of the results with this population. The results obtained from students who subsequently took the test are then compared with those norms.

Nonstandardized tests do not have rigid administration procedures and do not provide norms for comparison or interpretation. These tests are generally considered to be informal assessment tools, as described in Chapter 3. Although nonstandardized tests generally have guidelines for administration, the evaluator is not held to specific standardized procedures and has more leeway for individualization. For this reason,

nonstandardized tests are typically more useful in assessing students who are blind or visually impaired.

Norm-referenced and Criterion-referenced Tests

When a student's performance on a standardized test is compared to that of the larger group on which the test was standardized, the test is considered norm referenced. In such cases, it is essential that the student's demographic characteristics are similar to those of the standardization sample and that the test is administered in a manner similar to the way in which it was administered to that norming group. If this is not the case, the validity and reliability of the test results (discussed in the next section) are questionable.

When students who are blind or visually impaired are included in a norming sample, demographic information should include the severity and age at onset of the visual impairment; reading mode, if appropriate; presence of additional impairments; and other relevant characteristics. Often, students with visual impairments are not included in the norming sample on standardized tests or may require significant modifications to the test-administration procedures and materials. In such cases, the evaluator must exercise caution when interpreting the results, relying on a careful analysis of the student's performance in relation to the type of task involved and the purpose for which the test was given, rather than solely on the test scores themselves. Such an analysis may or may not provide useful information on the student's abilities, services needed, or appropriate goals.

Criterion-referenced tests compare the student's performance to the overall mastery of the skill being evaluated; they can be either formal or informal. Success is judged against a predetermined level of mastery, often expressed in percentages. For example, *instructional level* usually suggests that the student is able to perform a skill with supports, such as the teacher's guidance, models, and examples. *Independent level* usually suggests that the student would be able to use a given skill on his or her own without the supports just described (and could be expected to use this skill in independent practice or homework). Another term for the acquisition of skills, *mastery level*, usually suggests that the student can use the skill independently and apply it to new situations as called for (Salvia & Ysseldyke, 1995). When percentages are used, they are often arbitrarily set and must be considered carefully when used as guidelines. For example, in the area of reading, a mastery level of 90 percent may be acceptable, but in the area of O&M, a 90 percent success rate in crossing busy streets safely and independently would not be considered mastery. In addition, since criterion-referenced tools are usually designed according to the scope and sequence of the skill area being evaluated, they can provide helpful guidelines as to the next level of the skill to target for instruction. Thus, these types of tests are often more useful in determining goals and objectives and in assessing progress in skill areas for students with visual impairments (Curry & Russo, 1998). The evaluator must also exercise caution in using these types of tools by carefully considering whether the skill in question and the sequence in which it is presented are appropriate for a particular student.

VALIDITY AND RELIABILITY

In addition to knowing something about the characteristics of different types of tests, evaluators should also have a fundamental understanding and appreciation of several basic concepts related to the design of tests. In particular, they should understand validity and reliability because any changes in standard procedures to formal tests will have an impact on these two factors.

Validity

The validity of a test refers to how well the test measures what it purports to measure, that is, how well it does what it says it will do. There are several different methods of determining validity. Each method can be important, depending on the specific reason for using the test.

Criterion-related Validity

Criterion-related validity is determined by comparing scores on the test with other criteria that are considered indicators of the same trait or skill as that which is to be measured (Overton, 1992). Two types of criterion-related validity are concurrent validity and predictive validity.

Concurrent validity is determined by comparing the student's performance on two or more tests within a short period, usually within a day. Of course, the multiple tests used to establish concurrent validity would be chosen because they purport to measure similar skills. If the coefficient is high (that is, if the student performs similarly on both tests), the evaluator can have some confidence that both tests are measuring similar skills.

Predictive validity refers to a test's ability to predict a student's success in a related area at a later time. For example, screening tests or aptitude tests are used to make predictions about how well a student will perform in particular areas, such as school or vocational situations. When assessment tools are used to make decisions about a student's future success and opportunities, it is extremely important that these measures have strong and relevant predictive validity that is based on a strong research base and that this validity is not significantly compromised by modifications in administration.

Other Types of Validity

Content validity refers to how clearly the items sampled on the test represent the content that the test purports to measure (like reading, math, listening, and basic concepts). To have good content validity, a test must have a wide representation of items related to the content that it is attempting to measure. For example, a math test would need to have a range of math items across domains and levels of skills; it could not simply include addition and subtraction problems. Likewise, a reading test would have to include a range of domains and skill levels, rather than simply word-recognition items (Overton, 1992).

Construct validity describes a test's ability to measure certain psychological constructs, traits, or theoretical characteristics (Overton, 1992). Since these constructs (such as intelligence) are usually abstract and even hypothetical, they must usually be assessed by measuring the outcome, products, or results of the construct, rather than the construct itself. Determining construct validity may involve a variety of methods, including correlations with other tests (as with criterion-related validity), pre- and posttest comparisons, factor analysis, and so forth. Construct validity is relatively difficult to determine. However, this type of validity can be especially relevant in the use of formal tests with students with visual impairments, since changes in test items, materials, and administration can significantly alter what is actually being measured.

Reliability

The reliability of a test refers to the consistency with which a student's performance on it is repeated over multiple administrations across time. Reliability also refers to the consistent measuring of a skill across various items on the test. Therefore, reliability indicates the confidence that one can have in getting consistent results from a test over time. It is common to have some error present during any administration of a test, and this error can be estimated statistically. The careful evaluator looks for a test with a low estimate of error and a greater degree of reliability in order to choose the most adequate instrument (Overton, 1992).

Reliability can be tested and expressed in many ways, but an understanding of correlation is necessary to understand and discuss reliability. Correlation is a method of determining the degree of relationship among variables. The greater the degree of the relationship (or correlation) of the results of different administrations of the test, the more reliable the instrument. A statistically determined correlation coefficient can be used to express the direction and degree of the relationship.

There are three primary methods for determining reliability, all of which involve correlating two sets of scores from the same test or from parallel forms of a test. These methods include the following:

◆ *Test-retest reliability,* in which the same test is administered to a group of students within a short period (usually two to three weeks);

◆ *Equivalent-forms reliability,* in which the test developer prepared two equivalent forms of a test and students take each form within a short period; and

◆ *Split-half reliability,* in which two forms of a test are created from one test by splitting it in half (generally, odd-numbered items form one test and even-numbered items form the other).

Selecting Tests

Although the evaluator attempts to select a test with good validity and reliability as reported in the test manual, he or she must carefully consider its use with students who are blind or visually impaired. The fact that these students are not typically included in standardization procedures of formal tests, and that modifications of the test are likely to be needed, has a considerable impact on the validity, reliability, and appropriate use of a test. Several questions that the evaluator may ask when selecting assessment tools include these:

◆ What is the purpose of the assessment? What information is needed? What is the test purported to measure?

◆ Is the test accessible to the student so as not to penalize him or her because of the visual impairment? Would necessary modifications be possible that would still maintain the content validity of the test?

◆ Will the test provide relevant information about the student's abilities and instructional needs? That is, although scores may have limited value because of the limitations of the standardization process with regard to students with visual impairments, will an analysis of the student's performance provide useful information related to the purpose of the assessment?

MODIFYING FORMAL ASSESSMENTS

Categories of Tests

Assessment tools have many different characteristics and can be grouped according to how and for whom they were designed. For example, some tests are designed for students without disabilities, but are sometimes used with students with visual impairments without modifications. They may be used without modifications because their visual format, size, presentation, style, content, response format, and so on make them appropriate for gathering valid information without penalizing the student's performance because of his or her visual impairment. An example of such a test is *KeyMath Revised: A Diagnostic Inventory of Essential Mathematics* (Connolly, 1988). Its large print, high contrast, lack of clutter in its diagrams, vertical easel presentation, criterion-referenced design, and individual administration make it appropriate for some students with low vision. Its criterion-referenced design allows the evaluator to use the student's performance in a constructive way to identify the current level of skills and to determine logical goals and objectives in the math content area.

Other tests that were designed for students without disabilities may be used appropriately with students who are visually impaired if certain modifications are made. Such modifications may include enlarging the print, transcribing printed material into braille, or allowing more time to take the test. The KeyMath is an example of this category as well. The printed material has been transcribed into braille, and the pictures and diagrams have been simplified and modified into tactile dis-

plays (Duckworth & Willis, 1996), though this simplification somewhat limits the amount of information available to the student with a visual impairment. Again, the criterion-referenced design of the test allows the teacher to relate the student's performance to classroom skills and to identify specific goals in the area of mathematics. If the student is to use this modified version of the Key-Math test, however, it is critical that he or she knows the necessary Nemeth Code of Braille Mathematics to read the transcribed problems and is able to explore and read the tactile displays effectively. In addition, before the test is given, the evaluator needs to assess the student's use of the Nemeth Code itself, use of the abacus, and other special skills related to the visual impairment.

Tests can be grouped into still a third category—those that are designed specifically for students with visual impairments. Several obvious examples are tests that are designed to assess the student's functional vision. Other examples include tests that address areas of the expanded core curriculum (see Chapter 6) and tests of developmental skills that do not penalize students with visual impairments. Such tests present visual items in an optimum manner or omit them altogether, present items with well-thought-out tactile or auditory renditions, and include students with visual impairments in the norming or field test sample.

Types of Modifications

A variety of modifications can influence the accessibility and fairness of the testing experience for a student with a visual impairment. Several of these modifications are discussed in the following sections.

Materials

Students with low vision may need enlarged materials (such as large print and larger diagrams or pictures). Some tests are available in a larger format from the test's publisher or from the American Printing House for the Blind (APH; see the Resources for this chapter and at the end of this volume). Informal materials can sometimes be enlarged by using copying machines, as long as high-quality and sufficient contrast can be provided. Low vision devices, including magnifiers and closed-circuit televisions (CCTVs), can also be used to provide enlarged images, as can computer technology, in the form of scanners, screen-enlarging software, and larger monitors. Students who are blind or visually impaired may require materials in braille or in an auditory format.

Other equipment may be appropriate as well. For example, reading stands can allow closer viewing without postural strain, thus reducing fatigue. Adjustable reading lamps can provide more individualized lighting, typoscopes can provide added structure and tracking assistance on cluttered pages, and work trays can help students keep track of their materials and of the area in which they must work. Acetate sheets may increase the contrast of printed materials for some students with low vision (yellow is usually most effective), but care must be taken that surface glare is controlled.

In addition, drawings or diagrams may be rendered in a tactile medium for students who are blind. This rendering must be done with extreme care, since some concepts (like three-dimensional perspective) and complicated pictures cannot be effectively presented with raised-line diagrams, and attempting to do so would only confuse the student and greatly affect the validity of the assessment tool. Actual three-dimensional objects or models may sometimes be substituted for otherwise inaccessible pictures or drawings; again, however, the selection of these objects must be done with caution to maintain the critical features of the original display and not to negate the validity of the test. Many students with severe visual impairments are not efficient at exploring and reading tactile displays, so the use of these displays may further penalize them, rather than make the material accessible.

An abacus can be used for math calculations (see Chapter 10). However, calculators should not be used if the purpose of the assessment is to evaluate the student's ability to carry out calculations. Braille rulers, clocks, marked scales, and other mathematical or scientific equipment may also be appropriate for students who are blind.

Time

Expanding the time limits for completing an assessment may be necessary for several reasons. The logistics of the assessment process themselves are likely to take longer for a student who is blind or visually impaired. For example, it may take students with low vision additional time to use low vision devices or large print, as well as regular print, and to scan a page or work area to locate specific information or items or response formats. Furthermore, such students may fatigue more easily from extended visual tasks than many of their peers, and this fatigue may also affect the time needed for testing. The functional vision and learning media assessments should provide information on the extent to which fatigue may be a factor.

It is sometimes mistakenly thought that providing large-print versions of materials or other devices will speed up the reading process for students with low vision. In actuality, although magnification may increase accessibility, it may not increase a student's reading speed to that of the student's sighted peers. Since getting very close to the material or enlarging it physically or with a low vision device will limit the field of view, the student with low vision may need more time simply to explore the material.

Reading and writing braille, tactilely scanning to orient to a task, and locating and manipulating materials may also require additional time by students who are blind. Variations in the time that is needed will depend on an individual student's visual impairment, the medium used, and the materials involved (Bradley-Johnson, 1994).

Response Format

Sometimes the manner in which the student responds to test items requires some modification. Simple adaptations, such as the use of special writing tools, bold-line paper, and felt-tip pens, may be all that is needed to enable the student to read and monitor his or her own responses. However, students may need to type answers or use special computer software or produce their answers on a braillewriter or slate and stylus. Preformatted answer sheets with push pins (available from APH) may be helpful. If writing or spelling skills are not being tested, answers may be recorded on audiotape.

Administration

On occasion, the way in which a test is administered to a student with a visual impairment may differ from its original design. For example, perhaps only the verbal section of a test of cognitive abilities is administered, and the performance section is omitted because of its reliance on visual information. Some items on an achievement test may be skipped when they repeat the content of other items and the evaluator judges that fewer selected problems would provide appropriate data on the student's abilities. Breaking the assessment into several sessions may also be done when much additional time is required or if the student fatigues easily.

Guidelines for Selecting Modifications

When deciding which modifications would be the most appropriate for a particular student, the evaluator must consider several factors, including the following:

- The type and severity of the student's visual impairment;

- The presence of additional disabilities that may require modifications;

- The demands of the test's presentation and response formats;

- The student's familiarity with the modifications being considered (such as tactile graphics, an abacus, a CCTV or other low vision devices, and the Nemeth Code); and

- The effect of the modifications on the test's validity and ability to meet the desired purpose of the assessment.

Whenever modifications are made to a test or assessment process, special care must be taken to consider how the changes may affect the information gathered. Since the validity of a test or task relates to what is being tested, modifications that change the task itself or the way in which the student can carry out a procedure may have major implications. For example, if the original test provided a series of two-dimensional drawings and asked the student to number them according to a certain sequence, but the modified version provided the student with a three-dimensional model that could be tactilely explored and manipulated, the task might have been made accessible, but it might also have been made easier because of the concrete hands-on quality. Likewise, if speed is an integral part of performing a task, then eliminating any time requirements may be fairer to the student whose visual or tactile approach necessitates more time than adhering to the regular time limits; however, it may also be changing part of what the task was originally designed to measure.

The evaluator must exercise caution when deciding which modifications are important. The goal is to modify what is necessary to make the assessment tool fair, but not to change significantly the purpose, content, or difficulty level and thus the validity of the task. Considering information from the student's functional vision evaluation, observations, and pertinent records, as well as keeping in mind the purpose of the assessment, can assist in making such decisions. Whatever modifications may be considered, it is critical that the student is competent in using any specialized equipment (such as an abacus) or modified presentation (like tactile displays). Otherwise, these modifications will hinder accessibility.

Whenever modifications are used, it is important that they be recorded and described in the written assessment report to provide an accurate picture of the conditions under which the student performed. Without such information, incorrect assumptions can be made by parents and relevant professionals not only about the student's performance, but about the validity and reliability of the assessment process itself.

ASSESSMENT AREAS

This section focuses on assessment issues that should be considered when assessing students with visual impairments. Specific skill areas that are appropriate for school-age students, young students, and students with additional disabilities are discussed, along with relevant concerns. A selection of assessment tools, both formal and informal, that are commonly used by teachers of students with visual impairments, and others who are involved in assessing these students, is found in Tables 2.1, 2.2, and 2.3; this selection is not intended as a comprehensive list but rather as a sampling of those frequently used. The reader is also referred to Chapter 3, on ongoing assessment, as well as Chapter 4, on specialized assessments, and other chapters throughout the book that address individual skill areas. Additional sources of assessment tools include Bradley-Johnson (1994), Sacks and Silberman (1998), and Smith and Levack (1996).

Assessment of School-Age Students

Areas that should be considered in a comprehensive assessment of school-age students include functional vision, cognitive functioning, learning media assessment, educational achievement, motor skills, O&M, social skills, and independent living skills. Examples of such assessment tools appear in Table 2.1. At times, such as in the development of an IEP for a new student, all or most of these areas have to be addressed. At other times, only specific areas or skills need to be assessed, depending on the purpose of the assessment, as when monitoring the progress toward a particular objective or when a particular problem area is identified.

Functional Vision

Assessment of the student's functional vision complements information on the ocular report and provides information that is much more relevant to the teacher of students with visual impairments and the general education teacher in developing the student's IEP. The functional vision assessment identifies the student's visual needs with regard to lighting and glare control, size of print, figure-ground tolerance, and specific skills such as systematic search and tracking skills, eccentric viewing, and the use of low vision devices. It requires structured observation in relevant settings and the use of informal and possibly formal assessment tools. Usually, the teacher of students with visual impairments conducts the functional vision assessment, although some programs have specialists who gather this information in collaboration with general education teachers, parents, physical and/or occupational therapists, and the teacher of students with visual impairments. Chapter 4 provides details on functional vision assessments.

Learning Media Needs

The learning media assessment determines the student's preferred and most efficient learning style, approaches, materials, and literacy media. It also helps determine appropriate media (such as braille and print) and modifications (like enlarged print or pictures, tactile displays, and the use of low vision devices) for use in additional areas requiring assessment.

Such an assessment involves observing the student perform various relevant tasks and his or her responses to different sensory experiences, learning methods, and materials. If the student is reading, then it also includes evaluating reading and writing skills for accuracy and efficiency. A variety of observational techniques and formal and informal reading tests can be combined to gather such information. The learning media assessment can be part of an initial comprehensive evaluation or can be conducted in conjunction with a functional vision assessment to determine any changing needs that the student may have. Specific strategies for conducting the learning media assessment are presented in Chapter 4.

Intellectual and Cognitive Ability

The assessment of the intellectual and cognitive ability of any student, but especially a student with a visual impairment, requires much caution. In the first place, various definitions of intelligence exist, and over 100 different elements are related to intelligence. Therefore, assessment tools that are based on different definitions will sample different abilities and/or behaviors (Bradley-Johnson, 1994; Hall et al., 1986).

Second, students with visual impairments may have had different or limited background experiences. The way in which they develop concepts may also differ from that of sighted students. The students' concepts may have been formed from part to whole because of their smaller visual fields, need to get very close to objects or magnify them, or because of spatial restrictions resulting from tactile exploration.

Third, some items on intelligence tests are heavily based on information that has been specifically taught, and the lack of exposure to this information can result in further penalties. Furthermore, no multifaceted intelligence tests have included children with visual impairments in their standardization procedures. If a test is selected and adaptations (such as partial administration or substitution of materials) are made, additional interpretive questions arise, particularly those related to validity. All these situations make it especially important to use multiple measures and not to rely on one tool.

Qualified psychologists, preferably with experience with students with visual impairments, should administer intelligence tests. Teachers of students with visual impairments can provide valuable support by sharing information about the impact of a visual impairment on learning and appropriate modifications for individual students. Although intelligence tests are not used as extensively in placement and program decisions, they are required for eligibility for some special education services. Some examples of tests that are sometimes used with students with visual impairments to assess this area are included in Table 2.1.

Educational Achievement and Communication Skills

This area includes skills in the core curriculum (such as reading and math), as well as special or compensatory skills that are necessary because of the student's visual impairment (such as braille, abacus, O&M). A variety of assessment tools can and should be used, depending on the purpose of the test (for instance, participation in district program tests, development of an IEP, and remediation of skills) and the individual student.

Norm-referenced tests compare a student's level of skills to a larger standardized group. This type of test may provide information about the levels of skills in a school district, as well as the grade levels at which a student is performing, but it is likely to provide limited information for planning a sequenced instructional program or for monitoring a student's progress with specific skills. Furthermore, if some of the content on the test is not covered in the student's classroom, the test may actually become more of a test of intelligence.

Currently, there are no individual achievement tests whose norms include students with visual impairments. On the other hand, the *Woodcock-Johnson Psychoeducational Battery—Revised* (1989) could be quite useful in identifying specific areas for instruction for some students with visual impairments (Silberman & Sowell, 1998). Several norm-referenced group achievement tests have been transcribed into braille or large print. The Stanford Achievement Test Series (SAT–Form J, 1989) was adapted in braille and large print by the APH. As part of this adaptation, several items that could not be adequately transcribed into braille were eliminated, and the norms were readjusted to reflect the missing items.

The SAT is a reasonable choice for assessing academic achievement, although it is best to give it individually to students with visual impairments. While such a test may not be the best tool for pinpointing instructional objectives, it allows for the achievement of the student with a visual impairment to be compared with that of his or her sighted peers and may be useful in determining

Table 2.1. Instruments Commonly Used with School-aged Students with Visual Impairments

Instrument	Areas/Skills	Adaptations/Comments
LEA Symbols Flash Cards and Single Symbol Book (Vision Associates)	Young children, estimate of visual acuity	Requires matching or naming several basic shapes.
Lighthouse Flash Cards (Lighthouse International)	Young children, estimate of visual acuity	Requires matching or naming several basic shapes.
Colenbrander Low Vision Chart (Vision Associates)	Chart with letters on one side and continuous text on the other side; tests visual acuity	Requires matching and reading.
Sloan Test of Continuous Reading	Estimate of near visual acuity	Allows for use of context clues.
Visual Functioning Assessment Tool (Costello et al., 1980)	Range of basic and perceptual visual skills; functional skills in mobility, physical education; environmental variables	Evaluator selects sections as appropriate.
Program to Develop Efficiency in Visual Functioning: Diagnostic Assessment Procedure (Barraga & Morris, 1980)	Primarily visual perceptual skills related to early school near tasks	Designed for students with visual impairments.
Developmental Test of Visual Motor Integration (Beery & Buktenica, 1997)	2–18 years; copying designs	Not normed on students with visual impairments; use analysis of performance.
Motor-Free Visual Perceptual Test (Colarusso & Hammill, 1995)	Preschool–early grades; range of visual perceptual skills	Not normed on students with visual impairments; difficulty levels increase quickly.
Test of Visual-Perception Skills (nonmotor) (Gardner, 1982)	Preschool level–elementary grades; range of visual perceptual skills	Not normed on students with visual impairments; many difficult items.
Body Image of Blind Children (Cratty & Sams, 1968)	Young children, basic concepts of body image and directionality	No adaptation necessary.
Hill Test of Selected Basic Positional Concepts (Hill, 1981)	Preschool–elementary grades; basic concepts of body image, position, and environment	No adaptation necessary.
Tactile Test of Basic Concepts: A Tactile Analog to the Boehm Test of Basic Concepts, Form A	Preschool–early grades; basic quantity and spatial concepts	APH tactile supplement uses raised-line drawings; original test not normed on students with visual impairments.
Stanford Achievement Test Series—Form J (1989)	Range of grade levels and curricular areas	Should be administered individually; available in braille or large print from APH; blind students must be able to use braille codes and tactile displays.
Brigance Diagnostic Comprehensive Inventory of Basic Skills with APH Tactile Supplement (Brigance, 1983)	Range of grade levels and curricular areas	Not normed on students with visual impairments; APH tactile supplement necessary for some students.

(continued on next page)

Table 2.1. *(Continued)*

Instrument	Areas/Skills	Adaptations/Comments
KeyMath Revised: A Diagnostic Inventory of Essential Mathematics (Connolly, 1988)	Range of grade levels and math skills	Not normed on students with visual impairments; APH tactile supplement necessary for some students.
Iowa Tests of Basic Skills, Large Print Edition (Hieronymous, 1986)	Range of grade levels and curricular areas	Not normed on students with visual impairments; available in large print from APH.
Braille Unit Recognition Test (Caton & Duckworth, 1985)	Grade 2 Literary Code	No adaptation necessary.
Basic Reading Rate Scale—Braille Edition—Form A (Duckworth & & Caton, 1985)	Grade 2 Literary Code	No adaptation necessary.
Braille Unit Recognition Battery (Caton & Duckworth, 1985)	Grade 2 Literary Code, numbers, and mechanics	No adaptation necessary.
Minnesota Braille Skills Inventory (Godwin et al., 1995)	Grade 2 Literary Code; some Nemeth Code, Music Code, and Computer Code; reading and writing	No adaptation necessary.
Woodcock-Johnson Psychoeducational Battery—Revised (Woodcock & Johnson, 1989)	Range of grade levels and skill areas, 2 parts: cognitive ability and achievement	Not normed on students with visual impairments; evaluator must select sections as appropriate; good visual presentation for many students with low vision.
Color Vision Testing Made Easy (Waggoner, 1994)	Children and adults, uses simple shapes, Ishihara compatible	No adaptation necessary.
Blind Learning Aptitude Test (BLAT) (Newland, 1971)	6–12+ years; several subtests related to understanding of learning processes (such as matching, sequencing, matrices)	Does not require verbal responses or braille reading.
Revised Brigance Diagnostic Inventory of Early Development with Tactile Supplement (Brigance, 1991; Duckworth & Stratton, 1992)	Preschool–7 years; range of developmental and early academic skills	APH tactile supplement available.
Preparatory Reading Program for Visually Handicapped Children (Hall et al., 1981)	Young children, prereading and reading concepts	No adaptation necessary.
Basic Reading Inventory (Johns, 1997)	Preprimer–12th-grade reading skills, early literacy	Available in braille and large print through Texas School for the Blind.
Woodcock Reading Mastery Test (Woodcock, 1987)	K–adult levels, range of reading skills	Presentation appropriate for some children with low vision.
Wechsler Intelligence Scale for Children–III (Wechsler,1991)	6 1/2–16 years	Not normed on students with visual impairments; Performance Scale not appropriate; Digit Span could be substituted for Arithmetic (Bradley-

(continued on next page)

Table 2.1. *(Continued)*

Instrument	Areas/Skills	Adaptations/Comments
		Johnson, 1994); must be supplemented with other measures.
Adaptive Behavior Scale, Public School Version (Lambert et al., 1993)	Includes independent living skills, language development, vocational areas, limited math behaviors	Not normed on students with visual impairments; based on informant and performance; includes levels of skill.
Wechsler Individual Achievement Test (Wechsler, 1992)	Range of skills: reading, mathematics, listening comprehension, oral and written expression	Not normed on students with visual impairments; several areas require considerable vision.
Assessment Kit (Texas School for the Blind and Visually Impaired) (Sewell, 1997)	Range of special skills	Checklist format; evaluator must structure actual assessment tasks and materials.
Vineland Adaptive Behavior Scales (Sparrow et al. 1984)	Communication, daily living skills, socialization, motor skills	Loosely defined inclusion of students with visual impairments in norming sample; emphasizes typical behavior; many items require vision.

the student's eligibility for special education services in addition to those necessitated by the visual impairment alone (Bradley-Johnson, 1994). The test could also be used to identify areas that require more specific analysis and assessment so that appropriate objectives may be set.

For some students with low vision who are print readers, several individual achievement tests are sometimes used, even though they do not include such students in their standardization process. Several of these tests are included in Table 2.1. The appropriateness of their use would depend upon the student's ability to see the print and graphic displays, the presentation format of the test, and the adequacy and implications of any modifications that may have been made.

Criterion-referenced tests, curriculum-based measures, and portfolio reviews are usually more applicable to planning instructional programs. Such tools are built on a sequenced paradigm of progressive skills and reflect the specific skills of interest to the general education teacher and/or the special educator. These measures can also be used more frequently and appropriately for ongoing assessment. In addition, they typically allow for more flexibility in modifying materials or administering the tests than do norm-referenced tests (Bradley-Johnson, 1994). (The reader is referred to Chapter 3, on informal assessment, for additional information on such measures.)

Occasionally, a test used with students with visual impairments may be both criterion referenced and norm referenced. One such test is the aforementioned KeyMath, although its standardization did not include students with visual impairments. The evaluator would gain the most valuable information from both the student's performance on individual criterion-referenced items and a comparison of these individual items with the performance of the student's sighted peers, rather than simply from the test scores.

An assessment of reading and writing must include the range of skills commonly covered in this area of the core curriculum (such as comprehension and word attack skills and language arts). In addition, the teacher of students with visual impairments must evaluate the efficiency of learning and literacy media for individual students (visual, tactile, and auditory learning channels, as well as print, braille and auditory reading modes) (see Chapter 4 for information on learning media assessments). Such an assessment would also guide the teacher in providing the appropriate equipment, technology, and devices and in collaborating with the general education teacher with regard to teaching approaches. The student who is blind or visually impaired must also be assessed on his or her skills with relevant specialized equipment and media (like braille codes and writing tools, assistive technology, and listening equipment).

Since listening can be a major learning channel for many students, especially those with visual impairments, such skills should be included in an overall assessment. Skills to be assessed in this area include listening for specific sounds in the environment and in language, listening for the main idea and for specific facts, recalling auditory information, and critically interpreting the material.

In the area of mathematics, it is also important to assess a variety of concepts and skills, including Piagetian concepts (such as conservation, seriation and one-to-one correspondence), basic quantity concepts, operations, word problems, time, fractions, measurement, graphs, algebra, and geometry. In addition, special skills should be included in the assessment, such as mental math; the use of calculating tools, such as the abacus, braillewriter and calculator; the ability to handle visual and tactile displays; and knowledge of the Nemeth Code (Kapperman, Heinze, & Sticken, 1997 and Chapter 10).

Math-application skills must also be assessed, using both formal and informal assessment tools. The SAT is an example of a formal test that includes a range of math skills that are typically covered in the core curriculum. The KeyMath is an example of a norm-referenced and criterion-referenced test, which APH modified for use by students who are blind. Table 2.1 lists several additional tests that can provide useful information, with appropriate cautions. Additional criterion-referenced tests, checklists, and functional problem-solving situations should be used to assess specific elements of identified problem areas and the special skills that are essential to a student who is blind or visually impaired. Several of these are also listed in Table 2.1

Assistive Technology

Yet another area that must be evaluated for students with visual impairments is assistive technology. This assessment could include the use of computer hardware and software for screen enlargement, screen-reading braille production, note taking, and switch access or other adaptive devices. It is individualized and determines which strategies and technologies are needed to give the student access to the general curriculum and to provide the support needed for him or her to function as efficiently and independently as possible. An assistive technology assessment examines such areas as communication and academics, independent living skills, O&M, and vocational performance, as well as computer accessibility. It must involve relevant tasks in these areas and consider environmental variables. The resulting information should lead to appropriate choices of technology and strategies (both low and high tech). Evaluations should be done by teachers of students with visual impairments who are trained in and have experience with assistive technology; assistive technology specialists; therapists; physical occupational, or speech and language; or a combination of these professionals. (The reader is referred to Chapters 4 for more information on approaches to assistive technology assessments.)

Motor Skills and O&M

O&M skills are critical for a student's self-concept, opportunities for experiences and social contacts, control over his or her environment, and independence. Both the O&M specialist and the teacher of students with visual impairments are responsible for assessment in this area. The teacher is involved in assessing such concepts as body image, positional, and some environmental concepts; special needs related to physical education; and familiarity with the classroom, school, or home setting. The O&M specialist is responsible for assessing not only these areas, but precane skills, cane skills, use of specialized devices, and general independent travel. Ongoing collaboration between the O&M specialist and the teacher of students with visual impairments is needed in assessing this area.

Gross motor skills must also be assessed, especially in relation to their implications for movement, coordination, balance, and O&M. Often the teacher of students with visual impairments collaborates with the physical education teacher, the O&M specialist, and the physical therapist in the assessment of gross motor skills. In the case of young children or those with motor impairments, consultation with a motor development specialist or physical therapist is important. The teacher of students with visual impairments can assist with modifications in procedures and materials that are appropriate because of the student's visual impairment. The assessment of fine motor skills is especially important because of the role of these skills in writing, copying, using specialized equipment, and performing daily living tasks. The teacher of students with visual impairments can collaborate with an occupational therapist if the student has difficulties in this area.

Social Skills and Independent Living Skills

Social skills are often overlooked in programs for students with visual impairments, yet they are extremely important to the students' school experiences and overall quality of life. Furthermore, since many social skills are learned through observation and incidental learning, students with visual impairments are at a greater risk of having difficulties in developing them. Skills in this area may include turn taking, attending to others, initiating and continuing conversations, and understanding and using expressions and behaviors that are commonly used by children of the same age.

Teachers of students with visual impairments must include social skills in an overall assessment,

or when difficulties are observed, and develop relevant goals and objectives when appropriate. Assessment in this area is generally informal, relying on systematic observations and interviews with persons who know the student well. Some social skills are included in formal or informal adaptive behavior tests.

Independent living skills, such as eating, dressing, grooming, preparing food, cleaning, and managing money, should also be included in an overall assessment. As with social skills, independent living skills sometimes do not receive the attention they require in a student's program. Furthermore, they often develop with the assistance of incidental learning, which may be limited for students with visual impairments.

Useful techniques for assessing independent living and social skills include adaptive behavior scales, systematic observation during tasks, criterion-referenced checklists, and interviews with parents or other caregivers and others who are familiar with the student's abilities. When secondary sources are used, they should be supplemented with direct observation, since the degree of familiarity with the student can result in over-estimating or underestimating the student's abilities. Occasionally, formal behavior scales can be useful, although they are more useful for identifying general problem areas than for instructional programming. Ideally, such formal and informal tools should measure not only whether a skill exists, but also the level the student has attained. Several measures in this area are listed in Table 2.1.

Career Education Skills

There are several concerns with regard to career education skills that are especially important for students with visual impairments. For example, in addition to specific interests, aptitudes, and general work habits, specific skills in communication, social interaction, O&M, and daily living also play a critical role in preparing a student who is blind or visually impaired for success in a career. (See Chapter 19 for more information on career education.) Assessment in this area, as in other areas already discussed, involves a combination of strategies for gathering information. Specific tests related to dexterity, speed, interests, and aptitude can be formal or informal; assessment approaches for work habits, social skills, O&M, and independent living skills have already been discussed.

Assessment of Young Children

Working with young children, especially young children with visual impairments, requires special attention for several reasons:

♦ Young children have limited receptive and expressive language.

♦ They may be unable to follow the evaluator's directions.

♦ Much of the ability that is assessed at this age is typically picked up from incidental information or develops during the maturation process. Because much incidental information is visual and because their visual impairments can affect the developmental process, children with visual impairments may respond differently on early assessments.

♦ The assessment of young children is a relatively new area, and much is yet to be learned about appropriate processes (Bradley-Johnson, 1994).

There are many critical areas that must be examined when working with young children, including a variety of developmental areas, such as the following:

♦ Visual functioning skills,

♦ A broad range of sensory channels and learning media,

♦ Cognitive development and concept development,

♦ Language development and communication,

♦ Social skills and emotional development,

♦ Motor skills (including reflex levels, both gross motor and fine motor skills),

♦ Play skills and interaction with objects,

♦ Personal and daily living skills, and

♦ Initiation and problem-solving skills.

Examples of formal and informal assessment tools that are sometimes used, generally to assess the areas just listed, are presented in Table 2.2. (The reader is also referred to Chapter 3 for a more complete discussion of informal methods of assessment, generally the preferred approach for young children with visual impairments.)

An additional area that is critical to assess is parental and family involvement. Parental involvement is essential for understanding the child's behaviors; developing an Individualized Family Service Plan (IFSP) that identifies the family's strengths, sets goals, and recommends strategies and resources for the young child and his or her family members; and, in general, facilitating optimum learning experiences for the child and support for his or her parents. Such an assessment requires the evaluator to be sensitive to parents' concerns and cultural perspectives, and to have a flexible communication style.

Although the overall process of assessing young children may be similar to the process described for school-age children, several special considerations need to be kept in mind, such as the following:

♦ The evaluator must have a good understanding of the typical development of young children and how a visual impairment can affect a child's development (for example, differences in the way concepts may develop, risks for limited background experiences, effects of a visual impairment on the child's motivation to explore, and how these factors can lead to delays in motor and concept development).

♦ Multiple assessments over time are necessary to gain a more accurate profile of the

Table 2.2. Instruments Commonly Used with Young Children with Visual Impairments

Instrument	Areas/Skills	Adaptations/Comments
Batelle Developmental Inventory (Newborg et al., 1984)	Birth–8 years, developmental areas, generally used for determining eligibility for additional special services, rather than for instructional programming	Students with visual impairments not included in standardization; many items not usable with this population, some others can be adapted.
Bayley Scales of Infant Development (Bayley, 1993)	Infants; cognitive, motor, and infant behavior	Not normed on children with visual impairments; many items not appropriate, especially for children with severe disabilities.
Revised Brigance Diagnostic Inventory of Early Development, with APH Tactile Supplement (Brigance, 1991; Duckworth & Stratton, 1992)	Birth–6 years; developmental areas, basic reading, writing, and math	Not normed on children with visual impairments, APH Tactile Supplement necessary.
Carolina Curriculum for Infants and Toddlers with Special Needs (also Preschooler version) (Johnson-Martin et al., 1991)	Infants version: birth–2 years; preschooler version: 2–3 years; developmental areas	Some adaptations presented in manual; not norm referenced.
Developmental Activities Screening Inventory (DASI) (DuBose & Langley, 1977)	Birth–5 years, developmental areas	Geared for children with sensory disabilities; emphasis on performance, rather than language.
Family Assessment in Early Intervention (Bailey & Wolery, 1989)	Family needs and resources, critical events	Some individualizing would be appropriate.
Growing Up: A Developmental Curriculum (Croft & Robinson, 1990)	Birth–6 years, developmental areas	Designed for young children with visual impairments but not severe disabilities; not normed.
Hawaii Early Learning Profile (HELP) (Furono et al., 1979)	Young children; developmental areas	Not designed for children with visual impairments but can be useful.
Home Observation and Measurement of the Environment (HOME) (Caldwell & Bradley, 1972)	Physical, social, emotional, and cognitive support for children in the home	Some individualization would be appropriate.
Informal Assessment of Developmental Skills for Younger Visually Handicapped and Multi-handicapped Children (Swallow et al., 1978)	Infants and preschoolers; developmental areas	Adaptation not necessary.
Oregon Project for Visually Impaired and Blind Preschool Children (Anderson et al., 1991)	Birth–6 years; developmental areas, visual functioning, compensatory skills	Not appropriate for children with severe multiple disabilities; not normed.
Peabody Mobility Scale for Infants and Toddlers	Selected basic concepts and motor skills	Adaptation not necessary; limited skills covered.
Body Image of Blind Children (Cratty & Sams, 1968)	Selected body image and spatial concepts	Adaptation not necessary.

(continued on next page)

Table 2.2. (*Continued*)

Instrument	Areas/Skills	Adaptations/Comments
Receptive Expressive Language Assessment of the Visually Impaired B-6	Birth–6 years; receptive and expressive language	Designed for students with visual and multiple impairments.
Reynell-Zinkin Developmental Scales for Young Visually Handicapped Children (Reynell & Zinkin, 1979)	Birth–5 years; developmental areas	Normative information; not appropriate for children with severe disabilities.
Social Skills Rating Scale (Teacher and Parent Scale) (Gresham & Elliott, 1990)	Preschool through high school; social skills, problem behaviors, limited academic areas	Not normed on students with visual impairments.
Visual Evoked Response	Infants and children with multiple disabilities; estimate of visual acuity	Uses changes in brain activity while viewing changing designs to estimate acuity.
Preferential Looking	Infants and children with multiple disabilities; estimate of visual acuity	Based on premise that child will prefer to look at a design rather than a blank choice.
Hill Test of Selected Basic Positional Concepts (Hill, 1981)	Preschool–early grades	No adaptations needed.
Tactile Test of Basic Concepts: A Tactile Analog to the Boehm Test of Basic Concepts, Form A (Caton, 1980)	Preschool–first grade; basic concepts related to quantity and position	APH tactile supplement uses raised line drawings; original test not normed on students with visual impairments.
LEA Symbols Flash Cards and Single Symbol Book (Vision Associates)	Young children; estimate of visual acuity	Requires matching or naming.
Lighthouse Flash Cards (Lighthouse International)	Young children; estimate of visual acuity	Requires matching or naming.
Developmental Test of Visual-Motor Integration (Beery & Buktenica, 1997)	2–18 years; copying designs	Not normed on students with visual impairments; focus on analysis of performance.
Koontz Child Development Program (Koontz, n.d.)	Preschool; developmental areas	Not normed on students with visual impairments but some adaptations suggested for children with visual impairments.

child's ability and to note trends in growth (Bradley-Johnson, 1994).

◆ Systematic observations of the child should be supplemented with interviews with parents and other caregivers and the administration of more formal tests to avoid gathering biased information. Such observations require the evaluator to have experience with young children with visual impairments.

◆ The use of norm-referenced tools that do not include children with visual impairments in their norming samples is especially risky with these young children. Although sections of these tests are occasionally used, they typically require modification, which further reduces their validity. Therefore, careful observation and interpretation of the child's performance, rather than the use of scores, are essential.

◆ When selecting materials to use with young children, keep in mind that some children may react more to novel materials, while others may respond better to those for which they have already shown a preference.

◆ With the many different theories about the nature of intelligence and with the limited availability of appropriate tests for the population discussed here, it is more appropriate to focus on the assessment of skills needed for educational and life success than on intelligence testing (Bradley-Johnson, 1994). In any case, as with older children, if intelligence testing is attempted, it should be done by a fully qualified psychologist or psychometrist, preferably one with experience with young children with visual impairments. The teacher of students with visual impairments can play a collaborative and supportive role by describing the impact of a visual impairment on early development and by altering the evaluator to possible modifications that would be appropriate.

◆ There are many reasons why young children with visual impairments may show apparent delays in several skill areas. Unless evidence of additional difficulties (such as a hearing impairment or physical disability) is well founded, labels should be avoided, and the assessment should focus on areas for intervention.

Assessment of Students with Visual and Additional Impairments

Assessing students with visual and additional disabilities also requires special attention. The impact of multiple disabilities is not simply additive, but compounding; such disabilities affect a student in a great variety of ways. Students may have a visual impairment with a hearing impairment, a visual impairment or deaf-blindness with a cognitive disability, a visual impairment with learning disabilities, blindness with a physical impairment, or many other concomitant disabilities. Students may have syndromes that are not stable and present challenges that change over time. In addition, the severity of the concomitant disabilities can vary greatly among students—and from time to time. Such possibilities result in a great heterogeneity of learning approaches, accessibility issues, functioning levels, and ability to demonstrate skill and understanding. Students' methods of communication with others (expressive) and their understanding of others who are communicating with them (receptive) can also vary greatly among students with multiple disabilities. All these factors influence the assessment of these students.

Formal assessment is especially difficult, since the heterogeneity of these students severely limits the students' inclusion in norming samples or adherence to uniform administration procedures. If formal instruments are used (see Table 2.3), they must be used with great caution, since their validity and reliability are likely to be greatly compromised. Therefore, the assessment of a student with a visual impairment and additional disabilities requires an individualized approach and a combination of assessment techniques, including structured observation, interviews with persons who are familiar with the student, criterion-referenced measures, performance tasks that allow the student to demonstrate his or her abilities, and a prescriptive or diagnostic teaching approach, in addition to components of formal instruments when they can provide useful information.

Areas that should be assessed depend on the purpose of the assessment, the student's age and functioning levels, and the implications of the student's combined disabilities, among other considerations. Examples of areas that may require assessment include functional vision; developmental areas listed in the section on young children; cognitive abilities; functional academics, as well as appropriate traditional academic areas; communication styles, learning channels, and learning media; O&M; independent living skills; social skills; and compensatory skills. Regardless

Table 2.3. Instruments Commonly Used with Students with Visual and Multiple Impairments

Instrument	Areas/Skills	Adaptations/Comments
Callier-Azusa Scale (Stillman, 1978)	Birth–9 years; developmental areas	Students with deaf-blindness and multiple disabilities.
Carolina Curriculum for Infants and Toddlers with Special Needs (also version for preschoolers) (Johnson-Martin et al., 1991)	Infants version: birth–2 years; preschoolers version: 2–3 years; developmental areas	Infants, toddlers, and preschoolers with disabilities; may require adaptations for some skills.
Clinical and Educational Manual for Use with the Uzgiris and Hunt Ordinal Scales of Infant Psychological Development (Dunst, 1980)	Various scales for examining cognitive strategies, especially Relating to Objects	Students with visual impairments not included in the design; not all scales appropriate; supplementary manual by Dunst necessary.
Developmental Activities Screening Inventory (DASI) (DuBose and Langley, 1977)	Birth–5 years; screening for children with sensory impairments	Emphasis on performance, not language.
Functional Skills Screening Inventory (FSSI)	Basic skills, communication, personal care, homemaking, work skills and concepts, community and social awareness	Especially useful for older students with multiple disabilities; levels of environmental functioning.
Growing Up: A Developmental Curriculum (Croft & Robinson, 1990)	Birth–6 years; developmental areas	Designed for young children with visual impairments but not severe multiple disabilities, not normed.
INSITE Program (Hope, Inc.)	Young children with sensory and multiple disabilities; developmental areas	Assessment component refers to teaching activities from Oregon Project or Hawaii Early Learning Profile (HELP).
Hawaii Early Learning Profile (HELP) (Furono et al., 1979)	Young children; developmental areas	Not designed for children with visual impairments but can be useful.
Reynell-Zinkin Developmental Scales for Young Visually Handicapped Children (Reynell & Zinkin, 1979)	Screening/assessment for birth–5 years; developmental areas	Normative information; not for children with severe multiple disabilities; new normative studies being conducted independently at this writing.
Oregon Project for Visually Impaired and Blind Preschool Children (Anderson et al., 1991)	Birth–6 years; developmental areas, visual functioning, compensatory skills	Not appropriate for children with severe multiple disabilities; not normed.
Visual Evoked Response	Infants and children with multiple disabilities; estimate of visual acuity	Uses change in brain activity while viewing changing patterns to estimate acuity.
Preferential Looking	Infants and children with multiple disabilities; estimate of visual acuity	Based on the premise that child will prefer to look at a design rather than a blank choice.

(continued on next page)

Table 2.3. *(Continued)*

Instrument	Areas/Skills	Adaptations/Comments
LEA Symbols Flash Cards and Single Symbol Book (Vision Associates)	Young children and those with moderate multiple disabilities; estimate of visual acuity	Requires matching or naming several basic shapes.
Model Vision Functional Vision Inventory	Young children and those with multiple disabilities; basic visual skills (such as fixation, tracking, shifting gaze, and near and distant acuity estimates)	Includes training activities related to assessment.
Test of Visual-Perceptual Skills (nonmotor) (Gardner, 1982)	Upper preschool–elementary school; range of visual perceptual skills	Not normed on students with visual impairments; many difficult items; does not require motor or verbal response.
Motor-Free Visual Perceptual Test (Colarusso & Hammill, 1995)	Upper preschool–elementary school; range of visual perceptual skills	Not normed on students with visual impairments; many difficult items; does not require motor or verbal response.
Fieber Scales for Cognitive Skills (Fieber, 1977)	Sensorimotor level; based on Uzgiris and Hunt Ordinal Scales	Adapted for children with sensory or motor impairments.

of the area or areas that are assessed, some issues that require special attention by the evaluator are as follows:

◆ What is the effect of the multiple disabilities on the child's receptive and expressive communication? Are special communication systems or augmentative devices needed?

◆ How do the multiple disabilities affect the child's ability to perform, indicate, respond, or demonstrate during an assessment?

◆ What effects do medications have on the child's ability to attend or to demonstrate his or her abilities? What about fatigue, seizures, and positioning?

There are several other considerations to keep in mind when assessing a student with visual and additional disabilities. First, the student may have difficulty generalizing his or her skills to a variety of settings. Second, as with teaching activities, assessment activities should be carried out in the various settings in which tasks are needed and ecological factors should also be assessed. Third, multiple samplings of the student's performance are necessary to have confidence in the results, whether formal or informal approaches are used.

Furthermore, when working with a student with severe multiple disabilities, the evaluator must be sensitive to the student's behaviors and reactions, since they may provide the most accurate information. The evaluator may find that materials for which a student has already shown a preference are more effective in eliciting a response (Smith & Levack, 1996); however, novel materials may be more effective for some students. The evaluator must also be careful about making assumptions before or during the assessment and avoid underestimating the student's potential, either of which may serve to limit the student's present or future opportunities.

A collaborative approach is necessary when assessing a student with a visual impairment and additional disabilities. The combined expertise and experience of the teacher of students with visual impairments, and other special education teachers; psychologists; physical, occupational, and language therapists; O&M specialists; medical personnel; and parents are needed to facilitate the most effective testing approaches and appropriate interpretation of the results. The teacher of students with visual impairments should contribute expertise in the areas of the student's visual functioning and its implications for modifying the testing procedures or materials, the impact of the visual impairment on learning and performance, and interpretation of the results and their implications for services and programming.

There are few formal assessment tools that can or should be relied on to provide accurate and useful information on the abilities and skills of students with visual and additional disabilities. Typically, such students are not included in norming samples, and significant modifications are needed. Table 2.3 lists several approaches that are sometimes used. The reader is also referred to Chapter 20, on teaching students with visual impairments and additional disabilities.

SUMMARY

Teachers of students with visual impairments are integrally involved in assessing their students. They may conduct the assessments themselves or in collaboration with relevant professionals on the educational team. They may collaborate with psychologists or psychometrists, as well as with other teachers and therapists, in determining appropriate modifications to the environment, test materials, or procedures and in interpreting the results of assessments. To modify and use formal tests appropriately, teachers must have knowledge of the impact of visual impairments, educational needs, the purposes of conducting assessments, and the wide range of assessment tools and procedures that can provide important educational information.

ACTIVITIES

1. Compare and contrast two assessment tools that attempt to measure similar skills. Focus on the advantages and limitations of each and how using multiple measures will affect the information gathered.

2. Observe a teacher of students with visual impairments and a psychologist during an assessment procedure. Describe the modifications made, the rationale for using them, and their implications for the results.

3. Outline the appropriate uses and limitations of norm-referenced assessment tests for students with visual impairments.

4. Develop an annotated resource file of assessment tools in areas relevant to school-age students, young children, and children with visual impairments and additional disabilities.

5. Interview members of an educational team, including the teacher of students with visual impairments, O&M specialist, psychologist or psychometrist, physical therapist, child development therapist, general or special education teacher, and so forth. Focus on each individual's particular role in the assessment process and how each addressed his or her collaborative role. Share the findings with the class.

6. Observe an educational team meeting. Focus on assessment instruments and approaches used by the educational team and how the information was presented to facilitate decisions about eligibility, placement, and the development of instructional objectives.

7. Role-play the collaboration of the psychologist or psychometrist and the teacher of students with visual impairments. Outline the important issues

related to the impact of a visual impairment on learning and testing, appropriate modifications, implications of those modifications, and suggestions for interacting with the student.

8. Select a student with visual impairments. Observe the student in an appropriate environment and choose an area for an in-depth assessment. Then select and administer a formal instrument to the student once appropriate parental permission is obtained. In a written report, describe the cautions related to interpreting the results, the valid information that has been acquired, and the next step to be taken in the assessment process.

REFERENCES

Anderson, S., Boigon, S., & Davis, K. (1991). *Oregon Project for Visually Impaired and Blind Preschool Children.* Medford, OR: Jackson County Education Services.

Bailey, D., & Simeonsson, R. (1989). *Family assessment in early intervention.* Columbus, OH: Merrill.

Bailey, D., & Wolery, M. (1989). *Assessing infants and preschoolers with handicaps.* Columbus, OH: Merrill.

Barraga, N., & Morris, J. (1980). *Program to Develop Efficiency in Visual Functioning: Diagnostic Assessment Procedure.* Louisville, KY: American Printing House for the Blind.

Bayley, N. (1993). *Bayley Scales of Infant Development* (manual; 2nd ed.). San Antonio, TX: Psychological Corp.

Becker, H., Schur, S., Paoletti-Schelp, M., & Hammer, E. (1986). *Functional Skills Screening Inventory,* Austin, TX: Functional Resources Enterprises.

Beery, K., & Buktenica, N. (1997). *Developmental Test of Visual-Motor Integration.* Los Angeles: Western Psychological Corp.

Boehm, A. (1986). *Boehm Test of Basic Concepts.* San Antonio, TX: Psychological Corp.

Bradley-Johnson, S. (1994). *Psychoeducational assessment of students who are visually impaired or blind.* Austin, TX: Pro-Ed.

Bradley-Johnson, S. (1995). *Psychoeducational assessment of visually impaired persons* (videotape). Louisville, KY: American Printing House for the Blind.

Brigance, A. (1983). *Brigance Diagnostic Comprehensive Inventory of Basic Skills.* North Billerica, MA: Curriculum Associates.

Brigance, A. (1991). *Revised Brigance Diagnostic Inventory of Early Development,* North Billerica, MA: Curriculum Associates.

Caldwell, B.. & Bradley, R. (1972). *Home Observation and Measurement of the Environment Inventory.* Little Rock: Center for Child Development and Education, University of Arkansas at Little Rock.

Caton, H. (1980). *The Tactile Test of Basic Concepts: A Tactile Analog to the Boehm Test of Basic Concepts, Form A.* Louisville, KY: American Printing House for the Blind.

Caton, H., & Duckworth, B. (1985). *Braille Unit Recognition Battery: Grade 2 Literary Braille.* Louisville, KY: American Printing House for the Blind.

Colarusso, R., & Hammill, D. (1995). *Motor-Free Visual Perception Test-Revised.* Los Angeles: Western Psychological Services.

Connolly, A. (1988). *KeyMath Revised: A Diagnostic Inventory of Essential Mathematics.* Circle Pines, MN: American Guidance Service.

Costello, K., Pinkney, P., & Scheffers, W. (1980). *Visual Functioning Assessment Tool.* Wood Dale, IL: Stoelting Co.

Cratty, B., & Sams, T. (1968). *The Body Image of Blind Children.* New York, NY: American Foundation for the Blind.

Croft, N. B., & Robinson, L. W. (1990). *Growing up: A developmental curriculum.* Ogden, UT: Parent Consultants.

Curry, S., & Russo, R. (1998). In S. Sacks & R. Silberman (Eds.), *Educating students who have visual impairments with other disabilities* (pp. 39–71). Baltimore, MD: Paul H. Brookes.

Dodson-Burke, B., & Hill, E. (1989). *Preschool O&M screening.* Alexandria, VA: Association for Education and Rehabilitation of the Blind and Visually Impaired.

DuBose, R., & Langley, M. (1977). *Developmental Activities Screening Inventory,* Austin, TX: Pro-Ed.

Duckworth, B. (n.d.). *Braille edition of the Stanford Achievement Test–Form J.* Louisville, KY: American Printing House for the Blind.

Duckworth, B., & Abbott, D. (n.d.). *APH tactile supplement to the Brigance Diagnostic Comprehensive Inventory of Basic Skills—1983.* Louisville, KY: American Printing House for the Blind.

Duckworth, B., & Caton, H. (1985). *Basic Reading Rate Scale–Form A: Directions for Braille Edition.*

Louisville, KY: American Printing House for the Blind.

Duckworth, B., & Stratton, J. (1992). *APH Tactile Supplement to the Revised Brigance Diagnostic Inventory of Early Development.* Louisville, KY: American Printing House for the Blind.

Duckworth, B., & Willis, D. (1996). *Braille edition of the KeyMath Revised: A Diagnostic Inventory of Essential Mathematics–Form A* (1988). Louisville, KY: American Printing House for the Blind.

Dunst, C. J. (1980). *A clinical and educational manual for use with the Uzgiris and Hunt Scales of Infant Psychological Development.* Austin, TX: Pro-Ed.

Fieber, N. (1977). Cognitive skills. In N. Haring (Ed.), *Developing effective individualized education programs.* Washington, DC: Office of Education, U.S. Department of Health, Education, & Welfare.

Furono, S., O'Reilly, A., Hosaka, C., Inatsuka, T., Allman, T., & Zelsloft, B. (1979). *The Hawaii Early Learning Profile,* Palo Alto, CA: VORT.

Gardner, M. (1982). *Test of Visual-Perception Skills (nonmotor).* Burlingame, CA: Psychological and Educational Publications.

Godwin, A., Martin, J., Grafsgaard, K., McNear, D., Hanson, N., Rieber, C., Hooey, P., & Tillmanns, E. (1995). *Minnesota Braille Skills Inventory.* Little Canada, MN: Minnesota Educational Services.

Gresham, F., & Elliott, S. (1990). *Social Skills Rating System.* Circle Pines, MN: American Guidance Service.

Hall, A., Rodabaugh, B., & Smith, C. (1981). *Preparatory reading program for visually handicapped children.* Louisville, KY: American Printing House for the Blind.

Hall, A., Scholl, G., & Swallow, R. (1986). Assessment. In G. Scholl (Ed.), *Foundations of education for blind and visually handicapped children and youth* (pp. 187–214). New York: American Foundation for the Blind.

Harley, R., DuBose, R., & Bourgeault, S. (1980). *Peabody Model Vision Project.* Wood Dale, IL: Stoelting Co.

Hieronymous, A. (1986). *Large print edition of Iowa Tests of Basic Skills.* Louisville, KY: American Printing House for the Blind.

Hill, E. (1981). *The Hill Performance Test of Selected Positional Concepts.* Wood Dale, IL: Stoelting Co.

Hyvarinen, L. (n.d.). *Assessment of low vision for educational purposes.* Orlando, FL: Vision Associates.

Johns, J. (1997). *Basic Reading Inventory.* Dubuque, IA: Kendall/Hunt.

Johnson-Martin, N. M., Jens, K. G., Attermeier, S. M., & Hacker, B. J. (1991). *The Carolina Curriculum for Infants and Toddlers with Special Needs.* Baltimore, MD: Paul H. Brookes.

Kapperman, G., Heinze, T., & Sticken, J. (1997). *Strategies for developing mathematics skills in students who use braille.* Sycamore, IL: Research and Development Institute.

Koontz, C. (n.d.). *Koontz Child Developmental Program.* Los Angeles: Western Psychological Corp.

Lambert, N., Nihira, K., & Leland, H. (1993). *Adaptive Behavior Scales—School Edition.* Austin, TX: PRO-ED.

Langley, M.B. (1980). *Functional Vision Inventory for the Multiply and Severely Handicapped.* Wood Dale, IL: Stoelting Co.

Maloney, M. (1997). *The reauthorization of IDEA: What are your new responsibilities?* Knoxville, KY: Weatherly Law Firm.

Morgan, E. (1989). *Insite Model Checklist.* Logan, UT: Home-Oriented Program Essentials.

National Association of State Directors of Special Education. (1997). *Comparison of key issues: Previous law and P.L. 105-17 (1997 IDEA amendments).* Alexandria, VA: Author.

Newborg, J., Stock, J., Wnek, L., Guidubaldi, J., & Svinicki, J. (1984). *Battelle Developmental Inventory.* Allen, TX: DLM/Teaching Resources.

Newland, T. (1971). *Blind Learning Aptitude Test.* Urbana: University of Illinois Press.

NICHCY. (1997, August). The IDEA Amendments of 1997. *News Digest of the National Information Center for Children and Youth with Disabilities, 26.*

Overton, T. (1992). *Assessment in special education.* New York: Merrill/Macmillan.

Reynell, J., & Zinkin, P. (1979). *The Reynell-Zinkin Scales: Developmental Scales for Young Visually Handicapped Children.* Wood Dale, IL: Stoelting Co.

Sacks, S. Z., & Silberman, R. K. (1998). *Educating students who have visual impairments with other disabilities.* Baltimore, MD: Paul H. Brookes.

Salvia, J., & Ysseldyke, J. E. (1995). *Assessment.* Boston: Houghton Mifflin.

Sewell, D. (Ed.) (1997). *Assessment Kit.* Austin, TX: Texas School for the Blind and Visually Impaired.

Silberman, R., & Sowell, V. (1998). Educating students who have visual impairments and learning disabilities. In S. Sacks, & R. Silberman (Eds.), *Educating students who have visual impairments with additional disabilities.* Baltimore, MD: Paul H. Brookes.

Smith, M., & Levack, N. (1996). *Teaching students with visual and multiple impairments: A resource guide.* Austin: Texas School for the Blind.

Sparrow, S. S., Balla, D. A., & Cicchetti, D. V. (1984). *Vineland Adaptive Behavior Scales.* Circle Pines, MN: American Guidance Service, Inc.

Stanford Achievement Test Series–Form J (large-print ed.). (1989). Louisville, KY: American Printing House for the Blind.

Stillman, R. (1978). *The Callier-Azusa Scale.* Dallas: University of Texas at Dallas.

Swallow, R., Mangold, S., & Mangold, P. (1978). *Informal assessment of developmental skills for younger visually handicapped and multihandicapped children.* New York: American Foundation for the Blind.

Waggoner, T. (1994). *Color Vision Testing Made Easy.* Orlando, FL: Vision Associates.

Wechsler, D. (1991). *Wechsler Intelligence Scale for Children* (3rd ed.). San Antonio, TX: Psychological Corp.

Wechsler, D. (1992). *Wechsler Individual Achievement Test.* San Antonio, TX: Psychological Corp.

Woodcock, R. (1987). *Woodcock Reading Mastery Test—Revised.* Circle Pines, MN: American Guidance Service.

Woodcock, R., & Johnson, M. (1989). *Woodcock-Johnson Psychoeducational Battery—Revised.* Allen, TX: DLM.

RESOURCES

Suggested Resources for Conducting Comprehensive Assessments

Resource	Type	Source	Description
LEA Symbols Flash Cards, Single Symbol Book, Colenbrander Acuity Charts	Acuity Assessments	Vision Associates	Charts and symbol cards and books using LEA symbols and Colenbrander letters and continuous text; Color Vision Testing Made Easy; wide range of additional testing materials and videos for estimating activity and basic visual skills of young children.
Multiple-Choice, Multipurpose Answer Sheets	Assessment aid	American Printing House for the Blind	Braille or large-print multiple-choice answer sheets; numbers 1–20 and choices A–E for each number.
Psychoeducational Assessment of Students Who Are Visually Impaired or Blind: Infancy through High School (Bradley-Johnson, 1994)	Book	Pro-Ed	Written primarily to aid psychologists and educational consultants who perform psychoeducational assessments. Also useful for those who must read and use assessment reports to make decisions regarding educational programs for students.
Psychoeducational Assessment of Visually Impaired Persons (Bradley-Johnson, 1995)	Videotape	American Printing House for the Blind	Video and brochure targeted to teachers and school psychologists who have not had experience with people who are visually impaired.
Work-Play Trays	Equipment	American Printing House for the Blind	Trays in two sizes (11 ¾ × 17 inches, 13 ¼ × 21 ¼ inches) that will hold objects that otherwise may roll out of reach. Provides an enclosed work space for activities, such as sorting and counting.

Contact information for each of the resources listed will be found in the Sources of Products, Materials, Equipment, and Services section at the back of this book.

CHAPTER 3

Ongoing Assessments: Informal Techniques

Carol A. Layton

KEY POINTS

◆ Informal techniques personalize the assessment process. They use school settings, instructional techniques, vocational plans, academic and cognitive needs, social implications, and environmental factors that are helpful in accurately depicting the student in his or her environment.

◆ Informal assessment techniques are holistic in nature, focusing on the student, making assessment an indispensable part of educational teaming, planning, and instruction.

◆ Informal assessment, exemplified by a collaborative team approach, results in a multidisciplinary process with many participants. It is problem solving at its best.

VIGNETTE

Ms. Chavez sat in the back of the classroom, writing in her notebook. LaShondra's eighth-grade science class had completed a project in identifying trees using a leaf key from the state's forestry division. LaShondra had easily matched the shapes of the real leaves to the silhouettes in the leaf key. She had used her handheld magnifier occasionally to check the spelling of the name of a tree and had listed the names of the trees on her worksheet using a felt-tip pen. LaShondra had shared her magnifier with her team—in fact, students from other teams had come to look at the pores it revealed on the undersides of certain leaves. Ms. Chavez noted that LaShondra mentioned tactile differences in the leaves that the other students missed. Twice LaShondra had asked her teammates to read notes from the chalkboard to her. When the students returned to their desks to answer the summary questions written on the chalkboard, LaShondra first walked to the board to copy them. By the time she began to answer the first question, several students were almost finished with the task.

Overall, however, Ms. Chavez was pleased with LaShondra's progress. It was important to know that LaShondra placed at the 72nd percentile in science on the statewide assessment, but the wealth of information obtained from observation in the classroom—how LaShondra used her tools, her social skills, and her various senses to complete a task—was equally important. Observation also permitted Ms. Chavez to note ways in which a simple environmental change—provision of a copy of the summary questions—could facilitate LaShondra's classroom performance.

INTRODUCTION

A quote that reportedly hung in the office of Albert Einstein went something like this: "Not everything that counts can be counted and not everything that can be counted counts" (quoted in Ryan, 1994, p. 1). In the assessment of students with visual impairments, data often cannot be counted, but must be documented. Qualitative data count and make significant differences in the development of excellent programs for students with visual impairments. The assessment of students' growth is a necessary and valuable part of the educational process. Assessment techniques—both informal and formal—are used to identify strengths and needs and to provide the basis for the Individualized Education Program (IEP) for each student. Formal assessment techniques usually involve the use of standardized norm-referenced tests. Informal assessment techniques are not standardized and are easily modified for the unique needs of students with visual impairments. Often this information is not quantifiable; it is qualitative, exceptional, and significant.

Chapter 2 focused on assessment procedures that are typically used in a comprehensive individual assessment, often norm referenced in nature. This chapter focuses on informal assessment techniques that are applicable in classroom instruction and are extremely beneficial to the educational team for planning a student's IEP. When teachers use informal assessment techniques, they uphold a commitment to collect evidence that documents students' learning and growth in naturally occurring settings (Ryan, 1994), including the home, the school, and the community.

Informal techniques are teacher friendly and easily explained to parents and help teachers create practical and meaningful IEP goals. They are typically used to gather information from a variety of sources: parents; teachers and other school personnel; and, most important, the student. Informal techniques are often constructed by members of the educational team (parents, general and special education teachers, administrative personnel, assessment personnel, the teacher of students with visual impairments, the orientation and mobility (O&M) instructor, and any other re-

lated service teachers) and may take the form of observations, interviews, checklists, and so forth. In the 1997 amendments to the Individuals with Disabilities Education Act (IDEA; P.L. 105-17), the renewed emphasis on tying assessment information to instructional goals makes the use of informal assessment techniques valuable.

The 1997 amendments to IDEA increase parental participation and create a stronger, mandatory link between assessment, the development of an IEP, and educational programming, emphasizing evaluation as it relates to the general curriculum and general education setting (Turnbull & Turnbull, 1998). Classroom-based assessment is required to monitor a student's progress and current functioning and to deliver effective services in the general and special education setting. IDEA now requires a holistic evaluation of a student's strengths and needs and the educational team's use of informal and formal tools, as well as assessment strategies to meet the student's educational needs.

Information from parents—an integral component of informal data collection—is essential in the assessment process because parents are key experts on their child's strengths and needs and activities at home and in the community. As mandated by IDEA, parents must have a direct role in assessment planning and the IEP process. Interviewing parents regarding their goals for their child helps the educational team (also referred to as the assessment team) understand the parents' perception of their child. Parents may contribute other valuable data through such methods as a communication notebook or their responses to checklists (discussed later in this chapter).

Interviewing and devising other informal instruments to gain the perspective of general and special education teachers and other school personnel are powerful tools. When educational team members are actively involved in reflecting on the social behaviors, acquisition of skills, and classroom placement of individual students and putting together successful plans for students, their investment in the process becomes a forceful motivation to help the students achieve goals.

Most important, information from the student is critical to an effective assessment. It can be acquired through informal techniques, such as checklists, open-ended interviews (about vocational goals, leisure activities, study skills, and so forth), and self-evaluation. Diagnostic teaching, a process that integrates teaching and assessment, is also helpful in pinpointing difficulties that a student is experiencing in learning. Each lesson provides an opportunity to modify and refine instruction (Koenig & Holbrook, 1993). A student's preferences regarding cognitive styles of learning, academic strengths, and areas that need improvement can be documented through diagnostic teaching techniques. These components of informal assessments provide the rich background for interpreting the results of formal tests (as described in Chapter 2).

Informal assessments tend to provide a greater wealth of information on the student's functioning at home and school and in the community than do traditional and formal assessments. Traditional assessments focus on the student's responses to tests or sets of predetermined questions. Students with visual impairments often demonstrate splinter skills—that is, concepts that are not cognitively fully developed—and the limited responses available on formal tests may not reveal such a partial conceptual understanding. In contrast, informal techniques are tailored to each student to document the student's progress and growth and to address his or her needs and specific goals. These assessment tools become part of daily planning and instruction, guiding the teacher and student in making learning meaningful and placing all the data obtained in formal and informal assessments in a multifaceted context that is appropriate for planning. This chapter presents information on the use of informal assessment techniques.

ROLE OF THE TEACHER OF STUDENTS WITH VISUAL IMPAIRMENTS

To ensure high-quality, individual assessments, the teacher of students with visual impairments must participate in all stages of the comprehen-

sive assessment process. He or she is likely to be the only person on the student's educational team who is knowledgeable about the impact of the visual impairment on learning and the expanded core curriculum (see Chapter 6) for students who are blind or visually impaired. Therefore, this teacher needs to be directly involved in (1) determining the appropriate areas of assessment; (2) developing or adapting appropriate assessment techniques, both formal and informal; (3) conducting formal and informal assessments, when appropriate; (4) interpreting data, both formal and informal, to ensure the consideration and understanding of the educational, psychological, and social implications of the visual impairment; (5) conducting ongoing assessment and evaluation of a student's progress and documenting this progress; and (6) developing a strong working relationship among the student, parents, and school personnel for productive assessments and instructional planning.

Although the educational team determines which team members will collect data and administer tests, it is appropriate for the teacher of students with visual impairments to administer formalized tests and use informal assessment strategies when possible. However, intelligence tests and some individualized norm-referenced instruments must be administered by a trained psychologist or psychometrist. Furthermore, an understanding of the impact of a visual impairment is essential for achieving accurate IEP goals and making sound recommendations.

INFORMAL ASSESSMENT TECHNIQUES

Informal assessment techniques assess a student's progress in acquiring needed skills over time, and hence the student is the focus of assessment. Informal techniques may be used daily, as a component of a comprehensive assessment, or as a periodic check on current functioning at the end of a curriculum unit and the progress achieved since the previous assessment. In essence, these techniques guide instruction by ensuring that teaching, learning, and evaluation are integral parts of a continuous cycle and fulfill the mandate of IDEA to document a student's current functioning and evidence in achieving the goals of the IEP.

A teacher can either create informal assessment instruments for an individual student or use existing informal instruments to measure current functioning and progress. Since these tools are not norm referenced, they may be modified to fit individual needs without losing their effectiveness. A repertoire of existing instruments and uniquely created instruments is a vital part of a teacher's resource file. The informal assessment techniques and measures discussed in this chapter include these:

◆ Interviews and questionnaires—open-ended questions asked orally and recorded by the examiner or presented in written format and recorded by the respondent;

◆ Observational methods—watching and recording behaviors to help understand the student through anecdotal records, running records, and event records;

◆ Checklists—lists of skills of increasing difficulty or related to a set of objectives that are used to monitor the progress of students;

◆ Communication notebooks—records of events at school and at home made by teachers, parents, and students;

◆ Environmental assessments—analysis of the student's school environment;

◆ Curriculum-based assessment—content from the student's curriculum used to evaluate progress;

◆ Diagnostic teaching—teacher-initiated problem solving that occurs during daily instruction; and

◆ Portfolios—collections of the results of various assessments and samples of the student's work used to evaluate and provide a holistic view of the student's progress.

Teachers of students with visual impairments face a constant challenge of adapting assessments and instruction to meet the unique needs of their students. Informal assessment techniques offer ways to collect bountiful information on students' progress. This chapter discusses a variety of options for conducting ongoing assessments using these informal strategies. To clarify these techniques and give examples of their usage, case studies of students called Joshua and Anna, are presented at various points in the chapter to illustrate how the different techniques work to document functioning and progress, clarify educational needs, and influence instruction. Summations of the case examples of Joshua and Anna are included after all the techniques are presented. The following descriptive information is given to introduce the case studies.

Joshua

Joshua, age 10, is in the fourth grade in a general education setting. From ages 3 to 5, he attended an early childhood program that provided a specialized curriculum for students with visual impairments. He then entered a general education setting and since kindergarten has received daily support from an itinerant teacher of students with visual impairments.

Joshua's vision records from his ophthalmologist indicate that he has no light perception in the right eye and glaucoma in the left eye and that the acuity in his left eye fluctuates between 20/500 and 20/1200 (6/150 and 6/360 metric). The teacher of students with visual impairments states that Joshua makes good use of his vision. Currently, Joshua reads print with a closed-circuit television (CCTV) and uses a handheld scanner for reading print at home. As a result of a recent learning media assessment, Joshua has begun braille instruction to facilitate his ease and rate of reading.

Joshua was evaluated by the school psychologist using a verbal intelligence test, which indicated that he is functioning in the above-average range, and according to the school records, he earned "all A's and B's" in the first, second, and third grades. Joshua listens to audiotaped texts for science and social studies classes and relies heavily on his parents to read assignments to him. He is acquiring braille skills quickly, but is reluctant to use braille or print in the classroom.

Anna

Anna, age ten, is in a self-contained classroom in her neighborhood school and attends physical education, art, and music classes in the general education classroom with her same-age peers. From birth, Anna has received special services for mild cognitive delays and a visual impairment. She attended early childhood programs and following kindergarten was placed in a setting that concentrated on functional skills. She is currently learning Grade 1 braille and can read labels and functional signs in braille. Her instruction in braille is progressing, and Anna is beginning to write and read notes from her teachers and parents.

Anna's records from her ophthalmologist indicate that she is cortically blind, and according to the functional vision assessment, she has no light perception in either eye. Anna receives services from an itinerant teacher of students with visual impairments.

Anna is currently functioning in a mildly intellectually deficient range as measured on a developmental scale and a verbal intelligence scale. On the bases of adaptive behavior measures, an intelligence quotient derived from a verbal intelligence test, and information from the developmental scale, Anna qualifies for services as a student with mild mental retardation. Because of the combination of impairments (mental retardation and blindness), Anna is listed as a student with multiple impairments.

The remainder of this chapter is devoted to helping teachers construct informal assessment instruments. The discussion of each type of instrument includes: (1) a description; (2) advantages; (3) step-by-step directions; (4) continuing case studies of Joshua and Anna, accompanied by sample instruments when appropriate; and (5) an example of a commercially available informal instrument, when applicable. At the conclusion of the

chapter, summaries of the information acquired through each selected informal assessment technique are provided for Joshua and Anna.

INTERVIEWS AND QUESTIONNAIRES

Interviews and questionnaires use open-ended questions to investigate and gather information about specific areas of interest and give parents, students, and teachers opportunities to express their experiences, interests, and concerns. Interviews are generally recorded in a written format by the interviewers, and questionnaires are completed by the persons who are responding to the questions. Conducting interviews with students and parents can be an appropriate and worthwhile part of a comprehensive assessment, but for gathering information from teachers, questionnaires are often more efficient, followed by interviews if needed. However, both interviews and questionnaires are used basically for the same purpose: to gain meaningful information that can be used to construct an effective educational program.

To be effective, interviews and questionnaires must be well designed. The principles of well-designed interviews suggested by Sattler (1992) include the following fundamental components:

◆ They have a definite purpose.

◆ The interviewer takes responsibility for the interaction and content.

◆ There is a nonreciprocal relationship between the interviewer and interviewee—the interviewer asks questions, and the interviewee shares his or her thoughts and answers.

◆ The interviewer accepts the interviewee's responses.

◆ The interviewer maintains his or her attention throughout the interview.

◆ The interview takes place at an agreed-upon time and place where the interviewee is comfortable and not fatigued or rushed.

- The interviewer does not avoid unpleasant facts and feelings.

With just slight modifications these principles apply to the construction of productive questionnaires. The following common components serve as guidelines for preparing questionnaires:

- There is a definite purpose.
- The questions are open ended.
- The reader accepts the responses.
- The reader regards the responses as valuable input.
- The reader obtains a release from the person completing the questionnaire so the information can be used for assessment purposes.

Interviews and questionnaires are most useful when they are constructed with open-ended questions, questions that cannot be answered with one-word responses. The following questions are typical open-ended questions asked of a parent in an interview setting:

- How would you describe your child's experience at school?
- How does your child spend leisure time outside school?
- How does your child get along with others at school and at home?
- What opportunities has your child had to develop responsibilities at home?
- How does your child study at home?
- What are your concerns regarding your child's educational programming?
- What goals has your child achieved during the current school year?
- What are your goals and plans for your child when he or she graduates from high school?

Although qualitative in nature and time-consuming to collect and analyze, the information obtained from interviews and questionnaires gives the educational team knowledge of curricular areas based on the observations of others to determine a student's strengths and needs. Ideally, the team will place these comments in a contextual framework that will pinpoint and verify the need for further assessment.

Constructing Interviews and Questionnaires

Interviews and questionnaires are not difficult to design. A basic 8 to 10 question interview can evolve into a lengthy discussion. Often interviews are preferable to questionnaires, especially for parents, since the interviewer can immediately verify what he or she has heard and ask more questions should the need arise, whereas questionnaires often limit the respondent to the space provided beneath a question. Whatever the choice, the following guidelines for interviews (guidelines for questionnaires are presented later) should help yield useful information:

1. Construct open-ended questions that are easy to understand. If one question can be answered in a few words, couple it with a question that requires more information.

2. Explain the purpose of the interview and obtain the person's written consent to use the information in an education team meeting. Remind the interviewee that all the information will be recorded as valuable data.

3. Encourage the respondent to give additional comments if the question elicits a new idea or some related information.

4. Respect the time constraints of respondents; conduct interviews at appropriate times when they are not rushed or fatigued.

5. Verify a respondent's answer by reading it aloud and restating or rephrasing the response. Preface this restatement with a question or statement, such as "Is this

what you mean?" or "Let me see if I understand what you are saying."

6. Respect the person being interviewed. Be courteous and a good listener and recorder.

Joshua

Joshua is having difficulty with reading at school. His teacher of students with visual impairments and other members of the assessment team want to help Joshua develop his reading skills as a powerful tool to aid his academic progress and to make reading an enjoyable leisure-time activity. The members of the team are cognizant of Joshua's strong intellectual potential. They are also motivated to help Joshua learn to use reading as a leisure activity so that reading can reinforce conceptual information that he may lack because of his visual impairment. The team designs an interview for Joshua (see Figure 3.1), and the school counselor interviews him about his reading tasks at school. The following is a summary of the information acquired from Joshua during the interview:

◆ Joshua likes being with his friends at school—playing games and talking with them. Since he likes being with his friends, he does not like to use his CCTV because it prevents him from sitting with his friends.

◆ He is taking math, physical education, art, social studies, science, and language arts. Joshua likes math, PE, and art classes best, and they are his easiest subjects. He likes these classes because little reading is required, and he finds reading braille to be very slow.

◆ Ms. Brown is his favorite teacher because she gives projects to complete instead of tests. Joshua does not like to take tests. He would rather participate in group activities or make a product to demonstrate his understanding.

◆ Joshua asks his parents to read all his assignments to him at home.

This information substantiates a number of points that the educational team surmised: Joshua is still experiencing difficulty with reading assignments, dislikes his CCTV and views it as an obstacle in social interactions, and is not enthusiastic about reading with braille in the classroom because of his lack of speed. The team brainstorms methods to help Joshua improve his reading skills for academic progress and leisure activity. The information gleaned from the interview affirms the team's decision to switch to braille as Joshua's primary reading medium.

Anna

Anna's teacher of students with visual impairments wants to create a productive working link between home and school. Typically, Anna's parents attend meetings of the educational team, but are reluctant to put forth their own ideas and allow professionals to make the decisions. The educational team wants Anna's goals to be generalized from home to school to increase her potential for learning across settings. Therefore, the teacher of students with visual impairments develops an interview to help elicit important goals from Anna's parents (see Figure 3.2). The following is a summary of the information acquired from Anna's mother.

◆ Anna is the oldest of four children, ranging in age from 1 to 10 years. She lives at home with her mother and father, siblings, and grandmother.

◆ Anna was born prematurely (eight weeks early); her Apgar scores were low, and she remained in the neonatal unit for six weeks. She easily develops respiratory infections and has been hospitalized four times during her 10 years for pneumonia.

◆ Anna loves to listen to tapes and CDs and enjoys playing with her brothers and sister.

◆ Anna can make her own bed and helps pick up toys.

◆ Anna listens and follows directions well.

Student Interview

Interviewer _Marcia Davis_

Name: Joshua Martin	Date: 8-12-00	Grade: 4th

1. What do you like best about school? _Being with my friends, playing games, and talking with them_

2. What subjects are you taking this year? _Math, phys. ed., art, social studies, science, language arts_

   What subjects do you like best? _Math, P.E., and art classes best_

   Why do you like these best? _Little reading is required in these classes._

3. Who are your favorite teachers? _Ms. Brown_

4. What kinds of things or subjects are easiest for you to learn? _I'm learning braille—it is a little slow right now, but I'm catching on._

   Why are they easier? _Nonreading classes are a breeze. No reading and school is a breeze._

5. What do some teachers do to make learning easier? _Ms. Brown gives projects instead of tests._

6. Do you have trouble with tests? If so, tell me what gives you problems? _Having to read the items, the CCTV is so big and it's slow to use._

   What kinds of tests do you like the best? _Tests with little reading and writing are the best._

   How could the tests be better? _Multiple choice tests! Things would be better if I never had to use that CCTV. It keeps me from my friends._

7. Do you ever ask for help with your school work? What kind of help do you like? _Yes, my parents read my assignments to me._

Figure 3.1. Sample Student Interview Form

Parent Interview

Interviewer _Julia Smith_

Name of Interviewee: _Mary Fields_	Student's Name: _Anna Fields_	Date: _7-1-00_

1. Where and with whom does your child reside? _Anna lives at home with her mother (me) and her father._

2. Who lives in your child's home? _Anna's grandmother lives with us. We have three other children._

3. What are the ages of the siblings? _Chris, age 6, David, age 4, and Natalie, age 1_

4. Describe your child's health history? _Low Apgar scores - Anna was very ill as an infant. She was born 8 wks premature. She was in the neonatal unit 6 wks._

5. What is the current status of your child's health? _Anna has respiratory problems every winter._

6. What does your child like to do in her free time? _She plays with her brothers and sister. She loves tapes!_

7. What activities does your family do together? _We go places together - camp together._

8. What chores and responsibilities does your child have at home? _Anna makes her bed and helps pick up toys._

9. What do you consider to be your child's strengths? _Anna listens well and follows directions well._

10. What do you consider your child doing at age 22? _I want Anna to be able to live independently with some assistance._

11. What goals would you like for your child to work on this year at school? _I would like for Anna to be able to fix snacks & clean up._

Figure 3.2. Sample Parent Interview Form

- At the present time, Anna's mother wants Anna to learn how to prepare simple snacks and clean up after herself.

- In the future, Anna's mother would like Anna to be able to prepare her own meals and perform daily living tasks independently.

Interview information guides the IEP team in selecting goals that are meaningful for Anna. Daily living experiences, such as simple snack preparation and cleanup, will enable Anna to develop skills that can be increased in the level of difficulty. Anna's mother is already thinking about Anna's future independence. Well-planned goals that encompass cooking experiences at home and school can lead to more complex tasks that will prepare Anna for greater independence.

The following are guidelines for questionnaires:

1. At the beginning of the questionnaire, include a note that explains the purpose of the questionnaire, provide a space for the respondent's signature for written consent to use the information in an educational team meeting, and emphasize that all information will be recorded as valuable data.
2. Construct open-ended questions that are easy to understand, varying questions that can be answered in a few words with those that require more information. Provide plenty of space for answers.
3. Encourage the respondent to give additional comments on the back of the questionnaire if a question elicits a new idea or some related information.
4. Provide an envelope for the respondent to return the questionnaire to the school. Remember that this information is assessment data and should be treated as confidential information.
5. Give the respondent a due date for returning the questionnaire.
6. Determine the person who is responsible for collecting questionnaires from teachers or parents. This person is typically the one who compiles the information from questionnaires for the next team meeting.

Joshua

The educational team wants to evaluate Joshua's use of reading across the curriculum. The members begin to collect comprehensive data on his current skills and needed areas of development. To obtain additional information, the team assigns the teacher of students with visual impairments the responsibility of constructing a questionnaire to gain information from all of Joshua's current teachers (see Figure 3.3).

The teacher of students with visual impairments distributes and collects the questionnaires. The following information summarizes the thoughts of Joshua's teachers.

- Joshua learns best in small-group situations. He is a great team leader and loves to participate with others in group activities.

- Joshua does not like to read silently or to work independently. Some teachers thought that he worked so slowly that he never had time to finish his work in the time allotted to other students, although the work that he does is good.

- Cooperative learning and group projects are best for Joshua. When possible, group projects and cooperative learning are incorporated into the classroom setting.

- Joshua likes to have time to do good work. He often asks for reading assignments a week ahead of time, so he can have his mother read them to him over the weekend. He sometimes uses audiotapes to listen to material from the text.

On the basis of the information from the questionnaires, the team notes that Joshua is having difficulty keeping up with reading assignments and works well in cooperative group activities. Joshua's assessment teams decides that further assessment information is needed on Joshua's braille literacy skills. Assignments are made to gather more information in that area.

August 15, 2000

Teacher Questionnaire

The following questions are an important part of the assessment of _Joshua Martin_. The assessment team needs your feedback in regard to _Joshua's_ current level of functioning in the classroom. Please regard this written questionnaire as confidential. Upon completion, please place the questionnaire in the enclosed envelope and return it to me by October 1. Thank you for your time.

Margaret White
Teacher of Visually Impaired Students

1. What are _Joshua's_ learning strengths?

   Joshua works well in a group. He is a leader!

2. What are _his_ learning weaknesses?

   He does not like silent reading assignments. He works slowly.

3. What classroom learning strategies work best for _Joshua_?

   Cooperative learning group projects.

4. What strategies is _he_ using to complete reading assignments in your class?

   1. asks for assignments early
   2. uses taped texts

5. What type of learning situations are the most beneficial to _Joshua_?

   1. Group projects
   2. Group work with other students reading orally.

6. Is the quality of _his_ work comparable to others in the classroom?

   He reads slowly; his work quality is good!

7. What additional modifications or adjustments in scheduling do you perceive _Joshua_ needs?

   Extra time for assignments requiring reading. Give assignments early.

Signature _Bill Waters_   Date _8-19-00_

Figure 3.3. Sample Teacher Questionnaire Form

OBSERVATIONAL METHODS

Teachers and other school personnel constantly observe students in the school setting. These observations provide valuable information to the educational teams regarding students' skills, behaviors, and interactions with others. Observing students while they interact in the classroom and throughout the school day adds another dimension to ongoing assessments. It is a tool to use while monitoring the effectiveness of a lesson, as well as assessing students' attainment of IEP goals. Since preschool students and students with visual impairments and additional disabilities are often difficult to assess with formal instruments, observational methods are an excellent source of documenting their strengths and needs.

Observational methods provide feedback to teachers and parents on specific behaviors that are interfering with a student's learning, as well as clues to cognitive processing. They also allow comparisons to be made between behaviors that occur in classroom settings and other environments throughout the day. These methods provide a written record of a student's behavior and a description of how the student is reacting in certain situations. Observations can be used to change instructional techniques that may alleviate some difficult behaviors.

Sattler (1992) described several methods of recording observations. Among them are narrative records including anecdotal records and running records, and event records.

Narrative Records

There are two basic types of narrative records: anecdotal records and running records (Sattler, 1992). Anecdotal records are written records of anything that appears significant in regard to a student's learning that occurs throughout the school day. Organizing and writing these records are often a challenge for teachers. Teachers are reluctant to stop and record these observations because doing so interrupts the lesson, but valuable information is lost when records are not made as they occur. To use these general observations

most efficiently, the teacher needs to develop a system that is unobtrusive. The following are two examples of simple systems that are designed to facilitate the recording of general observations.

◆ Keep adhesive-backed notes in a pocket, along with a pen, and record observations as they occur (see Figure 3.4). This system enables the teacher to jot down information and place the notes on a page with the correct date in the individual student's folder or in a file in an index box under the student's name. These records can be written without stopping a lesson.

◆ Use a general classroom observation form, such as the one in Figure 3.5. A clipboard is often a handy place to keep these forms. The form provides a space for the teacher to record the event and the student or students involved. After class, the teacher transfers these handwritten records into the students' individual folders.

The following are guidelines for recording anecdotal information:

1. Record behaviors that may provide insights into the student's pattern of learning or behavior at school.

2. If several similar observations of behavior (for example, positive behaviors, such as reading and talking appropriately with other children, and negative behaviors, like body rocking, thumbsucking, and eye poking) are made, consider targeting these behaviors to document their frequency and setting in an event record.

Joshua

During science and social studies, Joshua continually avoids using his CCTV. The teacher records this observation because it is becoming more frequent (see Figure 3.5). Later, she places the observation form in Joshua's file and makes a note to monitor this behavior closely to see if it is occurring in other subjects and to inquire if he

Results of Activities

Name of Observer _Julia Smith_   Date _10-4-99_

Anna-

–Needs prompting to wash hands.

Anna-

–Had trouble recognizing braille words for

Mayo
Mustard

–Needs to review food labels.

Anna-

–Left work island messy in the kitchen.

–Needs instructions on cleaning work area.

–Needs help with putting dishes in dishwasher.

Figure 3.4. Sample Anecdotal Record

General Observation Record

Name of Observer _Margaret White_

Student's Name: _Joshua Martin_		
Date	Observation	Setting
_8-20-00_	_Tells teacher that he has already listened to the chapter! Does not want to read with CCTV in class._	_Social Studies_
_8-21-00_	_Asks teacher for permission for student near him to read out loud. He does not want to use the CCTV._	_Science_

Figure 3.5. Sample Observation Record

is avoiding the CCTV in other classrooms. After noting Joshua's reluctance to use the CCTV in all settings, the teacher and Joshua discuss his avoidance of the CCTV. Joshua tells the teacher that the CCTV keeps him from being with his friends. The teacher and Joshua decide to re-arrange the room so Joshua can still have his CCTV available but be in closer contact with his friends. The teacher shares her simple solution with other school personnel, who help Joshua arrange the use of the CCTV in their classrooms, so it is less obtrusive and more conducive to interaction with friends.

Running Records

A running record is a rich description of a student in a natural setting that attempts to capture behavior as it is occurring (Sattler, 1992). These are typically records of lengthy episodes of a student's behavior (observations over a class period or extended amount of time). The entire episode is recorded, not just an isolated behavior, and is recorded without an analysis. It is a "telling" of a student's behavior in sequence.

The following is a synopsis of Sattler's (1992) comprehensive instructions for reading assessments:

1. Identify the child.
2. Describe the setting and the time of day.
3. Record events as they occur.
4. Be cognizant of verbal and nonverbal cues generated by the student.
5. Write down important verbalizations verbatim.
6. Preserve the sequence of events.
7. Attempt to be accurate, objective, and as complete as possible.
8. Describe the behavior; do not interpret it.
9. Integrate the information into a descriptive picture of the student.

Anna

Anna's teacher of students with visual impairments noted from the interview with Anna's mother that cooking skills and working in the kitchen are two areas of learning that can be generalized from the home to the school. Therefore, she plans to observe Anna using a running record to learn more about how Anna functions at school in cooking activities in the daily living center (see Figure 3.6).

Information gained from the running record of Anna's behavior in the functional skills classroom will aid Anna's teacher in planning future lessons. The synopsis of the running record indicates that Anna follows directions, needs encouragement to finish tasks, and responds well to teacher-student interaction. Her teacher deduces that Anna likes cooking and will probably benefit from extended experiences in cooking. Through the use of a running record the teacher of students with visual impairments knows that, although Anna enjoys cooking experiences, she requires encouragement to follow through with tasks. This information enables Anna's teacher to make future lesson plans that she knows will be enjoyable and beneficial learning experiences for Anna.

Event Records

Event records focus on specific targeted behaviors as they occur within an observational period, for example, 15 or 30 minutes (Sattler, 1992). A targeted behavior (such as reading, working, talking appropriately, smiling, shouting, screaming, making noise, thumb sucking, and head rocking) must be defined clearly so that the observer will be able to recognize it when it is occurring. Not all targeted behaviors are negative; it is appropriate and beneficial to graph the frequency of positive behaviors to encourage students to demonstrate desired behaviors more often. A frequency count—the number of occurrences of a target behavior within a specified observational period—is valuable quantitative information. The following are guidelines for recording targeted behaviors:

1. Determine the number of times that the student will be observed.
2. Designate the length of the observation period.

Student's Name _Anna Fields_   Date _8-15-00_

Setting _Functional Skills Classroom_   Name of Observer _Julia Smith_

Activity _Making Cookies_   Time _9:00 a.m._

Anna, a 10-year-old student who is blind, is seated at a table in the daily living center eating breakfast by herself. The other students, finished with breakfast, are at an adjacent table cutting out cookie dough to make cookies. The group is conversing about the shapes of the cookies. Anna is seated where she can hear the other students' conversations. The teacher invites Anna to join in the group activity. "Anna, come and help us make cookies." Several of the students join in. "Come on, Anna; this is fun." Anna continues to eat her breakfast slowly. Five minutes later, Anna gets up from the table and takes her plate to the sink. She rinses her glass and places it in the sink. Anna walks to the restroom and washes her hands. She goes to the table where the students are cutting out cookie dough that they prepared the day before. The teacher directs Anna to an empty chair. Anna sits down. The following conversation occurs. "Anna, do you remember what kind of cookies we mixed yesterday?" the teacher asks. Anna responds, "Sugar cookies, and we put them in the refrigerator." The teacher says, "That's right. Today we are cutting out our cookies and we will bake them in the oven for 10 minutes at 350 degrees. Would you like to cut out some cookies?" Anna says yes. The teacher sets a sheet of wax paper in front of Anna. She talks to Anna about the paper, the way it feels, and why it is placed on the table. She places a ball of cookie dough on the paper and explains to Anna how to roll the dough out so that it will be flat. The teacher gives Anna a small container of flour and a rolling pin. The teacher helps Anna flatten the dough, and roll the dough with the rolling pin. Anna listens closely to the teacher and is cooperative. The teacher asks Anna, "What shapes would you like your cookies to be? We have circles, hearts, stars, and rectangles." Anna responds, "Heart, please." The teacher gives her a heart cookie cutter, and Anna cuts five cookies out of the dough. The teacher comes by with a cookie sheet and helps Anna place her cookies on the pan. Anna smiles and talks about making other things in the kitchen all by herself. Anna says, "I cook at home. I make toast. I like to cook and eat." She listens to her teacher talk about cleaning up. Anna takes her cookie scraps and places them in the trash. She walks to the sink to wash her hands.

Synopsis

- Anna is comfortable in her classroom. She knows her routine. She takes her time finishing tasks.
- When motivated, Anna listens and follows directions.
- She responds well to her teacher.
- She is learning cooking tasks in the classroom that can be transferred to her kitchen at home.
- She enjoys cooking.

Figure 3.6. Sample Running Record

3. Target the specific behavior that needs to be observed.

4. Define the behavior clearly, so the observer or observers will immediately recognize it.

5. Choose the method for recording data (such as paper and pencil, electronic counter).

Joshua

As has been noted in previous glimpses of his reading behavior, Joshua is trying to avoid reading either braille or with his CCTV at school but is unaware of his determined tactics to avoid reading at school. The teacher of students with visual impairments decides to observe Joshua in his classes and monitor the number of times that he avoids reading assignments when he is directed to begin reading.

A generic form like the one in Figure 3.7 is used to monitor Joshua's behavior regarding reading. Frequency refers to the number of times the target behavior occurs, setting refers to where the behavior occurs, and length of observation is the time spent observing the student in the classroom. After collecting the information shown in Figure 3.7, Joshua's teacher discusses with him his reluctance to read in school. Joshua hadn't been aware of the number of times that he avoided reading tasks. After discussing the situation, Joshua agrees to initiate reading tasks and to record in a small notepad each time he avoids a reading assignment. Daily, Ms. White and Joshua will discuss his record of avoidance. If there are reasons for the avoidance that Ms. White can circumvent, she will make the adaptation so that Joshua is more comfortable with reading assignments. Examples of such adaptations would be placing the CCTV in such a way that Joshua can sit with his friends or providing reading assignments ahead of time so Joshua can have his parents read to him at home and then be able to simply skim the material in school. Joshua agrees to try to initiate reading when asked.

Information gained from forms such as Figure 3.7 gives the educational team and, when appropriate, the student, documentation to motivate change in classroom behavior and to initiate changes in the IEP. It is a simple, yet good example of assessment guiding instruction.

CHECKLISTS

A checklist is a list of items to be observed, monitored, and noted. Checklists are often presented in the form of a series of questions or statements requiring a yes-or-no answer to document whether a student has mastered a specific skill in the area being investigated, such as braille literacy skills, or various academic or vocational skills. Checklists, used effectively, pinpoint areas of instruction and modification that require focus and emphasis. They are typically linked with the curriculum and are sensitive measurements of progress that can be used to safeguard the IEP process, such as by monitoring parental involvement.

A checklist is an efficient tool to use with a student who has unique needs because it documents behavior. It indicates a student's own progress between two points in time and does not compare the student's progress with that of others. Checklist items are easy to understand, facilitate communication among members of the educational team, and can be used to develop IEP goals. The following are directions for creating a checklist:

1. Select the behavior, skill, series of skills, or type of activity to be assessed. To be appropriate for use with a checklist, the behavior must be observable, for example, getting dressed for school, eating lunch at school, demonstrating specific personal hygiene habits.

2. Organize the list of tasks in a logical format.

3. Use a verb (such as *wash, dry, brush, shave,* or *style*) as the initial word in a listing to help ensure that the behavior is observable.

Observation Form for Event Records

Name of Observer *Margaret White*

Name of Student: *Joshua Martin*			
Definition of Target Behavior: *Avoids reading when asked to read*			
Frequency	Setting	Date	Length of Observation
//// *(4 requests)*	*Science*	*8-27-00*	*45 minutes*
// *(2 requests)*	*Social Studies*	*8-27-00*	*30 minutes*
/// *(3 requests)*	*Language Arts*	*8-29-00*	*45 minutes*

Figure 3.7. Sample Observation Form for Event Records

4. Decide on the criteria for marking the checklist. A format indicating "yes" or "no" is the most simple choice. Others could include: "yes," "no," or "sometimes" or "allowed to do," "can do," "does habitually," or "skill emerging." Another useful response is "no opportunity to observe."

5. Insert blank lines at the end of each subset or subcategory to allow the parents, teachers, and the student to record alternative tasks.

6. Include space for the teachers and parents to write comments about their observations, if appropriate.

7. Incorporate dates into the checklist design to give a benchmark regarding the amount of progress within a specified period.

Joshua

Joshua, his teacher of students with visual impairments, and other members of the educational team are concerned about providing many opportunities for Joshua to develop his braille- and print-reading skills as a literacy tool and as a leisure-time activity. The teacher develops a checklist designed specifically for Joshua that includes different types of reading materials (see Figure 3.8). Since Joshua is using both print and braille at the current time, he marks on the checklist the medium which he is reading. He reads a selection to a listener and records the listener's name and the amount of time he spent reading.

To demonstrate the versatility of this type of tool, the following scenario demonstrates a different type of checklist (see Figure 3.9).

The educational team at Joshua's school works diligently to involve parents in the assessment process. The form shown in Figure 3.9 was developed by examining current state regulations regarding special education, the school district's special education handbook, and new federal law. This checklist's purpose is to ensure that the educational team is cognizant of the parents' needs and the requirements of state and federal law in conjunction with the school district's policy. The leader of the assessment team uses this checklist to ensure that parental safeguards have been addressed to help parents participate fully in the IEP process.

In this type of checklist, include a signature line for the parent and the person filling out the checklist and a space for the date when the form was completed.

Criterion-referenced Checklists

A criterion-referenced checklist is designed to measure a student's progress in a specific skill (Gredler, 1999) by indicating his or her mastery of a specific criterion or a set of objectives (Overton, 1996). An example of a criterion-referenced item may be reading words with a consonant, long vowel, consonant, and silent *e* pattern, such as *lake, bake, slide,* and *hide.* The criterion may be to decode 10 words at 100 percent accuracy. Many criterion-referenced assessments are presented in the form of checklists. They differ from the previously mentioned checklists in that they address a defined domain, such as naming body parts or identifying colors, with a specified criterion level, such as 90 percent of the items must be correct to indicate mastery. According to Gredler (1999), the word *criterion* is interpreted to mean a standard of performance on a particular domain or a level of mastery in a particular skill. These instruments allow teachers to compare a student's performance with a preset standard or level of accepted mastery (Stiggens, 1997).

A criterion-referenced checklist measures an individual's performance on a particular skill, and the information derived from it indicates the student's mastery of a skill. Mastery levels can be selected in a variety of ways such as 95 percent and above as mastery of the objective and 85 to 94 percent as instructional level. Below 85 percent needs more instuction and practice. A teacher can easily construct a criterion-referenced checklist by using the goals that are listed in the curriculum

Checklist of Reading Opportunities

Student's Name ___*Joshua Martin*___

Name of Recorder (if other than the student) _____

Week of ___*Aug. 25, 2000*___ (Monday to Monday)

Type of Reading Material	Date	Format Braille	Print	Listener/Length of Time Read
Library books	10/25	✓		Jan Martin 30 min.
Directions on games				
Labels	10-27		✓	Bob Martin 10 min.
Magazines				
Joke books	10-30		✓	Bob Martin 30 min.
Cereal boxes				
Recipes				
Newspapers				
Comic books				

Textbooks
  Science
  Social studies
  Science
  Reading
  Reading
	10/25
	10/26
	10/27
	10/28
	10/29
		✓
		✓
		✓
		✓
		✓
				Jan Martin 45 min.
				" " 30 min.
				" " 30 min.
				" " 45 min.
				" " 45 min.

Mail				
Advertisements				
Letters and notes				
Riddles				
Other				

Figure 3.8. Sample Checklist

Parental Postassessment Checklist

Name of Student _____

Parents ...	Yes	No
Read or listened to Parent Rights Booklet.		
Indicated their understanding of their rights.		
Participated in preassessment planning.		
Contributed assessment data (interviews, checklists, and the like).		
Understood the results of all the data collected.		
Accepted the results of the assessment team.		
Made recommendations for the IEPs.		
Agreed with the IEP goals selected.		
Agreed with the placement decisions.		
Received a copy of their child's IEP.		
If desired, received a copy of their child's assessment report.		

_____   _____
Parent or Guardian   Date

_____   _____
Recorder   Date

Figure 3.9. Sample Checklist

as items. By doing so, the teacher can ensure a good match between the checklist and the content of instruction. A commercially available test may have valuable content but not match the curriculum, so that the use of such an instrument would be invalid. Testing what you teach is a valid measurement of classroom instruction.

Gredler (1999) made the following recommendations regarding the construction of criterion-referenced checklists:

1. Choose a particular skill or group of competencies to assess.
2. List objectives that state particular capabilities.
3. Include items on the checklist in an observable format.
4. Report performance in terms of the objectives or skills.
5. Provide a mastery level or a continuum of performance such as novice to expert.

Joshua

The teacher of students with visual impairments constructs a criterion-referenced checklist (see Figure 3.10) to ascertain Joshua's competencies in reading comprehension. This checklist is directly tied to a district-mandated scope and sequence in reading. The criterion is 90 percent mastery on homework and in-class assignments. Because of his previous slow reading with print, comprehension was often a problem. In the past, Joshua had relied on his parents to read orally material that was difficult to understand. With his acquisition of braille skills, his teacher of students with visual impairments wants to monitor comprehension-related tasks. On the basis of the results of the checklist, the educational team is able to determine Joshua's status in comprehension using reading with braille. The team makes the following recommendations for Joshua's educational plan:

1. Continue daily instruction in braille skills.
2. Begin using braille as a tool in the classroom.

Commercially Available Criterion-referenced Assessments

Numerous commercially available checklists can assist the assessment team and facilitate effective teaching and assessment. These checklists are in general efficient and easy to use, and the following section describes several useful resources. In addition to the checklists that follow, the teacher can use self-made checklists or those developed by colleagues. These instruments become valuable tools and should be placed in a resource file for future use.

The Brigance Inventories.   The Brigance Inventories are widely used criterion-referenced assessments that are often referred to as extensive checklists and are considered a "system" of inventories that span various levels of skills. They are designed to record a student's progress over a number of years. Each inventory is intended to assess the mastery of certain concepts so that a teacher can choose areas that need thorough documentation. The system consists of large notebooks that are used in conjunction with student record books. The teacher uses various colors of pens or pencils to denote specific assessment dates; a color-coded key is kept on the first page of each student record book. Each time the teacher assesses a student, he or she records the answers in a different-colored lead pencil. The instructions are easy to understand and include the verbal directions that the teacher gives to the student. Although these instruments are not designed for students with visual impairments, these criterion-referenced instruments produce an available system for evaluating IEP goals and objectives. The Brigance system includes four criterion-referenced tests for different ages and skill levels:

◆ *The Brigance Diagnostic Inventory of Early Development-Revised* (Brigance, 1991).

◆ *The Brigance Diagnostic Inventory of Essential Skills* (Brigance, 1981).

◆ *The Brigance Diagnostic Inventory of Basic Skills* (Brigance, 1999).

Checklist of Comprehension Skills

Student: *Joshua Martin*   Name of Recorder *Margaret White*

Date: *August 31, 2000*

Student must achieve an average of 90 percent on homework and in-class assignments for a check in "yes" column for each activity.

Activity	Yes	No	N/O	Comments
Answers explicit questions (literal, factual, and recall)	✓			
Retells stories in sequence	✓			
States the main ideas of stories	✓			
Identifies significant details in stories	✓			
Draws conclusions		✓		*Jumps to wrong conclusion*
Predicts outcomes		✓		*Often is unrealistic*
Summarizes a story in one or two sentences	✓			
Understands cause–effect relationships		✓		*Finds this difficult*
Distinguishes between fact and fantasy	✓			
Understands the feelings of characters in the story	✓			
Answers questions that involve critical or evaluative response	✓			
Reads and follows written directions	✓			
Locates important details in content material	✓			
Understands the meaning of specialized vocabulary in science and social studies	✓			

N/O = No opportunity to observe

Figure 3.10. Sample Criterion-referenced Checklist

◆ *The Brigance Diagnostic Life Skills Inventory* (Brigance, 1994).

Tactile supplements to the *Brigance Diagnostic Inventory of Basic Skills* and *The Brigance Diagnostic Inventory of Early Development* are both available from the American Printing House for the Blind (APH). These tactile supplements include braille reading passages. To use these supplements, a teacher must already have the original inventory in print. Large print is not provided in the supplements.

Assessment of Braille Literacy Skills (ABLS).   The ABLS, by Koenig and Farrenkopf (1995), is a convenient, systematic checklist for monitoring braille literacy skills that covers unique features of braille reading. A student's progress is recorded by scoring skills as D = Developing, I = Independent, and NA = Not applicable.

Independent Living: A Curriculum with Adaptations for Students with Visual Impairments, Volumes 1, 2, and 3.   Although these books were designed as a resource and curriculum guide, they include well-developed checklists that are designed to record students' progress in independent living skills (Loumiet and Levack, 1991). This curriculum is intended for use with persons who will eventually live independently.

The Assessment Kit: Kit of Informal Tools for Academic Students with Visual Impairments. Compiled by Sewell (1997), this compilation identifies checklists and other informal tools that are appropriate for assessments. Areas addressed are the abacus, braille calculator, career readiness, communication, concept development, daily living skills, classroom behavior, communication, family environment, math, organization and study skills, keyboarding, reading, science, social studies, script writing, slate and stylus, social skills, and technology. Also included is a list of instruments used in many of these designated areas.

COMMUNICATION NOTEBOOKS

A communication notebook is a written account of activities, as well as reflections, in a natural setting that can be shared among several parties, such as the student, teachers, and parents, and used in several ways. First, the student can use it to record activities and reflective thoughts throughout the day. However, for a communication notebook to be used as a part of the assessment process, the student must be aware that it will be read by others. For students who write in braille, the communication notebook can be produced on a computer, printed out in braille and print, and stored in a binder so that the student can read and reflect on previous entries and the teacher can read the print version and add his or her comments and responses to the student. This notebook can be used not only to document activities, but as a purposeful activity that integrates reading and writing.

Second, parents can add valuable information by keeping a communication notebook of leisure skills, self-help, or home-living skills that the student routinely performs. This written account of what the student is doing at home and in the community helps the assessment team determine the skills that the student has or needs to acquire. The added reflective component gives insights into the parents' concerns regarding these skills. The combination of the written account and the parents' reflections and reactions help the educational team design goals that will enable the student to become better prepared for life experiences. Again, sending the notebook to school for the teacher to comment on activities during the school day and returning it to the parents helps link the school and the home. It also expands the potential for generalizing skills mastered in either setting.

A communication notebook provides a wealth of qualitative, detailed, reflective information. As was stated previously, it is an excellent tool for enhancing communication between the home and school and lends a valuable perspective on the student's progress. If the communication notebook is written by the student and teacher, it can link writing and reading to everyday activities. By looking for links between skills developed at home and generalized at school, and vice versa, the assessment team can use the communication notebook to create IEP goals that foster instructional connections across the curriculum.

Here are a few basic directions for using a communication notebook that the teacher of students with visual impairments needs to give to the student, parent, and general education teacher:

1. Target the type of behaviors that will be recorded in the communication notebook. For example, if the team's concerns center on the student's ability to perform daily living skills at home, then the parent may be asked to record the types of appliances and daily living activities that the student typically uses.

2. Supply the parent, general education teacher, or student with a small notebook with the target behaviors listed. Spend a few minutes explaining the target behaviors and the need to record any reflective thoughts regarding them.

3. Give the parent or student an idea of how many days to record information and instructions about sending the notebook to school for the teacher's input.

4. Remind the parent, student, and general education teacher that the notebook will be read by others.

5. Maintain the communication notebook for as long as it is helpful for the student, parent, or general education teacher.

6. Integrate the information into the assessment data by recording the dates, the name of the recorder, and a summary of the qualitative information disclosed in the communication notebook.

Anna

Anna's parents want her to be able to fix simple snacks and clean up in the kitchen after the snacks. They believe that the acquisition of these skills will help prepare Anna to learn the skills she will need to live independently later in life. The team asks the parents if they would be willing to record Anna's ability to find things in the kitchen and her knowledge about snacks, including Anna's preferred snacks, where things are kept in the kitchen, and the ingredients in certain snacks. Anna's parents agree that this information would be valuable in planning IEP goals that will assist Anna now and in the future.

For six weeks, Anna's mother records entries in the communication notebook regarding Anna's likes and dislikes and Anna's knowledge of where things are in the kitchen and the ingredients in the snacks. She also records her thoughts about Anna's choices and what may be appropriate for home and school instruction. The entry in Figure 3.11 demonstrates the type of information needed for planning Anna's IEP; it is also evident that Anna's mother has some valuable ideas about where to begin to help Anna develop a repertoire of snacks.

ENVIRONMENTAL ASSESSMENTS

An environmental assessment evaluates the learning environment of a student. It enables the educational team to identify conditions that support the student's academic success and behavioral competence (Salvia & Ysseldyke, 1995). Examples of these conditions include such teacher-initiated behaviors as establishing classroom rules that are clear and consistent, providing directions with sufficient information and delivering them to the student in several modalities, and giving immediate appropriate feedback. Traditional assessment practices have often focused on a student's deficits. Environmental assessment focuses on designing an instructional environment to help the student learn. At times, these environmental concerns affect the organization of rooms in the student's home. Teaching parents to make their homes accessible and organized often

Date: *July 1, 2000*

Entry by: *Mary Fields (Anna's mother)*

Anna's favorite snacks:
Popcorn
Peanut butter and jelly sandwiches
Apple smiles
Chocolate pudding
Toasted cheese sandwiches
Peanut butter and crackers
Mini pizzas
Chips
Cookies
Twinkies

Anna can find the following things in the kitchen:
Milk in the refrigerator
Glasses in the cabinet
Plates in the cabinet
Forks, knives, and spoons
Peanut butter in the pantry
Jelly in the refrigerator
Fruit in the fruit bowl
Chips in the pantry
Cereal in the cupboard

Things that Anna can make on her own:
Cereal with milk
Peanut butter and crackers
Chips and dip (can find them and put them together to eat)

Reflections
I want Anna to be able to prepare healthful simple meals. I would like her to learn to follow a simple recipe in braille. I think that it would make her feel so important to be able to make snacks for her younger brothers and sister. I also want her to be able to clean up after herself in the kitchen. Someday, Anna will need to cook for herself; we should start now.

Figure 3.11. Sample Communication Notebook Entry

facilitates the student's acquisition of daily living skills and helps the student generalize skills from the daily living center at school to the home environment. The remediation of an impairment is not always appropriate or probable. Adjusting the learning environment is often manageable and an easy step toward greater student success.

An assessment team can design its own environmental assessment tools that are appropriate for the particular school and programs. These tools should address aspects of learning, such as instructional match (the match between the student's ability and the demands placed on the student, in other words, the appropriateness of the learning objectives and level of instruction), instructional presentation, expectations of the student and teacher, classroom environment, motivational techniques, appropriate feedback, and adaptations for effective instruction.

Often changes in the learning environment are the easiest to make and the most effective way to promote successful educational programs, especially for preschool students and students with visual impairments and additional disabilities who may not be able to accommodate themselves to the existing learning environment or indicate when the environment of the classroom is interfering with their learning. These students are dependent on the teacher's and parent's observational skills to determine factors that are distracting them or otherwise inhibiting them from learning. Structuring the learning environment, at home or at school, to fit instructional goals may be the easiest approach to achieving progress toward IEP goals.

Environmental assessments are easy to design. Here are the steps in doing so:

1. Select the factors that the team wishes to assess, such as the classroom setting, kitchen in the daily living center, kitchen at home, class schedule, lighting, or noise.

2. Develop questions or indicators that establish the success in changing each factor.

3. Evaluate the presence of these indicators through observation.

4. Determine strategies to address needed changes in the learning environment.

The assessment shown in Figure 3.12 is typical of those for students who are included in the general education curriculum. It contains some factors, most of which are teacher initiated, that one educational team thought important to help a student achieve success in the classroom. A general education teacher who has never had a student with a visual impairment in the classroom may find it helpful to look at a checklist similar to this one before the beginning of the school year, so he or she can make appropriate adaptations before the first day of class. The teacher of students with visual impairments will need to discuss the checklist with the general education teacher. By developing a cooperative working relationship, the two teachers can team to provide an appropriate environment for the student.

Anna

Anna is having difficulty generalizing the skills she attained at school to the home environment. After talking with Anna's parents, the teacher of students with visual impairments helps them perform an environmental assessment of their kitchen at home. As a team, they develop the indicators for each category of the learning environment listed in Figure 3.13. After they complete the checklist, the parents reorganize their kitchen cabinets and labeling system to facilitate Anna's ability to transfer skills she acquired at school to her home. The parents will monitor Anna's progress to see if the changes in the kitchen help Anna do so.

CURRICULUM-BASED ASSESSMENT

Curriculum-based assessment involves the use of chapter or unit tests and chapter objectives to ascertain whether a student has mastered the objec-

Recorder _____ Date _____		

Student Name:	Yes	No
Instructional Match		
Student's abilities are similar to classroom peers.		
Curriculum matches the student's needs and abilities.		
Instructional Presentation		
Instruction is clear.		
Instruction is presented effectively.		
Directions contain sufficient information for the student.		
Student's understanding is checked.		
Teacher's Expectations		
Teacher's expectations are clear.		
Student is aware of the amount of work required.		
Teacher is consistent in requiring a level of accuracy.		
Teacher has high, yet appropriate expectations for the student.		
Classroom Environment		
Classroom is well organized.		
Aisles are kept clear of chairs.		
Student is located near the teacher's desk.		
Arrangement of furniture rarely changes.		
Motivational Techniques		
Positive behavioral management techniques are used.		
Techniques are effectively motivating for this student.		
Appropriate Feedback		
Teacher gives appropriate feedback immediately.		
When the student makes mistakes, correction is provided.		
Adaptations for Effective Instruction		
Modifications of learning activities are provided.		
Reading materials are provided in braille.		
Writing assignments are adaptable to a braillewriter.		
Pictures are provided through actual items or models.		
Teacher makes learning accessible to the student.		
Videos are used with a descriptive narrator.		
Student is able to participate fully in all learning activities.		

Figure 3.12. Sample Environmental Assessment Form

Recorder _Julia Smith_   Date _August-15-00_

Student's Name: *Anna Fields*	Yes	No
Student Can Locate Appliances in the Kitchen		
Stove	✓	
Refrigerator	✓	
Sink	✓	
Dishwasher	✓	
Microwave	✓	
Student Can Locate Items in the Cabinets		
Glasses	✓	
Plates	✓	
Forks	✓	
Spoons	✓	
Knives	✓	
Pots and Pans		✓
Kitchen Environment		
Kitchen is well organized.		✓
Items are labeled in braille.		✓
Items are within reach of the student.		✓
Arrangement of kitchen items rarely changes.	✓	
Pantry		
Items are arranged in the pantry for easy access.	✓	
Items are labeled in braile.		✓
Recipes		
Snack recipes and directions are located in the student's cookbook.	✓	
The cookbook is maintained, and additional items are added as learned.		✓
Adaptations for Effective Use		
Knobs on all appliances are labeled in braille.		✓
Markings on measuring utensils are in braille.		✓
Dangerous items, prior to instructional use, are in locked cabinets.	✓	
Hazardous cleaning materials are placed in locked cabinets.	✓	
Medicines are located in locked cabinets.	✓	
Hot water heater is regulated not to scald.	✓	

Figure 3.13. Sample Environmental Assessment—Anna's Kitchen at Home

tives taught in a curriculum. The use of chapter tests and chapter objectives found in an assigned textbook is a direct measurement of the curriculum studied and is appropriate for developing IEP goals. Logically, if a student is placed in a fourth-grade science class and the objectives of the class are not altered, then the chapter tests and objectives are appropriate for assessment.

Few instructions are needed for the teacher of students with visual impairments to use curriculum-based measures. The teacher should remember that if modifications are in place while instruction is delivered, then the same modifications need to be in place during the assessment (see Chapter 5). The important concept to stress in curriculum-based assessment is the expected mastery of concepts. If the educational team has placed a student in a class where he or she is expected to achieve objectives other than those related to curricular content—such as working with same-age peers and making friends with other students—then those goals need to be outlined in the IEP objectives. If the goals for the student's participation and mastery of concepts are the same as those of other classmates in the general curriculum, however, then, with modifications for the student's visual impairment, the student should be expected to master all the components of the curriculum. If such a student is unable to take the chapter assessments with the appropriate modifications, then the educational team needs to review the student's IEP. Perhaps the curriculum is not appropriate for this student, and he or she may need to be placed in a classroom where learning is feasible, or the objectives for the student may need to be modified to ensure that instruction and pacing are appropriate to enable mastery.

Examining curricular expectations is vital to the success of students with visual impairments in integrated settings. Lowering expectations for these students is inappropriate. However, appropriate goals can be selected and achievement can be fostered by evaluating the results of the students' curriculum-based assessments. The following are directions for conducting this type of assessment:

1. Examine the concepts presented in the chapter and determine the appropriateness of the test items.

2. When writing objectives for a general education setting, be cautious about lowering mastery levels. Mastery below 70 percent on curricular measures reflects low expectations for the student's outcomes. A 60 percent or 50 percent mastery level does not indicate that the student has mastered the content.

3. Prepare assessment measures in an accessible format using all modifications recommended for instruction in the curriculum-based assessment.

4. Present the chapter test in the student's appropriate learning medium (large print, braille, or regular print with a low vision device, if needed).

5. If the student successfully completes curriculum-based tests, such as chapter tests, successfully, then the curriculum is probably appropriate for the student. If he or she does not, then the assessment team must look at the student's current levels of functioning and ascertain appropriate goals and settings to implement them.

Joshua

The educational team is planning Joshua's schedule for the coming year. While reviewing Joshua's science chapter tests from the preceding year, the team members note that Joshua passed all curriculum-based tests at 90 percent mastery or above. The team used the form presented in Figure 3.14 to record the information gleaned from this review. It recommended that Joshua should continue in a mainstream setting for science with appropriate modifications for his visual impairment. The team members, including Joshua's parents, were pleased with the documentation that Joshua is mastering grade-level material in science.

Textbook and Core Curriculum Expectations

Person completing form _Bill Waters_   Date _5-5-2000_

Student's name _Joshua Martin_

Subject: _Science_		Textbook: _Exploring the Universe_		
The student ...			Yes	No
1. read the previous textbook			✓	
2. participated in all classroom activities enhancing the textbook			✓	
3. took chapter tests and achieved or surpassed 70 percent mastery			✓	
Adaptations needed for success:				
Textbook on tape			✓	
Low vision device			✓	
Oral descriptions			✓	
Extended time for tests			✓	
Access to a computer for written work			✓	

Figure 3.14. Sample Checklist Used in Curriculum-based Assessment

DIAGNOSTIC TEACHING

The process of combining instruction and assessment is often referred to as diagnostic teaching. It is an effective method of monitoring instruction and its effectiveness. Koenig and Holbrook (1993) listed the following principles of diagnostic teaching:

◆ Effective instruction and assessment are linked and should not be separated.

◆ A student's learning should be evaluated on an individual basis, not on the basis of group outcomes.

◆ When assessment data indicates that the student is not learning a specific concept, then instruction is immediately altered.

◆ The teacher engages in problem-solving techniques to explore an individual student's needs.

Through each instructional interaction, the teacher assesses the student's response to learning. The teacher needs to demonstrate good observational skills and is involved in ongoing problem-solving techniques, reacting to the student's response to classroom-assigned tasks.

Diagnostic teaching requires ongoing interaction between the teacher and the student. When a problem arises, the teacher immediately focuses on alternatives or seeks solutions to change the method of instruction to meet the student's needs and hence makes instruction more efficient and effective.

The following suggestions may facilitate diagnostic teaching:

1. Observe the student's response to learning and record general observations of behaviors that need to be noted.

2. Ask questions during instruction, listen attentively to the student's responses, and evaluate these responses.

3. Ask the student questions, such as "How did you get that answer?" If the student is unable to respond, then say "Show me how you worked the problem" or "How did you learn to do that?" The student's memorization strategies are often explored using these questions.

4. Observe a student performing tasks to identify student's favored learning modality. Remember that students with low vision occasionally process visual information more easily than information presented in other modalities, so do not assume that the auditory channel is always the best modality for learning. To determine the influence of a modality, switch to a different format. For example, if a student has difficulty writing responses, then ask for oral responses.

5. Ask the student probing questions, such as "Tell me more about that" or "Can you explain this to me?" Determining the extent of a student's conceptual information often requires the use of such questions. The student's responses can give the teacher clues to the extent of a student's conceptual foundation.

Anna

Anna mastered making her favorite snack, a peanut butter and jelly sandwich, a few weeks ago. Now she is learning how to make toasted cheese sandwiches. The teacher of students with visual impairments relies on Anna's ability to recall the steps in making a peanut butter and jelly sandwich to teach Anna how to make a toasted cheese sandwich. The teacher asks Anna what she remembers about making a peanut butter and jelly sandwich. Anna responds by doing the following:

1. Washes her hands.
2. Gets out the ingredients (bread, peanut butter, and jelly).
3. Gets a plate out of the cabinet.
4. Gets a knife from the drawer.
5. Places the bread on the plate.
6. Spreads one piece of bread with jelly and the other piece with peanut butter.
7. Places the two gooey sides together
8. Cuts the sandwich into rectangles and eats it.

The teacher then proceeds to teach Anna about the ingredients in toasted cheese sandwiches. She shows Anna where the cheese slices are located in the refrigerator. When she demonstrates how to pull the plastic wrapping off the cheese, she discovers that Anna is unaware that cheese slices are sometimes wrapped in plastic. She and Anna practice peeling the plastic away from the cheese. Then the teacher shows Anna how to spread either butter or mayonnaise on the bread before placing cheese on the bread. Anna practices this step and practices reading the braille label on the mayonnaise jar. The teacher helps Anna prepare several more sandwiches that they will serve as a snack to other students. Before Anna toasts the sandwiches in the toaster oven, the teacher talks with her about the toaster oven and discovers that Anna does not know what a toaster oven is or how to use one and thought she could use a toaster to make the sandwiches. Therefore, the teacher shows Anna the correct way to use a toaster oven and how the controls work. Anna feels the tactile markings on the controls and places a sandwich in the oven. By observing Anna using the toaster oven and discussing the difference between a toaster oven and a toaster, Anna's teacher discovered, through diagnostic teaching, that Anna did not know the difference between these two appliances.

Diagnostic teaching sometimes occurs after a breakdown occurs in performing a task. However, it can be used to analyze a skill or task as the student is learning or mastering it and prevents the student from making mistakes or misconstruing concepts.

PORTFOLIOS

An assessment portfolio is a collection of products that demonstrate a student's current and past levels of competence (Salvia & Ysseldyke, 1995) and provides information that supplements the information obtained from other assessment methods. The products include samples of the student's work in addition to any of the informal measures discussed in this chapter and standardized instruments. The portfolio is a measure of progress that documents a student's skills, interests, ideas, and accomplishments (Hart, 1994). It is a way to collect, organize, and evaluate work.

An evaluation statement (a summary of the important findings) must be attached to each piece in the portfolio that clearly tells why each piece was selected. A portfolio may be in the form of a notebook of writing samples, a collection of the student's art, documentation of needed job skills, or a collection of work to demonstrate the student's reading skills. From the outset, the student is involved in the project; he or she selects the items that will go in the portfolio and critiques and evaluates each one.

There are many advantages to a portfolio. First, because a portfolio contains a student's actual work, the parents and teacher can use it to discuss the student's progress. Second, the integration of assessment and instruction is a highly motivating factor that facilitates learning, and portfolios provide an easy link among learning, motivation, and assessment. Third, because the student is involved in selecting and critiquing the pieces, the portfolio is a way to monitor the student's own progress (through checklists, graphs, or charts and selections of writing), and the student becomes a self-critic and is motivated to improve. A portfolio embodies a dynamic that is cyclical—self-selected goals, followed by self-selected components that demonstrate progress toward the mastery of goals, and, finally, self-analysis and evaluation of each piece and the overall goal or purpose of the portfolio. Most important, the student becomes a partner of the teacher in assessing his or her progress.

Portfolios can be designed for a variety of purposes. It is important for the teacher to tell the student the purpose of a particular portfolio and to include a written statement of the purpose in the portfolio. Here are the steps in developing a portfolio:

1. Determine the purpose of the portfolio. What area of functioning and subsequent progress will it measure?

2. Develop a profile—a list of the competencies to be demonstrated—for the portfolio, together with the student, to indicate what the student is demonstrating. If it is a reading portfolio, many sections can be developed, each demonstrating a different reading competence. For example, a list of different types of books the student read for leisure could be included, along with a short report about each book. Other items that may be included in this type of portfolio are an audiotape of oral reading to demonstrate the student's oral reading skills and copies of tests to indicate the student's progress.

3. Have the student fill out a self-evaluation form for each piece that includes the reason the student selected the piece and the

Student's Name: _____   Date: _____

1. What do I like about this selection of work or demonstration of skill?

2. What was my reason for selecting this piece?

3. What competence does this selection demonstrate?

Figure 3.15. Sample Self-Evaluation Form

competence the piece is demonstrating (see Figure 3.15).

4. Give the student an opportunity to share the portfolio with numerous people. Some schools use this format in addition to more traditional reporting methods, such as report cards, to give the parents more insight into the student's progress.

Joshua

The teacher of students with visual impairments and Joshua decide that they will demonstrate his braille skills and reading ability by preparing a portfolio that can help document his progress. The teacher explains to Joshua that this will be an ongoing project that will encompass selected items of his work throughout the year. Assessment and instruction are tightly linked throughout this portfolio. With these pieces, Joshua will demonstrate his capability in skill areas, and the evaluation statement of each piece will document why Joshua selected it. The teacher ensures that Joshua has documented each area with observable data that demonstrate his abilities. She also tells Joshua that he will show the portfolio to his parents and others and will be critiquing his own work as well as monitoring his own progress.

Profile and Portfolio of Joshua's Braille Reading

SKILL AREA	DOCUMENTATION IN PORTFOLIO
Basic Reading Skills	
Increases reading rate with independent level materials	Graphs of reading rate measured daily
Increases reading levels	Results of an informal reading inventory in braille
Comprehends reading passages	Journal record of the themes of reading passages
Reads orally with expression and fluency	Audiotape recordings of oral reading passages
Reading as a Leisure Activity	
Reading for pleasure	Log of books read for pleasure
Variety of reading materials	Reading checklist developed for Joshua
Reading as a Learning Tool	
Participates in reading when involved in group activities	Videotapes and teacher's observation
Reads textbook chapters	Audiotapes and chapter tests
Reads assignments	Communication notebook for parent assignments completed based on reading

Sidebar 3.1 presents a profile (list of competencies or skill areas) and the items selected to document Joshua's work. Joshua helps create the profile and is involved in selecting documentation to support it. He and the teacher agree that if Joshua acquires all the skills listed in the profile and documents them in his portfolio, he should be able to show his parents and others his competence as a braille reader. This portfolio will contain documentation in each of the three areas listed in the profile: reading skills (reading rate and comprehension), reading as a leisure activity, and reading as a learning tool.

Joshua selects items to place in his portfolio to document his success in demonstrating the skills listed on the profile. These items are chosen from a variety of sources: videotapes, written pieces, reports of work, audiotapes, descriptions, diagrams, graphs and charts, and computer printouts. A self-evaluation page will accompany each work sample.

Anna

Anna's teacher of students with visual impairments sees great potential in constructing a format for Anna to use in developing a portfolio. She envisions several purposes for Anna's portfolio:

◆ Documentation of Anna's repertoire of snack recipes,

◆ Communication between the home and school,

◆ A generalized link between the skills acquired at school and practiced at home,

◆ An opportunity for Anna to express her thoughts about each snack made at home,

◆ Practice in reading and writing braille, and

◆ A purposeful collection demonstrating Anna's progress in acquiring cooking skills and communicating in braille.

Anna's teacher plans for Anna to put the portfolio together as she acquires skills in the kitchen. She wants Anna to read the portfolio recipes and the reflective thoughts of her siblings, parents, and teachers, as well as her own. By reading the portfolio often, Anna will engage in a repeated reading exercise (rereading material daily to develop fluency and gain needed reading practice) that will enhance her braille skills, as well as her ability to read recipes and recall instructions. The teacher develops an outline for Anna's portfolio (see Sidebar 3.2).

The teacher talks with Anna about Anna's collection of recipes and the cooking Anna does at home for her brothers and sister. With the teacher's help, Anna places, as she acquires new cooking skills, copies of her recipe cards (written in grade 1 braille) in a looseleaf folder, and she and the teacher discuss each recipe. Anna's parents are pleased that Anna can read these recipes and is beginning to make many of the snacks for herself and her siblings. They agree to write down Anna's siblings' comments about each recipe that she makes, such as "I liked the cookies!" "They are my favorite snack." The par-

ents use a communication notebook to record all these comments and write entries about their own feelings, including "I am so proud of Anna. She cleans the kitchen area after she prepares a snack." Anna also writes her own reflective and evaluative statements on the brailler. All these comments are placed in the looseleaf notebook under the recipes that are being discussed. Although these comments are brief and sometimes simple, they reinforce Anna's braille communication skills, cooking skills, and ability to make evaluative statements about her work.

CASE EXAMPLE: SUMMARIES

As is evident from the following summaries, informal assessment techniques provide valuable information for planning instruction and measuring progress. When students are viewed holistically, their personalities and goals emerge, creating an atmosphere in which members of educational teams work together to foster the student's success. Informal techniques require the participation of many players in the IEP process; in essence, all players become stakeholders supporting the student in effective instruction and evaluation.

Joshua

Joshua, a fourth-grade student, is mainstreamed in his neighborhood school. The teacher of students with visual impairments and other members of the educational team are seeking to provide Joshua with the tools he needs in a competitive academic setting. Through the use of informal assessment techniques, they have discovered much information that is pertinent to Joshua's goals.

In interviews, the general education teachers have indicated that Joshua has compelling leadership abilities and good interpersonal skills. He likes working with others in cooperative situations and gains pleasure and satisfac-

---

SIDEBAR 3.2

Portfolio of Anna's Cooking Skills and Braille Communication

COOKING SKILLS
Sources
Braille recipe cards of snacks mastered by Anna

BRAILLE COMMUNICATION
Sources
Braille recipe cards
Statements from parents, teacher, siblings, Anna

EVALUATIVE STATEMENTS
Source
Anna's own reflective statements

tion from interacting with them. Joshua has a strong desire to be a part of his classroom social environment. Although his reading rate is slow, Joshua's other academic skills are commensurate with those of other students in the classroom. He has good organizational skills and his adaptations have helped him stay current with reading assignments in the classroom. In an interview, Joshua told of his desire to fit in with his classmates and his dislike of being isolated from others when using his CCTV.

The questionnaires indicate that Joshua's general education teachers have discovered his excellent learning potential in cooperative group activities. The teachers noted that Joshua has good ability and requires little modification for success in the classroom. Through observations, Joshua's teacher of students with visual impairments determined that Joshua was reluctant to use the CCTV, and she discussed his rationale for not using the CCTV with him. Together, they have initiated steps to build his reading rate and to use braille as his primary learning medium.

The use of checklists and a portfolio have motivated Joshua to strive to become competent in braille reading—a goal that is shared by the educational team. Joshua's progress is monitored through curriculum-based assessments and portfolio evaluations. Joshua is highly involved in his own endeavor to achieve success. Through the use of informal assessment techniques, his IEP is constructive and effective. His parents are productively involved in his program, which will help him achieve his personal goals that will increase his ability to compete in his academic setting and prepare for life as a literate adult.

Anna

Anna, a fourth-grade student who has a mild cognitive impairment and is blind, attends her neighborhood school, where she receives services as a student with multiple impairments. Anna participates in a functional curriculum at school and is learning uncontracted braille. She attends several classes in the general education curriculum: art, physical education, and music.

In an interview, Anna's mother described her home, Anna's health history and tendency to develop upper-respiratory infections, and the kinds of things that Anna likes to do at home. She noted that when Anna is home, she likes to listen to audiotapes and CDs and to play with her younger siblings. With regard to Anna's future and what she thinks is important for Anna to learn in school now, Anna's mother stressed the need for Anna to be able to generalize the skills she is acquiring at school to the home setting. She also said that she wants Anna to develop skills that will help her to be as independent as possible when she reaches adulthood and knows that independence must begin with small steps now.

Anna's teacher of students with visual impairments, Mrs. Smith, is concerned about Anna's ability to generalize skills to the home setting. After examining Anna's functional skills and the parents' goals for Anna, she monitors Anna's cooking skills, which she thinks are an important link between the home and the school. Through tools like narrative observations, Mrs. Smith scrutinizes Anna's abilities and determines that Anna is a good listener, a learning strength that the educational team can use as a strategy to drive Anna's goal of independence.

In a communication notebook, Anna's mother examines and records Anna's favorite snacks and notes Anna's ability to locate kitchen appliances, cooking utensils, and foods. Anna's mother would like Anna to be able to prepare snacks for herself and her siblings and states in the communication notebook that Anna must start preparing now to achieve independence as an adult. After Mrs. Smith does an environmental assessment of Anna's kitchen at home, she and Anna's parents reorganize the kitchen cabinets and label items, so Anna can more readily transfer her skills from school to her home.

By selecting what Anna already likes to eat and coupling it with her desire to play with her siblings, the educational team enhances Anna's program by encouraging Anna to make snacks for her siblings. The portfolio developed by Anna and her teacher demonstrates Anna's expertise in the kitchen, her ability to make evaluative statements about her work, and her progressing braille skills, which she uses to read and write simple recipe cards and functional labels and the items in her portfolio. As a result of her ability to prepare simple snacks for her siblings independently, Anna's self-esteem has increased. In addition, Anna's parents feel a strong link between the school and the home because they have been encouraged to express their ideas regarding Anna's future and have mutual goals with the rest of Anna's educational team. Instruction and assessment, a cyclic connection, are being used to tie Anna's steps toward independence in the kitchen to function and effectiveness.

SUMMARY

Informal techniques are powerful tools for assessing student's strengths and needs, tools that yield qualitative information appropriate for determining educational goals. With a wealth of qualitative information derived from informal assessment techniques, the educational team can put all the data in a contextual framework that is conducive to efficient and productive goal setting in a healthy educational environment.

Informal techniques are uniquely appropriate for monitoring a student's achievement in the classroom. They inform the teacher of students with visual impairments of the effectiveness of instruction and enable school personnel to modify and change instructional strategies. Since informal techniques are student centered and goal directed, they help the educational team to create educational opportunities that enable each student to achieve his or her personal goals.

ACTIVITIES

1. Select a student for observation during a 30-minute segment of instruction. Record narrative information and prepare a written report that could be used in a meeting of the educational team.

2. Write open-ended questions for an interview with a student that focus on the student's vocational plans. Administer the interview and summarize the information obtained in a written report.

3. Prepare a questionnaire for the teachers of a student with a visual impairment in an inclusive setting. Give copies of the questionnaire to the teachers, collect the completed questionnaires, and write a summary of the information that has been obtained.

4. Develop a criterion-referenced checklist for a specific skill domain. Indicate the percentage of correct responses needed to indicate mastery. Duplicate the checklist and distribute the copies to your classmates.

5. Begin a file of informal checklists. Organize the materials in an assessment file system for later use.

6. Design a portfolio profile pertaining to the skills needed by beginning high school or college students. Include suggestions of the types of documentation needed for each component of the outline.

7. Create a system for organizing general observations in the classroom. Demonstrate in a class presentation the usefulness and efficiency of the system.

REFERENCES

Brigance, A. H. (1981). *Brigance Diagnostic Inventory of Essential Skills.* North Billerica, MA: Curriculum Associates.

Brigance, A. H. (1991). *Brigance Diagnostic Inventory of Early Development—Revised.* North Billerica, MA: Curriculum Associates.

Brigance, A. H. (1994). *Brigance Diagnostic Life Skills Inventory.* North Billerica, MA: Curriculum Associates.

Brigance, A. H. (1999). *Brigance Diagnostic Inventory of*

Basic Skills. North Billerica, MA: Curriculum Associates.

Caton, H. (1991). *Print and braille literacy: Selecting appropriate learning media.* Louisville, KY: American Printing House for the Blind.

Duckworth, B. J., & Abbot, D. (1983). *Tactile supplement to Brigance Diagnostic Inventory of Basic Skills.* Louisville, KY: American Printing House for the Blind.

Duckworth, B. J., & Stratton, J. M. (1992). *APH Tactile Supplement to Revised Brigance Diagnostic Inventory of Early Development.* Louisville, KY: American Printing House for the Blind.

Godwin, A., Martin, J., Grafsgaard, K., McNear, D., Hanson, N., Rieber, C., Hooey, P., & Tillmanns, E. (1995). *Minnesota Braille Skills Inventory.* Little Canada, MN: Minnesota Educational Services.

Gredler, M. E. (1999). *Classroom assessment and learning.* New York: Longman.

Hart, D. (1994). *Authentic assessment: A handbook for educators.* Menlo Park, CA: Addison-Wesley.

Koenig, A. J., & Farrenkopf, C. (1995). *Assessment of braille literacy skills.* Houston, TX: Region IV Education Service Center, Special Education Department.

Koenig, A. J., & Holbrook, M. C. (1993). *Learning media assessment of students with visual impairments: A resource guide for teachers.* Austin: Texas School for the Blind and Visually Impaired.

Loumiet, R., & Levack, N. (1993). *Independent living: A curriculum with adaptations for students with visual impairments* (Vols. 1–3). Austin: Texas School for the Blind and Visually Impaired.

Overton, T. (1996). *Assessment in special education: An applied approach.* Englewood Cliffs, NJ: Merrill.

Ryan, C. D. (1994). *Authentic assessment.* Westminster, CA: Teacher Created Materials.

Salvia, J., & Ysseldyke, J. E. (1995). *Assessment* (6th ed.). Boston: Houghton Mifflin Company.

Sattler, J. M. (1992). *Assessment of children: Revised and updated* (3rd ed.). San Diego, CA: Jerome M. Sattler, Publisher.

Sewell, D. (1997). *Assessment kit: Kit of informal tools for academic students with visual impairments.* Austin: Texas School for the Blind and Visually Impaired.

Stiggins, R. J. (1997). *Student-centered classroom assessment* (2nd ed.). Upper Saddle River, NJ: Prentice Hall.

Swallow, R., Mangold, S., & Mangold, P. (1978). *Informal assessment of developmental skills for younger visually handicapped and multihandicapped children.* New York: American Foundation for the Blind.

Turnbull, H. R., & Turnbull, A. P. (1998). *Free appropriate public education* (5th ed.). Denver, CO: Love Publishing.

RESOURCES

(continued on next page)

Suggested Resources *(Continued)*

Resource	Type	Source	Description
Brigance Diagnostic Inventory of Essential Skills (Brigance, 1981)	Checklist	Curriculum Associates	A criterion-referenced checklist of essential skills for secondary students with special needs, including reading, writing, spelling, math, and special areas like schedules, forms, money and finance, time and transportation, and telephone skills.
Brigance Diagnostic Life Skills Inventory (Brigance, 1994)	Checklist	Curriculum Associates	An extensive criterion-referenced checklist, addressing speaking and listening, money and finance, food, functional writing, words on common signs, clothing and labels, health, telephone skills, travel and transportation.
Independent Living: A Curriculum with Adaptations for Students with Visual Impairments (3 vols.) (Loumiet & Levack, 1993)	Checklist	Texas School for the Blind and Visually Impaired	Well-developed checklists encompassing independent living skills and other areas of the curriculum.
Informal Assessment of Developmental Skills for Visually Handicapped Students (Swallow, Mangold, & Mangold, 1978)	Book	American Foundation for the Blind	The text includes informal checklists and inventories to aid teachers in determining students' special needs. Covers tactile perception, braille and letter recognition, listening, visual functioning, vocational skills, and more for children from birth to senior high school.
Minnesota Braille Skills Inventory: A Resource Manual (Godwin et al., 1995)	Book	Minnesota Educational Services	A resource manual and student braille components used in completing an assessment of a student's knowledge of literary braille, basic and advanced Nemeth Code, braille computer code, braille music code, and dictionary and foreign language symbols.
Print and Braille Literacy: Selecting Appropriate Learning Media (Caton, 1991)	Booklet	American Printing House for the Blind	Guidelines to help ensure that every student with a visual impairment will have adequate opportunities for learning to use the medium or media most appropriate for his or her needs. Available in print, large print, or braille.

(continued on next page)

Suggested Resources *(Continued)*

Resource	Type	Source	Description
Revised Brigance Diagnostic Inventory of Early Development—APH Tactile Supplement (Duckworth & Stratton, 1992)	Tactile supplement to *Diagnostic Inventory of Early Development—Revised*	American Printing House for the Blind	The braille edition of student pages necessary to use Brigance Diagnostic Inventory of Basic Skills with students who are braille readers. Must have the print edition to use.
TOOLS for Selecting Appropriate Learning Media (Caton, 1994)	Book	American Printing House for the Blind	A manual designed to help parents, teachers, and administrators make decisions concerning students' use of braille, print, or both as their primary reading medium or media. Extension of the booklet *Print and Braille Literacy: Selecting Appropriate Learning Media* (Caton, 1991).

Contact information for each of the resources listed will be found in the Sources of Products, Materials, Equipment, and Services section at the back of this book.

CHAPTER 4

Specialized Assessments for Students with Visual Impairments

Alan J. Koenig, M. Cay Holbrook, Anne L. Corn, Linda B. DePriest, Jane N. Erin, and Ike Presley

KEY POINTS

- ◆ Students with visual impairments use sensory information to gain an understanding of their environments.

- ◆ Specialized assessments are needed to determine the student's efficiency in using sensory information and his or her potential to improve its use for the purposes of learning.

- ◆ The teacher of students with visual impairments has the primary role in conducting specialized assessments and offering recommendations based on the findings.

- ◆ The functional vision assessment focuses on the student's efficiency in using vision and his or her potential to increase this efficiency.

- ◆ The learning media assessment focuses on the student's use of all sources of sensory information and yields recommendations on the student's literacy medium or media.

- ◆ The assistive technology assessment focuses on selecting the various options for using technology to complete tasks and to facilitate learning.

VIGNETTE

Jana Darling, the teacher of students with visual impairments, sat across the table from Jacob Lee, the state's assistive technology specialist. Mr. Lee had come to Jana's school district to complete a series of assistive technology assessments for students in special education, three of whom were Ms. Darling's students.

Luis was a 10th-grade student whose learning media assessment and functional vision evaluations had revealed excellent braille skills and a limited ability to read 4-inch letters on the computer monitor. Luis had learned to use a Braille-'n'-Speak in elementary school; now Ms. Darling was delighted with Mr. Lee's recommendation that Luis should be provided with a note-taking device with a refreshable braille display. Although cost was always a consideration, Ms. Darling agreed that Luis, who would be attending the state university in three years, was ready for and would truly benefit from learning to use the more sophisticated device. Besides, the Braille-'n'-Speak could then be passed on to a younger student.

Mandy, a seventh-grade student with deaf-blindness, was the second student Ms. Darling and Mr. Lee discussed. In the past, Mandy had written legibly using a black felt-tip pen and had been able to read back what she had written. However, at the beginning of this school year, Ms. Darling had discovered, through a recent learning media assessment, that Mandy could no longer read her own writing. Ms. Darling had referred Mandy to her ophthalmologist for a reexamination; Mr. Lee recommended a new clinical low vision examination as well. Meanwhile, Mr. Lee suggested that Mandy should be taught to use the capacity of her word-processing program to make adjustments in fonts and font sizes. He also gave Jana a catalog of both fiction and nonfiction books available on disk; perhaps some of Mandy's assigned readings could be found among these selections. With the books on disk, viewing or printing them in a comfortable-size print would be easy.

Finally, Mr. Lee and Ms. Darling discussed Eli, a 3 year old attending a regular preschool class while receiving services from the school system for his multiple disabilities. Eli had low vision[1] and motor impairments, both resulting from anoxia at birth. Although he seemed to understand what was said to him, attended to stories, moved his head to indicate yes or no, and greeted friends with happy vocalizations, Eli could not speak. Mr. Lee had several recommendations for Eli, including a simple switch to operate toys, an audiotape recorder, and similar devices, which Eli would probably learn to use quickly. Teaching Eli to use a communication board was a more ambitious objective, but certainly an important one. They would begin with a simple board, perhaps one with four large, clear pictures and prerecorded messages, that would allow Eli to greet friends, request a snack or drink, ask for a story, and request a favorite toy.

---

[1]A person with low vision is one "who has difficulty accomplishing visual tasks, even with prescribed corrective lenses, but who can enhance his or her ability to accomplish these tasks with the use of compensatory visual strategies, low vision and other devices, and environmental adaptations" (Corn & Koenig, 1996, p. 4).

It was an important step on the road toward communication.

INTRODUCTION

The efficiency with which a student with a visual impairment uses sensory information in the learning process is essential and indispensable information that is needed to develop an appropriate Individualized Education Program (IEP). Specialized assessments that focus on the unique sensory needs of students who are blind or visually impaired are used to gather this information, thereby providing the foundation for designing and delivering high-quality instruction. Since a visual impairment directly influences the learning process and creates disability-specific needs, a professional with specialized knowledge of the impact of visual impairments must conduct these specialized assessments.

Students who are blind or visually impaired gain information about the environment and learn in ways that differ from students with typical vision. For example, a student who is blind will gather information about plants in a garden by tactilely exploring the leaves, stems, and roots. To gain an understanding of the way in which plants are arranged in rows and by type, he or she will examine the plants row by row and section by section, listen to someone describe how the garden is arranged, and then synthesize many pieces of information into a meaningful whole to form a concept of a garden. A student with low vision may use visual cues, along with tactile and auditory information, to gain knowledge of the concept of a garden. The process of exploring the garden may be largely visual, with minimal reliance on other cues; largely tactile and auditory, with minimal or no use of vision; or anywhere between. The extent to which vision will assist in this process depends on the nature of the student's visual impairment and the efficiency with which he or she uses vision.

The student's efficiency in using sensory information and his or her potential to increase that efficiency informs all aspects of the student's education. A student who is blind, for example, typically learns concepts using concrete objects, learns with physical prompts and guidance, learns to read and write in braille, and gains access to computers via synthesized speech or braille. A student with low vision, on the other hand, may learn concepts primarily visually, primarily tactilely, or both. He or she may use visual prompts or tactile and auditory prompts, may use visual imitation to learn skills, or may need to rely on other alternatives to gather information. A student with low vision may read print, print with an optical device, large print, and/or braille and may gain access to a computer visually or through synthesized speech or a combination of options.

The student's efficiency in using sensory information and the implications for instructional programming are determined through specialized assessment processes that are unique to the needs of students who are blind or visually impaired. These specialized assessments in the school setting include the following:

◆ *The functional vision assessment,* which determines the student's efficiency in using vision and potential for increasing the use of vision and forms the basis for recommendations on using vision for the purpose of learning;

◆ *The learning media assessment,* which determines the student's efficiency and preferences in using visual, tactile, and auditory senses and forms the basis for selecting general learning media (such as rulers, maps, and real objects) and specific literacy media (print and braille); and

◆ *The assistive technology assessment,* which determines the appropriate options for using technology to meet individual needs and for selecting access devices for computer input and output.

There are many interrelationships and overlaps among the three specialized assessments. For example, determining a student's reading efficiency rate (that is, the speed at which he or she can read with understanding and comprehen-

sion) is part of all three assessments. In the functional vision assessment, a measure of reading efficiency typically assesses reading speed in print reading, with or without low vision devices. In the learning media assessment, reading efficiency is measured in all media, including braille and other options. In the assistive technology assessment, reading efficiency is measured using the technological output devices that the student uses or is learning to use (for example, measuring print reading speed with electronically enlarged text on the screen or braille reading with a refreshable braille display).

In the United States various federal and state laws and regulations govern the way in which the specialized assessments are used to identify students with visual impairments and/or to develop students' IEPs. Specific provisions in the 1997 amendments to the Individuals with Disabilities Education Act (IDEA; P.L. 105-17) related to learning media and assistive technology assessments are addressed later in this chapter. Functional vision and learning media assessments are typically used for the dual purposes of identifying students who are blind or visually impaired and program planning. An assistive technology assessment is used primarily for program planning after a student has been identified as visually impaired.

Although there are generally specific time lines within which specialized assessment should be conducted, these assessment processes should occur ideally on an ongoing basis. Each opportunity that a teacher of students with visual impairments has to interact with a student should be considered a time to observe, identify needs, note progress, and make plans for subsequent instruction. When assessment and instruction are paired in this manner, changes in a student's instructional program can be made immediately, without waiting until a predetermined point in time (such as an annual IEP planning meeting).

This chapter presents guidelines and strategies for conducting functional vision, learning media, and assistive technology assessments. First, the role of the teacher of students with visual impairments is presented. Next, the importance of organizing medical and clinical low vision evaluations is discussed. Then the process of conducting each of the three specialized assessments is described. This chapter also presents resources for conducting these assessments, along with selected assessment checklists.

ROLE OF THE TEACHER OF STUDENTS WITH VISUAL IMPAIRMENTS

The teacher of students with visual impairments has the primary responsibility for conducting specialized assessments. This specialist takes the lead in conducting the functional vision assessment and learning media assessment. Other professionals, such as general special education teachers or diagnosticians, do not have the specific preparation needed or the understanding of the needs of students with visual impairments to do so. However, these professionals and the student's parents contribute valuable information (such as observations of the student's use of sensory information in a variety of environments and strengths and needs related to academic and social skills) to the assessment process. The assistive technology assessment may be conducted by the teacher of students with visual impairments or by a specialist who has specific preparation in the technological needs of students with visual impairments. In the latter case, the teacher of students with visual impairments usually conducts a screening of technology skills and needs to identify those that necessitate a more comprehensive and specialized assessment.

The teacher of students with visual impairments gathers information from the specialized assessments and uses it to design an appropriate IEP for a student. The specific role of the specialist is to do the following:

◆ Conduct the functional vision assessment;

◆ Conduct the learning media assessment;

◆ Conduct a screening of assistive technology needs;

◆ Ensure that a comprehensive assistive technology assessment is conducted;

◆ Collaborate with parents and other team members to gather objective and useful information on the student's strengths and needs related to the use of vision and other senses;

◆ Offer recommendations for instructional programming, literacy media needs, and assistive technology needs on the basis of the results of the specialized assessments; and

◆ Ensure that the needs of students are assessed on an ongoing basis using the specialized assessments to gather and synthesize information at least annually.

VISUAL ASSESSMENTS

Students with visual impairments participate in three types of evaluation related to the nature and extent of their visual impairments: medical and optometric evaluations, clinical low vision evaluations, and functional vision assessments. The medical and clinical low vision evaluations contribute important information to the overall assessment. The functional vision assessment extends the clinical data by providing information on the student's efficiency in using visual information; this is the focus of this section and, therefore, is presented in detail.

Because a visual impairment is a medical condition, the ophthalmologic or optometric eye care evaluation is almost certainly the first evaluation to be conducted. If the functional vision assessment precedes the clinical low vision evaluation, it provides the clinical low vision specialist with information on the individual's current functioning in the visual environment, such as the classroom, which will be useful in determining prescriptions.

In many cases, the clinical low vision evaluation precedes the functional vision assessment, enabling the educator to incorporate optical devices and other clinical information into an analysis of how the student is using vision with the best available optical and nonoptical systems. There is no standard, universally accepted sequence for when a clinical low vision evaluation is conducted in relation to the functional vision assessment. However, best practice would suggest that a functional vision assessment should be conducted in a systematic fashion when a child enters a school system and updated every year, according to the requirements of a state or school system, or if there is a suspected change in functional vision. Since the clinical low vision evaluation provides important information about optical and nonoptical devices, it may be preferable to conduct a functional vision assessment after a clinical low vision evaluation.

When a functional vision assessment is conducted after a clinical low vision evaluation, it can determine the change in a student's functional vision by means of optical and nonoptical devices. This information can be incorporated into instructional programs to help the student adjust to new methods of gaining access to the visual environment. For example, a student who at one time relied on a paraeducator to copy algebra problems from the chalkboard to a dry-erase board that the student could view up close may now be able to complete the assignment independently by using a monocular telescope to observe the teacher working the problems on the chalkboard.

Ophthalmology and Optometry Assessments

The primary eye care provider is responsible for diagnosing and treating an individual's eye condition. (While it is important that all children with low vision receive an ophthalmology examination, families may choose either an ophthalmologist or an optometrist to provide ongoing care if the child's condition does not require continuing ophthalmology interventions.) Usually, the emphasis is on the medical and optical aspects of the eye condition, as well as the individual's visual status and prognosis. The primary eye care provider is concerned with medical treatment and general

optical treatment (such as eyeglasses) but does not generally address the functional effects of the condition—that is, how it affects the individual's use of vision to perform everyday tasks—or techniques that may improve visual functioning. Therefore, when a student has been diagnosed by the primary eye care provider as having low vision, a referral for a clinical low vision evaluation should be made as well.

With the parents' permission, the primary eye care provider sends a report or the student's diagnosis, clinical measures, prognosis, and treatment to the educational program. This information is used to prepare for the functional vision assessment and to make other determinations about the student's eligibility for special education services.

Clinical Low Vision Assessments

The clinical low vision evaluation is conducted by an ophthalmologist or an optometrist who has specialized training in assessing the use of vision in students and adults. This evaluation is typically intended for three populations:

◆ Students for whom standard procedures do not result in clear clinical measures because of cognitive, expressive, or other attributes that preclude performance on traditional measures;

◆ Students with congenital or adventitious visual impairments for whom optical devices and instructional programs for visual efficiency may be needed; and

◆ Adults who had normal vision before a sudden or gradual loss of vision.

Referrals for the clinical low vision evaluation may be made by the primary eye care provider, the teacher of students with visual impairments, an orientation and mobility (O&M) specialist, a physician, or family members. With the family's permission, information from the clinical low vision evaluation is shared with the student's primary eye care provider, the student (if appropriate) and family members, the teacher of students with visual impairments, and other members of the educational team. At times, the clinical low vision evaluation may indicate the need for ophthalmologic or other medical assessments, in which case the clinical low vision specialist refers the student to the appropriate physicians.

Parents and educational personnel often ask how frequently a student should be seen by a clinical low vision specialist. Although there is no set time for reevaluations, the authors recommend that children be examined first at approximately age 3 for the potential benefit of optical devices. Following an initial evaluation, students should receive follow-up evaluations or be referred back to the clinical low vision specialist at the recommendation of the specialist when the visual demands of the classroom or outdoor environments change, when functional vision assessments indicate a need for such an evaluation, or approximately every two to three years.

Clinical low vision specialists also evaluate students for the prescription of low vision devices for near, intermediate, and distance tasks. This type of evaluation determines whether a student with low vision can benefit from optical and nonoptical devices and adaptive techniques to enhance visual function. The evaluation generally follows a sequence described by Wilkinson (1996) and includes the following components:

◆ A comprehensive case history, which addresses the individual's visual problem as well as visual goals and objectives;

◆ A review of the functional vision assessment (when available);

◆ A review of medical eye information, including ocular and general medical history;

◆ An evaluation of near and distance vision;

◆ An evaluation of color vision;

◆ An assessment of contrast sensitivity;

◆ An assessment of the student's visual field;

◆ A prescription of appropriate optical, nonoptical, and/or nonvisual techniques;

◆ Initial instruction in the use of optical devices and a recommendation for follow-up;

◆ A recommendation of accessory or nonoptical devices;

◆ A report of clinical findings.

Results from the clinical low vision evaluation are important to the educational team. Although the evaluation does not address educational issues, such as learning and literacy media, the information received can assist the educational team in preparing for a learning media assessment (or assistive technology assessment) and the subsequent development of an educational plan. This plan includes goals pertaining to the use of optical devices, instructional programs for visual efficiency, and accommodations that may need to be available (such as seating preferences) to enable a student to use his or her vision.

Functional Vision Assessments[2]

The purpose of a functional vision assessment is to provide information on how a student uses vision in real-life familiar and unfamiliar surroundings. This assessment also yields information about the impact of a student's visual impairment on learning. The results of the functional vision assessment delineate factors that help or hinder function and provide recommendations to the educational team about how to increase and enhance the student's visual efficiency.

Conducting a functional vision assessment is a key responsibility of the teacher of students with visual impairments. Although clinical acuity measures[3] (such as 20/200, 20/400) describe one

---

[2]*Parts of this section on functional vision assessment were adapted from J. N. Erin & B. Paul, "Functional Vision Assessment and Instruction of Children and Youths in Academic Programs," in A. L. Corn and A. J. Koenig, Eds.,* Foundations of Low Vision: Clinical and Functional Perspectives *(New York: AFB Press, 1996, pp. 185–220).*

[3]*Clinical measures of distance acuity are specified with Snellen notation. Typical vision is noted as 20/20. The first number represents the distance in feet from the eye chart, while the second number represents the smallest size symbol that can be recognized on a standard eye chart by a person with 20/20 (typical) vision. The notation of 20/200 indicates that the individual sees at 20 feet*

aspect of visual functioning—how well a person reads a standardized chart at a specified distance—they do not address other measures of visual functioning. Therefore, to provide for high-quality instruction for students with low vision, the results of a functional vision assessment are essential. Information from a functional vision assessment is used to do the following:

◆ Identify a student's visual skills with and without optical devices in a variety of environments and with a variety of levels of visual difficulty;

◆ Identify visual skills that need to be learned;

◆ Convey information to the student and other members of the educational team about how the student uses vision;

◆ Identify preferred environmental cues that the student can modify to enhance visual functioning;

◆ Help the student identify ways in which visual fatigue or discomfort can be alleviated or minimized;

◆ Make recommendations for referrals for other assessments as needed, such as O&M or clinical low vision evaluations; and

◆ Determine eligibility for services from a teacher of students with visual impairments and/or an O&M specialist.

The functional vision assessment provides an organized plan for observing how a student uses vision. Although a prescribed format is not required or recommended, several assessments with established formats are commercially available. Readers are encouraged to evaluate and choose which, if any, are most applicable and comfortable to use and to select informal assessment activities that provide for a sufficient sampling of visual behaviors that are pertinent to a child's visual condition. For example, a child with achromatopsia (a visual condition related to total color blindness

_____

what a person with 20/20 vision sees at 200 feet. In metric measurement, 6/6 represents typical vision; 6/60 is equivalent to 20/200.

and severe sensitivity to light) requires activities related to the use of lighting and acuity. The teacher may choose selected portions of formal instruments and informal activities that pertain to specific needs, as well as those that are important for the child's participation in school and community activities. Generally, teachers record their observations in a notebook or on the assessment forms and then use these notes as a basis for preparing the written report. The written report (discussed later) must be based on objective data and observations and must provide a sound basis for recommendations for the educational team to follow in instructional programming, as well as for referrals for additional tests or assessments.

The procedures for conducting functional vision assessments vary with the needs of the student and environmental factors. But in general, the following guidelines may be used:

◆ Arrange to conduct the assessment over a number of sessions using a variety of activities in different environments.

◆ Observe the student in his or her general education or special education classroom first, then observe the student in outside activities.

◆ Plan additional activities and observation opportunities that relate to problem areas detected through initial indoor and outdoor observations.

◆ Make sure that the student uses his or her typical optical devices, eyeglasses or contact lenses during the functional vision assessment activities.

A listing of the sections of a typical functional vision report are found in Sidebar 4.1. This may provide structure for writing the report.

Components

Reason for Referral

Knowing the reason that a student is referred for a functional vision assessment will help the teacher

Typical Components of a Functional Vision Assessment

- Background information, including visual history, medical history, and educational history;
- Description of the environments in which the assessment takes place;
- Pertinent information related to the structure of the eyes and reflexes, near vision, distance vision, color vision, fields of vision, motility, and other visual responses (such as to lighting and contrast);
- Results of any formal functional vision assessments used;
- Results of informal assessments of visual responses to selected activities;
- Summary and discussion;
- Recommendations and referrals; and
- Statements of eligibility for special educational services as appropriate.

- Does the student have difficulties reading or looking at things that are close to him or her?
- Does the student recognize people at a distance?
- Does the student hesitate more than is typical when moving from a lighted room to a darkened room or from the classroom to the bright outdoors?
- Does the student tilt his or her head to the side when looking at something?
- Does the student get very close to his or her work in order to see it?

Background Information

The teacher of students with visual impairments first reviews previous assessments that have been conducted, including:

- Ophthalmological and optometric reports,
- Educational history and academic achievement results,
- Clinical low vision evaluation,
- O&M assessment, and
- Learning media assessments.

The teacher should also review the student's previous IEP goals and accommodations pertaining to visual functioning. Age at onset, diagnosis, prognosis, medical and optical treatments, and the most recent clinical measures (of visual acuity) should also be noted. General information related to the student's developmental and educational history should be reviewed to identify any additional impairments, current functional levels, and how these impairments have influenced the student's use of vision.

Description of Environments

The environment in which the functional vision assessment is conducted is important, since envi-

of students with visual impairments select instruments and plan activities. For example, if a student is having difficulty locating steps, a general education teacher may refer a child to the school's special education program, and a functional vision assessment will be performed. The teacher of students with visual impairments may determine that a functional vision assessment is needed to determine whether the child needs a referral for further medical care or whether the child is not using previously learned visual skills, such as visually attending behaviors.

If the reason for the referral is not clear or if additional information is needed, the teacher of students with visual impairments may consider contacting the student's classroom teachers and parents with specific questions that may help clarify the student's visual difficulties. The questions may include:

ronmental issues may play a critical role in the student's ability to use his or her vision. Teachers of students with visual impairments should use the following guidelines for noting environmental issues:

- Note the approximate distances in the observation area. For example, note the distances between the student's desk and the area where visual information is typically presented and the distances from the student's desk to the windows and the area or areas where the teacher generally provides instruction to the class.

- Describe the physical attributes of the classroom, as well as all other areas in which the student will be observed, such as the cafeteria, library, and playground. These descriptions detail the available environmental cues, distractions, and other conditions under which the assessment will be conducted.

- Note the time of day, lighting, and general weather conditions.

- Include a sketch of the observation site that indicates the location of the doors, windows, student's desk, and other pertinent features. Make note of furniture and equipment; the presence of storage places for nonoptical, optical, and electronic devices; and access to electric outlets for additional illumination.

- Indicate the color and pattern of the floor and walls; the reflection of light sources on dry erase boards, overheads, and other surfaces where the student is expected to retrieve visual information; and the amount of visual clutter, distraction, and reflective glare in the room.

- Consider the visual demands of specific academic tasks. For example, note if the student is using a workbook with low-contrast print or if the student needs to read a graphing calculator to accomplish the same tasks as other students in the class.

- Describe the teacher's routines and patterns. Does the teacher stay in one place for instruction or circulate around the room? Does the teacher use facial expressions or gestures to convey essential information? Does the teacher tend to move close to the student when presenting visual information? Does the teacher tend to stand in areas that have high- or low-contrast background or in front of a window where glare could be a problem?

- List the daily schedule of activities in the student's classroom that form a framework for the visual demands during the day, as well as the degree of independence and consistency that the student demonstrates throughout daily routines. For example, is the student able to negotiate stairs visually both indoors and outdoors? Is the student able to tolerate changes in lighting in a hallway that has skylights with intense areas of sunlight?

Pertinent Information

Pertinent information includes all factors that may have an impact on the student's functioning. For example, if a child is on medications that are known to have possible ocular side effects, this information should be reported. A child who has recently experienced a personal trauma, such as the divorce of his or her parents or the death of a family member, may not perform well. This chapter emphasizes a student's use of sensory information, but other factors may be equally relevant to a student's performance.

Structure of the Eyes and Reflexes. The functional vision assessment should include a description of the appearance of the eyes and related structures. Since it is not the teacher's role to make a medical diagnosis, diagnostic terms should be avoided unless these terms are included in medical reports and are appropriately referenced. For example, a teacher may note, "Frank's right eye turns in consistently when he is reading," but should avoid using the clinical term "right esotropia." Other observations may relate to cloudiness of the eye, irregularities in the pupil and iris, deviations of either eye, irregularities of eye color, and any abnormalities of the lid or redness in or discharges from the eyes. If new or other unexpected characteristics are observed, the student should be referred to his or her primary eye care provider for evaluation.

The evaluator should check for pupillary responses. Although not necessarily an indicator of the presence or absence of vision, pupillary responses can provide information about whether the student may have unusual reactions to light. The information obtained can be used as a basis for choosing specific functional activities for further observation. For example, if the student has difficulty with pupillary reflexes, the teacher of students with visual impairments needs to observe the student when changing environments, such as when walking from a well-lit hallway to a darkened auditorium. To assess the student's eyes and reflexes, use the following strategies:

♦ Ask the student to sit in front of you in a darkened room and position a penlight in front of the student. Note how the student's pupils change when the light is turned on and off. Do not shine the light directly in the student's eye; rather, shine it on the bridge of the nose, the forehead, or the cheek.

♦ Ask the student to watch as you move an object from left to right, right to left, up and down, and in a circular motion. Make note of how the student's eyes move.

Near Vision.   Near vision generally refers to the use of vision within 12 to 14 inches from the eyes. Although the teacher may have a primary eye care provider's measures for near visual acuity, it is important to take a less formal measure in an environment in which the student is asked to function daily. This is not a definitive acuity measure since lighting, distance, and size of objects cannot be controlled as in a primary eye care provider's office. Rather, this measure provides a means by

which in-class functioning can be noted. If a large difference is noted, a referral to the primary eye care provider is necessary to determine the reason for the discrepancy. There are various ways to assess near visual acuity:

♦ Use commercially produced acuity cards that have letters, numbers, or pictures.

♦ Use actual objects of various sizes that roughly correspond to the size of the letters or pictures.

♦ Use cards with pictures instead of letters or numbers for preschool children or for children who do not know letters or numbers.

♦ Use matching symbols or pattern cards for students who are nonverbal and unable to respond by naming letters, numbers, or pictures.

♦ Assess the student's reading ability using not only typical school materials, but materials that vary in contrast and format, including magazines, comics, newspapers, labels on food and clothing, and telephone books.

♦ Take anecdotal notes by describing the student's behaviors during near-point activities. Examine how the student performs at other near tasks that involve seeing things up close, including eating, sewing, artwork, and electronics. Note how far away the student places materials, whether the student alters the angle at which materials are placed, and what types of background and lighting are chosen.

♦ Evaluate the student's handwriting ability by asking the student to read material that he or she has written, especially material that was written several days before and is no longer familiar.

♦ Explore how quickly the student writes. The student's writing speed may be slower than that of his or her sighted peers, and this fact should be noted so that instruction in handwriting or alternatives for note taking can be considered.

Distance Vision.   Distance vision refers to the use of vision from 18 inches and beyond. Intermediate vision is usually considered to be between 14 and 18 inches and is generally discussed within the context of distance vision. When optical devices are prescribed for intermediate use, they typically include telescopic components used for distance vision.

A distance-screening procedure should be included in the functional vision assessment to provide a comparison with clinical measures. Many materials are readily available, portable, and easy to administer, such as the Feinbloom Chart, the Lighthouse Distance Visual Acuity Charts or the LEA Symbols. An example of a formal assessment for distance vision is presented in *Beyond Arm's Reach* (Smith & O'Donnell, 1992).

The assessment of functional distance vision needs to be varied and to reflect the range of the student's interests and capabilities. The following guidelines should be used when assessing functional distance vision:

◆ Include indoor and outdoor activities, such as reading a banner in a hallway; recognizing a friend; catching a ball in a physical education class; or identifying the bus after school by its number, rather than its location.

◆ Take note of the student's visual environmental awareness, that is, whether the student notices objects (without the teacher's direction) in all visual quadrants (top left, bottom left, top right, bottom right); in the central, mid- and far periphery (to the sides, top, and bottom); and at levels at, above, or below the eye. Environmental awareness is important for gaining incidental visual information as well as for O&M purposes. Also ascertain the extent to which the student uses incidental visual information (that is, objects in the environment to which the student's vision has not been directed). The teacher will need to determine the best approach for individual students to communicate that which they notice. For example, one student may call out the names of objects he sees while another student may point to objects.

◆ Examine how the student uses distance vision in the classroom. For example, is he or she able to use dry-erase boards or chalkboards and overhead transparencies?

◆ Include an assessment of the student's ability to locate and read brief phrases, such as the next day's homework assignment; locate classmates and his or her desk; observe a teacher's demonstration of a science or math concept; see the teacher's facial expression; and retrieve dropped objects from the floor.

◆ Indicate the student's preferred seating position for these activities, including the approximate viewing distance from the material and lighting.

Color Vision.   Color vision is the ability to discriminate various hues and saturations of colors. The Ishihara Color Plates is a formal measure that screens for color deficiencies by asking the student to identify numbers or symbols or follow a winding line embedded in a patterned background. Another test, Color Vision Testing Made Easy, is based on the Ishihara but uses simple shapes that may be more appropriate for preschoolers and students who are nonverbal. The Holmgrem Wool Test is another formal measure consisting of a collection of yarn samples that the student must sort on basis of shade. The Farnsworth D15 is a diagnostic test used to determine the type of color deficiency; it has colored chips that the student arranges in chromatic similarity.

An assessment of color vision can be completed informally with a variety of activities:

◆ Organize a set of cards that includes lighter and darker shades of the same hue and ask the student to arrange them from lighter to darker or in families of related hues.

◆ Give the student a box of crayons of various shades of colors and ask him or her to put the crayons in order according to hue.

◆ Take note of the student's use of color in daily activities. Ask the parents and general education teachers if the student has difficulty completing tasks in which color plays a part.

Field of Vision.   Field of vision refers to the area of the environment that an individual can see. The visual field is divided into the central field, midperiphery, and far periphery. Formal assessments of the visual field should be conducted in the primary eye care provider's office. These assessments typically include the use of equipment and procedures that require special training.

An informal assessment of the visual field yields a gross estimate of the student's field, as well as how a student compensates for individual differences. How a student scans an array of objects (that is, shifts the gaze from one object or visual target to the next) or searches for a missing object can demonstrate his or her functional visual field at near point. For example, a compensatory turn of the head toward the right may suggest a peripheral field restriction to the right, since the student has learned to compensate by moving the usable visual field toward the side where information is missing. Observing how a student turns his or her head while performing activities, such as scanning a map or doing a word-search puzzle, can also suggest where scotomas (areas of diminished vision) may be located. Students who walk with their heads turned to one side or with a downward gaze may be compensating for a difference in visual fields.

Many students with low vision have vision in only one eye or use only one eye at a time. When binocular vision (vision using two eyes) is not available, the visual field and depth perception are affected. Students who use only one eye experience a field loss (approximately 35 degrees) on the side where vision is not present. (Whereas a person with one eye may have a horizontal visual field of approximately 155 degrees, someone with a typical visual field may approximate 185–190 degrees.) They also have an impaired ability to judge the distance of objects at close range. The teacher of students with visual impairments can help the student find ways of compensating for this loss of peripheral vision and inability to use depth perception at close ranges. Compensations may include scanning from side to side while walking down a crowded hallway and switching to tactile means when applying makeup to the eye through which the person sees.

Motility.   Motility refers to the coordinated movements of the eyes to conditions in which irregular eye movements occur (such as nystagmus). Eye movement, which allows a student to scan a broad array or follow a moving object can be observed in activities that require tracking (visually following a moving object), such as watching a squirrel move about outdoors. The smoothness of horizontal tracking movements should be noted, such as when following a slowly moving car or watching friends walk by in the hall. Some students have a jerky tracking movement, while others track without coordinated and smooth movements across their midline. Vertical eye movements can be observed as a student follows a bouncing basketball or the direction of a dropped object. Again, the focus of this observation is whether the student can follow a bouncing basketball and locate a dropped object, rather than taking measurements of eye movements or tracking ability.

The performance of tasks that involve combinations of eye movements, such as scanning a bookshelf for a particular book, can provide valuable information to the observer about the student's use of eye and/or eye movements. It should also be noted whether both eyes move together during tracking activities and whether the student typically moves his or her head and eyes while tracking and scanning. Generally, the lower the student's visual acuity, the more the student will move his or her head, rather than eyes, when visually searching (Jan, Ferrell, Wong, & McCormick, 1986).

Lighting.   A functional vision assessment should address the student's ability to discern the presence or absence of light, sensitivity to brightness and other lighting conditions, and need for increased or reduced levels of illumination. The

Cone Adaptation Test is often used to assess the student's ability to adapt to lighting changes. The task requires the individual to sort red, blue, and white squares in the least amount of light necessary to complete the task. Measures of light tolerance and glare may be conducted by the primary eye care provider.

The comfort levels of students with low vision may vary with different amounts and types of lighting. Some students, particularly those with specific retinal conditions, prefer bright lighting. However, other students, especially those with ocular media opacities (areas in which light does not have a clear pathway through the eye), such as cataracts, may be more comfortable with moderate lighting. Because of these differences, the teacher should take special care in gathering a wide variety of information about a student's lighting preference:

♦ Include both indoor and outdoor activities in the assessment.

♦ Observe the student when he or she is moving into and out of bright lighting.

♦ Note if the student prefers or benefits from light-absorption lenses, eyeglasses with shields on the side and above to block ambient light, lenses prescribed for low-contrast sensitivity, or darkly colored or therapeutic contact lenses for light control.

♦ Experiment with the use of visors, hats, or other items to shield the student's eyes from light.

Students who require more than average amounts of light should be assessed in different situations, including dimly lit rooms, at dusk, or on cloudy days, as well as in situations in which they may obtain more than available lighting (for example, when they have the option of using a lamp at a work space or working near a window). The teacher should determine if additional light at a desk or work area makes a difference in the student's functioning.

Contrast Sensitivity.   Contrast sensitivity refers to the ability to detect difference in grayness and background. Formal measures of contrast sensitivity are generally conducted by the primary eye care provider or during the clinical low vision evaluation. They require specific levels of illumination on charts that are designed to plot an individual's sensitivity to different levels of contrast.

The LEA Symbol Low Contrast Test assesses environmental contrast sensitivity by presenting the student with an acuity card of low-contrast print symbols. For students who are unable to respond to print symbols because of their age or cognitive level, the Hiding Heidi test consists of low-contrast cards used to assess face-to-face visual contact. As part of a functional vision assessment, a teacher's observation of how a student works with low-contrast materials (such as low-contrast pictures) or functions in low-contrast environments (such as a sandy playground with light-colored stepping-stones) can provide information on contrast sensitivity.

Summary and Discussion.   Conclusions that are included in the report of the functional vision assessment should be based on a synthesis of the teacher's observations. They should relate specifically to the student who has been assessed and should be included in the descriptions of visual behaviors and skills that will give direction to the recommendations. The following should be included:

♦ An explanation of the environmental conditions and other factors that help or hinder visual functioning;

♦ The student's potential for increasing efficiency in using vision;

♦ The student's best and typical visual functioning, as well as any differences from expected visual functioning; and

♦ Changes in functional vision since the last assessment.

Recommendations.   Recommendations should be based on the findings of the formal instruments and/or informal assessments, observations of a variety of activities, and conclusions in the preceding sections. No recommendation should be made without objective information, or without assessing its potential effectiveness. For example, if a teacher recommends that a student should use bold-line paper, there should be a preceding observation that standard-line paper cannot be used, that there is reason to believe that the student cannot learn to use standard-line paper efficiently at this time, and that bold-line paper was tried and made a difference in the student's performance, comfort, and/or stamina. If a teacher only surmises that something will be helpful, but it has not been tried, the recommendation should include a referral for further assessment.

The functional vision assessment should provide clear recommendations that can be put into practice. Because instruction in the efficient use of vision is more fully realized in the activities of the student, family, and other members of the educational team, the recommendations should be specific, easy to understand, and practical. Several types of recommendations can be included in the report:

◆ Adaptations and accommodations: the use of materials to facilitate visual learning, such as bold-line paper and environmental adaptations, such as a lamp with a rheostat or other variations in lighting, color, contrast, distance, and other characteristics, that enhance a student's visual efficiency;

◆ Compensatory strategies: the development of specific visual skills with or without the use of equipment or optical devices (such as teaching a student what "in focus" with an optical device looks like at a distance), the use of instructional and compensatory strategies to enhance visual functioning (like teaching a child with nystagmus to tilt his or her head to read the name of a store across a street), instruction in the use of optical devices and other low vision devices (for instance, manipulating a monocular and a pen with sufficient speed to complete a task like copying from a chalkboard), combining the use of functional vision with other senses (such as using a recorded text

while looking at diagrams using a magnifier and using vision to locate a keyhole and using a tactile approach to placing the key in the keyhole);

◆ Referrals for additional evaluations: an O&M evaluation, a learning media assessment, a clinical low vision evaluation, or an assistive technology assessment; and

◆ Services and eligibility statements: recommended services and eligibility statements (such as the student's eligibility to be registered with the American Printing House for the Blind or to receive services from a teacher of students with visual impairments).

Functional Vision Assessments of Students with Additional Disabilities

Functional vision assessments can provide valuable information for teachers of students with visual impairments and additional disabilities. Understanding a student's use of functional vision can help teachers and parents plan daily activities that will optimize the student's abilities. When assessing students who have visual impairments and additional disabilities, consider the following suggestions:

◆ Involve all members of the student's educational team in the assessment so that unique physical, motor, or speech needs are addressed.

◆ Make sure that the student's assessment is conducted at a time when his or her performance is not affected by medication.

◆ Provide assessment activities that are motivating to the student. Make sure that observations are conducted at a variety of times throughout the day. Some students with additional disabilities fatigue as the day goes on and may perform differently in the morning and in the afternoon.

◆ Provide plenty of time for the student to respond to requests. Some students with additional disabilities take more time to process visual information and need to have additional time to respond to visual stimuli.

◆ Follow up on areas of concern with additional observations or assessment. If it is difficult to determine how the student responds to a particular part of the functional vision assessment, provide multiple opportunities for the student to participate in the activity and observe his or her response over time.

◆ Use diagnostic teaching techniques to make sure that the student's responses are based on visual ability, not on an understanding of the task.

◆ Examine the student's use of functional vision regularly and throughout the day to understand how the student responds visually to a variety of daily tasks.

LEARNING MEDIA ASSESSMENT[4]

A learning media assessment is a process of systematically gathering objective information to provide a basis for selecting appropriate learning and literacy media for students who are blind or visually impaired. Whereas the functional vision assessment focuses on the visual channel, the learning media assessment examines the student's efficiency and needs in using all sensory channels, especially vision, touch, and hearing. In addition, a learning media assessment targets both the broad range of visual, tactile, and auditory learning media (such as pictures, globes, and eating utensils) and specific literacy media (including braille, regular print with low vision devices, and large print). Findings from the learning

media assessment guide instructional planning to ensure that each student gains solid literacy skills in a conventional literacy medium or media (print and/or braille) and develops a wide repertoire of literacy tools (see Table 4.1) to accomplish the daily demands of school, employment, and life.

One of the 1997 amendments to IDEA addresses the need to provide braille literacy instruction to students who are blind or visually impaired and mandates a targeted assessment process. This amendment requires that the educational team consider "special factors" when developing a student's IEP. The specific text is as follows:

[I]n the case of a child who is blind or visually impaired, provide for instruction in Braille and use of Braille unless the IEP Team determines, after an evaluation of the child's reading and writing skills, needs, and appropriate reading and writing media (including an evaluation of the child's future needs for instruction in Braille or the use of Braille), that instruction in Braille or the use of Braille is not appropriate for the child. [IDEA Section 1414(d)(3)(B)(iii)]

On the basis of this amendment, an educational team must presume that a student who has been identified as blind or visually impaired will receive instruction in braille literacy skills. However, if the results of an appropriate assessment indicate that braille is not an appropriate reading medium for the student—either now or in the future—then braille literacy instruction is not required. A complete and thorough learning media assessment provides objective documentation to support sound decisions and should address the following three elements identified in the IDEA amendment:

◆ An evaluation of the student's reading and writing *skills* (that is, achievement in these skill areas);

◆ An evaluation of the student's reading and writing *needs* (that is, literacy skills areas that need to be taught, expanded, or improved);

---

[4]*Parts of this section were adapted from A. J. Koenig, "Selection of Learning and Literacy Media for Children and Youths with Low Vision," in A. L. Corn & A. J. Koenig, Eds.,* Foundations of Low Vision: Clinical and Functional Perspectives *(New York: AFB Press, 1996, pp. 246–279).*

Table 4.1. Literacy Tools for Students with Visual Impairments

Visual Tools	Tactile Tools	Auditory Tools
Regular-print materials	Braille materials	Aural reading from audiotapes
Large-print materials	Braillewriter	Aural reading from CDs
Nonoptical devices	Slate and stylus	Audiocassette books
Optical low vision devices	Typewriter	Live readers
Regular writing paper	Signature guide	Radio Reading Service
Bold-line writing paper	Check-writing guide	Talking dictionary
Signature guide	Paper line guide	Synthesized speech
Print as a supplement to braille	Braille as a supplement to print	Audiocassette recorder (for notes)
Typewriter	Tactile graphics	Word-processing skills
Regular computer monitor	Electronic braille note taker	Telecommunication skills
Large computer monitor	Braille display	
Enlarged print on screen	Braille input device	
Inkprint printer	Braille embosser	
Keyboarding skills	Keyboarding skills	
Word-processing skills	Word-processing skills	
Telecommunication skills	Telecommunication skills	

Source: Adapted from A. J. Koenig and M. C. Holbrook, *Learning Media Assessment of Students with Visual Impairments: A Resource Guide for Teachers,* 2nd ed. (Austin: Texas School for the Blind and Visually Impaired, 1995).

◆ An evaluation of appropriate reading and writing *media* (that is, literacy media—braille, print, large print, and so forth—that are needed or are anticipated to be needed in the future), including the future need for braille.

The traditional learning media assessment has focused primarily on the final element—selecting appropriate literacy media—which is the focus of this section. The broader aspects of assessing literacy skills and determining literacy needs to be addressed through instruction are typically gathered through informal measures, such as checklists and observations (see Chapter 8).

A learning media assessment consists of two broad phases: (1) the selection of the initial literacy medium, which encompasses a short time from infancy to the beginning of formal literacy instruction (generally in kindergarten or first grade), and (2) the continuing assessment of literacy media, which begins immediately after the initial literacy medium is selected and continues throughout the student's school career. In each phase, there are a variety of observations to be conducted, data to be collected, and decisions to be made. The foundation of a learning media assessment is making sound, reasoned decisions on each student's learning and literacy needs that are based on objective data.

Although there are a number of learning media assessment processes, the one described here is based on *Learning Media Assessment of Students with Visual Impairments: A Resource Guide for Teachers* (Koenig & Holbrook, 1995). This is a comprehensive assessment process that includes specific guidelines for the teacher to follow and a series of checklists and forms to facilitate the collection of data and analyses in the following essential areas:

- ◆ Documenting the student's use of sensory channels;

- ◆ Selecting general learning media, including both instructional materials and teaching methods;

- ◆ Choosing the initial literacy medium for beginning formal instruction in reading and writing; and

- ◆ Conducting continuing assessments of the initial decision and determining when to provide instruction in additional literacy tools.

The basic elements are presented in the next section, and the reader is referred to the complete resource guide for detailed information and guidelines. Other assessment procedures are presented in the Resources section of this chapter.

Phase 1: Initial Selection Phase

Determining Preferred Sensory Channels

A cornerstone of the initial selection phase is documenting objectively the student's use of sensory channels—that is, the senses through which the student acquires information. This procedure involves observations in a variety of environments to determine how the student naturally chooses to use his or her sensory channels to complete tasks. Observed behaviors are documented as they occur, and the sensory channels that are in each behavior are recorded, thereby providing several samples of the student's behaviors under various conditions. After multiple observations, the teacher of students with visual impairments can evaluate all observation forms to determine the primary and secondary sensory channels that the student uses naturally. The student's primary and secondary sensory channels can be noted on the "General Student Information" form (see Appendix A to this chapter). This form can be used to summarize other key findings of the learning media assessment as well as background information from the student's file. The specific guidelines for this procedure (Koenig & Holbrook, 1995) are as follows:

1. Arrange three or more observation sessions of 15 to 20 minutes each. Given that students with visual impairments use sensory information differently under various conditions, it is suggested that the observations include structured times (such as a teacher-directed lesson) and unstructured times (such as recess), familiar settings (such as the student's classroom) and unfamiliar settings (such as a store in the community that the student has not visited), and indoor settings (such as a gymnasium) and outdoor settings (such as a city park).

2. Include parents and other members of the student's educational team in conducting observations. Teach them to use the observation and coding procedures and practice with them using videotapes before they conduct real-life observations. Including parents and other team members allows for additional observations in other environments and settings, including the home.

3. Observe and record all behaviors as they occur and in the sequence that they occur throughout the observation period. Record only observable, concrete behaviors. For example, "turns on faucet" and "picks up toy" are observable behaviors and should be recorded, whereas "wants a drink of water" and "seems restless" are not observable and should be avoided. (The actual behaviors, though, *should* be recorded, such as "picks up glass" and "fidgets in chair.")

4. Record a continuous behavior (like "swings on a swing" or "walks down the sidewalk") only once. Then code any unique behaviors that are observed within the continuous behavior. For example, a student who is swinging on a swing may wave to a friend and turn his or her head toward the sound of a whistle. In this situation, three behaviors would be recorded: "swings on swing," "waves to friend," and "turns head toward whistle."

5. Code each behavior immediately after it is recorded according to the sensory channel or channels (V for visual, T for tactile, and A for auditory) that were involved in accomplishing the task. This determination is made quickly on the basis of the observer's judgment. Code the primary channel (that is, the sensory channel that was primarily used to accomplish the task) with a square. Code any secondary channels that were involved with a circle. If unsure of which was primary, simply circle all sensory channels that were involved.

6. Record and rate 15 or more behaviors in each setting. Continue this procedure in other settings until a consistent pattern in the use of sensory channels is evident.

Figure 4.1 presents an example of a coded sensory channels observation form.

After all the observations are completed, the teacher of students with visual impairments should gather all the coded observation forms, including those from the other team members. The primary sensory channel will be the one that has been coded the most consistently with a square. The secondary channel or channels will be the one or ones that have been coded with a circle. This information should be noted in the file and included later in the assessment report.

If an inconsistent pattern of sensory use is found, then the teacher may wish to separate near behaviors from distance behaviors. Often, students with low vision use their senses differently on near tasks and distant tasks, and this procedure will help to identify such a pattern. If a consistent pattern of sensory use is still not found, the teacher of students with visual impairments will need to conduct additional observations under carefully selected conditions in an effort to identify the factor that is influencing the inconsistency. For example, the teacher may compare the student's behavior outdoors in sunny conditions versus cloudy conditions.

Findings related to the student's use of his or her sensory channels are used for two purposes.

First, they provide a basis for selecting appropriate general learning media, as described in the next section. For example, if a student is found to use touch as a primary channel, using real objects to develop concepts may be preferable to using pictures. Second, the student's preferred sensory channel will help inform, but will not dictate, the decision on the student's literacy medium or media. That is, students who use vision as a primary sensory channel, especially for near tasks, are more likely to be print readers, and students who use touch as a primary channel are more likely to be braille readers. However, additional information (described later) is needed before a decision on the student's literacy medium or media can be made.

Caution must be exercised in using information gained from the observation of sensory channels, because the findings will reveal the primary sensory channel that the student *prefers* to use, not necessarily the channel that is the most efficient. Some students, especially those with low vision, may struggle to use visual information even when this channel is inefficient and results in their obtaining misinformation. Many of these students have been encouraged to use vision and reinforced for doing so (such as, "nice looking!"), but have not had similar positive experiences and/or received positive reinforcement for using touch. When the teacher of students with visual impairments thinks that a student is showing a preference for an inefficient sensory channel, the course of action is to provide rich experiences in the other senses and to conduct another observation after a lengthy period of time (such as a semester or a year). Using diagnostic teaching (see Chapter 3) to provide instruction and providing opportunities to complete tasks using various senses is part of the procedure for selecting the initial literacy medium (discussed in a following section).

Considering General Learning Media

Another aspect of the initial selection phase is considering the general learning media (apart from literacy media) that are the most beneficial for the student. These media include both in-

Use of Sensory Channels: Observation Form

Student _David Smith_

Setting/Activity _Language arts class and O&M lesson_

Date _1/25/96_   Observer _Jane Holland_

Observed Behavior	Sensory Channel		
Class	Located desk	[V]	T	A
	Reached for recorder	[V]	T	A
	Placed disk in disk drive	[V]	T	A
	Turned on computer (switch in back)	V	[T]	A
	Switched on plug-in strip	[V]	(T)	A
	Gathered papers together	[V]	T	A
	Walked to reading circle	[V]	(T)	(A)
	Glanced around room	[V]	T	A
	Put on glasses	[V]	T	A
	Looked at book	[V]	T	A
	Took off glasses	V	[T]	A
	Listened to story	V	T	[A]
	Stared at overhead light	[V]	T	A
	Clapped hands	(V)	(T)	(A)
O&M	Identified parts of the cane	[V]	(T)	A
	Located office	[V]	T	A
	Walked in a straight line	[V]	T	A
	Waved at friends in hall	[V]	T	A
	Turned corner	[V]	(T)	A
	Looked behind self	[V]	T	A
	Went to office door	[V]	T	A
	Located office number	[V]	T	A
	Shook hands with teacher	[V]	(T)	A
	Examined poster on bulletin board	[V]	T	A
	Located specific room number	[V]	T	A
	Located drinking fountain	[V]	T	A

☐ Probable Primary Channel: _Visual_

○ Probable Secondary Channel(s): _Tactile and auditory_

Figure 4.1. Use of Sensory Channels: Observation Form

Source: Adapted from A. J. Koenig and M. C. Holbrook, *Learning Media Assessment of Students with Visual Impairments: A Resource Guide for Teachers,* 2nd ed. (Austin: Texas School for the Blind and Visually Impaired, 1995).

structional materials (such as pictures, calendars, puzzles, and clocks) and teaching methods (including demonstrations, gestures, prompts, and modeling). Also, both near and distance needs should be taken into account. General learning media are chosen on the basis of the student's use of his or her sensory channels, as just described, as well as the student's instructional goals for the coming year. If a goal is to increase daily living skills, for example, then the team needs to consider the appropriate materials and teaching methods that will match the student's use of visual, tactile, and auditory cues.

The outcome of this portion of the assessment is the generation of recommendations for general learning media that will be used for instructional purposes in the classroom to meet the student's individual needs. This is important and necessary information to share with parents, preschool teachers, and other educators.

Selecting the Initial Literacy Medium or Media

The process of selecting the initial literacy medium begins in infancy and continues through the preschool years. Throughout this time, the teacher of students with visual impairments, the student's parents, and others on the educational team systematically collect data on the student's use of his or her sensory channels, preferred approach to learning, interest in pictures and books, and so forth. To determine the student's preferred or most efficient approach, the teacher of students with visual impairments needs to offer the student both visual and tactile opportunities to complete the tasks. When the student is demonstrating behaviors closely associated with literacy—such as scribbling and reading back the message, saying the alphabet, attempting to write his or her name, and noting likenesses and differences between print or braille words—it is time to select the initial literacy medium.

Components of the initial selection process include documenting the student's use of sensory channels, choosing general learning media (both discussed previously), and selecting the literacy

medium or media. With regard to selecting the initial literacy medium, Koenig and Holbrook (1995) suggested that educational teams gather data in the following areas:

◆ The student's use of the visual sense for gathering information,

◆ The student's use of the tactile or other senses for gathering information,

◆ The smallest size of objects that the student can efficiently identify at a comfortable working distance (that is, the distance from the eye to the object),

◆ The stability and prognosis of the eye condition, and

◆ The influence of additional disabilities on learning to read.

Other information that is specific to the individual student is also considered, such as the student's and parents' attitudes toward or preference for a certain medium.

The first area in which data are gathered is related to the student's use of sensory information for learning. At this point, the educational team needs to consider the student's use of visual or tactile and other senses to complete a variety of specific tasks, including early literacy events, such as these:

◆ Recognition of others,

◆ Initiation of the reaching response,

◆ Exploration of a toy or other object,

◆ Discrimination of likenesses and differences in objects or toys,

◆ Identification of objects,

◆ Confirmation of an object's identity,

◆ Use of visual-motor and fine motor skills,

◆ Interest in pictures,

◆ Interest in books,

◆ Interest in scribbling or writing, and

◆ Identification of names or simple words.

Through diagnostic teaching (discussed in Chapter 3), the student is given both visual and tactile experiences, and the teacher assesses his or her preference for completing tasks with the visual sense or with the tactile and/or other senses. The process of gathering information through diagnostic teaching occurs over a lengthy period, and should begin in infancy. The actual decision about which learning medium to use is generally made when the student enters a conventional literacy program, usually in kindergarten.

Again, a word of caution is needed. To assess the efficiency of various senses in a nonbiased manner, the teacher of students with visual impairments must provide experiences to the student that are equal in intensity and quality. Recall the previously mentioned concern that students with low vision are often reinforced for using vision but do not receive the same level of reinforcement for using other senses. When a student's sensory experiences are unequal in intensity or quality, an assessment of the student's efficiency in using the various senses will be tainted. During this early diagnostic teaching phase, the educational team should seek to stimulate all the student's senses and reinforce the student accordingly.

Although the student's efficiency in using different forms of sensory information is important in making the initial decision about learning media, it must be considered within a larger context of objective data. For students with low vision, the information on efficiency in using the visual sense needs to be paired with the objective information on the size of objects that can be comfortably identified and viewing distances for identifying an object. For example, if a student is efficient in using visual information, but does so at such a close working distance that a sustained working time is not possible, tactile media may be more efficient. The educational team must consider the implications of combinations of factors and must never take isolated pieces of information out of context.

Other factors that are crucial in making the initial decision are the prognosis and stability of the eye condition. A stable eye condition allows the educational team to focus the initial decision primarily on the data they have gathered on sensory efficiency. A progressive or unstable eye condition, on the other hand, may necessitate a focus on the future implications of the condition. The educational team must consider both the immediate and future needs of the student, to ensure that the student is making meaningful progress toward establishing literacy skills. Some students with progressive or unstable eye conditions begin to learn braille reading and writing at a time when their visual efficiency is still high. In such instances, it is essential for the teacher of students with visual impairments to cultivate a positive environment for teaching braille and to nurture the student in the present and future value of learning braille reading and writing. (See Chapter 8 for more information on teaching literacy skills.)

Before the student enters a formal literacy program, members of the educational team review and synthesize all the information they have gathered. This synthesis and interpretation of the objective data should occur in a holistic manner, with deliberate care not to take any individual piece of information out of the context of all the others. In their deliberations, team members focus on whether the student demonstrates the characteristics of a visual learner who will make efficient use of print or a tactile learner who will make efficient use of braille. Some characteristics to consider in deciding on the initial literacy medium are presented in Sidebar 4.2. In some instances, the team may decide to implement formal reading instruction in both print and braille and use the upcoming semester or year to engage in diagnostic teaching to resolve any lingering questions. Thereafter, the educational team may decide to concentrate on one medium or continue with both media.

Phase 2: Continuing Assessment

As soon as the initial literacy medium is selected, the educational team begins the long-term process of continuing assessment of literacy media needs that continues throughout the student's school career. This phase has two purposes: (1) to con-

SIDEBAR 4.2

Profiles of Students for Braille Literacy and Print Literacy Programs

The characteristics of a student who may be a likely candidate for a *print*-reading program may include the following:

◆ Uses vision efficiently to complete tasks at near distances.

◆ Shows an interest in pictures and demonstrates the ability to identify pictures and/or elements within pictures.

◆ Identifies his or her name in print and/or understands that print has meaning.

◆ Uses print to perform other prerequisite reading skills.

◆ Has a stable eye condition.

◆ Has an intact central visual field.

◆ Shows steady progress in learning to use his or her vision as necessary to ensure efficient print reading.

◆ Is free of additional disabilities that would interfere with progress in a conventional reading program in print.

The characteristics of a student who may be a likely candidate for a *braille*-reading program may include the following:

◆ Shows a preference for exploring the environment tactilely.

◆ Uses the tactile sense efficiently to identify small objects.

◆ Identifies his or her name in braille and/or understands that braille has meaning.

◆ Uses braille to perform other prerequisite reading skills.

◆ Has an unstable eye condition or a poor prognosis for retaining his or her current level of vision in the near future.

◆ Has a reduced or nonfunctional central field to the extent that print reading is expected to be inefficient.

◆ Shows steady progress in developing the tactile skills that are necessary for efficient braille reading.

◆ Is free of additional disabilities that would interfere with his or her progress in a conventional reading program in braille.

Source: Adapted from A. J. Koenig and M. C. Holbrook, *Learning Media Assessment of Students with Visual Impairments: A Resource Guide for Teachers,* 2nd ed. (Austin: Texas School for the Blind and Visually Impaired, 1995), p. 43.

sider on an ongoing basis the appropriateness of the initial decisions and (2) to address the student's need to develop new literacy skills, such as aural reading, slate-and-stylus skills, and technology skills. The continuing assessment phase is a safety net that ensures that the student with a visual impairment will continue to develop functional literacy skills that he or she will need for independent living and employment. If the educational system has prepared the student to gain self-sufficiency and to serve as an advocate for

himself or herself, the student will then take over the process of continually assessing his or her literacy needs throughout life.

To guide the continuing assessment phase, Koenig and Holbrook (1995) suggested that the educational team should collect and synthesize *objective* data at least annually on the following:

◆ The result of ophthalmologic, optometric, clinical low vision, and functional low vision evaluations, to determine whether there has been a change in visual function-ing since the last review;

◆ Reading efficiency rates and reading grade levels, to determine whether the student reads with sufficient efficiency to perform academic tasks successfully and comfort-ably;

◆ Academic achievement, to determine whether the student is continuing to make academic progress in the current medium or media;

◆ Handwriting skills, to determine whether the student is able to read back his or her own handwriting even after a lapse of time and whether handwriting is an effective ex-pressive communication mode; and

◆ The effectiveness of the student's existing repertoire of literacy tools, to determine whether instruction is needed in additional literacy tools to meet the demands of pres-ent and future literacy tasks.

Table 4.2 summarizes these five areas of the con-tinuing assessment phase, possible sources of ob-jective information, and possible actions. Each area is also described in the following sections.

Areas to Be Assessed

Visual Functioning. The teacher of students with visual impairments should gather informa-tion from reports in the student's file related to vi-sual functioning, including the findings of oph-thalmologic, optometric, clinical low vision, and functional vision evaluations, and review and syn-thesize it to determine if any changes in the stu-dent's visual functioning have been noted. Of par-ticular importance is whether the student's eye condition is progressive or deteriorating, since the status of the eye condition may have a direct im-pact on the decision to continue to use print as the primary literacy medium. In the rare cases in which a student's visual condition has improved, it may be appropriate to move from a more re-strictive print option (such as the use of a closed-circuit television [CCTV]) to a less restrictive op-tion (such as the use of regular print with a low vi-sion device).

Reading Efficiency. The teacher of students with visual impairments gathers objective infor-mation to document whether the student is com-pleting academic tasks efficiently in the current medium or media and is making appropriate aca-demic progress within a reasonable time when compared to his or her peers with typical vision.

Data on reading efficiency should be col-lected in the student's habitual primary reading medium: regular print, large print, or braille. For example, if the student habitually uses regular print with a 2.5x stand magnifier (see Chapter 13), he or she should be tested under these conditions. If the student uses print as a secondary reading medium to supplement braille reading and writ-ing, he or she needs to be tested in braille, since this is the student's habitual primary reading medium. In this case, the use of print reading should be assessed as a literacy tool (discussed later) on the basis of how successful the student is in completing those supplementary literacy tasks.

It is essential to collect objective data on a stu-dent's reading efficiency annually. In the authors' opinion, every student's cumulative record should contain a graph that plots annual reading effi-ciency rates—that is, reading speed for material at the student's instructional level that is read with comprehension. Sidebar 4.3 presents a simple and time-efficient procedure for gathering these data using any commercially available informal reading inventory. The Basic Reading Inventory (Johns, 1997) and the Informal Reading Inventory (Burns & Roe, 1993) are particularly useful, since they contain reading passages for kindergarten through 12th-grade reading levels. These are in-formal measures, so the inventories can be em-bossed in braille or placed in large type[5] without invalidating their usefulness. These instruments

---

[5]*Although the copyright law allows many copyrighted materials to be placed in braille or large type without the permission of the publisher, this does not extend to as-sessment instruments. Permission must be obtained from the publisher before any assessment instrument (even an informal test) is placed in an accessible medium.*

Table 4.2. Components of the Continuing Assessment of Literacy Media

Questions	Sources of Information	Possible Actions
Does available information indicate a change in visual functioning?	◆ Functional vision assessment reports ◆ Clinical low vision evaluation reports ◆ Ophthalmological evaluation reports ◆ Observations of sensory usage	If yes, consider the impact on current primary literacy medium.
Does the student read at a sufficient rate and with adequate comprehension to complete academic tasks successfully?	◆ Results of an informal reading inventory ◆ Objective data on reading rate ◆ Reading rate and comprehension levels in content reading materials ◆ Feedback from classroom teacher on level of reading efficiency relative to peers ◆ Feedback from others on the educational team, including the parents ◆ Objective data on reading in various print media	If no, explore possible reasons through diagnostic teaching, consider need to expand literacy tools, and consider the impact of the findings related to reading efficiency on the primary medium.
Is the student able to complete academic tasks in the current medium or media successfully and in a reasonable amount of time in comparison with peers without visual impairments?	◆ Results of chapter tests and other informal assessments ◆ Grade cards and other feedback from members of the educational team ◆ Results of achievement tests or state competence examinations ◆ Observations of the student in the classroom ◆ Feedback from the parents on the amount of time spent completing homework	If no, consider the areas identified earlier, especially the need to add additional literacy tools that may increase overall efficiency.
Is the student able to read his or her own handwriting and use it as a viable mode of written communication?	◆ Writing samples ◆ Accuracy of rereading writing samples after a period of elapsed time	If no, consider expanding the student's repertoire of writing modes, especially the use of word processing.
Does the student have the repertoire of literacy tools, including technological tools, to meet his or her current educational needs? To meet his or her future educational and/or vocational needs?	◆ Checklist of literacy tools to document existing skills and to guide future needs ◆ Observations of the student using tools ◆ Feedback from members of the educational team on the student's success in using tools ◆ Long-range goals to guide selection of additional tools	If no, consider adding literacy tools first to meet current needs and then to meet anticipated future needs.

Source: Adapted from A. J. Koenig, "Selection of Learning and Literacy Media for Children and Youths with Low Vision," in A. L. Corn and A. J. Koenig, Eds., *Foundations of Low Vision: Clinical and Functional Perspectives* (New York: AFB Press, 1996), p. 255.

A Procedure for Documenting Reading Efficiency

SIDEBAR 4.3

1. Select a published informal reading inventory that provides reading passages of increasing grade-level difficulty and that includes at least five comprehension questions for each passage.
2. Prepare the reading passages in the student's primary reading medium. If the student typically uses a low vision device for reading, he or she should use that device during testing.
3. Have the student read the passages orally. Begin at a level that the student will be able to read with ease. Record with a stopwatch the time (in seconds) that the student spent reading each passage.
4. Read the comprehension questions for each passage aloud and score the student's response according to criteria provided by the publisher.
5. Then have the student read a parallel form of each passage silently. (Some students in the early grades may wish only to read aloud, and this practice should be permitted.) For silent reading passages, tell the student to begin reading when you say "start" and to look up at you when he or she is finished. Record with a stopwatch the time (in seconds) that the student spent reading each passage.
6. Read aloud the comprehension questions for each passage read silently and score the student's response according to criteria provided by the publisher.
7. Continue testing until the student reaches the frustration reading level in oral reading steps (steps 4–5) and then in silent reading (steps 5–6), as determined by the criteria provided by the publisher. Typically, this level is indicated by comprehension of less than 75 percent.
8. Calculate the rate of reading for each passage in which the student demonstrated 75 percent comprehension or higher. Some informal reading inventories provide equations to help determine the rate of reading. If not, count the words in each passage and apply the following formula:

$$\frac{\text{Number of words in passage}}{\text{Number of seconds spent reading}} \times 60 = \text{Number of words per minute}$$

9. Calculate the average words per minute for oral reading and the average words per minute for silent reading.

Source: Adapted from A. J. Koenig and M. C. Holbrook, *Learning Media Assessment of Students with Visual Impairments: A Resource Guide for Teachers,* 2nd ed. (Austin: Texas School for the Blind and Visually Impaired, 1995).

provide formulas that allow for the quick calculation of reading rates once the time required to read the passage is determined. Collecting reading efficiency data in this manner generally takes 30 to 45 minutes.

Although the procedure described in Sidebar 4.3 is easy and quick to use, the data have specific limitations. First, the rates are based only on the reading of short passages that typically are shorter than most reading assignments in a classroom. Second, given the short reading time, the rates do not indicate if visual fatigue is a concern for the student. Third, the rates are reflective of only "typical" narrative reading materials, commonly found in basal reading series and literature books.

The first two concerns can be addressed by having the student read for a sustained period (such as 20 or 30 minutes) from a lengthy, cohesive passage. Reading materials can be selected from a basal reader or a library book that is at the student's instructional reading level. A reading rate can be calculated for the first half of the reading episode and another for the second half using the formula in Sidebar 4.3, step 8. The number of words in each half of the story need to be counted first. A substantial gap between the two reading rates, with the second being lower, is evidence of visual fatigue. In contrast, some students with low vision will increase their rate of reading in the second half of the episode because they have gained basic knowledge of the story and thus are more efficient at predicting the author's message.

Stamina can also be measured by collecting a reading sample at the beginning of the school day and another at the end of the day and comparing the two rates. Another reading sample could be taken during the evening in the student's home to document reading efficiency during the time a student is expected to complete homework assignments.

The third concern can be partially addressed by measuring the student's efficiency in reading content from the textbooks in various subject areas that he or she is expected to read daily. Here are the steps in gathering such data for content materials:

1. Select passages that can be read in about 3 to 5 minutes from the student's science, social studies, and other content-area textbooks. Use passages that have not been previously read or studied in class.

2. Have the student read either silently or aloud and document the time he or she has spent reading with a stopwatch.

3. After the student has finished reading a passage, either ask several questions about the content of the passage or have the student tell what the passage was about in his or her own words. Document the level of comprehension as a percentage of questions answered correctly or

with a general descriptor, such as "average" or "inadequate."

4. Count the number of words in the passage and calculate the rate of reading using the formula in Sidebar 4.3.

After all the data are gathered, the educational team considers whether the student is making appropriate gains in reading efficiency. Since there is no formula to determine "appropriate" gains, the educational team must rely on sound reasoning and professional judgment. Some guidance in this regard is provided later in the section on interpreting data.

Academic Achievement.   General indicators of academic achievement (such as appropriately adapted and interpreted state competence tests, criterion-referenced tests from textbook series, chapter tests, and so forth) can be used to determine if the student is continuing to make progress in an academic program (see Chapters 2 and 3 for more information on academic assessments). Such indicators require a comparison between the performance of the student with a visual impairment and his or her sighted classmates. Although some educators are reluctant to make such comparisons, it is difficult to judge otherwise whether the student is continuing to make adequate academic progress. If the student is not making academic gains similar to those of his or her sighted classmates, the team needs to consider whether a change in the literacy medium is warranted or whether additional literacy tools are needed.

A particularly important aspect of academic achievement relates to reading skills. Screening information on a student's reading achievement can be gained from an informal reading inventory (used to document reading efficiency), which can determine the student's independent, instructional, and frustration reading levels. Although the teacher should follow the specific directions included in the inventory, Burns and Roe (1999) provided the following general guidelines for determining each level:

- Independent level—the level at which the student can read without any assistance or instruction, typically measured by a comprehension level of 90 percent or above and a word-recognition accuracy level of 99 percent or higher;

- Instructional level—the level at which the student can read with assistance and instruction by a teacher, typically measured by a comprehension level of 75 percent or higher and a word-recognition accuracy level of 85 percent or higher in Grades 1 and 2 and 95 percent or higher in Grades 3–12;

- Frustration level—the level at which a student is unable to read adequately (even with instruction) because of the difficulty of the reading material, typically measured by a comprehension level of less than 50 percent or a word-recognition accuracy level of below 85 percent for Grades 1 and 2 and below 90 percent for Grades 3–12.

This screening information should be viewed only within the context of other data on literacy achievement, such as scores from state or district competency tests, criterion-referenced tests, curriculum-based assessments, writing samples, and appropriately administered standardized achievement tests. Converting reading achievement tests to large print or braille, although common, does not, by itself, guarantee a nondiscriminatory assessment. Given the concerns about validity, data from standardized tests should only supplement many other sources of data from informal instruments; standardized tests should never be the sole source of information on the reading achievement of any student with low vision. Duckworth (1993) provided valuable guidelines for appropriately adapting standardized tests for use by students with visual impairments. The reader is also referred to Chapter 2 for more information on the appropriate use of formal assessment instruments.

Handwriting.　For a student with low vision, two aspects of handwriting should be assessed:

- The efficiency with which the student can use handwriting as a tool for personal communication, and

- The effectiveness with which the student can use handwriting to communicate with other people (such as his or her parents and classroom teacher).

Both areas can be assessed through informal writing samples using the following steps:

1. Gather some handwriting samples that the student completed two to three weeks prior to the assessment.

2. Hand the samples to the student and ask him or her to read them aloud. Note the student's efficiency and comfort in reading back the information.

3. Give the student's handwriting samples to another teacher or adult and ask him or her to read them. Note whether the samples are read easily and quickly or whether the samples are read with difficulty.

If concerns about the writing instruments or paper used to complete the writing assignment arise, diagnostic teaching can be used to explore other options (such as using felt-tip pens, bold-line paper, or a reading-writing stand). If the tools used for writing seem adequate, but the writing is not legible, then some targeted lessons in penmanship may be helpful. Adults who work with students with low vision sometimes expect that the students' handwriting will be sloppy or illegible, and the students often meet those expectations. With proper expectations and instruction in targeted skills, handwriting skills are likely to improve. However, some students will need other options—either apart from handwriting or as a complement to handwriting—such as the use of word-processing or braille-writing skills.

Literacy Tools. The teacher of students with visual impairments examines the range of literacy tools that the student can use and the efficiency with which the student uses them in daily tasks. These tools range from traditional tools (such as large print, signature guides, slate and stylus, and recorded textbooks) to technological tools (including screen-enlargement software, computer or word-processor keyboards, refreshable braille display, and synthesized speech; see Chapter 14; see also Table 4.1 for other literacy tools). In this area, the teacher of students with visual impairments needs to do the following:

1. Take an inventory of the literacy tools that the student uses independently;
2. Note the student's effectiveness in using the tools and in choosing among the various options to complete daily tasks;
3. Identify literacy tools in which instruction has been provided, but for which additional instruction is needed; and
4. Identify literacy tools for which new instruction is needed to meet daily demands.

Some of this information can be gained through interviews with the student, but general education teachers, parents, and the teacher of students with visual impairments need to extend this information with observations and the direct assessment of skills. For example, if a general education teacher states that a student uses keyboarding and word-processing skills efficiently in class, the teacher of students with visual impairments can follow up with a direct assessment of the student's accuracy and speed in keyboarding and use of word-processing features and procedures.

The goal is for the student to be able to use a wide range of literacy tools to perform current school tasks. A goal for the teacher is to anticipate the student's *future* needs and to provide instruction in the literacy tools that the student can use to meet those needs. For example, a fifth-grade student who will be moving to a middle school in the sixth grade, where he or she will change classes throughout the day, should start learning to use tools that are easily transportable (such as a braille note-taking device, slate and stylus, low vision device, and laptop computer) before he or she needs these devices.

Interpreting Data

All data gathered in the continuing assessment process should be reviewed holistically and interpreted with sound, reasoned professional judgment. The focus should be on whether the student is doing the following:

◆ Establishing efficient reading and writing skills in an appropriate primary literacy medium that matches his or her level of visual functioning,

◆ Acquiring a variety of literacy tools for the efficient completion of tasks that require reading and writing to maintain his or her current academic progress and to complete functional tasks,

◆ Acquiring skills in additional literacy tools that will be appropriate for meeting future academic and vocational demands, and

◆ Developing and using skills in making appropriate choices among communication options to accomplish specific tasks effectively and knowing when and how to acquire additional literacy tools (Koenig & Holbrook, 1995).

Perhaps the most challenging decisions involve making judgments on whether a student's print-reading efficiency is appropriate, given the present and future academic or vocational demands and given the reading rates of peers without visual impairments. There is no formula for determining whether a student's reading efficiency is "appropriate" or whether time requirements to complete academic tasks are "reasonable," so professional judgment, based on objective findings, is the primary means of making such determinations. The following general guidelines and examples may be helpful:

1. Consider the magnitude of the gap, if any, between the reading efficiency rate of a student with low vision and his or her classmates with normal vision relative to the grade-placement level using a table of typical rates for students with typical vision (see Table 4.3). For example, in first grade, when many children are just learning to read and there is great variation in the reading skills of students, if a student with low vision is reading silently at 65 words per minute and others are reading silently at 81 words per minute, the team may consider such a gap to be reasonable. However, if a seventh grader with low vision is

reading silently at 65 words per minute and others are reading silently at about 180 words per minute, this gap is not likely to be considered reasonable at a time when there are likely to be considerable academic demands on his or her reading skills.

2. On the basis of the student's documented reading efficiency rate and the average reading efficiency rate of his or her sighted classmates, consider the time required to read a short story of a given number of words. For example, a typical first-grade story, late in the school year, may have 500 words. A student with low vision who is reading at 65 words per minute would take about 8 minutes to read the story, compared to 6 minutes for classmates with normal vision who are reading at 81 words per minute. At this grade level, the additional time taken by the student with low vision is reasonable. However, if the first grader with low vision reads at 15 words per minute, it would take about 33 minutes to read the story. Most educators would consider the additional 27 minutes for the student with low vision to be unreasonable for a first grader. On the other hand, if the same additional time of 27 minutes was required of a seventh grader (on an appropriately longer text), this difference would be considered reasonable.

3. Consider whether the student is continuing to increase his or her reading efficiency from year to year. By collecting and graphing reading efficiency rates on an annual basis, the educational team can objectively determine whether meaningful gains are being made. Steadily increasing gains in reading efficiency indicate that the student is reading in an appropriate medium and is receiving appropriate instruction. On the other hand, some students may reach a plateau for a number of reasons, such as these: (1) the quality and intensity of reading instruction may be inadequate to promote steady gains; (2) the primary literacy medium may not be appropriate, given the student's needs; (3) instruction may not have been provided to increase the reading efficiency rate; (4) the student may have reached his or her potential for reading efficiency, given his visual condition. Diagnostic teaching is needed to deter-

Table 4.3. Typical Oral and Silent Reading Rates for Individuals with Normal Vision (in words per minute)

Grade Level	Minimum Oral Reading Rates	Typical Silent Reading Rates
1	60	< 81
2	70	82–108
3	90	109–130
4	120	131–147
5	120	148–161
6	150	162–174
7	150	175–185
8		186–197
9		198–209
10		210–224
11		225–240
12		241–255
College		256–333+

Sources: Adapted from R. P. Carver, "Silent Reading Rates in Grade Equivalents," *Journal of Reading Behavior, 21,* 155–166; and F. J. Guszak, *Diagnostic Reading Instruction in the Elementary School,* 3rd ed. (New York: Harper & Row, 1985).

mine which factor or factors are contributing to the plateau.

4. Consider whether the student has sufficient stamina to complete all required academic tasks with relative comfort throughout the school day and evening. The objective data on fatigue obtained by having the student read lengthy passages—both in a session and at different times of the day—is one source of information in this regard. These objective data, however, need to be completed by information from a wide variety of sources, including reports from teachers and parents, the student's self-reports and behavioral observations (such as rubbing the eyes, acting-out behavior, and the avoidance of visual tasks). Fatigue is heavily influenced by one's psychological set, which is an important and necessary factor to consider in judging a student's stamina for visual tasks. A student's comfort level and general level of pleasure and enjoyment in reading should also be considered.

5. Consider whether the student is making gains in reading achievement and academic achievement, in general, from year to year. With a variety of data on reading achievement, members of the educational team can examine yearly gains to determine that the student is making continual progress in this area. Judging progress in reading should be embedded in the larger context of general academic achievement, since the two are likely to be highly correlated.

Making Appropriate Decisions

After critically reviewing the assessment data, the educational team makes decisions to ensure the continued development of literacy skills. If the student is making documented progress in reading efficiency and achievement, then the team will probably decide to continue instruction in the student's primary literacy medium and to expand, as appropriate, the student's repertoire of literacy tools. If the student is not making the desired progress, the team must act to change the current course of action to address the identified areas of difficulty. Among the many possible decisions are to do the following:

◆ Continue with the existing primary literacy medium and add additional literacy tools—such as audiotaped books and the services of a live reader—to the student's repertoire;

◆ Continue with the existing primary literacy medium, but provide targeted and intense instruction in reading skills to improve the student's reading efficiency and achievement;

◆ Begin instruction in an alternate literacy medium, typically braille reading and writing, but continue to use print and other options until braille becomes either the primary or a secondary literacy medium.

If a student is reading inefficiently in print and/or not making appropriate gains in reading achievement, a decision to change the primary literacy medium is not automatically necessary. The student may lack an appropriate experiential background or specific reading skills, such as decoding or comprehension, or may not have received high-quality reading instruction. In such instances, changing the medium will not eliminate the underlying problems. However, if the student's progress is hampered or restricted by a literacy medium that does not match his or her sensory functioning, then a deliberate change may indeed be required.

If a student is not making appropriate gains in braille reading and writing, the first course of action is to examine the range, intensity, and quality of the braille literacy instruction that is being provided. In some instances, teachers and others may think that a student's lack of progress is due to a learning disability or some other "explainable" problem, when the real cause may be sparse, fragmented, or weak instruction. In such cases, the decision is often to emphasize or overemphasize the use of audiotaped materials as a substitute for braille, when the appropriate course of action is to provide sufficient and appropriate instruction in braille literacy skills (see Chapter 8 for details on teaching braille literacy skills). If a student truly has a learning disability, then the teacher of students with visual impairments needs to consult with a specialist in learning disabilities to identify and try alternate approaches to teaching literacy skills.

Learning Media Assessments of Students with Additional Disabilities

Students who are blind or visually impaired and have additional disabilities also benefit from learning media assessments. Some of these students participate in conventional literacy programs with modification, whereas others, especially those with severe cognitive disabilities, participate in functional literacy programs, in which the goal is to use reading and writing to accomplish daily practical tasks, such as reading a tactile label on a can of soup or using a visual symbol to identify the appropriate time card in an after-school work program. Regardless of the way they will use literacy in their lives, all students, including those with additional disabilities, have the right to a comprehensive assessment of their potential for and use of literacy skills. The basic process of conducting a learning media assessment for a student with additional disabilities for whom functional literacy is appropriate parallels the process of doing so for a student without additional disabilities.

Koenig and Holbrook (1995) offered three major points to keep in mind when conducting a learning media assessment for a student with additional disabilities:

- Consider all literacy options and avoid making decisions on the basis of preconceived notions of the abilities of students with additional disabilities.

- Examine the student individually and make decisions on the basis of his or her unique needs and abilities.

- Determine the student's literacy goals. If the goal for functional literacy is to read environmental signs, then the importance of gathering information visually is increased, since environmental signs (such as exit, street, and store or restaurant signs) are, for the most part, visual signs. However, if the goal is to use a communication board (see Chapter 20), either visual or tactile symbols can be used.

Use of Sensory Channels

The educational team needs to begin the learning media assessment by examining the student's use of sensory channels. Observation procedures described earlier are also appropriate for use with a student with additional disabilities. However, several issues must be considered during the observation that may be unique to such a student:

- Choose an activity that is motivating to the student. Although this suggestion is true for all students, it is especially pertinent for a student with additional disabilities because of the complexity with which these students perform tasks.

- Observe the student at a time of day when he or she is most alert, that is, when the student is not fatigued and the effects of medication are not strong.

- Work closely with the physical therapist and/or occupational therapist to make sure that the student's physical positioning and motor control will allow the student to participate in the activity to the maximum.

Choosing an Initial Literacy Medium

The decision to begin functional literacy instruction using tactile or visual symbols is based on the way the student uses sensory information and the quality of his or her visual and tactile explorations. However, it is also important to keep the goals of functional literacy in mind. The teacher of students with visual impairments must take the lead in finding appropriate and creative ways to increase the student's use of tactile and visual symbols to achieve functional goals. Before the initial selection of literacy media, the educational team should address the following questions (Koenig & Holbrook, 1993):

◆ Would the student benefit from instruction in literacy skills for functional purposes?

◆ Would functional literacy skills facilitate the development of independent living and work skills?

◆ Would teaching functional literacy skills be justified, given other areas of need?

Continuing Assessment of Functional Literacy Media

It is especially important to conduct such continuing assessments because students with visual impairments and additional disabilities may not be developmentally ready for literacy instruction until well past the time when typically developing students are beginning to learn to read and write. The following suggestions will help members of the educational team continue to examine a student's learning media:

◆ Create an environment in which tactile or visual symbols are meaningful. Label the student's work space, storage space, and daily classroom materials. Provide labels that allow the student to use both touch and vision and observe student's use of each over time.

◆ Provide daily opportunities for the student to participate meaningfully in literacy activities, such as reading daily menus, the calendar of daily activities, or the schedule of classroom events. Ask the student to point to or recognize functional symbols during these literacy activities.

◆ Provide direct instruction so the student

can expand his or her use of functional literacy into all areas of life.

While the student is being taught and encouraged to use functional literacy, the educational team should continue to examine the efficiency with which the student participates in these activities, as well as any changes in visual functioning or the need for additional literacy tools.

ASSISTIVE TECHNOLOGY ASSESSMENT

There are many useful technological tools for students who are blind or visually impaired, and their number and usefulness will increase in the future. These tools can help students with visual impairments gain access to information—both print and electronic—and facilitate written communication. (See Chapter 14 for a discussion of the different types of technology mentioned in this section.) The key to taking advantage of the opportunities these tools offer is to give students access to the appropriate ones when needed. Determining the most appropriate technological tools for current and future educational tasks is the purpose of the comprehensive assistive technology assessment.

The 1997 amendments to IDEA (P.L 105-17) require a student's educational team to address the need for assistive technology, and a comprehensive assessment is generally the way to establish this need. A comprehensive assistive technology assessment identifies the technology that a student will need to complete different required tasks in the educational program. An effective assessment should be a team process. Team members may include the student (when appropriate); the student's parents; the teacher of students with visual impairments; the general education teacher; the physical, occupational, and speech therapists; the assistive technology specialist; the rehabilitation engineer; the general technology specialist; the rehabilitation counselor; and possibly a vendor or product representative. These additional team members are crucial to the successful completion of the assessment, especially for a student with a visual impairment and additional disabilities.

The comprehensive assistive technology assessment includes a review of background information and an initial assessment by a teacher of students with visual impairments, together with a follow-up assessment and recommendations by an assistive technology specialist or rehabilitation engineer. Once the technology has been put in place, the teacher of students with visual impairments and other members of the educational team conduct ongoing assessments and periodic reevaluations to ensure that the student's needs are continually addressed and appropriate changes in the student's educational program are made expeditiously.

Background Information

The first step in completing the assessment is to obtain the parents' permission for the evaluation and gather background information, a task typically completed by the teacher of students with visual impairments. Information from the student's permanent records, combined with functional data from informal evaluations and observations of the student, are essential, as is any information about the student's use of assistive technology in the past. The teacher should also compile a list of related questions and concerns raised by various people who have been involved with the student, such as these:

- ◆ "Would it be helpful for Scott to use a computer with speech synthesis? He really has a hard time seeing the screen even when we make the print bigger."

- ◆ "I'm concerned that Shondra can't use the keyboard with enough accuracy to do her schoolwork. She doesn't seem to keep her fingers on the home-row keys and can't see the screen well enough to catch her mistakes."

- ◆ "Is a switching device available that could make it easier for Marcus to activate the drill press at his job site? His cerebral palsy is hampering his output, and he's getting frustrated that he can't keep up with his co-workers."

- ◆ "After two weeks of using speech synthesis in our computer programming class, I can say that it doesn't work! Kindra is a great student, but she has to know each and every symbol on the computer screen, and the speech program just isn't good enough. Isn't there a way she can use braille to check her work?"

The student must have many related or prerequisite skills to maximize the value of assistive technology. For example, the student needs to have an adequate level of fine motor skills to use a keyboard, braille literacy skills to use a computer braille display, listening skills to use speech synthesis, and cognitive and conceptual skills to complete assigned tasks. Previous evaluations should have provided much of the information needed to determine the student's level of skill in this regard. If not, team members will have to obtain these data before they proceed with the assessment. To prepare for the assessment, they need to gather information from the following sources:

- ◆ Medical eye examination: information on near and distance acuities, visual fields, and the stability and prognosis of the eye condition;

- ◆ Clinical low vision evaluation: information on prescribed near and distance optical and nonoptical devices;

- ◆ Functional vision assessment: information on the student's use of vision for everyday tasks, both academic and nonacademic, and efficiency of basic visual skills, preferred font size, comfortable reading distance, position of materials, lighting preferences, and visual stamina;

- Learning media assessment: information on the primary literacy medium, additional literacy tools, reading efficiency and comprehension;

- General medical, psychological, and academic evaluations: information on the student's motor, auditory, cognitive, behavioral, and academic functioning that may affect the student's use of technology;

- Informal assessments and observations by teachers: information on the student's current use of assistive technology and strengths and needs in the major subject areas of reading, writing, spelling, mathematics, study skills, oral communication, activities of daily living, recreation and leisure, prevocational and vocational, and mobility, as well as typical modifications used in the classroom.

Additional background information is related to the quantity of printed information that the student needs to gain access to and the settings in which the information are to be accessed (for example, the length of the assignment and where the student will complete it). Since a variety of technological tools can be of assistance in completing a task, it is helpful to know the magnitude of the task and if it is to be completed in class, in a media center, in a computer lab, or at home.

A simple example illustrates this point. A seventh-grade student with low vision is unable to read most regular-print materials. The teacher prefers to give only short reading assignments in class and have the students complete longer ones at home. The class is assigned to read an eight-page story at home and to respond in small groups the next day to discussion questions that the teacher devised. Knowing the quantity of material to be read and the settings in which the student will work allows the teacher of students with visual impairments to offer the student a choice of assistive technology for each task. The student may use large-print or audiotaped books for the longer reading tasks at home and a magnifier for reading the discussion questions in school.

An often-overlooked issue during an assistive technology assessment is the school district's instructional program and course offerings in the field of technology. The assessment should address how a student with a visual impairment will gain access to the technology instruction that is offered to the other students. It is imperative that the teacher of students with visual impairments and other members of the student's educational team be proactive in this area to ensure that the student has the appropriate assistive technology and related skills to participate in the technology instruction offered in the general curriculum.

Initial Assistive Technology Assessment

Once the background information has been collected and reviewed, the assistive technology assessment can begin. The teacher of students with visual impairments can conduct the initial assessment, which typically involves the determination of the student's strengths and needs in these areas:

- Gaining access to print information through regular print, large print, optical devices, nonoptical devices, braille, auditory modes;

- Producing written communication through standard tools and technological devices;

- Gaining access to computers through visual, auditory, and tactile modes; and

- Inputting information into computers using keyboards or other devices.

The teacher can use the Technology Assessment Checklist for Students with Visual Impairments (shown in Appendix B to this chapter) to guide the assessment. Some of the information requested in the checklist may be available from the evaluations discussed in the previous section. If it is not, then direct assessment of the items is necessary. If the teacher of students with visual impairments does not have access to some technologically advanced options discussed in the checklist, these options can be evaluated by the assistive technology specialist or the rehabilitation engineer as part of a comprehensive assistive technology assessment. All items not assessed should be marked NA to indicate not attempted or not applicable; otherwise, it may be assumed that the student cannot perform the task.

In preparing for the initial assistive technology assessment, the teacher needs to locate a quiet room where the teacher, the student, and an observer can work without visual and auditory distractions and environmental factors, such as lighting and glare, are easily controllable. Since the assessment requires the student to perform many tasks that may lead to visual or physical fatigue, it may be advisable to conduct it over several days, depending on individual circumstances.

Gaining Access to Print

Many technologies can assist a student who is visually impaired to gain access to print. Information obtained in the learning media assessment will guide the teacher of students with visual impairments to the student's primary literacy medium, but a thorough assessment investigates the student's ability to use additional literacy tools, too. The teacher needs to review the Technology Assessment Checklist thoroughly before the assessment starts to determine what materials need to be gathered and which parts may require assistance from a general technology specialist or an assistive technology specialist.

Many variables need to be evaluated and controlled if a student is to gain access to materials visually. Print size, use of optical aids, lighting, glare control, and fatigue affect both the student's learning environment and the assessment environment. Considering such environmental factors and making appropriate modifications will help ensure that the student who is visually impaired will benefit from both the assessment and instruction. Sidebar 4.4 presents a summary of issues associated with many of these and other environmental factors.

Regular Print. Many students with low vision are able to use regular print to complete some reading tasks. The teacher of students with visual impairments should determine if the student is able to function effectively with regular-print materials and under what conditions. Two major issues to consider are the viewing distance and the quantity of viewing before visual or physical fatigue occur.

Large Print. Point size and font preference are two factors that the teacher of students with visual impairments needs to assess regularly because a student's preferences can change over time. The teacher needs simple samples of text in various point sizes and fonts and a tape measure for gauging viewing distance. For some students 18-point type—typically considered large type—is adequate. For others, it is not large enough, and for still others, it is too large. Ideally, large print is used to display as much text as possible in a size that the reader can view at a comfortable distance. This ideal font size may vary from task to task, so it is necessary to measure the viewing distance for several point sizes. Many users of large print indicate a preference for a particular font. Arial, Antique Olive, Tahoma, and Verdana are popular fonts because of their lack of ornamentation and the openness of their characters.

Optical Devices. The student should use his or her optical device or devices during the assistive technology assessment when appropriate. However, the teacher may want to take this opportunity to assess the student's ability to read print without a device. This type of information can be helpful to the student and the teacher when the aids are broken or not available.

Electronic Low Vision Device. The CCTV is the most widely used electronic low vision device. A small television system with a camera and monitor in one unit that sits on top of a desk or table, it electronically enlarges onto a monitor the images of text, pictures, or other materials placed on the X/Y table beneath the camera. The X/Y table is so named because it allows the materials placed on its surface to be moved freely in any direction. The

Environmental Considerations for Assistive Technology

Several environmental factors need to be considered before a teacher of students with visual impairments provides a student who is visually impaired with assistive technology. The following outline should help guide the teacher's thinking about the environment in which the student will use this technology.

I. What is the environment?
   A. The classroom the student is in for his or her classes
   B. The resource room the student may use
   C. The special education resource room
   D. Any other room the student uses for classes or studying
II. What aspects of the environment are important for the student with low vision?
   A. Lighting
      1. Is there too much light and/or glare?
      2. Is there not enough light?
      3. Is it the correct kind of light for the task?
         a. Fluorescent
         b. Incandescent
         c. Window lighting
      4. Can the ambient overhead and window lighting be controlled by shields around a computer monitor (top and sides)?
   B. Space
      1. Is there enough room for the recommended equipment?
      2. Are the tables at an appropriate height for the student's size?
      3. Do the student's feet rest solidly on the floor?
      4. Is the computer or CCTV monitor at the appropriate height for viewing?
   C. Positioning
      1. Where is the student positioned in relation to overhead lights: under or between?
      2. Where is the student positioned in relation to the windows, blackboard, and/or overhead projector?
      3. What color and kind of paint is on the wall beside the student?
   D. Electricity
      1. Is electricity available near the student?
      2. Is the equipment on a surge protector?
   E. Portability
      1. Can the student physically carry the portable device?
      2. Is there sufficient space on the student's desk?
   F. Accessibility
      1. How many different printers are available for printing in-class assignments, and where are they located?
      2. If a cart is being considered as a means of transporting the device, are there stairs in the school?
      3. How good are the student's mobility skills?
III. What aspects of the environment are important for a student who is totally blind?
   A. Sound
      1. How disruptive is the noise made by a braille printer?

(continued on next page)

Environmental Considerations for Assistive Technology (Continued)

2. Can the printer be kept somewhere else?
3. Is some type of noise-reduction equipment available?

B. Space
1. Is there enough room for the recommended equipment?
2. Are the tables at an appropriate height for the student's size?
3. Do the student's feet rest solidly on the floor?
4. Is the table at an appropriate height for braillewriting and typing?

C. Positioning
1. Where is the student positioned in relation to his or her braille books?
2. Is the student positioned appropriately in relation to the teacher so he or she can hear the teacher's instructions?
3. How is the room laid out: in rows, clusters of desks, an orderly grid pattern, or large open areas?

D. Electricity
1. Is electricity available near the student?
2. Is the equipment on a surge protector?

E. Portability
1. Can the student physically carry the portable device?
2. Is there sufficient space on the student's desk?

F. Accessibility
1. How many printers are available for printing in-class assignments, and where are they located?
2. If a cart is being considered as a means of transporting the device, are there stairs in the school?
3. How good are the student's mobility skills?

_____

Source: Adapted from:
http://www.tsbvi.edu/technology/environment.htm

CCTV user can adjust the zoom control to get the desired letter size and a polarity control to view white letters on a black background, or vice versa. Some CCTVs are available with color monitors and may offer other options, such as the ability to split the screen between two tasks or to mask out lines of print on the screen to show only the line (or a few lines) being read. The device is simple to use, and a teacher of students with visual impairments can gain basic mastery of it in a brief demonstration from an experienced CCTV user or a company vendor.

A student with low vision needs basic motor and cognitive skills to take advantage of a CCTV, although reading skills are not mandatory. The teacher needs a collection of simple monochrome line drawings and appropriate reading selections to conduct the assessment. Starting with drawings, pictures, and even objects can generate interest for both nonreaders and readers. Sidebar 4.5 lists the steps in conducting a CCTV assessment to determine if a student has the potential to use the device effectively as a tool to gain access to printed information.

Nonoptical Devices. Many students benefit from nonoptical approaches, like dark felt-tip pens and bold-line paper, as well as controlling and enhancing lighting and controlling glare. The students may have a definite preference for a type

Steps for Completing the CCTV Assessment

1. Position the student in a chair with his or her feet on the floor and sitting up straight.
2. Move the student's chair or CCTV so that the student's eyes are approximately 13 inches from the screen. *It is imperative that this viewing distance remain constant when measurements are made during the assessment.*
3. Adjust the height of the CCTV to the student's eye level.
4. Place a 1-inch-square line drawing under the camera, turn on the CCTV, zoom to maximum enlargement and focus the image. Adjust the brightness and contrast, if necessary.
5. Reduce the magnification of the image until the entire drawing fits on the screen and ask the student to identify the object. Allow the student to move closer to the screen, if necessary, but note the approximate viewing distance.
6. Show the student how to control the zoom lens to adjust magnification. Ask the student to adjust the size of the image to the largest magnification and then the smallest magnification, make the drawing fill up the screen, and change the magnification to that point where he or she can see it best.
7. Check the student's distance from the screen to ensure that the student is approximately 13 inches from the screen.
8. Ask the student to adjust the size of the image to the smallest magnification. Place a different 1-inch-square line drawing under the camera. The image should remain in focus because the distance between the camera lens and the image has not changed.
9. Ask the student to adjust the magnification to the best viewing size.

Make sure the student does not lean forward. Ask the student to identify the drawing.

10. Measure the approximate height of the image the student was able to identify and note it on the checklist. Also note the size of the screen being used.
11. Repeat these steps with a page of text.
12. Adjust the magnification to its maximum. Adjust the focus to make the image out of focus. Place a different image of text under the camera.
13. Ask the student to adjust the focus until the image is clear and then adjust the magnification of the image until it is at the size he or she can see best. On the checklist, note the student's ability to adjust the size and focus of the image.
14. Show the student the controls for polarity of the image—black on white, or white on black. Show the student both settings with a graphic image and a text image. Note his or her preference on the checklist.
15. Explore the CCTV's feature that allows the user to set various color combinations of the image being enlarged. If the CCTV being used has this feature, note the student's preference.
16. Place a single sheet of reading material that is of interest to and of the appropriate grade-level difficulty for the student under the camera and ask the student to adjust the magnification to the desired size.
17. Adjust the friction brake so the top-to-bottom movement of the page is stiff but movable. Set the left and right margin stops so only the desired images are viewable on the screen.
18. Ask the student to move the X/Y table to locate the target image on the left and

(continued on next page)

Steps for Completing the CCTV Assessment *(Continued)*

then move the X/Y table to locate the same image in the row.

19. Ask the student to move to the next row and repeat the task.

20. Repeat this process for all four samples. Note how the student manipulates the X/Y table while viewing from right to left and how he or she returns to the left edge and moves down to the next line. Many young students are not able to perform this task efficiently. However, the information gained from observing the young student performing this task will give an idea of whether the student has the potential to master the physical and cognitive skills required to use the device. Note the observations on the checklist.

21. Place a regular sheet of notebook paper under the camera and readjust the margin stops accordingly.

22. Ask the student to write his or her name on one line and a sentence on the next line.

23. Replace the regular writing paper with bold-line paper and ask the student to write his or her name on one line and a different sentence from the one he or she wrote on the regular paper on the next line. Record the legibility of the print on the checklist.

24. Remove the writing assignment and replace it with an appropriate grade-level reading selection that will take 2–3 minutes for the student to read. Select a passage that is just one column of text. Ask the student to adjust the magnification to the desired size.

25. Adjust the friction brake and the margin stops for this reading selection. Conduct an informal reading rate assessment to be used later for comparison and note it on the checklist.

26. Place the writing samples that the student completed earlier under the camera and ask the student to read them. Note the student's ability to read his or her own handwriting under the CCTV with regular and bold-line paper.

---

of lighting (incandescent, fluorescent, or natural light through a window) and the location of the lighting source in relation to the materials being viewed. The improper placement of the lighting source may result in excessive amounts of glare reflecting off the viewing surface.

Students with low vision often work with materials at distances of approximately 6 inches or less. The student may hold the material close to the eyes or place the material on a tabletop and bend over to view its contents. Both options may soon result in physical fatigue. As part of the assessment, the teacher of students with visual impairments should give the student an opportunity to view materials on a reading stand and evaluate the student's response by observing the student using the stand and by asking him or her for feedback. The teacher may also explore the use of a flexible arm copy holder that clamps onto the edge of a table for lighter materials and for those to be viewed when entering information into a computer.

Gaining Access to Braille and Other Tactile Materials

This section of the assessment begins with an evaluation of the student's ability to gather information efficiently using braille and other tactile materials. Teacher-made tactile graphics or commercial products (such as the Mangold Program for Tactile Perception and Braille Letter Recognition) can be used to determine the student's ability to obtain information tactilely. The teacher acquires the results of any braille assessments that have been conducted with the student or if none has been administered, conducts a braille assessment at this time to support the assistive technology assessment. The teacher pays particular attention to the student's mastery of the mechanics of braille reading, reading rate, and writing rate. These data will help the teacher and the assistive technology specialist to determine the appropriateness of recommending a refreshable braille display for the student.

A refreshable braille display contains 40 or 80 braille cells, with retractable pins forming the dots of the braille characters, and provides line-by-line output of information presented on a computer monitor (see Chapter 14). The student's ability to use a refreshable braille display is assessed by first introducing the student to the concept of the display, and giving the student some basic information on using the device and some simple reading materials. Then, in a brief diagnostic teaching session, the teacher determines the student's response to receiving output from a computer via braille (rather than synthesized speech). The teacher notes the student's tactile sensitivity to the pins used to display the dots and ability to manipulate the control keys and the extent to which the student understands the basic procedures of using a refreshable braille display.

Gaining Access to Auditory Materials

Before the teacher administers this part of the assessment, he or she examines the student's file for information on the student's use of auditory and listening skills. Informal inventories and checklists are typically used to assess auditory and listening skills. They provide information on the student's auditory discrimination, auditory memory, and listening comprehension. If information on the student's auditory and listening skills is not available, data can be gathered using the following techniques:

◆ Read aloud to the student an appropriate grade-level passage from an informal reading inventory (see Chapter 3). Ask the questions provided and evaluate the student's responses according to the criteria in the inventory. Also, ask the student to relate some details of the story and to answer some simple factual questions. Note if the student is able to paraphrase the information presented in the sentence or story. Continue with additional passages until the student's highest listening level is found.

◆ Dictate some simple sentences and ask the student to braillewrite, write, or type the sentences. Note the student's ability to remember what was dictated and how many times the information must be repeated.

◆ Assess the student's ability to gain information from recorded books or books on CD-ROMs. Passages from an informal reading inventory of short stories that are of interest to the student can be used for this purpose.

◆ Expose the student to the variable speed and pitch controls on an audiotape player with these features. Gradually increase the speed of the audio information, adjust the pitch control, and scrutinize the student's ability to comprehend compressed speech. Note the student's ability to gain information when these variables are changed.

Examining Reading Rates

This is an optional section that is used when needed to demonstrate to the student, the student's parents, teachers, or administrators the benefits of using various technological and nontechnological devices when reading. Using certain equipment and techniques may make some students feel conspicuous and, therefore, uncomfortable. Since a student's level of comfort in using such adaptations is a personal matter and may vary from setting to setting, it is difficult to know which adaptations will be acceptable to the student and which will not. The adaptation that provides the student with the greatest reading efficiency may not always be used for every reading task and in every environment, but the data on reading rate may help the student understand the efficiency of using the adaptation in private. Several of the adaptations may require additional practice before their efficiency is evident.

Basic reading efficiency rates in braille or print should already have been gathered as part of the learning media assessment. For the initial technology assessment, the focus is on the student's reading rate while using various technological options, such as a CCTV, a refreshable braille display, and screen-enlargement software. Objective rates, along with the accompanying levels of comprehension, should be noted in the assessment report. A degree of diagnostic teaching may be appropriate if a particular technological device is new to the student. For example, if the teacher wishes to know if using screen-enlargement software will increase efficiency and accuracy in word-processing skills, he or she can give a lesson or two on its use and determine the student's response to this instruction.

Using Other Tools

Calculators with enlarged displays and speech output are valuable tools for students. The teacher of students with visual impairments needs to determine the size of the numeral display a student can view comfortably by exposing the student to a variety of calculators and asking him or her to complete a few simple mathematical tasks. The teacher also needs to assess the student's ability to understand the speech produced by a talking calculator and to manipulate the keys and buttons on a calculator. To determine if the student has the cognitive skills necessary to operate a calculator, the teacher asks the student to perform a variety of basic tasks and notes if the student performs them independently or needs to be prompted.

Talking dictionaries are a highly efficient way to gain access to information. Some speak only

the target word and its spelling, but do not speak the definition and hence are of limited value. However, one company[6] offers an elementary-level model (the Franklin Homework Wiz) and a high school–college-level model (the Franklin Language Master Special Edition), both of which are fully speaking and offer many features. The teacher needs to assess the student's ability to comprehend the speech produced by this device, determine the student's manual dexterity in manipulating the keys, and observe whether the student has the cognitive ability to perform tasks with the device. Asking the student to complete several school-related tasks using the talking dictionary is an authentic way to evaluate its potential usefulness.

The final part of the section on accessing print requires the examiner to ascertain how the student gains access to information presented in class on the chalkboard or an overhead projector. The teacher of students with visual impairments, the general education teacher, and the student will be able to provide this information, which is usually also available in the functional vision assessment.

Written Communication

Technology offers students with visual impairments many options for producing written communication. Writing by hand is often a laborious task, and materials written by the student are frequently not legible to the student and others. The initial assistive technology assessment can explore the student's ability to write by hand and to use different tools to do so. The examiner first asks the student for a short writing sample in manuscript (that is, print) and cursive, if appropriate. A timed writing sample, either dictated or copied, may also be valuable to collect during a direct assessment. If the writing sample is to be copied visually during the timed assessment, the teacher should ensure

---

[6]*Franklin Learning Resources, One Franklin Plaza, Burlington, NJ 08016-4907; 800-525-9673, 609-239-4333; FAX: 609-386-250; www.franklin.com*

that it is of a sufficient point size and font for the student to read comfortably. In addition, the student should be allowed to choose to write either in manuscript or cursive during this test. While the student is writing, the teacher notes any physical difficulties the student is exhibiting. After collecting the writing samples, the teacher reviews them for legibility, spacing, and logical content. Then the student reads the samples and signs his or her name, and the teacher notes the student's efficiency in completing these tasks.

Braille writing and embossing can be performed with a variety of tools. If braille writing and embossing were not part of the braille assessment noted earlier, then the teacher asks the student to produce writing samples with a manual braille-writer, a slate and stylus, and an electronic braille-writing device. If the student exhibits motor difficulties with the manual braillewriter, then the teacher may substitute a unimanual braillewriter (designed for one-handed use) or extended keys for a standard braillewriter and assess the student's ability to write braille with these adaptations.

Electronic writing tools, such as personal computers and personal note takers allow students with visual impairments to produce high-quality and efficient written communication. A personal computer with a word-processing program is probably the most common electronic writing tool available. As is explained in the next section, input may be in print, using a traditional QWERTY typewriter-style keyboard, or in braille using a six-key braillewriter-style keyboard. This assessment may have to be done by the assistive technology specialist or rehabilitation engineer because of the lack of assets to the specialized equipment. Or a regional representative from a company that manufactures such devices may schedule a visit to the school to demonstrate these devices.

Computer Access

A computer system with the appropriate adaptations is an ideal tool for a student with a visual im-

pairment to use to gain access to information and produce written communication. The teacher of students with visual impairments needs to assess the most efficient input and output method to be used by the student.

Visual Factors.   Before beginning this stage of the assessment, the teacher determines whether the student will use an optical device, such as eyeglasses or contact lenses, and makes sure the student is using it. Most students with visual impairments need some type of adaptation to work efficiently with a computer system, but some choose not to use an adaptation. The student may choose to lean over close to the monitor to see the display; however, doing so usually causes the user's abdomen to push against the wrists and hands and results in inefficient keyboarding and possible discomfort. Such options as using a keyboard drawer or placing the keyboard in the student's lap would allow the monitor to be brought to the edge of the table, thereby increasing visual access. All of these options have negative aspects, however, and are considered poor practice. The student may wish to use one of these, but the end result will be increased fatigue and inefficient performance. Finding the appropriate adaptations for each individual is the key to successful and efficient use of technological tools.

The teacher needs to assess the student's functioning with and without adaptations. First, he or she notes the viewing distance at which the student can read and identify menus, icon titles, and dialog boxes and the size of the monitor. Next, the teacher opens a prepared word-processor file containing a few words or sentences of various point sizes and fonts and asks the student to read the text, noting the viewing distance and point size and font that the student prefers.

Adaptations that enlarge the image on a computer monitor are available as either hardware attachments or software applications. One such adaptation is a screen magnifier, which is attached to the front of the monitor and magnifies the screen's image approximately 1.25 times its original size; if this adaptation is used, the teacher measures the viewing distance and notes it on the checklist. Another adaptation is a monitor stand with a flexible arm, a standard office accessory that allows the monitor to be placed on a platform that floats above the table and whose height and the distance from the viewer's eyes can be easily adjusted for maximum viewing. Still another adaptation is to use a 19-inch, 21-inch, or even larger monitor. Because of the added expense of these monitors it is imperative that the teacher determine the effectiveness of this option by measuring the viewing distance required at all four corners of the monitor. In many cases the gains made in image size will be offset by the fact that the viewer is physically farther from some sections of the monitor. This is especially noticeable with younger or smaller users.

New computer operating systems include accessibility software at no additional cost that enlarge most, but not all, of the displayed text. The teacher will need to become familiar with these features prior to the assessment. During the initial assessment, the teacher of students with visual impairments teaches the student to use these features of the operating system and assesses the student's response to using them. If the student is able to work efficiently with this level of adaptation and the enlarged fonts of a word processor, then this combination can be an effective and affordable writing tool. However, caution is advised. These free accessibility features do not work with some programs, and in others they only enlarge system features such as menus, not the actual content of the program. If the tool needed is something more than a large print word processor, then a dedicated screen-magnification program is necessary.

Dedicated screen-magnification software provides the larger degrees of magnification that some students need. In addition, it offers many features for customizing how the information is displayed on the screen. Some models contain an automatic reading or review mode, and others offer paired synthesized speech with the review mode. Basic steps in assessing the use of screen-enlargement software are presented in Sidebar 4.6.

Auditory Factors. All modern computers produce synthesized speech with the appropriate hardware and software. A compatible sound card or dedicated speech synthesizer actually produces the sound, and a software program, called a screen reader, directs the text displayed on the screen to the synthesizer. An assessment of a student's potential for using auditory access to the computer must answer two questions:

◆ Can the student understand and comprehend the synthesized speech?

◆ Does the student have the physical and cognitive ability to execute the commands that control the program?

Speech synthesizers are either hardware or software based, and the teacher needs to assess the student with several types. (A software synthesizer is usually available as part of an application program that talks and uses the computer's sound card.) The objective of the assessment is to determine what quality of synthesizer the student can work with efficiently. If no software or hardware synthesizer is available, a talking calculator or talking dictionary can be used—two types of synthesizers that are at the low end of the quality scale. Thus, if the student is able to understand and comprehend the low-quality speech from a talking calculator or talking dictionary, he or she will probably be able to work with computer-based synthesized speech, which is of a higher quality.

To assess this area, the teacher can prepare files with software that ask such questions as, "What is your name?" "How old are you?" and "What is your favorite food?" Since most screen-reading programs speak punctuation, it is best to turn this feature off to make the speech more understandable. If the student is able to answer the questions correctly, then he or she will be able to work with that quality of speech. Most students who do not have physical hearing losses or auditory processing deficits are able to learn to understand synthesized speech and use it efficiently.

The teacher demonstrates to the student the commands to read through a document by words,

Steps for Completing the Assessment of Screen-Magnification Software

1. Open a prepared word-processor file with the text displayed in 12 point in the student's preferred font. This file should contain several paragraphs, enough to fill up about three-quarters of the screen. Also open an application that will display a graphic, picture, or map.

2. Open the screen-magnification program. During this section, switch between the two applications—the text displayed in the word processor and the graphics displayed by the other program—to demonstrate the flexibility of the various features of the screen-magnification software.

3. Leave the computer display set on the graphics application for now.

4. Ask the student to sit up straight in the chair with his or her back against the back of the chair.

5. Measure the viewing distance to ensure that the student is approximately 13 inches from the display.

6. Switch the computer to the word-processor application.

7. Adjust the magnification of the image until the student is able to read the text and view the material without having to lean forward.

8. Demonstrate the polarity options and ask the student if he or she prefers black text on a white background or white text on a black background.

9. Note the student's preferred magnification size and polarity choice (dark on light or light on dark) on the checklist.

10. Demonstrate the different viewing modes—full, lens, area, horizontal split, and so forth—offered by the program and explain to the student how these modes

affect spatial orientation. When the image or text is enlarged, only a portion of it can be viewed at any time. A full-screen viewing mode at 2× magnification will allow the user to view only one-fourth of the unmagnified image. Ask the student to move the mouse around to change the image being displayed and to notice how only part of the paragraph is viewable at any time.

11. Ask the student to move back to the left edge of the screen and read a line of the text. Note if the student has any difficulty locating the left edge and how well he or she is able to track across the line of text.

12. Ask the student to find the beginning of the second paragraph. Note the strategy he or she uses to locate it. Does the student get lost, or can the student reorient himself or herself?

13. Move the mouse so the display is in the middle of the line of text and about halfway down the unenlarged screen of text. Explain to the student how easy it is to get disoriented and that when using this type of computer-access program, the user must reorient himself or herself by returning to a known point, such as the top left corner of the screen.

14. Ask the student to use this strategy and then move to the beginning of the third paragraph. Note the student's ability to maintain or regain his or her orientation.

15. Switch to the graphics application.

16. Ask the student to navigate around the image and verbally identify the information being displayed.

17. Ask the student to locate specific parts of

(continued on next page)

Steps for Completing the Assessment of Screen-Magnification Software (Continued)

the image: top right corner, bottom left corner, middle of the image, and so forth. Again, note the student's ability to stay oriented.

18. Change the screen-magnification software to the lens setting. The lens mode will display the entire image, but only a small rectangular area will be enlarged. Point out to the student how much easier this mode is for navigating around the graphic image.

19. Switch to the word-processor program and ask the student to read a line of text. Note how much more difficult it is for the student to stay on track.

20. Change the screen-magnification software back to the full viewing mode.

21. Instruct the student to open a menu and select items from it, choose items in a dialogue box, and select icons on a toolbar.

22. Set up the parameters for the review or panning mode for automatic reading and have the student read a paragraph of text. Adjust the speed so the student can read the text easily. Note the speed setting for this option. (This may be a step that the assistive technology specialist needs to perform.)

---

characters, and sentences. He or she also instructs the student to move forward and backward through the text by characters, words, and sentences and notes the student's responses.

Tactile Factors. Electronic or refreshable braille displays are becoming more affordable and for many braille readers, they are the ideal way to gain access to computerized information. However, their use is not widespread, so many teachers of students with visual impairments do not have access to them. If a portable note taker with a braille display is available, it can serve as an indicator of the student's potential to use a computer braille display effectively. The objective is to determine whether the student has the tactile sensitivity to read the refreshable braille and the cognitive ability to execute its commands.

In assessing the use of a refreshable braille display, the teacher asks the student to read some prepared sentences on the braille display and notes the results. The other factor that the teacher observes is the student's ability to understand cognitively the concepts involved in navigating around the text displayed in the computer

file. The teacher demonstrates the commands required to move a word, character, and sentence and then asks the student to execute some of these commands. The student enters a couple of sentences and then reads them back to the teacher.

Computer Input

Entering information into a computer can be accomplished in several ways. However, the most readily available input devices are still the traditional typewriter-style keyboard and the mouse. Alternative keyboards, switch input, and voice recognition are other options and, if needed, should be assessed by someone who is experienced in their use. Most students are able to use the standard keyboard and a mouse, so an evaluation of their use is a necessary part of the assistive technology assessment.

Keyboard. The teacher should open a blank word-processor file and ask the student to enter some simple text, such as the student's name, two to three short sentences, and the alphabet. The teacher can then observe the student's ability to locate the alphanumeric keys, and to hold down the shift key to make a capital letter, as well as the number of fingers on each hand the student uses when entering text. While the student is typing, the teacher should observe his or her posture (feet on the floor, sitting up straight), the angle of the student's wrists and hands in relation to the keyboard, and the curvature of the student's fingers. The teacher can assess the student's ability to strike the intended key or its neighbor ("miss-hit") and his or her ability to lift a finger before the letter is repeated (key repeat). Finally, the teacher can determine if the student looks at the keys while typing or can enter text without looking at the keys.

If the student demonstrates physical difficulties while using the standard keyboard, there are various hardware and software adaptations that can be of assistance. Students with low vision and a physical impairment that prevents them from doing touch typing may benefit from enlarged identifying letters on the keys, referred to as "zoom caps." If the teacher is not comfortable assessing the student's ability to use some of the adaptations listed on the checklist, he or she can ask the occupational and physical therapist to do so. If the student is unable to input text using a standard keyboard with or without adaptations, then he or she needs to be referred to the assistive technology specialist, rehabilitation engineer, or occupational or physical therapist for a computer access evaluation.

Pointing Devices. The most commonly used pointing device is the mouse, although some people prefer to use a trackball or a touch pad. The teacher first asks the student to perform the tasks listed on the checklist with a mouse. If difficulties are noted, he or she asks the student to use a trackball or another pointing device. If difficulties persist, the teacher refers the student for a computer access evaluation. Students who are blind and some students with low vision use computer keystrokes to navigate the screen.

Assistive Technology Assessments for Students with Additional Disabilities

Students with visual impairments and additional disabilities also benefit from assistive technology assessments. Although the type of technology these students use may be different from that used by students in academic programs, careful consideration of their abilities and potential for using technology is still important. The structure of assessment for students with additional disabilities is similar to that discussed for visually impaired students without additional disabilities. However, teachers also need to pay attention to the following:

- Involve all members of the student's educational team when examining assistive technology needs.

- If the student uses assistive technology for communicating, examine all the components of the communication system and determine the most appropriate access, either visual, tactile, or auditory.

- Consult with a physical therapist to determine the student's positioning and other considerations for assessing access to technology.

- Work with the student's parents to assess how the student uses assistive technology at home or at other places in the community.

- Provide information to other members of the student's educational team regarding the impact of the student's visual impairment on the use of assistive technology.

Follow-up Assessment

The teacher of students with visual impairments gives the information compiled in the initial assistive technology assessment to the assistive technology specialist or rehabilitation engineer, who can assess the student's potential for using more sophisticated devices and systems not available to the teacher. This follow-up may also include any additional assessments that other specialized personnel, such as the occupational therapist, physical therapist, or speech therapist, may need to conduct. For example, a physical therapist and an occupational therapist may work in collaboration with an assistive technology specialist to examine switch options for a student who is blind and has severe physical disabilities. Since such devices are typically custom-made, they are probably not available to teachers of students with visual impairments.

Recommendations and Decisions

All the members of the educational team who have conducted parts of the assistive technology assessment need to submit written reports of their findings, together with their recommendations, to the team. These recommendations should be based on practical considerations and functionality. They then meet to decide which technology tools may be most beneficial for the student. After reviewing all the information compiled, this assessment team devises a plan for the student. Sidebar 4.7 presents general guidelines for making decisions about assistive technology. Once these decisions are made, a final written report, containing a summary of the assessment and the recommendations, is compiled and submitted to the entire educational team, along with an addendum that specifies the reasons why the student needs the technological tools that are recommended and the skills that the student will need to use the tools effectively. This report should explain the benefits of these tools, and indicates their costs and where they may be obtained. If possible, devices should be provided on a trial basis to determine if they should be purchased.

The recommendations section of the Technology Assessment Checklist for Students with Visual Impairments (Appendix B to this chapter)

lists the issues to be considered when addressing the student's needs in the areas of accessing printed materials, producing written communication, and computer access. Space is provided for requesting any additional equipment that is needed to produce materials in an accessible format for the student.

It cannot be emphasized enough that the student needs to use a variety of tools to perform the required educational tasks and to meet the legal mandate, as spelled out by IDEA, for the student's access to a free and public education. Students, parents, teachers, and administrators need to realize that there is no one solution for a student's access to information, just as there is not a single solution for all low vision students or for all braille readers.

Implementing Recommendations

The next step is to implement the recommendation. The team develops a plan that identifies the technological tools that need to be tried on loan or purchased immediately and those that the student will need in years to come. Many of the recommendations are designed to be implemented over a period of perhaps two or three years so the student can become comfortable with the tools before their use becomes mandatory for meeting his or her educational objectives. During this time, other technological tools may be developed that will better meet the student's needs, but the assistive technology assessment establishes the priority of needs and makes recommendations about how to address them.

As with the other specialized assessments, the comprehensive assistive technology assessment should be looked at as an ongoing process. Even though the assessment may take a long time, all of it does not have to be completed immediately. It can be spread out over several weeks or even months, depending on the student and his or her needs.

The teacher of students with visual impairments will be able to conduct parts of the assess-

SIDEBAR 4.7

Factors to Consider in Making Decisions about Assistive Technology

The basic task in an assistive technology assessment is to match an individual student with tools that will meet his or her needs as efficiently and effectively as possible. After all the information is compiled, the team needs to convene to develop a plan for the student, using the following steps to guide the process:

1. Identify the problem: What does this student want or need to do that he or she cannot currently do?

2. Generate solutions through brainstorming, keeping the following points in mind:

   ◆ Attempt to alter the environment to enable the student to function independently.

   ◆ Ensure that the device is age appropriate and has the capability of accommodating growth and development.

   ◆ Ensure that the device meets the student's expectations.

   ◆ Ensure that the student is motivated to use the device.

   ◆ Ensure that the goals are comparable with the student's ability.

   ◆ Begin with low-tech devices to develop the skills and motivation necessary for the student to master high-tech devices.

3. Evaluate alternatives by answering the following questions:

   ◆ What financial resources are available?

   ◆ Would a device or modification help the student to do what he or she wants or needs to do?

   ◆ Are there limitations to or risk in using a particular device? Is it comfortable to use? Is it ready to use?

   ◆ What skills are needed to use the technology, and how long will it take the student to master these skills? Is outside training necessary or available, reasonable, and convenient? Is it included in the purchase price?

   ◆ How will the technology be maintained and repaired? How reliable is the device? What is its average life expectancy? How will the device withstand the intended use? Is there a warranty and/or service contract? What maintenance is required; are special maintenance services necessary? What is the upgrade or trade-in policy? What is the service record of the vendor and the manufacturer? What is the time required for returning the equipment when repairs are needed? Is there a loaner policy if a device needs to be sent for repair?

GAYLEN KAPPERMAN and JODI STICKEN
Northern Illinois University , Dekalb

ment with little preparation and only minimal expenditures for materials. Other members of the student's educational team listed earlier will also contribute, depending on their expertise in various areas. Assessing the student on the special-

ized hardware and software will probably require finding an assistive technology specialist who is knowledgeable about these technologies and can work with the team to complete the assessment. It may take longer to complete this part of the assessment, but in the meantime, recommendations from other sections of the assessment can be implemented.

Several universities are beginning to offer programs in the area of assistive technology, and their number is likely to continue to grow. Assistive technology specialists are required to have a general knowledge of many areas of assistive technology, including some basic information on assistive technology for students who are visually impaired. Many assistive technology specialists find vision technology intriguing and are interested in expanding their knowledge in this area. It is important to remember, however, that a specialist in visual impairment should always be involved in the assessment.

Assistive technology specialists are being hired by state departments of education or regional programs to serve as resources for local school systems; many metropolitan school districts already have such specialists on their staffs. To find an assistive technology specialist, contact the local school district or check at the state level. If an assistive technology specialist is not available, ask about a rehabilitation engineer. In many states, state schools for students who are visually impaired have personnel who are knowledgeable in this area, so if the local school district or state department of education cannot recommend a specialist, a representative of the state school may be able to conduct parts of the assessment at the neighborhood school or ask for the student to be taken to the state school for the assessment.

Another option is to hire an assistive technology specialist as a consultant. Before the consultant is hired, the teacher of students with visual impairments and his or her supervisor need to meet with the consultant to ensure that he or she has experience with technology designed for students who are visually impaired—the different areas listed on the assistive technology assessment checklist. If the assistive technology specialist is not familiar with vision technology, then other candidates should be interviewed.

Specialized technology for students with visual impairments is usually provided by companies with a network of representatives or distrib-

utors who often have access to high-tech devices and a general working knowledge of their features. However, since a vendor representative frequently knows only the products that the vendor manufactures, it would be wise to ask the representatives of several vendors to assist with the assessment.

A final option is to gather as much information as possible and then ask an experienced assistive technology specialist to review the information and recommendations in the written report. An experienced specialist will be able to confirm many of the recommendations and spot any areas that may have been overlooked. All these approaches, though not ideal, will allow the assistive technology team to establish a plan and provide the student with some technological tools that will assist the student in fulfilling his or her educational objectives.

WRITING ASSESSMENT REPORTS

After an assessment has been completed, the results should be presented in a written report. If the functional vision assessment, learning media assessment, and assistive technology assessment were conducted as parts of a more comprehensive assessment by the teacher of students with visual impairments, then the results of all three assessments should be included in a comprehensive report. However, if the assessments were conducted separately, each report should be written and signed by the individual who conducted the assessment.

An assessment report is the primary written source of information on the student's strengths and needs in the areas of functional vision, learning media, and assistive technology. As a record of the findings and recommendations, the report should be *specific*, with details about the student's performance on individual tasks in clearly described situations; *factual*, with conclusions based on clear, objective observations, rather than opinions or broad generalizations; and *ap-

plicable, with direct links to the tasks and activities that the student normally performs or that the student can learn to perform with vision.

The report should be detailed but clearly understandable to the student (when appropriate), the student's family, and other members of the educational team. Typically, it is in narrative form, although checklists and the results of formal instruments and forms can be included or attached. The report should offer clear, practical recommendations that will be immediately useful to members of the educational team and that can be used in developing the IEP.

SUMMARY

The functional vision, learning media, and assistive technology assessments provide the basic foundation for designing an IEP for a student who is blind or visually impaired. Given the specialized nature of these assessments, the teacher of students with visual impairments takes the primary role in conducting them, reporting the findings, and offering useful recommendations. These assessments typically rely on informal measures, observations, and interviews, but their findings and recommendations must be based on objective data. A students with a visual impairment will benefit from these assessments, since they explore and document the student's unique use of sensory information. This information, in turn, is used to develop a comprehensive and individualized educational plan.

ACTIVITIES

1. Observe a teacher of students with visual impairments conducting a learning media assessment, functional vision assessment, and assistive technology assessment, and note the areas involved in the assessments. Then ask the teacher to provide his or her thoughts on the outcome and how the results will be used to plan an appropriate literacy program for the student.

2. Collect several different learning media assessment procedures and forms. Compare the various procedures and select the most important elements from each one. If possible, conduct a learning media assessment under the supervision of a qualified teacher of students with visual impairments.

3. Interview a teacher of students with visual impairments regarding the need for and use of learning media assessments, functional vision assessments, and assistive technology assessments. Ask the teacher for suggestions for conducting these assessments, including issues of scheduling, record keeping, and report writing.

4. Observe a meeting of a student's educational team in which the results of specialized assessments are being discussed. Follow up on your observation by meeting with the teacher of students with visual impairments and discussing the procedure.

5. Meet with a classmate and develop a series of fact sheets on the three types of assessments for parents, administrators, or general education teachers. Make sure that these fact sheets include explanations of the specialized assessments, along with statements of their importance and brief summaries of the procedures.

6. Develop a kit that contains all the materials necessary for conducting a functional vision assessment. These materials may include a variety of lights (penlights, flashlights, colored lights), a variety of print materials (newspaper articles, magazine articles, and samples of print in different fonts and sizes), and toys with various levels of contrast and color.

7. Conduct an informal reading inventory with three students at different literacy levels. Prepare a short assessment report

for each student, along with recommendations for further assessments.

REFERENCES

Barraga, N. C., & Morris, J. E. (1980). *Program to develop efficiency in visual functioning.* Louisville, KY: American Printing House for the Blind.

Blazie, B. J., & Dote-Kwan, J. (1997). *Braille 'n' Speak teaching curriculum.* Forest Hill, MD: Blazie Engineering.

Burns, P. C., & Roe, B. D. (1999). *Informal Reading Inventory.* (5th ed.). Boston: Houghton Mifflin.

Carver, R. P. (1989). Silent reading rates in grade equivalents. *Journal of Reading Behavior, 21,* 155–166.

Caton, H. (1991). *Print and braille literacy: Selecting appropriate learning media.* Louisville, KY: American Printing House for the Blind.

Caton, H. (1994). *Tools for selecting appropriate learning media.* Louisville, KY: American Printing House for the Blind.

Chen, D. (1997). *What can baby see? Vision tests and intervention strategies for infants with mutiple disabilities* (Videotape). New York: American Foundation for the Blind.

Corn, A. L., & Koenig, A. J. (1996). Perspectives on low vision. In A. L. Corn & A. J. Koenig (Eds.), *Foundations of low vision: Clinical and functional perspectives* (pp. 3–25). New York: AFB Press.

Duckworth, B. J. (1993). Adapting standardized academic tests in braille and large type. *Journal of Visual Impairment & Blindness, 87,* 405–407.

Erin, J. N., & Paul B. (1996). Functional vision assessment and instruction of children and youths in academic programs. In A. L. Corn & A. J. Koenig (Eds.), *Foundations of low vision: Clinical and functional perspectives* (pp. 185–220). New York: AFB Press.

Guszak, F. J. (1985). *Diagnostic reading instruction in the elementary school* (3rd ed.). New York: Harper & Row.

Jan, J., Ferrell, K., Wong, P., & McCormick, A. (1986). Eye and head movements of visually impaired children. *Developmental Medicine and Child Neurology, 28,* 285–293.

Johns, J. (1997). *Basic Reading Inventory* (7th ed.). Dubuque, IA: Kendall/Hunt.

Koenig, A. J. (1996). Selection of learning and literacy media for children and youths with low vision. In A. L. Corn & A. J. Koenig (Eds.), *Foundations of low vision: Clinical and functional perspectives* (pp. 246–279). New York: AFB Press.

Koenig, A. J. & Farrenkopf, C. (1994–1995). *Assessment of braille literacy skills.* Houston, TX: Region IV Education Service Center.

Koenig, A. J., & Holbrook, M. C. (1995). *Learning media assessment of students with visual impairments: A resource guide for teachers* (2nd ed.). Austin: Texas School for the Blind and Visually Impaired.

Langley, M. B. (1999). *Individualized systematic assessment of visual efficiency.* Louisville, KY: American Printing House for the Blind.

Levack, N. (1994). *Low vision: A resource guide with adaptations for students with visual impairments.* Austin: Texas School for the Blind and Visually Impaired.

Mangold, S. (1977). *The Mangold developmental program of tactile perception and braille letter recognition.* Castro Valley, CA: Exceptional Teaching Aids.

Sanford, L., & Burnett, R. (1997). *Functional vision and media assessment* (3rd ed.). Hermitage, TN: Consultants for Visually Impaired.

Sewell, D. (1997). *Assessment kit: Kit of informal tools for academic students with visual impairments.* Austin: Texas School for the Blind and Visually Impaired.

Smith, A. J., & Cote, K. S. (1982). *Look at me: A resource manual for the development of residual vision in multiply impaired children.* Philadelphia: Pennsylvania College of Optometry Press.

Smith, A. J., & O'Donnell, L. M. (1992). *Beyond arm's reach: Enhancing distance vision.* Philadelphia: Pennsylvania College of Optometry Press.

Wilkinson, M. E. (1996). Clinical low vision services. In A. L. Corn & A. J. Koenig (Eds.), *Foundations of low vision: Clinical and functional perspectives* (pp. 143–182). New York: AFB Press.

General Student Information

Identifying Information

Student _____ Birth Date _____ Age _____

Grade/Placement _____ School _____

Components of Learning Media Assessments Conducted

_____ Use of Sensory Channels

_____ Selection of General Learning Media

_____ Selection of Literacy Media

_____ Initial Decision on Literacy Medium

_____ Continuing Assessment—General

_____ Continuing Assessment—Selection of Print Media

_____ LMA for Student with Additional Disabilities

Date(s) of Learning Media Assessment _____

Evaluator(s) _____

Presence of Additional Disabilities

_____ Motor Impairment: _____

_____ Cognitive Disability: _____

_____ Other Sensory Disability: _____

_____ Other Disabilities: _____

For Students with Established Literacy Skills

Primary Literacy Medium _____

Secondary Literacy Media _____

(continued on next page)

Appendix A. General Student Information Form

General Student Information (*Continued*)

Information on Eye Condition

Date of Most Recent: Ophthalmological Examination _____

                              Clinical Low Vision Evaluation _____

                              Functional Vision Evaluation _____

Cause of Visual Impairment _____

Age at Onset _____   Visual Fields _____

Near Acuity	Right Eye	Left Eye	Both Eyes
Without Correction	_____	_____	_____
With Correction	_____	_____	_____
With Low Vision Device	_____	_____	_____
Near Device(s) Used	_____	_____	_____

Distance Acuity	Right Eye	Left Eye	Both Eyes
Without Correction	_____	_____	_____
With Correction	_____	_____	_____
With Low Vision Device	_____	_____	_____
Distance Device(s) Used	_____	_____	_____

Stability of Visual Condition: Stable   Deteriorating

Visual Functioning: Stable   Fluctuating

Possibility of Secondary Visual Impairment(s) _____

_____

Additional General Information

_____

_____

_____

_____

_____

(continued on next page)

General Student Information (*Continued*)

Summary

Findings of Learning Media Assessment

Sensory Channels: Primary _____

     Secondary _____

General Learning Media: Visual _____

     Tactile _____

     Auditory _____

Literacy Media: Primary Medium _____

     Secondary Media _____

Instructional Implications

Type of Literacy Program: _____ Conventional literacy program (for academic student)

     _____ Prereading or readiness program

     _____ Formal literacy program

     _____ Functional literacy program (for student with additional disabilities)

     _____ Other communication program (for student with additional disabilities who is functioning at a level such that a conventional or functional literacy program is not now appropriate)

Implications of: Prognosis _____

_____

     Additional Disabilities _____

_____

_____

Literacy Objectives: 1. _____

     2. _____

     3. _____

Technology Assessment Checklist
for Students with Visual Impairments

Student Name _____   Date of Assessment _____

Person Completing Checklist _____   Position _____

During this assessment, informal measures were utilized to evaluate the student's ability to print, produce written communication, access the computer and use various assistive technologies. Some of the information requested may be obtained from the Learning Media Assessment, the Clinical Low Vision Evaluation or the Functional Low Vision Evaluation.

Accessing Print

Regular Print

When accessing printed information, the

_____ Student is able to read print materials at _____ inches *without* adaptations.

_____ Student is able to read regular print materials *with* adaptations.

_____ using prescribed glasses or contacts

_____ materials enlarged on photocopying machine—Specify (i.e. 130%, 3 times)

_____ Student is able to read regular print materials *with* or *without* adaptations for

_____ min before experiencing either visual or physical fatigue.

Large Print

When accessing large print *with* prescribed optical aid (if appropriate) the student is able to read:

72 point print at approximately _____ inches.

60 point print at approximately _____ inches.

48 point print at approximately _____ inches.

36 point print at approximately _____ inches.

30 point print at approximately _____ inches.

24 point print at approximately _____ inches.

18 point print at approximately _____ inches.

(continued on next page)

Appendix B. Technology Assessment Checklist for Students with Visual Impairments

Technology Assessment Checklist (*Continued*)

14 point print at approximately _____ inches.

12 point print at approximately _____ inches.

Student's font preference _____ Arial, _____ Antique Olive, _____ Tahoma, _____ Verdana

Student's preferred point size *without* prescribed aids.

_____ 14 _____ 18 _____ 24 _____ 30 _____ 36 _____ 48 _____ 60 _____ 72

Optical Aids

When accessing printed materials with the use of an optical aid, the student is able to use

_____ glasses _____ contact lens

_____ handheld/stand magnifier, power_____

_____ telescope, power_____

Closed-Circuit TeleVision (CCTV)

_____ inch graphic _____ inch text on a _____ inch monitor at approximately 13 inches

polarity preference; _____ dark on light _____ light on dark

color combination preference (if available) _____

Use of CCTV controls—The student is able to:

_____ adjust size of image.

_____ focus image.

_____ independently use X/Y table for viewing materials with friction brake and margin stops adjusted by examiner.

_____ write their name and a short sentence legibly on regular writing paper.

_____ write their name and a short sentence legibly on bold line paper.

_____ read approximately _____ wpm orally when the friction brake and margin stops are adjusted properly by the examiner.

_____ read the sentence they wrote on regular writing paper.

_____ read the sentence they wrote on bold line writing paper.

Use of the VisAbility program with optical scanner connected to computer

preferred magnification _____ for viewing at approximately 13–16 inches

polarity preference; _____ dark on light _____ light on dark

color combination preference _____

(continued on next page)

Technology Assessment Checklist (*Continued*)

Use of VisAbility features—The student was able to:

_____ select menu items and tools from the toolbar with the mouse.

_____ navigate around the magnified image with the mouse.

_____ read text in the panning/review mode with a speed setting of_____.

Non-Optical Aids

When accessing information through the use of non-optical aids, the

_____ student reads materials produced with felt-tip pen on bold line paper.

_____ student prefers __ incandescent lighting, __ fluorescent lighting __ window lighting.

_____ student experiences glare problems from __ overhead lighting __ window lighting.

_____ student prefers less lighting than currently available.

_____ student prefers to have materials placed on a reading stand or copy holder.

Braille and Tactile

When accessing information through braille and tactile graphics, the

_____ student is able to use simple tactile graphics.

_____ student is able to read materials in braille. Attach results of formal/informal Braille Assessments conducted by TSVI.

_____ student's oral braille reading rate is _____ wpm.

_____ student is able to read braille on an electronic/refreshable braille display.

Auditory

When accessing printed information auditorally, the

_____ student is able to demonstrate comprehension by answering simple questions & relating details about a passage when it is read to him/her.

_____ student is able to paraphrase information presented orally (sentence or story).

_____ student is able to write, type, or braille what he/she heard (sentence dictation) without having it repeated more than twice.

_____ student is able to put tape in and remove tape from player/recorder.

_____ student is able to activate play, pause, stop, fast forward and rewind functions (please underline those demonstrated).

_____ student is able to understand and comprehend compressed or "fast" speech.

(continued on next page)

Technology Assessment Checklist (*Continued*)

_____ student is able to manipulate variable speed and pitch controls.

Reading Rates (This is an *optional* section used when needed to demonstrate to the student, parents, teachers, or administrators the benefits of using adaptations when reading.)

When reading printed information, the

    student is able to read _____ wpm orally when provided with 12 point materials.

    student is able to read _____ wpm orally when provided with materials in the optimum size for viewing at 10–13 inches (_____ point print).

    student is able to read _____ wpm orally when using a CCTV.

    student is able to read _____ wpm orally when using VisAbility.

    student is able to read _____ wpm orally when provided with materials in braille.

    student is able to read _____ wpm orally when provided with recorded materials.

Other

When using a large print calculator, the

_____ student is able to see _____ inch numerals displayed on a large print calculator.

_____ student is able to accurately manipulate keys on a large print calculator.

_____ student is able to perform basic functions __ with, __ without instruction.

When using a talking calculator, the

_____ student is able to understand synthesized speech produced by a talking calculator.

_____ student is able to accurately manipulate keys on a talking calculator.

_____ student is able to perform basic functions __ with, __ without instruction.

When using a talking dictionary, the

_____ student is able to understand synthesized speech produced by a talking dictionary.

_____ student is able to accurately manipulate keys on a talking dictionary.

_____ student is able to perform basic functions __ with, __ without instruction.

When accessing information presented on a blackboard or overhead projector, the student reported that he/she

_____ sits close enough to read board.

_____ gets a copy from the teacher.

_____ gets a copy from other students.

(continued on next page)

Technology Assessment Checklist (*Continued*)

_____ uses a handheld or spectacle mounted telescope.

_____ has information read aloud to student and

_____ writes information on paper.

_____ types information into computer or portable note taker.

_____ brailles on braille writer.

_____ records on tape recorder.

_____ Other, please specify_____

Are these options working adequately? _____ yes _____ no Explain briefly: _____

_____

Producing Written Communication

When using standard writing tools, the

_____ student's manuscript writing is legible.

_____ student's cursive writing is legible.

_____ student's spacing is intact.

_____ student's writing is labored and difficult.

_____ student is able to write _____ wpm from __ dictation, __ copy.

_____ student is able to read his/her own writing.

_____ student is able to sign his/her name legibly in cursive __ with, __ without a signature guide.

When writing with the following adaptation the student's _____ manuscript, _____ cursive writing is legible.

_____ a screen board   _____ bold line paper

_____ raised line paper   _____ a felt-tip pen

_____ a white board and erasable marker

_____ Other modifications _____

When using a braille writing device, the

_____ student is able to use a manual braille writer to emboss characters, words, and sentences at _____ wpm from __ dictation, __ copy.

(continued on next page)

Technology Assessment Checklist (*Continued*)

_____ student is able to use the slate & stylus to emboss characters, words and sentences at _____ wpm form __ dictation, __ copy.

_____ student is able to use the Mountbatten brailler to emboss characters, words and sentences at _____ wpm from __ dictation, __ copy.

_____ student is able to use a portable note taking device such as the Braille 'n Speak to emboss characters, words, and sentences at _____ wpm from __ dictation, __ copy.

When using an electronic writing device, (computer, portable note taker) the

_____ student is able to write characters, words, and sentences.

_____ student is able to perform basic functions __ with, __ without instruction from the examiner.

Comments: _____

_____

_____

Computer Access

Visual

When accessing electronic information on a stand alone computer or in the computer lab, the

_____ student is able to read menus and other system text items on a _____ inch monitor at approximately _____ inches.

student is able to read bold _____ point print in an __ Arial, __ Antique Olive, __ Tahoma, __ Verdana font displayed on a _____ inch monitor at approximately 13 inches.

_____ student is able to see information on the standard computer monitor with

_____ screen magnification hardware (CompuLenz) at approximately _____ inches.

_____ flexible arm monitor stand at approximately _____ inches.

_____ screen enhancements provided with computer operating system.

_____ WIN 95/98 High Contrast

_____ WIN 95/98 Large

_____ WIN 95/98 Extra Large

_____ screen magnification software with _____ magnification.

(continued on next page)

Technology Assessment Checklist (*Continued*)

When accessing the computer through the use of screen magnification software, the

_____ student is able to read 12 point print enlarged to _____ x magnification at a viewing distance of approximately 13 inches.

_____ student expressed a polarity preference for; _____ dark on light, _____ light on dark.

_____ student is able to locate and select menu items, buttons and icons with the mouse/pointing device.

_____ student is able to navigate around the magnified image with the mouse/pointing device.

_____ student _ is, _ is not able to maintain orientation when navigating around the screen.

_____ student is able to read text in the panning/review mode with a speed setting of _____.

_____ student expressed a viewing mode preference. Specify _____

_____ student is *unable* to access the computer visually. (If checked, skip to Auditory section)

Auditory

When accessing computer based information auditorily, the

_____ student is able to understand synthesized speech produced by

Software synthesizer

_____ Kids Time Deluxe _____ Write Outloud _____ Other

_____ Flextalk   _____ TrueVoice

_____ Dectalk Access 32 _____ Eloquence

Hardware synthesizer

_____ Braille/Type 'n Speak   _____ Double Talk   _____ Other

_____ Accent SA   _____ Dectalk

_____ student is able to execute navigation commands with instruction.

Tactile

When accessing computer based information tactually, the

_____ student is able to read braille text displayed on an electronic refreshable braille display.

_____ student is able to execute navigation commands with instruction.

_____ student is able to enter text through the braille keyboard.

(continued on next page)

Technology Assessment Checklist (*Continued*)

Input Devices

Keyboard Use

_____ The student is able to use a standard keyboard without adaptation.

    _____ The student is able to locate and identify alphanumeric keys.

    _____ The student is able to locate and identify function keys.

    _____ The student is able to activate two keys simultaneously.

    _____ The student does not demonstrate excessive miss-hits or key repeats.

    _____ The student uses good mechanics when typing. (Posture, wrist elevation, etc.)

    _____ The student types with __ fingers of right hand and __ fingers of left hand.

    _____ The student demonstrates keyboard awareness (has a general knowledge of the key locations).

    _____ The student is able to touch type while looking at his/her hands.

    _____ The student is able to touch type without looking at his/her hands.

_____ The student is able to utilize a standard computer keyboard *with adaptations.* (Seek assistance from occupational and physical therapist as needed.)

    _____ zoop caps   _____ keyguard   _____ finger guard/pointer

    _____ keylatch   _____ wrist/arm support   _____ head pointer

    _____ moisture guard   _____ tactile locator dots   _____ mouthstick

    _____ other   Specify _____

The student is able to utilize a standard computer keyboard with the following keyboard utilities. (Seek assistance from general technology specialist, OT or PT to complete this section.)

    __ sticky keys __ repeat keys __ slow keys __ toggle keys __ mouse keys

_____ The student is *not* able to utilize a standard keyboard with or without adaptations. (If checked, refer student for a Computer Access Evaluation.)

Use of a Pointing Device

_____ The student is able to navigate the desktop with the standard mouse/trackball.

_____ The student is able to maintain the mouse position while clicking/double-clicking.

_____ The student is able to maintain eye contact with the screen while navigating the desktop.

(continued on next page)

Technology Assessment Checklist (*Continued*)

_____ The student is able to access pull-down menus with the standard mouse.

_____ The student is not able to use a standard mouse. (If checked, please request a Computer Access Evaluation.)

Additional Assessment Information: _____

_____

_____

_____

_____

_____

_____

_____

_____

_____

_____

Recommendations for Assistive Technology

Based on the results of this assessment, the following recommendations are made regarding assistive technology to support this student's educational objectives.

Accessing Printed Materials (Students with visual impairments will use a combination of strategies to access printed information. Some will be appropriate for short reading assignments and others will be necessary for longer passages.)

Check all that apply

_____ Student should use regular print materials for

 _____ short reading assignments.

 _____ most reading assignments.

_____ Student should use regular print materials with optical aids.

 _____ glasses/contact lenses

 _____ handheld magnifier

 _____ stand magnifier

(continued on next page)

Technology Assessment Checklist (*Continued*)

_____ Student should use materials written with felt-tip pen on bold line paper.

_____ Student should use regular print materials enlarged on a photocopying machine.

_____ Student should use large print books.

_____ Student should use regular print materials scanned into a computer, edited and printed out in _____ point print.

_____ Student should use regular print materials with CCTV (Closed-Circuit Television).

_____ Student should use regular print materials with the VisAbility program.

_____ Student should use materials in braille.

_____ Student should use recorded materials.

_____ Student should use a computer assisted reading system such as Kurzweil 1000, Open Book, etc.

_____ Student should use a _ basic, _ scientific calculator with at least 1/2 inch numeral display.

_____ Student should use a _ basic, _ scientific talking calculator.

_____ Student should use calculator program on computer.

_____ Student should use a large print dictionary with at least 18 point print.

_____ Student should use dictionary/thesaurus program on computer.

_____ Student should use a talking dictionary.

_____ Student should use crayons and a screen board to develop basic tactile skills using tactile graphics.

_____ Student should use tactile graphics to access maps, charts, diagrams, etc.

Comments: _____

_____

Producing Written Communication (Students with visual impairments will use a combination of strategies to produce written communication. Some will be appropriate for short writing assignments and others will be necessary for longer assignments.)

Check all that apply

_____ Student should use pen/pencil and paper

_____ for short writing assignments.

_____ for most writing assignments.

(continued on next page)

Technology Assessment Checklist (*Continued*)

_____ Student should use felt-tip pen and bold line paper.

_____ Student should use bold line graph paper for math.

_____ Student should use crayons and a screen board for beginning handwriting.

_____ Student should use a white board with erasable markers.

_____ Student should use a computer with the word processing software most commonly used in the student's school.

_____ Student should use computer with form filling software such as VisAbility.

_____ Student should use manual braille writer.

_____ Student should use manual braille writer with extended keys.

_____ Student should use a unimanual braille writer.

_____ Student should use slate & stylus.

_____ Student should use an electronic braille writer. Specify: _____

_____ Student should use portable word processor (Braille 'n Speak/Type 'n Speak, etc.)

Comments: _____

_____

_____

_____

_____

_____

Computer Access

Input Method

_____ Student should use a standard keyboard.

_____ Student should develop/improve keyboarding skills.

_____ Student should use a standard keyboard with adaptations. Specify _____

_____ Student should use an alternative keyboard. Specify _____

_____ Student should use a standard pointing device like a mouse or trackball.

_____ Student should use an alternate point device. Specify _____

_____ Student should have access to a copy holder that allows printed materials to be positioned at a comfortable viewing distance.

(continued on next page)

Technology Assessment Checklist (*Continued*)

Output Mode

_____ Student should use a standard computer monitor—Optimal size: _____

_____ Student should use a standard computer monitor with hardware adaptations.

     _____ adjustable monitor arm _____ Compu Lens

_____ Student should use screen magnification software.

     _____ CloseView _____ inLarge _____ WIN xxx Accessibility enlargement

     _____ Dedicated screen magnification software—Specify _____

_____ Student should use a talking word processing. Specify _____

_____ Student should use a speech synthesizer/sound card and screen reading software.

     Specify _____

_____ Student should use an electronic braille display. Specify _____

Additional Hardware & Software

Student should be provided with access to the following hardware & software:

_____ Macintosh computer system with

     __ Mb memory __ hard drive __ CD drive __ modem

_____ IBM compatible computer system with

     __ MB memory __ hard drive __ CD drive __ modem

_____ Optical Scanner __ Printer

_____ Word processor used in student's school __ Internet access

_____ CD Encyclopedia __ Dictionary __ Atlas

_____ Other: _____

Equipment needed to produce materials for student in appropriate format.

_____ Mac or IBM compatible computer system

_____ Optical scanner _____ OCR software

_____ Word processing software _____ braille translating software

_____ Inkjet or laser printer _____ braille embosser/printer

_____ Tactile graphics production equipment, specify _____

(continued on next page)

Technology Assessment Checklist (*Continued*)

Additional comments/recommendations: _____

_____

_____

_____

_____

_____

_____

_____

The recommendations made above do not all have to be implemented immediately. The suggestions are designed for a 2–3 year plan in which the student masters certain skills and is provided access to additional technologies that can facilitate his/her educational program. During that time, new technologies will become available that will enhance his/her ability to maximize his/her educational potential. The specific devices recommended may no longer be the most appropriate, but the assistance that they provide will continue to be a need for this student.

_____   _____
Assessment Completed by (*Signature*)   Position

R E S O U R C E S

Suggested Resources for Conducting Specialized Assessments

Resource	Type	Source	Description
Assessment Kit: Kit of Informal Tools for Academic Students with Visual Impairments (Sewell, 1997)	Book	Texas School for the Blind and Visually Impaired	A kit that includes informal checklists and other assessment materials that are useful with students with visual impairments. Addresses technology skills, among many others.
Assessment of Braille Literacy Skills (Koenig & Farrenkopf, 1994–1995)	Assessment Instrument	Region IV Education Service Center	A tool for the meaningful assessment of braille literary skills.
Beyond Arm's Reach: Enhancing Distance Vision (Smith & O'Donnell, 1992)	Book	Pennsylvania College of Optometry Press	A program of sequential lessons from which a child can build a visual foundation and then solidify skills commensurate with his or her visual potential.
Braille 'n Speak Teaching Curriculum (Blazie & Dote-Kwan, 1997)	Book	Blazie Education Services	A curriculum designed to provide a comprehensive, well-sequenced series of instructional lessons in using Braille 'n Speak. The controlled vocabulary permits students with limited knowledge of the braille code to begin using Braille 'n Speak.
Foundations of Low Vision: Clinical and Functional Perspectives (Corn & Koenig, 1996)	Book	AFB Press	This textbook includes three chapters that are relevant to special assessments. "Functional Vision Assessment and Instruction of Children and Youths in Academic Programs" (Erin & Paul) *(continued on next page*

Resource	Type	Source	Description
			and "Functional Vision Assessment and Instruction of Children and Youths with Multiple Disabilities" (Erin) provide thorough discussions of vision, its development, and means of functional assessment for students in academic programs and those with multiple disabilities. "Selection of Learning and Literacy Media for Children and Youths with Low Vision" (Koenig) presents a thorough discussion of selecting learning media for students with low vision.
Functional Vision and Media Assessment (3rd ed.) (Sanford & Burnett, 1997)	Assessment Instrument	Consultants for the Visually Impaired	A comprehensive instrument for a functional vision assessment and a learning media assessment. Appropriate for students in preacademic and academic programs in kindergarten through Grade 12.
Individualized Systematic Assessment of Visual Efficiency (Langley, 1999)	Assessment Instrument	American Printing House for the Blind	A functional vision assessment tool developed for use with both sighted and visually impaired infants, the developmentally young, and other difficult-to-test and severely physically impaired children.
Learning Media Assessment of Students with Visual Impairments (Koenig & Holbrook, 1995)	Book	Texas School for the Blind and Visually Impaired	A description of the process and presentation of forms necessary to complete a learning media assessment of a student with a visual impairment. For students from preschool through secondary school, as well as students with multiple disabilities. LMA Form 7 is a literacy tools inventory that provides a useful checklist of technology tools and computer applications that are appropriate for students with visual impairments.
Look at Me: A Resource Manual for the Development of Residual Vision in Multiply Impaired Children (Smith & Cote, 1982)	Book	Pennsylvania College of Optometry Press	This book on the evaluation of vision in children with multiple impairments presents teaching strategies to help these children achieve their optimum levels of visual functioning.

(continued on next page)

Suggested Resources *(Continued)*

Resource	Type	Source	Description
Low Vision: A Resource Guide with Adaptation for Students with Visual Impairments (Levack, 1994)	Book	Texas School for the Blind and Visually Impaired	This book presents specific directions and an assessment tool for conducting a functional vision evaluation. Guidelines for implementing programming that will enhance students' visual functioning. A reference guide for information on low vision.
Print and Braille Literacy: Selecting Appropriate Learning Media (Caton, 1991)	Booklet	American Printing House for the Blind	Guidelines to help ensure that every child with a visual impairment will have adequate opportunities for learning to use the medium or media most appropriate for his or her needs. Available in print, large print, or braille.
Program to Develop Efficiency in Visual Functioning (Barraga & Morris, 1980)	Diagnostic and training kit	American Printing House for the Blind	Materials for assessing visual functioning and lessons for training in visual efficiency. For students aged 3 and older.
TOOLS for Selecting Appropriate Learning Media (Caton, 1994)	Book	American Printing House for the Blind	A manual designed to help parents, teachers, and administrators make decisions concerning students' use of braille, print, or both as their primary reading medium or media. Extension of the booklet *Print and Braille Literacy: Selecting Appropriate Learning Media* (Caton, 1991).
What Can Baby See? Vision Tests and Intervention Strategies for Infants with Multiple Disabilities (Chen, 1997)	Videotape	American Foundation for the Blind	A presentation of common vision tests and methods used with infants and young children to help identify visual impairments that require early intervention services. Also addresses ways of working with families and early intervention strategies.

Contact information for each of the resources listed will be found in the Sources of Products, Materials, Equipment, and Services section at the back of this book.

CHAPTER 5

Basic Techniques for Modifying Instruction

M. Cay Holbrook and Alan J. Koenig

KEY POINTS

◆ The appropriate adaptation of instructional materials and teaching methods is essential to ensure that students with visual impairments have full and equal access to educational opportunities.

◆ Teachers of students with visual impairments work collaboratively to decide on and provide instructional modifications.

◆ Visual, tactile, and auditory modifications of classroom instruction and materials need to be based on a comprehensive functional vision assessment and learning media assessment of the student who is visually impaired.

◆ Teachers of students with visual impairments need to provide insightful modifications of instruction that address their students' individual needs without fostering overdependence on adaptations.

◆ Students with visual impairments should be held to the same academic and social standards as their sighted classmates in order to be prepared for adult life.

VIGNETTE

Sue Whitman's mailbox held a print copy of an English test and a completed math assignment in Nemeth Code, both from the sixth grade, and a request from Cesar Reyes for a consultation. She dropped these papers into her bag and placed yesterday's interlined math work in the sixth-grade teacher's box. She would prepare a braille copy of the English test and interline the new math papers this afternoon and place them in the sixth-grade teacher's box in the morning. Managing the print-to-braille and braille-to-print materials exchange was an important part of her daily routine as a teacher of students with visual impairments.

Ms. Whitman walked to Mr. Reyes's classroom. Kevin—a third-grade student with a visual impairment, mild cognitive delays, and mild motor impairments—was Mr. Reyes's student. For counters in math activities, Kevin had been given the same colorful plastic disks his classmates used, but he had difficulty picking them up. After consulting with Kevin's occupational therapist, Ms. Whitman had brought a bag of one-inch wooden cubes that would be easier for Kevin to handle.

Today, Mr. Reyes was eager to share his enthusiasm for the audiotaped social studies textbook Sue had provided for Kevin. Mr. Reyes had set up a listening center for Kevin and two classmates with learning disabilities; the three boys listened to the tape and read along in their textbooks. Mr. Reyes told Ms. Whitman with delight that he thought this tape was not only helping the students learn their social studies content, but was having a positive influence on their reading skills.

Ms. Whitman's last stop that morning in Wildwood School was in the fifth grade, where Lisa's class was scheduled to complete a science activity that required the measurement of liquids. Ms. Whitman had brought a set of beakers and syringes that allowed accurate measurement without sight. Ms. Whitman and Lisa had used these tools before. Today's visit was to demonstrate their use to Ms. Albertson, Lisa's general education teacher, so she would understand how Lisa could participate in the learning activity.

INTRODUCTION

The academic success of students with visual impairments depends, to a great extent, on the students' access to instruction and materials. Although the amount of time necessary to complete assignments may vary, students with visual impairments who are enrolled in educational programs for primary academic instruction should be required to accomplish the same educational tasks as students who are sighted. For them to do so, teachers of students with visual impairments must be diligent in their adaptation of instruction and educational materials for use in specialized and general education settings. This chapter addresses general strategies for adapting the presentation of instruction and materials for students who are visually impaired.

It is impossible to determine one method of adaptation that will work for all students who are visually impaired because each student has unique needs and abilities. The modification of instruction and materials will depend on the following:

- The functional implication of the student's visual impairment (such as photophobia or tunnel vision),
- The student's level of adaptive skills (including the student's ability to use an abacus and the student's level of listening-comprehension skills),
- The student's personal preference, and
- The primary and secondary goals of each academic assignment.

ROLE OF THE TEACHER OF STUDENTS WITH VISUAL IMPAIRMENTS

In general, it is the responsibility of the person providing instruction to ensure that all students, including the student with a visual impairment, have full access to instruction and all materials used in a lesson. However, since most instruction for students who are visually impaired in inclusive settings is conducted by a general education teacher with little or no knowledge of or experience in modifications for students with visual impairments, it is essential for the teacher of students with visual impairments to be involved in each part of the planning, implementation, and evaluation of modifications. The specialist in visual impairments provides assistance to general education teachers by suggesting these materials and modifications:

- Commercially available, specially adapted materials that are helpful for instruction in certain topics,
- Modifications of teacher-made materials to meet a student's individual needs,
- Modifications of teaching methods and strategies to meet a student's individual needs,
- Modifications of a student's output and completion of assignments,
- Modifications of feedback to a student, and
- Collaborative efforts for effective communication about a student's need for modifications.

This chapter presents guidelines to teachers of students with visual impairments in providing these kinds of suggestions and making appropriate adaptations. Some suggestions for working with a general education teacher appear in Sidebar 5.1. As noted, in addition to collaborating with the general education teacher on specific materials to be used,

Strategies for Collaborating with General Education Teachers

- Explain the student's sensory abilities and skills to the general education teacher; demonstrate the use and care of any assistive devices as well as adapted materials.

- Discuss the student's academic abilities with the general education teacher and stress the student's need to be a full participant in the class and all its associated laboratories, field trips, and other activities.

- Discuss general modifications that will be necessary for the student to be a complete participant in the class.

- Explain the system by which adapted materials are provided to the student on an ongoing basis. That is, are adapted materials prepared by a paraprofessional who is at the school full time or a braillist who visits once a week? How much lead time is necessary? Overnight may be enough time to prepare one braille worksheet, but preparing a tactile graphic may require two weeks or more.

- Explain that you will work directly with the student on compensatory skills and want to be alerted if the student appears unable to perform any needed task.

- In the case of students who read braille, meet at least once with the general education teacher midway through the *previous* year, to determine which textbooks will be needed and to allow time for them to be obtained. Although computer technology is speeding up the production of braille textbooks, you do not want to risk *not* having books on hand when needed.

- Identify new skills that the student will need in the coming year, to allow time for you to prepare or obtain necessary adaptive materials and equipment and to enable you to schedule time to preteach the necessary compensatory skills. You may find, for example, that the student will need to read a thermometer in chemistry or will need a tactile map of North America in history. Such discoveries made several months in advance of need allow *you* and the student to feel confident and successful. When such discoveries are made days before—or worse, after—the materials and skills are needed, there can be no truly positive outcome.

- Teachers who have never taught a student with a visual impairment often express some apprehension about this new challenge. Although assuring them of your ongoing support is helpful, it may also be effective to put them in contact with teachers who have worked successfully with the particular student in the past.

DAVID B. ROSS
Kutztown University, Kutztown, Pennsylvania

MARGARET C. ROBINSON
Texas Tech University, Lubbock

the teacher of students with visual impairments will have suggestions for strategies to promote the student's learning and facilitate his or her inclusion in the classroom. Sidebar 5.2 presents some suggestions for helping general education teachers include students who are visually impaired.

GENERAL PRINCIPLES FOR ADAPTATIONS

The adaptation of instruction and materials involves many complex issues. One of the most com-

Facilitating Inclusion

- Arrange seating in the classroom in a way that fosters friendships. Place the student who is visually impaired with other students. If electricity is required to operate necessary equipment, seat the group near an electrical outlet on the floor or use a taped-down extension cord so the student is able to sit with the class or within a group.

- Encourage the general education teacher to call on the student who is visually impaired, just as he or she would call on any other student.

- Make it possible for the general education teacher to place feedback on braille worksheets. Supply her with sticky notes bearing braille messages, such as "Good Work!" "See Me," or letter grades. Notes can be made of clear adhesive-backed laminating material or blank return address labels printed with floral or cartoon images (both available at office supply stores).

- Prevent problems: An ounce of prevention really *is* worth a pound of cure. Remaining aware of new skills to be introduced in general education classrooms allows you to teach those skills ahead of time that could cause difficulty for students with visual impairments, and the students will be more confident and successful as a result. A few examples include the first use of a glossary or index or a key in map reading and introduction to the table of elements.

- Help the student become an active part of the class by providing the appropriate adapted materials, models, and equipment to facilitate full participation. Success with equipment, such as tactile graphics, tactile measuring devices, and an electronic note taker promotes self-esteem and increases motivation.

- Discourage the student from becoming dependent on his or her sighted classmates. For example, completing a lab with a classmate is appropriate; allowing the classmate to do all the measuring, mixing, timing, and observing is not. The provision of appropriate adaptive equipment is an essential prerequisite to independence.

- Have the student who is visually impaired demonstrate specialized equipment to the class. This activity will open the door for classmates to approach him or her.

- Have the student teach others to use specialized equipment in science or social studies. Using a video camera connected to a microscope is "really cool."

- Teach the braille alphabet to a braille-reading student's classmates. Young students often find secret codes appealing. Provide a set of inexpensive plastic slates and styluses for the classroom's writing center. Ask the general education teacher to allow any student to complete certain assignments, such as short answers to fill-in-the-blank questions, in braille.

- Help foster friendships among students who have visual impairments. Young students benefit from having older friends who are successful and can serve as positive role models. Older students benefit from the self-esteem they gain from serving as role models. If possible, allow an older student to demonstrate the use of various new adaptive aids to a younger student, describing both the techniques for their use and their advantages over other methods.

DAVID B. ROSS
Kutztown University, Kutztown, Pennsylvania

MARGARET C. ROBINSON
Texas Tech University, Lubbock

plex is determining the primary goal of instruction. Many lessons contain extraneous or supplemental objectives that may be confused with the primary goal. For example, if students are asked to circle nouns in a sentence with a red pen and underline verbs with a blue pen, then teachers must be able to determine that the primary goal of the lesson is to identify nouns and verbs, *not* the ability to use different colors of ink or know the difference between a circle and an underline. The student with a visual impairment needs only to respond to the primary goal of this lesson to meet the goal of instruction. If the instruction includes more than one goal, then modifications must be made to make sure that the student can meet each goal.

Wholesale adaptation of materials should be avoided in preference to deliberate decision making regarding the need for and application of modifications. Students who are given adapted materials without careful consideration may find that these modifications, although temporarily helpful, have done little to enhance their ability to participate as fully as possible in future educational and employment opportunities. Close consideration should be given to the restrictiveness of materials and the development of a student's skills to use as many adaptations as possible so that the adaptations are not only helpful, but appropriate.

Stratton's (1990) hierarchy from least-restrictive to most-restrictive materials reflects the importance of providing instruction in a meaningful way that can be directly and naturally transferred to the requirements of daily life (see Figure 5.1). She pointed out that adapted materials "should serve as a means to an end . . . should be a way to build skills that will be a bridge toward learning in the natural environment" (p. 3). Level 1 of the hierarchy reflects a student's ability to learn from the natural environment with no special adaptations. Level 1 is the least intrusive and allows the student to participate most fully in regular activities using standard materials. Level 2 requires the teacher to assist the student as he or she uses natural learning materials. Level 3 refers to the need to adapt materials as a means of developing skills that later can be used in the natural environment. Level 4, the most intrusive level, is the complete replacement of standard materials with adapted materials.

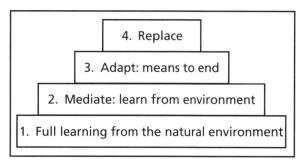

Figure 5.1. Stratton's Hierarchy for Adapting Materials

Source: Reprinted, with permission, from J. Stratton, "The Principle of Least Restrictive Materials," *Journal of Visual Impairment & Blindness* 84 (1990), p. 3.

Stratton (1990) pointed to the need to analyze a student's skills and the requirements of a particular task to make sure that the appropriate amount of adaptation is provided. She stated that "to adapt more than is necessary separates the child from the environment; to adapt less may inhibit learning" (p. 5). In using Stratton's hierarchy, teachers of students with visual impairments should focus first on the student's ability to use materials that are not adapted and then provide adaptations to match the student's needs on a temporary basis (for example, using bold-line graph paper to help the student learn to align numbers in a multidigit multiplication problem) or more permanently (for instance, using a talking calculator to compute problems) if necessary. The key is to respect both the need for adaptation (as well as the child's ability to use standard materials) and to work so that the least-intrusive option is used.

Koenig and Holbrook (1989) referred to the need to fill a student's "toolbox" with a variety of tools for accomplishing a particular task. In this analogy, "tools" refer to the range of options— bold-line writing paper, closed-circuit television (CCTV), felt-tip pens, braille tests, braille note takers, handwriting, keyboarding, and so forth—for completing tasks. A student who is able to perform a task only by using adapted materials is limited to the use of those materials. When the adaptation is not available, the student is unable to participate in the activity. For example, if a student's only option for gathering daily news is to use enlarged materials provided by the teacher of students with visual impairments, the student access to the amount and availability of news will be limited. If, however, the student has a variety of ways to gather news (such as enlarged news materials, use of low vision devices, use of live readers, or use of radio reading services), the student will be more prepared to participate in this activity regardless of the availability of adapted materials.

MODIFICATION OF INSTRUCTION

The task of fully including a student who is visually impaired in a general education classroom sometimes seems daunting because of the vast amount of visual information presented throughout the school day. It may be especially intimidating to general education teachers who do not have experience working with students who are visually impaired. The following guidelines present some of the modifications needed during typical classroom activities. Some modifications that are especially suited to specific subject areas are discussed in the relevant chapters in this text.

Use of Chalkboards and Overhead Projectors

Teachers commonly use chalkboards or overhead projectors as instructional tools. These tools can be difficult for students who are visually impaired who may not be able to see the information being placed on them. Here are some strategies to suggest to general education teachers with regard to writing on chalkboards or overhead projectors:

- Say everything as it is being written. This may take a little practice, but will help all the students in class and will provide an initial overview for a student with a visual impairment.

- Provide an advance copy of work that will be written on the board or overhead transparency (such as daily assignments) in the student's primary reading medium. In some

cases, it may be possible to do so even for work that is written during a lecture if the text is prepared ahead of time.

- Encourage a student with low vision to walk up to the chalkboard or screen to get a closer look if that would be helpful. Students who use optical devices should be allowed to position themselves so they make the best use of their devices.

- Ask the student who is visually impaired what seating arrangement would be the most helpful and then provide it. It may be necessary to allow the student to move to different locations in the classroom, depending on the visual or auditory requirements of the task.

- Encourage the student to ask when he or she thinks that something was missed from the chalkboard or screen. As the student is learning to determine his or her need for additional information, it may be necessary for the teacher to spot-check the student's understanding of material on the chalkboard or overhead projector.

- Experiment with using a blackboard with white chalk, a green board with white or yellow chalk, or a white dry-erase board with a variety of colored dry-erase pens. At times, it is useful to use flip-chart paper so that after the board work is completed, the paper can be removed from the flip chart and given to the student to examine more closely or to the teacher of students with visual impairments to transcribe in an accessible medium.

- Experiment with the position of the overhead projector to vary the size of print projected on the screen. The student should be able to help determine the size of print that is most helpful.

Demonstrations

Another classroom activity that may require adaptation is the use of demonstrations. Demonstrations are a powerful tool in education and it is critical to make these experiences available to students who are visually impaired. The following are some strategies to use during classroom demonstrations:

- Try to reduce glare and visual confusion by standing away from the window and in front of an uncluttered wall.

- Allow the student to stand close to the demonstration. If the student uses a low vision device, encourage him or her to use it during the demonstration. At times, it may be helpful to include the low vision device as a part of the demonstration. For example, placing an insect under the camera of a CCTV would allow all students to see the details and small parts of the insect more clearly.

- Allow the student to participate in the demonstration, if possible, and/or to explore the materials before and after the demonstration.

- Use creative ways to include multisensory input so that the student with a visual impairment can participate on an equal footing. For example, when examining the differences among the leaves of plants, examine not only the way they look, but the way they feel and the way they smell.

- Allow students to work with partners, making sure to pair the student who is visually impaired with a student who is particularly good at providing verbal descriptions.

Modeling

Teachers model a wide variety of behaviors and skills. They use modeling to help students learn handwriting skills, some mathematical calculations, and music techniques and to demonstrate physical education activities. Any time a teacher says "Watch me" to a class and then expects the students to imitate what he or she is doing, the teacher is using modeling techniques. Specific suggestions for teaching handwriting, mathematics, art, music, and physical education can be found in subse-

quent chapters of this book. However, the following are some general guidelines for using modeling with students who are visually impaired:

- Allow the student to stand close to the model and to use a low vision device when it is helpful.

- Talk through the activity, saying, for example, "I am going to start with the ends of the jump rope in each hand and the rope touching the back of my legs. Then I will swing my arms in back of me and over my head as I hold on to the ends of the rope."

- Use multisensory approaches to modeling. For example, when modeling handwriting, it may be helpful to have the letter made of puff paint so the student can examine it as the teacher is describing and writing it.

- Allow the student to touch your hand lightly as you model a technique, such as the motion to use in flipping a pancake.

- Provide physical guidance to the student throughout a specific activity (like placing your hands over the student's hands to show how to align a braille ruler by matching the appropriate end of the ruler with the beginning of the object to be measured).

Lectures

Relatively few adaptations can be made for students who are visually impaired during classes that use the lecture as the primary format. However, these are a few noteworthy adaptations (see also Chapter 9 for a discussion of note taking during lectures):

- Pay close attention to the use of gestures during lectures, since they are used almost unconsciously while speaking. Make sure that gestures that provide important meaning are accompanied by verbal clarification. It may be helpful to record lectures on audiotape and listen to them to detect which gestures would not be understandable without visual input.

◆ Use such words as "look" and "see" freely during lectures because avoiding such words is awkward, and the use of these words is generally not offensive to individuals who are visually impaired.

◆ Use questioning techniques throughout the lecture to ensure that all students in the class are engaged.

Class Discussions

Class discussions may be difficult for students who are visually impaired, especially if they are unstructured. Since students with visual impairments generally do not have the option to use eye contact or visual cues, it is often difficult for them to follow the discussion—that is, to know who is speaking or to hear all the comments when several people speak at once—and to enter the group by adding their comments. During class discussions, it may be helpful to use these suggestions:

◆ Require students to raise their hands and wait until their names are called before commenting.

◆ Avoid pointing to students or using eye contact to indicate who is to talk. When calling on students, make sure to use their names, so the student who is visually impaired will know who is speaking and when he or she is being called on to make a comment.

◆ Summarize comments after they are made, to make sure that all students, including the student who is visually impaired, heard them. It may be helpful to spot-check understanding by asking students to repeat or restate the comments of other students.

Field Trips

Field trips are essential for students with visual impairments to gain basic experiences but may provide a unique challenge for their teachers (see also Chapters 9 and 11). The challenge may include all areas of adaptation and specialized instruction, from orientation and mobility to demonstration to accessible media. Some general guidelines for modifying field trips are as follows:

◆ Plan carefully. Planning is the key for the successful inclusion of a student who is visually impaired on a field trip. The teacher of students with visual impairments should be closely involved in planning the field trip so that situations that need modification can be anticipated.

◆ Visit the field-trip site in advance. The teacher of students with visual impairments should examine the environment for necessary adaptations. The visit may also include an in-service session for the staff of the site, along with specific suggestions for modifications and the gathering of materials that need to be adapted for the student. During this visit, the teacher of students with visual impairments will ask the staff questions concerning the actual field-trip experience: How much of the demonstration can be tactilely accessible for the student, where will the primary activities of this field trip take place, are prerecorded audio presentations available that describe any part of this experience?

◆ Provide pamphlets and other forms of public information from the field trip in accessible media.

◆ Provide braille or large-print labels for signs and posted information at the field-trip site.

◆ Provide scale or full-size models for items that are tactilely inaccessible (for example, items protected by glass cases can be provided in an alternate form).

Guest Speakers

Guest speakers are typically used to supplement or enhance instruction. However, because they are not usually a part of the school, they are probably not aware of the modifications that are necessary for including a student who is visually impaired in their activity. The following steps should be taken to help guest speakers provide the most effective instruction for all students, including the student who is visually impaired:

◆ Contact the guest speaker well in advance to discuss the adaptations needed for the presentation. Let the speaker know that assistance will be provided to modify materials and decide on a date to gather the materials that need to be adapted.

◆ Ask the speaker to arrive a little early on the day of the presentation so the student who is visually impaired can examine any manipulative materials in advance of the speaker's presentation.

◆ Make sure that there is adequate assistance during the guest speaker's presentation. It may be necessary for someone to provide individual assistance to the student throughout the presentation.

MODIFICATIONS OF EDUCATIONAL MATERIALS

Educational materials can be modified in three ways: visually, tactilely, and auditorily. The results of learning media and functional vision assessments can help teachers determine which adaptations are appropriate for a particular student. Functional vision and learning media assessments are conducted by a qualified teacher of students with visual impairments or an orientation and mobility specialist. These informal assessments provide information about how a student uses his or her senses to accomplish various tasks and guidance in making appropriate sensory modifications of the environment to help the student use his or her senses efficiently to gather information and complete daily living and educational tasks. (See Chapter 4 for a more comprehensive discussion of functional vision assessments and learning media assessments.)

Approaches to Adapting Materials

Visual Adaptations

Modifications of educational materials can sometimes be made so that a student with low vision is more successful using his or her vision to complete a task. Visual adaptations are the result of enlarge-

ment, increased clarity and contrast, increased illumination, decreased glare and decreased visual clutter.

Photocopying. There are three ways to enlarge materials: photocopying enlargements, using magnification devices, and holding material closer to the eye. A common enlargement method is photocopying. Large-print books are commercially available from the American Printing House for the Blind (APH) and other sources. Teachers also use photocopy machines to enlarge regular-print classroom materials, tests, and teacher-made materials.

The more significant issue related to large print is whether the use of such materials is essential for a student to make optimal progress in school. Large-print books are commonly ordered for students with low vision, even when their use is unnecessary or restrictive (Koenig, 1996). If a student becomes dependent using large print when low vision devices or nonoptical approaches would allow him or her to read print efficiently, then the student's access to print materials is restricted to those situations when large print is available.

Whether a student will benefit from large print is answered by comprehensive functional vision and learning media assessments. Students with low vision may need enlargement, but enlargement may be gained through the use of optical devices or nonoptical techniques (discussed next). By providing a variety of tools to gain access to print materials, the teacher is applying the principle of filling a student's toolbox with a variety of tools. Some students, given the functional implications of their eye condition, will actually be hampered by unnecessary enlargement. Therefore, the notion that "bigger is better" for students with low vision is not always true.

Using Magnification Devices. The second strategy for enlarging materials is to use magnification devices. Two primary categories of devices are used for magnification: CCTVs and optical low vision devices. CCTVs are electronic devices that use a small mounted camera to project an image onto an attached television monitor. This image or size of print can then be enlarged to meet the individual needs of the user. Students with visual impairments use CCTVs to read, write, do mathematical calculations, and enlarge classroom materials. The CCTV is typically located in the classroom and is used by the student throughout the day as a tool for completing work in class.

Optical low vision devices can be handheld or spectacle mounted, depending on the purpose for their use. Handheld optical devices are typically used for reading or studying close work, while spectacle-mounted lenses or handheld telescopes are used to complete distance work, such as reading from a chalkboard. (Chapter 13 presents methods for teaching students to use optical devices.)

The third strategy for enlarging materials is to bring them closer to the eye. This is the simplest and easiest strategy to use, since it requires no equipment or specialized materials. By bringing material closer to the eye, the image of the material on the retina becomes bigger. Although looking at print close to the eye does not damage the eye, it may cause eye strain and muscle tension. To prevent the strain caused by sitting close to reading material, students who are visually impaired can take advantage of many of the bookstands or reading stands available commercially or those that are made by their teachers.

Increasing Clarity and Contrast. Increasing clarity and contrast often can make materials more useful for students with visual impairments. Some classroom materials are difficult to read because they have been produced from old master copies. It is especially difficult for students who are visually impaired to participate in activities that use purple ditto materials. It may also be difficult for them to use photocopied material if the original copy was in poor condition. Contrast and clarity can be manipulated using the following techniques; the teacher should keep in mind, however, that the needs of individual students must be considered before making any adaptations to classroom materials:

- When possible, use photocopied materials, rather than purple dittos, for the student who is visually impaired.

- Use a dark felt-tip pen when writing something specifically for a student with low vision.

- Use colored overlays to change contrast and make materials easier to see if such a modification is indicated by the functional vision assessment.

- Allow a student with low vision to use a pen or felt-tip marker to complete assignments.

Some students need increased lighting to use classroom materials successfully. However, their needs in this regard vary according to their functional vision skills and preferences. Thus, it is essential to work directly with a student who is visually impaired to find the lighting that is most appropriate and most helpful for him or her. It is also important to consider the placement of lights. Is the student more comfortable with lighting that comes from behind him or her? Can lighting be placed in such a way to produce the fewest shadows? A variety of lighting options (including natural lighting, incandescent lighting, and fluorescent lighting) should be available to allow a student to use different lighting for different educational tasks.

It is important to remember that not all students with low vision benefit from increased lighting and that for some students, increased lighting actually hampers their visual productivity and comfort. Since this is the case, a careful consideration of the results of a functional vision assessment, along with a deliberate analysis of a student's needs and preferences, is critical.

Decreasing Glare. Students with certain types of visual impairments have difficulty with glare. When glare is a problem, a student's visual functioning may fluctuate. This can be frustrating to the student and decrease his or her visual comfort and efficiency. Teachers of students with visual impairments help students adapt their educational environment and materials to compensate for this increased sensitivity to light and glare. Furthermore, the students need to know when and why they need these adaptations so they can effectively advocate for themselves, that is, learn how to request what they need comfortably and effectively. The following suggestions have been found to be helpful in controlling light and decreasing glare:

♦ Have the student wear a visor indoors and outside to help decrease the amount of light. Students may need to wear visors or baseball caps with the bills facing forward to control light. Since wearing caps is sometimes prohibited inside school buildings, it may be necessary to make sure that the faculty and staff of a school know of this adaptation and permit the student to wear a cap or find an alternate way to control glare.

♦ Use sunglasses both indoors and outside.

♦ Provide preferential seating for a student who is sensitive to light, making sure that he or she is located away from windows or doors that let in sunlight. It may also help to put miniblinds or curtains on classroom windows so that light can be controlled.

♦ Use a file-folder shield in front of or over material that is being worked on to control light and glare.

Decreasing Visual Clutter.   In order for students to isolate visual information that is critical to an educational task, it is important to have options for decreasing visual clutter. Some students benefit from using typoscopes, which allow them to block out part of a page by placing a piece of cardboard or paper with a hole that reveals only the important information. Students can also use their hands to cover visual clutter on a page.

A teacher may use clear overlays to isolate certain pieces of information and add to the overlays as a student is ready for more complex visual information. For example, if a teacher is teaching a student the underground system in London, she may want to make overlays with each line printed on a different plastic overlay and start with a simple map, adding overlays until the student can interpret the entire tube system.

Another strategy is to simplify visual materials for students with low vision. For example, if a third grader with low vision is learning to read a map, it

may be appropriate to eliminate some unimportant elements in the map to allow the student to make better use of his or her vision. Or if a preschooler is improving his or her fine motor skills by coloring with crayons, then removing some extraneous information from the coloring books may be helpful. However, the teacher should guard against establishing an expectation that visual materials are always "simple." Rather, the teacher needs to foster knowledge of the range of complexities in visual materials and teach the student appropriate visual or alternative skills for gaining information.

If simplifying materials is a means to an end and will allow the student to learn more sophisticated visual skills, then it serves an important instructional purpose. However, if the simplified materials represent "the end," then the teacher should look for alternative strategies to accomplish the same task. For example, if the third grader just mentioned will eventually learn to use regular maps to navigate a city bus route, then the intermediary process of simplifying maps will be beneficial. However, if the student will not be able to do so, given his or her level of existing or potential vision, then the teacher may teach the student to gain information from maps by using a live reader or a bus company's telephone information line.

Tactile Adaptations

The most common tactile adaptation of classroom materials is the transcription of text, handouts, tests, and other written materials into braille. Teachers of students with visual impairments must also be skilled in modifying maps, graphs, diagrams, and simple pictures into tactile representations. Chapters 9 and 10 address strategies for providing tactile graphics for students with visual impairments. Some specific strategies for modifying classroom materials are discussed in the next section.

Auditory Adaptations

The use of auditory materials is critical for the success of students with visual impairments, especially for large quantities of written material that must be read in a short time. However, the provision of auditory material to the exclusion of tactile or visual adaptations must be avoided. Students need to balance their use of auditory materials with their use of print or braille materials, so they can continue to develop and expand their reading and writing skills. Teachers need to consider the following questions to help them determine the appropriateness of using auditory adaptations:

◆ Is the purpose of the assignment primarily to gather large amounts of information efficiently?

◆ Will there be limited requirements to go back to the text to search for answers to specific questions?

◆ Is the text continuous, without the need to skip from one section to the next or to read footnotes?

◆ Is the student's interpretation of mood and inflection unimportant?

If the answers to these questions are yes, the student may benefit from the auditory modification of materials without losing primary instructional goals. The auditory modification of materials is *not* appropriate under the following conditions:

◆ The primary goal of the assignment is to develop reading skills.

◆ Extensive reference to written material is required throughout an assignment (such as a vocabulary assignment that requires students to determine the definitions of words by locating the words in the text).

◆ Auditory materials are provided as a substitute for braille materials because of the school's inadequate resources.

General guidelines for taping classroom materials and texts can be found in Sidebar 5.3. More detailed information on describing tables, charts, and graphs is presented in Sidebar 5.4.

Modification of Textbooks, Videos, and Pictures

Students with visual impairments may require adaptations of all or most classroom texts and materials. Some classroom materials must be adapted by the teacher of students with visual impairments, since they are not available from any other source. Other materials are commercially available (see the Resources at the end of this and other relevant chapters) or are available on loan from centralized resource centers that exist in most states and provinces to provide specialized materials, often on loan, to students and teachers in specific geographic areas. Classroom materials that need to be adapted should be given to the teacher of students with visual impairments well ahead of the time they will be needed. The general education teacher and teacher of students with visual impairments must work together closely to develop a system for communicating about these materials.

Textbooks

Textbooks for students with visual impairments are adapted into print, braille, and auditory formats. The specific needs of each student determine the type of adaptations that are provided.

Large-Print Textbooks.   Print adaptations of textbooks generally involve enlarging the text. The most common method of enlarging print today is by photocopying. Standard large print is typically 18-point type (Corn & Koenig, 1996), although a common practice is to enlarge the text up to the size that will fit onto an 11×17-inch sheet of paper. Since the level of enlargement is dependent on the size of the original print, the large print that is actually generated may be more or less than the standard 18 points. Teachers should assess the size of print that a student needs to ensure that the actual large print is sufficient to meet the student's needs.

Large-print books are plagued by a number of problems. First, since they are typically photocopied onto 11×17-inch sheets of paper, the

Guidelines for Audiotaping Classroom Materials

SIDEBAR 5.3

◆ Read the material in advance to be sure of the correct pronunciation of words and to identify special concerns related to pictures, tables, or charts, and so forth.

◆ Use a good audiotape recorder with a clear cassette tape. After tapes have been reused a number of times, they may start to have static in the background. Discard such tapes and purchase new ones.

◆ Use a microphone, if possible, to ensure the highest-quality sound. Read at a comfortable pace using clear speech.

◆ Identify the material clearly at the beginning of the recording, for example, the book from which it was excerpted, the title of the worksheet, the title of the text, and the page number if appropriate.

◆ Describe pictures if they are necessary to understand the materials. Write these descriptions in advance, rather than speak extemporaneously. Consider whether to supplement the audiotape with real objects or models.

◆ Describe tables and charts if the description will be useful to the student (see Sidebar 5.4 for additional guidelines). Often, a tactile supplement of essential information is important and necessary. An audio version of a table or chart may provide accurate information, but may not be helpful in completing an assignment.

◆ Provide tone indexing for the beginning of pages, sections, or chapters as appropriate if the tape recorder offers this option. Tone indexing is a method for coding a tape in which a high-pitch tone is heard when the tape is in fast-forward mode; this tone helps the student to locate new pages, sections, or chapters. Tone indexing is important for finding one's place in extended recorded passages or books. Teach the student to use these tones to search for specific locations in the tape or to review information.

Source: Adapted from *NBA Tape Recording Manual*, 3rd ed. (Rochester, NY: National Braille Association, 1979.)

---

books are large and cumbersome to carry and handle. Teachers can make some books smaller by folding the sheets in half, thereby making them easier to carry. However, the student must then unfold each sheet to its original size, which creates similar problems in handling the books. Second, pictures in large-print books are generally in black and white and lack the clarity of the originals.

Braille Textbooks. Braille textbooks are usually produced by certified braille transcribers. In most states and provinces, state resource centers provide braille transcription services. It is essential for teachers to submit textbook orders early in the spring semester before the books are needed or, if possible, even earlier because it takes several months to transcribe books, and the student must not be placed at a disadvantage by not having a braille book when other students in their class have print books. Some large school districts, regional programs, and special education cooperatives also provide braille transcription services, for consumable materials, such as worksheets, tests, and other instructional materials, but generally not for entire textbooks. If such services are not available through a centralized resource center, then the teacher of students with visual impairments is responsible for transcribing consumable braille ma-

Guidelines for Describing Tables, Charts, and Graphs

SIDEBAR 5.4

TABLES AND CHARTS

◆ Read the title, source, captions, and any explanatory keys.

◆ Describe the physical structure of the table or chart, including the number of columns and the heading of each column (and subcolumn, if any). Read from left to right.

◆ Explain whether the table will be read by rows or columns. Reading by rows is usual, but in some cases, reading by vertical columns better conveys the content.

◆ If there are only a few rows, you may wish to repeat the column headings when you read the figures beneath them. If there are many rows, repeat the column headings as you read every fifth row.

◆ Indicate the last row by saying, "and finally . . ." or "the last row. . . ."

GRAPHS

◆ Name the type of graph: line graph, bar graph, circle graph, and so forth. Read the title, source, and caption (if any).

◆ For line and bar graphs, announce what quantities are measured along the x and y axes and their limits. Say, for example, "The x axis is months in 1995 from January to December. The y-axis is the average temperature in Hawaii from 0 to 120 degrees."

◆ For line graphs, start at the left and give the coordinates (x and y values) of significant points—highs, lows, and points where the line changes direction. Always read the horizontal coordinate first.

◆ For bar graphs, first mention any clear trends in the graph by saying, for instance, "Moving from left to right, each bar is taller than the one before it." Then, start at the left and give the value of each bar as measured on the y axis.

◆ A listener can visualize a circle graph more easily if you announce at which o'clock position you are starting and whether you are traveling in a clockwise or counterclockwise direction. For example, "Starting at 9:00 and reading clockwise, the largest wedge of the circle is housing, with 40 percent. . . ."

◆ In school textbooks, wedges of a circle graph are often shown in different colors. mention the colors, since they may be referred to in class.

◆ Always mention when you have completed the description of the graph.

Source: Adapted from *NBA Tape Recording Manual,* 3rd ed. (Rochester, NY: National Braille Association, 1979.)

terials. If there is a great need for such materials, the teacher of students with visual impairments should approach the school administrators about hiring or training a braille transcriber.

Braille textbooks have several unique features. First, since it takes more space to write braille than print, they are often in several volumes. For example, the braille version of a typical third-grade mathematics textbook may be in 5 to 10 volumes. Second, the braille textbooks contain braille numbers in the upper right-hand corners corresponding to the page numbers of the inkprint book. If more than one braille page is needed for an inkprint page (as is common), then the subsequent page numbers are preceded by the letters "a," "b," and so forth. For example, the first braille page containing inkprint page 115 will be designated "115," the second page will be designated "a115," the third page will be designated "b115," and so forth. Third, when new inkprint pages start in the middle of a braille page, a braille line (using the two lower dots in the braille cell) is drawn across the entire width of the page, and the page number of the inkprint book is placed in the far-right cells. Fourth, textbooks with multiple volumes that are transcribed according to the conventions established by the U.S. Library of Congress contain preliminary pages to each volume with the inclusive page numbers and a separate contents page containing information in each specific volume. Fifth, pictures, maps, tables, and other graphic displays may be omitted from the braille text. If they are, a transcriber's note (that is, a note from the transcriber that is not part of the original text), such as "Picture omitted. Ask the teacher," is generally provided. In such instances, the teacher of students with visual impairments is responsible for providing information about the graphic that was omitted. Sixth, the glossary for a textbook is typically located in a separate volume, even if that volume has fewer pages than the others. Here are some hints for using braille textbooks:

- Teach the general education teacher braille numbers and how to use inkprint page numbers so that the teacher can help the student find the appropriate volume and page for an assignment.

- Have the student keep the volume containing the glossary at his or her desk to use while he or she uses the text.

- Teach the student to look for the transcriber's note that describes the pictures and diagrams that have been omitted and provides other important information for interpreting the text.

- Store braille books in bookshelves sitting on their end, not stacked on top of one another, which could harm the braille by flattening it.

- Provide the braille reader with a print copy of the textbook, so he or she can obtain assistance from people who do not use braille.

Some braille textbooks are produced by a Thermoform process, which copies braille onto plastic paper using a heating device. Thermoform paper is slicker than braille paper, and students sometime complain that the Thermoform braille dots are less distinct or that the Thermoform paper makes their hands perspire. Putting talcum powder or cornstarch on a student's fingers may make reading Thermoform more comfortable. Textbooks in Thermoform are less common today, since most textbooks are produced in hardcopy paper form using braille embossers.

Braille textbooks are typically put together using plastic comb bindings, which allows students to open the books flat for easier access to the pages. However, comb bindings are not as durable as book bindings and often need special care, including proper storage. Some wide-comb bindings have locks at the top and bottom combs. When these locks are used, they help keep the combs from becoming snagged on something that would pull out the pages.

Audiotaped Textbooks. As was noted earlier, adaptations of textbooks on audiotapes can be a valuable tool for students who are visually impaired. When using a textbook on audiotape, a student who is visually impaired typically uses a special four-track audiotape player that allows for audio indexing and variable speed control. Although these features may help make the gathering or retrieval of auditory information more efficient, it is still difficult to find specific pages or specific information on a page, review material efficiently, scan material, and skip unnecessary information.

Textbooks for students who are visually impaired must be available in accessible media at the same time as they are available in regular print for students who are sighted. Large-print and braille textbooks are produced commercially by APH and other companies and are available for purchase through federal quota funds and loan programs. Individuals who have been certified as braille transcribers by the Library of Congress produce braille textbooks. Specific rules are used for textbook formats that cross subject areas. The precision and accuracy of textbooks produced in braille is critical. Books on audiotape or in electronic formats are available through APH, Recording for the Blind and Dyslexic, the Library of Congress National Library Service for the Blind and Physically Handicapped, the Canadian National Institute for the Blind, and other sources. (See Sidebar 5.5 for more information.)

Videos

The use of videos in classrooms is challenging for teachers who work with students who are visually impaired. A limited number of videos (mostly commercial movies) are available with accompanying audio descriptions that are designed to assist people with visual impairments. In these videos, a narrator verbally describes the visual action on the screen as part of the background to the regular audio track of the movie. However, most videos that are used in classrooms do not include audio descriptions. Therefore, certain adaptations are useful when videos are used in the classroom:

- ♦ Arrange for a classmate to serve as a narrator to answer the student's questions about the visual information presented in the video.

- ♦ Provide accessible copies of outlines, lists, descriptions, and definitions that are posted on the screen before the video is shown.

- ♦ Allow the student who is visually impaired to take advantage of preferential seating to maximize his or her use of visual and auditory information.

Pictures

Classroom materials usually contain pictures. These pictures make the material more visually appealing and may illustrate points that are made in the text. Sometimes the text is dependent on the pictures for meaning, as in early literacy books with predictable language (such as "I see a cat, I see a dog, I see a bird, . . .") and art appreciation books that contain pictures of artwork or architecture and descriptions of the work.

When pictures are critical to the text, they must be represented in some form. In some cases, it is appropriate to have actual objects available for the student to explore. If it is not possible to do so, providing a tactile model of the object or raised-line drawing may be helpful. A raised-line drawing is an embossed or tactile representation of something, typically made with raised dots (similar to braille dots) or in a less sophisticated manner, such as with glue or puff paint.

However, great care should be given in providing raised-line drawings of pictures in texts. Typically, raised-line drawings are not an adequate substitute for pictures, since they have little tactile relationship to the pictures they represent. For example, if a young child's braille book has a picture of a bunny with a carrot in his mouth, it would not be appropriate to outline the picture with a tactile substance, such as puff paint or glue, because the child would not be able to recognize either the bunny or the carrot simply by touching the outlined drawing. Children who are sighted gather a great deal of information from pictures because the pictures "look like" the real objects. Even though a tactile drawing may "look like" the real object, it may not be beneficial as a tactile representation. Similarly, the same picture of the bunny and the carrot would not be adequately represented simply by cutting a bunny shape out of a piece of furry material, using a cotton ball for the bunny's tail, and cutting a carrot shape out of cardboard. Remember that the essence of a bunny for a child who is blind is not just how that bunny's fur feels, but how the bunny moves, how it smells, and the noises it makes. Therefore, a hands-on experience with a live bunny is the best substitute for the picture in this case. The following are some suggestions for dealing with pictures in texts:

- ♦ Make sure that the student has a strong experiential base to reinforce concepts that are included in books. For example, if the student is reading a story about a picnic, make sure that he or she has been on a picnic.

- ♦ Use a guided preview of the story before the student begins to read, discussing

Sources of Adapted Materials

Students are able to obtain books and other educational materials produced by the American Printing House for the Blind (APH) through a federal program, known as the Federal Quota Program, first enacted in 1879. The program is administered by APH through designated agencies in each state, including the state department of education, the state instructional resource center, residential schools, and other agencies serving people with visual impairments. Congress appropriates an annual amount, allocated on a per capita basis, depending on an annual census of eligible students. Individuals of any age are eligible to obtain materials through the program if they fit the definition of legal blindness and are students working below the college level.

Materials available from APH include textbooks in braille, large type, electronic media, and recorded form; assessment materials; braille teaching programs; talking computer software; low vision simulation programs; infant intervention materials; and commercially unavailable educational aids, tools, and supplies, such as adapted audio recording equipment, devices for writing braille, talking computer hardware, and consumable materials like braille paper, bold-line paper, and special binders and notebooks.

Most states have instructional resource centers (also known as instructional materials centers) that provide adapted materials, such as textbooks in braille or large print or on audiotape. The operation and funding of these centers differ; most are affiliated with state departments of education, but some are affiliated with residential schools, state departments for persons with visual impairments, or regional libraries that are part of a network administered by the National Library Service for the Blind and Physically Handicapped of the Library of Congress. Most of the centers use funds from the Federal Quota Program to obtain materials for students, but their resources vary widely from state to state, as do the systems for delivering the materials. Most of the centers operate as distribution centers, lending books for the duration of the school year. Others operate as clearinghouses. Some centers only purchase books, while others have their own braille presses and provide additional services. The *AFB Directory of Services for Blind and Visually Impaired Persons in the United States and Canada* (American Foundation for the Blind, 1997) lists instructional resource centers across the nation. Teachers can also contact their state department of education or state vision consultants to find out if a materials center exists in their state.

An additional source for reading material is the Library of Congress National Library Service for the Blind and Physically Handicapped, based in Washington, DC. This service lends free reading materials on tape or disk or in braille through a network of regional libraries throughout the United States. It also provides information on other sources of braille books and braille transcription and other materials and equipment.

---

the information contained in visual pictures and introducing tactile representations.

◆ Have the general education teacher or classmates describe pictures as a natural part of the process of reading stories and books. In the early grades, it is typical for teachers to take time to discuss pictures before they read the text.

◆ Use a "book bag" (Miller, 1985) approach to gather real objects that are related to stories and keep the objects together with the book so that the student experiences consistency each time the book is read.

TEACHER-STUDENT COMMUNICATION

Providing Assigned Work

Students who use braille as their primary literary medium must develop a repertoire of skills for providing their work in a format that they can give to their teachers. The teacher who assigns the work should be responsible for grading and providing feedback to the student who is blind, just as he or she grades and provides feedback to all the other students in the class.

While a student is learning braille (either in the early grades or later, in the case of a student who loses his or her sight after having developed literacy skills), it is important for the teacher of students with visual impairments to interline the student's work (that is, write print above the braille text). This technique gives the teacher of students with visual impairments the opportunity to examine the student's braille literacy skills within a natural assignment. Also, the paper can then be graded by the general education teacher when he or she is grading the other students' papers.

As a student becomes more sophisticated in using adapted equipment and once his or her braille literacy skills are fully developed, the student needs to be taught various options for providing homework and classwork in an accessible manner for the instructor. These options include using a word processor (with or without a braille printer), a typewriter, an audiotape recorder, and other technological devices. Chapter 14 provides more information about teaching assistive technology skills to students with visual impairments.

Providing Feedback

All students require timely and constructive feedback. The provision of such feedback is particularly difficult for students who are visually impaired and their teachers because to be useful, the feedback must be given in an accessible form. It is important to establish a consistent system of feedback so that a student knows when and where to find it. The suggestions discussed in the following sections can be incorporated into the personal feedback system for any student.

Visual Feedback. Some students benefit from feedback in print. If a student can use print to gather feedback from teachers, the following suggestions may be helpful:

◆ Make sure that the print feedback for students with low vision is clear and legible. Handwritten notes may be more easily seen if they are carefully written with a dark (black or blue) felt-tip pen or in a contrasting color to the student's own work.

◆ Avoid visual clutter by writing the student a separate feedback note instead of providing feedback directly on the student's paper. One approach is to use Post-it notes, which can be placed on the student's work at the location appropriate for feedback.

◆ Use a yellow highlighter to draw attention to visual feedback.

Tactile Feedback. Students who use braille require tactile feedback, but providing such feedback may be difficult for teachers who do not know braille, but want to provide tactile notes to their students who use braille. There are several techniques for providing tactile feedback:

◆ Give the general education teacher a supply of index cards with grades, such as A, B, C, and general comments, such as "Good Job!," "Excellent!," "Needs Work," and "See Me," written in both braille and print. Be sure to inkprint each card. These cards provide the general education teacher with an immediate way of communicating with the student. Such feedback can be supplemented with more comprehensive auditory feedback (see the next section).

◆ Use a braille-translation software program and a braille embosser to provide written comments to students in braille. This combination of software and hardware allows the teacher to input comments in print, translate it into braille, and then emboss the comments on a special braille embosser. This system allows the general education teacher to provide comments immediately for the student.

◆ Provide comments to the student on a computer disk. The student can then generate braille or auditory output using the appropriate technology.

Auditory Feedback. There are three primary ways to provide auditory feedback. The first is simply to discuss a student's work with him or her. Although this can be a time-consuming process, it gives the student the opportunity to clarify what the teacher means and allows the teacher to determine the student's understanding of an assignment. This is also a helpful time for the student and teacher to discuss the effectiveness of adaptations in meeting the student's needs. An occasional joint conference with the general education teacher, the teacher of students with visual impairments, and the student can help clarify areas of unique concern.

The second technique is to use an audiotape recorder. It may be helpful to use microcassette tapes for feedback, since feedback generally takes little room on a tape. The use of these tapes requires a student to have a microtape recorder that accommodates the smaller-size tape. A teacher can keep a basket of used tapes to use when needed, and the student can place the rewound used tapes into the basket after he or she listens and responds to the feedback.

Third, students who use voice output on a personal computer may prefer to receive feedback on disk. With this technique, the teacher simply responds to the student's work using a computer. Labeling the disks in print and braille as feedback disks and recycling them helps organize this system.

EXPECTATIONS FOR STUDENTS

Students who are visually impaired and have no additional disabilities should be held to the same academic and social standard as students who are sighted. It is important for a teacher to expect success and excellence from a student who is visually impaired. In order to make sure that these expectations are communicated to the student, the guidelines presented in the following sections should be considered.

Amount of Work

Students who are visually impaired should be required to complete the same amount of work as students who are sighted. The amount of time allowed to complete this work may vary, but the amount of work should not. There are three major reasons why the amount of work should not be compromised. The first relates to the assumption that assigned class work helps students acquire or practice skills presented in the lessons. If this is not the case (in other words, if the class is assigned "busy work"), then a change should be made for the entire class, not just for the student who is visually impaired. The elimination or reduction of class work or homework will give the student less of an opportunity to master the concepts taught in class.

The second reason is the social consequences of such an alteration. These consequences include not just the immediate ones that may affect how the student interacts with his or her peers, but also the impact of such differential treatment on the student's interactions with others in the future. By consistently allowing the student who is visually impaired to complete less work for the same grade, both the student who is visually impaired and his or her peers receive the message that people with visual impairments are "less than" people without visual impairments: less efficient, less competent, less capable. Such a message may influence both the overall confidence of the student who is visually impaired and the willingness of classmates to establish working or social relationships with him or her.

The third reason is that it is important for students with visual impairments to know that when they are adults, they will be held to the same employment standards as others in competitive employment environments. If they are taught throughout school that they do not have to complete all assignments or that they can do only half the assignments that other students are required to do, it may be difficult for them to change their behavior to accommodate the requirements of employment.

To address the complex issue of time requirements, the teacher of students with visual impairments, in collaboration with the general education teacher and the student, should carefully analyze the aspects of each assignment that will necessitate additional time. For example, a student may need more time to complete an assignment because of the amount of reading required and the student's reading speed. In that case the teacher and student can determine how much extra time the student will need on the basis of the student's reading rate. In other cases a student may need extra time to manipulate material or equipment (producing mathematical problems on a braillewriter, for example, takes more time than writing the problem with paper and pencil). The teacher and student can estimate the additional time needed on the basis of the time requirements of the task. In both of these examples, adaptations may decrease the amount of extra time required (a live reader or audiotaped materials may be used for a reading assignment, or an abacus or talking calculator may be made available for a mathematics assignment).

Social Behavior

Students who are visually impaired must also be held to the same standard of social behavior as their peers. They must be taught to be responsible for their own actions, to consider the feelings and needs of others, and to take the initiative in making social situations rewarding. Teachers of students with visual impairments must feel comfortable discussing social issues with them and brainstorming and using role-modeling as techniques to solve social issues. Students with visual impairments are likely to need direct instruction in social skills. (See Chapter 17 for details on teaching social skills to students with visual impairments.)

SUMMARY

One of the most important tasks that a teacher of students with visual impairments performs is to modify materials and methods so a student who is visually impaired can participate fully in classroom activities. In an inclusive setting, this task is accomplished collaboratively with the general classroom teacher and the student. In determining the level and type of modification a student needs, the teacher of students with visual impairments conducts a functional vision assessment and a learning media assessment, as well as an assistive technology assessment, and updates these assessments regularly, depending on changes in the student's visual condition and academic requirements. All areas of the student's education are affected by the student's need for instructional modification. The remaining chapters in this book address specific areas of the curriculum and guide teachers through unique situations in each area.

ACTIVITIES

1. Bring an instructional game or kit to class. Work in small groups to plan appropriate modifications of these materials for students who are blind and students who have low vision. Share the outcome of the small-group work with the entire class and gather additional ideas for modifying the materials.

2. Visit a school supply store or a teacher resource center. Examine the materials available for a student who is totally blind and categorize them according to Stratton's hierarchy: (1) materials that require no adaptation; (2) materials that require no adaptation, but would require intervention by a teacher of students with visual impairments; (3) materials that require modification as a means to an end; and (4) materials that require complete adaptation.

3. Observe a general education teacher for one instructional period and record a running narrative of his or her teaching episode. Later, note those aspects of instruction that would require modification for students with low vision and students who are blind. Then recommend two or three modifications for each of the identified areas.

4. Interview a teacher of students with visual impairments. Discuss how he or she prepares adapted materials. Determine the teacher's strategies for ensuring the timely delivery of appropriate adapted materials.

5. Write to at least 10 companies that specialize in adapted materials and equipment for people with visual impairments. Use the *AFB Directory of Services for Blind and Visually Impaired Persons in the United States and Canada* (American Foundation for the Blind, 1997) to find companies and their addresses. Begin an address file of these specialized companies and a resource file of the materials you receive.

REFERENCES

American Foundation for the Blind. (1997). *AFB Directory of Services for Blind and Visually Impaired Persons in the United States and Canada* (25th ed.). New York: Author.

Bishop, V. (1996). *Teaching visually impaired children* (2nd ed.). Springfield, IL: Charles C Thomas.

Braille Authority of North America. (1997). *Braille formats: Principles of print to braille transcription.* Louisville, KY: American Printing House for the Blind.

Corn, A. L., & Koenig, A. J. (1996). *Foundations of low vision: Clinical and functional perspectives.* New York: AFB Press.

Koenig, A. J. (1996). Selection of learning and literacy media for children and youths with low vision. In A. L. Corn & A. J. Koenig (Eds.), *Foundations of low vision: Clinical and functional perspectives* (pp. 246–279). New York: AFB Press.

Koenig, A. J., & Holbrook, M. C. (1989). Determining the reading medium for students with visual impairments: A diagnostic teaching approach. *Journal of Visual Impairments & Blindness, 83,* 44–48.

Mangold, S. (1982). *A teacher's guide to the special educational needs of blind and visually handicapped children.* New York: American Foundation for the Blind.

Miller, D. (1985). Reading comes naturally: A mother and her blind child's experiences. *Journal of Visual Impairment & Blindness, 79,* 1–4.

National Braille Association. (1979). *NBA tape recording manual* (3rd ed.). Rochester, NY: Author.

Olmstead, J. E. (1991). *Itinerant teaching: Tricks of the trade for teachers of blind and visually impaired students.* New York: American Foundation for the Blind.

Stratton, J. (1990). The principle of least restrictive materials. *Journal of Visual Impairment & Blindness, 84,* 3–5.

Torres, I., & Corn, A. L. (1990). *When you have a visually handicapped child in your classroom: Suggestions for teachers* (2nd ed.). New York: American Foundation for the Blind.

Willoughby, D. M., & Duffy, S. L. M. (1989). *Handbook for itinerant and resource teachers of blind and visually impaired students.* Baltimore, MD: National Federation of the Blind.

RESOURCES

(continued on next page)

Suggested Resources for Modifying Instruction

Resource	Type	Source	Description
A Teacher's Guide to the Special Education Needs of Blind and Visually Handicapped Children (Mangold, 1982)	Book	American Foundation for the Blind	A multidisciplinary approach to the education of students with visual impairments. Addresses instruction in basic academic skills, as well as many skills taught outside the regular classroom.
AFB Directory of Services for Blind and Visually Impaired Persons in the United States and Canada (25th ed.) (American Foundation for the Blind, 1997)	Book	AFB Press	List of companies that specialize in adapted materials and equipment for people with visual impairments.
Braille Formats: Principles of Print to Braille Transcription (Braille Authority of North America, 1997)	Code book	American Foundation for the Blind	Provides detailed guidelines on formatting braille textbooks, tests, worksheets, tables, and so forth.
Foundations of Low Vision: Clinical and Functional Perspectives (Corn & Koenig, 1996)	Textbook	AFB Press	A comprehensive textbook on low vision, including detailed information on visual modifications of materials, environmental modifications, use of low vision devices, and so forth.
Handbook for Itinerant and Resource Teachers of Blind and Visually Impaired Students (Willoughby & Duffy, 1989)	Book	National Federation of the Blind	Practical, comprehensive, and creative advice about the education of blind students. Helpful to both new and experienced teachers.

Suggested Resources *(Continued)*

Resource	Type	Source	Description
Itinerant Teaching: Tricks of the Trade for Teachers of Blind and Visually Impaired Students (Olmstead, 1991)	Book	American Foundation for the Blind	Practical suggestions for the itinerant teacher of students with visual impairments.
NBA Tape Recording Manual, 3rd ed. (Rice, 1979)	Guide book	National Braille Association	Provides detailed guidelines for audiotaping textual materials, including tables and charts.
Oh, I See!	Videotape	American Foundation for the Blind	Offers a lively seven-minute video presentation on common strategies for modifying instruction and activities for students who are visually impaired in general education classrooms.
Teaching Visually Impaired Children, 2nd ed. (Bishop, 1996)	Book	Charles C Thomas	A comprehensive resource for the general education teacher for working with a visually impaired child, as well as a systematic overview of education for the specialist in visual disabilities.
When You Have a Visually Handicapped Child in Your Classroom: Suggestions for Teachers (Torres & Corn, 1990)	Booklet	American Foundation for the Blind	A practical, easy-to-read guide for including students who are visually impaired in general education classrooms.

Contact information for each of the resources listed will be found in the Sources of Products, Materials, Equipment, and Services section at the back of this book.

CHAPTER 6

Planning Instruction in Unique Skills

Alan J. Koenig and M. Cay Holbrook

KEY POINTS

- Students with visual impairments should receive effective, specialized instruction in the unique areas that constitute the expanded core curriculum in addition to instruction in the core curriculum required for all students.
- Areas of the expanded core curriculum are targeted for instruction on the basis of the student's needs as identified by a comprehensive assessment.
- Special methods for teaching students with visual impairments involve providing concrete experiences, learning by doing, and unifying instruction.
- The Individualized Education Program (IEP) for each student clearly specifies what is to be taught in measurable annual goals and short-term objectives or benchmarks.
- Students should be afforded opportunities to acquire new skills efficiently, practice skills to a proficient level, maintain skills, and generalize skills to new environments and conditions.

VIGNETTE

Ron Kowalsky frowned at his schedule. What he *really* needed was some way to stretch it. LeAnn needed more time! LeAnn was a new student whose congenital glaucoma was causing a rapid loss of vision. Sometimes she could read the print in her second-grade books, but trying to read often led to a headache. Ron had taught LeAnn to use the closed-circuit television (CCTV), hoping it would help her read print more comfortably until braille could become her primary literacy medium. LeAnn enjoyed her braille lessons and could read several "emergent reader" books independently. She and Ron usually had time every day to do some writing on the Perkins braillewriter, too. Ron's biggest concern was math. LeAnn needed to learn the Nemeth Code, as well as literary braille, and he did not know how he would find the time to teach it to her.

Ron's next stop was Manuel, a third grader with low vision. One of Manuel's goals for the next year was to learn to type on a computer keyboard. Students in Manuel's school usually learned touch typing in the sixth grade, in the computer lab. However, the educational team had agreed that Manuel should not wait that long because although Ron could usually read what Manuel wrote with a felt-tip pen, Manuel usually could not! Thus, learning to use a computer word processor was an essential skill for Manuel. Manuel looked forward to being able to type, but needed lots of prompting to complete the necessarily repetitive practice of sentences like "That lady has a glass flask."

Next, Ron phoned the guidance counselor at the high school. John Ware, a 10th grader in a career education class, was expected to interview an adult who was employed in a "desired" occupation. Ron had obtained the name and phone number of a computer programmer who was blind. Although Ron had talked to the programmer and could have arranged the appointment himself, he thought it was important for John to do so. The guidance counselor, who taught the class, would pass the information on to John.

At 10 o'clock, Ron visited Yvonne, a seventh grader with low vision. Ron had recently obtained a monocular for Yvonne and taught her the techniques for using it in the classroom—locating material at a distance, scanning a line, and locating the beginning of the next line. Ron wondered if Yvonne was more comfortable with the monocular now that she had had time to practice with it. Could she use it to read material presented on the board, the overhead projector, and the flip charts her teacher often used? If so, did using the monocular allow Yvonne to complete her work faster? Ron smiled. Yvonne would like anything that let her work faster. Ron made a note to himself to ask Yvonne's orientation and mobility (O&M) instructor to address the uses of the monocular in indoor and outdoor travel situations.

Just in time, Ron met Martin's class in the lunch line. Martin, who was totally blind and moderately mentally retarded, received educational services in a developmental disabilities class. Using a "learning-by-doing" approach, Ron ate lunch with Martin each day and used the opportunity to teach Martin independent living skills. He had recently used a backward-chaining technique to teach Martin to open a milk carton. Martin was proud of his new skill and was eager to succeed on his next objective: using a knife to spread butter or jelly on bread. The lunchroom staff was supportive of their work. If the prepared lunch did not include a roll and butter, they would give Ron a plastic-wrapped paper plate holding two pieces of bread and something "spreadable." Ron found people's unexpected generosity to be one of the greatest pleasures of his work.

As Ron left Martin's school, he thought about the gains that each of his students had made this year. But he also wondered how much more progress the students could make if he continued to have barely enough time to teach all the skills they really needed.

Ron came to the painful realization that he was short-changing his students to accommodate his heavy caseload. He knew that he needed lots of time to teach special skills to his students, and he had to get this message across clearly and convincingly to his supervisor. To help make the case that the skills he was teaching his students were essential, he would get some much-needed support from a journal article on the expanded core curriculum for students with visual impairments. With this plan of action in mind, he was eager to get back to the office to arrange a meeting with his supervisor.

INTRODUCTION

Planning and delivering instruction in unique, disability-specific skills is a key role of the teacher of students with visual impairments. Much of a specialist's time is devoted to modifying instruction and materials for general education teachers and other professionals, as described in Chapter 5. In such instances, the instruction is designed by someone else, and the task is to make it meaningful and accessible for students with visual impairments. The teacher of students with visual impairments must also be prepared to design and deliver original instruction in unique skills that are specific to the needs of individual students.

Students who are blind or visually impaired receive instruction in two equally essential and interrelated curricula. The first is the "core curriculum," which consists of skill areas that are common to all students, such as reading and writing, mathematics, social studies, and physical education (Hatlen, 1996). This curriculum is established by states, provinces, and local school boards. The second curriculum, which students with visual impairments must also learn, is the "expanded core curriculum," involving such skills as independent living skills, compensatory academic skills, and orientation and mobility (O&M) skills. This term was coined by Hatlen (1996) to reinforce the idea that the unique skills taught to students with visual impairments are an integral and indispensable component of the core curriculum, not skills that are considered extra or for enrichment. (See Sidebar 6.1 for an overview of the core curriculum and the expanded core curriculum.)

The elements of the expanded core curriculum serve as the basis for *what* teachers of students with visual impairments teach. However, *how* teachers instruct students with visual impairments is also unique. For example, these specialists use more direct instruction and physical guidance to teach new skills, rather than rely on visual modeling and imitation, as is typical of general instruction. Lowenfeld (1973), who developed a comprehensive theoretical framework for teaching students who are blind, presented the unique principles of instructional methodology for working with these students (discussed later in this chapter).

This chapter begins with a discussion of the role of the teacher of students with visual impairments in planning and delivering specialized instruction. It then presents an overview of the principles of special methods for teaching students with visual impairments, which the authors consider to be the foundation of specialized instruction, followed by a description of a process for designing unique instruction. If a teacher of students with visual impairments knows how to perform the required special skills and can skillfully apply the principles of special methods through solid instructional strategies, then he or she can teach the range of unique skills in the expanded core curriculum to a student with a visual impairment. The information that follows is a process to guide the teacher. (Specific strategies that are unique to individual skill areas are presented throughout this book.) The final section of this chapter provides guidance on delivering effective instruction.

ROLE OF THE TEACHER OF STUDENTS WITH VISUAL IMPAIRMENTS

The teacher of students with visual impairments plays a primary role in teaching the skills included in the expanded core curriculum. Other profes-

---

SIDEBAR 6.1

Components of the Core and Expanded Core Curricula

CORE CURRICULUM

- ◆ English language arts and other languages, to the extent possible
- ◆ Mathematics
- ◆ Science
- ◆ Health and physical education
- ◆ Fine arts
- ◆ Social studies and history
- ◆ Economics and business education
- ◆ Vocational education

EXPANDED CORE CURRICULUM

- ◆ Compensatory or functional academic skills, including communication modes
- ◆ Orientation and mobility
- ◆ Social interaction skills
- ◆ Independent living skills
- ◆ Recreation and leisure skills
- ◆ Career education
- ◆ Use of assistive technology
- ◆ Visual efficiency skills

Source: Reprinted, with permission, from P. Hatlen, *Core Curriculum for Blind and Visually Impaired Children and Youths, Including Those with Additional Impairments* (Austin: Texas School for the Blind and Visually Impaired, 1996). Also available on-line at http://www.tsbvi.edu/education/corecurric.htm

---

sionals on the educational team are not likely to have the special knowledge or preparation to teach these skills, nor do they generally have the responsibility to do so. Therefore, the role of the teacher of students with visual impairments in providing instruction in the expanded core curriculum is to do the following:

♦ Take a leading role on the educational team to identify areas of the expanded core curriculum that the student needs, on the basis of the results of the comprehensive assessment (discussed in Chapters 2, 3, and 4);

♦ With the other members of the educational team, develop measurable annual goals and accompanying short-term objectives or benchmarks to ensure that the student's educational program is cohesive and individualized;

♦ Understand and apply the principles of special methods for teaching students with visual impairments;

♦ Use appropriate teaching approaches, especially direct instruction, effectively, to teach unique skills to a student with visual impairment;

♦ Use a variety of instructional tools and strategies—task analysis, prompting, guidance, chaining, and so forth—to promote optimal learning; and

♦ Use evaluation procedures on an ongoing basis to ensure that a student is benefiting from the instruction that is provided and, if not, make appropriate changes in instructional procedures.

PRINCIPLES OF SPECIAL METHODS

Given that 60–80 percent of the information that students use in learning is visual (MacCuspie, 1996), one can clearly understand that special methods are required to teach students who are blind or visually impaired effectively. Lowenfeld (1973) delineated three limitations that are imposed by a visual impairment:

♦ Restriction in the range and variety of experiences as a result of the limitations of the tactile and auditory senses to provide

the same quality and quantity of information about the environment that vision provides instantly and holistically.

♦ Restriction in the ability to get about, which influences opportunities both for gaining access to experiences and for developing social relationships.

♦ Restriction in interaction with the environment, as a result of the lack of ready control over the environment, leading to detachment from physical and social environments.

To minimize or eliminate these restrictions, Lowenfeld (1973) proposed three principles of special methods for teaching students with visual impairments: (1) the need for concrete experiences, (2) the need for learning by doing, and (3) the need for unifying experiences. Table 6.1 presents examples of how the principles of special methods can be used to teach unique skills. Although Lowenfeld suggested that these principles apply primarily to students who are functionally blind (that is, who rely primarily on tactile and auditory information in learning), the authors believe that the principles apply equally to students with low vision, who, though visually impaired, may use vision in developing concepts and learning about their environment.

Concrete Experiences

Children with visual impairments need rich, varied, and consistent experiences with concrete objects to gain a thorough knowledge of the environment around them and to develop meaningful concepts. Such experiences help them overcome, to some extent, the restriction in the range and variety of experiences (Lowenfeld, 1973). To provide concrete experiences, Lowenfeld says, the teacher needs to do as follows:

♦ Use real objects in the natural environment, when possible;

♦ Use real objects outside the natural environment only when learning in the natural

Table 6.1. Applications of the Principles of Special Methods

Unique Skill	Principles of Special Methods		
	Concrete Experiences	**Learning by Doing**	**Unifying Experiences**
Making lemonade	Use real ingredients, real utensils, and real dinnerware.	Make the lemonade, completing each step in the process with or without guidance or prompting from the teacher.	Purchase ingredients from a grocery store. Integrate measurement concepts learned in math class. Drink lemonade as part of an after-school party for peers and parents.
Writing with slate and stylus	Use the actual slate and stylus. Use slate instructional tool from the American Printing House for the Blind to introduce cell-configurations.	Use the slate and stylus with guidance from the teacher, as needed. Explore other specialty slates, such as one-liner notecard slate, full-page slate, and cassette-labeling slate.	Use the slate and stylus to jot assignments. Use the slate and stylus to take notes in a classroom. Use a slate and stylus at home to label CDs.

environment is not possible (for example, bringing seashells to class when the school is in Iowa); and

◆ Use scale models of objects when the real objects are unavailable (such as dinosaurs) or inaccessible (like snowflakes that are too fragile, skyscrapers that are too large, and constellations that are not tactilely accessible).

Additionally, the following suggestions are offered as strategies for providing concrete experiences:

◆ Provide ample time and physical guidance to allow a child to explore real objects fully using all the available senses, including vision for students with low vision (on a field trip to a museum, for instance, make sure that a student is not rushed through exhibits, but has time to explore them tactilely);

◆ Avoid the overuse of tactile drawings to substitute for real objects in developing

conceptual understanding because such drawings do not accurately or meaningfully represent the reality of three-dimensional objects (for example, a raised-line drawing of a tree will not help a student who is blind understand the characteristics of a tree);

◆ Use scale models of large objects after a real-life experience to give the child a sense of its spatial arrangement and wholeness (that is, have the child explore a model of a barn *after* he or she has climbed up the ladder, played in the hayloft, and explored the animal pens);

◆ Teach directly those skills that are typically learned incidentally through visual observation and imitation (like shaking hands, maintaining eye contact with communication partners, and performing activities of daily living); and

◆ Continually expand the child's repertoire of common experiences with activities that are typical in daily life (such as playing in a city park, cleaning up a garage, and playing at a miniature golf course).

Providing rich, concrete experiences in meaningful contexts will help a child with a visual impairment avoid the use of "verbalisms," that is, using words without an experiential basis to make them meaningful. According to Lowenfeld (1973, p. 43), "Giving blind children a knowledge of the realities around them is not a question of enriching the [children's] vocabulary, but of giving [them] a sense of reality about the environment."

Learning by Doing

Learning by doing is achieved simply by engaging a child who is visually impaired in completing the task that is the focus of instruction, rather than presenting only a lecture or discussion. It is easy to understand that a lecture on how to tie one's shoelaces or to make a mini-pizza would be devoid of any (or much) meaning for the child. In many instances, a lecture followed by the actual experience would be somewhat better, but one might question the value of the preceding lecture.

For most special skills that students with visual impairments need to acquire (such as daily living skills, recreational skills, and vocational skills), the ideal approach is to guide and prompt a child through the steps needed to complete the actual task or skill being taught. Any explanations of the steps that are important will then occur naturally within the actual experience. As the task is repeated on several occasions, the child will gain more independence in completing the task, relying less on prompts and guidance from the teacher. A later section presents strategies for using prompting and graduated guidance strategies.

Lowenfeld (1973) cautioned against the practice of doing things for children with visual impairments to save time, rather than have them do things for themselves. "Make me a doer, not a done-to-er"—a common saying in the field of visual impairments—is a basic principle that teachers need to follow. Teaching unique skills and expecting children to complete the skills for themselves is a process that requires time for systematic instruction, practice, and application.

A best-practices approach to educating students with visual impairments upholds the need for and provides the optimum instructional time to develop unique skills that are required for achieving a fulfilling life. Ensuring appropriate instructional time may require extending instruction beyond the normal school hours (for example, instructing a child in daily living skills before or after school or on weekends) or beyond the typical school year (using extended-year programs or summer camps to expand instruction in unique skills). Although students have sometimes been pulled out of subjects, such as science or physical education, to be taught unique skills, this approach eliminates essential areas of the core curriculum and is not an acceptable practice. The approach should be to establish priorities among and plan instruction in unique skills throughout the school year and to schedule additional time to provide such instruction.

Unifying Experiences

Providing unifying experiences gives students with visual impairments opportunities to gain a sense of the totality and wholeness of objects and situations. Since a visual impairment restricts one's opportunities to experience things holistically, specific strategies must be used to compensate for this restriction. Lowenfeld (1973) suggested the following strategies:

◆ Teach in study units to allow connections to be made between and among the topic of instruction (such as using logical reasoning skills learned in mathematics to figure out a problem posed for a novice detective in a story read in language arts class).

◆ Use field trips to provide real-life applications of skills and concepts learned in the classroom (for instance, using computation skills to estimate the total of one's grocery bill and the sales tax while shopping for candy for a class party).

The provision of unifying experiences is extremely critical; however, it is an aspect of specialized methods that is frequently overlooked. It may be helpful to think of unifying instruction from two standpoints: within the lesson and throughout a child's life.

To unify within the lesson, make sure that sequential tasks (like the tasks involved in most daily living skills) are completed from the first to the last steps, even if the teacher must prompt or guide the student in the steps that the student cannot complete independently. This practice gives the student an idea (and the reality) of the entire task, not only of a fragmented portion or portions. For example, if a child completes only two of the steps in baking cookies, then he or she may think that making cookies involves just beating batter and putting the tray in the oven, without learning the nature of the ingredients, how to measure, and how to shape the dough. In general education programs, in which each student gets to do one of the steps, the specialist in visual impairment or another skilled adult needs to be available to conduct a parallel lesson with the student who is blind or visually impaired so the student can complete each step in the sequence.

Another aspect of unifying within the lesson is related to the completeness of tactile and sensory explorations. Young students with visual impairments need to be taught to explore objects systematically so they can observe all the features of the objects using all their available senses. For children with low vision, the use of vision should be paired with tactile observation, to prevent the children from gaining inaccurate or incomplete visual information about objects. For example, when a young student encounters a rocking horse in the classroom for the first time, the teacher of students with visual impairments can guide his or her hands to the head, neck, body, saddle, two handles on either side of the horse's head, two stirrups (pegs for the feet), four legs, and two rockers, as well as the area surrounding the horse. This procedure will give the student an idea of the wholeness of the rocking horse, and the subsequent enjoyment of the rocking will be the ultimate application of this lesson. However, if the student haphazardly explores the rocking horse and gets on the saddle without locating the handles or stirrups, he or she will not only fail to gain a total sense of the rocking horse, but the resulting awkward rocking motion undoubtedly will minimize the enjoyment of "riding" the horse.

For nonsequential tasks (such as learning to advocate for oneself), the teacher can unify within the lesson by using sound strategies for presenting instruction (discussed later), beginning by connecting the lesson with previous lessons to provide a context within which a new skill or concept will be developed. Linking the new information to other areas of the curriculum through study units and field trips, as Lowenfeld (1973) suggested, is another strategy for unifying within the lesson.

Providing unifying experiences throughout a student's life is one way to ensure generalization—that a task learned in an instructional setting is applied under different conditions and in various real-life environments. One ideal strategy for achieving generalization is to teach skills in a number of real environments or to provide follow-up applications of skills in real environments. For example, if the student is learning to use an abacus to estimate sums, he or she can use the abacus during a shopping lesson to keep a cumulative total of the nearest dollar amounts for the items being purchased. The strategy is to provide clear and meaningful links between classroom instruction and real-life applications. If classroom instruction has no meaningful, real application, then the teacher must consider whether it is an important task to teach.

PROCESS OF DESIGNING INSTRUCTION

The process of designing and delivering unique instruction has eight components: (1) specifying measurable annual goals, (2) specifying short-term objectives or benchmarks, (3) analyzing the task, (4) selecting an appropriate instructional approach or approaches, (5) choosing appropriate instructional strategies, (6) selecting appropriate instructional materials, (7) addressing increased levels of proficiency, and (8) planning appropriate evaluations of instruction. An overview of these components and what they entail is presented in Sidebar 6.2.

After a course of instruction is designed, the teacher of students with visual impairments delivers the instruction, as described later in this chapter. As part of the instruction and evaluation processes, the specialist considers modifying the instructional approach, implementing additional lessons, providing ongoing assessments, and continuing the cycle. Given this cyclical procedure, it is easy to understand that designing and delivering unique instruction is not a linear process. For example, when an ongoing assessment finds that a young child has mastered the skills involved in eating finger foods as part of daily living skills instruction, the teacher may begin to teach the child to eat selected foods with a spoon.

Specifying Measurable Annual Goals

The first step in designing unique instruction is to specify measurable long-term goals for the student. This is the natural outcome of conducting the comprehensive educational evaluation and developing the IEP, in which a student's strengths and needs are identified and goals are written to address those needs through appropriate educational intervention. Measurable long-term goals are statements about the growth a student is expected to achieve in an extended period, typically one year. Rosenberg, O'Shea, and O'Shea (1998, p. 91) recommended that long-term goals contain the following five components:

1. *Direction* of the desired gain (e.g., increase, decrease, maintain).
2. *Deficit area* from which the student is operating (e.g., reading, written language, social skills).
3. *Starting point* for instruction (typically, similar to the student's present level of performance).

4. *Ending point* for instruction (level of performance the student is expected to attain in one year).
5. *Resources* (instructional methods or techniques from which the student is most likely to benefit, given the student's individual learning characteristics).

Here are some examples of measurable long-term goals that address areas of unique need for students with visual impairments:

◆ Sally will increase her social interaction skills from interacting only with adults to interacting with her same-age peers using verbal prompts from her teachers and parents.

◆ Craig will increase his use of functional literacy skills, from relying on adults to assist him to completing tasks independently, through the teacher's use of direct instruction in community settings.

◆ Carlos will develop basic computation skills with the Cranmer abacus, from having no abacus skills to performing addition and subtraction problems on the abacus, through the teacher's use of direct instruction.

◆ Kirstin will increase her time on task, from staying on task 20 percent of the time to staying on task 80 percent of the time, through the teacher's use of indirect verbal prompts, a self-management program, and tangible reinforcers.

Educational goals for students with visual impairments typically are based on areas of the expanded core curriculum, which addresses unique needs that are associated with visual impairment, rather than simply specifying what is already in the core curriculum. The educational team needs to focus on those skills that will allow the student to have full access to the educational and social opportunities that are expected of all students. Therefore, the team may specify a goal of acquiring skills in using the abacus, for example, rather

Important Points to Consider in Planning Specialized Instruction

SPECIFY MEASURABLE LONG-TERM GOALS

- ◆ Base goals on the ultimate level of functioning that is desired.
- ◆ Consider the student's and family's wishes.
- ◆ Use a one-year time frame for specifying goals.
- ◆ Write goals in measurable terms, specifying the beginning and ending points for instruction.

SPECIFY SHORT-TERM OBJECTIVES OR BENCHMARKS

- ◆ Link objectives to the student's mastery of specified long-term goals.
- ◆ Include the student's name, conditions under which the behavior will be demonstrated, the behavior, and evaluation criteria in each objective.
- ◆ Identify only observable, measurable behaviors.

ANALYZE SKILLS OR TASKS

- ◆ Break down the task into teachable parts, if necessary and desirable.
- ◆ Use a traditional task analysis for sequential tasks.
- ◆ Identify the component skills or tasks for nonsequential tasks.

USE AN APPROPRIATE INSTRUCTIONAL APPROACH OR APPROACHES

- ◆ Consider the use of one or a combination of instructional approaches: lecture, demonstration, questioning and guided discussion, experiential learning, and direct instruction.
- ◆ Integrate within any approach the principles of special methods by providing concrete experiences, learning by doing, and unifying experiences.

USE APPROPRIATE INSTRUCTIONAL STRATEGIES

- ◆ Use single or multiple strategies to support the learning process: modeling and guidance, prompts, shaping, and chaining.
- ◆ Prompt or guide only to the extent necessary for the student to complete the task.
- ◆ Fade prompts and assistance as soon as possible.

USE APPROPRIATE INSTRUCTIONAL MATERIALS

- ◆ Match the instructional materials needed to teach the skill or task with the developmental needs of the student.
- ◆ Modify materials only to the extent needed to teach the lesson effectively.

INCREASE THE STUDENT'S PROFICIENCY IN COMPLETING TASKS

- ◆ Ensure an increase in the student's proficiency by facilitating acquisition, fluency, maintenance, and generalization.
- ◆ Ensure that the student has had adequate practice to build fluency.
- ◆ Ensure that the task generalizes across conditions, people, and settings.

EVALUATE THE EFFECTIVENESS OF INSTRUCTION

- ◆ Link daily evaluation with the evaluative component in short-term objectives.
- ◆ Ensure the student's overall progress by using a variety of informal assessment techniques.
- ◆ Use the daily evaluation and diagnostic teaching to plan subsequent lessons.

than outline the elements of the standard mathematics curriculum. By learning to use an abacus (and other unique skills), the student will be equipped with the tools to benefit from the standard mathematics class.

The expanded core curriculum provides a valuable framework with which to structure the comprehensive educational assessment and the resulting establishment of goals (and later, objectives) to address identified needs. Sidebar 6.3 outlines an example of specific skills within each of the basic examples of components of the expanded core curriculum. A best-practices approach to assessment and program development supports a process that addresses each of the areas in this expanded core curriculum.

Specifying Short-Term Objectives or Benchmarks

Short-term objectives, also called "benchmarks" in the Individuals with Disabilities Education Act (IDEA), provide the essential framework for achieving long-term goals. When instruction follows a series of carefully planned objectives and the student attains these objectives, the long-term goal is achieved. Since objectives are stated in observable, measurable terms, they also serve an essential evaluation function. According to Alberto and Troutman (1995), an objective typically has four components:

◆ The student (which they call the "learner");

◆ The conditions under which the behavior will be demonstrated;

◆ The behavior, stated in observable terms; and

◆ The criterion for mastery.

Sidebar 6.4 provides examples of each component of short-term objectives and then shows various formats for writing complete objectives. The following is a brief discussion of each of the four components.

Student.   In developing an IEP for a student with a visual impairment, the focus is always on the student's needs. This basic tenet is reinforced by clearly specifying the student's name in the objective. Objectives that do not identify the student fail to reinforce the individualness of the educational plan (Alberto & Troutman, 1995).

Conditions.   A well-written objective clearly specifies the conditions that are antecedents to performing the skill or task that is being taught (Alberto & Troutman, 1995). Will the student be asked orally to select appropriate clothing, given current weather conditions? Be presented with a worksheet to practice abacus skills? Be prompted to pick up ingredients tactilely to make chicken soup? Be seated at a computer station to begin using a word-processing program? The conditions under which a given task is to be performed can significantly influence the difficulty of the task. For example, asking for an oral response from a child to demonstrate knowledge of rhyming words is generally easier than asking for a written response.

Behavior.   Objectives written for IEPs are often referred to as "behavioral objectives," since the term *behavior* indicates that the activity is observable and, therefore, measurable. For example, "runs a 100-yard dash" is an observable behavior. "Knows the 50 states" is not, but restating it as "recites the names of the 50 states" makes this behavior observable.

The verb that is used in the objective is often the factor that makes the behavior observable. Examples of action verbs that are observable include *mark, remove, point to, put on, circle, say,* and *read orally;* verbs that are ambiguous or not directly observable include *inquire, find, summarize, develop, be aware, think, feel,* and *perceive* (Alberto & Troutman, 1995). Since areas of the expanded core curriculum for students with visual impairments are usually skill based (rather than knowledge based), they are generally easy to observe: to use the sighted-guide technique, to maintain eye contact, to comb one's hair, to track a line of braille smoothly, and so forth.

Areas of the Expanded Core Curriculum and Examples of Specific Skills

COMPENSATORY OR FUNCTIONAL ACADEMIC SKILLS AND COMMUNICATION MODES

- ◆ Concept development
- ◆ Study and organizational skills
- ◆ Speaking and listening skills
- ◆ Adaptations for gaining access to areas of the core curriculum
- ◆ Braille reading and writing
- ◆ Use of large print
- ◆ Use of print with optical devices
- ◆ Communication modes for students with additional disabilities (such as tactile symbols, a calendar system, sign language, and recorded materials) (Hatlen, 1996)

ORIENTATION AND MOBILITY SKILLS

- ◆ Body image
- ◆ Environmental concepts
- ◆ Spatial concepts
- ◆ Precane mobility skills
- ◆ Independent travel skills

SOCIAL INTERACTION SKILLS

- ◆ Interpersonal communication
- ◆ Requesting information from persons in the general public
- ◆ Self-advocacy
- ◆ Maintaining eye contact
- ◆ Taking turns in conversations

RECREATION AND LEISURE SKILLS

- ◆ Competitive sports (such as bowling, goalball, and marathon running)
- ◆ Noncompetitive sports (like swimming and jogging)
- ◆ Hobbies
- ◆ Choosing recreational activities

CAREER EDUCATION

- ◆ Time management
- ◆ Organizational skills
- ◆ Knowledge of various occupations
- ◆ Work habits and discipline
- ◆ Effective communication skills
- ◆ Specific vocational skills

TECHNOLOGY

- ◆ Keyboarding skills
- ◆ Braille access devices
- ◆ Visual access software and devices
- ◆ Auditory access software and devices
- ◆ Choosing appropriate options
- ◆ Device maintenance and troubleshooting

VISUAL EFFICIENCY SKILLS

- ◆ Use of nonoptical low vision devices
- ◆ Use of optical low vision devices
- ◆ Use of a combination of senses
- ◆ Use of environmental cues and modifications
- ◆ Recognizing when not to use vision

Components and Examples of Short-Term Objectives

COMPONENT

- Learner and Conditions

  Sally: when verbally reminded by an adult
  Craig: upon hearing from the cashier the amount of the bill
  Carlos: when presented with an abacus and 10 addition problems transcribed in braille
  Kirstin: after the bell rings for the second period

- Behavior

  Sally: will make eye contact with the person speaking to her
  Craig: will write a legible and legal check
  Carlos: will use the abacus to calculate the sums
  Kirstin: will be seated at her desk

- Evaluation or Criterion for Mastery

  Sally: on 4 out of 5 occasions
  Craig: within 45 seconds in 4 out of 5 opportunities
  Carlos: with 90 percent accuracy
  Kirstin: within 5 seconds

APPROPRIATE FORMATS FOR COMPLETE SHORT-TERM OBJECTIVES

1. When verbally reminded by an adult, Sally will make eye contact with the person speaking to her on 4 out of 5 occasions.
2. Craig, upon hearing from the cashier the amount of the bill, will write a legible and legal check within 45 seconds in 4 out of 5 opportunities.
3. When presented with an abacus and 10 addition problems transcribed in braille, Carlos will use the abacus to calculate the sums with 90 percent accuracy.
4. Kirstin will be seated at her desk within 5 seconds after the bell rings for second period.

Criterion.   The criterion component of the objective clearly states the level of accuracy or mastery that is required of the student for the teacher to conclude that the objective has been achieved. Typical criterion measures are percentage correct, number correct, rate, duration, and latency. Table 6.2 presents examples of each.

When establishing a criterion level, a teacher of students with visual impairments needs to match the behavior of interest with an appropriate measure. For example, tasks that require a student to make repeated responses (such as completing math problems) lend themselves well to a measure that notes the percentage correct or the number correct out of the total possible responses. However, it is not meaningful to say that a student will make a peanut butter sandwich with 90 percent accuracy. A teacher may specify that the student will make an edible peanut butter sandwich on four out of five trials or that 90 percent of the steps in a task analysis (described later) will be completed in sequence. The important point is to specify the criterion clearly so that anyone who works with the student knows exactly what is expected for mastery.

Such criteria as the percentage correct and

Table 6.2. Typical Criterion Measures, Definitions, and Examples

Criterion	Definition	Examples
Percentage correct	The proportion of correct responses to the total number of responses.	Completes addition problems with 90 percent accuracy. Answers comprehension questions with 80 percent accuracy.
Number correct	A simple count of the number of correct responses.	Recites the alphabet in the correct sequence in 4 out of 5 trials. Places nuts on bolts in 8 out of 10 trials.
Rate	The speed at which a task or behavior is demonstrated; generally given in rate per minute.	Reads aloud at 85 words per minute. Completes 10 division problems in 5 minutes.
Duration	The total length of time that a task or behavior is demonstrated.	Jogs around the track for 10 minutes. Interacts with peers for 5 minutes.
Latency	The length of time between a directive (or another antecedent) and the initiation of a task or behavior.	Begins work within 20 seconds of the teacher's request. Sits at the desk within 1 minute of hearing the bell.

number correct are useful for evaluating the mastery of skills in the initial acquisition phase. At this level, the teacher of students with visual impairments is concerned that the student can accomplish the task, not necessarily that the task must be accomplished within a certain amount of time. However, after the student initially acquires the skill, the specialist then becomes more interested in efficiency or fluency. At this point, adding a measure of rate, duration, or fluency is often appropriate.

For example, if a student has mastered the steps in writing a check to pay a bill, then the teacher might include a criterion, such as "within one minute." The student would then practice the skills until the task was accomplished within the specified time frame. The specialist should prepare objectives that ensure that the student has not only acquired a new skill, but that the skill is performed efficiently within a suitable time. For example, if the student was able to write a legible and legal check for a purchase at a store, but

needed five minutes to do so, mastery of this skill would not facilitate his or her assimilation into the real environment in which the completion of such a task is expected to take only a minute or less.

Analyzing the Task

Traditional Task Analysis. The next step in designing unique instruction is to analyze the task or skill. For sequential tasks—such as baking a cake, doing the laundry, traveling to the school cafeteria, and using the telephone to call 911—a traditional task analysis is the ideal approach. This analysis involves listing the steps that are required to complete the task in their proper sequence. To ensure that the sequence is complete and in the correct order, it may be helpful for the teacher of students with visual impairments actually to perform the task that is being analyzed and to write down each step as it is completed.

One aspect of task analysis that must be addressed is the degree of specificity in the steps. A cursory task analysis of brushing one's teeth, for example, may take about 10 steps; however, a detailed task analysis of the same skill may take up to 30 steps. In general, the characteristics of the student dictate how specific the analysis needs to be. For academic students without additional disabilities, a concise task analysis is often appropriate. As the severity of additional cognitive and physical disabilities increases, the detail that is needed in the task analysis also increases. A more detailed task analysis allows the specialist to pinpoint smaller parts of the overall task for targeted instruction. Table 6.3 presents an example of the difference between a concise and a detailed task analysis.

Component Analysis. Some tasks that students with visual impairments need to accomplish are not sequential tasks and, therefore, do not lend themselves to a traditional task analysis. Examples of such tasks include communicating with others, advocating for oneself, and using functional literacy tools to acquire information. Although such a task may have typical starting and ending points, much of it is not accomplished in a set sequence. In such instances, listing the essential components of the task may be more helpful. As an example, consider the following components of the task of making small talk at a party:

♦ Mingling with others in search of a conversation partner or partners;

♦ Gaining entry to a conversation that is already in progress;

♦ Approaching someone who is not already engaged in a conversation;

♦ Introducing oneself;

♦ Acknowledging others as they enter the conversation;

♦ Shaking hands, if appropriate;

♦ Maintaining eye contact with a communication partner or partners;

♦ Taking turns speaking without monopolizing a conversation;

♦ Introducing a new appropriate topic;

♦ Leaving a conversation with one other participant; and

♦ Leaving a conversation with two or more participants.

This approach allows the teacher of students with visual impairments to target the various components at different times during instruction, and then work with the student to pull all the components together in real-life situations. It should be noted that many of these components (such as introducing oneself and shaking hands) are common to other social interactions, and the specialist should make appropriate linkages to these situations. (See the discussion on providing unifying experiences earlier in this chapter.)

Selecting an Appropriate Instructional Approach

Once the goals and objectives have been specified and the task has been analyzed in some way, the teacher of students with visual impairments needs to consider the approach that he or she will use to teach the new task or skill. Basic instructional approaches include lecture, demonstration, questioning and guided discussion, experiential learning, and direct instruction. The choice of an instructional approach—or, in reality, generally a combination of approaches—is based on the task or skill that is being taught and the characteristics and needs of the student.

Lecture. In using the lecture approach, the teacher mainly provides verbal information in a fairly linear fashion, that is, the teacher talks, and the students listen. Effective lectures engage students by asking for their input, posing a question to spark discussion, giving a puzzle or dilemma to solve, and so forth. In other words, to be effective, lectures must generally be combined with other approaches to ensure a high-quality learning experience. Lectures are typically used in academic subjects to provide students with information about 18th-century poets, the chemical proper-

Table 6.3. Task Analyses: Making a Ham-and-Cheese Sandwich

Concise Task Analysis	Detailed Analysis
1. Gather the needed ingredients and the plate.	1. Get the package of bread from the pantry and place it on the counter.
	2. Get the package of ham from the refrigerator and place it on the counter.
	3. Get the package of cheese from the refrigerator and place it on the counter.
	4. Get the squeeze bottle of mustard from the refrigerator and place it on the counter.
	5. Get a plate from the cabinet and place it on the counter.
2. Place one slice of bread on the plate.	6. Open the bread wrapper.
	7. Grasp one slice of bread.
	8. Place the slice of bread on the plate.
3. Place a slice of ham on the bread.	9. Open the package of ham.
	10. Grasp one slice of ham.
	11. Place the slice of ham on top of the slice of bread.
4. Place a slice of cheese on the ham.	12. Open the package of cheese.
	13. Grasp one slice of cheese.
	14. Place the slice of cheese on top of the slice of ham.
5. Apply mustard to the second slice of bread.	15. Open the mustard squeeze bottle.
	16. Grasp the second slice of bread and place on the plate next to the first slice.
	17. Squeeze the mustard on the second slice of bread.
6. Place the second slice of bread on top of the cheese with the mustard side down.	18. Pick up the second slice of bread.
	19. Place the second slice of bread on top of the cheese with the mustard side down.

ties of acids, or the philosophical and historical foundation of the "enlightened society," for example. When students with visual impairments are instructed through lectures, these lectures are typically offered by general education teachers in the core curricular areas. In such instances, the suggestions for modifying instruction in Chapter 5 should be consulted.

Given the unique nature of the disability-specific skills needed by students with visual impairments, lecturing is rarely the approach of choice in teaching areas of the expanded core curriculum, since these areas typically represent skills instead of knowledge. One can imagine the absurdity of lecturing a student on raking leaves in a yard and then expect that he or she will go out after school and carry out the instructions. Even if it was possible for the student to do so, another instructional approach (such as demonstration and/or direct instruction) would probably be more effective and enjoyable.

Demonstrations. Demonstrations involve the teacher's modeling of something that the students observe and then imitate, as described in Chapter 5. Since such demonstrations rely primarily on receiving visual information to imitate, this approach must be used selectively in providing unique instruction to students with visual impairments. Some students with low vision may be able to gather information visually from a demonstration and later imitate what was demonstrated. A thorough functional vision assessment is necessary to determine if it would be possible for a particular student to do so. However, for most students with low vision and all students who are blind, the use of other instructional strategies will make demonstrations more effective.

Physical guidance (full physical contact and cooperative action to perform a task), physical prompting (limited physical contact only as necessary to perform a task), graduated guidance (a steady decrease in physical contact over time to increase a student's independence in accomplishing a task), and other prompting procedures allow the teacher of students with visual impairments to use a form of demonstration or modeling to teach many skills. For example, using a hand-over-hand approach (physical guidance) to teach a student to spread peanut butter on a slice of bread, to form the capital letter *G* properly, or to insert a CD into a CD player is a modified form of demonstration—a strategy typically used in direct instruction. Such strategies are addressed in more detail later in the chapter.

Questioning and Guided Discussion. A teacher uses questioning and guided discussion to permit students to explore topics for themselves, with the teacher serving a guiding—rather than a directing or dictating—role. This teaching approach can be used effectively with students who are blind or visually impaired by having them explore areas that involve problem solving, self-advocacy, and other social skills. Such a discussion and/or questioning session may center, for example, on why a birthday party was not an enjoyable event for a student. If it is determined through questioning and discussion that the student was unable to locate his or her friends to talk with them, then this determination may lead the

teacher to suggest strategies to address this problem in the future and/or may lay the foundation for future specialized lessons in specific areas of social skills.

One often hears that teachers need to listen more to students with visual impairments, to allow the instructional process to be more of an interactive experience than a linear, one-way event. If students are asked appropriate questions and guided to explore their thoughts and feelings in a nonjudgmental and supportive manner, they will greatly contribute to an active and enabling learning process. Often, questioning and guided instruction (facilitating instruction with verbal prompts) are used to supplement other teaching approaches. For example, an effective lecture combines strategic questioning and discussion so the students are truly engaged in learning the content of the lecture.

Experiential Learning. In experiential learning, the environment is arranged to motivate children to explore, investigate, ponder, and question so they can construct knowledge for themselves. This approach is consistent with the Montessori approach to learning, in which teachers are facilitators of learning, rather than directors of it; it may also be called discovery learning. A fundamental element that is critical to the success of experiential learning is the use of visual motivation, observation, and imitation. Because of the key role of vision in experiential learning, this approach is not usually relied on in teaching students with visual impairments.

Experiential learning, though, should not be confused with providing children with opportunities for learning by doing, an approach that *is* used and should be used often by teachers of students with visual impairments. However, when the specialist uses actual experiences to teach a unique skill, the approach is called direct instruction. The actual experience is simply the technique or tool that is used to deliver the instruction.

Direct Instruction. Direct instruction is often the instructional approach of choice for teaching students with visual impairments, since a visual impairment can restrict the natural types of learning that occur through modeling, observation, and imitation. Direct instruction is an active approach to addressing areas of the expanded core curriculum, rather than leaving these areas to chance development.

Diagnostic teaching can be considered a variation of direct teaching. This instructional approach originated with the teaching of students with learning disabilities and other learning problems. The notion was that the behavior of these students was so complex that the only way truly to assess their needs was to engage the students in instruction and assess their responses to strategic changes in specific instructional techniques. Diagnostic teaching skillfully interweaves the processes of instruction and assessment. Since each teaching session is viewed as an opportunity to gain further understanding of a student's needs and abilities, the maximum use of instructional time is ensured. If a particular teaching technique is not found to be effective, then the teacher—through the use of diagnostic teaching strategies—determines this fact quickly and changes the teaching technique. If, as in traditional instruction the teacher waits until the end of an instructional unit or the next examination to assess the skill and then finds that the student has not been making appropriate progress, much valuable learning time will have been lost.

Integrated within the use of direct instruction are the principles of the special methods discussed earlier in this chapter: providing (1) concrete experiences, (2) learning by doing, and (3) unifying experiences. Also, the basic strategies for modifying materials and instruction that were presented in Chapter 5 need to be applied as appropriate in specialized instruction. For example, if a teacher was teaching a student to cut an apple pie into equal slices, he or she might use a simple raised-line drawing to preview the process, thereby providing a "dry run" before the real activity. Furthermore, in direct instruction, the specialist can use various instructional strategies, described next, to promote learning: modeling and guidance, prompting, shaping, and chaining.

Choosing Appropriate Instructional Strategies

The teacher uses a variety of instructional strategies, often in combination, to teach new skills to students with visual impairments and to foster higher levels of proficiency and independence in use of those skills. Specific instructional strategies include modeling and guidance, prompting, shaping, and chaining. The teacher should select the strategy or strategies that will best assist the student in learning a particular task. For example, if a student is learning to launder clothes, the teacher may teach sequential steps in the task (chaining), accompanied initially with physical guidance through the various steps. Later, after the student has gained a basic level of proficiency, the teacher may need only to provide minimal verbal prompts. The teacher should be well versed in all strategies, but should select carefully those strategies that match both the task or skill being taught and the student's functioning level.

Modeling and Guidance

In modeling, a teacher of students with visual impairments provides a model or demonstration of the task or skill, and the student uses this model as a guide to attempt to perform the task or skill. For students with visual impairments, hand-over-hand (the teacher's hands on top of the student's) and hand-under-hand (the teacher's hands beneath the student's)—both forms of physical guidance—are common techniques. The teacher of students with visual impairments stands or sits behind the student, places his or her hands over or under the student's hands, and guides the student through the steps in the task. In this approach, the model provided by the teacher and the application by the student occur simultaneously, not sequentially.

Physical modeling or physical guidance is an extremely efficient way to teach new skills. A lesson that uses physical modeling to teach a student to put peanut butter on a slice of bread, for example, can be accomplished quickly, whereas a lesson that relies on oral guidance would probably be inefficient and is less likely to yield success. Oral guidance may be used to supplement physical guidance and, as such, is actually a form of prompting (described next) unless the skill being taught is an oral skill (such as how to use voice inflection to convey a message). Visual modeling may be used with some students with low vision, but even then is most often paired with some physical and verbal guidance.

The technique called *graduated guidance* varies the amount of oral and/or physical guidance that a student needs to complete the task. As the student is provided with instruction and repeated practice in the task, he or she will require less and less guidance from the specialist. The amount of guidance is "graduated" from full guidance to less and less guidance as the student is ready. At some point, the amount of guidance is so minimal that it actually becomes a prompt. The exact point at which one leads to the other is immaterial; the important factor is that the specialist provides less and less intervention as the student is able to complete more of the task himself or herself.

Prompting

Prompts allow a teacher of students with visual impairments to provide minimal assistance—visual, tactile-physical, and/or auditory—to a student so the student can complete a task that he or she has not yet completely mastered. Oral prompts are commonly used in learning situations in which the teacher will provide a "hint" that will remind or stimulate the student to complete the task. Prompts may start out with direct hints and then later move to general ones. For example, if a student is selecting the appropriate tool to saw a board into two pieces, the teacher may provide an overt prompt, such as "Do you need a saw or a hammer?" As the student becomes more skilled in the task, the teacher may offer a less specific prompt: "What tool do you use to saw a board in two?" After the student has mastered the task, the teacher may need only to say, "What do you need to do next?"

Oral prompts are often effective with students who are blind, since these students use a sensory channel (hearing) that is most often intact. Visual prompts, on the other hand, may be effective for some students with low vision, depending on their usable working distance, visual efficiency, acuity, field, and so forth. For example, pointing to a saw in the workshop may offer an effective visual prompt to some students with low vision. A thorough functional vision assessment is needed to determine what types of, and under what conditions, visual prompts are effective for a given student with low vision.

Various types of prompts are frequently combined—visual with physical, oral with visual, and so forth—and for students with visual impairments, this practice often provides the optimum level of information that a student needs to complete a task. For instance, if a student is learning to select a favorite beverage from a soft-drink vending machine, the teacher may say "Find the top right button" while guiding the student's hand to the top row of buttons. If a student with low vision is learning to integrate the use of visual skills into this task, the teacher may pair the same oral cue with a visual prompt, such as illuminating the correct button with a flashlight. Then as the student begins to master the skills, the teacher will eliminate one of the prompts and/or reduce the specificity of both—a technique known as fading.

Teachers should be vigilant in providing only the minimal level of prompts that is necessary and continually working toward fading prompts. The goal is to have students complete tasks independently. Alberto and Troutman (1995) offered four approaches to fading prompts:

- ◆ Decreasing assistance—providing fewer or less specific prompts as the student is able to complete more of the task independently,

- ◆ Graduated guidance—gradually reducing the physical pressure applied when providing the prompts,

- ◆ Time delay—waiting for an increasing

amount of time before providing a prompt, and

♦ Increasing assistance—moving from no prompt to the minimal prompt that is necessary to allow the student to complete the task.

One has only to observe teachers and students working together to see numerous examples of overprompting. In many cases, overprompting allows students to use a teacher's prompt to know the answer or the next step in the process without learning the subject matter or task. For example, when a teacher says "are you sure?" only after a student responds incorrectly, the student quickly learns that when the teacher questions the response, it is wrong. Although prompts are an important tool in a teacher's repertoire of instructional strategies, they can also promote learned helplessness or slow learning in a student. Therefore, adhering to the strategies just discussed for fading prompts is a way for a teacher to monitor his or her use of prompting procedures.

Shaping

Shaping is an instructional procedure in which a teacher permits a student to move gradually toward mastering a given task by accepting and reinforcing the student for the successive approximations. Consider the way shaping is used in teaching a student to spread peanut butter on a piece of toast. At first, the teacher positively reinforces the student's placement of a spoonful of peanut butter anywhere on the toast. After the student demonstrates this ability, the teacher reinforces the student for placing the peanut butter in the middle of the toast. Later, the teacher requires the student to spread the peanut butter partially to receive reinforcement. Eventually, the student needs to spread the peanut butter smoothly and evenly on the toast to receive reinforcement.

Chaining

For sequential tasks—such as making a sandwich, doing the laundry, and putting on a T-shirt—a teacher of students with visual impairments may benefit from using a chaining procedure to structure the lessons needed to learn a particular task. Chaining is a way to target a specific step in a sequential task for instruction and to teach that step until a student masters it before the teacher adds the next step in the sequence. Typically, when a teacher uses chaining, all other steps in the sequence other than the targeted (or mastered) steps are either completed by someone else or the student is "prompted through" them, often with direct physical guidance. This is a way to make a multistep task seem manageable and learnable, rather than overwhelming, for the student. Since chaining is used with sequential tasks, the teacher typically conducts a traditional task analysis (discussed earlier) before implementing instruction.

There are two types of chaining procedures: forward and backward. The *forward chain,* as the name implies, starts at the beginning of a sequence; the teacher targets the first step for instruction but completes the remaining steps for the student. For example, in the concise task analysis presented in Table 6.3 for making a ham-and-cheese sandwich, the teacher, using a forward chain, would first target the gathering of ingredients for instruction. When the student mastered that step, the teacher would target placing one slice of bread on the plate and expect the student to continue to gather the ingredients independently. This process would continue until the student completed each step in the sequence independently. During instruction on the targeted step, the teacher would make use of the prompting procedures presented earlier to guide the student's mastery of each step.

Although it may seem reasonable always to start with the first step in a sequential task, it is sometimes better to start with the last step. For example, if the teacher targets the last step in the process of making a ham and cheese sandwich—placing slices of bread together—then this step is followed immediately by the naturally reinforcing process of eating the sandwich. Targeting the last step in a sequential task for instruction is called *backward chaining.* Teachers need to evaluate each sequential task to determine if a backward chain would be more advantageous than a forward chain for a given student.

A variation of the chaining procedures is *total task presentation* (Alberto & Troutman, 1995). In this procedure, the teacher targets all the steps in the sequence for instruction, providing whatever level of prompting is necessary for the student to complete each step until the entire sequence is mastered. Alberto and Troutman suggested that this approach may be the most effective for a student who knows some or all the steps in a task but is unable to perform them in the appropriate sequence.

Selecting or Designing Instructional Materials

As part of the planning process, a teacher of students with visual impairments considers the instructional materials needed to provide high-quality specialized instruction. A primary consideration in selecting materials is whether the materials directly address, and will facilitate the teaching of, specific objectives on the student's IEP. If there is no direct match between objectives and materials, the use of such materials will be an unnecessary distraction in the instructional process.

Issues of quality and durability should also be considered. Since many instructional materials are repeatedly manipulated and explored tactilely by students with visual impairments, the materials need to be more durable than those that are explored or used visually. For example, a model of a snowflake made of flimsy, translucent tissue paper will not provide the tactile cues needed by a young student who is exploring it primarily through touch. For this student, a sturdier model, created with posterboard, will provide tactile details and needs to be coupled with exploration of real snow (if available in the student's geographic region) or snow created in a science lab.

Some materials used in unique instruction are specially designed and commercially available. Examples include slates and styli for writing braille, abaci for computing in mathematics, braille or large-print rulers for measuring, beeper balls for recreation or physical education, speech synthesizers to provide access to computers, and braille timers for use in cooking. These specialized devices and materials are identified throughout the remaining chapters of this book, along with information on where they can be obtained.

Other materials need to be modified by the teacher of students with visual impairment prior to their use in instruction. For example, before a lesson on using a key to interpret a tactile map, the teacher of students with visual impairments may adapt an existing diagram of the student's classroom in a tactile format. In such instances, the guidelines for modifying materials presented in Chapter 5 are helpful. Instructional materials should be modified to the extent needed not only to promote efficient instruction, but to facilitate a student's integration into a regular education classroom. For example, a student with low vision may use bold-line paper in an integrated classroom to benefit from instruction in penmanship provided by the general education teacher. The principle of least-restrictive modification (presented in Chapter 5) provides guidance on how to plan modifications of instructional materials.

Occasionally, the teacher of students with visual impairments needs to design a unique instructional device or material to achieve a specific objective on a student's IEP. For example, if a student with severe visual, cognitive, and physical disabilities is learning to sort recyclable materials to prepare for a community work placement, the specialist may need to construct a set of bins, place them in strategic positions to accommodate the student's physical disability, and label the bins with appropriate tactile or visual markers to facilitate efficient and accurate sorting. The design, production, and placement of these bins would probably be done in collaboration with other individuals, such as a physical or occupational therapist and a carpenter.

Addressing Increased Levels of Proficiency

Throughout all aspects of the instructional design process, a teacher of students with visual impairments needs to consider and address a student's need to increase the level of proficiency in completing tasks. Alberto and Troutman (1995) identified four levels of proficiency in students' learning:

♦ Acquisition—initial mastery of a task or skill,

♦ Fluency—the rate at which a task or skill is performed,

♦ Maintenance—continuing to perform the task or skill over time, and

♦ Generalization—performing the task or skill under various conditions.

Acquisition.   Teachers tend to concentrate their instructional efforts on having students acquire new skills or learn new tasks. The instructional approaches and strategies presented in the earlier sections of this chapter can be used to help students initially acquire skills or tasks. However, teachers often fail to provide the level of practice needed to bring a skill to a fluent level or to ensure that the skill will be maintained and generalized to other environments and under other conditions.

Fluency.   The importance of gaining sufficient fluency in a skill or task (and therefore increasing proficiency) is often overlooked in instruction. The repeated practice of acquired skills is the key to gaining fluency. Think for a moment about the kinds of routine tasks that pervade adult life: doing laundry, making a pot of coffee, lighting a fire in the fireplace, writing a check for groceries, and shampooing hair. These tasks become so routine that adults often perform them with little or no concentration. These seemingly effortless tasks become so because of ample practice.

Children share the same need for practice; they develop true mastery by having adequate time to practice skills they already know. Without adequate practice, the performance of a task is more difficult than is necessary and more inefficient. When a student can complete a task without errors and without concentrating on specific steps, he or she has practiced the task sufficiently.

Maintenance.   After a student has gained an appropriate level of fluency through daily practice, then practice sessions can be offered periodically to ensure that he or she maintains the skill. If the teacher finds that a student is not maintaining the skill, then it will be necessary for the teacher to reteach the skill and provide more frequent (less "periodic") practice sessions. The key is to find an appropriate pace of review and frequency of practice sessions that will ensure that the student maintains the skill, but not to the extent that the student becomes bored with the instruction.

Generalization.   The ultimate level of learning is generalization, that is, applying skills or tasks in new environments, with different materials or under new conditions. For example, if a student learns and maintains the task of meeting unfamiliar people with a verbal greeting and a handshake in the school environment in the presence of the specialist, then the student would show generalization of this skill when he or she greets unfamiliar people in the community in the presence of his or her parents and, finally, when alone.

A basic condition that must be met before a teacher of students with visual impairments promotes generalization is that the student has acquired, practiced, and maintained the skill or task under consideration. After this condition is met, the teacher takes steps to promote the generalization of the skill or task. Mastropieri and Scruggs (1994, p. 41) offered the following strategies for promoting generalization:

Train sufficient examples. This strategy involves using a variety of different examples during instruction. For example, if a student is learning to microwave frozen meals, then he or she should be exposed to a number of different microwave ovens, other than the one used at school. Ideally, the microwave oven used at home should be included.

Train loosely. This strategy involves allowing the student to respond in a variety of ways and under different conditions during instruction, rather than being overly structured (as is likely to be the case in initial instruction). For example, if teaching a student to greet friends, the teacher needs to allow and encourage him or her to use a variety of greetings, such as "Hello," "Howdy," "Hey," "What's going on?" "How's it going?" and "What's up?"

Use indiscriminable contingencies. This strategy is typically applied as part of a highly structured approach to teaching and reinforcing a student's behaviors (see the next section on applied behavior analysis). It involves arranging a variety of learning situation so a student is less certain about when he or she will receive reinforcement for good work. For example, a teacher may arrange several different opportunities for a student to use turn-taking skills, rewarding him or her when these skills are displayed.

Use role-play activities. In this strategy, the teacher arranges situations that are typical of nonclassroom or "real-life" environments in which students can act out what they would do in given situations. For example, the teacher may use role-playing activities to allow the student to practice telephoning 911 in a simulated emergency.

Promote self-monitoring. This strategy involves teaching the student to monitor and manage his or her own behavior in various settings. For example, a student who is attempting to increase eye contact with others may be given a counter to hold in his or her pocket. Each time the student uses eye contact throughout the day, he or she can click the counter once. At the end of the day, the student can chart the total number on a line chart to measure his or her progress.

Reinforce generalization. This strategy involves providing overt feedback and reinforcement when a behavior is used in another setting or under different conditions. For example, if a student is

learning to stay on task during special instructional time, he or she may be specifically reinforced for the same behavior by other teachers or his or her parents throughout the day.

Retrain. This strategy involves teaching the targeted behavior or skill in other settings and under different conditions. For example, if a student is learning eating skills at lunchtime at school, the same teaching techniques are used during a field trip to a local restaurant, at dinnertime at home, on a school picnic, and so forth.

Applied Behavior Analysis. Most students respond to high-quality instruction in which reinforcement is "casually" provided, that is, they receive feedback and praise when the teacher feels it is appropriate to give them, but not according to a specified schedule. Other students need a more systematic approach to learning in which strict procedures are followed for presenting tasks or steps in an instructional session, prompting and reinforcing students, and charting students' progress.

If a student needs a more systematic approach to learning, the teacher should consider using the strategies of applied behavior analysis. Applied behavior analysis incorporates the principles of behavior modification and structured reinforcement procedures to increase desired behaviors in students. The term *behavior* is defined broadly to include both academic skills (such as fluent reading, accurate spelling, and the classification and categorization of objects) and social skills (like taking turns, interacting appropriately with others, and following directions) or any other actions that can be defined objectively and observed repeatedly. Applied behavior analysis uses specific instructional (or "experimental") designs to determine whether an intervention is responsible for the resulting changes in a student's behaviors. See Sidebar 6.5 for a case study on the use of applied behavior analysis.

There are many resources on applied behavior analysis. However, *Applied Behavior Analysis*

Case Study: Using Applied Behavior Analysis

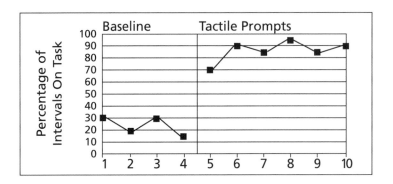

Fred is a 17-year-old student with multiple impairments, including low vision (20/400 OU), moderate cognitive impairments, and motor impairments (mild hemiplegia). His IEP states that he will participate in vocational training at school, designed to teach skills identified as prerequisites for the transition to supported employment. Fred's teachers have noted that Fred shows frequent off-task behaviors during his vocational training sessions. They believe that these off-task behaviors contribute to the lack of progress Fred has shown in achieving the prerequisite skills.

The educational team decided to implement a simple AB design intervention. "AB" refers to the two stages of the design: "A" refers to the baseline stage and "B" to the intervention stage. If a change in the level of on-task behavior is seen between the baseline and intervention phases, then the intervention was successful. The advantage of using applied behavior analysis is that the student's behavior is charted each day to show the effects of the intervention and to signal if changes are needed in the intervention program.

Baseline data for Fred were collected for four days using the interval recording method. The teachers divided one daily 15-minute skill session into 90 10-second intervals. During each 10-second interval, a plus sign was recorded if Fred was on task at any point in the interval, and a minus sign was recorded if Fred was off task during the entire interval. The "percentage of intervals on task" was determined for each day's session and recorded as baseline data. These data were plotted on a line chart and found to be fairly stable across the four days. During the baseline phase, Fred was shown to be on task no more than 30 percent of the time.

Intervention consisted of a simple tactile prompt. The teacher would gently touch Fred's shoulder whenever Fred was observed to be off task. The program was explained to Fred, who readily agreed to accept this signal as a reminder to return to task. Interval recording was again used to collect data. The percentage of intervals on task was recorded for the intervention period as shown on the graph.

This relatively simple intervention allowed Fred to increase his time on task during skill-training sessions to around 90 percent. Continued intervention is needed to achieve a level closer to 100 percent and to ensure that this behavior is maintained and, ultimately, generalized to other settings and conditions. To facilitate generalization, plans were made to place Fred in a half-day supported employment position in the next school term.

MARGARET C. ROBINSON
Texas Tech University, Lubbock

for Teachers, by Alberto and Troutman (1995), is suggested as an initial text, since it is comprehensive, practical, and easy to read.

Planning Appropriate Evaluations of Instruction

Each lesson should include an evaluation to determine if or to what extent the student benefited from the instruction. The daily evaluation should be tied directly to the behavioral objective. If the objective was stated properly, the evaluation component will indicate how the lesson should be evaluated and the criterion for mastery.

For example, consider the students presented in Sidebar 6.4. Sally needs instruction in maintaining eye contact. The condition states that when she is reminded by an adult, she will make eye contact on four out of five occasions. So within the lesson, the teacher will provide instruction on the importance of eye contact, along with at least five occasions and reminders for Sally to make eye contact. Then the teacher will chart Sally's success in doing so. These behaviors can be recorded as a simple frequency count. If Sally is successful in making eye contact on four out of the five occasions with a reminder, then she has met the criterion. In situations in which she does not make eye contact, the teacher may want to use a more direct prompting method, such as a physical prompt (by lightly touching Sally's chin). Noting the earlier discussion on the importance of practice, the teacher would want to see Sally demonstrate eye contact over a period of several days, then with no reminder, and then under different circumstances and in various environments.

Generally, daily evaluation involves tallying or charting behaviors in some systematic way as described in the example just given. However, other informal assessment techniques may be helpful in evaluation, such as using checklists of skills, interviews with students and others, and observations. (See Chapter 3 for a detailed discussion of informal assessment techniques.) It should be kept in mind, though, that daily evaluation should be tied directly to the objective for the lesson, and

the evaluation method should assess the effectiveness of that lesson and thus the student's mastery of the lesson's objective.

DELIVERING INSTRUCTION

After appropriate planning and preparation, the next step in instruction is to deliver the lesson. The approach should be to deliver the desired content, engage the student actively in learning, and have the student master the objective of the lesson. To deliver instruction, consider the following guidelines:

1. State the purpose and importance of the lesson. The student should know clearly the focus of the lesson and should not have to wonder what is being taught.

2. Review previous material or lessons as appropriate. If this is a continuing lesson, one may start with: "Yesterday we . . ."

3. Connect the lesson to the student's experiential background. Learning is more efficient and meaningful when it builds on a student's background experiences. Without this link, the student may not have the understanding or conceptual knowledge for the lesson.

4. Present the lesson, providing guided practice and prompts as appropriate. Ensure that the student is staying on task and is engaged in the lesson. If not, redirect him or her to the task at hand. Check whether the student understands by asking questions and periodically reviewing the important points of the lesson. Praise the student appropriately, but do not overpraise him or her.

5. Give the student an opportunity for independent practice. Avoid overprompting the student during practice time.

6. Conclude the lesson with an evaluation component and provide the student with feedback on his or her performance. Tie the lesson to the next

lesson by telling the student what can be expected the next day.

SUMMARY

Teachers of students with visual impairments are responsible for designing and delivering effective instruction in the areas of the expanded core curriculum. To do so, they must develop goals and objectives on the basis of a student's assessed needs and design lessons to meet the established objectives. Although much of the work of a specialist in visual impairment is done in collaboration with other members of the educational team, the specialist must be well prepared to deliver direct instruction as appropriate and needed. The general strategies presented in this chapter will help the teacher with this important role. The remainder of this book presents information on teaching specific content areas.

ACTIVITIES

1. Prepare a detailed task analysis for a daily living skill and a recreation skill. Select one of these task analyses and present the lesson to a classmate to ensure that all the steps are included in the correct sequence.

2. Observe a teacher of students with visual impairments conducting a lesson with a child who is blind or who has low vision. Note the special techniques and materials that the teacher uses and the student's response to the instruction. Later, discuss the lesson with the teacher to gain his or her insights into its effectiveness.

3. For the student observed in Activity 2, write a measurable long-term goal and three to five short-term objectives or benchmarks that would allow the student to achieve the long-term goal. Share the goal and objectives with the child's teacher of students with visual impairments to gain his or her perspective on their appropriateness.

4. Prepare a detailed lesson plan for teaching a specific skill in the expanded core curriculum. Include the goal and objective, prerequisites, special materials, detailed steps in presenting the skill, and an evaluation procedure.

5. With permission from the parents and school administrators, observe an IEP meeting for a student who is blind or who has low vision. Make note of the specific references to the expanded core curriculum and whether the resulting IEP appropriately addresses the unique skill areas.

REFERENCES

Alberto, P. A., & Troutman, A. C. (1995). *Applied behavior analysis for teachers* (4th ed.). Columbus, OH: Merrill.

Hatlen, P. (1996). *Core curriculum for blind and visually impaired students, including those with additional impairments* [On-line]. Available: http://www.tsbvi.edu/education/corecurric.htm

Lowenfeld, B. (Ed.). (1973). T*he visually handicapped child in school.* New York: John Day.

MacCuspie, P. A. (1996). *Promoting acceptance of children with disabilities: From tolerance to inclusion.* Halifax, NS: Atlantic Provinces Special Education Authority.

Mastropieri, M. A., & Scruggs, T. E. (1994). *Effective instruction in special education* (2nd ed.). Austin, TX: Pro-Ed.

Rosenberg, M. S., O'Shea, L., & O'Shea, D. J. (1998). *Student teacher to master teacher: A practical guide for educating students with special needs.* Columbus, OH: Merrill.

Willoughby, D., & Duffy, S. (1989). *Handbook for itinerant and resource teachers of blind and visually impaired students.* Baltimore, MD: National Federation of the Blind.

R E S O U R C E S

Suggested Resources for Planning Instruction in Unique Skills

Resource	Type	Source	Description
Applied Behavior Analysis for Teachers (Alberto & Troutman, 1995)	Textbook	Merrill	A comprehensive, practical, easy-to-read text on the principles of and strategies for using applied behavior analysis with students with special needs.
Core Curriculum for Blind and Visually Impaired Students, Including Those with Additional Disabilities (Hatlen, 1996)	Article	On-line: Available: http://www.tsbvi. education/corecurric. htm	An in-depth discussion of the expanded core curriculum for visually impaired students and its delivery.
Handbook for Itinerant and Resource Teachers of Blind and Visually Impaired Students (Willoughby & Duffy, 1989)	Book	National Federation of the Blind	Practical, comprehensive, and creative advice about the education of students who are visually impaired. Helpful to both new and experienced teachers.
Student Teacher to Master Teacher (Rosenberg, O'Shea, & O'Shea, 1998)	Textbook	Merrill	Practical guidelines for planning and delivering instruction to students in special education programs, emphasizing processes and general strategies, rather than specific disabilities.

Contact information for each of the resources listed will be found in the Sources of Products, Materials, Equipment, and Services section at the back of this book.

PART TWO

Modifying and Designing Instruction

CHAPTER 7

Early Childhood

Virginia E. Bishop

KEY POINTS

- ◆ The foundation for everything that is learned in school and in adult life is established during the early childhood years, typically from birth through age 5.
- ◆ Children who are visually impaired need early and ongoing intervention to address their unique developmental needs.
- ◆ Parents and other family members play a key and essential role in fostering the early development of a child who is visually impaired.
- ◆ The teacher of students with visual impairments must play an active part on the educational team to ensure that the assessment and intervention activities for a child who is visually impaired are appropriate throughout the early childhood years.
- ◆ High-quality intervention and appropriate educational and family services during the early childhood years help ensure that a child with a visual impairment will enter kindergarten or first grade with the necessary skills to be successful.

VIGNETTE

Jan Ferris, a teacher of students with visual impairments and now a consultant for the county's infant intervention program, watched with genuine pleasure as Toby Cordele mouthed the soft, blue-and-white, rubberlike penguin. Toby, 8 months old and with light perception only, sat on the floor between his mother's legs. At the moment, he leaned back against her in comfort, clutching the penguin with both hands and happily chewing its yellow beak, but Jan considered this a well-deserved break. Toby's mother, Alicia, had been eager to show Jan Toby's latest accomplishment. When Jan had seen Toby two weeks ago, he could maintain a propped sitting posture only as long as both hands were on the floor. Today, Toby maintained his position with one hand while he used the other to follow and then grasp the little penguin as Alicia moved it about on the floor.

Alicia next grasped the penguin and moved it just a bit—perhaps an inch—away from Toby. Toby kept his grip on it. Alicia moved it again, and then again, each time just a bit farther from Toby. Toby chortled and gripped the penguin. When Alicia had moved the penguin perhaps 6 inches, Toby's left hand slipped off it. Alicia held the penguin steady and waited. Toby's left hand waved for a moment

225

and then relocated the penguin. Alicia let go, and Toby pulled the penguin back for another chew. Jan watched with interest. Was Toby building the concept of object permanence? Did it "count" if his right hand remained in contact with the penguin when his left came off? How long would it be before Toby would reach for the penguin when *neither* hand retained contact with it?

Next, Alicia placed Toby on his stomach on a small quilt on the floor. Quickly, Toby pushed himself up into a hands-and-knees position. From this position, he rocked enthusiastically, but his hands did not come off the floor. Toby was not ready to try to crawl yet. Jan thought of the connection between reaching for a lost object and crawling forward to retrieve one. She decided to recommend that Alicia give Toby lots of "floor time" and interact with him using favorite toys, such as the soft penguin. Maybe by the next time Jan saw him, Toby would be able to use one hand to grasp the penguin from a hands-and-knees position. "Tiny steps like these lead to big milestones," she thought.

INTRODUCTION

The early childhood years lay the foundation for everything that is learned throughout school and adult life, so it is imperative that the educational opportunities and experiences provided during this period are designed to promote a child's optimum growth and development. Teachers of students with visual impairments typically have responsibilities for students from infancy through high school. Although most of these teachers are prepared as elementary or secondary teachers, they must also have knowledge and skills to provide educational services to infants and preschoolers who are visually impaired. Collaboration and teamwork with families, caregivers, early childhood intervention specialists and others are essential for addressing the needs of young children with visual impairments.

A number of basic assumptions support the importance of intervention programs for infants, toddlers, and preschoolers with visual impairments. These assumptions center on the role that vision plays in early development and provide clear justification for early intervention services:

◆ Vision is the primary data-gathering system of humans, providing both near and distance information and integrating information holistically. All the other senses together cannot provide equal information to the brain (Gesell, Ilg, & Bullis, 1949).

◆ Vision is the feedback system for many other developing systems in young children (Als, Tronick, & Brazelton, 1976). When the visual system is impaired, other body systems do not have a monitoring system to ensure their smooth and timely development.

◆ Vision occurs in the brain. The eyes simply collect data and send it to the brain for processing. The two systems are interrelated, interconnected, and interactive.

◆ Vision cannot be "conserved." Vision must be used and practiced to be effective, and the most critical time for visual "practice" is in the first few years of life when eye–brain connections are being made.

◆ Age at onset of the visual impairment is a critical factor in development. Visual impairments that exist at birth (i.e, are congenital) are more likely to cause developmental delays than are visual impairments that occur later (i.e, are adventitious).

◆ At least 60 percent of the current population of young children with disabilities have multiple disabilities, and visual impairments are likely to be among those disabilities (Bishop, 1991b). Since the visual system is neurologically based, any impairment of the neurological system (including the brain) can also affect vision.

◆ Hearing is not a motivator equal to vision in encouraging an infant to reach for objects. There is a mismatch in the timing between when an infant is physically ready to reach (by about 5 months) and when his or her auditory processing ability can attach some meaning to sound (the last quarter of the first year) (Barraga & Erin, 1992). The development of reach is especially critical for infants with visual impairments, since the use of hands to explore the environment and attach meaning to the world is even more important for them than it is for infants who make greater use of vision.

◆ Development occurs in sequential steps, but the timing varies with the individual child. Also, development proceeds in an organized, predictable way—both for children with visual impairments and for those who are sighted.

◆ The early years, from birth to about age 6, are especially critical for the development of children with visual impairments. Sighted children learn a great deal spontaneously and incidentally during these years, but visual impairment interferes with the natural ability to observe and imitate and to understand relationships between objects and actions.

◆ There are windows of opportunity for development and learning. The first 6 to 8 weeks of life are critical in stimulating retinal function, and the early childhood years are crucial in learning most other skills.

Given the importance of the early years for children with visual impairments, early intervention is essential. Frequently children and youths with visual impairments who did not receive early intervention services have gaps in their knowledge, experience, and understanding of the world. It is difficult for these children to catch up with their peers who are sighted unless these gaps are addressed at home and in their school programs. Early intervention services are now mandated by law in recognition of the importance of these services to children who are visually impaired.

This chapter begins by discussing the role of the teacher of students with visual impairments in facilitating early learning of infants and pre-schoolers with visual impairments. It then presents several unique aspects of early childhood intervention programs: federal mandates and policy, special teams and teamwork, individualized program plans, and work with families. The remainder of the chapter focuses on strategies for assessment and evaluation, intervention, and transition. Although some of these topics were addressed in earlier chapters of this book, there are unique aspects of each area that apply to services for infants and preschoolers with visual impairments. For this reason, each topic is addressed here within the context of visual impairment and early childhood.

ROLE OF THE TEACHER OF STUDENTS WITH VISUAL IMPAIRMENTS

The teacher of students with visual impairments plays a vital role in ensuring that infants and preschoolers receive high-quality early childhood services. The role of the teacher is to do the following:

◆ Participate in and facilitate the initial screening, comprehensive assessment, and ongoing assessments;

◆ Participate in the development of the child's Individualized Family Service Plan (IFSP);

◆ Collaborate with families and other caregivers, early childhood intervention specialists, medical personnel, and others concerning the impact of a visual impairment on development and learning and concerning appropriate intervention strategies;

◆ Provide resources, information, and referrals to families and others who are involved in the child's early education;

◆ Provide direct instruction in areas of the expanded core curriculum (such as concept development and prebraille skills) as appropriate; and

◆ Ensure a coordinated transition from home- to school-based programs and from preschool to kindergarten.

The teacher also plays an essential role in working with students with additional disabilities; strategies focusing on students with visual impairments and additional disabilites and resources for teachers appear later in this chapter.

ASPECTS OF EARLY CHILDHOOD INTERVENTION

Federal Mandates and Policy

Eligibility for Programs

Early childhood special education is not just a downward extension of special education. Whereas special education is concerned with modification, remediation, and rehabilitation, early childhood special services generally provide intervention to prevent or minimize delays in development. The focus is on maximizing capabilities at an age when foundations are being laid for future growth and learning. Therefore, the regulations and standards that govern special education may not always be appropriate for young children.

P.L. 99-457 (the 1986 amendments to the Education for All Handicapped Children Act of 1975, P.L. 94-142) mandated preschool special education from birth to age 3, but individual states were allowed considerable latitude in designing their programs. Each state had to designate a "lead agency" to oversee programs for children with disabilities from birth to age 3, but was allowed to define *developmental delay* and other criteria for eligibility for these services. Furthermore, disability-related categorical labels were not required, and visual impairment often fell under the broad term *sensory impairment* or the description "at risk for delay." Early intervention services had to include a multidisciplinary assessment, an IFSP, and the monitoring of each plan by a "case manager," to ensure the timely delivery of all services described in the IFSP. (Programs for children aged 3–5 followed special education guidelines that required an Individualized Education Program [IEP] and all procedural safeguards guaranteed to school-age students with disabilities.)

The division in policy between children from birth to age 3 and those aged 3–5 led to different service plans for the two age groups. The states that designated their departments of education as their lead agencies (less than half the states) were able to develop smoother transitions between their early intervention and preschool programs. However, the states where the lead agency was *not* the state department of education, where it was, for example, the state department of health, have had to make extra efforts to coordinate services and personnel between the two groups.

In 1990, the Education for All Handicapped Children Act was renamed the Individuals with Disabilities Education Act (IDEA), P.L.101-476. The 1997 amendments to IDEA (P.L. 105-17) shifted the Early Intervention Program for Infants and Toddlers with Disabilities to Part C of IDEA, and early intervention programs are sometimes referred to as Part C programs. Under the 1997 regulations, early intervention is to be provided for children under age 3 who are experiencing developmental delays or who have any physical or mental conditions that have a high probability of causing developmental delays (20 U.S.C. 1432). The IFSP focuses on infants and toddlers and their families and must include a number of statements and time lines that clearly outline why intervention is needed, what kind of intervention it will be, who will provide it and how often, and in what environment it will be provided. The IFSP must also designate a service coordinator (formerly called a case manager) who will ensure that the plan is implemented and will coordinate the participation of all agencies involved. Sidebar 7.1 summarizes the current requirements for IFSPs.

Identification and Referral

Part of the legal mandate for services to young children with disabilities and their families is what is known as a "child find" system. According to this system, each state is required to have a plan for locating and evaluating all children (including infants and toddlers) with disabilities and referring them for service. Each state is also responsible for providing "full educational opportunity" to these children, from birth to age 21. Local school districts must implement their state's plan and are

Federal Requirements for IFSPs

SIDEBAR 7.1

1. "A statement of the infant's or toddler's present levels of physical development, cognitive development, communication development, social or emotional development, and adaptive development, based on objective criteria;

2. A statement of the family's resources, priorities, and concerns relating to enhancing the development of the family's infant or toddler with a disability;

3. A statement of the major outcomes expected to be achieved for the infant or toddler and the family, and the criteria, procedures, and timelines used to determine the degree to which progress toward achieving the outcomes is being made and whether modifications or revisions of the outcomes or services are necessary;

4. A statement of specific early intervention services necessary to meet the unique needs of the infant or toddler and the family, including the frequency, intensity, and method of delivering services;

5. A statement of the natural environments in which early intervention services shall appropriately be provided, including a justification of the extent, if any, to which the services will not be provided in a natural environment;

6. The projected dates for initiation of services and the anticipated duration of those services;

7. The identification of the service coordinator from the profession most immediately relevant to the infant's or toddler's or family's needs (or who is otherwise qualified to carry out all applicable responsibilities under this part), who will be responsible for the implementation of the plan and coordination with other agencies and persons; and

8. The steps to be taken supporting the transition of the toddler with a disability to preschool or other appropriate services."

Source: 20 U.S.C. 1436, § 636(d) (June 4, 1997).

---

thus responsible for finding, evaluating, and providing appropriate educational programs. In the case of infants and toddlers, these educational programs include services to families.

When an infant or toddler with a suspected disability is located, he or she is referred to a local early intervention agency. Although different agencies may have different intake procedures, all should have personnel who are knowledgeable about visual impairments, review the child's and parents' medical histories or family records, and note any indicators in these records that suggest the possibility of a visual impairment. Vision screening should follow, conducted by personnel who have been trained to do this. If a visual impairment is suspected, the child should be further evaluated by an eye care specialist (preferably a pediatric ophthalmologist). After this, the teacher of students with visual impairments needs to conduct a functional vision assessment and a learning media assessment. This multistep screening process establishes the child's eligibility for services. Figure 7.1 illustrates this process.

Definitions of the various eligible disabilities may vary from state to state, and there are few regulations governing the expertise of service providers in early intervention programs. When and how visual impairments are identified and the process followed to bring in a teacher who has special training in visual impairments may vary from state to state and district to district. Regardless of a state's procedures, it is crucial to involve the teacher of students with visual impairments as soon as a visual impairment is suspected.

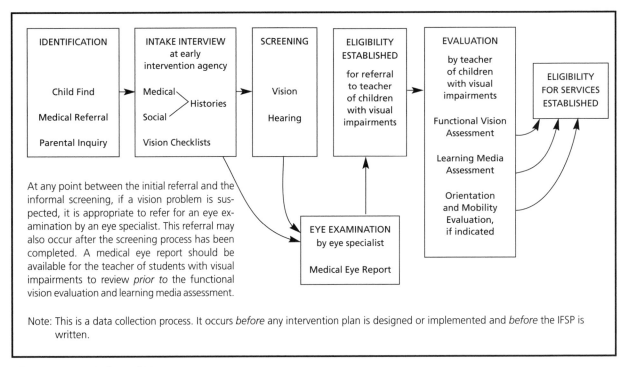

Figure 7.1. Referral Process

Types of Placements

The 1997 amendments to IDEA require early intervention for infants and toddlers to be delivered in a "natural environment"; that is, "the home and community settings in which children without disabilities participate." They also require a "continuum" (or array) of placement choices to be available and mandate parental choice and individualized planning. For an infant or toddler, the child's own home should be one of the choices available to parents, with early intervention professionals providing services there. Another option is a center-based program geared to children who need early intervention that can offer unique vision-related expertise, materials, and equipment to facilitate early learning. Placement in a regular preschool program with support from early intervention professionals is another option in the continuum.

The ideal choice of environment for an infant or toddler depends on the specific needs of the child, as well as the needs and desires of the par-

ents. The infant and toddler years are often fragile, emotional times for parents of children with visual impairments, whose priority is determining the best learning environment for their child. Parents may receive the highest level of support from center-based programs, where they have contact with other parents with similar concerns and where techniques can be modeled by uniquely trained professionals. Parents of infants and toddlers with visual impairments may require a high level of guidance and education that is not easily obtained outside these programs.

The nature of visual impairment itself suggests that other factors may need to be considered when selecting learning environments. Lack of vision may prevent the acquisition of information beyond arm's reach, affect the child's ability to imitate behaviors, and interfere with spatial orientation. Thus, specific and structured environments that offer predictability, minimal distractions, consistency, and safety may be the optimum early learning environments for infants and toddlers with visual impairments. Such structured sites can also enhance specific interventions (such as intensive experience with sequenced sensory stimulation activities and exposure to braille readiness experiences) that are unique to these children. A description of why a particular environment would be natural *and* most appropriate for an infant or toddler with a visual impairment should be included in the child's IFSP.

When a severe visual impairment has been identified, it is critical for a teacher of students with visual impairments to be a functioning member of the program planning team. This specialist can explain the important role that vision plays in early development, interpret the results of assessments in terms of the kind and degree of visual impairment, suggest programs that maximize functional vision, and assist in modifying instructional strategies to help the child make the best use of his or her other senses. The earlier intervention begins, the greater the chance that there will be minimal or no delays as a result of the visual impairment.

As was mentioned earlier, a unique characteristic of a special early childhood intervention program is the service coordinator (who may be, but is not necessarily, the teacher of students with visual impairments). Because services are family focused and may involve multiple agencies or resources, the coordinator monitors the services to be sure they are timely, appropriate, and coordinated; the coordinator also keeps all the team members informed by giving them progress reports and alerts the team members when six-month reviews are needed. This careful coordination allows a number of diverse support systems to be combined into a single, but multifaceted and effective program of services.

Special Teams and Teamwork

Teams and Plan Focus

A special team for an infant or toddler may include professionals from many disciplines, including various medical specialists who submit reports and monitor the child's growth and development, as well as an early childhood interventionist, public health nurse, social worker, nutritionist, occupational therapist, and physical therapist. Educational specialists may include a teacher of students with visual impairments, a teacher of students with hearing impairments, an orientation and mobility (O&M) specialist, a speech and language therapist, and a diagnostician or school psychologist. Since coordinating the contributions of all these specialists is a critical part of the IFSP, a capable service coordinator is essential. (For more on teams, see Chapter 1.)

As has been stated, there is a difference in the focus of programs for young children with disabilities from birth to age 3 and those for children from 3 to 5 years. Programs for infants and toddlers focus on the family, whereas programs for preschoolers focus on individual children. As a result, the written service plans—IFSPs for children up to age 3 and IEPs for 3 to 5 year olds—take different forms. A comparison of these two plans is presented in Table 7.1.

Working with Families

Parents' Roles on Educational Teams. Parents and families, especially of infants and toddlers, are an important part of the special education process. The IFSP reflects that focus, and includes a written plan designed to meet both the family's needs and the child's needs. In this way, the family becomes both a participant in and a recipient of services.

When a meeting is held to develop either an IEP or an IFSP, at least one parent must be present. That parent has the right to question, delete, expand, or disapprove the goals and objectives recommended by the other members of the educational team and must approve the plan before it is implemented. The inclusion of both parents and service providers in the special education process has benefited families and professionals. Not only is there better communication among and between team members, but there is greater understanding of the feelings of parents, whose reactions may be an important factor in the success of their children's educational plans.

Table 7.1. A Comparison of the IFSP and the IEP

IFSP	IEP
Must focus on the needs of the family as well as the child.	Must address the educational needs of the child.
The local ECI Program, under the supervision of the state's lead agency, either provides services directly or arranges for and coordinates services from other organizations.	School district is responsible for providing service.
Services are provided year-round.	Services are generally provided during the school year.
Eligibility is based on developmental delays in one or more of five developmental areas, established risk conditions that have a high probability of resulting in a developmental delay, or high risk for substantial developmental delay.	Eligibility is based on educational needs.
Families are protected by procedural safeguards described in Part C of IDEA.	Families are protected by due process, as outlined in Part B of IDEA.

Parents' Reactions and Needs. As early as the 1940s, researchers examined how parents of children with visual impairments responded to the news about their child's disability (Sommers, 1944). Researchers during this time concluded that parents needed ongoing support during the early years as they learned to raise a child with a visual impairment. Without such support, denial, overprotectiveness, or a number of other reactions may develop. Denial closes parents off from positive suggestions and may interfere with intervention strategies, and overprotectiveness insulates the child with a visual impairment from the environment that he or she needs to discover.

There is no clear method of helping parents to resolve problems of denial, overprotectiveness, or other emotional or behavioral patterns. Ongoing support is one resource that the professional can offer. Teachers of students with visual impairments should not attempt to provide "therapy" for parents. Rather, if severe emotional problems seem to exist (for example, the family seems to be in danger of "falling apart"), professional counseling and, possibly, respite care (short-term placement to relieve parental stress) should be recommended.

Socioeconomic status may be a factor in parents' reactions to having a child with a visual impairment (Collins, 1982). As the socioeconomic situation improves (for example, there is at least one wage earner in the family), the ability to deal with stress also seems to improve. Conversely, if there are few resources to address the basic needs of food, shelter, clothing, and medical care, in some instances the parents' ability to manage their emotional reactions to having a child who is visually impaired may be stretched to the breaking point. Since financial assistance can make a contribution toward balancing parents' emotional levels, it is an important consideration in an IFSP.

Like other children, to feel secure and develop a strong self-image and self-esteem, a child with a visual impairment needs to feel accepted in his or her family and be treated "like other kids." Nurturing parents, regardless of their socioeconomic status, are important for all children, but they are particularly helpful for children with visual impairments. Pride in the child's achievements and praise for the child's efforts can build a sense of accomplishment.

Since services for infants and toddlers focus on the family, every effort should be made to assess each family's specific and unique needs. The teacher of students with visual impairments can be helpful in this regard by suggesting strategies for intervention and for the cooperative provision of service. Such strategies and services are especially critical in the early years, when parent-child bonding is taking place, since a visual impairment can interfere with bonding because the child may not make eye contact, may startle when touched, or may turn his or her head away when approached (Ferrell, 1985). Moreover, a child with early medical problems may have spent considerable time in a hospital separated from caregivers or had uncomfortable experiences with physical contact (such as injections and invasive procedures). Thus, the child may require special handling and the parents or caregivers may need extra support and counseling. Ongoing support for the family can help resolve miscommunications and ensure the necessary bonding between the child and his or her parents.

Diversity.   An important consideration in working with families is diversity. Today's communities are ethnically, racially, and religiously diverse; mobile; and often disparate economically. There are single-parent (both male and female) families, two-parent families, extended families, and combined families with both parents and stepparents. Because each culture has its own values, family structures, and attitudes toward disabilities, the service provider needs to be sensitive to a family's values and beliefs and attempt to establish rapport with the family before a service plan is implemented. Taking time to listen, talking *with* (not *to*) family members, building trust, and respecting a family's values will help build the kind of relationship with a family that will facilitate discussions about services. Families who feel comfortable as team members may ultimately become highly effective contributors to the team.

ASSESSMENT

Assessing the capabilities and needs of infants and toddlers with visual impairments (and their families) is different from assessing those of school-age children with visual impairments. Many young children are functioning with incompletely developed language, motor, and cognitive systems, and they may not cooperate with evaluators. Therefore, assessments must be done in

short, multiple sessions and require exceptionally good observational skills.

Complicating the assessment process is the fact that few teachers of students with visual impairments are prepared or experienced in assessing young children. Furthermore, few instruments are designed for children with visual impairments, and no standardized test has norms for these children. (See Chapters 2, 3, and 4 for discussions of assessment issues and practices.) Thus, assessing children with visual impairments is a complex process. The following sections present unique issues in assessment for preschool children.

Vision Screening

Vision screening, the first level of evaluation for children with visual impairments, largely involves the collection of information and observation of young children by someone in the early childhood agency or program. At the time of referral, a medical and social history of the family is usually taken. (Appendix A in this chapter presents a questionnaire that can be used to obtain information from the parents during an initial interview.)

An observation of the child's visual functioning (noting such elements as eye contact and accurate reach), and visual appearance (noting such items as excess tearing, cloudy looking pupils, redness, or discharge) can also provide indicators of a visual impairment. Sidebar 7.2 lists a variety of signs of possible eye disorders, and Appendix B presents a checklist that can be used to monitor the appearance of the child's eyes during a vision screening. The person performing the screening should assess such factors as pupillary response, ocular muscle balance, fixation, tracking, and ability to shift gaze.

Since most preschool children with visual impairments do not know they see differently from everyone else, an experienced evaluator is required to recognize and note unusual or abnormal visual behaviors during a vision screening. The teacher of students with visual impairments can

Signs of Possible Eye Disorders in Children

PHYSICAL SIGNS

- Eyes that are red rimmed, crusty looking, or swollen.
- Eyes that are frequently inflamed or watery.
- Eyes that do not look properly aligned.
- Sties that recur frequently.
- Pupils that look "cloudy."

CHILD'S BEHAVIORS

- Is unable to make eye contact.
- Attempts to brush away a blur.
- Rubs eyes excessively.
- Frowns constantly.
- Shuts or covers one eye for visual tasks.
- Tilts or turns the head when looking at something.
- Leans forward to see better.
- Blinks excessively.
- Is unduly sensitive to light, or gazes at lights.
- Is excessively irritable during close work.
- Stumbles or trips over objects.
- Is clumsy in reaching.

CHILD'S COMPLAINTS[1]

- Statements such as "I can't see that."
- Dizziness, nausea, and headaches after close work.
- Statements such as "I see two of them" (when there is only one object present).

MEDICAL EMERGENCIES[3]

- Complaint of pain in the eyes.
- Foreign object (such as dirt, sand, "speck") in the eye.
- Injury from being hit in the eye with an object.
- Puncture wound to the eye.
- Chemical injury to the eye (such as that caused by the splashing of lye or other caustic materials).
- Eyes that appear infected (reddened, crusted, or swollen, or containing pus or other exudate).

---

[1]Most children, especially young children, do not usually complain that they are unable to see; children typically do not realize that other people see differently from the way they do.
[2]An ophthalmologist or other medical personnel need to be consulted for medical emergencies.

---

assist with vision screening, when needed, or can train an early childhood interventionist to do so. The screener should have a clear understanding of normal visual development to determine that a particular child's visual status is not typical. For example, if a child's eyes do not appear to be aligned at age 2 or 3 months, it would not be unusual, since ocular muscles are not normally fully coordinated until about 6 months. Eyes that are not aligned *after* 6 months should be checked by an eye care specialist.

Functional Vision Assessment

A functional vision assessment is an important part of the assessment process for all students with visual impairments, including young children. In addition to the information presented here and in Chapter 4, some excellent guidelines are available (see the Resources at the end of this chapter).

In evaluating functional vision, the teacher of students with visual impairments answers several general questions regarding an infant or toddler with a visual impairment:

◆ Does the child react to light? If so, how?

◆ Does the child react to black-and-white designs (such as a bull's eye, checkerboard pattern, wide diagonal, or jagged lines)? If so, how and at what distance?

◆ Does the child react to *silent* human faces? If so, how, and at what distance?

◆ Does the child make any attempt to *maintain* a gaze at *silent* people or *silent* objects? If so, at what distance?

◆ What size and color of *silent* objects does the child try to look at, at what distance, and under what lighting conditions?

The teacher also notes behaviors that are related to or are monitored by vision, such as these:

◆ Ability to hold the head erect and steady, allowing the visual system to operate at whatever level it is able;

◆ Interest in people, their facial expressions, and body movements;

◆ Interest in objects and attempts to obtain them;

◆ Ability to reach accurately for objects and people; and

◆ Ability to imitate facial expressions (such as sticking out the tongue, opening the mouth wide, making a silly face) or gestures (like finger wiggling and playing peek-a-boo).

The results of these observations are indicative of how the child uses whatever vision is available to him or her.

Learning Media Assessment

After a child has been identified as visually impaired, a learning media assessment will be conducted, which will examine the child's use of sensory information, readiness to begin formal reading and writing instruction, use of general learning media and, during the later preschool years, an appropriate literacy medium or media. Chapter 4 contains a discussion of learning media assessments.

Developmental Assessment

Developmental scales, commonly used by psychologists, diagnosticians, and early childhood interventionists, present some serious problems when used with children who are visually impaired. Many of the earliest developmental milestones (such as controlling the head and tracking) are visual skills or require vision and visual experience, and others (such as reaching) depend on visual monitoring.

For example, the Battelle Developmental Inventory (BDI), an instrument that measures a child's developmental level (Newborg, Stock, Wnek, Guidubaldi, & Svinicki, 1984), has been analyzed extensively in relation to the performance of preschool children with visual impairments aged 12–73 months (Hatton, Bailey, Burchinal, & Ferrell, 1997). The analyses found that although patterns of development were related to the amount of useful vision, as well as the presence of mental retardation or developmental delay, children with no other disabilities with the poorest vision scored significantly lower on all the BDI scales and had slower rates of development over time on the motor and personal-social scales. Therefore, the BDI would be an inappropriate measure to use with young children with visual impairments unless these limitations were factored into the results and reported.

The report of Project PRISM (Ferrell, 1998), a five-year study of the developmental process, sequences, and ages of acquisition of "milestone" developmental skills, suggested that developmental sequences may differ for young children with visual impairments. The study found that the delays were not only expected and predictable for some of these children, but were more marked for children with multiple disabilities. Again, any developmental assessment of children with visual impairments must recognize the critical role that vision plays in early development, and any apparent developmental delays should be reported with this role in mind.

Adaptive scales should be used with caution with young children who are visually impaired, since reduced or absent vision can cause delays in many of the skills (such as self-help, independent functioning, and social interaction) measured by such scales. Social maturity scales may have the same flaws. The Maxfield-Buchholz Social Maturity Scale, a measure of the social development of children who are blind, is considered obsolete. It was developed a long time ago and has not been updated, not because of its age, but because the standardizing population is not representative of most children with visual impairments today.

A number of checklists designed to be used with children who are visually impaired are available for evaluating such early skills as listening, the acquisition of basic concepts, self-help, social skills, braille readiness, sensory awareness, and body image (Sewell, 1997). Any appropriate program of services should be based on a child's current level of functioning, which can be determined by using one or more of these checklists.

Cognitive testing of children under age 4—whether sighted or visually impaired—is probably inappropriate. Moreover, there are no cognitive norms for children with visual impairments *above* that age. Many diagnosticians and psychologists choose the earliest level of the Wechsler series—the *Wechsler Preschool and Primary Scale of Intelligence–Revised* (WPPSI–R, n.d.) to estimate the cognitive level of older preschool children with visual impairments (aged 4–6) because it has a split-scale format (verbal and performance). Although the verbal portion may give a closer estimate than the full scale, the results should still be interpreted cautiously. Verbal answers may be overrated if the child has language skills that are not firmly based in meaning. Information from multiple sources, such as selected subtests from the WPPSI, supported by additional information from the *Developmental Activities Screening Inventory* (Fewell & Langley, 1984), *Growing*

Up (Croft & Robinson, 1986), or the Oregon Project scales (discussed next) can yield a reasonable *estimate* of cognitive range and should be reported as such.

The Oregon Project (Anderson, Boigon, & Davis, 1994), developed from the early Portage materials, is a developmentally based curriculum developed in Portage, Wisconsin (Bluma, Shearer, Frohman, & Hilliard, 1976) that has been revised several times. This instrument has undergone field testing with young children who are visually impaired. Its portability and stated applications for infants and toddlers with visual impairments are its strength, as are the many suggestions for early language development. The weaknesses of the Oregon Project are the segmented format of the evaluation booklet and a profile format that may be difficult to understand and translate. An extensive set of curriculum guidelines is linked directly to the assessment results.

Growing Up (Croft & Robinson, 1986) is an assessment and programming kit designed for preschool children with visual impairments. The assessment procedure involves a card-sort done by parents and a detailed, sequential, double-page profile of the results. The curriculum is directly related to the behaviors assessed and is based on a Piagetian theory of development. Although the scale is not standardized, it is based on other standardized scales. Several studies (Markland, 1979; Wright, 1980) have supported both its reliability and concurrent validity. The data from Project PRISM (Ferrell, 1998) also support the ages of acquisition that the assessment assumes for a great many of the milestone skills, particularly in the 1- to 3-year range.

Any discussion of assessment during the preschool years cannot omit reference to the means of evaluating a family's needs. Several checklists, interview protocols, and parent-needs inventories are available for this purpose (see the references and resources at the end of this chapter). Although a family's needs may be evaluated by a social worker or health care provider in the earliest years, the teacher of students with visual impairments may want to explore the family's needs and attitudes in relation to their child's visual impairment. Since the IFSP requires a focus on the family, a structured data collection system would seem appropriate.

INTERVENTION STRATEGIES

Children develop different skills from year to year, and strategies for intervention and the rationales for them follow the changing needs of the child. Although it should be noted that no system of the body develops in isolation, the rate of growth appears greater in one or two areas each year. The following sections address specific areas of growth in each age level.

Early Reflexive Behaviors

Many early reflexes are precursors to later skills. They appear as involuntary reactions to external stimuli, seem to disappear, and later return as voluntary behaviors. The early reflexes seem to be preliminary practice for later learning and may even create early preparatory patterns in the brain. Examples of these early precursor reflexes are the crawling, stepping, and grasp reflexes.

Other reflexes serve developmental purposes. They are either self-preservative (as in protective-defensive reflexes) or provide a basis for the system to grow. "Rooting" (searching for a nipple) and sucking reflexes and the hand-to-mouth reflex are survival behaviors, whereas the asymmetrical tonic neck reflex (ATNR) creates just the right stimulus (the infant's hands at just the right viewing distance) for visual practice. The ATNR exists from about birth to 4 months, when it disappears (Caplan, 1978; Gesell et al., 1949). Not coincidentally, the child discovers and looks at his or her own hand just before the ATNR disappears. This convenient progression is not accidental; it ensures the practicing of emerging visual skills at just the right time and at just the right distance with a visual target of just the right size.

When vision has not been practiced in the first few months (via the ATNR), "hand regard" may be a meaningless milestone. One of the purposes of hand regard is to bring the infant's hands together at the midline. Without useful vision, hand regard may not even occur, and intervention strategies must be used to encourage certain behaviors (such as playing pat-a-cake or placing the infant's hands on a bottle). Playing with the infant's hands and helping the infant play with his or her own hands can help the infant become aware of both hands. This ability to "finger" his or her own hands will help later when tactile exploration becomes a necessary means of exploring the world.

The First Year

Although social and prelanguage foundations are being laid in the first year, the emphasis is primarily on sensory maturation and motor development. Visual impairment in an infant is a serious impediment to motor development, so it is not surprising that this is the year when the most marked delays occur. As a result, the most urgent need for intervention also occurs in the first year.

Motor Skills

In an infant who is sighted, vision is a powerful motivator for head and neck control, upright posture, and accurate reach. When an infant is visually impaired, these three developmental milestones are likely to be delayed if intervention is not provided. Without head control, upright posture, and accurate reach, the infant cannot use any available vision effectively or efficiently.

Head and Neck Control. Although the normal visual system is not mature at birth and needs much of the first 6 months to become useful, enough visual stimuli reach the developing brain to make vision a motivator for head and neck control. The infant wants to see what is in his or her environment and learns quickly that it is easier to do so if the head is held upright. Repeated attempts to achieve an upright head position strengthen the neck muscles. Intervention for an infant with a visual impairment should imitate this process within the first 6 months of life. The following are strategies to help infants achieve head control:

◆ Gently lift the infant's head while the infant is on his or her stomach. Lift with one hand under the chin and the other behind the head. Stroke the back of the neck and talk in soothing tones to the infant. Withdraw manual support gradually as the infant is able to lift his or her head independently.

◆ Continue brief periods of supervised prone position to allow the infant to practice head lifting.

◆ Provide trunk support with a rolled towel under the infant's chest. Begin positioning the infant's forearms under his or her upper torso with the elbow-to-shoulder portion of the arm perpendicular to the body for weight bearing. This position provides support and preparation for independent lifting of the head, neck, and chest.

Many infants who are visually impaired are not motivated naturally to lift their heads while in the prone position (on their stomachs) and will fuss when placed in that position. A caregiver may worry that an infant will not be able to breathe when prone or may be uncomfortable with the infant's fussing and crying. Part of this first intervention involves reassuring the caregiver that short periods (perhaps 5–10 minutes a day) of monitored time in the prone position are important for the child. The baby needs to develop head and neck control first, before the next steps of upright posture can be achieved.

Upright Posture.   To achieve an upright orientation (sitting alone), a number of interrelated factors must be present: a complex system of nerves and muscles must be operational; head and neck control must be achieved; the use of the arms and hands must be refined enough to be independent of posture (sit without hand or arm support); and balance must be achieved. Sitting alone takes much of the first year to achieve. Vision plays an important role in the development of the precursor skills (head control, orientation in space, and balance), and a visual impairment can interfere with the development of those skills.

It is important to remember that an infant who is blind can learn to sit alone when he or she has the physical ability and strength to do so. Motivational factors and orientation in space are most affected by the lack of vision. Indirectly, muscle tone and stamina may also have been affected if the baby does not have the opportunity to move and is not encouraged to do so from the beginning.

Infants with visual impairments need to learn to sit at as near a developmentally appropriate time as possible. Their beginning exploration of the environment (such as the floor around them and the tray of the high chair) depends on the availability of their hands, which must be free to move and must move independently of the torso. Sitting alone is a major milestone for infants with visual impairments and a critical one for cognitive growth to come. Sitting can be encouraged by the following:

◆ Prop the infant (from about 3 months) with pillows in the corner of a chair, couch, infant seat, or crib for only a few minutes at a time. The infant should not be totally vertical until he or she has head control and the back muscles are mature. A backward-leaning position is preferable at first.

◆ Place the infant at around 6 months (if torso and head control are present) in a sitting position between an adult's legs (with the infant's back to the adult's stomach). Gently place the infant's hands, palms down, in front of him or her to provide independent support. Praise the infant and practice daily.

◆ Place toys in front of the infant between his or her legs (once balance improves), and encourage the infant to play with the toys. The child will have to lift one hand to get the toys. Provide cushions or pillows for support until the infant can sit without them, which may take several months.

To build torso control, the teacher of students with visual impairments should consult with a physical therapist, if necessary. The following suggestions may also be helpful:

- Encourage rolling over from the stomach to the back (at about 3 to 4 months) by tucking the infant's bent arm under the chest and helping the infant to roll over when he or she is prone. Praise the infant and practice this exercise daily.

- Encourage rolling over from the back to the stomach (at about 5 to 6 months) by extending one of the infant's arms up next to his or her head. Gently roll the infant's head over this arm while lifting the opposite leg with the knee bent and crossing over the other leg. Gently press the knee to the floor, and the hip should follow. Roll the infant over to his or her stomach, provide praise, and practice this exercise daily.

Accurate Reach. The ability to use hands independently is a crucial skill for a child who must use touch to learn about and explore the world. An infant who is blind may not have the motivation to reach, grasp, and explore an object unless intervention is provided early. When the infant discovers that there is something interesting in the environment and tries to attain it, the first hurdle has been cleared. The refinement of hand skills (that is, the use of the hands at the midline to manipulate and explore objects and the development of finger dexterity and the use of fingers indepen-dently) follow later, and much practice is needed to achieve these goals at developmentally appropriate times.

The selection of appealing materials and toys is critical for infants and toddlers with visual impairments as they learn to reach. Attention should be given to texture and sound. Sound becomes a useful lure late in the first year. Many plastic toys, though visually appealing, are not appropriate for infants who are visually impaired. The preferences of individual children should be observed and followed. These are some techniques to help achieve reach:

- Suspend objects with interesting and varied sounds and textures within arm's reach of the infant, so that accidental swipes will make contact with them. Make sure that the objects are securely attached.

- Guide the infant's hands toward the objects, if necessary, to let the infant know they are there.

Techniques to encourage hand use are as follows:

- Encourage the use of hands at the midline by placing the infant's hands on a bottle.

- Play pat-a-cake and other midline finger plays.

- Place the infant's hands on the caregiver's face while the caregiver is standing in front of and talking to the infant.

- Place interesting objects in the infant's hands for exploration and manipulation. If the infant has vision, the objects should be high contrast (black and white for the first few months; and reds, yellows, and oranges at around 3–5 months). If the infant is blind, the objects should be tactilely appealing and sound producing.

- Encourage the infant to grasp, rub, shake, bang, finger, probe, and otherwise explore the objects.

Creeping and Crawling. Sometimes in the second half of the first year, babies attempt to move themselves toward a desired object or person. Some infants creep using forward or backward movements with the stomach still on the floor. Others crawl on their hands and knees. Some infants do both, and a few do neither. If an infant has not attempted to creep or crawl by 9–10 months, intervention may entice him or her to do so. Readiness to creep entails both physical orientation (the head, shoulders, and upper torso raised when in the prone position) and motivation (the desire to move).

Readiness for crawling is indicated when the infant gets up on his or her hands and knees, can "rock" back and forth in that position, and is motivated to reach. Motivation can be gauged by whether the infant makes any attempt to reach toward a preferred object or person. The key to motivation is the type of lure that is provided. Generally, the lure is a favorite toy, but it could be a new and interesting object. For infants with vision, high contrast and bright colors will probably be appealing. For infants with little usable vision or who are blind, interesting objects may include those with sustained sound (such as music boxes, bells, and wind-up toys) and novel textures. When possible, use objects with multisensory appeal (for instance, those with bright colors, a variety of textures and intriguing sounds). To encourage crawling:

- ◆ Place the objects just out of reach, and encourage the infant to try to obtain them.
- ◆ If necessary, touch the infant's hand with the object first and then pull it slowly to arm's distance and then just beyond reach. The infant should stretch to reach the object.
- ◆ Using a toy that produces a sound, coax the infant to "get it" or say "where is it?"

Standing. The next level of upright posture—standing—requires both control of the torso and balance. Standing is the precursor to walking. For some children who are blind, standing may represent the lessening of body contact with the environment, which may be frightening. Once the child is standing, only the soles of the feet are rooted to the ground. The child must let go of the world he or she has become sure of through contact with nearly half the body (back, buttocks, and legs) and suddenly knows only what touches his or her feet. The process may be slow and may require a great deal of transitional support through hand holding, under-arm assistance, or something to hold on to. Independent standing is an important milestone for a child with a visual impairment and should be a goal to achieve within the first year, when possible.

To encourage standing, these techniques may be useful:

- ◆ Put the infant (around 10–11 months), in a standing position next to a couch or heavy

overstuffed chair. Put toys on the chair or couch within easy reach.

- ◆ Encourage the infant to play with the toys while standing (leaning on the couch or chair if necessary). Limit the time to only a few minutes at first and extend the time as the child is able. The child may need assistance in sitting down. Practice standing daily, but not for long periods that will tire the child.

Additional ideas to enhance motor development can be found in Filan (1992).

Sensory Development

When a young child has a visual impairment, he or she may have to rely on senses other than vision to provide information about the world. The development of the senses should be encouraged beginning in infancy. Many opportunities for sensory stimulation occur during daily events and in natural environments. The following suggestions may be helpful in developing early sensory awareness and beginning discrimination:

- ◆ Gently rub and name body parts (such as the arms, hands, tummy, back, legs, and toes) while bathing the infant (or while massaging him or her with lotion after a bath).
- ◆ Name the body parts in the process of dressing (for example, *arms* go into armholes, *legs* go into leg openings, and snaps and zippers cover up the "*tummy*").
- ◆ Use a variety of textures (including satin, flannel, wool, and velvet) to massage the infant's feet and hands.
- ◆ Provide toys that make a variety of sounds (such as rattles, bells, and squeaky squeeze toys).
- ◆ Name unique sounds (like water running in the sink, the doorbell and telephone ringing, a dog barking).

- Provide a variety of textures and tastes when solid foods are introduced.

- Provide a variety of textures for finger feeding (such as crackers, bananas, and pasta of different shapes).

- Provide for children with useful vision high-contrast (black-and-white) designs with edges and angles (such as a checkerboard design) to look at for a few months; at around 3 to 4 months, bright colors in high-contrast designs may be more interesting.

As the child gets older, provide a wider variety of experiences with sensory stimuli, including:

- Books with diverse textures on each page (such as swatches of carpeting, wood or plastic, rubber, fur, and cloth).

- Foods with different textures, temperatures, and tastes.

- Stickers, especially the "scratch-and-sniff" variety.

- "Sniff bowls" (plastic margarine tubs containing cotton sprinkled with different scents, including lemon, peppermint, vanilla, orange, and chocolate; the tops of the tubs should have holes to allow the smells to be sniffed).

- Toys with a variety of textures, sounds, and configurations.

- Floor surfaces of different textures to be explored when the child begins to creep or crawl and while walking barefoot when the child begins to walk.

Language, Social, and Cognitive Skills

Since the sensory and motor systems mature and the neurological system develops during the first year, the language, social, and cognitive systems are occupied in building bases for future growth. The infant with a visual impairment coos, babbles, and imitates sounds, just as babies who are sighted do, but most such language is prepara-tional. However, this is not to say that the infant does not communicate feelings and needs, since caregivers learn to discriminate infants' sounds as signals.

The first year of language development builds a base for the future acquisition of language, and intervention should be viewed within this context. Talking to an infant with a visual impairment serves a dual purpose; it provides a linguistic intonation pattern for later imitation and establishes an auditory link with the child (an equivalent to "eye contact" for a child who is blind). The caregiver's voice is both familiar and reassuring, in contrast to voices on television or radio, which do not provide the same emotional reassurance.

Establishing social contact with an infant who is visually impaired may be difficult for some parents, who may be accustomed to having eye contact with infants and smiling at them. For parents of infants with visual impairments, social contact can include touching (such as snuggling, nuzzling, tickling, and holding), making sounds (like singing, talking, reciting rhymes), and any combination of the two (including finger plays, talking and snuggling at the same time).

Most cognitive scales begin with object permanence (that is, the awareness that an object continues to exist even if it is no longer visible). Object permanence occurs for sighted children sometime in the second half of the first year. For infants with low vision, however, it may not occur until late in the first year, and for those who are blind, it is a particularly difficult milestone to achieve. The following suggestions may help parents encourage the development of language, social, and cognitive skills:

- Parents and other caregivers need to be mindful that some infants and toddlers may stop an activity to listen and that there will be periods of quiet when the children are thinking, exploring, or problem-solving.

- Reassure parents and other caregivers that the lack of eye contact does not mean that their child is ignoring them or their presence.

◆ Reassure parents that touch and voice are appropriate substitutes for eye contact.

◆ Play games with the child to encourage the establishment of object permanence. One example is a game in which an object that has a sustained sound or vibration (like a wind-up toy) is hidden under a cover while the child remains in physical contact with the object; the infant is encouraged to remove the cover with the opposite hand.

The Second Year

During the second year of life, the child begins to project beyond himself or herself. Increasing gross motor ability and the refined use of the hands and fingers allow the child to move out into the world and start building concepts. Intervention activities will enhance these expanding abilities.

Motor Skills

Walking. Toddlers who are sighted usually walk sometime between age 12 to 18 months. However, children with visual impairments are more likely to walk unassisted between 16 and 22 months (Ferrell, 1998). This is a major milestone for children with visual impairments, and every attempt should be made to provide timely intervention. The major indicator of readiness for walking is the ability to stand alone with reasonably good balance. Intervention may begin around 11 or 12 months if the child appears to be ready, but should certainly be started by 15 months. Much practice will be needed, and an O&M instructor may need to be consulted for support and additional ideas for intervention. The following are some suggestions for encouraging a child to walk:

◆ Place the child in a standing position next to a couch or low table. Place toys just out of reach to the left or right of the child. Encourage the child to step to the side to attain the toys. Provide daily practice.

◆ Place the child in a standing position with his or her back against the wall. Offer a hand or finger to the child for support. Keep physical assistance minimal and lessen it gradually as the child gains confidence. Provide verbal reassurance.

◆ Use a small chair, cardboard box, or walker (to push) for support. Some toddler push toys (such as a toy shopping cart, lawnmower, and wagon) can also be used. Consult with the O&M instructor for additional ideas.

Fine Motor Skills. The development of fine motor ability depends on the opportunities a child has to practice hand- and finger-exploration activities, so he or she can experience the world of objects firsthand. The names of items must be matched with their unique appearance, sound, and feel. The challenge for intervention is to provide as many objects as possible, along with their names, including both environmental objects (such as spoons, combs, shoes, pots and pans, clothespins, keys, and cups) and toys. In order for the child to learn the functions of objects, as well as their characteristics, the uses of the objects should be explained (for example, "This is a spoon; we eat cereal with it") when possible. The names of objects (nouns) and how they are used or what they do (verbs) are the beginning of useful language.

An extension of the refining of fine motor ability is the functional use of hands and fingers. In this regard, the goals of intervention should be to provide opportunities for functional applications of fine motor skills. Examples include the following:

◆ Removing objects from a container (both pouring out and reaching into the container),

◆ Putting objects into a container,

◆ Putting pegs into holes,

◆ Putting shapes into a form board,

◆ Turning pages of a heavy cardboard book,

◆ Opening and closing lids,

◆ Unwrapping loosely wrapped food,

◆ Nesting containers, and

◆ Stacking blocks.

Self-Help Skills. Part of developing motor abilities is the emergence of self-help skills. Intervention in this area may simply involve the following:

◆ Suggest that the child help in dressing and undressing (for instance, putting his or her arms up to remove or put on a shirt, pulling off his or her own socks or shoes, and putting on a hat).

◆ Encourage the child to begin to take responsibility for eating activities (for example, beginning to drink from a cup and using a spoon).

◆ Encourage the child to cooperate in games (such as pointing to major body parts and clapping to music).

◆ Practice fine motor skills that lead to the acquisition of self-help skills and encourage independence.

Language and Cognition

In addition to the expansion of motor skills, there is a major growth spurt in language and cognition in the second year of life. Children who are sighted learn many nouns and verbs spontaneously through observation during this time. However, with children who are visually impaired, service providers and parents often need to make extra, intentional efforts to create specific opportunities for the child to experience firsthand the objects in the world around him or her, such as the following:

◆ Alert parents to the importance of talking about cause-effect events (for example, "Where does the water go when it goes down the drain?" or "What happens if I turn this switch?").

◆ Encourage parents to watch for situations in which they can help their children to learn causal relationships.

◆ Create an alternate-sense equivalent for an event (for instance, pouring water through a funnel and feeling the water coming out the bottom can approximate the situation of water going down a drain).

The Third Year

Between the ages of 2 and 3, a child's motor skills expand, and there is an explosion in language, which helps to develop cognitive skills. The child's growing independence also supports an expansion in self-help and social skills. For the toddler who is visually impaired, opportunities must be intentionally provided for exploring and interacting with people and the environment, and encouragement must be given for practicing self-help skills. This year is crucial in building self-esteem, self-confidence, and emerging independence.

Motor Skills

During the third year, the child is primarily involved in coordinating and refining motor skills that require a more complex coordination of legs, arms, wrists, hands, and fingers than earlier, and self-help skills use the child's growing ability to coordinate muscles. The toddler with a visual impairment whose vision may not be providing adequate feedback to the brain needs extra practice or modified procedures for coordinating these muscles and learning new skills.

Throwing, Kicking, and Catching. The ability to kick or throw a ball may require only physical strength and a perception of direction, but catching a ball—a task based largely on visual anticipation—may be extremely difficult. The use of a large beeper ball can facilitate ball play, but auditory anticipation is never as accurate and instantaneous as visual anticipation. Throwing and kicking may be learned more easily than catching. Throwing a large, soft ball (such as a beach ball) into the child's outstretched arms is an appropriate activity to help a child who is blind learn to catch.

Jumping. Jumping is another difficult skill for a toddler with a visual impairment because it requires a total separation (though momentary) from reality (that is, the child's feet must leave a secure surface). The easiest way to teach jumping is to begin by teaching the child to step off a low board or box. When the child has learned one-footed descent, he or she can be assisted—by holding the child under his or her arms or holding the child's hands—to use both feet at once.

Stepping Up and Down. Going up and down steps and climbing or descending a ladder may be taught simultaneously with jumping. Generally, children may need physical assistance or demonstrations of the movement of their limbs to learn these skills. Hopping (jumping on one foot) and skipping (a combination of hopping and skipping) are based on the ability to jump and should be taught only after a child has mastered jumping.

Riding a Tricycle. The opportunity to ride a tricycle should not be denied to a toddler who is visually impaired, but it requires close supervision and both physical coordination and conceptual organization. The brain must tell the legs and feet to push alternately and in a circular motion. The child must understand pedals, wheels, around, push, steer, and stop. The child must also have the chance to explore the parts of a tricycle to understand what happens when the pedals go around. A clear and unobstructed area is necessary for tricycle practice. A child who is blind can learn to ride a tricycle given adequate motivation, orientation, and practice.

Refining Fine Motor Skills. Fine motor skills continue to involve functional movements. Activities like filling and dumping things out of containers can build such concepts as full, empty, or "all gone." Scribbling with a writing instrument builds motor coordination, which is a prerequisite to handwriting. If the child has little or no usable vision, the use of a screenboard and wax crayons can provide tactile feedback while scribbling. In addition, increasing thumb–finger opposition allows the child to learn to use scissors. Children who are blind can learn to cut narrow strips of construction paper with proper instruction and use the pieces of paper later to make a collage. The developing coordination of the wrists and hands allows the wrists to rotate, the movements needed for turning doorknobs, putting nuts and bolts together, and turning screws.

Encouraging Self-Help Skills. In the domain of self-help, motor development provides a level of readiness that allows the child to undress and dress (for example, pull off socks, shoes, hats, and pants; pull on socks, pants, jackets), wash hands, brush teeth, and scoop with a spoon. Toilet training may even begin during this time. Toddlers with visual impairments should be expected to acquire the same skills, but the instructional methods may differ.

Most self-help skills can be taught with physical demonstration (hand-over-hand), and much repetition may be needed. Toilet training will depend on whether the child is aware of and can control his or her bowels and bladder (that is, when the child knows he or she has to go to the toilet and asks for help). Physical maturation of the bladder and bowel systems and an awareness of alternatives to diapers (such as using a potty) are obvious prerequisites to toilet training. Toddlers with visual impairments may be afraid of a toilet because of the flushing noise or the puzzle of why it is necessary to dispose of bodily wastes. Emphasis should be placed on the physical comfort of being dry and clean and the fact that this is what grown-ups do. Flushing can be a kind of closure or reward for "big-kid" behavior.

Cognitive and Language Skills

Cognitive memory becomes not only useful, but important, during this period and needs to be practiced. For children with visual impairments, memory will be a critical capability both academically and socially, and lots of practice during this preschool period will lay a strong foundation for it. Verbal games (such as "Tell me about . . ." or "Remember when we . . . ? What happened?"), repeating short two-word shopping lists (like milk and eggs), and encouraging pretend play (for instance,

"*You* be the Mommy now") can provide pleasurable practice of memory.

The domain of language and communication is the area of greatest growth in this age range. At 24 months, the toddler has an expressive vocabulary of around 300 words, but by 36 months, this vocabulary more than triples to 1,000 words or more with a receptive vocabulary of twice that number (Nuttall, Romero, & Kalesnik, 1999). Although the 2-year-old's vocabulary is made up primarily of nouns, verbs, and noun-verb combinations (such as "baby go"), the expanding experiences of the 2–3 year old provide a variety of descriptors using adjectives and adverbs. In addition, the emerging independence of this age group underscores the separation of "me" from "you," so pronouns are added to the vocabulary base.

For toddlers with visual impairments, the experiences that build a descriptive vocabulary and the describing words may have to be provided intentionally. The service provider must add words like *big, little, fuzzy, warm, soft,* and so forth, to objects (for example, *fuzzy bear*) and should use opportunities to generalize experiences (for instance, "Your teddy bear is fuzzy like your bunny"). Even though the 2–3 year old may not yet internalize these generalizations, the foundation is being laid for the future cross-applications of words.

Most 2–3 year olds are learning to use gestures as a form of communication. The use of gestures not only enhances normal social skills, but expands the scope of available communication choices. Since visual impairment interferes with the ability to observe others using gestures, intervention is needed to teach such alternative ways of communicating. Service providers must intentionally teach such gestures as waving bye-bye, raising the arms to indicate up, nodding the head to mean yes, and shaking the head to indicate no.

Transition from Home to School

At the close of this period, the child may undergo a transition from the family-focused early childhood program to the child-centered public school program. During this time, it is essential for as many of the service providers as possible to continue intervention with no interruption. Any change of instructional environment could interfere with the child's progress, unless the instructional personnel remain consistent and assist with the transition to a center- or school-based preschool program.

The Preschool Years

Ages 3–5 are the years of concept building, perhaps the most critical ones for children with visual impairments. Basic concepts build foundations for meaningful language, provide spatial orientation for mobility, and expand the cognitive base needed for reasoning and decision making. Although the motor system, particularly the use of the hands and fingers, is still being refined and the language domain is expanding in sentence structure and syntax, it is the cognitive area that requires the greatest intentional intervention.

Cognitive Skills. Much of the regular preschool program is designed to build basic concepts, but children with visual impairments need more reinforcement and extra experience and practice to make up for their lack of ability to observe spontaneously. The time spent strengthening basic concepts during the preschool years will pay off later, when the child who is visually impaired is able to compete academically and socially with sighted children. Meaningful language and a wide range of acquired concepts will become tools both for learning and for formal reasoning (see Sidebar 7.3 for a list of basic concepts).

A unique area of cognitive development is the acquisition of the concept of one-to-one correspondence. Children with visual impairments, who may not observe "one for each," need to be given specific experiences to build this concept, such as matching one peg to one hole, dropping one object in each container, passing out straws (one to each child), counting classmates by touching each one on the shoulder, and counting objects by touching each one in order. The acquisition of this concept is a vital prerequisite for even the simplest math skills, so care should be taken

Basic Concepts[1]

SIZE
- Big-little
- Large-small
- Long-short
- Tall-short
- Thin-thick
- Wide-narrow
- Fat-skinny
- Heavy-light

SHAPE
- Round, ball
- Square, block
- Triangle, cone, pyramid
- Rectangle
- Diamond
- Cross
- "X" shape
- Star shape

QUANTITY
- Some
- A few
- Several
- More-less
- Most-least
- Whole-part
- None-one
- Half
- Pair
- As many as
- Equal

TIME
- Yesterday
- Today
- Tomorrow
- Night-day
- Spring, summer, fall, winter

ORDER
- First-last
- Middle
- Second, third, and so forth
- Next
- Then

LOCATION
- Top-bottom
- In-out
- Inside-outside
- Next to
- Middle-in the middle
- Center
- Through
- Far-near
- Around
- Over
- Between
- Corner
- Behind
- Below-under
- In front of
- Forward-backward
- After-before
- Left-right
- In a row
- Side

TEMPERATURE
- Hot-cold
- Warm-cool

MISCELLANEOUS PROPERTIES
- Hard-soft
- Smooth-rough
- Wet-dry
- High-low
- Loud-soft
- Fast-slow
- Sweet-sour

MISCELLANEOUS TERMS
- Begin-beginning
- End-ending
- Separated
- Another
- Always-never
- Every
- Almost
- Sometimes

FOLLOWING DIRECTIONS
- Stop, go, start
- Follow-trace
- Return
- Match

---

[1]When opposites have been mastered, the comparative versions should be taught, such as big*ger* and big*gest*. The child needs to understand the terms "like" and "different" before comparisons can be taught.

that it is a secure concept before math skills are taught.

During the latter half of the preschool years, an important extension of basic concepts occurs: Children begin to group objects by properties or function (that is, to classify). Children with visual impairments often need structured and supervised sorting experiences until they understand the idea of groups with similar characteristics. Until the concept of similarities or differences is firmly established, they should be taught to sort by single properties (such as shape, size, texture, or function). Multiple property grouping (like sorting large, round objects) requires a higher level of cognitive ability than most preschoolers have achieved.

The teacher of students with visual impairments needs to evaluate the level of basic concepts that kindergartners and first graders with visual impairments have attained and include enrichment activities in the IEP to strengthen any weak areas. Grouping experiences (that is, sets and subsets) can then be built on a strong foundation.

Motor Skills. Preschoolers generally spend a great deal of time refining motor skills, particularly the use of their fingers. Preschoolers with visual impairments, especially those who may become braille readers, also need activities (and extra experiences) in strengthening their fingers, so that their fingers can move independently, as well as in a coordinated manner. The use of clay or Play-Doh helps strengthen their hands, and experience with a variety of tools (such as a hammer, saw, screwdriver, hole punch, and stapler) and fasteners (including locks, bolts, hooks, buttons, snaps, and zippers) helps build the finger and hand coordination necessary for operating technical equipment later.

Language and Social Skills. Additional gestures and body language are usually learned spontaneously during the preschool years but they must be intentionally taught to children with visual impairments. Using the index finger to point, raising a hand to gain the teacher's attention, and shaking hands when introduced to a new person are examples of age-appropriate gestures that preschool children with visual impairments need to learn.

Actual language skills may include manners words (*please, thank you, excuse me,* and *you're welcome*) and how to ask questions. Some children with visual impairments sit quietly in class because they do not know how to phrase a question to acquire information. This skill should be taught early, and the preschool years are an appropriate time to do so.

An area not usually addressed in regular preschool programs is the extinguishing (or minimizing) of inappropriate behaviors. The preschool years are the times to address such behaviors of children who are visually impaired. Socially inappropriate behaviors, such as rocking, eye poking, and finger flicking, should be eliminated, if possible, before a child enters school. These behaviors may be self-stimulative before age 2, but can become avoidance techniques during the preschool years (Troster, Brambring, & Beelmann, 1991). Sometimes the solution to the problem of inappropriate behaviors could be as simple as giving the child something else to do with his or her hands. Other children may need a more structured behavior modification plan to minimize or extinguish these behaviors (see Chapter 6 for a discussion of applied behavior analysis).

Socially inappropriate behaviors should not be tolerated because of sympathy for the child's visual impairment since they can only give people who are sighted a negative impression of the child and do not enhance the child's image among his or her peers. Every attempt should be made to enhance the child's image, and eliminating or reducing unacceptable mannerisms can be a step toward that end.

Sensory Skills. Although sensory skills (awareness, discrimination, and applications) have been emphasized from the first year of life, structured experiences to refine sensory capabilities should continue in the preschool years. Children with low vision need to practice and apply visual skills to increase efficiency and to use touch as a supplementary sense. For children who are blind or have severe visual impairments, touch should be considered the major exploratory sense.

Although most sensory experiences will be provided as part of a strong concept-development program, listening skills may need a separate emphasis. It is hoped that the preschooler has already been encouraged to identify, discriminate, and imitate sounds. During the preschool years, the focus should be on the sounds of letters and on similar words (rhyming), relating details of a story in sequence, and following directions (both single step and multistep). The ability to learn by listening to recorded materials is not an automatic skill and it must be specifically taught. A strong preschool program of activities to develop auditory skills is needed to ensure a child's later success.

Self-Help Skills. One area of self-help that is often overlooked for children with visual impairments is cleaning up after oneself. This is an appropriate skill to work on during the preschool years. A child who is visually impaired can learn to use a sponge to wipe off a table, find the trash can to deposit empty milk cartons, and put toys away in their proper places. If they learn orderliness and neatness early, children with visual impairments will be able to acquire more easily the organizational skills they will need throughout life.

TRANSITION

Most people think of transition as it applies to school-age children and youths, but there are also transition periods in the early years. The first transition usually occurs when services become less home based and more community or center based (usually around age 2 or 3). This transition period should be as individualized as possible and be based on the readiness of both the child and his or her family for change. During this transition, service providers need to consider which services can be better provided outside the home.

For young children with visual impairments, environmental change must be carefully planned. Consistency and predictability—of both people and environments—are critical for children who are visually impaired. The availability of special materials or a structured, consistent, safe, and predictable environment may be factors in transition, but the readiness and needs of the individual child should govern the timing.

A child who is visually impaired should have the opportunity to visit and explore any new setting prior to actual placement. Familiar service providers (such as the teacher of students with visual impairments and the O&M instructor) can assist both the child and his or her parents in becoming familiar with the new environment, and should do so gradually over several visits. In some cases, services may continue for a period in both the home and the new setting until the child has become accustomed to the new environment and feels comfortable in it. It cannot be stressed too strongly that the needs of the child, not the convenience of service providers, should determine the environment in which services are provided.

If a special education center-based program is being considered, it is important to match the child to the class. Generally, children with visual impairments who have no other disabilities benefit from being placed with nondisabled peers. Such a placement affords them opportunities to model peer-appropriate behaviors and to participate in age-appropriate activities. Support services from the teacher of students with visual impairments and O&M instructor can be provided within the structure of the normal preschool environment.

For children with visual impairments and additional disabilities, a special education center may be appropriate. Generally, the more severe the disabilities, the more appropriate the special program. Individual needs should determine each child's placement. The teacher of students with visual impairments (and possibly the O&M instructor) can still act as consultants or service providers as the child's individual needs dictate.

When a child with a visual impairment reaches age 3 and there is an administrative transition from early childhood intervention services to a public school program, the shift from family-focused planning to child-centered programming should occur as smoothly as possible. There may be fewer direct services to the family, but many of the same team members may still be available to the child. The more the team remains constant, the more consistent will be the services. The goal is to make the transition as seamless as possible, and the educational team is responsible for ensuring that it is.

Depending on a child's functional level, there may be yet another transition period in the early years. When the child reaches school age (enters kindergarten or first grade), his or her readiness for school needs to be evaluated. In addition to the developmental skills that have been the focus of services from birth to age 3 or 4, a number of other school-readiness skills should be addressed, as indicated in Sidebar 7.4.

True success in a mainstreamed or inclusive setting may depend on the mastery of skills that will allow a child who is visually impaired to compete with children who are sighted and to be personally independent. Although inclusion implies simply placement among peers, real success in that environment requires interaction, independence, and initiative. Efforts at the preschool level to ensure that children with visual impairments acquire these abilities should result in increased confidence, positive self-esteem, and both academic and social success. The time spent in developing school-readiness skills during the preschool years will have positive results later on.

SUMMARY

The early childhood years are crucial to overall development, since the skills and knowledge that are acquired during this period provide the foundation for all later learning. Infants, toddlers, and preschoolers with visual impairments need access to coordinated and specialized services because they cannot use imitation and modeling to learn new skills, as do their sighted counterparts. Working collaboratively with family members is especially important during the early childhood years. With ongoing collaboration to address the unique needs of young children with visual impairments, these children will be prepared to

---

SIDEBAR 7.4

School-Readiness Skills

◆ Taking care of own physical needs (toileting, dressing, eating, washing own hands, and the like).

◆ Following directions (listening, waiting, carrying out simple instructions, and so forth).

◆ Taking turns and cooperating with rules.

◆ Playing interactively and cooperatively.

◆ Using fine motor skills to handle tools (such as a marker or crayon, scissors, paste or glue, eating utensils, and a straw), unwrap foods and open a milk carton, and manipulate fasteners (including buttons, zippers, hooks, latches, doorknobs, and slide-bolts).

◆ Using gross motor skills and spatial understanding to get from one place to another in a socially acceptable manner and to participate in playground activities.

◆ Pressing keys on a braillewriter, if appropriate.

◆ Communicating needs and ideas, answering questions, and knowing and responding to own name.

◆ Understanding a wide variety of basic concepts (like up-down, little-big, tall-short, early-late, right-left, rough-smooth, top-bottom-middle, forward-backward, back-front, high-low, loud-soft, and hard-soft).

◆ Concentrating on and completing a task.

make the transition to a school program in kindergarten or first grade.

your classmates and look for commonalities among the suggestions.

ACTIVITIES

1. Visit a toy store and examine the toys that are appropriate for children under age five. List and describe the toys that would be the most motivating for young children with visual impairments. Categorize the toys according to their visual, tactile, auditory, and overall multisensory qualities.

2. Observe an early childhood program for students without disabilities and note areas that would require modification for young children who are blind and also for those who have low vision (make two separate lists). Then prepare two sets of recommendations that would be appropriate for general education teachers and other service providers to ensure that children with visual impairments would benefit from classroom activities.

3. Attend an IFSP meeting and an IEP meeting. Compare the basic elements of these two types of team meetings.

4. Adapt a commercially available game (such as Chutes and Ladders) for young children with visual impairments. Be sure to include modifications for children who are blind and for children with low vision. Arrange to have a play session with a preschooler who is visually impaired to try out the adapted game. Report your experiences to your classmates.

5. Interview parents of a child with a visual impairment who is in elementary school. Have the parents recount their early interactions and experiences with various professionals, focusing on the experiences that were helpful and those that were not. Prepare a list of suggestions that will help facilitate effective teaming with parents who have infants and preschoolers with visual impairments. Share the list with

REFERENCES

Als, H., Tronick, E., & Brazelton, T. (1976). Affective reciprocity and the development of autonomy: The study of a blind infant. *Journal of the American Academy of Child Psychiatry, 19,* 22–40.

American Printing House for the Blind. (n.d.). *Playing the crucial role in your child's development.* [Video]. Louisville, KY: Author.

Anderson, S., Boigon, S., & Davis, K. (1994). *Oregon Project for Visually Impaired and Blind Preschool Children.* Medford, OR: Jackson Education Service District.

Anthony, T., Armenta, F., Chen, D., Fazzi, D., Hughes, M., McCann, M., Nagaishi, P., Segal, J., Simmons, S., & Stout, A. (1993). *First steps: A handbook for teaching young children who are visually impaired.* Los Angeles: Blind Children's Center.

Barraga, N., & Erin, J. (1992). *Visual handicaps and learning.* Austin, TX: PRO-ED.

Bishop, V. (1991a). *Preschool children with visual impairments.* Unpublished manuscript. Austin, TX: Author.

Bishop, V. (1991b). Preschool visually impaired children: A demographic study. *Journal of Visual Impairment & Blindness, 85,* 69–74.

Bishop, V. (1996). *Teaching visually impaired children.* Springfield, IL: Charles C Thomas.

Bishop, V. (1998). *Infants and toddlers with visual impairment.* Unpublished manuscript. Austin, TX: Author.

Blind Children's Center. (n.d.). *Heart to heart* [Video]. Los Angeles: Author.

Blind Children's Center. (n.d.). *Let's eat.* [Video]. Los Angeles: Author.

Bluma, S., Shearer, M., Frohman, A., & Hilliard, J. (1976). *Portage guide to early education.* Portage, WI: Cooperative Educational Service Agency #12.

Bradley-Johnson, S. (1986). *Psychoeducational assessment of visually impaired and blind students.* Austin, TX: PRO-ED.

Caplan, F. (Ed.). (1978). *The parenting advisor.* New York: Anchor Books.

Chen, D. (1997). *What can baby see? Vision tests and intervention strategies for infants with multiple disabilities* [Video]. New York: AFB Press.

Chen, D. (Ed.). (1999). *Essential elements in early intervention: Visual impairment and multiple disabilities.* New York: AFB Press.

Chen, D., & Dote-Kwan, J. (1995). *Starting points: Instructional practices for young children whose multiple disabilities include visual impairment.* Los Angeles: Blind Children's Center.

Chen, D., & Orel-Bixler, D. (1997). *Vision tests for infants* [Video]. New York: AFB Press.

Collins, M. (1982). Parental reactions to a visually handicapped child: A mourning process. *Dissertation Abstracts International, 43,* 867A. (University Microfilms International 82–17, 840).

Croft, N., & Robinson, L. (1986). *Growing up: A developmental curriculum.* Ogden, UT: Parent Consultants.

Dunst, C. (n.d.). *Family-focused intervention rating scales.* Morganton, NC: Family, Infant & Preschool Program Western Carolina Center.

Dunst, C. J., Trivette, C. M., & Deal, A. G. (1988). *Enabling and empowering families: Principles and guidelines for practice.* Cambridge, MA: Brookline Books.

Ferrell, K. (1985). *Reach out and teach.* New York: American Foundation for the Blind.

Ferrell, K. (1998). *Project PRISM: A longitudinal study of developmental patterns of children who are visually impaired* (Final Report CFDA 84. 0203C, Field Initiated Research. HO 23C10188). Greeley, CO: Author.

Fewell, R., & Langley, B. (1984). *Developmental Activities Screening Inventory.* Austin, TX: PRO-ED.

Filan, S. (1992). Motor development. In E. Trief (Ed.), *Working with visually impaired young students: A curriculum guide for birth–3 year olds* (pp. 98–121). Springfield, IL: Charles C Thomas.

Gesell, A., Ilg, F. & Bullis, G. (1949). *Vision: Its development in infant and child.* New York: Harper & Bros.

Hatton, D., Bailey, D., Burchinal, M., & Ferrell, K. (1997). Developmental growth curves of preschool children with visual impairments. *Child Development, 68,* 788–806.

Holbrook, M. C. (1996). *Children with visual impairments: A parent's guide.* Bethesda, MD: Woodbine House.

Koenig, A. J., & Holbrook, M. C. (1993). *Learning media assessment of students with visual impairments: A resource guide.* Austin: Texas School for the Blind and Visually Impaired.

Levack, N. (1991). *Low vision: A resource guide with adaptations for students with visual impairments.* Austin: Texas School for the Blind and Visually Impaired.

Lighthouse International. (n.d.). *A special start* [Video]. New York: Author.

Lueck, A., Chen, D., & Kekelis, L. (1997). *Developmental guidelines for infants with visual impairments.* Louisville, KY: American Printing House for the Blind.

Markland, M. (1979). *Assessing kindergarten children with Project Vision-Up: A comparative study using selected standardized measurements.* Doctoral dissertation, Department of Educational Psychology, Brigham Young University.

Moore, S., (1985). *Beginnings.* Louisville, KY: American Printing House for the Blind.

Newborg, J., Stock, J., Wnek, L., Guidubaldi, J., & Svinicki, J. (1984). *Battelle Developmental Inventory (BDI).* Allen, TX: DLM Teaching Resources.

Nuttall, E. V., Romero, I., & Kalesnik, J. (1999). *Assessing and screening preschoolers: Psychological and educational dimensions* (2nd ed.). Boston: Allyn & Bacon.

Pogrund, R., Fazzi, D., & Lampert, J. (Eds.). (1992). *Early focus: Working with young blind and visually impaired children and their families.* New York: American Foundation for the Blind.

Robinson, L., & De Rosa, S. (1980). *Parent Needs Inventory.* Ogden, UT: Parent Consultants.

Sewell, D. (1997). *Assessment kit: Kit of informal tools for academic students with visual impairments, Part 1.* Austin: Texas School for the Blind and Visually Impaired.

Sommers, V. (1944). *The influence of parental attitudes and social environments on the personality development of the adolescent blind.* New York: American Foundation for the Blind.

Trief, E. (Ed.). (1992). *Working with visually impaired young students: A curriculum guide for birth–3 year olds.* Springfield, IL: Charles C Thomas.

Troster, H., Brambring, M., & Beelmann, A. (1991). The age dependence of stereotyped behaviors in blind infants and preschoolers. *Child: Care, Health and Development, 17,* 137–157.

Visually Impaired Preschool Services. (n.d.). *Can do* [Video series]. Author.

Wechsler Preschool and Primary Scale of Intelligence—Revised. (n.d.). San Antonio, TX: Psychological Corp.

Wright, F. (1980). *Project Vision-Up assessment: Validity and reliability.* Doctoral dissertation, Department of Educational Psychology, Brigham Young University.

Parent Questionnaire

Child's Name _____   Parent's Name _____

Date _____   Observer's Name _____

Family History

Does anyone in your family have a severe vision loss or eye disease (such as albinism, amblyopia, cataracts, glaucoma, strabismus, or retinoblastoma)?

_____ Yes   _____ No   If so, what? _____

Did the child's mother have any serious infections or diseases (such as rubella, cytomegalovirus, toxoplasmosis, syphilis, herpes) during pregnancy?

_____ Yes   _____ No   If so, what? _____

Did the child's mother use drugs or alcohol during pregnancy?

_____ Yes   _____ No   If so, which: _____

Was the child's mother exposed to any environmental hazards (like chemicals, radiation) during pregnancy?

_____ Yes   _____ No   If so, what? _____

Birth History

Was the child born prematurely?   _____ Yes   _____ No

If so, how early was he [she]? _____

What was the child's birthweight: _____ (3 pounds or under is a cause for concern).

Were there any postnatal infections (e.g., meningitis, encephalitis, hydrocephalus, prolonged fever, or convulsions)?

_____ Yes   _____ No   If so, what? _____

Was there any kind of head trauma at birth (or shortly thereafter)?

_____ Yes   _____ No   If so, describe: _____

Other Relevant History

Has any syndrome been identified?

_____ Yes   _____ No   If so, what? _____

(continued on next page)

Appendix A. Sample Parent Questionnaire

Parent Questionnaire *(Continued)*

Has cerebral palsy been identified?   _____ Yes   _____ No

Has any neurological disorder been identified (such as seizure activity)?

_____ Yes   _____ No

Does your child take any medications (such as anticonvulsive medication)?

_____ Yes   _____ No   If so, what? _____

Has a hearing problem been identified or suspected?   _____ Yes   _____ No

Are there any other medical problems known?   _____ Yes   _____ No

If so, what? _____

Do you have any concerns about your child's vision?   _____ Yes   _____ No

If so, what? _____

Functional Skills	Yes	No	Age of Typical Achievement
Looking			
Does your child look at your face, even momentarily?	_____	_____	(1 month)
Does your child look at his [her] own hands?	_____	_____	(3–4 months)
Does your child look at toys?	_____	_____	(3–4 months)
Does your child notice small objects (like raisins, Cheerios, lint)?	_____	_____	(4 months)
Does your child watch people at 6 feet away?	_____	_____	(6 months)
Does your child look for toys that have been dropped?	_____	_____	(9 months)
Is your child interested in pictures or picture books?	_____	_____	(12 months)
Reaching			
Does your child bat at objects that are suspended above him [her]?	_____	_____	(3 months)
Does your child try to reach out and grasp toys or objects?	_____	_____	(6 months)

(continued on next page)

Parent Questionnaire *(Continued)*

Functional Skills	Yes	No	Age of Typical Achievement
Reaching			
Does your child try to pick up small objects (such as raisins, Cheerios, lint)?	_____	_____	(8 months)
Does your child try to grab at your eyeglasses or jewelry?	_____	_____	(9 months)
Does your child reach into a container and try to pull out an object?	_____	_____	(12–18 months)
Locomotion			
Does your child notice an interesting object at least 5 feet away and indicate an interest/desire to have it (such as by pointing, waving arms, babbling, making hand movements)?	_____	_____	(6–7 months)
Does your child move, by any means, toward an interesting object at least 5 inches away?	_____	_____	(7–8 months)
Social			
Does your child react differently to different faces or people?	_____	_____	(6 months)
Does your child react to facial expressions (such as a smile, frown, or "funny face")?	_____	_____	(10–12 months)

Source: Reprinted, with permission, from V. Bishop, *Infants and Toddlers with Visual Impairments.* (Unpublished manuscript; available from author, 1998).

Appearance-of-the-Eyes Checklist

Child's Name _____   Observer's Name _____
Date _____

Eyelids
(check all those that apply)

_____ swelling of either eyelid

_____ drooping of one or both lids

_____ redness

_____ discharge (either watery or puslike)

_____ excess blinking

_____ scaly or crusted appearance

White part of eyes
(check all those that apply)

_____ yellowish appearance

_____ bloodshot, reddish appearance

_____ mucous discharge

_____ excess tearing

_____ scarring

Eyeballs
(check all those that apply)

_____ appear to be excessively large

_____ appear to be unusually small

_____ appear to be "sunken" into
        the eye socket

Overall Appearance of the Eyes
(check all those that apply)

_____ appears to be a "cloudy" film over the
        front of the eye

_____ pupil appears cloudy or whitish

_____ abnormal constriction or dilation of the
        pupil or pupils

_____ appearance of the eyes is normal
        (i.e., none of the above were observed)

Source: Reprinted, with permission, from V. Bishop, *Infants and Toddlers with Visual Impairments.*
(Unpublished manuscript; available from author, 1998).

Appendix B. Sample Assessment Checklist

Strategies for Teaching Preschoolers with Visual Impairments and Additional Disabilities

The preschool years for children who have impairments in addition to vision are a critical time to establish skills that serve as the foundation for communication, mobility, independence, and socialization and to prevent the patterns that interfere with the acquisition of these skills. Knowledge of gaps and problems that may occur in the development of children who may have postural, cognitive, or other sensory impairments enables teachers and parents to intervene as early as possible to facilitate an organized, integrated, and sequential progression of skills; to encourage functional compensatory behaviors; and to engage the children in the same playing and learning experiences as their peers.

Many families of young children who have cognitive impairments in addition to a visual impairment experience two grieving and acceptance processes: first for the loss of vision; and second, at the realization that the child is also mentally challenged. These processes sometimes overlap as families continue to experience some aspect of these processes with each transition the child makes. Although the integration of developmental skills may vary for a child with a visual impairment only, the learning rate and sequence should closely parallel that of his or her sighted peers, particularly toward the second year of life. There are signs, however, that may indicate dysfunctional or impaired learning processes. Identification of these indicators early will help the interventionist better plan for educational transitions and counsel parents to seek other appropriate services. Some of these indicators are

- Intense light gazing, which is preferred almost exclusively to other forms of information;
- The presence of self-injurious behaviors;

- The use of maladaptive behaviors (such as biting or head-banging) rather than speech to communicate;
- Self-stimulation with toys rather than appropriate play behavior;
- Resistance to organized learning sessions, despite consistency of rich learning opportunities;
- Acquisition of "splinter" skills, especially in the area of speech development, which is a relative developmental strength; and
- Development of expressive speech more than understanding and concepts.

Providing high-quality educational services to preschool children who are visually impaired and have additional disabilities is a challenging endeavor. Teachers of students with visual impairments must work closely with the child's parents and with other professionals to ensure that the child's unique, individual needs will be met. Both assessment and intervention should be addressed in relation to preschool services to children with visual impairments and additional disabilities.

Assessment

When children have deficits or dysfunction in multiple learning systems, assessments that provide for an understanding of the interrelationship of all developmental domains may yield the most helpful information for planning intervention strategies. A number of scales have been developed expressly for the purpose of looking at functional behaviors so that concerns may be addressed and strategies designed to help integrate learning systems. Chapter 2 discusses as-

(continued on next page)

sessments that may be appropriate to this population.

Assessments should include a consideration of the child's visual functioning as well as the influence of the child's posture, cognitive level, behavior state, and medication on the quality, level, and consistency with which he or she responds to items on the assessment. When the child is severely involved, assessments should not be conducted until the child's organizational, postural, and attentional qualities are addressed. An occupational therapist should be consulted for handling ideas and suggestions as to how to better integrate the child's sensory system prior to the assessment procedure.

Intervention

Teachers of students with visual impairments have an important role to play when determining appropriate instructional interventions for preschool children with visual impairments and additional disabilities. Implications of the child's visual impairment as well as all other disabilities should be considered when planning. This is a complex process that requires all team members to examine the child in a holistic manner. The following sample of suggestions to assist in specific developmental tasks for children who are visually impaired and have additional disabilities demonstrates the coordination of planning to address the implications of the child's multiple disabilities.

◆ When the infant's postural systems reflect either too much or too little muscle stiffness, the child may lack sufficient stability at the trunk and pelvis to lift his or her head. When the child does not have sufficient control to lift the head, motor movements cannot develop (such as sitting and reaching). In addition,

the child who is visually impaired often lacks the visual motivation to lift the head. Gentle, firm pressure into the pelvis and gentle, subtle shift of weight toward the feet with your hand will provide proprioceptive cues to lift the head. Hold this posture for several seconds and then let the baby rest. Simultaneous gentle, intermittent support at the forehead to assist with the head lift may also be helpful but this cue should be faded as soon as the baby begins to take control.

◆ As soon as the infant demonstrates sustained control of the head from a prone prop position, the parent can be shown how to shift the child's weight laterally by exerting control at the pelvis. Gentle lateral cues at the pelvis or trunk to shift weight in prone to one side assist the child in gaining mobility of the non-weightbearing side to reach. This is a component many infants who are visually impaired miss because they lack sufficient vision to elicit head rotation in prone to shift weight laterally. This lateral shift is essential to the development of a more sophisticated diagonal shift used as the infant crawls.

◆ To facilitate organization of midline, functional hand skills, and integration of primitive, protective touch (and avoid tactile hypersensitivity), parents should be encouraged to offer the infant firm, deep pressure into the palms with the parent's thumb. As the infant's hands relax, the pressure can move toward the fingers. Once the infant's hands are open the parent should play with placing the infant's hands on his or her own face, and then on the

(continued on next page)

parent's face, and then facilitate the infant to achieve palm to palm contact. The infant should be encouraged to reach his or her open hand to the foot in supine, to bring the hand to the mouth and bring a firm toy to the mouth while holding it. The pressure of the parent's hands against the infant's simulates weight bearing. As the parent holds the infant, he or she can provide the input to the palms and to the soles of the feet.

The pressure to the bottom of the feet also simulates weight bearing to get the infant ready to take weight when posturally appropriate. Other strategies include placing the infant in supine position and bending the knee to place the foot on a firm squeak toy. As pressure is exerted over the knee through the foot, the infant's foot activates the noise of the toy.

◆ As many children with visual impairments have low tone, they tend to sit with their knees bent and legs extended behind them, a posture referred to as "W" sitting. This posture provides the child the stability he or she lacks because of poor trunk muscles. Parents can be shown how to help the child play in side sit or circle sit to avoid the "W" sit, which places stress on ligaments and can lead to hip dysplasia.

◆ When the child sits with peers in a circle at preschool, "W" sitting and sitting on the low back (sacral sit) can be avoided by having the child sit on a low bench or stool rather than on the floor. Children with less control should be at the same level as their sighted peers during circle time. Providing support to the trunk allows the child to use his or her hands to perform finger plays and to reach toward a peer to shake hands.

◆ There are very appropriate toys on the market now for children with visual impairment. Selection of toys for children with multiple disabilities should focus on toys that will afford opportunities to develop a range of cognitive abilities and simultaneously encourage refinement of hand skills, social cause-effect, and communication.

◆ When encouraging the development of children with significant neurological impairment, olfactory stimulation should be avoided because of the possible reactions that may occur because of inadvertent stimulation to the trigeminal nerve. The sense of smell must be addressed only in natural settings so that the child learns to use smell for orientation within the environment, for anticipation of an activity, and for safety, avoiding poisons, fire, and other noxious substances. There are multiple natural opportunities throughout the day in which the child is exposed to smells that are associated with family, areas of the home, and routine, familiar activities.

◆ Particularly for the most severely involved children with visual impairment, all activities must occur within meaningful, natural contexts. Sitting the child in a highchair as mom and dad prepare dinner allows the child tactile explorations while smearing mashed potatoes around the tray, chomping on a frozen green bean, and responding to the sounds of water running and pots and pans clanging. Because skill acquisition and generalization is so complex for a

(continued on next page)

Strategies for Teaching Preschoolers *(Continued)*

child who has limited access to information, experiences need to approximate as closely as possible those contexts in which the child will function.

◆ Eating difficulties are often pronounced in children with visual impairments and with additional disabilities. Although each child is different, the problems are similar. The child may resist textures, refuse to chew, and protest gooey substances on the hands, preferring to be fed rather than to feed him- or herself. While bringing a loaded spoon to the mouth may be readily accomplished, the child has difficulty scooping, partially because of a lack of wrist extension and rotation sighted peers developed as they rotated toys in their hands and fingers while visually exploring them. If the child has not yet developed the cognitive skills of object permanence and tool use, he or she may not realize there is food in the bowl or dish and a spoon may have little meaning as a means of transferring the food from the bowl to the mouth.

◆ As food becomes increasingly more textured, time and patience are needed and the parent should be encouraged to continue to expose the infant to different textures, even though the child may spit them out the first time. If feeding continues to be difficult, the expertise of an occupational or speech therapist should be sought as early as possible to encourage functional eating behaviors and happy meal times.

◆ Parents should be encouraged as early as possible to provide the infant with as much oral and facial stimulation as possible with their hands, washcloths, and toys of various textures.

◆ Within a preschool setting, the child with multiple disabilities should participate in the same activities as his or her peers. Playing within the different learning centers, the nonverbal child who has limited hand control should be provided with single switch communication devices or with devices that allow him or her to make choices to learn to attract a peer's attention, or to request or choose a toy.

M. BETH LANGLEY
Pinellas County Schools
St. Petersburg, FL

RESOURCES

Suggested Resources for Early Childhood Intervention

Resource	Type	Source	Description
A Special Start	Videotape	Lighthouse International	Describes model preschool programs that include a child who is visually impaired.
Assessing and Screening Preschoolers: Psychological and Educational Dimensions, 2nd ed. (Nuttall, Romero, & Kalesnik, 1999)	Book	Allyn & Bacon	Guidelines for assessing and screening preschool children; includes a description of normal and abnormal development and a chapter on assessing preschool children with visual impairments.
Beginnings (Moore, 1985)	Book	American Printing House for the Blind	Presents ways of building critical skills such as reaching, grasping, midline coordination, and walking, in children birth to 2 years with visual impairments. Companion to *Playing the Crucial Role in Your Child's Development.*
Books, pamphlets, and newsletters	Books, pamphlets, and newsletters	Blind Children's Center	Books and pamphlets.
		Blind Children's Fund	Newsletter and pamphlets.
		National Association for Parents of Children with Visual Impairments	Newsletter and pamphlets.
		Oregon School for the Blind	*The National Newspatch* (newsletter)
		Texas School for the Blind and Visually Impaired	*SEE/HEAR (newsletter)*

(continued on next page)

Suggested Resources *(Continued)*

Resource	Type	Source	Description
Can Do (Series)	Videotapes	Visually Impaired Preschool Services	A set of 11 short videotapes that help parents and professionals to understand how to enhance early development in such areas as beginning concepts, motor development, self-help, social skills, and O&M; also includes parental reactions, low vision, adapting the preschool environ-ment, and braille readiness.
Children with Visual Impairments: A Parent's Guide (Holbrook, 1996)	Book	Woodbine House	A text written for parents; addresses all areas of development for children with visual impairments.
Developmental Activities Screening Inventory (DASI-II) (Fewell & Langley, 1984)	Assessment instrument	PRO-ED	A developmental assessment screening for preschool children (birth to age 5); adaptations given for children with visual impair-ments but no scoring adjustments.
Developmental Guidelines for Infants with Visual Impairments (Lueck, Chen, & Kekelis, 1997)	Book	American Printing House for the Blind	A manual for professionals working with infants with visual impairments from birth to age 2; describes what is known about the development of infants with a wide range of visual impairments. Addresses critical issues and over-all perspective of intervention concerns.
Early Focus: Working with Young Blind and Visually Impaired Children and Their Families (Pogrund, Fazzi, & Lampert, 1992)	Book	American Foundation for the Blind	Clear descriptions of early intervention techniques with students with visual impairments; stresses benefits of family involvement and transdisciplinary teamwork. Valuable information on working with families of various ethnic-minority groups.
Enabling and Empowering Families: Principles and Guidelines for Practice (Dunst, Trivette, & Deal, 1988)	Book	Brookline Books	In this text is the Family Needs Scale and Family Resource Scale.
Family-Focused Intervention Rating Scales (Dunst, n.d.)	Assessment instrument	Family, Infant, & Preschool Program, Western Carolina Center	A family-focused interactive tool for an ecologically relevant and functional approach to assessment and intervention with families of children who are severely disabled.
First Steps: A Handbook for Teaching Young Children Who are Visually Impaired (Anthony et al., 1993)	Book	Blind Children's Center	Textbook addressing knowledge and skills necessary for teaching young children with visual impairments.

(continued on next page)

Suggested Resources *(Continued)*

Resource	Type	Source	Description
Growing Up: A Developmental Curriculum (Croft & Robinson, 1986)	Assessment instrument and curriculum	Parent Consultants	Assessment and programming kit designed for use with preschool children with visual impairments. Based on a Piagetian theory of development.
Heart to Heart	Videotape	Blind Children's Center	Presents the parents' viewpoint on having a child with a visual disability.
"Infants and Toddlers with Visual Impairment" (Bishop, 1998)	Unpublished manuscript	Author (Virginia Bishop)	Description of the development of and appropriate interventions for infants and toddlers with visual impairments.
Learning Media Assessment of Students with Visual Impairments: A Resource Guide (Koenig & Holbrook, 1993)	Book	Texas School for the Blind and Visually Impaired	Guidelines and forms useful in assessing sensory channels and learning/literacy media.
Let's Eat	Videotape	Blind Children's Center	Describes the process of learning to eat and self-feed for children with multiple disabilities and visual impairment.
Low Vision: A Resource Guide with Adaptations for Students with Visual Impairments (Levack, 1991)	Book	Texas School for the Blind and Visually Impaired	A comprehensive guide to low vision for professionals and parents. Reflects current philosophies, medical and technical information, and methodologies and adaptations that are practical. Includes useful assessment forms.
Oregon Project for Visually Impaired and Blind Preschool Children (Anderson, Boigon, & Davis, 1994)	Assessment instrument and curriculum	Jackson County Education Service District, Medford, OR	A criterion-referenced assessment for children with visual impairments from birth through the preschool years; includes compensatory education activities.
Parent Needs Inventory (Robinson & De Rosa, 1980)	Assessment instrument	Parent Consultants	A unique and systematic process for identifying parents' needs, priorities, and suggestions for intervention. Allows parents to explore and examine their own feelings and attitudes.
Playing the Crucial Role in Your Child's Development	Videotape	American Printing House for the Blind	Suggestions for parents in creating a positive environment to enhance early development. Presents ways of building critical skills, such as reaching, grasping, midline coordination, and walking, in children from birth to 2 years with visual impairments. Companion to *Beginnings*.

(continued on next page)

Suggested Resources *(Continued)*

Resource	Type	Source	Description
Psychoeducational Assessment of Visually Impaired and Blind Students (Bradley-Johnson, 1986)	Book	PRO-ED	Survey of assessment instruments used with students with visual impairments across ages and assessment areas.
Reach Out and Teach (Ferrell, 1985)	Guide	American Foundation for the Blind	A guide for parents of preschool children who are visually impaired. Includes two parts—an instructional guide and companion workbook—that address all areas of child development.
Starting Points: Instructional Practices for Young Children Whose Multiple Disabilities Include Visual Impairment (Chen & Dote-Kwan, 1995)	Book	Blind Children's Center	Textbook addressing knowledge and skills necessary for teaching young children with multiple disabilities including visual impairments.
Teaching Visually Impaired Children (Bishop, 1996)	Book	Charles C Thomas	A textbook addressing the knowledge and skills necessary for teaching children with visual impairments; covers all age groups.
Wechsler Preschool & Primary Scale of Intelligence–Revised (n.d.)	Assessment instrument	Psychological Corporation	An intelligence test for preschool children; should be used only by a trained, experienced diagnostician. May need modification for children with visual impairments.
What Can Baby See? Vision Tests and Intervention Strategies for Infants with Multiple Disabilities (Chen, 1997)	Videotape	AFB Press	Presents common vision tests and methods used with infants and young children with multiple disabilities; helps identify visual impairments that require early intervention services. Also addresses early intervention and strategies for working with families.
Working with Visually Impaired Young Students: A Curriculum Guide for Birth–3 Year Olds (Trief, 1992)	Book	Charles C Thomas	A curriculum guide for children from birth to age 3 with visual impairments. Primary emphasis is on sensory, motor, and language development.

Contact information for each of the resources listed will be found in the Sources of Products, Materials, Equipment, and Services section at the back of this book.

CHAPTER 8

Literacy Skills

Alan J. Koenig and M. Cay Holbrook

KEY POINTS

- The acquisition of literacy skills provides the foundation needed for achieving in school, as well as in many other areas of life, including employment.
- The assessment of literacy media needs and literacy skills is crucial for designing an appropriate, individual literacy instruction program for each student with a visual impairment.
- The teacher of students with visual impairments has the primary responsibility for providing direct instruction in braille and other compensatory literacy skills to students who are blind.
- Students with low vision have specific needs and challenges in developing literacy skills that must be addressed through direct instruction and consultation with general education teachers.
- Students who receive literacy instruction in general education classrooms must be supported through consultative services, supplementary direct instruction, and ongoing assessment to ensure that they develop optimal literacy skills.

VIGNETTE

While riding the bus to the high school, Joel had finished the chapter assigned for homework in civics.

Civics was the first period, and Mr. Bryan, Joel's civics teacher, sometimes gave pop quizzes just to see who had done the reading. Joel was really glad he had learned braille. He could still read print, if it was big enough and the passage was short enough, but he could *never* have read an entire social studies chapter in the uncertain lighting and bouncing motion of a school bus. However, with his braille book, he had read half the chapter going home yesterday and the second half this morning. "Look, Ma! No homework!" he chuckled to himself.

Teresa and Ms. Powell, the teacher of students with visual impairments, sat side by side reading *The Little Red Hen* again, with Teresa taking the parts of all the selfish animals. "'Not I!' said the cat. 'Not I!' said the dog. 'Not I!' said the mouse." Teresa read with delight. "'Then I'll do it myself!' said the Little Red Hen, and she did!" read Ms. Powell. A few hard grains of wheat lay scattered on the table amid a dusting of flour, so that Teresa could examine the difference. Later Teresa and Ms. Powell would look more closely at the braille signs for *said* and *not,* and Ms. Powell would teach Teresa to write these words in braille and to give their full spelling. Ms. Powell had already added homemade cards for *sd, said, n,* and *not* to their card deck, and if there was time, she and Teresa would play a game of Go Fish with braille contractions.

On the playground, 9-year-old Devon slid an index card into his plastic slate. While Luther, his fourth-grade classmate, said the numbers one at a time and watched in fascination, Devon carefully wrote Luther's phone number. On the bottom row of the card, he wrote, "Luther." He put the card in his shirt pocket. He would take it home and put it in his file box. The next time he wanted to call Luther, he would have the right number.

That afternoon, Ms. Powell sat in the library at the junior high school with Cassandra, an eighth-grade student with low vision. Cassandra was using her magnifier to examine the diacritical marks indicating the pronunciation of the word *exemplary.* After she noted the marks, she and Ms. Powell looked together at the pronunciation key at the bottom of the right-hand page. Cassandra was making a list of diacritical marks and some simple words that would help her remember the meanings of each one. On other afternoons, Ms. Powell and Cassandra had come to the library and explored a thesaurus, an almanac, and how to use the index volume of an encyclopedia. The school library was in the process of changing to a computerized card catalog system. When the change-over was complete, Ms. Powell and Cassandra would learn to use the new system together. Ms. Powell felt strongly that students need to use many resources to "unlock the power" of the library.

INTRODUCTION

The importance of well-developed literacy skills for all individuals is reflected in the value placed on reading and writing in schools and throughout this society. Instruction in literacy skills can justifiably be considered the cornerstone of education. Achievement in all other subjects—such as mathematics, science, and social studies—is linked to reading and writing skills and the ability to gather, use, and convey information. Without question, literate individuals can excel in school and enter adulthood with a competitive advantage in employment and in life that is less possible for individuals with low or no literacy skills.

For individuals who are blind or visually impaired, the value of literacy skills is equally important. The way in which students with visual impairments develop literacy skills may differ, but the goal is the same: to use reading, writing, and

other literacy tools to gather and understand important information and to convey important information to themselves or to others. The information contained in this chapter is based on a broad definition of literacy that encompasses three major facets:

◆ Emergent literacy skills—the earliest attempts by young children to bring meaning to reading and writing;

◆ Academic literacy skills—the basic reading and writing skills taught in a conventional literacy medium (print or braille) during the elementary and middle school years; and

◆ Functional literacy skills—the application of literacy skills and the use of a variety of literacy tools (such as listening and technology) to accomplish daily tasks in the home, school, community, and work settings (Koenig, 1992).

Each facet of literacy constitutes an essential component of the expanded core curriculum for students who are blind or have low vision (see Chapter 6). For instructional purposes, these three areas can be divided into more discrete units. Sidebar 8.1 presents a framework that delineates specific areas of literacy instruction for students in braille literacy programs and students in print literacy programs. This division is arbitrary, however, since a portion of the population of students with low vision will benefit from instruction in braille literacy skills, as determined through appropriate assessments.

This chapter begins by discussing the important role of the teacher of students with visual impairments in ensuring the growth of literacy skills for students who are blind or visually impaired and describing informal assessment approaches to measure this growth. It then presents detailed information on strategies for teaching literacy skills to students who are blind and students who have low vision. Finally, it describes the integration of students with visual impairments in literacy programs within general education classrooms.

SIDEBAR 8.1

Areas of Instruction in Literacy Skills for Students with Visual Impairments

NEEDS OF STUDENTS IN BRAILLE LITERACY PROGRAMS

- Emergent braille literacy skills
- Formal early braille literacy skills ("prebraille")
- Beginning braille literacy skills
- Beginning literacy skills in dual media (print and braille)
- Intermediate braille literacy skills
- Advanced braille literacy skills
- Braille literacy skills for students with print literacy skills
- Listening, aural reading, and live reader skills
- Keyboarding and word-processing skills
- Technology skills
- Slate and stylus skills
- Signature-writing skills

NEEDS OF STUDENTS IN PRINT LITERACY PROGRAMS

- Emergent print literacy skills
- Integrated use of visual skills
- Beginning print literacy skills

- Beginning literacy skills in dual media (print and braille)
- Use of optical devices in near environments
- Use of optical devices in distant environments
- Braille literacy skills for students with print literacy skills
- Listening aural reading, and live reader skills
- Keyboarding and word-processing skills
- Technology skills
- Intermediate and advanced print literacy skills

———————————

Sources: Adapted from A. L. Corn and A. J. Koenig, *Assuring Quality Literacy Instruction for Students with Low Vision,* Manuscript in preparation (2000); A. J. Koenig and M. C. Holbrook, "Assuring High-Quality Literacy Instruction for Students in Braille Literacy Programs," *Journal of Visual Impairment & Blindness,* in press; and A. J. Koenig and E. J. Rex, "Instruction of Literacy Skills to Children and Youths with Low Vision," in A. L. Corn and A. J. Koenig, Eds., *Foundations of Low Vision: Clinical and Functional Perspectives* (New York: AFB Press, 1996), pp. 280–305.

ROLE OF THE TEACHER OF STUDENTS WITH VISUAL IMPAIRMENTS

The teacher of students with visual impairments plays a direct role in ensuring that all students with visual impairments attain solid literacy skills. Although the specialist's specific role and responsibilities change as students progress from home to preschool and from elementary school through high school, the specialist's involvement remains relatively constant throughout the school years. The specialist's responsibilities also differ somewhat for students who are blind and for those with low vision. In general, students who are blind receive more direct instruction, while students with low vision receive more consultation and short-term instruction. However, the nature of the instructional services (direct or consultative) and the amount of time devoted to direct instruction depend on the needs of each individual student determined by the results of assessments. The responsibilities of the teacher of students with visual impairments are the following:

◆ Provide initial and ongoing assessments of students' needs for literacy media;

◆ Collaborate with and model for family members and others the strategies needed to facilitate the development of emergent literacy in students who are blind and students with low vision;

◆ Provide direct, consistent, daily instruction in prebraille skills and beginning braille literacy skills throughout preschool and the early elementary grades;

◆ Provide direct instruction in unique literacy skills, including slate and stylus skills, signature writing, aural reading (gathering information from audiotaped materials), live reader services, keyboarding, word processing, and technology skills;

◆ Provide direct instruction in braille reading and writing for students who are learning braille as a complementary medium to print or who are moving from print to braille;

◆ Teach the integrated use of vision skills and the use of optical and nonoptical devices to students with low vision; and

◆ Collaborate with general education teachers and others to integrate students with visual impairments in literacy instruction within general education classrooms.

The teacher also plays an essential role in working with students with additional disabilities; strategies focusing on students with visual impairments and additional disabilities and resources for teachers appear later in this chapter.

ASSESSMENT

Two aspects of assessment in the area of literacy skills need to be addressed. The first is related to selecting appropriate learning and literacy media for students, a process commonly referred to as learning media assessment (see Chapter 4 for a detailed description of this process). The second, which is the focus of this section, is related to the general assessment of growth in and achievement of literacy skills in whatever medium or media the student uses. Both assessment processes require the expertise of a teacher of students with visual impairments and demand ongoing attention throughout the school years.

To complete assessments of literacy skills, the teacher draws on a variety of informal assessment techniques and checklists (see Chapter 3). Such informal assessment procedures may include informal reading inventories, observations and interviews of the student's reading interests, analyses of miscues made during reading aloud, measures of comprehension and vocabulary skills, and measures of reading achievement. In addition, the results of appropriately modified standardized assessments that may be administered on a district- or statewide basis in some areas may be used as a source (but never the sole source) of information to document the student's continued progress in developing braille literacy skills.

The informal instruments related to the unique aspects of reading and writing in braille, such as the Minnesota Braille Skills Inventory (Godwin et al., 1995) and the Assessment of Braille Literacy Skills (Koenig & Farrenkopf, 1995), should also be used. The former checklist assesses the student's mastery of specific braille contractions, short-form words, and symbols of the Nemeth Code (math). The latter checklist also assesses braille code skills, but encompasses braille literacy skills. Appendix A of this chapter presents a checklist for conducting a diagnostic assessment of braille reading skills, and Appendix B includes a checklist for assessing mastery of the braille slate and stylus. Checklists are also available for assessing a student's use of visual skills and low vision devices in literacy tasks (see Chapter 13).

There are a variety of resources to assist the teacher of students with visual impairments in conducting high-quality literacy assessments. Separate chapters are devoted to this topic in *Instructional Strategies for Braille Literacy* (Wormsley & D'Andrea, 1997; specifically see Layton,

1997), *Communication Skills for Visually Impaired Learners* (Harley, Truan, & Sanford, 1987), *Beginning with Braille* (Swenson, 1999), and *Foundations of Braille Literacy* (Rex, Koenig, Wormsley, & Baker, 1994). Assessment strategies for students with low vision are addressed in *Foundations of Low Vision* (Corn & Koenig, 1996). Finally, the general assessment strategies discussed in Chapter 3 of this book are helpful in designing and using informal assessment strategies.

EMERGENT LITERACY SKILLS

The early years of a child's life provide the foundation for developing literacy skills during the school years. During this period, infants and toddlers are developing language and concepts and gaining rich experiences that will make literacy events meaningful to them. For example, visiting a local petting zoo to explore real livestock will make "writing" a letter to Grandma about the trip (an early literacy event) a meaningful experience. Later, when the child reads *Charlotte's Web* by E. B. White in elementary school (another literacy event), the earlier experiences gained through the petting zoo, coupled with other experiences, will help ensure that he or she has the understanding of animals needed to bring meaning to this children's classic.

Emergent literacy skills comprise the child's earliest interactions with print, braille, and other abstract symbols and the meaning that the child begins to attach to these abstract symbols. For example, a child who pretends to read from a newspaper or scribbles on a page and "reads" back the message is demonstrating emergent literacy. Although the child cannot read or write the words in a conventional sense, he or she is learning that printed words have meaning and that reading allows one to unlock meaning.

Young children who are sighted begin to learn the functions of reading and writing by observing experienced readers and writers carrying out these tasks. They also learn through interactions with the environment, by associating abstract

symbols (such as the "golden arches" of a McDonalds fast-food restaurant) with a meaningful event (like eating hamburgers). Because vision plays a dominant role in the development of emergent literacy skills, children who are visually impaired need to have unique learning experiences so that emergent literacy events are addressed directly, not left to chance development.

During the infant and toddler years, the teacher of students with visual impairments works with children in the home and in early childhood settings to model appropriate techniques for fostering emergent literacy and to provide direct instruction as needed. Parents and other family members play a key and essential role, since much of the development of emergent literacy occurs in the home or community before children enter a center-based preschool program. The following are some important strategies for ensuring that young children with visual impairments gain emergent literacy skills:

◆ Expand the child's range of early experiences. Arrange for field trips and community excursions to encounter new things and activities. Sidebar 8.2 presents a list of 22 areas of fundamental experiences to undergird early reading and writing experiences (Koenig & Farrenkopf, 1997). The child should be presented with rich and varied activities like these, using sound principles of multisensory learning. The child needs to have time to explore objects using the available senses (for example, experiencing a frog in its natural habitat by feeling, smelling, hearing, and looking) and to engage directly and actively in activities (for instance, climbing on a jungle gym at the park or pulling weeds from a flowerbed). Parents and teachers need to encourage active exploration and participation through physical modeling, hand-over-hand guidance, and other techniques (see Chapters 5 and 6). These experiences take longer than those that are gained primarily through vision, so the teacher and parents should allow ample time for them.

SIDEBAR 8.2

Common Experiences to Undergird Early Reading and Writing Experiences

EXPERIENCES TYPICALLY GAINED THROUGH DAILY ACTIVITIES

- Exploring nature, plants, insects
- Experiences with living creatures
- Experiencing emotions and a sense of well-being
- Experiences with family and family traditions
- Experiences in the community
- Experiences at home
- Experiences with friends or pretending
- Experiences with eating
- School experiences
- Experiences with books
- Experiences with weather
- Using different forms of transportation
- Enjoying the arts
- Going to a farm
- Working together, sharing, helping
- Doing or making things
- Learning about people who are different
- Getting into trouble
- Looking for or finding something
- Traveling or visiting others

EXPERIENCES TYPICALLY GAINED THROUGH INSTRUCTION

- Understanding specific concepts
- Learning and content areas

Source: Reprinted, with permission, from A. J. Koenig and C. Farrenkopf, "Essential Experiences to Undergird the Early Development of Literacy," *Journal of Visual Impairment & Blindness, 91* (1997), p. 18.

- Stress the quality and depth, not merely the quantity, of experiences. For sequential tasks, such as washing the family car, make certain that the child experiences each step in the sequence. For nonsequential activities, such as participation in a birthday party, ensure that the child is actively involved in all of the various aspects. Include multiple opportunities to engage in the same or similar experiences to allow for practice and generalization.

- Provide daily opportunities to read aloud to the child. Reading aloud is one of the most important components of emergent literacy activities and has a direct impact on literacy learning throughout the school years. Work with the parents to gather a wide range of interesting and motivating books in accessible media. Print-braille books—those containing both print and braille on the same pages or superimposed pages—are ideal for reading aloud, since they expose the child to both media and it may not be possible to determine whether an infant or toddler will be a print reader or a braille reader.

- Use "book bags" (Miller, 1985) to accompany books while reading aloud. These bags or boxes contain key objects from the story that are a substitute for pictures for children who are blind, and a supplement to the pictures for children with low vision. While reading aloud, present the objects to the child at appropriate times in the story and encourage the child to manipulate and explore them. See Sidebar 8.3 for more suggestions for reading aloud.

◆ Model for the parents and encourage them to involve the child directly in literacy events throughout the day. For example, while looking through the daily mail, the parent can "read through" the mail with the child by sorting bills, reading cards, and discarding junk mail. The teacher of students with visual impairments can help make this experience more meaningful by

---

SIDEBAR 8.3

Suggestions for Reading Aloud

INFANCY

- ◆ Read to a child in a cozy place.
- ◆ Read and sing rhymes to help soothe a child.
- ◆ Use your voice in a dramatic way to make the words of the story exciting.
- ◆ Read anything, as long as you enjoy it.
- ◆ Choose books with simple, bright illustrations in case the child has some vision; outline the illustrations with a dark felt-tip pen to provide contrast, if necessary.

TODDLER YEARS

- ◆ Give the child objects to feel in place of the pictures that may be in the books.
- ◆ Collect objects in a story box to accompany stories; explore the objects before reading a story.
- ◆ Make your own books with objects for each page, using sturdy cardboard for the pages.
- ◆ Give the child plenty of opportunities to handle books.
- ◆ Look for and use commercial books that have items for touching and looking.
- ◆ Keep books in a location where the child can have access to them.
- ◆ Involve the child in the story; encourage him or her to repeat words or rhymes and ask the child simple questions.

ALMOST PRESCHOOL

- ◆ Read stories that are predictable.
- ◆ Use tactile symbols for the covers of books.
- ◆ Use books with tactile illustrations that are in print and braille.
- ◆ Let the child's interest in braille develop naturally.
- ◆ Let the child know what you use print for.

PRESCHOOL

- ◆ Enroll the child in a preschool story-hour program at a local library.
- ◆ Review books to see if they depend on pictures before reading them to the child.
- ◆ Consider if the concepts presented in the books are familiar to the child; if not, help the child learn the concepts by relating them to things the child knows. Books then begin to broaden the child's learning.
- ◆ Use tactile-visual storybooks or books with raised-line drawings, such as those published by APH.
- ◆ Use print-braille books.

Source: Reprinted, with permission, from D. P. Wormsley, "Fostering Emergent Literacy," in D. P. Wormsley and F. M. D'Andrea, Eds., *Instructional Strategies for Braille Literacy* (New York: AFB Press, 1997), p. 44; adapted, with permission, from *Discovering the Magic of Reading: Elizabeth's Story* [Videotape] (Louisville, KY: American Printing House for the Blind, 1995).

periodically sending the child cards and messages in braille and/or print.

♦ Provide a variety of appropriate writing tools in the home, such as a braillewriter, slate and stylus, markers, soft-lead pencils, and a screen board (that is, a piece of heavy cardboard or a board with wire screen stretched over the surface, which provides tactile feedback when a child colors or scribbles on paper placed over it). For a child who is blind, the teacher and parents need to provide direct exposure to braille writing devices, starting with the brailler. Making personal lists (such as a grocery list) is an excellent activity for this purpose, since it involves short writing episodes and is something that is meaningful for the child. A shopping list may include two or three items that the child wants from the store; at the store, the child can "read" the list, relying primarily on memory.

♦ Provide models of proficient readers, especially for a child who will read braille. The teacher should put parents in contact with proficient braille readers, so the child has experience of "reading" with or being read to by someone who uses braille. During this activity, the child's hands need to be in direct, physical contact with the page and the reader's hands, so while the adult reader continues to read fluently, the child can explore the page with his or her hands. Models of proficient readers are also important for children with low vision. Generally, the only modification that is needed is to place the child in close proximity to the proficient print reader, so he or she can observe and experience the process. The adult with low vision can also model the effective use of low vision devices. For both children who are blind and those with low vision, adults should model the writing process as well.

♦ Provide opportunities and resources for the parents and other caregivers to learn braille. The uncontracted braille code can be learned easily and will allow parents to have knowledge of the code that the child will use for literacy activities. *Just Enough to Know Better* (Curran, 1988) was written specifically for parents and provides concise, motivating lessons to learn the braille alphabet or the entire braille code.

♦ Encourage the use of listening during the early years, since listening will be a major source of information during the school years. For example, listening for the garage door to open signals a parent's arrival from work, the sound of animals in the neighborhood provides cues to the extended environment, and traffic sounds and other cues assist with orientation and facilitate movement. Also, by listening to others, the child can gather important information. In practicing this skill, a parent may have a child remember one or two things that are needed at the store and then request this information later when the two are shopping.

♦ Provide a wide variety of early literacy activities throughout the early years. Sidebar 8.4 lists motivating activities that can be included naturally as part of the child's day. Students who are blind will complete early reading and writing activities in braille, and those with low vision will complete the same activities in print or in both print and braille.

♦ In the early years, use diagnostic teaching to gather information on how the child uses his or her senses and to determine the appropriate reading medium or media for beginning reading. In this approach, the teacher provides instruction in both print and braille and then observes the child's responses to the instruction within a variety of rich literacy events (such as scribbling to convey a message, looking at pictures to make up or review stories, "helping" an adult as he or she reads aloud, and acting out stories). Chapter 4 presents more information on strategies for selecting the initial literacy medium.

Early Literacy Activities

- Provide a variety of tactile books for the child to explore.

- Read from "Twin Vision" books that contain both print and braille.

- Adapt print books by placing braille above or below the lines of print.

- Adapt book covers to make them meaningful, perhaps by gluing on an object from the story.

- Make "book bags" that contain objects from the story. While reading aloud, let the child explore the objects that go with the various parts of the story.

- Act out stories with the child after reading aloud.

- Let the child scribble with a braillewriter, after or in conjunction with repeated modeling of the use of braille writing equipment.

- Let the child use a raised-line drawing kit for drawing and scribbling.

- While the child dictates, write stories in braille about the child's experiences or

keep a journal; then read these stories together.

- Make an "auditory experience album" by recording events and experiences on audiocassette tapes; review the album occasionally as you would a book or picture album.

- Leave off the ends of sentences in predictable stories and let the child finish them.

- Have the child practice tracking in real braille books while you read aloud; when the child stops tracking, you stop reading.

- Work with the child on the prerequisites to reading and book-related conventions and behaviors: moving left to right, turning pages, and recognizing the top and bottom of pages, for example.

Source: Adapted from D. D. Miller, "Reading Comes Naturally: A Mother and Her Blind Child's Experiences," *Journal of Visual Impairment & Blindness, 79* (1985); adapted from E. J. Rex, A. J. Koenig, D. Wormsley, and R. Baker, *Foundations of Braille Literacy* (New York: AFB Press, 1994), p. 11.

The teacher of students with visual impairments can draw on a wide variety of resources to promote emergent literacy. *The Bridge to Braille* (Castellano & Kosman, 1997) and *Growing into Literacy* (Koenig, 1996a) were written specifically for parents of young children who are visually impaired. *On the Way to Literacy* (Stratton & Wright, 1991), written for both parents and teachers, addresses the emergent literacy needs of children with visual impairments. *Beginning with Braille* (Swenson, 1999) and *Instructional Strategies for Braille Literacy* (Wormsley & D'Andrea, 1997) are comprehensive books for teachers that address the literacy needs of children who are blind from in-

fancy through the school years. See the Resources for descriptions of these and other materials.

EARLY BRAILLE LITERACY SKILLS

At the beginning of the preschool years (around age 3), a student who is blind begins a series of formal instructional activities that address early braille skills. This phase generally extends through kindergarten, although the child should move seamlessly into more formal early braille literacy skills as appropriate for his or her developmental level. The purpose of this special sequence of instruction is to teach students the hand movements and tactile skills—called mechanical skills—required for efficient braille reading. These skills are sometimes referred to as "prebraille" skills, indicating that they precede formal reading and writing instruction in braille. In addition, the specialist should continue to develop the early literacy skills to ensure that the child applies the mechanical skills in meaningful contexts and activities.

The teacher of students with visual impairments plays a direct and ongoing role in teaching prebraille skills. Professionals in braille literacy instruction recommend that children should receive prebraille instruction for a half hour to an hour each day (Koenig & Holbrook, in press). Given the short attention span of children at this age, this instructional time may be divided between two or more short instructional sessions. The specialist in visual impairments also continues to collaborate with the parents and the preschool teacher to ensure that appropriate prebraille activities are integrated throughout the day and evening.

Mechanical Skills

During the time when prebraille skills are being taught, the teacher of students with visual impairments focuses on developing skills that lead to efficient braille reading. Since efficiency in braille skills during the early years has a direct impact on a child's efficiency in braille literacy skills throughout the school years (Olson, 1981), the teacher needs to keep the goal of efficient literacy skills in mind while providing instruction. Mangold (1994b, p. 8) stated that the following characteristics are typical of good braille readers:

- Exhibits few regressive[1] hand movements (either vertically or horizontally).

---

[1] *Regressive hand movements are those in which the hands and fingers move back and forth or up and down unnecessarily on the braille line and hamper efficient tracking skills. In early literacy activities, these movements may indicate that the student needs additional practice in tracking lines while tactilely discriminating likenesses and differences between characters and words.*

- Uses very little pressure when touching the braille dots.

- Utilizes a two handed reading technique in which the left hand locates the beginning of the next line, while the right hand finishes reading the previous line.

- Uses at least four fingers at all times.

- Demonstrates the ability to scan efficiently when reading both vertical and horizontal format.

- Demonstrates the ability to read letters accurately without confusing letters that are mirror images of other letters.

Olson (1981) recommended that the specialist in visual impairment focus on four areas of mechanical skills:

Finger Dexterity and Wrist Flexibility. Sorting, stacking, stringing beads, punching holes in paper, screwing lids on jars, putting nuts and bolts together, and many other activities in which a child engages throughout the day provide opportunities to practice finger dexterity and wrist flexibility. The key is to teach these activities and then expect the child to do them on his or her own.

Hand Movement Skills and Finger Positions. These skills are taught through specific activities related to braille or tactile materials. The teacher can model these skills by standing or sitting behind the child and placing the child's hands over his or her hands. Then the teacher provides braille lines or other tactile lines for the child to track, keeping multiple fingers on the lines, tracking smoothly, and returning efficiently to the next line. Generally, the teacher starts with double-spaced lines of equal length and then goes to double-spaced lines of unequal length, single-spaced lines of equal length, and single-spaced lines of unequal length. A typical progression of tracking movements is presented in Sidebar 8.5. A variety of materials are available to help the teacher provide instruction in hand-movement skills, as discussed later in this section.

SIDEBAR 8.5

Sequence for Tracking Skills

TRACKING LINES (EARLY SKILLS)

- Moves fingers from left to right.
- Moves fingers from top to bottom.
- Detects breaks in lines.
- Detects end of lines.
- Keeps fingers on lines without moving paper.
- Tracks double-spaced lines with fluidity.
- Tracks single-spaced lines with fluidity.

TRACKING PATTERNS (FOR BOTH DOUBLE-SPACED, AND SINGLE-SPACED LINES)

- Reads with both hands together, retraces line with hands together, and drops hands to next line together.

- Uses left pointer finger as a line marker while the right hand reads the line; right hand returns on same line and both hands drop together.

- Uses left pointer finger as a line marker while the right hand reads the line, and left pointer finger drops to the next line while the right hand lifts to meet it.

- Left hand reads to the middle of the line, the right hand continues to read from there to the end of the line, the left hand drops down to the next line and begins reading (independent two handed reading).

Source: Reprinted, with permission, from A. J. Koenig and C. Farrenkopf, *Assessment of Braille Literacy Skills (ABLS)*. (Houston, TX: Region IV Education Service Center, 1995).

Light Finger Touch.   This skill is encouraged and reinforced in every lesson. If a teacher observes that the child is placing too much pressure on the fingertips, he or she reminds the child orally or models a light finger touch. Sometimes a child tries to compensate for the lack of discrimination skill by pressing more heavily on the braille characters to gain more tactile information. If the child exhibits a heavy finger touch while completing discrimination activities, then reminders and modeling alone may not be sufficient. In this case, it is necessary to provide instruction in efficiently discriminating and/or identifying braille characters.

Tactile Perception and Discrimination Skills. These skills are taught through a series of special activities geared to the needs of students who read braille. Although there is no established sequence to follow in developing tactile perception skills, the sequence provided by Mangold (cited in Olson, 1981) demonstrates careful attention to increasing the level of difficulty in small steps, as presented in Sidebar 8.6. To develop efficient and effective tactile perception and discrimination skills, this area of instruction must be integrated with hand movements, as Mangold's sequence clearly indicates.

Instructional Materials

There are several sources of instructional materials for specialists in visual impairment to use in developing prebraille skills. The most comprehensive program is *The Mangold Developmental Program of Tactile Perception and Braille Letter Recognition* (Mangold, 1994a). This extensive set of materials is based on the sequence provided in Sidebar 8.6 and uses principles of precision teaching (including timed activities, working to a preestablished criterion, and charting progress). Furthermore, it skillfully integrates the development of hand movements with tactile perception and includes discrimination and recognition of individual braille letters. The package includes a teacher's manual, as well as one set of consumable worksheets for the student and supplementary

Sequence for Tactile Perception and Discrimination Activities

1. Tracking from left to right across like symbols that follow closely without a space between them.
2. Tracking from left to right across unlike symbols that follow closely without a space between them.
3. Tracking from left to right across like symbols that have one or two blank spaces between them.
4. Tracking from left to right across unlike symbols that have one or two blank spaces between them.
5. Tracking from top to bottom over like symbols that follow closely without a space between them.
6. Tracking from top to bottom over unlike symbols that follow closely without a space between them.
7. Tracking from top to bottom over like symbols that have one blank space between them.
8. Tracking from top to bottom over unlike symbols that have one blank space between them.
9. Identifying two geometric shapes as being the same or different.
10. Identifying two braille symbols as being the same or different.
11. Identifying two braille symbols as being the same or different when they are preceded and followed by a solid line.
12. Identifying the one symbol that is different within a line of like symbols, using the letter *l* and the letter *c*.
13. Identifying the one symbol that is different within a line of like symbols using a variety of braille symbols for different lines.
14. Identifying the one symbol that is different within a group of three symbols, two of which are identical.
15. Identifying the letters of the alphabet in the following sequence: *c, g, l, d, y, a, b, s, w, p, o, k, r, m, e, h, n, x, z, f, u, t, q, i, v,* and *j.*

Source: Adapted from S. S. Mangold, cited in M. R. Olson, *Guidelines and Games for Teaching Efficient Braille Reading* (New York: American Foundation for the Blind, 1981), pp. 45–46.

materials, such as push pins and a rubber mat. This instructional program was extensively field-tested in an empirical study and was found to be effective (Mangold, 1978).

The *Patterns Prebraille Program* (Caton, Pester, & Bradley, 1987) and *Patterns: The Primary Braille Reading Program* (Caton, Pester, & Bradley, 1980) are additional resources for teachers. The *Patterns* series was specifically designed for students who are learning to read braille. The prebraille program includes activities for emergent braille literacy, as well as for prebraille skills, and leads to the more comprehensive reading series. Unlike the Mangold program, the *Patterns* series

integrates mechanical skills with literacy and language skills, with more emphasis on the latter.

Integration of Literacy Skills

Because of the prominent role of teaching mechanical skills in prebraille instruction, the teacher of students with visual impairments may tend to overemphasize mechanics. Rather, an equal or even greater emphasis should be placed on the continued development of the early literacy skills that began in infancy and preschool. The key is to balance mechanics with meaningful literacy experiences. For example, Miller (1985) recommended having a young child track along in a braille book while an adult reads the book aloud. This approach provides opportunities for fluent tracking and is a meaningful literacy activity.

Lamb (1996) suggested a number of ways to integrate prebraille experiences with language and literacy activities using whole-language strategies. Whole-language strategies use meaningful, natural opportunities to link language and literacy, such as when a child uses "pretend" reading or writes in a journal using pictures and invented spellings. Lamb's approach uses symbolic or actual braille words that are based on a child's language to practice prebraille skills. This approach is best understood by reviewing the examples presented in Figure 8.1. In addition, Mc-Comiskey's (1996) *Braille Readiness Skills Grid* helps the teacher focus on all the skill areas needed in developing early literacy, rather than concentrating on mechanical skills (see Figure 8.2). These skill areas include tactile, fine motor, listening and attention, conceptual, and book and story skills. By continually looking across all skill areas and placing an appropriate balance on each, the teacher ensures that the child receives a cohesive early literacy program.

During the prebraille phase, the teacher of students with visual impairments needs to start making links to beginning braille literacy skills. Although formal instruction typically begins in kindergarten or the first grade, the time to set the stage and prepare for a smooth, seamless transition is during the preschool years. To make this transition, the teacher may find that shared reading and language experience stories are helpful, as described next.

Shared Reading. Shared reading is a whole-language strategy in which the teacher and child read together in a risk-free environment with no predetermined expectations by the child (Routman, 1991). This strategy is "risk free" because the child does not have to worry about saying words correctly or being put on the spot to read any of the words. Similarly, there are no specific expectations of the child; he or she can read none, any, or all the words without any judgment by the

teacher. Whatever contributions the child makes to the shared reading experience are encouraged and reinforced by the teacher. Such a risk-free environment facilitates the child's participation in this enriching literacy activity.

To use the shared reading strategy, the teacher of students with visual impairments should find appropriate and motivating books in braille that match the child's experiential background. Books or stories with predictable patterns (such as "Brown bear, brown bear, what do you see? I see a tiger looking at me. Tiger, tiger, what do you see? . . ."; Martin, 1996) are ideal to use at first, as are short books that are read repeatedly over a number of days. In this approach, the student puts his or her fingers on the braille lines and tracks along during reading. Initially, the teacher reads most or all the words and reads slightly louder than the child. Over time, the child begins to pick up familiar words or words with unusual configurations. The trust between the teacher and the child is fundamental to the success of shared reading. The child needs to know that he or she is free to contribute many, few, or none of the words in the story and that the teacher will read all the rest.

Language-Experience Approach. The language-experience approach uses the child's actual experiences as the basis for written stories; these stories are then used to teach reading. Because this approach uses the child's experiences, the teacher is assured that the child has appropriate background knowledge to bring meaning to the story. The steps in the language-experience approach are as follows:

1. Arrange for and carry out a special event or activity for the child (or a group of children), such as a visit to the town's post office or a nearby farm. A naturally occurring experience like a classmate's birthday or a school assembly, may also be used but it is also important to continue to expand the child's experiences through unique and special activities (such as attending a circus or riding in a rowboat). Use a multisensory approach and active

learning to immerse the child fully in the experience.

2. After the activity, have the child tell a story about what happened. If he or she has trouble getting started, use some brief prompts (like "What happened first?"). As the child tells the story, write it down word for word with a braillewriter. Generally, the stories are relatively short at this stage in the student's literacy development. Three important points need to be emphasized at this point:

◆ Use a braillewriter (rather than a computer) to write the story, so the child knows that what he or she is saying is being recorded through writing. Have the child follow along with his or her finger just behind the embossing head, if appropriate.

◆ Write the story in braille as the child is speaking. It is not instructionally effective to write it in print and then later transcribe it into braille. Writing immediately in braille makes the child aware of the natural relationship between spoken words and written words.

◆ Write down the child's words exactly as he or she says them. Do not fix grammatical errors or attempt to control the vocabulary in any way. Part of the success of this approach is building trust with the child. If the child thinks that his or her story needs to be "fixed," then this feeling of trust is interrupted, and the child may be less willing to share his or her experiences and stories in the future.

3. Reread the story immediately with the child using the shared reading strategy just discussed. The child will remember much of the story and will be able to read along, saying many of the words. Do not stop or pause during this step to have the child sound out or analyze words. The immediate rereading should be a holistic experiences to recount the child's story.

4. Continue rereading the story through shared reading on subsequent days. Soon, the child will independently know more of the words and may even begin to recognize some of the words out of context.

5. Arrange contextually appropriate reading-strategy lessons based on the story, especially as the child approaches kindergarten. For example, if the story has several *p* words in it, talk about the initial /*p*/ sound. The child can scan to find the *p* words in the story and make a list, perhaps in a shared writing experience, of other *p* words. A comprehension activity may involve writing a new ending of the story by changing one feature (for example, "How would your story have ended if . . ."). Also, art activities or binding the story into a book may be fun and motivating for the child.

Balancing mechanical skills with literacy skills is a major key to ensuring a good foundation for formal beginning literacy instruction in braille. If the teacher spends a consistent and appropriate amount of time doing so during the early years of a child's life and in preschool, the child will be ready for the transition to more formal braille literacy instruction.

BEGINNING BRAILLE READING SKILLS

The teacher of students with visual impairments has a direct and consistent role in teaching beginning braille literacy skills to students from kindergarten through the third grade. Professionals recommend providing one to two hours of instruction each day to teach these skills (Koenig & Holbrook, in press). Instructional patterns that provide less direct contact and fewer hours of instruction or use nonqualified personnel (such as paraeducators) to deliver literacy instruction do

Exercise 1 demonstrates different levels of representation of key elements (e.g., gold).

1. **Child's Language:** "We went to Sovereign Hill and found some gold."

   (a) distinctive pattern to represent *gold*

   (b) initial letter or contraction

   (c) whole word

Exercise 2 demonstrates how the task of discriminating the *eggs* can be made more difficult by increasing tactual complexity.

2. **Context: Easter theme.**
   The Easter bunny hops through the grass leaving eggs for the children to find. The eggs are increasingly difficult to find as the grass gets thicker and longer, requiring finer discrimination.

   Activity: Look for the eggs. Go carefully (lightly) so you don't step on them. Can you count the eggs? (Establish *grass* before looking for *eggs*.)

grass

egg

Exercise 3 illustrates how the same patterns could be used to represent different text or elements within text.

3. **Child's Language:** "We found some mushrooms in the school ground."

   Activity: Child is asked to look in the grass to find the mushrooms. Step lightly so as not to squash them. Count the mushrooms. (Establish *grass* before asking the child to locate *mushrooms*.)

   The same pattern could be used to represent the following text:

   People standing on the platform at the station.
   Houses in the street.
   Rocks in the water.

Sequential elements can be added to maintain story line as in Exercise 4.

4. We found some mushrooms growing in the school ground.

   We picked all the mushrooms.

   OR   People standing on the platform at the station.
   The people caught the train.

   OR   Rocks in the water.
   The tide has covered them.

Figure 8.1. Examples of Lamb's Approach to Integrating Early Literacy Activities

Source: Reprinted, with permission, from G. Lamb, "Beginning Braille: A Whole Language-Based Strategy," *Journal of Visual Impairment & Blindness, 90*, p. 188.

5. **Child's Language:** "We went to the beach and I swam in the waves."

   Activity: See how far out you can swim. See how fast you can swim.

sand   waves

child

   The same pattern could be used to represent the following text:
   A beach ball washed away by the waves.
   A car on a bumpy road.
   Sailing in a yacht.

Exercise 6 focuses on tracking and word matching.

6. **Child's Language:** "My mum's in the hospital. I went to visit her."

   Activity: Find mum in the hospital. Show example at left of line. Fingers have to walk/track along the hospital passage looking for mum. Go quietly so as not to wake other people.

Exercises 7, 8 and 9 use significant words from the study to promote word recognition.

7. **Child's Language:** "Jason went to the beach and he had a swim and built a sand castle."

   Activities: Read together aiming for good tracking and location skills, concepts of words and space, and/or for identification of key words.

   Jason went to the beach.

   Jason had a swim at the beach.

   Is Jason having a swim or building a sandcastle?

8. **Child's Language:** "My dad came to the concert last night."

   Activities: 1. Find dad in the audience.

   2. Find Alan on the stage.

   3. Find dad and Alan in the audience.

   4. Count the people in each row.

   OR

9. **Child's Language:** "My friend's got a budgie. He keeps it in a cage."

   Activity: Find the bird in the cage. Track each line to find the bird.

Figure 8.1. (Continued)

Tactile	Tolerates Being Touched	Enjoys Being Touched	Examines Objects by Touch	Matches and Sorts Objects	Touches Braille in Exploration	Matches Gradations of Sandpaper, etc.	Locates Tactile "Mark" on Paper	Uses Pad of Index Finger to Touch	Participates in Mangold's Activity Sheets & Units
	Traces 3-Dimensional Outline of Shape	Traces 2-Dimensional Outline of Shape	Traces Left to Right Continuous Line with Sticks, Glue, etc.	Traces Left to Right Using: a. Braille Cell w/no space b. Braille Cell w/space c. Dot 2,3,5,6 w/no space d. Dpt 2,3,5,6 w/space		e. Dot 3,6 w/no space f. Dot 3,6 w/space g. Dot 1 w/no space h. Dot 1 w/space		Uses Two Hands Cooperatively in Tracing (Place Marker & Reader Hand)	

Fine Motor	Holds Objects in Each Hand	Uses Pincer Grasp	Opens and Closes Books	Turns Cardboard Pages	Uses Two Hands Cooperatively	Uses Appropriate Grasp with Stylus	Makes Stylus Art with Construction Paper	Turns Pages One at a Time	Copies Patterns with Pegs, Muffin Tins, Geo Boards, etc.
	Shows Hand Strength and Flexibility	Shows Finger Strength and Dexterity	Places Individual Finger on Braille Key	Manages Paper into Slate	"Scribbles" with Slate and Stylus	Manages Paper in/out of Brailler with Help	Positions Fingers on Braille Keys Appropriately	Manages Paper in/out of Brailler Independently	Operates all Keys of Brailler Appropriately

Listening and Attention	Alerts to Sound	Listens to Interaction Songs	Socially Sits with Adult 5–10 Minutes	Listens to and Enjoys Rhymes	Participates in Finger Plays and Songs	Follows 2-Step Directions	Matches Sound Cans	Shows Interest in Short Stories About Self	Shows Interest in Short Stories about Others, with Participation
	Shows Interest in Stories About Others Without Participation		Uses Jargon and Imitation on Phone	Tells Simple Event (Idea)	Makes up Simple Stories (3 ideas)	Listens to Simple Story Tape	Manages Tape Recorder with Help	Manages Tape Recorder Independently	Attention to Task Completion (5–20 Minutes)

Concept

Identifies Body Parts	Names Body Parts	Identifies Objects and Actions	Names Objects and Actions	Shows Object Permanence Concept	Searches for Dropped Objects	Shows Same and Different Concept Awareness	Demonstrates Number Awareness of Quantities to 3	Shows More/Less, Big/Small, Long/Short, Wide/Narrow Concepts with Objects	Plays Symbolically
Shows Concepts of: Above/Below, Left/Right Back/Front, Up/Down Top/Bottom, Middle/Sides (with Objects)		Understands Positional Concepts with Marks on Page	Shows Rote Knowledge of Alphabet	Shows Letter/Cell Awareness Using Balls, Marbles and Braille		Says Letters of Name (Rote)	Says Names of Brailler Keys	Shows Awareness of Touch Patterns Representing Word; i.e., Name	

Book and Story

Uses Books as Toys (Squeak, Pull, etc.)	Identifies Parts of a Book (Cover, Pages, Margin, etc.)	Holds Book and Turns Pages	Explores Tactile Books Using Pad of Fingers	Purposefully Traces Marks in Tactile Book from Start to End	Participates in Object "Book" Story	Daily TWIN-VISION Book Lap Time	Dictates and Reads "Sentence" Book
Selects Favorite Book and Stories	"Touch and Tell" and "Patterns" Series Completed (APH)	Enjoys "On the Way to Literacy" Series (APH)					

DIRECTIONS: Reading and writing braille is achieved by systematic building of skills in many areas of development. This literacy readiness grid enables parents and teachers to identify accomplished skills and target other skills for educational programming.

Using observation and informal assessment identify which skills in each area a child has accomplished. Highlight the accomplished skill box entirely. Emerging skills are partially filled with highlighter. Non-highlighted skill boxes are skills targeted for the child's educational program. This is a flexible tool. Add or delete boxes for individual children. Remember: FUN IS THE KEY INGREDIENT.

Name:
DoB:
Vision:

Figure 8.2. The Braille Readiness Skills Grid

Source: Reprinted, with permission, from A. V. McComiskey, "The Braille Readiness Grid: A Guide to Building a Foundation for Literacy," *Journal of Visual Impairment & Blindness, 90* (1996), p. 142.

not adequately address the intensity of needs of beginning readers who are blind.

Students who do not receive high-quality, intense instruction during the early elementary school years are at a serious risk of entering middle school with fragmented or weak braille literacy skills, which makes progress in other academic subjects much more difficult. Furthermore, these weak literacy skills carry over to and are compounded in high school and then in adult life, having a direct impact on opportunities for competitive employment. Therefore, it is essential that teachers of students with visual impairments take every opportunity to advocate for and provide daily instruction in braille literacy skills to beginning readers.

Instructional Approaches

Given that the teacher of students with visual impairments is likely to have the primary responsibility for teaching beginning braille literacy skills, he or she is free to choose the instructional approach. A number of options are available, including *Patterns: The Primary Braille Reading Program* (Caton et al., 1980), a standard basal series, whole-language instruction, or a combination of these approaches.

Basal Readers

Patterns is a comprehensive basal reader program (that is, a sequenced set of instructional materials with a defined scope and sequence and accompanying stories and activities) that was designed specifically for students who are learning to read and write in braille. It uses a controlled vocabulary based on the difficulty of braille letters, contractions, and short-form words. The choice and introduction of vocabulary words is carefully planned and coordinated from story to story and level to level to provide sufficient practice.

This series begins with *Patterns Prebraille Program* (Caton et al., 1987), discussed previously, and continues with instructional materials at the readiness level, preprimer level, primer level, level 1, level 2, and level 3. Although the authors of

Patterns state that the levels do not correspond to grades, professionals in the field typically consider that the program will be completed by the end of the third grade. After level 3, the student is ready to start using a standard basal reader or whatever literacy program is offered in the school district.

Patterns is comprehensive in that at each level it contains student readers, worksheets, mastery tests, short leisure reading books in the *Patterns Library Series,* and teacher's guides. Also, *Patterns: The Primary Braille Spelling and English Program* (Caton et al., 1993) includes instructional materials for teaching the language arts in braille. Beginning teachers of students with visual impairments may view *Patterns* as a good choice for initial instruction because of its comprehensiveness.

Another approach—the one used before *Patterns* was developed and one that continues to be a popular option, especially for experienced teachers—involves the use of a standard basal reader series that is appropriately modified and transcribed in braille. There are two major challenges with this approach: (1) the vocabulary is controlled on the basis of factors that make words easy or more difficult to read in print, but this does not necessarily correspond to the difficulty of reading the words in braille, and (2) these materials generally rely a great deal on pictures to convey or supplement meaning, especially in the early grades. Despite these disadvantages, many teachers prefer this approach because the stories tend to be more interesting than those in *Patterns.* This approach also allows students in inclusive classrooms to read and participate in the same stories and literacy activities as their classmates. The use of this approach requires careful attention in several areas:

- ◆ New vocabulary words and any accompanying braille contractions should be introduced in meaningful contexts and before the student reads a new story.

- ◆ Appropriate substitutes must be made to address the lack of pictures in the braille edition, such as previewing the pictures or substituting real objects or models.

◆ Appropriate experiences may need to be arranged before the student reads a new story to ensure that he or she has the essential background knowledge to bring meaning to the stories.

◆ Supplementary activities need to be included in instruction to address the unique aspects of reading braille, such as continuing to refine mechanical skills and learning various braille formats and conventions.

◆ Ongoing assessment must be provided to ensure that the student is gaining academic literacy skills, as well as learning the unique aspects of reading braille.

Whole-Language Strategies

Another approach is the use of whole-language strategies. This approach provides a rich, exciting, and meaningful learning environment, but requires the teacher to have a solid grounding in whole-language theory, philosophy, and practice. If the teacher does not have such a background, then he or she is strongly encouraged to select another teaching approach. Instruction based on the whole-language approach includes reading authentic literature (that is, actual children's literature, rather than stories with controlled vocabularies) and using naturally occurring opportunities for reading and writing (such as reading daily announcements from the school principal or writing a thank-you card to a classroom guest). Instruction in specific reading skills occurs after or, if appropriate, during a holistic reading experience. *Beginning with Braille* (Swenson, 1999) presents comprehensive guidelines for integrating and balancing whole-language strategies with other approaches for students in braille literacy programs.

Selecting an Approach

Although each teacher selects an approach for the direct instruction of braille literacy skills, a teacher may wish to give strong consideration to the approach used in the school district in which the student resides. For example, if the school district uses a certain basal reader series, then the teacher may choose to use this approach to facilitate the student's transition to and inclusion in a general education classroom reading program at an appropriate time. Regardless of the primary approach, elements of all these approaches can be used in a holistic literacy program.

Eight basic whole-language strategies offer valuable and enriching ways to teach reading and writing skills: reading aloud, shared reading, guided reading, independent reading, writing aloud, shared writing, guided writing, and independent writing (Routman, 1991). These strategies can be used with students in braille literacy programs with simple modifications. They can also be used with students in print literacy programs with appropriate modifications to ensure access to printed text. Table 8.1 describes these techniques and ways to modify them for students who are blind and students with low vision.

Basic Areas of Instruction

Apart from the approach that is used to teach beginning braille literacy skills, there are several areas of instruction that are fairly common to all approaches. Olson (1981) outlined four key areas of skills to target in beginning reading instruction:

◆ Decoding skills—understanding and using sound-symbol relationships (phonics), sight vocabulary (words recognized instantly without analysis), context cues (use of meaning or sentence structure), and structural analysis (breaking words into units) to identify words;

◆ Vocabulary development—expanding the use of meaningful vocabulary with appropriate and rich background experiences;

◆ Comprehension skills—understanding the author's message, inferring meaning from information presented in the text, and making personal judgments about what was read; and

◆ Flexibility skills—scanning to locate specific information (such as looking in a

Table 8.1. Basic Whole-Language Strategies and Modifications

Strategy	General Procedures	Modifications
Reading aloud	Reading aloud is considered "the single most influential factor in young children's success in learning to read" (Routman, 1991, p. 32). In reading aloud, the teacher simply reads aloud from books that are of interest to the students. This strategy should be used on a daily basis with students at all grade levels (Routman, 1991).	◆ Take time to preview and/or describe and discuss pictures if the teacher is showing them to the class. ◆ Supplement with real objects, scale models, acting out of events. ◆ Ensure that the student has gained appropriate background experiences to bring meaning to the story.
Shared reading	In shared reading, the student "sees the text, observes an expert (usually the teacher) reading it with fluency and expression, and is invited to read along. The learner is in the role of receiving support, and the teacher-expert accepts and encourages all efforts and approximations the learner (the novice) makes" (Routman, 1991, p. 33). After shared reading, the student should have a chance to read the story by himself or herself (Routman, 1991).	◆ Ensure that the student has all stories and books used for shared reading in an appropriate medium. ◆ When pointing, the teacher of students with visual impairments moves the student's fingers to the specific word. ◆ Ideally the student, the teacher of students with visual impairments, and the general education teacher are using shared reading simultaneously. ◆ Shared reading can be used as part of special instructional time or to supplement shared reading in the classroom.
Guided reading	According to Routman (1991, p. 38), "Guided reading is the heart of the instructional reading program. Here we meet with students to think critically about a book. Selections that have been assigned for silent reading are discussed, with the children responding to the text in open-ended and personal ways." This strategy can be used with the whole class, in small groups, or on an individual basis. Instruction in reading skills, such as vocabulary or word attack skills, occurs during guided reading within meaningful contexts (Routman, 1991).	◆ Ensure the availability of books and other materials in appropriate media. ◆ Ensure that the student has an adequate repertoire of background experiences to allow meaningful comprehension. ◆ The teacher of students with visual impairments collaborates with the general education teacher to ensure the appropriate development of unique braille skills or use of visual skills within guided reading instruction. ◆ The teacher of students with visual impairments may assist with teaching phonics by presenting contracted and uncontracted versions of stimulus words. ◆ The teacher of students with visual impairments may supplement instruction in the general education classroom using guided reading to teach unique aspects of braille.

(continued on next page)

Table 8.1. *(Continued)*

Strategy	General Procedures	Modifications
Independent reading	Routman (1991, pp. 41–42) explains that "In independent reading students are in charge of their own reading—by choosing their own books, by doing their own reading, and by taking responsibility to work through the challenges of the text." The teacher guides (but does not direct) the student to select books that are at his or her independent reading level. Time should be set aside each day for independent reading, using special times such as "SSR" or sustained silent reading (Routman, 1991).	◆ Make sure that a wide variety of braille books are available from which the student may choose. ◆ Incorporate the practice and use of low vision devices for students with low vision. ◆ Be available at times to "observe, acknowledge, and respond" to the unique features of braille.
Writing aloud	Writing aloud is a strategy that is used to model the writing process. According to Routman (1991, p. 51), "Writing aloud occurs when the teacher writes in front of students and also verbalizes what he or she is thinking and writing," which provides opportunities for "demonstrating various aspects of writing." The teacher talks through his or her thoughts on the writing episode, addressing issues of format, spelling, vocabulary, and so forth (Routman, 1991).	◆ The teacher of students with visual impairments or a blind adult transcribes the writing with a braillewriter as a student feels braille as it is being produced. ◆ Technology can be used to produce braille: refreshable braille display, Mountbatten brailler. ◆ The teacher of students with visual impairments reinforces skills and conventions that are unique to braille, such as 2-cell indentation and the use of contractions. ◆ Can be used during specialized instruction to model unique aspects of writing with a brailler, slate and stylus, and the like. ◆ Make appropriate environmental modifications for students with low vision to allow ready visual access to the writing.
Shared writing	In shared writing, the students and teacher write collaboratively "with the teacher acting as a scribe and expert to her group of apprentices. . . . As in shared reading, in shared writing the teacher's role is an enabling, supportive one that encourages and invites students to participate and enjoy writing experiences they might not be able to do on their own" (Routman, 1991, p. 60).	◆ In the classroom, the teacher of students with visual impairments transcribes the text in braille as it is written by the general education teacher. ◆ Encourage the student to contribute to the writing process. ◆ Ensure that all products of shared writing are transcribed in braille. ◆ Can be used in individualized instruction with the student who is blind and the

(continued on next page)

Table 8.1. *(Continued)*

Strategy	General Procedures	Modifications
Shared writing *(cont.)*		teacher of students with visual impairments, allowing them to focus on the unique aspects of writing in braille. ◆ Use appropriate nonoptical and optical low vision devices for students with low vision.
Guided writing	According to Routman (1991, p. 66), "The teacher's role in guided writing is to guide students, respond to them, and extend their thinking in the process of composing text." Unlike writing aloud and shared writing, during guided writing "the student holds the pen and does the writing" (p. 66), while the teacher serves as the facilitator. Instruction on specific skills is provided when necessary and occurs within meaningful writing episodes (Routman, 1991).	◆ Collaborate with the general education teacher to create a three-way writing session. ◆ Make sure that writing is generated in an accessible print form—interlining, print output from a computer, print on the computer screen—so the general education teacher can provide guidance. ◆ The teacher of students with visual impairments provides guidance in the unique aspects of writing in braille. ◆ Use appropriate nonoptical and optical low vision devices for students with low vision.
Independent writing	In independent writing, the student chooses what he or she wishes to write about and does so without intervention by the teacher. Routman (1991, p. 67) explains the purpose of independent writing: "To build fluency, establish the writing habit, make personal connections, explore meanings, promote critical thinking, and use writing as a natural, pleasurable, self-chosen activity." Journal writing is a common form of independent writing (Routman, 1991).	◆ No modifications of basic procedures are needed. ◆ *If* the student chooses to share any part of his or her free writing, the teacher of students with visual impairments should interline braille and/or use technology to generate print. ◆ The student should have opportunities, *if desired,* to share his or her writing with adults who are braille readers. ◆ Have low vision students use appropriate optical and nonoptical devices.

Sources: General procedures adapted from R. Routman, *Invitations: Changing as Teachers and Learners K–12* (Portsmouth, NH: Heinemann, 1991).

Modifications adapted from D. McNear, M. C. Holbrook, and A. J. Koenig, "Enhancing Literacy Skills Through a Whole Language Approach," in A. J. Koenig and M.C. Holbrook, Eds., *Proceedings of the Second Biennial Conference of Getting in Touch with Literacy* (Alexandria, VA: Association for Education and Rehabilitation of the Blind and Visually Impaired, 1997), pp. 93–107.

letter for the time an event begins) and skimming to get an overview of a passage (that is, getting the "gist" of a reading passage without understanding the specific details).

In addition to these skill areas, students in braille literacy programs need continued instruction to refine and expand the unique skills needed for reading braille: both mechanical skills and learning new braille contractions and unique braille formats. Teaching new braille contractions and short-form words should be integrated meaningfully into literacy activities. For example, when introducing new vocabulary words for a story, the teacher of students with visual impairments can make note of new braille signs and introduce them while presenting the new words, rather than drilling isolated braille contractions. Doing so provides a meaningful context. The teacher also provides appropriate practice of new contractions in other words as they are encountered.

Increasing Fluency and Rate of Reading

Students may need special attention to increase their fluency and rate in braille reading. Two of the many techniques that can increase reading fluency are described next (Tierney, Readence, & Dishner, 1990).

Repeated Readings.   Repeated readings involves reading and rereading a short passage until a predetermined criterion (that is, rate of reading) is met. To use this strategy, select a short passage from a story or book that represents a complete unit of thought and transcribe the passage into braille. Have the student read the passage aloud. Immediately calculate the rate of reading and set a criterion level that is higher but that will be attainable in two or three rereadings. Tell the student the reading rate and remind him or her of the criterion rate. Then have the student continue reading the passage until that rate is achieved. As the student continues to read the passage, his or her fluency will increase, and (according to the theory on which this technique is based) attention will be refocused from reading the words to comprehending the meaning. This strategy should be used daily with short sessions over an extended period (a semester, a year, or more).

Paired Reading.   In paired reading, a proficient reader models reading a passage and then a novice reader reads the same passage. This approach is best used with a complete story or sections of a book. Before the session, transcribe the reading material in braille. Begin by reading aloud a paragraph or two short paragraphs, as the student follows along. Then have the student read the same passage. Continue for a comfortable amount of time. This strategy provides a model of fluent reading for the student and is an easy reading experience (since the teacher's reading always precedes the student's). Paired reading should be used in short sessions over an extended period. The teacher can collect data on fluency each day to ensure that the strategy is improving the student's fluency.

WRITING SKILLS IN BRAILLE

Braille writing skills are generally introduced informally in preschool or even earlier in the home with exposure to the braillewriter and braille slate. Encouraging the child to scribble or share writing experiences with a parent or teacher are important ways to show the use and value of writing. In kindergarten, the teacher of students with visual impairments begins to provide more formal instruction in writing skills using the Perkins braillewriter.

Perkins Braillewriter

Formal instruction on using the braillewriter typically starts with the teacher modeling the use of the keys to produce certain braille letters and signs. An ideal first lesson is to teach the student to write his or her name; it can be done even before the student recognizes his or her name in braille. In this lesson, the teacher stands or sits behind the student and physically guides the student to place his or her fingers properly on the six keys and then to press the keys in the proper sequence. Since the student's fingers are also on the braillewriter keys, he or she soon learns the sequence through repeated trials.

The teacher may prefer to discuss the relationship between the dot numbers in the braille cell and the corresponding cells on the braillewriter. Another option is to use the American

Printing House (APH) for the Blind Swing Cell. This device allows the students to place large pegs in the cell that correspond to the dots in the letter or sign and then to swing each side out and up to denote the keys on the braillewriter. Other early lessons can focus on inserting the paper, changing lines, backspacing, and so forth, using physical guidance at appropriate times during writing experiences.

The teacher can use the whole-language strategies of writing aloud and shared writing (Routman, 1991) to guide the development of beginning writing skills (see the next section for more details). With writing aloud, the teacher shares the steps in the writing process orally, and the process provides a model for using the process of writing in braille. Shared writing involves the teacher and student writing together while the teacher provides guidance in the unique features of braillewriting. This may actually be a preferred strategy over writing aloud, since the student actively participates (whereas writing aloud relies primarily on an oral model of the writing episode).

Spelling instruction is an additional component for students who read and write in braille. When students learn new spelling words, they need to practice them in both the contracted and uncontracted forms. They will use the contracted forms for general reading and writing purposes and the uncontracted forms for keyboarding and word processing. Because of the relationship to keyboarding skills, the practice of spelling words in both contracted and uncontracted forms during spelling instruction (and during some skills instruction in a reading class) should begin early in the primary grades.

Slate and Stylus Skills

Writing with the braille slate and stylus is an essential skill for students who are blind. The braille slate is a quick, portable, inexpensive, and functional means of taking notes, jotting telephone numbers and addresses, making lists, and so forth. To use this device, the writer places a sheet of paper in the slate and then uses the stylus to press each dot in each braille character successively. Since the

dots are pressed through the paper, writing on the slate proceeds from right to left; thus, on the braillewriter, dot 1 is in the upper left-hand corner of the braille cell, whereas with the braille slate, it is in the upper right-hand corner. The change in direction when forming characters on the braille slate is easy to learn with proper instruction.

Typically, students learn to write with the slate and stylus after they have established basic writing skills on the braillewriter. Most professionals recommend introducing the braille slate in grades 3 or 4, with several days of instruction each week in sessions of less than a half hour to an hour, depending on the student's individual needs (Koenig & Holbrook, in press). This practice does not preclude students' earlier exposure to or familiarization with the slate in preschool or the early elementary grades. Indeed, students are likely to be more receptive to learning to write with the slate if they have had experiences with the device, either directly or through modeling by others. Direct instruction in using the braille slate is provided by the teacher of students with visual impairments as part of the expanded core curriculum. Sidebar 8.7 presents some instructional strategies for teaching the braille slate and stylus.

To teach a student to use the braille slate, the teacher of students with visual impairments can begin by familiarizing him or her with the device and how to load the paper. To load paper in a traditional slate (one with a hinge that connects the front and back), Mangold (1994c) suggested the following steps:

- Open the slate so the front and back sides form a wide-open angle;

- Tip the slate away from you so that it sits upright on the table;

- Insert a sheet of paper upright into the corner of the slate with the top edge of the paper lying flat against the table;

- Close the slate, checking to make sure that the pins that hold the paper in place have torn through the paper; and

- Place the slate (with the paper loaded) flat on the table and begin writing.

Techniques for Teaching the Slate and Stylus

◆ Develop in the student an understanding of the value and uses of the slate and stylus through modeling before instruction is begun (for example, use the slate and stylus to jot down feedback and grades on tests).

◆ Use the hand-over-hand method to introduce the mechanics of forming characters and contractions with the slate and stylus. Some teachers may prefer to use dot-number formations if the student learned to write with a braillewriter this way.

◆ Avoid unnecessary drill and practice in forming characters and contractions. Emphasize the effectiveness of communication and the efficiency with which successful communication takes place.

◆ Begin using the slate and stylus for functional writing purposes as soon as possible:
  1. Jotting down homework assignments;
  2. Writing notes to teachers of students with visual impairments;
  3. Making personal lists, such as things to buy at a store;
  4. Labeling personal items like CDs, cassettes, and clothes;
  5. Writing the name and telephone number of a friend;
  6. Taking notes in a class;
  7. Jotting short notes or letters to friends who are blind;
  8. Signing a birthday card or other greeting cards; and
  9. Writing recipes and labeling canned goods.

◆ Incorporate the use of the slate and stylus into activities throughout the school day and in the evening. Start with tasks that do not require a high degree of accuracy (such as making personal lists) and move toward those that require accuracy (for example, jotting down a telephone number).

◆ Emphasize the development of speed in taking notes as instruction advances. Earlier instruction in note taking on the braillewriter is necessary. Again, avoid an overemphasis on accuracy.

◆ Practice note-taking skills from an audiocassette recording of a class lecture.

◆ Discuss with the student the difference between writing for personal uses and for uses in which accuracy and neatness are judged by others.

◆ Discuss with the student the tasks for which the slate and stylus should be used and those for which another mode of writing is more appropriate. For example, a computer word-processing program would be more appropriate for completing a term paper.

◆ Reinforce the student's appropriate selection of one mode of writing over other options. If the student chooses an inappropriate writing mode, use problem-solving techniques with the student, so he or she can gain an appreciation of the use of an alternative mode.

◆ Incorporate the study of grade 3 braille and/or personal contractions for taking notes with the slate and stylus when the student enters high school.

◆ Familiarize the student with a variety of different types of slates and styli and their uses (for example, a one-liner for labeling).

Source: Adapted from E. J. Rex, A. J. Koenig, D. Wormsley, and R. Baker, *Foundations of Braille Literacy* (New York: AFB Press, 1994), pp. 104–105.

In initial instruction, the teacher may choose to use the Janus slate, available from the APH. The front and back of the Janus slate are permanently connected, so the slate does not open or close. The user simply inserts a 3 × 5-inch index card into the slate and begins to use it. This is an ideal way to focus initially on writing with the slate, rather than on the process of loading and advancing the paper.

After the paper is loaded, the teacher can introduce the sequencing of dots within the braille cell using hand-over-hand guidance. With hand-over-hand guidance, the teacher grasps the student's hand—after requesting permission to do so—and then presses dots in the slate using a systematic pattern within the cell and between cells. Two basic methods can be used for this purpose:

1. Use dot numbers if this approach was used in teaching writing on the brailler. Begin with dot 1 in the upper right-hand corner of the cell and proceed downward with dots 2 and 3; then go to the upper left-hand corner of the cell and press dot 4, followed downward by dots 5 and 6. Say each dot number as it is pressed. Then go to the upper right-hand corner of the adjacent cell and continue. After several cells, the student will easily grasp the concept of writing on the slate.

2. Use the approach suggested by P. N. Mangold (1993) and S. Mangold (1994c) that uses specific terms to denote each dot rather than dot numbers. Both authors recommend using the terms *first side* and *second side* to refer to the two parts of the braille cell and the terms *top dot, middle dot,* and *bottom dot* to refer to the position of the individual dots within the cell. For example, the configuration of the letter *l* is top, middle, and bottom dots on the first side. The only difference between the braille slate and the braillewriter is the starting position. If the student did not use dot numbers to learn to write with the braillewriter, it is likely

that this approach will make the most sense. Again, use hand-over-hand guidance and the terminology just mentioned to introduce the student to writing with the slate. Even if the student used dot numbers on the brailler, the Mangold method still may be considered the preferred approach.

The APH Peg Slate can be used with either of the two approaches to introduce the student to the concept of writing on the slate. This plastic device contains a short line of enlarged braille cells. The braille dots are pegs that can be pushed downward through the Peg Slate. To use the device, the student presses down the dots that are contained in the character that he or she wishes to write. Then when the Peg Slate is turned over, it shows the position of the dots to press in the conventional slate. The Peg Slate is used only for the purpose of familiarization and is not a writing device in itself.

To provide initial practice on the slate, the teacher of students with visual impairments may ask the student to make a row of full cells, using a systematic approach to pressing the dots. The teacher can provide feedback on keeping the stylus positioned straight up (not slanted) and on moving rhythmically from dot to dot and cell to cell. Then the teacher may want to use physical guidance again in writing the student's name, writing the alphabet, or writing rows of repeated letters. Let the student's needs and interest govern what to write and for how long.

The concept and mechanics of writing with the braille slate are easy to grasp in a few sessions. The challenge for teachers is to move as expeditiously as possible to meaningful, functional writing tasks. Making lists, jotting down assignments, and labeling personal items present short, but meaningful tasks that are useful to most students. To label personal items, the teacher should familiarize the student with a special type of slate that has openings on each end to hold a piece of plastic labeling tape. The student threads a piece of labeling tape through the two openings, writes the label, trims the tape to an appropriate length, and attaches it to the item being labeled. After simple tasks are mastered, the student then can work on note-taking skills.

The teacher's attitude toward using the braille slate will have a direct influence on the student's attitude toward using it. If the teacher of students with visual impairments shows a positive regard for the value and practical use of the braille slate, the student will respond positively. One way to nurture this respect is for the teacher to consistently model the uses of the braille slate before the formal instruction begins. The teacher can keep a braille slate handy to use for jotting notes to the student, providing feedback or grades on the student's work, and for writing personal notes (such as recording the time and date for an upcoming Individualized Education Program (IEP) meeting). The sound of the braille slate is distinctive from the braillewriter, and the child will know when the teacher is using the slate. If he or she hears this sound consistently over an extended period, the child will learn the value of this device.

Signature Writing

Students who are blind need to develop a basic level of print-writing skill in order to have a legal signature. Signature-writing instruction typically begins sometime between grades 5 to 7, although some professionals advocate beginning instruction in grades 3 or 4. The teacher of students with visual impairments provides the direct instruction in this skill in moderate to short sessions (an hour or less) several days per week (Koenig & Holbrook, in press). Most students probably respond best to sessions of around 15 to 30 minutes on a consistent basis.

Prior to instruction, the teacher needs to gather a variety of writing instruments and raised-line paper. He or she also needs to check with local authorities (such as bank personnel) to determine the criteria for a legal signature. Such a signature may be a student's full name, initials, or a combination of initials and a last name, as long as it is consistent and the student can replicate it (Mangold & Pesavento, 1994). Then the teacher needs to consider the approach that he or she will use to teach signature writing.

Forward Chaining.   This approach was recommended by Mangold & Pesavento (1994). Begin by delineating the individual strokes that are needed to write the student's legal signature. A stroke is defined as one movement that either ends or changes directions. The cursive letter *a*, for example, has two strokes: (1) an oval shape starting and stopping near the top right and (2) a downward stroke to the baseline. After delineating the strokes, the teacher provides instruction in the first stroke until the student masters it. He or she then teaches the first two strokes, followed by the first three strokes, and so forth, until the student has learned to write his or her signature completely. Mangold and Pesavento (1994) recommended that the student should learn to write his or her signature in the size that it ultimately will be used, rather than start with a large signature and decrease its size later.

Spatial Configuration of the Braille Cell.   In this method advocated by Weis and Weis (1978), letter formations are based on the dot numbering system in the braille cell. For example, to make the cursive capital letter *A,* the student starts at dot 4; proceeds in sequence to dots 1, 3, 6, 4, and 6; and then connects to dot 3 on the adjacent cell. To form descenders, the student imagines connecting to the top dots (1 or 3) of the next row. There are no actual dots on the page; the student uses his or her memory of the spatial arrangement of the cell as a guide. The signature that is formed is a type of "squarehand," but the teacher can concentrate on teaching the student to curve the edges of the letters after the basic pencil strokes are learned. The strategy of forward chaining can also be used to teach signature writing with this approach.

Signature Template.   In this approach, the teacher prepares an enlarged template of the student's signature so the student can trace within the template to learn the pencil strokes. To prepare the template, the teacher glues yarn on a mirror image of the signature and then duplicates the image on a Thermoform machine.[2] The Thermoform version has inset grooves representing the signature. With the teacher's guidance, the student places his or her pencil at the appropriate starting point and traces the grooves throughout the signature using sequential strokes. The template is used until the student has learned the sequential pencil strokes. Then the student is taught to transfer these strokes to raised-line paper. Since the template is larger than an actual signature, the teacher must teach the student to use a smaller and smaller size signature until the appropriate size is attained.

The student needs to have opportunities to sign his or her name in appropriate situations, so he or she understands the value of signature writing. During the learning phase, the student can be encouraged to sign papers that are handed in to the general education teachers or to sign learning contracts if such contracts are used in the classroom. Once the signature is established, the student can sign his or her social security card, which all children now receive early in life. Then the teacher or parents may take the student to a bank at an appropriate time to establish a savings account, sign an existing savings account application, or establish a checking account. Such field trips help to integrate the use of literacy skills into the student's life and thus enhance the importance, meaningfulness, and usefulness of these skills.

---

[2] *The Thermoform machine duplicates tactile materials from paper or a metal sheet onto a thin sheet of plastic. The plastic sheet is placed on top of the master and clamped into the machine. Then a heating element is pulled over the top of the materials being duplicated and held there for a few seconds. After the heating element is pushed away, a vacuum device is activated that pulls the plastic sheet down over the master. After a few seconds, the vacuum process is stopped, and the plastic duplicate is separated from the master. Since Thermoform machines are not in widespread use today, the teacher may need to contact a braille duplication agency and ask it to create several copies.*

INTERMEDIATE AND ADVANCED BRAILLE LITERACY SKILLS

Students who are blind need to continue to develop and expand their braille literacy skills throughout middle school and high school. The involvement of the teacher of students with visual impairments in teaching these expanded braille skills will depend on the skill that is being taught and the needs of the student. This instruction may involve sessions of 30 minutes to two hours one to five days per week (Koenig & Holbrook, in press). For example, if the student is increasing his or her fluency in braille reading, the teacher may work with him or her in 30-minute sessions five days per week. On the other hand, if the student is learning a new software program for writing reports, the teacher may choose to have two-hour sessions over a couple of days and then follow up periodically.

As part of a study on the instructional needs of students in braille literacy programs, areas of emphasis in braille skills were outlined for students at the intermediate and advanced levels (Koenig & Holbrook, in press; D. P. Wormsley, personal communication, 1998). The study found that for students in grades 4 through 8, the specialist needs to do the following:

- Teach and reinforce the use of literacy skills as a tool for learning, especially in the content subject areas;

- Teach the student to use reading strategically and flexibly to meet the demands of a given reading assignment, such as skimming to get the gist of a passage, scanning to find specific pieces of information, or studying to learn and assimilate information;

- Teach the use of references, such as dictionaries, encyclopedias, and other library resources;

- Teach the use of editing marks for refining writing drafts (paired with instruction in word-processing skills, described later in this chapter);

◆ Continue to develop and reinforce fluent reading, using such strategies as paired reading and repeated readings (described earlier);

◆ Continue to refine the student's accurate recognition of braille contractions and other elements of the braille code, as needed;

◆ Develop a wide variety of literacy skills, such as use of the slate and stylus and technology (the computer, assistive technology, and other electronic devices), and integrate these skills into the student's activities throughout the day and evening; and

◆ Apply literacy skills and tools in authentic contexts, such as using signature writing to sign checks, word-processing skills to write to sighted friends, and slate skills for labeling CDs at home.

As students progress through high school, they will continue to refine and expand their braille skills, preparing them for postsecondary education or employment. In grades 9 through 12, the teacher of students with visual impairments needs to do the following:

◆ Teach specialized braille codes, such as foreign language (see Sidebar 8.8) and computer braille codes, depending on the individual student's needs;

◆ Continue to expand the student's Nemeth Code skills (see Chapter 10) to support mathematics instruction in high school and, if appropriate, college;

◆ Continue to expand student's knowledge of and skills in using various formats, such as time lines, plays, graphs, and tables;

◆ Teach the grade 3 braille code (a highly contracted braille code that is used only for taking personal notes) as an option for a student who is college bound, although

many students prefer to adopt their own set of personal contractions;

◆ Continue to develop and expand technology skills to accomplish tasks that involve printed information; and

◆ Teach the student to select wisely among various literacy tools to accomplish given tasks (for example, using synthesized speech to obtain large amounts of information over the Internet, using braille to revise and edit a term paper, and using a live reader to review the daily mail) and to apply literacy skills within authentic tasks.

UNIQUE CONSIDERATIONS IN BRAILLE LITERACY INSTRUCTION

The preceding sections addressed the needs of students who are introduced to braille as a primary literacy medium during the preschool years and continue expanding their skills throughout their school careers. There are three unique situations, however, in which the approaches differ from this traditional approach: (1) teaching uncontracted braille in initial instruction; (2) teaching literacy skills in dual media (that is, print and braille); and (3) teaching braille skills as a complementary medium to, or replacement for, print literacy skills.

Teaching Uncontracted Braille

The traditional approach to teaching braille literacy skills is to introduce contracted braille (that is, the 189 braille contractions and short-form words, also known as grade 2 braille) from the beginning of instruction. Some experts believe that one complication of teaching braille to children with visual impairments is the use of braille contractions. However, the success of countless efficient braille readers contradicts this belief. Students who begin learning to read and write using

Braille Symbols for Selected Foreign Languages

Students who are blind will study a foreign language at some point during their schooling. To assure integration in foreign language classes, the teacher of students with visual impairments should provide braille copies of all instructional material and provide instruction to the student in the braille symbols used to represent the special accented letters. The symbols used in French, German, Italian, and Spanish are presented in the accompanying chart. The convention for transcribing foreign language instructional materials in braille is to use uncontracted braille (letter-by-letter spellings using the standard alphabet in braille), substituting the braille symbols for each accented letter. Prior to the beginning of the foreign language class, the teacher of students with visual impairments should preteach the special braille symbols as part of direct, specialized instruction. Thereafter, the specialist's role is largely one of collaborating with the classroom teacher and providing textbooks, workbooks, and other materials in braille. For additional information on transcribing foreign words in an English context refer to *English Braille American Edition 1994* (BANA, 1994) and *Braille Formats: Principles of Print to Braille Transcription 1997* (BANA, 1998).

FRENCH

ç	⠯
é	⠿
à	⠷
è	⠮
ù	⠾
â	⠡
ê	⠣
î	⠩
ô	⠹
û	⠱
ë	⠫
ï	⠻
ü	⠳
æ	⠜
œ	⠪

GERMAN

ä	⠜
ö	⠪
ü	⠳

ITALIAN

à	⠷
è	⠮
ì	⠌
ò	⠬
ù	⠾
â	⠡
ê	⠣
î	⠩
ô	⠹
û	⠱

SPANISH

á	⠷
é	⠿
í	⠌
ó	⠬
ú	⠾
ü	⠳
ñ	⠻

PUNCTUATION MARKS

¿ ?	⠢
¡ !	⠖
— —	⠤⠤

braille successfully integrate the entire braille code into their reading and writing process.

Approaches

Although it is clear that contracted braille can be learned efficiently from the outset, there is some trend toward teaching uncontracted braille (grade 1 braille) in initial instruction, either as a step in the process of teaching the entire braille code or as a sole approach for some students. The uses of uncontracted braille include the following:

♦ The use of braille as a supplement to print with students whose primary literacy medium is print (see the next section) can be helpful in labeling, writing personal communications, and writing notes used for public speaking. Some students with low vision benefit from coordinated instruction in both braille and print and thus will learn the contracted braille code at some point in instruction.

♦ With students who are learning braille after having established some level of print literacy skills (see a later section), the teacher may choose to teach the alphabet first, so students can write any word. This approach makes it possible for the students to write text that is motivating to them, rather than the stilted text that would result from using only previously learned contractions. After the students learn the alphabet, integrate the teaching of contractions as quickly as possible into holistic literacy experiences to ensure that the students become efficient in reading the entire braille code and continue to expand their literacy skills.

♦ Students who are braille readers can use uncontracted braille to communicate in writing with their parents, siblings, and classmates. Encourage social interactions by teaching the braille alphabet to others who are important in the students' lives. General education teachers can use un-

contracted braille to write short notes or feedback on class assignments to the students.

♦ Some students who are blind and have additional disabilities can use uncontracted braille to attain functional literacy. Write uncontracted braille labels, words on communication boards, and short notes. In some cases, students with additional disabilities may benefit from the use of some contractions but not others. For example, if a student's name has a contraction in it, it may be easier for the student to recognize his or her name using the contraction. The teacher of students with visual impairments should closely examine a student's abilities when deciding on the extent to which contractions should be used with these students.

Which approach to use in teaching uncontracted braille depends on a student's needs. For preschoolers, the language-experience approach, described earlier, can be used. The only departure from the standard procedure would be that the stories would be written in uncontracted braille. Teaching the names of individual letters could be integrated naturally into the literacy experiences. For example, if a child's first name is Theresa, the child may be asked to read through the story and find all the words that start with (or that contain) the letter *t*. This approach could be combined with *The Mangold Developmental Program of Tactile Perception and Braille Letter Recognition* (Mangold, 1994a). As the student advances in this program, individual lessons are presented on tactilely discriminating individual letters. The names of letters can be taught at that point and integrated meaningfully with activities when using language-experience stories.

Issues

There are two primary issues related to teaching uncontracted braille. The first is the availability of reading materials. Since most braille materials—

even for young students—are embossed in contracted braille, finding suitable stories and books in braille will be a challenge, although a few commercial producers of braille (such as Seedlings, a publisher of children's books in braille) have begun to produce some limited materials in uncontracted braille (see the Resources for this chapter). Thus, if the teacher of students with visual impairments decides to teach in uncontracted braille, he or she also must make the commitment to provide suitable and extensive reading materials for the student. That is, the specialist or a braille transcriber hired by the school district will have to transcribe most materials.

The second issue is when and how to make the transition to contracted braille. In the absence of research on this issue, the teacher of students with visual impairments and others on the student's educational team will have to make this decision. Students who begin literacy instruction in braille and will use braille as their primary reading and writing medium need to master the braille code by the end of the third grade or the beginning of the fourth grade. This timing is important because by the fourth grade, sighted students in general education classrooms receive less-intense instruction in reading and writing and are expected to have well-developed, basic literacy skills. If this end point is used as a general guideline, then instruction in braille contractions may begin in the middle of the first grade or early in the second grade. The individual needs of the student, though, must guide this decision.

To introduce contractions, the teacher can present a few new contractions in each new story so the student learns them in a meaningful context. The major braille translation software packages allow a person to control the use of contractions in the text, so the teacher of students with visual impairments can provide materials to the student with only those contractions. One disadvantage of this approach is that as soon as the student has learned additional contractions, the materials produced earlier become virtually unusable. As was mentioned previously with respect to uncontracted braille, if the specialist prepares materials with some, but not all, contractions, he

or she will be responsible for transcribing all the braille materials the student uses. For this reason, the transition to fully contracted braille should occur as expeditiously as possible, but in a manner that allows contractions to be meaningfully integrated into the student's developing braille literacy skills.

Students who will continue to use only uncontracted braille throughout school and life are generally those students who have disabilities in addition to visual impairments. The use of uncontracted braille may provide a viable option for self-communication (for example, writing messages to oneself, labeling objects, and keeping an address book). If the student develops reading skills in uncontracted braille, then he or she can use braille-translation software to create documents in uncontracted braille as an adult. However, the decision to teach only uncontracted braille will limit a student's options for using braille in adult life, so this option should be used mainly for the students just mentioned.

Teaching in Dual Media

Some students with low vision benefit from learning both braille and print as complementary literacy media. The decision to teach literacy skills in dual media is made on the basis of the results of a comprehensive learning media assessment (see Chapter 4). In the past, teachers struggled over the decision to teach braille to students who had the capacity to use print. However, students who were inefficient in print reading and writing had no alternative other than to struggle with that inefficiency.

This practice is changing. Now students who have low vision—appropriately identified in learning media assessments—are given the option of learning to read and write braille before weak print-reading skills would interfere with their progress in school. If the educational team is unsure of whether a student with low vision will develop a high level of reading efficiency in print as a sole medium, the student should be afforded the opportunity to learn braille literacy skills during the early grades. Then the student will truly have a choice during the later grades and in adulthood for the most efficient medium to use to accomplish a given task.

The educational team must decide when to introduce instruction in dual media and how much to emphasize each medium. Holbrook and Koenig (1992) suggested two instructional options for teaching dual media to students with low vision:

◆ Parallel instruction: teaching braille and print concurrently and with the same level of intensity. This option is generally used with young students who are beginning literacy instruction in the early grades and hence are developing initial literacy skills.

◆ Nonparallel instruction: teaching braille skills at some point after students have acquired basic print literacy skills. This option is typically used if a student has not gained sufficient efficiency in print literacy skills or has an acquired or progressive visual condition such that print is no longer adequate as a sole medium.

In practice, a student's needs may fall somewhere between these two approaches. For example, a young student may have had more exposure to print than to braille during the preschool years, so his or her relative knowledge of print and braille may differ. In this case, the development of literacy skills will not be truly parallel during initial instruction, but the intensity of instruction can and should be similar.

When the decision is made to teach a student in dual media, appropriate levels of instruction need to be provided. Students who are learning to read in dual media typically need one to two hours of specialized instruction each day, five days per week, by the teacher of students with visual impairments, for an extended period (that is, throughout one or more school years) (Koenig & Holbrook, in press). The actual amount of direct instruction from the specialist will depend on the arrangement that is used to teach the two media. If the general education teacher is responsible for teaching print literacy skills and the specialist is responsible for teaching braille literacy skills, a significant portion of the specialist's time will be spent coordinating literacy instruction with the general education teacher. If the specialist is responsible for teaching literacy skills in both media, instructional time is maximized and unnecessary duplication is prevented, since general literacy skills (such as vocabulary and comprehension skills) are taught once and reinforced in each medium.

The educational team should evaluate each option regularly and choose the one that best meets the student's needs. Thereafter, the team should explore options and select the approach that will be used to teach literacy skills. If the general education teacher is responsible for teaching print literacy skills, then the approach will probably have been selected by the school district. The teacher of students with visual impairments generally decides on the approach to teaching braille literacy skills, although some approaches better meet the needs of students who are receiving parallel instruction (that is, a similar intensity of instruction in both media) during the early grades. Table 8.2 lists the advantages and disadvantages of several of the approaches to teaching reading and writing skills presented in this chapter and indicates whether each approach is suited to parallel or nonparallel instruction.

When the teacher of students with visual impairments is teaching both print and braille literacy skills, he or she can evenly distribute the concentration on each of the two media. For example, the first part of a story can be read in braille and the rest read in print, and skills lessons can be taught in different media. The meaning that is derived from reading a story or completing related activities will occur independently of the medium, so it is not necessary to repeat activities in each medium. The development of word-identification skills is a notable exception to this general rule: Students should be introduced to new words and given sufficient practice in each medium. During this time, the teacher of students with visual impairments can introduce any new braille signs in the new words.

Table 8.2. Summary of Selected Instructional Approaches for Teaching Braille Reading to Students with Low Vision

Approach	Advantages	Disadvantages	Type of Instruction[a]
Basal reader	Efficiency of instructional time Comprehensive, sequential approach	No control over the introduction of braille contractions	Ideal for parallel instruction Useful for nonparallel instruction
Language experience	No concerns about the student's experiential background Highly motivating to student Flexible—useful for teaching reading in print and/or braille	No control over the introduction of vocabulary and braille contractions May appear unstructured	Equally valuable for parallel and nonparallel instruction
Whole language	Highly motivating to the student Opportunities for reading and writing activities with peers The student has opportunities to select appropriate tools	Provision of adapted materials Incompatible with the itinerant teaching model	Ideal for parallel instruction May be useful for nonparallel instruction
Patterns	A comprehensive program Controlled introduction of vocabulary and contractions Not dependent on pictures	Incompatible with other approaches Prevents the student's integration with peers during reading classes Limits reading materials outside the *Patterns* program	May be useful for parallel instruction Limited usefulness for nonparallel instruction
Read Again	Designed to teach the braille code to individuals with adventitious blindness A comprehensive program	Age appropriateness is restricted to older students Beginning exercises appear contrived	Useful for nonparallel instructions only

[a]Parallel instruction: Both print and braille reading skills are being developed at the same time and with the same intensity. Nonparallel instruction: Basic print-reading skills have been established, and braille code skills are being introduced.

Sources: Adapted from M. C. Holbrook and A. J. Koenig, "Teaching Braille Reading to Students with Low Vision," *Journal of Visual Impairment & Blindness, 86* (1992), pp. 44–48; reprinted, with permission, from A. J. Koenig, "Selection of Learning and Literacy Media for Children and Youths with Low Vision," in A. L. Corn and A. J. Koenig, Eds., *Foundations of Low Vision: Clinical and Functional Perspectives* (New York: AFB Press, 1996), p. 271.

In most situations, however, the general education teacher will probably be responsible for print literacy instruction, and the teacher of students with visual impairments will be responsible for braille literacy instruction, so the two teachers will have to collaborate and coordinate their efforts closely. The specialist will not only discuss with the general education teacher the appropriate ways of teaching print literacy skills, using optical and nonoptical devices, and reinforcing the use of braille in the general education classroom, but will deliver a parallel instructional program in braille literacy skills. If the specialist chooses *Patterns* to teach braille literacy skills, then the links between the print and braille instructional programs will be limited. If he or she uses the approach used in the general education classroom—a more desirable approach—then he or she can reinforce the skills learned in print while teaching the unique aspects of braille.

For example, if a language-experience story is being used in the general education classroom, then the teacher of students with visual impairments can transcribe the story in braille. Doing so will give the student additional experiences in reading the story and allow the specialist to introduce vocabulary words and new contractions in braille. The specialist would not duplicate all the instruction in the classroom, but would focus on the unique skills used in braille reading. For example, if the general education teacher used the story to teach the difference between the hard and soft *c* sounds, the specialist would not need to do so again in braille because the medium makes no difference in learning this new skill. However, the specialist might reinforce this skill while integrating a braille-related skill. He or she could have the student skim the braille passage to find words that start with a hard *c* sound and then skim the story again to find the words with a soft *c* sound. This approach would promote fast, efficient skimming in braille and reinforce the phonics lesson taught in the general education classroom.

Students who are accustomed to using their eyes to read may want to look at the dots at first. Although some adults may feel uncomfortable about allowing them to do so, students who are used to visual input may find it helpful to have a visual representation that they can use as they become comfortable reading with their fingers. Students who have low vision may also feel more comfortable using their vision to orient them to the page or a sentence. This reliance on vision typically fades as students become more confident in their tactile skills.

Students who are learning to read in dual media need to have regular, consistent, and intense instruction in each medium during the primary grades. If a student receives ongoing instruction in print literacy skills but sporadic instruction in braille literacy skills, the educational team may

believe that he or she prefers to use print for literacy tasks, when the student may simply be using the medium in which he or she has acquired the greatest level of skill, regardless of efficiency. For students to use dual media appropriately and efficiently, they must receive similar levels of instruction in each medium. Then in the middle school grades and beyond, they can choose the medium that is truly the most efficient or preferred for a given task.

Teaching Braille as a Replacement for Print

Some students learn braille skills as a replacement or substitute for print. Generally, these students became blind sometime after the early grades or have progressive, deteriorating eye conditions. In either situation, they have some level of print literacy skills on which to base the new braille skills to be taught. The intensity of instruction will depend on whether a new medium is needed immediately (as in the case of a student who had a traumatic injury that caused sudden, functional blindness) or is needed at some point in the future (as in the case of a student with retinitis pigmentosa, which progresses over an extended period).

In teaching braille as a replacement for print, the teacher of students with visual impairments must consider whether an emphasis on literacy skills is more appropriate than an emphasis on braille code skills. The main need of young students in the primary grades (kindergarten through the third grade) is to continue to strengthen their literacy skills and to develop integrated braille code skills at the same time. After students attain a fourth-grade reading level or higher, they have a basic level of literacy skills, and the emphasis may appropriately be placed on braille code skills. However, even these students must use their braille code skills to accomplish meaningful literacy tasks, or they will be hampered in gaining an appreciation of using braille as a communication medium. That is, drilling a student on individual letters, contractions, or short-form words in braille is of limited value unless these braille skills are integrated into holistic literacy tasks, such as reading for pleasure or writing notes to oneself.

For students in the primary grades who need an emphasis on literacy skills while they are learning braille, the teacher of students with visual impairments can use any approach designed to teach beginning literacy skills, with appropriate modifications if needed. If the students are in kindergarten or the first grade, the specialist could consider using *Patterns*. This approach may be of limited usefulness for students in the second or third grades (since the beginning stories were written for younger students) and should *not* be used with students in the fourth grade or higher. Another option is to continue the approach that has been (or is being) used in the general education classroom, such as a basal reader or whole-language approach, although the ways of teaching these approaches need to be modified, as was described earlier in the section on beginning braille literacy skills. Regardless of the approach, the student needs to learn the unique tactile discrimination and hand-movement skills used in braille reading.

For students in upper middle school or high school who have gained basic literacy skills, two commercial programs are available: *Read Again* (Caton, Pester, & Bradley, 1990) and *Braille Too* (Hepker & Cross-Coquillette, 1995). These programs were designed for adolescents who are learning braille for the first time, and each contains worksheets and teacher's guides. If one of these series is selected, the teacher of students with visual impairments will probably find that using portions of the *The Mangold Developmental Program of Tactile Perception and Braille Letter Recognition* (Mangold, 1994a) will be helpful.

It should be noted that it takes much less time to teach the braille code to students who have established print literacy skills than to those who receive instruction in braille along with initial instruction in reading and writing. Although students who begin initial literacy instruction in braille take up to three to four years to develop basic literacy skills and a complete knowledge of the braille code, students who learn braille as a code

should be able to begin using the code efficiently in less than a year. It is important to consider the needs of each student carefully, but, in general, teaching the braille code as quickly as a student can comfortably learn it will allow the student to integrate braille more quickly into his or her daily life. The teacher of students with visual impairments should take direct steps to ensure that braille code skills are meaningfully integrated with the student's literacy skills (for instance, by encouraging the student to read for pleasure and asking the student to braille a speech that he or she is going to give in class).

In providing braille literacy instruction as a replacement for print, the teacher of students with visual impairments and other members of the educational team need to consider the total context within which the instruction is provided. These students are likely to be experiencing either a decrease in visual functioning or to have suddenly become blind, both of which will affect all aspects of their lives. They need to acquire compensatory skills for daily living and travel, as well as the skills needed to regain literacy and to continue learning academic subjects. Given this context, two important points should be acknowledged. First, the students probably have psychosocial issues and challenges that must be addressed, perhaps through counseling with qualified professionals and by learning alternative techniques for skills previously accomplished visually. Second, they need to see that the compensatory skills they are learning are valuable, so the skills must have real-life meaning and utility for them. In regard to learning braille reading and writing, D'Andrea (1997) offered the following suggestions to create, sustain, and increase motivation:

- ◆ Find stories and books that relate to the student's specific interests and that the student can read comfortably, to guarantee immediate success.

- ◆ Find functional uses for braille, such as labeling personal belongings (lockers, notebooks, CDs, and so forth), recording telephone numbers, and writing homework assignments or shopping lists.

◆ Use braille access technology, such as computers and personal note takers (see Chapter 14), as a motivating factor.

◆ Introduce the student to an adult braille reader who can serve as a mentor.

◆ Give the student directions in braille to follow, such as the steps in a treasure hunt or a description of a route in an O&M lesson.

◆ Encourage the student to subscribe to and read braille magazines that are of interest to him or her.

◆ Use a peer tutor to pair an experienced braille reader with a novice braille reader.

◆ Write braille notes to the student and place them in unexpected places to create interest and a sense of excitement in using braille. Later, the student can be encouraged to write notes to the teacher of students with visual impairments and others.

◆ Play enjoyable, motivating games, including those that are commercially available (such as Monopoly and Scrabble) and those that the teacher made or adapted with the student.

◆ Encourage the student to teach braille to his or her sighted classmates.

◆ Encourage the student to keep a log of the braille books he or she read.

◆ Encourage the student to enter contests, including those that are available to all students through school or library activities or those for students who are blind (such as Braille Readers Are Leaders, the annual contest held by the National Federation of the Blind).

◆ Model the use of braille (as when reading aloud to the student) and use braille for sending messages and other functional purposes.

Some of the materials used by students who are learning braille as a replacement for print will probably need to be provided in recorded form or electronically for reading through synthesized speech (discussed later). During the time that the student is gaining braille skills, he or she must have a way to keep up with the demands of daily classroom instruction, and recorded media are an important component of this process. However, the teacher of students with visual impairments should provide consistent instruction in braille literacy skills so the student can increase his or her use of literacy skills for classroom instruction in a timely manner, rather than overly on the use of recorded media.

PRINT LITERACY SKILLS

In many respects, students with low vision in print literacy programs have needs that are more complex to understand than are those of students in braille literacy programs. First, the ways in which students' eye conditions and levels of visual efficiency influence print reading are extremely complex and individualized. Therefore, generalizations across groups of students cannot be made, and careful assessment and attention to individual needs for instruction and modification are essential. Second, whereas the areas of instruction for students in braille literacy programs are readily apparent and definable, this is not the case for students with low vision in print literacy programs. In print literacy programs, the dividing line is often not clearly established between providing specialized instruction and providing consultation to a general education teacher, nor is there a clear distinction between compensatory skills training and tutoring.

Providing Instruction in Unique Skills

Although many students with low vision receive most of their literacy instruction in general education classrooms (see a later section), they have specific needs that must be addressed to ensure the optimal growth of their print literacy skills. To support and facilitate the development of literacy skills for students with low vision, the teacher of students with visual impairments needs to do the following:

♦ Teach the integrated use of visual skills in interpreting pictures, reading, and writing (see Chapter 13 for teaching strategies);

♦ Teach the use of optical and nonoptical low vision devices for completing near and distance literacy tasks (see Chapter 13 for teaching strategies);

♦ Teach keyboarding and word-processing skills if they are introduced later than the third grade in the standard curriculum;

♦ Build fluency and stamina in reading extended passages with or without low vision devices (see Sidebar 8.9 for suggested strategies).

♦ Teach the effective use of listening, aural reading, and live reader skills (see the next section); and

♦ Teach braille as a complementary medium to print or as a replacement for print when the results of a comprehensive learning media assessment indicate such a need.

As the teacher of students with visual impairments provides instruction in unique literacy skills to students with low vision, he or she should ensure that this instruction is integrated within meaningful literacy experiences. Most of the strategies mentioned earlier in this chapter (specifically, language-experience stories, repeated readings, shared reading, and all the whole-language strategies outlined in Table 8.1) are appropriate and important to use with students with low vision. Generally, the only modifications needed are to ensure that materials are presented in an appropriate medium (such as large print or regular print with or without a low vision device) and that the student is encouraged and prompted to use efficient visual skills.

Providing Primary Literacy Instruction

The question may arise as to when, if ever, the teacher of students with visual impairments should assume primary responsibility for teaching print literacy skills to a student with low vision. The authors of this chapter recommend such direct instruction when any of the following conditions prevail:

♦ Collaboration with the general education teacher and supplemental teaching by the specialist in visual impairment have failed to promote steady gains in the development of literacy skills;

♦ The lack of progress in developing literacy skills is thought to be due to a learning disability;

♦ The student is receiving fragmented, poor-quality instruction in the general education classroom;

♦ The student is having difficulty integrating the use of optical devices during classroom reading instruction; or

♦ The student is learning both braille and print as complementary media, and the educational team wants to provide a holistic literacy program that skillfully interweaves learning in both media.

To address any of these areas, the teacher of students with visual impairments may provide a period of brief, concentrated instruction (such as daily for one to several weeks or a quarter) or extended instruction (such as daily over an entire school year). For all the conditions just presented (except teaching reading in dual media), the specialist needs to provide high-quality, intense literacy instruction using the principles of diagnostic teaching (see Chapter 3 for a description). This approach is the most powerful way to determine the cause of certain difficulties and to implement strategies to address them.

Furthermore, diagnostic teaching is perhaps the only way to determine whether a student is experiencing difficulties because of a learning disability or fragmented instruction. If a period of high-quality instruction promotes steady gains in a student's literacy development, then the difficulties are not the result of a learning disability. However, if progress is not appar-

Strategies for Promoting Fluency and Stamina

- Use easy reading materials that appropriately match the student's experiential background and interests;

- Document the student's reading efficiency rate and maintain objective documentation throughout the school years;

- Determine an objective level of stamina both within a single session and throughout the school day, using sustained reading samples and supplement this information with interviews with the student, parents, teachers, and others;

- Use objectively gathered baseline data to set reasonable goals for continually increasing the student's reading efficiency rate and stamina to levels of "just manageable difficulty," a general concept for learning suggested by Hobbs (1965);

- Check that the student has demonstrated a consistent and comfortable degree of mastery of a given goal before setting the next goal;

- Involve the student directly in setting goals and in monitoring the results of instruction;

- Provide feedback to the student on the student's progress in increasing his or her reading efficiency rate and stamina using line charts or tables as appropriate;

- Use real opportunities for increasing the student's reading efficiency rate and stamina, such as repeatedly reading a text to be read aloud in a school program;

- Encourage the student to assess continually whether the visual environment is conducive to reading and have him or her make adjustments in lighting, position of the book, and other factors, according to the student's preferences;

- Encourage the student to monitor continually his or her use of any optical devices while reading, and to make needed adjustments in focal distance, working distance, viewing angle, and so forth;

- Teach the student to recognize the signs of visual fatigue and offer strategies for dealing with it, such as taking short breaks, changing from reading a text to listening to a recorded version, or changing his or her physical position;

- Teach the student to read for specific purposes: scanning quickly to find needed information, skimming to get the gist of a passage, and studying to understand and remember details; and

- Encourage the student to read for pleasure, generally with easy reading materials of high motivational value.

Source: Adapted from A. J. Koenig and E. J. Rex, "Instruction of Literacy Skills to Children and Youths," in A. L. Corn and A. J. Koenig, Eds., *Foundations of Low Vision: Clinical and Functional Perspectives* (New York: AFB Press, 1996), pp. 293–294.

---

ent, then the teacher of students with visual impairments needs to collaborate with a teacher of students with learning disabilities (commonly employed by school districts) to develop and implement targeted strategies for increasing literacy skills and to assess the effects of these strategies.

In some circumstances, it may be determined that the teacher of students with visual impairments should continue to provide primary literacy instruction to a student with low vision. If so, the specialist must make a commitment to provide instruction one to two hours each day. If these difficulties arise while the student is in a general education classroom, then the ultimate goal should be to reintegrate the student into the general literacy program at some point.

LISTENING, AURAL READING, AND LIVE READER SKILLS

The efficient use of auditory information is important for both students who are blind and students with low vision. Auditory information in the environment facilitates independent travel and social interactions and allows a student to gather information efficiently in the classrooms. Students with visual impairments make use of auditory information by developing listening, aural reading, and live reader skills. The specialist collaborates with the students' parents, teachers, and others to facilitate the use of listening to gather information and works directly with the students to teach aural reading and live reader skills.

Listening

The development of listening skills generally occurs naturally for students with visual impairments without special or targeted instruction. Parents are the initial teachers of listening skills as they interact with infants in their cribs and give simple directions to toddlers and preschoolers. Preschool teachers often emphasize listening skills in activities, such as show-and-tell, in which young children listen to their classmates tell about experiences and show favorite objects from home. Perhaps the most direct teaching of listening skills occurs in orientation and mobility (O&M) instruction (see Chapter 15), in which auditory cues are used for orientation to the environment and for safe travel.

Aural Reading

Aural reading refers to gathering information from audiotaped materials and books. Recording for the Blind and Dyslexic provides numerous recorded textbooks, and the National Library Service (NLS) for the Blind and Physically Handicapped provides a wide variety of materials—novels, newspapers, magazines—in Talking Book (recorded) format. These recordings are placed on special four-track tapes that require a specific tape player provided by the NLS or purchased from APH or other companies. In addition to agencies and organizations that prepare recorded books and materials, general education teachers often make their own recordings. Students with visual impairments need to learn the strategies both for using tape players and for gathering information from recordings.

Teaching the mechanical aspects of the tape players is relatively easy if the teacher is familiar with the specific brand of tape player that the student will use. The student should first be oriented to the various controls and keys and allowed to try each feature. Typical features include controls for volume, speed, and ejecting a cassette, as well as keys for stopping, starting, pausing, forwarding, and rewinding. It is particularly important to teach the student to switch tracks on a four-track tape and to adjust the speed control to provide a comfortable rate of reading.

In addition, the teacher of students with visual impairments needs to teach the student strategies for efficiently understanding and gathering information presented on an audiotape. Although the use of audiotaped materials may seem straightforward at first, there are challenges. First, the listener has little control over the presentation of the information. Second, the material is presented linearly, and it is not easy to scan ahead or review recorded information. Third, specialized tape players that were designed for use by readers who are blind (such as those from the Library of Congress and APH) offer a tone-index feature. When an indexed tape is placed in fast-forward mode, a high-pitched sound is heard at the beginnings of chapters, sections, or pages. The specific way in which a tape is tone indexed generally is described at the beginning of the tape. Using the tone-indexing feature allows the reader a measure of control in scanning ahead and locating specific sections or pages, but the method is imprecise, and further forward and reverse searches generally are needed to locate specific information. Fourth, no spatially presented materials, such as tables and graphs, accompany audiotaped books. Although these displays are described by a professional narrator (as on the NLS tapes), it is difficult to listen to information from a spatial format in a linear sequence. Finally, since listening tends to be a passive activity, it is not uncommon for the listener to daydream. To promote efficient aural reading, the following suggestions are offered:

◆ Begin by giving the student a question or questions to answer on the basis of a short, recorded passage to give the student a specific purpose in "reading" the passage. It may be preferable to use materials that are easy for the student, rather than those at his or her instructional level.

◆ Provide an outline of the elements of a recorded passage in braille or an accessible print format. Encourage the student to follow along with the outline as he or she listens to the passage. Then ask literal and inferential comprehension questions that are based on the passage as a follow-up activity.

◆ Have the student take brief notes on the passage as he or she listens to the recording.

◆ As the student becomes skilled in using audiotaped materials with external prompts and cues (as indicated earlier), have him or her move to a more independent level. Start by having the student pause the tape player occasionally to review the key elements of the passage. Later, have the student continually review in his or her mind the key elements as the tape is playing. This technique makes a passive activity more active.

Ultimately, the goal of aural reading is to gather the specific information that is needed from the passage with the most efficient use of time and with as few external prompts as neces-

sary. If the student can listen to a recorded passage and complete whatever assignment is needed afterward, then no external cues or prompts may be needed. If the student needs to take notes to stay focused on the materials, then he or she should be encouraged to do so.

With the increased use of computers in today's schools, it is likely that students with visual impairments, especially those who are blind, will use synthesized speech—that is, the use of computer software and hardware to convert the words on the screen into spoken language—to gather information. This process is a form of aural reading. However, screen-reading software allows the user more control over the reading episode by using search capabilities and strategic cursor movements (such as move ahead one sentence, move back one sentence, move ahead one paragraph, and move back one paragraph). Also, most screen readers have more sophisticated capabilities for changing the speed and quality of the speech. Although synthesized speech is computer generated and does not sound exactly like human speech, students generally can learn to understand it at faster and faster rates. (See Chapter 14 for more information on the use of screen readers and synthesized speech.)

Live Readers

Most individuals who are blind, as well as some with low vision, make some use of live readers to gather information from print materials, although the expanded use of technology has decreased this usage somewhat. A live reader works under the direction of the person with a visual impairment to read aloud information from printed materials, such as mail, memos, bills, and textbooks. To use a live reader efficiently, a student needs to be given specific instructions, practice, and feedback from a teacher of students with visual impairments. It is important for the student to learn to control and direct the live reader, not to expect the reader simply to read without direction. The student also needs to learn that when using a live reader, all work completed must be the student's work, not that of the live reader.

The obvious advantage of using a live reader over recorded materials is that the individual with a visual impairment is in direct control of the reading episode. He or she can ask the reader to read the table of contents or the headings in a chapter, to skip to the next section or the next chapter, to review specific parts or to search for certain pieces of information, to consult the index to locate a topic of interest, and so forth. The major disadvantage is that using a live reader requires the presence of another person who has his or her own schedule and commitments and thus may not always be available when the student needs his or her services.

To teach the efficient use of a live reader, the specialist may find the following sequence (Iowa Department of Education, 1986) helpful:

1. *Listening to a live reader:* Have the student listen as you read aloud. Stop occasionally to ask questions and to check for understanding. This technique is typically used with young children from toddlerhood through the early elementary grades.

2. *Directing a live reader:* In elementary school and throughout middle school, start giving the student some control over the reading situation. Prompt the student for specific directions and sequencing for the reading activity. Suggest techniques, such as reviewing a table of contents or index, to pinpoint certain information. Give the student guidance on how to use a live reader effectively and provide appropriate prompts and reinforcement, decreasing them as the student progresses. After the student is effectively using the specialist as a live reader, have him or her gather information from other teachers and eventually from his or her classmates.

3. *Managing a live reader:* In late middle school and throughout high school, discuss with the student the importance of seeking, hiring, and managing a live reader. Generally, the student will not pay a live reader during the school years, but it

is necessary to discuss this matter to prepare him or her for college and adult life. Also discuss the characteristics of a live reader that are desirable and help the student to find and "hire" classmates as live readers. In addition, discuss and plan reading schedules, along with backup plans for instances when live readers fail to keep their commitments to read. These activities should intensify as the student gets closer to high school graduation and prepares to enter college or employment.

A Cautionary Note

Using effective listening skills is an important and necessary tool for gathering information for students with visual impairments. However, the teacher of students with visual impairments must ensure that an appropriate balance is maintained between the use of listening skills and the development of literacy skills in braille and/or accessible print. In most cases in which this cautionary note is applicable, the overuse of listening at the expense of developing literacy skills is the issue. Students learn to read and write by reading and writing, *not* by listening.

Audiotaped materials and live readers must not be habitually used to take the place of instructional materials in braille or accessible print. The occasional use of an alternative medium (like listening) to take the place of braille or print is appropriate in that it reflects the hectic pace and unpredictability of the real world. However, if listening is used because accessible materials are routinely not provided in braille or print in a timely fashion, then the student's literacy skills are placed at risk. In such circumstances, the teacher of students with visual impairments must address the real issue of how to provide braille or accessible print at the time it is needed in the classroom. The teacher should bring such issues to the attention of his or her administrator, so additional human or technological resources are provided to meet the demands of providing instructional materials in accessible media.

KEYBOARDING, WORD-PROCESSING, AND TECHNOLOGY SKILLS

Students who are blind or have low vision need to acquire a range of technology skills that will give them options for gathering and conveying information. Typically, they gain their first introduction to computers through instruction in keyboarding. This is an essential first step, since the keyboard allows the students to control the computer, as well as to use it for writing and gathering information from electronic sources. Keyboarding instruction begins in the first, second, or third grade, with the second grade a good general starting point (Koenig & Holbrook, in press); instructional sessions tend to be from less than 30 minutes to an hour, depending on a student's needs. Word-processing skills follow as a natural extension and application of keyboarding skills.

A teacher of students with visual impairments provides direct instruction in keyboarding and word-processing skills to a student who is blind. He or she may provide direct instruction to a student with low vision, or the student may receive instruction from another teacher or computer specialist in collaboration with the specialist in visual impairment. An essential starting point for all students with visual impairments is to gain access to the computer screen. Students who are blind generally make use of speech synthesis and screen readers, refreshable braille displays, and hard-copy braille output. Students with low vision benefit from programs or hardware that enlarge the image on the screen, and some may prefer to use synthesized speech as a supplement to or a replacement for print on the screen. Chapter 14 explains this technology and presents strategies for teaching its use.

The importance of well-developed computer and technology skills for students with visual impairments cannot be overstated. These skills provide access to the vast amount of information that is available in electronic format, much of which is readily available through the Internet. Technology can provide equal opportunities in school and employment, and students with visual impairments must have the advantages afforded by technology skills when they exit the school system and enter adult life.

INCLUDING STUDENTS IN LITERACY INSTRUCTION IN THE GENERAL EDUCATION CLASSROOM

Students in Braille Literacy Programs

Beginning Braille Reading and Writing Skills

Some students who are blind receive a portion of their instruction in literacy skills in a general education classroom. This approach assumes that the teacher of students with visual impairments is providing direct, daily instruction to ensure that integrated literacy experiences are meaningful and successful. It also assumes that the teacher of students with visual impairments is engaging in close, daily collaboration with the general education teacher. Specific strategies to ensure a student's positive inclusion are as follows:

◆ Provide braille and other modified instructional materials on time. All print materials that are used to teach reading and writing should be available in braille or other tactile forms to a student who needs them. Clearly mark papers and worksheets in print for the general education teacher. Cross-reference the pages of braille materials with those of inkprint pages, especially those in the teacher's manual. Work with the general education teacher to design a system for identifying early those materials that need to be transcribed or modified, so they will be ready for the student when he or she needs them. If instructional materials are not provided in braille and accessible formats, the student will not be afforded comparable reading and writing experiences, and the lack of these experiences will interfere with his or her learning literacy skills.

◆ Ensure that the student who is blind has appropriate background experiences to bring meaning to the stories used for classroom instruction. Review the stories in advance, making a list of the key experiences. Work with the student's parents and others to provide important experiences for the student before he or she reads the stories in the classroom. When appropriate or necessary, arrange these experiences for the student or integrate the experiences into O&M lessons.

◆ Review the student's stories in advance to identify new words and contractions and devote additional instructional time to introducing these new elements in meaningful contexts before these elements are taught in the general education classroom. Having advance knowledge of new words and braille contractions will allow the student to focus on other aspects of the reading lesson, such as comprehending the story, taking turns when reading, and so forth.

◆ Discuss with the general education teacher a number of options for handling the content of pictures in the stories. The options may include previewing the pictures in a special instructional period, substituting some real objects for pictures, or having the teacher or classmates describe the pictures before the class reads the story.

◆ Establish a procedure for handling written work. Generally, students in the early elementary grades write their class work and assignments on a Perkins braillewriter. A student should be encouraged to specify the worksheet or activity at the top of the braille page and place the papers in a designated place so the teacher of students with visual impairments can collect them, inkprint (or interline) them, and return them to the general education teacher for grading the same day or the next day. As the student learns to use appropriate technology, he or she will be able to submit homework assignments in print independently.

◆ Promote independence in the classroom. In literacy activities, as well as other school activities, the student should be given appropriate instruction and should gain the skills he or she needs to function independently. A paraeducator or classmate should not do things for a student who is blind that the student can do for himself or herself. The key is to provide instruction in the needed skills before they are required in the classroom. Interactions with classmates should focus on mutually beneficial learning activities, such as "buddy reading" and writing conferences. Paraeducators should be assigned to teachers, not students, and should prepare adapted materials and assist the teacher with classroom activities, not "hover" unnecessarily over the student who is blind.

◆ Provide ongoing collaboration with the general education teacher, observe the student in the classroom regularly, and provide ongoing literacy assessment. Staying involved in daily classroom activities and knowing what the student is learning are paramount. The student should be routinely engaged in meaningful braille literacy activities throughout the school day.

Intermediate and Advanced Braille Literacy Skills

With a solid foundation in braille literacy skills acquired from kindergarten through the third grade, the student should be prepared to engage in literacy activities in middle school and high school with less direct involvement from the teacher of students with visual impairments. During this time, the specialist ensures that the student receives appropriately adapted materials on time. If any new or unusual formats or braille signs appear, they should be introduced in preteaching activities before they are needed in the classroom. The specialist stays involved in the student's braille literacy program by addressing the student's need for direct instruction in the areas discussed earlier in this chapter.

Students in Print Literacy Programs

To integrate students with low vision in regular print literacy programs, the teacher of students with visual impairments must collaborate with the general education teacher on a regular basis. Even with close collaboration, the specialist should assume the ultimate responsibility for ensuring that a student with low vision receives a high-quality literacy program. To do so, the specialist teacher will teach the unique skills needed by a student with low vision (described earlier) and collaborate with the general education teacher to support and facilitate the growth of a student's literacy in the general education classroom.

In some situations, a teacher of students with visual impairments may presume that the general education teacher is responsible for instruction in literacy skills and hence may focus on other skills (such as social skills or daily living skills). Or the general education teacher may presume that the specialist is responsible and thus may not hold the same expectations for the student with low vision or may judge the student's progress by a separate, lower standard than for the sighted students in the classroom. Either situation puts the student with low vision at risk of not making steady progress in developing literacy skills.

The key to ensuring that each student with low vision develops solid literacy skills is effective and ongoing collaboration between the specialist and the general education teacher. Here are some suggestions for doing so:

- ◆ Share information from the learning media assessment and functional vision assessment, especially the implications for the student's development of literacy skills, with the general education teacher.

- ◆ Involve the general education teacher in gathering data for the ongoing learning media assessment, noting his or her concerns, as well as the student's strengths in and needs for further instruction in literacy skills.

- ◆ Demonstrate the use of optical and nonoptical devices to the general education teacher and make sure that he or she is comfortable integrating the use of these devices into literacy instruction.

- ◆ Make suggestions for modifying the environment to make literacy activities comfortable and enjoyable.

- ◆ Observe the student in the general education classroom regularly to ensure that the student is making appropriate use of optical and nonoptical devices and environmental modifications and is continually engaged in literacy activities.

- ◆ Conduct ongoing assessments of the student's literacy skills and literacy media to ensure that the student's placement in a print literacy program remains appropriate.

When the teacher of students with visual impairments needs to provide direct, primary instruction in literacy skills for students with low vision, he or she should proceed expeditiously to do so, working in concert with other members of the educational team. Often, the literacy needs of students with low vision are overlooked, since it appears that they are or should be making progress in a print literacy program. Not all students make adequate progress with this instruction alone, and those who do not should be given the opportunity to have direct instruction from a teacher of students with visual impairments. Providing direct, primary instruction in print literacy skills in a timely and consistent manner helps ensure that these students with low vision gain the solid literacy skills needed to make progress throughout school and life.

SUMMARY

Providing high-quality literacy instruction to students with visual impairments and ensuring the students' continued growth in these essential skills is a significant role for the teacher of students with visual impairments. Each student must receive an individualized assessment of his or her need for literacy media to determine the appropriate literacy medium or media. Students who are blind need direct instruction in beginning braille literacy skills and other areas, such as aural reading, keyboarding, word processing, and the use of the slate and stylus. When students who are blind are included in literacy instruction in the general education classroom, the specialist must maintain daily and ongoing involvement and collaboration with the general education teacher to ensure that the students benefit from all literacy activities. Students with low vision have unique and complex needs that must be addressed by specialists in visual impairment, both through direct instruction and through collaboration with general education teachers.

ACTIVITIES

1. Select a picture book that was written for young children. Assemble a "book bag" and create a print-braille version of the book. Read the book to your classmates.

2. Interview an adult with low vision and an adult who is blind. Note the ways in which they use print and/or braille throughout their daily lives. Ask them to explain their strategies for gaining access to information that is initially inaccessible to them (such as print that is too small for a person with low vision or mail in a printed format for a person who is blind).

3. Select an article from a journal, such as *The Reading Teacher,* that presents a strategy for teaching literacy skills to sighted students. Prepare a brief handout with modifications of this strategy for students who are blind and students with low vision. Present the strategy and modifications to your classmates and give them copies of the handout for their resource files.

4. Observe a general education classroom in which the teacher uses principles of whole-language instruction. Note the various activities that the teacher uses and specify the modifications that would be needed to allow a student who is blind and a student with low vision to participate fully in all activities.

5. Select a unit from the teacher's manual that accompanies a standard basal reading series. Modify each activity and learning experience presented in the manual. Prepare all braille materials that will accompany the unit, including any charts and supplementary materials.

REFERENCES

American Printing House for the Blind. (1998). *Discovering the magic of reading: Elizabeth's story.* [Videotape]. Louisville, KY: Author.

Braille Authority of North America. (1994). *English braille American edition 1994.* Louisville, KY: American Printing House for the Blind.

Braille Authority of North America. (1998). *Braille formats: Principles of print to braille transcription 1997.* Louisville, KY: American Printing House for the Blind.

Castellano, C., & Kosman, D. (1997). *The bridge to braille: Reading and school success for the young blind child.* Baltimore, MD: National Organization of Parents of Blind Children.

Caton, H., Pester, E., & Bradley, E. J. (1980). *Patterns: The primary braille reading program.* Louisville, KY: American Printing House for the Blind.

Caton, H., Pester, E., & Bradley, E. J. (1990). *Read again: A braille program for adventitiously blinded print readers.* Louisville, KY: American Printing House for the Blind.

Caton, H., Pester, E., & Bradley, E. J. (1987). *Patterns prebraille program.* Louisville, KY: American Printing House for the Blind.

Caton, H., Pester, E., Bradley, E. J., Modaressi, B., Hamp, E. P., & Otto, R. (1993). *Patterns: The primary braille spelling and English program.* Louisville, KY: American Printing House for the Blind.

Corn, A. L., & Koenig, A. J. (Eds.). (1996). *Foundations of low vision: Clinical and functional perspectives.* New York: AFB Press.

Corn, A. L., & Koenig, A. J. (2000). *Assuring quality literacy instruction for students with low vision.* Manuscript in preparation.

Curran, E. (1988). *Just enough to know better: A braille primer.* Boston: National Braille Press.

D'Andrea, F. M. (1997). Making the transition from print to braille. In D. P. Wormsley & F. M. D'Andrea (Eds.), *Instructional strategies for braille literacy* (pp. 111–143). New York: AFB Press.

Edman, P. K. (1992). *Tactile graphics.* New York: American Foundation for the Blind.

Freund, E. D. (1967). *Longhand writing for the blind.* Louisville, KY: American Printing House for the Blind.

Godwin, A., Grafsgaard, K., Hanson, N., Hooey, P., Martin, J., McNear, D., Rieber, C., & Tillmanns, E. (1995). *Minnesota braille skills inventory: A resource manual.* Little Canada: Minnesota Educational Services.

Harley, R. K., Truan, M. B., & Sanford, L. D. (1987). *Communication skills for visually impaired learners.* Springfield, IL: Charles C Thomas.

Hepker, M. L., & Cross-Coquillette, S. C. (1995). *Braille too.* Cedar Rapids, IA: Grant Wood Area Education Agency.

Hobbs, N. (1965, October). *The professor and the student or the art of getting students into trouble.* Paper presented at the 48th annual convention of the American Council on Education, Washington, DC.

Holbrook, M. C., & Koenig, A. J. (1992). Teaching braille reading to students with low vision. *Journal of Visual Impairment & Blindness, 86,* 44–48.

Iowa Department of Education. (1989). *Guidelines for programs serving students with visual impairments: Field test version.* Des Moines: Author.

Koenig, A. J. (1992). A framework for understanding the literacy of individuals with visual impairments. *Journal of Visual Impairment & Blindness, 86,* 277–284.

Koenig, A. J. (1996a). Growing into literacy. In M. C. Holbrook (Ed.), *Children with visual impairments: A parents' guide* (pp. 227–257). Baltimore, MD: Woodbine House.

Koenig, A. J. (1996b). Selection of learning and literacy media for children and youths with low vision. In A. L. Corn & A. J. Koenig (Eds.), *Foundations of low vision: Clinical and functional perspectives* (pp. 246–279). New York: AFB Press.

Koenig, A. J., & Farrenkopf, C. (1995). *Assessment of braille literacy skills* (ABLS). Houston, TX: Region IV Education Service Center.

Koenig, A. J., & Farrenkopf, C. (1997). Essential experiences to undergird the development of early literacy. *Journal of Visual Impairment & Blindness, 91,* 14–24.

Koenig, A. J., & Holbrook, M. C. (in press). Assuring quality literacy instruction for students in braille literacy programs. *Journal of Visual Impairment & Blindness.*

Koenig, A. J., & Rex, E. J. (1996). Instruction of literacy skills to children and youths with low vision. In A. L. Corn & A. J. Koenig (Eds.)., *Foundations of low vision: Clinical and functional perspectives* (pp. 280–305). New York: AFB Press.

Lamb, G. (1996). Beginning braille: A whole language-based strategy. *Journal of Visual Impairment & Blindness, 90,* 184–189.

Layton, C. A. (1997). Assessing the literacy skills of students who are blind or visually impaired. In D. P. Wormsley & F. M. D'Andrea (Eds.), *Instructional strategies for braille literacy* (pp. 231–268). New York: AFB Press.

Lowenfeld, B., Abel, G. L., & Hatlen, P. H. (1969). *Blind children learn to read.* Springfield, IL: Charles C Thomas.

Mangold, P. N. (1993). *Teaching the braille slate and stylus: A manual for mastery.* Castro Valley, CA: Exceptional Teaching Aids.

Mangold, S. (1978). Tactile perception and braille letter recognition: Effects of developmental teaching. *Journal of Visual Impairment & Blindness, 72,* 259–266.

Mangold, S. (1994a). *The Mangold developmental program of tactile perception and braille letter recognition.* Castro Valley, CA: Exceptional Teaching Aids.

Mangold, S. (1994b). *The Mangold developmental program of tactile perception and braille letter recognition: Teacher's manual.* Castro Valley, CA: Exceptional Teaching Aids.

Mangold, S. (1994c). *Teaching the braille state and stylus.* [Videotape]. Castro Valley, CA: Exceptional Teaching Aids.

Mangold, S., & Pesavento, M. E. (1994). *Teaching signature writing to those who are visually impaired* [Videotape]. Castro Valley, CA: Exceptional Teaching Aids.

Martin, B. (1996). *Brown bear, brown bear, what do you see?* New York: Henry Holt.

McComiskey, A. V. (1996). The braille readiness grid: A guide to building a foundation for literacy. *Journal of Visual Impairment & Blindness, 90,* 190–193.

McNear, D., Holbrook, M. C., & Koenig, A. J. (1997). Enhancing literacy skills through a whole language approach. In A. J. Koenig & M. C. Holbrook (Eds.). *Proceedings of the second biennial conference of Getting in Touch with Literacy* (pp. 93–107). Alexandria, VA: Association for Education and Rehabilitation of the Blind and Visually Impaired.

Miller, D. D. (1985). Reading comes naturally: A mother and her blind child's experiences. *Journal of Visual Impairment & Blindness, 79,* 1–4.

Olson, M. R. (1981). *Guidelines and games for teaching efficient braille reading.* New York: American Foundation for the Blind.

Rex, E. J., Koenig, A. J., Wormsley, D., & Baker, R. (1994). *Foundations of braille literacy.* New York: AFB Press.

Routman, R. (1991). *Invitations: Changing as teachers and learners K–12.* Portsmouth, NH: Heinemann.

Sharpe, M. N., McNear, D., & McGraw, K. S. (1996). *Braille Assessment Inventory.* Columbia, MO: Hawthorne Educational Services.

Stratton, J. M., & Wright, S. (1991). *On the way to literacy.* Louisville, KY: American Printing House for the Blind.

Swallow, R. M., Mangold, S. S., & Mangold, P. (Eds.). (1978). *Informal assessment of developmental skills for visually handicapped students.* New York: American Foundation for the Blind.

Swenson, A. M. (1999). *Beginning with braille: First-hand experiences with a balanced approach to literacy.* New York: AFB Press.

Understanding braille literacy [Videotape]. (1993). New York: AFB Press.

Weiss, J., & Weiss, J. (1978). Teaching handwriting to the congenitally blind. *Journal of Visual Impairment & Blindness, 72,* 280–283.

Wormsley, D. P., & D'Andrea, F. M. (Eds.). (1997). *Instructional strategies for braille literacy.* New York: AFB Press.

Diagnostic Assessment of Braille Reading Skills

Name _____ School _____ Grade _____

Teacher _____ Date _____

Note: The teacher who provides direct instruction in braille must have the following:

1. Adequate knowledge of the braille reading code in order to analyze the reading errors of the child.
2. A thorough understanding of the major reading methods to match the braille reading approach to the child's reading skills and learning style.
3. Specific skills in adapting and modifying reading strategies based upon the assessed needs of the child.
4. Pertinent information relative to the teaching of braille reading to ensure proper skills development.

A. Child is able to:

	Yes	No
1. Easily locate		
1.1 Top of page	_____	_____
1.2 Braille page number	_____	_____
1.3 Print page number	_____	_____
1.4 Beginning of each braille line	_____	_____
1.5 End of each braille line	_____	_____
2. Position braille book correctly	_____	_____
3. Track evenly across every page with		
_____ two hands	_____	_____
_____ one hand	_____	_____
3.1 Does not backtrack	_____	_____
3.2 Does not use regressive hand movements	_____	_____
3.3 Tracks without scrubbing letters	_____	_____
3.4 Uses light pressure	_____	_____

(continued on next page)

Appendix A: Diagnostic Assessment of Braille Reading Skills

Diagnostic Assessment of Braille Reading Skills *(Continued)*

	Yes	No
4. Maintain correct posture		
4.1 Hands relaxed	_____	_____
4.2 Fingers curved	_____	_____
4.3 Sitting	_____	_____
5. Maintain page turning procedures		
5.1 Turns braille pages easily	_____	_____
5.2 Reads last line with left hand and turns page with right hand	_____	_____

B. Finger mentoring

  1. Describe fine-motor development.

    1.1 Finger strength:

    1.2 Manual dexterity:

    1.3 Manipulative behavior:

    1.4 Grasp behavior:

    1.5 Thumb/index finger opposition:

  2. Describe finger sensitivity to braille line

left   right

    2.1 Left hand:

    2.2 Right hand:

C. Braille reading-type errors

  1. Reversals or rotations (circle errors)

d/f	e/i	h/j	m/sh
n/ed	o/ow	p/th	r/w
s/wh	t/ou	z/the	ar/gh
_____	_____	_____	_____
ed/the	m/u	s/gh	er/with
_____	_____	_____	_____

(continued on next page)

Diagnostic Assessment of Braille Reading Skills *(Continued)*

2. Whole-word signs (such as *can, rather, that, this, which*)

   _____   _____   _____   _____

   _____   _____   _____   _____

   _____   _____   _____   _____

   _____   _____   _____   _____

3. Short-form words (such as *across, also, good, perhaps*)

   _____   _____   _____   _____

   _____   _____   _____   _____

   _____   _____   _____   _____

   _____   _____   _____   _____

4. Two-cell contractions (fill in errors)

   4.1 Initial letters (like *day, here, part, right*)

   _____   _____   _____   _____

   _____   _____   _____   _____

   _____   _____   _____   _____

   4.2 Final letter contractions (*-sion, -tion, -ation*)

   _____   _____   _____   _____

   _____   _____   _____   _____

   _____   _____   _____   _____

5. Confusions

   5.1 Letter similarity (lr h = *have, here, his, had*)

   _____   _____   _____   _____

   _____   _____   _____   _____

   _____   _____   _____   _____

   5.2 Braille position errors (such as *t,* from, *ff, !*)

   _____   _____   _____   _____

   _____   _____   _____   _____

   _____   _____   _____   _____

(continued on next page)

Diagnostic Assessment of Braille Reading Skills *(Continued)*

    5.3 Words with two braille symbols (*to, was, were, his*)

    _____   _____   _____   _____

    _____   _____   _____   _____

    _____   _____   _____   _____

D. Word-recognition skills (use of a reading skills assessment is recommended)

    1. Sight word recognition (Dolch):

    APH Dolch list _____ percent correct.   Date: _____

    2. Phonetic analysis: *Yes*   *No*

    The child is able to:

    2.1 Recognize the following single consonants
and name a word containing each consonant.
(Circle errors)   _____   _____

    b, c, d, f, g, h, j, k, l, m, n,

    p, q, r, s, t, v, w, x, y, and *z*

    2.2 Recognize a consonant blend and give a word
containing one of them.
Example: *brick, flower,* or *spring*   _____   _____

    2.3 Recognize a consonant digraph and give a word
containing one of them.
Example: *ship, chain,* and *those*   _____   _____

    2.4 Recognize each single vowel and give a word
containing the long vowel sound.
Example: *a, e, i, o, u,* and *y*   _____   _____

    2.5 Recognize each single vowel and give a word
containing the short vowel sound.
Example: *a, e, i, o, u,* and *y*   _____   _____

    2.6 Recognize a diphthong and give a word containing it.
Example: *boy, ouch,* and *boil*   _____   _____

    2.7 Understand how *r* after a vowel affects the sound
of the vowel.
Example: *her, skirt,* and *fur*   _____   _____

(continued on next page)

Diagnostic Assessment of Braille Reading Skills *(Continued)*

2.8 Understand how *w* before a vowel affects the sound of the vowel.
Example: *wall* and *worm*

Yes _____   No _____

2.9 Understand how a vowel sounds when it is followed by *l.*
Example: *ball, doll,* and *fall*

_____   _____

2.10 Understand the following rules:

a. When two vowels are together, the first is often long and the second is silent.
Example: *tail, fear,* and *goal*

_____   _____

b. A single vowel in a word or syllable is short.
Example: *ran, dot,* and *sun*

_____   _____

c. A single *e* at the end of a word is silent and makes the preceding vowel long.
Example: *rake, date,* and *tape*

_____   _____

3. Structural analysis:

The child is able to:

Yes   No

3.1 Recognize a base or root word.
Example: *walks, walked,* and *walking*

_____   _____

3.2 Understand the function of suffixes.
Example: *s, ed, ing, y, en,* and *es*
         ly, ful, les, ness, er, en

_____   _____

3.3 Understand the function of prefixes.
Example: *a, un, in,* and *be,*
         b, pro, and *re*

_____   _____

3.4 Recognize the number of syllables in words pronounced aloud

Two-syllable words

_____   _____

Three-syllable words

_____   _____

Four-syllable words

_____   _____

3.5 Apply these rules of syllabication:

a. A word usually contains as many vowels as there are syllables in the word.

_____   _____

(continued on next page)

Diagnostic Assessment of Braille Reading Skills *(Continued)*

	Yes	No
b. When two consonants come between vowels, one consonant goes with each vowel. Example: *let/ter*	_____	_____
c. When one consonant comes between two vowels, the first syllable usually ends with the vowel, and the second syllable begins with the second consonant. Example: *ta/ble*	_____	_____
d. When the first of two vowels separated by a single consonant has a short sound, the single intervening consonant ends the first syllable. Example: *cam/el*	_____	_____
e. Divide a compound word correctly. Example: *fire/men, play/ground*	_____	_____
f. Apply the principle of dropping the final *e* and adding *ing.* Example: *raking*	_____	_____
g. Apply the principle of doubling the final consonant before adding *ing.* Example: *running*	_____	_____
h. Apply the principle of changing *y* to *i* and adding *es.* Example: *babies*	_____	_____
i. Understand contractions. Example: *doesn't*	_____	_____

4. Context clue usage:

The child is able to:

	Yes	No
4.1 Decide the braille contractions with limited braille clues. Example: *Sally is coming to the car.*	_____	_____
4.2 Apply context-clue usage effectively in determining the meaning of an unknown word.	_____	_____
4.3 Complete a context-clue exercise. Example: Mary wants to go for a (*red, ride, rake*) on a train.	_____	_____

(continued on next page)

Diagnostic Assessment of Braille Reading Skills *(Continued)*

5. Dictionary usage:
The child is able to: *Yes*   *No*

    5.1 Use a braille dictionary to locate the meaning of unknown words.   _____   _____

    5.2 Use a simplified dictionary to locate the pronunciation and meaning of unknown words.   _____   _____

E. Comprehension skills:
The child is able to: *Yes*   *No*

1. Answer literal or factual questions that have been asked from stories read.   _____   _____

2. Answer interpretive questions that are based on stories read.   _____   _____

3. Answer questions that require critical or evaluative judgment.   _____   _____

4. Follow up the reading in a problem-solving situation, such as by creative writing, role-playing, or creative dramatics.   _____   _____

F. Silent reading:
The child is able to: *Yes*   *No*

1. Enjoy silent reading.   _____   _____

2. Maintain proper posture and book position.   _____   _____

3. Not move the lips or whisper.   _____   _____

4. Use proper hand movements while reading silently.   _____   _____

5. Read at a functional (reasonable) rate.   _____   _____

G. Oral reading:
The child is able to: *Yes*   *No*

1. Enjoy oral reading.

    1.1 With the teacher of students with visual impairments   _____   _____

    1.2 In the general education classroom   _____   _____

(continued on next page)

Diagnostic Assessment of Braille Reading Skills *(Continued)*

	Yes	No
2. Read with good oral expression.	_____	_____
3. Observe punctuation marks while reading orally.	_____	_____
4. Read in phrases or groups of words.	_____	_____
5. Read with few additions or omissions (reading-type errors).	_____	_____
6. Read without repeating words or phrases.	_____	_____

H. Reading rate is _____ wpm.

Reading comprehension is _____ grade level.

I. Justify reading series or method selected.

Check

_____ Sight   _____ Linguistic

_____ Phonics   _____ Multisensory

_____ Experiential

State the reasons for selection and relate them to the child's assessed skills.

State the reading objectives for _____ year in behavioral terms.

1.

2.

3.

4.

5.

Source: Adapted from R. M. Swallow, "Diagnostic Assessment of Braille Reading Skills," in M. R. Olson, *Guidelines and Games for Teaching Efficient Braille Reading.* (New York: American Foundation for the Blind, 1981), pp. 100–105.

Assessing Mastery of Braille Slate and Stylus Skills

Name _____   Date _____

Teacher _____   Age _____

Yes	No	The student will demonstrate the ability to:
+	−	1. Identify equipment
_____	_____	1.1 slate
_____	_____	1.2 stylus
_____	_____	1.3 slate paper
		2. Orally identify several uses of the slate
_____	_____	2.1 note taking
_____	_____	2.2 letter writing
_____	_____	2.3 labeling
_____	_____	2.4 making shopping lists
_____	_____	3. Correctly position paper in slate for writing
_____	_____	4. Properly grip stylus
_____	_____	5. Correctly write the letters and words (an entire line with no more than one mistake. Circle errors)

(1) a   (2) c   (3) k   (4) l   (5) all   (6) call   (7) little   (8) cad   (9) lack
(10) cab   (11) ball   (12) fall   (13) m   (14) p   (15) g   (16) h   (17) d
(18) e   (19) u   (20) x   (21) v   (22) s   (23) y   (24) z   (25) j   (26) i
(27) o   (28) q   (29) r   (30) t   (31) w

Yes	No	
		6. Correctly read a braille character and duplicate it on the slate
_____	_____	6.1 letters of the alphabet
_____	_____	6.2 braille contractions and signs
_____	_____	7. Correctly write his [her] name
_____	_____	8. Correctly write short sentences

(continued on next page)

Appendix B: Assessing Mastery of Braille Slate and Stylus Skills

Assessing Mastery of Braille Slate and Stylus Skills *(Continued)*

Yes   No

_____ _____   9. Correctly write short paragraphs from dictation

                  10. Compose mentally and write on the slate

_____ _____   10.1 sentences

_____ _____   10.2 paragraphs

_____ _____   10.3 short stories

_____ _____ 11. Take notes from recorded or braille text

_____ _____ 12. Take notes from lecture given in regular class

_____ _____ 13. Write at _____ braille characters per minute

Instructional Record

This student receives _____ minutes per week/month of slate and stylus instruction.

Date	Time (in minutes)	Objective	Evaluation

Source: Adapted from P. Mangold, "Assessment of Slate Skills," in R. M. Swallow, S. S. Mangold, & P. Mangold (Eds.), *Informal Assessment of Developmental Skills for Visually Handicapped Students.* (New York: American Foundation for the Blind, 1978), pp. 56–57.

Strategies for Teaching Literacy Skills to Students with Visual Impairments and Additional Disabilities

In the broadest sense, literacy is communication, especially when the concepts and issues are applied to students with visual impairments and additional disabilities. In this respect, then, literacy is the most basic foundation for all learning, for receiving and imparting information, and for initiating interactions with others. What is more important for students with visual impairments and additional disabilities is that literacy opens the doors to personal relationships, shared interests, leisure activities, learning strategies, partial to full independence at home and in the community, and vocational possibilities.

As with other students with visual impairments, the first steps to designing literacy programs and discovering methods for ensuring appropriate literacy opportunities for students with additional disabilities are a comprehensive assessment of the need for literacy media and a functional analysis of the student's response options and of opportunities for embedding literacy instruction and practice—whether reading, writing, or the use of other literacy tools—in all learning environments. These steps should lead to the functional and age-appropriate design, adaptation, and application of materials and strategies that will enable the student to engage in literacy activities along with his or her peers.

Regardless of age, all students should experience the shared closeness, rhythm, resonance, variety of expressions, and multiple sensory sensations derived from being read to. Opportunities for choice making, reciprocal communication, the development of vocabulary, and the enhancement of fine motor and tactile perception all can be embedded in even five minutes of reading together.

YOUNG STUDENTS

With a young student, several tactile books with sound, flaps, or textures to explore may be needed to maintain attention as the student learns that reading can be an enjoyable time with another person. The parents should be encouraged simply to let the child explore pages and to provide simple labels, phrases, or descriptions of the child's reactions, rather than feel pressured to "read" an entire story. An infant, toddler, or preschooler needs to be encouraged to scan each of two books tactilely or visually to indicate his or her choices. If the books are to be scanned tactilely, they should be opened to a favorite tactile symbol to increase recognition and recall and help the student to select one of them.

A student with limited motor control or one who may need to augment his or her voice can signal a favorite poem, song, or fingerplay during circle time by placing a distinguishable hand puppet, a small stuffed toy, or another small textually significant object on an augmentative device. When it is the student's turn to select, he or she does so by pulling off the puppet or object and offering it to the teacher or classmate who asked him or her to make a choice. The student may want to wear the hand puppet or hold whatever object was chosen as a further reinforcement of his or her selection.

OLDER STUDENTS

Reading to a student inherently implies to others that the student is competent. Skills acquired through practice, such as attending, turning pages, responding to statements or questions in some manner as one is read to are seen as "typical behaviors" of both infants and older children who are visually impaired. Even if a student does not necessarily process all the content, he or she enjoys the social and auditory pleasures of reading age-relevant material. Reading such material to older students while waiting at public places,

(continued on next page)

such as an airport, physician's office, or car service, impresses on unfamiliar others that the student is competent to understand what is being read. Giving the student every opportunity to "read" the same materials as more cognitively aware students enhances others' perceptions of his or her abilities.

- Ask for a brailled menu at a fast-food restaurant, encourage the student to "read" it, orally confirm what the student has read, and ask the student to indicate his or her choice.

- Comment on the braille on a bank's ATM and elevators and doors of public buildings and encourage the student to scan it. Practice in these different venues will encourage the student's familiarity with and independence in scanning.

SUGGESTED ACTIVITIES

- Encourage an elementary-age student to "read" books that have a button sound strip down their right-hand edges and pictures that correspond to the stories, by having the student press the appropriate button. The more a book is read, the more a student will recall the general approximation of the familiar buttons (top, middle, and bottom) with respect to the vertical strip. The pictures in one such book about Stevie Wonder are brailled. Other electronic books are interactive and require the student to locate specific items. The reinforcers for repairing or maintaining holes punched in paper or puffy glue or paint can be used to indicate the location of the sound cells on the pages, so the student can read and play with the books independently.

- Teach a student with limited hand control to participate in spelling activities by using devices with raised letters. On one such device, as a letter is pushed, the name of the letter is spoken.

- Show a student how to use an inexpensive speaking augmentative device, so he or she can remind a parent or peer of the items on a shopping list. Samples of appropriate items or parts of items and labels on items (such as a bottle cap, nonperishable food, or a scouring pad) may be Velcroed to the buttons to help a student who needs more support. Prior to shopping, the student should select the symbols of the items that are needed, adhere them to the buttons, and then practice identifying them. As each item is procured during shopping, the student should pull off the symbol, pair it with the object, and place both the symbol and the item in the shopping cart or basket. Other symbols may be kept in a hip pack until they are needed, and the used ones may be returned to the hip pack.

- To help a student refine tactile perception and ensure that his or her favorite CDs are in the proper place, teach the student to scan the outside of each box and the surface of each CD to check that they match or to scan two cases to locate the one that matches the CD.

- Help a student learn to prompt himself or herself about the steps in a task by "reading" the strips recorded on Language Master cards. Each step is recorded on a card, and the cards are placed sequentially upright in a letter

(continued on next page)

holder. The student takes the first card, runs it through the Language Master, follows the prompt, places the card in a "finished" box, and proceeds until he or she has completed all the steps and there are no more cards in the letter holder. large paper clips or clothespins may be attached to the cards to facilitate dexterity for a student who needs additional support.

◆ Encourage a student to share a book report with the class by having the student select (with a classmate's assistance, if necessary) favorite parts of the book and asking the classmate to record the selections on a word processor. The student with low vision may want to illustrate the report using a special input device for a graphics program on a computer. The student can share the book report by inserting the disk into a computer and activating the voice output.

◆ Encourage a student with a visual impairment and additional disabilities in a child development class at a high school to "read" a storybook to preschoolers with his or her augmentative system. The student can be assisted in this activity by having a classmate or a preschooler hold the book and turn the pages when the student activates the augmentative system to signal that it is time to do so.

◆ Teach a preschooler or older student with low vision who can hold a crayon in his or her hand to use Magna Doodle to practice writing his or her name. The student rubs a crayon over a sheet of paper that is placed on top of a small card on which the cut-out letters of the name were glued. As the child rubs the crayon over the paper, the letters appear.

◆ Make a stencil of the student's name by cutting letters from oak tag or cardboard and clamping or taping the letters on paper. Encourage the student to move a marker, crayon, or paintbrush back and forth across the stencil until the letters are filled in. Consult with an occupational therapist to determine if wrist weights will give a student with low postural tone better proprioceptive feedback to direct hand movement.

◆ Teach an older student for whom coloring may not be age relevant, to "scribble" with a brailler as his or her classmates engage in writing or drawing assignments associated with a story that was read during library time. A classmate or paraeducator can help the student to load the paper and braille his or her name.

◆ A student may learn to write his or her name on credit card receipts, assignments, gym clothes, and so forth using a name stamp. A strip of Wikki Stix may be placed on the paper or object to help the student align the name stamp.

◆ Elevate the surface on which a student with limited postural control is writing to afford postural alignment, decrease the distance the student must reach, and avoid the need constantly to readjust the focal length or head control. Lying prone over a wedge often facilitates better hand and arm control and eye–hand coordination and limits distractions.

M. BETH LANGLEY
Pinellas County Schools
St. Petersburg, FL

RESOURCES

Suggested Resources for Teaching Literacy Skills

Resource	Type	Source	Description
Beginning with Braille: Firsthand Experiences with a Balanced Approach to Literacy (Swenson, 1999)	Book	AFB Press	Presents creative and practical strategies for designing and delivering quality braille instruction and teacher-friendly suggestions for such areas as reading aloud to young children, selecting and making early tactile books, teaching tactile and hand-movement skills, teaching braille-writing skills, and more.
Blind Children Learn to Read (Lowenfeld, Abel, & Hatlen, 1969)	Book	Charles C Thomas	Explores the status of braille reading in local classes and residential schools for blind children. Discusses the character-istics of efficient braille readers and the methods of instruction that are likely to produce them.
Books in braille, large print, and recorded formats	Books	American Action Fund for Blind Children and Adults	American Action Fund offers print-braille (Twin-Vision) books to children from pre-K through high school. Also provides free braille calendars.
		National Braille Press	National Braille Press offers a "book of the month club" for young braille readers; also offers braille calendars, *Just Enough to Know Better,* and other braille books.
		National Library Service (NLS) for the Blind and Physically Handicapped	NLS provides large-print, braille, and recorded magazines, novels, and other general reading *(continued on next page)*

Resource	Type	Source	Description
			materials at no cost. Works in cooperation with state and regional libraries for the blind.
		Recording for the Blind and Dyslexic	Recording for the Blind and Dyslexic provides textbooks on cassette tape and in electronic format for persons who cannot read standard print because of visual, physical, and perceptual disability. Maintains a lending library of recorded books.
		Seedlings	Seedlings has a growing catalog of braille books for children, including a number of classics and popular series.
Braille Assessment Inventory (Sharpe, McNear, & McGraw, 1996)	Assessment instrument	Hawthorne Educational Services	This instrument is helpful both in selecting appropriate literacy media and in monitoring students' progress in braille. Helpful in planning instructional interventions.
Braille Too: An Instructional Braille Reading and Writing Program for Secondary Students (Hepker & Cross-Coquillette, 1995)	Instructional materials	Grant Wood Area Education Agency	A comprehensive program for teaching braille reading and writing to adolescents who have been print readers. It is assumed that students have at least minimum competence in reading and writing skills.
Foundations of Braille Literacy (Rex, Koenig, Wormsley, & Baker, 1994)	Book	AFB Press	Addresses teaching braille reading and writing in the context of literacy in general and the whole-language approach. Provides both a theoretical framework and practical applications for instruction in braille literacy. Companion videotape: *Understanding Braille Literacy.*
Guidelines and Games for Teaching Efficient Braille Reading (Olson, 1981)	Book	American Foundation for the Blind	Presents effective games and guidelines for designing and delivering a reading program to the needs of braille readers. Based on research in the areas of reading and precision teaching.
Instructional Strategies for Braille Literacy (Wormsley & D'Andrea, 1997)	Book	AFB Press	A user-friendly, comprehensive handbook on teaching braille literacy skills provides instructors with specific creative strategies and methods for teaching braille. Includes information on working *(continued on next page)*

Suggested Resources *(Continued)*

Resource	Type	Source	Description
			with students with additional disabilities and students who are speakers of English as a second language.
Longhand Writing for the Blind (Freund, 1970)	Teaching materials	American Printing House for the Blind	An embossed workbook for practicing the cursive alphabet, a Tactile Marking Mat, a pad of paper with embossed lines, and a detailed teaching manual in both regular type and braille. Helps students learn traditional cursive writing.
Mangold Developmental Program of Tactile Perception and Braille Letter Recognition (Mangold, 1994a)	Instructional materials	Exceptional Teaching Aids	A program designed to promote good two-handed braille reading and decrease scrubbing and back-tracking, as well as errors in braille character recognition. Teaches letters of the alphabet.
On the Way to Literacy: Early Experiences for Visually Impaired Children (Stratton & Wright, 1991)	Books	American Printing House for the Blind	A print handbook for parents and teachers, accompanied by a separate series of tactile/visual storybooks to be read to young children.
Patterns Prebraille Program (Caton, Pester, & Bradley, 1987)	Instructional materials	American Printing House for the Blind	Designed to help children before they begin a basic braille reading program; helps build a child's auditory, tactile, conceptual, and language abilities.
Patterns: The Primary Braille Reading Program (Caton, Pester, & Bradley, 1980)	Basal reading series	American Printing House for the Blind	A complete basal reading series for preschool and early elementary students who are learning to read braille; includes student books, worksheets, competency tests, and instructor's manual.
Patterns: The Primary Braille Spelling and English Program (Caton et al., 1993)	Instructional materials	American Printing House for the Blind	A program to teach complete spelling and language skills to primary-grade students who use braille as their primary literacy medium. Includes textbooks, worksheets, posttests, and teacher's editions.
Read Again: A Braille Program for Adventitiously Blinded Print Readers (Caton, Pester, & Bradley, 1990)	Instructional materials	American Printing House for the Blind	Program to present the braille code to teens who were print readers and now need to use braille as their reading medium. Worksheets, reading selections and activities, tests, review materials, *(continued on next page)*

(continued on next page)

Suggested Resources *(Continued)*

Resource	Type	Source	Description
			cassette tape instruction for student use, and teacher's editions.
State Libraries for the Blind and Physically Handicapped	Books	Library of Congress	A federally funded source of reading material in braille and recorded media for children and adults. Contact LOC for information on locating your State Library for the Blind and Physically Handicapped.
Tactile Graphics (Edman, 1992)	Book	American Foundation for the Blind	An encyclopedic handbook on translating visual information into a three-dimensional form that students who are blind can understand. Essential for teachers who produce their own materials.
Teaching Signature Writing to Those Who are Visually Impaired (Mangold & Pesavento, 1994)	Videotape	Exceptional Teaching Aids	A 35-minute video and supplementary booklet available in print, large print, or braille. Offers a creative teaching method that will help students to make an acceptable legal signature.
Teaching the Braille Slate and Stylus: A Manual for Mastery (P. N. Mangold, 1993) and *Teaching the Braille Slate and Stylus* (S. Mangold, 1994c)	Book and videotape	Exceptional Teaching Aids	A print manual and a 25-minute video presenting specific techniques for teaching writing with the braille slate.
Teaching tools for braille instruction: braillewriters, slates, braille paper, Swing Cell, Peg Slate, Tactual Discrimination Worksheets	Equipment	American Printing House for the Blind	The American Printing House for the Blind offers equipment and materials for instruction in braille lliteracy. Provides materials to school systems based on "quota funds."
		Howe Press of Perkins School for the Blind	Howe Press offers the Perkins braillewriter and an assortment of related tools, including slates and styli.
The Bridge to Braille: Reading and School Success for the Young Blind Child (Castellano & Kosman, 1997)	Book	National Organization of Parents of Blind Children	An easy-to-read, practical book of strategies for parents and teachers who are working with young children who are blind. Includes an extensive list of resources.
Understanding Braille Literacy (1993)	Videotape	AFB Press	A motivational and instructional video that covers all aspects of a successful braille education program.

Contact information for each of the resources listed will be found in the Sources of Products, Materials, Equipment, and Services section at the back of this book.

CHAPTER 9

Social Studies and Science

David B. Ross and Margaret C. Robinson

KEY POINTS

◆ Students with visual impairments, like all students, need access to science and social studies instruction and activities.

◆ Science and social studies instruction and activities often rely on information presented visually. Therefore, academic compensatory skills and modifications are needed to allow students with visual impairments to gain full access to them.

◆ The teacher of students with visual impairments plays a key role in providing adapted materials and teaching the compensatory academic skills, such as how to read tactile maps and employ adapted measuring devices, that facilitate the use of the materials.

◆ The teacher of students with visual impairments collaborates with general education teachers regarding methods of instruction and the need for adapted materials and instruction in compensatory skills.

VIGNETTE

Ming, a kindergartner, put the huge fireman's hat on her head. It was so big it covered most of her face. "Look at me!" she called. "I'm a fireman!

Rrrrrrrrrrrr! I'm putting out the fire!" Giggling, she put the heavy red hat back in the Community Helpers Box and pulled out another. "What's this?" she asked her neighbor. Holding it close, she saw that it was blue and had a silver shield on the front. Quickly she put the cap on her head. "I'm a policeman! I'll help you across the street!" she exclaimed.

LeVon, a second grader, carefully removed a bean seed from the sprouter and replaced the lid. Carrying it to his desk, he set it on a square of black construction paper and slid it under his stand magnifier. He leaned down for a good look and then reached over and touched his neighbor's arm. "Look, Terry—it's got hairs!"

Penny, a ninth grader, slid the map under the closed-circuit television (CCTV) camera and carefully focused the lens. *List the countries that border France.* "There can't be that many," she thought. "France isn't all that big." Locating the Atlantic coastline of Europe, she began to search northward for France.

Carter, an 11th-grade braille student, examined the complex shape of the DNA model again. Mr. Fields, his teacher of students with visual impairments, had explored the model with him earlier and helped him identify each of the four tactilely different molecules: *adenine, cytosine, guanine,* and *thymine.* At the top of the model, the two strands of molecules were repeatedly linked across the middle and twisted into a shape Mr. Fields called a double helix. Beginning halfway down, the strands separated, "just like a zipper," Carter thought. The complexity of the model was challenging, but it was certainly easier to understand than the description in his textbook.

INTRODUCTION

Students who are blind or visually impaired with no additional disabilities are expected to master the same academic subject matter as are students without visual impairments. Science and social studies classes are challenging for students with visual impairments, since instruction in these subjects often involves the use of illustrations, maps, and diagrams, and the students often need to use adapted and modified instructional tools to understand the concepts that are involved.

Social studies is the "integrated study of the social sciences and humanities to promote civic competence. . . . The primary purpose of social studies is to help young people develop the ability to make informed and reasoned decisions for the public good as citizens of a culturally diverse, democratic society in an interdependent world" (National Council for the Social Studies, 1993, p. 3). Students with visual impairments need to work toward this goal, as do students who are sighted.

Social studies content is taught in the study of self, home, family, neighborhoods, community, U.S. history, world history, geography, and world cultures. In the elementary grades, these content areas are generally taught as interdisciplinary social studies, organized by topic, rather than as separate courses. Secondary social studies (grades 7–12) are typically taught in specialized classes in history, economics, and American government, as well as more contemporary courses like global education, environment studies, and conflict resolution (Brophy & Alleman, 1996).

Science education is meant to help students understand the natural world in which they live and to understand and recognize the importance of scientific developments in the world today and in the future. Science is often taught through a hands-on approach involving laboratory investigation, problem solving in the various scientific areas, and critical and creative thinking. With the use of hands-on instruction, students are expected to learn critical thinking skills and processes, such as observing, classifying, identifying, measuring, inferring, and predicting. According to Gega (1994, p. 19), "Good science teaching develops in children the kinds of attitudes, ways of thinking, and a solid knowledge base that promote success in the real world." The expectations for a student with visual impairment should be no less.

In books such as this one, mention is frequently made of the opportunities for incidental learning available to sighted children. Nowhere are these opportunities more evident than in science and social studies. Depending on where they live and what they have seen on television, sighted children may have observed "community helpers" at work, the space shuttle, bees visiting flowers, birds building nests, killer whales, kangaroos, an automobile factory, a Scottish kilt, a desert oasis, a river in flood, a volcano erupting, the slow movement of arctic glaciers, and the Earth from space. Even cartoons and comic books play a role in this incidental learning, in that they depict clothing styles and traditional architecture from around the world to indicate the locations of episodes. Even without the intervention of adults, sighted children have many opportunities to learn a great deal about the world around them.

Students with visual impairments are unable to take full advantage of such unplanned learning. However, this observation merely underscores the importance of ensuring that they receive the most effective social studies and science education possible because these subjects can help them compensate for the absence of incidental learning. After all, each item listed in the previous paragraph as being available to sighted children through incidental learning is addressed at one point or another in science or social studies curricula. By making this planned education accessible to students with visual impairments, teachers of students with visual impairments can help their students achieve a greater understanding of the world in which they live.

ROLE OF THE TEACHER OF STUDENTS WITH VISUAL IMPAIRMENTS

Much of the role of the teacher of students with visual impairments involves collaborating with and providing resources to general education teachers who have the primary responsibility for teaching the content of science and social studies courses. The role of the specialist is to do the following:

- Collaborate with general education teachers and content-area teachers in science and social studies to provide guidance on including students with visual impairments in their classes;

- Provide adapted materials, models, and equipment for the students to use;

- Prepare tactile maps, charts, and diagrams when these materials are unavailable from other sources; and

- Teach the prerequisite skills and compensatory academic skills needed in science and social studies (such as reading a tactile map or using adapted measuring devices) before lessons are taught in the content-area classroom.

The teacher also plays an essential role in working with students with additional disabilities; strategies focusing on students with visual impairments and additional disabilities and resources for teachers appear later in this chapter.

ASSESSMENT

It is the responsibility of the content-area teachers to assess the student's achievement of objectives in science and social studies. The role of the teacher of students with visual impairments is to measure the student's mastery of compensatory skills. Compensatory education refers to the knowledge and skills that make it possible for a student with a visual impairment to achieve educational objectives at a rate and level that are commensurate with his or her sighted classmates. The goal of assessment is to determine which compensatory skills must be taught for the student to succeed in classroom activities and his or her progress in developing these skills. Informal assessment instruments, such as teacher-made checklists of skills, are often the most appropriate for this purpose.

In both science and social studies, students are frequently expected to use reference sources. A glossary, dictionary, and encyclopedia should not be vast mysteries to students with visual impairments. Appendix A at the end of this chapter is a simple checklist for assessing a student's skill in using these references. When using this assessment, Use of Reference Sources, the teacher may assign the student to research words and topics of real interest to the student, to increase the intrinsic motivation for this task.

The *Assessment Kit: Kit of Informal Tools for Academic Students with Visual Impairments* (Sewell, 1997) is a useful resource. Two assessment checklists from the *Assessment Kit* are presented in the appendixes to this chapter. The first, Science and Social Studies Survival Skills (see Appendix B), found in the Science and Social Studies Category, is a checklist that assesses a student's use of spatial information, models, and tactile graphics.

The second checklist, the Measurement Assessment (see Appendix C), found in the Math Category, addresses a student's knowledge of measurement terms, including linear dimensions, volume, and weight. It assesses how well a student understands the practical applications of these terms by asking questions such as: "Which unit of measurement would you use to measure the distance to another city?" In addition to using this Measurement Assessment, it would be helpful to evaluate a student's ability to perform actual measurements using the tools he or she will be expected to use in the next school year. In elementary school, this latter assessment could include asking a student to use a braille or large-print ruler or yardstick to measure the width of his or her textbook or the height of a set of shelves or to use a balance and a set of gram weights to determine the weight of a marker. The teacher of students with visual impairments may want to assess the ability of an older student to use adapted measurement tools to time an interval of 30 seconds, to determine the temperature of a beaker of water, or to measure 50 milliliters of water.

Another type of assessment is conducted throughout the year as the teacher of students with visual impairments observes the student work in the classroom. Although not unique to the science and social studies curricula, student behaviors are directly related to success in academic settings. The *Assessment Kit* includes several checklists that are applicable to this area, such as the Observation Guidelines (created by C. M. Cowan) found in the Classroom Category. This checklist asks a number of pertinent questions such as "Does the student get up to get his own materials?" "Does the student raise a hand to participate and ask questions?" and "Can the student fully operate any equipment given to him?" Because many lab activities are performed in small groups, you might wish to ask other questions such as, "Does the student participate actively in lab sessions, rather than consistently recording results reported by other students who complete all active tasks?" and "What tasks, if any, does the student appear to consistently avoid?"

Assessments continue as the teacher of students with visual impairments works with the student. For example, after the student is taught to use tactile graphics, the specialist observes areas of improved skill as well as areas of continuing need. These observations guide the specialist's subsequent instruction of the student. The specialist may observe that a fourth-grade student has learned to distinguish most of the tactile symbols available in the graphics kit but frequently does not distinguish between the raised *X* and a hollow star. He or she responds to this observation by creating an activity for the next tactile graphic session that offers many opportunities to distinguish between these symbols and rewards the student for successes.

INSTRUCTIONAL CONSIDERATIONS

Much of the teaching that takes place in science and social studies classes is done through the presentation of visual materials—photographs, diagrams, graphs, and maps. Therefore, the teacher of students with visual impairments needs to enable the student to have full access to the content of the science and social studies curricula. To accomplish this the teacher should:

♦ Establish and maintain close cooperation and communication with the content-area teacher.

♦ Help the student acquire a full array of basic concepts.

♦ Consider the need to make accommodations for various teaching methods, remembering that instruction should be based on real experiences when it is practical and safe to do so.

♦ Provide adaptations of visual displays that are used as teaching aids in content-area classrooms in an accessible medium.

♦ Obtain or create adapted equipment to help the student complete class activities and form accurate concepts.

Each element is addressed in this chapter. Suggestions are offered for communicating with content-area teachers, maximizing the student's acquisition of basic concepts, making accommodations for various teaching methods, providing adaptations of visual displays, and adapting laboratory activities. These guidelines can serve as a beginning point for teachers of students with visual impairments. References are suggested to enable the reader to explore various topics further (see the References and Resources sections).

Communicating with Content-Area Teachers

The teacher of students with visual impairments needs to establish and maintain frequent contact with the social studies and science teachers. Collaboration should involve all personnel who work with the student. (See Chapter 5 for suggestions on working with general education teachers.) General education teachers are key to helping students feel at home in the classroom and to facilitating their inclusion. There are as many different ways to facilitate inclusion as there are classrooms and teachers, but the teacher of students with visual impairments will be able to make important suggestions in this regard. (See Chapter 5 for specific tips on facilitating inclusion.)

The teacher of students with visual impairments often has valuable information to share with the teacher, and perhaps students, in an inclusive classroom. For example, a class that is studying Spain may find it interesting to learn about the Organización Nacional de Ciegnos Españoles, Spain's economic organization for people who are blind (see Vaughan, 1998, pp. 167–189). A civics course could include information about White Cane Day, held every October. A lesson on the importance of the Americans with Disabilities Act might be supplemented with guest speakers on disabilities. A course on environmental studies could adapt an outdoor lesson on the exploration of the environment by having the class discuss observations made while they were wearing blindfolds. Steps such as the ones suggested in this chapter help to create a climate of belonging for the student with a visual impairment.

Maximizing the Acquisition of Basic Concepts

Certain basic concepts and abilities are necessary for a student to benefit fully from instruction in science and social studies. Teachers of students with visual impairments expect to work with young children on basic concepts, such as *big* and *little*, but they sometimes forget that older students may need to learn basic concepts at a more mature level. Teachers must remain aware of the concepts and vocabulary that are important for various grade levels and subject areas and monitor their students' progress and needs in this area.

As discussed in Chapter 7, children with visual impairments may not develop basic concepts at the same rate as sighted children because their visual impairments may hamper incidental learning. Children with poorly developed basic concepts cannot take full advantage of instruction in science and social studies. Even in the lower elementary grades, it is usually assumed that students understand such terms as *empty* and *full, few* and *many, half* and *whole* and the nature of comparisons like *cold, colder,* and *coldest.* Young children with visual impairments may not have formed clear concepts of these terms. They may also be confused by such terms as *firehouse* and *city hall* if they have not visited these places.

The need to understand essential vocabulary affects older students, too. A middle school student who has had no experience with a balance scale may not understand such terms as *equal, in balance,* and *unbalanced* in reference to this device; thus, the student may not fully comprehend a description of a class demonstration involving the use of a balance. Some students with visual impairments have only vague concepts of terms like *river* or *border,* although they may use the words appropriately in some situations. The word *border,* when used in terms of states and nations, is an abstract term; a state border is not a concrete object and is difficult to "experience directly." Although *river* refers to a concrete object, even the experience of wading in a river may not be enough to help a student understand the differences between a river and a lake.

Concepts related to orientation in one's own environment are also important. Chapter 15 discusses concepts of orientation in some detail. For a student to profit from a study of geography, he or she must first have firm concepts of directionality in his or her own environment. The student who does not know whether Susan sits on his left or his right or who cannot "keep walking south down this hallway and turn east at the first intersection" is not likely to gain much real understanding from statements such as, "Texas lies west of Louisiana."

Teachers of students with visual impairments need to watch for such gaps in basic concepts and vocabulary, to test for them before a unit of study begins, and to help remediate any deficits that are found. They can monitor their students' understanding of appropriate terms by asking probing questions: "What does your teacher mean when she says 'the scale is in balance'?" "Can you describe a state border?" and "Can you stand so that I am on your left?" In most cases, direct, hands-on experience with real objects is the most reliable way to build understanding. It is not difficult to provide a student with experience in using a balance scale, but direct experience with a *river* or a *border* can be difficult or impossible to provide. In such cases, models, such as topography maps that can be "flooded" with water, and tactile graphics are useful. (More information about models and tactile graphics is presented later in this chapter.) Concepts of directionality are best learned through movement and are often addressed by orientation and mobility (O&M) instructors.

An important "basic concept" that teachers of students with visual impairments must teach their students who read braille is the Nemeth Code for math and science. This code is not only essential for competence in math, it is equally essential in science. For students to be successful in using braille textbooks in any area of science, they must be able to identify the specific symbols used in the Nemeth Code. Some examples are shown in Sidebar 9.1. The teacher of students with visual impairments teaches new Nemeth Code symbols to students as part of compensatory skills instruction before these symbols are introduced or used in the general education classroom.

Making Accommodations for Teaching Methods

General education teachers may use a variety of methods for teaching the content of a social studies or science lesson. They are not limited to the traditional approaches of lecture, reading mate-

---

Examples of the Nemeth Code for Science

SIDEBAR 9.1

The Nemeth Code is commonly thought of as a "math" code. However, it is also the code used in science. The following are some of the symbols that students with visual impairments may encounter:

212° C

lat. 30° 20' N

1000 g = 1 kg

1l = 1,000ml

1 light-yr.

6 ft.-lbs.

I/O (Input/Output)

Hydrogen-3

heat
$\longrightarrow$

ergs/cm³

---

rial, worksheets, and class discussion. Common alternatives include the presentation of videotapes, role-playing, guest speakers, field trips, and research by students. Science classes usually include demonstrations or laboratory experiences. Thus, the needs of the student with a visual impairment must be considered in light of the instructional approach chosen by a particular content-area teacher. Some adaptations are presented here; others are discussed in Chapter 5.

Lecture

Science and social studies are usually the first subjects in which students encounter the lecture format. When the lecture format is used, a student with a visual impairment must be prepared to take notes as his or her sighted classmates do. The teacher of students with visual impairments must determine from the science and social studies teachers when they expect students to begin taking notes, so he or she can teach this important skill to the student with a visual impairment before it is needed. Some points about taking notes include these:

- Students take notes to facilitate later study of the material presented. Notes should be brief and should highlight main ideas. Instruct the student to listen for the main ideas and to record key words, rather than attempt to write complete sentences. Noting sequence clues, such as first, second, and third, often helps identify the main ideas, as does noting concepts that the lecturer finds important enough to repeat.

- Appropriate means of taking notes may be to use a felt-tip pen, a slate and stylus, or an electronic note-taking device. If a slate and stylus or an electronic note-taking device is used, the teacher of students with visual impairments needs to provide compensatory education in using it.

- Taking notes with a braillewriter is an option, but should not be the only means of taking notes that a student learns. Note-taking skills should be transferable to college classes and various other sites where a braillewriter cannot be provided for the student's convenience. Carrying a braillewriter to college classes and other locations where notes may need to be taken would be inconvenient; a more portable device, such as a slate and stylus, is necessary.

- The use of a tape recorder to record the entire lesson is rarely appropriate because it will still take an hour to review an hour-long lecture and a recording gives no indication of the main ideas. Thus, the benefits of taking notes—brevity of review and recall of the main ideas—are lost.

Textbooks

The first "real test" of a student's reading skill is in the content areas of science and social studies. For a student to understand the material in a science or social studies textbook, his or her reading skills must be on or near grade level. Furthermore, science textbooks, in particular, often include a great deal of unfamiliar terminology, which increases the challenge of reading comprehension. Therefore, teachers of students with visual impairments need to provide textbooks in a timely manner in an accessible medium, and be sure that their students are able to use the textbooks' glossaries efficiently.

Large-print textbooks include illustrations, maps, charts, and diagrams. However, because of copier technology, these items may appear as incomprehensible shapes of various tones of gray. Braille textbooks frequently omit these items completely. Thus, the teacher of students with visual impairments needs to augment these textbooks with appropriate adaptations, either material obtained from various suppliers (for example, a braille atlas from the American Printing House for the Blind [APH]) or items the teacher has made to meet a specific need. The methods for making these adapted materials are described later in this chapter.

Some students with visual impairments whose reading skills are below grade level (perhaps because they have recognized reading difficulties or have recently lost their vision and are undergoing a change in literacy medium) are unable to use a science or social studies textbook independently. Teachers of students with visual impairments not only help these students develop appropriate reading skills, but enable the students to achieve the objectives of the science or social studies curriculum. They may provide support to the students by previewing vocabulary and conceptual knowledge, prereading a chapter and examining essential visual or tactile diagrams, providing textbooks on audiotape, or helping the students make arrangements to use live readers. (See Chapters 5 and 8 for more information on using recorded textbooks and live readers.)

Worksheets

Worksheets are as valuable for a student with a visual impairment as they are for a sighted student. Copies of worksheets must be provided to the student with a visual impairment in an accessible media. Science and social studies worksheets often require that a student have access to and skill in using various reference materials, including a glossary, encyclopedia, globe, map, or other tactile graphic, to complete an activity. The teacher of students with visual impairments provides the necessary adaptive aids and the compensatory education that will allow the student to use them.

For the most part, worksheets should be provided to the student in an accessible medium so that he or she can work independently. However, if the sighted students in the class are to complete worksheets in cooperative learning groups, the student with a visual impairment must be able to function as a capable member of such a group. It is not acceptable for the student always to be the group recorder; he or she should also be able to retrieve information from various sources as the other participants do. The student may also have to learn to take turns in conversation or to have the assertiveness to volunteer in a group. Thus, the teacher of students with visual impairments may need to work with the student on appropriate social skills as well as academic ones.

Demonstrations

The classroom demonstration has long been a part of general education practice and is an effective method in the instruction of students. It is particularly common in science classes, as when teachers model the techniques that students are to use in lab activities or provide dramatic demonstrations of the combination of hydrogen and oxygen. Since students with visual impairments may not be able to see demonstrations from their place in the classroom or lab, some modifications may be necessary, such as these:

- ◆ A lab station near the demonstration.

- ◆ A clear verbal explanation, either by a lab partner or the demonstrator.

- ◆ A written description prior to the demonstration.

- ◆ Exploration of a three-dimensional model, tactile graphic, or enlarged diagram with the student before the demonstration.

- ◆ Demonstration of the equipment to be used or complete demonstration of the experiment prior to the class during a study period or another appropriate time.

Videotapes

Videotapes provide vivid images of places and events that most students will never experience in person. However, a student with a visual impairment may not be able to see these images clearly, if at all. Therefore, the teacher of students with visual impairments should ask the general education teacher to view videotapes before he or she presents them in class to note whether the narration on the videotape provides an adequate explanation for the student with a visual impairment. If the narration is not adequate, the student will need the assistance of a narrator (the teacher or an eloquent classmate) who will quietly provide a concise description of the essential visual elements of the videotape. After the videotape is shown, the class discussion should include descriptions of key visual images.

Guest Speakers

Guest speakers are frequently invited to address students in science and social studies classes. For example, an employee of a local zoo may present unusual animals, such as a hedgehog or a boa constrictor; a civic leader may talk about city government; or a member of a particular cultural group may show special clothing, photographs, and artifacts from his or her country of origin. The general education teacher should determine in advance whether a guest speaker will use visual displays in the presentation. If visual displays are to be used, the teacher of students with visual impairments may need to provide adaptations, such as enlargements and braille handouts. Also, if appropriate for the subject of the speaker's presentation, the general education teacher may suggest that the speaker bring tangible objects that can be safely touched and explored, rather than use only visual presentations.

Role-playing

Role-playing is an effective method of teaching social studies. Young students often role-play adults in their own culture and community, such as a fireman, police officer, teacher, physician, construction worker, and librarian. Students who are studying another culture may role-play by dressing in the traditional clothing of that culture, when available; listening to music and learning a traditional dance, such as the hula during a study of Polynesian countries; or preparing and eating traditional foods in the classroom while role-playing people from that culture. A student with a visual impairment will notice differences in music and the taste of foods, but may need physical assistance to learn a dance or to help prepare a meal.

Field Trips

In science and social studies classrooms, students often leave the classroom to study phenomena in various environments in the community. Much of the study is based on visual observation. Students with low vision may use optical devices to enhance their ability to observe directly, and those who are blind may work with a partner who can describe the objects or events that the students cannot see or explore tactually.

Field trips offer excellent learning opportunities in science and social studies, but require careful planning, as the description of the highly effective field trip to a fine arts museum in Chapter 11 demonstrates. Because of such planning, the museum was able to arrange for a sufficient number of docents to be present to meet the group's needs. Furthermore, personnel at the museum were familiar with the needs of visitors with visual impairments. If other locations, such as a

farm or factory, do not provide such well-trained docents, the teacher of students with visual impairments can help make the trip more meaningful by sharing certain tips with the host or hostess, such as these:

- Wait until all the students are in place before beginning to speak.
- Use specific terms. "The bottle capper is on your right, about six feet away," is much more helpful than "That's a bottle capper over there."
- Allow as much hands-on examination of items as possible. At a farm or zoo, there are many animals that students can safely touch.
- When items being pointed out are too far away, too fragile, too dangerous, or otherwise inaccessible to touch, give the clearest verbal description possible. Allow time for questions to clarify uncertainties.
- Items that a host may consider ordinary may be exotic to a student with a visual impairment. For example, on a farm, students with visual impairments might benefit from having an explanation paired with hands-on experience with common tools, such as a shovel, hoe, pitchfork, and rake.

Singleton (1972, p. 34) recommended verbally orienting students with visual impairments to the place they will be visiting before a trip. Describe the building or environment and the experiences the students are likely to have. Such an orientation helps the students construct an image of the whole from discrete parts, which sighted students do with vision.

Research

Students at various levels of schooling often do some type of research in science and social studies classes by searching a library—or the Internet—for information on a given topic. A student with a visual impairment must not be "excused" from this important activity. To assist the student in performing such research, the teacher of students with visual impairments needs to do the following:

- Familiarize the student with the library's resources. Even a braille reader who lacks direct access to certain resources needs to be familiar with their presence and typical contents. Introduce the student to encyclopedias, an almanac, an atlas, the card or computer catalog, and the wealth of books on innumerable topics. Read illustrative contents to the student, such as an article on a given subject from both *World Book* and *Britannica,* to allow the student to compare the readability levels and extent of coverage of the topic of the two encyclopedias.

- Teach the student how to ask for help from a sighted assistant in the library. The student who can say, "I need an encyclopedia article on George Washington Carver. I'd prefer one from *World Book,* and can I make a copy of it, please?" will be more successful than one who can only say, "I'm supposed to do research on George Washington Carver."

- Teach the student to use the resources of the state library for the blind. With a toll-free phone call, the student can arrange home delivery of several resources, including books in braille and on audiocassette.

- Help the student use the *Rose Project,* managed by Seedlings Braille Books, which provides encyclopedia articles in braille for students' projects and reports (see the Resources for this chapter).

- Keep technological skills up to date, and stay informed about the development of new technology for individuals with visual impairments. The teacher of students with visual impairments needs to be able to help a student develop technological skills, including the ability to gain access to information on the Internet.

Providing Adaptations of Visual Displays

Science and social studies instruction frequently involves the use of illustrations, diagrams, maps, time lines, and other visual displays of information. When such displays are large enough, are uncluttered, and show good contrast, they may be used by some students with low vision without adaptation. However, students with more severe visual impairments often need a form of modification to understand the concepts that are presented.

Some adaptations, such as an enlarged copy of a diagram of the human circulatory system, may be simple to produce. Others, like a tactile map of Africa showing important geographic features, national borders, and major cities, may be more complex. To use such adapted displays effectively, a student may need instruction in compensatory skills. Whatever the modification or adaptation provided, it is essential that the teacher of students with visual impairments, who has training in special adaptations and teaching methods, remain closely involved to ensure that appropriate learning occurs once an adaptation or modification has been made.

Before the teacher of students with visual impairments decides which materials need to be modified and which modifications are necessary, he or she should review the student's educational folder to determine, from the results of eye examinations, functional vision assessments, and learning media assessments, the student's use of visual and tactile methods for gaining information. These reports may also contain information on the preferred print size and recommended or prescribed optical devices.

Describing Visual Displays

Although much of this chapter addresses methods for creating modifications of visual displays, it should first be said that it is not necessary to modify *every* visual display presented in a classroom. As was noted earlier, both science and social studies textbooks are full of pictures, graphs, maps, and diagrams that may appear as mottled areas of shades of gray in a large-print textbook, while braille textbooks often replace these items with such statements as, "Picture—Ask your teacher." Even if a teacher had time to make an adaptation for each visual display, few students would have the time to explore them all.

One appropriate solution is to describe the visual displays to the student orally. Singleton (1972, pp. 21–22) pointed out that *all* students benefit from hearing thoughtful descriptions and offered guidelines to help teachers describe pictures effectively. Because science and social studies teachers usually describe pictures, the teacher of students with visual impairments may wish to share these guidelines with them:

◆ Think about the purpose of describing the picture. Identify the most important people and objects first, in relation to their action or state and the immediate environment. Say, for example, "A mother and father and two children are standing beside a picnic table in a park, looking very unhappy." Do not clutter the initial description by describing the table, the barbecue grill, the trees and birds, and the parking lot in the background.

◆ Next, relate other objects and people who are pictured to the key people and objects. Include details that clarify what is happening in the picture and give additional related information, as in the following example: "Empty marshmallow bags and hot dog wrappers, soft drink cans, and wadded-up napkins are scattered all around the table. The table has spilled ketchup on it."

◆ In describing the picture, use terms for things that the students have personally experienced or manipulated. Simply naming an unfamiliar object will not convey much meaning.

◆ Describe what the picture shows—not what you assume or conclude about it. It is important to allow students with visual impairments to have the opportunity to complete the same cognitive processes that sighted students do. In the example of the picnic, for instance, one would not explain that previous picnickers were poor citizens who left a mess. It is better to allow the students to draw their own conclusions.

◆ Describe pictures matter-of-factly, addressing the entire class rather than just the student with a visual impairment. A good oral description will help all students.

Enlarging Materials

Materials may be enlarged in several ways. The simplest way is for the student with low vision to move closer to the work. Materials may also be enlarged on a copier or by having the student use an optical device such as a telescope, magnifier, or closed-circuit television (CCTV) (see Chapter 13). Students who are familiar with several methods of enlargement and are able to choose among them for various tasks will be more independent and successful in the classroom and the lab.

Moving closer to a classroom demonstration may provide effective enlargement for some students with low vision. In activities that require students to manipulate objects, the student with low vision can simply hold the objects closer or move closer to them. However, there are times, such as during certain chemistry experiments, when close proximity to the materials may be dangerous. Therefore, the teacher of students with visual impairments and the general education teacher need to teach the student when it is appropriate to view something up close and when it is not.

Enlarging printed text on a copier is a common adaptation for students with low vision; it is also effective for some maps, diagrams, and charts. The teacher should be sure to use a copier that provides sharp, clean copies and should experiment with several sizes of enlarged text to determine a size that the student can read comfortably and efficiently. However, it should be noted that enlargement is not appropriate for all students with low vision.

To enlarge visual displays, such as maps, charts, and diagrams, it is necessary to have good contrast, both in the original material and in the enlargement. Print materials in color turn to shades of gray when copied on most copiers. If *everything* is gray, it may be difficult for the student to distinguish the various areas of a map, diagram, or chart. In such a case, outlining the sections with a black marker may be helpful. The use of color copies is helpful when a student is able to distinguish colors and see them clearly, as determined by the student's functional vision and learning media assessments. Again, it is important to experiment with the student to determine whether black-and-white or color copies are the most effective.

Low vision devices may be an effective means of enlarging print material, and may assist in viewing objects. A student may be able to use a telescope to view hawks in an ecology sanctuary during a field trip and to see maps, videos, and visual displays presented at a distance during a lecture. A magnifier or CCTV may help a student see diagrams, maps, and small objects at his or her desk. If the student is able to see color, then a color CCTV may be the most effective method of enlarging maps and diagrams in textbooks. However, some students work more efficiently with the greater contrast of a black-and-white CCTV screen. Finally, the ultimate "low-tech" low vision device may be a sheet of colored acetate, often yellow, placed on printed material, which makes the images appear brighter and sharper for some students. The functional vision assessment will determine whether use of acetate sheets is appropriate for the student and, if so, what color is most useful. (See Chapter 13 for more information on low vision devices.)

Using Three-Dimensional Models

Three-dimensional models are appropriate for almost any student. Students with visual impairments benefit from models when they cannot examine the real objects. A three-dimensional model of a coiled strand of DNA provides a clearer image to a student who is blind than a tactile graphic of the same molecule. A taxidermist's recreation of a bear, life size and in a natural stance, tells a blind student far more about a bear than the best two-dimensional rendering. Science-supply catalogs are often good sources of three-dimensional models. Local natural history museums and hunters' supply stores may also have many preserved species that students can explore tactilely.

Young students can begin to learn about three-dimensional models by comparing the models to familiar real objects. For example, comparing the body of a doll to their own bodies may help make models meaningful, as may physically comparing a toy car or dollhouse furniture to the family's car and furniture. It is essential to help the student understand that although a model is similar in shape to the real object that it represents, it is different in size and usually in texture.

Students may benefit from instruction in the systematic exploration of models. One method is to establish a point of reference. If a model of DNA includes a portion that is "split," the point at which the split occurs may be taken as a point of reference. The student then explores above and below this point of reference, using the point as a way to "anchor" discoveries in their relative positions. Symmetry, if it exists in the model, can help a student organize his or her perceptions. For example, in exploring a life-sized model of a skeleton, the student may place one hand on each shoulder, move both hands outward and down each respective arm, and so forth and then use both hands together to explore the details of small areas of the model. A final helpful approach is to compare the model to a similar, more familiar item. For example, in exploring the preserved body of a bear, a student whose family has a dog may be helped to identify similarities and differences between the bear and the dog.

Creating Tactile Graphics

Science and social studies texts frequently present data in graphic form: maps; diagrams; and graphs, including pictographs, bar graphs, line graphs, and circle graphs. As was mentioned earlier, in braille textbooks, these items are often replaced with such statements as, "Map omitted—ask your teacher." If a science class visits a planetarium, where celestial images are projected above and around the students in a dark room, the student with a visual impairment is unlikely to be able to see these images. Nevertheless, map- and graph-reading skills and knowledge of stars and constellations are important for the student with a visual impairment, so this information must be made available in some accessible manner, such as a tactile graphic.

When a three-dimensional object or model is not available or is not an option, a tactile graphic can help a student organize and review information. The teacher of students with visual impairments often has to produce tactile graphics and provide the compensatory education the student needs to learn to interpret them.

Producing Tactile Graphics. The production of and instruction in the use of tactile graphics, diagrams, and maps is an essential component of the job of the teacher of students with visual impairments. This section presents basic information on preparing tactile graphics, as described by Edman (1992, p. 8). A tactile graphic may be necessary under the following circumstances:

- When the actual object (such as the stars, the solar system, a skyscraper, an elephant, a mountain, or a tree) is too large or otherwise unavailable to study,

- When the actual object (like an atom or a blood cell) is too small for detailed study,

- When a phenomenon (for example, the Northern Lights or smoke from a campfire) is difficult to put into words,

- When the actual object (such as electrical current or a soap bubble) cannot be touched or examined,

- When two points on a route need to be clarified (using an orientation map), and

- When the size relationships of two objects (for instance, the size of a man and of a dinosaur) need to be compared.

Before the teacher creates a tactile graphic, there are several issues to consider. First, is the tactile graphic necessary? Sometimes the information can be given to the student in an equally or more effective manner, such as by using real objects, models, or an oral description.

Another issue is whether a commercially produced tactile graphic will serve as well. APH produces a variety of inexpensive tactile maps and graphics, including those of the solar system, seasons, continents, oceans, countries, regions, and states of the United States. In addition, it produces the seven-volume *National Geographic Picture Atlas of the Fifty States,* which includes a political map of major cities; a physical map of mountains, rivers, and landmarks; and a road map of major interstate and highway routes for each state. Relief maps for desk use, tactile and visual globes, and *The Braille World Atlas* are also available from APH, as is *Graphic Aid for Mathematics,* which allows a student to construct many different types of graphs. Another product from APH is the *Basic Tactile Anatomy Atlas,* a two-volume set of graphics that presents a comprehensive overview of the human body.

Finally, the teacher of students with visual impairments should consider whether NOMAD (available from APH) could be used. The NOMAD work surface is a high-resolution touch-sensitive pad with 9,600 individual points that can be programmed with speech. NOMAD may be connected to a personal computer on which files describing the graphics are loaded. A student can then touch various points on the graphic, and NOMAD will describe them with synthetic speech. Graphic packages may be purchased or maps and graphs may be custom designed by the teacher.

After considering these issues, the teacher of students with visual impairments will have a clearer idea of whether he or she needs to produce the tactile graphic or whether one that is commercially available can be used. Basic guidelines for preparing tactile graphics are presented in Sidebar 9.2.

Teaching Tactile Graphics. Students who are blind need compensatory instruction in interpreting tac-

Suggestions for Creating Tactile Graphics

♦ The quickest and simplest graphic images may be created on a raised-line drawing board, which resembles a clipboard with a rubber coating, with plastic sheets clipped to the board. By drawing with a ballpoint pen, one creates a raised line. This approach meets many immediate needs, such as the quick illustration of an unfamiliar shape or a short route in orientation and mobility. The line-drawing kit also allows children with visual impairments to draw and feel their productions.

♦ Other materials create more substantial tactile graphics. For example, use sheets of heavy metal foil (available from APH) into which lines and symbols can be impressed from the back. A tactile image enhancer creates raised lines or areas from any black line or area drawn or copied on special microcapsule paper. A "heat pen" may be used to produce raised hand-drawn images, using the same paper. More common materials, such as cardboard, poster board, and sheets of braille paper, may serve as a base on which an almost limitless variety of materials can be glued to create a tactile image: string, wire, strips of solder, puff paint or fabric paint, shapes cut from craft foam or balsa wood, cross-stitch canvas, assorted fabrics, wire or plastic screen, different grades of sandpaper, seeds, rubber washers, and so forth.

♦ Use low-tech approaches, such as outlining maps with puff paint or thick fabric paint available in craft stores, as appropriate. Colors may help students with low vision to interpret tactile graphics.

♦ When preparing tactile graphics think in terms of tactile presentation, not visual presentation. Proofread the work with the fingers, not the eyes. The goal is not beauty but clarity of meaning.

♦ Include only the parts that are essential to make the point; omit all unnecessary lines, words, or images.

♦ "Variation in height is the trait of a relief display that gives the greatest amount of information to the blind or visually impaired reader" (Edman, 1992, p. 14). Use materials of different thicknesses and textures. Changes in color or contrast are helpful for students who can see them.

♦ Consider the student's age, print- or braille-reading ability, and previous experience with tactile graphics. Use simple graphics with young students and more complex ones with older students. Include new elements, such as a key or compass, and teach the skills for using them before they are needed in the classroom.

♦ A graphic can be more complex if the student has assistance from a sighted adult or classmate. Use print, large-print, or braille labels, or an audiotaped message to explain challenging elements of the graphic.

♦ Consider the size and durability needed for the graphic. Graphics that are intended for in-class use by only one student can be made of paper. A map of the school neighborhood that an orientation and mobility instructor expects to use with several students or

(continued on next page)

Suggestions for Creating Tactile Graphics *(Continued)*

for several years should be durable, waterproof, and portable.

♦ The size of the tactile graphic may not match the size of the original, to permit tactile recognition. For example, a map of the United States printed on a single sheet of 8 1/2 × 11-inch paper could be reproduced on microcapsule paper without enlargement if the lesson is on

the size and shape of the United States as a whole. However, if the lesson is on regions and state capitals, the map should be enlarged or divided into several sections and enlarged to provide details within regions and states.

♦ Recommended resources include *Tactile Graphics* (Edman, 1992) and the *Tactile Graphics Kit* (APH).

---

tile graphics, beginning in the early grades. By starting with simple graphics, a student can develop the skills needed to interpret more complex displays later. These skills take time to develop. As Singleton (1972) pointed out, sight is a unifying sense. Rather than observe the whole and then consider the parts, the student with a visual impairment must observe the parts and mentally construct the whole, which is a more challenging way to learn.

The map-reading methods taught by a general education teacher have little applicability to a student who is reading a tactile map. Therefore, the teacher of students with visual impairments needs to provide specialized instruction in advance of lessons in the classroom in such areas as tactile exploration of a map with an organized scanning system, tactile identification of various features on a map (like plains, mountains, rivers, and cities), and how a map should be stored so the raised portions are not damaged. Even students who are experienced in reading tactile graphics may benefit from a preview of a new or complex tactile graphic before it is used in the classroom. This preteaching will help the student focus on the purpose of the lesson to a greater extent. Sidebar 9.3 presents a systematic approach to teaching tactile graphics.

Time Lines

Time lines are often introduced to students in elementary social studies when the students create time lines of their own lives "so far." In print, time lines are generally presented as a horizontal line with small print indicating events and dates. For some students with low vision, it may be appropriate to enlarge horizontal time lines on a copier or through the use of a low vision device. Other students may work more efficiently with time lines rewritten in a vertical format, with dates and events written to the left and right of a vertical line. For students who read braille, the teacher of students with visual impairments may make tactile time lines. Generally, a braille time line is designed so that dates and events are presented in a vertical list, rather than horizontally. When a student's time line differs in orientation from those of the other students in the class, the teacher of students with visual impairments should preteach the time line to the student and explain the braille time line to the general education teacher, so the braille student can be included more easily in the classroom activities related to the time line. (For detailed information on constructing time lines in braille, see *Braille Formats, Principles of Print to Braille Transcription, 1997* [Braille Authority of North America, BANA, 1998].)

Tables

In a table, information usually intended for reference is presented in vertical columns and horizontal rows. Because of the space required for braille writing, only the most compact print tables

Suggestions for Teaching Tactile Graphics

◆ To introduce tactile graphics, have the student participate in copying a variety of familiar objects—his or her hand or a circle and square from a familiar-shapes kit—on a raised-line drawing board. By helping to create these images and then examining them and matching them to the objects they represent, the student learns that a two-dimensional line drawing can represent a known object.

◆ Next, introduce tactile images of familiar objects that are too large to be copied in a same-size drawing. *Tactile Graphics* (Edman, 1992) presents good examples for beginners, such as a full-front image of a person or side views of a chair or a table.

◆ Introduce maps by working first on a map of a familiar area, such as the classroom. If a map of the entire classroom would be too cluttered, it is best to map only a small area of the classroom at first. Some teachers begin with a three-dimensional model, using, for example, a rectangular block to represent the teacher's desk, a tuna can for a round table, and smaller blocks to represent the students' desks. These objects may later be traced on a raised-line drawing board to create a tactile map. Have the student walk routes in the real area, identifying the objects that he or she passes, and then trace these routes on the model or tactile map.

◆ To introduce maps of unknown places, begin with a simple map with no more than three symbols, such as a triangle with "house" brailled next to it, a large circle with "pond" brailled inside it, and a straight line with "road" brailled next to it. Have the student trace the path a person leaving the house would follow to go fishing in the pond. Gradually increase the complexity of these maps.

◆ APH produces a series of map-study programs. *Map Study I: Maps Represent Real Places* contains materials and guidelines for introducing basic map concepts using a classroom and other known environments. *Map Study II: Basic Map Reading Concepts* presents 30 map-reading concepts, including directions; location; finding corners; diagonal, vertical, horizontal movement; and so forth. *Map Study: Recognizing Landforms* includes such concepts of geography as distinguishing mountains from valleys and channels from bays.

◆ Standard, commercially produced tactile maps and graphics use small tactile symbols to represent key places. Assess the students' ability to distinguish these shapes. With the *Tactile Graphics Kit* (APH), straight and curved lines of various widths and solid- and hollow-center circles, squares, rectangles, and multiple-sided shapes can be produced. Teach the student to recognize the shapes that he or she does not know.

◆ Teach the student to use a key to learn what the map or graphic is "all about" and for assigning meaning to the shapes presented on standard tactile maps and graphics.

◆ Teach the student to explore a graphic in an organized manner by scanning the figure from top to bottom, using both hands, to determine overall dimensions and layout. Singleton (1972)

(continued on next page)

Suggestions for Creating Tactile Graphics *(Continued)*

recommended teaching the student to think first about the overall shape or area presented and then about smaller, specific areas within the major boundaries.

♦ Singleton (1972) also suggested teaching students to locate a point of reference from which to work. The student can mark the point of reference by keeping a finger on it or marking it with a pushpin or sticker. If the student becomes confused while exploring the graphic, he or she can return to the point of reference. It may be helpful to choose the most important element from the key and locate it on the graphic to use as a point of reference. The student can then continue locating and identifying other textures and symbols, working outward

from the point of reference. This systematic technique can be applied to any illustration.

♦ Many map-reading tasks involve following lines (such as rivers and boundaries). A useful line-tracing technique is to follow a line with both hands. When the line branches, the student can keep one hand on the branching point and explore the various options with the other hand. In this way, the place will not be lost if a wrong branch is followed.

♦ As the student's skill increases and he or she encounters more complex graphics, it may be helpful to teach him or her to divide a graphic mentally into quadrants or regions to simplify exploration. Remind the student to refer to the key as often as necessary.

---

can be transcribed into braille and retain their original row-and-column structure. An alternate format is often used in braille. Once again, compensatory education is necessary, since most of the explanation and instruction given by the science or social studies teacher will not be meaningful to the braille reader. A simple table is presented as an example in Figure 9.1. (For information on how to construct tables in braille, see *Braille Formats, Principles of Print to Braille Transcription, 1997* [BANA, 1998].)

Some of the factors discussed so far are illustrated in the following case study of Amy's experiences in writing a social studies report.

Case Study: Amy

Amy, an eighth-grade student who is blind and has no light perception, is studying world geography. The end-of-the-year assignment is to cre-

ate her own country. Her country is to have a name, a capital, at least three major cities, mountains or a desert, rivers, and lakes. It can be a coastal country, an inland country, or an island.

Amy is to describe the country in a written report. She is to discuss the people, their culture (which cannot be the same as hers), their occupations, political system, and leaders, and to include information about the country's primary and secondary crops and natural resources. Amy also has to produce a map of the country, and must include a key.

The following are several options for completing the assignment. Some options require assistance or participation from others, while some allow Amy to work independently. Some of Amy's options for researching ideas for her country are:

♦ Discuss the project with her parents and classmates,

◆ Listen to prerecorded tapes or CDs about life in different countries and about the geography of different regions,

◆ Have live readers read books or encyclopedia articles to Amy or record them on audiotape for her to listen to,

◆ Read braille material about life in different countries and about the geography of different regions,

◆ Do similar research using a computer encyclopedia program,

◆ Search the World Wide Web for information about countries and emboss information in braille or use synthesized speech output,

◆ Study tactile maps previously given to Amy by her teachers,

◆ Work independently, or

◆ Form a study group with other classmates and share any information gathered with the group and receive similar information in return.

Amy may use several options for taking notes. These options will be influenced by the setting and the number of notes she has to take:

◆ Rely on memory,

◆ Use a tape recorder,

◆ Use a slate and stylus,

◆ Use a braillewriter,

◆ Use an electronic note taker (such as Braille Lite, Type 'n Speak), or

◆ Use a desktop or laptop computer.

Amy's options for completing the written assignment include these:

◆ Working from her notes, dictate the report to her older sister, who will write it in ink for her;

◆ Write the report with a braillewriter and ask the teacher of students with visual impairments to inkprint it;

◆ Use an electronic note taker, save a text file, print an ink copy for the teacher, and a braille copy for herself; or

◆ Use a desktop or laptop computer and a word-processing program (like MS Word or WordPerfect), import the file to a braille translator program (such as MegaDots or the Duxbury Braille Translator), save a text file, and print an ink copy for the teacher and a braille copy for herself.

Amy's options for making a tactile map include:

◆ Use a surface, such as foam or poster board, with fabric paint, strips of solder, and a selection of different kinds of cloth to form the images. A parent or peer could help with the cutting and gluing under Amy's direction, and Amy would attach symbols for geographic features and cities. Amy would label the map and key in braille, writing on labeling tape with a slate and stylus or on adhesive laminating material with a braillewriter. A parent or a peer could assist by providing labels in print.

◆ Produce the map image by hand or by computer (she may or may not need assistance in doing so) and use a tactile image enhancer to produce the map. She could label the map and key in braille and use a computer program to make print labels to attach.

◆ Use a tactile graphic kit (such as the APH Tactile Graphic Kit) to produce the map. She could attach braille labels to the map and key and use a computer program to make print labels to attach.

◆ Use NOMAD and a computer to produce a map of her country. She would require the assistance of her teacher of students with visual impairments to complete this activity.

Adaptations for Lab Activities

When it is necessary to modify a learning task for a student with a visual impairment, it is essential that adaptations be chosen so that the activity remains equivalent to that of the sighted students. For example, if one objective of a science lab activity is for students to use a balance to weigh materials accurately before the materials are

A. The original table

LAND BIOMES

Biome	Characteristics	Rainfall	Common Plants	Common Animals
Tundra	Harsh cold most of year, almost treeless	20 cm	Lichens, grasses, mosses, small shrubs	Arctic hares, caribou, snowy owls, wolves
Grassland	Four seasons, few trees, many grasses, less rain than temperate forests	50 cm	Tall and short grasses	Prairie dogs, bison, coyotes, pronghorn
Tropical Rain Forest	No seasons, hot all year, much rain, heavily forested	200 cm	Lianas, orchids, palms, ferns, tall broadleaf trees	Beetles, parrots, monkeys, frogs, snakes, jaguars

Source: Adapted from M. R. Cohen, T. M. Cooney, C. M. Hawthorne, A. J. McCormack, J. M. Pasachoff, N. Pasachoff, K. L. Rhines, and I. L. Siesnick, *Discover Science 6* (Glenview, IL: Scott, Foresman, 1989), pp. 126–133.

B. How columns and rows are arranged in braille

LAND BIOMES

Transcriber's Note: Print column form changed as follows:

Biome

    Characteristics

        Rainfall

            Common Plants

                Common Animals

Tundra

    harsh cold most of year, almost treeless

        20 cm

            lichens, grasses, mosses, small shrubs

                arctic hares, caribou, snowy owls, wolves

Grassland

    four seasons, few trees, many grasses, less rain than temperate forests

        50 cm

            tall and short grasses

                prairie dogs, bison, coyotes, pronghorn

Tropical Rain Forest

    no seasons, hot all year, much rain, heavily forested

        200 cm

            lianas, orchids, palms, ferns, tall broadleaf trees

                beetles, parrots, monkeys, frogs, snakes, jaguars

(continued on next page)

Figure 9.1. Changing a Table from Print to Braille

C. How the material looks in braille

Figure 9.1. (*Continued*)

combined, it would *not* be appropriate to provide premeasured materials for the student with a visual impairment to mix. Instead, a balance with tactile indications of balance must be provided. A number of appropriate modifications are discussed next. Sidebar 9.4 presents additional ideas.

Safety considerations must be addressed when *any* student, including a student with a visual impairment, works in a science lab. Many

SIDEBAR 9.4

Modifications for Lab Activities

METHOD

- ◆ Orient the student with a visual impairment to the work area, materials, equipment, and the like, and provide a controlled, well-organized work space.
- ◆ Set up instructional environments or areas to ensure the most advantageous physical distance between the teacher and student for effective monitoring.
- ◆ Develop science activities to meet the student's needs after assessment and modify standard experiments for meaningful, multisensory experiences.

STRATEGY

- ◆ Encourage every student to be involved in every step of the lesson. Do not encourage the student who is visually impaired to play a passive role or to act only as the recorder in experiments with sighted partners.
- ◆ Select a sighted team member carefully to work along with the student who is visually impaired. Rotating partners for the entire class may be an appropriate strategy.
- ◆ Periodically observe the student who is visually impaired participating in the science class. After the class, offer suggestions to both the student and the science teacher.
- ◆ Maintain a close working relationship with the science teacher to encourage frequent feedback and mutual consultation.

MATERIALS

- ◆ Provide real objects, organisms, and materials for classroom use and experiments as often as possible.
- ◆ Use sturdy objects and organisms of appropriate size for tactile examinations, such as beans, rather than radish seeds, and crayfish, rather than butterflies.
- ◆ Describe or provide alternatives to chalkboard work, printed diagrams, photographs, and so forth. Provide clear, high-contrast printed materials for a student with low vision.
- ◆ Germinate seeds in a seed sprouter rather than in soil, so that all students can observe the seeds growing using various senses.
- ◆ Adapt or modify tools and materials for effective use by a student who is visually impaired. For example, fix a physical stop to a large syringe so the plunger can be pulled out to a preset measure, or cut tactile notches in the edges of the plunger of a syringe to determine a variety of volumes.
- ◆ Acquire specialized tools, data-recording materials, and other materials, when necessary, including braille rulers and thermometers, speech-output calculators, braille or auditory scales, and three-dimensional models of cells.
- ◆ Use organizational containers, such as muffin tins or divided trays.

(continued on next page)

Modifications for Lab Activities *(Continued)*

◆ Use stable and unbreakable materials.

◆ Label containers and materials in braille and large print using a one-line slate with ordinary labeling tape.

◆ Use high contrast between materials and work surfaces when possible.

◆ Be certain that written materials, including textbooks, articles from science journals, and the teacher's handouts, are

accessible to the student with a visual impairment.

◆ Make use of braille, audiotapes, large print, and sighted readers for the student, as appropriate.

Source: Adapted from K. M. Huebner, L. DeLucchi, L. Malone, and M. R. Olson, in G. Scholl, Ed., *Foundations of Education for Blind and Visually Handicapped Children and Youth* (New York: American Foundation for the Blind, 1986), p. 380.

---

things found in a lab (such as electrical current, knives for dissecting, acids, and chemicals) are harmful or deadly if touched, mishandled, or ingested by taste or smell. These concerns are not a reason to keep the student with a visual impairment out of a lab. However, they *are* a reason to think ahead and determine methods for completing activities that will maximize both safety and learning.

Adopting a Multisensory Approach

For science and social studies to have depth of meaning and for students with visual impairments to learn and use the skills of the scientific process, a multisensory approach must be used. Sighted students learn a great deal through incidental and planned observation of materials and activities in the classroom and in laboratory investigations. Students with visual impairments, however, must use an approach that does not rely predominantly on sight. The key to such an approach is to use all available senses—tactile, auditory, olfactory, and taste in an efficient and safe manner.

Students with visual impairments may not be able to *see* the changes as a tiny radish seed sprouts, but they can feel the planting and sprouting of a larger bean seed. They can smell the soil, hear the rustling of the leaves of the bean plant

that grows, and taste the beans that ultimately grow on the plant they raise. Together, these elements constitute an experience of "sprouting seeds" that is as worthy as a visual one. In fact, all students in the class will benefit from the multisensory approach—the teacher should not consider it something for only the student with a visual impairment. It is important to teach and encourage students to use all their senses at the appropriate time. For example, a student may choose to use vision to observe an earthworm under a CCTV but prefer to use a tactile representation to study a complex electron micrograph.

The multisensory approach encourages students to use all their senses in exploring and learning and results in a rich learning experience. However, since many substances used in chemistry and other sciences are harmful or deadly if touched or ingested, it is essential to teach students when to use and not to use all their available senses.

Setting Up a Lab Area

A lab area for a student with a visual impairment will need some modifications, often requiring space. For example, ample space may be needed for a microvideo station for microscope work and for a CCTV, if applicable. If tactile graphics are to be used, the student will need a wide, flat area to support the graphic while he or she examines it. Even a braillewriter or electronic note taker will need a moderate amount of extra space. Each of these items must be kept away from water and other spills. Other considerations include additional electric outlets to permit the operation of a student's special equipment; storage space for braille or large-print references, if used; and adjustable lighting.

Working with Lab Partners

All students who work with partners in group activities are more successful if they have learned certain interpersonal skills. For example, all group members should be able to take turns and assume their share of responsibilities. In addition, a student with a visual impairment may need to be able to assert himself or herself as an active member of the lab partnership and to ask for assistance when needed.

Lab work should be divided fairly among the lab partners. In the case of two lab partners (one sighted and one visually impaired) who must mix two predetermined chemicals and observe the reaction, the work might be divided in two ways. First, the student with a visual impairment could record the results of the experiment as the partner performs and describes the interaction. Second, the student with a visual impairment could measure and mix the chemicals, using adapted measuring tools and techniques he or she has been taught, as the sighted partner describes the interaction of the mixed chemicals and records the results. Either approach is appropriate at times, but the first approach must not be used exclusively.

Schools in the United States, as well as teachers of students with visual impairments, have typically worked to foster independence in students. However, the increased use of cooperative group learning and inclusive practices in special education reflect a growing appreciation for the advantages of interdependence. Cooperative learning groups are often used in science and social studies classrooms to complete various laboratory and learning activities. This opportunity for shared learning may prompt teachers to consider whether students with visual impairments must always strive for complete independence. This question does not have a "one-size-fits-all" answer. With regard to the case study of Amy presented earlier, the options for completing a social studies project included opportunities to be dependent on others or to work interdependently and independently.

Employing Measurement Tools

Students in science classes often measure volumes, weights, lengths, and intervals of time. Measuring devices that have been adapted for persons with visual impairments include braille rulers and yardsticks; containers adapted for measuring liquid volume; various digital timekeeping devices; and weighing systems with a tactile indication of balance or a large-print, tactile, or voice output of numerical weight. Teachers of students with visual impairments need to be sure that their students have frequent experience with these devices, so the students can develop and maintain expertise in their use. The Resources section at the end of this chapter suggests some sources for these items.

Not every student needs an adapted form for every measurement device. A student with low vision may be able to measure some objects, such as the width of the room or the height of a desk, with an ordinary ruler or yardstick and use a CCTV to facilitate the measurement of very small items. A braille-reading student can measure the approximate length of a hallway using an ordinary yardstick or meter stick, or learn to estimate distances by pacing them off. For accuracy, though, this student will appreciate braille rulers with a caliper slide or the Click Rule from the National Federation of the Blind, which permits accurate measurement to sixteenths of an inch.

For measuring harmless liquids, Lawrence Hall of Science (LHS) at the University of California at Berkeley developed a series of simple but accurate adapted tools, included in its SAVI/ SELPH science module kits and available individually. (For more information about the SAVI/

SELPH program, see Sidebar 9.5.) For example, LHS produces a series of graduated-size beakers, each with an "overflow hole." To measure a liter of water accurately, a student places the liter beaker in a large plastic pan and pours water into the beaker until it seems full. Excess water will drain out of the overflow hole. Because water is a harmless liquid, the student can check tactilely for overflow. When the water stops flowing out of the hole, the beaker contains a liter of water. However, with chemicals, measuring with an overflow hole

beaker may expose the student to drops of caustic liquid clinging to the outside of the beaker, so the student must wear protective gloves. This approach also requires that steps be taken to dispose of the overflow liquid remaining in the pan safely. Other approaches to liquid measurement that have been suggested include these:

◆ Using a liquid level indicator that hangs over the lip of a container and buzzes or vibrates when the liquid is approximately

---

The SAVI/SELPH Science Program

SIDEBAR 9.5

The SAVI/SELPH (Science Activities for the Visually Impaired/Science Enrichment for Learners with Physical Handicaps) materials were developed by the Lawrence Hall of Science (LHS) at the University of California at Berkeley. Originally designed for use by students with visual or physical impairments, the program and its materials may also be used with students without disabilities.

The SAVI/SELPH program includes nine modules, or teaching units: Measurement, Structures of Life, Scientific Reasoning, Communication, Magnetism and Electricity, Mixtures and Solutions, Environments, Kitchen Interactions, and Environmental Energy. Each module addresses a different content area in science and has four or more activities that can be used by a small group of students under the close supervision of a teacher. The modules, which may be purchased separately or as a group, present instructions for the teacher, the tools and equipment needed for each activity, including the specially designed or adapted tools for use by students with visual impairments, and appropriate braille and print charts and labels.

When students with visual impairments are in inclusive settings, the teacher of students with visual impairments may or may not have an opportunity to teach the content of any given

SAVI/SELPH module. Nevertheless, the adapted measurement tools available separately from LHS are valuable for promoting active participation in the science activities scheduled in the science classroom. The following are brief descriptions of some of these tools:

◆ A balance with tactile markings and a variety of gram weights for measuring weights in grams.
◆ Graduated cylinders for measuring from 5 to 50 milliliters of liquids. A disk of foamlike material floats on the liquid in the cylinder, supporting a notched strip of plastic that extends above the rim of the cylinder. By counting notches above the rim, a student can determine the volume of liquid in the cylinder.
◆ Syringes with notches cut in the plungers for measuring liquids.
◆ Overflow beakers that measure 100 to 1000 milliliters of liquid.
◆ A dial-shaped thermometer, with print and tactile markings, that floats in liquid.
◆ Flexible metersticks marked in braille and print with which a student can measure the circumference of a tree or lengths along an uneven surface.

1 inch from the top of the container. This method is safe, but the measurement is not accurate.

- Using measuring devices that have been designed to hold an exact amount, such as measuring spoons and droppers.

- Using syringes with fixed stops for the plunger, so a set amount of liquid is pulled out.

- Using syringes with tactile notches cut in the edges of the plunger.

- Directing a lab partner to measure chemicals; both partners should know what is being measured and the amount that is being measured. This method should not be used exclusively.

Students with visual impairments can use a variety of timekeeping devices. Braille and talking watches make it simple to observe the passing of hours or intervals of five minutes with adequate accuracy, and simple dial timers are available with numbers in large print or marked for tactile identification. For more accurate timing, digital timers are available that give readouts in large print or voice and can identify precise intervals, such as 15 seconds.

For measurements of weight, different approaches may be followed. Talking, large-print-readout, or tactile scales are available, although they are most appropriate for measuring large amounts, such as may be used in a kitchen. For weighing small amounts, such as a gram in a chemistry lab, a student with a visual impairment may learn to use a balance adapted with tactile markings. The student should understand the principles of using this device, even if he or she must rely on a sighted partner for accuracy in judging balance. A tactile balance appropriate for elementary school students is included in the SAVI/SELPH materials mentioned earlier.

Noting Directionality

In some social studies activities, students use compasses to identify the cardinal directions in their immediate environment. A braille compass is an intriguing device that is simple to use and requires no batteries or electricity. It consists of a freely rotating dial, with a raised arrow that points north and the letters *S, E,* and *W* for south, east, and west, enclosed in a small case. The user faces any direction, holding the compass flat in front of him or her. After waiting a moment to allow the compass dial to locate and point north, the user opens the lid of the case. Opening the lid causes the dial to be stabilized; that is, it will no longer turn. The user can then tactilely read the arrow and letters on the surface of the dial to determine the direction. The user must be careful not to alter the position of the compass after opening the case. Any braille-reading student whose class is working on activities involving cardinal directions should have access to a braille compass (available from several suppliers; see the Resources section at the end of this chapter).

Charting Information

Students in science classes often record data by completing charts. A student with a visual impairment should complete all chart work that is required of the other students, although he or she may sometimes need a lab partner to give verbal descriptions as an experiment is proceeding so it may be recorded.

The teacher of students with visual impairments should receive charting forms from the general education teacher in time to permit any needed modifications to be made. He or she may provide compensatory education, modified materials, and special equipment to allow the student to use the following:

- The standard recording chart provided by the general education teacher used with a magnifier or CCTV;

- A recording chart with bold lines or one that has been enlarged;

- A recording chart that has been produced in braille, inserting answers with a braille-writer, or indicating "check marks" by inserting pushpins in a chart mounted on a cork board or applying adhesive dots (for example, Bumps-On from Exceptional Teaching Aids);

◆ A braillewriter, slate and stylus, or electronic note taker to record information that can be charted later; or

◆ A tape recorder to record results and translate data to a print or braille format later.

Using a Microscope

The use of a microscope is often difficult for students with visual impairments. However, by increasing light and magnification, some students will be able to use a microscope. Others can use a desktop microvideo camera or microscope video system that projects the image under the microscope onto a television monitor for easier viewing. For a student who cannot view a projected image, the microscope session may be adapted by allowing the student to learn the parts of a microscope and how it works, participate in setting up the lab station with the microscope and slides, learn to prepare some simple slides and the safety issues involved with glass slides, and then to be given an oral or written description or tactile graphic of the materials being viewed under the microscope. It is *not* appropriate simply to excuse a student with a visual impairment from the microscope lab.

Participating in Dissection

The dissection of animals in biology can be modified by allowing a student with a visual impairment to explore a model, tactile graphic, or actual specimen tactilely before the actual dissection. During the dissection, a lab partner could describe the process of dissection, doing the cutting in phases while the student who is visually impaired tactilely explores the specimen between phases. A student with a visual impairment may participate in cutting the specimen with guidance from the lab partner or teacher. This approach works best if the student has an opportunity to explore a previously dissected specimen prior to cutting. The following case study describes the options for two students in dissecting the eye of a cow.

Case Study: Tom and Teresa

Tom and Teresa, two students who are visually impaired, are in an inclusive 11th-grade science class. Their class will be dissecting cow eyes next week. Tom has coloboma of the iris, a visual acuity of 20/200 for distance and 20/50 for near with reduced lower vision, and uses a 2x magnifier. Teresa has Grade 4 retinopathy of prematurity with light perception. The students will be working with lab partners. The following lesson plan from the science teacher lists some adaptations that the two students will use.

1. Present an eye model, demonstrating parts of the eye.

   ◆ Tom: Examine the model prior to class, using a handheld or stand magnifier for detail, if necessary, and include a verbal description.
   ◆ Teresa: Tactilely explore the model prior to class; include a verbal description.

2. Present the eyeball to the students (individually wrapped) and have the students unwrap them.

   ◆ Tom: No adaptation.
   ◆ Teresa: The lab partner may help Teresa find the location of the wrapper opening only if necessary.

3. Identify the optic nerve and muscles.

   ◆ Tom: No adaptation; use a handheld or stand magnifier for detail, if necessary.
   ◆ Teresa: Tactilely explore; the lab partner may use verbal descriptions, if necessary.

4. Locate the front of the eye.

   ◆ Tom: No adaptation.
   ◆ Teresa: Tactilely find the optic nerve; the front of the eye is at the opposite end.

5. Dissect the sclera with a scalpel.

   ◆ Tom: No adaptation; use a stand magnifier, if needed (see the following note).
   ◆ Teresa: Lab partner may assist, if necessary.

(Some students, including sighted students, may need assistance with the scalpel. The teacher of students with visual impairments may assist the science teacher and student during the lesson on safety and use of a scalpel. If the student is not proficient in using a knife for cutting food, then the lab partner should use the scalpel.)

6. Slice the eyeball in half (vitreous will flow out).

   ◆ Tom: No adaptation; use a stand magnifier, if needed.
   ◆ Teresa: The lab partner may assist, if necessary.

7. Explore the front half of the eyeball and identify the parts.

   ◆ Tom: No adaptation; use a handheld or stand magnifier for detail, if needed.
   ◆ Teresa: Tactilely explore the parts, comparing them to the model; the lab partner may use verbal description. Encourage Teresa to share her findings about tactile characteristics with her lab partner.

8. Explore the back half of the eye and identify the parts.

   ◆ Tom: No adaptation; use a handheld or stand magnifier for detail, if needed.
   ◆ Teresa: Tactilely explore the parts, comparing the eye to the model; the lab partner may use verbal description.

9. With the tip of the scalpel, pull the retina away.

   ◆ Tom: No adaptation; use a stand magnifier, if needed.
   ◆ Teresa: Tactilely find the location where the scalpel will be inserted, carefully insert the scalpel and separate the retina; the lab partner may assist in placing the scalpel, if necessary, while Teresa continues to separate the retina.

10. Summarize the activity.

   ◆ Tom: No adaptation.
   ◆ Teresa: No adaptation.

SUMMARY

Social studies and science are two critical content areas in the academic curriculum. In most cases, the teacher of students with visual impairments collaborates with general education teachers and content-area specialists to ensure that students who are visually impaired benefit from the classroom instruction. The specialist in visual impairment provides adapted materials and equipment and teaches special skills prior to their use in the classroom.

The teacher of students with visual impairments will also provide information to the content-area teachers on modifications in the presentation of material. He or she will make suggestions on ways to ensure the inclusion of the student in all aspects of the class and on ways to make learning as rewarding for the student who is visually impaired as it is for other students.

ACTIVITIES

1. Develop and demonstrate a sequence of activities appropriate for introducing tactile graphics to young elementary students. Begin with basic activities using a raised-line drawing board, include at least one classroom map using three-dimensional materials, and conclude with a simple map of an area surrounding a school. Test the materials for clarity with classmates who are blindfolded.

2. Produce three maps of your state for a sixth-grade student who is blind. Include major cities and key landforms. Use three methods of adaptation: the Tactile Graphics Kit from APH, a tactile image enhancer, and an assortment of materials with different textures. Have blindfolded classmates examine the maps and use them to answer simple questions. Discuss

the advantages and disadvantages of each map with the classmates.

3. Select a chapter from a social studies or science textbook that includes at least one table, one graph, and one important diagram or illustration. Prepare adaptations and modifications for two students, one who is blind and one with low vision.

4. Obtain a variety of adapted measurement tools. Suggestions include a balance (with a set of gram weights); overflow beakers; syringes with notched plungers; a cylinder with floating volume indicator; a floating or talking thermometer; a braille ruler, yardstick, or meterstick; and a Click Rule. Teach a blindfolded classmate to make accurate measurements. Demonstrate the use of these tools to the class. Share up-to-date information on sources for these tools with your classmates.

5. Prepare a 30–45-minute presentation on a topic of interest from this chapter for the class. Include handouts as appropriate that will be of use to your classmates in their role as teachers of students with visual impairments.

REFERENCES

Braille Authority of North America. (1998). *Braille formats: Principles of print to braille transcription, 1997.* Louisville, KY: American Printing House for the Blind.

Brophy, J., & Alleman J. (1996). *Powerful social studies for elementary students.* Fort Worth, TX: Harcourt, Brace.

Cohen, M. R., Cooney, T. M., Hawthorne, C. M., McCormack, A. J., Pasachoff, J. M., Pasachoff, N., Rhines, K. L., & Siesnick, I. L. (1989). *Discover science 6.* Glenview, IL: Scott, Foresman.

Edman, P. K. (1992). *Tactile graphics.* New York: American Foundation for the Blind.

Gega, P. C. (1994). *Science in elementary education* (7th ed.). New York: Macmillan.

Huebner, K. M., DeLucchi, L., Malone, L., & Olson, M. R. (1986). Science. In Scholl, G. (Ed.), *Foundations of education for blind and visually handicapped children and youth* (pp. 375–381). New York: American Foundation for the Blind.

National Council for the Social Studies. (1993). *The social studies professional.* Washington, DC: Author.

Sewell, D. (1997). *Assessment kit: Kit of informal tools for academic students with visual impairments.* Austin: Texas School for the Blind and Visually Impaired.

Singleton, L. R. (1972). *Social studies for the visually impaired child: MAVIS sourcebook 4.* Boulder, CO: Social Science Education Consortium.

Vaughan, C. E. (1998). *Social and cultural perspectives on blindness.* Springfield, IL: Charles C Thomas.

Use of Reference Sources

Student's Name: _____   D.O.B.: _____

Assessor: _____   Assessment Date: _____

	+/-	Comments
1. Glossary		
Describes purpose/contents of glossary		
Locates glossary in text		
Finds section of glossary for given initial letter		
Uses alphabetical order to locate word in glossary		
Identifies definitions of entry word		
Uses glossary to define unfamiliar words; integrates definitions into understanding of passages read		
2. Dictionary		
States purpose/contents of dictionary		
Locates dictionary in classroom		
If necessary, locates correct volume of dictionary		
Finds section of dictionary for given initial letter		
Uses alphabetical order to locate word in dictionary		
Identifies definition of entry word		
Uses dictionary to define unfamiliar words; integrates definitions into understanding of passages read		
Uses diacritical marks to determine pronunciation of unfamiliar words		
3. Encyclopedia		
States purpose/contents of encyclopedia		
Locates encyclopedia in: a. classroom b. library		
Identifies "key word" for locating article: a. person's last name b. key word for other topics		
Locates correct volume of encyclopedia		
Uses alphabetical order to locate article		
Reads and comprehends article; applies information		

Appendix A: Checklist on Use of Reference Sources

Science and Social Studies Survival Skills

Student's Name: _____   Date: _____

Student uses the following spatial information:

1. Directional terms:
   - ☐ left
   - ☐ right
   - ☐ center/middle
   - ☐ up
   - ☐ down
   - ☐ top
   - ☐ bottom
   - ☐ upper left
   - ☐ upper right
   - ☐ lower left
   - ☐ lower right

2. Compass directions:
   - ☐ North
   - ☐ South
   - ☐ East
   - ☐ West
   - ☐ NW
   - ☐ NE
   - ☐ SW
   - ☐ SE

3. Columns:
   - ☐ can find information in various columns

4. Rows:
   - ☐ can find information in various rows

Student uses information from oral descriptions:

1. To understand the main idea of:
   - ☐ texts
   - ☐ films
   - ☐ field trips

2. To understand the details of:
   - ☐ texts
   - ☐ films
   - ☐ field trips

Student uses the following to understand illustrations:

1. ☐ Oral descriptions
2. ☐ Real objects
3. ☐ Three-dimensional representations

4. Graphic representations:
   - ☐ two-dimensional objects
   - ☐ solid embossed shapes
   - ☐ outlines of objects
   - ☐ raised line representations
   - ☐ symbols/letters

Student uses the following to read and interpret maps and graphics:

1. ☐ Map key/legend
2. ☐ A point of reference to start tactile or visual examination
3. ☐ Examination of overall area
4. ☐ Examination of detailed areas
5. ☐ A structured approach to examination (top to bottom, left to right)

(continued on next page)

Appendix B: Science and Social Studies Survival Skills Checklist

Science and Social Studies Survival Skills *(Continued)*

Student interprets information from graphs and tables:

1. ☐ Pictographs
2. ☐ Vertical Bar Graphs
3. ☐ Horizontal Bar Graphs
4. ☐ Line Graphs
5. ☐ Circle Graphs
6. ☐ Tables

Student uses a tape recorder:

1. ☐ To "read" textbook
2. ☐ To complete assignments or complete class projects, such as interviews

Student uses reference materials:

1. ☐ Glossary
2. ☐ Dictionary
3. ☐ Encyclopedia

Source: Reprinted, with permission, from D. Sewell, *Assessment Kit: Kit of Informal Tools for Academic Students with Visual Impairments* (Austin: Texas School for the Blind and Visually Impaired, 1997).

Measurement Assessment

School Year(s): _____

Student's Name: _____   D.O.B.: _____

Assessor: _____   Date(s) of Assessment(s): _____

Directions:
> The teacher or residential instructor interviews the student and records the answers.
> This assessment may be used for three consecutive school years.
> Color-code each school year and mark the approximate boxes using this key:

☒ Generalized Use: Does this frequently with minimal support in at least 3 different contexts.

☐ Emerging Use: Does this infrequently, and/or only with support, and/or in less than 3 contexts.

☐ Not observed or not addressed.

Linear Dimensions

1. Understanding terms:

   long .... ☐   short .... ☐
   tall .... ☐   length .... ☐
   width ...... ☐   height .... ☐
   linear .... ☐

2. 1 foot = _____ inches
   1 yard = _____ inches
   1 yard = _____ feet
   1 mile = _____ feet

3. Name familiar objects which are approximately equal in length to:

   1 inch .... ☐
   1 yard or 1 meter .... ☐
   1 millimeter .... ☐
   1 foot .... ☐
   1 centimeter .... ☐

4. When given various linear measure-ments, state which measurement is shorter and which is longer .... ☐

Volume/Capacity

1. Understand terms

   volume .... ☐
   liquid .... ☐
   gaseous .... ☐
   capacity .... ☐
   solid .... ☐

2. Name familiar containers (fluid) which are approximately equal in volume or capacity to:

   1 milliliter ...... ☐
   1 cup .... ☐
   1 liter .... ☐
   1/2 gallon ...... ☐
   1 fluid oz ...... ☐
   1 pint .... ☐
   1 quart .... ☐
   1 gallon ...... ☐

3. When given various units of volume, state which one contains more liquid .... ☐

(continued on next page)

Appendix C: Measurement Assessment Checklist

Measurement Assessment *(Continued)*

Weight/Mass

1. Understand terms:

   weight ....□

   heavy ....□

   large ....□

   mass ....□

   light ....□

   small ....□

2. Name familiar objects which are approximately equal in weight to:

   1 milligram ....□   1 gram ....□

   1 ounce ....□   1 pound ....□

   1 kilogram ....□   1 ton ....□

3. When given various units of weight, state which one is heavier ....□

Which unit of measurement would you use:

1. To tell you about the size of the bag of flour you bought at the store? ......□
2. To take some cough medicine? ....□
3. To tell how much you weigh? ....□
4. To tell how much milk you bought at the store? ....□
5. To measure the distance to another city? ....□
6. To tell the barber how much to cut off your hair ....□
7. To tell how tall you are? ....□
8. To tell how much a car would weigh? ....□
9. To talk about the size of yogurt container you bought? ....□
10. To talk about how much water a bathtub holds? ....□
11. To tell someone how much Coke to buy at the store? ....□
12. To measure your waist? ....□

Abbreviations of Measurement Units

1. Recognizes (customary) abbreviations of:

   fl. oz. ....□   c. ....□

   pt. ....□   qt. ....□

   gal. ....□   oz. ....□

   in. ....□   lb. ....□

   ft. ....□   yd. ....□

   mi. ....□

2. Recognizes (metric) abbreviations of:

   ml ....□   l ....□

   mg ....□   mm ....□

   g ....□   cm ....□

   kg ....□   m ....□

   km ....□

___

Summary/Recommendations:

___

Source: Reprinted, with permission, from D. Sewell, *Assessment Kit: Kit of Informal Tools for Academic Students with Visual Impairments* (Austin: Texas School for the Blind and Visually Impaired, 1997).

Strategies for Teaching Social Studies and Science to Students with Visual Impairments and Additional Disabilities

Strategies involving students with visual impairments and additional disabilities in science and social studies instruction require planning, creativity, and common sense. Emphasis should be placed on teaching students the concepts and strategies they need for exploring, discovering, and applying information that will increase their competence in performing tasks of daily living and in meeting the social expectations of their communities.

In teaching these students science and social studies content, the key is to provide life-based experiences, use adapted equipment and materials that will promote generalization across contexts, embed communication and choice-making opportunities throughout instruction, and ensure that instructional content is relevant and functional to the student's needs. Learning about life and the world "firsthand" through frequent and multiple examples and contexts is even more critical to this group of students than to students whose only impairment is visual. The following are strategies for doing so:

◆ Although class trips and experiences may have no apparent long-term relevance for the students, such opportunities may provide exposure to vocabulary, friendships, support resources, topics for communicative exchange, and simple sensory enjoyment. In addition, science and social studies lessons may encourage the expansion and refinement of other skills, such as greater attention to task, socialization, navigating transportation, mobility, reading, and mathematics. As promoted in this chapter, the students should be expected, either independently, with supervision, or through partial participation, to get their own materials, raise their hands or otherwise seek the instructor's attention appropriately, participate in discussions, and safely manipulate materials and equipment. Many of the materials and equipment recommended in this chapter may be used with students with additional disabilities with minor adjustments in the instructional process.

◆ The student should be expected to be an active participant in activities, making choices to select subtopics, materials, and classmates with whom to work; matching, sorting, sequencing, and assembling information relevant to the topic; and assuming responsibility for some component of a demonstration or report.

◆ Typical activities of a preschool science center are appropriate, fun, and relevant for preschoolers with visual impairments and additional disabilities. A student with limited postural and motor control can readily participate in activities that require decisions about the types of materials that are attracted by magnets and the types of materials that sink or float. The mediums of magnets and water require little physical effort, and often all that is needed is appropriate positioning equipment so that the student has sufficient stability to use his or her hands. A preschooler can also practice needed physical skills of postural control and arm-hand function by feeding fish and petting rabbits or gerbils. Many a

(continued on next page)

physically limited preschooler has been motivated by attempting to keep up with a hamster as it rolls about within a protected ball that contains a small bell. The use of a magnifying lens to view bugs and the structure of leaves may also be relevant to a preschooler with low vision and additional disabilities.

◆ Elementary school students may be involved in preparing plaster of paris or papier-mâché for the construction of a class-made volcano, communicating choices for colors and acknowledging whether more water is needed. Switch mechanisms to activate the volcano can be controlled by the student via either a simple jelly bean or motion-sensitive switch or an environmental control unit built into an augmentative system. Units on the rain forest may culminate in the construction of rain sticks. The student with limited hand function may team with a classmate who pours rice into an adapted measuring cup that pours the rice into prepared cardboard tubes when the student activates the switch that rotates the cup.

◆ Students at all levels can benefit from units on machines. For example, a student with additional disabilities may be paired with a classmate to read a print-braille book about selected machines. Similarly, in a lesson on constructing simple switches, the student may demonstrate the use of the switches to operate lights, fans, radios, paper shredders, and blenders.

◆ During a dissection or chemistry lesson, nonverbal students may be called on to direct critical components of the lesson by successively communicating the steps of the task through an augmentative device, such as a Four Frame Talker. Using such a device, the student presses each of four squares to which a picture or object symbol associated with the component of a task is attached. The step is spoken when the student presses the picture or object symbol.

◆ Elementary school students can respond to discussions about continents, oceans, animals, and land forms by interacting with their classmates through electronic teaching toys, such as the VTECH Little Smart Light-Up Map, which can be easily activated with minimal pressure and control.

◆ Middle- and high school students with visual impairments and additional disabilities can participate in projects designed to promote civic responsibilities by recruiting, sorting, packaging, and delivering donated toiletries to homeless shelters. A classmate may provide two samples of a needed item from which the student selects one.

◆ A nonverbal student may contribute to a lesson on civil rights by operating a computer that plays a selected portion of Martin Luther King's famous speech.

◆ Classmates can work together to program a student's augmentative system with responses to be used during a game of Jeopardy that is designed to reinforce lessons from a chapter on the Industrial Revolution. A teaching assistant or classmate may cue the student when to activate the system to respond to a specific question.

(continued on next page)

Strategies for Teaching Social Studies and Science *(Continued)*

◆ Contact the precinct in which the student would vote to determine when there may be less congestion during various elections. Give the student the experience of sitting in a voting booth and using a stylus to make choices. Often a sample ballot is available for others to familiarize them with the procedure. The student may practice social interaction, fine motor, scanning, and orientation skills during this experience in addition to practicing skills he or she may apply in voting at age 18. Follow-up activities could include visiting the courthouse to pick up a voter's registration application, completing the application, and mailing or returning it in person to the courthouse.

M. BETH LANGLEY
Pinellas County Schools
St. Petersburg, FL

R E S O U R C E S

Suggested Resources for Teaching Social Studies and Science

Resource	Type	Source	Description
Assessment Kit: Kit of Informal Tools for Academic Students with Visual Impairments (Sewell, 1997)	Teaching aid	Texas School for the Blind and Visually Impaired	A kit of assessment instruments addressing all areas of the curriculum for students with visual impairments, including science and social studies.
Basic Tactile Anatomy Atlas; Braille World Atlas; Graphic Aid for Mathematics; National Geographic Picture Atlas of the Fifty States	Learning aids	American Printing House for the Blind	A sample of the numerous tactile graphics materials available for instructing students.
Braille Formats: Principles of Print to Braille Transcription	Book	American Printing House for the Blind	Essential reference for braille formats. Describes and illustrates tables, boxed material, tests, time lines, and more.
Braille Lite and Type 'n Speak	Computer	Blazie Engineering	Electronic notetakers that work like a laptop computer with voice output in place of a screen.
Bumps-On	Learning aid, activity of daily living aid	Exceptional Teaching Aids	Raised "bumps" in two sizes, with adhesive backs; useful in recording data on charts in lab exercises, and for marking dials and touch buttons on appliances.
CCTV	Optical device	LS&S Group Lighthouse International Maxi Aids	Camera and "television" system in color or black and white, allows printed material, graphics, or small objects to be enlarged for viewing on a monitor.

(continued on next page)

Suggested Resources *(Continued)*

Resource	Type	Source	Description
Click Rule	Learning aid	National Federation of the Blind	A device for accurately measuring length; useful in many situations, including shop classes; other measuring devices are also available.
Compass (directional)	Learning aid, mobility aid	LS&S Group Maxi Aids Ann Morris Enterprises, Inc	Braille or talking compass indicates cardinal directions; useful for learning basic concepts, social studies concepts, and orientation and mobility skills.
Four Frame Talker	Augmented communication device	Program Development Associates	Augmented communication device with four message capability, using pictures and illustrations to active speech.
Graph sheets and progress charts	Learning aid	American Printing House for the Blind	Graph paper with raised lines; may be inserted in a braillewriter; useful for charting results in lab work. Bold-line version available as well.
Liquid level indicator	Learning aid, activity of daily living aid	LS&S Group Lighthouse International Maxi Aids	A device that hangs over the rim of a drinking cup or beaker in science labs; sound indicates when poured liquid nears the rim of the container.
Low vision and tactile graphics	Learning aids	TAEVIS (Tactile Access to Education for Visually Impaired Students) Purdue University, Office of the Dean of Students	An online source of 3,000+ diagrams useful in secondary-level biology, chemistry, physics, and math. Large-print versions for use by students with low vision; braille versions must be processed in a tactile image enhancer for use by braille readers.
Map Study I: Maps Represent Real Places Map Study II: Basic Map Reading Concepts Map Study: Recognizing Landforms	Learning aids	American Printing House	An assortment of tactile maps for the study of geography.
Mega Dots and Duxbury Braille Translators	Computer software	Duxbury Systems	Software for translating print to braille for printing on a braille computer.
NOMAD	Learning aid	American Printing House for the Blind	A touch-sensitive work surface used with tactile graphics and programmed speech.
One-Line Slate	Writing implement	Howe Press	A slate designed for writing on labeling tape; allows labels for maps and other tactile graphics to be produced.

(continued on next page)

Suggested Resources *(Continued)*

Resource	Type	Source	Description
Raised Line Drawing Kit	Learning aid	Howe Press	Similar to a clipboard with a rubber surface. Writing on plastic sheets with a ballpoint pen produces a raised line. Used for the quick production of tactile graphics; also allows students to draw.
Raised tactile image systems	Tactile graphics production equipment	Repro-Tronics HumanWare American Thermoform Corporation	A tool used to produce tactile graphics using microcapsule paper and black-and-white graphic images; a heat pen, also available, permits freehand drawing of raised images.
Rose Project	Student resource	Seedlings Braille Books	Provides encyclopedia articles in braille for students' projects and reports.
SAVI/SELPH modules	Science curriculum and materials	Lawrence Hall of Science, University of California, Berkeley	Units of instruction in science concepts and skills primarily for students with visual or physical impairments in grades 4–7; an assortment of tactile measurement tools accompany the modules or are available separately.
Science Curriculum for Deaf-Blind (Department for Deaf-Blind Children, n.d.)	Curriculum	Howe Press at Perkins School for the Blind	A curriculum guide, at four levels, to be used with students with cognitive development from ages 2 to about 9. Addresses Living Things, Earth and the Universe, Fantasy versus Reality, and more.
Tactile globes; world maps	Learning aid	American Printing House for the Blind Exceptional Teaching Aids	Globes and maps with tactile markings; check catalogs for details of the available maps.
Tactile Graphic Kit	Learning aid	American Printing House for the Blind	A kit for producing tactile images, including many tools and materials.
Tactile Graphics (Edman, 1992)	Book	American Foundation for the Blind	An encyclopedic handbook on translating visual information into tactile form that students who are visually impaired can understand. Essential for teachers who produce their own materials.
Tactile measurement tools	Learning aid	Lawrence Hall of Science, University of California, Berkeley	An assortment of adapted measurement aids, including overflow beakers, a graduated cylinder, syringes with fixed stops or notches cut in plungers, a balance with tactile marks, a *(continued on next page)*

Suggested Resources *(Continued)*

Resource	Type	Source	Description
		LS&S Group Maxi Aids	flexible meterstick, and a floating thermometer for liquids. Tactile kitchen scales and more. Syringes for measuring smaller fixed amounts of liquid, from 5 to 1 cc., among other items.
Tactile and talking timers	Learning aids, activity of daily living aids	LS&S Group Lighthouse International Maxi Aids	An assortment of clocks, watches, and timers, including "dial-types" appropriate for cooking, and digital devices for accurate measurement of small intervals, such as 10 seconds.
Videomicroscopy systems; microscope video systems	Optical device	Carolina Biological Supply Company Frey Scientific Science Products	Useful in biology lab work, several varieties of camera systems allow enlarged images of small objects or views through the lens of a microscope to be viewed on a computer monitor, television screen, or projection screen.
VTECH Little Smart Light-Up	Learning Aid	VTECH	A toy that provides visual, tactile and auditory stimulation.

Contact information for each of the resources listed will be found in the Sources of Products, Materials, Equipment, and Services section at the back of this book.

CHAPTER 10

Mathematics

Gaylen Kapperman, Toni Heinze, and Jodi Sticken

KEY POINTS

- ◆ An understanding of mathematics is essential for full participation in society.

- ◆ Students with visual impairments can gain a comprehension of basic mathematical concepts through the use of real objects and manipulatives.

- ◆ Students with visual impairments should be taught a number of options for performing arithmetic computations, including use of the braillewriter, abacus, and calculator.

- ◆ A thorough grounding in the Nemeth Code is essential for teachers of students with visual impairments, so they can teach this braille code for mathematics to their students and prepare accurate materials.

- ◆ Teachers of students with visual impairments teach the unique skills related to mathematics (such as using an abacus and tactile graphics) and collaborate with general education teachers to ensure that each student gains sound mathematical skills.

Portions of this chapter are reprinted from G. Kapperman, A. Heinze, & J. Sticken, Strategies for developing mathematics skills in students who use braille. *(Sycamore, IL: Research & Development Institute, 1997).*

VIGNETTE

"Give me the *big* cup, Eddie," said Ms. Powell. Eddie examined the cups, and held up the largest one. "Good, Eddie! That's the *big* one." Ms. Powell made a check on her checklist. Across the table, Mr. Day, the teacher of students with visual impairments, expressed satisfaction that Eddie was developing basic math concepts of size and number along with his preschool classmates.

Mr. Day remembered when Danielle was Eddie's age. Today, Danielle was in the fourth grade and keeping up with her class in math. She was adept at using the abacus and braillewriter for computation. She was learning how to interpret tactile line and bar graphs, and was using fraction models to aid in understanding equivalent fractions.

Mr. Day was contacted by Mr. Getz, the high school math teacher, regarding a situation that had arisen in one of his classes. Amber, one of the students enrolled in his second-year algebra class, was totally blind. Mr. Getz was about to introduce the topic of three-dimensional graphing. In the ensuing conversation, he asked Mr. Day for recommendations for helping Amber to master the concepts. Mr. Getz was at a loss as to how to present the concept to Amber in a meaningful way. Mr. Day realized that he could not use raised-line drawings to present a three-dimensional concept in a meaningful way to Amber. Thus he decided to construct a model of a three-dimensional graph using a shoe box. Three strings would represent three straight lines on the graph.

The next day Mr. Day returned with a shoe box and the necessary strings. He met with Amber and Mr. Getz. Mr. Day encouraged Amber to explore the model while he explained the concepts. Mr. Getz described the mathematical concepts he wanted Amber to grasp. After some discussion, both teachers were satisfied that Amber understood the general principles underpinning three-dimensional graphing.

INTRODUCTION

A thorough grounding in mathematics enhances educational and occupational opportunities for all people, whether sighted or visually impaired. In day-to-day routines, a practical understanding of mathematics allows a person to function more successfully and independently. People who have adequately developed mathematics skills are easily able to calculate the correct change they should receive when making a purchase, calculate the amount of interest one may pay on a loan, or add one-half cup and three-fourths cup to measure ingredients in a recipe. They can choose the basic mathematics operation or combination of operations to solve common problems in daily life. For example, they can balance their checkbooks or calculate the total travel time in a given bus route that involves one or more transfers.

Furthermore, effective instruction in mathematics provides students with access to the widest possible range of educational and employment opportunities. Examinations to assess educational progress as well as examinations administered to determine admission to various vocational and educational programs on every level usually contain quantitative subtests. Moreover, fundamental mathematics skills are essential for entry into the technical areas of employment that are and probably will continue to be fertile areas for career opportunities in today's world. In a society with an ever-increasing reliance on technology, the study of mathematics—the discipline that underpins all aspects of the broad field of technology—is increasingly important.

Because many aspects of mathematics are visual in nature, persons with visual impairments need to be able to integrate individual units of information mentally into an abstract whole. Thus, for students who are visually impaired to benefit from a thorough understanding of mathematics, their teachers of students with visual impairments must have a basic understanding of mathematics and know how best to present its concepts to them. In addition, these teachers must be skilled in collaborative consultation to work effectively with general education teachers and mathematics specialists.

In the case of students who read braille, it is essential that teachers of students with visual impairments be well prepared in the Nemeth Code, the braille code used for mathematics and science notation, to teach their students to read and write the symbols that underpin the study of mathematics and to direct the preparation of braille materials (Kapperman, 1994; Wittenstein, 1993). These teachers also need to understand the basic principles that guide the production of tactile materials, to ensure that their students have appropriate educational materials, such as graphs, charts, and diagrams.

In the case of students with low vision who read print, the study of mathematics follows an approach similar to that used by sighted students. The enlargement of printed materials or the use of low vision devices enables these students to master the subject more easily. Depending on a student's visual skills, basic mathematics concepts may be taught using manipulatives and concrete experiences in much the same way as they are taught to students who are blind.

This chapter explores the many issues involved in the study of mathematics by students with visual impairments, beginning with the role of the teacher of students with visual impairments. It describes strategies for assessing mathematics concepts and skills; teaching mathematical concepts, number facts and operations, the Nemeth Code, and calculation strategies; using mental arithmetic; making tactile displays; and including students in regular mathematics classes. It also includes an array of resources that can be used by those who wish to help students with visual impairments learn mathematics.

ROLE OF THE TEACHER OF STUDENTS WITH VISUAL IMPAIRMENTS

The teacher of students with visual impairments plays an essential role in ensuring that students who are visually impaired receive appropriate mathematics instruction and make steady gains in mathematics concepts and skills. The specialist must be fully cognizant of the unique aspects of mathematics for students with visual impairments—an abacus, tactile displays, the Nemeth Code, and so forth—and be able to teach these skills to his or her students. The key responsibilities are to:

♦ Use formal and informal strategies to assess mathematics concepts and skills, particularly those that are unique to students who are visually impaired (such as calculation with an abacus or braillewriter and the use of tactile displays);

♦ Teach students specialized computation methods, using an abacus, braillewriter, talking calculator, and mental math;

♦ Teach students the Nemeth Code sequentially and in meaningful contexts;

♦ Teach students to interpret and use tactile graphs, charts, and other displays;

♦ Provide consultation to general education teachers on appropriate methods for teaching mathematics to students who are visually impaired; and

♦ Provide general education teachers and students with appropriately modified learning materials and equipment for mathematics instruction, including tactile graphics.

The teacher also plays an essential role in working with students with additional disabilities; strate-

gies focusing on students with visual impairments and additional disabilities and resources for teachers appear later in this chapter.

ASSESSMENT

A subject-centered mathematics assessment, which may be administered by a general education teacher or a teacher of students with visual impairments, helps pinpoint a student's current level of functioning (see Chapters 2 and 3 for more information on assessments). In addition, it will provide information about specific areas in which the student needs targeted instruction (Meltzer et al., 1996). Many published achievement tests have mathematics subsections. In addition, criterion-referenced tests (tests containing questions or exercises pertaining to specific criteria or skills in a particular curriculum) are incorporated into mathematics textbooks and instructional materials. Any of these tests can be adapted by the teacher of students with visual impairments, using a combination of large print, braille, and/or oral administration, as appropriate, to assess a student's general level of performance in mathematics. Since some adaptations involve the use of manipulatives (concrete materials, such as blocks of various shapes and sizes, that can be used for counting, forming sets, comparing attributes, and computation) or graphic displays, it is important to ensure that a student has the ability to read and interpret such graphics before an assessment is conducted. It is also important for the teacher of students with visual impairments to review tests before the assessment to ensure that examples and graphics are meaningful to the student who is blind and to determine the need for manipulatives.

Students who are visually impaired may exhibit a high level of verbal fluency and auditory memory, which may be falsely interpreted as indications of a full understanding of concepts. Therefore, it is important for the specialist to consider carefully a student's mastery of mathematical concepts. Having students use skills to solve problems in everyday situations and explaining the steps they take and the rationale for those steps will provide evidence of their understanding. For example, a trip to a store to purchase items for use in teaching daily living skills can be used to teach and assess basic mathematical concepts. Estimation of the total cost, addition of the prices of items as they are added to the shopping cart, and checking that the change received is accurate are real-life challenges. The student must have mastered the concepts, as well as the facts in addition and subtraction, to succeed at such tasks.

In addition to analyzing specific areas in mathematics (through achievement and criterion–referenced tests) that may require further development, it is important to determine a student's mathematics learning style. As in other areas of study, many students have preferred means of mastering information. Some are auditory learners, some are visual or kinesthetic learners, and some are a combination of all three. Students have various levels of ability to master abstract concepts; many require manipulatives or practice in real-life applications to comprehend a particular concept, whereas others have a facility for abstract reasoning and problem solving. For example, some of the fundamental skills necessary for achievement in mathematics, such as learning to interpret material presented graphically, lend themselves more easily to a visual presentation and may be difficult to grasp for a student who has a primarily auditory learning style. Thus, the teacher of students with visual impairments needs to have a variety of strategies for presenting information to students.

If a student's learning style is known, effective instruction can be designed. To be successful in learning mathematics, a student must do the following:

♦ Develop the ability to retain (memorize) facts,

♦ Recognize patterns,

♦ Recognize relationships (part to whole and sequential and spatial concepts),

♦ Categorize and classify,

♦ Organize mathematical information,

♦ Have a basic awareness of when an answer is reasonable or possible,

♦ Think through a problem,

♦ Plan a solution and predict an outcome,

♦ Differentiate essential information from superfluous and irrelevant information, and

♦ Use mental flexibility to identify multiple ways to solve a problem.

The student's knowledge and use of the Nemeth Code and of appropriate calculation tools must also be assessed. Checklists, such as the Minnesota Braille Skills Inventory (Godwin et al., 1995) and the Braille Recognition Level Tests for Mathematics (Czerwinski, 1982), or teacher-designed checklists to address specific skills can provide information to document progress or pinpoint areas for instruction.

The teacher of students with visual impairments needs to understand that in some cases student's difficulty with mathematics may stem from seemingly unrelated learning difficulties, including problems with reading skills, language and communication skills, and attention problems. These difficulties may also create mathematics anxiety that, in turn, can impede learning. If a student is not progressing in mathematics at an appropriate rate, it would be wise to assess these areas to determine any contributing factors. Such an assessment may be accomplished by thinking through the following list to determine if a particular student does the following:

♦ Analyzes patterns,

♦ Recognizes part-whole relationships,

♦ Identifies relevant information and ignores irrelevant information,

♦ Understands mathematics-related vocabulary,

♦ Processes information and responds in an appropriate amount of time,

♦ Understands verbal directions,

♦ Reads problems independently,

♦ Accurately interprets words with multiple

meanings according to the context in which the words are used, and

- Understands the relationship among words, graphs or line drawings, and objects.

To determine whether a student has these skills, the teacher of students with visual impairments needs to use the principles and strategies of diagnostic teaching (see Chapter 3). With this approach, the teacher provides mathematics instruction and through this instruction explores areas of difficulty. For example, if a student is having difficulty completing word problems, the teacher can work through several problems with the student to see if the difficulty lies in reading and understanding the words or in computing the answer. Having the student "talk through" the completion of the problem and asking him or her questions will help identify the difficulty.

TEACHING MATHEMATICAL CONCEPTS

Strategies for Enhancing Mathematics Instruction

For children who are blind, direct teaching of mathematics concepts is essential; that is, the development of concepts must not be left to incidental learning. In some cases, the teacher of students with visual impairments should teach students specific mathematics concepts before they are introduced in the mathematics class to identify and address difficulties. In other cases, the specialist teaches with the general education teacher, demonstrating appropriate, hands-on techniques and the use of adaptive materials. For example, when the general education teacher is preparing to introduce concepts of measurement or money, the specialist can give the student who is visually impaired some prior experience in using the tools of measurement or identifying coins and currency.

The teacher of students with visual impairments should also encourage a student to be a self-advocate by teaching the student to articulate clearly what the general education teacher needs to do to allow him or her to participate in learning activities. An effective method for teaching a student to be a self-advocate is to set up situations in which the student can practice overcoming typical barriers to learning and participating in the general education setting. An occasional one-on-one lesson presented in the traditional format by the teacher of students with visual impairments (such as the teacher solving a problem on the chalkboard while the student "observes" and asks questions) can be used to generate problem-solving strategies and to practice the communication of special needs.

A topic that is rarely addressed is the issue of speaking about mathematics accurately so that a student who is blind can understand a sighted reader. In the *Handbook for Spoken Mathematics,* Chang (1983) presented a system to standardize the verbalization of mathematics. For example, the expression $a(b^4 + c)^2$ should be read: "*a* open paren *b* to the fourth power plus *c* close paren to the second power." The guidelines dictate that spoken mathematics should be consistent and unambiguous, using a fixed vocabulary that is not impromptu. Each individual mathematical symbol must have *only one* specific name. It is recommended that this system be taught to students who are blind. In that way, they can train readers in the use of the system once they use higher-level mathematics independently.

Number Sense

Number sense is a largely intuitive ability to attach meaning to numbers and number relationships; to understand the magnitude of numbers, as well as the relativity of measuring numbers; and to use logical reasoning for estimation. Although some ability to understand numbers may be intuitive, this ability also uses many visual referents. A sighted child can immediately compare and analyze groups of objects; the child who is blind or visually impaired must explore the same groups in parts before being able to draw conclusions about similarities and differences. For this reason, although there are many incidental opportunities for young children to use number sense in their daily lives, children with visual impairments need to be deliberately guided through opportunities for exploring, comparing, ordering, and problem solving in the real world to allow for a natural development of number sense. Such opportunities also cultivate a positive attitude toward mathematics and facilitate a child's achievement and confidence. The following are a few suggestions:

◆ Provide many opportunities for students to explore groups of objects that can be perceived with one or two hands to compare the relative size of groups of things.

◆ Provide many opportunities for students to count both small and large groups of objects.

◆ Provide extensive opportunities to match the number of objects to fingers.

◆ Talk about numbers: how many, how many more or less, how many more are needed.

◆ Assign number names to groups of objects that are dissimilar in size or shape for experience with the concept of quantity and the comparison of quantity.

For students to understand and work with formal mathematical concepts successfully, they must understand these concepts:

◆ Classification (discrimination, matching, categorizing);

◆ Seriation (ordering objects, quantities, and numbers according to specific criteria);

◆ Conservation (a given amount remains the same though its appearance may change); and

◆ Position in space (such as top, bottom, around, beside).

Students must first work with and understand these concepts on the basis of quality or attributes (such as shape, size, and weight), then different criteria (such as more or less), and finally number attributes (for example, $100 = 10 \times 10$, $4 + 1 = 1 + 4$). For instance, for the concept of conservation, a student could be given a certain amount of clay (an example of size or weight). He or she could then reshape it or break it into two pieces and be asked whether he or she has more or less or the same amount. Finally he or she could work with numbers, such as 4 ounces = 2 + 2 ounces or 1 + 3 ounces.

To develop mathematical concepts, students must have numerous and varied interactions with their environment—exploring, comparing, and arranging real sets of concrete objects—before they move to symbolic representations. As was stated earlier, these interactions must be deliberately guided for a student who is blind, not left to incidental learning. Responsibility for routine chores in the home or classroom can provide opportunities for comparing the size of towels, plates, boxes, and clothing. Guiding students in matching and categorizing everyday items (such as eating utensils, grooming tools, foods, and toys) according to function is also helpful, as is arranging items according to sets and then rearranging these sets to be smaller, larger, or empty.

When students have demonstrated a basic sense of numbers, including one-to-one correspondence, and are ready to develop the skill of counting, they can benefit from learning several counting strategies. Three strategies are:

◆ Scanning—moving one's hands across the top of each item to gather information about the objects and their arrangement;

◆ Organizing—moving randomly displayed items to one side in preparation for counting or locating the first item in a linear series and scanning to confirm the arrangement; and

◆ Separating or partitioning—keeping track of items that have been counted by placing them in a separate area on a tray or touching each item as it is counted while the other hand keeps track of the next item to be counted.

Students sometimes develop one or more such strategies on their own, but it is beneficial to provide training in this area. As with any concept or skill, it is important to start working with real objects and manipulatives and to continue providing them as learning aids for students who are visually impaired. Another technique is to pair the use of manipulatives, oral counting, and number statements with the representation of these numbers on paper. For example, students can act out word problems and can arrange materials in sets or express number statements and then write these number statements on a braillewriter or set them on an abacus. Students with low vision can write the number statements on paper or arrange stickers with numbers and signs of operation to correspond to the number statements.

TEACHING THE USE OF MEASUREMENT TOOLS

It is critical to teach students about the availability and appropriate use of tools of measurement, such as those that measure length, weight, and volume. Ideally, students should be exposed to a broad range of tools, including those that are not specifically produced for use by persons with visual impairments but that can be inexpensively modified if necessary, such as by marking a standard ruler with braille. Mainstream, unadapted tools should be used, whenever possible, since they are the least expensive and easiest to obtain, but students need to be aware of all that is available so they can make informed choices in the future. Instruction should include background information on the purpose of the tool, where or how to purchase it, and the approximate cost. (Sources of adapted tools and measuring devices appear in the Resources section in this chapter.) Specific in-

struction in the proper use of the tool should be followed by multiple opportunities to use it in a functional application, either in the direct solution of mathematics problems or in activities of daily living.

Teaching students with visual impairments to use measuring devices requires students to have hands-on experiences with real objects. For example, to teach a student who is blind to measure with a braille ruler, the teacher of students with visual impairments can begin by having the student measure a three-dimensional object with a flat edge, such as a textbook or shoe box. Using hand-over-hand guidance, if needed, the teacher can then have the student align the ruler along the edge of the object being measured, making sure that the starting point of the ruler is placed exactly at one end of the object. Holding the ruler with one hand, use the other hand to find the opposite end of the object. Finally, move the finger that has located the end of the object over the top of the ruler and read the braille number. After the student has mastered the basics of measuring three-dimensional objects, measuring raised lines is generally the next step.

A caliper slide—a small metal clip that is attached to a braille ruler that slides (with enough resistance to hold its position) back and forth along the length of the ruler—is ideal for measuring an object precisely. After one edge of the ruler is aligned with one end of the object being measured, the caliper slide is moved to a position that matches the other end of the object. Then the ruler can be taken away to allow a student who reads braille to examine the numbers and marks between the numbers. If a caliper slide is not available, a rubber band twisted securely around the ruler and positioned at the far end of the object makes a good substitute.

TEACHING BASIC NUMBER FACTS AND OPERATIONS

It is important for students to consider mathematics and the calculations they perform as part of their daily lives. Providing opportunities to apply basic concepts and operations in real-life situations reinforces students' skills and motivates them to progress in mathematics. Emphasis should be placed on the development of concepts, as well as processes and rote memorization. A primary area of attention for mathematics instruction for students who are visually impaired is that of fractions and decimals.

Grasping the fundamental concepts underlying the addition, subtraction, multiplication, and division of fractions is difficult for many students. Students with visual impairments need ample experience with manipulatives depicting concepts related to fractions. Such models should represent a variety of examples. For instance, a model of a circle divided in half does not provide sufficient experience with the concept of one-half. Students also need to have experience with tactile models of other shapes, such as triangles, hearts, stars, squares, or rectangles, that can be divided in half vertically, horizontally, and diagonally to demonstrate this concept.

A teacher can teach a student to calculate the correct answers to problems containing fractions, but being able to complete the operations correctly does not guarantee that the student has a fundamental understanding of the meaning of the four basic mathematical operations as they pertain to fractions. The use of manipulatives to illustrate the basic operations in which fractions are involved enhances the understanding of all students, but especially that of students who are blind. The following strategies illustrate that point:

◆ The student should be instructed that the symbols between the opening fraction indicator (dots 1–4–5–6) and the fraction line (dots 3–4) constitute the entire numerator and the symbols between the fraction line and the closing fraction indicator (dots 3–4–5–6) constitute the entire denominator.

◆ With regard to the order of operations, students need to learn that all computations above the horizontal fraction line are to be completed and all computations below the horizontal fraction line are to be completed before they divide the numerator by the denominator.

◆ To teach a student to add 3/4 and 1/2, the teacher may use two cardboard circles divided into fourths. Three pieces from one circle represent 3/4, and two pieces from the other circle represent 1/2. Bringing the three pieces (3/4) together with the two other pieces (1/2) results in a total of five pieces (5/4). The pieces can be reassembled into one whole circle comprised of four pieces, with an additional single piece representing 1/4. The answer is thus 1 1/4. The manipulation of the pieces provides concrete evidence of the concept of adding fractions.

◆ In subtracting 1/2 from 3/4, a similar activity would be effective. In this case, three pieces would be displayed. To subtract 1/2 from 3/4, one would simply remove two of the pieces, representing 2/4 (1/2). The remaining piece, then, is the answer: 1/4.

The multiplication and division of fractions are more complex operations for all students to understand because their meanings are not intuitively apparent. The use of manipulatives makes these concepts much easier to grasp.

◆ Multiplying 1/2 times 3/4 actually is asking the question, What is 1/2 of 3/4? To illustrate this point, a cardboard circle is divided into eighths. To convert the fraction 3/4 to 6/8, six pieces of the circle are used, each of which constitutes 1/8 of the circle. One-half of 6 is 3. Thus, multiplying 1/2 times 3/4 is 3/8.

◆ Dividing 3/4 by 1/2 is really asking, How many 1/2s are in 3/4? Once again, the teacher can display a partial circle with three 1/4 pieces. Two of these 1/4 pieces are removed, representing one 1/2. The remaining piece represents 1/4. The fraction 1/4 is one-half of 1/2; thus, there are 1 1/2 1/2s in 3/4.

TEACHING ADVANCED MATHEMATICS

Several important points should be considered when students with visual impairments study advanced mathematics. The first and most important is that the students must be proficient in the Nemeth Code. Without a good command of Nemeth Code symbols and the rules that govern their use, it is nearly impossible to master algebra, geometry, trigonometry, or calculus. The tasks required in the study of these subjects cannot be carried out mentally. (For further information, see the next section on teaching the Nemeth Code.)

The second point to keep in mind is that, when possible, efforts should be made to illustrate the problems for students who are blind or severely visually impaired in such a fashion that they have experience with the principles involved. To make the problems more meaningful, students may be asked to reenact the actions represented in the problems. For example, two students may be asked to reenact a problem in which two trains leave the station at different times, each train traveling at a different rate. The question to be answered is: How long will it take the second train, traveling at a faster rate, to overtake the first train? The two students can represent the two trains. The first student begins walking at a slow pace from the starting point (such as one wall of the classroom). Shortly thereafter, the second student, beginning at the same point, walks forward at a faster pace. It is then noted how long it took the second student to overtake the first student.

In other situations, students can manipulate objects that represent the concepts being studied. When students cannot see printed material and graphic displays, other methods can be used to enable them to grasp the underlying concepts. If visual displays, for example, depict three-dimensional objects, then real objects should be used to represent them. Attempting to illustrate a three-dimensional object on a two-dimensional plane in tactile form is not sufficient to enable the tactile reader to discern the meaning of the display. Likewise, verbal description alone is inadequate to convey such underlying visual concepts. Thus, students who cannot view graphic displays visually must be given the opportunity to examine tangible representations of those graphic displays.

Because geometry is highly visual, it poses a particular challenge to instructors attempting to represent the various visual concepts in a form that can be appreciated by students who cannot see them. Two-dimensional concepts can be represented in tactile form on a two-dimensional plane fairly easily. However, it must be kept in mind that these depictions should be produced in relatively simple form. A tactile display that is too complex is often so difficult to analyze tactually that it is of little or no value.

The greater challenge is to represent three-dimensional concepts that cannot be adequately represented on a two-dimensional plane. Thus, tangible objects must be used. In exploring both two-dimensional and three-dimensional concepts, a knowledgeable person should guide the student. It is unwise merely to give a student the tangible objects without accompanying them with detailed, guided explanations. This is a time-consuming procedure, but without the explanation, the student will benefit little from access to the materials.

For example, the following strategy can be used to help a student who is severely visually impaired grasp the concept of three-dimensional graphing. This concept cannot be depicted in tactile form (a raised-line drawing) on a two-dimensional plane (a piece of paper). A shoe box can be used to represent the three-dimensional graph. Three strings can be attached at different points on the sides of the shoe box and positioned so they intersect. The student can explore the model using his or her hands and fingers. The point at which the three strings cross represents the solution of the three equations that the strings represent. This method does not produce the exact solution to the equations, but, rather, helps the student to grasp the concept of three-dimensional graphing.

For students with low vision who can visualize graphic displays, adaptations or modifications should be made as necessary to ensure that the students have access to the materials that display the visual concepts. Students who have severe visual impairments, however, experience some of the same challenges in studying mathematics as do those who are totally blind. In these cases, the students will benefit from two- and three-dimensional models. Students with low vision can be assisted by the following:

◆ Providing a defined work area by presenting materials on a high-contrast mat or work tray.

◆ Teaching a student to search the field systematically, to ensure that all parts are accessed.

◆ Using a logical sequence of difficulty in presenting tasks:

1. Begin with a whole object such as a three-dimensional model with removable pieces representing volume. Instruct the student to remove parts and then replace them correctly.

2. Present the same object with several parts removed. Instruct the student to reconstruct the whole.

3. Present only the parts; instruct the student to build the whole.

Adaptations for a student with low vision may include teaching the student to carry out systematic search patterns similar to those recommended for tactile readers. The visibility of the materials can be enhanced by enlarging them, darkening certain lines, or changing the color to suit a student's needs. In addition, by experimenting with lighting, contrast, and various levels of magnification, the teacher of students with visual impairments can provide the optimum conditions for a particular student. In the case of complex graphic patterns, the display can be simplified by eliminating unnecessary visual information.

The final point about the study of advanced mathematics is that it should be as efficient as possible. Since students with visual impairments generally require more time to study and to complete exercises than do their sighted counterparts, steps should be taken to enable them to complete their work efficiently. One way to do so is to allow the students to use calculators to carry out the computational portions of problems in advanced mathematics, rather than to use braillewriters to accomplish this task. (For more information, see the later section on the use of calculation tools.) One must bear in mind that the goal should be mastery of the underlying mathematical concepts. In advanced courses, students are not learning basic arithmetic operations, so the use of the calculator allows them to concentrate on higher-level skills.

TEACHING THE NEMETH CODE

The Nemeth Code of Braille Mathematics and Science Notation, developed by Abraham Nemeth to transcribe the symbols that underpin mathematics and science, was officially adopted for use in the United States in 1956 (Nemeth, 1962). It was subsequently revised and is updated periodically. The literary braille code consists of 63 different braille symbols using the six dots of the braille cell, along with the rules for their use. To write mathematics and science notation, it is necessary to use the same symbols governed by different rules. For example, the *th* sign (dots 1-4-5-6) in the literary code is the opening simple fraction indicator in the Nemeth Code. Sidebar 10.1 presents some common Nemeth Code symbols.

Students should always be presented with flawless braille mathematics. Furthermore, in teaching the structure and function of the symbols that make up the Nemeth Code, the teacher of students with visual impairments should strictly adhere to the code's rules. If a teacher changes the written forms of the symbols, considerable confusion will arise when students read properly transcribed mathematics. Therefore, no matter how awkward some of the symbols may appear when first encountered, their proper form should be maintained. When one reads material written in the literary code that contains errors, the correct meaning can usually be determined

Common Nemeth Code Symbols

Numeric indicator (dots 3-4-5-6)	⠼	no print equivalent
Numerals		
1 (dot 2)	⠼⠁	1
2 (dots 2-3)	⠼⠃	2
3 (dots 2-5)	⠼⠉	3
4 (dots 2-5-6)	⠼⠙	4
5 (dots 2-6)	⠼⠑	5
6 (dots 2-3-5)	⠼⠋	6
7 (dots 2-3-5-6)	⠼⠛	7
8 (dots 2-3-6)	⠼⠓	8
9 (dots 3-5)	⠼⠊	9
0 (dots 3-5-6)	⠼⠚	0
Mathematical comma (dot 6)	⠠	,
Decimal point (dots 4-6)	⠨	.
Equals (dots 4-6, 1-3)	⠨⠅	=
Greater than (dots 4-6, 2)	⠨⠂	>
Less than (dots 5, 1-3)	⠐⠅	<
Addition (dots 3-4-6)	⠬	+
Separation line (dots 2-5, 2-5, 2-5,etc.)	⠒⠒⠒	___
Subtraction (dots 3-6)	⠤	−
Multiplication × (dots 4, 1-6)	⠈⠡	×
Multiplication dot (dots 1-6)	⠡	·
Division symbol (dots 4-6, 3-4)	⠨⠌	÷
Cent sign (dots 4, 1-4)	⠈⠉	¢
Dollar sign (dots 4, 2-3-4)	⠈⠎	$
Shape indicator (dots 1-2-4-6)	⠫	no print equivalent
Circle (dots 1-2-4-6, 1-4)	⠫⠉	○
Rectangle (dots 1-2-4-6, 1-2-3-5)	⠫⠗	▭
Triangle (dots 1-2-4-6, 2-3-4-5)	⠫⠞	△
Square (dots 1-2-4-6, 2-5-6)	⠫⠳	□

(continued on next page)

Common Nemeth Code Symbols *(Continued)*

Simple fraction indicator:

Opening (dots 1-4-5-6)	⠹	no print equivalent
Closing (dots 3-4-5-6)	⠼	no print equivalent
Horizontal fraction line (dots 3-4)	⠌	——
Diagonal fraction line (dots 4-5-6, 3-4)	⠸⠌	/

Mixed number indicator:

Opening (dots 4-5-6, 1-4-5-6)	⠸⠹	no print equivalent
Closing (dots 4-5-6, 3-4-5-6)	⠸⠼	no print equivalent
Degree[1] (dots 4-6, 1-6)	⠠⠡	°

Parentheses:

Opening (dots 1-2-3-5-6)	⠷	(
Closing (dots 2-3-4-5-6)	⠾	)
Percent (dots 4, 3-5-6)	⠈⠴	%
Punctuation indicator (dots 4-5-6)	⠸	no print equivalent
Radical sign (dots 3-4-5)	⠜	√‾
With termination sign (dots 1-2-4-5-6)	⠻	no print equivalent
Superscript indicator (dots 4-5)	⠘	no print equivalent
Subscript indicator (dots 5-6)	⠰	no print equivalent
Baseline indicator (dot 5)	⠐	no print equivalent

[1] Must be preceded by the superscript indicator (dots 4-5).

through the use of context clues. However, there are no context clues when reading mathematical symbols. Thus, it is essential that the braille mathematics symbols are precise and accurate.

There is one area of braille mathematics, however, in which changes should be made in both the form of the symbols and the format: the use of the braillewriter to calculate addition, subtraction, multiplication, or division problems that are spatially arranged. If one rigidly adheres to the strict transcription rules when using the braillewriter as a calculation tool (see the later section on calcula-

tion tools), the task will be much more challenging than necessary.

The mechanics of teaching Nemeth Code symbols is relatively straightforward, but requires preplanning and preteaching by the teacher of students with visual impairments. That is, the teacher needs to preview upcoming instructional units in a student's mathematics textbook to discover mathematical symbols that the student may have not yet learned and develop simple lessons to teach those braille symbols and their proper use before the student encounters them in his or her textbook. Such preteaching is especially important for symbols that do not have print equivalents, such as the baseline indicator (dot 5), the superscript indicator (dots 4-5), the subscript indicator (dots 5-6), the opening fraction indicator (dots 1-4-5-6), and the closing fraction indicator (dots 3-4-5-6).

In advanced mathematics courses, the teacher of students with visual impairments is not expected to know the precise meaning of each print symbol. Instead, he or she should consult with the regular mathematics teacher to ensure that the symbols have been correctly interpreted by the student who is blind. It is imperative that the specialist and the mathematics teacher collaborate in these situations.

Learning the Nemeth Code

As already indicated, well-developed knowledge of the Nemeth Code is essential for the delivery of effective instruction in mathematics for youngsters who are blind. Teachers who want to learn the code or refresh their skills can do so in several ways. One way is to obtain instructional texts from the American Printing House for the Blind (APH). Another is to use software tutorials, such as, *The Computerized Nemeth Code Tutor,* available from the Association for Education and Rehabilitation of the Blind and Visually Impaired (AER). (See the Resources section in this chapter for these and other options for learning the Nemeth Code.)

Production of Nemeth Code Materials

The knowledgeable teacher of students with visual impairments or braille transcriber can produce Nemeth Code materials using a braillewriter. In addition, braille translation software exists to translate mathematical information into the Nemeth Code. The two most commonly used programs are MegaDots and Duxbury Braille Translator by Duxbury Systems (see the Resources section in this chapter for the sources of these products). An individual can input mathematical

expressions into a computer using a keyboard, scanner, or voice-recognition software. The Mathematics Accessible to Visually Impaired Students (MAVIS) project, headquartered at New Mexico State University, developed software using Scientific Notebook, a common mathematics and science word-processing program, to make it possible to type higher level mathematical symbols using a standard keyboard. Those expressions can then be translated into accurate Nemeth code symbols with the use of braille translation software, and hard copy braille can be produced using a braille printer.

The computer keyboard can also be converted into a Perkins style keyboard, and Nemeth Code expressions can be directly inputted using six keys and the space bar of any keyboard. These methods have made the production of accurate Nemeth Code materials much more efficient than in the past.

TEACHING THE USE OF CALCULATION TOOLS AND AIDS

According to the National Council of Teachers of Mathematics (1989), all students need meaningful instruction in mathematics with appropriate tools. It is particularly important for students with visual impairments to be exposed to the use of multiple mathematics strategies and tools, including the braillewriter, abacus, talking calculators, mental mathematics, fingermath, and the calculator function of electronic note-taking devices. These strategies and tools should be introduced early in a student's educational program and continually reinforced throughout the school years.

This section describes the use of and recommended sequence of instruction in the various tools for arithmetic calculation and the specific advantages and disadvantages of each tool. In addition, it presents suggestions for integrating these tools into the overall mathematics instruction program.

The braillewriter is an essential calculation

tool for students who are blind to understand the fundamental steps involved in the four basic operations; those who rely solely on the talking calculator have no opportunity to learn these steps. The abacus is an excellent tool for teaching the steps involved in arithmetic operations, but it does not give a student the opportunity to emulate how sighted students perform these operations. Therefore, it should be taught simultaneously with the braillewriter. Similarly, as the mathematical concepts become more complex and after the student has mastered the basic operations, greater reliance can be placed on the talking calculator.

The Braillewriter

Of all the available tools, the braillewriter is the most time consuming and cumbersome to use to perform calculations (Kapperman, 1974). Using the braillewriter for this purpose is analogous to a sighted student completing mathematical calculations with a typewriter. Given this analogy, why spend the extra time and effort needed to teach the use of the braillewriter as a calculation tool? The answer is, as indicated earlier, that students who are blind benefit from knowing the steps that are required to carry out arithmetic calculations in this manner. In general, although the use of the braillewriter as a calculation tool should not be heavily emphasized, it should be introduced at the beginning of mathematics instruction, followed by instruction in the use of other tools.

The teacher of students with visual impairments should ensure that calculations with the braillewriter are accomplished as easily as possible. To do so, the teacher needs to make alterations in the format and the use of symbols. The recommended changes in the methods for performing arithmetic calculations, as well as in the strict rules for transcribing the Nemeth Code, make it easier for students to carry out the necessary steps to add, subtract, multiply, and divide with the braillewriter.

As an example, Sidebar 10.2 (item a) presents an addition problem that is transcribed in braille according to the strict rules for transcription. To simplify this problem using the braillewriter as a calculation tool, the following procedure is recommended. An addition problem is copied from the student's braille textbook. The item identifier (number of the problem) is written according to the Nemeth Code rules, beginning with the numeric indicator (dots 3-4-5-6), followed by the Nemeth Code number, the punctuation indicator (dots 4-5-6), and the period. Two spaces are left between the period and the first addend (the first number in the list of numbers). No numeric indicators are placed before any of the numbers in the problem, including the answer.

Immediately below the first addend, subsequent addends are brailled. These numbers are placed in the proper columns, as they would be in print. A blank line is left under the last addend. Neither the horizontal line that separates the addends from the answer (a line of dots 2-5) nor the sign of operation (such as a plus sign) are brailled, since it is clear from the written exercise that this is an addition problem. The principle to follow is to braille as little as possible in order to save time. However, sufficient symbols must be brailled to make the steps in the operation clear. To leave a blank line below the last addend, tap the paper advance key twice after the last addend has been brailled. The embossing head of the braillewriter should then be positioned in the units column. The student can use his or her finger to make certain that he or she feels the embossing head pointing to the units column.

After the embossing head of the braillewriter has been positioned correctly, the calculation can begin. The student reads the numerals in the proper column, adding them as they are read. He or she then writes the units number of the answer and backspaces twice to position the embossing head in the tens column. If there is a number to "carry over" (regroup), the student must remember that value. He or she then adds that value to the number at the beginning of the tens column and proceeds down the column, adding the numbers as they appear under his or her finger. If the student has difficulty holding the regrouped number in his or her memory, an abacus can be used to store it temporarily.

SIDEBAR 10.2

Sample Addition Problem in Nemeth Code

a. As written in a strict Nemeth Code format:

1. $\overset{1}{78}$
       $\underline{+37}$
       115

b. As written on the braillewriter by a student for computation purposes:

1.   78
       37

       115

       ans. = #115

The student then writes the number and backspaces twice. This procedure is repeated until the operation is complete. The teacher may wish to have the student clarify which number is the final answer by having the student rewrite it below the problem as follows: ans. = the number, with a numeric indicator preceding it. (See item b in Sidebar 10.2 for an example of this format.) For a detailed description of the recommended approach to be used in carrying out the four basic operations with whole numbers, decimals, and fractions, see Kapperman, Heinze, and Sticken (1997).

The Abacus

The abacus is a useful calculation tool—whether used alone or in conjunction with other devices—because of its speed, accuracy, portability, and flexibility. (See the Basics of the Abacus in Sidebar 10.3.) The Cranmer abacus is adapted for efficient use by persons who are blind. These adaptations include a felt liner under the rods and beads to prevent the beads from sliding if the abacus is accidentally moved, raised vertical notches to guide the placement of decimals and commas, and raised dots to reinforce place value. Since the Cranmer abacus is manipulated concretely, its use leads to a more meaningful understanding of numbers than does the use of calculators.

Familiarity with the abacus should start in the primary grades to develop number concepts as soon as a student acquires the fine motor skills necessary for manipulating the beads. A student who has difficulty in this area may begin instruction on an enlarged Cranmer abacus that has larger beads and greater space between the beads and makes the transition to a standard abacus when appropriate. The concepts of sets and place value can be reinforced with the abacus. A student can arrange and rearrange sets and then set numbers and number statements (for example, identify a set of 4 and set 4 on the abacus, identify a set of 6 using a bundle of 5 and a 6th item and then set 6 on the abacus, arrange a set of 4 by combining 2 and 2 and then set 2 + 2 on the abacus, and identify a set of 12 using a bundle of 10 and 2 more items and then set a 10 bead and 2 unit beads on the abacus).

Students should have many opportunities to discover the "partners" that make up numbers, that is, the various pairs of numbers that can be added together to make up a number. Because the abacus uses beads with a value of 5 as well as of 1, and because the columns are in multiples of 10, as in standard print notation, knowledge of the partners of the numbers 5 and 10 are absolutely necessary for understanding computational operations on the abacus. They can arrange and rearrange sets to discover that 5 = 2 + 3, 5 = 3 + 2, 5 = 4 + 1, or 5 = 1 + 4 and that 10 = 7 + 3, 10 = 5 + 5, 10 = 2 + 8 and so forth. After these number statements are set on the abacus, a student will be in a position to begin simple computation.

A teacher's competence and attitude have a great impact on a student's potential for success with the abacus. Therefore, a teacher must be skilled in the use of the abacus, convey a positive attitude toward it, and demonstrate its relevance to the student.

There are several approaches to teaching the use of the abacus. Since one method may not work as effectively for all students, teachers of students with visual impairments need to be familiar with several methods and can adapt or combine the methods, if necessary. Students can learn to work problems on the abacus in the traditional manner (moving from left to right) or they can move from right to left to coincide with the general education teacher's demonstration of problems on the chalkboard or with other students' writing with paper and pencil. The three commonly used approaches are partners or logic, secrets, and counting.

Partners or Logic. This approach focuses on understanding the "what" and "why" of the steps in solving a problem on the abacus and requires a student to know the partners or complements of

---

The Basics of the Abacus

SIDEBAR 10.3

The abacus is arranged in 13 columns, each consisting of one bead above the separation bar and four beads below it. The columns correspond to the columns in written numbers. Thus, the column on the far right is the units column, the next column to the left is the 10s column, the third column is the hundreds, and so on, with each column increasing by a value of 10.

The four beads below the separation bar each represent a value of 1. The single bead above the bar represents a value of 5. To represent numbers on the abacus, a person moves the beads toward the separation bar. To clear the numbers, he or she moves them away from the bar. Thus, the maximum value that can be set in a column, when the top bead is moved down to the separation bar and all four beads on the bottom are moved up, is 9, just as in a written column of numbers.

Source: Adapted from P. E. Ponchillia and S. V. Ponchillia, Eds., *Foundations of Rehabilitation Teaching with Persons Who Are Blind or Visually Impaired* (New York: AFB Press, 1996), pp. 201–202.

---

the numbers up to 10 (such as 5 = 2 + 3, 5 = 1 + 4) and to understand the logical concepts involved in computational processes. Verbalizing the steps and the reasons for each movement of the beads is an important feature of this approach. Initially, the teacher explains each step as the student works through a problem. Next, the student verbalizes the process; eventually, this "conversation" can be shortened until, ultimately, the process is internalized. The following two examples demonstrate two ways in which a teacher might verbalize the steps:

The problem is 3 + 4. What number comes first? The answer is 3. So we set 3 on the abacus. Now we need to add 4. Do we have 4 more ones to add? No. Since we don't have enough ones to add, we can add the 5 bead (set 5). But 5 is too many; we only want to add 4. So we'll have to clear the extra bead or beads. What is 4's partner in 5? The answer is 1. So we'll clear one extra bead. Now what is our answer? The answer is 7.

The problem is 3 + 4. What number comes first? The answer is 3. Set 3 on the abacus. Can you add 4 directly? No. What is the smallest amount that can be set that is greater than 4? The answer is 5. Set the 5 bead. How many more than 4 is 5? The answer is 1. Clear 1 bead. What is the answer? The answer is 7.

Secrets. The use of secrets focuses on the process of moving the abacus beads in a particular sequence, following a specific set of rules for different numbers and operations. This approach and terminology, taken from the original method developed in Japan, emphasizes rote memory of the bead movements, rather than an understanding of the logical process. It is an appropriate method to use with students who have difficulty understanding the principles behind each step of the process. The following example shows the use of secrets:

The problem is 3 + 4. What number comes first? The answer is 3. So set 3 (raise 3 "earth" counters, those beads below the separation bar). Now we want to add 4. To do that, we must set 5 (bring down a "heaven" counter, the bead above the separation bar) and clear 1 (clear 1 earth counter). What is our answer? The answer is 7.

Counting. Counting requires the student to count each bead as it is added or subtracted. There are specific rules regarding certain numbers and operations, but fewer than the full set of "secrets." This approach is another alternative for students who have difficulty understanding the principles behind each step of the process. The following example shows the use of counting:

The problem is 3 + 4. What number comes first? The answer is 3, so we set 3. Now we want to add 4. To do that, we push up another unit bead (count 1), then push down the bead above the counting bar (count 2), and clear all 4 beads under the counting bar. Then push up a bead (count 3). Finally, we push up 1 more unit bead (count 4). What is the answer? The answer is 7.

The specific techniques in using the abacus as a calculation device are beyond the scope of this chapter. However, a teacher can use a number of comprehensive resources in developing these skills. To learn more about using partners or logic, readers can refer to *The Abacus Made Easy* (Davidow, 1988) and *Use of the Cranmer Abacus* (Livingston, 1997). To learn more about the use of "secrets," readers can refer to *The Japanese Abacus: Its Use and Theory* (Kojima, 1955). For more about the counting method, *Abacus Basic Competency* (Millaway, 1994) and *Use of the Cranmer Abacus* (Livingston, 1997) are helpful sources of information. The sources of all these books are listed in the Resources for this chapter.

Talking Calculators

During initial instruction in arithmetic operations, manipulatives, paper and pencil or the braillewriter, and the abacus are the major tools used in calculations. The talking calculator should be used only as a reinforcer for skills learned using one of these approaches until a student masters the fundamental concepts involved in computation. Sighted students are typically expected to have mastered all the basic facts of addition, subtraction, multiplication, and division by the end of the fourth grade. This same expectation should exist for academically functioning students who are visually impaired. As a student demonstrates his or her understanding of basic mathematics concepts, progressively more emphasis should be placed on the use of the talking calculator.

Talking calculators may be used in educational settings to do the following:

◆ Practice basic facts;

- Improve the speed and accuracy of computational skills;

- Provide a competitive calculation tool for students who have mastered basic operations;

- Provide an alternative to the abacus;

- Offer an alternative for advanced mathematics and science calculations that are too complex for computation with the braillewriter;

- Provide benefits to students with motor disabilities that impede the use of the abacus or with cognitive disabilities that hinder the comprehension of mathematical concepts or rote learning;

- Offer the advantage of checking one's computation, whether using mental math or other aids, such as the abacus; and

- Assist with other school subjects, such as bookkeeping, business, geography, and cooking.

Eventually, the talking calculator is likely to be the student's major tool for performing calculations, especially in advanced mathematics (such as algebra), in which emphasis is placed on learning content far advanced from the simple performance of arithmetic calculations. The teacher of students with visual impairments needs to make sure that each student has the most efficient tool to use so he or she is not expending inordinate amounts of time performing arithmetic calculations, rather than mastering the subject matter.

Considerations for Use

A variety of calculators with distinct characteristics are available to help with a number of unique tasks, including the calculator functions of electronic note-taking devices. The following characteristics are desirable:

- Large separated keys for increased accuracy,

- Adjustable volume and speed of auditory output,

- Headphone or earbuds, and

- Consideration of size and contrast of the numbers in the visual display and on the keys for a student with low vision.

Although the talking calculator is the most efficient method of performing arithmetic calculations by students who are visually impaired, it has two major disadvantages. First, reliance on the talking calculator does not allow a student to practice and understand the underlying steps needed to perform a calculation. Second, heavy reliance on the talking calculator early in a student's schooling may result in the loss of instant recall of the basic arithmetic facts.

Graphing Calculators

Graphing calculators contain small visual displays that show the results of sophisticated calculations and graphs that illustrate the manipulation of various mathematical functions. These devices, commonly used in high school mathematics instruction, present a challenge for students who are blind or severely visually impaired because it is necessary to visualize the display to operate the calculators properly. Therefore, teachers of students with visual impairments need to make the images on the visual display perceivable by their students.

To visualize the images, students with low vision can use various low vision devices. They can use closed-circuit televisions (CCTVs), although for some students, the glare produced by the light source of the CCTV diminishes the visibility of the images. They can also use projection devices, such as a liquid crystal display (LCD) panel, which can be connected to a graphing calculator, to enlarge the images. Other options include using software installed in computers to develop graphs and larger-than-usual monitors or assistive technology software to magnify the images on the screen. (See the Resources section for sources of information on using these strategies.)

At this writing, truly suitable methods for providing the results from graphing calculators in a tactile or auditory form for students without usable vision are still under development. However, special software can be used to produce graphs in raised-line form on a braille printer. Software can also be used to reproduce graphs in auditory form through the use of tones of various frequencies to represent the shape of the graph. (See the Resources for information on these methods.)

Mental Math

The ability to calculate mentally with efficiency is an essential skill for all students, but especially for students who are visually impaired. Using the braillewriter and the abacus can be labor intensive and time consuming, and talking calculators have their own limitations. The more efficiently students can estimate, calculate, and check the reasonableness of answers in their heads, the more skilled they will be at using numbers. Strategies for doing so should be taught to students as soon as they begin to count and work with simple numbers.

Although there are many individual techniques for estimating and calculating mentally, most strategies involve one of the following four basic approaches:

◆ Rearranging numbers that can be easily recomposed into meaningful and useful units or groups using their complements or partners; for example, $54 + 23 = 54 + 20 + 3 = 74 + 3 = 77$.

◆ Putting numbers together that are easier to work with, often by changing the order of the numbers; for example, $3 + 86 + 7 = (3 + 7) + 86 = 10 + 86 = 96$.

◆ Replacing values with equal values that are easier to manipulate; for example, $.75 \times 32 = 3/4 \times 32$ (substituting a fraction for a decimal) $= (32 \text{ divided by } 4) \times 3 = 8 \times 3 = 24$.

◆ Rearranging numbers so they are easier to calculate, either by changing a number and then adjusting the answer or by adjusting both numbers so there is no need to change

the answer; for example: $23 + 29 = 23 + (30 - 1 = 53 - 1 = 52$.

Fingermath

Fingermath, or Chisenbop, is an alternative manipulative approach that allows students to be actively involved in carrying out arithmetic calculations by attributing specific values to their fingers and moving their fingers in a prescribed manner to carry out those calculations (Lieberthal, 1979). It may be introduced before the abacus or as a supplemental technique. Although fingermath requires some training, it may be easier to learn than the abacus, since the finger movements are simpler and no equipment is needed. A disadvantage of fingermath is the difficulty of writing the answer, since the student must remember the answer before he or she moves the hands to record it. It may also be difficult for some students to use this technique with numbers over 99.

Fingermath has numerous similarities to the abacus. For example, the values of the fingers correspond to the unit beads, the thumbs correspond to the five beads, and the hands correspond to the various columns on the abacus. The processes of setting, exchanging, and clearing numbers are also similar. For instance, using fingermath, a student would set 4 by pressing 4 fingers on the right hand and clear the 4 by raising those fingers, whereas using the abacus, the student would set 4 by pushing 4 unit beads up toward the separation bar and clear that 4 by pushing the unit beads down away from the separation bar.

Another example is the calculation of $4 + 6$. Using fingermath, the student would add $4 + 6$ by pressing 4 fingers on the right hand and add the 6 by using a method similar to the counting method for the abacus: pressing the thumb while raising the 4 fingers of the right hand (saying, "1"), then pressing those 4 fingers again (saying, "2, 3, 4, 5"), and then pressing the index finger of the left hand and raising all the fingers on the right hand (saying, "6"). The answer is 10 (1 finger on the left hand). Using the abacus, the student could add 4 + 6 by setting 4 unit beads on the abacus, then add 6 by bringing down a 5 bead and clearing the 4 unit beads (saying, "1"), setting the 4 unit beads again (saying, "2, 3, 4, 5"), and then setting a 10 bead and clearing the 9 unit beads (saying, "6"). With the abacus, the student could use either of the other abacus methods described earlier.

TACTILE DISPLAYS AND GRAPHICS

The use and complexity of graphics in education has grown dramatically. Although advances in technology have increased the accessibility of general information to persons who are visually impaired, major barriers continue to exist with regard to information presented graphically. Although creating tactile representations of graphic information is an effective way to make this information accessible to students who are blind or visually impaired, the key to this effort is to remember that tactile displays and graphics are meant to be felt, not seen. Information is not received in the same manner by the tactile and visual senses. For example, a three-dimensional drawing of a house cannot be rendered into an understandable tactile drawing that makes sense to a person who is blind. The three-dimensional drawing represents perspective that cannot be discerned tactually. Literal tactile renditions of visual images may cause confusion to students who are blind.

Guidelines for Designing Tactile Displays

There are a variety of situations that call for the information in graphic displays to be maintained as is, or suggest that modification in the size, scale, or layout of the information would make the tactile display more comprehensible. The guidelines presented in Sidebar 10.4 should be considered when creating a tactile rendering of a print graphic display.

The production of tactile images for use in mathematics instruction should follow similar procedures for the production of any type of well-designed tactile displays (see again Sidebar 10.4; see also the suggestions in Chapter 9). In addition to producing original raised-line drawings, charts, and graphs by adding a variety of materials, such as glue and string to paper, several thermal-based devices are used to produce replicable tactile displays. For example, a master copy of the tactile display can be placed in a Thermoform machine and covered with a piece of plastic paper. Through the use of heat and vacuum, the plastic conforms to the original image and becomes a durable copy. Another device allows graphs and other displays showing mathematical concepts to be drawn or photocopied on special heat-sensitive paper and then passed through the apparatus that heats the paper. The application of heat causes the lines to rise and thus to be perceivable by the tactile reader.

Extensive information on the production of tactile displays, equipment, and materials is available in the following resources: *Tactile Graphics* (Edman, 1992), *The Tactile Graphics Guidebook* (Barth & Berla, n.d.), *Tangible Graphics: Teacher's Guide* (Barth & Berla, 1986), *Guidelines for Mathematical Diagrams* (Braille Authority of North America, BANA, 1983), *Guidelines for Mathematics Diagrams Supplement* (BANA, 1983), and *Strategies for Developing Mathematics Skills in Students Who Use Braille* (Kapperman, Heinze, & Sticken, 1997).

Teaching Students to Use Tactile Displays

To teach students to be successful in handling and interpreting a variety of models and tactile graphics, teachers of students who are visually impaired must present them with many opportunities to handle real objects, then models, and finally two-dimensional representations with guidance from the teachers. The successful reading of tactile graphics requires knowledge of spatial and geographic concepts and strategies for exploring and interpreting the displays. Furthermore, students who are blind often do not see the whole (gestalt) at once as do sighted students, and they must ex-

Guidelines for Creating Tactile Displays

◆ Spacing between braille characters and other lines or symbols is critical. At least 1/4 inch space between items is necessary for the tactile reader to perceive them as separate; more space is needed if braille characters or symbols are placed next to information that is presented in especially high relief.

◆ The size of the symbols used must be considered. The absolute size of the symbol is important because a tactile reader cannot enlarge symbols the way a visual reader does by looking closer or using a magnifier to increase the size of the image. Furthermore, the relative size of the symbol makes a difference in the tactile reader's ability to recognize it efficiently. It is more difficult and takes more time to recognize shapes if they are of a different size from those originally presented. Avoid varying the size of repetitive symbols on displays or keys, unless the difference in size denotes a different meaning.

◆ The size of the diagram itself is important; generally, the area to be examined should be the size of one or two hands. If diagrams are small, they may appear cluttered and confusing; if they are large, it may be difficult to perceive that different areas are connected or related. Unless accurate scale is necessary, small diagrams with much detail may be rendered better using an enlarged version with an emphasis on critical features. Complex diagrams could be divided into several sections.

◆ If the need to enlarge the parts of a diagram results in having to divide the diagram into more than one part, these divisions should be made in such a way that they do not interfere with the concept being presented. Separated parts should be presented in a careful sequence, with instructions to help the student connect them. A diagram containing the pattern of the display (but with less detail) should be presented either as an introduction to the separate parts or as a summary.

◆ Scale is important only if it provides useful information or is necessary to solve a problem using the display. It may be effective to alter the scale, enlarging critical details so they can be perceived more accurately. If the scale is modified, the alteration should be described in the key.

◆ The relative position of symbols is an important consideration. A tactile reader may not readily recognize the same shape, presented in different positions, as being the same. Therefore, the position of symbols or pictures should not be changed, unless the change in position is necessary to denote different information.

◆ All symbols should be defined and explained. Descriptions or keys to accompany a tactile diagram could be placed on the same page, but not on the diagram itself, or on a separate facing page to reduce clutter on the diagram.

◆ Tactile displays must be presented in an uncluttered format so the reader can easily locate all significant information. Keep nonessential information to a minimum. It is often necessary to use simple shapes to represent complex pictures. Edit the printed display carefully before making it into a tactile display, identify critical features necessary to make it meaningful, and eliminate unnecessary elements that may be confusing.

◆ Proofread the tactile diagram with the fingers, not just the eyes.

perience many concepts sequentially. Thus, they may require more time than their classmates to complete assignments that involve such information because this synthesizing may be more difficult and time consuming. Students need to be taught to examine objects and graphics systematically to ensure that they experience the entire field and do not miss any important information.

Students need specific training in the concepts and skills necessary for interpreting tactile information, including the discrimination and tracking of real objects, two-dimensional symbols and lines, and the maintenance of spatial orientation while exploring models and tactile graphic displays. The following are some guidelines for teaching students to interpret tactile displays effectively:

♦ Use three-dimensional objects or models in conjunction with symbolic displays, when possible, particularly when introducing a new concept or type of graphic display. When selecting models to represent actual items or concepts, make sure that the critical features of each object or concept are present in the model to be used.

♦ Provide careful sequencing when moving from three-dimensional (concrete) to two-dimensional (symbolic) presentations. Use a logical sequence of simple-to-complex displays, emphasizing critical features and information.

♦ Teach students to use a systematic search pattern to explore tactile displays, using one or both hands to scan the entire field for the type of information presented, the layout and format, and the location of a key or other descriptive information.

COLLABORATIVE AND INCLUSIVE STRATEGIES

A major advantage to including a student who is visually impaired in mathematics instruction in the general education classroom is that the stu-

dent is taught mathematics by a mathematics teacher who knows the subject matter well, while the teacher of students with visual impairments is responsible for teaching any new information from the Nemeth Code, transcribing materials into braille or an enlarged format, and producing raised-line drawings and other tactile graphics. Each specialist uses his or her particular expertise, and the two work closely together as a team to facilitate learning.

In secondary-level mathematics classes, where coplanning and coteaching may be impractical, it is vital for the two specialists to develop an ongoing system for communicating with each other. This communication may take the form of memos, telephone calls, regularly scheduled instructional sessions for the teacher of students with visual impairments to teach prerequisite skills or clarify concepts that will be presented to the class, or assistance with administering and evaluating tests.

The following are some suggestions that the teacher of students with visual impairments may share with the mathematics teacher to facilitate the meaningful involvement of a student who is visually impaired in a mathematics class:

♦ During a lecture, words such as *this*, *that*, and *there* are meaningless for the student and should be avoided.

♦ The descriptions of problems or techniques should be worded carefully to avoid ambiguity; a copy of *The Handbook for Spoken Mathematics* (Chang, 1983) may be useful to the mathematics teacher.

♦ Whatever is written on the chalkboard should be verbalized, labels on diagrams should be described, and new words should be spelled as they are written.

♦ Transparencies and notes from the chalkboard should be given to the teacher of students with visual impairments to enlarge or transcribe into braille for the student's use at his or her desk, so the student has access to them at the same time as does the rest of the class.

- It is often helpful to give a student a print copy of a textbook and print handouts that his or her parents or a reader can use at home.

- If the class is completing problems on the chalkboard, a sighted classmate can write the work as the student who is blind explains it aloud.

- Mathematics assignments should be checked daily by someone who can read braille.

- Mathematics teachers may be taught how to make simple adaptations, such as using a tracing wheel or Wikki Stix (pliable, wax-covered string) for graphs that can be immediately available to the student.

SUMMARY

To prepare students for full participation in a society that is technologically based, the students must be given the opportunity to reach levels of achievement in mathematics to the extent that their abilities will carry them. In the case of students who are visually impaired, the study of this discipline is typically more challenging than it is for sighted students because of a variety of reasons, including the abstract nature of many essential concepts and the heavily visual presentation of the subject. These challenges can be met and overcome through the use of well-conceived strategies. The suggestions and strategies offered in this chapter can be used to good advantage in enabling students with visual impairments to reach levels of achievement commensurate with their abilities. The highly skilled, competent, well-informed teacher of students with visual impairments is essential in this effort.

ACTIVITIES

1. Present a blindfolded student with a raised-line drawing of a three-dimensional picture of a house, a car, or an animal. Instruct the student to examine the drawing tactually in an attempt to determine what it depicts. Once the student has made his or her judgment, instruct the student to remove the blindfold to view the picture visually. This activity vividly illustrates that three-dimensional pictures cannot be accurately perceived tactually.

2. Use at least three calculation tools—a braillewriter, abacus, talking calculator, fingermath, or mental math—to solve a series of addition, subtraction, multiplication, and division problems. Compare the efficiency of using each tool and note the advantages and disadvantages of each.

3. Present a blindfolded student with three-dimensional objects representing geometric shapes and solids and two-dimensional representations of shapes and solids in raised-line form. Ask the student to identify each. Observe the student's process and accuracy in completing these tasks. Formulate some possible guidelines for using objects versus raised-line drawings with students who are blind.

4. Present a student with a printed-line drawing of a geometric shape. Do not allow the student to view the drawing in advance of the exercise. Ask the student to make a hole with his or her pencil or pen in the center of a blank sheet of paper, place the paper with the hole over the picture of the shape without looking at the drawing, and view the drawing through the hole in the paper. Have the student reproduce the line drawing on a separate sheet by viewing the original drawing through the hole, moving the paper in such a manner as to view the separate parts of the drawing. Ask the student to compare his or her drawing to the original. This activity illustrates the difficulty of understanding concepts when one perceives only parts of the whole.

5. Using a raised-line grid, require a blind-

folded student to find the coordinates that represent the solution to the equation, $X + Y = 7$. Possible solutions are (2,5), (0,7), and (3,4). Place thumbtacks at those coordinates and position a string under the heads of the tacks. The string should form a slanted, straight line if the correct coordinates were selected. Have the student view a print version of the properly graphed points to compare his or her tactilely derived solution to the print version. This activity illustrates the skills required to carry out a tactile graphing task effectively.

REFERENCES

American Association of Workers for the Blind—Association for Education of the Visually Handicapped—National Braille Association (AAWB—AEVH—NBA) Braille Authority (1973). *The Nemeth braille code for mathematics and science notation, 1972 revision.* Louisville, KY: American Printing House for the Blind.

Barth, J. L., & Berla, E. P. (n.d.). *Tactile graphics guidebook.* Louisville, KY: American Printing House for the Blind.

Barth, J. L., & Berla, E. P. (1986). *Tangible graphs: Teacher's guide.* Louisville, KY: American Printing House for the Blind.

Braille Authority of North America. (1983). *Guidelines for mathematics diagrams supplement.* Rochester, NY: National Braille Association.

Chang, L. A. (1983). *Handbook for spoken mathematics: Larry's speakeasy.* University of California at Berkeley: Lawrence Livermore Laboratory.

Craig, R. (1987). *Learning the Nemeth braille code; A manual for teachers and students.* Louisville, KY: American Printing House for the Blind.

Czerwinski, M. H. (1982). *Braille recognition level test for mathematics* [elementary-level and high school level tests]. Newark: New Jersey Commission for the Blind and Visually Impaired, Education Services.

Davidow, M. (1988). *The abacus made easy.* Louisville, KY: American Printing House for the Blind.

Edman, P. K. (1992). *Tactile graphics.* New York: American Foundation for the Blind.

Godwin, A., Grafsgaard, K., Hanson, N., Hooey, P., Martin, J., McNear, D., Rieber, C., & Tilmanns, E. (1995). *Minnesota Braille Skills Inventory: A resource manual.* Little Canada: Minnesota Educational Services.

Kapperman, G. (1974). *A comparison of three methods of arithmetic computation by the blind.* Unpublished doctoral dissertation, University of Northern Colorado, Greeley.

Kapperman, G. (1994). [Survey of knowledge of the Nemeth code by special educators and rehabilitation teachers]. Unpublished raw data. Sycamore, IL: Research & Development Institute.

Kapperman, G., Heinze, A., & Sticken, J. (1997). *Strategies for developing mathematics skills in students who use braille.* Sycamore, IL: Research & Development Institute.

Kapperman, G., Henry, J., Cortesi, M., Heinze, A., & Sticken, J. (1997). *The computerized Nemeth Code tutor.* Sycamore, IL: Research & Development Institute.

Kojima, T. (1954). *The Japanese abacus: Its use and theory.* Rutland, VT: Charles E. Tuttle Co.

Lieberthal, E. M. (1979). *The complete book of finger mathematics.* New York: McGraw-Hill.

Livingston, R. (1997). *Use of the Cranmer abacus.* Austin, TX: Texas School for the Blind and Visually Impaired.

Meltzer, L. J., Roditi, B. N., Haynes, D. P., Biddle, K. R., Paster, M., & Taber, S. E. (1996). *Strategies for success: Classroom teaching techniques for students with learning problems.* Austin, TX: PRO-ED.

Millaway, S. M. (1994). *Abacus basic conpetency.* Morristown, PA: Eye-Deal Materials for the Visually Handicapped.

National Council of Teachers of Mathematics. (1989). *Curriculum and evaluation standards for school mathematics.* Reston, VA: Author.

Nemeth, A. (1962). *Nemeth Code of braille mathematics.* Louisville, KY: American Printing House for the Blind.

Ponchillia, P. E., & Ponchillia, S. V. (Eds.). (1996). *Foundations of rehabilitation teaching with persons who are blind or visually impaired.* New York: AFB Press.

Roberts, H., Krebs, B., & Taffet, B. (1978). *Introduction to braille mathematics.* Louisville, KY: American Printing House for the Blind.

Whigham, M., & Utsinger, D. (1996). *Preparing tactile adaptations for mathematics and science.* [Videotape]. Ames, IA: Iowa State University Media Resources Center.

Whigham, M., & Utsinger, D. (1996). *Using adaptations for mathematics and science* [Videotape]. Ames, IA: Iowa State University Media Resources Center.

Wittenstein, S. H. (1993). *Braille literacy: Preservice training and teacher attitudes: Report of a national study.* Unpublished doctoral dissertation, Teachers College, Columbia University.

Strategies for Teaching Mathematics to Students with Visual Impairments and Additional Disabilities

Opportunities to practice and apply basic mathematical concepts in meaningful and functional contexts are critical for students with visual impairments and additional disabilities. Concepts may best be facilitated, reinforced, and generalized through the strategies of embedded sequences, partial participation, and cooperative learning. Students should not be excluded from participating in mathematical activities with their classmates because of their limited ability to understand and carry out mathematical operations. However, instructional strategies should encourage the development of skills and operations that will have functional relevance for a particular student. The following are suggested instructional strategies:

- Reinforce concepts of size by providing familiar objects for the student to manipulate and explore. Pair a preschooler with a sighted peer in the housekeeping center to match lids to different sizes of pots and pans, stack and nest plastic containers, and sort and match silverware by size. A student with limited motor control can eye gaze to indicate which lid goes with a pan or where to place the big spoon. If the student's vision is significantly impaired as well, instruct the peer how to help the student touch and place materials to the extent that the student's motor capabilities will permit as the peer labels the sizes.

- With older students, reinforce differences in size by having the student match large and small socks or sort the family laundry, putting children's shirts in one pile and adults' shirts in another. Arranging materials such as art materials, books, and canned goods, by stacking them in descending order helps the student develop concepts of sequence and order. Give the student choices to clarify a task and encourage his or her efforts to communicate.

- Relate counting to real-life situations and contexts. To practice one-to-one correspondence, a student can count produce as a peer places it in a bag or container or the student reaches and grasps cans, boxes, or produce to release them into the grocery cart or plastic bag as a peer counts them. Playing a game of dominoes with regular-size or enlarged sets of dominoes encourages the student to count and match amounts. Provide a variety of materials, both commercially available and specially designed, to serve as jigs for a student who needs to count specific items for various packaging and assembly tasks. A student may package a dozen cookies for a bake sale by placing one cookie in each compartment of a 12-cup muffin tin and then transferring the cookies to a plastic bag. Concepts of empty and full, more, another, a few more, too many, and so forth can be developed through this type of activity.

- Have an elementary student with low vision practice counting with such materials as teacher-made vacuum-formed low vision number cards or those purchased from IEP Resources (see the Resources in this chapter). Also have the student participate in counting activities by pressing individual or combinations of numbers on the VTECH Little Smart Number Desk with voice output.

(continued on next page)

◆ Introduce the students to money and the concept of exchanging money as early as possible. While the first-grade classmates count money in workbooks, the student can improve his or her visual and/or tactile scanning and dexterity skills by picking up coins and inserting them in a bank. A student who has difficulty attending, even one with limited sight, can be engaged for longer periods by using a mechanical money-sorting machine to see or hear a coin as it moves into the appropriate chamber. Still other students may be able to sort by dollar bills versus coins. Cut slots in the lids of transparent plastic food containers so a student with low vision may sort visually and leave off the lids so a student with significantly limited vision may compare his or her choices tactilely. Securing the containers with Velcro, rubber shelving material, or Dycem matting will make it easier for the student to manipulate the money.

◆ Have a student sort coins into separate containers and then place them in change wrappers so that they are ready to be taken to a bank. Take the student on a field trip to the bank to pick up the wrappers and then to exchange the coins, so the student understands the purpose of the activity and has experience with conservation.

◆ As early as possible, give a student multiple opportunities to practice exchanging money for products. A student with limited motor control can choose between two quarters and a dollar bill to indicate which should be placed in a vending machine while another student inserts the money. The

same strategy can be used for purchasing any product. Provide a student who cannot count or manipulate money with alternative solutions, such as the "next-dollar" strategy or extending an envelope with a predetermined amount of money. As students approach graduation age, they may be eligible for credit cards with their parents as guarantors. Learning to discriminate, indicate, and manipulate a credit card eliminates the need to manipulate coins and paper money, requires a single step, and affords opportunities to practice "signing" their names.

◆ Use the Coin-u-lator, an electronic device available from IEP Resources, which contains realistic coin buttons in place of calculator numbers. With this device, a student can match the real coin to its facsimile to read/speak its value, can add and subtract, and can play money-value games.

◆ Have a student practice sequencing skills while shopping. A sighted peer can read the purchase price to the student so the student can locate and punch in the price on a talking calculator. A student with low vision may be able to read the price and sequence numbers on the calculator to input the amount.

◆ Reinforce literacy and math skills by having a student look through ads from a local supermarket to select pictures of items needed for preparing a meal with a sighted peer and cut out the pictures and prices of the items. Use an envelope for each item that is marked with the corresponding price and partial participation procedures so the student can count the money needed for the

(continued on next page)

envelope. The students can then scan the pictured items and prices to locate the item with the same price as that on the outside of the envelope. Construct the shopping list by attaching the pictured item and corresponding envelope with paper clips or staples.

◆ Use cooking and meal preparation activities to teach a student concepts related to measurement. A student can partially participate in cutting vegetables, fruits, or sandwiches in half; pouring 2 cups of water into a mixing bowl; and "filling" a measuring cup with flour or glasses with ice. These kinds of activities encourage the development of fine motor skills and tactile perception.

M. BETH LANGLEY
Pinellas County Schools
St. Petersburg, FL

RESOURCES

Suggested Resources for Teaching Mathematics

Resource	Type	Source	Description
The Abacus Made Easy (Davidow, 1988)	Book	American Printing House for the Blind	A manual with instructions on using the Cranmer abacus.
Braille 'n Speak	Education aid	Blazie Engineering	A talking calculator, clock, and word processor; can connect to a computer system to print both braille and print copies of files.
Complete Book of Finger Mathematics (Lieberthal, 1979)	Book	McGraw-Hill	An instruction book on using finger mathematics.
Computerized Nemeth Code Tutor (Kapperman, Cortesi, Henry, Heinze, & Sticken, 1997)	Computer program	Association for Education and Rehabilitation of the Blind and Visually Impaired	A tutorial program for teachers addressing the Nemeth Code.
Duxbury Braille Translator	Computer program	Duxbury Systems	A braille translation and word-processing program for computers; includes the Nemeth Code translation program.
Guidelines for Mathematical Diagrams (Braille Authority of North America)	Book	Braille Authority of North America (BANA)	A resource for producing tactile diagrams for use in math.
Introduction to Braille Mathematics (Roberts, Krebs, & Taffet, 1978)	Book	Library of Congress, National Library Service for the Blind and Physically Handicapped	An easily assimilated presentation of the special symbols and complex rules and procedures contained in the Nemeth Code for Mathematics and Science Notation. Lessons and exercises proceed in a step-by-step fashion. *(continued on next page)*

Suggested Resources *(Continued)*

Resource	Type	Source	Description
The Japanese Abacus: Its Use and Theory (Kojima, 1954)	Book	Charles E. Tuttle	A book that explains the "secrets" methods of using an abacus.
Learning the Nemeth Braille Code (Craig, 1987)	Book	American Printing House for the Blind	Nemeth braille code instruction manual for teachers.
Low vision and tactile graphics	Instructional materials	TAEVIS (Tactile Access to Education for Visually Impaired Students) Online	An online source of 3,000+ diagrams useful in secondary level biology, chemistry, physics, and math. Large-print versions for use by low vision students; braille versions must be processed in a tactile image enhancer for use by braille readers.
Mathematics Accessible to Visually Impaired Students (MAVIS)	Computer program	MAVIS	A Nemeth Code translator for conversion of math into braille; requires that math first be written in Scientific Notebook, a math word processor available at www.scinotebook.com.
MegaDots	Computer program	Duxbury Systems	A versatile braille translation program, word processor, and Nemeth Code translation program.
Nemeth Braille Code for Mathematics and Science Notation (American Association of Workers for the Blind, 1973)	Book	American Printing House for the Blind	The official code book for symbols and formats used in the Nemeth Code in mathematics and science.
Pictures in a Flash (PIAF)	Equipment	HumanWare	Equipment for producing tactile graphics from black-and-white print originals, using microcapsule paper that swells and raises where black ink is present when heated.
Preparing Tactile Adaptations for Mathematics and Science (Whigham & Utsinger, 1996).	Videotape	Iowa State University Media Resources Center	A videotape demonstrating techniques of preparing tactile adaptations for math and science.
Strategies for Developing Mathematics Skills in Students Who Use Braille (Kapperman, Heinze, & Sticken, 1997)	Book	Association for Education and Rehabilitation of the Blind and Visually Impaired	A discussion of techniques for math instruction; addresses topics, such as teaching mathematical concepts, basic number facts and operations, and advanced mathematics. Also includes Chang's *Handbook of Spoken Mathematics.*
Swell-Form Graphics Machine	Equipment	American Thermoform Corporation	Equipment for producing tactile graphics from black-and-white print originals, using microcapsule paper that "swells" where black ink is present when heated.

(continued on next page)

Suggested Resources *(Continued)*

Resource	Type	Source	Description
Tactile Graphics (Edman, 1992)	Book	American Foundation for the Blind	An encyclopedic handbook on translating visual information into tactile form that students with visual impairments can understand. Essential for teachers who produce their own materials.
Tactile Image Enhancer	Equipment	Repro-Tronics	Equipment for producing tactile graphics from black-and-white print originals, using microcapsule paper that swells and raises where black ink is present when heated. Thermo-Pen is also available, which allows teachers or blind students to create free-hand tactile drawings.
Talking calculators	Education aid	LS&S Group Maxi Aids Science Products for the Blind	Calculators with voice readouts for individuals with visual impairments.
Thermoform Machine	Equipment	American Thermoform Corporation	Equipment for producing multiple copies of tactile graphics pages using plastic sheets "Thermo-formed" over a teacher-made original.
Use of the Cranmer Abacus (Livingston, 1997)	Book	Texas School for the Blind and Visually Impaired (TSBVI)	An instruction book on using the Cranmer abacus, following the "counting" method and the "TSBVI" method. Covers all operations and provides sample problems.
Using Adaptations for Mathematics and Science (Whigham & Utsinger, 1996)	Videotape	Iowa State University Media Resources Center	A videotape demonstrating adaptations for math and science.

Contact information for each of the resources listed will be found in the Sources of Products, Materials, Equipment, and Services section at the back of this book.

CHAPTER 11

Arts Education

Donna McNear

KEY POINTS

- ◆ **Participation in arts activities is an essential area of study for all students, including students who are visually impaired.**

- ◆ **Appreciation of the arts is a value to be encouraged in the lives of students with visual impairments to enhance the students' participation in and enjoyment of our society.**

- ◆ **Teachers of students with visual impairments play a critical role in promoting arts education and helping students gain access to it.**

- ◆ **High-quality and effective instruction in the arts disciplines is provided to students with visual impairments using commonsense modifications and appropriate tools.**

VIGNETTE

For several years, Ms. McNalley, a teacher of students with visual impairments in a rural area, had a small group of students who were similar in age and needs to students in the neighboring rural area. She and the other vision specialists would periodically get the students together for group learning activities and field trips. After surveying the students one year, the specialists discovered that none of the students (all of middle school age), had been to the fine arts museum in the nearby city and so arranged a "touch tour" of the museum's sculptures to be led by trained docents.

During the touch tour, one docent and a teacher of students with visual impairments accompanied each group of two to three students. All the students and docents wore soft, white cotton gloves so they could feel the sculptures without leaving an oil residue from their skin. As the group that Ms. Mc-Nalley accompanied walked through the museum to the first sculpture, the well-trained docent described the museum and surroundings in specific terms that captured the students' interest.

Stopping by the first sculpture, the docent named the sculpture and artist, Rodin; described the sculpture; and gave facts about Rodin's life and related them to a time line and other historical events. As she spoke, she began to guide each student's hands in a tactile exploration of the sculpture. As Ms. McNalley watched the docent and children explore the sculpture, she began to view the sculptures in a new light. Imagining Rodin as he formed his sculpture and watching the details of the figure through the children's touch gave her insights into the form of the sculpture that added a different dimension to her way of seeing and interpreting.

At the end of the tour, the children took off their gloves and quickly reverted to schoolchildren who needed to eat and talk to each other about their latest CDs and other interests. As Ms. McNalley reflected on this teaching and learning experience later, she thought it was one of the most important field trips she had been on as a teacher. She also decided that she needed to examine her own priorities and widen her role with her students to have a far greater influence on them in relation to arts education.

INTRODUCTION

This chapter addresses the content and instructional strategies that encourage students with visual impairments to participate in arts education and increase their access to the arts curriculum, including dance, music, theater, and the visual and literary arts. The focus of instructional considerations is the basic knowledge and skills that beginning teachers of students with visual impairments need to provide to facilitate high-quality arts education experiences for their students.

Providing high-quality services to students in the arts disciplines is a multifaceted process and includes such issues as attitudes, access, and participation in meaningful activities that reflect the students' cultural experiences in today's society. Therefore, the instructional considerations include teaching strategies not only to modify the product and performance aspects of art—the tangible outcomes—but to promote the students' participation in the arts curriculum. These are the concepts and skills associated with making, responding to, and interpreting the various art forms (*Minnesota Frameworks for Arts Curriculum Strategies,* MFACS, 1997).

"All students deserve access to the rich education and understanding that the arts provide, regardless of their background, talents, or disabilities," according to the *National Standards for Arts Education* (NSAE) (Consortium of National Arts Education Associations, 1994, p. 4). The arts are important to *all* students, including students who are visually impaired, because they connect students' imagination to questions about human existence and present issues and ideas that teach, persuade, entertain, and adorn. All aspects of life (personal, social, economic, and cultural) are shaped by the arts and help students develop attitudes, characteristics, and intellectual skills to participate in this society.

Through participation in arts activities, students can develop personal-social skills, such as those relating to cooperation, feelings of belonging, sharing, leadership, courtesy, respect, responsibility, dependability, and membership in a group (Consortium, 1994). These areas are critical to the growth and development of students with visual impairments. As NSAE (1994, p. 4) emphasized, "students with disabilities, who are often excluded from arts programs, can derive great benefit from them—and for the same reasons that studying the arts benefits students who are not disabled."

Education in the arts is gaining prominence throughout the United States. Various art forms are being included in the core curriculum for all students and are being promoted as essential for living a satisfactory life. The arts are no longer being viewed as an optional field of study but as a necessary component of a comprehensive and high-quality educational experience. In line with this focus, educational standards and curricula in the arts are being studied and developed at the national, state, and local levels (Consortium, 1994; MFACS, 1997).

In the 1990s, several educational reform initiatives focused on the arts and their role in general education, including the following:

◆ The Goals 2000: Educate America Act acknowledged that the arts are a core subject area (National Education Goals Panel, 1990).

◆ NSAE, developed by the Consortium of National Arts Education Associations (1994), outline the knowledge and skills that students should acquire in the arts disciplines.

- ◆ The Interstate New Teacher Assessment and Support Consortium (INTASC), a program of the Council of Chief State School Officers, is developing model licensing standards for beginning teachers in the arts that will define what all beginning teachers and arts specialists should know and be able to do in regard to the arts ("Arts Education Standards," 1999).

- ◆ Individual states are developing teacher certification and licensing requirements, and institutes of higher education are developing personnel preparation programs in the arts.

These initiatives are important because they promote greater participation in the arts for all children and greater access to art education for students with visual impairments.

Because an arts education is necessary for all students, it is important to focus on the issues and strategies related to providing access to the arts to students with visual impairments. Yet there is a scarcity of information on the arts and teaching strategies in the field of visual impairments. Shaw (1986) reviewed the literature on arts education for children who are visually impaired, much of which dated from the 1950s to the 1970s. This literature provides a beginning base of knowledge on the importance of this area to students with visual impairments and validates the benefits of participation in the arts. The author's electronic searches of database documents revealed limited, more recent information on effective teaching strategies and other instructional considerations in this area.

This chapter presents issues and strategies for creating access to opportunities and resources in the arts, beginning with the role of the teacher of students with visual impairments. Other topics include assessment in the arts disciplines; instructional considerations in the areas of dance, music, theater, and the visual and literary arts for students with visual impairments; and resources for service providers.

ROLE OF THE TEACHER OF STUDENTS WITH VISUAL IMPAIRMENTS

In the opening vignette, Ms. McNalley asked herself critical questions about the relationship between students who are visually impaired, the arts, and her role as a teacher of students with visual impairments and concluded that she could have a greater influence on the arts education her students would receive. Her questions echo those of many teachers of students with visual impairments. For example, Corn and Bailey's (1991) study of music programs at residential schools for students who are visually impaired found that the teachers' major concern was scheduling conflicts because of the students' many needs and priorities, such as instruction in braille and orientation and mobility (O&M). Other major obstacles to providing arts education to students with visual impairments include the large caseloads of teachers of students with visual impairments, the limited research-based disability-specific teaching strategies and professional resources available in the field of visual impairments, and the fact that many schools provide arts education as extracurricular activities or as part of physical education programs and hence specialists may not be aware of these activities. Furthermore, because of negative societal attitudes toward the participation of people with visual impairments in arts activities and the lack of accommodations necessary for this participation, many students with visual impairments may not consider participating in these activities.

In general, the role of the teacher of students with visual impairments is to ensure that students have the opportunity to learn and participate in the arts curriculum (Napier, 1973). To ensure that students have opportunities in the arts, the specialist performs a multifaceted role and assumes responsibilities, as identified by Spungin and Ferrell (in press), that are similar to those in other curricular areas, as follows:

- ◆ Advocates with other members of the educational team, administrators, and teaching staff for the appropriate participation of students with visual impairments in all arts activities.

- ◆ Collaborates with art teachers to adapt lessons and decide on possible modifications of instruction.

- ◆ Ensures that the arts teachers and students have the appropriate materials, resources, and adaptations to allow the students to participate in arts activities.

- ◆ Exposes students to ideas, concepts, activities, and experiential learning that will enhance their understanding of the arts.

- ◆ Preteaches art skills (such as a dance step or the use of a tool) or specialty skills (such as braille music notation) as needed to prepare students for lessons in art disciplines.

- ◆ Narrates or describes performances and works of art.

The teacher also plays an essential role in working with students with additional disabilities; strategies focusing on students with visual impairments and additional disabilities and resources for teachers appear later in this chapter.

To facilitate students' participation in the arts and to collaborate effectively with others, the teacher of students with visual impairments needs to have knowledge in the following areas:

- ◆ A broad understanding of arts education,

- ◆ Familiarity with the arts curriculum in general education,

- ◆ An awareness of access issues in the arts for students with visual impairments, and

- ◆ Specific knowledge of the instructional content to provide a high-quality arts education experience for the students.

NSAE (Consortium, 1994) identified the content needed to develop a broad understanding of arts education. Sidebar 11.1 lists the standards in four areas: dance, music, theater, and visual arts. A fifth area—the literary arts—is included in this chapter because of its importance to literacy and self-expression for students with visual impairments. The standards for this area, based on those developed by MFACS (1997), are presented in Sidebar 11.2. A review of these standards enhances the teacher's perspective on the knowledge and skills expected of all students in the arts curriculum.

Issues related to the access of students with visual impairments to the arts curriculum encompass opportunities and experiences, learning activities, productions and performances, tools, concepts, materials, resources, and instruction. In addition, the expectations and attitudes of teachers, and society toward including students with visual impairments in the arts influence the students' attitudes toward participating in the arts and therefore affect the quality of the students' educational experiences (Land, 1998; Shaw, 1987).

The provision of high-quality services and effective instruction in the arts should include the following:

- ◆ Planning, managing, delivering, and evaluating instruction;

- ◆ Collaborating with other members of a student's educational team and teachers in various areas of the arts curriculum;

- ◆ Providing a variety of experiences and opportunities that encourage a student to participate and learn ways to interact in the environment;

- ◆ Including the concepts and skills associated with creating, performing, responding

National Standards for Arts Education: Content Standards

DANCE (GRADES K–12)

- Identifying and demonstrating movement elements and skills in performance dance.
- Understanding choreographic principles, processes, and structures.
- Understanding dance as a way to create and communicate meaning.
- Applying and demonstrating critical and creative thinking skills in dance.
- Demonstrating and understanding dance in various cultures and historical periods.
- Making connections between dance and healthful living.
- Making connections between dance and other disciplines.

MUSIC (GRADES K–12)

- Singing, alone and with others, a varied repertoire of music.
- Performing on instruments, alone and with others, a varied repertoire of music.
- Improvising melodies, variations, and accompaniments.
- Composing and arranging music within specified guidelines.
- Reading and notating music.
- Listening to, analyzing, and describing music.
- Evaluating music and music performances.
- Understanding relationships among music, the other arts, and disciplines outside the arts.
- Understanding music in relation to history and culture.

THEATER (GRADES K–12)

- Scriptwriting based on personal experience and heritage, imagination, literature, and history.
- Acting improvisations, scripted scenes, and informal and formal productions.

- Directing classroom dramatizations, improvised and scripted scenes, and informal and formal productions.
- Researching for classroom dramatizations, improvised and scripted scenes, and supporting artistic choices.
- Comparing art forms, such as film, television, electronic media productions, dance, music, visual arts, and new art forms.
- Analyzing and constructing meanings from classroom dramatizations, improvised and scripted scenes, and informal and formal theater in film, television, and electronic media.
- Understanding context by recognizing and analyzing the role of theater, film, television, and electronic media in daily life, other cultures, and in the community (past and present).

VISUAL ARTS (GRADES K–12)

- Understanding and applying media, techniques, and processes.
- Using knowledge of structures and functions.
- Choosing and evaluating a range of subject matter, symbols, and ideas.
- Understanding the visual arts in relation to history and cultures.
- Reflecting upon and assessing the characteristics and merits of their work and the work of others.
- Making connections between the visual arts and other disciplines.

Source: Adapted from Consortium of National Arts Education Associations, *National Standards for Arts Education: What Every Young American Should Know and Be Able to Do in the Arts* (Reston, VA: Author, 1994).

Literary Arts: Content Standards

1. Students explore, generate, and develop feelings, ideas, and values through writing stories, poems, and other works of creative writing.
2. Students demonstrate the skills of reflection, interpretation, assessment, analysis, and criticism applied to their own creative writing and that of other writers.
3. Students discover, acknowledge, and critically understand their own and others' preferences and aesthetic sensitivities in the literary arts.
4. Students experience various roles in the literary arts field, including writing, editing, publishing, and sharing literature with an audience.
5. Students acquire and demonstrate knowledge through creative writing of the historical, cultural and other contexts of the literary arts.
6. Students realize and make connections that demonstrate the relevance of the literary arts to other areas of learning and to their lives.

Source: Reprinted, with permission, from *Minnesota Frameworks for Arts Curriculum Strategies* (Golden Valley: Minnesota Center for Arts Education, 1997).

to, and interpreting various art forms—both the process and products;

◆ Utilizing skills and methods for gaining access to the arts curriculum; and

◆ Modifying and adapting instruction and materials (CEC Knowledge and Skills, 1998; Consortium, 1994; Spungin & Ferrell, in press).

As was true of Ms. McNalley in the vignette, helping students gain access to the arts can make the role of teachers of students with visual impairments more fulfilling and meaningful. It can also influence students to explore and attain goals that they previously did not believe they were capable of achieving and can generally enrich the quality of their lives (Kaplan, Mayerson & Sovin, 1998).

ASSESSMENT

Because there are no "formal" assessments in the arts that are specific to students who are visually impaired, a teacher of students with visual impairments needs to be knowledgeable about the issues involved in assessing the general population of students in the arts. Typically, these assessments involve reviews of portfolios in the visual arts and evaluations of students' performance skills in dance, music, and theater (Consortium, 1994).

According to the Arts Education Assessment Framework, developed by the National Assessment of Educational Progress (NAEP, 1997), knowledge in the various arts disciplines is assessed within personal, social, cultural, and historical contexts and, in the area of aesthetics, form and structure. Skills (cognitive, affective, and motor) in creating, performing, and responding to the arts are assessed within the perceptual, intellectual/reflective, expressive, and technical areas.

Measuring and evaluating students' skills in and knowledge of the arts constitute a challenge that is complicated by the presence of a sensory disability. Thus, it is critical for teachers of students with visual impairments to collaborate with other appropriate personnel (such as arts teachers, music and band directors, physical education instructors, and general education teachers) to modify and adapt assessments. If the teacher of students with visual impairments considers the components of assessment just described, in conjunction with these other personnel, he or she can develop appropriate accommodations, modifications, and adaptations that will allow a student who is visually impaired to be included in the arts curriculum and be held to appropriate standards.

For example, the student assessment for an art appreciation class on Impressionism might include comparing the painting styles of Monet and Gauguin. The assessment could be modified for a student who is blind by having the student compare the two artists' lives through biographical studies. In a third-grade art class students might be required to include a drawing of an animal in their assessment portfolio. Since the preferred medium for a student who is blind is clay, the assessment requirement for this student could be adapted to include slides of an animal sculpture in clay. Both the process and the final product could be demonstrated.

Since assessing students with visual impairments in some of the arts disciplines may be complicated, it is important for the teacher of students with visual impairments to be flexible, creative, and open to new ideas.

INSTRUCTIONAL CONSIDERATIONS

What does a teacher of students with visual impairments do to support students in the different arts disciplines? What instructional considerations and strategies encourage students to meet the goals and objectives in the areas of dance, music, theater, and the visual and literary arts? As the body of knowledge on effective instruction in the arts and teaching students with visual impairments develops, it is essential to consider the experiences of students within the arts curriculum. This chapter presents suggestions to make educational experiences more meaningful for students with visual impairments. In addi-

tion, the experiences of one student, named Tracey Kiel, will be described in order to illustrate the inclusion of a student with a visual impairment in the arts.

To develop effective instructional strategies in the arts for students with visual impairments, it is important to consider the knowledge and skills used by teachers in other academic areas. It is also necessary to consider the impact of a visual impairment on learning, including the effects on a student's range and variety of experiences, ability to get around, and interactions with the environment. Because of these effects on learning, the curriculum that teachers of visually impaired students teach should be based on three major areas—(1) skills needed to gain access to the academic curriculum, (2) skills learned incidentally by sighted students, and (3) skills specific to students with visual impairments—and the methods that specialists use to approach the curriculum need to be based on applying common sense, keeping expectations high, and adapting materials (Lewis, 1999). It seems appropriate that instruction in the arts also includes these considerations.

Land's (1998) research with high school students with visual impairments found that some students who had limited experiences and exposure to the visual arts had negative attitudes toward the visual arts and participation in them. Therefore, exposing these students to ideas, activities, and experiences in the arts that students who are sighted learn incidentally may increase their knowledge and skills and change their attitudes toward participating in the arts.

The following sections describe general instructional strategies that are common to all the arts disciplines, followed by strategies for each of the arts areas—dance, music, theater, and the visual and literary arts. For each area, educational and other issues that are important to the specific disciplines are discussed, to provide an appropriate context for the instructional strategies, and the comments of Tracy Kiel, a young woman who is congenitally blind and a graduate of Milaca High School in Milaca, Minnesota, are presented to illustrate the experiences of students who are visually impaired.

GENERAL INSTRUCTIONAL STRATEGIES

Planning is an important component of effective instruction (Algozinne, Ysseldyke, & Elliot, 1997). First, it is important to create an atmosphere for a student who is visually impaired in which the student is encouraged to participate in and to be inquisitive about various arts areas. To do so, the teacher of students with visual impairments exposes the student to ideas and concepts that are necessary for understanding the arts that students who are sighted learn incidentally (such as the characteristics of a theater and the layout of the stage area) and provides experiential learning activities (including visits to museums and attendance at musical and theatrical performances) that give the student concrete experiences with the arts.

Second, since arts activities are frequently integrated into other subject areas or are taught by specialist teachers, it is necessary to review the curriculum and standards of all subject areas to determine if arts activities are included. Third, it is essential to develop a plan for ensuring the student's participation. This planning may include meeting with arts and general education teachers to establish ongoing collaborative relationships and to learn the content of specific lessons. It also includes researching, ordering, and gathering materials and ensuring that the student has access to the materials (such as braille music and supplies for making raised-line drawings) when he or she needs them for a particular lesson and arranging to teach needed skills before the student will be required to use them in specific classes.

In addition, many arts activities are provided in extracurricular and enrichment programs through special clubs and organizations and in community education programs. Since many of these programs are held after school, in the evenings, or on weekends, the teacher of students with visual impairments needs to develop a flexible schedule for accommodating the student's instruction and for supervising the student's participation.

In collaborating with other personnel, the teacher of students with visual impairments should not assume that they have the knowledge, attitudes, and expectations that promote involvement of a student who is visually impaired in the arts. For example, some arts teachers may initially be unsure that the student will benefit from participating in certain activities, but, in time, may discover such benefits, especially if the specialist encourages them to express their misgivings and misperceptions and to try to include the student.

Depending on the student's individual needs and the requirements of a particular lesson, the teacher of students with visual impairments needs to collaborate with the arts teacher or general education teacher to adapt the objectives of a lesson if they seem inappropriate for the student with a visual impairment. As Napier (1973) noted, the artwork of a student who is visually impaired does not need to be like that of his or her sighted classmates in medium or theme. For example, if the student's classmates are using crayons, the student could create a tactile drawing using materials that create raised lines and shapes. If the class is focusing on clouds, the theme of rain might be more meaningful to the student who is visually impaired.

Preteaching (teaching skills before the student needs them for particular activities) is one of the key strategies for providing high-quality educational experiences in the arts, as well as in many other areas of the curriculum. The teacher of students with visual impairments needs to preteach the student the following:

◆ Skills that are needed for a particular class (such as specific braille music symbols for a music lesson or a dance step for a dance class);

◆ Tools and equipment that the student may need to use (like a potter's wheel for a ceramics class or an awl for working with leather); and

◆ Vocabulary specific to a particular art area, especially if the activity is language based, so the student can understand and communicate verbally about the discipline (Doyle, 1981).

Once the student is participating in an arts class, it is important to encourage him or her to be as independent as possible, such as by putting away an instrument after band practice and retrieving and replacing materials in a pottery class. To facilitate the student's independence, the teacher of students with visual impairments may collaborate with the O&M specialist to ensure that the student can move around the area easily and knows where various objects are located. If a support person (a paraeducator, sighted classmate, or trained volunteer) is needed to help the student participate, the specialist makes sure that this person understands his or her role in relation to the student and the activity and supervises the support person's involvement, such as in demonstrating a dance step or partnering a student, so that unnecessary dependence is not fostered in the student. For a student who is serious about a particular area of the arts and wants to advance in it, the teacher may arrange for a mentor to provide one-on-one instruction.

When observation skills are required for a learning task, such as watching a dance video or a theatrical performance or viewing other students' work, the teacher of students with visual impairments may also need to provide a narration or a description of the work. In addition, the specialist needs to monitor the student's participation in the arts activity periodically to ensure that the student is participating appropriately (that is, working as independently as possible, using the correct tools, and otherwise managing the learning environment) and to evaluate the student to determine what went well and what needs to be improved.

STRATEGIES FOR SPECIFIC ARTS

Dance

In dance, movement is the medium for sensing, understanding, and communicating (MFACS, 1997). Movement is a critical area of development for students who are visually impaired, and the dance curriculum includes activities that enhance a student's movement skills (Duehl, 1979; Emes, 1978; Kratz, 1977). A strong curriculum in dance can improve the quality of a student's movement, encourage creativity with movement, and expand a student's openness to exploring and taking risks in other activities that require physical skills. The skills gained through dance can increase a student's independence and success in other areas, such as O&M.

Dance is usually taught in physical education classes or extracurricular programs in public schools and is frequently limited to units in social dance. The instructional strategies for dance presented here are appropriate for both this traditional curriculum and the more formal dance curriculum that is being promoted in current arts reform initiatives (Consortium, 1994; NAEP, 1997).

The early elementary school years may be the most important time to influence movement through participation in dance activities, since young children are frequently willing to take risks, follow suggestions, and explore new ways of moving. Teachers of students with visual impairments should take advantage of the dance curriculum in the early years to encourage students to think, feel, and move. Even if a student is not interested in participating in dance, it is important to expose him or her to a variety of dance styles (jazz, tap, ballet, and folk) to increase the student's general understanding of dance and appreciation of dance performances. The following instructional strategies encourage access to dance activities:

◆ Collaborate with the O&M specialist, adapted physical education and physical education teachers, and dance instructors to learn which movement skills and locomotor skills need to be pretaught to a student. These specialists may need to participate in an assessment of the student's motor skills to determine which ones need to be pretaught. Sidebar 11.3 is a comprehensive checklist of movements that can be used as a guide for determining the movements that a student needs to learn before he or she participates in a dance class. Another important aspect of collaboration is to determine which aspects of motor skills the different specialists will teach, so that the various areas of instruction are coordinated (Kratz, 1977).

◆ Orient the student to the physical environment in which dance instruction takes place. Assist with any strategies for changing clothes and shoes or any other daily living skills that are required for participation.

◆ Allow students with low vision to have access to the dance instructor's movements and demonstrations by being in close proximity to the instructor or area of demonstration or receiving individual instruction, if needed.

◆ Physically guide the student who is blind through movements. During this instruction, the student can place his or her hands on the teacher to get a sense of the movement, or two sighted students can position themselves on either side of the student to help him or perform a movement (Doyle, 1981; Kratz, 1977; Loumiet & Levack, 1993).

◆ Teach movement and dance concepts by associating the concepts with those the student is familiar with, such as shapes (Kratz,

1997). They can also be taught by associating them with objects and language. For example, objects can be used to help children identify the quality of movement. Clay can suggest the infinite shapes of a child's body, wire has endless shapes but also encompasses hardness, rubber bands emphasize the stretching and contraction of muscles, and balloons represent lightness (Duehl, 1979).

◆ Use verbal prompts to keep a student oriented during movement activities and to provide directions and feedback to the student. A variety of auditory cues (such as instruments, music, whistles, and clapping) can also be used to facilitate a student's orientation while moving in space, and tactile clues (like mats) can be used to define space on the floor (Kratz, 1977). Guidance and prompting should be eliminated as the student becomes more comfortable with the skills, but for some advanced dance techniques, assistance may always be necessary.

◆ Allow the student to perform at a rate that is comfortable and do not expect the student to "keep up" with the other students until he or she is ready (Kratz, 1977).

◆ Pay special attention to aspects of movements, such as aggressiveness, tension, speed, resistance, and sustaining movement, which can pose challenges for students who are blind (Doyle, 1981; Emes, 1978; Kratz, 1977). Is important to collaborate with the dance instructor to develop creative teaching strategies for teaching these skills. If a student is challenged by a particular whole-body movement, isolate the individual movements involved and have the student practice them separately using various body parts before they are combined.

◆ Provide individual feedback and repetition for new movement and dance skills (Doyle,

Checklist of Movement Skills

GENERAL BODY MOVEMENTS

Walking
Running
Jumping
Hopping
Skipping
Tiptoeing
Shuffling
Skating
Crawling
Rolling
Stooping
Bending (backward,
    forward, and to the
    side while standing
    or sitting)
Squatting
Sitting
Swaying
Twirling
Turning
Lifting
Lying down
Standing up
Bending body parts while
    lying down

LOWER-BODY MOVEMENTS

Kicking
Swinging leg
Stamping
Standing on one foot
Bending knees
Tapping toes and heels
Wiggling toes

Standing on tiptoe
Clicking heels together

UPPER-BODY MOVEMENTS

Swinging arms
Clapping
Reaching
Stretching
Shrugging
Punching
Pulling
Throwing
Tugging
Catching
Winding
Folding
Waving
Clutching
Shaking
Grasping
Patting
Pounding
Rubbing
Bending arm
Raising arm up and down
Straightening arm
Moving chin up and down
Moving head in a circle
Putting arm across body
Shaking head
Nodding head

FINGER MOVEMENTS

Pinching
Pointing
Squeezing

Wiggling
Snapping
Scratching
Tapping
Lacing
Cutting
Tying

FACIAL MOVEMENTS

Squinting
Wrinkling
Grimacing

WAYS IN WHICH TO MOVE

Slowly
Quickly
Loudly
Quietly
Happily
Sadly

DIRECTIONS IN WHICH TO MOVE

Up
Down
Backward
Forward
Sideways
In a circle

MOVING IN RELATION TO AN OBJECT

Over
Under
In front of
In back of
Between
Beside

1981). Furthermore, the instructor should provide directions that are detailed and within the student's experience. As Doyle (1981, p. 25) noted, "defining swaying in terms of a tree doesn't mean much to a person who has never seen a tree." The dance teacher should also provide plenty of opportunities to practice an activity, since practice is critical in developing movement and dance skills.

◆ Assess progress realistically and frequently to provide adequate feedback to the student (Doyle, 1981).

◆ Analyze each activity to provide an appropriate level of intervention. Dance activities that require dancing with a partner often increase in middle school level. Such activities can be taught with few accommodations.

◆ Consider the personalities of the student and the student's individual abilities to determine the student's ability to perform. Since many dance concepts can be adapted and expressed in language, older students who have a greater ability to communicate ideas through language can describe, compare, and discuss dance concepts, rather than perform dances.

Tracy Kiel had this to say about her experiences with dance as a student who is blind:

I had limited experiences in dance. The only basic experience was in social dance in eighth grade physical education. It was hard to participate in class when the teacher gave instructions, such as, "Put your left foot here and turn like this." What helped me was when the adapted physical education teacher or the instructional assistant assisted me before and after class by physically guiding me through the movements. When I was pretaught the steps and movements, I could follow and understand the teacher during class and felt more confident. I felt capable when I could dance alongside my peers (and was not pulled out of class for instruction). I would

have liked some exposure to ballet, jazz, and tap dancing because I do not understand the concepts of these types of dances. Others have seen it so they have some idea of it, but I don't have any idea of how it is done. I really liked dance because I didn't feel different.

Music

Music is tonal-rhythmic sound moving through time and space (MFACS, 1997). Lowenfeld (1971, p. 89) believed that "there is no question that music is perhaps the most important art activity of the blind." Even if one takes issue with Lowenfeld's comment, there is still evidence to support the idea that more students with visual impairments participate in music than in any other area of the arts. Many aspects of the music discipline are the same for students with visual impairments as they are for students who are sighted (Napier, 1973; Shaw, 1986). Furthermore, students who are visually impaired and those who are sighted derive the same benefits from music (Corn & Bailey, 1991) and have the same learning outcomes. It is primarily the teaching modifications that need to be addressed. Initially, it may seem that few accommodations are needed to gain access to the music curriculum. However, the effective teacher of students with visual impairments may discover that many strategies can be used to ensure that a student who is visually impaired participates at the same level and achieves the same outcomes and benefits as his or her classmates who are sighted.

As is true for the other arts disciplines, a review of the literature reveals few instructional strategies for the beginning teacher of students with visual impairments. However, the following strategies may facilitate a student's access to the music curriculum:

◆ Expose the student to musical instruments at an early age to help him or her develop musical concepts by listening to instrumental music and learning about how music is produced (Napier, 1973). Also encourage the student to attend musical performances and familiarize him or her with the environment of concert halls, including the orchestra pit, stage area, and risers used for choirs.

♦ Meet with the music and general education teacher to answer any questions they may have about a particular student's musical ability. In addition, at the beginning of the year (or semester), review the upcoming activities and lessons with the music teacher and jointly plan whatever modifications and instructional materials are needed, especially if the student is to read music with braille.

♦ Review the need for nonvisual conducting and directing strategies for a student who will participate in a choir or band. Both audible cues and tactile prompts by peers are effective alternatives to visual cues. Sidebar 11.4 describes how to include a student who is blind in instrumental music in a variety of bands and how individual lessons and musical concepts are taught.

♦ Locate and use the services of a certified music transcriber to transcribe the music into braille (see the Resources section at the end of the chapter for suggestions).

♦ Allow a student with low vision to use enlarged music scores and lyrics that he or she may read from a distance while sight-reading or otherwise performing in a band or choir. A student who is blind may need to memorize a score before a lesson.

♦ Familiarize a student who is visually impaired with terms and conventions used by sighted students (Goldstein, 1998), even if the student is using braille music. Tactile graphics can be used to teach such concepts as clefs and scales.

♦ Become familiar with the technological advances in the production of braille music and the different ways that students can write, print, and record music. See Resources at the end of the chapter for companies that are involved with music and braille technology for people who are blind or have low vision.

♦ Teach conducting skills learned by advanced music students through manual guidance and extra practice.

♦ Refamiliarize the student with a variety of band instruments when he or she is about to enter middle school, where many students join bands. Explore how each instrument produces sound (Shaw, 1986). Collaborate with the band instructor, so each instrument can be demonstrated.

♦ Encourage an older student to be responsible for his or her own adaptations in musical activities by consulting the music teacher to learn what the student will need before a class begins. Encourage the student to order his or her own braille music materials.

Braille Music

A brief explanation of some of the unique characteristics of reading braille music may help teachers of students with visual impairments understand the strategies of teaching and integrating braille music into the music curriculum. The braille music score is laid out in a linear fashion. For example, a piano score must first be read for one hand and practiced and read for the other hand and practiced; only then can the student put the two together. This procedure requires memorization because students who are blind cannot sight-read music (Krolik, 1998; Lowenfeld, 1971). Students who are blind who participate in choirs cannot sight-read for the same reason. Thus, learning to sing and play an instrument using braille music takes more time than a sighted student needs with printed music scores.

A serious music student who is blind needs to read and write braille music to participate in advanced classes, such as those on music theory and sight-reading and to continue a formal education in music (Goldstein, 1998). The following suggestions focus on strategies for teaching students to read and write braille music:

Teaching High School Instrumental Music to Students Who are Blind: A Director's Perspective

The following is a summary of adaptations that can be used in the day-to-day musical training of a student whose preferred learning mode is auditory. It is based on a director's experience teaching a student to perform in various types of bands in a rural high school.

BAND
Correct Notation and Musical Phrasing

◆ To learn notation and musical phrasing aurally, a student who is blind needs to listen to many high-quality recordings (compiled by the director) of the performances of full bands and of individual musicians (preferably playing the same instrument the student plays) and spend considerable time learning the musical concepts.

◆ In listening to the recordings, the student needs to focus on the following in addition to notation and phrasing: intonation, correct rhythms, adjustments in articulation, dynamics throughout the piece, and stylistic considerations.

◆ The student also needs to spend time organizing and rehearsing these concepts using an audiotape player at home or during a free hour at school, depending on his or her schedule.

Communication

◆ If the director uses gestures and facial expressions to communicate musical ideas, the student will not grasp these concepts as quickly as other members of the ensemble. Therefore, the director needs to explain these concepts in detail verbally.

◆ The director needs to review the concepts that the student may not be aware of

without access to the music in braille or print. For example, when the printed music indicates ritardano or rallentando (a gradual slowdown in pace) the director should explain when it is to begin and its duration.

Director's Responsibilities

◆ The director needs to set aside regularly scheduled time for individual lessons for the student to concentrate on phrasing, difficult notation, dynamics, intonation and musical concepts. Scheduling these lessons before or after school seems to be the best solution because both the student and director have more time to ask and answer questions, and the director has enough time to provide individual assistance with musical styles and notation and to gain a better understanding of his or her expectations for the student.

◆ The director also needs to schedule sufficient time to prepare and record the instrumental parts the student will be performing. To record the best possible examples for the student, the director needs to pay attention to the details of the mechanics of recording, such as the position of the tape recorder and microphone.

Physical Awareness and Instrumental Techniques

◆ The student needs to understand the correct posture, embouchure placement, and physical features of an instrument. To help the student learn these concepts and features, the director provides touch and verbal directions and feedback.

(continued on next page)

◆ The director needs to try a variety of methods to help the student grasp such concepts as the correct means of creating a good-quality sound and the amount of air being forced through an instrument.

◆ Assist students with physical adaptations and changes that need to occur by using verbal directions and feedback, and placing the student in the correct position.

Facility Setup

◆ The student needs to understand the physical features of the rehearsal facility and should be oriented to the rehearsal facility and to any changes in the physical arrangements that occur during the school year by the teacher of visual impairments or the O&M specialist.

◆ The layout of the rehearsal facility needs to remain somewhat consistent so the student can move about it independently. In this regard, the facility should be set up so there is a clear pathway to the areas for seating, storing instruments and music folios, and other areas the student uses during rehearsals. Make sure that percussion instruments and chairs remain in a general area.

JAZZ EDUCATION

◆ The musical concepts and notation are the same as for a band.

◆ For jazz improvisation, a beginning student needs a detailed explanation of the chord structure and symbols. This explanation should include information on the style of chord progression, accidentals located in the key signature, and stylistic considerations of the piece, as well as guidelines for improvisation.

MARCHING BAND

◆ To facilitate the independent participation of the student who is blind, a guide bar can be attached to three students, with the blind student in the middle, using bungee cords strapped around the three students' waists and connected to the bar. This technique allows the blind student to remain in a straight line with those around him or her. The three students can be marching next to each other or one in front of the other. This technique can be used in a field as well as on a street.

◆ The student and director should decide whether to explain the use of this technique to the judges of any contests that the band enters. Some students do not want the increased attention.

◆ A sighted student can be placed in charge of the guide pole and various other marching accessories. Other sighted classmates can help the student learn difficult musical passages, marching steps, and choreography. This assistance creates a bond between the sighted classmates and the blind student that is beneficial for the entire band.

◆ The student needs to be taught how the uniform should fit and where and how the accessories are to be worn. He or she also needs to know where to locate the uniform and accessories for performances.

LEON SIEVE
Director of Bands
Milaca High School
Milaca, MN

◆ Teach a complementary tactile system for reading and notating music using different notating systems (syllables, numbers, and letters). Encourage a student to use tactile skills at an early age to influence the use and acceptance of braille music as the student develops literacy skills.

◆ Provide lyrics to songs in braille to encourage a student to use a variety of learning modes for participation. Students who are blind frequently learn to rely on memorization for singing and participating in choirs (Lowenfeld, 1971; Napier, 1973).

◆ Introduce the student who is blind to the braille music code at the same rate as for students who are sighted (Napier, 1973). Figure 11.1 presents selected elements of the braille music code.

◆ Encourage the student's use of braille music in classes, by reviewing the methods that are used to integrate literary braille and Nemeth braille into classes. Develop, create, and provide braille music materials to facilitate the student's immersion in braille music. Small books focusing on different braille music symbols, individual cards, and games may be helpful. Allow the student to take these materials home to practice with them at night and on weekends.

◆ Encourage the student to compose music using the braille music code.

◆ Encourage a student to develop both tactile and aural skills for participating in music. As the student advances, he or she may develop a preferred learning mode for music that the student chooses on the basis of his or her own strengths and needs.

Tracy Kiel's considerable experiences with music illustrate how students who are blind learn music from an early age through high school.

When I was young, I took piano lessons in grades 1 through 4. I was taught by the Suzuki method. The teacher brought tapes of different music se-lections so I could listen to the music and choose what I wanted to learn and play. This gave me the freedom to choose. In fifth grade, I started to play the sax, and I continued through high school. What worked well was to sit by someone who knew how to play because I could listen and hear how the music was supposed to sound. Friends really helped me. If I couldn't tell what notes were being played (if it went too fast or there was a weird interval jump), they would help me by telling me the notes and/or playing the part for me slower so I could hear the notes.

Although my band director usually gave group lessons, he made mine individual. The individual lessons were helpful because if I had questions about notes, articulation, and dynamics, I didn't feel like I was holding anyone back. For one semester I had group lessons, and I did not ask many questions because I was too self-conscious. Sometimes the band director recorded my part.

I also participated in a marching band. It took some time before we could work out a successful solution for my independent participation in marching band practices and performances. What we worked out (between myself, my dad, the mobility specialist, the teacher of visual impairments, and the band instructor) was a pole that extended between me and the marchers to either side of me (or in front or in back), depending on the marching requirements. The three of us were "attached" to the pole with bungee cords around our waists. The pole was covered with black tape, so it blended with our black uniforms. At first, I was kind of embarrassed because people could see the pole and asked questions about it. I could also hear comments made by people watching from the sidelines as we marched in parades. But I got used to these comments and I realized that people were just curious. The hardest things that I had to learn were routines, changing directions, and various body positions (including how to place my feet). I had a good friend in the sax section, and she would put me in the right positions and demonstrate positions for me so I wouldn't have to interrupt and ask the director questions.

Notes

	C	D	E	F	G	A	B	rest
8th, 128th	⠙	⠑	⠋	⠛	⠓	⠊	⠚	⠭
Quarter 64th								
Half, 32nd								
Whole, 16th								

Octave Marks

<1st	1st	2nd	3rd	4th	5th	6th	7th	>7th

RH	Fing:	1	2	3	4	5		LH

Intrvls:	2nd	3rd	4th	5th	6th	7th	8th	

Other Symbols

4 Meas. rest		fff		Bracket Slur (beginning)	
Double Bar		Mezzo-forte		Bracket Slur (End)	
Dot		Piano		Martellato	
Music Hyphen		Pianissimo		Swell	
Triplet		Mezzo-piano		Fermata on a note	
Repeat sign		Dim.		Fermata between notes	
Slur		Rallentando		Fermata over a bar line	
Tie		Ritardendo		Measure in-accord	
Chord Tie		Ritenuto		Part-measure in-accord	
Flat		Word apostrophe		Measure division sign	
Sharp		Word sign		Staccato	
Natural		Tenuto		Staccatissimo	
Dim. (shape)		Tenuto-Staccato		Crescendo (hairpin)	
Forte		Accent		Cresc.	
Fortissimo		Note: Articulation Marks (staccato, fermata, etc.) are shown as applied to a quarter note C (⠹).			

Figure 11.1. Selected Elements of the Braille Music Code

Source: http://www.estp.umkc.edu/personal/bhugh/brmintro.html

I also participated in choir. I sat by people who knew music well. The choir director had the lyrics typed up, and they were transcribed into braille. If I had access to the words, I was able to learn the songs by listening to the melodies. When I could hear that my section wasn't all together on a certain note, I would ask a friend what note we were supposed to be on. My friend would tell me about the phrasing and dynamics of the piece and if I was singing something wrong. She would also give me physical prompts (by elbowing me or tapping me for cutoffs) during rehearsals and performances so I could follow the director's conducting.

When the choir director would demonstrate techniques, such as breath support and how to shape your mouth, my friend would show me. She would physically shape my mouth, guide me manually, and give me verbal directions.

During voice lessons, the teacher would suggest a variety of positions, so I could feel what everyone else could see. For example, he suggested that I should bend over to realize the impact of correct breathing.

I used braille music, which helped with basic things, such as note values, but I learned more difficult pieces by ear. During the first two years when I was learning to play my sax, I used braille music in theory books. I found it frustrating because I had to read the music, stop and play, find my spot again, read, and then play again. It broke up the piece too much, and it was difficult to memorize. As the pieces grew harder, I started developing relative pitch, which allowed me not only to hear and interpret the notes being played but to hear the piece as a whole. Doing it auditorally gave me an overview of the music, as well as the details in it. My band director recorded my parts for fast pieces slower so I could hear all the notes being played. Many times, I had to rewind the tape and listen to a part to hear all the notes, but this technique was still faster than using braille music to learn the piece.

During high school, I didn't think I needed to use braille music because of the routine I had. Now I realize that it would have been more ef-fective if I had used both braille music and auditory learning. I would still have used primarily an auditory mode, but braille music would have helped me with notes and markings in the music that I never knew existed.

Theater

Theater and drama offer excellent benefits to students who are visually impaired (Shaw, 1986) and can help all students develop both external and internal personal resources. Theatrical expression "requires that the participants feel another's situation. The result—an intense learning experience that evokes our emotional, imaginative, and intellectual capacities" (MFACS, 1997, Theater, p.1). Theater is an excellent vehicle for students with visual impairments to reach beyond their own self-concepts and perceptions and experience situations from other perspectives.

Even though there are many anecdotal stories about drama instructors and troupes working with students with visual impairments, there is limited documented information on instructional strategies for including students in drama and other theater activities. There is some information on helping students gain access to formal theater productions (see Audio Description in the Resources at the end of the chapter), but little guidance on developing students with visual impairments as actors.

Sidebar 11.5 presents the strategies that a high school speech and drama director used to include a high school student who was blind in theater and speech activities. Speech is included because students who become interested in theater frequently begin their training in middle school and high school speech classes.

In addition to the instructional strategies suggested in Sidebar 11.5, the following are strategies for theater-related activities:

◆ Review each teaching unit with the regular education teacher for activities that involve drama. Suggest ways to include the student who is visually impaired in active roles.

Performing in High School Theater Productions and Speech Meets: A Director's Perspective

The following instructional considerations enable a student who is blind to participate in high school theatrical productions and speech meets.

THEATRICAL PRODUCTIONS

Auditioning

- Give the student the sections of the script that will be used in the audition (in braille or large print), but be aware that the use of braille or large print limits the student's flexibility to read spontaneously from other sections of the script during the audition.

- Discuss with the student what roles will be read during the audition, so he or she can be prepared.

- Provide a substantial part for the student to read, so he or she can have more variety in reading.

- Allow the student either to memorize the part or read from the braille script.

- Encourage the student to demonstrate initiative in preparing for the audition and allowing enough time to get the script, choose the sections to be read, and have the text transcribed into braille.

Rehearsal

- Arrange for an initial orientation to the rehearsal area, which can be conducted by a peer, the teacher of students with visual impairments, or the O&M specialist, depending on the student's abilities.

- Use a "buddy" or guide to facilitate the student's participation in rehearsals. The "buddy" can be a volunteer or can be selected by the student and does not necessarily have to be in the production.

- Use a guide to help the student learn the mechanics of the part faster and respond to the director's verbal or demonstrated directions immediately.

- Use the guide to verbally and/or manually guide the student through the directions and give the student clarification and feedback, so the director does not have to stop the rehearsal to do so. When the student learns the part, the guide may no longer be necessary. The decision to stop using the guide is made jointly by the student, the director, and the guide.

Entrances and Exits

- Tell both the student and the guide when the student needs to be on stage and where the student should enter from.

- Allow the student to enter on his or her own or with the guide.

Movement on Stage

- Facilitate the student's independence on stage by using many strategies. If the student makes entrances and exits independently, landmarks can be used on stage, such as the actual props that will be used in the performance.

- Use tactile surfaces on the floor such as nonslip area rugs.

Blocking

- Use of a sighted guide in the first three weeks of rehearsals will facilitate blocking (planning the expected movements of the actors) since blocking changes constantly while different strategies are being tried.

(continued on next page)

◆ Use strategies to limit the amount of blocking, including revising the blocking to fit individual actors and their abilities; allowing the student who is blind to remain fairly stationary because quick movements may disorient him or her; and limiting the number of props, especially hand props.

◆ Edit the script if an adjustment in blocking interferes with the meaning of the dialogue. Some editing can be done ahead of time; other editing can be done throughout the rehearsals, depending on the adjustments that are made.

Stage Directions

◆ Substitute sound cues for the traditional lighting cues for the student who is blind.

◆ Verbalize directions; do not rely on nonvisual cues, such as body language.

General Considerations

◆ Be flexible and adapt to the abilities of all the actors, not just the one with a visual impairment.

◆ Develop successful strategies by trial and error. If something does not work, simply try something else.

◆ Try the following process that was successful in training a blind student as a performer. The first year, the student received a speaking part off stage; the second year, the student had a nonspeaking part on stage; the third year, the student had a speaking part on stage; and the fourth year, the student had a major part.

◆ Encourage the student to participate in the camaraderie in the theater department that affects all the participants. During rehearsals and afterward, the students have many informal conversations, both on and off stage, and often develop close friendships.

SPEECH MEETS

◆ Encourage the student to be responsible for creating or copying the speech into an appropriate medium.

◆ Help the student learn to use body language and gestures while speaking.

◆ Teach gestures in a variety of ways: by trial and error, having an assistant stand behind the student and guide him or her through them, placing the student in different positions, and giving verbal directions and frequent feedback.

◆ Teach broad gestures, which may be easier to learn than small hand movements.

◆ Use a sighted guide at speech meets to help the student find the appropriate room and to read directions that are provided to the participants. A sighted guide can also help the student move to the speaking area if the student wishes.

Source: Based on an interview with
JACK PALMER
Director for Speech and Drama
Milaca Public Schools
Milaca, MN

◆ Familiarize the student with the features of a theatrical environment, including seating, the stage area, lighting, curtains, and the orchestra pit.

◆ Preteach theater concepts, such as scenery, costumes, makeup, and the use of lighting and sound and the purposes of these elements through concrete and experiential learning activities.

◆ Collaborate with the O&M specialist to determine the skills and techniques needed to engage in theater activities and to incorporate them into O&M lessons.

◆ Preteach the student about body language, facial expressions, and the variety of positions in which people stand, sit, and move. Sacks and Reardon (1992) offered strategies for developing physical skills, such as eye contact, gestures, and body language. They suggested rehearsing "gestures either by consistent sequences of motor-support intervention or through instruction and practice" (p. 159).

◆ Encourage the student to participate actively in classroom dramatizations beginning at an early age and to seek roles that require movement and props.

◆ Take the student to theatrical productions and arrange tours of the stage, if possible. Many theaters in urban areas provide audiocassettes of descriptions of productions specifically for people to use while attending performances.

◆ Collaborate with a theater director to teach the student about the elements of directing. When directing a play, the student may need assistance from a sighted classmate.

◆ Teach the student the various techniques for moving on a stage and in classroom productions, including using a sighted guide, a cane, and tactile cues and memorizing the set, and when to use specific techniques.

◆ Provide individual lessons for specific movements required for a part in a production. Give the student plenty of time to practice and provide frequent feedback.

◆ Ensure that the student is participating appropriately in a theater production by observing rehearsals periodically and offering suggestions for modifications.

◆ Encourage students to participate in theatrical productions by working on scenery, sound, lighting, costumes, and makeup. These are activities for which accommodations (e.g., tactile markings on lightboard switches) are easily provided.

Tracy Kiel participated in theatrical productions throughout high school:

> I participated in theater during my four years in high school. My director made accommodations for me but did not favor me. He gave me a little leeway, such as letting me sit so I could put my braille script on my lap, rather than stand as the others did. Having a "buddy" during rehearsals really helped. She would guide me when my stage directions said to move. At the beginning, the blocking would change frequently, and it would be hard to memorize. The buddy was helpful during this time, until the blocking became permanent.
>
> My buddy also helped me with my movements so that during an action, I was always facing the audience. For example, if I needed to turn to face the other direction, she showed me how to move so that I turned toward the audience, not away from it. She held my script for me, which freed me to be able to read and still walk around to move and act.
>
> My director eliminated movements that were unnesccessary to the plot and allowed me to do movements that were comfortable because some things did not seem natural to me. For example, when the stage directions indicated a long cross to a table to help clear it, the director changed the directions so I could make a shorter cross and sit on a couch.

Visual Arts

"Through the visual arts the student is trained in aesthetic perception, extracting rich meanings from the sights, sound, and experiences presented by art.... This aesthetic dimension is what gives the visual arts their educational power in such things as interpreting cultures, communicating feelings, and sharing human aspirations" (MFACS, 1997, Visual Arts, p. 3). This description of the visual arts provides a broad and meaningful context for including students with visual impairments in this curriculum.

The literature is dominated by discussions of the benefits of the visual arts for people with visual impairments and the meaning derived from these arts (Haupt, 1969; Lisenco, 1971; Lowenfeld, 1971; Napier, 1973; Shaw, 1987). There is a consensus on the benefits of the creative process, which allows "personal satisfaction received from the creative activity and the possibility of continued satisfaction after the completion of the work" (Lisenco, 1971, p. 59). The challenge for teachers of students with visual impairments is to provide meaningful experiences in the visual arts and adaptations that enhance students' participation in a way that expands their aesthetic knowledge and skills. Sidebar 11.6 presents one teacher's perspective on tactile art, and Sidebar 11.7 gives some ideas for tactile art activities.

The following teaching strategies encourage a student's participation in all aspects of the visual arts. It is important to consider the individual abilities, needs, desires, and interests of each student when providing services in this area:

- Meet with teachers of arts activities to discuss adapting the visual arts curriculum for a student who is visually impaired, including issues that sometimes cause dilemmas for teachers, such as color and two-dimensional art. Help teachers understand how the visual arts can be meaningful for the student.

- Consider the negative attitudes toward the visual arts revealed by students in Land's research (1998). Expose the student with a vi-sual impairment to experiential learning activities beginning at an early age that expand his or her thinking about the visual arts. Ensure that the student's experiences with visual art are meaningful and provide personal satisfaction. For example, take the student to museums to get a hands-on experience with works of art and to develop a sense of the history and culture of the visual arts.

- Note that Haupt (1969) suggested that teachers of students with visual impairments should help students use their hands efficiently, explore objects in depth, ask questions that provoke the spirit of inquiry, use a rich vocabulary for the remaining senses, know the importance of first-hand experiences, and be skillful in using analogies.

- Give students in the early grades ample opportunities to develop their fine motor skills, such as tearing, cutting, gluing, stringing, and stacking, using a variety of tools, including scissors, tools for drawing and making marks, and materials to "make things stick," like gluesticks, double-sided tape, and spray adhesives. For example, students who are blind can make tactile marks with such self-adhesive materials as Velcro, Wikki Stix (waxed string), and raised-line drawing materials.

- Adapt typical tools used in the classroom; for instance, label crayons of different colors in braille, so a student who is blind can work independently.

- Encourage students with low vision to use the same low vision devices (near, distance, and closed-circuit television [CCTV]) they use for literacy activities (see Feld & Hall, for the use of CCTVs) and a variety of materials, including fluorescent paper, paint, felt-tip pens, markers, light colors on dark backgrounds, and glow-in-the-dark materials (Wellman, 1994) for art activities. For younger students, monitor the environ-

Tactile Art: One Teacher's Perspective

People who are sighted can see all parts of an art object at the same time and how the parts are related to each other and to the whole. Although most people think of art in this spatial way, art also has a temporal aspect, which is the most obvious when large pieces of sculpture or buildings are viewed. As one walks around a sculpture or through a building, the parts reveal themselves sequentially. Then the flow of the parts, one into the next, becomes an important aspect of the art experience. There is both a static spatial and a flowing, temporal aspect. For people who are sighted, the spatial aspect of art seems to dominate the temporal aspect. In contrast, people who are blind experience an art object as their hands and fingertips move over it, so the experience is primarily a temporal, sequential one and only secondarily a spatial one.

The materials of which art objects can be made have many qualities: color, shape, texture, and others that are experienced kinesthetically, such as firmness, springiness, resistance to touch or movement, and weight. For sighted children, the most important quality is color. However, for children who are blind, the important qualities are texture, the surface's resistance to touch, variations in elevation from the surface, and weight.

Think of the things that are enjoyable and beautiful to touch and handle: a cashmere sweater, the handle and heft of a well-made and balanced tool, polished wood, a kitten's soft fur, a string of beads. The happiness and sense of well-being that one feels as one's hands and fin-

gertips move over such objects and the shape and weight of the objects as one holds them constitute tactile-kinesthetic art appreciation—art from the viewpoint of a connoisseur who is blind.

Consider the art materials of the preschool and the elementary classroom: crayons, paint, various kinds of paper, glue, paste, and Play Doh. Since all these materials except paper are either not perceptible by or offensive to the touch of children who are blind, what these children are likely to learn most powerfully in the early years is that art is unintelligible and unpleasant. Later they learn that they can make many art objects that are acceptable to their art teachers. They can glue paper shapes onto big pieces of paper. They can weave strips of paper through paper slits to make placemats. They can cut along raised lines. But what of art appreciation and artistic production from the children's point of view?

The activities in Sidebar 11.7 involve art objects and processes that are interesting, pleasurable, and fun to touch and handle, and many include sound to add another dimension to the art experience. They are designed to give children who are blind the opportunity to create art objects that they, themselves, can appreciate and enjoy and by making, can express their creativity.

Source: Adapted from Martha Pamperin, *Tactual Art (Draft)* (On-line). Available: www.tsbvi.edu/education/tactual.htm

ment to ensure that appropriate modifications are being used but expect older students to be responsible for appropriate modifications.

◆ Keep a container in the classroom with a variety of materials in different sizes and

shapes that promote many sensory experiences, such as feathers, buttons, string, paper, beads, and fabric (Mangold, 1982), including scented materials (like markers and stickers) that can be smelled and textured materials (like fabric and wallpaper)

STUFF-N-STUFF

Crumple an object, stuff it into a bag, and close up the bag. Do so with a different object in each of a number of bags and then assemble or arrange the bags in some way. These bags are fun to touch and squeeze. While the child is having fun, he or she will also develop finger and hand strength and wrist and finger dexterity and will learn more about the inside and outside of shapes of containers, the properties of various materials, a sequence of activities leading to a goal, and how to participate in a group.

Materials

1. Things to crumple: pieces of newspaper, pages torn from magazines, paper towels, sheets of plastic, aluminum foil, foam rubber, Kleenex, rags, leaves, and the like.
2. Kinds of bags: small paper bags, cloth bags, nylon stockings, socks, and so forth.
3. To keep the bags closed: twist paper bags closed or use tape, string, rubber bands, clothes pins, and so on.
4. A cardboard or plastic container for crumpled things that are ready for stuffing (unless each crumpled piece will be stuffed into a bag as soon as it is crumpled).

Activities

- Crumple the materials and toss them into a box. The child can climb or reach into the box and play with the materials.
- The child can squeeze or pound the bags, roll them between his or her hands, and roll over them.
- The find-it game: Have a child or all the children in a class crumple materials and toss the crumpled pieces into a box or other container. When the container is full, let the children take turns finding an interesting object that the teacher or another child has hidden in the box.

- Squeeze-me board or squeeze-me line: Each day have the child crumple a different material and stuff it into a different type of small bag. Vary the kinds and shapes of the bags and the kinds of "crumplebles." Tie each stuffed bag with a string and attach it to the side of a cardboard box, a bulletin board, or another firm surface. Let the child select the place where the bag will go on the board or other surface and give him or her the opportunity to explore the resulting display.
- Other games: Use the bags on strings as indoor balls or punching bags.

STRINGING THINGS

Materials

1. Stringables: cardboard tubes, beads, washers, nuts, macaroni, pieces of drinking straw, buttons, pieces of wood with holes, and so forth.
2. Stringers: pipe cleaners, pieces of wire coat hanger, dowels, drinking straws, shoelaces, thin wire, rope, string, and yarn (firm things are easier to use than wobbly things).

Process

For beginners, the teacher knots or otherwise secures one end of the stringer so that the stringables cannot slide off and leaves it free or inserts one end of the stringer through a hole in heavy cardboard, secures the stringer, and tapes it and the cardboard to a tabletop. The student then strings the stringables on the stringer. When the student is finished, the teacher secures the free end of the stringer or puts it through another hole in the cardboard and then secures it. The student explores and plays with his or her creation, moving the materials back and forth on the string; tipping the cardboard, so the materi-

(continued on next page)

als slide from one end to the other; turning the materials on the string; and so on. The child may also wish to wear the creation around his or her wrist or neck or hang it by one end from a bulletin board.

Extensions

◆ If a variety of stringables are available, the student can explore what happens when items with different-size holes are strung on the same stringer (they may slide over one another). Older children can make stringable tubes by rolling paper and securing it with tape, string or rubber bands, and decorate them.

◆ Flat shapes with small holes in them can be used as separators to prevent one item from sliding over another.

◆ Beads can be made from Play-Doh® or clay.

HIDDEN COLLAGE

Almost anything can be stuck to a flat surface to make a collage. The problem with most collages for students who are blind is that it is difficult to feel them without either getting the hands sticky with glue or dislodging the pieces. This problem can be solved by covering a collage with a piece of material, such as an old sheet or a lighter material, and having the student feel it through the material. Crayon rubbing or paint can be added to the material after the collage is finished for students with low vision.

Materials

1. A firm, flat surface: cardboard, heavy paper, or another firm material.
2. Thin objects to stick to the surface: cardboard shapes, leaves, grasses, fabric, foam, string and so forth.
3. An adhesive material: glue, paste, starch, or tape. Starch is much less offensive to handle than is glue.
4. A smooth, lightweight piece of material,

such as an old sheet, piece of nylon material, or sheet of paper toweling.

Process

1. Attach one edge of the material to the top back of the surface, so the material can be easily pulled down to cover the collage and then raised.
2. The student affixes each object with the adhesive and sticks the objects on the surface one by one or coats the entire surface with starch and then sticks the objects on it. With starch, the objects will stick but can be easily removed and put somewhere else. The student can cover and check the collage periodically while it is being made.

When the collage is completed, the material is stretched over it and folded under, and the edges are taped to the back so the material covering the picture stays in place, and the student feels it through the material. If paper toweling is used, the student can coat it with starch using is or her fingertips and press the toweling gently with the fingertips to mold it to the shapes below. If a visual effect is desired, the student can do a crayon rubbing on the material, which will not interfere with his or her tactile enjoyment of the collage.

PAPIER-MÂCHÉ

Papier-mâché can be made from any kind of shredded paper or paper strips mixed with any kind of liquid paste. Some combinations are much less pleasant to handle than others. Shredded paper toweling mixed with starch is minimally messy and fairly comfortable to handle. Papier-mâché can be used to build up contours or relief on a surface, such as on a mask, a map, or a picture.

Materials

1. Paper towels or other types of paper torn into small pieces.
2. Liquid starch or a thin flour paste.

(continued on next page)

Tactile Art Activities *(Continued)*

3. Cardboard or another firm, flat material for the surface.

Procedure

1. Shred the paper.
2. Add enough starch to get all the paper wet.
3. Mix until a moldable substance is achieved.
4. Squeeze out extra starch.
5. Place all or part of the mixture on the surface. Mold to the desired shape with the fingers.
6. Dry for several days.

Extensions

◆ Before the papier-mâché is put on the cardboard, cover the cardboard with construction paper, wrapping paper, or another covering. The starch may not stick well to a slick surface, so glue can be used after the papier-mâché is dry.

◆ Before the papier-mâché is put on the cardboard, cover the cardboard with a sheet of braille or a raised-line drawing on a heavy paper. Then mold the papier-mâché to the lines. This technique is good for making relief maps.

◆ Finish the papier-mâché relief by carefully pressing a large piece of paper towel moistened with starch over the entire surface so it adheres to the contours of the relief.

◆ Color the dried papier-mâché with watercolor, crayon or tempera.

◆ Spray the relief picture from an angle so the contours determine where the color will be.

◆ Make some kind of frame.

OTHER IDEAS

Paper sculpture. Cut or tear paper, fold or twist it, and affix it to a stable surface, such as a piece of heavy paper or cardboard, with tape, staples, or paste.

Sewing and weaving. Punch holes in paper, cardboard, or another surface. Weave or sew through the holes using pipe cleaners, yarn, string, or anything else that is pleasant to handle and can be poked through the holes.

Macramé. Start by using a firm base and three-strand braids made of heavy string, pipe cleaners, twine, rope of various textures and widths, laces, and ribbon. Teach the student various knots and knot sequences.

Building toys. Choose building toys that stick together, such as LEGOs, Lincoln Logs, Bristle Blocks, and many others that are commercially available.

Source: Adapted from Martha Pamperin, *Tactual Art (Draft)* (On-line). Available: www.tsbvi.edu/education/tactual.htm

---

for tactile experiences, from which a student may choose. Encourage an older student to collect, store, and organize his or her materials.

◆ Preteach how to use materials and tools, such as pointed instruments and knives, safely and how to organize a work space when working on an art project.

◆ Help students to "explore objects more efficiently by observing not only forms, but textures, temperatures, weights, odors, and sounds and their contrasting relationships" (Haupt, 1969, p. 42). Also discuss how different tactile materials can communicate different ideas and feelings (Mangold, 1982).

◆ Teach the concepts of color, associate colors with feelings, words, ideas, sounds, and textures by using books (such as *Hailstones and Halibut Bones* by Mary O'Neill), poems, and familiar experiences. For example, tell the student, "Yellow is the warmth felt when you bury your feet in the sand on a hot day." Other visual concepts that may need additional explanations are contrast, illusion, and depth.

◆ Review instructional adaptations that are specific to a painting unit. "Tactile paint" can be made by adding a different gritty material (such as sand) to each color of paint (Lisenco, 1971). A number of painting techniques, including fingerpainting, brush painting, string painting, spattering paints, blowing paint through a straw, painting with paint tubes, and painting within raised-line shapes (plastic stained-glass templates), can be tried. Painting objects can be more meaningful than painting paper (Loumiet & Levack, 1993). In addition, scented sprays and oils can be added to any materials.

◆ Review instructional adaptations that are specific to a drawing unit. There are a variety of materials for making tactile drawings: self-adhesive materials (such as Velcro and magnetic materials), Letraline (used by architects), glue, puffy paint, plastic templates, craft stencils, cookie cutters, and tracing wheels (on surfaces that retain the imprint of a tool). Raised textures can also be created by drawing with crayons over textured surfaces like a metal screen, plastic stitchery canvas, and corrugated cardboard (Lisenco, 1971; Loumiet & Levack, 1993). Scented markers and crayons can be used as well.

◆ Use technological tools to produce tactile materials for a student or for a student to create artwork. For example, the Thermo-Pen, which has a tip that is hot, makes a raised line or mark on capsule paper (or swell paper), a heat-sensitive paper on which black images are raised when the paper is heated using a stereo copier or Pictures in a Flash (another heating device). Images can also be created using a braillewriter and PictureBraille to produce

images on a braille embosser. A useful low-tech product is the Woolly Pen, which dispenses wool that sticks to a special drawing board.

◆ Teach students who are visually impaired about reliefs, sculpture, mosaics, graphic media (engraving, etching, and blockprinting) (Lisenco, 1971), printmaking collage (Loumiet & Levack, 1993), dioramas, photography, and computer art (Wellman, 1994). Many materials can be used with these techniques, such as found objects (natural and man-made), textured paint, paper, tile, clay, metal, leather, fiber, and wood. Kinetic sculpture (whose parts move in some way) and sound sculpture, such as a windchime (which produces interesting sounds), may also be meaningful art forms for a visually impaired student. Hobby stores have many materials to create moving parts (Wellman, 1994).

◆ Explore performance art, which mixes media and art forms and emphasizes the act of creating (Wellman, 1994) as an interesting alternative for students with visual impairments, as is multimedia art, in which a visual art piece is combined with another medium such as music or other audio outputs, to convey an idea or mood.

Crafts may have a negative connotation in the visual arts and among people with visual impairments because they are said to promote repetitive skills and are not creative or aesthetic (Napier, 1973; Shaw, 1986). This misperception of crafts may be due to the historical role they have placed as a vocation for people who are blind (Lowenfeld, 1971). Today, many people view crafts as having equal status with two-dimensional visual arts. Since crafts provide unlimited opportunities for artistic and creative expression for students with visual impairments (Napier, 1973), it is important for teachers of students with visual impairments to provide craft activities that promote an aesthetic experience as well as the development of skills. Expose students to the multitude of crafts that are available by visiting arts and crafts stores, hobby stores, and craft shows. The following comments indicate Tracy Kiel's experiences with the visual arts:

My experiences with drawing and painting were helpful in understanding some visual arts ideas. In the first grade, I had a piece of artwork—a snowman—in an art show. When I was little, I liked to draw dogs, and my friends really encouraged me and showed me what shapes to draw.

I was never interested in visual arts. Shading and colors were concepts that I could not comprehend. My friends have done a remarkable job trying to describe color, and I now have a small sense of what it is. I even have a favorite color—turquoise—that reminds me of a mix of blue and green, and when I picture the ocean it seems like a serene color, rich and cool. But I can't really identify with putting colors on paper. When I was little, I liked building three-dimensional things because they had texture and I had experience with them.

I also don't comprehend other visual concepts, such as views and perspectives. Simple things like drawing a cube on paper or even drawing the top of a sphere make no sense to me. I don't understand how a three-dimensional object can be represented in a two-dimensional way, like how a sphere is seen flat from the top.

Instead of drawing, my teachers often adapted projects for me. I remember making a three-dimensional map of the United States out of clay. When I had an assignment to draw a map of my house and yard, my father helped me put together a map using a wooden board for a base, carpet for grass, a three-dimensional house, screws with twist ties for trees, and a rippled material for our pond.

When I had to draw pictures in elementary art class, I used glue and string to put my ideas on paper. Visual art, like any art, is a way to express oneself. It must be adapted, or I must adapt it, so the main goal of art can still be achieved.

Literary Arts

"The literary arts is a field of endeavor where words and language are imaginatively used to explore, discover, and express feelings, ideas, and values in poetry, fiction, creative non-fiction, drama, and other creative writing" (MFACS, 1997, Literary Arts, p. 1). The literary arts, part of the language arts curriculum in which students acquire skills in reading, writing, speaking, and listening, gives students a vehicle for self-expression and the opportunity to develop literacy skills beyond the required reading and writing. A student with a visual impairment "will be strengthened in the link between the concrete and the abstract, between things and symbols, words and ideas" (Sennet, 1969, p. 84).

Given access to assistive technology, a student who is visually impaired can participate fully in the literary arts. Sidebar 11.8 presents a sample of the writing of Tracy Kiel when she was a high school student. In high school, Tracy was encouraged to develop her creative writing abilities and to explore and express her ideas about the physical enviroment.

Instructional strategies that support access to the literary arts for students who are visually impaired are as follows:

◆ Provide instruction and support in the early grades, when many activities for the literary arts are integrated during reading and writing instruction. The teacher of students with visual impairments should be available not just to assist with literacy instruction, but to facilitate the student's participation in literary arts activities. (See Chapter 8 on teaching literacy skills.)

◆ Exercise care in the early grades not to overuse oral and aural methods. They provide communication easily but can decrease the student's opportunities to read and write independently. Students who are visually impaired should use these methods with the same frequency as do their sighted classmates.

◆ Ensure that a young child who is visually impaired has a variety of appropriate low- and high-tech writing tools, such as a braillewriter, a slate and stylus, a computer with appropriate access technology (en-

A Creative Writing Sample

A MOUNTAIN MEADOW

A mountain view may be spectacular, but I've learned from experience that a mountain meadow itself is much more appealing. Sitting on an aging tree stump, I curiously surveyed my surroundings. Thousands of wild flowers danced in the sunlight, each one carefully painted with its own color and design. The delicate scent of the flowers filled my nose, an aroma softer and sweeter than any bottle of perfume could ever capture. I peered down to find a rippling stream flowing lazily at my feet. The crystal-clear water looked luscious, and I had difficulty believing the water was anything less than pure. Acting as a bridge, an unsturdy log lies across the stream. My fellow hikers had crossed this bridge with caution and uncertainty, fearful of its instability. I turned my attention upwards, to behold hundreds of birds soaring among the puffy white clouds. Their voices joined together to form a melodious song, like a chorus of angels singing majestically in the heavens. The meadow served as a place of serenity and peace, and I felt privileged to be a part of it.

TRACY JO KIEL
Student
Milaca Public Schools
Milaca, MN

♦ Provide students with a strong background in concept development and experiential learning activities to derive the most benefit from literary art activities. Provide students with ongoing experiences with these activities.

♦ Provide feedback to students in an appropriate medium (braille, large print, or orally) to help them develop appropriate skills in the literary arts.

♦ Ensure that students have methods (such as electronic formats or scanning) for gaining access to a greater volume of reading material as the requirements for reading other literary works increase.

♦ Pair a student who is blind with a sighted classmate and have the blind student report the assignment as a language-based activity. A background in creative writing may assist the student in communicating many ideas and concepts.

♦ Continue to provide experiences to develop vocabulary and other concepts to ensure that students are interpreting and using language that is meaningful.

Tracy Kiel's following comments illustrate her experience with the literary arts:

Having literary works in braille, rather than on tape or read aloud, helped me to form my own pictures or images and enhanced my creativity. Reading the literature to yourself helps *you* say it, which is different from how others would say it.

One of the most helpful creative writing techniques that was taught in school was to use the five senses in writing. It made me realize that even though I could not see, all my readers were sighted, so I wrote things that would appeal to them to help the audience and writer relate to each other. I realized that if I wanted to be a good writer, I needed to cover all the senses. Including the visual sense was easy because I used pictures in my head of what things would be like. Other times, however, it was much more difficult. I often sought help from my mother in such cases. She would describe the color, shape, size, and

larged print, voice, and braille), and a personal note taker.

♦ Encourage students with visual impairments and sighted students to have an immediate way of sharing their reading and writing with each other, such as with assistive technology like a Mountbatten braillewriter and CCTV, or other ways to read and write independently. Relying on live readers for literary art activities takes the personal experience away from the student.

physical features of an area. My mother would describe everything, from the color of a sunset to the type of weeds growing near our pond.

SUMMARY

The arts are playing a greater and greater role in the lives of people everywhere as technological and other changes are having an increasing effect on daily life. The disciplines of dance, music, theater, the visual arts, and literary expression are critical in helping people develop completely and relate to each other in a global environment (MFACS, 1997). It is through the arts that people may discover the common bonds among their multicultural communities.

To enable students who are visually impaired to have an equal opportunity to enhance their lives through the arts, teachers of students with visual impairments must take the initiative to include them in this area of the educational curriculum. Current educational initiatives, such as the *National Standards for Arts Education* (CNAEA, 1994), and teacher training and licensing in the arts, can help support student participation.

Instructional strategies for including students with visual impairments in the arts curriculum are built on common sense, high expectations, and adapting materials. They are for all students with visual impairments, not just the talented, because all students derive benefits from the arts. Through studying the arts, the joy of learning can become real, tangible, and powerful for students with visual impairments.

ACTIVITIES

1. Break into small groups of three or four. One individual should serve as the teacher, and the others should be blindfolded as the students. Complete one of the art activities described in Sidebar 11.7. Every 10 minutes, have someone else in the group be the teacher, so everyone has a chance to be a student. Share your experiences with each other.

2. Contact a residential school for students who are visually impaired and ask to speak with the art teacher. Interview this individual to find suggestions for integrating students with visual impairments into regular art classes. Prepare a handout on these suggestions and share them with your classmates.

3. Observe an art class in a local elementary, middle, or high school. Describe the activity or activities that you observed, and list possible modifications that would be needed to integrate a student who is blind into the class.

4. Read an autobiography or biography of an artist (painter, actor, musician) who was blind or had low vision. Write a short report on the role that art played in the artist's life. Include any specific adaptations that the artist used and share this information with your classmates.

REFERENCES

Algozzine, B., Ysseldyke, J., & Elliot, J. (1997). *Strategies and tactics for effective instruction.* Longmont, CO: Sopris West.

Arts education standards. (1999, Spring). *INTASC in Focus, 1,* 5–6.

Art history through touch and sound: A multisensory guide for the blind and visually impaired [Audiobook]. (n.d.). New York: Art Education for the Blind.

Bullard, S. (1993, Fall). New visions. *Teaching Tolerance,* 46–49.

Corn, A. L., & Bailey, G. L. (1991). Profile of music programs at residential schools for blind and visually impaired students. *Journal of Visual Impairment & Blindness, 85,* 379–382.

CEC knowledge and skills for all beginning special education teachers of students with visual impairments. (1998). In *What every special educator must know: The international standards for the preparation and licensure of special educators* (3rd ed., pp. 75–80). Reston, VA: Council for Exceptional Children.

Consortium of National Arts Education Associations. (1994). *National standards for arts education: What every young American should know and be able to do in the arts.* (Available from Music Educators National Conference, 1806 Robert Fulton Drive, Reston, VA 22091.) Available on-line at http://www.artsedge.kennedy-center.org./cs/design/standards/index.html

Doyle, D. (1981). Ballet for visually handicapped students. *Journal of Physical Education and Recreation, 52*(8), 25, 28–29.

Duehl, A. N. (1979). The effect of creative dance movement on large muscle control and balance in congenitally blind children. *Journal of Visual Impairment & Blindness, 73,* 127–133.

Dykema, D. (1986). *They shall have music: A manual for the instruction of visually handicapped students in the playing of keyboard instruments.* (Available from D. Dykema, 604 North Allen, Carbondale, IL 62901.)

Emes, C. G. (1978). Creative dance: A valuable process for blind children. *Education of the Visually Handicapped, 10,* 84–87.

Feld, G. F., & Hall, C. C. (1980). The CCTV as an art tool. *Journal of Visual Impairment & Blindness, 74,* 151–153.

Goldstein, D. (1998). Summer music institute for blind college-bound musicians. *RE:view, 29,* 163–167.

Haupt, C. (1969). Creative expression through art. *Education of the Visually Handicapped, 1*(2) 41–43.

Kaplan, T., & Mayerson Sovin, J. (Eds.). (1998). *I don't know where the nose is: Poetry and art by students from the California School for the Blind.* Fremont: California School for the Blind.

Koenig, A. J., & Farrenkopf, C. (1994–95). *Providing quality instruction in braille literacy skills,* a companion guide to R. Routman, *Invitations: Changing as teachers and learners K–12* (1991). Houston, TX: Region IV Education Service Center.

Kratz, L. E. (1977). *Movement without sight: Physical activities and dance for the visually handicapped.* Palo Alto, CA: Peek.

Krolick, B. (1998). *How to read braille music* (2nd ed.). San Diego, CA: OPUS Technologies.

Land, D. (1998). *Visual arts and students with visual impairments, A thesis in special education.* Unpublished master's thesis, Texas Tech University, Lubbock.

Lewis, S. (1999). Blindness and low vision. In A. Turnbull, R. Turnbull, M. Shank, & D. Teal, *Exceptional lives: Special education in today's schools* (pp. 662–710). Upper Saddle River, NJ: Prentice Hall.

Lisenco, Y. (1971). *Art not by eye.* New York: American Foundation for the Blind.

Loumiet, R., & Levack, N. (1993). *Independent living: A curriculum with adaptations for students with visual impairments. Volume 3: Play and leisure* (2nd ed.). Austin: Texas School for the Blind and Visually Impaired.

Lowenfeld, B. (1971). *Our blind children: Growing and learning with them* (3rd ed.). Springfield, IL: Charles C Thomas.

Mangold, S. (1982). Art experience is fundamental to creative thinking. In S. Mangold (Ed.), *A teacher's guide to the special educational needs of blind and visually handicapped children* (pp. 111–118). New York: American Foundation for the Blind.

Minnesota frameworks for arts curriculum strategies. (1997). Golden Valley: Minnesota Center for Arts Education.

Napier, G. (1973). Special subject adjustments and skills. In B. Lowenfeld (Ed.), *The visually handicapped child in school* (pp. 221–277). New York: American Foundation for the Blind.

National Assessment of Educational Progress. (1997). *NAEP 1997 Arts Report Card.* Washington, DC: U.S. Government Printing Office. Available on-line at http://www.nces.ed.gov/naep

National Education Goals Panel. (1990) *National education goals: Building a nation of learners.* Washington, DC: U.S. Government Printing Office. Available on-line at http://www.negp.gov/webpg130.htm

New International manual of braille music notation. (n.d.). San Diego, CA: OPUS Technologies.

Pamperin, M. (n.d.). *Tactual art (draft)* (On-line). Available: http: www.tsbvi.edu/education/tactual.htm

Sacks, S. Z., & Reardon, M. P. (1992). Maximizing social integration for visually impaired students: Applications and practice. In S. Z. Sacks, L. S. Kekelis, & R. J. Gaylord-Ross (Eds.), *The development of social skills by blind and visually impaired students* (pp. 151–170). New York: American Foundation for the Blind.

Sennet, E. L. (1969). Creative writing and the blind child. *Education of the Visually Handicapped, 1*(3), 81–85.

Shaw, R. (1986). Curricular adaptations: The creative arts. In G. Scholl (Ed.), *Foundations of education for blind and visually handicapped children and youth: Theory and practice* (pp. 385–395). New York: American Foundation for the Blind.

Siller, M. A., & Joffee, E. (1971). *Reaching out: A creative guide for designing cultural programs for persons who are blind or visually impaired* [Video]. New York: AFB Press.

Spungin, S. J., & Ferrell, K. A. (in press). The role and function of the teacher of students with visual impairments. In *Position papers of the division on visual impairments: 1990–2000.* Reston, VA: Division on Visual Impairments, Council for Exceptional Children.

Sykes, K. (1974). *Creative arts and crafts for children with visual handicaps.* Louisville, KY: American Printing House for the Blind.

Wellman, C. (1994). Art education and children with visual impairments. *B.C. Journal of Special Education, 18,* 132–139.

Strategies for Teaching Art to Students with Visual Impairments and Additional Disabilities

The complexity of needs and unique talents of students with visual impairments and additional disabilities complicate the identification of which experiences may be enjoyable and meaningful for an individual student and may enhance the student's social, leisure, or instructional repertoire. Multiple and varied exposure to the arts may unearth unexpected talents, identify motivational incentives, and facilitate a student's personal growth. The same issues and instructional strategies discussed for the student with a visual impairment are applicable as well to the visually impaired student with additional disabilities. As with other subject areas, modification of performance expectations, adaptations to materials and equipment, careful and thoughtful planning, instructional ingenuity, and the use of partial participation should facilitate the student's involvement in all arts venues.

Because dance, music, theater, the visual arts, and the literary arts are taught in instructional settings that diverge from more standard learning contexts, they may offer considerable benefits to a student, such as the following:

◆ A student with postural and movement limitations may be more motivated to practice movement control and the planning and sequencing of movement transitions in a dance class than in a physical therapy suite or classroom.

◆ Specific types of music, such as baroque and other forms of classical music, may enhance concentration, integration, and relaxation and may provide the background for better arm and hand control when played during art experiences that are designed to facilitate specific hand movements and finger dexterity.

◆ The rhythmic application and proprioceptive feedback of making a rubbing, painting on a large easel, or working with clay often calm and organize a student with the characteristics of autism.

◆ The resonance of an orchestra, combined with the movement of dancers and the colors of their costumes and the scenery against the darkness of the theater and highlighted with fluorescent lighting, excites and captures the attention of a student with dual sensory impairments or with low vision in addition to significant cognitive deficits.

◆ A student with significant sensory dysfunction who craves touch thrives in hands-on museums with touchable exhibits and may attend much longer than ever observed within the confines of a typical learning situation.

Because the very nature of the arts suggests that students' participation and products may be as diverse as the students' interests and needs, the emphasis on the process, rather than "products" gives students myriad opportunities for self-expression, control, and integration of sensory modalities. Attention to and consideration of critical issues that are relevant to students with visual impairments and additional disabilities make interactions with all aspects of arts intrinsically rewarding.

Instructional personnel must work closely with the teacher of students with visual impairments and the occupational therapist to identify factors in the arts contexts that may be contraindicated for a student's sensory needs. Prior to each arts class, the instructional team should

(continued on next page)

identify whether the setting is conducive to learning. For example, the team should question whether the student's sensory system enables him or her to tolerate and integrate the following:

- Loud and unexpected noises;
- The closeness of a mass of people in an enclosed setting;
- The multiple sensory inputs of an expansive and open museum, theater, or concert; and
- The textures or smells of art media used for specific activities.

The fragility of the respiratory and immune systems of many of these students prevents their exposure to perfumes, dyes, and scents associated with many art materials, costumes, or fabrics that may be appropriate for other students with visual impairments. Thus, before such students are exposed to fragrances or scents, instructional personnel should consult with the students' parents. They should also refrain from using glitter or sand with students who may rub their eyes or place their hands in their mouths and from using fruits and vegetables to make prints, since some students may not understand that these items are no longer edible and may be confused by the use of food in such a discrepant manner.

Any activity related to the arts should be enjoyable to students; therefore, students who initially communicate some anxiety or indicate that they do not want to participate should not be forced to do so. However, these students often react this way in response to the novelty of an activity and not knowing what to expect. Although a student's message should be honored, another invitation to participate should be extended, and the student should be given time to adjust. If the student continues to resist, then alternative activities need to be provided.

When students have significant cognitive challenges, instructional personnel should carefully plan art projects, since the students' mental imagery, symbolic behavior, and interpretive skills may be minimal. If the class is going to create trees with scrunched up tissue paper and construction paper, for example, instructional personnel or parents should take the student to explore many trees, big and little, thick and thin, with wide leaves and with small leaves and flowers. Then the student should make a tree with the actual parts of a tree—bark, branches, and leaves—and then have the chance to compare that tree with a real one. If the class is going to make snowmen from cotton balls, the student should help to shave ice and make snowballs to make a miniature three-dimensional "snowman." This art will not last like that of his or her peers, but the student will have gained so much more from the experience, including concepts from science as the student experiences the snowman melt and hence change from a solid to a liquid.

Very Special Arts festivals (see the Resources) are conducted across the nation to allow students with special needs and with all levels of artistic abilities to demonstrate their competence. At these festivals, literacy, math, and fine arts are integrated as preschoolers enact scenes from *Goldilocks and the Three Bears* after reading the story using clay bowls and boxes they created and decorated during an art activity and real porridge made during a cooking activity. Students with poor postural control and severe cognitive challenges participate by controlling switches that activate spin-art toys to decorate their boxes (chairs) and simple augmentative systems to verbalize their lines in the play.

M. BETH LANGLEY
Pinellas County Schools
St. Petersburg, FL

R E S O U R C E S

Suggested Resources for Teaching Arts Education

Resource	Type	Source	Description
"Art Experience Is Fundamental to Creative Thinking" (Mangold, 1982)	Book chapter	American Foundation for the Blind	A chapter in *A Teacher's Guide to the Special Education Needs of Blind and Visually Handicapped Children* (Mangold, 1982). Includes a compilation of art lessons by teachers of students with visual impairments.
Art History through Touch and Sound: A Multisensory Guide for the Blind and Visually Impaired (Art Education for the Blind, n.d.)	Audiobook	Art Education for the Blind, New York	An audiobook series from prehistory through contemporary times, including approximately 600 tactile illustrations of major monuments.
Association for Theatre and Accessibility	Group	National Arts and Disability Center	A membership-based organization whose mission is to foster full participation and involvement of individuals with all types of disabilities in drama and theater activities.
Axis Dance Company	Organization	Axis Dance Company, Berkeley, CA	A dance company that has pioneered a new dimension of dance—a collaboration between dancers with and without disabilities; since 1987, the company has created and performed an innovative body of work that has received praise and respect from an international audience. *(continued on next page)*

Suggested Resources *(Continued)*

Resource	Type	Source	Description
Correspondence courses in braille music	Instructional materials	Hadley School for the Blind	Correspondence courses in braille music that teach the symbols for notes, chords, time and key signatures, and symbols and formats for advanced music. Also available is a course on the history, terminology, and theory of music.
Creative Arts and Crafts for Children with Visual Handicaps (Sykes, 1974)	Book	American Printing House for the Blind	A book that presents 23 art and craft projects that are appropriate for students with visual impairments.
Descriptive videos	Videotapes	Descriptive Video Service	Videotapes of Public Broadcasting Service television programs, Hollywood movies, and other visual media in a format accessible to people who are visually impaired.
How to Read Braille Music, 2nd Ed. (Krolick, 1998)	Book	OPUS Technologies	A book that provides information on reading braille music.
Music Braille Code	Books and other education materials	American Printing House for the Blind	Books and other educational materials and products related to music education.
National Dance Association	Organization	National Dance Association	Activities include developing and disseminating information on dance pedagogy (teaching content, process and methodology) and the creative process and providing resources for curriculum and program development, professional development, and teacher preparation. An affiliate of Very Special Arts.
National Library Service for the Blind and Physically Handicapped	Service	Library of Congress	Persons interested in music materials may receive them directly from the Music Section of NLS. The collection consists of scores in braille and large print; textbooks and books about music in braille and large print; and elementary instruction for voice, piano, organ, guitar, recorder, accordion, banjo, and harmonica in recorded form. Music Circular No. 4 contains a list of certified music transcribers. A Music Fact Sheet provides information on music magazines; the music collection in braille, large print, and recorded formats; and courses for instruction. *(continued on next page)*

Suggested Resources *(Continued)*

Resource	Type	Source	Description
NBA Music Catalog	Catalog	National Braille Association	A catalog containing titles of books on music theory, as well as classical and popular compositions. NBA also publishes instructional materials in music braille and provides transcription services in music braille.
New International Manual of Braille Music Notation (OPUS Technologies, n.d.)	Book in print, braille, and CD-ROM formats	OPUS Technologies	A book containing the latest braille music signs and rules adopted as the worldwide standard.
Reaching Out: A Creative Guide for Designing Cultural Programs and Exhibits for Persons Who Are Blind or Visually Impaired (Joffee & Siller, 1997)	Videotape and manual	AFB Press	A video and accompanying manual that detail how to make information on cultural programs and facilities accessible to people who are visually impaired. Created especially for libraries, museums, historical societies, outdoor cultural facilities, corporations, and anyone whose mission involves providing information to the community; offers practical design and program solutions; includes information on staff and volunteer training.
Tack-Tiles	Equipment	Tack-Tiles	LEGO-type blocks that are interchangeable with standard LEGO blocks; includes a set of braille blocks with music notation.
They Shall Have Music (Dykema, 1986)	Book	Dykema	A resource for teaching braille music; covers many of the different tools and methods that can be used.
Very Special Arts	Organization	Very Special Arts, Washington, DC	An international organization with affiliates in 41 states, the District of Columbia, and 83 countries that provides a variety of festivals, programs, and other initiatives related to art for students with special needs; VSA also serves as a resource for a variety of arts, education, and disability-related information.

Web Site	Description
Access Expressed www.accessexpressed.net/index.htm	Web site created to bring access information to people with disabilities about the many arts and entertainment opportunities that have become available since the passage of the Americans with Disabilities Act.

(continued on next page)

Suggested Resources *(Continued)*

Web Site	Description
ARTSEDGE artsedge.kennedy-center.org./welcome/	The National Arts and Education Information Network. The mission of ARTSEDGE is to help artists, teachers, and students gain access to and/or share information, resources, and ideas that support the arts as a core subject area in the K–12 curriculum.
ArtsEdNet www.artsednet.getty.edu	An on-line service developed by the Getty Education Institute for the Arts that supports the needs of the K–12 arts education community. It focuses on helping arts educators, general classroom teachers using the arts in their curriculum, museum educators, and university faculty involved in the arts. Getty Education Institute for the Arts, 1200 Getty Center Drive, Suite 600, Los Angeles, CA 90049-1683; phone: 310-440-7315; FAX: 310-440-7704; E-mail: artsednet@getty.edu
Audio Description www.artswire.org/ArtsWire/ad/index.html	National Endowment for the Arts, 1100 Pennsylvania Avenue NW, Washington, DC 20506. Voice: 202-682-5591. Audio Description involves the accessibility of the visual images of theater, media, and museum exhibitions for people who are blind or have low vision. It is a free narration service that attempts to describe what the sighted person takes for granted.
Braille M Web Page www.cstp.umkc.edu/personal/bhugh/braillem.html	The Braille M Web Page designed to help beginners in braille music and give them a place where they can ask questions of more experienced braille music users on all aspects of braille music.
Converto-Braille Groupe Galarneau Group, Inc. www.converto.org/	Distributors of Concert-O-Braille, a program designed to facilitate the braille transcription of music scores.
Screen Actors Guild of America www.sag.com/disabilityfaqs.html	*Everything You Wanted to Know about Working with Performers with Disabilities But Were Afraid to Ask,* an on-line manual developed by the Screen Actors Guild of America to answer some frequently asked questions about hiring performers with disabilities.
Special Needs Opportunity Windows (SNOW) snow.utoronto.ca/index.html	A project aimed at supporting educators of students with special needs. The Web site serves as a clearinghouse of practical resources and curriculum materials and as a place for educators to meet and share ideas and to develop their professional skills. SNOW Project, c/o ATRC, Information Commons, University of Toronto, 130 St. George Street, Toronto, Ontario M5S 3H1, Canada, Phone: 416-978-4360; FAX: 416-971-2729; E-mail: snow.help@utoronto.ca

Contact information for each of the resources listed will be found in the Sources of Products, Materials, Equipment, and Services section at the back of this book.

CHAPTER 12

Physical Education and Health

Carol Farrenkopf and Duncan McGregor

KEY POINTS

- ◆ Physical education is an essential part of the curriculum for all students, including those who are visually impaired.

- ◆ Students with visual impairments need active physical education programs to help maintain their health and sense of well-being.

- ◆ Teachers of students with visual impairments may need to teach specific prerequisite skills so students can engage in physical education activities.

- ◆ Teachers of students with visual impairments collaborate with physical education teachers on appropriate modifications to allow students to participate fully and actively in physical education programs.

- ◆ Students with visual impairments benefit from health education programs with appropriate modifications, paired with specialized instruction when appropriate, to ensure privacy and dignity.

VIGNETTE

Lincoln Elementary School was planning its end-of-school field day, which created a challenge for Nathan Carter, the itinerant teacher of students with visual impairments. Rosa Mercado, a kindergartner, was totally blind, and Buster Gibbs, a sixth grader, had a distance acuity of 20/600. The physical education teacher had given Nathan a list of activities that were planned for each grade, and Nathan was considering ways to integrate these students.

Nathan thought that the kindergarten activities would be fun for Rosa. Rosa could participate in the Egg Race, in which relays of students raced while carrying a raw egg in a giant spoon, with her teammates calling her name to direct her to the finish line. A bigger challenge was the Backward Bunny Race, in which students jumped backward to the finish line. Rosa had *just* learned to jump forward; would it be better to allow her to participate by jumping forward or to have an adult walk with her and hold her hands to steady her while she jumped backward? The tug-of-war would not require any adaptation—Rosa could certainly pull on a rope with her classmates. The Tumbleweed Tumble, in which the students did a series of somersaults along a row of gym mats laid end to end, probably would not need any adaptation, either. Rosa could do somersaults, and although she sometimes veered toward the edge of a mat, she could feel the edge and redirect herself.

The sixth-grade activities were more competitive. The baseball throw, in which the students competed to see who could throw a baseball the farthest, would not need to be adapted for Buster, since it did not involve catching a baseball. Neither would the standing long jump, with its large landing bed of soft sand. However, the hundred-yard dash *would* need modification. Buster could run toward a sound target, but the noise level during that activity was likely to be so high that he would not be able to hear a beeper or anyone shouting his name from 100 yards away. Would a running partner be better or a fluorescent chalk line to outline Buster's running lane? Next was a competition in which students "shot baskets" from increasingly greater distances from the goal; Buster could participate in this activity with a beeper mounted on the goal behind the ring. He would *probably* not get so far from the goal that he could not hear the beeper above the noise of the crowd. Finally, the sixth grade planned a volleyball competition between classes. Nathan reluctantly decided that Buster would have to skip this activity. The danger of being hit in the head by a volleyball was too great for a student with a history of retinal degeneration.

INTRODUCTION

Physical education has long been recognized as an essential component of the educational curriculum for all students. Students who are visually impaired have a right to high-quality physical education programs, regardless of whether they are in a general education class, a special class, or a residential school. Moreover, active physical education throughout the school years is essential for students' health and well-being and to their development into well-rounded individuals. The many benefits of physical education are often denied students with visual impairments, however. Too often, these students do not participate fully, if at all, in physical education activities. With appropriate modifications, students with visual impairments can participate in physical education programs.

Physical education has been mandated for children with special needs since 1975, when the Education for All Handicapped Children Act was implemented. If the regular physical education program is not appropriate for a student with a visual impairment, specific goals, adaptations, specialized instruction, and equipment should be included in the student's Individualized Education Program (IEP) (Block & Burke, 1999) to ensure that the student's physical education needs are met.

Mere enrollment in a physical education class is not enough; students with visual impairments must participate as much as possible in all activities. The degree of participation may depend, in part, on the attitude of the teacher of students with visual impairments and his or her encouragement of the student who is visually impaired. Furthermore, the attitude of a physical education teacher is influenced greatly by that of the teacher of students with visual impairments. If the specialist does not believe it is possible for a student to participate in physical education, it is likely that the physical education teacher will be reluctant to allow the student to do so.

In short, overanxious adults may too frequently be the reason that students with visual impairments are excluded from participating in physical education activities. These students can in general participate in most physical activities with appropriate modifications and do not need to be overprotected. They "recover from bumps, bruises, and scratches just like other children do; and have the right to acquire them" (Canadian Council of the Blind, 1993, p. 2).

Typically, people who are physically active tend to be healthier and live longer than do those who live sedentary lives (Hanna, 1986; Ponchillia, 1995), and physical activity during childhood and adolescence, through an effective physical education program, may lead to greater activity and better health later in life (Williams, Armstrong, Eves, & Faulkner, 1996). Children with visual impairments, however, tend to be less active and less physically fit than their sighted peers (Meek & Maguire, 1996) and often miss physical education classes to work on academic skills, orientation and mobility (O&M) skills, and other disability-specific skills that need to be taught on a one-to-one basis. Despite the importance of these other skills, physical education is not a class that a student with a visual impairment can afford to miss.

Physical education activities develop motor skills, strength, endurance, and agility (Modell &

Cox, 1999)—skills that are important in all areas of life, not just in sports and recreation. Since children who are visually impaired cannot learn skills incidentally by watching others and may not often play informally with other children, it is essential that they are taught physical education skills formally in school. However, before a teacher of students with visual impairments suggests modifications for a student with a visual impairment, he or she needs to familiarize himself or herself with the major content areas in general physical education. Table 12.1 outlines the content of typical physical education programs from kindergarten through high school.

Table 12.1. Contents of the Physical Education Curriculum

Lower Elementary School (K–3rd Grade)	Upper Elementary/Middle School (4th–7th Grade)	High School (8th–12th Grade)
Locomotor Patterns Run Jump Gallop Hop Skip Slide Leap Climb **Manipulative Patterns** Throw Catch Kick Strike **Body Management** Body awareness Body control Space awareness Effort concepts **Health and Fitness** Endurance, strength, and flexibility to perform locomotor and manipulative skills **Rhythms and Dance** Moving to a beat Expressing self through dance Singing games Applying effort concepts **Low-Organized Games** Relays and tag games Games with partners Games with a small group	**Locomotor Patterns for Sports** Locomotor patterns used in sports Combine 2 or more locomotor patterns Locomotor patterns used in dance **Manipulative Patterns for Sports** Throw Catch Kick Strike Volley Dribble Punt **Body Management for Sports** Gymnastics Body management skills applied to sports **Health and Fitness** Cardiorespiratory endurance Muscular strength and endurance Flexibility **Dance** Folk Modern Interpretive Aerobic **Lead-Up Games to Sports** Lead-up games to team sports	**Locomotor Sports** Track events Special sports applications of locomotor patterns Locomotor patterns used in dance Locomotor patterns used in leisure activities **Ball Sports** Basketball, soccer, softball, volleyball Bowling, golf, tennis, racquetball **Body Management for Sports** Body management skills applied to sports **Health and Fitness** Personal conditioning Lifetime leisure exercises Introduction to body composition concepts **Dance** Folk Modern Interpretive Aerobic and social **Modified and Regulation Sports** Modified sports activities Regulation sports

Source: Reprinted, with permission, from M. E. Burke and K. Burke, "Are Children with Disabilities Receiving Appropriate Physical Education?" *Teaching Exceptional Children, 31*(3) (1999), p. 20.

In addition to physical skills, students learn valuable social skills, including cooperation, competition, communication, turn taking, sportsmanship, and getting along with others, in physical education classes. Physical education affords students with visual impairments the opportunity to interact with other students in a positive and socially appropriate manner. If students who are visually impaired know the rules of a game (such as baseball), they can talk about the game with their friends at school, attend games with others on the weekend, watch or listen to games on television, or listen to sports events on the radio with family and friends (Willoughby & Duffy, 1989).

Finally, positive physical education experiences enhance a student's self-esteem (Luxton & Kelley, 1981). Successfully participating in a game may give a student with a visual impairment the feeling that he or she is competent and equal to students who are sighted. This feeling, in turn, may give the student a sense of confidence and a willingness to try other sports or games. This is an important step along the road to independence.

This chapter describes the role of the teacher of students with visual impairments in designing an appropriate physical education program for a student with a visual impairment and for the development of motor skills; individual instruction of prerequisite skills; and modifications of the teaching environment, teaching techniques, and activities. It also discusses instructional considerations such as safety and liability, the student's eye condition, assessment techniques, and ways to encourage a student to participate, and the application of the health education curriculum to a student who is visually impaired.

ROLE OF THE TEACHER OF STUDENTS WITH VISUAL IMPAIRMENTS

Teachers of students with visual impairments play a direct role in ensuring that students on their caseloads receive active and appropriate physical and health education programs. Typical responsibilities include these:

◆ Providing consultation to the physical education teacher on the student's eye condition, functional vision skills, restrictions on physical activities, and other factors that will affect the student's involvement in physical education;

◆ Recommending modifications of physical activities that will allow full or, when appropriate, partial participation of the student in physical education;

◆ Providing direct instruction (using appropriate special training methods) in prerequisite or disability-specific skills that the student needs to acquire before he or she can be fully involved in physical activities;

◆ Supplying adapted physical education equipment or information on where the equipment can be obtained;

◆ Advocating for a student's active and sustained involvement in physical education programs;

◆ Providing consultation to health education teachers on modifications needed for a student;

◆ Instructing a student in a separate setting for sensitive health topics (such as some aspects of sexuality education and personal hygiene); and

◆ Informing parents about the strategies that will be used to instruct the student in sensitive health topics.

The teacher also plays an essential role in working with students with additional disabilities; strategies focusing on students with visual impairments and additional disabilities and resources for teachers appear later in this chapter.

ASSESSMENT

In general, the physical education teacher, rather than the teacher of students with visual impairments, has the expertise to assess the physical ability of the student with a visual impairment. The physical education teacher is also best qualified to assess the student's understanding of the rules of a game and what qualities constitute sportsman-like behavior. Prior to the assessment, the specialist should tell the physical education teacher about the student's functional vision, medical considerations, safety restrictions, O&M skills (particularly in the gym, outdoor facilities, and locker room) and the student's understanding of vocabulary, adapted equipment, and safety issues related to physical education (Canadian Council of the Blind, 1993).

The issue of performance standards should be addressed thoughtfully when a physical education program and expectation are developed for a student who is visually impaired. Short and Winnick (1986) found that adolescents who were visually impaired scored lower than sighted adolescents on all six subtests of a physical fitness assessment (skinfold measurements to estimate the percentage of body fat, grip strength, sit-ups, sit and reach, 50-yard dash, and long distance run). Among the students who were visually impaired, those with visual acuities of 20/70 to 20/200 performed significantly better on the running subtests than did the students with acuities of 20/200 or worse.

Therefore, it is inappropriate to use sighted norms in assessing students with visual impairments for such purposes as grades, awards, and performance objectives in physical education. However, teachers should not view these lower scores as "acceptable." They should always strive to help their students achieve the same levels of fitness as sighted students (Short & Winnick, 1986).

DEVELOPMENT OF MOTOR SKILLS

Children with visual impairments may proceed through a different sequence of motor development than do children who are sighted, and there are often delays in this development (Ferrell, 1997;

Ferrell, Raver, & Stewart, 1999). Sighted children learn movement by observing and imitating others, but students with visual impairments usually cannot learn in this way. Furthermore, whereas children who are sighted are stimulated to move by their vision (that is, they see something and then move toward it), children who are visually impaired are less likely to want to move toward an object.

Warren (1994) stated that among infants who are blind, there is no generalized slowdown in overall development. However, young children with visual impairments appear to experience a delay in learning to walk that may be due more to the restriction of their opportunity to move around than to actual lags in their physical development. As children become older, delays are seen in other motor skills, some of which "can be attributed to lack of experience, particularly in gross motor interactions with the environment" (Schneekloth, 1989, p. 197). If children with visual impairments are encouraged to move about independently and interact with the environment, they will have well-developed patterns of movement.

Motor development may also be affected by the degree of vision loss and age of onset of the visual impairment (Heydt & Allon, 1992). In addition to severity of visual loss, motor development also depends on environmental experiences and the presence of additional disabilities (Ferrell, 1997). In other words, it is not just the child's vision (or lack of it) that affects developmental patterns. The greatest delays in motor development are generally found in children who are congenitally blind (who were born blind or who lost their vision in infancy), who do not have a visual memory to rely on when they engage in physical activity (Canadian Council of the Blind, 1993). These children do not know what it looks like when someone else performs an activity and, therefore, cannot imitate it, nor do they have a visual concept of performing the activity themselves. In contrast, students who lose their vision in adolescence have already developed movement skills that they can build on and can rely on their visual memory to assist them in performing higher-level motor skills.

INDIVIDUAL INSTRUCTION OF PREREQUISITE SKILLS

The goal of full participation in a physical education class is not always possible if a student with a visual impairment has not learned certain vital prerequisite skills. Thus, it is imperative for the teacher of students with visual impairments and/or the O&M specialist to be directly involved in preparing a student for upcoming physical education activities, in consultation with the physical education teacher.

It may be necessary for the teacher of students with visual impairments to remove the student from Physical Education class to work on prerequisite physical skills unless the student can work with the specialist at another time during the day. The benefits of withdrawing the student at this point outweigh the negative aspects because when the student returns to the class, he or she will be able to participate in the activity with classmates.

The following are suggestions that the teacher of students with visual impairments needs to consider in preparing a student with a visual impairment for participation in physical education activities:

- Establish a strong foundation. The student should be able to perform such basic skills as hopping, running, throwing, kicking, catching, skipping, jumping, and bouncing a ball. Without a reasonable level of proficiency in these areas, the student may be injured. For example, if a student cannot jump in place, he or she may be hurt when learning to jump rope.

- Proceed step by step. The specialist needs to teach physical activities in a systematic way, considering developmental prerequisite skills. Before a student can run, he or she must be able to walk. Likewise, before a student can play basketball, he or she must know how to bounce and catch a large ball.

- Teach sound-localization skills. A common adaptation for physical activities, especially ball sports, is to teach a student to localize sources of sound, such as beeping balls or balls with bells inside them. For instance, before a student who is blind plays goalball or dodgeball, he or she should be able to localize and auditorily track sounds made by a moving object.

- Teach the rules of the game. Some games have rules that children who are sighted have learned through observation. Students who are visually impaired may be unable to catch on to the subtle nuances of certain games and thus may not understand the rules. Therefore, the teacher of students with visual impairments needs to provide specific instruction in the rules and procedures of games. For example, different players on a football team are restricted as to where they line up on the playing field and what they are allowed to do. When a player goes offside, a penalty is called. The student who is sighted is able to understand why the penalty was called by watching the players, but the student with a visual impairment is left wondering what happened unless he or she knows the rules of the game.

- Build strength and endurance. A student must have sufficient strength and endurance to be included in rigorous physical activities. For example, if a student tires quickly and is unable to run for short periods, he or she will not be able to participate in soccer. Like all students, students with visual impairments should participate in some form of vigorous physical activity (such as walking, jogging, or aerobics) each day to develop greater strength and endurance.

MODIFICATIONS

Modifications are sometimes necessary to allow a student with a visual impairment to participate fully in physical activities. Three types of modifications can be made: environmental modifications, modification of teaching techniques and strategies, and modifications of a student's activities.

Environmental Modifications

Environmental modifications may be defined as physical modifications—tactile, auditory, or visual—to materials, equipment, or the field of play that allow a student with a visual impairment to participate in physical activities. Braille score sheets and rules are examples of modifications to materials, beeping balls or balls with bells in them are examples of modifications to equipment, and beeping goal posts and florescent pylons are examples of modifications to the field of play. Environmental modifications that could be made to enable a student who is blind to play soccer may include a ball with bells inside it, a sound source (such as music, a beeper, or another student clapping) at the goal, and moving the field of play so that natural boundaries (like a sidewalk or sand next to a grass field) can be used.

Some students with low vision may benefit from the same auditory and tactile modifications that are used for students who are blind. It should be noted that commercially available materials tend to be more durable than teacher-made materials, although they are generally more expensive and less readily available. (See the Resources section at the end of this chapter for sources of materials and equipment.) Sidebar 12.1 lists common environmental modifications.

Modifications of Teaching Techniques and Strategies

Skills should be introduced and taught sequentially to a student with a visual impairment. The teacher of students with visual impairments needs to work with the student on one skill at a time, rather than try to improve several skills at the same time. This practice should be followed when using the techniques and strategies that are discussed next.

Physical Guidance. For students who are blind and for some students with low vision, physical guidance through the movements of an activity, accompanied by the specialist's description of the action, allows them to experience how it feels to perform an action. The complete action should be demonstrated first, then its component parts. For this technique to work effectively, it is necessary to make the student as comfortable and relaxed as possible. Moving a student's arm stiffly through a throwing motion does not give the student a true idea of how it feels to perform the action correctly. Holding the student firmly and confidently helps create trust.

For example, when teaching a young student how to skip rope, the teacher of students with visual impairments should first demonstrate the entire action. To do so, the specialist should stand behind the student and guide his or her hands through the circular motion of moving the rope over his or her head. Once the rope has landed on the floor in front of the student, the specialist tells him or her to jump over the rope and begin the action again. Next, the specialist should review jumping over a rope and have the child practice turning the rope appropriately. Coordinating the two actions requires more practice and perhaps more physical guidance to refine the physical movements.

Tactile Modeling. Students who are blind and those with low vision may benefit from being physically in contact with the teacher of students with visual impairments as a movement is demonstrated. The specialist should also describe the action while demonstrating it. By feeling how the specialist moves, the student can better understand how he or she is to perform the skill. For instance, when teaching a student to dribble a ball, the specialist can dribble the ball while the student places his or her hand on top of the teacher's hand, so the student understands how the hand moves up and down and how the wrist remains flexible.

Visual Modeling. Many students with low vision are able to see and imitate movements in much

Common Environmental Modifications for Physical Activities

AUDITORY

- Balls with beepers or bells;

- Rice in a beachball or volleyball;

- Sound sources (beeps, music) for basketball hoops, bases, and relay batons;

- Beeping bases or sounding cones/pylons to help locate bases in baseball;

- Clappers or callers along the track for runners;

- Teammates calling or clapping as an indicator of the direction the play is going or should go (for example, where to throw the ball or where the ball is coming from); and

- Beepers or radios to locate targets, such as basketball hoops, goalposts, and the end of a swimming pool.

TACTILE

- Braille rules and procedures for games and activities;

- Braille team rosters;

- Braille score sheets;

- Tapper (a pole with a sponge on one end used to signal a swimmer, with a gentle tap on the head, that he or she is approaching the end of the lane);

- Lane markers for track and field (ropes or fences);

- Tactile boundary markers made of cord or rope placed under tape (2 or 3 lines of cords, spaced 3–4 inches apart, ensures that players will not miss the boundary while moving quickly);

- Foot-placement guides for field events (such as the long jump, or shot put);

- Natural boundaries on a playing field (like grass, dirt, asphalt); and

- Mats or carpets to mark boundaries indoors.

VISUAL

- Large-print rules and procedures for games and activities;

- Large-print team rosters;

- Large-print score sheets and modifications of the rules of play;

- Balls that are brightly colored or that contrast in color with the surrounding environment;

- A towel draped over a high-jump bar for a jumper with low vision;

- Colored or striped shirts or bibs to identify team members;

- Orange pylons beside bases for players with low vision;

- Padded and brightly colored goalposts for soccer, football, field hockey, and other games;

- Fluorescent tape to mark boundaries on a gymnasium floor, long jump takeoff board, balance beam, springboard, or diving board;

- Brightly colored pylons to mark field boundaries; and

- Lane markers for tracks (bright pylons).

OTHER MODIFICATIONS

- Modifications of the rules of play;

- Minimization of distracting noise;

(continued on next page)

Common Environmental Modifications *(Continued)*

- ◆ Sighted guide for running, soccer, basketball, football, baseball, and other children's games;

- ◆ A t-ball stand for playing softball or baseball;

- ◆ Plastic bottle for a puck in floor hockey;

- ◆ Simplification of the playing environment;

- ◆ A change in the number of players;

- ◆ Reduction in the field of play; and

- ◆ Simplification of scoring or how points may be earned.

---

the same way as do their sighted classmates. To maximize their ability to do so, a student with low vision should stand as close as necessary to the physical education teacher when the teacher is demonstrating and describing an action. If possible, the physical education teacher should wear clothing that contrasts with the background and makes him or her as visible as possible to the student. Some students also benefit from other appropriate environmental adaptations, such as glare control and lighting modifications, as well as low vision devices.

Physical education teachers frequently use visual modeling when teaching new skills. For example, swimming strokes are almost always taught out of the water first. The student with low vision will also benefit from the demonstration when the necessary adaptations have been made.

Verbal Direction.   Verbal directions should accompany all the techniques just outlined. Before giving directions, the physical education teacher makes sure the student knows that he or she is being addressed (that is, calls the student by name). He or she then gives complete, explicit directions before the student begins (to avoid giving directions in the middle of an activity) and checks to make sure that the student understands by having the student repeat the directions and then carry them out. In giving these directions, the specialist makes sure that directionality cues are specific to the student's position in space (for example, "Take one step to your left").

Other Techniques.   The student should be encouraged to move to an advantageous position near the physical education teacher as a way to take responsibility for gaining access to needed information by hearing instructions and observing, if possible, the demonstration of the activity. When asking a student with a visual impairment to perform a skill, the phsycial education teacher gives the student time to process the instructions before the student executes them and does not rush to help the student. The student should be encouraged to move freely throughout the gymnasium or playing field. A student who feels safe and comfortable will display more natural movements while engaging in formal physical education activities in open environments.

Modifications of Activities

Activities in each area of the physical education curriculum can be adapted to allow a student with a visual impairment to participate meaningfully in them. Some activities may need to be stopped to give the student instructions or to reorient the student to the field of play. Special commands (like Stop!) or a referee's whistle may be used to interrupt the game without penalty. For example, if a runner goes off course during a school meet, the clock is stopped while the runner is brought back on course. Once the runner is properly oriented, the clock is started again, without penalty.

The following examples are ideas for how to

adapt other physical education activities for students with visual impairments.

Running

The use of a sighted guide, trained by the teacher of students with visual impairments, may be helpful for a student who is blind. (See Sidebar 12.2 for suggestions on training a guide and on running with a guide.) In initial instruction, the basic sighted guide technique of grasping the guide's arm above the elbow may be the best option, since it is a technique that the student learned for O&M and thus will be familiar with. However, it inhibits the natural arm movement necessary for efficient running. Modification of the basic techniques by having the student hold the guide's wrist may allow for greater freedom of movement.

The tether method—in which a short rope or cord is held by the student and the guide—allows the student who is blind to run more freely and move more naturally. The rope, which is approximately 20 inches (51 centimeters) long and usually knotted at both ends, keeps the student and the guide close together and synchronized in their movements. Another type of tether is a baton or stick; this rigid tether may provide the student with more information than would a rope.

Running independently, without being in contact with a guide, allows the student who is blind to move naturally. In this method, the guide runs behind the student, giving verbal directions and gentle physical prompts when the student approaches a turn or begins to veer off the track.

In another method of independent running, callers standing at the halfway mark and at the finish line provide auditory cues that guide the student who is blind (Canadian Council of the Blind, 1993). Before the race begins, the student must be able to hear the callers so a few practice shouts are given. Only one student at a time races against the clock, and the spectators must remain quiet so that the student can hear the callers. As the race begins, the caller at the halfway mark shouts out "five, five, five" or "go, go, go." If the student veers off course, the caller provides clear directions to get him or her back on course. The caller at the finish line

A student who is blind (left) and a sighted peer run around a track together by using the tether method.

takes over immediately after the student has passed the halfway mark and does not move or stop calling out as the student approaches the finish line. It is the student's responsibility to run to the right or left of the caller at the finish line. Since this technique works only on straight courses, it is used only in sprints of up to 100 meters.

In some schools, primarily residential schools, the tracks have been adapted for students who are blind by the addition of handrails or guidewires that the students trail at their own pace and without assistance. These handrails are excellent for endurance training.

A student with low vision may be capable of running without a guide, particularly on a track or smooth surface. In cross-country running, however, the student may require a guide because the

Running with a Guide

The teacher of students with visual impairments should be involved in training all guide runners in sighted guide and other techniques before the guide and student who is blind begin running together. When training a guide, the specialist takes the role of the student (but is not blindfolded during practice sessions). Only when the specialist is convinced that the guide is competent should the guide and student attempt to run together. Initial running sessions should be at a comfortable pace and should be supervised by the specialist.

BASIC CONSIDERATIONS

- The guide should be aware of the student's unique needs.

- The guide must be able to communicate changes in the terrain, turns, obstacles, and so forth clearly and concisely while running.

- The guide and student need to establish rapport and to trust each other.

- The guide should be a faster runner than the student.

- The guide must be able to concentrate on keeping the student on the track instead of struggling to keep up with the student.

- Several guides should be trained for a student to ensure that a guide is always available.

TETHER METHOD

- When using the tether method the student and guide each hold one end of a flexible tether such as a short rope or cord, or a rigid tether, such as a baton or stick. The guide runs beside the student and does not pull or push the student.

- While running, the guide gives verbal directions to the student on turns, the location of other runners, changes in the terrain, or other relevant information.

INDEPENDENT RUNNING

- A student can run more naturally without being in physical contact with a guide.

- The guide runs behind the student and gives verbal directions and gentle physical prompts to indicate turns or to get the student back on track.

- When the guide is guiding on the student's left side and they are approaching a left turn, the guide presses lightly on the inside of the student's left arm to help initiate the turn. If the student veers left when he or she should be running straight or if the student is approaching a right turn, the guide presses lightly on the student's left hip to initiate movement to the right. If the student prefers to be guided on his or her right side, the procedure is reversed.

CROSS-COUNTRY RUNNING

- When guiding on cross-country courses or in road races, the guide provides additional information about changes in the terrain and the location of obstacles, other runners, mile markers, water stations, and family and friends who are cheering for the student along the route.

- For safety reasons, especially in crowded races, the student wears a bib or T-shirt that identifies him or her as a runner who is visually impaired. The guide may also wear identifying clothing.

- When possible, the guide and student run the route in advance of a race. During this run, they can familiarize themselves with the terrain and fine-tune their cues.

paths (in wooded areas or on busy sidewalks) may be harder to follow, and there may be uneven terrain and obstacles. However, it is generally unnecessary for the student to be in physical contact with the guide. The guide can run either beside or in front of the runner and give verbal instructions. It is beneficial for the guide to wear a brightly colored shirt or vest that should be reflective for night running.

Field Games

Field games, such as shot put, the standing long jump, and the running long jump, can be easily modified for a student who is visually impaired after the teacher of students with visual impairments teaches the student certain prerequisite skills.

Shot Put.   For the shot put, the student may need to build up his or her strength to throw the shot, which weighs about as much as a braillewriter. The teacher of students with visual impairments should work with the student on strength activities for several weeks prior to the commencement of the track and field unit. Next, the student needs to know how to place his or her feet in a stance that will maintain balance and where to position his or her hand and arm to throw the ball. The teacher of students with visual impairments may demonstrate the standing and throwing motion for the student by having the student explore the specialist's position tactilely. As the specialist throws the ball, the student should have his or her hand directly over the specialist's so he or she can feel the motion of the specialist's arm. The specialist may also use physical guidance to guide the student's throwing arm through the motion. Before throwing the shot put, the student must ask if he or she is facing the proper direction. Since the ball makes a "thud" sound when it lands, the student can determine how far he or she has thrown it. With practice and physical guidance, when necessary, the student should be able to participate in shot-put activities independently.

Standing Long Jump.   The standing long jump is an activity that requires few, if any, modifications

A student who is totally blind swings her arms to propel herself forward in the standing long jump.

but considerable practice. In this activity, students stand at the edge of a sand pit (on a hard surface), swing their arms, and then jump on the upswing. Since students with visual impairments are not usually confident jumpers, they may be reluctant to participate in this activity. However, if they have the opportunity to practice jumping in the sand pit and engage in different jumping games (such as leap frog without the frog or jumping on the spot when a horn is honked), their confidence may increase.

Once a student is comfortable jumping, the teacher of students with visual impairments may introduce the arm motions that help propel the body forward, using physical guidance and modeling to help the student develop the motor sequence necessary for jumping. If a student seems to have a great deal of difficulty swinging his or her arms and then jumping, two teachers may assist the student. That is, one teacher takes the student's left hand, while the other teacher takes the student's right hand. As the student swings his or her arms and prepares to jump, the teachers guide the student's hand and arms forward and provide support to the student while he or she lands in the sand pit. This technique works best with younger children.

Running Long Jump. In the running long jump, a student runs down a long, paved ramp and then jumps at a specific point, landing in a sand pit. With a great deal of practice, a student who is blind may run the length of the ramp and then jump independently at a verbal cue or tone or run and then jump with a sighted guide. However, this activity can be dangerous if the student veers off the track or jumps at the incorrect time, so it may be necessary to suggest that the running portion be reduced to two or three long strides.

For a student with low vision, the ramp can be highlighted by using florescent chalk along the vertical edges to indicate where the student should run, and a different colored florescent horizontal chalk line can be used to indicate where the student is to begin the jump. Verbal cues or tones may also be used to help the student determine when to jump.

Relay Games

Relay games can help young students with visual impairments develop motor skills, strength, endurance, balance, and agility (Lieberman & Cowart, 1996). Students in the elementary grades play a variety of relay games that follow the same general pattern: Teams usually line up at one end of the gym or field. Each member of the team runs, hops, skips, or rolls to the target area; performs some activity, returns to the line, tags the person next in line, and then goes to the end of the line. When each player has taken a turn and is seated in line, the team is finished. The first team to finish wins the game.

The student who is blind needs to be told where to stand in line and when it is time to move to the target area. The student may run, hop, skip, or roll to the target area independently if a beeper or some other sound source (including a person calling out to the student) provides direction, but noise from the other children may interfere with the student's ability to hear the sound source clearly. Alternatively, a sighted guide who is trained in the use of proper sighted guide techniques may travel with the student who is blind to the target area and back. Young children are generally not safe sighted guides in the excitement of a race.

When the student who is visually impaired is returning to the team line, teammates should be encouraged to shout out the student's name to provide direction. It is not enough for the teammates simply to chant, "Go, go!" "Hurry up!" "Faster!" because all the other teams are shouting out similar motivating phrases. With all the teammates calling out the student's name, it is not necessary to have an alternate sound source at the team line.

For a student with low vision, the route to the target area may be marked with pylons or brightly colored tape or may be located along a wall to assist the student to stay on course. The student's teammates should have the same colored bibs or shirts (that differ from those for the other teams) to help the student find his or her team at the finish line.

Baseball

Baseball is a challenging activity to modify for a student with a visual impairment, but the benefits gained from team participation and increased self-esteem justify the effort in making sure that the student is included in baseball games. During a game, a teammate can give the student verbal information about what is happening on the field, who is at bat, and who is next at bat. The following are specific activities that can help a student who is visually impaired participate fully:

◆ Use a batting tee or t-ball stand rather than pitch the ball to the student. The student may swing at the ball until he or she hits it, which is a modification of the three-strikes-and-you-are-out rule.

◆ Allow the student to throw the ball instead of batting, if necessary.

◆ Use a sighted guide to help the student who is blind run the bases or use beepers or other sound sources to indicate the location of bases. However, if more than one beeper with the same or similar sounds is sounding at the same time, it may confuse the student.

◆ Use a sighted partner when the student who is blind is in the field. The sighted partner catches the ball, passes it to the student who is blind, and then gives verbal directions for where to throw the ball. The partner may need to orient the student physically in the right direction. For safety reasons, the student with a visual impairment should play in the outfield, rather than the infield where he or she is more likely to be struck by a sharply hit ground ball.

◆ Consider using a beeping baseball in non-competitive games in which a student who is blind can take time to locate the ball independently. Beeping baseballs are of limited use in competitive baseball games.

◆ Change the entire game to one in which all the players are blindfolded. "Beep base-ball" is an adaptation of baseball for players who are visually impaired (see Chapter 18 for further information on this adaptation).

◆ Use an oversize, brightly colored utility ball in place of a white softball for a student with low vision or, if appropriate, a softball with fluorescent or black tape on it.

◆ Use orange pylons placed beside the bases and fresh, white chalk lines to indicate all the base paths, not just the first and third base lines, for a student with low vision.

Gymnastics

Gymnastics is an individual activity in which each student strives to build his or her skills. By partic-

ipating in gymnastics, students gain a variety of benefits: graceful movement, discipline, concentration, strength, and endurance.

When beginning gymnastics activities, allow a student who is visually impaired to explore the various pieces of equipment fully before he or she uses them. Also, for safety, orient the student to the area around the equipment so he or she knows where the other students will stand or sit while waiting their turn.

The majority of movement activities, particularly mat and climbing activities, do not need to be adapted for a student who is blind. Mat activities may include tumbling, simple balancing, and stretching, and climbing activities usually use ropes and ladders. However, if the student is unable to perform the skills involved in a movement activity, the techniques discussed in the section on Modifications of Teaching Techniques and Strategies may be used to teach the skills. It is essential that a trained spotter (an adult) is with the student at all times; it is not safe for a classmate to act as a spotter.

For balance-beam activities, a tactile strip on the floor may be used initially to teach the student how to walk and balance on a narrow path. As the student gets more proficient at this skill, the balance beam may be placed low to the ground (preferably on the floor) to allow the student to walk on the beam with confidence. If the student is nervous or unsure when walking on the balance beam, an adult may provide assistance and support. A student with low vision may benefit from having brightly colored tape at the edge of a springboard or a balance beam, as well as other environmental adaptations, such as appropriate lighting, glare control, and contrast enhancement.

Swimming

Swimming is a pleasant activity that students usually enjoy. For a student with a visual impairment to participate in swimming, the teacher of students with visual impairments needs to prepare the student in advance and make certain adaptations:

- Thoroughly orient the student to the locker rooms and swimming pool area.

- Maintain close proximity to the student, since the acoustics in swimming pools are often poor.

- Use lane ropes to help the student maintain his or her line of direction in the water. For a student with low vision, brightly colored flags or colored rope may be of benefit.

- Use a long pole with a sponge tip (a tapper) to signal when the student is swimming near the end of the pool by tapping him or her lightly on the head or shoulder.

- Teach new swimming strokes through physical guidance and tactile modeling. For a student with low vision, new strokes may be modeled visually first on the deck and then in the water. Keep in mind that when modeling in the water, the image is distorted. Verbal directions should be given along with the guidance and modeling.

- Provide a trained spotter to tell the student when it is safe to dive off the board or from the edge of the pool.

Aerobics

Aerobics is a lifelong physical fitness activity for many people, including those who are visually impaired (Ponchillia, Powell, Felski, & Nicklawski, 1992). A student with a visual impairment should be introduced to aerobics in the physical education program so that he or she may apply the skills learned in school in his or her recreational life. Many fitness clubs and television programs provide opportunities for aerobic workouts. When designing an aerobics program for a student who is visually impaired, the teacher of students with visual impairments needs to consider the following suggestions:

- Orient the student to the exercise area, noting where the equipment and mats are located.

- Position the student close to the aerobics

teacher so he or she can hear the instructions above the noise in the room.

- Describe the individual movements that make up a sequence of steps by using the techniques of physical guidance, modeling, and verbalization. Once the student has mastered the individual movements, use the same techniques to string the movements together, providing additional practice as needed.

- Make sure the student understands the terminology of aerobics, such as "Take a deep breath, hold it, and then let it out."

Basketball

A student who is blind can learn many of the skills involved in playing basketball—such as dribbling, shooting, and passing—and can play in noncompetitive situations or with modified rules. However, the student will probably not be able to participate competitively in basketball with sighted peers. As was previously mentioned, knowing the rules and basic procedures involved in basketball will enhance the student's enjoyment of this sport as a participant or a spectator and will provide opportunities for social interaction during the basketball season.

When playing basketball informally, a student who is blind benefits from passing drills with a partner. The partner can call for a pass (providing an auditory cue) and then pass the ball to the student when he or she is ready to receive the pass. A beeper or radio attached to a cord can be easily raised onto the metal plate between the hoop and the backboard to provide an audible cue for the student who is shooting a basket.

A student with low vision who has difficulty following the rapid movement on the basketball court may benefit from adaptation of the rules. For example, the players' movements may be limited by not permitting players to dribble or allowing them only three bounces before they must pass or shoot. Also, the student with low vision may be allowed to move closer to the basket when shooting a freethrow. Environmental modifications can also make the game more accessible to a student with low vision. For instance, the teams should wear easily identifiable, brightly colored jerseys or bibs, the basket can be lowered, the ball can be brightly colored or have a bell or beeper in it, and brightly colored tape can be used to mark the court boundaries. It also helps for a teammate to call the student by name before passing the ball.

Wrestling

Wrestling is a sport in which athletes who are blind or who have low vision can compete on an equal footing with sighted athletes, even at the national and international levels. Wrestlers start the match in contact with each other and must maintain contact with each other throughout the match. If contact is broken, the match is stopped and then restarted. A wrestler who is blind should have no difficulty determining when he or she is out of bounds because he or she can feel the edge of the mat. No modifications are necessary for a wrestler who has low vision.

IMPORTANT CONSIDERATIONS

Safety and Liability

Schools may be held accountable for injuries sustained in a physical education class if proper safety precautions have not been followed. Therefore, before a student engages in a specific activity, the teacher of students with visual impairments needs to consider several safety factors:

◆ Does the student have the skills necessary to participate safely? For example, does the student know how to swim? Does the student have sufficient balance to walk on a balance beam? Does the student know how to use a sighted guide when running?

◆ Does the student know what equipment,

people, boundaries, and so forth are in the environment? Has the student had the opportunity to explore the area beforehand?

◆ Is there sufficient supervision of the student? Keep in mind that the physical education teacher is responsible for the safety of all the students, not just the student who is visually impaired.

◆ Are the physical education teachers aware of the student's visual abilities and needs so they can help facilitate the student's safe participation in physical activities?

◆ Has the school been advised of potential safety issues related to the student with a visual impairment? For example, a student who has high myopia and is susceptible to retinal detachments should avoid contact sports and other activities, such as tumbling, that may cause further damage. Also, a student with a visual field restriction may not see a ball that is passed from outside his or her visual field, while a student with poor depth perception may not be able to determine the speed of a ball and catch it or get out of the way.

◆ Have the student's parents been informed of safety issues concerning the student's participation in physical education activities?

Student's Eye Condition

Ophthalmologists may recommend that students with certain eye conditions have restrictions placed on their physical activities because of the possibility of further vision loss, using statements like "student should avoid contact sports" or "student should wear protective lenses." Such statements should be heeded in determining whether a particular physical education activity is appropriate for a student with a visual impairment.

It is the responsibility of the teacher of students with visual impairments to inform the physical education teacher of any restrictions on a student's physical activity and of the warning signs of

S
I
D
E
B
A
R

1
2
.
3

Signs of Possible Eye Trauma

It is the nature of physical education activities that accidents occasionally happen and a student is injured. Of particular concern to a student who is visually impaired is an injury to the head or eyes resulting from a collision with another student, a fall, or being hit by a fast-moving object because trauma to the head or eyes may result in further damage to a student's visual functioning. The teacher of students with visual impairments should pay attention to any changes in the student's visual behavior or the physical condition of the student's eyes, as well as the student's complaints about his or her vision after such an injury. These changes may be indicators that a trauma has occurred and that the student's vision may be affected. If a change has occurred, the student should seek medical attention immediately.

Although such injuries are rare, the teacher of students with visual impairments must be aware of the potential results of trauma to the eye. For example, a student with severe myopia or a history of retinal degeneration may be susceptible to a retinal detachment if he or she is hit in the head with sufficient force. If the student complains of seeing flashing white lights or floaters, a retinal detachment may have occurred. Since visual functioning may not return to normal if part of the retina is out of contact with the choroid for a long period, it is essential that the student seek immediate medical attention (Bishop, 1996). A blunt injury or a puncture wound to the eye may also cause scarring, which may then cause cataracts (Bishop, 1996). Sec-

ondary glaucoma can be caused by trauma to the eye, and uveitis may also result (Pavan-Langston, 1996). A fracture of the bony orbit surrounding the eye may cause internal bleeding, a scratched cornea, a torn retina, or a dislocated lens (Pavan-Langston, 1996). The specialist needs to pay immediate attention to the following symptoms and student's complaints:

SYMPTOMS

- ◆ Squinting,
- ◆ Eye rubbing,
- ◆ Bloodshot eyes,
- ◆ Discharge or watery eyes, or
- ◆ Bumping into things more often than before.

STUDENT'S COMPLAINTS

- ◆ Flashing white lights, floaters (possible retinal detachment);
- ◆ Pain;
- ◆ Blurred vision;
- ◆ Dizziness;
- ◆ Sensitivity to light; or
- ◆ Double vision (diplopia).

Sources: Adapted from V. E. Bishop, "Causes and Functional Implications of Visual Impairment," in A. L. Corn and A. J. Koenig, Eds., *Foundations of Low Vision: Clinical and Functional Perspectives* (New York: AFB Press, 1996), pp. 86–114; and D. Pavan-Langston, *Manual of Ocular Diagnosis and Therapy* (Boston: Little, Brown, 1996).

eye trauma (see Sidebar 12.3 for signs of potential eye trauma). A student should also be aware of how the specific eye condition affects his or her participation in physical education activities and should be encouraged to communicate his or her own visual requirements as necessary.

Partial Participation

Sometimes an activity may be unsafe for a student with a visual impairment. Although full participation is the goal of modifying the physical education curriculum, if it is impossible, partial participation may still be valuable. The following suggestions may help the physical education teacher partially involve the student in a game or activity:

- ◆ Encourage the student to offer suggestions on how he or she may best participate.

- ◆ Provide alternate modifications to those that may be typically considered. For example, suggest playing a shooting game such as "horse" instead of competitive basketball.

- ◆ Provide intensive skill-based instruction related to the larger activity. For instance, teach the student to dribble instead of participate fully in a basketball game.

- ◆ Allow a student who is blind and cannot participate even partially in an activity (such as squash or badminton), which is a rare occurrence, to participate in a parallel activity like hitting a beeping baseball with a bat.

Support Personnel

It is often essential to have trained personnel—either the teacher of students with visual impairments or the O&M specialist—assist a student in a physical education class and teach specific skills. While working with the student, these specialists encourage the student to become as independent as possible in the activity because having an adult with the student at all times interferes with the student's social interactions with classmates. In short, the specialists need to balance the student's need for assistance with the student's need for independence.

Sighted peers may work with a student with a visual impairment, but should never have the responsibility of teaching the student skills. A peer may help the student as a sighted guide during running activities, as a partner practicing basketball passes, as a guide during warm-up exercises, and so forth. Before a peer can be effective in assisting a student with a visual impairment, he or she must be trained by the teacher of students with visual impairments, O&M specialist, or physical education teacher.

Advocacy for Participation

It is important for the teacher of students with visual impairments to obtain the support of the physical education teacher and other school personnel for a student's full participation in the physical education program. To do so, the following suggestions are offered:

- ◆ Inform the staff about the student's particular visual functioning. Stress what the student is able to do, not just what the student is unable to do.

- ◆ Make positive statements about the student and how he or she can benefit from participating in physical education.

- ◆ Give the staff information about including students with visual impairments in a physical education program—that students can participate fully in and benefit greatly from most physical education activities. A number of books, articles, and videos are available for this purpose (see the Resources at the end of the chapter).

- ◆ Invite the school personnel to observe another student with a visual impairment participating successfully in a physical education class at another school, such as a residential school for students who are visually impaired, as the first step in ensuring them that active participation in physical activities is possible.

- ◆ Consult with the physical education teacher in planning a program for a student with a visual impairment. If additional expertise or consultation is necessary, contact a physical education specialist at a residential school for students who are visually impaired.

- ◆ Take active steps to obtain more knowledge and skills in physical education and in adapting physical activities for students with visual impairments by accessing resources such as those included at the end of the chapter, and by attending workshops and in-services.

◆ Alleviate safety fears by providing specific suggestions for making physical education activities safe for the student with a visual impairment.

Scorekeeping Is Not Enough

Sometimes, a physical education teacher may be tempted to exclude a student with a visual impairment from an activity that is difficult to modify. He or she may assign the student to be the scorekeeper, thinking that keeping score involves the student in the activity more than being a mere spectator. Even though the teacher's intentions are understandable, this should not in general be considered an acceptable practice, although a student with a visual impairment certainly can learn to be a scorekeeper and occasionally take that role if the sighted students do so as well.

Some students with visual impairments welcome the opportunity to sit out a game, rather than participate in it, and some may even ask to keep score. However, students should always be encouraged to participate to the best of their ability. The teacher of students with visual impairments should try to determine why the student does not want to participate. Is it that, for example, the student is not capable of performing the activity, is afraid to participate, or feels awkward and embarrassed participating? Once the reason is determined, the specialist then needs to address the student's concerns accordingly through counseling, training in specific skills, or practice.

HEALTH EDUCATION

In many school districts, health education is part of the physical education curriculum. The health education curriculum is designed to influence positively the health knowledge, attitudes, and skills of students from preschool to grade 12. Health education includes the following areas:

◆ Consumer and community health;

◆ Growth and development;

◆ Environmental health;

◆ Family living;

◆ Mental and emotional health;

◆ The prevention of injuries and safe practices;

◆ Nutrition;

◆ Personal health;

◆ Communicable and chronic diseases; and

◆ The use of tobacco, alcohol, and other drugs.

Health education activities may involve no modifications other than to provide a student with materials in the appropriate learning medium, some modifications with the student remaining in the classroom, and major modifications in which the student is withdrawn for specialized instruction. For example, a student who is studying nutrition may follow along in his or her braille textbook as the other members of the class follow in their print textbooks, and a student who is learning about the effects of smoking on the heart and lungs may have the teacher of students with visual impairments help him or her explore a tactile model of the heart and lungs while the lecture is taking place. However, a female student who is learning about menstruation would benefit most from being withdrawn from the class and learning about feminine products by manipulating the actual products, with a female teacher of students with visual impairments; in such cases, it is imperative that the student's dignity and need for privacy be respected.

For the teacher of students with visual impairments to provide the appropriate tactile and visual modifications to a health lesson, he or she must work closely with the health teacher. Knowing what is coming up well in advance of the lesson that will be taught enables the specialist to gather, make, or modify the necessary materials to make the lesson meaningful and practical for the student with a visual impairment.

Curricular Content Areas

Consumer and Community Health. Common consumer and community health topics include food labeling, product advertising, and comparative shopping. Specific modifications that may be required in this area include having the information on food labels and in newspaper ads transcribed into braille or large print, bringing in actual food items (jars, cans, boxes, and so forth), or visiting a supermarket with the student. A student with a visual impairment requires hands-on experience with many of the products that sighted children have become familiar with through incidental observation, either through watching commercials on television; walking down the aisle of a supermarket; or reading labels on products, such as cereal boxes, at home.

Growth and Development. The growth and development unit includes learning about the senses, the body systems (like the circulatory system and the respiratory system), and the contribution of each system to the healthy operation of the human body. To illustrate to a student with a visual impairment where various body parts are located, the teacher of students with visual impairments can use tactile models. Many physical education and science departments have life-size skeletal models that the specialist may use for this purpose. The specialist should assist the student in exploring these models and relating each to the corresponding part of the student's body to ensure full understanding of the material being covered.

Environmental Health. This unit comprises such issues as air and water quality, allergies, ultraviolet radiation, and other environmental factors that affect people's health. Typical classroom modifications (for example, providing handouts in the appropriate reading medium, assisting the student with Internet searches, and verbally describing the contents of a video) are likely to be sufficient for most activities. When possible, the teacher of students with visual impairments should reinforce the concept being taught with real-life experiences. For example, a few minutes outside on an extremely smoggy day may be enough for a student to sense the difference in air quality.

Family Living. Cultural awareness, sharing traditions, parenting, discipline and guidance, respecting the rights and privileges of other family members, and sex education are a few of the topics discussed in this area. Given the sensitive nature of some of these topics, the teacher of students with visual impairments may wish to withdraw the student for individual instruction. For sex education, health teachers typically use diagrams, illustrations, photographs, and videos to teach about the male and female reproductive systems. However, a student who is visually impaired may need to explore tactile models, rather than these visual forms, and should do so with the assistance of the teacher of students with visual impairments. Since exploring models tactilely in the classroom may be embarrassing to the student, the student should be allowed to explore the models and ask questions in private. If possible, the specialist should be of the same sex as the student.

Mental and Emotional Health. The mental and emotional health component includes issues of self-esteem, confidence, expressing emotions appropriately, developing interpersonal relationships and self-awareness, and so forth. Specific issues involved in adjusting to or living with a visual impairment, including a student's low self-esteem, may require that the teacher of students with visual impairments take an active role in planning the program for this unit and acting as a counselor, especially since the health teacher and school guidance counselor may believe that they do not have the knowledge or skills to deal with these issues.

Prevention of Injuries and Safety Practices. Crossing roads safely, not talking to strangers, safe behavior on a school bus, and administering first aid are some of the topics that may be included in this component. For students with visual impairments, these issues are of the utmost importance. The O&M specialist and teacher of students with visual impairments should work together with the health teacher to create a program that will meet the unique needs of a visually impaired student. In fact, the O&M curriculum may overlap with this unit of the health curriculum, especially in the elementary grades, when children are taught how to travel safely and independently in the community.

Nutrition. The nutrition unit includes information on the basic food groups, vitamins and minerals, eating balanced meals, and making healthy food choices. Other than the provision of materials in an accessible medium, few modifications are likely to be necessary. However, the teacher of students with visual impairments may think that concrete objects may enhance the student's understanding of the concept being taught. For example, the specialist may bring in several brands of a particular type of food and have the student compare their nutritional content.

Personal Health. The personal health unit typically deals with the importance of maintaining a healthy lifestyle, including activities that will promote physical fitness and relieve stress. Standard modifications for students with visual impairments should be all that is required. Specific suggestions for promoting physical fitness were presented earlier in this chapter.

Communicable and Chronic Diseases. Students with disabilities tend to be less knowledgeable than those without disabilities about their bodies and their sexuality. They may also lack basic social skills and have low self-esteem (Birch & Marti, 1995). As a result, they may be vulnerable to the suggestions of their peers and engage in activities that place their health in jeopardy. Today, HIV and AIDS have reached epidemic proportions, so it is imperative that all students, including those who are visually impaired, be educated in the preven-

tion of HIV and AIDS. Typical classroom modifications, including tactile models, large-print or braille materials, audiotapes, and verbal descriptions, can be used. The teacher of students with visual impairments may also wish to involve a student's parents because they may not be aware of their child's need for specific instruction in this area. Just because a student is visually impaired does not mean that he or she will not be sexually active and, therefore, not susceptible to sexually transmitted diseases.

Tobacco, Alcohol, and Other Drugs. This portion of the health curriculum promotes awareness and the prevention of tobacco, alcohol, and drug abuse. It is important to recognize that some students with visual impairments, like sighted students, may abuse alcohol and other drugs (Leone, 1991). In fact, some students with visual impairments who have low self-esteem may be extremely susceptible to peer pressure to try drugs. Therefore, it is vital that these students take part in this unit and are not removed from class to work on other disability-specific skills. Typical classroom modifications, such as providing handouts in the appropriate reading medium, assisting the student with Internet searches, and verbally describing the contents of a video, are likely to be sufficient for most activities in this unit.

SUMMARY

Students with visual impairments need active physical education programs to develop physical fitness and a healthy lifestyle. Since they may be prone to inactivity, the importance of engaging in early and sustained physical activity needs to be emphasized. Teachers of students with visual impairments have a key role in consulting with physical education teachers to ensure the students' active involvement, providing adapted equipment and materials, and providing direct instruction in specific skills that will allow students to participate in various physical and health education activities.

ACTIVITIES

1. Select a physical education activity that was not described in this chapter and suggest modifications for a student who is blind.

2. Interview physical education teachers at the elementary, middle school, and high school levels. Ask them for their views of including a student who is blind and a student who has low vision in their physical education classes. Also ask them to name three activities in which they would feel the most comfortable including a student with a visual impairment and three activities in which they would feel the least comfortable. Finally, ask them for the type of information they would need to integrate a student with a visual impairment in their classes. Prepare a written report and share this information with your classmates.

3. On the basis of the concerns expressed by one of the teachers in Activity 2, design and present an in-service workshop to address the teacher's needs. Work in pairs or in small groups to carry out this activity.

4. A physical education teacher has refused to allow a healthy, active, 10-year-old girl who is blind to participate in any physical education activities because the teacher fears that the child will be injured and he will be held legally responsible. Prepare a written report on how a teacher of students with visual impairments would work with this teacher to enable the child to participate in physical education.

5. Observe a physical education class at the elementary level, middle school level, and high school level. Describe the activities that occurred during each period and list specific modifications that would be necessary to include fully a student who is blind. If full participation would not be possible, suggest a substitute or parallel activity.

6. Look through a catalog of physical education equipment. Identify 10 pieces of equipment that would need to be modified for students who are blind and students who have low vision. Provide suggested modifications or commercially available adapted pieces of equipment and their sources. Share copies of this work with your classmates.

REFERENCES

Blessing, D. L., McCrimmon, D., Stovall, J., & Williford, H. N. (1993). The effects of regular exercise programs for visually impaired and sighted schoolchildren. *Journal of Visual Impairment & Blindness, 87,* 50–52.

Block, M. E., & Burke, K. (1999). Are children with disabilities receiving appropriate physical education? *Teaching Exceptional Children, 31*(3), 18–23.

Birch, D. A., & Marti, R. (1995). *HIV/AIDS education for students with special needs: A guide for teachers.* Atlanta, GA: Association for the Advancement of Health Education.

Bishop, V. E. (1996). Causes and functional implications of visual impairment. In A. L. Corn & A. J. Koenig (Eds.), *Foundations of low vision: Clinical and functional perspectives* (pp. 86–114). New York: AFB Press.

Buell, C. E. (1992). *Physical education and recreation for the visually handicapped* (2nd ed.). Reston, VA: American Alliance for Health, Physical Education, Recreation and Dance.

Canadian Council of the Blind. (1993). *Active living through physical education: Maximizing opportunities for students with a visual impairment.* Gloucester, Ontario, Canada: Active Living Alliance for Canadians with a Disability.

De Pauw, K. P. (1981). Physical education for the visually impaired: A review of the literature. *Journal of Visual Impairment & Blindness, 75,* 162–164.

Ferrell, K. A. (1997). *Project PRISM: Final report to the United States Department of Education, Research in Education of Individuals with Disabilities Program.* Greeley: University of Northern Colorado, Division of Special Education.

Ferrell, K. A., Raver, S. A., & Stewart, K. A. (1999). Techniques for infants and toddlers with visual impairments. In S. A. Raver, *Intervention strategies for infants and toddlers with special needs: A team approach* (2nd ed., pp. 298–330). Upper Saddle River, NJ: Prentice Hall.

Hanna, R. S. (1986). Effect of exercise on blind persons. *Journal of Visual Impairment & Blindness, 80,* 722–725.

Hatlen, P. H., & Curry, S. A. (1987). In support of specialized programs for blind and visually impaired children: The impact of vision loss on learning. *Journal of Visual Impairment & Blindness, 81,* 7–13.

Heydt, K., & Allon, M. (1992). Motor development: Gross and fine motor skills. In C. Cushman, K. Heydt, S. Edwards, M. J. Clark, & M. Allon, *Perkins activity and resource guide: A handbook for teachers and parents of students with visual and multiple disabilities.* Watertown, MA: Perkins School for the Blind.

Lieberman, L. J., & Cowart, J. F. (1996). *Games for people with sensory impairments: Strategies for including individuals of all ages.* Champaign, IL: Human Kinetics.

Leone, P. E. (1991). *Alcohol and other drugs: Use, abuse, and disabilities.* Reston, VA: Council for Exceptional Children.

Loumiet, R., & Levack, N. (1993). *Independent living: A curriculum with adaptations for students with visual impairments.* Austin: Texas School for the Blind and Visually Impaired.

Luxton, K., & Kelley, J. D. (1981). Foundations and basis of recreation and leisure services for blind and visually impaired children. In J. D. Kelley (Ed.), *Recreation programming for visually impaired children and youth* (pp. 1–14). New York: American Foundation for the Blind.

Meek G. A., & Maguire, J. F. (1996). A field experiment of minimum physical fitness of children with visual impairments. *Journal of Visual Impairment & Blindness, 90,* 77–80.

Modell, S. J., & Cox, T. A. (1999). Let's get fit! Fitness activities for children with severe/profound disabilities. *Teaching Exceptional Children, 31(3),* 24–29.

Pavan-Langston, D. (1996). *Manual of ocular diagnosis and therapy* (4th ed.). Boston: Little, Brown.

Ponchillia, P. E. (1995). AccesSports: A model for adapting mainstream sports activities for individuals with visual impairments. *RE:view, 27(1),* 5–14.

Ponchillia, P. E., Powell, L. L., Felski, K. A., & Nicklawski, M. T. (1992). The effectiveness of aerobic exercise instruction for totally blind women. *Journal of Visual Impairment & Blindness, 86,* 174–177.

Schneekloth, L. H. (1989). Play environments for visually impaired children. *Journal of Visual Impairment & Blindness, 83,* 196–210.

Short, F. X., & Winnick, J. P. (1986). The influence of visual impairment on physical fitness test performance. *Journal of Visual Impairment & Blindness, 80,* 729–731.

Warren, D. H. (1994). *Blindness and children: An individual differences approach.* Cambridge, England: Cambridge University Press.

Williams, C. A., Armstrong, N., Eves, N., & Faulkner, A. (1996). Peak aerobic fitness of visually impaired and sighted adolescent girls. *Journal of Visual Impairment & Blindness, 90,* 495–500.

Willoughby, D. M., & Duffy, S. L. M. (1989). *Handbook for itinerant and resource teachers of blind and visually impaired students.* Baltimore, MD: National Federation of the Blind.

Strategies for Teaching Physical Education and Health to Students with Visual Impairments and Additional Disabilities

A student with a visual impairment and additional disabilities may engage in age-related activities with peers if materials and environments are adapted for better access, activities are modified to accommodate the student's means and level of participation, and expectations for the student are changed through the use of partial participation. The following are examples of these various means of involving a student:

◆ An obstacle course can be designed to accommodate any level of skill and to promote needed skills in a fun and interactive manner and gives a student many opportunities to practice the skills within a variety of situations and in a goal-directed manner. A number of spatial concepts; communicative skills; and foundation skills, such as climbing, jumping, and maintaining balance, may be enhanced as the student moves through the course and anticipates a targeted skill by the context of an activity.

◆ Students who may not have the balance and efficiency to participate in aerobics in a gym may find water aerobics less taxing and more fun. The resistance of the water allows students who may not otherwise remain upright without support to do so.

◆ Students with mental challenges in addition to blindness learn the necessary strokes for swimming in a pool more effectively than outside it because they typically have difficulty generalizing the strokes taught out of the water when they are in the water. Using the term *square up* in the pool directs a student's movement within lanes and does not require the student to learn yet another term or cue.

◆ Students should be encouraged to participate in community swim teams, such as those sponsored by the YMCA or YWCA. On such a team, a student may practice alongside his or her same-age peers, may enjoy the camaraderie of the team, and may support the team at meets by assisting, even through partial participation, with the team's equipment.

◆ Physical therapy for older students may better be addressed within the context of a community gymnasium under the guidance and assistance of a nondisabled high school student who serves as both a friend and a coach in this age-appropriate setting.

◆ Games, such as hockey and volleyball, are easily adapted so that participants of all levels may enjoy them. Traditional hockey can be turned into "broom hockey" using brooms and beach balls with bells inside, and traditional volleyball can be changed by stuffing hosiery or foam peanuts inside lawn garbage bags along with bells or other sound devices. Taping fluorescent colored tape around the "volleyball" bags may enable students with low vision to monitor the bags' movements.

◆ Students who are typically in wheelchairs may benefit from "walking" in parks or recreational areas with others through the use of adapted walkers, such as the Theratrek, which stabilizes and secures

(continued on next page)

the student in an upright posture and facilitates independent movement.

- ◆ A student can participate in an informal game of soccer by using a specially designed athletic ball with a smaller ball or bell inside it and running in tandem with a sighted partner who directs when to kick and stabilizes the student.

- ◆ Parachute activities require cooperation from all the participants and are an effective way to build a student's upper-

body strength while sharing in the fun with the other participants.

- ◆ Young children find learning to throw and catch more fun when the targeted object is the commercially available Hot Potato Musical Action Game™, which plays music as it is tossed from one player to another.

M. BETH LANGLEY
Pinellas County Schools
St. Petersburg, FL

RESOURCES

Suggested Resources for Teaching Physical Education and Health

Resource	Type	Source	Description
"AccessSports: A Model for Adapting Mainstream Sports Activities for Individuals with Visual Impairments" (Ponchillia, 1995)	Article	*RE:view*	A useful resource for adapting sports activities for students with visual impairments.
Active Living through Physical Education: Maximizing Opportunities for Students with a Visual Impairment (Canadian Council of the Blind, 1993)	Book	Active Living Alliance for Canadians with a Disability, Gloucester, Ontario, Canada	A comprehensive guide to the inclusion of students with visual impairments in physical education activities with their sighted peers.
"The Effectiveness of Aerobic Exercise Instruction for Totally Blind Women" (Ponchillia, Powell, Felski, & Nicklawski, 1992)	Article	*Journal of Visual Impairment & Blindness*	A study of the effects of aerobic exercise.
"The Effect of Exercise on Blind Persons" (Hanna, 1986)	Article	*Journal of Visual Impairment & Blindness*	A report of a study of the effects of exercise on persons who are blind.
"The Effects of Regular Exercise Programs for Visually Impaired and Sighted School Children" (Blessing, McCrimmon, Stovall, & Williford, 1993)	Article	*Journal of Visual Impairment & Blindness*	A report describing the advantages of regular exercise for students with visual impairments.
Independent Living: A Curriculum with Adaptations for Students with Visual Impairments (Loumiet & Levack, 1993)	Book	Texas School for the Blind and Visually Impaired	A curriculum that includes suggestions for instructing students with visual impairments in physical education.

(continued on next page)

Suggested Resources *(Continued)*

Resource	Type	Source	Description
"The Influence of Visual Impairment on Physical Fitness Test Performance" (Short & Winnick, 1986)	Article	*Journal of Visual Impairment & Blindness*	A study of the influence of visual impairment on physical fitness.
"In Support of Specialized Programs for Blind and Visually Impaired Children: The Impact of Vision Loss on Learning" (Hatlen & Curry, 1987)	Article	*Journal of Visual Impairment & Blindness*	An article addressing the impact of vision loss on learning; includes discussion of effects on health and physical development.
Physical Education and Recreation for the Visually Handicapped (2nd ed.) (Buell, 1982)	Book	American Alliance for Health, Physical Education, Recreation and Dance, Reston, VA	A textbook describing sports activities for students who are blind.
"Physical Education for the Visually Impaired: A Review of the Literature" (DePauw, 1981)	Article	*Journal of Visual Impairment & Blindness*	A resource for those who are interested in literature related to physical education for people who are visually impaired.
Sports equipment, such as balls with bells	Equipment	LS&S Group	A variety of sports equipment, such as beeping balls, balls with bells, and an audible "flying disc." Also provides health-related items like talking scales for weighing food.
Sports manuals	Books	Canadian Blind Sports Association	Coaching manuals for swimming, wrestling, and goalball and rules for track and field.

Contact information for each of the resources listed will be found in the Sources of Products, Materials, Equipment, and Services section at the back of this book.

CHAPTER 13

Visual Efficiency

Anne L. Corn, Linda B. DePriest, and Jane N. Erin

KEY POINTS

- ◆ **Students with low vision may not automatically develop visual skills and efficiency.**

- ◆ **A sequence of planned, direct instruction may be needed to facilitate the development of visual efficiency in students with low vision.**

- ◆ **Students with low vision may enhance their visual efficiency by using optical devices, nonoptical devices, environmental modifications, and other strategies.**

- ◆ **To develop their functional use of vision, students with low vision require instruction in natural tasks and daily routines.**

- ◆ **The teacher of students with visual impairments has a primary role in teaching visual efficiency skills to students with low vision.**

VIGNETTE

Jeanie, a second grader, entered the classroom and hung her pink baseball cap on the hook by the door. Her teacher of students with visual impairments, Ms. Carlyle, and her second-grade general education teacher, Ms. Burkette, had put up the hook so Jeanie would have a place to keep her cap and not have to

hunt for it each time she went out. In preschool, Jeanie had usually crouched in the shade at recess before it was discovered that she had ocular albinism and photophobia. Jeanie's visual acuity was 20/200. She wore tinted eyeglasses, and maybe when she was older she would wear contact lenses. With the tinted eyeglasses, indoor light almost never bothered her; but when outdoors, Jeanie really needed a cap with a visor as well. In the classroom, Jeanie sat at a desk in the front row, away from the windows. She read regular second-grade books, sometimes propping them on a reading stand, and occasionally used a handheld magnifier to view small print or the details of a picture. She was able to write using the same sort of pencil and paper as her classmates—and she could read what she had written, too.

Ms. Carlyle and Wes were practicing copying from the chalkboard with his handheld monocular. Wes had no trouble reading from the board with the device, but he habitually held the monocular in his right hand. The trouble was that Wes also *wrote* with his right hand, so he had to lay down the monocular and pick up his pencil each time he was ready to write. It was an inefficient process, and Wes was having trouble keeping up when Mr. Taylor, the mathematics teacher, wrote a series of problems on the board. Ms. Carlyle had written several typical problems on the board, and Wes was experimenting with holding the monocular in his left hand while he copied part of a problem with his right hand and then looking back at the board. This way, he did not have to put down either the monocular or the pencil. It was definitely a faster method, but Wes felt clumsy holding the monocular in his left hand. Ms. Carlyle told him that with practice, he might feel more comfortable and become more skilled in doing so.

INTRODUCTION

Students who are born with low vision (that is, who have congenital low vision) may not spontaneously learn to use and become efficient in using their available vision (Ambrose & Corn, 1997; Barraga, 1964; Sykes, 1971). Those with adventitious low vision (that is, who developed low vision later in childhood) may need to learn visual skills to retain visual approaches to carrying out day-to-day activities. Since most school-age students with visual impairments have vision that may be beneficial for learning, it is imperative that teachers of students with visual impairments know about and use instructional strategies that will allow these learners to use their vision efficiently.

A variety of terms are used to denote and describe visual functioning. Perhaps the most general term is *visual efficiency*. Barraga and Erin (1992, p. 28) defined visual efficiency as

> the most inclusive of all terms related to vision, . . . contingent on many personal and environmental variables. Visual acuity at a distance and at near range, control of eye movements, accommodative and adaptive capabilities of the visual mechanism, speed and filtering abilities of the transmitting channels, and speed and quality of the processing of the brain are all related to visual efficiency.

This definition underscores the fact that a person's sight can provide a measure of a person's visual capacity, but personal attributes may enhance the effectiveness of the visual system (the eyes, optic nerve, brain), and incorporate the totality of the experience of using vision. A student's

visual efficiency is affected by the following factors:

◆ Personal attributes, including age of onset of the visual impairment, self-concept, and experience with people who are visually impaired;

◆ Visual attributes, including type of visual impairment (such as central field versus peripheral field), severity of visual impairment, and other visual factors;

◆ Expectations for the student by people who are significant to him or her, including family members (see Sidebar 13.1 for a family's possible reactions to a child with low vision), other children, teachers, and eye care specialists;

◆ The presence of role models to allow a student with low vision to observe and receive information from others who have firsthand experiences in how to facilitate visual efficiency;

◆ The availability of instruction to enhance visual efficiency;

◆ The presence of additional disabilities (see Sidebar 13.2), which may be social, cognitive, communicative, neurological, or physical; and

◆ Cognitive and sensory factors, such as sensory stimulation, concept development, and communication.

The use of optical devices, nonoptical devices, and other techniques allow students to increase their use of vision for learning and for planning and completing tasks. To increase visual efficiency, medical, eye care, and educational specialists should provide appropriate assessments and instruction and help students to develop visual skills and understand visual information. Whereas vision can facilitate learning, learning can help to facilitate the use of vision.

Teachers of students with visual impairments should not assume that students will achieve visual performance that approximates normal vi-

Possible Reactions of a Family to a Child with Low Vision

◆ Family members may accept and treat their child as a person with low vision and encourage him or her to accept modifications and adaptations that will enhance visual efficiency. They convey the message that having a visual impairment is just one aspect of their child's total self. To enhance their child's functioning, they must advocate independence in and visual control of the environment and provide visual support when needed.

◆ Family members may deny that the visual impairment exists and expect their child to function as a normally sighted child with no modifications or adaptations made to the environment.

◆ Family members may acknowledge that their child has low vision and provide so much support that the child becomes overly dependent on them and others for visual supports and does not seek visual independence.

◆ Family members may perceive their child as an individual who is functionally blind, not realizing that variations in visual functioning exist.

◆ Family members may send mixed messages to their child regarding his or her low vision and may inconsistently acknowledge that the child has low vision. For example, a child who is encouraged by his or her parents to use optical devices at home is learning that adaptations are available to assist with optimal visual functioning and that it is acceptable to be a person who has low vision. However, if the child is discouraged by family members from using the same optical devices in public settings because of their desire for him or her to "pass" as a sighted person, the underlying message is that in certain circumstances it is not acceptable to have low vision.

sual functioning. Nor should they convey the message that to be visually oriented or to appear as a fully sighted individual is more important than functioning without visual input. Three important factors need to be considered in this regard:

◆ Not all students choose to extend the effort it may take to function visually over time.

◆ Students who are more efficient and comfortable using nonvisual approaches, alone or in combination with vision, should consider these approaches valid and worthy of their pride.

◆ Some students' visual capacity may not be sufficient for visual functioning to be comfortable, efficient, or preferred.

Teachers of students with visual impairments should respect the preferences of students who want to enhance their visual abilities, as well as of students who find that functioning as visual learners is unproductive or unimportant. They need to be sensitive to how students feel about their efforts to increase their visual functioning.

At one time, visual efficiency was not a concern of educators in the field of visual impairments. Methods that worked for students who were blind were used with students who had low vision. It seemed logical that if methods used with students who were blind were successful, it would be easier and more comfortable for people with low vision to be able to complete tasks without using vision. Also, from the early 1900s through the 1960s, these educators generally believed that a person with low vision should conserve his or her available sight and would further harm his or her eyes by using them. However, as early as 1930, ophthalmologists knew that this belief was without merit (Goodrich & Sowell, 1996).

In 1964, Barraga demonstrated through a systematic set of instructional activities that students who had low vision could increase the efficiency with which they used their vision. With these findings, teachers of students with visual impairments began to emphasize the use of vision over other methods, sometimes to the exclusion of nonvisual methods.

Today, educators need to find a more central position between the two extreme practices. It is understood that students with low vision can improve their functioning with individually designed instructional programs that may involve optical devices, nonoptical devices, and other techniques. It is also accepted that some students with low vision may increase their overall efficiency by combining visual methods with nonvisual approaches, such as the use of braille and other tactile approaches.

This chapter begins by describing the role of the teacher of students with visual impairments in

---

Issues Related to the Impact of Additional Disabilities on Visual Functioning

SIDEBAR 13.2

♦ The presence of an additional disability may influence how a student receives and responds to visual information. Although the presence of a disability in isolation may have little impact on a student's visual efficiency, the combination of an additional disability and a visual impairment may affect a student's ability to maintain control of the environment. Since variations in the range and combination of disabilities, as well as the impact of additional disabilities on visual functioning are endless, collaboration with professionals who are experienced in observing the visual functioning of this population is essential.

♦ Determining a student's capacity for visual functioning may be difficult, since students who have low vision and additional disabilities may not respond to traditional assessment measures that can be used to develop programming for instruction in visual efficiency for students without additional disabilities. Data-based observations may be used in describing how and under what circumstances these students appear to use vision.

♦ A student's visual functioning may be masked by more obvious and easier-to-identify characteristics of his or her additional disabilities. For example, with a student who has a severe motor deficit, as well as low vision, educational programming may focus on such areas as positioning for optimal comfort because the motor deficit has more overt characteristics that require attention and efforts to address. Thus, the student's attempts to promote visual efficiency may not have been recognized or addressed. Therefore, students with other disabilities should always be included in visual screenings and teachers of students with visual impairments should be available to provide direct and/or consultative education services.

providing instruction in visual efficiency. It then presents common terminology, along with factors that influence how visual efficiency develops. Next, it describes assessment processes and subsequently presents the strategies for designing unique instructional programs in visual efficiency for children and youths with low vision.

ROLE OF THE TEACHER OF STUDENTS WITH VISUAL IMPAIRMENTS

The teacher of students with visual impairments plays a primary role in ensuring that students with low vision develop visual efficiency. Instruction in visual efficiency is a component of the expanded core curriculum for students with visual impairments, so there is no direct counterpart in the regular curriculum (Hatlen, 1996). The primary responsibilities of the specialist are to do the following:

◆ Conduct functional vision assessments to determine students' levels of skill and to identify the types of instruction that students need to increase their visual efficiency (see Chapter 4 for information on functional vision assessments);

◆ Provide direct instruction in the use of optical low vision devices;

◆ Provide instruction and consultation in the use of nonoptical devices, environmental modifications, and other techniques;

◆ Ensure that visual skills instruction is integrated, as appropriate, throughout students' educational programs;

◆ Promote, provide corrective feedback on, and reinforce students' choices in using a visual approach, nonvisual approach, or a combination of approaches to perform tasks; and

◆ Continuously monitor and evaluate students' use of visual skills and future needs.

The teacher also plays an essential role in working with students with additional disabilities; strategies focusing on students with visual impairments and additional disabilities and resources for teachers appear later in this chapter.

TERMINOLOGY

Numerous terms have been used to describe vision, low vision, and blindness. Some terms relate to legal criteria, while others relate to the ways in which a person uses his or her senses to gather information from the environment and to learn. This section defines some of the most commonly used terms in the field of educating students with visual impairments.

Sight and Vision

Sight refers to the capacity of the visual system to receive originating or reflected light from objects. The light is transmitted through the eye, converted into information sent through the optic nerves, and deposited in the appropriate parts of the brain, where the image is interpreted and linked to other sensory, physical, emotional, cognitive, and experiential information.

Vision is the ability to interpret what is seen. Through the use of vision, the observer knows that something seen is a truck or a box of cereal or an object or a shadow. Vision also provides information with which to make decisions about what is seen. It allows the individual to answer such questions as, "Is the object coming toward me, or is it turning?" "Is the object small enough for me to pick up?" "Is that something I can walk under?"

Low Vision

The term *low vision* is used by many professionals and persons with visual impairments, and various definitions exist, but to date, there is no commonly used or legal definition of the term. Corn and Koenig (1996, p. 4) defined a person with low vision as one "who has difficulty accomplishing visual tasks, even with prescribed corrective lenses, but who can enhance his or her ability to accomplish these tasks with the use of compensatory visual strategies, low vision and other devices, and environmental modifications." In this definition, low vision is a descriptor of how one functions with vision, so the specialist does not rely on clinical measures to indicate whether a person meets a standard, such as legal blindness. Therefore, students and adults can have low vision and meet or not meet the definition for legal blindness, which is discussed below.

The World Health Organization's (WHO's) definition of a person with low vision is "one who has impairment of visual function, even after treatment and/or standard refractive correction, and has a visual acuity of less than 6/18 (20/60) to light perception or a visual field of less than 10 degrees from the point of fixation, but who uses or is potentially able to use, vision for the planning and/or execution of a task" (quoted in Best & Corn, 1993, p. 309). In this definition, visual functions are measures that coincide with international classifications of diseases, although not all low vision is the result of disease.

The term *partially sighted* has been used to describe the population of students and adults who have impaired sight and who use vision as their primary learning mode. At one time, this term referred only to a person whose best visual acuity in his or her better eye was between 20/70 and 20/200. In some instances, persons whose visual acuity is from 20/70 to minimal levels of vision that have allowed them to use vision have also been referred to as partially sighted. Today, this term is rarely used; still, professionals need to be aware of its meaning.

Legal and Functional Blindness

In 1934, the American Medical Association formulated a definition to help determine which persons in the United States were in need of economic support because of their visual impairments. In 1935, this formulation became known as the definition of *legal blindness* and was incorporated into the Social Security Act. *Legal blindness* was defined as follows:

Central visual acuity of 20/200 or less in the better eye with corrective eyeglasses or central visual acuity of more than 20/200 if there is a visual field defect in which the peripheral field is contracted to such an extent that the widest diameter of the visual field subtends an angular distance no greater than 20 degrees in the better eye (quoted in Koestler, 1976, p. 45).

A person is legally blind under standard conditions when with standard corrections (eyeglasses or contact lenses), he or she cannot resolve images smaller than the letter or symbol designated on a chart for 20/200 or has a visual field that does not exceed 20 degrees. A limitation of the definition is that it does not encompass other aspects of visual functioning, such as fluctuating vision, tolerance for lighting, visual fatigue, or contrast sensitivity. Furthermore, it does not indicate whether a person will function as if he or she is functionally blind or whether he or she is oriented visually to the physical environment.

Functional blindness is generally used to describe persons without usable vision who perform tasks primarily without visual input and whose knowledge of the environment is supplied by other than visual means. In other words, a person may have some level of vision, but use other sensory cues (auditory or tactile) to plan or complete tasks comfortably or efficiently.

Related Terms

Visual capacity refers to an individual's potential to develop visual efficiency. Because there are no data to illustrate what can be accomplished at the highest levels of visual efficiency for an individual's capacity, it is not possible to know whether a person has reached his or her highest level of visual efficiency. Therefore, it is difficult to say that if an instructional program were implemented, a child with specific clinical measures would reach a prescribed level of visual efficiency for his or her visual capacity and be able to accomplish a specific set of tasks under prescribed environmental conditions.

Visual environmental awareness refers to the

extent to which children and adults with low vision are aware of objects in their environment. For example, some young children with low vision may have little, if any, spontaneous interest in what is occurring at a distance. Older children with normal visual fields who meet their state's required visual measures to become low vision drivers may not attend to information in their far periphery, which could result in dangerous situations. Still others who have the visual capacity to see objects that are of specific sizes and shapes may not notice a specific object without someone directing them to look at it.

Visual functions refer to the abilities of the visual system, such as visual acuity, visual field, color discrimination, dark adaptation, contrast sensitivity, and the like, as measured by performance on standardized tests of sight. For example, an ophthalmologist will describe visual function and state a visual acuity or describe the extent and shape of a visual field. *Functional vision* and *visual functioning,* on the other hand, are defined as "the use of vision for purposeful behavior" (Hall & Bailey, 1989), and are more often used as educational or rehabilitative terms. These terms refer to what a person can do with his or her available vision.

THEORIES OF VISUAL FUNCTION

Barraga's (1964) research followed a developmental approach assuming that students with low vision go through the same milestones as sighted students in their development of functional vision. It is now understood that not all students follow all the steps seen in students with "normal development" (for example, many students who cannot use smooth eye movements are able to learn to read). However, the more of these milestones a student achieves, the better his or her foundation for visual functioning will be.

This developmental foundation is seen in other theories of visual function for people with low vision. In Corn's (1983) model, functional vision is depicted as a pliable cube (see Figure 13.1). This model combines the developmental ap-

proach with environmental features and interactions of various personal elements that lead children to elicit, maximize, or compensate for visual functions that do not approximate typical sight. Although the visual acuity of all infants at birth is not fully developed, since babies are not born with 20/20 acuity, contributions from the other dimensions facilitate infants' further development and use of vision. In Corn's model, altering one or more of the environmental cues, addressing the physical and emotional concerns of using vision, and seeing how the three dimensions interact lead to an understanding of how low vision is used daily under changing visual or environmental circumstances.

Hall and Bailey (1989) developed a theoretical model specifically for training young children in the use of low vision (see Figure 13.2). Their model begins with visual cue control, which leads to three domains: visual environment management, visual skills training, and visually dependent task training. In each domain, visual attending behaviors, visually guided motor behaviors, and visual examining behaviors can be trained, resulting in maximizing visual functioning. (See the discussion of Instructional Strategies for more details on using this model for instruction.)

ASSESSMENT

A student's efficiency in using and potential to use vision and his or her progress in increasing visual efficiency are determined by a functional vision assessment (see Chapter 4 for a detailed explanation of this assessment). A functional vision assessment provides information on how a student uses vision in familiar and unfamiliar surroundings, the impact of vision on learning, and the factors that help or hinder visual function and presents recommendations to the educational team on how to increase and enhance a student's visual efficiency.

The functional vision assessment has two major purposes: (1) to determine a student's eligibility for services; and (2) to describe visual functioning, assess progress, and identify ways in which the use of vision may be facilitated. In many states, the

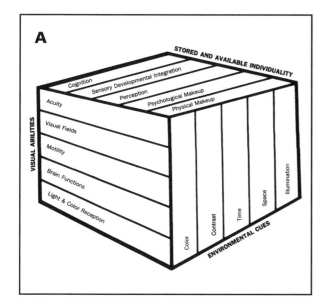

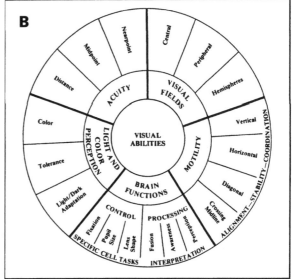

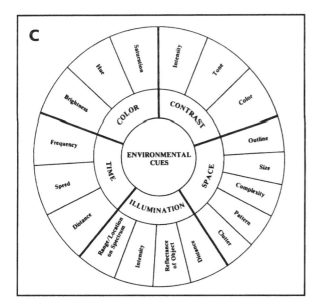

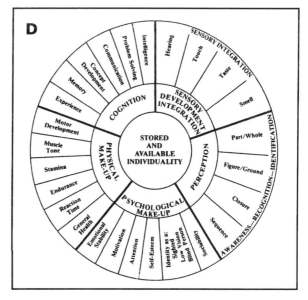

Figure 13.1. Corn's Model of Visual Functioning

A. Model of Visual Functioning
B. Components of the Visual Abilities Dimension
C. Components of the Environmental Cues Dimension
D. Components of the Stored and Available Individuality Dimension

Source: Reprinted, with permission, from A. L. Corn, "Instruction in the Use of Vision for Children and Adults with Low Vision," *RE:view, 21* (1989), pp. 26–38.

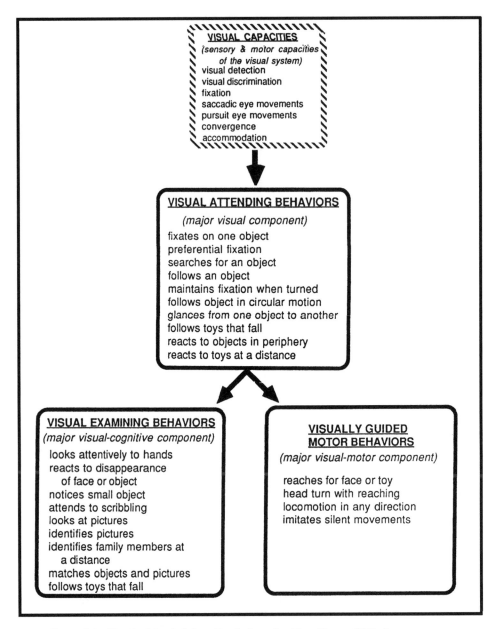

Figure 13.2. Hall and Bailey's Model for Training in the Use of Vision

Visual Behaviors of Visually Impaired Children from Birth to Age 2

Source: Reprinted, with permission, from A. Hall and I. L. Bailey, "A Model for Training Vision Functioning," *Journal of Visual Impairment & Blindness, 83* (1989), pp. 390–396.

functional vision assessment has a legal role in determining what students who are visually impaired require specialized services. These assessments are generally conducted at specific intervals, such as every year or every three years.

More specific to this chapter, though, is that a teacher of students with visual impairments con-

ducts an ongoing functional vision assessment, using specific activities, informal checklists, and observations to monitor and evaluate a student's progress in developing visual efficiency. For example, if the teacher is teaching a student to use a monocular telescope to gather distant information (see the section on Instruction in the Use of

Optical Devices), he or she would use a checklist of the steps in the process. As the student masters each step (such as spotting objects through the monocular, focusing for distances of less than 20 feet), the teacher would note that the task was mastered. Another use of checklists is to delineate and monitor the specific tasks and activities within which the use of vision is appropriate and the student's efficiency in using vision to accomplish those tasks. This information, then, is used to guide future instruction in developing visual efficiency or to change approaches, if necessary.

INSTRUCTIONAL STRATEGIES

This section describes a general approach to identifying needed visual skills and delivering instruction to teach those skills. The initial area of instruction is the use of visual skills without optical low vision devices. Then, because the use of optical devices by children with low vision has been largely underrepresented in the literature on visual impairment, the final section of the chapter, presents detailed strategies for teaching the use of optical devices (for additional information, see D'Andrea & Farrenkopf, in press).

On the basis of the functional vision assessment, instructional goals and procedures are planned. Selecting appropriate materials, sequencing the learning, and creating a motivating learning environment ensure that the student has opportunities to learn to use vision efficiently. The teacher of students with visual impairments is the facilitator, encouraging the student to assume more and more responsibility and thereby gain independent control over the visual environment. This independence may include visual and other methods for obtaining sensory information.

Planning and Implementing Instruction

According to Hall and Bailey (1989), instruction in the use of low vision involves three primary areas: making environmental adaptations, enhancing visual skills, and integrating vision into activities.

The Individualized Education Programs (IEPs) of many students include goals in all three areas.

Making Environmental Adaptations.   Changes in the learning environment can maximize the use of vision. The appropriate adaptations that are identified in the functional vision assessment may include adjusting seating, lighting, and distance, as well as positioning, to use vision efficiently. Although the teacher of students with visual impairments can guide progress in ensuring that adaptations are part of students' IEPs, ultimately the goal is for the students to make the necessary adaptations themselves. This goal may require instructing students to recognize environmental difficulties and, in some cases, to use appropriate skills in requesting assistance or being assertive.

Enhancing Visual Skills.   A visual skill is a specific behavior that is needed in a variety of activities, such as scanning a busy department store to locate a cosmetics counter or a buffet table to select desired foods. Instruction involves learning to use visual skills, such as tracking, scanning, and attending to visual stimuli. Although these skills may be taught through highly controlled activities whose main purpose is to stimulate and encourage the use of vision, this type of instructional activity is of limited effectiveness for some students with low vision.

In most cases, responses should be encouraged through visually stimulating activities. The teacher of students with visual impairments identifies the visual skills that are needed to perform a task (e.g., to copy words from a chalkboard) and evaluates the student's competence in these skills using information from the functional vision assessment, as well as observations of the specific activity.

Integrating Vision into Activities.   Most students with low vision have educational goals that focus on the efficient accomplishment of classroom tasks and life skills. Visual skills should be integrated into the actual activities in which they are needed, rather than taught in isolation, so students learn to become more efficient in performing those tasks. For example, Ray may work on shifting attention by matching words from his social studies text to the worksheet on his desk. Ashley may practice shifting her gaze at a quicker speed by matching a picture card to the corresponding card on her communication device and then locating the next card.

To integrate vision into tasks, the teacher of students with visual impairments can use an ecological approach in which he or she analyzes a student's environment by domains and determines the skills in each domain that the student needs at present and will need in the future (Brown et al., 1979). The steps are as follows:

1. Identify the domains in which the student functions. Although these domains may vary, depending on the stage of the student and his or her unique needs and goals, the school, domestic, leisure, community, and vocational domains provide a structure in which to address instruction in visual efficiency.

2. Identify the tasks and activities that a student must perform to be successful in each domain. For example, Alexis may want to read a recipe in a standard print cookbook to make cookies.

3. Determine whether the student will learn the task using vision, another sense, or all the senses. For example, if the tenth-grade home economics class is using recipes from a variety of cookbooks, Marquita can practice scanning the indexes of the cookbooks for a particular recipe and locating the titles of recipes. The opportunity to practice using vision to locate the information she needs will enable her to participate in the activity. Although she will increase her speed by practicing, the ultimate goal is for her to perform the task efficiently.

4. Implement an instructional program to teach needed visual skills. Suggestions for sequencing and delivering instruction are presented next.

Sequencing Instruction in Skills

Designing and delivering effective instruction in visual efficiency require careful planning and skillful implementation. The following steps should be included in the instructional process: specifying objectives, modeling, guided practice, and independent practice.

Specifying Objectives. Objectives should be based on recommendations from the functional vision assessment and should be specific and measurable. Objectives should be stated behaviorally and indicate how a task is to be performed (with physical assistance or verbal assistance, independently, and so forth), the statement of the skill to be performed, and the criterion for evaluation. For example, "With verbal prompt, Erica will reach for her eating utensils (spoon, fork, and knife) when presented at a distance of 20 inches" is more appropriate than "Erica will reach for objects." (See Chapter 6 for more details on writing behavioral objectives or benchmarks.)

Instructional objectives for visual efficiency may be embedded in such unique instructional programs as those in photography, art, landscaping, and culinary arts, as well as in travel and attendance at sporting activities, all of which present opportunities for students with low vision to develop visual efficiency. For students with low vision who will become drivers, bicycle riding, playing ball, and other activities that require quick visual interpretations and decision making can be excellent opportunities for practicing visual skills.

For students with lower levels of visual functioning, art classes, playing with pets in enclosed spaces, and looking at the movements of animals at a distance can also provide opportunities for visual efficiency. If these activities are used as a context for embedded visual skills, they need to be presented within an instructional program that has systematic benchmarks to evaluate progress. These activities may remain within the recreational, leisure and independent living domains so that visual skills are seen not as the primary focus, but as a way to enhance the desired outcomes of using vision in pleasurable situations.

Modeling. It is essential for a student to see others using a skill to understand its importance and to observe the activity. If there are no other students with low vision in the school, the teacher should arrange for the student to meet others with low vision outside the school and to observe them functioning efficiently. The student can also learn techniques, such as the use of a prescribed monocular device for watching play or spotting the license plates of cars or the use of a handheld magnifier for applying makeup (see the discussion on strategies for teaching the use of optical devices).

Guided Practice.   Initially, students should receive enough prompting and instruction to accomplish a task and gain confidence as they learn a visual skill. They should experience some success during each teaching session, and the steps need to be discrete enough that the mastery of individual elements of the task can be identified. It is important to determine whether a student understands the sequence of steps involved in the task or activity because guided practice reinforces the development of correct skills. A student must demonstrate his or her successful mastery of the entire sequence of steps before he or she is expected to perform the task or activity independently.

For example, the student who is learning to use an optical device learns discrete elements, such as spotting and focusing, that later become well integrated into activities (see the later section on using optical devices). So the student does not have to learn a new visual skill at the same time as he or she is learning new information in the classroom, the teacher of students with visual impairments begins instruction by presenting the use of the optical device outside the class and then uses guided practice in the classroom, if necessary. For example, in an instructional sequence the child may learn to do a word search on a dry-erase board before he or she learns to use a monocular to copy notes in a fifth-grade classroom.

Independent Practice.   Only after the student experiences repeated success toward mastery is he or she ready to practice the task independently. Once the student reaches the level of independent practice, it is important for him or her to have frequent opportunities to use and reinforce the skill. In addition, the teacher of students with visual im-

pairments should maintain close contact with the general education teacher and the student's parents to monitor the student's use of the skill in various settings. For example, if the student's goal has been to copy homework assignments independently from a chalkboard, the teacher of students with visual impairments can check weekly to see that he or she is doing so, until this practice becomes routine.

In implementing an activity through this process, it is important to consider the student's motivation. Although some skills and activities naturally motivate some students, others may need the reinforcement of interesting materials. Whether a reward is the student's choice of an activity after he or she has performed a difficult task, the search for a dinosaur sticker with a monocular or the opportunity to earn points by maintaining orderly study materials, the student should associate his or her efforts with a pleasant result.

Some students have heard only negative or pitying comments about their vision, so it is particularly important for them to feel positive about their visual capabilities. When other students think that a student cannot perform certain tasks independently (such as using a microscope), they may question his or her current abilities or past inabilities when the student begins to do the task independently. When students present themselves as being more visually able than in the past, independent practice may present emotional risks, as well as the challenge of meeting visual demands.

INCORPORATING NONOPTICAL APPROACHES IN INSTRUCTION

Nonoptical approaches include devices or techniques that will alter the visual environment by altering the space, illumination, color contrast, or other physical features of the environment. The main environmental factors that can be manipulated to enhance visual functioning are these:

Illumination. Illumination is a key factor in enhancing visibility. Generally, additional lighting increases visibility; however, some individuals are sensitive to too much light. Care must be taken to avoid glare by adjusting the angle of light reflected to the eye and avoiding or covering shiny surfaces.

Contrast. Providing additional contrast is an easy way to enhance visibility. For example, a student may be able to play tennis using a bright green tennis ball, but not be able to locate a white ball in motion.

Size. Most objects cannot be made bigger, but large-print or such devices as telephones or timers with large numerals may be used. In addition, apparent size may be increased by getting closer to objects (for example by holding a magazine closer to the eyes or sitting closer to the chalkboard in the classroom). The use of optical devices, described in the next section, is a primary way of increasing the size of objects.

Making such changes in the environment may elicit or enhance functional vision. Nonoptical approaches are used for the following major purposes:

- ◆ To manipulate a student or the environment (such as repositioning a student with orthopedic needs to increase his or her visual field or moving a student to avoid glare or to view an object at a closer distance).

- ◆ To increase or decrease illumination (by using rheostats, high-intensity lamps, or sun visors).

- ◆ To facilitate the ease of accomplishing a task and to reduce visual fatigue. For example, to make writing easier, a student may use bold-line paper, and to make reading easier, a student can use a typoscope (black paper with a window cut out of it to isolate a single line of type) and a yellow acetate overlay to increase the contrast of print.

- ◆ To enhance functional vision (such as a student with a central scotoma turning his or her head to make better use of peripheral vision).

The use of nonoptical devices, interventions, and techniques should be incorporated into any instructional program of visual efficiency. Such devices and techniques provide additional options for students in making efficient use of vision.

INCORPORATING LOW VISION OPTICAL DEVICES IN INSTRUCTION

An optical device uses a lens or a combination of lenses to alter a visual image—making it larger or smaller or changing its position—thereby providing usable information to and access to the environment for a student with low vision. Optical devices are individually prescribed by clinical low vision specialists and result in image sizes that relate to a student's visual condition and to the visual demands of specific tasks. Common optical devices include magnifiers for reading and other near tasks and telescopes for gaining distant information. (See Sidebar 13.3 for a list of commonly prescribed optical devices.) In the following discussino of optical devices, it is assumed that a clinical low vision specialist will provide the prescription for the devices. The teacher of students with visual impairments should remain in contact with the clinician to discuss the provision of instruction in the use of prescribed devices and the progress that students make in developing efficiency with the devices. The following are some benefits of using optical devices:

- ◆ Being visually independent, rather than relying on others to assist in specific situations.

- ◆ Gaining control over the visual environment by choosing what visual image one wants to see and when one wants to see it.

- ◆ Obtaining immediate access to information, rather than waiting for enlarged materials.

- ◆ Gaining access to various types of information (such as information written on chalkboards, the number on a bus, and scenery at a distance).

Typically Prescribed Optical Devices

A wide variety of optical devices are available for use by individuals with low vision. The following are among those often used by students:

◆ *Handheld magnifiers.* These magnifiers are generally round or rectangular and have a handle. The person grasps the handle and positions it over the words or object to be viewed. He or she places the lens at the focal distance from the print or object to obtain the greatest magnification and clarity; this distance is determined by the power of the lens.

◆ *Stand, paperweight, and bar magnifiers.* Stand, paperweight, and bar magnifiers are placed directly on the print or object with a set focal length by nature of the design of the lens and its base. Bar magnifiers are generally half a cylinder, paperweight magnifiers are rounded with a flat bottom, and stand magnifiers are lenses placed in a frame, the bottom of which is a distance from the lens.

◆ *Illuminated magnifiers.* These are hand-held or stand magnifiers that include illumination. They may use batteries and/or be plugged into a wall socket. Various types of light are available, and different powers and handles accommodate different needs.

◆ *Closed-circuit televisions (CCTVs).* These devices, which electronically enlarge print, pictures, and objects, consist of a camera, lenses, and a monitor. They are available in a table format, in which the print is placed beneath a set of lenses, or with a mouse-type scanner that is run across a page. CCTVs are available in black-and-white or color models. Changes can be made in size, brightness, color, contrast, and other characteristics of print. These systems generally sit on desks although there are a few portable models.

◆ *High-plus lenses.* These magnifying lenses (also called microscopes) are either placed in the center of eyeglasses with a carrier lens (no magnification) surrounding the magnifier or take up the entire area of the eyeglasses frame (in which case they are called "full-frame" magnifiers). They may also come in a half-frame model that typically includes prisms to allow for binocular vision, so the viewer does not need to remove eyeglasses to look at a distance.

◆ *Bifocals.* Bifocals are prescribed when the person needs more power for reading but not the higher powers of other magnification systems.

◆ *Prism glasses.* Prism glasses are used to reposition the image entering the eye for people with peripheral field restrictions or areas of no vision.

◆ *Handheld monoculars.* These small telescopes, which can be held in the hand, are used with one eye. They come in various powers and can focus for intermediate distances until infinity. They are generally cylindrical, but some new versions are rectangular.

◆ *Bioptic telescopic systems.* These are small telescopes that are placed in a pair of eyeglasses. The telescopic portion may be positioned centrally and high in the frame or centrally and low in the frame. To use these systems, a person lowers his or her head and looks through the telescopes or glances downward into

(continued on next page)

Typically Prescribed Optical Devices *(Continued)*

the telescopes to see an image that is actually in front of his or her face. These positions allow the person to use the center and other portions of the eyeglasses for typical viewing and the telescopic portions for seeing a magnified image.

◆ *Light-absorptive lenses.* People with low vision who need reduced levels of light may use tinted lenses that are darker than those available to the general public and come in colors that address a person's individual need for specific levels of light transmission within the color spectrum. For a person with photophobia (extreme light sensitivity),

the lenses may be placed in eyeglasses that include side and top shields to prevent ambient light from entering the eyes.

◆ *Therapeutic contact lenses.* People who have severe photophobia may receive contact lenses that are "painted" to restrict the amount of light that enters the eyes. These lenses may also be used for cosmetic purposes when impairments result in what a person considers to be unattractive eyes.

◆ *Electronic magnifiers.* This category of devices consists of head-borne devices that function as near and distance magnifiers with a zoom capacity.

◆ Increasing awareness of the visual environment (such as by observing events and movements at a distance).

◆ Performing many activities of daily living and enjoying leisure pursuits (for example, reading cleaning directions on clothing and viewing sports events at a distance).

◆ Enhancing self-esteem (for students who believe that they can "read anything" with these devices).

◆ Providing increased options for employment.

◆ Reducing costs, since optical devices are less expensive than large-type books; and reducing time, because the teacher of students with visual impairments does not need to enlarge or order materials and deliver them.

◆ Allowing students in states where driving with low vision is legal and who meet the visual requirements of their states (with bioptic telescopic systems) to learn to drive and obtain driver's licenses.

Expectations and Use of Low Vision Devices

Whether optical devices are used for near tasks (reading a newspaper), intermediate tasks (reading music on a stand), or distance tasks (reading a chalkboard), expectations for a student's visual functioning with a device are often limited by others' perceptions rather than the student's visual capability. When asked whether a student will be able to read a standard newspaper, read for an hour at a time, or read a street sign standing across a street, parents and professionals may rely more on their own concepts of a student's disability (for example, that the student is legally blind), than on knowledge of what adults with similar visual functioning have shown they are able to do.

Before a student receives optical devices, he or she may have used only large type and had someone read to him or her from the chalkboard. After the student receives the devices, parents and professionals may need guidance from a teacher, O&M instructor, or other experienced professional as to what to expect for the student's future performance of tasks. Some adults may think it is easier for students to read large type, so it may be difficult for them to think of large type as a visually restrictive medium for reading (see Table 13.1 for a comparison of the advantages and disadvantages of optical devices and large type). It may be difficult for students and teachers to switch to a new method (independently using optical devices to obtain visual information) when tried and workable approaches (such as a paraeducator reading work from a chalkboard) have been successful. Therefore, training, support, practice, and reinforcement in the use of devices are essential.

Students may use optical devices to read with sufficient speed to keep up with classmates, or they may read print as a complementary or secondary medium to braille. As long as a student is capable of reading print, optical devices generally are preferable to reading large type. The use of optical devices does not preclude a student from learning braille as a primary or complementary reading medium if it is anticipated that reading

with braille will yield a more functional reading speed.

Many different factors determine how comfortable a student is when using an optical device in the company of family members, classmates, and the general public. The messages the student receives from family, physicians and other professionals, and peers can have a profound impact on the student's sense of identity and willingness to use a device. For example, if parents consider their child to appear "normal" with or without his or her standard eyeglasses, but believe that the child appears "different" when using a device, the message they may convey to their child is that he or she should get by without using a magnifier or monocular. If, however, a brother says how great a monocular is and how he wishes he could look through it to see the moon, then the device becomes a valued object.

Students with visual impairments and additional disabilities and those who are as young as 3 years old have been able to benefit from optical

Table 13.1. Advantages and Disadvantages of Optical Devices and Large Type

Reading Element	Advantages	Disadvantages
Optical Devices	◆ Are portable. ◆ Provide immediate access to print. ◆ Provide access to the standard visual environment. ◆ Allow for visual independence. ◆ Are less costly than large-type books. ◆ Prescriptions are individualized. ◆ Are available for near, intermediate, and distance vision.	◆ Require head and/or hand control. ◆ Some require maintenance (such as replacement of batteries and lightbulbs). ◆ Require a clinical low vision evaluation. ◆ Some require instruction. ◆ Make conspicuous the individual's need for visual assistance. ◆ There is no standard for quality. ◆ Requires time and effort to order and receive or produce.
Large Type	◆ Does not require head and/or hand coordination. ◆ Does not require instruction. ◆ Is available through educational resources. ◆ Allows for a greater working distance. ◆ Can be produced through standard copying machines.	◆ Large-print books are bulky and heavier than standard books. ◆ Generally not available in society and in employment settings after the school years. ◆ Most large type is not available in individualized sizes. ◆ Materials are more costly than optical devices.

devices. In preschool or the primary grades, optical devices can become a part of their everyday repertoire of strategies for using vision, and the children may think of the devices as an extension of themselves. Although students in the intermediate grades learn to use optical devices successfully, some find this time especially difficult to begin a new approach to obtaining visual information because they may be especially self-conscious about their appearance or feelings of being different. Thus, special attention may need to be given to students in these grades. Emphasis on choices for independence, rather than simply using or not using optical devices, can be helpful in facilitating an open discussion of their feelings about using the devices.

High school students often become acutely aware of the need for optical devices to achieve independence. Though not all high school students want to change the way they gather information, many think that the ability to use devices to read chalkboards, use the same texts as their classmates, watch sporting events, and so forth is a solution to many of their challenges. Those who will enter college or look for jobs after they graduate may consider that the ability to read standard print will give them greater visual independence. Students who have clinical visual measures (acuity and fields) within their state's legal regulations for driving with low vision may be motivated to begin developing skills with optical devices in middle school or high school that may lead to a driver's license.

With appropriate instruction, students can become efficient users of optical devices, which can lead to an extension of their visual capabilities. Without instruction, optical devices can become a hindrance to visual function and not be used. Although many factors need to be considered in establishing goals for visual function with optical devices (such as a student's age and initial clinical measures), the teacher needs to have expectations that a student will be successful in using a device before beginning instruction. One cannot predict with certainty what skills and functional abilities an individual student will be able to achieve. However, the authors believe that students can learn to use optical devices as functional tools.

Factors That Influence Acceptance of Devices

Cosmetics. Students need to feel comfortable with the appearance of optical devices. Although the design of a few handheld devices have taken cosmetic factors into consideration (such as that of a monocular in the shape of a rounded rectangle with yellow stripes), many devices are available only in black. Therefore, the teacher of students with visual impairments should encourage students to decorate and personalize their devices, for example, by placing stickers on a monocular and attaching a brightly colored lanyard to it. Since the way in which an optical device is carried is also important to its appearance, the device should be placed in an attractive carrier.

Choice of Mounting System. Different tasks require different mounting systems for optical devices. The mounting system pertains to the placement of the lens(es) in a device. Generally, mounting systems are as follows:

◆ Handheld devices that have a handle or area for the hand to grasp;

◆ Stand-mounted devices that have stands or mounts to provide a fixed distance between the lens and the object to be viewed; and

◆ Spectacle-mounted lenses that are contained in an eyeglass frame and that may incorporate a standard prescription to correct a refractive error, along with a magnifier, telescope, or other optical system.

These mounting systems may be used alone or in conjunction with standard prescriptions for eyeglasses or contact lenses. Some students choose to use one mounting system, while others prefer to use more than one device to accomplish several tasks. A student's preference should be a major consideration in selecting an appropriate mounting system. Each system has advantages for different tasks, as suggested in Sidebar 13.4.

Advantages of Various Mounting Systems

HANDHELD MAGNIFIERS

- Have flexible eye-to-lens distance.
- Have built-in illumination in some systems.
- Can be extended to arm's length to see objects.
- Can be used to change from near to distance tasks without removing eyeglasses.
- Can be used with standard corrections.
- Require fewer head movements than with spectacle mounts for high powers.
- Are more cosmetically acceptable to some students.
- May cause less fatigue because of longer working distances.
- Are less costly than spectacle-mounted high-plus lens.

SPECTACLE-MOUNTED NEAR VISION LENSES

- Can incorporate corrections for astigmatism and other refractive corrections.
- Can be used for hands-free tasks.
- Have a larger field of view.
- Are comfortable for people who are accustomed to wearing eyeglasses.
- Can incorporate two powers in bifocals.
- Are more cosmetically acceptable to some.
- Can have tints incorporated into the lenses.
- Can include lower powers in bifocals and half frames.

- Offer the user only one device (eyeglasses) with which to contend.
- Can be used with side shields and other light-controlling components.

STAND-MOUNTED MAGNIFIERS

- Have a fixed focal distance.
- Can make lighting sources available.
- Are easier to manipulate for people who have difficulty with hand movements.
- Can make larger fields available (although the powers may be lower).
- In some cases, have stands that can allow people to write beneath the lenses.

HANDHELD MONOCULAR TELESCOPES

- Can be stored in a pocket or purse.
- Require fewer head movements than spectacle-mounted telescopes or bioptic telescopic systems.
- Are less expensive than bioptic telescopic systems.
- Are more cosmetically acceptable to some people.
- In some cases, have a short-focus option for intermediate distance viewing.

BIOPTIC TELESCOPIC SYSTEMS

- Can be used for hands-free tasks.
- Can be used for extended periods without fatigue from holding monoculars.
- Are specified for driving in most states where driving with low vision is allowed.
- Can incorporate more than one prescription into the system.

A Student's Current Options for Obtaining Visual Information

Before a teacher of students with visual impairments begins to teach a student to use optical devices, it is important to know how the student gains access to information. Appendix A to this chapter presents a nonexhaustive checklist that asks students to indicate how they currently obtain visual information. For some tasks, the methods the student is using may be efficient, so the student may not want to alter his or her approach, but for other tasks, the use of optical devices can provide new options. For example, if a student always has someone else read the sizes of clothing in department stores, a handheld magnifier may give the student another way to shop. However, if a student likes having another student read the notes from the overhead projector in math class, then the student may not want to use an optical device in that class.

Parents', teachers', and the student's expectations for visual functioning should be considered. Appendix B to this chapter presents an instrument that may be used to ascertain the extent to which these individuals (including the student) foresee the student's becoming an independent gatherer of visual information. Comparing expectations may be helpful in learning whether similar or mixed messages are being given or received concerning future visual functioning. Although a high score on this form may or may not necessarily indicate a realistic set of expectations, it provides a framework for discussing beliefs concerning visual functioning and establishing goals for future functioning. The next section discusses specific strategies for introducing near vision devices.

NEAR VISION DEVICES

Handheld Magnifiers

For a person with typical vision, using a low-power magnifying lens appears to be a simple task. However, a student with low vision who is attempting to accomplish an academic task and who may not be familiar with seeing individual letters may need to acquire new skills to use a magnifier. These skills include retrieving the device, grasping the device, adjusting the angle of the lens, determining the focal length and power, adjusting the working distance, finding the optical center, and placing and stabilizing of material.

Skills in Using Near Devices

Retrieving the Device. Whatever the size or shape of a handheld magnifier, easy retrieval is essential so students are ready to begin work at the same time as their classmates. A young student may want to keep the handheld magnifier in a basket on the teacher's desk or in a convenient spot in his or her desk. An older student may keep it in a backpack, purse, fanny pack, a soft case on a belt loop, or inside a pencil case. Wherever the handheld magnifier is stored, the student should not need to unwrap or retrieve it from a complicated clasp. A student may also find that placing a piece of colored tape or a sticker on a handheld magnifier that is made of a clear substance or has a clear handle will help him or her locate the magnifier.

Caring for a handheld magnifier may be a concern, but there should be a balance between the student being able to retrieve the device rapidly and protecting the device from scratches and breakage. Most of the devices are sturdy, and minor scratches can be tolerated. Furthermore, since these devices are not very expensive, they may be replaced, if necessary.

Some students may want to have two handheld magnifiers, so they can leave one in school and carry the other with them to use while traveling and at home. Young students may not be ready for the responsibility of transporting a device, so having an extra one at home is important.

When students have just completed a near vision task and know they will be using their handheld magnifier again soon, they may want to place the magnifiers on their desks in one of two positions. The first position is to the side and toward the top of the desk from the writing hand, so they can learn the motor movement to retrieve the device quickly. The second position is on the last word read or written. This position is effective if a student is writing and copying from the chalkboard or is viewing at a distance. It will help the student retrieve or locate both the magnifier and the last word read or written. Since it is often difficult for students with low vision to scan a page and relocate the last word read, this approach reduces the time it takes to continue reading.

Grasping the Device. How a student holds a handheld magnifier may help or hinder reading efficiency. A student who has difficulty maintaining focal length (that is, the distance between the lens and the object as determined by the strength of the lens) or has hand tremors may grasp the handle so the fingers rest on the page, forming a base for distance and stability. A student who does not need this form of assistance can rotate his or her wrist so the hand is freer to move and it is easier to change lines.

Adjusting the Angle of the Lens. Some students may be bothered by reflections from ceiling lights or from the visual effect of having overhead ceiling fans or finding the horizontal position of the magnifier to the page to be unnatural. When reflections or other environmental distractions interfere with seeing words or pictures or when the head-to-lens position is uncomfortable, a student may wish to adjust the angle of the lens of the handheld magnifier. To do so, the student will need to take into consideration slight distortions in the apparent image in the periphery. He or she still needs to look through the optical center of the lens (see the discussion of optical center later in the section), but can create a more comfortable working angle.

Determining the Focal Length. The × notation of a near optical device refers to the strength of the lens, that is, the extent to which the image is enlarged. There is a direct relationship between the diopters and the × power of a lens: 4 diopters equals 1× power. Therefore, a 20-diopter lens (referred to as 20D) is a 5× lens. However, when one checks a manufacturer's ratings of the magnification of a lens, a different × level is often marked, so it is more precise to work with the dioptric measure.

The focal distance of a lens is the distance from the back of the lens to the point at which the rays of light passing through the lens meet—that is, where they are focused. When reading with a magnifier, the student should hold the lens so that the distance from the lens to the page is the focal length of the lens. This distance may be determined by finding the reciprocal of the dioptric power in meters. If a 20D lens is used for near vision, the focal length would be 1/20, which is 5 centimeters or approximately 2 inches. As a quick reference, Table 13.2 presents the focal distances for common powers of near optical devices.

One method for finding this distance in practice is to lay the magnifier flat on the page and then raise it slowly until the letters remain clear

Table 13.2. Focal Distances for Near Vision Devices

Diopters	Power		Focal Distance (in inches)	Focal Distance (in centimeters)
+ 2	0.5	×	20.00	50.00
+ 4	1.0	×	10.00	25.00
+ 5	1.25	×	8.00	20.00
+ 6	1.5	×	6.60	16.67
+ 8	2.0	×	5.00	12.50
+10	2.5	×	4.00	10.00
+12	3.0	×	3.30	8.30
+14	3.5	×	2.90	7.14
+16	4.0	×	2.50	6.25
+18	4.5	×	2.20	5.50
+20	5.0	×	2.00	5.00
+24	6.0	×	1.70	4.16
+32	8.0	×	1.20	3.10
+40	10.0	×	1.00	2.50
+48	12.0	×	.83	2.08
+56	14.0	×	.71	1.78
+64	16.0	×	.62	1.56
+72	18.0	×	.55	1.38
+80	20.0	×	.50	1.25

Source: Reprinted, with permission, from Bureau of Education for Exceptional Students, *A Resource Manual for the Development and Evaluation of Special Programs for Exceptional Students, Volume V-E: Project IVEY: Increasing Visual Efficiency* (Tallahassee: Florida Department of Education, 1987), p. 313.

and are magnified to the maximum extent. When the letters or the image begins to blur, the focal length has been exceeded. The focal distance of a lens is fixed for near vision devices and is the same for anyone who uses the lens; an individual's standard correction will not have an impact on the focal length of a lens. Although the lens-to-object distance needs to remain fixed, the eye-to-lens distance may be varied (see the next section on working distance).

As the power of the lens increases, the diameter of the manufactured lens tends to decrease, decrease results in fewer letters or less of a picture or object to be seen, otherwise known as a reduced visual field. For people with low vision, the power of the lens is crucial. While lower powers tend to provide a larger visual field and a longer working distance, the size of the letters and the skills needed to coordinate movements of the lens are important in the reading process. Some people with low vision use higher powered lenses to read materials, such as maps, stock market reports, and laundering directions on clothing tags, in smaller size print, rather than just those in standard size print.

Adjusting the Working Distance.   When a handheld magnifier is being used, the eye-to-lens distance may be varied to create a more normal working distance to the page and help reduce postural fatigue. The working distance refers to the distance between the eye and the object without regard to the distance of the lens to the eye or the object. The one drawback to moving one's head away from the page is that the visual field is reduced. In other words, the farther one's eyes are from the lens, the fewer letters will be seen. Efficient users of handheld magnifiers may vary their distance from the lens at different times of the day or depending on the task at hand.

Placing and Stabilizing Reading Material.   Four components are involved in using a handheld magnifier: the eye, the head, the lens, and the object. Choosing which of these components will remain steady and which will be moved has an impact on the visual efficiency and comfort of tasks, such as reading. Although typical readers use eye

movements for efficient reading without head movements, the teacher of students with visual impairments needs to consider what will be the most efficient combination of stabilizations and movements for an individual student.

Some students will use head movements initially because when they read with large print, they had to keep the actual print within a few inches of their eyes. With these students, the teacher of students with visual impairments needs to determine whether switching to eye movements alone will be functional and efficient or whether moving the object may be more efficient. Stabilizing the object tends to be important, but should not result in an uncomfortable posture for the reader. If a book stand is used to stabilize reading material, one with a movable shelf should be considered.

As was mentioned previously, the eye-to-lens distance may be varied with handheld devices, so that fewer or more letters can be seen through the lens. The tilt of the magnifier may also be varied to avoid reflections from overhead lighting, among other factors.

Other Considerations

Such skills as coordinated scanning across lines, making efficient return sweeps, and maintaining a straight line of movement across lines of print are also important for the efficient use of handheld lenses. When students are copying materials from texts into notebooks or using computers along with reading from books or pages, the placement of their materials and their magnifiers needs to be considered. Placing their magnifiers in the same position each time a task is performed makes it easier for students to retrieve the devices.

Speed, comfort, and stamina are three components of efficiency with optical devices. If a student does not obtain a functional speed in using the device to read the materials that he or she wishes to read, the device becomes more of a hindrance than a help. Thus, while a student is learning to use a handheld magnifier, the teacher of students with visual impairments needs to keep certain goals in mind. Along with the goals related to reading speed and retrieving the device, the teacher must ensure that the student is comfortable with the physical mechanics of using the device and is emotionally comfortable using it in school, at work, and at home. Another important consideration is stamina. A student may have been able to read with enlarged print for only 20 minutes, for example, before he or she experienced visual fatigue. However, through goal setting and practice with the optical device, the student's stamina may be increased to the point where school assignments can be accomplished without unusual stress or discomfort.

Instruction and short-term practice should always include reading materials such as receipts, comics, menus, and candy wrappers. Nonreading applications should also be included. These include such tasks as the application of makeup (when appropriate), threading needles, and setting dials on ovens. Helping students identify tasks for which a magnifier is helpful is part of the instructional process. If a student believes that a handheld magnifier is to be used only for reading schoolwork, he or she will not use it outside the class, and the device not become a part of his or her daily functioning.

Stand, Paperweight, and Bar Magnifiers

Stand, paperweight, and bar magnifiers (see Sidebar 13.3) are especially helpful for young students or those who have difficulty maintaining the focal distance with a handheld device. These magnifiers, which are available in a variety of shapes and powers, must be positioned so they "sit" on the page of print. The user looks down into the lens, which may have optics that are angled to permit the user to retain a comfortable working position.

Stand magnifiers have different attributes for light; some are designed to maximize the available light, while others have features that tend to reduce the available light. Illuminated magnifiers may be handheld or on a stand and use batteries or electricity to provide additional light. Some students choose illuminated magnifiers to have light available wherever they are reading, to re-duce the effect of light reflections off the magnifier, or to highlight the areas they are reading.

Bar magnifiers and paperweight magnifiers rest on the page. Bar magnifiers are helpful for those who want an entire column or line of print to be magnified without the need to move a handheld or other type of stand magnifier. There are limitations on the power of magnification for these devices.

Spectacle-Mounted Magnifiers

Spectacle-mounted magnifiers may be referred to as high-plus lenses. Three drawbacks to this type of lens are that a student must (1) move his or her head to read across lines when the focal length is short; (2) remove high-plus lenses when looking at a distance, and (3) maintain a prescribed distance from a page, which requires more precise positioning than with other types of lenses. The advantages of this system are that both hands are free and that eyeglasses are a familiar approach to reading. Still, as many students who have successfully used handheld lenses have demonstrated, most tasks in school can be accomplished with handheld devices, and their advantages should be considered when choosing a mounting system.

Within the category of high-plus lenses are half frames and lenticular lenses. Half frames allow students to look up without removing the lenses, but they may not be easy for young students to use. The lenticular lens is a small magnifier positioned in the middle of a frame. It is lighter than the full frame high-plus lens but has many of the same drawbacks.

The power of high-plus lenses indicates whether the prescription will be in one or both eyes. Although some students with low vision can use only one eye at a time or may have the use of only one eye, the power of the prescription may preclude the placement of lenses in both eyes. When prescriptions go above +14D, half-frame lenses and some full-frame high-plus lenses incorporate prisms to allow for binocular vision (both eyes being used). However, when it is not possible to incorporate prisms, as with lenses with much higher power, only one lens will include the high-plus prescription. In this case, the image from one eye needs to be suppressed or one lens has to be occluded.

Stabilizing the object is one approach to easing the physical demands on a student when using a spectacle-mounted device. It is also important that any book stand or structure to stabilize the object allows the materials to be moved as the student reads, so the student does not experience discomfort while reading print that is toward the surface of the desk or table.

DISTANCE VISION DEVICES

Distance vision devices consist of handheld monoculars (that use one telescope) and spectacle-mounted bioptic telescopes (that use one or two telescopes). The importance of these devices should not be overlooked. Even when a student is able to read standard print materials (with near vision), he or she may not be able to see a chalkboard or other objects in the distance. Preschoolers who are prereaders may benefit from devices that help them see objects (such as animals) at a distance.

Handheld Monoculars

Basic Characteristics

Handheld monoculars are used with students of all ages. Since a young student may not yet be responsible for carrying the device to and from school, it is important that he or she has two monoculars, one in school and one at home. Handheld monoculars are easily retrievable and can help students accomplish myriad tasks. Monoculars come in many powers. Those that are 2.5×, 2.8×, 4.0×, 6×, 8×, and 10× are typically prescribed for school-age students and are available in various designs.

A student may receive a prescription for a monocular for the eye that has the better visual acuity or for the eye that is on the same side as his or her dominant hand. This decision is made by the clinical low vision specialist. However, the teacher of students with visual impairments or orientation and mobility instructor may provide

instruction in using the monocular with the dominant or nondominant hand or with a crossover technique (that is, using the dominant hand with the other eye).

The student needs a monocular with both sufficient power and visual field to be able to accomplish what he or she wishes to accomplish. Although the clinical low vision specialist may recommend that the student begin with a lower-powered monocular to benefit from a larger field of view, if the student cannot read the chalkboard or see the characters in a play, he may not see the value of the device. If a student receives a device with a lower power and wider field, the teacher of students with visual impairments may provide experiences that allow the student to find objects quickly with the wider field of view and then refer the student for a higher-power device. Close communication with the clinical low vision specialist is essential in addressing and resolving such issues.

A prescription for a monocular has two numbers; for example, with a 6×20 monocular, the first number refers to the strength of the lens, and the second number refers to the amount of light that will be gathered by the monocular. In other words, a 6×30 appears brighter than a 6×20. However, it should be noted that monoculars that have higher numbers and gather more light tend to be larger than those with lower numbers that gather less light. Therefore, if a student prefers a monocular that provides more light, he or she needs to know that it will be a larger device.

If a student wears eyeglasses while using a monocular, he or she will not receive the largest possible visual field that is available through the device. Therefore, the student needs to remove his or her eyeglasses, especially when first learning to use the device, to bring the ocular lens of the monocular closer to the eye to get a wider field of view.

Component Skills

To use a monocular efficiently, the student should grasp the device in the same way each time, so he or she can anticipate the information that will be available through the lenses. In addition, the student needs to place the monocular on his or her desk in the same position each time so it is easily retrievable when the student wants to copy from a chalkboard or write notes after observing the general education teacher perform a demonstration.

Stabilizing a monocular is another important skill because any movement of the device will result in an apparent quivering or movement of the enlarged image. By holding the monocular with the fingers close to the ocular lens (closest to the eye) and resting the barrel of the monocular or the eye relief (the rubberized protection between the ocular lens and the eye) against the nose or orbit of the eye, the student can stabilize the monocular.

The teacher of students with visual impairments also needs to teach the student how to focus the monocular, but may first need to teach the concept of "in focus" at a distance. Some specialists prefer to show students how to focus with one hand, while others support two-handed focusing. Ultimately, the student should be able to focus and refocus rapidly. When a student switches from one object to the next at a near distance (within 20 feet), he or she needs to refocus the monocular, but when an object is beyond this distance (at infinity), refocusing is not needed. This is one reason, in addition to social reasons, why many students with low vision choose to sit farther back than the front row in academic classes.

Manipulating a monocular, a pen, and other objects while copying distance information from an overhead projector or dry-erase board, for example, needs to become routine. Thus, a student has to decide whether holding the monocular and a pen simultaneously or placing the monocular on a surface will make it easier to manipulate the device and various materials.

Spotting objects begins with the student being able to retrieve the monocular and bring it to his or her eye rapidly. (See Sidebar 13.5 for definitions of common terms used with telescopes.) First, the student looks in the general area where an object that he or she wants to have enlarged is located. During the moment of transfer—looking at the object with the unaided eye to looking through the monocular—the student may momentarily lose the object. This movement takes practice. Spotting

---

Training Terms for Telescopic Lenses

SIDEBAR 13.5

- *Spotting:* Aligning the eye, the telescope, and the object of regard.

- *Tracking:* After spotting an object, moving the telescope from that object to another object along a real or imaginary line of sight. For example, to see an airplane through a telescope, the person may first locate the roof of a house and move vertically upward to locate the airplane; spotting a moving airplane without visual reference points can be difficult.

- *Scanning:* Using a telescope to see a stationary object, such as reading a chalkboard or a menu posted on a wall.

- *Panning:* Using a telescope to follow a moving object. Once a baseball is hit, the user may follow the ball's motion through a telescope.

---

objects on a wall at a distance is generally easier than spotting objects in close proximity, and spotting objects on a surface that has other objects is also easier than spotting an object that has no information surrounding it. If the first thing that is observed is not the object that is sought, the student identifies the direction in which he or she must move the monocular to locate the desired object. Having other lines and shapes near the object will be helpful as the student tracks to the object. For example, when searching for a street sign, one approach is to scan the environment horizontally below the area where the street sign is anticipated. In this way, the viewer can locate the pole and then "track" up the pole to the sign. With practice in spotting, a monocular user is able to spot the street sign directly. Spotting may also involve aligning the eye and the monocular with an object that is heard but not seen, such as a barking dog, or looking for an object to which another person is directing one's attention (as when a companion tells the viewer to look toward third base where the batter just hit the ball) (see Sidebar 13.6).

Scanning a stationary object is used while reading words and sentences on a chalkboard. To do so, the viewer keeps the monocular steady and moves his or her head or keeps his or her head still while slightly moving the monocular and eyes.

Panning occurs when the viewer follows a moving object such as an animal that is running or a plane moving across the sky. A practiced optical device user may locate an airplane in the sky quickly, but a novice may choose to locate an object seen below the airplane (such as the roof of a house) and then "track" on an imaginary line upward to the airplane.

Skills in using a monocular may be as simple as spotting across the room to observe a picture that the teacher is holding to locating and reading a street sign while on a moving bus. Although some students readily learn to use monoculars, others need to practice and refine their hand and eye movements. The goal is for the monocular to become a part of a student's extension of his or her "visual reach" beyond the near environment.

Some monocular users are interested only in spotting and reading for brief periods, whereas others build stamina and use their monoculars to view an entire play, concert, or sporting event. When monoculars are attractive, used efficiently, and allow students with low vision to gather visual information independently, they become invaluable tools in the student's repertoire of strategies.

Reading caps (plus lenses placed on the objective lens, the lens closest to the object) allow a monocular user to see at intermediate distances. These caps increase the range of a telescopic system that would otherwise be set up for distance viewing. Some monoculars are designed for "short focus," that is, they allow the user to bring into focus objects within a short distance (such as 11 inches) and focus as far as infinity. For example, a short-focus telescope is helpful for reading a program at a concert, without the need to retrieve a near vision lens. A drawback in using this type of monocular is the short depth of field (the area in which the image is in focus); a small movement of the monocular closer to or farther from the image can result in an out-of-focus image.

A 10-Step Procedure for Using a Monocular Telescope

1. Always store the device in an area that is readily available and retrieve the device quickly
2. Grasp the device in the same way each time
3. Remove glasses to provide for a larger visual field through the device if preferred
4. Estimate the distance of the device and how much the barrel will need to be turned and begin to turn the barrel (with a beginning student, this may be done after the monocular is brought to the eye)
5. Anticipate where the monocular and face should be directed so the eye, the monocular, and the object are in alignment
6. Hold the monocular so the thumb and index finger are close to the eye and the ocular lens is stabilized against the orbit of the eye or cheek
7. Refine the focus if needed; one handed focusing is an efficient method
8. If the object to be spotted is not seen through the monocular, begin to track for the object
9. Use scanning (e.g., reading words on a chalkboard) or panning of the object (e.g., following an airplane in the sky), once it is seen through the monocular
10. Place the monocular down on a surface or in a position where it will be easily retrieved for the next task

Bioptic Telescopic Systems

Bioptic telescopic systems (BTSs) are spectacle-mounted telescopic devices that may be positioned in front of one or both eyes. BTSs are typically recommended for students who need both hands free, as when a student with low vision is playing in a marching band or learning to drive. They may also be useful in courses where students need to use telescopic lenses for longer periods.

With BTSs, the position of the telescopic portion determines how the viewer uses head or eye movements. In a BTS in which the telescopic portion is positioned in the upper central portion of the carrier lens (the lens with the standard prescription), the viewer lowers his or her head and looks through the telescope. In a BTS in which the telescope is positioned in the lower central position (called a behind-the-lens system), the viewer lowers his or her eyes and sees what is in a forward line of vision. For both types of BTS, the viewer must move his or her head to read across lines of print or view expanses of scenery (scanning) or to observe moving objects (panning). Bioptic systems may also be developed for near vision tasks. By using a certain combination of lenses in the inferior position, a person can read with a set working distance, for example, 16 inches. These items are sometimes referred to as telemicroscopic systems.

OTHER CONSIDERATIONS

Care of Devices

To protect their devices, students should carry them in attractive, readily available, and protective cases—either in small carrying cases made for this purpose or in backpacks or purses. Ease of retrieval should be the key factor, since a device that is so well protected that it takes a minute to retrieve will not be used as often as one that is always in the front pocket of a backpack.

Some devices require batteries or a source of electricity. Therefore, students should keep replacement batteries with a recharger and extra lightbulbs on hand to maintain the necessary level of illumination.

Although most devices are durable, any device that includes lenses may need to be repaired or replaced. Thus, many students acquire two sets of devices so they have a second in case a magnifier is unusable or a monocular is being repaired. School systems may keep a lending library for such situations.

Another consideration is the need to clean lenses. Although a handheld magnifier or monocular is usually easy to keep clean with similar processes used for cleaning standard eyeglasses, students who use bioptic telescopic lenses have to mail their devices to a manufacturer for cleaning. Since BTSs are expensive devices, it is more practical to have an alternative device handy (such as a monocular for tasks other than driving) when a BTS is sent to be cleaned.

Incorporation of Devices into a Student's IEP

For students who have received prescribed optical devices and are learning to use them, the educational team may establish goals in a student's IEP for using the devices to gain access to the common core curriculum. For example, the goal for John may be to copy all homework assignments in his seventh-grade social studies class. The objectives for this goal may include the following:

- Using an 8× monocular, John will demonstrate spotting, tracking, scanning, and panning of stationary and moving objects in indoor and outdoor environments.

- Within 2 minutes, using his 8× handheld monocular, John will read five sentences written on a dry-erase board located between 16 and 25 feet from his desk.

- John will be responsible for copying all homework assignments from the chalkboard in each academic class.

- John will be responsible for copying all work from dry-erase and overhead projections in all academic classes, completing his assignments within the same time frame as his classmates.

Goals may also be set for using optical devices in the expanded core curriculum. For Joan, the goal may be to use her handheld magnifier to complete all reading required in her independent living skills class. The objectives for this goal may include these:

◆ Joan will demonstrate the use of her 20D handheld magnifier for 5 tasks required in a kitchen domain that require reading 8 to 12-point print (such as reading recipes in a cookbook, measures on a measuring cup, and dials on an oven).

◆ Using her 20D handheld magnifier, Joan will read electric, gas, and water bills from her town and write sample checks to pay these bills.

◆ Joan will identify 20 out-of-school tasks that she can accomplish independently using her 20D handheld magnifier that she cannot accomplish without it.

A student needs to learn to use optical devices efficiently before he or she is expected to use them in school settings. To do so, the student can practice with the teacher of students with visual impairments or orientation and mobility specialist, as well as at home while doing homework assignments. A guiding principle may be that the student should be able to complete a task in school using a device within a similar amount of time as his or her sighted classmates. If the student is focused on the device, not on the teacher's lesson, the device may become a hindrance rather than a help.

SUMMARY

Since most students with visual impairments can use vision to plan or perform important tasks in their daily lives, it is important that they receive appropriate assessment and instruction in visual efficiency. The teacher of students with visual impairments has the primary responsibility for carrying out functional vision assessments, planning instructional programs, and collaborating with other members of a student's educational team to ensure that visual skills are integrated in appropriate academic and nonacademic activities. The teacher also provides direct instruction in the use of optical devices. When working with a student to increase visual efficiency, the specialist needs to respect the student's attitude toward using vision or other sources of sensory information.

ACTIVITIES

1. Observe a teacher of students with visual impairments teach a lesson on daily living skills to an academic student with low vision and to a student with low vision and additional disabilities. During each observation, note the various ways in which the teacher encourages the student to use his or her vision. Ask the specialist how he or she tailors instruction to meet each student's individual needs.

2. Read a short text passage using three near devices of identical power: a stand magnifier, handheld magnifier, and spectacle-mounted magnifier. Be sure to take breaks to avoid headaches or fatigue. Note the advantages and disadvantages of each device, as well as your efficiency in using each device.

3. Ask for permission to observe an IEP planning meeting for a student with low vision. Note the major components of the student's recommended educational plan and identify those that relate to increasing visual efficiency. Consider whether the student's IEP objectives relate to the areas of the expanded core curriculum for students with visual impairments. Discuss these observations with the teacher of students with visual impairments.

4. Observe a student with low vision in his or her typical classroom environment. Note the possible changes that you would recommend to make the environment more conducive to learning and more comfortable for the student and discuss these recommendations with the teacher of students with visual impairments.

REFERENCES

Ambrose, G. V., & Corn, A. L. (1997). Impact of low vision on orientation. *RE:view, 19,* 80–96.

Barraga, N. C. (1964). *Increased visual behavior in low vision students.* New York: American Foundation for the Blind, Inc.

Barraga, N. C., & Erin, J. N. (1992). *Visual Handicaps and Learning.* Austin, TX: PRO-ED.

Best, T., & Corn, A. L. (1993). The management of low vision in students: Report of the World Health Organization consultation. *Journal of Visual Impairment & Blindness, 87,* 307–309.

Brown, L., Branston, M. B., Hamre-Nietupski, S., Pumpian, I., Certo, N., & Gruenwald, L. (1979). A strategy for developing chronological age-appropriate and functional curricular content for severely handicapped adolescents and young adults. *Journal of Special Education, 13,* 81–90.

Chen, D. (1997). *What can baby see? Vision tests and intervention strategies for infants with multiple disabilities* (Video). New York: AFB Press.

Corn, A. L. (1983). Visual function: A theoretical model for individuals with low vision. *Journal of Visual Impairment & Blindness, 77,* 373–377.

Corn, A. L. (1989). Instruction in the use of vision for children and adults with low vision. *RE:view, 21,* 26–38.

Corn, A. L., & Koenig, A. J. (1996). Introduction. In A. L. Corn & A. J. Koenig (Eds.), *Foundation of low vision: Clinical and functional perspectives.* New York: AFB Press.

D'Andrea, F. M., & Farrenkopf, C. (Eds.). (in press). *Looking to learn: Promoting literacy for students with low vision.* New York: AFB Press.

Goodrich, G. L., & Sowell, V. M. (1996). Low vision: A history in progress. In A. L. Corn, & A. J. Koenig (Eds.), *Foundations of low vision: Clinical and functional perspectives* (pp. 397–414). New York: AFB Press.

Hall, A., & Bailey, I. (1989). A model for training vision functioning. *Journal of Visual Impairment & Blindness, 83,* 390–396.

Hatlen, P. (1996). The core curriculum for blind and visually impaired students, including those with additional disabilities. *RE: view, 28*(1), 25–32.

Koestler, F. A. (1976). *The unseen minority: A social history of blindness in the United States.* New York: David McKay.

Langley, E. (1999). *Individualized systematic assessment of visual efficiency (ISAVE).* Louisville, KY: Ameriacn Printing House for the Blind.

Smith, A. J., & Cote, K. S. (1982). *Look at me: A resource manual for the development of residual vision in multiply impaired children.* Philadelphia: Pennsylvania College of Optometry Press.

Smith, A. J., & O'Donnell, L. (1991). *Beyond arm's reach: Enhancing distance vision.* Philadelphia: Pennsylvania College of Optometry Press.

Sonksen, P. M., Petrie, A., & Drew, K. J. (1991). Promotion of visual development of severely visually impaired babies: Evaluation of a developmentally based programme. *Developmental Medicine and Child Neurology, 33,* 320–335.

Sykes, K. S. (1971). A comparison of the effectiveness of standard print in facilitating the reading of visually impaired children. *Education of the Visually Handicapped, 3,* 997–106.

Current Access to Information

Name: _____ Date: _____

Interviewer Helping to Complete the Form: _____

Directions: For each of the following tasks, indicate which method you use most often. If you cannot see something mentioned, or it is something you just don't need to see at this time, please let the interviewer know. Also, tell the interviewer if you have any special problems reading any of the items described.

D = don't use at this time   SR = someone reads to me

LT = large type   RT = regular type (no optical devices)

OD = optical devices (with regular type)   B = braille

Near Vision Reading

____ textbooks	____ workbooks
____ magazines	____ receipt from a store
____ boxes, cans	____ newspapers
____ paper menus	____ rulers
____ computers	____ print maps
____ graphs and diagrams	____ greeting cards
____ numbers on paper money	____ temperature on an oven
____ paperback books, comic books	____ cookbooks
____ cards (baseball, playing)	____ directions with appliances
____ telephone directory	____ dictionary
____ price tags in stores	____ unit pricing in grocery stores
____ clothing tags, care instructions	____ bank statements and utility bills
____ thermometer (body temperature)	____ wristwatch
____ photographs of people	____ handwritten notes from others

Comments regarding above items:

(continued on next page)

Appendix A: Current Access to Information Checklist

Current Access to Information *(Continued)*

Near Vision Tasks

Please check any of the following tasks you are able to do at this time.

____ read notes written by students	____ read notes written by adults
____ write checks	____ complete forms
____ write on standard lined paper	____ write own lists (such as a phone list)
____ write notes for other people	____ write letters
____ read own handwriting	____ find typed spelling errors

Comments regarding above items:

Distance Reading and Viewing

Please check any of the following tasks you are able to do at this time. Where there is a blank, please estimate the farthest distance at which you can complete the task comfortably.

____ read the chalkboard in front of you (from your seat)

____ read the chalkboard from the sides of the front board

____ read address numbers on businesses

____ read bulletin boards

____ read directories in buildings to locate a room

____ read words on street signs from _____ ft. away

____ watch television from _____ ft. away

____ identify colors of street lights at _____ ft. away

____ identify bus numbers from _____ ft. away

____ read menus on walls in fast-food restaurants

____ read numbers on houses from _____ ft. away

____ enjoy scenery or a building at a distance

____ see action at a sports event from the stands

____ see theater, concerts

____ ride a bicycle on roadways

____ drive a car

Comments regarding above items:

Expectations for Visual Function

Student's Name: _____   Date: _____

Teacher's Name: _____   School: _____

Name of Person Completing the Form: _____

The tasks listed below relate to the student's future visual functioning. Circle 1 to 5 to indicate how likely you believe the performance of each task will be with the student's vision when he or she reaches adulthood. *Do not consider the student's current reading level, only whether he or she will be able to see the object or complete the task described.* He or she may do these tasks with or without optical devices.

Task	Will probably not be able to accomplish this			Will probably be able to accomplish this	
Can read standard street maps	1	2	3	4	5
Can read prices on food products in the market	1	2	3	4	5
Can read a newspaper	1	2	3	4	5
Can read names of streets while standing across the street	1	2	3	4	5
Can read the number of a bus as it approaches	1	2	3	4	5
Can read for at least one hour at a time	1	2	3	4	5
Can read as fast as others his or her age	1	2	3	4	5
Can read paper menus in restaurants	1	2	3	4	5
Can read seat numbers in a theater or sports stadium	1	2	3	4	5
Can read sizes and washing directions on clothing	1	2	3	4	5
Can read standard print books	1	2	3	4	5
Can read paperback books	1	2	3	4	5
Can read a chalkboard in a classroom	1	2	3	4	5
Can recognize people at 20 feet	1	2	3	4	5
Can find an office using a building directory	1	2	3	4	5

(continued on next page)

Appendix B: Expectations Checklist

Expectations for Visual Function *(Continued)*

Task	Will probably not be able to accomplish this			Will probably be able to accomplish this	
Can look up a word in a standard dictionary	1	2	3	4	5
Can use a telephone directory	1	2	3	4	5
Can spot a bird in a tree	1	2	3	4	5
Can use a standard bicycle for recreation	1	2	3	4	5
Can identify a stop sign half a block away	1	2	3	4	5

If your student's visual acuity is 20/200 or better and if he or she has a normal visual field, do you believe the student will:

Drive a car	1	2	3	4	5

Comments:

Strategies for Teaching Visual Efficiency Skills to Students with Visual Impairments and Additional Disabilities

The visual efficiency of students with visual impairments and additional disabilities is influenced, in addition to factors delineated in this chapter, by the effects of medication, behavior states, and cognitive and perceptual processes. Often, significant contrast between the background and the target stimuli is a critical variable for such students because the contrast is more likely to elicit and maintain attention. Attention is often best directed and sustained when the context or task is novel and functionally relevant for a student and his or her global level of functioning. Teachers of students with visual impairments must become experts in embedding opportunities for students with additional disabilities to use vision in as many situations and contexts as possible, but should always do so in a manner in which the information pursued is meaningful and relevant for them.

Sonksen, Petrie, and Drew (1991) set forth and field-tested the parameters and guidelines for the development of a systematic early intervention program to enhance vision in young children with severe visual impairments. At all stages of the prescribed program, activities and strategies are incorporated that ensure that vision is used for reinforcing purposes. This instructional sequence and design, with age-appropriate modifications, is appropriate for students with additional disabilities. The stages of intervention focus on the following considerations:

◆ Introduction of visual information as early as possible,

◆ Reinforcement for looking is used from the beginning of the program,

◆ The same pattern and sequence of visual behavior observed in sighted children are followed,

◆ Intervention strategies use developmentally appropriate visual targets,

◆ Visual responses are reinforced through multisensory feedback, and

◆ The concepts and motor skills inherent in visual behavior are promoted.

A large majority of students with additional disabilities have been, often indiscriminately, labeled cortically visually impaired. In the past, when a student was inattentive and severely physically handicapped, the label cortically blind was assigned on the assumption that the student was simply too neurologically impaired to process visual information. It is now widely understood that these students have characteristic visual behaviors, typically display some level of functional vision, and often continue to develop functional vision into their teens. Hallmark visual behaviors include fluctuating vision, bringing items close to the face to block out extraneous distractions, turning the head on reaching for items, better visual processing when either the student or the visual information is moving, and extremely latent responses to visual information. Many of these students respond well to color used to prompt visual attention and processing, widely spaced but minimal visual information at a time, sufficient time to process visual information, extremely high contrasts between foreground and background, and physical facilitation to rotate their trunks for better coordination of the eyes and hands and the opportunity to contact visual targets to elicit gaze behaviors.

Students who are not labeled cortically visually impaired but who have significant cognitive and motor deficits also benefit from activities

(continued on next page)

that are designed to mobilize their bodies and limbs and to provide subtle and gentle vestibular information and proprioceptive input to organize their eyes better for attending, grasping, and processing. Teachers of students with visual impairments must be able to identify the critical postural foundations from which all functional visual behaviors emerge and seek assistance from physical or occupational therapists. Particularly for students who have great physical challenges, vision may not be functional until the neurological and postural systems have been organized and appropriately "primed."

Regardless of the diagnosis, all opportunities to enhance the visual potential of this group of students must have some functional meaning to their lives and be arranged to be an integral part of any task. The following are suggestions for strategies for eliciting specific targeted visual behaviors within natural contexts and learning situations:

Activity	Visual Skill	Examples of Strategies
Feeding	Awareness/orientation	A dim background; a high-intensity lamp behind the student, reflective tape on a spoon; the spoon is oscillated in the child's periphery to attract attention.
	Object pursuit	The child's hand is directed to the spoon as it is oscillated at the midline, and the child is facilitated to grasp and bring the spoon slowly through a large arc towards the mouth.
		A musical cup is moved slowly toward the child through an arc; the child's hand is directed toward the cup to grasp and assist with drinking.
	Shift of gaze	A cup and spoon are held before the child; each is alternately oscillated to encourage the child to choose.
	Eye-hand integration	Natural background lighting; small bits of food items are presented singly and at various positions on a well-contrasting tray that is illuminated from below or placed on top of an illuminated desk. The child is encouraged to grasp small bits of food and place them in his or her mouth.
Putting away clothes	Scanning	Several pieces of the child's clothes are marked with puffy, fluorescent paint designs and mixed in with other family members' clothing. A laundry basket is placed in the child's room with a low-wattage black light in the background. The child is encouraged to find his or her clothing in the laundry basket.

(continued on next page)

Activity	Visual Skill	Examples of Strategies
	Eye-hand integration, depth perception, stability of gaze	Natural lighting in a room is dimmed with drapes or blinds. The child's bureau drawers are partially opened and illuminated with a flashlight inside each one. The child must shift from locating sorted clothing to moving toward an open drawer and placing clothes inside it.
	Visual discrimination	Different colors of translucent paper are placed over a flashlight, and each flashlight is placed in a separate drawer (red in the top, green in the bottom, and so forth). The child must sort the clothing in the laundry basket into the appropriate drawer (socks and pants, shirts and shorts, and the like).
Assisting in school	Scanning, localization, eye-hand integration	Typical overhead lighting found in school buildings. The child must locate blank, brightly colored labels on incoming envelopes and stamp "received" with a small hand stamp.

M. BETH LANGLEY
Pinellas County Schools
St. Petersburg, FL

R E S O U R C E S

Suggested Resources for Teaching Visual Efficiency

Resource	Type	Source	Description
Beyond Arm's Reach: Enhancing Distance Vision (Smith & O'Donnell, 1991).	Book	Pennsylvania College of Optometry Press	Program providing sequential lessons from which a child with low vision can build a visual foundation and then solidify skills commensurate with his or her visual potential.
Foundations of Low Vision: Clinical and Functional Perspectives (Corn & Koenig, 1996)	Book	AFB Press	A textbook addressing the effects of low vision and other concerns of teachers of students with visual impairments.
Individualized Systematic Assessment of Visual Efficiency (Langley, 1999)	Assessment instrument	American Printing House for the Blind	A functional vision assessment tool developed for use with both sighted and visually impaired infants, the developmentally young, and other difficult-to-test and severely physically impaired children.
Look At Me: A Resource Manual for the Development of Residual Vision in Multiply Impaired Children (Smith & Cote, 1982)	Book	Pennsylvania College of Optometry Press	Evaluation of vision in children with multiple impairments; also presents teaching strategies to help these children achieve their optimum levels of visual functioning.
Optical and nonoptical devices	Equipment	American Printing House for the Blind	Variable intensity lamps, bold-line paper, reading stands, and other aids; available on quota funds from APH.
What Can Baby See? Vision Tests and Intervention Strategies for Infants with Multiple Disabilities (Chen, 1997)	Videotape	AFB Press	Presentation of common vision tests and methods used with infants and young children to help identify visual impairments that require early intervention services.

Contact information for each of the resources listed will be found in the Sources of Products, Materials, Equipment, and Services section at the back of this book.

CHAPTER **14**

Assistive Technology

Gaylen Kapperman and Jodi Sticken

KEY POINTS

- The effective use of technology provides access to an immense amount of information, which is essential for achieving success in school and in life.

- Students with visual impairments can benefit greatly from ready access to information afforded by technology.

- Students with visual impairments need appropriate assistive devices to use conventional technology effectively and independently.

- Assistive technology provides access to information on a computer monitor by interpreting the visual images on the screen, causing the simulation of speech, and providing information in braille.

- The use of assistive technology also gives students who are blind or visually impaired access to the Internet.

- Instruction in the use of technology and assistive devices extends throughout a student's school career, and the teacher of students with visual impairments plays a key role in ensuring that the student receives instruction in the necessary skills.

VIGNETTE

As Ms. Perez, the fifth-grade teacher, answered the few remaining questions students had about the assignment, Jacob carried his English book to the computer desk in the back of the room. He put on his earphones, turned on the computer, and waited a few moments. Almost by habit, Jacob typed a few commands to open a new file in the word-processing program. He typed his name, the date, and "English, page 64," and then located Part A, Sentence 1. "Bald eagles and peregrine falcons are birds of prey," it read. Jacob typed "1. Bald eagles and peregrine falcons."

Fifteen minutes later, with the assignment completed, Jacob typed a series of commands and waited as the braille embosser produced a braille copy of his work. Jacob checked the braille copy and, satisfied, typed the commands that produced an inkprint copy, which he would give to Ms. Perez. His final tasks were to save his work to a disk, close the file and then the program, and shut off the computer. Visitors to the classroom were sometimes surprised to see Jacob working on the computer without the monitor turned on. Jacob's teacher of students with visual impairments, Ms. Nagy, was proud of Jacob's skills and knew they were the result of positive attitude, effective instruction, and lots of practice.

"Members of the Key Club met at Ollinder Park on Saturday morning for a big clean-up marathon,"

500

typed Trina. Leaning down to get a better look at her laptop monitor, Trina backspaced and changed the last "m" to an "n." She enjoyed being on the staff of the school newspaper, but Mr. Green was a real *bear* about spelling. This word processor was a tremendous help. It put a wiggly red line under any words she misspelled. The word processor also let her make the background *black*, the letters *white*, and the font size really big—say 36 point—while she wrote and then easily reset things to more ordinary settings just before she turned the disk in to Mr. Green. It was the most comfortable kind of writing Trina had ever done. She was really glad Ms. Nagy had taught her to use a computer.

Ms. Nagy looked over the brochure again. "Technology for a New Century! Latest Innovations in Adaptation!" The state department of education was offering a weekend workshop on computer technology for teachers, but her intent was to determine just how much of this technology would be useful in working with her students with visual impairments. Ms. Nagy did try to keep up with "innovations in adaptation," but sometimes felt that *her* best information came from workshops focused on technology for people with visual impairments, rather than from generic sources of computer information. She looked back at the brochure to see if it listed the manufacturers who would be represented at the workshop—that would help her decide whether *this* was a workshop she wanted to attend. Ms. Nagy usually attended at least one workshop on technology each year. There was always something new to learn.

INTRODUCTION

Success in school, employment, and life is directly influenced by one's ability to gain access to information. An immense amount of this information is obtained or produced through the use of technology. In this society, in which access to information is essential for full participation, rapid progress will continue to be made in all aspects of technology. If students with visual impairments are to participate on an equal basis with their sighted peers, then they must be given the opportunity to take advantage of the enormous benefits provided by technology.

Specialized equipment, often referred to by the broad term "assistive technology," allows students who are visually impaired access to the same kinds of information as their sighted peers. This equipment, including a range of hardware and software innovations, enhances the ability of students with visual impairments to obtain vastly increased amounts of information. In an information-based society, this is an essential capability and opens the possibilities for unprecedented educational and vocational opportunities for students with visual impairments. It is the teacher of students with visual impairments who plays a key role in orchestrating the student's learning and use of technology, beginning at the earliest age and extending throughout the school years.

Teachers of students with visual impairments need to deal with various challenges making appropriate technology available to their students. Students with visual impairments need adaptations or special access technology to gain access to the images and visual information displayed on a computer screen. The effort to provide access to screen information has revolved around three major approaches:

- Enhancing visual images on the screen,
- Causing the computer to speak, and
- Providing information in braille.

For example, students with low vision can use software to increase the size of the print on the screen. Those who use screen-reading software and a speech synthesizer can cause the computer to speak some of the information that appears on the screen. Students who are tactile readers can transform the text on the screen into braille using a device called a refreshable braille display. Combinations of these three approaches can also be used. For example, a student with low vision may use strategies to enhance the visibility of the image, together with synthetic speech, or a braille reader may use synthetic speech and braille output. Details on all these procedures are presented later in this chapter.

The 1997 amendments to the Individuals with Disabilities Education Act (IDEA) mandate that assistive technology must be considered in planning each student's Individualized Education Program (IEP). In this legislation, two key terms are defined.

♦ "Assistive technology device" refers to any item or piece of equipment used to maintain or improve the functional capabilities of a person with a disability.

♦ "Assistive technology service" refers to any service that helps a person learn about, acquire, and use an assistive technology device (IDEA Amendments of 1997, Section 602).

IDEA requires local school districts to provide assistive technology assessments (see Chapter 4) and education-related technological devices and services for all children aged 3 to 21 if these devices and services are included in the IEPs. (See Sidebar 14.1 for more information on IDEA and assistive technology.)

Since advances in technology are occurring at an ever-increasing rate, hardware and software are often replaced by superior technology in a short time. Therefore, a lengthy list of specific brand names or models of hardware and software would soon be obsolete. As a consequence, this chapter

---

SIDEBAR 14.1

Assistive Technology Mandates in IDEA

According to IDEA, mandated assistive technology services include the following:

1. The evaluation of the needs of a child with a disability, including a functional evaluation of the child in the child's customary environment;

2. Purchasing, leasing, or otherwise providing for the acquisition of assistive technology devices for a child with a disability;

3. Selecting, designing, fitting, customizing, adapting, applying, retaining, repairing, or replacing assistive technology devices;

4. Coordinating and using other therapies, interventions, or services with assistive technology devices, such as those associated with existing educational and rehabilitation plans and programs;

5. Training or technical assistance for a child with a disability or, if appropriate, the child's family; and

6. Training or technical assistance for

professionals, including individuals providing educational or rehabilitation services, employers, or other individuals who provide services to, employ, or are otherwise substantially involved in the major life functions of children with disabilities.

Assistive technology can also be part of a Section 504 plan. According to Section 504 of the Rehabilitation Act of 1973, schools are required to ensure that students with disabilities are not discriminated against in gaining access to the full range of programs and activities offered by the schools. If, for example, computers are used in the general education curriculum, a school must take all reasonable steps to make those computers usable by students with disabilities.

Source: *Individuals with Disabilities Education Act Amendments of 1997*, Sec. 602, 20 USC 1401, CFR Sec.300.6.

focuses on general principles and instructional strategies that can be applied in any situation and with any brand of software or hardware.

The chapter starts by presenting the benefits and limitations of assistive technology and then describes the role of the teacher of students with visual impairments in helping visually impaired students to gain access to the technology that is generally available to sighted students. After a discussion of strategies for assessing a student's progress in mastering the use of assistive technology, instructional strategies for helping students gain visual, auditory, and tactile access to computers and the Internet are presented.

BENEFITS AND CHALLENGES OF ASSISTIVE TECHNOLOGY

The major benefit of assistive technology is that it gives people with visual impairments access to the printed word, which they hitherto had difficulty obtaining. The ability to process the written word, to either consume it or produce it, is essential in both educational and vocational endeavors, since most jobs require the ability to communicate in written form. With assistive technology, persons who are visually impaired can avail themselves of those employment opportunities. Among the numerous benefits of technology are the following:

◆ The provision of written information using assistive technology is considerably less expensive than older methods, such as braille and large-print books. In many cases, the vast amount of written material provided to sighted persons through computer technology can be made available to students with visual impairments using assistive technology.

◆ Students with visual impairments can independently transform printed information into a format or medium that meets their needs.

◆ Keyboarding skills and word-processing software allow students with visual impairments to produce written material easily and efficiently.

◆ Students can gain access to the vast resources of the Internet, communicate with others using E-mail, and gain access to information stored on CD-ROMs or in databases.

In short, students who are visually impaired have the opportunity to achieve much higher levels of independence through the use of technology.

Along with the considerable promise of assistive technology for students with visual impairments come a number of challenges for their teachers. Accessing graphical information on the computer screen is a major challenge because graphics cannot automatically be converted into speech or tactile images. Since the use of graphical displays in computer software may in all likelihood increase over time, it is crucial to teach students to operate in these environments. Because of the complexity of much assistive technology, learning to use technology effectively requires direct instruction from qualified and technologically competent teachers of students with visual impairments. To meet this need, specialists must obtain the additional training necessary to help their students become proficient in the use of that technology (Kapperman, Heinze, & Sticken, 1998).

Finally, as the severity of a student's visual impairment increases, the more sophisticated the assistive technology used to meet his or her needs may be, and, in turn, the more expensive it is.

ROLE OF THE TEACHER OF STUDENTS WITH VISUAL IMPAIRMENTS

Teachers of students with visual impairments have the ultimate responsibility for ensuring that their students receive appropriate assistive technology services and instruction. To carry out this responsibility, they need to understand the benefits and limitations of technology, the major strategies to gain access to information on the computer screen, the process of assistive technology assessment, and the methods in which technology skills are taught to students with visual impairments. Specifically, they need to do the following:

- Guide the provision of assistive technology services with the assistance or collaboration of general technology specialists or assistive technology specialists in the schools;

- Advocate for the provision of various types of technology and technology instruction for all students in their caseloads;

- Conduct appropriate assistive technology assessments (see Chapter 4) with the assistance or collaboration, if necessary, of the schools' technology specialists or specialists in assistive technology;

- Advise school district officials on the purchase of appropriate assistive technology;

- Guide the IEP team in determining the appropriate goals and instructional benchmarks with regard to assistive technology;

- Design and provide direct instruction in the use of the chosen assistive technology or train other school staff (such as a general technology specialist, assistive technology specialist, or paraeducator);

- Provide ongoing assessment of a student's skills, as well as changing needs; and

- Consult with the general education teachers to facilitate the inclusion of assistive technology in the general curriculum.

The teacher also plays an essential role in working with students with additional disabilities; strategies focusing on students with visual impairments and additional disabilities and resources for teachers appear later in this chapter.

Because new devices and software programs are being introduced at a rapid rate, teachers of students with visual impairments need to remain informed of advances in technology so they can teach the appropriate skills to their students. Side-bar 14.2 presents strategies for keeping up to date on the latest technologies. To teach a new technology skill to their students, specialists must first be competent in that skill. Then they can use the general principles of instruction outlined in Chapters 5 and 6 to teach their students.

ASSESSMENT

The technology needs and skills of a student with a visual impairment are assessed in two ways. First, the student receives an assistive technology assessment to determine which technologies or strategies can be used to improve his or her functioning during specific activities or tasks and to overcome any barriers that may exist in the general education curriculum. This specialized assessment is required by IDEA. Since the needs of students with visual impairments are unique and no device or combination of devices will work for all students or every situation, it is necessary to evaluate thoroughly a student's needs and capabilities as they relate to functional goals and to match them with appropriate devices and services. Details of the assistive technology assessment are presented in Chapter 4.

Referral procedures for assessment of a student's need for assistive technology differ from one school district to another. Therefore, the teacher of students with visual impairments should be familiar with the process in his or her district. An assessment may be requested in any of the following general life skills areas: mobility, seating and positioning, communication, computer access, switch access, aids for daily living, work-site modification, home modification, and recreation.

Typically, formal assessments are conducted by professionals who are certified in related fields, such as physical therapy, occupational therapy, speech therapy, or rehabilitation engineering, as well as by assistive technology specialists or consultants, who are recognized by funding agencies as providers of assistive technology, although no credentialing or licensing is currently available. Some funding resources require formal assess-

---

Keeping Up to Date

SIDEBAR 14.2

In the fast-moving world of technology, teachers of students with visual impairments can use the following strategies to help themselves stay informed:

◆ Subscribe to technology newsletters and journals. These can be periodicals specific to people with disabilities or about computers in general.

◆ Use the Internet to obtain up-to-date information on technology, communicate with others in the field, and design activities for students.

◆ Attend local, regional, and national conferences.

◆ Invite vendors to give demonstrations to groups of teachers, students, and parents.

◆ Create a list and develop contacts with teachers and assistive technology consumers at other schools and universities in the area.

Source: Adapted from F. M. D'Andrea and K. Barnicle, "Access to Information: Technology and Braille," in D. P. Wormsley and F. M. D'Andrea, Eds., *Instructional Strategies for Braille Literacy* (New York: AFB Press, 1997), pp. 293–294.

---

ments to verify the need for technology to maintain or improve children's functioning and to ensure that the technology selected meets the needs of individual children.

An informal assessment, conducted by a member of a student's educational team who is not recognized as an assistive technology specialist, is acceptable for devices that do not require personalized fitting or prescription. These "off-the-shelf" items can be appropriately dispensed on the basis of common sense and practical considerations. Any device that requires personalized fitting or prescription needs to be evaluated and recommended by a professional who is experienced and knowledgeable in assistive technology. After appropriate technology and applications have been selected, the student receives ongoing assessments of his or her developing and expanding skills. A student's progress in mastering technological skills is generally assessed using informal checklists that include lists of component skills, generally in a sequence, that are needed to use a piece of technology, software program, or application appropriately. Appendix A to this chapter presents a checklist of generic compo-

nent technology skills (such as operating menus, creating and writing files, using editing commands, and using advanced editing features) and a means of recording a student's progress. Within each section of the checklist, specific subskills are listed. For example, under "calculator functions," the teacher notes whether the student can enter and exit the calculator mode, enter calculations, conduct basic computation functions, and so forth.

The teacher of students with visual impairments may also find it helpful to use checklists that are designed for specific technological devices, such as the sample checklist for using the Braille 'n Speak that appears in Appendix B to this chapter. As the specialist provides instruction and observes the student, he or she notes when skills (such as being able to create a file, insert text, or check spelling) are introduced and when they are mastered. When the student has mastered the skills on the checklist, he or she has gained basic mastery of the device.

Since new technology is being introduced rapidly, it may not always be possible to find checklists that are designed for specific devices or applications. The teacher of students with visual impairments may need to teach an application that is specific to an individual student (such as gaining access to a medical transcription database to simulate a work experience). In such instances, the specialist may need to create his or her own checklists (for additional information, see Chapter 3), to ensure that the assessment instrument matches the student's specific needs. Since a sequence of steps is generally important for the effective use of technology, the specialist may benefit from developing a task analysis of a particular skill (see Chapter 6) and using these steps as the basis for an informal checklist.

As part of the ongoing assessment, the teacher of students with visual impairments considers whether the instruction in assistive technology that is being provided is meeting the student's current and future needs and addresses the following issues when reassessing the suitability of a particular device:

- ◆ Spontaneity: Does the student use the device independently?

- ◆ Function: Is the device equipped with all necessary options? Should it be modified?

- ◆ Frequency of use: Are teachers and parents expecting the student to use the device on a regular basis?

- ◆ Speed and accuracy: Is the device cumbersome, or does it enable the student to perform at an age- and ability-appropriate level?

When a technological device is providing benefits to a student, instruction should be continued or expanded. If a device is not beneficial, instruction either needs to be modified to address the student's needs or discontinued in favor of another form of technology that would better address the identified needs.

Although formal assessment instruments are generally not available for assessing technological skills, the mastery of technology is often best demonstrated through the actual use of the technology. The use of targeted checklists to assess an individual student's mastery of technology may also be of immediate benefit in the instructional process.

INSTRUCTIONAL STRATEGIES

General Strategies

Assistive technology should be considered a tool that fosters a student's participation in an inclusive setting. It can be listed on the IEP as special education, a supplementary aid, or a related service, to allow a student to achieve reasonable educational progress in the least-restrictive environment. It is a means of facilitating inclusion, rather than a task or skill area that must be accommodated in an inclusive setting.

Technology needs to be introduced to students with visual impairments at least as early as it is presented to sighted children in the general education program. Adaptations or modifications can then be taught by the teacher of students with visual impairments or any school personnel who are trained in the use of the specialized hardware or software at the same time as sighted students are instructed in the unmodified versions of the technology. If the adaptations are complex, it may be helpful to schedule additional sessions with a student to promote the mastery of the specialized system. To teach a new technology skill, the teacher of students with visual impairments should:

1. Conduct an assessment to determine which assistive technology is most appropriate;
2. Facilitate the acquisition of the new technology;
3. Become thoroughly familiar with the use of the technology;
4. Develop observable and measurable objectives or benchmarks (see Chapter 6) for each skill to be taught to the student;
5. Analyze the operation of the assistive

technology to develop steps or tasks to sequence instruction to reach the goals; and

6. Deliver instruction in the use of the assistive technology, using the steps developed through a task analysis to plan and sequence instruction.

Once the appropriate technology has been acquired, the actual task of providing instruction in its use follows the strategies presented in Chapter 6 using these general steps:

1. Orient the student to the equipment and software;
2. Demonstrate the operation of the assistive technology;
3. Provide guided practice, using real tasks and materials;
4. Encourage independent use of the assistive technology for assignments or personal use; and
5. Conduct periodic evaluations of the student's progress in the use of the assistive technology and determine if remedial instruction or additional technology skills are needed.

Scope and Sequence

The process of gaining technological skills begins early in a child's life and continues throughout the child's school career and well into adulthood, since advances in technology occur rapidly and continually. During the school years, teachers of students with visual impairments focus on developing solid basic technology skills and meaningful applications of those skills and on helping students recognize the importance of learning new applications of technology when needed. Sidebar 14.3 presents an overview of the range of technological skills that may be beneficial for students from elementary school throughout high school.

The importance of well-developed keyboarding skills cannot be overemphasized. To operate computers equipped with assistive technology,

students with visual impairments (both those who are blind and those with low vision) need to master typing skills. Students must be able to strike the correct keys by touch without searching haphazardly. Appropriate methods should be used to ensure that they can view the screen and thus profit from the feedback that they receive while practicing typing, as described in the section Enhancing Visual Images on the Screen. Students who cannot see the images on the screen can use "talking" typing-instruction programs that provide immediate feedback.

In addition to basic instruction in how to use a computer, including the fundamentals of taking care of a computer, students with visual impairments need to be trained in the use of appropriate assistive technology and a word-processing program, as well as the capabilities of the computer's operating system. With regard to a word-processing system, a student with sufficient sight can learn to use a mouse as well as keyboard commands; a student who cannot see the screen needs to learn keyboard commands. It is particularly important that students who are blind are given information on the layout of the screen and the actions that take place on the screen as they perform a given command.

Once students have mastered keyboarding skills and basic computer skills, the focus of instruction changes to applications of those skills. Advanced skills may include the use of advanced word-processing features, braille note-taking devices, braille displays and screen readers, databases and reference materials, and Internet applications, as explained later in this chapter. The goal is to equip students with a range of needed and useful technology tools, so they can continue to progress in school and to enter young adulthood with the skills necessary to live independently and gain meaningful employment.

THREE MAJOR APPROACHES TO SCREEN ACCESS

In general, it is suggested that teachers use the least complex strategies that will enable a student

Scope and Sequence of Technology Skills and Applications

PRIMARY GRADES (K–3)

In these grades, the teacher of students with visual impairments needs to teach or foster the following:

- An awareness of technology, by having students explore the layout of equipment and how components are connected.

- The basic rules of computer use, such as shutting the computer down properly.

- How to navigate the screen using screen readers with synthesized speech or a refreshable braille display.

- Prekeyboarding activities using touch tablets and tactile overlays.

- Keyboarding skills when a student has the necessary motor and academic skills for the task using "touch-typing" techniques.

- Early word-processing skills, such as naming, saving, and printing files; inserting and deleting text; and completing written assignments.

- The use of screen-enlargement features, including built-in features of word-processing programs and specialized software.

- The use of screen-reading programs to read sentences, then words and characters; spell out individual words; adjust voice and punctuation settings; and so forth.

- The use of refreshable braille displays, either alone or in conjunction with speech synthesis, when a student is proficient in uncontracted braille.

MIDDLE SCHOOL (GRADES 4–8)

In these grades, the specialist instructs students in these skills:

- More advanced word-processing skills, such as cutting and pasting text, using a spell checker, using formatting features (including centering and underlining), and using the dictionary feature.

- More advanced screen-reading skills, such as using customized screen-reading settings and skimming long documents with search-and-find features.

- The use of portable note takers, beginning with simple applications (such as word-processing file management, and using the calendar and calculator functions).

- Internet applications, such as using E-mail, a Web browser, off-line browsing, and search engines.

- The use of braille-translation software and braille embossing.

HIGH SCHOOL (GRADES 9–12)

In high school, the specialist helps students master advanced skills:

- Advanced functions of applications.

- More detailed use of the Internet and World Wide Web, such as using advanced E-mail features and creating Web pages.

- The use of scanners and optical character recognition (OCR) software to create braille documents from print materials.

- Higher-level functions, including advanced mathematics and computer programming.

- The use of an electronic brailler and other types of specialized equipment.

Source: Adapted from F. M. D'Andrea and K. Barnicle, "Access to Information: Technology and Braille," in D. P. Wormsley and F. M. D'Andrea, Eds., *Instructional Strategies for Braille Literacy* (New York: AFB Press, 1997), pp. 269–307.

to maximize his or her access to the information displayed on the screen. There are several major advantages in following this principle. It minimizes: the time and effort spent by the teacher and student in learning to use technology; the cost of the technology; and potential technical difficulties. Thus, in selecting assistive technology for a student, the minimum amount that will accomplish the goal is likely to be the most efficient.

As was noted earlier, students who are visually impaired can use three major approaches to gain access to information on the computer screen: (1) enhancing visual images on the screen, (2) causing the computer to speak, and (3) providing information in braille format. Students may choose to use one or a combination of approaches and may need to use different approaches (or different devices) in different situations.

Enhancing Visual Images on the Screen

Options for Enhancing Screen Images.   The vast majority of students with visual impairments who use computers have low vision. The strategies described next, listed in order from those involving the least to those involving the greatest degree of adaptation, have proven to be beneficial for these students (see Chapter 13 for additional information on increasing the use of vision of students with low vision):

- Control lighting, contrast, and glare. Place the monitor in the location where it is possible to control lighting. The screen should not face or be close to uncontrolled window lighting. Control overhead lighting to avoid reflections and glare on the screen. Adjust lighting in the area in relation to the contrast and brightness of the monitor screen. Adjust the angle of the screen for optimal glare control.

- Use an adjustable monitor stand. The major advantage of this approach is to bring the monitor closer to the student while the student maintains good posture and com-

fort. An adjustable stand provides for increased control over distance, height, and angle of viewing.

- Use a large monitor. The increase in the size of the image on the screen is directly proportional to the increase in the size of the monitor screen. For example, the size of the image on a 15-inch screen is about 1.4 times larger on a 21-inch screen. All software operates normally with a large screen; no technical difficulties will be encountered because a large monitor is used. A variety of large monitors are readily available from various mainstream computer vendors.

- Use low vision devices. The teacher of students with visual impairments includes computer tasks in functional vision assessments and learning media assessments (see Chapter 4); often the low vision specialist includes them in low vision exams to determine which devices may be the most useful for such tasks. A student with low vision should be equipped with the most effective low vision devices possible for use with the computer (see to Chapter 13 for strategies on teaching the use of low vision devices).

- Use standard features in word-processing software. Using these features, a student with low vision can change the size of the letters that appear on the screen. Once the document has been completed and is ready for printing, the student can decrease the size of the print to a standard size before printing the document.

- Use screen-enlargement software. If a combination of the strategies listed above does not result in the information being sufficiently visible, screen-enlargement software can be used to increase the size of the images on the screen. Screen-enlargement software is designed for operation on specific computer systems and generally does not operate on other systems. Because this option involves additional learning and expense, other strategies should be considered first.

Using Screen-Enlargement Software.   The operation of screen-enlargement software follows certain general procedures. After the software is installed in the computer, a student can then invoke specific commands to enlarge the images to predetermined sizes. In addition, a student can increase the size of certain sectors of the screen while keeping the images in the background in the normal size, and can enlarge the size of the images in the vicinity of the cursor while following its movement. In general, the software can be configured to meet the specific needs of an individual student. To explore and determine the most efficient level of enlargement for an individual student, follow these general guidelines:

◆ Be thoroughly familiar with the student's level of visual functioning using the results of a current learning media assessment, functional low vision assessment, and clinical eye examination.

◆ Try various strategies, such as simple adjustments in the physical equipment, low vision devices, and specialized software in a setting in which the student feels comfortable, such as his or her home or classroom.

◆ Determine the least amount of enlargement that enables the student to function at his or her highest level.

◆ Have the student perform typical tasks to observe him or her carrying out the activities using the screen-enhancement strategies that have been determined to be the most efficient.

◆ Make modifications in the screen-enhancement strategies if the student does not function at his or her highest level.

◆ Periodically reevaluate the student's level of functioning with regard to the screen-enhancement strategies that are currently in use.

Causing the Computer to Speak

Speech Synthesis and Screen-Reading Software. Another method by which students with visual impairments can gain access to information on the computer screen is the use of speech synthesis and screen-reading software. This approach requires two components:

1. Software that converts the electronic signals that produce the letters and words that appear on the screen into electronic impulses that can be converted into spoken language by a speech synthesizer, and

2. A speech synthesizer, which is activated by electronic signals that emanate from the software.

Any computer can be made to "talk," given the appropriate software and hardware specifically designed to operate on a particular computer system. In general, the screen-reading software and hardware for all computer systems function similarly.

With regard to the selection of external speech synthesizers, the more humanlike the speech, the more costly the synthesizer. Within reason, however, the quality of the speech is not required to be humanlike; most students with visual impairments can learn to understand robotlike speech with little difficulty. Learning to understand the speech emanating from a synthesizer (which does not emulate the human voice) is similar to learning to understand a foreign speaker of English who has a considerable accent.

Basic Procedures for Screen Reading.   First, the software must be installed in the computer. Then the synthesizer must be connected to the computer if it is not already an integral part of the machine. Once the software and hardware have been configured to work together, the student can learn to operate the screen-reading software, prompting it to speak the letters and words that are displayed. In addition to learning to use the screen-reading software, the student must learn to use the operating system, as well as application software.

To use the screen-reading software, the student moves the cursor to an area of the screen and uses a command to cause it to speak the text it encounters. Most software can be configured to meet a student's specific needs. For example, predetermined portions of the screen can be set aside for access by the student, who then invokes certain commands to cause the information within the predetermined portion to be spoken.

The software can be configured to speak whenever the information changes within a certain sector of the screen, so the student can monitor the information that appears on the screen. For example, the screen-reading software can be configured to monitor the portion of the screen that displays the "insert/overwrite" condition in a word-processing program, so that when the software is changed from insert to overwrite, the software notes this change and causes the synthesizer to announce the change. Without knowledge of whether the word processor is in the insert or overwrite mode, a student who is visually impaired could accidentally overwrite already inputted material without knowing that he or she did so. Thus, this feature of the software is essential in performing word-processing tasks.

Advantages and Limitations. Screen-reading software enables a student who is visually impaired to gain access to information on the computer that would otherwise be inaccessible to him or her. The expert user of speech synthesis can operate the computer effectively in many application programs, given the limitations of not being able to cause graphics to speak.

As was noted earlier, synthetic speech systems cannot translate graphics, whether static or animated. However, some screen-access programs, such as those that have been designed for Windows, have features that can identify that a graphic is of a certain type, such as a button that needs to be selected to proceed with a task, as well as its color. In addition, Windows screen readers can label Windows icons so they can be spoken in meaningful terms. A picture of a wastebasket can be labeled "Delete," for example (AFB National Technology Center, 1998, 1999).

Since the passage of the Americans with Disabilities Act and the Telecommunications Act of 1996, a number of government agencies, organizations, and software companies have developed accessibility guidelines that highlight the need to make new software accessible for screen-access programs.

Providing Information in Braille Format

There are two methods for transforming the printed information on the computer screen into braille. The first is to use an electronic refreshable braille display, and the second is printing braille from a braille printer.

Refreshable Braille Display. An electronic refreshable braille display is hardware that is attached to the computer and driven by special software. The software converts the signals producing the print on the screen into signals that can be recognized by the refreshable braille display. The display is comprised of a series of six- or eight-dot braille cells made up of small pins, which are usually positioned just in front of the keyboard. Commonly, the braille displays contain 20, 40, or 80 cells. Each cell contains actuators that drive small pins in an upward motion when stimulated by electronic signals.

The software sends the signals to each cell to produce the appropriate braille symbol by causing the correct pins to move up. As the student commands the braille display to move across lines of print on the screen, the print located in those sectors is displayed on the electronic braille display. The student can immediately discern the details of the print that appears on the screen. The display has controls that the student can operate to cause the print on selected portions of the screen to be displayed. As the tactile reader invokes the commands, the braille that is displayed changes to represent the newly selected print. The student reads the braille tactilely by moving his or her fingers across the display. Capital letters and all punctuation are also displayed.

It should be noted that these pieces of hardware are costly; they sometimes cost more than the basic computer system to which they are connected. Once again, a considerable amount of learning is necessary to use these devices.

Braille Translation Software and Braille Printers. Another technology for producing braille is specially designed braille translation software, along with a braille printer that can be used by both students who are blind and their teachers. The software translates computer text files into braille. It drives braille printers that can be used to print the files in nearly flawless braille.

Teachers of students with visual impairments have found the use of braille translation software and braille printers to be extremely helpful in the production of braille materials for their students. They can enter the information to be converted into braille using the following three methods:

♦ Typing the material into a word processor, then using the braille translation software to convert it into braille and sending the translated information to the braille printer.

♦ Using a scanner and optical character recognition (OCR) software to input the information. In this case, the printed material is scanned into the computer. Depending on the quality of the original printed material and the quality of the OCR software, errors in the material may have to be corrected. Once the errors have been corrected, the printed material is translated into braille and sent to the braille printer.

♦ Retrieving the original material from a diskette or downloading it from the Internet or some other electronic source. In this case, the inputting has already taken place. In some cases, the format of the original printed material may need to be altered. Then the material is translated into braille and printed. This strategy has proved to be efficacious.

Itinerant teachers of students with visual impairments may find braille translation programs especially helpful if they cannot meet with their students every day. In this situation, the necessary software and hardware can be situated in the school that the student is attending, and the specialist can train a paraeducator to produce braille materials as the student needs them.

Finally, it should be noted that braille translation software is not limited to translating material into literary braille. It can be used to produce braille materials for use in studying mathematics and foreign languages as well.

A student who is blind can use the methods just described for producing braille materials for his or her own use. In addition, the student can use a braille note taker (see the section on portable note takers) to complete homework assignments; take tests; and, in general, produce braille materials independently. The materials the student produces in braille can also be printed in inkprint for general education teachers and other sighted individuals who do not know how to read braille.

The production of braille using braille translation software and braille printers has several advantages:

♦ It is an extraordinarily efficient method for producing high-quality braille, and it is not difficult to learn to use.

♦ Sighted persons who have no knowledge of braille can use the software and hardware to produce high-quality braille after a short period of training.

♦ The student who reads braille can transform computer files into hard-copy braille without assistance.

However, it should be noted that the braille produced is not immediately accessible. It must be printed using a braille printer before it can be read. In addition, to translate computer files into braille, a student who is blind needs to be skilled in using speech synthesis. Therefore, the computer that he or she uses for this purpose must be equipped with a speech synthesizer and screen-reading software, as well as braille translation software and a braille printer.

Specially designed computers exist which have braille keyboards that can be used to input information using the braille code, rather than a regular keyboard. However, the individual who uses this method must be knowledgeable in braille, whereas the individual who uses a regular computer keyboard and braille translation software need not know braille to produce it.

ACCESS TO THE INTERNET

The Internet—the global network of interconnected computer networks in constant communication—is perhaps the most flexible, convenient, and inexpensive form of long-distance communication ever developed. One can search the hundreds of thousands of computers on the Internet for information on any topic in which one is interested and can find a discussion group composed of individuals with similar interests, including live connections to chat groups, conferencing, and gaming forums. Public database access and retrieval services, as well as large software libraries, are also available. When a student finds the information he or she is seeking, it can be easily downloaded from other computers directly to his or her personal computer. Examples of specific types of activities in which one can engage using the Internet include these:

♦ Sending electronic mail (E-mail) to other users. E-mail arrives at its destination nearly instantaneously, whether it is going to other users on the Internet or any other networks with electronic mail.

♦ Keeping abreast of the latest information using Usenet, the world's largest bulletin board. This forum contains nonstop discussions of an enormous number of different subjects. If one has a question, one needs only to post it to the appropriate newsgroup.

♦ Obtaining answers to one's questions by posing them to hundreds of thousands of individuals who exchange messages with members of special-interest mailing lists called listservs.

♦ Exploring the vast array of resources through the World Wide Web. The most popular feature of the Internet, the Web allows one to link multiple documents without having to use menus.

Benefits for Students with Visual Impairments

Providing Access to Printed Information. Mastery of the appropriate assistive technology can enable students who are blind or visually impaired to gain access to the immense quantity of information available on the Internet and to transform that material independently into formats (such as braille, large print, or synthesized speech) with which they can deal effectively. Thus, access to the Internet holds great promise in helping to solve one of the longstanding problems faced by students who are visually impaired: having immediate access to large amounts of information.

It is imperative that students with visual impairments are trained in the procedures for gaining access to the information resources on the Internet during the school years for two reasons: First, students can use the skills in their day-to-day academic work in school. Second, the training will prepare them for the transition to college and job-related activities. At no other time in their lives can such training be more easily provided. In college, students can also use their skills to good advantage by, for example, gaining access to such databases as those that are provided by libraries.

In the 21st century, more and more jobs will require proficiency in handling information effectively. Students who have had several years of experience in honing these skills in school will be well equipped to deal with these types of tasks on the job. Thus, they will be more employable and better prepared to take their rightful place in the workforce.

Enhancing Social Participation. The Internet affords students with visual impairments opportunities for social participation. According to the results of a wide-ranging study on the transition of youths with disabilities (Wagner, D'Amico, Marder, Newman, & Blackorby, 1992), young people with visual impairments were the most isolated of all the youths with disabilities after they left school. On the Internet, everyone participates on an equal basis. This is, then, an unprecedented opportunity for people who are visually impaired to participate with others without disadvantage or discrimination.

What Students Need to Access the Internet

Equipment. In addition to the same hardware and software that sighted individuals use to gain access to the Internet (that is, a computer with sufficient speed and memory to operate the necessary software, a modem that operates at the current standard rate, a word-processing program, a dial-up program, an E-mail server, and a Web browser) a student who is visually impaired needs the appropriate assistive technology that meets his or her needs.

Training. A student with a visual impairment needs specific instruction from a knowledgeable teacher of students with visual impairments (or a general assistive technology specialist) to use the Internet effectively. In addition to mastering keyboarding and an appropriate word-processing program (discussed earlier), the student needs to learn to use the dial-up software that connects the computer to other computers over the telephone lines, the E-mail software that enables the computer to send and receive messages, and the Web browser that searches for and connects to sites on the Internet (Kapperman, Hahn, Heinze, & Dalton, 1997).

After learning to use the appropriate hardware and software, a student should be capable of gaining access to the vast resources found on the Internet. For students who cannot see the computer screen, the graphical displays that may appear will remain inaccessible, but all text-based information will be available.

OTHER COMPUTER-BASED ASSISTIVE TECHNOLOGY

OCR. The use of OCR technology holds great promise for students with visual impairments. It enables a student who is visually impaired to scan written information and thereby input it into the computer using OCR software that transforms the "pictures" of the letters and words into text. The student can then use assistive technology to convert the information into a medium that he or she can use. For example, the user of assistive technology can listen to the text being spoken by a speech synthesizer. A student with low vision can increase the size of the print on the monitor using screen-enlargement software and can produce hard copy large print by adjusting the font size in the document and using a standard printer. Using an electronic braille display, the student who is blind can read the material tactilely and use a braille printer to produce a hard copy of the document in braille.

CD-ROM. CD-ROM (compact disk read-only-memory) technology can also be used by students with visual impairments (Kapperman, Hahn, Heinze, & Dalton, 1996). If the information on the CD-ROM is in text form, it can be converted to a medium that meets the needs of the student (that is, speech, braille, or large print). Graphics that are embedded in the material cannot be made to speak, but they can be increased in size using screen-enlargement software.

Portable Note Takers. Portable note takers have proven to be useful for individuals who cannot see the computer screen. These devices are equipped either with a small standard keyboard or a braille keyboard. They also have speech synthesizers incorporated in them that enable the devices to speak the information being manipulated. One of the salient features of these devices is that they operate on rechargeable batteries, as well as regular electrical current, and thus can be carried about easily and used in many different situations where portability is essential. Printers can be connected to the devices; with braille note takers, either braille printers or inkprint printers can be used, enabling the student to print his or her documents in braille and/or print. Note takers can also be connected to computers in order to transfer files back and forth.

A prerequisite for using braille note takers is knowledge of braille; for note takers that are equipped with a standard print keyboard, knowledge of the keyboard is essential. Many teachers of students with visual impairments have found that these devices work well with beginning braille students, as well as those who have already mastered the code. It is common practice to begin instruction in the use of portable note takers at an early age.

SUMMARY

The importance of providing appropriate assistive technology training for students with visual impairments cannot be overstated. Students who are well equipped and receive up-to-date training in the most appropriate technology to meet their individual needs will have a significant advantage in their postsecondary educational and vocational endeavors. Consequently, teachers of students who are visually impaired need a firm understanding and constant updating in their own technology skills, and all those who provide educational services for students with visual impairments need to make every effort to make the best possible training available to their students.

ACTIVITIES

1. Invite vendors of assistive technology to demonstrate equipment and software or attend a conference for professionals or consumers and view the technology exhibits. Gather information on products and begin a resource file that also includes funding sources.

2. View videotapes showing assistive technology devices being used in a variety of environments. Note the strengths and limitations of various devices, given the demands of a particular setting.

3. Interview persons with visual impairments who are successful users of assistive technology about their use of assistive technology. Share the results from the interviews with other class members.

4. Try various assistive technology devices and software while blindfolded; for example, use a screen reader and speech synthesizer to gain access to a specified piece of information from the Internet.

REFERENCES

AFB National Technology Center. (1998, June). *Creating applications accessible to people who are visually impaired* (Fact sheet). New York: American Foundation for the Blind.

AFB National Technology Center. (1999, May). *Synthetic speech systems* (Fact sheet). New York: American Foundation for the Blind.

Assistive technology assessment: Summary for students with visual impairments. (1999). Austin: Texas School for the Blind and Visually Impaired. Available on-line: http://www.tsbvi.edu/technology/vieval.htm

Blazie, B. J., & Dote-Kwan, J. (1997). *Braille 'n Speak teaching curriculum.* Forest Hill, MD: Blazie Education Services.

Closing the gap annual resource directory. (1999). (Available from Closing the Gap, P.O. Box 68, 526 Main Street, Henderson, MN 56044.)

D'Andrea, F. M., & Barnicle, K. (1997). Access to information: Technology and braille. In D. P. Wormsley & F. M. D'Andrea (Eds.), *Instructional strategies for braille literacy* (pp. 269–307). New York: AFB Press.

Gill, J. M. (n.d.). *Equipment for blind and partially sighted persons: An international guide.* London: Royal National Institute for the Blind, Scientific Research Unit.

Individuals with Disabilities Education Act Amendments of 1997, Section 602 (1997, January 7).

Kapperman, G., Hahn, S., Heinze, A., & Dalton, S. (1996). *Project CD visROM: Remote access to CD ROM by visually impaired students* (Report No. EC304754). Sycamore, IL: Research and Development Institute. (ERIC Document Reproduction Service No. ED394234)

Kapperman, G., Hahn, S., Heinze, A., & Dalton, S. (1997). *Project VISION: Visually impaired students and Internet opportunities now* (Report No. EC305414). Sycamore, IL: Research and Development Institute. (ERIC Document Reproduction Service No. ED406762)

Kapperman, G., Heinze, T., & Sticken, J. (1998). *Survey of assistive technology use by Illinois students.* Unpublished manuscript, Northern Illinois University.

Rocklage, L. A., Peschong, L. A., Gillett, A. L., & Delohery, B. L. (1996). *Good junk + creativity = great low-end technology.* (Available from L. Rocklage, P.O. Box 971022, Ypsilanti, MI 48197).

Sewell, D. (1997). *Assessment kit: Kit of informal tools for academic students with visual impairments. Part 1: Assessment tools for teacher use.* Austin: Texas School for the Blind and Visually Impaired.

The Rehabilitation Act, 45 C.F.R. Section 504, Part 84 (1973).

Wagner, M., D'Amico, R., Marder, C., Newman, L., & Blackorby, J. (1992). *What happens next? Trends in postschool outcomes of youth with disabilities.* Washington, DC: Office of Special Education Programs, U.S. Department of Education.

Wormsley, D. P., & D'Andrea, F. M. (Eds.). (1997). *Instructional strategies for braille literacy.* New York: AFB Press.

Skills Needed to Operate Equipment

Student's name: _____

Instructor's name _____

Training date(s) _____

Name and version of device _____

The following checklist will serve as an indicator of the tasks that this student has learned:

* I - independently performs task

* N - uses notes ( )% of the time to complete tasks

* V - needs verbal coaching ( )% of the time to complete task

* U - unable to consistently perform the task assigned

* — student has not been shown that particular feature of the device

	Pretest Date						Posttest Date
Major Components The student can							
— identify and locate all the alpha keys							
— identify and locate all the number keys							
— identify and locate the special function keys such as help							
— identify and connect the power charger							
— describe and perform the charging procedure							
— state name and manufacturer of device							
— find information in the manual							
— get technical support							
Operating the Menus The student can							
— select menu choices							
— exit menus and return to document							
Creating and Writing a File The student knows the procedures for							
— creating a new file							
—opening an existing file							

(continued on next page)

Appendix A: Checklist of Skills Needed to Operate Equipment

Skills Needed to Operate Equipment *(Continued)*

	Pretest Date						Posttest Date
— describing the cursor and its function							
— moving the cursor to the top or bottom of a file							
— quitting and saving a file							
Editing Command							
The student knows the procedures for							
— positioning the cursor for properly inserting letters, words, and sentences							
— deleting the current word							
— deleting the current character							
— deleting the previous character							
— deleting to the end of a sentence							
— deleting to the end of a paragraph							
— deleting from the cursor to the end of a file							
New Pages, Search Procedures, and Place Markers							
The student knows the procedures for							
— starting a new page							
— searching forward for a specific string of text							
— searching backward for a specific string of text							
— searching and replacing text forward							
— searching and replacing text backward							
Operating the Disk Drive							
The student knows the procedures for							
— touching the disk properly without affecting its storage capability							
— positioning and inserting a disk							
— formatting a disk							
— removing the disk safely from the disk drive							

(continued on next page)

Skills Needed to Operate Equipment *(Continued)*

	Pretest Date					Posttest Date	
— setting the write-protect tab on the diskette							
— transferring files between the device and the disk drive							
File Commands The student knows the procedure for							
— reading the disk directory							
— reading subdirectories on disks							
— spelling file names or directory names							
— copying from disk to memory							
— erasing files from memory or disk							
— renaming files							
Printing a File The student knows the procedure for							
— loading the paper into the printer							
— connecting the printer cables to the device and the printer							
— selecting a specific print driver (if appropriate)							
— printing a single page							
— printing multiple pages							
— printing a single file							
— printing groups of files							
Calculator Functions The student knows the procedures for							
— entering and exiting the calculator mode							
— entering calculations							
— operating adding, subtracting, multiplying, and dividing fractions							
— operating negation, percentages, and parentheses							
— operating trigonometric functions (if available)							

(continued on next page)

Skills Needed to Operate Equipment *(Continued)*

	Pretest Date						Posttest Date
— operating the square and square-root functions (if available)							
— operating the logarithmic functions (if available)							
— operating the power and root functions (if available)							
Advanced Editing Features The student knows the procedures for							
— moving a block of text							
— copying a block of text							
— deleting a block of text							
— merging documents							
— centering text							
— underlining text							
— making a line right justified							
— moving to the start of the next line							
— moving to the next tab setting							
— inserting the time and date into a file							
— inserting the calculated result							
— editing directly from disk							
— exiting a file without saving text							
Other Features The student knows the procedures for							
— using spell checking, if available							
— adding, deleting, and changing a word in the dictionary							
— saving and retrieving a dictionary file to disk							
— deleting the current dictionary							
— running another application program							
— setting the time and date							

(continued on next page)

Skills Needed to Operate Equipment *(Continued)*

	Pretest Date						Posttest Date
—formatting disks							
—renaming disks							
—copying disks							
Using the Help Key The student knows the procedures for							
—entering and exiting the help mode							
Miscellaneous The student knows the procedures for							
—reinitializing, resetting, warm-booting the device							
—installing new application programs							
—updating software							

Source: Reprinted, with permission, from D. P. Wormsley and F. M. D'Andrea, Eds., *Instructional Strategies for Braille Literacy* (New York: AFB Press, 1997).

Braille 'N Speak Checklist

Student's name: _____ Date: _____

	Mastery		
	Introduced	Yes	No
Speech Parameters			
Set volume, pitch, rate			
Set key echo, click, or silent			
Set pronunciation of numbers			
Set punctuation level			
Files			
Create a file			
Delete a file			
Move down a file list			
Move up a file list			
Open a file			
Open a "pointed to" file			
List files			
Turn on/off grade 2 translation			
Print a file			
Spell a file's name			
Delete a "pointed to" file			
Tell name of currently active file			
Insert and Delete Commands			
Insert text			
Delete x number of characters			
Delete x number of words			
Delete x number of lines			
Block delete (able to set mark)			
Use the clipboard			
Delete from the cursor to the end of the file			

(continued on next page)

Appendix B: Sample Braille 'N Speak Checklist

Braille 'N Speak Checklist *(Continued)*

	Introduced	Mastery Yes	No
Cursor Movement			
To end of chapter (4 5 6-Chord)			
To beginning of chapter (L-Chord)			
Forward one sentence at a time (4-Chord)			
Backward one sentence at a time (1-Cord)			
Forward one word at a time (5-Chord)			
Backward one word at a time (2-Chord)			
Forward one character at a time (6-Chord)			
Backward one character at a time (3-Chord)			
Backward and erase one character (B-Chord)			
Create a carriage return (4 6-Chord)			
Status Menu			
Set baud, parity, duplex, data bits, stop bits, handshaking			
Set printer type			
Set printer margins			
Append linefeed			
Miscellaneous			
Check spelling			
Set windows			
Set format commands			
Transfer information to/from disk drive			
Connect Braille 'n Speak to inkprint printer			
Connect Braille 'n Speak to braille printer			
Safely charge Braille 'n Speak			

Source: Reprinted, with permission, from D. Sewell, *Assessment Kit: Kit of Informal Tools for Academic Students with Visual Impairments* (Austin: Texas School for the Blind and Visually Impaired, 1997).

Strategies for Teaching Technology Skills to Students with Visual Impairments and Additional Disabilities

Assistive technology is often the link that enables students with visual impairments and additional disabilities to enjoy the same activities as students without disabilities. It improves the functional capacities of these students and gives them a means of controlling their environments. With assistive technology, these students demonstrate increased motivation; initiation; attention to task; independence; and communication, motor control, and social interaction skills.

The assessment, design, selection, and purpose of assistive technology for a student with a visual impairment and additional disabilities requires a team approach and consideration of the student's cognitive-perceptual, visual, and motor skills in addition to medical status and endurance. It is essential that whatever assistive technology is chosen offers a means for the student to expand his or her control of and interaction with the environment and independence. In this regard, careful consideration of the function of the assistive device and generalization of the concepts it enhances will prevent it from becoming simply a vehicle for self-stimulation or a source of frustration.

The least amount of assistive technology that will meet a student's needs is the most effective. Because assistive technology is often extremely expensive, the educational team must weigh the potential benefits for the student and the range of skills or functions that may be enhanced against the cost. Other factors to consider include these:

♦ Can a more readily available, "typical" device or equipment be just as effective with minor adaptations?

♦ Does the device significantly set the student apart from the other students?

♦ Does use of the device lead to functional outcomes, influence the acquisition of other needed skills, or enable the student to be perceived as more competent?

♦ Is the device's level of complexity commensurate with the student's ability?

♦ Will the quality and nature of the device allow the student to attain immediate success or feedback and/or reduce physical effort and fatigue?

The primary forms of assistive technology for students with visual impairments and additional disabilities are as follows:

♦ Adaptive switches that provide sensory feedback, such as music, speech, sounds, vibration, items in motion, light, and air.

♦ Adaptive switches that are interfaces to and a means of activating toys and entertainment devices; appliances; communication, self-care, and mobility devices; and computers.

♦ Adapted multifunction toys similar to infants' busy boxes.

♦ Toys that are adapted so appropriate interaction is reinforced with illumination, vibration, or music (for example, shapes in a formboard complete a circuit that results in music or blocks that are stacked activate a series of lights).

♦ Switches that are designed to develop or increase specific motor skills (such as mercury switches to increase head control or wrist extension, pinch or squeeze switches to improve grasp, and pressure switches to encourage weight bearing).

(continued on next page)

- Communication devices.
- Environmental control units.
- Adapted or alternative computer keyboards and input devices (Intellikeys, Touch Windows, and Kidboards).
- Adaptive software.

The following are suggested strategies and considerations for using assistive devices with these students:

- When a student is physically capable, he or she can be exposed to cause-effect relationships by learning how to activate a switch on a garage door, a light switch, a doorbell, elevator buttons, a button on a handheld massager, a remote control for opening doors on a car, or a remote control for a CD player.

- As quickly as possible, activation of a simple cause-effect switch must be generalized via a different switch requiring the identical effort and level of activation; the same switch used to activate a variety of toys or appliances; and/or a different switch requiring a slightly different movement, pressure, or use of another movement strategy.

- The switches selected for initial instruction of cause-and-effect relationships should provide a clear connection between the activating source and the result. For example, if a student is given a switch with dangling beads that produces music and vibration simultaneously, he or she may not be able to distinguish that it is the pressure against the switch (not the beads) that is the means of activation and may not be able to attend to both

auditory and proprioceptive feedback. A better choice may be a roller switch that produces only music.

- Once the student understands cause and effect, he or she can be given opportunities for choice making and scanning.

- The student's ability to tolerate/integrate sensory information must match that of the feedback provided by a toy to be used with an adaptive switch. For example, children who startle readily or have difficulty tolerating loud or high-pitched sounds need quiet, calm toys, not those with repetitive movement and sounds. Additionally, toys and feedback must be carefully chosen for students with seizure disorders.

- If sensory feedback is too strong, students may be either overwhelmed or so attracted to the stimulus that it detracts from their ability to understand the effects of their behavior on the switch.

- Communication devices must be practical, meaningful to individual students, and allow them to get their messages across quickly to both adults and other students. For students with severe cognitive and perceptual impairments, communication systems with distinguishable buttons, levers, or panels are much more functional than are those that have flat overlays. For example, a nonverbal student may use an inexpensive, single-button memory device attached to a belt or kept in a pocket to respond to the question, "What is your name?"

- Auditory scanning, which requires a student to hold information in memory

(continued on next page)

Strategies for Teaching Technology Skills *(Continued)*

while scanning, anticipate when a desired message is forthcoming, and precisely time a response, is a very difficult skill for students with significant cognitive limitations. At least initially, a two- to four-panel communication device may be the most practical; if a student activates a message accidentally, he or she can quickly repair the communication by activating another panel without waiting for an auditory cue.

◆ Digitized speech is difficult for a student with impaired cognitive function to interpret. Therefore, the speech of the communication device should be clear, and the voice should approximate that of the student (for example, if the student is male and aged 18, someone of that age and sex could record the message).

◆ Few software programs offer a student who is blind and has significant cognitive impairments the opportunity to learn more than simple cause-and-effect relationships. Three exceptions, all designed by R. J. Cooper & Associates, are *Find the Buttons,* which encourages a blind student to scan with a mouse, and *101 Animations* and *RadSounds,* which encourage more complex skills. In lieu of more appropriate programs, students with similar needs should be paired with classmates without disabilities who can facilitate their partial participation in more relevant and motivating software programs.

M. BETH LANGLEY
Pinellas County Schools
St. Petersburg, FL

RESOURCES

Suggested Resources for Teaching Assistive Technology

Resource	Type	Source	Description
Assistive Technology Assessment: Summary for Students with Visual Impairments (Texas School for the Blind and Visually Impaired, 1999)	Checklist	Texas School for the Blind and Visually Impaired Website (http://www.tsbvi.edu/technology/vieval.htm)	A downloadable checklist-style summary of technology skills achieved by students with visual impairments. Includes assessments of use of optical aids, talking calculators, tools for writing, and other aids, in addition to computer access skills.
Braille 'n Speak	Equipment	Blazie Engineering	The Braille 'n Speak is sometimes referred to as an electronic note taker. It is much more. This and other technological devices are available from Blazie Engineering.
Braille 'n Speak Teaching Curriculum (Blazie & Dote-Kwan, 1997)	Book	Blazie Education Services	A curriculum designed to provide a comprehensive, well-sequenced series of instruction lessons in the use of the Braille 'n Speak. The controlled vocabulary permits students with limited knowledge of the braille code to begin using the Braille 'n Speak.
Center on Disabilities	Organization	Center on Disabilities	The center maintains a Web site and sponsors conferences on technology for individuals with disabilities.
Closing the Gap Annual Resource Directory	Resource directory	Closing the Gap	A source of information on computer technology in special education and rehabilitation.

(continued on next page)

Suggested Resources *(Continued)*

Resource	Type	Source	Description
Equipment for Blind and Partially Sighted Persons: An International Guide (Gill, n.d.)	Guide	Royal National Institute for the Blind, Scientific Research Unit	A guide to equipment for individuals with visual impairments.
Good Junk + Creativity = Great Low-End Technology (Rocklage, Peschong, Gillett, & Delohery, 1996)	Book	L. Rocklage	Each section of the book provides an overview and discussion of the topic, as well as instructions, diagrams, and photos of materials, devices, and strategies. Although the suggestions in this book are not meant to be inclusive of the wide array of low-end technology possibilities, they serve as a starting point for individual creativity and designs.
Stereo tape recorder, "Speech Expressor," accessories	Equipment	American Printing House for the Blind	Equipment for making and playing recordings of lectures, meetings, and so forth.
Trace Center	Organization	Trace Center, University of Wisconsin	A center that provides selected disability documents and resources.

Contact information for each of the resources listed will be found in the Sources of Products, Materials, Equipment, and Services section at the back of this book.

CHAPTER 15

Orientation and Mobility

Nora Griffin-Shirley, Sharon Trusty, and Rachel Rickard

KEY POINTS

- ◆ Orientation and mobility (O&M) skills provide freedom of movement and enhance the independence of students who are blind or visually impaired.

- ◆ An O&M curriculum is varied and includes activities that are used throughout students' lives.

- ◆ Teachers of children with visual impairments play a critical role in this area by promoting the development of concepts in young children and by teaching basic O&M skills and other essential travel skills.

- ◆ A certified O&M specialist teaches formal O&M skills and collaborates with other members of the educational team to promote safe and efficient travel for a student with a visual impairment.

- ◆ A team approach is needed to promote and teach safe and effective O&M skills.

VIGNETTE

Suzanne Tallant, a certified O&M specialist, stirred her coffee and smiled. "Miguel is learning landmarks and clues around the school very well for a 3 year old. He pointed out the lunchroom to me as we passed it this morning, but really, that was too easy. You could smell the fried chicken all the way down the hall. He knows the office, too, by the carpet square in front of the door and the sounds of printers and telephones. And he knows the library is the first door past the water fountain."

Lamar Jefferson, a teacher of students with visual impairments, nodded. "He's well oriented to his classroom, too, and is pretty good about using that 'bumper' self-protective technique you taught him. He's also making good progress on body parts. He showed me his elbows today. How's Tanya doing?"

Ms. Tallant frowned as she considered what to say about the 9 year old. "She does just fine when I'm with her. The problem is when I'm *not* with her. Several teachers have complained that she trips children with her cane. Apparently she swings it so far to the left that it's almost perpendicular to her line of travel, so *of course* she trips people. But she never does it when I'm there."

"I've seen her do it," said Mr. Jefferson. "I spoke to her about it, as I'm sure you have. Do you think we should ask the teachers on her hallway to remind her to use her cane safely whenever they see her swinging it so widely?"

"Yes, more frequent reminders would help," Ms. Tallant answered. "On a more positive note, though, Tanya is doing well on crossing streets. When I see her next Thursday, we're going to walk up to the Quick Mart three blocks away. She's pretty excited about off-campus travel. I don't know if it's getting out of the school building or the candy we'll buy at the Quick Mart, but she can't wait to go!"

INTRODUCTION

A significant and immediate consequence of visual impairment is the restriction in one's ability to travel through physical and social environments and to anticipate and exercise control over potentially hazardous situations. The skills needed to move safely and confidently through the environment are developed through instruction in orientation and mobilitiy (O&M) (Tuttle & Tuttle, 1996). In the *National Agenda for the Education of Children and Youths with Visual Impairments, Including Those with Multiple Disabilities* (Corn, Hatlen, Huebner, Ryan, & Siller, 1995, p. 12), O&M was described as "the first disability-specific need to be isolated, described, and offered as a school subject in public schools. It was recognized that for most children with normal vision, the ability to travel safely and with ease in the environment was learned in a casual, unconscious, and natural manner. Visually impaired children could also travel safely and with ease, but they needed careful, systematic instruction to accomplish this." In recognition of the essential importance of O&M, this body of skills was identified as a related educational service in the 1997 regulations governing the implementation of the Individuals with Disabilities Education Act (IDEA).

Students who receive O&M instruction and use these skills to travel independently may receive psychological, physical, and social benefits, including a stronger self-concept from traveling by oneself, improved health from walking, increased social interactions, and the better performance of daily living skills (Hill, 1986). For example, students who are independent travelers can go to stores to get their own toiletries, thereby exercising control over this aspect of their lives, which leads to a better self-concept and provides opportunities for exercise, which, in turn, improves fitness. The long-term benefits of independent travel may include a greater likelihood of employment and a greater variety of experiences.

O&M training can be broadly defined as teaching the concepts and skills necessary for students to travel safely and efficiently in their environments. *Orientation skills* enable people with visual impairments to use sensory information to know their location in different settings, and *mobility skills* enable them to travel in different areas. People travel to different destinations using different techniques (such as the sighted guide or trailing techniques) or by using assistive devices (like the long cane and wheelchair).

Both students mentioned in the vignette at the beginning of this chapter have educational needs for O&M training. Miguel is learning to use orientation skills to learn the layout of his school and to use mobility skills to travel safely from place to place within the school using a mobility aid. Tanya's needs relate primarily to mobility skills in the community. She needs to learn to use her cane more effectively to be safe while traveling and not to interfere with the movement of her classmates and other sighted persons.

O&M training encompasses much more than teaching students to use a long cane. It begins early with concept development and continues with training in auditory skills, safety issues, and problem solving and in the use of assistive technology, community resources, and public transportation systems. O&M instruction is equally important for students who are blind and for those with low vision. To be effective, it should be an integral part of a student's day; that is, a student should use O&M techniques for many activities (such as using a map to complete an assignment, walking to the cafeteria, or meeting the school bus). Students who have well-established O&M skills are able to incorporate what they have learned in O&M training to travel in their environments safely and efficiently.

This chapter begins by discussing the roles of the O&M specialist and the teacher of students with visual impairments and the ways in which these two professionals, as well as others on a student's educational team, collaborate in teaching O&M skills. The remainder of the chapter focuses on the instructional strategies that teachers of students with visual impairments can use to teach specific, but limited, aspects of O&M skills. The chapter does not provide detailed information for O&M specialists; the reader is referred to other textbooks for such information (see, for example, Blasch, Wiener, & Welsh, 1997).

ROLE OF THE TEACHER OF STUDENTS WITH VISUAL IMPAIRMENTS

O&M is a unique area of the expanded core curriculum (see Chapter 6) in that a professional other than the teacher of students with visual impairments is largely responsible for instruction. Therefore, to understand the role of the teacher, the reader first needs to understand the role of the O&M specialist, the areas in which the O&M specialist provides direct instruction, and the areas that can be taught by the teacher of students with visual impairments.

O&M specialists receive unique university preparation and clinical experiences to prepare them to teach O&M skills to students with visual impairments. They generally receive professional certification from the Academy for Certification of Rehabilitation and Education Professionals and, in a few states, from their states' certification programs. Some O&M specialists hold dual certification as O&M specialists and teachers of students with visual impairments, although states, provinces, or local authorities do not generally require it. However, many states require dual credentials or other "teaching" credentials to teach O&M in public schools. The O&M specialist's responsibilities include the following:

◆ Conducting assessments, designing programs, and providing instruction in O&M skills to students with visual impairments in various environments;

◆ Teaching the use of the long white cane or assistive mobility devices;

◆ Holding workshops for parents, teachers, and paraeducators;

◆ Reporting students' progress in O&M skills; and

◆ Serving as a consultant to related service personnel, teachers, administrators, and other members of the educational team on O&M issues and practices.

The teacher of students with visual impairments is responsible for doing the following in relation to O&M:

◆ Teaching skills that enable students to maximize the use of their remaining senses, such as through the localization of sounds and tactile discrimination;

◆ Teaching basic O&M skills (the sighted guide technique, protective techniques, trailing, and familiarization with a room);

◆ Monitoring students' safety when traveling independently within and around the school;

◆ Collaborating with parents, students, the O&M specialist, and general education teachers regarding O&M issues and concerns; and

◆ Promoting attitudes among school personnel and members of the community that foster independent travel by students with visual impairments.

The teacher also plays an essential role in working with students with additional disabilities; strategies focusing on students with visual impairments and additional disabilities and resources for teachers appear later in this chapter.

The O&M specialist and the teacher of students with visual impairments must work closely together to ensure that students receive effective O&M instruction. Table 15.1 presents the various components of an O&M curriculum, arranged in a hierarchy from the simplest to the most complex. The italicized skills are the sole responsibility of the O&M specialist. All other skills can be taught collaboratively by the teacher and the O&M specialist.

The O&M specialist has the sole responsibility for teaching the use of the long cane, adaptive mobility devices, and electronic travel devices.

Table 15.1. Selected Components of an O&M Curriculum

Component of the O&M Curriculum	Hierarchy of O&M Concepts and Skills		
	Infants/Preschoolers	**Elementary School Students**	**Secondary School Students**
Concept development	Names of body parts	Functions of body parts	Body image
	Names of areas or items in environments (home, neighborhood, park, stores, house of worship)	Generalization of concepts	Spatial concepts
		Names of spatial concepts	All environments (all areas of the school; home; workplace; airport; train, subway, and bus stops and stations; stores; bank; house of worship)
		Familiar environments (school, home and neighborhood; bank, stores, house of worship)	
Sensory training	*Auditory*	*Auditory*	*Auditory*
	Awareness of sounds	Awareness of sounds that may not be common to the environment (in a factory, zoo, train, farm, pier, and so forth)	Use of sounds that are not common to the environment (complicated traffic intersections)
	Recognition of common sounds in the environment		
	Localization of sounds	Awareness of sounds of traffic	Ability to follow written or verbal directions for complex routes
		Ability to follow written and verbal directions	
	Visual	*Visual*	*Visual*
	Use of vision (shapes, sizes, color)	Identification of visual references (landmarks, clues) with or without low vision devices	Independent use of vision
	Use of vision to locate landmarks		Independent use of low vision devices
	Tactile	*Tactile*	*Tactile*
	Detection of textures and sensations, indoors and outdoors	Discrimination of textures with hands and fingers	Description of tactile differences used in following routes
		Discrimination of textures with feet and shoes	
Mobility skills	Sighted guide with modified grip	Sighted guide with appropriate grip	Sighted guide
	Trailing	Trailing	Trailing
	Upper protective	Upper protective	Upper protective
	Lower protective	Lower protective	Lower protective
	Use of appropriate terms		
	Adaptive mobility device, precane or long cane	*Adaptive mobility device, precane or long cane*	*Adaptive mobility device, precane or long cane*
			(continued on next page)

Note: Items in italics are taught *only* by the O&M specialist.

Table 15.1. *(Continued)*

Component of the O&M Curriculum	Hierarchy of O&M Concepts and Skills		
	Infants/Preschoolers	**Elementary School Students**	**Secondary School Students**
Orientation systems	Familiarization to the home, day care	Use of the following in familiar environments:	Use of the following in all environments:
	Use of selected landmarks in the home, day care	◆ Clock system	◆ Clock system
	Clues in the home, day care (sounds, smells)	◆ Measurement of time and distance	◆ Measurement of time and distance
	Weather (sun, wind, rain, snow, sleet)	◆ Room-familiarization skills	◆ Room-familiarization skills
	Use of sun and wind as outdoor clues	◆ General map skills	◆ Specific map skills
	Select landmarks	*Use of landmarks and clues in routes*	*Use of landmarks and clues in routes*
	Introduce mapping concepts	*Use of sun and wind in outdoor travel*	*Use of sun and wind in outdoor travel*
		Compass directions	*Compass directions*
		Numbering systems	*Numbering systems*
		Develop orientation aids, including maps	*Develop orientation aids, including maps*
Solicitation of aid	Questions and answers with adult modeling ("How do you get to school?" "I ride a bus." "Have you ridden in a taxi?" "Yes, from the airport.")	Questions for information and appropriate responses about travel options, routes, and the like, without supervision	Complex questions, problem solving ("I have $5. What is my best transportation option to get to the mall?" or "Can I get a driver's permit?")
	Questions and answers with adult supervision, if needed	Knowledge of from whom and when to ask questions	*Independently selecting and standing at an appropriate place to ask for assistance*
		Learning where to stand on the corner to ask for assistance	
Use of community resources and public transportation	Discussion of a variety of modes of transportation (family car, buses, airplanes, trains, subways, boats, ships, canoes)	Experience with a variety of modes of transportation with adult supervision (family car, city buses, airplanes, trains, subways, boats, ships)	Knowledge of travel tools (identification, passport, and so on)
	Familiarization to school bus	Development of resource list (commission for the blind office, library for the blind office)	Independent use of resources on list
	Discussion of and experience with modes of movement within a building (elevators, escalators, moving sidewalks, stairs)	Deciding what method to use to record resource information (print, braille, audiotape, note taker)	Discussion of and experience with community resources
			Independent use of transportation to leisure and school activities

(continued on next page)

Note: Items in italics are taught *only* by the O&M specialist.

Table 15.1. *(Continued)*

Component of the O&M Curriculum	Hierarchy of O&M Concepts and Skills		
	Infants/Preschoolers	**Elementary School Students**	**Secondary School Students**
Safety issues	Maintaining an upright posture	Physical intervention (self-defense: posture, assertive physical movements to deter an assailant)	A larger repertoire of physical intervention techniques
	Knowing the difference between safe and dangerous activities (playing in the yard is safe; playing in the street is dangerous)		
	Common safety rules		
	Understanding "stranger"		
	Knowing the difference between appropriate and inappropriate touch		
Assistive technology[1]	Money skills	Monitored use of precane/mobility device or long cane on school routes	Monitored use of precane/mobility device or long cane
	Appropriate clothing (in reference to the weather)	Responsible for use of fanny pack or backpack to carry necessary items (money, water, identification, medications, tools for note taking)	Responsible for use of fanny pack or backpack to carry necessary items (money, water, identification, medications, tools for note taking)
	Low vision devices	Appropriate clothing	Appropriate clothing
	AMDs, long cane	Use of watch (analog, digital, auditory, braille)	Use of watch (analog, digital, auditory, braille)
		Low vision devices	Low vision devices
		AMDs, long cane	
		Travel with low vision devices	*Information about dog guides, support dogs*

Note: Items in italics are taught *only* by the O&M specialist.

[1]Assistive technology is "any item, piece of equipment, or product system, whether acquired commercially off the shelf, modified, or customized, that is used to increase, maintain, or improve functional capabilities of the individual with a disability" (*Individuals with Disabilities Education Act Amendments of 1997,* sect. 602 [22]).

However, the teacher of students with visual impairments, the student's parents, general education teachers, and the paraeducator have the responsibility of supporting the student as he or she strives to become an independent traveler (Pogrund et al., 1995). In addition, the teacher of students with visual impairments has many responsibilities in teaching prerequisites to and concepts for O&M and facilitates communication between the O&M specialist and the other team members. Some important questions that a teacher may ask an O&M specialist to determine areas in which they may collaborate include the following:

- How much help does the student need to get to destinations in the school?

- When the student travels to class, what techniques is the student expected to use?

- What are the landmarks and clues that the student uses to travel?

- Will artwork displayed on the walls of a hallway distract the student from his or her route?

- How does the student respond to light? Is glare and lighting an issue with this student when traveling?

- What techniques should be used to travel across wide, open spaces (such as the cafeteria, gymnasium, auditorium, and playground)?

- Is the student a route traveler who must go the same way each time?

- Does the student have the skills to solve problems in unique situations?

- Is the student able to use his or her near and distant low vision devices independently?

- What O&M skills are appropriate for the student's regular education teachers, paraeducator, or parents to teach?

Ultimately the O&M specialist is responsible for the outcome of the instruction in the form of the O&M skills provided to the student who is visually impaired.

Specific areas in which the teacher and the O&M specialist work collaboratively include concept development, street safety, basic O&M skills, and sensory training. (These areas are discussed in more detail in the section on Instructional Strategies later in this chapter.) For example, the teacher of students with visual impairments may teach a student how to familiarize himself with his classroom, while the O&M specialist will teach the same child how to familiarize himself with the city block where his house is located. Likewise, the teacher of students with visual impairments may expose a student to the importance of listening to

sounds made by different objects in her school, whereas the O&M specialist may teach her the importance of listening to and identifying sounds along the street in front of her house.

COLLABORATION AMONG TEAM MEMBERS

Once the educational team has determined that O&M is necessary for a student, the O&M specialist becomes part of the student's team and recommends goals for the student's Individualized Education Program (IEP) on the basis of an O&M assessment. When the student masters O&M skills, the O&M specialist trains other members of the team (the parents, general education teachers, teacher of students with visual impairments, and so forth) to reinforce and monitor those skills throughout the student's life.

Effective O&M instruction requires close and ongoing collaboration among all members of a student's educational team. Collaboration can be nurtured by doing the following:

- Recognizing that students and parents are equal partners in O&M training,

- Teaching O&M skills in the manner that is considered the best practice by recognized professionals,

- Adhering strictly to a student's educational goals and objectives in O&M instruction,

- Documenting the student's ongoing progress in developing O&M skills,

- Adhering to ethical practices that delineate the specific O&M skills that are taught by O&M specialists and those that are taught by teachers of students with visual impairments,

- Following the school district's policies on transporting students in one's personal vehicle, and

- Adhering to established policies and ethical guidelines on maintaining confidentiality related to students' programs (Banja, 1994; Marsh, 1995).

To facilitate teamwork, the members of the educational team will find it helpful to follow the guidelines presented in Chapter 1.

ASSESSMENT

A thorough assessment of a student's O&M skills is the basis for establishing the need for O&M services, as well as the development of appropriate and relevant goals and objectives. Generally, the O&M specialist takes the lead in conducting this assessment, although the teacher of students with visual impairments, the student's parents, and other team members also play roles in a comprehensive assessment. An assessment of O&M skills may involve observations of the student's O&M skills by the parents or other caregivers and teachers; using formal assessment instruments, such as those listed in Sidebar 15.1, to collect data; and obtaining information from the informal assessment checklist compiled by the O&M specialist. The assessment process also entails reviewing all the student's records and previous assessments, interviewing the student, and requesting the student to demonstrate O&M skills.

After all this information is collected and synthesized, the O&M specialist writes an O&M assessment report and presents it to the educational team. The team members select goals related to O&M that are incorporated into the student's IEP and indicate the frequency, duration, and location of the O&M services that are to be provided (Pogrund et al., 1995).

INSTRUCTIONAL STRATEGIES

Itinerant and center-based programs are the primary models for providing O&M services. In itinerant programs, O&M specialists travel to schools, communities, or homes to work with students who are visually impaired, whereas in center-based programs, O&M specialists are based at schools, residential facilities, or rehabilitation centers to which students travel to receive instruc-tion. In either delivery model, O&M instruction may be provided in a student's home, school, or in the community (Smith & Levack, 1996).

The O&M curriculum is varied and includes activities that are used throughout a student's day and life. The components of this curriculum (see Table 15.1) are applicable to students of all developmental levels. This section presents information on O&M instruction in specific O&M skills and in relation to other academic and nonacademic skills.

Play

Play is an excellent way for young children to develop an understanding of space and the mobility skills to move safely in the environment (Simmons, 1996). Physical and psychological environments need to be designed and structured to promote independence. For example, a play environment (that is, a physical environment) can be specifically designed for young children with visual impairments (see the Appendix to this chapter) or an environment can be modified to promote safe travel (discussed later). Psychological environments begin with children's first interactions with others. If these interactions are reinforcing, then children are motivated to initiate movement. To encourage continued movement, parents and other caregivers need to present stimuli that appeal to the children's senses, so the children are encouraged to move.

Participation in play activities is important for children's growth and development (Levine, 1990; Schneekloth, 1989). Schneekloth (1989) advocated play environments for children with visual impairments that are complex, safe, and accessible and in which the children can learn that they have control over their own bodies.

An infant or preschooler can be assessed and taught O&M skills while he or she is playing. Direct observation during a play activity and a review of a videotape recorded while the child was playing can provide information on the child's motor skills, including strength and coordination; visual functioning; use of toys as mobility tools; orientation skills; language development; and social skills. The teacher of students with visual impair-

Formal Instruments to Assess Concept Development

- *Assessing Infants Who Are Visually Impaired or Deaf-Blind for Functional Vision and Orientation and Mobility* (Davies, 1989–90). Can be used by parents and other caregivers or others who know the child. Assesses a child's functional vision, O&M skills, use of senses, concept development, communication skills, and gross and fine motor skills.

- *The Basic Concept Inventory* (Engelmann, 1967). Designed for sighted, culturally disadvantaged preschool and kindergarten children, and those who are slow learners, emotionally disturbed, and mentally retarded. Can be used to assess a child's understanding of common words and imitation of movement patterns.

- *The Tactile Test of Basic Concepts* (Caton, 1980). Measures the mastery of visual and auditory concepts by children in kindergarten and grades 1 and 2. Identifies both the child who has not mastered concepts and the concepts on which the child needs to work. The categories of concepts are space, quantity, time, and miscellaneous.

- *The Body Image of Blind Children* (Cratty & Sams, 1968). Primarily assesses a child's ability to identify body parts, planes, directionality, and functioning.

- *The Hill Performance Test of Positional Concepts* (Hill, 1981). Assesses a child's ability to identify the positional relationships of body parts, moving body parts, and body and objects to demonstrate concepts of position.

- *Preschool Orientation and Mobility Screening* (Dodson-Burk & Hill, 1989). Used to assess the O&M skills of children with visual impairments from birth to age 5, with or without additional multiple disabilities.

- *Manual for the Stanford Multi-modality Imagery Test* (Dauterman, 1972). Designed to assess the functional imagery of children who are blind.

- *TAPS Comprehensive Assessment and Ongoing Evaluation* (Pogrund et al., 1995). Assesses the level of functioning in O&M of students aged 3–21. Includes orientation skills, mobility skills, and concept development.

- *The Oregon Project for Visually Impaired and Blind Preschool Children* (Brown, Simmons, & Methvin, 1991). Assesses developmental levels in eight areas (cognitive, language, socialization, vision, compensatory skills, self-help, fine motor skills, and gross motor skills), guides the selection of educational goals, and documents the acquisition of skills.

---

ments should allow sufficient time for an observation and may find it helpful to prompt a play activity and then withdraw a few feet, so the child can play independently.

As children mature, they engage in various types of play: solitary, parallel, functional-manipulative, symbolic, dramatic, and cooperative (Rettig, 1994). (See Table 15.2 for definitions of each type of play, along with strategies for developing play behaviors.) Since children with visual impairments cannot observe and imitate play in the same way as do sighted children, they need their parents and teachers to guide them through these types of play. The following suggestions facilitate the development of play in a young child with a visual impairment:

Table 15.2. Types of Play and Strategies for Developing Play Behaviors with Children Who Are Visually Impaired

Type of Play	Definition	Strategies for Teachers of Children with Visual Impairments
Solitary play	A child plays alone	Allow the child time to play—at least 30 minutes. Verbally reinforce the child's activity. Encourage make-believe. Go with the child's ideas, and do not interject your own. Avoid letting the child be pulled out of a play period. Include both indoor and outdoor play periods. Choose toys in a variety of sizes and both tactile and auditory qualities. Provide an area that is large and has a soft surface to facilitate active movement.
Parallel play	A child plays near another child but not with this child.	Place the child close to other children who are playing. Describe the area and what the other children are doing. Allow time for the child to play (at least 30 minutes).
Functional-manipulative play	A child uses a plaything in the way it is supposed to be used (e.g., drinking tea from an empty teacup).	Provide concrete objects for the child to play with. Use the real objects (e.g., spoon for eating, a cup for drinking) that the child uses for activities of daily living (ADLs). When the child is engaging in ADLs, allow him or her to explore objects while you verbalize what is occurring.
Symbolic play	Two children pretend that an object is another object (e.g., the kitchen table draped with a blanket over it is a fort).	Model what the child is doing. Imitate the child's action. Reinforce, make suggestions, and model again. Take a toy dog and pretend it is a dog guide and you are putting its harness on. Encourage turn taking. Assist the child to enter group play. Start with one playmate. Try to pair a movement of the child's body with that of a toy (for example, swing arms while playing with a toy swing).
Dramatic play	A child role-plays another character (e.g., pretends to be Count Dracula).	Provide props (e.g., hose, firefighter's helmet, toy ax, fire truck), time, and space. Encourage interaction among a group of children. Provide a play theme (in this case, a fire station) that the child is familiar with. Verbally reinforce the children's verbal interactions.
Cooperative play	Children engage in organized play.	Read books on different types of games (such as football, softball, and goalball). Provide materials to play the game (e.g., a ball and blindfolds for the sighted children). Explain the rules of the game. Teach the child the discrete motor activities to play the game (catching a ball, running, and localizing sound to identify where the ball is being rolled or thrown). Have a group of children play the game.

Source: Adapted from M. Rettig, "The Play of Young Children with Visual Impairments: Characteristics and Interventions," *Journal of Visual Impairment & Blindness, 88* (1994), p. 410.

◆ Encourage the child to use his or her body parts for play and show the child that toes can wiggle, hands can shake, feet can kick, and hands can grasp and drop and find objects.

◆ Take time to explore a bus, truck, or car inside and out with the child.

◆ Use brightly contrasting colored household items as toys (such as a red plastic mixing bowl and a green plastic mixing spoon) to enhance the use of vision of a child with low vision.

◆ Pretend with the child (for example, have a tea party without tea and snacks).

◆ Discuss daily routines with the child (such as getting ready for a baby-sitter or taking a bath before bedtime) and include descriptions of body parts, appropriate clothing, and weather conditions.

◆ Use suction cups to secure toys or place toys in a shallow baking pan or on a tray to provide a boundary for a child with orthopedic problems.

◆ Arrange furniture to encourage independent movement inside the house and, if possible, allow the child to move independently in a fenced-in yard or an enclosed playground.

◆ Place a sound source (such as bells on doorknobs or wind chimes on the outside of the front and/or back doors) to facilitate the child's localization of sound and orientation as to where the doors are located.

◆ Use high contrast on objects (such as dark dishes with light food and dark towels in a light bathroom) that the child with low vision uses.

◆ Hang a patterned mobile for an infant with low vision at hand level to encourage hand-eye or hand-ear coordination and to enhance visual efficiency.

◆ Use contrasting colors and/or textures to help a child identify feeding utensils, tools for personal grooming (such as comb and towels), and furniture, pillows, bedspreads.

◆ Mark a staircase with appropriate lighting using a contrasting color or texture and place a fan or wind chimes at the entrance to the stairs and gate until the child becomes a safe traveler at home and in school.

◆ Place a visual or tactile marker at the door of the child's classroom so the classroom can be easily identified. Place it at hand level for trailing or at eye level for a child with low vision.

◆ Use objects and furniture at home and in school to teach concepts. For example, use a coffee table to teach such concepts as under, around, top, and back by having the child crawl under, walk around, climb on top of, and put his or her back to the table (Uriegas, 1996).

◆ Allow the child to play alone in a safe, supervised area.

◆ Model appropriate activities for each type of play.

◆ Arrange classroom areas to facilitate play activities (for example, provide a playhouse and access to clothes and costumes for dressing up).

Concept Development

The development of concepts, or mental ideas of things, is the building block for independence and is therefore essential in O&M training (Welsh & Blasch, 1987). For O&M purposes, concepts can be divided into three categories: body concepts, spatial concepts, and environmental concepts.

Body concepts are necessary because the body is often used as a primary reference point (Welsh & Blasch, 1987) in O&M training. For instance, a teacher of students with visual impairments could use a student's body for orientation to a room (by saying, for example, "the table is on your left, and the sofa is on your right"). Body concepts include the parts, movements, planes (front, behind, above, and below), and directionality (right side, left side) of the body. Along with these concepts, the student needs to know the functions of body parts and how the parts relate to each other.

Spatial concepts, including directionality, shapes, actions, distances, amounts, time, weights and volumes, widths, lengths, and sizes, are important for safe travel (Hill & Blasch, 1987). Some words that are included in spatial concepts are: *into, clockwise, front, inch, full, empty, second, day, triangle, thick, move, creep, run,* and *push.*

Environmental concepts enable people to understand how their surroundings are laid out and organized. The list of environmental concepts is almost endless; some of these concepts include *town, state, traffic light, sidewalk, grass, building, railroad, window, car, telephone booth, water fountain, slope, pavement, icy, smooth, hot,* and *bumpy.*

At the beginning of O&M training, it is important to assess how well the student understands basic concepts and to determine whether the student has only a verbal understanding of the concept or whether he or she has a concrete, functional, and generalizable understanding as well. For instance, if a young child learns the features of a wooden block, can he or she generalize the features to a block of ice and to a neighborhood block?

A student's understanding of concepts can be assessed both formally and informally. Formal assessments—such as those presented in Sidebar 15.1—use standardized administration procedures and are interpreted using normative data. Informal assessments are not standardized, and they have no normative data (Turnbull, Turnbull, Shank, & Leal, 1999; see also Chapters 2 and 3). Such instruments may include checklists or observation scales and may have been developed by the teacher of students with visual impairments or the O&M specialist. Informal assessments may also consist of structured observations of the student during regularly occurring activities (for instance, during play or at lunchtime).

Once a student's needs in concept development are identified, members of the educational team can incorporate targeted goals and objectives in the student's IEP. Table 15.3 presents examples of such goals and activities.

Basic O&M Skills

Most children develop ambulatory skills in the same general way; they roll over, sit, crawl, cruise along furniture (that is, move from object to object using the objects for support; Smith & Levack, 1996), and then walk independently. The motivation to move in many cases is that the child sees something out of reach that he or she wants. This type of learning, called "incidental learning," is acquired without guidance or instruction. Incidental learning is a "by chance" process, commonly

Table 15.3. Examples of Educational Goals Related to Concept Development

Concepts	Goal	Activity	Environment
Body concept	Quince will be able to touch parts of his body when asked.	When the song, "Head, Shoulders, Knees, and Toes" is sung, Quince will point to the specified parts of his body.	Home Day care
Spatial concept	Grant will be able to tell the difference among whole, half, and quarter turns of his body.	Grant will practice making whole, half, and quarter turns with his body.	School
Environmental concept	Kelsey will be able to identify and apply concepts of floor level, intersection, and bus.	Kelsey will cross an intersection, ride the city bus, and walk to the second floor of the Biology Building to get to her class.	School Work Home

obtained by watching other people perform tasks (Turnbull et al., 1999). Children who are blind or visually impaired do not have the same visual information, motivation to move, or ability to avoid obstacles while moving as do sighted children and thus may choose to stay in the same, safe place.

Children with visual impairments may develop ambulatory skills at a slower pace than do sighted children, and for those with additional disabilities, the development may also be different. Early intervention with O&M skills helps children with visual impairments learn and build the skills they need to move through the same motor development as sighted children. The teacher of students of visual impairments and family members may need to provide more structured guidance to ensure that the children have the necessary language, conceptual knowledge, and skills to move safely and independently.

To enable a child who is visually impaired to move safety through the environment, the teacher of students with visual impairments should teach the sighted guide, trailing, and protective arm techniques—skills that are commonly referred to as "precane skills" or basic O&M skills because they are usually taught before the long white cane is introduced. These skills are generally used in indoor environments or for short distances. In some cases, the O&M specialist may introduce and teach skills that the teacher of students with visual impairments will monitor and reinforce.

Sighted Guide Technique

A student with a visual impairment may move from one place to another, using a sighted guide (that is, a person who walks just in front of and is in constant contact with the student; see Figure 15.1). This technique is a safe and efficient way for students to travel across large open spaces, such as a cafeteria, gym, auditorium, or playground.

To make initial contact, the sighted guide stands to one side of the student and touches the student's hand (see Figure 15.2). The student then moves his or her hand along the outside of the guide's arm, stopping just above the guide's elbow (see Figure 15.3). Next the student grasps the

Figure 15.1. A frontal view of the sighted guide technique

guide's arm, with the thumb on the outside and the fingers on the inside of the guide's arm (see Figures 15.4 and 15.5). If the student is too short to grab the guide above the elbow, he or she can grasp the sighted guide by the wrist or by the guide's index and middle fingers. When the two are walking, there is a short distance—about half a step—between the guide and the student that allows the student time to react to the guide's movements and gives the guide a full field of vision. Generally, this distance does not prevent the guide and the student from conversing and should not draw attention to the student.

When there is not enough room for the guide and the student to walk side by side, a system called the *narrow passageway technique* is helpful. In this technique, the guide positions the arm the student is holding in the middle of his or her back,

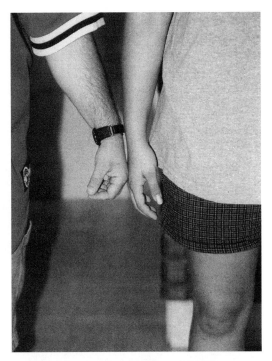

Figure 15.2. A guide establishing physical contact with a student to initiate the sighted guide technique

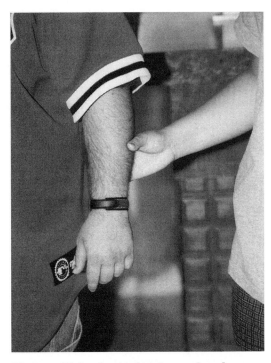

Figure 15.3. A student moving her hand up a guide's arm to grasp his elbow

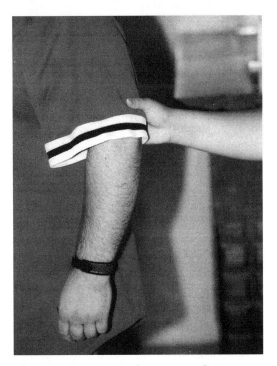

Figure 15.4. A student grasping a guide's elbow

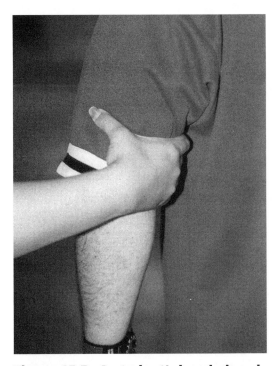

Figure 15.5. A student's hand placed in a "c" cup position when grasping a guide's arm

so the student is almost directly behind the guide, and returns the arm to his or her side once the way is clear (see Figures 15.6, 15.7, 15.8, and 15.9).

The advantages of the sighted guide technique are the efficiency and speed in which a student can move to his or her destination. The drawbacks are that the student is dependent on someone else to move from place to place, and does not gain much information about the environment.

Trailing

When a student becomes more familiar with a route, he or she can use two techniques to reinforce his or her orientation and travel: trailing (discussed here) and protective techniques (discussed in the next section). Trailing (see Figure 15.10) can be used to move safely from one location to another by maintaining contact (using the arm and hand) with a wall, furniture, or surroundings. It can also be used to travel around furniture and obstacles in a classroom, to detect the number of doors from the building entrance to the classroom, and so forth.

To trail a wall, the student extends one arm down, slightly in front and out from the body and touches the wall at his or her side. Generally, the hand that is used in this technique is the one that allows the student to move with the flow of traffic. The side of the hand opposite the thumb touches the wall, and the fingers of the hand trailing the

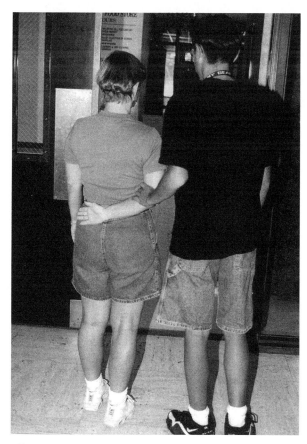

Figure 15.6. A guide placing her arm behind her back to forewarn a student that they are going to be walking through a narrow space

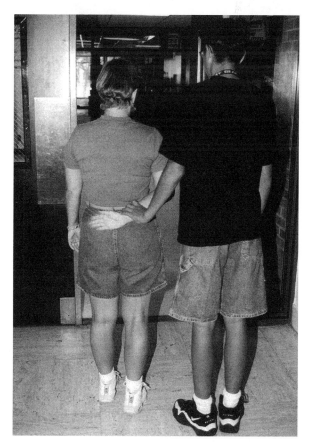

Figure 15.7. A student moving his grip down to a guide's wrist while using the narrow passageway technique

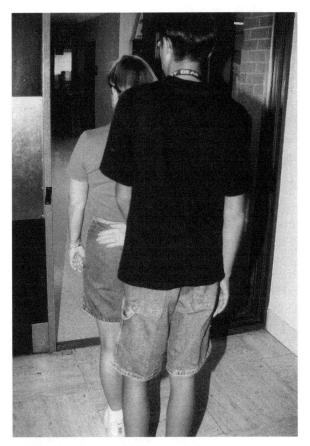

Figure 15.8. A student moving his body behind a guide for the narrow passageway technique

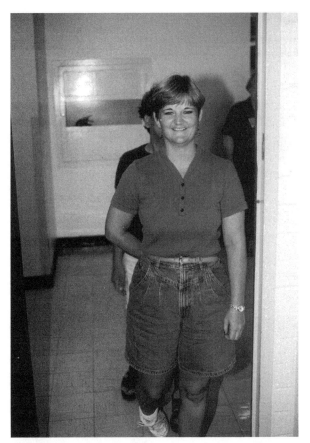

Figure 15.9. A student and guide using the narrow passageway technique to walk through a narrow space

wall are curled under as the student moves forward to prevent injury when the student encounters architectural features (such as door frames). As a teaching tip, the teacher can have the student imagine that he or she is grasping an apple in the trailing hand.

Trailing can be used to meet a variety of needs. For example, students who are learning their way around a new school may trail the walls from class to class or to locate their lockers. They can also trail a wall while holding their long canes in their trailing hands or when using protective techniques.

Protective Arm Techniques

There are two protective arm techniques: cross-body or upper-body protection and lower-body

protection. These techniques are important because not all obstacles in a traveler's path are against a wall, and some obstacles may be at head or shoulder height (such as tree limbs, hanging plants, coat racks, and shelves) and at waist or groin level (like water fountains, telephones, and display tables).

To use the *upper-body protective technique* (see Figures 15.11 and 15.12), the student raises one arm to shoulder height with the palm of the hand facing outward beyond the opposite shoulder and the fingers slightly curled and 2 inches beyond the opposite shoulder. The raised arm is slightly bent across the student's body, thus the name "cross-body" technique.

When bending over to pick up a dropped object, the student needs to use the upper-body

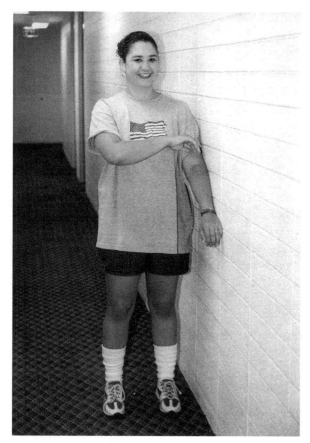

Figure 15.10. A student trailing a wall

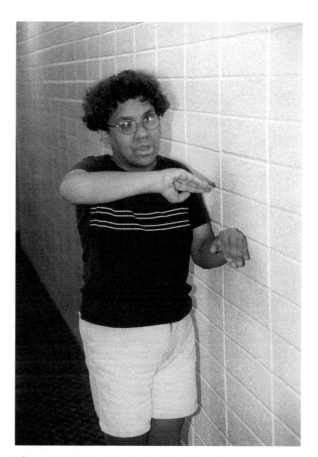

Figure 15.11. A student using the upper-body protective technique while trailing a wall

technique to avoid bumping his or her forehead. To locate the object, the student can use the fingertips of a cupped hand to find a reference point near where he or she thinks the object is located and move the hand in a small circle, increasing the size of the circle until he or she finds the object. To protect the face or upper body, the hand is in front of the student's face with the palm facing outward and the elbow bent slightly less (about a 120-degree angle). To protect the chest, the student moves the arm and hand to chest level in the same position mentioned earlier.

The *lower-body protective technique* (see Figure 15.13) is used to protect the lower body. To use this technique, the student's arm is extended downward, straight from the shoulder, fingertips pointed toward the ground, and held 6 to 8 inches in front of the opposite hip area. Sometimes, it may be appropriate for the upper and lower body techniques to be combined to provide maximum protection.

If a student is young or has low muscle tone, then the protective techniques can be modified. For example, the student can extend both arms in front of his or her body with the fingers interlaced to protect the upper body. To protect the lower body, a student can extend both arms downward in front of his or her body overlapping the hands with the palms toward the body.

Combining Precane Techniques

Trailing may be used in conjunction with either upper-body or lower-body protection, depending

Figure 15.12. A student finding a door while using the upper-body protective technique

Figure 15.13. A student using the lower-body protective technique

on the expected obstacles on the route. For example, in a classroom filled with desks and chairs, a student may use lower-body protection to trail around the room or down an aisle to his or her desk. When a student is traveling in a hall where few desks and chairs are located, upper-body protection offers protection from open classroom doors and other obstacles mounted in the hallway (see again Figure 15.10). If a student is traveling in an unfamiliar area, the O&M specialist needs to be consulted to decide the most appropriate technique or combination of techniques and the routes that the student can travel.

The sighted guide technique is generally taught before the protective techniques. Common strategies for teaching these skills are verbal and physical prompting. As skills improve and students become more independent in traveling, fewer verbal and physical prompts are needed. Some teaching tips for the sighted guide and upper- and lower-body protective techniques are presented in Sidebar 15.2.

Auditory Training

Objects in the environment that produce sounds provide essential clues to a student (Pogrund et al., 1995) because of the distinctive volume, pitch, and quality of the sounds. Auditory training improves the ability of students who are visually impaired to orient themselves (that is, to determine their location in space), to localize sounds (to use

Strategies for Teaching Precane Mobility Techniques

SIGHTED GUIDE TECHNIQUE

◆ The guide needs to make sure the student follows slightly behind him or her at all times. A good method for checking whether the student is doing so is to have the student take his or her free hand and check the guide's shoulder to make sure it is in front of his or her shoulder.

◆ Teach the technique in an open area that is free of obstacles, like a hallway.

◆ The guide can carry on normal conversation without describing in detail the area they are walking through.

◆ Once a skill is mastered, practice the skill in a variety of areas (including crowded malls and outdoors around the school grounds) and with different guides.

UPPER-BODY PROTECTIVE TECHNIQUE

◆ Introduce the technique in an open area.

◆ When the student masters the skill, add obstacles at head, shoulder, and waist heights for the student to detect.

◆ Limit practice to short periods, since this can be a physically tiring technique. Increase the practice time as the student's strength and endurance improve.

◆ Introduce the modifications of these techniques for young students and those with low muscle tone and endurance (see the text for suggestions).

LOWER-BODY PROTECTIVE TECHNIQUE

◆ When the child masters the skill, add obstacles at waist and groin level for the student to detect. Once the student detects an obstacle, he or she should explore it, to decide the best way to go around it.

◆ Introduce the modifications of these techniques for young students and those with low muscle tone and endurance (see the text for suggestions).

---

the sounds to pinpoint the location of objects, as for finding dropped objects), to determine "the exact bearing or line of direction of a sound" (Hill & Ponder, 1976, p. 115), and to travel safely. For example, when a student wants to cross a street, he or she listens to the oncoming traffic and waits until the sounds cease before crossing.

Welsh and Blasch (1987) suggested that auditory training should focus on the auditory skills necessary for independent travel. Students need to understand the following conditions that can occur when sound is emitted from an object:

◆ A *sound echo* is reflected sound from a sound source, like the chirping sound from

an audible pedestrian signal alerting a child when it is time for the walk signal.

◆ *Echolocation* occurs when sound is reflected off objects. For example, the sound of the cane tapping the ground changes when the traveler walks past an open area, such as an alleyway or an open doorway. This change in sound assists the student in identification of an alleyway, open door, or overhang.

◆ *Sound masking* occurs when another sound blocks the sound a person needs to hear. For example, since an airplane flying overhead makes it difficult to hear traffic, a student needs to learn to wait until he or she can hear the traffic again to decide when it is safe to cross a street.

- A *sound shadow* occurs when an object between a sound source and a person causes a change in the originating sound. For example, because passing a telephone booth changes the sound of parallel traffic, a student needs to learn to continue to travel in the same direction until he or she can hear the traffic clearly again.

According to Brothers and Huff (1975), students should be taught to localize sounds in four stages: (1) to become aware of sounds, (2) to interpret sounds, (3) to localize sounds, and (4) to convert sounds for orientation purposes. They suggested the following sequence for teaching students how to localize sound:

- The student and the sound source (such as a radio or a music box) remain stationary. The student points to where the sound source is located as the instructor turns it on.
- The student remains stationary while the sound source (like a windup toy or a toy bear that laughs and bounces) moves. The student indicates the path of the movement with his or her hand.
- The student moves, and the sound source remains stationary. For example, the student walks or runs toward or away from a radio that is playing.
- The student moves while the sound source is moving. For instance, the student walks beside a moving toy train.

An auditory training curriculum needs to include all the aforementioned concepts. Training can focus initially on the auditory identification of grossly different objects, such as a dog barking and a door opening. Once the student can associate meaning with the sounds, then he or she can be taught higher-level skills, such as reacting to sound masking and then sound shadow. The fol-

lowing suggestions may be helpful in teaching a student to use auditory information:

- Ask the student to make a list of the different sounds he or she hears to increase the student's awareness of the role that hearing plays in travel.
- Have the student audiotape sounds at home, in the yard, and at school. (What sound does a refrigerator make when making ice? What sound does a washing machine make when washing clothes?) To increase the student's knowledge of sounds from various environments (such as a barnyard and a train station), have the student's classmates listen and identify which objects are making sounds on another audiotape.
- Hide a sound source in the classroom and have the student find it within one minute. Vary the amount of time and the number of sound sources that are hidden.
- Ask the student to walk parallel and perpendicular to an object, such as a radio, that is making a continuous sound.
- Place a radio that is playing in a trash can and throw bean bags into the trash can to improve the student's sound-localization and motor skills (and to improve hand-ear coordination). The radio may be used as a sound source to aid the student in locating the trash can.
- Place a radio that is playing on a table and have the student walk toward, away from, and around the radio, as well as parallel and perpendicular to it.
- Play games like ring-around-a-rosy, farmer in the dell, dodgeball, seven-up, and tug-of-war to improve the student's motor-coordination and sound-localization skills in a group setting.
- Set up an obstacle course using sound sources at each control point along a course and have the student find each control point by using his or her hearing.

Orientation Systems

Orientation is defined as "the process of using the senses to establish one's position and relationship to all significant objects in one's environment" (Hill & Ponder, 1976, p. 3). In other words, students with visual impairments use sensory information to know where they are in their environments, where they want to go, and how they intend to travel to their destinations. To improve a student's orientation to the environment, it is important to increase his or her skills with various orientation systems: landmarks and clues, the clock system, the self-familiarization process, compass directions, numbering systems, and measuring items and distances.

Landmarks and Clues. *Landmarks* are objects in homes or classrooms that are easily identified, permanent, and unique to their particular setting (Hill & Ponder, 1976). A fireplace in a living room or a carpeted play area in a classroom are examples. *Clues* are bits of temporary sensory information that can be used to tell where one is or the direction in which one wants to go. For example, a child can use the smell of steaks cooking on a grill to determine his or her location in the backyard and the sun and wind to identify the direction in which he or she is walking.

When showing a student where food is placed on a plate and where eating utensils are located on a tray, the teacher of students with visual impairments can use the clock system. For example, a teacher may say, "Your potatoes are at 12 o'clock, the meatloaf is at 3 o'clock, the carrots are at 6 o'clock, and the milk is beside you at 9 o'clock." The clock system can also be used to identify the location of furniture in a child's classroom. Suggestions for teaching landmarks and clues are presented in Sidebar 15.3.

Self-Familiarization and Room Familiarization. Young children with visual impairments can learn techniques to familiarize themselves to rooms in their homes and to their classrooms. Once they learn the *self-familiarization* technique, they can

use it to familiarize themselves in any unfamiliar area.

To use the self-familiarization technique, the student walks with an adult around the perimeter of a room and identifies the pieces of furniture or the architectural features (such as a door or window) along each wall. This is known as the perimeter method. Each wall is given a label or name on the basis of the architectural feature or piece of furniture that was found while walking (for example, window wall or bureau wall). Over time, the labels for the walls can become compass directions. For instance, the window wall can be called the west wall. To familiarize themselves with the interior of a room, students can use either a crisscross or a grid pattern (see Figure 15.14).

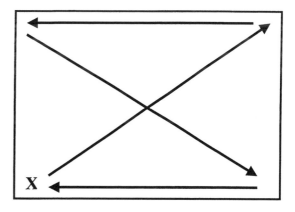

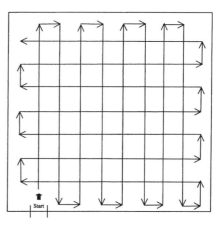

Figure 15.14. Patterns a student can use for familiarization with the interior of a room

Strategies for Teaching Landmarks and Clues

GENERAL STRATEGIES

◆ Walk around the house or classroom with the student and discuss objects that can be used as landmarks and clues.

◆ Divide the students into groups of two, provide them with a list of landmarks and clues in braille or large print, and send them on an orienteering course, a timed raced where participants use a tactual map and a braille compass to locate checkpoints on an unfamiliar course. Reward the group who finds the most controls.

◆ While the students are sitting at their desks, have them write down the different types of landmarks and clues they can see, hear, or smell.

◆ Have a student make a model or map of a room, noting the location of specific landmarks.

USE OF SUN AND WIND

◆ Walk in a park or on the playground with a student. Discuss the direction and sensations that come from the sun and wind.

◆ Read a book about the sun and wind to learn how they can be used for orientation. For example, since the sun rises in the east and sets in the west, when the student is traveling west at dusk, the sun should be in front of him or her.

◆ To facilitate the use of the sun and wind as orientation clues, have the student keep a weather diary of windy and sunny days for a week. Have the student include comments about how the weather affected him or her, for example, "My hat blew off my head on the way to the bus."

◆ With the student, walk down a street with skyscrapers, so the student can experience the wind-tunnel effect when he or she crosses an alley, an empty lot, or reaches a corner. Discuss with the student that this is a clue as to the distance he or she has traveled.

CLOCK SYSTEM

◆ Make a model of a clock out of art supplies. Use either braille or large print, depending on the student's vision. Use times with calendar activities and have the student schedule activities for the day. The student can learn about the importance of time and how to develop routes that are time efficient.

◆ Teach the student to tell time using a watch face; include different types of watches (braille, large print, and an APH analog clock model).

◆ Practice using the clock system with the student when describing where furniture is placed in a classroom or home, where food is on a plate, and so forth.

Learning to use *compass directions* is important for independent travel because north, south, east, and west never change, whereas left and right are relative positions that change with the direction the individual is facing. A student will learn later to rely on compass directions when traveling in his or her neighborhood and town. Some strategies for teaching the use of compass directions are as follows:

◆ Have the student relate compass directions to a clock face during initial instruction. Call the four cardinal directions Never Eat Sour Watermelons for north, east, south, and west.

◆ Explore with the student how compass directions are used on a map and on a globe.

◆ Use a braille compass or a regular compass to teach compass directions, depending on the student's level of vision.

◆ Have a Boy Scout or a Girl Scout from the student's class discuss how he or she uses compass directions on a hike.

◆ Have students read about the invention of compasses.

◆ Have the student plan a route using compass directions for classmates to follow.

Numbering Systems. The system of sequential numbering of school classrooms and houses on a street is called a *numbering system.* Numbering systems enable a student who is visually impaired to understand that there is order to his or her environment. The use of the numbering system allows students to find classrooms or a friend's house on a city block. Strategies for teaching the use of numbering systems are as follows:

◆ Walk down a school corridor with the student and discuss how the rooms are numbered. Look at the braille signage.

◆ Walk along a street with the student and discuss how the houses are numbered on each side of the street (that is, the numbers

follow in sequence, one side of the street has even numbers while the other side has odd numbers).

◆ Have the student read a book on city planning to understand how cities use numbering systems to organize large areas of land.

◆ Make a map with the student of a school corridor placing all the numbered rooms on the map.

Measurement. To measure is to "[ascertain] the exact or approximate dimensions of an object or space, using a given unit" (Hill & Ponder, 1976, p. 8). This technique can help students who are visually impaired understand the size of objects, the distance between them and the objects, the distance between different objects, and the approximate distance they walk on a route. Students may use measurement to determine, for example, whether a route walked is long or short, how far they need to walk to locate the corridor that leads to the principal's office, and the size of a room. The following are some strategies for teaching the use of measurement:

◆ With the student, measure various objects at home and at school using nonconventional measuring systems, such as the student's fingers, hands, or arms. Then measure the same objects with standard measures, such as braille/large print rulers, yardsticks, and measuring tapes. Make the point that all things are measurable.

◆ Show the student the length of his or her pace by having the student walk on a braille/large print tape measure. Have the student count the number of paces to specific, familiar locations, such as the principal's office or the rest room. Then ask the student to estimate distances from his or her desk to the other locations and time how long it takes the student to travel each route. This activity enhances time-distance judgment.

◆ Construct with the student a model of his or her home. Have the student measure distances from objects in the home (using braille/large print ruler or tape measure, depending on visual functioning) and discuss the concept of scale. This activity provides a framework to illustrate the differences between maps and models and how size and distance are portrayed in each item.

Community Resources and Public Transportation

It is essential that students with visual impairments become skilled in using the resources in their environments and communities to increase their independence. For example, to be able to plan a route, travel to a job interview, and arrive on time, the student needs to know how to use public transportation. This process may involve locating a telephone booth, calling the bus terminal to find out when and how long it takes to travel to the site of the job interview, and then locating the correct bus and getting off at the correct stop.

To help a student with this task, the teacher of students with visual impairments can begin by teaching him or her to ask others for assistance or to refuse assistance gracefully when it is not needed. Expectations for requesting or refusing assistance must be matched with the student's age and, even more important, with the student's skills as a traveler. If a high school student is going for a job interview and has been dropped off at a corner by a cab driver, the student can ask the driver how to find a specific address from the corner. On the other hand, a kindergarten student may be expected to ask a fellow student where the rest room is located in the corridor in which the two are walking.

The teacher of students with visual impairments can teach a student to ask for assistance initially by modeling effective questions to obtain important travel information and then by helping the student to develop his or her own questions. For instance, a student can learn to ask specific questions, such as "Is the library north or south of me?" instead of a general question like "Where is the library?" Additional strategies for teaching

students to ask for assistance are presented in Sidebar 15.4. Since people sometimes offer assistance to a person with a disability when none is needed, the student also needs to learn to refuse this type of help politely but firmly.

Furthermore, the teacher of students with visual impairments needs to explore a variety of transportation options with the student, including school and city buses, trains, airplanes, and subways. By exposing a student to different modes of transportation, the teacher is preparing him or her for formal O&M training in the use of public transportation. Some strategies for teaching the use of public transportation are these:

♦ Have the student, teacher, or parent read books about various transportation systems, so the student becomes aware of these different forms of public transportation.

♦ Have models of airplanes, trains, and automobiles available, so the student can examine their differences and similarities to actual vehicles. Have the student explore actual airplanes and trains as well. Discuss the advantages and disadvantages of various types of public conveyances.

♦ Ride in elevators and escalators at a mall and in office buildings with the student. Have the student compare the time it takes to ride an elevator and escalator to the time it takes to climb a set of stairs.

♦ Have the student telephone the bus station, train station, or airport and ask a customer service representative about any special services that may be offered to travelers with visual impairments.

Safety Issues

For students with visual impairments to travel independently, it is essential for them to be aware of safety issues. Pava, Bateman, Appleton, and Glascock (1991) stated that persons with visual impairments need to have a heightened awareness of personal safety issues for the following reasons:

Suggestions for Teaching a Student How to Ask for Assistance

BEGINNING TRAVELERS

♦ Model the questions the student should ask and give the student many opportunities to practice asking questions.

♦ Have the student telephone a bus station or movie theater to ask about scheduled times in preparation for an upcoming outing.

INTERMEDIATE TRAVELERS

♦ Teach the student whom he or she should ask for help (teachers, adults, bus or taxi drivers).

♦ Teach the student how to use technology (including the redial feature on a telephone, a note taker, or an audiotape recorder).

♦ Have the student use the information he or she obtained to travel to a destination on a city bus.

ADVANCED TRAVELERS

♦ Help the student learn to phrase questions to obtain specific, detailed information (such as: "I am at Fourth and Green Streets. I need to locate the bus terminal. What is the correct street address? What is the north/south or east/west intersecting street?").

♦ Give the student opportunities to practice skills with assistive technology. For example, if a student is moving to a new city to attend college and needs to find out the available bus routes, he or she can use the Internet to locate the Web page for the city's bus company information.

♦ They use mobility devices that label them as potential targets;

♦ They use public transportation that puts them at bus or subway stops where they may be waiting alone;

♦ They may travel at times of the day when fewer travelers are using public transportation, due to work schedules;

♦ They may not be aware that someone is watching their daily routines;

♦ They have less or no access to general safety precautions (such as looking through a peephole or out a window to identify who may be at the door or reading identification cards or asking for identification);

♦ They may ask fellow travelers for directions and thus may be misguided by a potential attacker; and

♦ They may not be able to identify and describe an assailant visually.

Safety rules and procedures should be introduced early in a student's life and be extended throughout formal schooling. Parents and teachers need to teach preschoolers their full names, addresses, and telephone numbers and to whom and when to disclose this information. Recognizing emergency situations, such as fire or severe weather, and taking appropriate actions when emergency situations arise are crucial. To know the appropriate actions, the students must practice the drills independently and in a group.

As students become independent travelers, they become more vulnerable. Thus, with freedom of movement come responsibilities to maintain their own safety. Although the O&M specialist teaches a student how to cross streets safely, the teacher of students with visual impairments can help to prepare the student for this instruction by discussing street and car safety. A self-defense expert can introduce the use of physical self-defense to all students in a physical education class and then discuss special self-defense issues for people with disabilities (with guidance provided by the teacher of students with visual impairments), followed by small-group or individual demonstrations and practice. Here are some strategies for teaching safety issues:

◆ Discuss with the student the impact that a visual impairment can have on a student's personal safety.

◆ Discuss with the student the importance of wearing appropriate clothing (that is, clothing that is easily viewed by a driver or wearing a reflective armband, headlamp, or vest) (Pogrund et al., 1995).

◆ Discuss the importance of carrying belongings in one bag (rather than in multiple bags), carrying a whistle, and carrying a rape-repellent capsule (such as mace) (Pogrund et al., 1995).

◆ Have the student and teacher, together and separately, read general books on street safety and discuss how the general public crosses streets (using such adages as "Stop, Look and Listen" and "Cross at the Corner").

◆ Teach the student how to walk, stand, and appear confident when conversing with others and when traveling.

◆ Discuss what constitutes appropriate and inappropriate touching. The student needs to understand that physical prompting by teachers as part of the instructional process is considered appropriate, whereas touching personal places on a student's body without permission is inappropriate.

◆ Discuss appropriate conversations to have when traveling and during interactions with strangers. For example, the student should know that he should not give out personal identifying information to strangers at any time.

◆ Use role-playing to practice requesting and refusing assistance (such as directions to a building).

◆ Teach the student ways to recognize when someone is following him or her and what to do to get help (for example, enter a store or business).

◆ Have the student practice requesting and receiving information by telephone, over the Internet, and using other resources.

◆ Invite self-defense experts to speak to a physical education class and help the student to practice self-defense strategies using physical prompting and guidance as needed.

◆ Encourage the student to enroll in a community self-defense course and provide resources and consultation to the instructor.

◆ Help the student obtain appropriate identification cards and documents.

◆ Suggest to the student strategies for carrying identification and money when traveling, such as in a wallet or fanny pack.

◆ Teach the student problem-solving skills to ensure safe decision making in familiar and unique situations (such as what to do if the student misses his or her stop while on a bus).

◆ Use role-playing to practice what the student might do in potentially dangerous situations (as when the student's ride does not show up after school, the student is being followed home from school, a date is becoming aggressive, and a conversation on the Internet is becoming inappropriate).

◆ Teach the student to recognize when and how to phone the emergency number, 911 (as when a stranger is outside the student's home late at night or there is smoke in the house).

◆ Teach the student strategies to increase his or her safety (for example, conceal one's name on clothing, do not travel alone at night if it can be avoided, do not wait alone at a subway or bus stop, and learn physical self-defense skills).

♦ Invite community experts to lecture on such topics as date rape.

Assistive Technology Devices

The Technology-Related Assistance to Individuals with Disabilities Act of 1988 jdescribes assistive technology as any device or system, whether purchased, modified, or created, that improves or maintains a student's educational programming (Turnbull et al., 1999). The assistive technology used in O&M instruction includes mobility tools and orientation devices.

Mobility tools enable a student to move out in the environment as independently as possible by providing protection, gathering information about the area the student is walking in, and detecting obstacles in the environment. Mobility tools range in complexity from electronic travel aids (ETAs) and adaptive mobility devices (AMDs, such as push toys, instructor-made devices constructed from PVC pipe) to long canes, walkers, and wheelchairs. An ETA is usually used with a long cane; it indicates obstacles in the environment by emitting sounds or vibrations and can assist with orientation. The use of these mobility tools is taught by O&M specialists. Teachers of students with visual impairments can help by teaching prerequisite skills and concepts, as well as reinforcing the skills taught by the O&M specialists.

A long cane is used to detect obstacles directly in front of the traveler—curbs, stairs, and changes in surface textures—and identifies the person as visually impaired. However, a cane does not offer protection for the upper body and may miss such obstacles as a lantern hanging from a building or a mirror on the side of a pickup truck. Older students may choose to use dog guides, rather than canes, to travel independently.

Low vision devices can assist students with low vision to orient themselves to the environment and to accomplish other O&M tasks. For example, students can use the following devices for these purposes:

♦ A magnifier to read a bus schedule;

♦ A telescope to read street signs, Walk/Don't Walk signs, and house numbers;

♦ A telescope to read the menu at a fast-food restaurant; and

♦ A telescope to see bus numbers.

(See Chapter 13 for strategies on teaching students with low vision to use near and distance optical and nonoptical devices.)

Other orientation devices, such as a braille compass and a map, provide many types of information about a student's present location. A map gives the student a visual or tactile representation of the route he or she is to take. Directions and details about a destination can be available to the student on an audiotape recorder or a braille note taker made either by the O&M specialist or by the student. These devices, as well as a slate and stylus, can be used to take notes. High-tech devices combine satellite technology and computers with speech access to tell the traveler the name of the nearest street and the number of streets from the present location to the destination.

Low-tech aids, such as fanny packs or backpacks, hold identification, money, snacks, water, medications, and other items that are necessary to the student and free the student's hands to hold a cane or to trail a wall. The student may use a watch with large-print numerals or with speech to help reach destinations on time and a cellular telephone to summon assistance or transportation.

The use of assistive technology is taught collaboratively by the teacher of students with visual impairments and the O&M specialist. For example, the teacher can teach the student to use a slate and stylus to take down directions to the grocery store while on a mobility lesson. If the student has taken down the information accurately and can interpret these directions, then he or she has the information to get to the destination. If not, then the O&M specialist can confer with the teacher of students with visual impairments to develop a remediation plan.

MODIFICATIONS THAT PROMOTE TRAVEL IN SCHOOL

Teachers and other school personnel can modify the environment in the classroom and other parts of the school in a variety of ways to promote safe and independent travel for students with visual impairments, beginning in infancy and continuing through adolescence (see Sidebar 15.5 for some examples). The modifications may vary as the student learns to be more independent and will depend on the student's sensory abilities and travel skills. Modifications promote learning by changing methods and objects in the environment to address individual sensory needs. The teacher of students with visual impairments should consult with the O&M specialist to determine the modifications and strategies that will best promote effective travel for individual students. The following are some common environmental modifications and strategies:

◆ Provide an organized environment in the classroom to help the student learn his or her way around more efficiently. Familiar objects and landmarks can give the student information about where he or she is in the room. In addition, since the student needs a generally consistent environment to promote independent travel, the furniture should be kept in the same place, and the regular education teacher should let the student know of any changes that have been made in the arrangement of the room to which the student needs to be familiarized.

◆ Provide storage for the AMD or cane. Select a consistent place to hang it up or place it alongside a cubbyhole.

◆ Use changes in color, contrast, lighting, or texture to assist the student with low vision in traveling.

◆ Prepare the student for a fire or disaster drill by walking through the procedures prior to the actual drill. During the drill or an emergency, a guide should explain to the student where he or she is and what to expect and should follow established procedures. The guide should receive training as well, prior to the drill.

◆ Limit the number of obstacles in commonly traveled routes to keep the student moving forward toward the destination. Too much information from a number of obstacles can be distracting to the student.

◆ Mark classroom areas with different floor textures: ceramic tile, linoleum, concrete, carpet, or wood. Observe whether the student notices the difference and if the student can use this information to discover where he or she is in the classroom. The student needs to be taught how to use these differences in texture as landmarks.

◆ Identify the landmarks and clues that the student contacts as he or she travels on familiar routes. It is vital that all the educational team members use the same terms to lessen confusion and frustration in communication, especially with a student with a visual impairment and additional disabilities.

◆ Teach the student to explore and organize work consistently from left to right. This skill is necessary in reading and math activities. It reinforces laterality and position in space for near activities that can be generalized to gross motor activities.

◆ Reduce glare for a student with low vision by tilting objects, using preferential seating and desk placement, avoiding laminated materials, using theater gels over reading materials, and so forth.

◆ Create a greater contrast and visual background by having the student work on a sheet of black or dark construction paper.

◆ Keep hall doors completely closed or, if necessary, completely open to prevent painful collisions when traveling in the halls.

Modifications to Promote Travel in the School

INFANTS AND PRESCHOOLERS

- ◆ Organize the environment with furniture that can be trailed and with familiar objects to provide landmarks.
- ◆ Mark various areas of the classroom with different floor textures.
- ◆ Mark or identify landmarks and clues on routes.
- ◆ Reduce or limit the number of objects to simplify the route.
- ◆ Provide high contrast using white paper on black or dark construction paper for maps, directions for a route, diagrams, and the like.
- ◆ Reduce glare from laminated surfaces, shiny objects, sunlight through windows, and overhead lighting by using sunglasses, baseball caps worn inside the building, tilted objects like lamps, window coverings, and alternate lighting sources.
- ◆ Keep doors completely open or completely closed to prevent collisions.
- ◆ Mark the classroom door with a floor mat.

ELEMENTARY SCHOOL STUDENTS

- ◆ Provide a consistent, organized environment.
- ◆ Involve the student in arranging furniture.
- ◆ Allow ample storage space for a student's cane, AMDs, maps, braille compass, and low vision devices.
- ◆ Refrain from displaying artwork at the waist level of children in classrooms and hallways where it may be disturbed if a student who is blind trails over it.
- ◆ Close hallway doors.
- ◆ Make the classroom door tactilely and visually distinctive from other doors in the hallway.
- ◆ Use ADA-approved signage in the building.
- ◆ Discuss with the O&M specialist the mobility skills that the student should use. Ask the best way to monitor some of these skills. Also communicate progress and problems. If working with other staff, try to adhere to the O&M specialist's suggestions.
- ◆ Relate academic skills to independent travel (for example, have the student use a Braille 'n Speak to jot down notes on how to get to the airport on the subway system).

ADOLESCENTS

- ◆ Close hallway doors.
- ◆ Make the classroom door tactilely and visually distinctive from other doors in the hallway.
- ◆ Use ADA-approved signage in building.
- ◆ Discuss with the O&M specialist the mobility skills that the student should use. Ask the best way to monitor some of these skills. Also communicate progress and problems. If working with other staff, try to adhere to the O&M specialist's suggestions.
- ◆ Allow the student to decide the most appropriate O&M skills to use.

◆ Since a student who is trailing a wall as he or she moves to a different location may disturb art displays on walls, it may be necessary to raise the artwork to promote efficient trailing.

◆ Place distinctive floor mats (bumpy textured rugs) outside specific classroom doors to help the student locate each room.

SUMMARY

O&M skills provide freedom of movement and independence for students who are visually impaired, which in turn, promote high self-concept and offer increased opportunities for social interactions and employment. The teacher of students with visual impairments plays a critical, though limited, role in teaching O&M skills by promoting early concept development, providing instruction in basic O&M skills, and teaching other essential travel-related skills. However, the O&M specialist is responsible for teaching a student to travel in the community with a long white cane or with other mobility devices. A team approach is needed for promoting safe and effective O&M skills, with all members of the educational team working collaboratively to foster travel skills.

ACTIVITIES

1. Interview people who are receiving O&M services. Identify the purpose of the O&M training they are receiving, how their travel skills have changed since training began, the challenges they have experienced during training, and how they dealt with the challenges.

2. Observe an O&M specialist teaching lessons to children of various ages and with different needs (such as infants and elementary school children with visual impairments and additional disabilities). Share your observations and questions with your classmates and college instruc-

tor and telephone the O&M specialist to gather any additional information that is needed.

3. Interview a teacher of children with visual impairments and an O&M specialist to identify how they assess children and develop instructional programs. Note the similarities and differences.

4. Obtain sample O&M goals and objectives from O&M specialists. State the different roles and responsibilities the teacher of children with visual impairments and the O&M specialist would have in providing instruction to assist a child to meet these goals and objectives.

5. Pair up with a classmate. Take turns using a blindfold or low vision simulator to practice basic O&M skills. The "nondisabled" classmate is responsible for ensuring the safety of the individual who is wearing the blindfold or low vision simulator. Keep a journal about your experiences and attitudes and share these reflections with your classmates.

6. Develop an in-service training package for parents, general education teachers, or people in the community on the importance of O&M training for the independence of children with visual impairments.

REFERENCES

Banja, J. D. (1994). The determination of risks in orientation and mobility services. Ethical and professional practices. *Journal of Visual Impairment & Blindness, 88,* 401–410.

Blakely, K., Lang, M. A., & Hart, R. (1991). *Getting in touch with play: Creating play environments for children with visual impairments.* New York: The Lighthouse.

Blasch, B., Wiener, W., & Welsh, R. (Eds.). (1997). *Foundations of orientation and mobility* (2nd ed.). New York: AFB Press.

Brothers, R. J., & Huff, R. (1975). *Sound localization. Suggested activities for the development of sound lo-*

calization skills. Louisville, KY: American Printing House for the Blind.

Brown, D., Simmons, V., & Methvin, J. (1991). *The Oregon Project for Visually Impaired and Blind Preschool Children.* (Available from Jackson Service Center, 101 North Grape Street, Medford, OR 97501.)

Carruthers, A., & North, J. (1989). Towards general competence. *Conference Papers: Australian Early Intervention Association Seventh Annual Conference.* (pp. 5–61). Sydney, Australia: Sydney University.

Caton, H. R. (1980). *The tactile test of basic concepts.* Louisville, KY: American Printing House for the Blind.

Corn, A., Hatlen, P., Huebner, K., Ryan, F., & Siller, M. A., (1995). *The national agenda for the education of children and youths with visual impairments, including those with multiple disabilities.* New York: AFB Press.

Cratty B. J., & Sams, T. A. (1968). *The body image of blind children.* New York: American Foundation for the Blind.

Dauterman, W. L. (1972). *Manual for the Stanford Multimodality Imagery Test.* New York: American Foundation for the Blind.

Davies, J. (1989–90). *Assessing infants who are visually impaired or deaf-blind for functional vision and orientation and mobility.* San Diego, CA: Programs for the Visually Impaired.

Dodson-Burke, B., & Hill, E. W. (1989a). *An orientation and mobility primer for families and young children.* New York: American Foundation for the Blind.

Dodson-Burke, B., & Hill, E. W. (1989b). *Preschool orientation and mobility screening.* Alexandria, VA: Association for the Education and Rehabilitation of the Blind and Visually Impaired, Division IX.

Engelmann, S. E. (1967). *The basic concept inventory.* Chicago: Follett Educational Corp.

Foy, C. J. (1991). *English/Spanish basics for orientation and mobility instructors.* New York: American Foundation for the Blind.

Huebner, K. M., Joffee, E., Prickett, J. G., & Welch, T. R. (1995). *Hand in Hand: Essentials of communication and orientation and mobility for your students who are deaf-blind* (2 vols.). New York: AFB Press.

Hill, E. W. (1981) *The Hill Performance Test of Positional Concepts.* Chicago: Stoelting.

Hill, E. W. (1986). Orientation and mobility. In G. T. Scholl (Ed.), *Foundations of education for blind and visually handicapped children and youth* (pp. 315–340). New York: American Foundation for the Blind.

Hill, E. W., & Ponder, P. (1976). *Orientation and mobility techniques: A guide for the practitioner.* New York: American Foundation for the Blind.

Individuals with Disabilities Education Act Amendments of 1997, Section 602 (22).

Jacobson, W. H. (1993). *Art and science of teaching orientation and mobility to persons with visual impairments.* New York: AFB Press.

Lang, M. A., & Dietz, S. (1990). Creating environments that facilitate independence: The hidden dependency trap. *Children's Environments Quarterly* 7(3), 2–6.

Leary, B., & von Schneden, M. (1982). *"Simon says" is not the only game.* New York: American Foundation for the Blind.

Levine, L. M. (1990). *Child's play: From birth to age 3.* San Antonio, TX: Communication Skill Builders.

Lydon, W., & McGraw, L. (1973). *Concept development for visually impaired children.* New York: American Foundation for the Blind.

Marsh, R. A. (1995). *Legal implications of providing orientation and mobility to school children in the state of Texas.* Unpublished manuscript.

North, J. (1992). Play for children with sensory disabilities. *Conference Proceedings of the Royal Australian Institute of Parks and Recreation,* (pp. 87–93). Sydney: Royal Australian Institute of Parks and Recreation.

Pava, W. S., Bateman, P., Appleton, M. K., & Glascock, J. (1991). Self-defense training for visually impaired women. *Journal of Visual Impairment & Blindness, 85,* 397–401.

Pogrund, R., Healy, G., Jones, K., Levack, N., Martin-Curry, S., Martinez, C., Marz, J., Roberson-Smith, B., & Vrba, A. (1995). *TAPS—Teaching age-appropriate purposeful skills: An orientation and mobility curriculum for students with visual impairments* (2nd ed.). Austin: Texas School for the Blind and Visually Impaired.

Rettig, M. (1994). The play of young children with visual impairments: Characteristics and interventions. *Journal of Visual Impairment & Blindness, 88,* 410–420.

Sauerburger, D. (1993). *Independence without sight or sound: Suggestions for practitioners working with deaf-blind adults.* New York: American Foundation for the Blind.

Schneekloth, L. (1981). *Play environments for handicapped children: Design guidelines.* Buffalo: State University of New York.

The seven-minute lesson [Video]. (1978). New York: American Foundation for the Blind.

Simmons, S. (1996, January). Personal communication.

Smith, M., & Levack, N. (1996). *Teaching students with visual and multiple impairments: A resource guide.* Austin: Texas School for the Blind and Visually Impaired.

Turnbull, A., Turnbull, R., Shank, M., & Leal, D. (1999). *Exceptional lives.* Upper Saddle River, NJ: Prentice Hall.

Tuttle, D. W., & Tuttle, N. R. (1996). *Self-esteem and adjusting with blindness* (2nd ed.). Springfield, IL: Charles C Thomas.

Uriegas, O. (1996). *Infant and toddler orientation and mobility around the house.* (Available from Region XI Education Service Center, 3001 North Freeway, Fort Worth, TX 76106.)

What do you do when you see a blind person? [Video]. (1971). New York: American Foundation for the Blind.

Welch, T. R. (1995). *Hand in Hand: It Can Be Done* [Video]. New York: AFB Press.

Welsh, R. L., & Blasch, B. B. (1987). *Foundations of orientation and mobility.* New York: American Foundation for the Blind.

Designing Play Environments

Schneekloth (1989, p. 201) stated that play environments that are appropriately designed for children with visual impairments need to be "accessible, safe, exciting and complex." However, the desire to make play areas accessible and safe sometimes eliminates the challenges that make the areas exciting and complex. "Although intended to facilitate independence and development, adaptations can create huge barriers because they nurture dependent behavior" (Lang & Dietz, 1990, p. 4). The challenge is to design play environments (whether a school playground or a child's backyard) that provide interactions with the environments, through natural or planned opportunities, that sustain and/or elaborate on a child's behavior (Carruthers & North, 1989) yet are safe and accessible. For children with low vision, color, contrast, and lighting are crucial for learning concepts and encouraging independent mobility. In addition, a variety of play spaces need to be available: "active areas, quiet areas, pathway, enclosed spaces, open spaces, well-defined areas and those that lack definition" (North, 1992, p. 87). The following guidelines need to be considered in designing these play spaces. The suggestions are from Schneekloth (1989) and Blakely, Lang, and Hart (1991), and the examples are from playgrounds designed for the Royal New South Wales Institute for Deaf and Blind Children under the supervision of Jan North.

Design Element	Considerations	Example
Child scale	The sizes of the children who will use the play area must be considered, so the area can be used safely. Older and younger children can be separated by creating play areas with developmentally appropriate activities and equipment. The design of the equipment should be flexible to allow for the changing needs of children. Different standards of leg length, arm length, stepping height, and crawl-over height are required to adapt equipment for comfortable use by young children.	Use swing sets that have replaceable swings for children of different sizes and physical needs, rather than fixed swings of one size. Design spacing on ladder steps to fit the children who will use the equipment.
Understandable order	Organize play structures and equipment to create a unified play space. Make a consistent plan for the use of colors, textures, sound devices, and structures. Design or designate a particular landmark in each play section that will help children identify an activity area. Provide distinctive boundaries for each area. Provide storage areas with ample space for loose materials.	Use different textures in a path to indicate specific play areas. Design circular play-area paths, so that each section leads to another and back to the beginning of the path, with no need to backtrack to get to another area.

(continued on next page)

Appendix: Guidelines for Designing Play Environments

Designing Play Environments *(Continued)*

Design Element	Considerations	Example
Circulation	Place play areas in relation to one another in such a manner as to permit the easy flow of movement between sections. Include circulation paths that run around, rather than through, the different play areas. Recess large stationary objects.	At the bottom of a slide, provide options of routes and methods to return to the top of the slide or to move on to other equipment, rather than isolate the equipment. Have paths go around trees.
Graduated challenges	Offer a variety of ways to gain access to equipment for more complex play behaviors and to promote various levels of mastery.	Ladders, ropes, tunnels, ramps to the tops of slides offer variety of challenges.
Safe fall areas	Provide impact-absorbent surfaces for equipment that will permit children to run, step up, and climb without being injured. These surfaces will maximize safety and foster greater confidence for risk taking.	Soft-fall materials (such as rubber and bark mulch) under climbing equipment minimize injuries if children fall.
Safe paths	Create barriers around swings, slides, ropes, and other equipment that propels children in space, so the children will not wander in front of them.	Hedges planted in front of swings keep children from running in front of others who are swinging.
Defined boundaries	Use different ground coverings to provide information about children's location on the playground, as well as to help with the transitions from one activity to another. Indicate changes in elevation visually and tactilely.	Use a grassy area for running with a gravel path defining the edge of the area and aromatic plants surrounding the sand-play area. Place textured rubber tiles in contrasting color on the edges of steps.
Adventure	Provide a variety of surface textures, including raw materials like sand or mud, and water-play areas. Include facilities where the staff and children can take care of animals.	Provide an area for digging in dirt, as well as in sand. Include a water source for experimenting with wet and dry substances.
Running space	Include open spaces, both flat areas and hills and mounds, that eliminate obstacles or barriers. Use soft ground coverings. Provide boundaries that enclose the area and keep moving objects from escaping.	Use a large, open grassy area bordered with soft hedges to stop balls and make them easily retrievable.
Real-world objects	Cultivate plants and shrubbery with different fragrances and textures. Natural land formations provide a range of experiences.	Plant a small garden or orchard.

(continued on next page)

Designing Play Environments *(Continued)*

Design Element	Considerations	Example
Variety of configurations (alone, small-group, large-group)	Provide a small, shaded semi-enclosed space to which a child can retreat and watch or listen but that gives adults a partial view of the child.	Provide a small partially enclosed area with a bench for one or more children to gather. Provide tables and benches in shaded areas for rest.
Variety of spatial experiences	Create structures that permit opportunities for children to experience their bodies in different types of spaces.	Provide small and large spaces with different materials. Include climbing areas and a slide that is surrounded with scented plants.
Variety of textures	Create structures of different sizes and shapes that stimulate all the senses and encourage exploration.	Use different shapes and colors in play areas to define the areas. For example, outline the sand-play area with contrasting rocks.
Sound	Design the area to reduce ambient sound that may interfere with the use of sound for orientation. Components that produce sounds when children interact with them allow children to locate and encourage them to play with objects.	A hedge or wall blocks traffic noise. Animal noises indicate the location of the animal enclosure.
Indoor and outdoor	Design both shaded areas and sunny spaces. If possible, provide a contiguous indoor play space to which children can retreat in cold or inclement weather.	A shaded porch leads to the outdoor play area.

PAT KELLEY
Texas Tech University
Lubbock, TX

Strategies for Teaching O&M Skills to Students with Visual Impairments and Additional Disabilities

For students with visual impairments and additional disabilities, instruction in O&M encompasses the same basic components as for students with only visual impairments. The O&M specialist may have to design and adapt assistive devices to meet the students' unique O&M needs and work closely with physical and occupational therapists to ensure consistency in instructional expectations, to become familiar with adaptive positioning and mobility equipment, and to learn how to design equipment that provides the necessary stability for effective mobility.

ASSESSMENT

The assessment of these students must incorporate an analysis of the environments in which the students function and in which they are anticipated to function during the school year, including the school, areas in which field trips are scheduled, community-based instructional settings, and vocational training settings. The manner in which many of these students travel is dependent on the nature of the activity associated with each instructional setting, as well as the structure and arrangement of the context and composition of surface areas. The O&M specialist should lead the educational team in determining when a student may need to use a less sophisticated form of travel to ensure safety and efficiency when moving in a busy hallway; climbing up and down steps; traveling on sand, grass, or dirt; or traveling in emergency situations, such as during fire or tornado drills.

USE OF SENSORY INFORMATION

Developing and expanding the use of vision, hearing, touch, and smell must be integrated into meaningful routines to encourage the use of senses for identifying locations and guiding movement to accomplish a needed function. For example, a student can be taught to scan for light streaming through an open door as he or she moves along a hallway to locate the gymnasium or to move toward the smell of food being prepared for lunch to locate the cafeteria. Consistently pairing concepts of, for example, stop and listen, communicates that the student needs to respond to noise by waiting until he or she can identify where he or she is and when it is safe to move. Since many students with visual impairments and additional disabilities cannot do two things at once, these directions need to be emphasized separately but tangentially within the sequential context of an activity. In addition, instruction in tactile scanning should be embedded within trailing lessons so when the student encounters a different texture or object, he or she can make the appropriate decision about how to proceed. Because routines build anticipation, memory, and initiation skills, routes, cues, prompts, and directing attention to natural contextual cues must be consistent and repeated often. Regardless of their level of ability, students with visual impairments and additional disabilities can develop some degree of motor memory.

Teaching a student to use naturally occurring sounds to direct his or her movement will facilitate generalization to similar contexts. For example, a student may be encouraged to move from the toilet toward the sound of water running in a sink, rather than to the voice commands of the instructor, or to orient to a pool area by listening for the sound of splashing water and the vibrations of the diving board (as well as the smell of chlorine). In addition, young children whose movement is severely limited should be encouraged to localize to the sound of a favorite toy to initiate rolling over to find and retrieve it or to pull themselves short distances when they hear the sound of crackers being opened for a snack.

(continued on next page)

If a student moves about in an electric wheelchair, the O&M specialist needs to teach orientation to auditory and visual cues simultaneously with operating the directional controls of the wheelchair. The student can be taught to use peripheral vision to take note of changing colors in the hallway or the bright orange cones in the parking lot to anticipate that he or she needs to stop the wheelchair, to turn the wheelchair to the left or approaching an intersection in the hallway to go to the lunchroom, or to go straight to move toward the sound of telephones and copying machines in the school office.

O&M TECHNIQUES

The O&M specialist needs to recruit guides with as many different body types as possible when teaching a student the sighted guide technique. When a classmate's, sibling's, or teacher's height and weight are different from that of the O&M specialist, some students balk and cannot follow the lead of the sighted guide. Thus, it is important to use a number of people to show the student how to adjust when walking with a younger, smaller child or a taller, heavier person. Repeated trials with a variety of people will help the student learn the appropriate grasp to use with a person who is not familiar with the sighted guide technique. The O&M specialist may need to consult with a physical therapist or an occupational therapist to adapt a modified sighted guide technique for a student in a gait trainer.

Students with low postural tone may lack sufficient shoulder girdle stability to use the standard trailing technique. These students should be taught to trail either by facing the wall and maintaining contact with both palms against the surface and sidestepping or by rotating the arm outward so the palm and forearm maintain contact with the wall and they walk forward; this arm position naturally encourages upright posture. The O&M specialist may need to help the students monitor the environment for safety as they travel. Students in wheelchairs and gait trainers need to be taught to trail in a modified manner if they are independent travelers.

A critical role of the O&M specialist working in programs that serve a number of students who require special equipment, such as wheelchairs and mobility devices, is working with the administrative staff to determine where to store equipment when not in use in a location other than hallways where the students must travel. Although it can be beneficial to encounter some hazards along the way, when the entire hallway is lined with wheelchairs and other equipment—obstacles that are not encountered in more typical environments—a student's route is interrupted too frequently.

A student's first premobility device may be a tricycle, a Cozy Coupe, a walking toy, or a push toy, such as the Fisher Price Cornpopper or a toy vacuum cleaner or lawn mower. For a student who is still learning to grade his or her gait, these devices may be weighted with another child, when appropriate, or with sandbags. An older child may hold on to the back of a wooden chair and push it, and an older student with a traumatic brain injury can readily learn to push a shopping cart in the appropriate contexts.

Many students who lack the cognitive skill and/or balance to use a standard cane are successful with one of the many variations of precanes constructed from PVC pipe. The rectangular form of the devices encourages bilateral function and alignment of the student's body, particularly for a student who has a weaker side. A student with additional disabilities, such as an orthopedic problem, may temporarily use a precane that is similar to a walker until he or she develops sufficient balance and confidence to use a more streamlined model.

M. BETH LANGLEY
Pinellas County Schools
St. Petersburg, FL

RESOURCES

Suggested Resources for Teaching Orientation and Mobility

Resource	Type	Source	Description
Art and Science of Teaching Orientation and Mobility to Persons with Visual Impairments (Jacobson, 1993)	Book	AFB Press	A text on O&M. Unit 1 covers basic skills, such as environmental and spatial concepts, traversing familiar indoor environments, and walking with a sighted guide. Unit 2 discusses how the O&M instructor teaches the use of the cane in various familiar and unfamiliar indoor and outdoor settings.
Canes, low vision aids, independent living equipment	Equipment	Anne Morris Enterprises LS&S Group Lighthouse International	Teaching supplies, games, toys, and other products used by persons who are blind or visually impaired.
Concept Development for Visually Impaired Children (Lydon & McGraw, 1973)	Book	American Foundation for the Blind	A text on the development of basic concepts and methods of teaching. Addresses the importance of concept development, children who are blind and have additional disabilities, the body image of blind children and screening, room orientation, and more.
English/Spanish Basics for Orientation and Mobility Instructors (Foy, 1991)	Book	American Foundation for the Blind	A teaching aid for O&M instructors that includes vocabulary they may need to teach students in Spanish.
Foundations of Orientation and Mobility, 2nd ed. (Blasch, Wiener, & Welsh, 1997)	Book	AFB Press	A comprehensive textbook on O&M: origins, history, and present state of the field. Covers the field *(continued on next page)*

Suggested Resources *(Continued)*

Resource	Type	Source	Description
			in depth, with much background information and its relevance to O&M instructors.
Getting in Touch with Play: Creating Play Environments for Children with Visual Impairments (Blakely, Lang, & Hart, 1991)	Book	Lighthouse International	A book about creating play environments for students with visual impairments.
Hand in Hand: Essentials of Communication and Orientation and Mobility for Your Students Who Are Deaf-Blind (Heubner, Joffee, Prickett, & Welch, 1995)	Book	AFB Press	A textbook on development, education, and transition to adult life of students with deaf-blindness. Addresses O&M skills and strategies for teaching. Provides a list of resources.
Hand in Hand: It Can Be Done (Welch, 1995)	Videotape	AFB Press	Part of a package created by the AFB Deaf-Blind Project; designed to develop resources for educators of children who have both visual and hearing impairments. Emphasis on the communication and mobility skills crucial to independence.
Independence Without Sight or Sound: Suggestions for Practitioners Working with Deaf-Blind Adults (Sauerburger, 1993)	Book	American Foundation for the Blind	A book about methods and techniques for teaching people with deaf-blindness, as well as an integrated study of their needs. Presents numerous examples from actual experience and discussions of practical applications. Includes sections on O&M training, street crossings, and teaching O&M to people with limited language skills, communication with strangers and the public, and a survey of dog guide schools.
Infant and Toddler Orientation and Mobility Around the House (Uriegas, 1996)	Book	Region XI Education Service Center, Fort Worth, Texas	Information on O&M for young children.
Oregon Project for Visually Impaired Children (Brown, Simmons, & Methvin, 1991)	Assessment instrument	Jackson Service Center, Medford, Oregon	An instrument for assessing the overall development of children with visual impairments. Addresses early development of O&M skills, among others.
An Orientation and Mobility Primer for Families and Young Children (Dodson-Burke & Hill, 1989a)	Book	American Foundation for the Blind	A book explaining the basics of O&M to families of children with visual impairments.

(continued on next page)

Suggested Resources *(Continued)*

Resource	Type	Source	Description
Orientation and Mobility Techniques: A Guide for the Practitioner (Hill & Ponder, 1976)	Book	American Foundation for the Blind	A textbook on teaching techniques for the O&M practitioner. Some sections are useful for sharing with regular education teachers, rehabilitation teachers, and other professionals.
The Seven-Minute Lesson (1978)	Videotape	American Foundation for the Blind	A brief introduction to the basic techniques used by a sighted guide for a person who is visually impaired.
"Simon Says" Is Not the Only Game (Leary & von Schneden, 1982)	Book	American Foundation for the Blind	A compilation of activities that teach various concepts necessary for traveling without vision, among them body awareness, body planes and parts, and laterality and directionality.
TAPS—Teaching Age-Appropriate Purposeful Skills: An Orientation and Mobility Curriculum for Students with Visual Impairments (2nd ed.) (Pogrund et al., 1995)	Book	Texas School for the Blind and Visually Impaired	Curriculum for students aged 3–21 who are blind or have low vision; also appropriate for students with additional disabilities. Can be used in all settings. Screening instrument, comprehensive assessment and ongoing evaluation, functional mobility tasks, educational goals and objectives, teaching strategies.
Videotape Series: 1. *Seeing Things in a New Way* 2. *Learning About the World* (concept development) 3. *Becoming a Can-Do Kid* (self-help) 4. *Making Friends* (social and play) 5. *Going Places* (O&M)	Videotape	Visually Impaired Preschool Services	A series of videotapes on various aspects of the early development of preschoolers who have visual impairments.
What Do You Do When You See a Blind Person? (1971)	Videotape	American Foundation for the Blind	A humorous look at myths and misconceptions about people who are blind. Illustrates that courtesy and common sense generally provide the answers.

Contact information for each of the resources listed will be found in the Sources of Products, Materials, Equipment, and Services section at the back of this book.

CHAPTER 16

Independent Living Skills

Pat Kelley and Pat Smith

KEY POINTS

◆ Independent living skills encompass a broad range of activities and skills and are key components of the expanded core curriculum for students with visual impairments.

◆ Each family has its own expectations and values related to a child's independent living skills that must be considered when planning instruction.

◆ The teacher of students with visual impairments provides direct instruction and collaborative consultation to ensure that students develop independent living skills.

◆ Independent living skills are best assessed and taught in natural environments within functional, daily routines.

◆ Students with visual impairments use a variety of techniques to perform various independent living skills; each student has the right to choose the strategy that works best and that he or she prefers.

VIGNETTE

Coming out of the boys' restroom, Eric spotted Ms. Donne. "It works!" he exclaimed. Eric was a first-grade student with low vision and mild motor prob-lems. Until two weeks ago, he had been unable to zip his jeans independently. That was when Ms. Donne, his teacher of students with visual impairments, had talked with his parents about using zipper pulls after she saw a set of zipper pulls decorated with colorful plastic dinosaurs in a catalog. These zipper pulls were too expensive for the parents to buy, but they gave Ms. Donne the idea of simply putting the metal ring from an inexpensive key ring through the hole in the zipper tab of each pair of Eric's jeans. Eric's mother even found brass rings to match the brass zippers. Now it was easy for Eric to grip the ring and zip his jeans.

"Hi, Mr. Getz!" said 10-year-old Elaine, as the little bell on the door jingled behind her. With her cane, Elaine quickly maneuvered around the table and chairs by the front window and located the display case. This bakery smelled better than anyplace else in the world!

Mr. Getz gave her his usual warm greeting and asked, "And what do you want today?"

"Have you got any thumbprint cookies?" Elaine asked. Mr. Getz said that he did, and Elaine asked for a dozen. She carefully located two dollar bills in her wallet and paid for the cookies and then counted the change Mr. Getz gave her—a quarter and a dime—and placed it in the wallet pocket. Elaine knew, and Mr. Getz probably knew, that her mother was waiting outside in the car for her, but she really liked coming into the bakery and making purchases by herself.

Mike flipped to the third section of his braille card file: *Agencies.* The other sections contained telephone numbers and addresses of friends and relatives. This section held addresses and telephone numbers for all sorts of organizations and companies, from the corporation that sold (and warranted) his talking alarm clock to the local movie theater. Today he needed the telephone number of the state library for the blind. He would call and request a braille copy of *The Sword in the Stone* (by T. H. White), a book he hoped to read to satisfy a 12th grade English requirement.

Ms. Giacomo and her tenth-grade home economics students were in the kitchen making soup, and Mr. Springer, the teacher of students with visual impairments, had joined them. Kia had read the recipe, using the closed-circuit television (CCTV). She had gathered implements and scrubbed the carrots and celery confidently, but now she hesitated before the cutting board and knife. At home, her mother would hardly let her in the kitchen, but in school, Kia and Mr. Springer had practiced with a knife and softer items several times. Under Mr. Springer's encouragement, Kia felt the first carrot. Suddenly, she decided this was not such a big deal after all; she could feel the end of the carrot perfectly well. Carefully, she placed the knife half an inch down from the end. She steadied the carrot with her left hand, made sure her fingers were out of the way, and cut. Discarding the cut end, Kia smiled. Just wait until she told her mother she had sliced carrots!

INTRODUCTION

The term *independent living skills* is a broad label that encompasses every skill that an individual needs to have at some time in his or her life to be as independent as possible (Hatlen, 1996), as illustrated in the vignettes at the beginning of this chapter. These activities are often referred to as *activities of daily living, daily living skills, adapted living skills, functional skills,* or *life skills,* but each of these terms is descriptive of only a portion of the overall concept of independent living skills, so the more global term is used in this chapter. Indepen-

dent living skills may include other categories of skills, such as academic skills or orientation and mobility (O&M), since all these skills overlap and support other areas. Independence is the ability to make informed choices and the knowledge and skills to act on those choices successfully.

The term *independent living skills* is so broad that it is impossible to cover the topic comprehensively in one chapter; entire books and volumes of books have been written on this subject. Therefore, this chapter presents a brief overview of issues related to the instruction of independent living skills and offers selected suggestions on particular areas of concern. The level of competence achieved in any given skill may be largely determined by an individual's abilities. Since the population of students with visual impairments is heterogeneous, all levels of skill cannot be addressed within one chapter. Thus, suggestions included here are targeted for students who have no disabilities in addition to their visual impairment and are of elementary school age.

Generally, independent living skills are divided into five categories: personal management, home management, communication, leisure and recreation, and O&M. Since communication, O&M, and leisure and recreational skills are addressed in other chapters of this book (see Chapters 8, 15, and 18, respectively), this chapter concentrates on the categories of personal management and home management. Personal management includes eating, grooming, hygiene, the care and identification of clothing, medical care and management, the identification and management of money, and telling time and time management. Home management includes food and diet management, cleaning, basic household repairs, measurement, shopping, and gardening.

Children who are sighted typically learn what to do and how to act by watching their parents and others and then imitating what they observe. For example, by watching others eat and then imitating motions and manners, they learn the socially acceptable eating skills used in their particular culture. However, children with visual impairments must learn these skills without the benefit of observing others and learning from their behaviors. Since visual imitation is restricted for these children, it must be supplemented or replaced by other sources of information (Barraga, 1986; Warren, 1994).

Teachers of students with visual impairments and the students' parents need to be actively involved in the instruction of independent living skills using a variety of multisensory approaches, primarily direct instruction using both physical and verbal prompts. Instruction should foster independence; ensure safety; encourage efficiency; use real experiences and materials; be age appropriate; and respect a student's abilities, differences, and privacy (Loumiet & Levack, 1991).

This chapter begins by describing the role of the teacher of students with visual impairments in providing instruction in independent living skills and then presents a number of issues related to this area of the expanded core curriculum (see Chapter 6 for a discussion of the expanded core curriculum). Next, suggestions are offered for assessing independent living skills, followed by suggestions for teaching these skills to students with visual impairments.

ROLE OF THE TEACHER OF STUDENTS WITH VISUAL IMPAIRMENTS

As was mentioned earlier, independent living skills are typically learned incidentally through visual observation and modeling. Since students with visual impairments frequently miss such opportunities, the area of daily living skills is considered part of the expanded core curriculum, and the teacher of students with visual impairments has the responsibility for ensuring that independent living skills are taught. The specialist's role is to do the following:

◆ Conduct assessments of independent living skills to determine skill areas that need to be included in a student's Individualized Education Program (IEP);

◆ Collaborate with a student's parents and other caregivers, other specialists, and general education teachers to develop strategies for teaching independent living skills;

◆ Provide direct instruction in independent living skills in natural environments as specified in a student's IEP;

◆ Gather resources and adapted materials for teaching independent living skills to share with the parents and other members of the student's educational team; and

◆ Explore and plan additional opportunities to expand a student's opportunities for instruction in independent living skills, such as home-based instruction and attendance at a summer camp.

The teacher also plays an essential role in working with students with additional disabilities; strategies focusing on students with visual impairments and additional disabilities and resources for teachers appear later in this chapter.

ISSUES RELATED TO INSTRUCTION

Including Independent Living Skills in the Curriculum

Periodically, school administrators question the practice of including independent living skills in the curriculum of students with visual impairments, since these skills are not generally part of the curriculum of sighted students. However, these skills are considered part of the expanded core curriculum (see Chapter 6) and should be included in the IEPs of students who are visually impaired because, as Rosen (1993, p. 18) noted:

Life skills are as important as academic skills in preparing children and youth with visual handicaps for future employment, social integration and participation in the community. The ability to perform life skills as independently as possible also enhances self-esteem and feelings of self-worth that are central to the psychosocial development of children with visual handicaps.

In a study of adults with visual impairments, Beach, Robinet and Hakim-Larson (1995, p. 536) found that "higher self-esteem is significantly related to lower levels of dependence on others in performing daily living skills."

In a position statement ratified by the Division on Visual Impairments of the Council for Exceptional Children, Spungin and Ferrell (1992) indicated that to ensure that children with visual impairments have access to any area of the curriculum, the teacher of students with visual impairments is responsible for providing direct or collaborative instruction in 21 areas, including activities of daily living. Furthermore, the standards for the preparation and licensure of special educators (Council for Exceptional Children, 1998, p. 78) states that teachers of students with visual impairments should have knowledge of "methods to develop social and daily living skills that are normally learned or reinforced by visual means" and "functional life skills instruction relevant to independent, community, and personal living and employment for individuals with visual impairments."

The *Functional Academic Curriculum for Exceptional Students, Revised* (FACES), developed for students with developmental disabilities (Cardwell et al., 1998), includes independent living skills in respective parts of its academics curriculum. That is, the skills of meal preparation, clothing care, housekeeping, calendar, plant life, temperature, body parts, and animal life are part of the science curriculum; feeding, toileting, dressing, grooming, safety, nutrition, wellness, self-concept, ecology, and human growth and development are part of the health curriculum; and numeration, time, measurement, money, and computation are part of the mathematics curriculum. Tying independent living skills to academic subjects can help justify use of academic time to teach these skills.

For children with low vision or those with low vision and additional disabilities, one skill area that can be identified as being clearly within the expanded care curriculum is the efficient use of vision. Downing and Bailey (1990) and Goetz and Gee (1987) demonstrated that the goals for using vision are best learned by integrating them into a natural routine of functional activities that are meaningful and age appropriate, encourage a student to participate, and provide reinforcement and regular practice.

It is important for a teacher of students with visual impairments to be able to explain clearly and justify the inclusion of independent living skills instruction in a student's IEP. To do so, the specialist must demonstrate the student's need for independent living skills by assessing the student's abilities in this area, as discussed in a later section. In addition, with the greater emphasis on planning for transitions, the need for independent living skills can become an integral part of the transition plans for most students.

Committing Instructional Time

Although teachers, parents, students, and administrators may recognize the need for instruction in independent living skills, the demands of academic instruction often leave little time to address these skills. When the majority of students with visual impairments attended residential schools, specialized teachers addressed these issues in the dormitories and in home management or vocational classes. As more and more students were included in general education settings, the opportunities for instruction throughout the student's day (from dawn to dark) were reduced, and much of the specialized expertise was lost as teachers retired and the focus of instruction shifted to academics. As Hatlen (1990, p. 80) commented, "By the late 1960's this nation began graduating from high school a generation of youth with visual impairments who had spent every school day of their young lives with sighted classmates"; these students "could solve binomial equations but not make change for a dollar." Now there is a trend toward including instruction in areas of the expanded core curriculum, including independent living skills, for students with visual impairments in general education settings.

Suvak (1999), found that teachers of students with visual impairments in Colorado spent a mean of 5.8 hours per month providing instruction in daily living skills: 13 hours for students in residential settings, 5.4 hours for students attending general education classes part time, and 4.37 hours for students attending general education classes full time. Thus, students in residential settings continue to receive far more instruction in independent living skills than do those in local public schools. In order to make sure that students have adequate independent living skills, teachers of students with visual impairments in general education settings need to devote more time to these skills. This is especially true for older students who generally take greater responsibility for these activities (Curry & Hatlen, 1988).

Teachers can assist parents in teaching these skills to young children, and some older students take home economics courses in the general curriculum. In some school systems, special classes on independent living skills for students with visual impairments can be arranged for high school credit. Since independent living skills need to be taught at the time they are used, other options for scheduling instruction in independent living skills should be considered. For instance, eating skills can be taught at lunchtime, and dressing skills can be taught in physical education classes.

Creative scheduling before or after school can give the teacher of students with visual impairments time to teach personal or household management skills in a student's home. Teachers' unions in some states have regulations about work hours and times that need to be considered when developing alternative scheduling options for teaching independent living skills. Summer camps at residential schools or other camp programs (such as the Boy Scouts and Girl Scouts) offer opportunities for instruction in a wide range of independent living skills. In some states, rehabilitation teachers employed by state agencies provide instruction during nonschool hours.

Using Appropriate Facilities

Because independent living skills should be taught in natural environments, the school and classroom are often inappropriate for teaching these skills. For example, a cafeteria-style kitchen or a lounge area in a school may have the equipment (such as a refrigerator and microwave oven) necessary to prepare a meal, but such areas do not have the same equipment and arrangements as those of a kitchen in a student's home. Likewise, setting the table in a cafeteria using plastic utensils and trays is not the same as setting the table at home. Thus, instruction may have to take place in the student's home before or after school.

Another option for providing instruction in appropriate facilities is to use the "train-the-trainers" approach, that is, training parents or other caregivers in the methods of teaching independent living skills to students with visual impairments, as discussed later in this chapter. These individuals then take on the primary role of instructors of these skills.

Reviewing Sensitive Areas of Instruction

Many areas of personal management (such as hygiene) need to be treated sensitively. The teacher of students with visual impairments must be aware of this issue and of students' cultural or family values that are relevant to this area of instruction and find creative solutions to dealing with these skills. Bathing, toilet training, shaving, and feminine hygiene often are difficult topics to approach and may best be addressed by parents with the specialist's assistance with instructional strategies. Often these topics are too sensitive for parents to discuss in a large group meeting, so details need to be discussed in private before an IEP meeting. Instruction in such areas may be improved by consultation with and assistance from the school nurse or sex education, home economics, or health teachers.

Attending to Cultural Considerations

Cultural diversity has an impact on all areas of independent living skills. For example, people from some cultures eat the majority of foods with their fingers, and in many Muslim cultures, males and females never touch each other. Therefore, the teacher must be careful about how he or she approaches instruction.

Cultural or family values regarding independence must also be considered. Lowrey (1987) outlined the differences between the values and components that underlie the field of rehabilitation and the cultural values of the Navaho people. Whereas the notion of rehabilitation tends to emphasize individual responsibility, concern for the future, individualized services, and a sequential approach, the Navaho culture values interdependence, concern for the present, community services, and a nonsequential approach. Lowrey noted the following for many students who are visually impaired from a Navaho background: "although their home may have no indoor plumbing and heating and cooking may be done with wood, they will be taught daily living and mobility skills that are relevant to life in a middle-class urban community" (p. 164). As a result, these individuals were not prepared for life at home and became dependent on things like electricity and running water. Such a situation can be avoided by teaching independent living skills in students' natural environments, rather than in school.

A family's expectations for independence are also important in the development of independent living skills. Age, gender, status in the family, the amount of reciprocity in the family, and the degree to which family members are linked all affect such expectations. In a qualitative study of three adolescents, Sacks and Wolffe (1998) found that all three students performed a range of independent living skills that were similar to, but less frequent than, those performed by their sighted peers; however none used a stove or oven without support from an adult.

In a quantitative study that compared students who were blind, those who were sighted, and those with low vision, Wolffe and Sacks (1997) found that the students with visual impairments were more like than different from their sighted peers, with the most obvious differences in the area of home management and the greatest discrepancies in cooking, yard work, and simple clothing repair. Furthermore, students with greater levels of responsibility had greater amounts of vision. In anticipating the time when their children would live independently, the parents of the children with visual impairments thought that their children would always need assistance with household and personal management and transportation in addition to financial assistance. These expectations may be low, given that Ponchillia and Kaarlela's (1986) study of 60 adults with visual impairments found that nearly all participated in personal care and household chores and more than 58 percent prepared hot meals.

Information on cultural and family expectations can be gathered from discussions with the family and representatives of cultural organizations and exploration of the World Wide Web. Such information should then be used when designing instruction in the area of independent living skills.

ASSESSMENT

For instruction in daily living skills to be effective, it is critical that the teacher of students with visual impairments and other members of the educational team conduct thoughtful, ongoing assessments to determine a student's current level of functioning and level of need for specific daily living skills. In conducting these assessments, members of the educational team must carefully consider a variety of issues, such as cultural issues, family concerns and values, developmental readiness, fine and gross motor skills, cognitive ability, responsibility, judgment, and future needs for independent living skills.

The assessment of a student's independent living skills cannot be easily conducted in a school because the natural environment for performing these skills (such as dressing) is the home or the community, not the school. Thus, it is necessary to conduct assessments outside school settings, and members of the student's educational team need to plan assessments carefully, so the student's true levels of skills are apparent. Chapter 3 of this book discusses the development of informal instruments that may be helpful in assessing independent living skills.

Few commercially available assessment instruments focus on independent living skills, although *Independent Living: A Curriculum with Adaptations for Students with Visual Impairments, Vol. 1: Social Competence* (Loumiet & Levack, 1991) has an assessment section. Most commercial assessments are checklists of skills and are not normed or validated on students with visual impairments. The *Scales of Independent Behavior* has been adapted for students with visual impairments (Woo & Knowlton, 1992), and the *Instrument to Measure the Activity Level of the Blind (IMALB)* asks the individual to rate the difficulty of the activity, independence, and motivation to learn (Becker, Lambert, Schulz, Wright, & Burnet, 1985).

Many developmental scales address independent living skills in the gross motor and fine motor sections, and some may have self-care sections, but they do not group the skills together. However, it is not always necessary to use an existing assessment instrument; some teachers of students with visual impairments and parents have found that constructing their own assessments is the most helpful. Chapter 6 contains information on the development of a task analysis (a step-by-step list of skills incorporated into an activity) that could be constructed for any independent living skill. The Appendix to this chapter includes a sample checklist for evaluating personal and household management skills.

One useful technique for determining a student's level of functioning in activities of independent living is to conduct a comprehensive analysis of a student's daily schedule or an ecological inventory and, in doing so, examine skills that are developmentally appropriate and a natural part of the student's activities. Such an analysis involves observing the environments in which the activities are performed, identifying usual activities, and observing sighted peers to deter-

mine the skills needed for participation (Chen & Dote-Kwan, 1999; Downing, 1996). The next step is for the teacher of students with visual impairments to conduct a discrepancy analysis of the activities to determine those typically done by children of the same age as the student with a visual impairment and what the student can currently do. Then the specialist determines how the student can accomplish those tasks; the student may simply need an explanation, may need adaptations to methods or materials, or may need assistance.

Another method of assessment may be to interview and observe the student and his or her general education teachers and parents throughout a typical day, listing necessary skills of independent living and the student's competence in performing these skills and rating the student's competence by levels of independence (for example, independent, with minimum assistance, with partial participation, with extensive assistance, unable to complete). An example of a checklist used by an educational team to analyze the skills of an elementary-aged student with low vision for part of a day is presented in Table 16.1.

The educational team needs to discuss the best way to gather this assessment information. Since most of the activities occur naturally in the home environment, the student's parents will provide most of the information on independent living skills. In summary, some strategies for assessment include interviewing parents and students, observing students performing activities, and conducting environmental assessments.

INSTRUCTIONAL STRATEGIES

Once a comprehensive assessment has been conducted, the members of the educational team need to determine appropriate goals and objectives based on the student's current level of functioning and needs. They then have to decide how instruction will be delivered, including when and where it will occur and who will be responsible for delivering it. (See Sidebar 16.1 for suggestions for workshop activities for parents and caregivers.)

Table 16.1. Sample Routine Analysis: A Student's Morning Routine

Activity	Independent	Minimal Assistance	Partial Participation	Extensive Assistance	Unable to Complete
Getting Up in the Morning					
Sets wake-up time on alarm clock the night before (judges the amount of time needed to get ready)					
Turns on the alarm					
Turns off the alarm					
Brushing Teeth					
Identifies toothbrush and toothpaste					
Applies toothpaste to the brush					
Brushes teeth					
Rinses and puts toothbrush and toothpaste away					
Bathing or Showering					
Turns on water					
Adjusts the temperature					
Identifies soaps and shampoo					
Bathes					
Turns off the water and drains the water from the tub if applicable					
Dressing					
Selects appropriate clothing					
Puts clothing on					
Eating breakfast					
Chooses the cereal, bowl, spoon, and glass					
Pours cereal, milk, and juice					
Eats appropriately					
Rinses the bowl, glass, and spoon or places them in the dishwasher					

Suggestions for Workshop Activities for Parents and Caregivers

◆ Assess the needs of individual students in independent living skills so the suggestions made to parents are appropriate for their children.

◆ Incorporate role models who have visual impairments in workshops, so parents can observe people who are visually impaired completing independent living skills using adaptive techniques.

◆ Practice activities with the equipment and materials that most closely approximate what is available in the home environment and is appropriate for the child.

◆ Provide hands-on activities so parents learn adaptive techniques in such areas as eating, labeling clothing, identifying clothing, using search patterns, and locating dropped objects.

Once again, the nature of independent living skills makes these decisions more complex. Some parents are comfortable teaching independent living skills and have a natural ability to adapt activities to meet their child's unique needs. Other parents may be hesitant to teach specific skills and are less comfortable making adjustments to compensate for their child's visual impairment. Still others may be uncomfortable teaching independent living skills and need extensive support and assistance as they work with their child on such activities. Therefore, the specialist must recognize these differences and provide support to parents where and when they need or request it.

Since most parents of children with visual impairments do not have firsthand experience performing independent living skills without vision, a primary responsibility of the teacher of students with visual impairments is to teach the parents alternative techniques for working with their child in this area. This instruction can be done in workshops or one-on-one. As the parents and specialist work together, adaptive techniques of living skills can be incorporated into the instruction when a new skill is introduced.

Sidebar 16.2 lists some basic principles and strategies for teaching independent living skills.

The specialist can apply these fundamental principles and strategies to teaching nearly any independent living skill and can explain the fundamentals to parents to help them teach their child.

The following sections present suggestions for instructional strategies that can be used to teach specific independent living skills to students who are visually impaired. Many independent living skills are first learned when a child is young and then refined as the child grows older. For example, when a child begins to use a spoon, he or she holds it in the fist, and much of the food ends up scattered around the room. As the child grows older, he or she learns to use spoons, knives, and forks correctly and eventually even learns to eat spaghetti without spilling the sauce.

As was mentioned before, independent living skills encompass a wide variety of activities. A number of helpful resources address the many areas more fully (see the Resources), some of which are written with young children or those with additional disabilities in mind and may need to be adapted for older students. As was noted earlier, this chapter focuses on two areas of daily living that commonly pose challenges for students who are visually impaired: personal management and home management. However, since organization

SIDEBAR 16.2

Basic Strategies for Teaching Independent Living Skills

- Start young.
- Simplify tasks initially.
- Teach organizational skills, which are the key to independence in all areas.
- Maintain consistency and routines.
- Provide sequential instruction.
- Use task analysis, backward chaining, and repetition.
- Teach skills in appropriate settings.
- Adjust standards to a child's capability.
- Allow a child time to learn and practice new skills.
- Focus on one specific priority at a time while maintaining other skills.

- Use minimal adaptations to equipment and the environment; it is better to adapt a technique than a piece of equipment.
- Develop a system for identifying or labeling items.
- Share responsibilities between the home and the school.

Source: Adapted from G. Gale, P. d'Apice, K. Freeman, R. Payne, & L. Tierney, "Life Skills," in P. Kelley and G. Gale, Eds., *Towards Excellence: Effective Education for Students with Vision Impairments* (North Rocks, New South Wales, Australia: North Rocks Press, Royal Institute for Deaf and Blind Children, 1998), p. 229.

---

is essential in all areas of life, including personal and home management, it is discussed first.

ORGANIZATION

Organization is key to the development of independent living skills and should be taught from an early age. Unless students have it modeled for or presented directly to them, they may not understand how the world is organized. Since a child with a visual impairment cannot scan a room to locate an object, organization is an essential skill. The following are some suggestions for teaching organizational skills in the home:

- Encourage the student to retrieve and replace toys from the storage area, such as a toy box, starting at an early age. Verbal suggestions may be given on how to organize the toys more safely or efficiently, but the child, not the adult, should be the one to arrange the play area and place materials.

- Teach the student to arrange objects for maximum effectiveness and efficiency. Adequate storage space and consistent locations for items help the student to do so.

- Establish routines within the day (such as consistent meal and sleep times and a routine for bathing and brushing teeth before bedtime).

- Have the student share some responsibilities at home (for example, participating in cleaning, taking out the trash, and setting the table).

Organizational skills extend outside the home. Here are suggestions to give students to help them learn organizational skills in the community:

- Keep a file (notebook or data disk) with information on ordering and repairing materials (like canes, braillers, and adaptive devices).

- Keep a file on important telephone numbers.

- Keep bus and transportation schedules in one place.

- Ask the location and nearest major cross street when calling a business for directions.

- Make a list of needed items before going shopping and take the list to the store.

PERSONAL MANAGEMENT

Hygiene

Personal hygiene and grooming can have a strong impact on a student's social acceptance. Activities in this area, such as bathing and toileting, require sensitivity and respect for privacy, and instruction is often best addressed at a young age. Furthermore, the teacher of students with visual impairments should obtain permission from the student and his or her parents before teaching such skills.

Washing Hands and Body.   A common concern for a student with a visual impairment is how to determine if all parts of the hands or body are clean. For example, ink from a computer printer stays on the hands and has no texture or smell to help the student determine if his or her hands are clean. Therefore, students need to be told that certain materials are difficult to remove from their hands and that extra scrubbing with soap, including under the nails, may be necessary. Hand washing can be addressed during various parts of the school day. Bathing and showering are best addressed by the parents, since initial instruction may require hand-over-hand modeling paired with verbal instruction. The development of a sequence for washing all parts of the body will ensure that all are clean.

Shaving.   For both boys and girls, the need to shave indicates growth into adulthood. Students with visual impairments should have opportunities to examine various products that remove hair (such as electric razors, disposable razors, and cream hair removers) (Loumiet & Levack, 1991). Electric razors are good choices for shaving, since there is no risk of nicks or cuts. Initially, however, the teacher of students with visual impairments can introduce a student to shaving and the use of pattern techniques by using shaving cream and a double-edged razor without a blade to ensure safety. Systematic procedures (such as using overlapping strokes from the top of the cheekbone to the chin or from the ankle to the knee) can help the student cover all the areas.

Feminine Hygiene.   In addition to the usual information young girls need about menstruation, girls with visual impairments require specific instruction in gaining access to information that is normally obtained through sight. For example, a girl with a visual impairment may need instruction in such aspects as these:

- Developing a written system for tracking the sequence of her menstrual periods to be prepared for the onset of the next menstrual cycle;

- Using a sanitary napkin or tampon vending machine;

- Knowing how often to change napkins or tampons; and

- Identifying and removing stains.

It is important to work in tandem with a girl's parent or guardian at home so that all familial concerns regarding feminine hygiene are appropriately addressed, both at home and in school.

Eating Techniques

A person's eating techniques are determined primarily by the person's culture, not necessarily by what is most functional. For example, one of the most inefficient methods of eating is the American style of using just a fork to "chase" food around a plate and keeping the other hand in one's lap. Points to consider when teaching eating skills include the following:

◆ Cultural factors (such as eating style and which items are accepted as finger foods) are important to recognize;

◆ Manners and skills are situational (for example, how one eats in a formal restaurant is different from the way one eats at home when one is alone);

◆ Consistent skills can be learned even for foods that one eats only occasionally (such as learning how to crack crab legs); and

◆ Eating skills improve and expand with age and practice (that is, more refined fine motor development and eye-hand coordination are required for eating with a knife and fork than for scooping with a spoon).

Many of the beginning difficulties in learning to eat independently are common to all children. However, there are also predictable areas of concern for students who are visually impaired, such as those described next.

Locating Food on a Plate. Some foods, such as peas, are more difficult than others to load on a fork or spoon and keep in place. The following are some suggestions that can assist with this skill and make mealtimes less stressful:

◆ Use a placemat of contrasting color to the plate to help a student with low vision locate items on the table.

◆ Use solid color plates to assist a student with low vision in locating food on a plate. Designs on plates can often be mistaken for food.

◆ Teach the student to orient himself or herself to the place setting by using a relaxed hand position with the fingers slightly curled and moving the hand slowly around the place setting.

◆ Provide an orientation to the place setting if the student desires such information. Compass directions; standard clock-face directions; or other directions, such as left and right, near the edge of the table and

away from the edge of the table, can be used to indicate the location of various foods on a plate.

◆ Teach the student to use a buffer or pusher (like a knife, a piece of bread, a carrot, or celery stick) to load the fork.

◆ Prompt the student to keep moving food from the outer edge of the plate to the center to keep him or her from pushing food off the edge of the plate.

Using Condiments. Identifying condiments and controlling the amount used can be difficult for a student with a visual impairment. For example, it is important to be able to determine the difference between salt and pepper shakers and to control the amount applied to food. The following suggestions may be helpful in adapting methods, strategies, or equipment for a student who is visually impaired:

To identify salt and pepper, the student can do as follows:

◆ Smell the shakers to identify the difference, making sure to keep the shakers a discreet distance from the nose to avoid offending other diners.

◆ Use tactile information, such as the tactilely discernible letters *S* and *P* on the tops or sides, if available, to identify the shakers.

◆ Sprinkle a small amount in the palm of the hand and identify the salt or pepper by smell, taste, or touch.

To apply salt and pepper to food, the student can use these techniques:

◆ Locate the position of the food to be seasoned on the plate with the tines of the fork.

◆ Put a small amount of seasoning in the palm of the hand and, with the fingers of the other hand, pinch the seasoning and sprinkle it over the food.

◆ Hold one hand just above the food to be seasoned, with the palm facing down toward the plate and the fingers spread slightly apart. Sprinkle the seasoning over the fingers, feeling the amount of seasoning being added to the food.

To apply sauces, salad dressings, and condiments, the student can do the following:

- Dip a spoon into a wide-mouth container.

- Pump or squeeze a glass or plastic bottle.

- Position the tip of the finger just under the lip of a bottle when pouring. After the desired amount of salad dressing has been poured, discreetly wipe the finger on a napkin in the lap.

Using a Knife. A student with a visual impairment can learn to use a knife safely and effectively. The following are some suggestions for teaching a student how to use adaptive methods for cutting:

- Have a young student practice cutting a banana or other soft substances with a plastic knife.

- Use children's safety knives and similar pumpkin-carving knives to teach cutting techniques.

- Teach the student to grasp the handle of the knife, so the cutting edge is down and the index finger is on the back of the blade.

- Begin to teach cutting techniques with real knives using soft substances, such as pancakes, hot dogs, and hamburgers. The student may find it easier to cut if the plate is turned so the food is located at the six o'clock position.

- Have the student move the food toward the center of the plate and away from the edge—especially with a plate that has a beveled edge—so the plate does not slip when he or she is cutting.

- Teach the student to use the tines of the fork to determine the shape of the food and the location of a bone, if applicable.

- Have the student cut a circle around the fork and pull the fork toward him or her to be sure that the piece is severed or cut a vertical strip and then smaller pieces of that strip.

Dressing

Teachers of students with visual impairments are frequently asked questions about how to teach students dressing skills. Although some students come to school clean and neatly dressed, this does not necessarily mean that the students (regardless of their age) have the skills necessary to dress independently. In fact, some specialists find out that their students have difficulty dressing only when the students enter junior high school and must participate in physical education activities that require them to change into gym clothes.

Since it is best for students to learn independent dressing skills at appropriate ages, the teacher of students with visual impairments needs to keep in close contact with students' parents during the early school years to answer their questions and provide assistance. Many of the beginning problems of dressing are common to all children. But there are also predictable areas of concern for students who are visually impaired. The following section presents suggestions for working with students and parents in various areas of concern related to dressing.

Recognizing the Right Side of the Garment. A manufacturer's tag or label is a good indicator of the inside, back, and front of a garment, as are the locations of pockets and zippers.

Tying Shoes. Students who are sighted generally learn to tie shoelaces just before or shortly after they enter elementary school. The teacher of students with visual impairments generally teaches a student this skill while the student is wearing the shoe or the shoe is in the position as if he or she was wearing it. One method of teaching a student to tie shoelaces was presented by Swallow and Huebner (1987): tying two laces of contrasting colors or textures together, with the knot centered in the middle of the shoe. Then the steps should be taught in this order:

♦ Tie a simple knot with the two laces;

♦ Make a loop in each side of the lace (that is, two loops) and hold one loop in each hand;

♦ Hold the base of each loop between the thumb and index finger of each hand; and

♦ Cross one loop over and under the other and then tie as a simple knot.

Coordinating Clothing.   Making sure that clothing is appropriate to the occasion and that colors, patterns, and styles are compatible can be difficult for students who are visually impaired. Color coordination can be addressed through the use of a labeling system. Sidebar 16.3 presents sugges-

---

SIDEBAR 16.3

Coordinating Colors of Clothing

DECIDE ON A LABELING SYSTEM

♦ Determine what information the student wants to have before determining a system for labeling clothing for color coordination. For example, does the student want to know the actual color and pattern or simply which garments may be worn together?

♦ Consider whether labels are needed. Some garments may be identified by their styles or unusual types of fabric and thus do not require tactile labels.

SELECT COMMON ITEMS USED TO LABEL CLOTHING

♦ Consider using small, brass safety pins. A particular number can represent a color (for example, one pin means the garment is blue and two pins means the garment is red), or the pins can be arranged in different positions to represent different colors.

♦ Consider using embroidery floss. French knots can be sewn in seams, or facings or on tags, with particular numbers of knots representing different colors, or knots can be sewn in different patterns (lines or shapes) for different colors. The floss can be sewn in different patterns. This method is often more comfortable

than using safety pins when garments are worn, since there are no hard objects to irritate the skin.

♦ Consider using small buttons of different shapes to represent different colors.

♦ Consider marking the tags already sewn into the clothing. For a student who is not bothered by clothing tags at the nape of the neck or prefers clothing tags, the edges of the tags can be cut in different patterns to represent different colors.

♦ Consider using commercially available materials from specialty catalogs, such as Do-Dots, Matchmakers, braille clothing tags made of aluminum or cloth, geometrically shaped buttons, and safety pins with raised dots.

PLACE THE LABELS

♦ Place a tactile label in an inconspicuous location where it will not irritate the skin.

♦ Use consistent locations in similar garments so the student can quickly find the information.

♦ Prepare a legend written in an accessible medium when a labeling system is first developed and until the student is comfortable with the coding system. The legend can also include cleaning directions and information on accessories.

tions for developing a labeling system for clothing. Systems for labeling other items are presented in the next section.

Understanding Current Fashion. Because many students with visual impairments are not able to learn visually about current fashions or the types of clothing that are worn for different functions, it may be necessary for the teacher of students with visual impairments to work with the students' parents to teach them other socially appropriate ways of obtaining this information. The specialist can address this issue by teaching students to participate in common social conversations to learn what friends are going to wear to a party, or to discuss the clothing worn by performers in favorite television shows and by popular musicians, or the clothing shown in fashion magazines. The specialist or parents may want to address directly which types of clothing are appropriate in the workplace.

Ensuring Privacy. Young children with visual impairments often find it difficult to understand that they need to dress and undress in private. They do not realize that even though they do not see others, others may still be able to see them. Thus, they may dress and undress in front of open windows because they do not yet have the concept of what others see or realize that window shades are up or curtains not drawn. Developing a routine to check that windows are covered and doors are closed can alleviate this problem. Young students may benefit from discussions on the concept of sight and what sighted people can and cannot see.

Labeling

Much of the information that students need in their daily lives can be obtained via simple tactile or visual labels. Appropriate labeling of commonly needed objects (see Sidebar 16.4) is one way to maintain organization and complete daily living tasks efficiently. To decide which of a student's items need to be labeled and how they are to be labeled, the teacher of students with visual

---

SIDEBAR 16.4

Labels

LABEL COMMON ITEMS

- Foods (such as canned goods, boxed goods, and frozen food packages)
- Personal care products (like toothpaste, shampoo, and hair conditioner)
- Medicines (including the name of the medication, amount of each dose, and number of daily dosages)
- Audiocassette tapes, CDs, and books
- Print copies of homework
- Clothing
- Dials on equipment (such as a microwave, a stove, a clothes washer, clothes and hair dryers, and a thermostat)

USE COMMON OR LOCALLY AVAILABLE MATERIALS FOR LABELING

- Puff paints or embossing paints
- Glue or glue with glitter
- Rubber safety tread tape (rolls in various widths and colors that can be purchased in any length in hardware stores)
- Clear contact paper (to make tactile lines or shapes with slate and stylus or brailler; does not retain a sharp image as long as does heavier plastic, such as Braillabel from the American Thermoform Corporation)
- Contact paper over braille paper or an index card
- Scrap plastic
- Plumber's epoxy

impairments needs to consider the following questions:

- Does the label need to be permanent or temporary?

- How many people will be using the label, or can it be individualized?

- What are the sensory options of the people who will be using the label? Do they discriminate tactilely, have functional vision, read in braille or large print, and distinguish colors?

- Where will the item be used (for example, in a freezer, near the burner of a stove, outdoors in inclement weather)?

- On what type of surface material will the label be placed (for example, wood, plastic, or metal), and will color contrast be necessary?

- How much space is available for the label?

- What is the student's preference with regard to a label?

The student should be directly involved in deciding what and how to label objects of importance to him or her. Sidebar 16.4 presents some options for labeling.

HOME MANAGEMENT

Managing Money

Money management involves a broad range of skills, from understanding that money has value to investing one's earnings. It also includes organizing money in a wallet or purse and holding and carrying money safely (for instance, not displaying money in public; carrying money in a wallet or purse, not just stuffing it in a pocket; and placing a wallet in an inside pocket of a coat or jacket and holding a purse at all times when traveling in the community).

On the most basic level, all children should be able to identify currency. Because U.S. currency is all the same color and design, differentiated only by the denominations of bills and coins, individuals who are blind and those with low vision need special strategies to distinguish the denominations. The following sections present suggestions for working with students and parents on the identification of coins and bills.

Identifying Coins.   Students with visual impairments should be taught to identify coins quickly and accurately. A coin purse with metal or plastic slots for each type of coin (quarters, dimes, nickels, and pennies) will facilitate quicker access to desired coins than will carrying all coins loose in a pocket or coin compartment. Coins of a similar size (such as a dime and penny) may be difficult to identify, so relying on tactile cues may be the most efficient. The following are the tactile characteristics of U.S. coins:

- A penny has an unmilled edge;

- A nickel has an unmilled edge but is larger than a penny;

- A dime has a milled edge and is slightly smaller than a penny;

- A quarter has a milled edge and is much larger than a dime;

- A half dollar has a milled edge and is larger than a quarter;

- A silver dollar has a milled edge and is larger than a half dollar; and

- A Susan B. Anthony silver dollar is difficult to differentiate from a quarter because it has a milled edge, but it has a face edge with a texture different from that of a quarter.

Identifying Bills.   Bills are often kept in order through some form of folding system. A student who is visually impaired may need to ask a sighted person to identify bills initially and then devise a folding system that suits him or her. Once the student devises a system, it is important to use it consistently. The following is an example of a system for folding the various denominations of bills:

◆ A $1 bill is left unfolded;

◆ A $5 bill is folded end to end to make a square;

◆ A $10 bill is folded in half lengthwise to make a long rectangle (and inserted in a wallet with the folded side up, so other bills are not inserted in the crease and lost when a $10 bill is pulled out); and

◆ A $20 bill is folded into fourths (and may be placed in a separate compartment of the wallet).

Students with low vision may choose to use a folding system, such as the one just described, or visual cues to identify bills. Given the optimum environmental lighting conditions, many students with low vision can use the patterns of light and dark on the backs of bills to identify the bills. The front of the bills have the same pattern: a dark oval in the middle of the bill, surrounded by a large light area with a small dark border. However, the backs of U.S. bills can be discriminated according to the following characters:

◆ A $1 bill has a small rectangle of light in the center surrounded by a large dark border;

◆ A $5 bill has a large rectangle of light in the center with dark lines in the middle;

◆ A $10 bill has a large oval of light in the center, with a gray area in the middle;

◆ An old $20 bill has a large rectangle of light with two dark areas in each end of the rectangle; and

◆ A new $20 bill has large, dark numbers at the lower right-hand corner and a large, light border with a dark strip across the bottom third of the bill.

Preparing and Cooking Meals

Many of the beginning challenges of cooking are common to all children. But there are also predictable areas of concern for students who are visually impaired. Learning meal-preparation skills and helping with related chores in the kitchen should begin at an early age. Sidebar 16.5 presents suggestions that may be offered to parents of children with visual impairments to encourage the development of these skills at home. This section provides guidelines for teachers who are working with students and parents on areas of concern related to cooking.

Pouring. Regarding pouring, two issues are of concern: lining up the two containers and over-pouring. During instruction, a short-sided tray or pan can be used as a work surface for ease of cleanup and to confine spills. Using the index finger, the student can align the pouring spout with the receiving container. He or she can gauge the level of liquid in several ways:

◆ Place a finger near the top of the glass to provide a tactile clue when pouring cold liquids;

◆ Hold a finger slightly over the top and stop pouring when warmth is felt from hot liquids;

◆ Monitor the change in sound as the liquid nears the top of the container;

◆ Monitor the increase in weight of a container as it fills up; or

◆ Use liquid-level indicators and hot beverage dispensers that dispense a set amount of liquid (Paskin & Soucy-Moloney, 1994).

Most students, regardless of the severity of their disabilities, can learn to pour. Taylor (1987) reported on the process used to teach a young woman with severe disabilities, including deaf-blindness, who had no speech, but was mobile, to prepare cereal, chocolate milk, and juice. The instructional sequence and strategies included the following steps:

◆ Tactile recipes were prepared by gluing miniature objects to cards that were placed in a tray in sequence.

◆ The student was presented with the materi-

Developing Skills for Preparing Meals

18 TO 24 MONTHS

◆ Let the child open and close cupboards and drawers and explore other movable kitchen objects, such as an ice cream scoop with a flipper, a manual can opener, food tongs, flip lids (as on an empty spice box), and a push top of a detergent bottle.

2 TO 3 YEARS

◆ Allow the child to experience the functions of movable parts by, for example, spraying plants, squirting detergent in a bowl, opening cans, and helping to scoop ice cream.

◆ Begin household chores, such as carrying napkins to the table. Also, place frequently used utensils, such as pans, measuring cups, and serving spoons, where the child can reach them and have the parent ask the child to give him or her a specific utensil.

3 TO 4 YEARS

◆ Encourage the child to assist in cooking by stirring batter and sauces, shredding lettuce, mixing powder with liquid for chocolate milk or pudding, and so forth. The child will need to check his or her progress in mixing with his or her fingers, which are the most efficient tool, especially for a child who is blind who learns to substitute touch for sight. The wise parent quickly accepts what may appear to be messy and unsavory as an essential learning step. During the child's third year, when a child is gaining independence in washing hands, helping in the kitchen provides many opportunities to clean hands.

◆ Use cooking and baking activities (such as baking cookies, cooling pudding,

and freezing ice cubes) to help the child become aware of time. Use a kitchen timer to alert the child to the time period. Adapt a timer by raising dots or enlarging minute signs with nail polish or glue.

◆ Teach other household chores by having the child help fold napkins (with instruction and guidance at first), bring utensils to the table, return dirty dishes to the kitchen after mealtime, push food scraps off plates into a garbage pail, and hand dishes to an adult to be loaded into a dishwasher.

4 TO 5 YEARS

◆ Encourage the child to complete such simple food-preparation tasks as putting cheese on crackers or meat on bread and spooning out jelly on bread. The latter task probably will be messy, but it will prepare the child for later tasks.

◆ Teach the child how to set a table. Use left- and right-side orientation skills: the knife goes on the right side of the plate, the fork goes on the left, the cup goes in front of the knife, and the chair goes behind the plate.

5 TO 6 YEARS

◆ Encourage the child to perform other, simple food preparation tasks like spreading butter, peanut butter, and jelly on bread and pouring beverages into glasses, with assistance, from quart containers or pitchers.

◆ Supplement cooking tasks by discussing how the textures of foods change during the cooking process; for example, tell the child that cookies change from soft (when they are dough) to hard after they have been baked and cooled. Encourage

(continued on next page)

the child to touch, mold, smell, and taste foods to find out how they change. Incorporate the making of pudding and ice cubes into a child's science education. Later, ask the parents and siblings to chart these activities and talk about the chemical and physical properties of foods.

♦ Have the child mop up spilled liquids with a sponge, cloth, or paper towel. Keep needed supplies in a consistent place and within easy reach, so the child can learn where to find the sponge or cloth or to take a paper towel from the roller. Keep this job pleasant and do not strive for perfection.

6 TO 7 YEARS

♦ Allow the child to help prepare salads or other vegetables by dicing or slicing them and breaking them up.

♦ Teach the child to squeeze oranges, lemons, and limes for juice or to add to other foods.

♦ Have the child set the table with little or no guidance.

7 TO 8 YEARS

♦ Encourage the child to complete such simple food-preparation tasks as using a can opener, fixing hot dogs, making lemonade from frozen concentrate, and preparing beverage mixes.

♦ Have the child help dry dishes or unload them from the dishwasher and put them away.

8 TO 9 YEARS

♦ Let the child assist with cooking and baking activities by measuring required amounts using 1 cup, 1/2 cup, 1/3 cup, and 1/4 cup braille or large-print

measures, as appropriate. Use only level, dry ingredients for measuring in the beginning.

♦ Have the child practice cracking eggs in a bowl for scrambled eggs.

♦ Have the child help wash dishes by filling a sink or a pan with hot, soapy water; filling a second sink or pan with clean water; and washing dishes with a sponge or cloth, feeling the surface with a hand to check for and eliminate grease or grit; rinsing the dishes; drying the dishes; and putting the dishes in the proper cupboard. Allow the child plenty of time to complete these tasks and give him or her plenty of help. At first, assign the child to be a helper, teaching him or her to dry and put away dishes. Then gradually increase the child's responsibilities over a period of years. At age 8, the child can wash dishes, and someone else can finish the pots and pans. When dishes are put into the rack unclean, cheerfully tell the child to rewash them. Maintain standards and cut down on quantity if the child has difficulty.

9 TO 10 YEARS

♦ Teach the student to use an electric or gas stove like any other skill. This is the age to start teaching a student to use a stove for cooking and baking. Alleviate the parents' fears that the child will be burned and encourage the parents not to overprotect the child to the point that he or she is unable to learn this essential skill.

♦ Introduce the range by pointing out the location of all parts. When the range is

(continued on next page)

cold, orient the child to all burners, emphasizing the concepts of front and back and left and right. Ask the child to find the right burners, left burners, left front burner, left rear burner, and so forth. This is a difficult concept for many children and requires a lot of practice.

◆ Identify the knobs that turn on the heat. Depending on the child's level of knowledge, it is important to explain the connection of the switches to the source of power. Correlate each knob with each burner (omit the oven knob for the time being). Have the child turn each knob on.

◆ Expose the child to heat from the burners. With a gas stove, place the child's hand under yours near the burner, but not close enough to scorch; have the child listen for the sound of the pilot igniting the burner; and move his or her hand away and toward the burner to feel the intensity of the heat. With an electric burner, tell the child that it takes longer to heat up and change temperature and teach him or her some cues, such as listening for a click when the knob is turned, increasing the level of heat by turning the knob one direction, and decreasing the level of heat by turning the knob the opposite direction.

◆ With the burner off, have the child practice placing various size pans on a burner. Remind the child that when cooking, the food must be in a pan before the burner is turned on. Teach appropriate levels of heat for particular cooking jobs.

◆ To begin to teach oven cooking, mark or raise the spots on a circular temperature range (250, 350, and 450 degrees are recommended) and place a raised

mark on the pointer. Teach the child to match the pointer with the degree of temperature (at or between the raised marks). Have the child experiment with the feel of low, medium, and high oven settings. It is particularly important for the child to experience the heat that is felt when the oven door is opened.

◆ Keep pot holders at a location that is easily accessible to the oven. With a cold oven, practice putting various sizes of pots and pans in the oven. Some pans require one hand, while others require two hands. After practicing with a cold oven, start to teach the child to bake cookies and layer cakes.

10 TO 11 YEARS

◆ By this time, the child should know how to peel bananas and oranges independently and dispose of the peels. Now introduce paring and dicing of apples and pears, providing a great deal of practice using a peeler, which is a difficult instrument to use well. Also teach the child to use a corer for preparing more than one apple or pear. Having a child prepare a fruit salad gives him or her the opportunity to use washing, peeling, coring, cutting, and dicing skills.

◆ Have the child practice draining excess liquids off noodles and pasta through a colander. Ladling soups and sauces requires a great deal of practice in removing the soup pot from the stove, placing a soup bowl next to the pot, and transferring the soup from the pot to the bowl. (Have the child practice with cold and warm soups before he or she ladles hot liquids.) Teach the child to place a finger on the rim of the bowl to gauge

(continued on next page)

the correct position of the spoon and the height of the liquid in the bowl.

◆ Give the child more opportunities to measure dry and liquid foods using a metal cup measure with a handle and bending the handle so the measure becomes a scooper. Teach the child to scoop the measuring cup into the flour or sugar bin and level it with a finger and, later, a knife. The same technique may be used with measuring spoons. To measure salt, place salt in a wide-mouth container and have the student scoop it out with a measuring spoon or teach him or her to pour salt over a sink. Use the same metal cup for measuring liquids, either scooping it from a large container or pouring it into a measure that has been placed in a larger bowl or on a plate to handle any spills and overflow.

11 TO 12 YEARS

◆ Label canned goods and boxes in braille (or large print) so the child can easily find them.

◆ Have the child practice stewing meat following the guidelines provided earlier for introducing burners and the oven. Teach the child about different uncooked meats. Broiling can begin with hot dogs and hamburgers before steak and pork chops are tried. Encourage the child to note changes in texture and temperature that occur during cooking. Provide practice in trimming fat from raw and cooked meats.

◆ Teach the child to pare potatoes and carrots using the same peeler used for apples and pears.

12 YEARS AND UP

◆ Have the child establish a braille or large-print cooking file. The first section may contain directions that are frequently used for preparing standard package items, such as orange juice, frozen dinners, pot pies, hamburger mixes, and macaroni and cheese. Another section should contain recipes, starting with the easiest (such as hot dogs and popcorn) and building as the child gains experience. As the child's skills and interest increase, cooking may become not only a rewarding experience, but a life-long hobby.

◆ Introduce electrical appliances (such as a can opener, orange juicer, mixer, blender, ice crusher, coffee maker, hot dog maker, and hamburger maker) after a child has experienced and mastered the motions of mechanical devices. The only differences between electrical appliances and mechanical devices are the speed of automation and safety rules.

Source: Adapted from F. Naughton and S. Z. Sacks, *Hey! What's Cooking? A Kitchen Curriculum for the Parents of Visually Impaired Children* (Harvey, IL: South Metropolitan Association for Low Incidence Handicapped, n.d.).

als and ingredients to prepare cereal, along with the tray with the sequenced cards.

◆ Signed prompts were used along with physical guidance, to guide the student's hands in the correct sequence to the needed item or ingredient. Physical guidance was gradually removed and then signed prompts were gradually removed.

◆ Once the student acquired the first skill (preparing cereal), she was introduced to the next skill (pouring chocolate milk). When the student mastered that skill, the next skill (preparing juice) was introduced. After the initial training, each subsequent skill required fewer training sessions.

This example illustrates the value of teaching students in manageable steps, using sound instructional principles and building on each preceding step. The use of physical guidance and prompts allowed the student to complete the entire sequence of steps. Later, the prompts were faded, and she was able to complete this skill independently.

Using a Stove. Although cooking programs for young children or children with developmental disabilities may provide guidance, some aspects of cooking have to be adapted in detail for students with visual impairments. A lesson on cooking may need to be broken down into lessons on orientation to the top of the stove while it is cool, including manipulating the controls and size of burners; centering pots and pans on the burners; gauging temperature; turning foods; and detecting when liquid is boiling or food is sufficiently cooked (Ponchillia & Ponchillia, 1996). The section on students 9 to 10 years old in Sidebar 16.5 presents detailed suggestions on introducing students with visual impairments to using the stove.

Cooking utensils and equipment may also need modifications (such as tactile markers on temperature controls, cutting guides, and tactile or large-print timers). Dickman (1983), Paskin and Soucy-Molony (1994), and Ponchillia and Ponchillia (1996) presented more detailed suggestions

for adapting cooking and other household methods and materials for individuals who are blind or have low vision. The important point to remember is that students who are visually impaired can cook on a stove safely and efficiently.

Opening Packages.   Opening packages can present a challenge for all people at one time or another. For a student who cannot see the "open here" label, this skill may need to be explicitly addressed. Although many packages can be opened by feeling for the perforated strip along a box, trying to open school milk cartons and bags of snacks (like potato chips) can be frustrating for anyone and should be practiced with students. The following guidelines may be helpful in opening a milk carton:

◆ Locate the side that opens, which is slightly thicker than the sealed side;

◆ Insert both thumbs in the opening at the top of the triangle;

◆ Using the fingers on the rest of the carton as a brace, move the thumbs away from each other;

◆ Locate the juncture of the *V* (where there should be a small opening), insert a finger or fingernail at the top of the *V* and pull the spout to the front.

Bags of snacks may have a notch at the top that can be tactilely located and torn. Another option is to grasp each side of the bag and pull both sides apart gently to break the seal.

Learning Food Concepts. Children need to learn food concepts at an early age by being exposed to where foods come from and how they grow and are made. A child whose only experience with carrots is as round slices does not recognize the original shape of a carrot and does not know that carrots grow in the ground. Gardening and preparing foods that one has grown can help develop these concepts, as can visits to farms and grocery stores, as well as cooking.

Cleaning. When cleaning the home, systematic patterns and overlapping should be used. For example, start to wipe the table on the left, overlap the first swipe when making the second, continue to the right edge of the table. Routine wiping of surfaces, mopping, vacuuming, and dusting can ensure that all areas are cleaned, even when it may not be evident to a person with a visual impairment that cleaning is necessary (Ponchillia & Ponchillia, 1996). At an early age, students can be introduced to cleaning concepts by being given the responsibility for putting away their toys or making their beds. However, a particular family's level of cleanliness and neatness needs to be considered. For example, if no one in the family makes his or her bed and an unmade bed does not bother the child or other family members, then there is no need to make this skill a priority.

SUMMARY

Independent living skills encompass a wide range of skills and activities that are performed daily. The teacher of students with visual impairments can facilitate the development of these skills in a student who is visually impaired in cooperation with the student, his or her parents, and others in the student's life and by teaching some skills directly. Instruction in independent living skills is essential for students who are visually impaired, since the students will not gain information incidentally by observing others perform these tasks. Assessment and instruction in these skills need to occur in natural environments during normal routines to ensure that they are integrated into students' daily lives.

ACTIVITIES

1. Collect simple recipes that require few skills and can be prepared in a short time; write a task analysis of the skills required and share it with your classmates.
2. Make samples of various ways to label clothing, canned goods, and dials. The samples can be used to explain to students how items can be labeled. Since some substances (e.g., glue, paint) that are used to make labels need to dry for several days before they can be affixed to surfaces, students can determine if a particular substance is appropriate for them before they use it.
3. Compile, organize, and evaluate resources and equipment related to personal management and household management, such as catalogs, manuals, informational resources (people or places), evaluations of books (including cookbooks), adaptive techniques, simple recipes, lesson plans, teaching materials, or projects for specific tasks. Include class notes, outside readings, and so forth. The resource file should be well organized and arranged to allow for future expansion.
4. Choose a comfortable, casual restaurant. Pair up with a partner to experience eating in a restaurant with simulated blindness. One person in the pair wears a blindfold, while the other person (with no blindfold) assists, when necessary, and ensures the partner's safety. Afterward, make notes of the experience, especially the factors that helped or hindered enjoyment of the meal. The next day or week, change roles, so the other partner can experience eating while blindfolded.
5. Interview a teacher of students with visual impairments about strategies that have worked for providing essential instructional time for independent living skills. Also ask the specialist about his or her thoughts on the importance of balancing academic skills with nonacademic skills for students with visual impairments.

REFERENCES

Baker, B., & Brightman, A. (1989). *Steps to independence.* Baltimore, MD: Paul H. Brookes.

Barraga, N. (1986). Sensory perceptual development. In

G. Scholl (Ed.), *Foundations of education for blind and visually handicapped children and youth* (pp. 83–98). New York: American Foundation for the Blind.

Beach, J. D., Robinet, J. M., & Hakim-Larson, J. (1995). Self-esteem and independent living skills of adults with visual impairments. *Journal of Visual Impairment & Blindness 89,* 531–540.

Becker, S. W., Lambert, R. W., Schulz, E. M., Wright, B. D., & Burnet, D. L. (1985). An instrument to measure the activity level of the blind. *International Journal of Rehabilitation Research 8,* 415–424.

Canter, P., Cole, M., Hatlen, B., & LeDuc, P. (no date). *Beyond TV dinners. Three levels of recipes for visually handicapped cooks.* San Pablo, CA: Living Skills Center for the Visually Handicapped.

Cardwell, K., Grappe, S., Novian-Rojas, E., Pike, K., Thomas, R., & Wheat, P. (1998). *Functional academic curriculum for exceptional students, revised (FACES).* Lubbock, TX: Region 17 Education Service Center.

Chen, D., & Dote-Kwan, J. (1999). Evaluating a preschooler's skills, performance, and learning needs in daily activities. In K. Wolffe (Ed.), *Skills for success: A career education handbook for children and adolescents with visual impairments* (pp. 71–76). New York: AFB Press.

Cleary, M. E. (Ed.). (1994*). Diabetes and visual impairment: An educator's resource guide.* Chicago: American Association of Diabetes Educators.

Council for Exceptional Children. (1998*). What every special educator must know: The international standards for the preparation and licensure of special educators.* (3rd ed.). Reston, VA: Council for Exceptional Children.

Curry, S., & Hatlen, P. (1988). Meeting the unique educational needs of visually impaired pupils through appropriate placement. *Journal of Visual Impairment & Blindness 82,* 417–424.

Cushman, C., Heydt, K., Edwards, S., Clark, M. J., & Allon, M. (1992). *Perkins activity and resource guide: A handbook for teachers and parents of students with visual and multiple disabilities.* Watertown, MA: Perkins School for the Blind.

Dickman, I. (1983). *Making life more livable: Simple adaptations for the homes of blind and visually impaired older people.* New York: American Foundation for the Blind.

Downing, J., & Bailey, B. (1990). Developing vision use within functional daily activities for students with visual and multiple disabilities. *RE:view 21,* 209–220.

Downing, J. E. (1996). *Including students with severe and multiple disabilities in typical classroom: Practical strategies for teachers.* Baltimore, MD: Paul H. Brookes.

Duffy, M. A. (1997). *New independence! Environmental adaptations in community facilities for adults with visual impairments.* Mohegan Lake, NY: Associates for World Action in Rehabilitation and Education.

Elder, V. (1999). *Money handling and budgeting.* Louisville, KY: American Printing House for the Blind.

Gale, G., d'Apice, P., Freeman, K., Payne, R., & Tierney, L. (1998). Life skills. In P. Kelley & G. Gale (Eds.), *Towards excellence: Effective education for students with vision impairments* (pp. 227–238). North Rocks, New South Wales, Australia: North Rocks Press, Royal Institute for Deaf and Blind Children.

Goetz, L., & Gee, K. (1987). Teaching visual attention in functional contexts: Acquisition and generalization of complex visual motor skills. *Journal of Visual Impairment & Blindness 81,* 115–117.

Griffin-Shirley, N., & Groff, G. (1993). *Prescriptions for independence: Working with older people who are visually impaired.* New York: AFB Press.

Hatlen, P. (1990). Meeting the unique needs of pupils with visual impairments. *RE:view 22,* 79–82.

Hatlen, P. (1996). *The core curriculum for blind and visually impaired students, including those with additional disabilities.* Austin: Texas School for the Blind and Visually Impaired. Available on-line: http://www.tsbvi.edu/education/corecurric.htm

Inkster, W., Newman, L., Weiss, D. S., & Yeadon, A. (1997). *Rehabilitation teaching for persons experiencing vision loss* (2nd ed.). New York: CIL Publications.

Loumiet, R., & Levack, N. (1991). *Independent living: A curriculum with adaptations for students with visual impairments Vol. 1: Social Competence.* Austin: Texas School for the Blind and Visually Impaired.

Lowrey, L. (1987). Rehabilitation relevant to culture and disability. *Journal of Visual Impairment & Blindness 81*(4), 162–164.

Mangold, P. (1980). *Pleasure of eating for those who are visually impaired.* Castro Valley, CA: Exceptional Teaching Aids.

Naughton, F., & Sacks, S. Z. (n.d.). *Hey! What's cooking? A kitchen curriculum for the parents of visually impaired children.* Harvey, IL: South Metropolitan Association for Low Incidence Handicapped.

Paskin, N., & Soucy-Moloney, L. A. (1994). *Whatever works.* New York: The Lighthouse.

Ponchillia, P. E., & Kaarlela, R. (1986). Post-rehabilitation use of adaptive skills. *Journal of Visual Impairment & Blindness 80,* 665–669.

Ponchillia, P. E., & Ponchillia, S. V. (1996). *Foundations of rehabilitation teaching with persons who are blind or visually impaired.* New York: AFB Press.

Rosen, S. (1993). Academics are not enough: Incorporating life skills in the curriculum for children and youth with visual handicaps. *DVH Quarterly 39*(1), 18.

Sacks, S. Z., & Wolffe, K. E. (1998). Lifestyles of adolescents with visual impairments: An ethnographic analysis. *Journal of Visual Impairment & Blindness 92*, 7–17.

Spungin, S. J., & Ferrell, K. A. (1992). The role and function of the teacher of students with visual handicaps. *DVH Quarterly 37*(2), 19–24.

Stenquist, G., & Robbins, N. (1978). *Curriculum for daily living.* Watertown, MA: Howe Press at Perkins School for the Blind.

A Step-by-step guide to personal management for blind persons (2nd ed.). (1974). New York: American Foundation for the Blind.

Suvak, P. A. (1999). What do they really do? Activities of teachers of students with visual impairments. *RE:view 30*, 181–190.

Swallow, R., & Huebner, K. M. (1987). *How to thrive, not just survive: A guide to developing independent life skills for blind and visually impaired children and youths.* New York: American Foundation for the Blind.

Taylor, R. G. (1987). Teaching a severely handicapped deaf-blind young woman to prepare breakfast foods. *Journal of Visual Impairment & Blindness, 81*, 67–69.

Warren, D. (1994). *Blindness and children: An individual differences approach.* New York: Cambridge University Press.

Wolffe, K., & Sacks, S. Z. (1997). The lifestyles of blind, low vision, and sighted youths: A quantitative comparison. *Journal of Visual Impairment & Blindness 91*, 245–257.

Woo, I., & Knowlton, M. (1992). Developing a version of the Scales of Independent Behavior, adapted for students with visual impairments. *RE:view 24*, 72–83.

Yeadon, A. (1978). *Toward independence: The use of instructional objectives in teaching daily living skills to the blind.* New York: American Foundation for the Blind.

Evaluation of Independent Living Skills
for a Student with a Visual Impairment

Student's name: _____ D.O.B. _____ School _____

Evaluator(s) _____ Date of Evaluation _____

General Information

To establish the criteria for acceptable (functional) performance for this student, list on a separate page the significant factors that have or will have an impact on the student's needs and abilities.

I. Learning Factors

    A. Does the student have any physical, sensory, or health impairments that would require the use of adaptive techniques, materials, or services to complete independent living tasks? Please describe.

    B. What is the student's learning rate? How much repetition is usually required for mastery of a task? Is the student able to generalize classroom learning to a real environment? Please describe.

    C. What is the student's motivation for learning and performing independent living tasks? Are caretakers encouraging or overprotective? What reinforcers have worked well for this student in the past to get him or her to initiate or continue an activity?

    D. Does the student have any behaviors that affect his or her acquisition or performance of independent living skills? What behavioral management techniques have been successful?

    E. Describe the student's ability to self-evaluate (that is, to determine appropriate solutions to problems, to "read" a social situation and act accordingly, to determine the "correctness" of his or her own responses).

II. Expectations of the Living Situation

    A. Current
       1. Describe the student's current living situation.

       2. Describe the standards for independence in the current living situation.

    B. Transitional
       1. Describe the student's transitional living situation.

       2. Describe the standards for independence in the transitional living situation.

(continued on next page)

Appendix: Evaluation of Independent Living Skills for a Student with a Visual Impairment

Independent Living Skills *(Continued)*

C. Projected

   1. Describe the student's target living situation (projected maximum independence).

   2. Describe the standards for independence in the projected target living situation.

Performance Evaluation

Directions: For each of the following independent living skill areas, indicate the appropriate rating for each item according to the following key:

Level of Independence

Student consistently performs:

   5 = without assistance
   4 = following multistep verbal or written directions
   3 = with verbal prompting
   2 = with step-by-step verbal prompting
   1 = with physical guidance
   0 = does not perform

Organization

Student consistently:

   5 = selects appropriate equipment, methods, and products for tasks and organizes his or her work environment efficiently
   3 = needs assistance to select and/or organize equipment, methods, and work area
   0 = does not select or organize equipment, methods, or work area

Safety

Student consistently:

   5 = completes tasks in safe manner
   3 = needs prompting to perform tasks safely
   0 = is unaware of safety needs

Motivation

Student consistently:

   5 = is self-motivated to initiate and perform tasks
   3 = needs external reinforcement to perform tasks
   0 = will not perform tasks

Time to Complete Task

Indicate the time required to complete each task:

(continued on next page)

Independent Living Skills (Continued)

Personal Management

A. Personal Hygiene and Grooming

Task	Level of Independence	Organization	Safety	Motivation	Time to Complete
Self toilets	5 4 3 2 1 0	5 4 3 2 1 0	5 4 3 2 1 0	5 4 3 2 1 0	
Takes bath or shower	5 4 3 2 1 0	5 4 3 2 1 0	5 4 3 2 1 0	5 4 3 2 1 0	
Cares for teeth (brushes, flosses)	5 4 3 2 1 0	5 4 3 2 1 0	5 4 3 2 1 0	5 4 3 2 1 0	
Maintains proper nasal hygiene	5 4 3 2 1 0	5 4 3 2 1 0	5 4 3 2 1 0	5 4 3 2 1 0	
Shampoos and dries hair	5 4 3 2 1 0	5 4 3 2 1 0	5 4 3 2 1 0	5 4 3 2 1 0	
Maintains menstrual hygiene	5 4 3 2 1 0	5 4 3 2 1 0	5 4 3 2 1 0	5 4 3 2 1 0	
Uses deodorant	5 4 3 2 1 0	5 4 3 2 1 0	5 4 3 2 1 0	5 4 3 2 1 0	
Trims and cleans nails	5 4 3 2 1 0	5 4 3 2 1 0	5 4 3 2 1 0	5 4 3 2 1 0	
Maintains proper hair appearance	5 4 3 2 1 0	5 4 3 2 1 0	5 4 3 2 1 0	5 4 3 2 1 0	
Shaves facial, leg, and underarm hair	5 4 3 2 1 0	5 4 3 2 1 0	5 4 3 2 1 0	5 4 3 2 1 0	
Uses makeup	5 4 3 2 1 0	5 4 3 2 1 0	5 4 3 2 1 0	5 4 3 2 1 0	
Cares for low vision aids	5 4 3 2 1 0	5 4 3 2 1 0	5 4 3 2 1 0	5 4 3 2 1 0	
Cares for ocular prostheses	5 4 3 2 1 0	5 4 3 2 1 0	5 4 3 2 1 0	5 4 3 2 1 0	
Cares for limb prostheses	5 4 3 2 1 0	5 4 3 2 1 0	5 4 3 2 1 0	5 4 3 2 1 0	

1. Does the student consistently perform personal hygiene tasks at the appropriate level and with appropriate frequency?

2. Describe the student's previous experiences that may help or hinder the acquisition of personal hygiene and grooming skills?

3. Describe any special equipment and/or environmental conditions that the student requires to perform the task independently.

4. Of the tasks the student is *not* performing independently, describe how the personal hygiene and grooming need is being met.

(continued on next page)

Independent Living Skills (Continued)

B. Eating Skills

Task	Level of Independence	Organization	Safety	Motivation	Time to Complete
Drinks from a cup or glass	5 4 3 2 1 0	5 4 3 2 1 0	5 4 3 2 1 0	5 4 3 2 1 0	
Locates food on a plate	5 4 3 2 1 0	5 4 3 2 1 0	5 4 3 2 1 0	5 4 3 2 1 0	
Uses appropriate utensil to					
◆ scoop food	5 4 3 2 1 0	5 4 3 2 1 0	5 4 3 2 1 0	5 4 3 2 1 0	
◆ spear food	5 4 3 2 1 0	5 4 3 2 1 0	5 4 3 2 1 0	5 4 3 2 1 0	
◆ cut soft foods	5 4 3 2 1 0	5 4 3 2 1 0	5 4 3 2 1 0	5 4 3 2 1 0	
◆ cut meat	5 4 3 2 1 0	5 4 3 2 1 0	5 4 3 2 1 0	5 4 3 2 1 0	
◆ butter bread	5 4 3 2 1 0	5 4 3 2 1 0	5 4 3 2 1 0	5 4 3 2 1 0	
Uses condiments					
◆ from shakers	5 4 3 2 1 0	5 4 3 2 1 0	5 4 3 2 1 0	5 4 3 2 1 0	
◆ (salt/pepper)	5 4 3 2 1 0	5 4 3 2 1 0	5 4 3 2 1 0	5 4 3 2 1 0	
◆ from squeeze bottles	5 4 3 2 1 0	5 4 3 2 1 0	5 4 3 2 1 0	5 4 3 2 1 0	
◆ from bottle/jar	5 4 3 2 1 0	5 4 3 2 1 0	5 4 3 2 1 0	5 4 3 2 1 0	
Serves self from					
◆ serving bowl	5 4 3 2 1 0	5 4 3 2 1 0	5 4 3 2 1 0	5 4 3 2 1 0	
◆ meat platter	5 4 3 2 1 0	5 4 3 2 1 0	5 4 3 2 1 0	5 4 3 2 1 0	
Uses napkin	5 4 3 2 1 0	5 4 3 2 1 0	5 4 3 2 1 0	5 4 3 2 1 0	
Maintains erect posture	5 4 3 2 1 0	5 4 3 2 1 0	5 4 3 2 1 0	5 4 3 2 1 0	
Chews bite-size mouthfuls	5 4 3 2 1 0	5 4 3 2 1 0	5 4 3 2 1 0	5 4 3 2 1 0	
Chews with his or her mouth shut	5 4 3 2 1 0	5 4 3 2 1 0	5 4 3 2 1 0	5 4 3 2 1 0	
Completes a meal	5 4 3 2 1 0	5 4 3 2 1 0	5 4 3 2 1 0	5 4 3 2 1 0	

1. Does the student consistently perform eating skills at the appropriate level and with appropriate frequency?

2. Describe the student's previous experiences that may help or hinder the acquisition of eating skills?

3. Describe any special equipment and/or environmental conditions that the student requires to perform the tasks independently.

4. Of the tasks the student is *not* performing independently, describe how the eating need is being met.

(continued on next page)

Independent Living Skills *(Continued)*

C. Dressing/Undressing Skills

Task	Level of Independence	Organization	Safety	Motivation	Time to Complete
Removes pants or shorts	5 4 3 2 1 0	5 4 3 2 1 0	5 4 3 2 1 0	5 4 3 2 1 0	
Removes shirt, blouse, coat	5 4 3 2 1 0	5 4 3 2 1 0	5 4 3 2 1 0	5 4 3 2 1 0	
Removes shoes	5 4 3 2 1 0	5 4 3 2 1 0	5 4 3 2 1 0	5 4 3 2 1 0	
Removes socks	5 4 3 2 1 0	5 4 3 2 1 0	5 4 3 2 1 0	5 4 3 2 1 0	
Identifies the front and back of garment	5 4 3 2 1 0	5 4 3 2 1 0	5 4 3 2 1 0	5 4 3 2 1 0	
Turns garment right-side out	5 4 3 2 1 0	5 4 3 2 1 0	5 4 3 2 1 0	5 4 3 2 1 0	
Uses fasteners:					
Buttons	5 4 3 2 1 0	5 4 3 2 1 0	5 4 3 2 1 0	5 4 3 2 1 0	
Zippers	5 4 3 2 1 0	5 4 3 2 1 0	5 4 3 2 1 0	5 4 3 2 1 0	
Snaps	5 4 3 2 1 0	5 4 3 2 1 0	5 4 3 2 1 0	5 4 3 2 1 0	
Hooks	5 4 3 2 1 0	5 4 3 2 1 0	5 4 3 2 1 0	5 4 3 2 1 0	
Velcro closures	5 4 3 2 1 0	5 4 3 2 1 0	5 4 3 2 1 0	5 4 3 2 1 0	
Puts on undergarments	5 4 3 2 1 0	5 4 3 2 1 0	5 4 3 2 1 0	5 4 3 2 1 0	
Puts on pants or shorts	5 4 3 2 1 0	5 4 3 2 1 0	5 4 3 2 1 0	5 4 3 2 1 0	
Puts on shirts, blouses, coats	5 4 3 2 1 0	5 4 3 2 1 0	5 4 3 2 1 0	5 4 3 2 1 0	
Puts on gloves or mittens	5 4 3 2 1 0	5 4 3 2 1 0	5 4 3 2 1 0	5 4 3 2 1 0	
Puts on hat	5 4 3 2 1 0	5 4 3 2 1 0	5 4 3 2 1 0	5 4 3 2 1 0	
Puts on belt	5 4 3 2 1 0	5 4 3 2 1 0	5 4 3 2 1 0	5 4 3 2 1 0	
Laces and ties shoes	5 4 3 2 1 0	5 4 3 2 1 0	5 4 3 2 1 0	5 4 3 2 1 0	
Matches clothing by color and pattern	5 4 3 2 1 0	5 4 3 2 1 0	5 4 3 2 1 0	5 4 3 2 1 0	
Selects appropriate clothing for the weather	5 4 3 2 1 0	5 4 3 2 1 0	5 4 3 2 1 0	5 4 3 2 1 0	
Selects clothing appropriate for an activity or situation	5 4 3 2 1 0	5 4 3 2 1 0	5 4 3 2 1 0	5 4 3 2 1 0	

1. Does the student consistently and independently handle all dressing and undressing tasks appropriate to his/her age and situation?
2. Describe the student's previous experiences that may help or hinder the acquisition of dressing/undressing skills?
3. Describe any special equipment and/or environmental conditions that the student requires to perform the tasks independently.
4. Of the tasks the student is *not* performing independently, describe how the dressing and undressing need is being met.

(continued on next page)

Independent Living Skills (Continued)

D. Clothing Care Skills

Task	Level of Independence	Organization	Safety	Motivation	Time to Complete
Organizes closet and drawers	5 4 3 2 1 0	5 4 3 2 1 0	5 4 3 2 1 0	5 4 3 2 1 0	
Folds linens, flat items	5 4 3 2 1 0	5 4 3 2 1 0	5 4 3 2 1 0	5 4 3 2 1 0	
Folds clothes	5 4 3 2 1 0	5 4 3 2 1 0	5 4 3 2 1 0	5 4 3 2 1 0	
Hangs up shirt, dress, coat	5 4 3 2 1 0	5 4 3 2 1 0	5 4 3 2 1 0	5 4 3 2 1 0	
Hangs slacks, skirts	5 4 3 2 1 0	5 4 3 2 1 0	5 4 3 2 1 0	5 4 3 2 1 0	
Does laundry:					
◆ Sorts clothes	5 4 3 2 1 0	5 4 3 2 1 0	5 4 3 2 1 0	5 4 3 2 1 0	
◆ Removes stains; "pretreats"	5 4 3 2 1 0	5 4 3 2 1 0	5 4 3 2 1 0	5 4 3 2 1 0	
◆ Measures soap, softener	5 4 3 2 1 0	5 4 3 2 1 0	5 4 3 2 1 0	5 4 3 2 1 0	
◆ Sets dials on washer and dryer	5 4 3 2 1 0	5 4 3 2 1 0	5 4 3 2 1 0	5 4 3 2 1 0	
◆ Uses coin-operated machines	5 4 3 2 1 0	5 4 3 2 1 0	5 4 3 2 1 0	5 4 3 2 1 0	
◆ Hand washes	5 4 3 2 1 0	5 4 3 2 1 0	5 4 3 2 1 0	5 4 3 2 1 0	
Selects and prepares clothes for dry cleaning	5 4 3 2 1 0	5 4 3 2 1 0	5 4 3 2 1 0	5 4 3 2 1 0	
Cleans/polishes shoes	5 4 3 2 1 0	5 4 3 2 1 0	5 4 3 2 1 0	5 4 3 2 1 0	
Hand mending:					
◆ Threads needle	5 4 3 2 1 0	5 4 3 2 1 0	5 4 3 2 1 0	5 4 3 2 1 0	
◆ Sews on button	5 4 3 2 1 0	5 4 3 2 1 0	5 4 3 2 1 0	5 4 3 2 1 0	
◆ Mends rips and tears	5 4 3 2 1 0	5 4 3 2 1 0	5 4 3 2 1 0	5 4 3 2 1 0	
◆ Does machine mending	5 4 3 2 1 0	5 4 3 2 1 0	5 4 3 2 1 0	5 4 3 2 1 0	
Ironing					
◆ Sets temperature and steam	5 4 3 2 1 0	5 4 3 2 1 0	5 4 3 2 1 0	5 4 3 2 1 0	
◆ Irons clothing	5 4 3 2 1 0	5 4 3 2 1 0	5 4 3 2 1 0	5 4 3 2 1 0	
Packs a suitcase	5 4 3 2 1 0	5 4 3 2 1 0	5 4 3 2 1 0	5 4 3 2 1 0	
Shops for own clothing	5 4 3 2 1 0	5 4 3 2 1 0	5 4 3 2 1 0	5 4 3 2 1 0	

1. Does the student consistently perform clothing care tasks at the appropriate level and with adequate frequency?
2. Describe the student's previous experiences that may help or hinder the acquisition of clothing care skills?
3. Describe any special equipment and/or environmental conditions that the student requires to perform the tasks independently.
4. Of the tasks the student is *not* performing independently, describe how the clothing care need is being met.

(continued on next page)

Independent Living Skills *(Continued)*

E. Medical Management Skills

Task	Level of Independence	Organization	Safety	Motivation	Time to Complete
Identifies medication	5 4 3 2 1 0	5 4 3 2 1 0	5 4 3 2 1 0	5 4 3 2 1 0	
Takes medication in proper dose:					
◆ Tablets	5 4 3 2 1 0	5 4 3 2 1 0	5 4 3 2 1 0	5 4 3 2 1 0	
◆ Liquid	5 4 3 2 1 0	5 4 3 2 1 0	5 4 3 2 1 0	5 4 3 2 1 0	
◆ Injections	5 4 3 2 1 0	5 4 3 2 1 0	5 4 3 2 1 0	5 4 3 2 1 0	
Takes medications on schedule	5 4 3 2 1 0	5 4 3 2 1 0	5 4 3 2 1 0	5 4 3 2 1 0	
Gets refill of medication	5 4 3 2 1 0	5 4 3 2 1 0	5 4 3 2 1 0	5 4 3 2 1 0	
Wears or carries emergency information	5 4 3 2 1 0	5 4 3 2 1 0	5 4 3 2 1 0	5 4 3 2 1 0	
Makes doctor's appointments	5 4 3 2 1 0	5 4 3 2 1 0	5 4 3 2 1 0	5 4 3 2 1 0	
Cares for assistive equipment:					
◆ Visual aids	5 4 3 2 1 0	5 4 3 2 1 0	5 4 3 2 1 0	5 4 3 2 1 0	
◆ Hearing aids	5 4 3 2 1 0	5 4 3 2 1 0	5 4 3 2 1 0	5 4 3 2 1 0	
◆ Mobility aids	5 4 3 2 1 0	5 4 3 2 1 0	5 4 3 2 1 0	5 4 3 2 1 0	
Treats minor cuts	5 4 3 2 1 0	5 4 3 2 1 0	5 4 3 2 1 0	5 4 3 2 1 0	
Treats minor burns	5 4 3 2 1 0	5 4 3 2 1 0	5 4 3 2 1 0	5 4 3 2 1 0	

1. Does the student consistently perform medical management tasks at the appropriate level and with the appropriate frequency?

2. Describe the student's previous experiences that may help or hinder the acquisition of medical management skills?

3. Describe any special equipment, services, and/or environmental conditions that the student requires to perform the tasks independently.

4. Of the tasks the student is *not* performing independently, describe how the medical needs are being met. Are these methods or systems that can be provided in the transitional or target living situation?

(continued on next page)

Independent Living Skills *(Continued)*

F. Time-Management Skills

Task	Level of Independence	Organization	Safety	Motivation	Time to Complete
Tells time on a clock	5 4 3 2 1 0	5 4 3 2 1 0	5 4 3 2 1 0	5 4 3 2 1 0	
Tells time on a watch	5 4 3 2 1 0	5 4 3 2 1 0	5 4 3 2 1 0	5 4 3 2 1 0	
Sets time on a clock	5 4 3 2 1 0	5 4 3 2 1 0	5 4 3 2 1 0	5 4 3 2 1 0	
Sets time on a watch	5 4 3 2 1 0	5 4 3 2 1 0	5 4 3 2 1 0	5 4 3 2 1 0	
Sets alarm/uses alarm on a clock	5 4 3 2 1 0	5 4 3 2 1 0	5 4 3 2 1 0	5 4 3 2 1 0	
Arrives at appointments on time	5 4 3 2 1 0	5 4 3 2 1 0	5 4 3 2 1 0	5 4 3 2 1 0	
Uses a timepiece to determine length of activity	5 4 3 2 1 0	5 4 3 2 1 0	5 4 3 2 1 0	5 4 3 2 1 0	
Estimates the passage of time	5 4 3 2 1 0	5 4 3 2 1 0	5 4 3 2 1 0	5 4 3 2 1 0	
Uses a timer	5 4 3 2 1 0	5 4 3 2 1 0	5 4 3 2 1 0	5 4 3 2 1 0	
Reads a calendar	5 4 3 2 1 0	5 4 3 2 1 0	5 4 3 2 1 0	5 4 3 2 1 0	
Uses a calendar to plan a schedule	5 4 3 2 1 0	5 4 3 2 1 0	5 4 3 2 1 0	5 4 3 2 1 0	
Has a system to remember special dates (such as birthdays)	5 4 3 2 1 0	5 4 3 2 1 0	5 4 3 2 1 0	5 4 3 2 1 0	

1. Does the student consistently manage time concepts and skills at the appropriate level?

2. Describe the student's previous experiences that may help or hinder the acquisition of time-management skills?

3. Describe any special equipment and/or environmental conditions that the student requires to perform the tasks independently.

4. Of the tasks the student is *not* performing independently, describe how the time-management need is being met and whether that system could be provided in the next living situation.

(continued on next page)

Independent Living Skills *(Continued)*

Household Management

A. Cooking

Task	Level of Independence	Organization	Safety	Motivation	Time to Complete
Pours cold liquids into a cup or glass	5 4 3 2 1 0	5 4 3 2 1 0	5 4 3 2 1 0	5 4 3 2 1 0	
Pours hot liquids into a cup or glass	5 4 3 2 1 0	5 4 3 2 1 0	5 4 3 2 1 0	5 4 3 2 1 0	
Opens jars, boxes, pull-top cans, and bottles	5 4 3 2 1 0	5 4 3 2 1 0	5 4 3 2 1 0	5 4 3 2 1 0	
Uses a can opener	5 4 3 2 1 0	5 4 3 2 1 0	5 4 3 2 1 0	5 4 3 2 1 0	
Identifies package contents	5 4 3 2 1 0	5 4 3 2 1 0	5 4 3 2 1 0	5 4 3 2 1 0	
Spreads	5 4 3 2 1 0	5 4 3 2 1 0	5 4 3 2 1 0	5 4 3 2 1 0	
Cuts, slices, dices	5 4 3 2 1 0	5 4 3 2 1 0	5 4 3 2 1 0	5 4 3 2 1 0	
Measures liquid ingredients	5 4 3 2 1 0	5 4 3 2 1 0	5 4 3 2 1 0	5 4 3 2 1 0	
Measures dry ingredients	5 4 3 2 1 0	5 4 3 2 1 0	5 4 3 2 1 0	5 4 3 2 1 0	
Uses oven:					
◆ Sets temperature	5 4 3 2 1 0	5 4 3 2 1 0	5 4 3 2 1 0	5 4 3 2 1 0	
◆ Inserts/removes items	5 4 3 2 1 0	5 4 3 2 1 0	5 4 3 2 1 0	5 4 3 2 1 0	
◆ Lights gas oven	5 4 3 2 1 0	5 4 3 2 1 0	5 4 3 2 1 0	5 4 3 2 1 0	
◆ Positions racks	5 4 3 2 1 0	5 4 3 2 1 0	5 4 3 2 1 0	5 4 3 2 1 0	
◆ Bakes	5 4 3 2 1 0	5 4 3 2 1 0	5 4 3 2 1 0	5 4 3 2 1 0	
◆ Broils	5 4 3 2 1 0	5 4 3 2 1 0	5 4 3 2 1 0	5 4 3 2 1 0	
Cleans oven	5 4 3 2 1 0	5 4 3 2 1 0	5 4 3 2 1 0	5 4 3 2 1 0	
Uses stovetop:					
◆ Sets temperature	5 4 3 2 1 0	5 4 3 2 1 0	5 4 3 2 1 0	5 4 3 2 1 0	
◆ Lights gas burners	5 4 3 2 1 0	5 4 3 2 1 0	5 4 3 2 1 0	5 4 3 2 1 0	
◆ Centers pan on burners	5 4 3 2 1 0	5 4 3 2 1 0	5 4 3 2 1 0	5 4 3 2 1 0	
◆ Heats convenience items	5 4 3 2 1 0	5 4 3 2 1 0	5 4 3 2 1 0	5 4 3 2 1 0	
◆ Boils	5 4 3 2 1 0	5 4 3 2 1 0	5 4 3 2 1 0	5 4 3 2 1 0	
◆ Fries	5 4 3 2 1 0	5 4 3 2 1 0	5 4 3 2 1 0	5 4 3 2 1 0	
◆ Drains (pasta)	5 4 3 2 1 0	5 4 3 2 1 0	5 4 3 2 1 0	5 4 3 2 1 0	
Cleans stovetop and burners	5 4 3 2 1 0	5 4 3 2 1 0	5 4 3 2 1 0	5 4 3 2 1 0	
Transfers food to serving dishes	5 4 3 2 1 0	5 4 3 2 1 0	5 4 3 2 1 0	5 4 3 2 1 0	
Sets and clears the table	5 4 3 2 1 0	5 4 3 2 1 0	5 4 3 2 1 0	5 4 3 2 1 0	
Washes dishes	5 4 3 2 1 0	5 4 3 2 1 0	5 4 3 2 1 0	5 4 3 2 1 0	

(continued on next page)

Independent Living Skills *(Continued)*

A. Cooking *(continued)*

Task	Level of Independence	Organization	Safety	Motivation	Time to Complete
Dries dishes	5 4 3 2 1 0	5 4 3 2 1 0	5 4 3 2 1 0	5 4 3 2 1 0	
Stores food properly	5 4 3 2 1 0	5 4 3 2 1 0	5 4 3 2 1 0	5 4 3 2 1 0	
Disposes of garbage	5 4 3 2 1 0	5 4 3 2 1 0	5 4 3 2 1 0	5 4 3 2 1 0	
Wipes off work surfaces	5 4 3 2 1 0	5 4 3 2 1 0	5 4 3 2 1 0	5 4 3 2 1 0	
Uses cooking timer	5 4 3 2 1 0	5 4 3 2 1 0	5 4 3 2 1 0	5 4 3 2 1 0	
Uses small appliances	5 4 3 2 1 0	5 4 3 2 1 0	5 4 3 2 1 0	5 4 3 2 1 0	
Uses microwave oven	5 4 3 2 1 0	5 4 3 2 1 0	5 4 3 2 1 0	5 4 3 2 1 0	
Uses dishwasher	5 4 3 2 1 0	5 4 3 2 1 0	5 4 3 2 1 0	5 4 3 2 1 0	
Defrosts refrigerator	5 4 3 2 1 0	5 4 3 2 1 0	5 4 3 2 1 0	5 4 3 2 1 0	
Plans meals:					
◆ Follows recipe	5 4 3 2 1 0	5 4 3 2 1 0	5 4 3 2 1 0	5 4 3 2 1 0	
◆ Plans nutritious meals	5 4 3 2 1 0	5 4 3 2 1 0	5 4 3 2 1 0	5 4 3 2 1 0	
◆ Plans a balanced diet	5 4 3 2 1 0	5 4 3 2 1 0	5 4 3 2 1 0	5 4 3 2 1 0	
◆ Plans within budget	5 4 3 2 1 0	5 4 3 2 1 0	5 4 3 2 1 0	5 4 3 2 1 0	
◆ Prepares a complete meal	5 4 3 2 1 0	5 4 3 2 1 0	5 4 3 2 1 0	5 4 3 2 1 0	
◆ Prepares a grocery list	5 4 3 2 1 0	5 4 3 2 1 0	5 4 3 2 1 0	5 4 3 2 1 0	
◆ Shops for groceries	5 4 3 2 1 0	5 4 3 2 1 0	5 4 3 2 1 0	5 4 3 2 1 0	
Organizes and cleans cabinets	5 4 3 2 1 0	5 4 3 2 1 0	5 4 3 2 1 0	5 4 3 2 1 0	

1. Does the student consistently perform cooking skills to be independent in the preparation of all meals?

2. Describe the student's previous experiences that may help or hinder the acquisition of cooking skills?

3. Describe any special equipment and/or environmental conditions that the student requires to perform the tasks independently.

4. Of the tasks the student is *not* performing independently, describe how the cooking need is being met and whether this system can be provided in the next living situation.

(continued on next page)

Independent Living Skills *(Continued)*

B. Cleaning Skills

Task	Level of Independence	Organization	Safety	Motivation	Time to Complete
Makes the bed	5 4 3 2 1 0	5 4 3 2 1 0	5 4 3 2 1 0	5 4 3 2 1 0	
Changes the linen	5 4 3 2 1 0	5 4 3 2 1 0	5 4 3 2 1 0	5 4 3 2 1 0	
Stores cleaning equipment/supplies	5 4 3 2 1 0	5 4 3 2 1 0	5 4 3 2 1 0	5 4 3 2 1 0	
Dusts furniture using a spray and cloth	5 4 3 2 1 0	5 4 3 2 1 0	5 4 3 2 1 0	5 4 3 2 1 0	
Sweeps with a broom and uses a dustpan	5 4 3 2 1 0	5 4 3 2 1 0	5 4 3 2 1 0	5 4 3 2 1 0	
Uses a vacuum cleaner	5 4 3 2 1 0	5 4 3 2 1 0	5 4 3 2 1 0	5 4 3 2 1 0	
Cleans the tub, sink, and toilet	5 4 3 2 1 0	5 4 3 2 1 0	5 4 3 2 1 0	5 4 3 2 1 0	
Cleans mirrors, windows	5 4 3 2 1 0	5 4 3 2 1 0	5 4 3 2 1 0	5 4 3 2 1 0	
Scrubs the floor	5 4 3 2 1 0	5 4 3 2 1 0	5 4 3 2 1 0	5 4 3 2 1 0	
Dry mops the floor	5 4 3 2 1 0	5 4 3 2 1 0	5 4 3 2 1 0	5 4 3 2 1 0	
Wet mops/waxes the floor	5 4 3 2 1 0	5 4 3 2 1 0	5 4 3 2 1 0	5 4 3 2 1 0	
Washes walls/baseboards	5 4 3 2 1 0	5 4 3 2 1 0	5 4 3 2 1 0	5 4 3 2 1 0	
Cleans cabinets	5 4 3 2 1 0	5 4 3 2 1 0	5 4 3 2 1 0	5 4 3 2 1 0	
Cleans and empties wastebaskets	5 4 3 2 1 0	5 4 3 2 1 0	5 4 3 2 1 0	5 4 3 2 1 0	
Uses garbage bags/ties	5 4 3 2 1 0	5 4 3 2 1 0	5 4 3 2 1 0	5 4 3 2 1 0	
Cleans up after pets	5 4 3 2 1 0	5 4 3 2 1 0	5 4 3 2 1 0	5 4 3 2 1 0	
Cleans up broken glass	5 4 3 2 1 0	5 4 3 2 1 0	5 4 3 2 1 0	5 4 3 2 1 0	

1. Does the student consistently perform household cleaning tasks at the appropriate level and with adequate frequency?

2. Describe the student's previous experiences that may help or hinder the acquisition of household cleaning skills?

3. Describe any special equipment and/or environmental conditions that the student requires to perform the tasks independently.

4. Of the tasks the student is *not* performing independently, describe how the cleaning need is being met and whether this system can be provided in the next living situation.

(continued on next page)

Independent Living Skills *(Continued)*

C. General Household Tasks

Task	Level of Independence	Organization	Safety	Motivation	Time to Complete
Locates dropped objects	5 4 3 2 1 0	5 4 3 2 1 0	5 4 3 2 1 0	5 4 3 2 1 0	
Locks/unlocks doors	5 4 3 2 1 0	5 4 3 2 1 0	5 4 3 2 1 0	5 4 3 2 1 0	
Uses keys	5 4 3 2 1 0	5 4 3 2 1 0	5 4 3 2 1 0	5 4 3 2 1 0	
Knows if lights are on/off	5 4 3 2 1 0	5 4 3 2 1 0	5 4 3 2 1 0	5 4 3 2 1 0	
Opens, shuts, locks windows	5 4 3 2 1 0	5 4 3 2 1 0	5 4 3 2 1 0	5 4 3 2 1 0	
Plugs in appliances	5 4 3 2 1 0	5 4 3 2 1 0	5 4 3 2 1 0	5 4 3 2 1 0	
Uses extension cords appropriately	5 4 3 2 1 0	5 4 3 2 1 0	5 4 3 2 1 0	5 4 3 2 1 0	
Chooses/inserts batteries	5 4 3 2 1 0	5 4 3 2 1 0	5 4 3 2 1 0	5 4 3 2 1 0	
Selects and uses glue	5 4 3 2 1 0	5 4 3 2 1 0	5 4 3 2 1 0	5 4 3 2 1 0	
Selects and uses tape	5 4 3 2 1 0	5 4 3 2 1 0	5 4 3 2 1 0	5 4 3 2 1 0	
Uses scissors	5 4 3 2 1 0	5 4 3 2 1 0	5 4 3 2 1 0	5 4 3 2 1 0	
Wraps packages for mailing	5 4 3 2 1 0	5 4 3 2 1 0	5 4 3 2 1 0	5 4 3 2 1 0	
Wraps packages for gifts	5 4 3 2 1 0	5 4 3 2 1 0	5 4 3 2 1 0	5 4 3 2 1 0	
Hangs pictures and curtains	5 4 3 2 1 0	5 4 3 2 1 0	5 4 3 2 1 0	5 4 3 2 1 0	
Measures for rugs, curtains, and so forth	5 4 3 2 1 0	5 4 3 2 1 0	5 4 3 2 1 0	5 4 3 2 1 0	
Sets the thermostat	5 4 3 2 1 0	5 4 3 2 1 0	5 4 3 2 1 0	5 4 3 2 1 0	
Turns radiators off/on	5 4 3 2 1 0	5 4 3 2 1 0	5 4 3 2 1 0	5 4 3 2 1 0	
Uses a portable heater	5 4 3 2 1 0	5 4 3 2 1 0	5 4 3 2 1 0	5 4 3 2 1 0	
Use an air conditioner	5 4 3 2 1 0	5 4 3 2 1 0	5 4 3 2 1 0	5 4 3 2 1 0	
Uses a fan	5 4 3 2 1 0	5 4 3 2 1 0	5 4 3 2 1 0	5 4 3 2 1 0	
Uses smoke detectors	5 4 3 2 1 0	5 4 3 2 1 0	5 4 3 2 1 0	5 4 3 2 1 0	
Changes lightbulbs	5 4 3 2 1 0	5 4 3 2 1 0	5 4 3 2 1 0	5 4 3 2 1 0	
Fixes blown fuse/circuit breaker	5 4 3 2 1 0	5 4 3 2 1 0	5 4 3 2 1 0	5 4 3 2 1 0	
Cleans the sink and tub drains	5 4 3 2 1 0	5 4 3 2 1 0	5 4 3 2 1 0	5 4 3 2 1 0	
Turns off water supply	5 4 3 2 1 0	5 4 3 2 1 0	5 4 3 2 1 0	5 4 3 2 1 0	
Clears clogged drains with a plunger	5 4 3 2 1 0	5 4 3 2 1 0	5 4 3 2 1 0	5 4 3 2 1 0	

(continued on next page)

Independent Living Skills *(Continued)*

C. General Household Tasks *(continued)*

Task	Level of Independence	Organization	Safety	Motivation	Time to Complete
Clears clogged drain, with chemicals	5 4 3 2 1 0	5 4 3 2 1 0	5 4 3 2 1 0	5 4 3 2 1 0	
Repairs a flush tank to stop dripping	5 4 3 2 1 0	5 4 3 2 1 0	5 4 3 2 1 0	5 4 3 2 1 0	
Cares for indoor plants	5 4 3 2 1 0	5 4 3 2 1 0	5 4 3 2 1 0	5 4 3 2 1 0	
Arranges furniture/room	5 4 3 2 1 0	5 4 3 2 1 0	5 4 3 2 1 0	5 4 3 2 1 0	
Takes garbage to the dumpster/can	5 4 3 2 1 0	5 4 3 2 1 0	5 4 3 2 1 0	5 4 3 2 1 0	
Shovels snow	5 4 3 2 1 0	5 4 3 2 1 0	5 4 3 2 1 0	5 4 3 2 1 0	
Mows lawn	5 4 3 2 1 0	5 4 3 2 1 0	5 4 3 2 1 0	5 4 3 2 1 0	
Rakes leaves	5 4 3 2 1 0	5 4 3 2 1 0	5 4 3 2 1 0	5 4 3 2 1 0	
Trims bushes	5 4 3 2 1 0	5 4 3 2 1 0	5 4 3 2 1 0	5 4 3 2 1 0	
Waters garden/lawn	5 4 3 2 1 0	5 4 3 2 1 0	5 4 3 2 1 0	5 4 3 2 1 0	

1. Does the student consistently perform general household tasks at the appropriate level and with adequate frequency?

2. Describe the student's previous experiences that may help or hinder the acquisition of general household skills?

3. Describe any special equipment and/or environmental conditions that the student requires to perform the tasks independently.

4. Of the tasks the student is *not* performing independently, describe how the need is being met and whether the system or method could be provided in the next living situation.

(continued on next page)

Independent Living Skills *(Continued)*

D. Telephone Skills

Task	Level of Independence	Organization	Safety	Motivation	Time to Complete
Dials 911, 0, or another emergency number	5 4 3 2 1 0	5 4 3 2 1 0	5 4 3 2 1 0	5 4 3 2 1 0	
Gives appropriate information in an emergency	5 4 3 2 1 0	5 4 3 2 1 0	5 4 3 2 1 0	5 4 3 2 1 0	
Dials a pushbutton phone	5 4 3 2 1 0	5 4 3 2 1 0	5 4 3 2 1 0	5 4 3 2 1 0	
Dials a rotary phone	5 4 3 2 1 0	5 4 3 2 1 0	5 4 3 2 1 0	5 4 3 2 1 0	
Uses a pay phone accurately	5 4 3 2 1 0	5 4 3 2 1 0	5 4 3 2 1 0	5 4 3 2 1 0	
Dials directory assistance	5 4 3 2 1 0	5 4 3 2 1 0	5 4 3 2 1 0	5 4 3 2 1 0	
Records telephone numbers accurately	5 4 3 2 1 0	5 4 3 2 1 0	5 4 3 2 1 0	5 4 3 2 1 0	
Uses proper telephone manners	5 4 3 2 1 0	5 4 3 2 1 0	5 4 3 2 1 0	5 4 3 2 1 0	
Takes/retrieves telephone messages	5 4 3 2 1 0	5 4 3 2 1 0	5 4 3 2 1 0	5 4 3 2 1 0	

1. Does the student consistently use the telephone at the appropriate level?

2. Describe the student's previous experiences that may help or hinder the acquisition of telephone skills?

3. Describe any special equipment, services, and/or environmental conditions that the student requires to perform the tasks independently.

4. Of the tasks the student is *not* performing independently, describe how the telephone communication needs are being met and whether this system can be provided in the next living situation.

(continued on next page)

Independent Living Skills (Continued)

E. Financial Management

Task	Level of Independence	Organization	Safety	Motivation	Time to Complete
Demonstrates basic number concepts	5 4 3 2 1 0	5 4 3 2 1 0	5 4 3 2 1 0	5 4 3 2 1 0	
Identifies coins	5 4 3 2 1 0	5 4 3 2 1 0	5 4 3 2 1 0	5 4 3 2 1 0	
Counts mixed denominations of coins	5 4 3 2 1 0	5 4 3 2 1 0	5 4 3 2 1 0	5 4 3 2 1 0	
Counts out exact coins for given amount	5 4 3 2 1 0	5 4 3 2 1 0	5 4 3 2 1 0	5 4 3 2 1 0	
Identifies paper currency	5 4 3 2 1 0	5 4 3 2 1 0	5 4 3 2 1 0	5 4 3 2 1 0	
Organizes wallet	5 4 3 2 1 0	5 4 3 2 1 0	5 4 3 2 1 0	5 4 3 2 1 0	
Makes change	5 4 3 2 1 0	5 4 3 2 1 0	5 4 3 2 1 0	5 4 3 2 1 0	
Counts change given in store	5 4 3 2 1 0	5 4 3 2 1 0	5 4 3 2 1 0	5 4 3 2 1 0	
Reads cent and dollar amounts	5 4 3 2 1 0	5 4 3 2 1 0	5 4 3 2 1 0	5 4 3 2 1 0	
Makes simple purchases	5 4 3 2 1 0	5 4 3 2 1 0	5 4 3 2 1 0	5 4 3 2 1 0	
Follows a budget	5 4 3 2 1 0	5 4 3 2 1 0	5 4 3 2 1 0	5 4 3 2 1 0	
Cashes checks	5 4 3 2 1 0	5 4 3 2 1 0	5 4 3 2 1 0	5 4 3 2 1 0	
Writes checks/money orders	5 4 3 2 1 0	5 4 3 2 1 0	5 4 3 2 1 0	5 4 3 2 1 0	
Records expenses	5 4 3 2 1 0	5 4 3 2 1 0	5 4 3 2 1 0	5 4 3 2 1 0	
Fills out deposit/ withdrawal slips	5 4 3 2 1 0	5 4 3 2 1 0	5 4 3 2 1 0	5 4 3 2 1 0	
Balances checkbook	5 4 3 2 1 0	5 4 3 2 1 0	5 4 3 2 1 0	5 4 3 2 1 0	
Uses a savings account	5 4 3 2 1 0	5 4 3 2 1 0	5 4 3 2 1 0	5 4 3 2 1 0	
Pays bills on time	5 4 3 2 1 0	5 4 3 2 1 0	5 4 3 2 1 0	5 4 3 2 1 0	
Uses a credit card appropriately	5 4 3 2 1 0	5 4 3 2 1 0	5 4 3 2 1 0	5 4 3 2 1 0	
States information needed for tax forms	5 4 3 2 1 0	5 4 3 2 1 0	5 4 3 2 1 0	5 4 3 2 1 0	
Uses other banking services	5 4 3 2 1 0	5 4 3 2 1 0	5 4 3 2 1 0	5 4 3 2 1 0	
Contacts financial aid when needed	5 4 3 2 1 0	5 4 3 2 1 0	5 4 3 2 1 0	5 4 3 2 1 0	

1. Does the student consistently manage his or her finances at the appropriate level and with adequate frequency?

2. Describe the student's previous experiences that may help or hinder the acquisition of financial management skills?

3. Describe any special equipment, services and/or environmental conditions that the student requires to perform the tasks independently.

4. Of the tasks the student is *not* performing independently, describe how the need is being met and whether this system can be provided in the next living situation.

(continued on next page)

Independent Living Skills *(Continued)*

Summary Sheet

Personal Management

1. What is the student's overall level of independence? What objectives does the student need to complete to increase his or her independence in the following:
   a. Personal hygiene and grooming
   b. Eating
   c. Dressing/undressing
   d. Clothing care
   e. Medical management
   f. Time management

2. What strategies may be effective in increasing the student's organizational skills?

3. What strategies may be effective in increasing the student's efficiency?

4. What is the student's overall motivation to initiate and complete personal management skills? What strategies or reinforcement may be effective in increasing the student's willingness to initiate and complete tasks?

5. Describe any special equipment, services, and/or environmental conditions that the student requires to perform the task without the teacher's or caregiver's assistance.

6. Of the tasks that the student is *not* performing independently, describe what systems are currently being provided to meet the personal management needs. Are these systems in the transitional or target living settings?

Household Management

1. What is the student's overall level of independence? What objectives does the student need to complete to increase his or her independence in the following:
   a. Cooking
   b. Cleaning
   c. General household tasks
   d. Telephone skills
   e. Financial management

2. What is the student's overall motivation to initiate and complete household management skills? What strategies or reinforcement may be effective in increasing the student's willingness to initiate and complete tasks?

3. Describe any special equipment, services, and/or environmental conditions that the student requires to perform the task without the teacher's or caregiver's assistance.

4. Of the tasks that the student is *not* performing independently, describe what systems are currently being provided to meet the household management needs. Are these systems in the transitional or target living settings?

Source: Adapted from J. Matsuoka and P. B. Smith, *Foundations of Education of Students with Visual Impairments.* Unpublished manuscript.

Strategies for Teaching Independent Living Skills to Students with Visual Impairments and Additional Disabilities

Instruction that facilitates students' ability to do as much for themselves as their capabilities allow and decreases students' reliance on others may be the most relevant for students with visual impairments and additional disabilities. As is true for all students with visual impairments, these skills are taught in natural and functional routines and are evaluated in ongoing assessments. In addition, opportunities for enhancing the development and efficiency of communication, social, movement, and vocational skills are incorporated into the facilitation of the instruction of independent living skills. Goals for these students may involve learning a wide variety of skills, such as indicating preferences for foods; sustaining one's weight long enough to assist with a transfer from a wheelchair to a toilet; and selecting, purchasing, and laundering clothing. The ability to eat and toilet with only minimal assistance may allow a preschooler to participate in a community preschool with nondisabled classmates and the student who is of transition age to gain access to mainstream vocational opportunities.

Chapter 7 of this volume presents suggestions related to early self-feeding skills. Older students who have difficulty managing eating utensils, especially those with poor proprioceptive feedback and minimal wrist strength in addition to the lack of vision, may benefit from using an adapted spoon, that provides sufficient stability to scoop but whose bowl stays level regardless of how a student orients his or hand. In addition, Dycem matting or Rubbermaid rubber shelving material stabilizes plates and other utensils. Students who need assistance with scooping may need only a raised-edge plate, such as the divided Rubbermaid plates used for storing and transporting meals.

An efficient way to encourage independence is to use routines that revolve around necessary skills. Toileting or changing children's diapers can serve as a springboard from which other skills are facilitated. A carefully thought-out changing or diapering routine is functional, offers natural contexts in which other critical skills can be performed, typically occurs frequently during an instructional day, and hence provides multiple opportunities for learning. The skills fostered in a changing routine for a young student with postural deficits may include the following:

◆ Weight bearing in supported standing to transfer from a wheelchair to the changing area;

◆ Sitting upright and maintaining balance with minimal support;

◆ Gesturing to indicate the need to have a diaper changed;

◆ Raising the pelvis so pants can be lowered and the old diaper can be removed and again so the new diaper can be put on and the pants can be pulled up;

◆ Using two hands to pull pants over knees;

◆ Visually localizing the new diaper;

◆ Reaching for, grasping, and releasing the diaper;

◆ Visually localizing the diaper pail or trash can to throw a dirty diaper away;

◆ Gesturing "finished";

◆ Visually establishing gaze with the teacher to ask to sit up; and

◆ Choosing which learning center to go to after being changed.

(continued on next page)

Skills that may be fostered in an elementary school child during toileting may include:

♦ Responding to natural signals, transition times, or gestured requests to indicate whether he or she has to use the toilet;

♦ Recognizing an object or picture symbol of a toilet;

♦ Indicating the need to toilet by pointing to or touching the objects or picture symbol of the toilet or signing;

♦ Locating and moving toward the bathroom using a walker or by trailing;

♦ Manipulating the handle of a door;

♦ Undressing;

♦ Toileting;

♦ Performing skills related to toileting (wiping himself or herself and flushing the toilet);

♦ Signaling or gesturing "finished";

♦ Dressing;

♦ Indicating the next step on a sequence chart;

♦ Localizing the sink to wash one's hands;

♦ Localizing the soap;

♦ Imitating the actions of washing hands;

♦ Localizing the towel; and

♦ Indicating the next activity on a schedule or a preferred activity.

Although such routines require a careful analysis of the needed behaviors and a well-organized plan of instructional strategies, in addition to the extra time to do more than toilet a student, the benefits far outweigh the amount of time they take.

Students of all relevant ages can assume responsibility for their clothing. Toddlers with postural deficits can be encouraged to help pull off their socks as their parents hold them in their laps and help them pull the socks from their left feet with their right hands. This routine not only promotes self-dressing skills but helps children with motor difficulties plan the process of bringing one leg up, crossing it at the midline, and coordinating the hand with the foot. Preschoolers should be expected to locate, open, and toss dirty clothes into a hamper. Those with light perception can be assisted initially to locate the hamper by placing a flashlight in it and dimming the background lights. Teenagers can practice bilateral skills, spatial relationships, and assembly tasks by hanging up shirts.

Students who are resistant to performing self-care tasks, such as brushing hair or teeth, accept these tasks more readily when they are allowed to do them with electric- or battery-operated toothbrushes or hairbrushes. Older boys can safely shave themselves with electric razors, such as the Norelco Reflex, which is a safe, effective shaver.

An older student can be self-prompted to initiate toileting by the beep or verbal announcement of the time by the alarm on a talking watch. The watch prompt may also be used to alert a student to other needed self-care tasks, such as checking to ensure that their mouths are dry if the control of saliva is a concern. For students who want to pursue vocational interests in the community, it is especially important to master toileting, self-feeding, and personal hygiene.

Students with limited hand control can be expected to help prepare meals, and remote-control devices may be used to activate coffee bean grinders, popcorn poppers, electric can openers, blenders, and juicers. Toddlers can be facilitated

(continued on next page)

Strategies for Teaching Independent Living Skills *(Continued)*

to place chopped or sliced vegetables in a salad bowl and in so doing, practice both localization and grasp-release skills. Students who are more mobile can assist with sorting and placing groceries in appropriate areas. Flashlights may be used inside cabinets and on shelves to cue the students to the location of canned versus boxed goods. Learning to place cold items in a refrigerator and boxed items in dry storage areas facilitates tactile discrimination, classification, and memory skills in addition to functional mobility and postural adjustment skills.

Students can practice all levels of hand function by assuming responsibility for washing the dishes they used during lunchtime at school. Unzipping a backpack, taking out a lunch box, and opening food and drink containers involve many different needed motor and sequencing skills. The use of a soap applicator with a knob or handle provides more stability for washing than does a dishcloth or hands and reinforces the use of a practical tool to achieve a desired result. In addition, students can call friends or family by simply pushing an oversized, programmed button that depicts the photograph of the desired recipient. Tactile cues may be added to the buttons for students with more limited vision.

M. BETH LANGLEY
Pinellas County Schools
St. Petersburg, FL

RESOURCES

Suggested Resources for Teaching Independent Living Skills

Resource	Type	Source	Description
Adaptive equipment for independent living skills	Equipment	Ableware AdaptAbility Ann Morris Enterprises Carolyn's LS&S Group Maxi-Aids	Sources for all types of adaptive equipment for individuals with visual impairments and those with physical impairments.
Adaptive spoons, utensils	Equipment	Sammons Preston	Adaptive equipment for individuals with physical impairments.
Beyond TV Dinners: Three Levels of Recipes for Visually Handicapped Cooks (Canter, Cole, Hatlen, & LeDuc, n.d.)	Book	Living Skills Center for the Visually Handicapped	A recipe package for students who need recipes geared to their cooking abilities. The three levels of cooking are directly related to the cooking evaluations that are included in the book.
Braillabel	Labeling material	American Thermo-form Corporation	Plastic with adhesive on the back can be brailled upon.
Braille labels for clothing	Equipment	American Printing House for the Blind	Adaptive equipment for individuals with visual impairments.
Curriculum for Daily Living (Stenquist & Robbins, 1978)	Curriculum	Howe Press at Perkins School for the Blind	A curriculum for use with deaf-blind students, designed for use by teachers, child care workers, houseparents, or others who are responsible for helping students develop daily living skills. Includes goals and objectives.

(continued on next page)

Suggested Resources *(Continued)*

Resource	Type	Source	Description
Diabetes and Visual Impairment: An Educator's Resource Guide (Cleary, 1994)	Book	American Association of Diabetes Educators	Information on diabetes and visual impairment.
Do-Dots, Matchmakers, etc.	Equipment	Independent Living Aids Lighthouse Enterprises Consumer Products Division	Equipment for independent living adaptation.
Foundations of Rehabilitation Teaching with Persons Who are Blind or Visually Impaired (Ponchillia & Ponchillia, 1996)	Book	AFB Press	A textbook on all aspects of rehabilitation teaching with individuals who are visually impaired.
How to Thrive, Not Just Survive: A Guide to Developing Independent Life Skills for Blind and Visually Impaired Children and Youth (Swallow & Huebner, 1987)	Book	American Foundation for the Blind	Guidelines and strategies for helping children with visual impairments to develop, acquire, and apply skills that are necessary for independence in socialization, orientation and mobility, and leisure-time and recreational activities.
Independent Living: A Curriculum with Adaptations for Students with Visual Impairments, Volume 1: Social Competence (Loumiet & Levack, 1991)	Book	Texas School for the Blind and Visually Impaired	The first of a three-volume set that addresses the nonacademic, disability-specific needs of students with visual impairments. For many areas of social competence (self-concept, emotions, nonverbal communication, personal social skills, and sexuality) the text presents goals and skills and a rich variety of useful resources.
Making Life More Livable: Simple Adaptations for the Homes of Blind and Visually Impaired Older People (Dickman, 1986)	Book	American Foundation for the Blind	A book that shows how simple adaptations in the home and environment can make a big difference to individuals with visual impairments. Numerous specific recommendations: how to mark food cans for greater visibility, furniture arrangement, use of appliances, and much more.
Money Handling and Budgeting (Elder, 1999)	Book	American Printing House for the Blind	A resource guide with an adapted practice checkbook that helps adolescents and young adults learn vital money-handling skills; based on the premise that daily living skills must be learned in natural settings and with real-life applications when possible. Includes how to identify coins and bills, count money and make change, budgeting and banking skills, and more.

(continued on next page)

Suggested Resources *(Continued)*

Resource	Type	Source	Description
New Independence! Environmental Adaptations in Community Facilities for Adults with Visual Impairments (Duffy, 1997)	Book	Associates for World Action in Rehabilitation and Education	Resources guide for adapting environments for individuals with visual impairments.
Perkins Activity and Resource Guide: A Handbook for Teachers and Parents of Students with Visual and Multiple Disabilities (Cushman, Heydt, Edwards, Clark, & Allon, 1992)	Book	Perkins School for the Blind	A reference on activities and teaching strategies for those who work with students with visual impairments and additional disabilities.
Pleasure of Eating for Those Who are Visually Impaired (Mangold, 1980)	Book	Exceptional Teaching Aids	A book designed to help children and adults who are blind or have low vision master the complex skills of eating. Contains many practical suggestions. Available in braille, large type, and audio-cassette.
Prescriptions for Independence: Working with Older People Who Are Visually Impaired (Griffin-Shirley & Groff, 1993)	Book	AFB Press	An easy-to-read manual on how older persons with visual impairments can pursue their interests and activities in community residences, senior centers, and other settings. Topics include signs of vision loss, recreation, personal care, orientation and mobility, and modifications in the environment.
Rehabilitation Teaching for Persons Experiencing Vision Loss (Inkster, Newman, Weiss, & Yeadon, 1997)	Book	CIL Publications	Textbook for rehabilitation teachers. Provides information and teaching tips for working with individuals with visual impairment.
Steps to Independence (Baker & Brightman, 1989)	Book	Paul H. Brookes	A book that describes steps in teaching daily living skills.
Toward Independence: The Use of Instructional Objectives in Teaching Daily Living Skills to the Blind (Yeadon, 1978)	Book	American Foundation for the Blind	A book that presents detailed instructional objectives to teach a variety of daily living skills; for example, "table behavior" is broken into 23 separate behaviors.
Whatever Works (Paskin & Soucy-Moloney, 1994)	Book	Lighthouse International	A book that describes steps in teaching daily living skills.

Contact information for each of the resources listed will be found in the Sources of Products, Materials, Equipment, and Services section at the back of this book.

CHAPTER 17

Social Skills

Sharon Zell Sacks and Rosanne K. Silberman

KEY POINTS

- ◆ Effective social skills are crucial for progressing in school, being integrated into society, and finding and maintaining employment.

- ◆ Social skills are typically learned through visual observation, imitation, and experiential learning.

- ◆ Students who are blind or visually impaired do not have ready access to visual models on which to base the development of social skills.

- ◆ Authentic assessment and targeted instruction in social skills are needed to ensure that students with visual impairments gain the social competence they need to lead successful lives.

- ◆ Teachers of students with visual impairments play a primary role in teaching social skills, since this is an area of the expanded core curriculum.

VIGNETTE

"Ms. Carol!" cried Kaleigh, a preschooler who is blind, as she entered the classroom carrying a small brown bag.

"Kaleigh, please hold your head up," said Ms. Carol.

Kaleigh raised her head. "Ms. Carol!" she exclaimed again.

"Good, Kaleigh! I like to see your smile! Now, what is it? Is there a surprise in your bag?"

Rachel, a seventh-grade student, raised her hand.

"Yes?" asked Mr. Sedwell, the substitute English teacher.

"Mr. Sedwell, I'll need a braille copy of this test. Ms. Vernon keeps a file of braille materials for me in the cabinet by the door. My vision teacher, Ms. Craft, makes braille copies and files them there. I'm sure my test is in there."

Mr. Sedwell opened the cabinet, and sure enough, there was a small file box with a number of inkprint and braille papers in it. In the front was a copy of the English test with several braille pages clipped to it. Intrigued, he took it out and felt the dots as he walked to Rachel's desk. "I guess this is yours!" he said. "I'm glad you spoke up!"

"Mr. Darrow, can I talk to you?" asked Luis. It was lunchtime, and Luis, an eleventh grader, had come to Mr. Darrow's tiny office next to the library.

"Hi, Luis, come on in. Sure. What's up?" replied Mr. Darrow, the teacher of students with visual impairments.

Luis looked uncomfortable for a moment and then said, "Mr. Darrow, you know I like Janie. I want to ask her out. How can I ask her out when I don't have a car?"

After a serious discussion, Luis and Mr. Darrow generated several choices. Luis *did not* want to ask his parents to drive them, but his best friend Stuart had a car—they could go somewhere with Stuart and his girlfriend. Or, depending on where they were going, they could take a bus. A taxi was too expensive. "And Luis, you might ask if *she* has a car. There's no reason that *only you* should provide the transportation."

INTRODUCTION

Most sighted people attain and maintain the multiple and complex skills needed to achieve social competence naturally through observation, imitation, and experiential learning. According to Hill and Blasch (1980), almost 85 percent of what is learned socially is mediated through the visual sense. The absence of vision or limited visual functioning may make it more difficult for students with visual impairments to acquire accurate information about their social environment, the context in which social activities occur, and the interpretation of social concepts or nuances that are abstract rather than concrete. Children, particularly those with congenital visual impairments (that is, who have been visually impaired since birth), are more dependent than sighted children on others to provide valuable information about the social environment, as well as the intricacies involved in obtaining and maintaining social relationships with family members, friends, and acquaintances.

Perhaps of all the developmental processes, socialization is the most strongly affected by vision. How students with visual impairments perceive their environment and initiate and respond to interactions with others is directly related to their ability to use sensory information effectively to obtain information on appropriate social behavior. Also, how others react to and interact or do not interact with them can directly affect the students' ability to develop positive self-concepts, a sense of autonomy and independent functioning,

and opportunities to enhance social competence through risk-taking experiences. As Scott (1969, p. 1025) noted:

> Without vision the person is cut off from a larger segment of the physical and social environment to which he must adapt. He cannot easily relate to the environment; he can only infer and therefore misses meanings and intentions which are created when words are combined with the rich vocabulary of expressive gestures.

The acquisition of social skills by students with visual impairments (both those who have been visually impaired from birth and those who lost vision later in life) is an ongoing process. For a child to be successful in social contexts, he or she must be motivated to reach out to others and to use additional information (auditory, olfactory, and tactile) to assist in the mediation of social exchanges. He or she also needs consistency in feedback from others and opportunities to practice a repertoire of socially acceptable behaviors and skills in natural contexts. When a child with a visual impairment receives little or no visual information from others or is unwilling or unable to take risks to achieve social inclusion, he or she may be susceptible to social isolation and a greater dependence on others.

This chapter describes the role of the teacher of students with visual impairments in this area and the unique socialization needs of students with visual impairments, including definitions of important terms and models for understanding social skills. It also presents assessment and intervention strategies that the specialist and others may use to promote social inclusion and integration.

ROLE OF THE TEACHER OF STUDENTS WITH VISUAL IMPAIRMENTS

The teacher of students with visual impairments plays a primary role in teaching appropriate social skills to students who are visually impaired. The area of social interaction skills is part of the expanded core curriculum (Hatlen, 1996; see Chapter 6). Since there is no counterpart in the general education curriculum, the specialist, working in collaboration with others on the educational team, is responsible for addressing this area. Given the unique educational needs of students with visual impairments and the differences in these students' social development, it is crucial for each professional who works with these students to teach and facilitate the instruction of social skills throughout the students' education. The specialist's role in providing social skills instruction is to do the following:

♦ Work with parents of infants and preschoolers in their homes and in school programs to promote early social behaviors and skills;

♦ Assess each student's social skills using a variety of strategies to determine areas in which instruction is needed;

♦ Work with the other members of a student's educational team to design and plan an intervention program for increasing social skills;

♦ Provide direct and targeted instruction in social skills;

♦ Provide accurate and constructive feedback on each student's social skills and competence to the student and his or her family;

♦ Implement strategies to ensure that social skills that are learned in specialized settings will generalize to other environments (school, home, and community);

♦ Work with other members of the educational team, including the family, to facilitate and reinforce appropriate social skills in all environments;

♦ Provide opportunities for a student to participate in a variety of experiential learning activities throughout the student's educational career;

♦ Provide opportunities for a student to meet and interact with role models and mentors who are visually impaired; and

♦ Ensure that social skills instruction is written into a student's educational program.

The teacher also plays an essential role in working with students with additional disabilities; strategies focusing on students with visual impairments and additional disabilities and resources for teachers appear later in this chapter.

DEFINITIONS AND MODELS

Definition of Terms

Terms like *self-concept, self-esteem, self-perception,* and *social competence,* which are often used interchangeably, are defined in this section so the reader has a consistent basis for understanding and synthesizing the information provided in this chapter. Terms such as *locus of control, learned helplessness,* and *learned optimism* are also used throughout the literature to describe how persons with visual impairments function in social contexts, so definitions of these terms are presented here as well.

Self-concept is the foundation on which social skills are developed. How a person feels about himself or herself is central to the development of a positive self-image. Fitts (1967, p. 1) defined *self-concept* as "the perceptions and feelings the individual has about the self whether realistic or not. The image, the picture, the set of perceptions and feeling he has of himself is reflected through self-concept." Tuttle and Tuttle (1996) suggested that the development of self-concept is influenced by two dimensions of personality:

♦ The cognitive component, which relates to factual information about oneself (such as height, hair color, and gender), and

♦ The affective component, which relates to how one feels about oneself (such as, "I'm too tall" or "I'm too short").

Family members and professionals are pivotal in helping students acquire and maintain a positive sense of themselves. How families perceive the capabilities of their children who are visually impaired and promote positive attitudes toward visual impairment can have a strong impact on the socialization process.

Self-esteem focuses more on the affective dimension of self-concept. Self-esteem is part of, and emerges from one's self-concept. It is the evaluative component of self-concept. According to Coopersmith (1967, pp. 4–5), self-esteem is defined as follows:

> The evaluation that the individual makes and customarily maintains with regard to himself: it expresses an attitude of approval or disapproval, and indicates the extent to which the individual believes himself to be capable, significant, successful, and worthy. In short, self-esteem is a personal judgment of worthiness that is expressed in the attitudes the individual holds toward himself.

Social competence, in contrast, is the ability to demonstrate a repertoire of behaviors and actions that promote positive relationships and that are accepted by the culture or society to which the person belongs. To exhibit socially competent behavior, a child must have a positive sense of self and be able to demonstrate a repertoire of socially acceptable behaviors. Since students with visual impairments from culturally diverse backgrounds may exhibit different social amenities or customs, professionals who work with these students need to be sensitive to and aware of the social values and behaviors of various social groups. It is critical that an individual student has a clear understanding of his or her visual impairment, has a sense of control over the environment, has had experiences that promote social understanding and self-esteem, and has a realistic understanding of his or her strengths and limitations.

Self-perception is influenced by how others view a person's abilities and disability. When a child or young adult with a visual impairment is able to make decisions, travel independently, and experience a range of activities in daily life, then he or she may have a sense of control over his or her environment and feel less dependent on others for support or assistance. This phenomenon, *locus of control,* allows the individual to take responsibility for his or her actions and activities and to take advantage of opportunities to achieve a greater sense of independence.

Learned helplessness is a form of depression (Seligman, Reivich, Jaycox, & Hillham, 1995). It may occur when a person learns to become dependent on others for support and assistance, frequently because few expectations are placed on him or her to participate or to achieve. When individuals are faced with adversity and frustration, some may respond by giving up and allowing others to make choices or perform tasks for them, so that there are fewer demands placed on them. Some students with visual impairments may feel that performing daily chores, traveling independently, and completing classroom and homework assignments with little assistance is overwhelming. If they do not have the inner motivation or family support to learn to be independent, they may find it easier to allow others to assume responsibility for performing these activities.

Learned optimism (Seligman et al., 1995), the direct opposite of learned helplessness, is based on positive thinking about events in one's life. Children acquire learned optimism by having positive life experiences. Persons who are optimists view the obstacles of life with a can-do attitude: "Optimism is seeing the glass half full or always seeing the silver lining" (Seligman et al., p. 52).

Models for Defining Social Skills

It is often difficult for professionals to define clearly what is meant by social skills. Some view social skills as innate personality traits. Others believe that social skills are learned behaviors that are influenced by environmental and familial factors. Still others conceive of social skills as a set of social rules set forth by the culture or society in which a person resides. The following three models that attempt to define social skills all have value when determining how best to improve the social competence of students with visual impairments.

The *trait model* is based on the assumption that "skillfulness" in social behavior is predetermined and embedded in one's personality structure (Sacks, Kekelis, & Gaylord-Ross, 1992). This model assumes that an individual's social behavior remains stable and consistent over time and across settings. According to this model, prior experiences, family and environmental factors, and cultural values do not influence how a person reacts or interacts socially.

In the *molecular* or *component model,* social skills are viewed as observable units of behavior that, when combined, can facilitate successful interactive experiences (McFall, 1982). Furthermore, because social skills are learned behaviors that occur in specific situations, an individual will exhibit different social behaviors in different social situations. According to this model, the environment reinforces behavior, or as Kelly (1982, p. 3) explained it, social skills are "those identifiable learned behaviors that individuals use in interpersonal situations to obtain or to maintain reinforcement from their environment."

The *process model* has two general assumptions. The first assumption is that social skills are the component behaviors that make up specific actions (such as looks or nods) or sequences of behaviors that create specific encounters (for example, a greeting). Proponents of this view believe that the use of certain behaviors in specific social contexts is contingent upon rules. According to Trower (1982, p. 418), "Such components are learned by experience or observation, retained in memory in symbolic form, and subsequently retrieved for use in the construction of episodes." The second assumption is that goals are used to attain a set of socially skilled behaviors. That is, the individual monitors the immediate social situation and evaluates his or her own behavior according to external feedback (verbal or nonverbal cues from others) and internal assessment (cognitive representation or logical thinking). This approach relies on a person's ability to perceive the physical environment as well as the internal needs of others.

For children with congenital visual impairments, the molecular and process models of social skills may be particularly difficult to master without direct intervention from a teacher of students with visual impairments. Incidental learning and modeling of specific behaviors are highly contingent on visual observation and imitation. Varied experiences, direct instruction, and realistic feedback from teachers and family members are necessary to develop social skills in and enhance the socialization process of students who are visually impaired.

The way one interprets or defines social skills or social competence is highly dependent on one's culture, values, and socioeconomic background. However, professionals often judge how students or clients should perform or act in the sighted world on the basis of their own values or cultural norms. Therefore, it is critical that during assessments and interventions, professionals take individual differences and family preferences into consideration. Although a set of "societal rules" governs appropriate social behavior in this society, professionals must not dismiss the unique differences that individuals from different cultures bring to Western culture. Professionals also need to acknowledge and respect the attributes of blindness or low vision that are part of a person's identity. Thus, for example, although teachers of students with visual impairments strive to teach students to direct their gaze toward people with whom they are interacting, they need to be aware that in some cultures children do not establish eye contact with adults because doing so is a sign of disrespect.

Schema for Social Skills Development

The impact of a visual impairment, whether congenital or acquired, may impede a student's ability to establish and maintain social contacts with others. The development of social relationships begins even before young children are able to process or react to the information being presented. However, the social functioning of young children with visual impairments is restricted by their inability to acquire information through the visual sense. Therefore, these students may need specific assistance and interventions to acquire typical social behaviors that are part of children's daily routines.

Figure 17.1 displays a schema that depicts social development in children and adolescents with visual impairments as a process with three levels. As students progress from one level to the next, the teacher of students with visual impairments can assist by providing appropriate experiences and using appropriate intervention strategies, as explained throughout this chapter.

At the first level, students develop an awareness of social behavior. For example, infants who are blind may not readily smile or laugh appropriately unless their parents and the specialist work together to initiate and generalize the desired behavior.

At the next level, students become aware of and use strategies to develop positive social interactions after they become aware of other people's needs in social situations. For instance, children who are congenitally blind may not realize that they are keeping their heads down when they speak to others unless they are told that sighted people talk to one another face to face.

At the third level of social development, students with visual impairments are able to interpret social encounters, evaluate these encounters, and use strategies to enhance their social competence. For example, older students with visual impairments may need to learn how to flirt using nonverbal cues, as well as when and where it is appropriate to flirt and how to evaluate the effectiveness of flirting. The assessment and intervention strategies described throughout this chapter are based on this model of cognitive social understanding.

ASSESSMENT

In assessing social skills, the teacher of students with visual impairments examines the student's social abilities in relation to those of sighted chil-

Level I

> Self-Identity + Social Awareness
>
> =
>
> Behavioral Social Skills

Level II

> Awareness of Other People's Needs + Strategies for Positive Interactions
>
> =
>
> Interactive Social Skills

Level III

> Interpretation of Social Situations + Awareness of Social Needs of Others + Strategies to Enhance Social Competence
>
> =
>
> Cognitive Social Understanding

Figure 17.1. Social Development Schema

dren and adolescents, as well as of other students with visual impairments. The specialist also keeps in mind that each student has unique attributes and limitations and that personality traits, family values and culture, and additional disabilities influence a student's level of social skills.

Solid assessment is necessary to determine which social skills need to be taught to a student and in what sequence. The specialist uses a variety of strategies and techniques to gather information on a student's social skills: observation, interviews, checklists, role-playing, problem solving, a student's self-evaluation, and video- and audiotapes. With this information, the specialist can work with other members of the student's educational team, including the parents, to develop appropriate instructional strategies and techniques.

Observation

One widely used form of social skills assessment is structured observation. That is, the teacher of students with visual impairments, school psychologist, school counselor, social worker, and others observe a student interacting with other children in many different social environments: the playground at recess, the cafeteria, the classroom during free time or unstructured activities, and the home and neighborhood.

When developing an observation protocol to assess a student's social skills, the evaluator (the teacher of students with visual impairments or another member of the educational team) begins by observing children without visual impairments to determine a baseline for assessment. This pre-evaluative phase allows the evaluator to gain insight into and a realistic perspective on the social world and culture of sighted children and adolescents. Having knowledge of "typical" social standards gives the evaluator a basis for judging the social skills that students with visual impairments need most to interact with others. Observation is a particularly useful assessment tool for evaluating the social skills needed by students with visual impairments who have additional disabilities.

Observing a student who is visually impaired at play or simply hanging out with other children can tell the evaluator a great deal about the student's personality and ability to communicate effectively in a group. Observing a student during free-play periods over a consistent period of time can determine whether the student has a tendency to play with large groups of children; small, more intimate groups; or alone. The types of play activities in which the student engages may indicate how outgoing the student is and whether he or she has the potential to make friends. It is also important to observe students in more structured social environments, such as the classroom or workplace, to determine how they deal with adult authority, structured group projects, and unstructured work time. The following questions (Wolffe & Sacks, 1997) may guide the evaluator in structuring the observation:

- In a group, does the student initiate contact with others?
- Is the student able to communicate his or her needs, wants, and desires effectively?
- Is the student able to maintain conversations with others?
- Does the student take turns during social encounters?
- Is the student open to the ideas of others, or does the student insist on getting his or her own way?
- Does the student demonstrate a willingness to compromise and share?
- Does the student listen when others are talking and know when to interrupt a speaker?
- Can the student maintain an interactive conversation?
- Can the student work effectively for an extended period when working on a group project?
- Has the student grasped many of the social nuances used by age-mates and adults in school, at home, and in the community?

Interviews

Interviews are another tool that teachers, counselors, residential staff, and related services professionals can use to assess social skills. The purposes of these interviews are to determine the student's typical responses to social demands and what the student feels about himself or herself and other children and to gain insights into what the student, his or her parents, and other family members view as important social skills to be learned. Because teachers of students with visual impairments and other professionals develop close and trusting relationships with students, it is natural for them to have frequent informal discussions with the students regarding self-concept, interactions with age-mates, and issues related to visual impairment, such as driving and dating. The following questions (Wolffe & Sacks, 1997) may help the evaluator to learn more about a student and the student's level of social competence during an interview:

♦ What has been going on in your class the past few days?

♦ What have you been doing at home?

♦ What have you been doing after school?

♦ Can you describe a typical day in your life?

♦ How do you interact with your sighted classmates?

♦ What attributes do you look for in a friend?

♦ How would you describe the most popular person in your school?

♦ How are you the same as or different from the most popular person in your school?

♦ How would your friends describe you?

♦ How would your family describe you?

♦ What are your strengths (and weaknesses) in social situations?

Social Skills Checklists

Social skills checklists help members of the educational team determine specific social skills for instruction by evaluating a student's performance using an established set of behavioral criteria. Usually, these checklists provide the basis for an expanded curriculum. Numerous social skills checklists are commercially available for students with disabilities and provide a solid foundation for assessments. They include *The Social Skills Rating System* (Gresham & Elliot, 1990), *School Social Behavior Scales* (Merrell, 1993), and *The Walker McConnell Scale of Social Competence and School Adjustment* (Walker & McConnell, 1995).

Few social skills checklists have been developed specifically for students with visual impair-

ments. However, two protocols have been written to meet the unique educational needs of these youngsters. *Independent Living: A Curriculum with Adaptations for Students with Visual Impairments: Volume. 1. Social Competence* (Loumiet & Levack, 1991) contains an excellent checklist for assessing social skills. The *Santa Clara County Social Skills Curriculum for Children with Visual Impairments* (McCallum & Sacks, 1993) also includes a checklist that is divided into three parts: basic social behaviors, interpersonal relationships, and cognitive social behaviors. This checklist—*Social Skills Assessment Tool for Children with Visual Impairments*—is presented in Figure 17.2.

Situational Role-Plays

Situational role-plays allow the evaluator to define specific scenarios that are natural and typical of a student's social world. The purpose of a role-play assessment is to determine the student's strengths and weaknesses in responding to a given social situation. A situational role-play can also be used to evaluate whether structured social skills training has improved a student's social behavior. Allowing a student to assume the role of another person in a situational role-play can help the student understand how age-mates may perceive the student or handle a similar situation.

Using age-mates without disabilities as partners in situational role-plays provides an element of reality in an assessment that is missing when an adult is a partner. Furthermore, positive support and influence from peers can help a student with a visual impairment to develop and maintain socially competent behavior at home, in school, and in the community.

Although age-mates without disabilities may not have expertise in assessing or teaching social skills to others, they give the student who is visually impaired realistic information about the peer culture in which they engage (Sacks & Gaylord-Ross, 1989; Sacks & Wolffe, 1992). Peers are excellent models for helping a child to learn how to gain access to play groups (Corsaro, 1985), attract and direct the attention of other children (Putallaz & Gottman, 1982), resolve conflicts (Shantz, 1986),

Social Skills Assessment Tool for Children with Visual Impairments

Student: _____ Assessor: _____ Date: _____

Rate each item as: 1 = absent; 2 = poor; 3 = fair; 4 = adequate; 5 = good; 6 = excellent

BASIC SOCIAL BEHAVIORS

A. Body Language

1. _____ Maintain appropriate eye contact.
2. _____ Demonstrate appropriate body posture.
3. _____ Maintain appropriate personal body space.
4. _____ Utilize and respond to gestures and facial expressions.
5. _____ Refrain from engaging in socially unacceptable mannerisms.

B. Communication Skills

1. _____ Positively initiate interactions with others.
2. _____ Exhibit age-appropriate interactions and conversations.
3. _____ Expand conversations.
4. _____ Listen well.
5. _____ Take turns and share.
6. _____ Compliment.
7. _____ Interrupt appropriately.
8. _____ Demonstrate empathy and sympathy.
9. _____ Respond appropriately to positive and negative feedback from peers and adults.

C. Cooperative Skills

1. _____ Demonstrate cooperation and an understanding of group dynamics.
2. _____ Demonstrate respect for the group leader.
3. _____ Sustain group involvement.
4. _____ Share in group activity.
5. _____ Initiate joining a group.
6. _____ Lead a group activity.

INTERPERSONAL RELATIONSHIPS

A. Interactions

1. _____ Interact appropriately with others: _____ adult _____ disabled peer
   _____ nondisabled peer _____ younger children _____ older children.

   Comment on type and style of interaction:

2. _____ Play with others: _____ one _____ small group _____ larger group.

   Comment on quality of play:

(continued on next page)

Figure 17.2. Social Skills Assessment Tool for Children with Visual Impairments

Social Skills Assessment Tool *(Continued)*

3. _____ Demonstrate ability to engage in a variety of play activities.
4. _____ Can compromise.
5. _____ Show awareness of common activities and interests.
6. _____ Encourage the efforts of others.
7. _____ Demonstrate gratitude toward others.

B. Sustaining Relationships

1. _____ Demonstrate an understanding of differences among family, friends, acquaintances, and strangers.
2. _____ Make friends and be liked by peers.
3. _____ Demonstrate appropriate behaviors for attending social events.
4. _____ Interact with peers outside school.
5. _____ Understand the needs of others.
6. _____ Demonstrate an age-appropriate awareness of human sexuality, including concepts of public versus private, and societal values and attitudes.
7. _____ Demonstrate an age-appropriate awareness of job-related concepts, including assuming responsibility and relating to others in work situations.

COGNITIVE SOCIAL BEHAVIORS

A. Self-Identity

1. _____ Demonstrate an understanding of visual impairment.
2. _____ Demonstrate an awareness of personal competencies and limitations.
3. _____ Demonstrate an awareness of possible adaptations.
4. _____ Advocate for self in school, home, and community environments.
5. _____ Demonstrate assertiveness in an appropriate manner.

B. Interpreting Social Situations

1. _____ Observe and identify opportunities for social interactions.
2. _____ Interpret social cues and generate strategies for interaction.
3. _____ Anticipate the consequences of strategies and select the most desired one.

C. Performance of Social Skills

1. _____ Initiate and perform appropriate behaviors.
2. _____ Generalize social skills to a variety of situations.
3. _____ Sustain social competence over time.

D. Self-Evaluation

1. _____ Demonstrate an ability to evaluate and monitor own social performance realistically.
2. _____ Demonstrate an ability to adjust own behavior accordingly.

Source: Adapted from B. J. McCallum and S. Z. Sacks, *The Santa Clara County Social Skills Curriculum for Children with Visual Impairments* (Santa Clara, CA: Santa Clara County Schools, 1993); and K. E. Wolffe and S. Z. Sacks, *Focused on . . . Assessment Techniques* (New York: AFB Press, 2000).

engage in fantasy play (Corsaro, 1985), and maintain friendships with others (Corsaro, 1985). Adolescents with visual impairments depend on close friends and family members to interpret visual cues from others and to obtain verbal feedback regarding gestures or social nuances made by others (Sacks, 1996). The following are three typical role-play scenarios in which sighted age-mates could offer support to a student with a visual impairment during an assessment:

♦ You are the only visually impaired student in your elementary school. Your teacher insists that you must go to recess with a sighted classmate. Each day she assigns a different classmate to you at recess. Today, you want to play on the climbing equipment, but the classmate wants to jump rope. How do you handle your teacher and your classmates?

♦ While sitting in your math class, you realize that your teacher is writing examples of math problems on the board without verbally describing them. You have already asked the teacher to describe what is written on the board. How do you handle this situation?

♦ Whenever you stand in the cafeteria line at lunch, a few students always come up and tease you. They call you "blindy" and wave their hands in front of your face. What do you do, and what do you tell them?

Problem-Solving Scenarios

This form of social skills assessment allows the evaluator to determine if the student can solve a problem or dilemma in a logical manner. The student has to be able to identify the social problem, determine how to react to the social situation, and decide if the action taken was the correct one. Usually, problem-solving scenarios involve moral decisions and an awareness of appropriate social behavior. Again, using sighted age-mates during these scenarios can be an effective evaluation and intervention tool. The following examples of problem-solving scenarios (Wolffe & Sacks, 1997)

provide the evaluator with valuable information about how a student with a visual impairment may perceive certain social situations:

♦ A classmate takes your hat (or pen, pencil, long cane, and so forth) and will not return it. What do you do?

♦ You are late to class because you could not get into your locker. What do you tell your teacher?

♦ A classmate asks you to share your notes (provided to you by your teacher) because he was not paying attention in class. What do you do?

♦ You are at a fast-food restaurant, and two acquaintances cut in line in front of you. What do you do?

Student's Self-Evaluation

A self-evaluation allows a student with a visual impairment to judge his or her social abilities and skills in relation to age-mates with and without visual impairments. It gives the student an opportunity to examine objectively how he or she acted or reacted in a specific situation. The student may ask the following questions:

♦ How did I do in that situation?

♦ What would I do differently the next time?

♦ Did I receive a positive or negative response from my classmates, teachers, and others, and why?

A self-evaluation can also include a rating system by which the student ranks himself or herself in relation to others using a rating scale. For example, adolescents may be asked to rate how they get along with other students using a rating of 1 (excellent) to 5 (poor). Young students with low vision may be asked to rate themselves using pictures or drawings that represent themselves and their feelings.

Another strategy for helping students to evaluate their own social behavior is to have them write about themselves, their friends, and their families with an emphasis on feelings, which gives the evaluator insight into the students' self-concepts and motivations for establishing social relationships. Young students with low vision can be asked to express their feelings about themselves, their families, and their friends through drawings, and students who are functionally blind can do so by making sculptures out of clay. Assessments of drawings and sculptures by young students often require open-ended discussions.

Video- and Audiotaped Evaluations

Students with visual impairments are often unaware of their social behavior because they have limited access to visual feedback. Unless they are given auditory or visual feedback from family members or friends, they may not realize that the way they act socially appears awkward or unconventional. Videotaping or audiotaping a student in an age-appropriate activity with other students can provide information about how the student converses with others, what type of actions and gestures the student uses to gain and maintain access to a group, and the level of reciprocal interaction among peers. It also provides information about a student's voice tone and quality, voice latency (length of response), and physical and age-appropriate appearance.

GENERAL INSTRUCTIONAL STRATEGIES

After assessment information is gathered and instructional priorities are established, the teacher of students with visual impairments begins to provide instruction and other opportunities to address targeted needs. Instructional priorities for social skills interventions are usually determined by a student, his or her parents and other family members, and other members of the student's educational team. Assessment data are used to assist the educational team in determining what skills need to be taught. In the sections that follow, guidelines and suggestions are provided for helping students establish a sense of identity and for

promoting the development of social skills in young students, school-age students, and adolescents. Many of the interventions described in these sections can be modified for students with visual impairments and additional disabilities. Structured interventions and peer-mediated models are particularly useful for this population.

Establishment of a Sense of Identity

An individual's social competence is based, in part, on his or her sense of identity. Therefore, the teacher of students with visual impairments and the student's family members need to encourage the student to establish a strong sense of identity as a person with a visual impairment. Many students with visual impairments perceive themselves as being either sighted or blind, so it may be difficult for students with low vision to establish a strong social identity. In addition, societal values about blindness and low vision may prevent students from feeling adequate and self-sufficient.

Students who are visually impaired may feel isolated from the sighted world and have limited opportunities to identify with other persons with visual impairments. They are often the only students in their schools or local communities who are blind or have low vision. Because they may expend a great deal of energy keeping up with schoolwork or trying to fit in with the sighted students, they may not feel good about their skills or accomplishments and may need support from others to help establish a sense of identity by enhancing their self-esteem and understanding their visual impairments.

Strategies to Enhance Self-Esteem

Creating Opportunities

Parents and professionals must create opportunities that are success oriented to enhance the self-esteem of students with visual impairments. Allowing students to make decisions, to assume responsibilities for household chores and school assignments, to take risks, and to experience everyday activities with greater independence can promote a positive sense of self. Mangold (1982) suggested several strategies for nurturing self-esteem:

◆ Tell the student when he or she is doing something correctly, rather than emphasize negative behavior (say, for example, "I like the way you are looking at me");

◆ Provide honest feedback about observed behavior (for instance, tell the student that it is socially unacceptable to stand with one's back to another person);

◆ Make lists of the tasks and activities that the student *can do;*

◆ Encourage the student to engage in activities that he or she performs better than his or her sighted age-mates (such as using a computer, playing a musical instrument, keyboarding, and memorizing valuable information in group projects or activities);

◆ Give the student opportunities to compare his or her accomplishments with those of sighted peers or siblings (for example, "I skied down the expert slope this weekend; how did you do?" or "I mastered the third level in Zelda, my favorite computer game; what level are you on?");

◆ Encourage the student to perform household chores and simple cooking activities at home;

◆ Encourage the student to engage in risk-taking activities (like climbing play structures and doing downhill or cross country skiing, river rafting, wall climbing, and a ropes course);

◆ Encourage the student to explore and engage in after-school activities (such as a dance class, drama club, gymnastics, ice-skating, karate, wrestling, cheerleading, and swimming).

Helping Students Understand Their Visual Impairment

To establish a positive sense of self, students need to understand their visual impairments and be able to communicate their needs to others. Those who can effectively tell others about what they can and cannot see and effectively demonstrate a repertoire of age-appropriate activities with peers tend to feel good about themselves and their abilities. Sidebar 17.1 provides strategies for enhancing students' understanding of their visual impairments.

Disclosing One's Visual Impairment. Students who understand their visual impairments may feel less conspicuous or ashamed about their impairments and begin to accept themselves as capable individuals. Even preschool-age children should be encouraged to let others know about their visual impairments by saying the following, for example:

◆ "When I was a baby, I was very small, and my eyes don't work right."

◆ "I can't see; I'm blind. Can you help me find the ball?"

◆ "My eyes move a lot, 'cause it helps me see."

Older students must determine for themselves when and where to disclose their visual impairments to others. Telling others about one's visual impairment is a real art. A student needs to determine how much and what type of information to disclose and be prepared to describe his or her visual needs and abilities succinctly. It is not always necessary to describe in detail the nature and scope of the visual impairment. For example, a young student who is being teased in an elementary school classroom because she wears magnification lenses to read regular print might explain: "I use my glasses to help me read. They make the letters in the book larger so I can read easily." When students are describing the cause of their visual impairments to close friends or teachers, they may choose to describe their visual status in greater detail, saying, for example, "I was born two months early. I weighed 2 pounds and 2 ounces. The oxygen they gave me in the incubator damaged my retina. That's why I can't see."

When students with visual impairments inter-

Activities to Enhance Students' Understanding of Visual Impairment

◆ Have the students with low vision examine their own eyes in the mirror (placing a magnifier on the mirror may be helpful). Ask them to pay attention to the color and shape of the eyes and to any difference they observe with respect to structure or function.

◆ Let the students with low vision compare their eyes with those of others.

◆ Use a pull-apart model to help the students learn the location of different parts of the eye.

◆ Devise matching games or board games to help the students become familiar with different parts of the eye (for example, a concentration matching game in which the students match the description of an eye condition with the name of the condition).

◆ Provide opportunities for the students to discuss and learn about their own visual impairments (for instance, those who use computers can search the Internet for information on their eye conditions and present five-minute oral reports).

◆ Once the students become familiar with the parts of the eye, have them name and identify the sources of their visual impairments (using models or drawings).

◆ Develop role-play scenarios in which the students need to give information about their visual impairments to other children or to general education teachers.

◆ Provide opportunities for the students to meet other children or adults with similar visual impairments. Have them develop lists of interview questions about their visual impairments to ask others.

◆ Let the students share information about their visual functioning. For example, create a scavenger hunt around the school campus or in the community. Instead of finding items, the students have to compare how objects (such as stairs, buildings, and floor surfaces) appear in different light and with different levels of contrast.

◆ Develop a board game in which students who are sighted and students who are visually impaired can learn more about vision and low vision (for instance, a Trivial Pursuit type of game that has several categories related to visual impairments and eye conditions).

◆ Have the students create a story in which the main character is a person with low vision.

◆ Have the students create television or radio commercials for adaptive equipment used by persons with specific visual impairments.

◆ Have the students keep journals as persons with low vision, recording positive or successful accomplishments or adaptations used throughout the school year.

_____

Source: Adapted from S. Z. Sacks, "Psychological and Social Implications of Low Vision," in A. L. Corn and A. J. Koenig, Eds., *Foundations of Low Vision: Clinical and Functional Perspectives* (New York: AFB Press, 1996), p. 37.

act with a range of individuals in the community, the level of disclosure is much different. They need to be brief, yet direct, in providing information while asking for assistance, as in the following statements: "Can you read the ice cream flavors to me. I can't see very well" or "Could you assist me in completing this deposit slip? I can't see the numbers on the check." In job situations, adolescents with visual impairments have to educate and provide information about their visual impairments, job adaptations, and need for assistance to employers and co-workers. However, to be treated as equals, they must demonstrate poise, social competence, and a sense of independence.

Providing Mentors and Role Models. Since students with visual impairments are frequently the only students in their schools or communities who have visual impairments, they can come to feel more comfortable and at ease with their disabilities if they are introduced to adults who are visually impaired and have similar visual etiologies to theirs. Through casual and consistent social interactions with these adults, the students can begin to identify with others with visual impairments, and their feelings of inadequacy or embarrassment may shift to a stronger sense of social competence. Role models and mentors can provide information about the progression of a visual impairment and strategies for performing independent living and travel tasks and can model appropriate social behaviors in a variety of situations. They can also help the students enhance their self-confidence and social competence through discussions, question-and-answer sessions, and exposure to organizations of and for persons who are blind or have low vision.

Promoting Self-Advocacy. Once students feel comfortable discussing their visual impairments freely and openly, they begin to feel a sense of control over their ability to interact effectively with others. They quickly learn that advocating for themselves is an effective strategy for promoting interdependence and prosocial behavior. If students can communicate their needs or desires effectively to peers and adults using age-appropri-

ate social behavior, they are likely to gain greater acceptance and support from others at school and in the community.

A student who uses assertive statements develops a sense of competence and capability that is critical in the socialization process. For example, "I really like it when you verbalize what's on the white board; it helps me learn the information" gives the general education teacher valuable information and helps ensure that the teacher will continue to use this effective strategy. However, statements like "You have to read what's on the white board so I can get the information; if you don't, I'll do poorly in class" or "It's hard to get the information; you know I can't see," are less effective. Students can be taught to rephrase aggressive or passive statements through role-playing or problem-solving scenarios or by analyzing audiotaped social interactions.

SOCIAL SKILLS INSTRUCTION FOR SPECIFIC AGE GROUPS

Infants and Preschoolers

Early socialization experiences begin with interactions between infants with visual impairments and their parents, siblings, and other close relatives. These experiences facilitate cognitive growth and development and promote interactions with other people and with objects in the environment. Children learn to interact with the environment through play and other early experiences that provide opportunities to enhance socially competent behavior, expand the use and function of language, and encourage the expansion of creative and critical thinking abilities.

Enhancing Positive Social Behavior

Parents are the first teachers of social skills. For young children with visual impairments, promoting prosocial behavior involves consistency, responsibility, and expectations. Early learning of social skills can be facilitated by families through physical modeling, verbal feedback, and tactile cues and by teaching their children to explore the environment through coactive movement and through manipulation of materials and objects during activities. One cannot assume that a young child with a visual impairment will naturally exhibit appropriate social behavior unless the social world and its experiences are brought to him or her. Skellenger, Hill, and Hill (1992) found, for example, that to facilitate play, it is beneficial to limit the play area and number of toys provided to young children with visual impairments. (See Chapter 15 for additional strategies on designing play environments.) They also suggested that teachers and family members should demonstrate and model the use and function of toys to promote the children's interaction with their sighted peers.

Sidebar 17.2 presents several examples from the *Santa Clara County Social Skills Curriculum for Children with Visual Impairments* (McCallum & Sacks, 1993) that illustrate how teachers and family members can infuse social skills instruction into daily activities and routines for young children. These examples focus on activities to foster appropriate social behaviors, such as eye contact, facial expressions and gestures, body posture and body space, the use of amenities, and the initiation of social interactions.

Promoting Social Language and Expression

Teachers and families facilitate the development of social language in young children with visual impairments through hands-on experiences, auditory modeling of reciprocal expression (that is, listening and paying attention to others), turn taking, and auditory descriptions of actions and activities performed by others (siblings and other children). According to Kekelis and Sacks (1988), young children with visual impairments need the support of others to promote positive social communication. To make sense of their social environment, they tend to ask many more questions than do their sighted peers, and their responses may be limited because of their lack of social experiences. To promote social communication ac-

tivities for a young child with a visual impairment, Kekelis and Sacks suggested doing the following;

◆ Begin by making certain that the child with a visual impairment understands what other children are doing. Describe the children who are present and the activities in which they are engaged.

◆ Remind the child to take a moment to listen to a group at play before he or she jumps in with a question or comment that disrupts the group.

◆ Remind the child that he or she is expected to answer questions and respond to comments made by friends. Point out that listening and taking turns will help the child make and keep friends.

◆ Help the child to find alternate ways other than questions to keep in touch with a play partner. For example, when two young children are playing with blocks, the teacher can model appropriate descriptions for the sighted partner to use when engaging in pretend play with the student with a visual impairment: "Lindsay, you might want to say to Brian, 'Help me build the road around the town so we can race our cars.'"

Promoting Social Inclusion at Home and in School

During the early years and beyond, parents and other family members need to be actively involved in designing activities and experiences that promote social integration of their children with visual impairments in the community and the school. Therefore, it is critical for them to view themselves as essential members of the school community even if their children attend specialized schools for students who are visually impaired or special day classes outside the local school districts. Sidebar 17.3 presents strategies for helping young children with visual impairments participate in social activities that promote interdependence, decision making, turn taking, and sharing with peers.

Ways to Infuse Social Skills Instruction in Daily Activities

Goal: The child will maintain appropriate eye contact when engaged in interactions with adults and peers:

- Hold the child in your arms and encourage him or her to face toward adults when they are talking.

- Get down close to the child's level when talking to him or her. Verbally or physically prompt the child to turn his or her body toward you when you are speaking.

- Encourage the child to turn his or her body and head toward a person who is speaking. Reinforce verbally throughout the day when the child spontaneously looks and faces a person.

- Encourage the child to maintain appropriate eye contact throughout a conversation or interaction.

Goal: The child will demonstrate appropriate body posture while sitting and standing by holding his or her head up and back straight without reminders:

- Give the child opportunities to engage in a variety of activities that can be done while seated (such as eating or playing with clay). Verbally or physically prompt the child to maintain an upright position.

- Provide opportunities for the child to practice appropriate body space and posture through partner games, such as London Bridge or pretend play.

Goal: The child will maintain appropriate personal body space without disturbing or disrupting others:

- During floor or table play, identify the child's defined space verbally, visually,

and tactilely. Comment on and reinforce the child when he or she remains within the identified space.

- Give the child opportunities to become familiar with materials in new environments with direction from an adult.

- Give the child opportunities to explore and become familiar with materials and environments with other children present and have an adult describe the space around the child while emphasizing such words as *mine, his, hers, theirs,* and *yours.*

- Give the child opportunities to be in close proximity to other children and reinforce the child when he or she plays without disrupting the other children's materials or food.

- Remind the child to back away from or not to touch another person when he gets too close to the other person. Verbally reinforce the child when he or she complies and comment when appropriate space is established.

Goal: The child will use and respond to common gestures and facial expressions:

- Throughout the day comment on feelings (such as happy, angry, sad, and sleepy) as they occur, emphasizing facial expressions. Encourage the child to explore facial expressions tactilely and visually.

- Use gestures to indicate to the child to sit, come, stop, and so forth, paired with language. If appropriate, do not use spoken language cues.

(continued on next page)

Social Skills Instruction *(Continued)*

Goal: The child will take turns or share with others:

- During informal group conversations (at the lunch table), encourage the child to respond to simple questions asked of several children in turn, by saying, for example, "John, it is your turn to answer."

- During a group or circle activity, encourage the child to take a turn by raising his or her hand without talking. Reinforce, comment or prompt as appropriate.

- Encourage a variety of adult–child and child–child reciprocal interactions with toys (such as rolling a ball back and forth, talking on the telephone, and playing simple board or card games).

- Give sets of toys with similar items to small groups of children (for example, five cars for three children, three cars for three children, or one car for three children) and give the children specific, positive feedback for sharing items.

Goal: The child will use appropriate and positive comments during social interactions:

- Model specific positive feedback (for example, "Marc, you're sitting up straight!" "Michelle, I like your new dress!").

- Model appropriate times to say "please," "no thank-you," "you're welcome," "I'm sorry," and "excuse me." Reinforce the child and his or her peers when they approximate and/or spontaneously use these amenities.

Source: Reprinted, with permission, from B. J. McCallum and S. Z. Sacks, *The Santa Clara County Social Skills Curriculum for Children with Visual Impairments* (Santa Clara, CA: Santa Clara County Schools, 1993).

Strategies to Promote Social Inclusion at Home and at School

- Encourage the child to explore the environment by providing many hands-on experiences. Take him or her on outings to various community sites (such as parks, playgrounds, and restaurants), and on shopping trips (to the grocery store, shopping mall, or video store), for example.

- Allow the child to be an active participant in each hands-on experience. For example, when grocery shopping, have the child choose a favorite snack or select a favorite fruit from the produce section.

- Provide opportunities for the child to participate in structured group activities that facilitate socialization, such as swimming lessons, gymnastics, story hour at a public library, and rhythm and music groups. Many of these activities can be done with a parent or other family member.

(continued on next page)

Strategies to Promote Social Inclusion *(Continued)*

◆ Encourage the child to take risks and try new activities. Provide opportunities for the child to experience a variety of multisensory activities (such as tasting new foods and feeling a variety of textures; playing rough-and-tumble games; engaging in climbing activities; and playing in water, sand, and snow).

◆ Provide opportunities for the child to assume responsibility for classroom jobs or home chores on a consistent basis.

Young children can be responsible for putting away their toys, putting their dirty clothes in a clothes hamper, helping to set the table for a family meal, clearing the table after eating a meal, or helping to take out the trash or recycle bins.

◆ Form partnerships with other parents and teachers and become involved in play groups and community groups (such as a church, Tiny Tots, dance classes, music lessons, ice-skating, and skiing).

Elementary and Middle-School Students

School provides a framework for students with visual impairments to initiate and maintain friendships and a structure for students to learn and practice a range of social behaviors. Children learn quickly what is acceptable social behavior in the school community through modeling and feedback from teachers and other children. The culture of a school establishes boundaries for acceptable social behavior. For example, in classrooms, students are expected to sit in their seats, raise their hands when answering questions or responding to requests, and cooperate with others. Students are also expected to establish eye contact and maintain a level of personal distance when interacting with others in play and academic activities.

Sighted students learn early about the importance of sharing and taking turns in group activities. However, it is not enough for students with visual impairments to know how to gain access to a peer group or use positive social initiations with peers. They must learn the intricacies of the peer culture, including all the visual cues and nuances that make up the social rules and behaviors that children follow in social contexts. To integrate these skills, most students with visual impair-

ments need to have support from others and the desire to engage with others. Parents, siblings, teachers, and other professionals play an integral role in helping a student learn the nuances of the peer culture by providing hands-on experiences and consistent feedback about the environment.

Promoting Risk Taking and Decision Making

Students with visual impairments must be encouraged to take risks and motivated to engage with others. Providing opportunities for them to participate in activities, such as wall climbing, river rafting, skiing, hiking, and other physical endeavors, fosters a positive sense of self and a willingness to try new and challenging experiences. In addition, the students must learn to integrate cognitive, motor, and linguistic skills while incorporating feedback and other types of input from others. Sidebar 17.4 presents ways in which students can become more socially interactive and assertive with peers.

Fostering Development of Friendships

Few studies have examined the impact of visual impairment on the development of friendships. One such study, by MacCuspie (1992, p. 88), found

Activities to Promote Interaction with Peers

◆ Encourage the student to participate in reciprocal, interactive conversations that focus on turn taking and sharing ideas and opinions.

◆ Provide opportunities for the student to engage in imaginative play that fosters sharing with other students.

◆ Introduce the student to "in" games and activities. Spend time teaching the student how to play the games or manipulate the toys (such as Magic cards, Pokémon cards, Nintendo or Sega video games).

◆ Teach the student to use the vocabulary of his or her peers when playing with them. Record other children's dialogue, if necessary, to provide a model for the student with a visual impairment.

◆ Encourage the student to accept invitations to birthday parties, sleep-over parties, and after-school play.

◆ Encourage the student to participate in group activities that promote sharing and team building: music groups (chorus, orchestra, and band), school and community drama clubs, athletic experiences (swimming, gymnastics, soccer, and wrestling), and dance groups (folk dance, ballet, tap, and jazz).

◆ Provide opportunities for the student to make decisions about which play or academic activities he or she wants to participate in and to follow through on the choice, regardless of the outcome.

◆ Encourage the student to participate in activities in which he or she has to select a partner during group activities in the classroom or during recreational activities in school or in the community.

◆ Create real or imaginary situations in which the student has to make a decision independently. Help the student to evaluate the choice he or she has made by using problem-solving strategies. For example, a teacher can provide the following scenario to a student: "You are in a line at a fast-food restaurant, and someone cuts in front of you. What do you do?" The student may choose to ignore the situation; say something to the person like, "You butted in line; the end of the line is over there"; or tell someone in authority. After a choice is made, the student and teacher discuss the possible outcomes of such a response or action. The student then evaluates the response and, if appropriate, may choose another option.

---

that students with visual impairments (both those who were blind and those with low vision) had few friends and perceived friends as "those who helped them." Although the students in MacCuspie's study wanted to play and interact with popular sighted students, none routinely did so.

MacCuspie (1992) also found that, for the most part, the students believed that they were "special" and entitled to privileges, such as standing in front of the cafeteria line, and did not have to obey rules created by sighted students and teachers. Many of the children said that they had few opportunities to reciprocate or support other children and considered themselves to be the ones who needed help. Although the students recognized the importance of reaching out to others and reciprocating for assistance given by others, they often thought that certain types of assistance or support were the benefits of their visual impairments that were to be expected, not requested.

According to Kekelis (1992), students with visual impairments may require more practice and experience in developing friendships. She noted that children who are liked by their peers and who successfully participate in play activities and conversations have learned to determine and to respond to their peers' interests. They also have personal characteristics that are essential for inclusion in social groups, such as physical attractiveness, academic success, athletic abilities, and interactive language abilities.

Kekelis and Sacks (1992) found that the most socially adept child in their ethnographic study of kindergartners and first graders with visual impairments exhibited personal characteristics that made other children want to interact with him. He was outgoing, physically attractive, academically successful in his first-grade classroom, and understood the function and repertoire of play activities and the topics discussed by his classmates. However, for this boy to have truly interactive social experiences, he required assistance from his teachers to set up situations in which he could demonstrate his social competence. For example, during recess, he played with Matchbox cars and action figures, which enticed other children to come to him, so he did not have to search for others on an extremely busy and active playground. Although the sighted students genuinely enjoyed interacting with this student, his teacher and family had to work hard to expand social activities beyond school. They enrolled him in a variety of after-school activities (a karate class, swimming class, and chess club) that promoted friendships and social competence.

It is not enough for children to interact with one another; they must learn to engage in social exchanges that promote and foster friendship and equality in their relationships. Kekelis and Sacks (1992) noted that many of the social exchanges between one kindergarten boy who was blind and his sighted classmates were negative and did little to promote active friendships. The sighted classmates often teased the boy by calling out his name and then running away when he tried to find

them. The social milieu of the classroom and the lack of cooperation between the general education teacher and the teacher of students with visual impairments prevented this boy from developing positive social relationships with his sighted classmates. The sighted children also needed and desired information about the boy's visual status. Helping sighted students understand how their classmate who is visually impaired functions in the classroom and in play activities and providing alternative strategies to enhance group interactions may promote positive social exchanges among them.

Although research on the development of friendships by students with visual impairments is sparse, it seems clear that direct steps should be taken to encourage and nurture friendships. Sidebar 17.5 presents suggestions that teachers can make to students with visual impairments to foster friendships with their sighted peers.

Providing Structured Social Skills Interventions

Although the strategies provided thus far are practical and useful for students, teachers, and families, students with visual impairments may require more structured interventions to learn the skills that are necessary to become socially interactive with sighted children and adults. Structured social skills training takes many forms and can parallel many of the strategies used for social skills assessments (discussed earlier), as well as the following additional strategies:

◆ *Structured social skills training* uses direct teaching based on behavioral techniques, including the teacher's modeling of the skills and providing opportunities to practice the skills and feedback on the student's use of the skills. This strategy is particularly useful for students with visual impairments and additional disabilities.

◆ *Peer-mediated social skills training* uses age-mates to provide interventions with the guidance from the teacher.

◆ *Peer-support social skills models* use sighted

Strategies for Students to Use to Foster and Promote Friendships

- Display positive orientation skills (smile, orient toward the speaker, pay attention to what the speaker says, and do not refocus attention on yourself or insignificant details).

- Demonstrate reciprocity (give and take). Share in activities and conversations. Wait for responses from others without dominating the interaction.

- Communicate openly and honestly, but with sensitivity toward others. Recognize and be attentive to the wishes of others. Demonstrate flexibility when selecting an activity or game.

- Reinforce others when they demonstrate positive interactions. Use words that express praise and compliments (for example, "Hey, thanks for the ride; it was fun!" or "Wow! You really know how to use that Gameboy!").

- Initiate thoughtful interactions. Compliment others or share something special with them (such as food, cards, or a small gift).

- Be a good listener.

- Share feelings and belongings.

- Select peers who have similar likes and dislikes (food, dress, games, radio and television programs, music, and the like) as you do.

- Pay attention to the effect of your behavior on others. Be sensitive to the needs and feelings of others.

- Consider others' feelings, values, and interests. Be open minded in trying new foods, activities, or experiences.

- Be trustworthy and loyal. Keep information told in confidence to yourself.

- Understand your peer culture (dress, language, and customs).

- Be prepared to relate an array of experiences and share them with others.

- Find opportunities to experience new activities that foster interaction with peers or enhance the peer culture.

- Be willing to try new experiences. Take risks.

- Show a positive attitude about yourself and the impact of visual impairment on your behavior and abilities.

peers to help the student with a visual impairment engage in social experiences throughout the day.

- *Cognitive social skills interventions* use role-playing and stories to promote thinking, self-evaluation, and planning by the student.

- *Audiovisual approaches* use audiotaped or videotaped social interactions as the basis

for promoting self-evaluation and planning by the student.

- *Adults who are blind or have low vision act as role models* by demonstrating effective social skills and answering the student's questions.

More information on using each of these approaches is presented in Sidebar 17.6.

Social Skills Intervention Strategies

STRUCTURED SOCIAL SKILLS TRAINING

This model is based on behavioral techniques. The behavior for training is identified and defined for the student. The teacher models the appropriate behavior (such as maintaining eye contact, using positive initiations, joining a group). The student practices or rehearses the target behavior. The teacher provides verbal and physical feedback. The student practices the behavior using a role-play scenario of a typical situation in the student's life. The teacher provides feedback. The student is given a homework assignment to practice the behavior with peers in the real environment.

PEER-MEDIATED SOCIAL SKILLS TRAINING

In this model, a same-age sighted peer is recruited to provide the intervention. With the help of a teacher, the sighted peer identifies the social skill to teach the student who is visually impaired. The sighted peer receives initial instruction from the teacher about the student's visual impairment and his or her visual functioning. The peer and the teacher brainstorm about activities the two students can do together. The teacher reminds the peer that the relationship is an equal one and that the activities are to be mutually determined. The teacher demonstrates the targeted behavior to the sighted peer and offers a variety of prompt and feedback strategies to help the student with a visual impairment learn the skill. The two students meet at least three times a week for 30 minutes. During a session, they select a social activity they can engage in together. During the activity, the sighted peer works with the student with a visual impairment by providing positive, and sometimes honest, feedback about the student's use of the targeted social skill. The peer may model the desired behavior. After each session, the teacher works with the sighted peer to provide suggestions.

PEER-SUPPORT SOCIAL SKILLS MODELS

Peer-support models enlist a sighted classmate to help the student with a visual impairment engage in positive social encounters in the classroom, at recess, and at lunch. Peer supports can take three forms: (1) help with interpreting or doing assignments or reminding the student to use appropriate social behavior (for example, prompting the student to raise his or her hand instead of talking out loud), (2) assistance with equipment and materials in the classroom, and (3) assistance in engaging in social games or activities on the playground or with conversations while eating with a group at lunch.

COGNITIVE SOCIAL SKILLS INTERVENTIONS

Act out scenarios and stories that are specifically related to the student. Initially have the student identify the behavior or problem that requires intervention. Have the student engage in a role-play or real-life experience in which the social behavior is to be used. After the activity has taken place the student must ask himself or herself, "How did I handle the behavior?" "Was my reaction to the situation positive or negative?" "What could I have done differently?" Have the student try the interaction again with a new strategy and then evaluate himself or herself. For students to evaluate their own behavior, they must understand and internalize the specified rules of using the behavior correctly.

AUDIOVISUAL APPROACHES TO TEACHING SOCIAL SKILLS

Encourage the students to listen to and analyze audiotaped conversations with peers, paying

(continued on next page)

Social Skills Intervention *(Continued)*

special attention to the tone and quality of the voices and analyzing the length of the exchanges.

- Record a public television program, such as *Wonder Works* or *After School Special,* and discuss behaviors and social encounters the program depicts, including friendship, discord, cooperation, flirtation, embarrassment, and testing.

- Discuss popular movies that the students have seen (with a peer, teacher, or family member interpreting visual information). Analyze the social skills content: How was anger handled? How did the characters show that they liked one another? How did the

characters use nonverbal behaviors to express emotions?

- Take photographs or videotape students engaged in social activities. Develop a discussion centered on interpreting actions, body language, and gestures.

USE OF ADULT ROLE MODELS TO PRACTICE SOCIAL SKILLS

Invite adults with the same visual impairments as the students to come to the classroom or visit them in the community to provide a natural way to promote social exchanges and encourage dialogue related to social competence. Encourage the students to ask questions related to typical social encounters, such as dating, interviews, and interpreting nonverbal behavior.

Promoting Interdependence through Responsibility and Expectations

As students with visual impairments reach middle-school age, it is critical for them to establish a sense of interdependence, that is, to understand that no one is totally independent and that each person requires assistance and support from others, regardless of the presence or absence of a disability. A sense of interdependence allows students to achieve independence by accepting responsibility for their actions and fulfilling expectations of their teachers, peers, and family members. At the same time, it emphasizes that asking for help when one needs it to complete a task is desirable.

Structured social skills interventions give students with visual impairments the tools to interact effectively with others. Teachers, family members, and friends must be vigilant in expecting the students to act appropriately and to use the skills they learned in a consistent way. Giving the students opportunities to assume responsibility for

their actions, belongings, and chores, both in school and in the community, helps to promote social competence and self-esteem. Whether students are responsible for using a specific social behavior (such as keeping their heads up or maintaining eye contact while talking to others) or following through on specific tasks (like placing dirty clothes in a clothes hamper or taking out the trash), it is critical that family members and teachers do the following:

- Be consistent in their approach,
- Give positive feedback every time the students successfully complete an action or activity,
- Expect the students to complete a given task or action regularly once they have learned it.

The activities presented in Sidebar 17.7 promote responsibility and interdependence throughout the elementary and middle school years.

SIDEBAR 17.7

Strategies to Foster Responsibility and Interdependence

◆ Encourage the student with a visual impairment to be responsible for his or her belongings in school, such as lunch money, a backpack, magnifiers and other optical devices, an adapted computer, and note-taking equipment.

◆ Have the student assume responsibility for obtaining classroom and homework assignments by using a homework log prepared in print or braille.

◆ Encourage the student to participate in classroom or school jobs, such as taking the attendance list to the office, watering plants, working in the school office or cafeteria, assisting a general education teacher with a project, and helping students with assignments through peer tutoring or cross-age peer support groups.

◆ Expect the student to perform specific chores around the house. Suggest that the parents reward the student's work with a weekly allowance or a special treat.

◆ Encourage the student to assist with chores that could be considered paid work in the future (like washing cars, mowing lawns, and recycling cans and plastic bottles).

◆ Encourage the student to volunteer to help support others (for example, caring for a household pet, baby-sitting, assisting with child care, serving food at a homeless shelter, reading to younger children, and picking up litter at a local park).

◆ Give the student ongoing opportunities to make choices about which clothes to wear for school or special occasions, which foods to select from a menu at a restaurant, or which peers to invite to a birthday party or sleep-over party.

◆ In situations in which the student needs to ask for assistance or support, show the student alternative ways of handling a situation, rather than provide the support automatically. For example, if classmates in a general education classroom are taking notes from an overhead transparency, encourage the student to think of ways to obtain assistance in getting the notes from the overhead. Challenge the student to think of alternatives and reinforce the student when he or she comes up with a solution.

High School Students

Social Relationships

Few studies have examined the lifestyles and social networks of adolescents with visual impairments. The Social Network Pilot Project (SNPP) (Sacks, Wolffe, & Tierney, 1998; Wolffe & Sacks, 1997) compared the lifestyles of 48 adolescents (16 who were blind, 16 who had low vision, and 16

who were sighted) over a one-year period. Quantitative data were gathered using interview questionnaires and time-diary protocols, and qualitative data were obtained through observations of a subset of the total sample. Some key findings of this research were as follows:

◆ The parents of adolescents with low vision had lower expectations for their children's success in school than did the parents of students who were blind and of students who were sighted.

◆ Both students who were blind and students with low vision spent more time in school completing homework and class assignments than did their sighted peers. They also depended on their parents and teachers to assist them, whereas the sighted adolescents depended almost exclusively on their friends.

◆ The adolescents who were blind or who had low vision were more like their sighted peers than different when performing money management, time management, and personal management tasks. However, their parents believed that their children would need support with these tasks in early adulthood.

◆ The adolescents with low vision appeared to be involved in the fewest leisure and social activities and were less likely to be involved in social situations that included a group of people.

◆ More than 75 percent of the adolescents who were blind or who had low vision indicated that they spent their time after school alone or with one friend.

◆ The adolescents who were blind were more greatly involved in passive activities (such as watching television, talking on the telephone, and listening to the radio or to music) than were those who had low vision and those who were sighted.

◆ The sighted adolescents had almost four times as many social interactions as the adolescents with low vision and twice as many as the adolescents who were blind.

◆ The adolescents with low vision reported that they spent greater amounts of time sleeping than did those who were blind or those who were sighted.

◆ Although almost all the participants (92 percent) reported having paid jobs, the majority of adolescents with visual impairments obtained jobs with the help of their teachers or rehabilitation counselors, and worked in the human service professions (as teacher's aides) or in office-clerical work (receptionists), whereas the sighted adolescents found their own jobs and worked in a greater variety of employment settings.

Facilitating the Development of Autonomy

Given the findings just presented, it seems evident that adolescents with visual impairments require social skills interventions that promote interdependence, assertive behavior, clear decision making, advocacy skills, and strategies to enhance the likelihood of dating and successful employment in adulthood. Adolescence is a time when children move from the protection and influence of their families and begin to structure lifestyles that are highly influenced by input from peers and by community values.

Adolescents are expected to make decisions and to take greater responsibility for their actions and belongings than they did when they were younger. In addition, they are less influenced by feedback from adults and strive to move away from their families by attending social and athletic events with peers, dressing according to the rules set by the peer culture, and making decisions independent of their parents or other caregivers. Adolescents with visual impairments must be given opportunities to experience clear expectations and age-appropriate responsibilities, use verbal feedback to describe social nuances, and experiment with social skills. They also need to explore issues that have an impact on their social competence and well-being, such as these:

◆ How to determine how others perceive them on the basis of their physical appearance and physical stature;

◆ How to move through space with confidence and assurance;

- How to cope with transportation issues, including nondriving;

- How to flirt and date without creating misconceptions or misinterpretations of their intended social behavior;

- How to experiment with personal freedom when it is difficult to blend in with the crowd; and

- How to cope with interdependence by finding a balance between being helped too much and asking for assistance when needed.

Fostering Interdependence

For students with visual impairments to gain acceptance and social support in their transition from school to adult life, they must develop a repertoire of social skills that promote positive interactions with others. Learning to be interdependent, rather than striving for total independence or dependence, is the key. Interdependence is a socioemotional status in which an individual does some tasks without assistance and other tasks with assistance. Inherent in interdependence is the concept of reciprocity: individuals sharing what they do best by exchanging energy, assistance, or skills. It is important for adolescents with visual impairments to analyze their strengths and assets and to recognize all the attributes that make them unique and worthwhile to others.

Promoting Affective Communication

Perhaps the most difficult social skills that students with visual impairments need to acquire are those that involve nonverbal communication—that is, actions, gestures, visual gaze, and body posture that have meaning to those who view them (for example, people who frown and whose body stance is rigid exude anger). Adolescents with visual impairments would not be privy to such information without an auditory cue or a verbal description from another person. There-

fore, they must develop alternative strategies to cope with nonverbal communications, such as the following:

- Ask a trusted peer or adult to interpret social situations in which nonverbal information is being communicated.

- Use auditory skills to figure out the members of a social grouping at a party, a dance, or any other social gathering.

- Incorporate the use of hand and facial gestures when interacting with others.

- Learn to face others when being spoken to and to switch body stance, according to the direction of the speakers' voices.

- Exhibit emotions and feelings when interacting with others using verbal skills—laughter, surprise, anger, and disbelief (for example, "Oh, John, what a nice surprise. I didn't know you were here!").

- Enlist support from others to help interpret nonverbal cues and emotions that can be misinterpreted, especially in a flirting or dating situation.

- Enlist a sighted friend, sibling, family member, or teacher to provide descriptive information about flirting—what it is, how to do it, what it accomplishes—and to explain different styles of flirting, for example, that some females giggle, smile, and purposely ignore and some males simply try to establish eye contact and continue gazing until they receive feedback.

Fostering Dating Skills

A much greater emphasis is placed on the development of relationships with opposite-gender peers during adolescence than earlier in student's lives. Students with visual impairments are no different from their sighted age-mates when it comes to dating; they want to be accepted and feel that they are attractive and desirable. However, acquiring skills that promote good social communication, mutual interests, attention to age-appropriate physical appearance and dress, and a positive sense of identity as a person with a visual impairment are essential for enhancing this aspect of socialization. Dating occurs naturally when adolescents are given opportunities to interact with groups of peers in casual social situations.

Generally, adolescents with visual impairments have to take the first step to initiate social contacts that may lead to dating, such as by joining school clubs, athletic teams, community organizations, performing arts groups, and volunteer groups where they can meet other adolescents. They also need opportunities to meet and engage with other adolescents with visual impairments. Encouraging them to attend weekend groups, summer camps, and leadership groups for adolescents who are visually impaired and to become involved in consumer organizations of and for people with visual impairments allows them to expand their networks of social contacts.

Adolescents with visual impairments also need to be aware that dating, as exemplified on television shows or in the movies, may be unrealistic. It is important to help them understand that not all sighted adolescents date; that many adolescents attend social events in groups, rather than in couples; and that close personal relationships begin with solid friendships. The following activities can be included when working with students individually or in small groups:

◆ Develop a list of conversation topics to engage peers in interesting discussions. Practice and role-play various conversations emphasizing turn taking, sharing information, and using animated gestures.

◆ Role-play scenarios in which a student with a visual impairment asks a peer for a date.

◆ Develop strategies and options for not being able to drive when out on a date. Explore several ways to inform a date about one's visual status: the nature of assistance and support needed when at a dance, a movie, or a concert and in a restaurant.

Teaching Problem-Solving Strategies to Enhance Socialization

The ability to solve problems and to make decisions are skills that can influence a student's success in future work or social situations. People with visual impairments are often not given the opportunity to speak or act on their own behalf and hence become dependent on others to complete tasks or to make crucial life choices. Carkhuff and Berenson (1977) presented a model that supports a cognitive-behavioral strategy for examining problem solving. Wolffe (1998) explained that there are four steps in this strategy:

1. Engage in self-exploration (the student with the problem explores his or her feelings).

2. Understand the problem, both internally and externally (the student analyzes how he or she, others, and the environment contribute to the problem).

3. Brainstorm ideas and develop a plan (the student obtains information on how to solve the problem by himself or herself and from others and decides on a plan of action).

4. Implement the plan of action (the student chooses to act on his or her decision and risks the consequences of his or her actions).

One of the hardest decisions an adolescent with a visual impairment has to make is when and how to disclose his or her visual impairment to others and how much information he or she wants to disclose. Disclosing one's visual impairment is a personal matter and takes a lot of skill and social confidence. Disclosing and describing one's visual impairment and the needs required to act and function with interdependence are situation specific. For example, at a dance where many of the peers are strangers or acquaintances, giving brief, casual information like, "Sorry I bumped into you. It was dark and I couldn't see you" may alleviate embarrassment or confusion. However, if a student is at a fast-food restaurant with friends who do not recognize that he or she has a severe visual impairment, the student can either choose to "mask" the visual impairment (not disclose any information) or can matter-of-factly explain, "I use this little telescope to see the menu on the wall. I was born with this condition that affects my lenses, and my vision isn't great." Giving students permission and opportunities to practice real-life problem-solving scenarios in a safe and caring environment helps them feel more comfortable with their visual impairments and their social relationships with others.

Helping Students Cope with the Impact of Not Driving

An important rite of passage among adolescents is obtaining a license to drive a car. Adolescents look forward to that day with great anticipation because it signifies true independence. There is great social value in being able to transport oneself and others and to run errands independently. Adolescents view this stage in their lives as the threshold to adult responsibilities and ultimate freedom from parental control.

Adolescents with visual impairments may view their inability to drive as an obstacle, and it may influence their locus of control and self-worth. Although they are certainly more dependent on others (parents, siblings, or friends) for rides to and from school or community events, they need to find alternative ways to feel independent and autonomous. The following strategies may help to promote and support alternatives to driving:

- ◆ Encourage the student to use alternate modes of transportation, such as buses, paratransit, or taxis to school and social events.

- ◆ Encourage the parents to allow the student to work for pay or to give the student an allowance to reciprocate others for driving, paying for gas, or sharing taxi or paratransit fares.

- ◆ If the parents have purchased a car or have allowed their sighted children to drive the family regularly, suggest that they give their adolescent with a visual impairment the financial equivalent so he or she can use the funds to hire a driver or use alternative modes of transportation without their permission or supervision.

- ◆ Provide opportunities for students with visual impairments to experience driving a car in a safe and protected environment (such as a parking lot or on country roads). Motor bikes, golf carts, or go-carts provide similar experiences and can help students feel that they have been exposed to driving.

- ◆ Introduce and encourage the student with a visual impairment to attend a driver's education course. Having knowledge about the rules of the road, makes and models of cars, and safe driving practices can help them engage in social conversations and interactions.

Promoting Self-Advocacy and Assertiveness

Two other critical elements of the socialization process for adolescents with visual impairments are self-advocacy and assertiveness—the ability to communicate to others in a straightforward, nonjudgmental manner and to make one's needs and preferences known and achieve one's goals. Assertiveness skills can complement advocacy efforts. By being exposed to and interacting with adults and adolescents with visual impairments who exhibit assertive behavior and promote advocacy for themselves and others, a student can learn these skills and use them in employment and independent living situations in the future. By participating in consumer organizations of and for people who are visually impaired (such as the American Council of the Blind and the National Federation of the Blind), the student can have opportunities for leadership and mentoring experiences.

When adolescents use self-advocacy strategies in an assertive manner, rather than an aggressive or passive manner, others are more willing to listen to them and respect their needs. When they use an aggressive or passive communication style, they are often viewed as angry, vengeful, pitiful, or less than adequate. Wolffe (1998) compiled a number of suggestions for fostering assertiveness among adolescents with visual impairments. The strategies in Sidebar 17.8 encourage and promote self-advocacy as a means of enhancing social competence and self-worth.

Strategies to Promote Self-Advocacy in Adolescents

SIDEBAR 17.8

MAINTAIN EYE CONTACT OR FACIAL ORIENTATION

For students who are blind or students with low vision, this is a skill that must be taught and reinforced by using auditory and tactile cues. Verbal feedback is a must.

DEMONSTRATE CONFIDENT BODY POSTURE

Without visual cues, students must also be taught to keep their heads up and their bodies erect and may need tactile or verbal cues to remind them to do so. Teaching students to lean forward to position themselves close (but not too close) to a speaker may help. Students with severe visual impairments may also need to be taught what certain nonverbal signals mean to sighted observers. For example, arms folded across the chest may indicate that the speaker is angry or taking control of a situation.

USE APPROPRIATE GESTURES

Gestures have to be demonstrated and taught and explained to students who are blind using hand-over-hand techniques. For example, these students need to know that having one's palms up at shoulder height and raising one's shoulders indicate a question and should be able to demonstrate this gesture.

USE APPROPRIATE FACIAL EXPRESSIONS

This is another set of skills that has to be described and "shown" by allowing students to feel sculpted images and the faces of live models and giving them feedback on their own facial expressions.

USE APPROPRIATE VOICE TONE AND INFLECTION

These skills are the easiest for students with visual impairments who do not have hearing difficulties to master; however, deaf-blind students require extensive instruction and, depending on the amount of residual hearing, may not be able to learn these skills at all. Students must understand the differences in the impressions made by a speaker who uses a well-modulated voice versus one who screams, whines, whispers, or uses sarcasm.

EXHIBIT HONEST EXPRESSION OF FEELINGS

This is the cornerstone of assertive communication skills, and students need to be taught how to state their feelings in non-aggressive ways by using "I" messages, since "you" messages put others on the defensive. For example, they need to say, "I feel frustrated when appointments with me are missed," rather than, "You make me angry when you don't show up for your appointments with me."

TIME MESSAGES APPROPRIATELY

Although spontaneous communication is usually the most assertive, it is sometimes more appropriate to wait and share a message in private. Judging situations that are conducive to assertive

(continued on next page)

Strategies to Promote Self-Advocacy *(Continued)*

communication is a skill that can be taught by modeling and role-playing.

UNDERSTAND THE PURPOSE OF ASSERTIVENESS

Using the assertive communication style does not mean that one always gets what one wants; rather, it means that one expresses what one wants and feels and extends the same courtesy to others. Students learn this skill best by role-playing, engaging in problem-solving scenarios, modeling, and receiving feedback related to their communication strengths and weak-

nesses. Examples from popular movies or television or radio shows can also help students understand the differences among assertive, passive, and aggressive communication styles and the consequences of using one style or another.

_____

Source: Reprinted, with permission, from K. Wolffe, Transition Planning and Employment Outcomes for Students Who Have Visual Impairments with Other Disabilities. In S. Z. Sacks and R. K. Silberman, Eds. *Educating Students Who Have Visual Impairments with Other Disabilities* (Baltimore, MD: Paul H. Brooks, 1998), p. 351.

SUMMARY

Children with visual impairments either are unable to learn or have difficulty acquiring social skills through observation and imitation, as sighted children do. Therefore, they need ongoing assistance from their parents and the teacher of students with visual impairments to develop the self-esteem, self-confidence, and sense of identity that they need for social competence—the repertoire of behaviors and actions that are necessary for developing meaningful social relationships. The teacher of students with visual impairments assesses a student's social skills and uses strategies to promote the student's skills in interacting with others and being assertive in expressing his or her needs and preferences.

ACTIVITIES

1. Observe sighted children in a social situation (such as on a playground, at lunch, or at a birthday party). Note the number of social exchanges they make among themselves in 20 minutes. Also note their topics of conversation and the way they interact with each other.

2. Observe a student with a visual impairment at any age level in a play situation or a group activity at school, at home, or in the community. How does the student join the group? How does the student move from one activity to the next? How does the student gain attention from his or her peers using verbal or nonverbal cues?

3. Observe an elementary school child, middle school child, and adolescent with visual impairments in their schools or homes. With the information gained from this chapter, select three behaviors or skills you would teach each student. Are the behaviors similar or do they vary for each age group?

4. Develop a role-play scenario and a problem-solving scenario for a middle school or adolescent student with a visual impairment. Both scenarios should be reflective of the student's school or community life.

5. Select a partner and target a specific social skill for training. Teach the partner a social skill using a structured behavior strategy or a cognitive behavioral strategy. Obtain feedback from the partner.

Switch roles and discuss the outcomes of training.

REFERENCES

American Foundation for the Blind. (1975). *Sex education for the visually handicapped in schools and agencies: Selected papers.* New York: Author.

Carkhuff, R. R., & Berenson, B. G. (1977). *Beyond counseling and therapy* (2nd ed.). New York: Holt, Rinehart, & Winston.

Coopersmith, S. (1967). *The antecedents of self-esteem.* San Francisco: W. H. Freeman.

Corsaro, W. A. (1985). *Friendship and peer culture in the early years.* Norwood, NJ: Ablex.

Fitts, W. H. (1967). *The self-concept as a variable in vocational rehabilitation.* Nashville, TN: Mental Heath Center.

Gresham, F. M., & Elliott, S. N. (1990). *The social skills rating system.* Circle Pines, MN: American Guidance Service.

Hatlen, P. (1996). *The core curriculum for blind and visually impaired students, including those with additional disabilities.* Austin: Texas School for the Blind and Visually Impaired. Available on-line: http://www.tsbvi.edu/education/corecurric.htm

Hill, E. W., & Blasch, B. B. (1980). Concept development. In R. L. Welsh & B. B. Blasch (Eds.), *Foundations of orientation and mobility* (pp. 265–290). New York: American Foundation for the Blind.

Kekelis, L. S. (1992). Peer interactions in childhood: The impact of visual impairment. In S. Z. Sacks, L. S. Kekelis, & R. J. Gaylord-Ross (Eds.), *The development of social skills by blind and visually impaired students: Exploratory studies and strategies* (pp. 13–35). New York: American Foundation for the Blind.

Kekelis, L. S. & Sacks, S. Z. (1988). Mainstreaming visually impaired children into regular education: The effects of visual impairment on children's interactions with peers. In S. Z. Sacks, L. S. Kekelis, & R. J. Gaylord-Ross (Eds.), *The development of social skills by visually impaired children.* San Francisco: San Francisco State University.

Kekelis, L. S., & Sacks, S. Z. (1992). The effects of visual impairment on children's social interactions in regular education programs. In S. Z. Sacks, L. S. Kekelis, & R. J. Gaylord-Ross (Eds.), *The development of social skills by blind and visually impaired students: Exploratory studies and strategies* (pp. 59–82). New York: AFB Press.

Kelly, J. A. (1982). *Social skills training: A practical guide for interventionists.* New York: Springer.

Loumiet, R., & Levack, N. (1991). *Independent living: A curriculum with adaptations for students with visual impairments, Vol. 1: Social Competence.* Austin: Texas School for the Blind and Visually Impaired.

McCallum, B. J., & Sacks, S. Z. (1993). *The Santa Clara County social skills curriculum for children with visual impairments.* Santa Clara, CA: Santa Clara County Schools.

MacCuspie, P. A. (1992). The social acceptance and interaction of visually impaired children in integrated settings. In S. Z. Sacks, L. S. Kekelis, & R. J. Gaylord-Ross (Eds.), *The development of social skills by blind and visually impaired students: Exploratory studies and strategies* (pp. 83–102). New York: American Foundation for the Blind.

MacCuspie, P. A. (1996). *Promoting acceptance of children with disabilities: From tolerance to inclusion.* Halifax, NS: Atlantic Provinces Special Education Authority.

McFall, R. M. (1982). A review and reformation of the concept of social skills. *Behavior Assessment, 4,* 1–33.

Mangold, S. S. (1982). Nurturing high self-esteem in visually handicapped children. In S. S. Mangold (Ed.), *A teacher's guide to the special educational needs of blind and visually handicapped children* (pp. 94–101). New York: American Foundation for the Blind.

Merrell, K. W. (1993). *School social behavior scales.* Brandon, VT: Clinical Psychology.

Putallaz, M., & Gottman, J. M. (1982). Conceptualizing social competence in children. In P. Karoly & J. J. Steffen (Eds.). *Improving children's competence* (pp. 1–33). Lexington, MA: Lexington Books.

Sacks, S. Z. (1996). Psychological and social implications of low vision. In A. L. Corn & A. J. Koenig (Eds.), *Foundations of low vision: Clinical and functional perspectives* (pp. 26–42). New York: AFB Press.

Sacks, S. Z., & Gaylord-Ross, R. J. (1989). Peer-mediated and teacher-directed social skills training for visually impaired students. *Behavior Therapy, 20,* 619–638.

Sacks, S. Z., Kekelis, L. S., & Gaylord-Ross, R. J. (Eds.). (1992). *The development of social skills by blind and visually impaired students: Exploratory studies and strategies.* New York: American Foundation for the Blind.

Sacks, S. Z., & Wolffe, K. E. (1992). The importance of social skills training in the transition process for students with visual impairments. *Journal of Vocational Rehabilitation, 2*(1), 46–55.

Sacks, S. Z., Wolffe, K. E., & Tierney, D. (1998). Lifestyles of students with visual impairments: Preliminary studies of social networks. *Exceptional Children, 64,* 463–478.

Scott, R. A. (1969). Socialization of blind children. In D. Goslin (Ed.) *Handbook of socialization theory and research.* New York: Rand McNally.

Seligman, M. E. P., Reivich, K., Jaycox, L., & Hillham, J. (1995). The fundamentals of optimism (pp. 49–66). *The optimistic child.* New York: Houghton Mifflin.

Sex education for the visually handicapped in schools and agencies: Selected papers. (1975). New York: American Foundation for the Blind.

Shantz, D. W. (1986). Conflict, aggression, and peer status: An observational study. *Child Development, 51,* 1322–1332.

Skellenger, A. C., Hill, M. M., & Hill, E. (1992). The social functioning of children with visual impairments. In S. L. Odom, S. R. McConnell, & M. A. McEvoy (Eds.), *Social competence of young children with disabilities: Issues and strategies for intervention* (pp. 165–188). Baltimore, MD: Paul H. Brookes.

Swallow, R., & Huebner, K. M. (Eds.). (1987). *How to thrive, not just survive: A guide to developing independent life skills for blind and visually impaired children and youths.* New York: American Foundation for the Blind.

Trower (1982). Toward a generative model of social skills: A critique and synthesis. In J. P. Curan & P. M. Monti (Eds.), *Social skills training.* New York: Guilford Press.

Tuttle, D. W., & Tuttle, N. (1996). *Self-esteem and adjusting with blindness* (2nd ed.) Springfield, IL: Charles C Thomas.

Walker, H. M., & McConnell, S. (1995). *The Walker-McConnell Scale of Social Competence and School Adjustment: Adolescent version* (pp. 35–36). San Diego, CA: Singular Publishing.

Wolffe, K. (1998). Transition planning and employment outcomes for students who have visual impairments with other disabilities. In S. Z. Sacks and R.K. Silberman (Eds.), *Educating students who have visual impairments with other disabilities* (pp. 339–370). Baltimore, MD: Paul H. Brookes.

Wolffe, K., & Sacks, S. Z. (1997). The social network pilot project: A quantitative comparison of the lifestyles of blind, low vision, and sighted young adults. *Journal of Visual Impairment & Blindness, 91,* 245–257.

Wolffe, K., & Sacks, S. Z. (2000). *Focused on . . . assessment techniques.* New York: AFB Press.

Strategies for Teaching Social Skills to Students with Visual Impairments and Additional Disabilities

Students with visual impairments and additional disabilities can fulfill the social competencies of making choices, traveling as independently as possible, and engaging in a range of activities when supported through modifications in equipment, adaptive switches, changes in level of participation, engineered environments, and augmentative systems and devices that promote control over their environments.

Students with significant cognitive and physical impairments in addition to limited vision can participate in such family, neighborhood, and community activities as these:

◆ Taking the family trash to the curb by hooking a trash can onto an adapted tricycle;

◆ Caring for the garden of a neighbor who is on vacation—filling water jugs, watering flowers, and raking and bagging leaves—through partial participation;

◆ Working with a neighborhood friend to recycle, using an augmentative system to inquire whether neighbors have items for recycling and then sorting glass, newspaper, and plastic items before extending the items to the friend to place in the appropriate bins; and

◆ Assisting older persons at the grocery store by using a CheapTalk augmentative device to offer to reach items from a high shelf.

Through careful planning and the use of a variety of assistive devices for mobility and communication, students of all ability levels can participate with their peers in age-relevant leisure, work, and community service activities:

◆ The use of specialized gait-training equipment, such as the Theratrek, allows students with poor balance and coordination to walk independently as they accompany friends from high school to a movie and shopping.

◆ Modifications made to a scanner at a library may enable students with minimal hand use and severe visual field losses to scan and check out library books as part of career-exploration or vocational training activities. Augmentative devices of various levels of sophistication can be used to communicate with peers and patrons.

◆ Even a student with significant cognitive and communication limitations in addition to blindness can accompany peers in a high school glee club to the local hospital to rock babies whose families cannot be with them. The peers serve as a natural support for the student, who may need to be supervised to ensure the infants' safety. The student could activate an audiotape recorder to sing a lullaby to the infants.

◆ Single-step communication devices, such as the Big Mac switch, can be programmed so a student can serve as a greeter at a church or synagogue. The natural cues of a door opening can prompt the student to activate the switch to express a welcome.

◆ A preschool child with significant physical and communication deficits in addition to hearing and vision losses can be an active participant in circle time in a community

(continued on next page)

preschool by using a Big Mac switch to indicate "my turn" during show-and-tell and then a Pocket Talker augmentative system to "share" a show-and-tell experience that a sibling recorded for circle time.

The use of systematic training opportunities in functional settings is critical when training students to use assistive devices that will promote independence and perceptions of competence within the community. A student who cannot verbalize his or her name may use a simple memo-recording device kept in a pocket or attached to a purse that will speak the name when the student activates the button in response to being asked who he or she is. The use of a name stamp to sign invitations; greeting cards; sales receipts; and school documents, such as an Individualized Education Program, a permission slip for going on a field trip, and a Special Olympics form, gives the student a sense of accomplishment and conveys to others the student's level of independence in carrying out an age-expected skill.

M. BETH LANGLEY
Pinellas County Schools
St. Petersburg, FL

R E S O U R C E S

Suggested Resources for Teaching Social Skills

Resource	Type	Source	Description
Development of Social Skills by Blind and Visually Impaired Students: Exploratory Studies and Strategies (Sacks, Kekelis, & Gaylord-Ross, 1992)	Book	American Foundation for the Blind	A book that links theoretical constructs of social development to the unique process that children who are visually impaired undergo to learn and maintain social skills. Also includes research and strategies for establishing social skills training in schools, at home, and in the community.
How to Thrive, Not Just Survive: A Guide to Developing Independent Life Skills for Blind and Visually Impaired Children and Youths (Swallow & Huebner, 1987)	Book	American Foundation for the Blind	A book that presents guidelines and strategies for helping children who are visually impaired develop, acquire, and apply skills that are necessary for independence in socialization, orientation and mobility, and leisure-time and recreational activities.
Independent Living: A Curriculum with Adaptations for Students with Visual Impairments, Volume 1: Social Competence (Loumiet & Levack, 1991)	Handbook	Texas School for the Blind and Visually Impaired	The first of a three-volume set of curriculum guides, this volume addresses the nonacademic, disability-specific needs of students with visual impairments. For many areas of social competence (self-concept, emotions, nonverbal communication, personal/social, sexuality, and so forth), the text presents goals and skills and a rich variety of useful resources.

(continued on next page)

Suggested Resources *(Continued)*

Resource	Type	Source	Description
"Nurturing High Self-Esteem in Visually Handicapped Children" (Mangold, 1982)	Book chapter	American Foundation for the Blind	This chapter in Mangold's book *A Teacher's Guide to the Special Educational Needs of Blind and Visually Handicapped Children* (pp. 94–101) includes many practical suggestions on the ways in which parents and teachers can help children with visual impairments develop high self-esteem.
Promoting Acceptance of Children with Disabilities: From Tolerance to Inclusion (MacCuspie, 1996)	Book	Atlantic Provinces Special Education Authority	This study of the social lives of children with visual impairments in public schools uncovered many obstacles to social integration. It discusses the intricacies of peer group interactions and provides suggestions for parents, educators, and administrators on how to promote understanding in the classroom.
Santa Clara County Social Skills Curriculum for Children with Visual Impairments (McCallum & Sacks, 1993)	Curriculum	Santa Clara County Schools	A curriculum designed to assist teachers of students with visual impairments, general education teachers, related service personnel, and family members in designing social skills intervention strategies to help students with visual impairments develop social skills. Divided into preschool, elementary school, and secondary school age groups.
Sex Education for the Visually Handicapped in Schools and Agencies: Selected Papers (Author, 1975)	Book	American Foundation for the Blind	A collection of articles on sex education for students with visual impairments.

Contact information for each of the resources listed will be found in the Sources of Products, Materials, Equipment, and Services section at the back of this book.

CHAPTER 18

Recreation and Leisure Skills

Duncan McGregor and Carol Farrenkopf

KEY POINTS

- ◆ The discovery of an array of enjoyable recreation and leisure skills is an important part of growing up.

- ◆ Students with visual impairments may not know the range of recreation and leisure skills that are available, since knowledge of these activities is gained largely through visual observation.

- ◆ Teaching recreation and leisure skills to students with visual impairments is an essential component of the expanded core curriculum.

- ◆ Teachers of students with visual impairments, parents, and other members of students' educational teams should expose students to a wide variety of recreation and leisure activities, so students can choose those that are of most interest to them.

- ◆ Teachers of students with visual impairments are responsible for providing instruction in recreation and leisure skills and for collaborating with recreation specialists to determine the students' needs.

VIGNETTE

"Ms. Scott!" exclaimed Billy. "Mom and Dad are taking me bowling again on Saturday! We're taking my friend Jason, too!"

Samantha Scott, who taught students with visual impairments, was delighted. She had arranged a visit to Westside Bowling Lanes the past weekend for her elementary school students with visual impairments. Ms. Scott had arranged for the students to arrive at the bowling alley a half hour before the usual opening, and the manager had taken the children behind the scenes and showed them the bowling pins and the mechanism that arranged them. Ms. Scott and the parents who had stayed kept busy helping seven beginners locate their bowling balls, orient to the lane, and deliver the balls. "Bumper guards" had kept the balls in the lanes, ensuring greater success. The children all seemed to enjoy the activity, and now, it seemed that at least one student would benefit even further, through continued recreation with his family.

Ms. Scott thought of other students who had discovered recreation or leisure-time activities that they had come to enjoy: a sixth grader who liked to fish with his grandfather, a ninth-grade girl who knitted luxurious sweaters, and the high-school senior who excelled at tae kwon do. She also had students who often went to plays, movies, and concerts and who were involved in youth groups at their houses of worship or in Scouting. Activities of this sort gave such a flavor to life! Unfortunately, Ms. Scott also had students who seemed to do nothing. Well, this month's newsletter to parents would certainly include the story of the bowling trip, along with the location and hours of the bowling alley. Perhaps one or more other families would decide to try it for themselves. Now, what should she plan for their *next* outing?

INTRODUCTION

The ultimate goal of education for students who are visually impaired is healthy growth toward adulthood. As a part of this goal, students work to accomplish objectives related to intellectual, emotional, and physical growth. Recreation and leisure skills are also important for achieving this goal and need to be a part of the educational programs of students with visual impairments (Hatlen & Curry, 1987). In fact, they should be part of a student's Individualized Transition Plan (ITP) if the student hopes to participate in community-based recreation and leisure programs (Stopka, Pomeranz, Siders, Dykes, & Goodman, 1999).

Recreation and leisure activities are those in which one chooses to engage during one's free time, including physical, cultural, artistic, social, technological, and intellectual pursuits (Recreation Council on Disability in Nova Scotia, 1991). Sighted children are exposed to a wide variety of recreation and leisure activities through observation. They may see children playing catch, watch downhill skiing on television, observe a sibling making a model airplane, or learn about canoe-tripping in the backcountry by looking at pictures in a magazine. From the vast array of possible recreation and leisure activities, sighted children may choose those that are of interest to them, even though they have not yet participated in the activities. Children with visual impairments usually do not learn recreation and leisure skills incidentally by observing others and imitating them. These skills must be taught directly.

To develop an interest in a similarly wide array of recreation and leisure activities, students with visual impairments must be directly exposed to many activities, both as participants and as spectators. Students who learn the prerequisite skills for an activity, such as tandem cycling, and are successful in it enjoy the activity and are prepared to participate at it again. Students can also learn about an activity to enjoy it as spectators, even though they may not enjoy or be successful participating in it. For example, a student who does not have exceptional musical ability or an interest in playing an instrument can still learn to appreciate music and enjoy attending concerts.

Even if students do not want to participate in a particular recreation or leisure activity, knowledge of how to perform some of the component skills may enhance their enjoyment and understanding of it as spectators. For example, while play wrestling and roughhousing with their friends and classmates, young children with visual impairments are learning some of the component skills of professional wrestling and participating in an age-appropriate recreation activity. The theatrical style of wrestling typical of the World Wrestling Federation is probably not a reasonable career goal for students with visual impairments, nor is it something they will participate in recreationally as adults. However, these childhood experiences can enhance their enjoyment of attending professional wrestling events as adults.

This chapter discusses the role of the teacher of students with visual impairments and how he or she can integrate the teaching of recreation and leisure skills into a student's educational program. Many possible recreation and leisure activities are described, including noncompetitive and competitive sports, games, arts and crafts, participation in youth groups, and independent leisure activities.

ROLE OF THE TEACHER OF STUDENTS WITH VISUAL IMPAIRMENTS

Recreation and leisure skills are part of the expanded core curriculum for students with visual impairments (for information on the expanded core curriculum, see Chapter 6). Therefore, the teacher of students with visual impairments must assume responsibility for ensuring that opportunities for developing these skills are provided. These responsibilities may include direct instruction in specific activities or prerequisite skills, consulting with or training recreation specialists, and providing adapted materials and equipment. The role of the specialist is to do the following:

♦ Expose students to a variety of recreation and leisure activities so they can choose those that best match their individual interests;

♦ Provide direct instruction in recreation and leisure activities or their prerequisite skills, as appropriate;

♦ Provide consultation to recreation specialists that will allow the students to participate in regular, community recreation programs; and

♦ Create meaningful links with the academic curriculum to foster the development of enjoyable recreation and leisure skills.

The teacher also plays an essential role in working with students with additional disabilities; strategies focusing on students with visual impairments and additional disabilities and resources for teachers appear later in this chapter.

ASSESSING AND TEACHING RECREATION AND LEISURE SKILLS

Recreation and leisure skills should be taught as part of the educational programs of students with visual impairments. In some cases, these skills may be related to activities in the physical education, art, drama, or music programs, but they are more likely to be related to extracurricular activities, such as a school's outdoor club, chess club, or bowling league. To participate in these activities, students who are visually impaired need to be taught the prerequisite skills for the activities. For example, a teacher of students with visual impairments may use an adapted chessboard to teach a student the rudiments of chess, so the student may join the chess club.

The teacher of students with visual impairments first determines what skills a student needs to learn. As in any other area of the curriculum, instructional goals for students must be based on assessments of the skills they already have. Check-lists may be used to guide the assessment of a student's recreation and leisure skills. Some of the areas the teacher of students with visual impairments may wish to assess include managing leisure time; playing independently; playing with friends; and skills related to physical games and sports, arts and crafts, music, and dance. A comprehensive assessment checklist of these skills is included in *Independent Living: A Curriculum with Adaptations for Students with Visual Impairments. Vol. 3: Play and Leisure* (Loumiet & Levack, 1993).

After the specialist has determined which skills need to be taught, he or she then schedules time for instruction. Since instruction in recreation and leisure skills is not part of the general school curriculum, the specialist has to find time in the student's day when these skills can be taught (before or after school, during lunch hour, during an extra period or study period, or in a class where a similar activity is being taught) without removing the student from other essential classes (such as art, science, braille literacy instruction, and physical education). It may also be possible to enlist the help of others, including parents, friends, and recreation specialists, to help teach and reinforce these skills.

Before students with visual impairments can choose which recreation and leisure activities in the community are most interesting to them, however, they must first know what activities are available. Teachers of students with visual impairments often organize social outings for groups of students to introduce students to a wide range of possible leisure activities of which they may otherwise be unaware.

Recreation activities tie together several areas of the curriculum, including orientation and mobility (O&M), money management skills, social skills, and independent living skills. For example, a student may first have to learn to use the telephone to obtain information about an activity's hours of operation, cost, and location; then learn to plan and travel the route between home or school and the activity independently; and once there, may have to pay for the activity. In addition, the student needs to learn what constitutes so-

How to Encourage Students to Participate in Recreation and Leisure Activities

◆ Describe activities in a positive manner.

◆ Stress the enjoyment experienced by participants in various activities.

◆ Involve the student's friends and/or family members with the student in recreation and leisure activities.

◆ Discuss possible recreation and leisure activities with the student's parents.

◆ Teach the appropriate prerequisite skills that will enable the student to participate in an activity confidently and independently.

◆ Become part of the cheering section at one of the student's games.

◆ Videotape a performance or game that can be viewed with the student and his or her family and friends at a later date.

◆ Create a scrapbook with the student who is visually impaired of items related to leisure activities that he or she can share with sighted friends and relatives.

cially appropriate behavior while traveling and participating in the activity.

Many students with visual impairments need to be motivated to participate in recreation and leisure activities other than those organized by their schools. Sidebar 18.1 lists some ways in which the teacher of students with visual impairments can encourage a student to participate in such activities. Most recreation and leisure activities can be modified or adapted for students with visual impairments. The next section describes some noncompetitive activities that students with visual impairments may enjoy, along with suggested modifications for use when needed.

NONCOMPETITIVE SPORTS

Noncompetitive sports are those in which one participates primarily for enjoyment. They are often informally organized. If times or scores are kept, they are usually gauges of the individual's performance. Some noncompetitive sports (such as swimming, downhill skiing, canoeing, scuba diving, and sailing) need to be taught by certified instructors, whereas others (like playing miniature golf, bicycling, ice-skating, in-line or roller skating, bowling, and fishing) are typically taught by teachers, parents, older siblings, or friends who are skilled in the activities. For an activity that must be taught by a certified instructor, the teacher of students with visual impairments needs to work with the instructor to design a program of instruction for a student with a visual impairment. The specialist may also assist the instructor with modifications of teaching techniques and strategies, as discussed in Chapter 12. In some cases, the instructor of a specific activity may be required to have special training in teaching individuals who are visually impaired, in addition to being a certified instructor of the sport (see the later discussions on water skiing, downhill skiing, and scuba diving).

Bicycling and Running

Students who are visually impaired often enjoy tandem bicycling, that is, riding in the backseat of a tandem bike while a sighted partner (captain) rides in the front seat. The captain steers the bike, orally indicates turns and changes in speed, and warns of changes in the terrain (such as hills, bumpy roads, and puddles) while both cyclists pedal.

Some verbal direction by the teacher of students who are visually impaired helps the student with low vision play miniature golf.

A young student who is blind spends some leisure time tandem cycling with her father, who, as "captain," rides in the front seat.

A student with low vision may also be able to cycle independently on a regular bicycle if he or she has sufficient vision, skills, and knowledge to travel safely or rides only in an area that is safe and confined (that is, away from vehicular traffic) and with supervision (Connor, 1992). A student with low vision may prefer to follow another cyclist who is wearing a brightly colored shirt or vest and have this cyclist provide auditory cues when turning or stopping. Whether they ride in tandem or alone, all cyclists should wear helmets, which are required by law in many jurisdictions.

Running for fitness and pleasure is a recreation activity that many people with visual impairments enjoy. However, some students may not feel comfortable running alone. They may find running partners by participating in school-sponsored cross-country teams and track teams or local running clubs. Techniques for running with and without a sighted guide are presented in Chapter 12.

Orienteering

Orienteering involves traveling over unknown terrain with the aid of a map and compass to locate specified landmarks, known as "controls." When a control is located, a symbol on the control is recorded on the participant's score sheet as proof that he or she has found it. In a sense, orienteering is similar to a treasure hunt. Although it is generally considered a competitive sport, it can be organized less competitively and students with visual impairments can participate with appropriate modifications.

To participate in orienteering meets, students must have mastered skills and concepts in five areas: time, distance, direction, map-reading, and physical concepts and skills (Bina, 1986). For students with visual impairments, orienteering can be adapted by using tactile maps and braille or auditory compasses or by eliminating maps and compasses altogether. The controls may be objects to be picked up by the students. A student can travel with a sighted guide who helps him or her navigate rough terrain and spots the controls.

A student uses a tactile map with braille labels to participate in an outdoor activity. Tactile and auditory cues are used throughout to help the student navigate the chosen course.

When introducing orienteering to a student who is visually impaired, the teacher of students with visual impairments or O&M specialist may begin with a course that is set up in one room. The game can take the form of a treasure hunt in which the student has to find objects placed at specific locations in the room. Directions can be written in either braille or large print or on a tactile or large-print map. Later, the course can be expanded to include larger areas in the school and then to shopping malls (Bina, 1986). In mall orienteering, the controls can be pieces of information obtained from salespersons in stores or edible evidence that one has located a business.

Once a student has demonstrated proficiency in indoor orienteering, simple courses can be set up outdoors, using sidewalks and other pathways in residential neighborhoods. A student who is blind may use his or her O&M skills to locate large controls (such as mailboxes, telephone booths, and fire hydrants) independently.

For orienteering on a course that covers rough terrain and often on indoor and residential courses, team orienteering is recommended. For example, a student who is blind, a student with low vision, and a sighted student may work together as a team. The first may read a tactile map or braille instruction sheet, the second may help locate the control and mark information on a large-print score sheet, and the third may act as a sighted guide. Working together toward a common goal facilitates cooperation, interdependence, and social interaction (Bina, 1986).

Swimming

Recreational swimming can take place in a swimming pool or in a lake or other natural body of water. For safety reasons, all swimmers, including those who are visually impaired, should never swim alone. In open water, where there are no boundaries to provide the swimmer with a visual impairment with a line of direction, it is especially important for the swimmer with a visual impairment to be accompanied by a sighted swimming partner, who can provide essential information on landmarks. Swimmers with visual impairments also need to know that in emergencies, swimming in the direction of the waves will eventually take them to the shore. That waves travel to the shore is a concept that must be taught to any swimmer who is visually impaired who will be swimming in open water. Other cues to the direction of the shore are natural sound sources on the shore (such as people talking, dogs barking, lawnmowers, music and cars) for both swimmers who are blind and those who have low vision and natural visual cues (like buildings, trees, flags, and lights) for swimmers with low vision.

Canoeing and Sailing

Before a student with a visual impairment begins canoeing, he or she must first learn how to paddle. The teacher of students with visual impairments may bring a paddle to school and have the student practice kneeling on the floor with the paddle to one side. The specialist can demonstrate the strokes using physical guidance and tactile modeling so the student feels the flow of the motion or can use visual modeling for a student with low vision. Next, the student copies the motion while the specialist corrects his or her motion and body position. Once the student feels comfortable with the stroke, the specialist may bring a canoe to the school or community swimming pool, and the student can practice sitting and balancing in it. When the student is comfortable sitting in the canoe, he or she can move into the kneeling position and practice maintaining his or her balance. Finally, the student is given a paddle, and he or she begins paddling.

Navigating strokes (such as ruddering, turning, and slowing down) can be taught using the same method just described. It is important that the student feels the resistance of the water on the paddle and the direction in which the canoe travels as a result of moving the paddle. A sighted partner, seated in the steering position in the back of the canoe, can give the student oral instructions about the type, intensity, and direction (forward or backward) of the paddle strokes that should be used. Only after the student is proficient in and comfortable with maneuvering the canoe in a restricted environment should he or she venture into open water.

A student who is visually impaired should always be accompanied by a sighted partner who can warn him or her of rough water, rocks, swimmers, watercraft, and other obstacles in their path. All canoeists should always wear personal floatation devices (PFDs) and be able to swim.

A student who is visually impaired may participate in sailing with a sighted partner giving directions or as a passenger on or a member of the crew of a large sailboat. Like all passengers and crew members on a sailboat, the student should always wear a PFD and be able to swim. On a large sailboat, a crew member with a visual impairment must be attentive to the activity around him or her to avoid accidents, such as falling overboard or being hit by the boom, and a passenger who is visually impaired should be seated in a location where he or she will be out of harm's way and has something on which to hold.

Before a student boards a sailboat, the teacher of students with visual impairments should review basic sailing terminology with him or her, including such directional concepts as fore and aft and port and starboard, and basic parts of the boat, like bow and stern, rudder, deck, mast, and boom. The specialist should also orient the student to the sailboat before sailing, using the terminology previously taught in conjunction with the actual parts of the sailboat. A few trips in a sailboat as a passenger will help the student become familiar with the sailing experience. If the student enjoys the experience and wishes to learn more about sailing, the teacher of students with visual impairments can help him or her to enroll in a sailing school.

Water Skiing, Scuba Diving, and Snorkeling

Water skiing requires little modification once the student has learned how to water ski. There must be a sighted "spotter" in the boat who watches the student at all times; tells the student when the driver is ready; and tells the driver when the student falls or wants to speed up, slow down, or stop. The skier typically signals to the spotter by using hand signals. Water skiers should always wear PFDs and be able to swim.

Water skiing should be taught by a qualified instructor who has been trained to work with students who are visually impaired. Alternatively, the teacher of students with visual impairments can work with a qualified instructor to design an appropriate instructional program. Local agencies for persons who are blind may be of assistance in locating water-skiing clubs that welcome skiers with visual impairments.

The various sensations experienced under water while scuba diving and snorkeling may be pleasurable for a student with a visual impairment who is able to swim. Previous experience in swimming with fins and/or snorkeling is beneficial. Since the combination of the water and the diver's mask causes a magnification of approximately 25 percent (PADI, 1988), students with low vision may see better under water.

Only individuals who have been trained and certified by professional dive instructors may scuba dive. As in any swimming activity, a student with a visual impairment must always dive with a sighted partner. A scuba diver who is blind always needs to maintain physical contact with his or her sighted partner, and a scuba diver with low vision may swim alongside the sighted partner, who should wear a brightly colored wet suit and/or fins and may carry an underwater flashlight so he or she is easier to see. Hand signals that are normally used for communication between sighted scuba divers must be adapted for divers who are visually impaired, or a system of tactile prompts or radio communication may be used instead.

The teacher of students with visual impairments can work with a qualified scuba-diving instructor to design an appropriate instructional program and may also teach basic sighted guide techniques to the instructor. Local agencies for persons who are blind may be of assistance in locating scuba-diving clubs that welcome divers with visual impairments.

Snorkelling provides much of the same enjoyment of swimming and exploring underwater as scuba diving, but at much less expense and without the requirement of formal certification by a professional dive instructor. A student with a visual impairment must snorkel with a sighted partner. The adaptations mentioned above for scuba diving apply equally to snorkelling.

Downhill Skiing

Downhill skiing allows students with visual impairments freedom of movement and the ability to control speed without being in physical contact with anyone or anything. Training must be con-ducted by certified ski instructors who have been trained to teach skiers who are visually impaired (Lusher & Lusher, 1987). A skier with a visual impairment should always ski with a trained, sighted guide who is a better and more experienced skier.

Most organizations for skiers with disabilities can provide information about training and guiding skiers with visual impairments. The teacher of students with visual impairments may assist the student in contacting these organizations and may even wish to become a guide.

Sighted ski guides and skiers with visual impairments typically wear easily identifiable jackets or bibs. A bib worn by the skier who is visually impaired may have the caption "Blind Skier" or a picture of an eye with a line through it to make the skier more recognizable to the public, and the guide may wear a bib with the caption "Guide."

The sighted guide must be constantly aware of his or her own skiing, the skier's skiing, the terrain, and other skiers on the hill. When guiding a skier who has little or no usable vision, the guide typically guides from behind and calls out clear, concise instructions (such as left, hard right, slow down, traverse the hill, and stop) to the skier in a loud voice. The skier and guide should discuss the commands before they begin skiing together. Also, the guide must tell the skier ahead of time on which side to exit the lift.

For a more advanced skier or racer who is blind, the guide skis in front of the skier and calls out turns over his or her shoulder. An advanced skier who is blind may prefer to ski down the center of the hill (if no other skiers are on the hill) and turn where he or she wishes without the guide calling out the turns. In such a case, the guide continues to follow the skier and calls out only when the skier strays too far from the center of the hill or approaches the bottom of the hill.

When guiding a skier with low vision who can follow the guide visually, a guide may ski approximately 10 feet in front of the skier, wearing clothing that is easily visible to the skier. The guide checks over his or her shoulder to make sure the skier is still following. If the skier strays from the guide's path, the guide calls out the necessary correction in a loud voice.

A specially trained guide directs the skier who is visually impaired from behind, using verbal signals.

The skier needs to be responsible for his or her own equipment, including renting or caring for the equipment (sharpening and waxing the skis independently), putting on the equipment independently, and describing what his or her equipment looks like so the guide can locate it. If the teacher of students with visual impairments is an experienced skier, he or she can teach the student how to sharpen skis by bringing a pair of skis to school. The specialist can demonstrate (using tactile or visual modeling and physical guidance) how to hold the file, how to sharpen the skis using an even back-and-forth motion along their length, and how to tell if the edges of the skis are sharp enough. When waxing the skis, the student may require assistance in choosing the correct wax for the snow conditions. A trip to a ski shop or sporting goods store is an excellent way to expose the student to equipment, clothing, and accessories used in skiing.

Ideally, a skier who is visually impaired will have friends or relatives who have been trained as guides to accompany him or her on ski vacations. However, large ski resorts may have volunteer guides available for skiers who do not have their own. The skier should call in advance to see if the resort provides guides and, if so, to arrange for one.

Cross-Country Skiing

Like downhill skiing, cross-country skiing must be taught by an instructor who has been trained to teach skiers who are visually impaired. Distinguishing ski jackets or bibs for the sighted guide and skier who is visually impaired are also used in cross-country skiing. The guide typically directs the skier from in front and calls out turns over his or her shoulder. However, a skier with low vision may prefer to follow the guide visually. The guide should also be able to ski better than the skier with a visual impairment because he or she must be able to keep up with the skier; protect the skier from collisions with others; and concentrate on guiding, rather than on his or her own skiing.

Many cross-country skiing facilities have groomed trails with tracks set for the skiers to follow. Since the tracks are pressed into the snow, the skier who is visually impaired can use them as a tactile aid to maintain orientation. If the skier skis out of the tracks, the guide can have the skier stop and step either left or right until he or she locates the indentations of the tracks tactilely with his or her skis. When two sets of tracks are available, the guide may also guide the skier from the side, so the two can socialize more easily while skiing.

Ice-Skating and In-Line Skating

Balance is a concern when teaching any form of skating to a student with a visual impairment. When ice-skating, the teacher of students with visual impairments orients the student to the ice surface and the boards around the rink while the student is wearing shoes or boots. The teacher may also wear shoes or boots rather than skates if he or she does not know how to skate. The student may prefer to have some form of support when he

Student with low vision can learn how to ice skate by using a chair for support.

or she is learning to skate. For example, the student may push a chair or hold the hand or arm of a sighted guide who is wearing shoes or boots, rather than skates. The student should also consider wearing a helmet to protect his or her head from falls. Once the student has learned how to skate, he or she may skate independently by trailing the boards or by skating next to a sighted guide who gives verbal directions.

Many of the same considerations for ice-skating apply to in-line skating; however, it takes some time to adjust to the sensation of moving on narrow wheels. While skating, the student with a visual impairment, like all in-line skaters, should wear protective knee and wrist pads and a helmet at all times. It may be helpful for a beginner to learn how to skate in a rink or another smooth, confined space, rather than on city streets or sidewalks. It is important for the student to have a sighted guide when skating in the community. The teacher of students with visual impairments may also encourage the student to read in-line skating magazines with a sighted friend or classmate.

Bowling

Many people who are visually impaired enjoy bowling as members of a bowling league or with friends and family members. In learning to bowl, a student with a visual impairment should first be oriented to the lane and the arrangement of the pins at the far end; the latter may be simulated at school before the first bowling experience. A bowler who is visually impaired may need oral feedback about which pins have fallen and which remain standing. A bowler who has low vision may use a brightly colored bowling ball to track the ball visually while it rolls down the lane.

A novice bowler who is blind needs to follow a rail or wall when learning to make an approach to the foul line. Many bowling alleys have rails available for this purpose. Alternatively, portable rails may be available through local agencies for people who are blind, or a trailing surface may be improvised using the back of a bench or chairs. Two other options are to make an approach with a

A student who is blind enjoys bowling as a leisure-time activity.

sighted guide or simply to stand at the foul line to deliver the ball. A bowler who has low vision may not need to use any of these options, but may benefit from having the foul line marked with high-contrast tape. However, permission must always be obtained from the bowling alley manager before tape is applied to the floor, because after the tape is removed, a sticky residue often remains that interferes with subsequent bowlers' footwork.

With experience, bowlers know how many steps to take on their approach. To assist bowlers who are blind, a tactile marker—two or three lengths of rope taped to the floor, placed 2 to 3 inches (5 to 8 centimeters) apart—may be placed before the foul line. If the foul line buzzer is deactivated, the automatic scoring equipment will not deduct pins for foot fouls.

Gutter balls can be frustrating for a bowler who is visually impaired. Many facilities have gutter guards made out of rails or inflatable rubber bumpers that are also used for young children. These gutter guards block off the gutters to ensure that the ball actually hits a pin and keep the ball in the bowler's lane.

Most bowling alleys now have automatic

scorekeeping terminals, thereby making paper-and-pencil scorekeeping unnecessary. However, it is still important to know how to score points. The teacher of students with visual impairments may choose to teach the student with a visual impairment how to keep score during a math class and can encourage the student to keep track of his or her own score on a large-print score sheet, abacus, slate and stylus, talking calculator, or braille note taker while bowling.

Hiking, Camping, Fishing, and Rock Climbing

Few modifications are necessary for students with visual impairments to enjoy hiking and camping activities. However, the teacher of students with visual impairments should teach the components of these activities before a camping trip. For example, a student needs to practice setting up a tent, rolling up a sleeping bag, packing a backpack, walking with a heavy backpack, lighting a fire, practicing fire safety, and performing basic first aid. It may also be beneficial for the student to take a first aid course through an accredited organization, such as the Red Cross, before the trip. An O&M specialist can help the student determine methods of travel (cane or sighted guide) over rough terrain.

The teacher of students with visual impairments may wish to prepare the student for a camping trip by developing a list of supplies and an itinerary with the student and by giving the student a map in the appropriate medium (braille or large print). The specialist may also help the student purchase supplies and pack his or her gear.

A student with a visual impairment requires no special equipment to fish. Some skills that are required in fishing, such as selecting lures and hooks, tying knots, baiting hooks with different kinds of bait, and safely casting the line, may be taught in advance during specialized instructional time or may be integrated into the fishing experience. A student should be taught to maintain a safe zone around himself or herself when casting the line to ensure that no one is injured by the hook. After mastering the basic techniques, the student may then fish independently or with a sighted partner. Having a sighted partner may enhance the social experience of fishing and may be helpful for untangling snagged lines and tying and baiting hooks. When storing hooks in a tackle box, the student needs to place corks over the ends of the hooks to prevent injury.

Rock climbing is a physically demanding activity that a student with a visual impairment who is physically fit can engage in. The student needs to learn the techniques of rock climbing in a controlled situation (such as climbing walls with a safety harness). Climbing techniques must be taught by a certified instructor who is familiar with the equipment and safety requirements and who has been informed by the teacher of students with visual impairments of the student's unique needs. The climber who is visually impaired should always wear a helmet and a safety harness.

Martial Arts

A student who is visually impaired can participate in regular classes in karate, judo, tae kwon do, and other martial arts disciplines, at school or in the community. These activities may be effective in promoting fitness, agility, and body awareness and can improve a student's self-confidence and self-esteem (Gleser & Brown, 1986).

Martial arts classes are taught by certified instructors with whom the teacher of students with visual impairments should work to design an appropriate program for the student with a visual impairment in which physical guidance, tactile or visual modeling, and oral directions (see Chapter 12) are used in teaching the techniques. In particular, the student may experience some difficulty maintaining his or her balance while learning certain movements. A student with low vision should stand close to, but at a safe distance from, the instructor when skills are being demonstrated, and a student who is blind should feel the instructor's movements (tactile modeling) in slow motion first and then try to replicate them. Once the student is comfortable with the movements, he or she can attempt to perform them at full speed.

COMPETITIVE SPORTS

Competitive sports are those in which one participates with and against others. Although one may participate in competitive sports for enjoyment, these sports are more formal in their organization than are noncompetitive sports. Times or scores are kept as a means of comparison among teams or competitors. Many of these sports are simply competitive versions of noncompetitive sports discussed earlier and in Chapter 12.

The International Blind Sports Association (IBSA) developed a classification system that categorizes athletes who are visually impaired according to their degree of visual impairment to promote fairness in competition. The three classification categories—B1, B2, and B3—are defined in Table 18.1. An athlete competes with other athletes in the same category.

Table 18.1. Sight Classification System of the International Blind Sports Association

Classification	Criteria
B1	No light perception in either eye up to light perception, but inability to recognize the shape of a hand at any distance or in any direction.
B2	From ability to recognize the shape of a hand up to visual acuity of 2/60 and/or visual field of less than 5 degrees.
B3	From visual acuity of 2/60 up to visual acuity of 6/60 and/or visual field of more than 5 degrees and less than 20 degrees.

Source: International Blind Sports Association, *Classification of B1, B2, and B3* [On-line]. Available: http://www.ibsa.es/rules/doc/cap-04d

Team Sports

Depending on the student's degree of visual impairment and the sport being played, the student may be able to play on school teams. Although a student who is blind cannot be expected to hit a pitched baseball or participate in a fast game of basketball, it may be possible for him or her to play the offensive line of a high school football team. More commonly, students with visual impairments participate in team sports with other athletes who are visually impaired. In this case, the rules of the game are sometimes adapted.

Beep Baseball. In beep baseball, each team has six players with visual impairments, arranged in two rows of three in the outfield (Ponchillia, 1995). In addition, two sighted players act as the pitcher and catcher when the team is on offense, and one sighted player acts as a spotter when the team is in the field (Lieberman & Cowart, 1996).

All the players are blindfolded, including the students with visual impairments. The pitcher is a member of the batting team who tries to pitch a ball that the batter can hit successfully. The ball emits a beeping tone that enables the batter and the fielders to locate it. When a batter comes to bat, audible signals at first and third base are activated to indicate fair territory and can be discriminated from each other on the basis of their location. The sighted spotter informs the players in the field of the direction of a fly ball and warns them of impending collisions between players (Ponchillia, 1995).

The pitcher signals to the batter that the pitch is coming by calling out in a consistent cadence, "ready-pitch" and releasing the ball on the word *pitch.* There are no walks in beep baseball; the batter remains at bat until he or she has either hit the ball in fair territory or has struck out. When the ball is hit, the runner can run to either first or third base. A run is scored if the runner reaches the base before the ball is picked up by a fielder. Since runners do not have to run around the bases or return to home plate to score a run, there is no second base.

Ice Hockey. A student with a visual impairment can play ice hockey if the team consists of players with visual impairments and sighted players. The function of sighted players is to keep the flow of play moving by passing the puck to the other players and by calling out directions to the players who are visually impaired. Only the players with visual impairments are permitted to score goals. Also, the goaltender is visually impaired. A metal puck somewhat larger than a standard hockey puck is used. It is filled with ball bearings to enable the players to hear it as it moves along the ice and is brightly colored to enable players with low vision to locate it.

Goalball. Goalball was created in Europe following World War II for veterans who were blinded during the war. It is a popular competitive sport among players with visual impairments and is fast becoming popular with sighted players. All players, including those who are totally blind, wear blindfolds to ensure that everyone is participating on an equal basis. Knee and elbow pads are also recommended to prevent bruises and floor burns. The audience must remain silent during the game to enable the players to hear the ball and other sound cues made by the players. Players are not allowed to talk to each other while on the court; however, they can signal to each other by patting the floor or signal a pass by making some other nonverbal noise.

The goalball is a heavy rubber ball with bells inside, weighs 2.75 pounds (1.25 kilograms), and is 30 inches (76 centimeters) in circumference. Goalball is played on a court 60 feet (18 meters) by 30 feet (9 meters), which is the same size as a volleyball court. For recreational goalball games, the size of the court may be altered to take into consideration the space available and the ages and skill levels of the players. Duct tape is used to mark the boundaries of the court and orientation lines. It provides a tactile cue to the players without interfering with the game and enables them to reorient themselves independently. Figure 18.1 depicts a standard goalball court.

Three players from each team—one center and two wingers—are on the court, lined up across the "team area" lines at their team's end of the court. One player attempts to throw the ball,

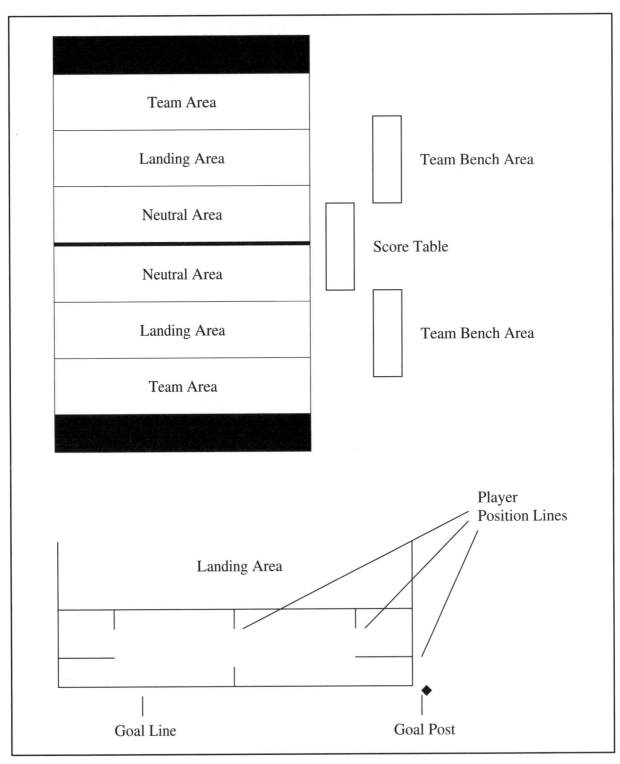

Figure 18.1. Layout of a Standard Goalball Court

Source: International Blind Sports Association [On-line]. Available: http://www.ibsa.es/rules/doc/sports/goalball.html

using a bowling action, past the opposing team's goal line to score a goal. The thrower may deliver the ball while either standing or kneeling. The ball must touch at least once in the neutral or landing area in the thrower's own team end, or the throw will be nullified. Team members try to prevent the opponents' shots from crossing their own goal line by extending their bodies in front of the oncoming ball. The game is 14 minutes long and is divided into 7-minute halves (Canadian Blind Sports Association, 1988).

Goalball can be an intensely competitive and physically demanding sport that requires excel-lent orientation skills. However, the game can be easily modified for young students with visual im-pairments and their sighted classmates. In Toronto, students (both those who are sighted and those who are visually impaired) compete against students in other schools in an annual goalball tournament. The tournament has been successful in providing competitive sports opportunities for students with visual impairments and in inte-grating sighted students into an activity for their classmates with visual impairments (Baxter, 1997). (See Sidebar 18.2 for suggestions for organ-izing such a goalball tournament.)

Organizing a Goalball Tournament for Students Who Are Visually Impaired and Their Sighted Classmates

SIDEBAR 18.2

♦ Introduce goalball in the student's physical education class. Organize a team of interested players (including the student who is visually impaired) and begin to practice.

♦ Discuss the possibility of getting another team together with another specialist in visual impairment. If two or more teams can be organized (each team with a student who is visually impaired), then it is possible to arrange a tournament.

♦ Reserve time in the gymnasium for the tournament (approximately 3 hours is needed to play a four-team round-robin tournament).

♦ Advertise the tournament in the school district, particularly in the school the student goes to, so that the teams can have an audience. Be sure to note in the advertisement that the audience must remain silent at all times, except when a goal is scored.

♦ Allow a maximum of five members on a team. It does not matter which positions the players take.

♦ Instruct all the players to wear blindfolds (including the students who are visually impaired) and protective elbow and knee pads.

♦ Modify goalball rules until all the teams are comfortable playing the game. Modified rules may include the following:

1. Using mats on the floor instead of duct tape to indicate the team areas (mats are easier for the students to detect and provide additional padding for their bodies);

2. Calling time out so the sighted spotters can adjust the mats that have been moved during the course of play;

3. Reducing the the size of the court to fit the particular gymnasium;

(continued on next page)

Organizing a Goalball Tournament *(Continued)*

4. Extending the 8-second time limit allowed in competitive goalball to take a shot to 15 seconds; and

5. Extending the 3-minute intermission to 5 minutes to help students reorganize themselves.

◆ Provide medals to winning teams and a trophy to the first-place finishers to make it exciting for the players and place goalball on a par with other school sports. The winning team keeps the trophy in its school's display case until the next tournament.

◆ Allow schools to develop rivalries among themselves over time. This rivalry is good for school spirit and promotes the sport.

GAMES

Active Games

Active games involve movement or physical activity. Unlike sports, active games are seldom, if ever, pursued in formal competition. Students with visual impairments enjoy participating in the same games as do sighted children, but some modification and teaching of prerequisite skills and concepts may be necessary for them to participate as fully and independently as possible. For example, a game of hide-and-seek will be successful only if the student with a visual impairment understands that standing behind a glass partition is not a good hiding spot because the sighted children can see through it.

Some additional active games include Twister, hopscotch, keep-away, dodgeball, Simon says, Mother may I?, tug-of-war, and jump rope. Since many of these games take place during recess, the teacher of students with visual impairments may wish to spend some time observing them. If the student does not know how to play any of the games, the specialist should teach him or her the necessary skills so the student can participate as fully and independently as possible. For example, the game Twister can be modified by adding textures to the colored circles. The lines on a hopscotch grid can be made bolder and thicker. A large, brightly colored ball can be used in dodgeball and keepaway. In the game Simon says, the student with low vision can stand close to the leader to observe the actions to be modeled.

Sedentary Games

Sedentary games require little or no gross physical movement. Most of the time, they are played with others and hence provide valuable opportunities for social interaction as well as recreation.

Card Games

Braille and large-print playing cards are available commercially; however, the teacher of students with visual impairments can use a braillewriter or a slate and stylus to braille the symbols for the denominations and suits on regular playing cards. The denominations are indicated by the number on the card (for example, a lower *e*, without the number sign, for the number 5) or the letters *j* (for jack), *q* (for queen), *k* (for king), and *a* (for ace), and the suits are indicated by the letters *s* (for spades), *h* (for hearts), *d* (for diamonds), and *c* (for clubs). Other card games (such as Uno) can be similarly adapted for students who read braille.

When teaching a student how to play card games, the teacher of students with visual impairments should make sure that the student understands that he or she must hold his or her cards so the other players cannot see them. If the student is unable to hold all his or her cards independ-

used to mark the score of the next hand. Using this method the student could also keep score for his or her opponent.

Another method of keeping score involves using a braillewriter and simply adding numbers underneath each other and then totaling them; the scores of several players can be kept in columns. Another option is to use an abacus to tally one player's score and two or more abaci if more than one player is playing. Keeping score on an abacus is an excellent way to reinforce the skills learned in math class.

Board Games

Braille or tactile versions of many popular board games, including Monopoly, Scrabble, checkers, chess, and cribbage, are available commercially. The modified Scrabble board, for example, has raised boundaries between the squares for the letters to fit into, braille captions to indicate double- and triple-word or letter squares, braille letter tiles with point values (without the number signs), and a peg board and large-print score sheets for score keeping. For the serious Scrabble player, *The Official Scrabble Player's Dictionary* is available in braille (see the Resources).

Other board games may be easily adapted by the teacher of students with visual impairments using various materials. For example, Chutes and Ladders can be modified by boxing in all the squares using puff paint, tactile tape, or other means of creating raised lines. Ladders may be made from toothpicks or popsicle sticks, and chutes can be made from felt strips, sandpaper, or some other textured material. A standard game of checkers can be adapted by gluing a textured surface to or drilling a hole through the center of either the red or black set of checkers.

Tactile dice may be purchased commercially, although some standard dice already have dots that can be detected tactilely. The rules of games and score cards need to be transcribed into braille for the student who is blind or enlarged, if needed, for the student with low vision. Braille and large-print bingo cards are also available commercially, but can be made using a photocopier, braillewriter, or slate and stylus.

The game Twister requires little modification for students with visual impairments—textures can be added to the colored circles to help students distinguish them.

ently, the student can use a card holder (two round pieces of plastic between which the cards are inserted and that can be held easily in one hand). Plastic card holders are available through vendors of specialized equipment.

A student who is blind can keep score in several ways. The most common method is to use a peg board, similar to a cribbage board, which can be purchased commercially or made with simple woodworking tools. The student places two pegs at the starting point. After the first hand or round, he or she counts the appropriate number of points and inserts one peg. This peg keeps the place of the current score, and the second peg is

Tactile and large-print bingo cards enable all players to enjoy the game.

If a student with a visual impairment is with a group of friends who want to play a board game and no adapted version is readily available, the student can still participate. The student can partner with a sighted friend who acts as the reader for the student and describes what is happening on the playing board and what the other players are doing. Both partners can participate equally in strategic decision making.

ARTS AND CRAFTS

Needlecrafts, such as knitting, crocheting, needlepoint, embroidery, and sewing, may be adapted for a student with low vision using large needles, thimbles, and needle guards on a sewing machine; enlarged patterns; and dark pattern lines (see Ludwig, Luxton, & Attmore, 1988). For a student who is blind, knitting and crocheting do not require modifications, although the instructions should be in braille.

The tactile nature of pottery makes it an ideal activity for students with visual impairments, who can experiment with texture and form just as sighted students do. More advanced students with

visual impairments may successfully use a pottery wheel with instruction.

Woodworking with hand or power tools is another activity that students with visual impairments can perform, provided they obey the safety rules for each piece of equipment. Students must always wear protective goggles and should be supervised at all times. A black marker, or tactile markings can be used to indicate where cuts are to be made. Braille labels can be applied to tools and their location on the tool rack to help a student who is blind to organize and identify the tools. The use of power tools in woodworking must be taught in advance by a skilled craftsperson or vocational education teacher with expertise in specialized techniques for teaching students who are blind or have low vision.

Despite their visual nature, painting and drawing are important recreation and leisure activities for students with visual impairments. Students with low vision may experiment with color, form, and texture, just as do sighted students. Students who are adventitiously blind (who lost their vision later in childhood) and have a good visual memory of the world may choose to express themselves through painting and drawing. Students who are congenitally blind (that is, who have been blind since birth) may experiment with painting and drawing using various colors of paint to which sand and other gritty substances have been added for texture for a tactile experience. Crayons, oil paint, and pastels can also be used. (See Chapter 11 for more information on fostering an appreciation for the arts in students with visual impairments.)

YOUTH GROUPS

Students with visual impairments should be encouraged to join organized, community clubs that match their particular interests. Clubs such as Boy Scouts, Girl Scouts, 4-H, religious youth groups, and community boys' and girls' clubs generally welcome members with disabilities. Other after-school activities may include joining a school or community sports club (like soccer, track and field, and gymnastics), dance group (ballet, jazz, or tap), choir, school band or orchestra, and a cultural or historical society. Since recreation and leisure skills and social interaction skills are an integral part of the expanded core curriculum, it is imperative that the teacher of students with visual impairments provide appropriate support for a student, such as presenting in-service workshops for group leaders and sighted members, accompanying the student to the first meeting, and teaching any prerequisite skills the student may need before he or she joins a particular group. (See Chapter 21 of this book for information on presenting information on visual impairments to members of the general public.) Not only will the student learn from the experience, but he or she will have the opportunity to make friends in his or her own neighborhood.

INDEPENDENT LEISURE ACTIVITIES

Students with visual impairments can read during their leisure time as long as the materials are available to them in the appropriate reading medium (regular print, large print, or braille). They need to learn how to obtain materials for themselves from the various agencies, including public libraries, that provide material in accessible media. Agencies for people who are blind are often the only place to obtain braille materials, whereas large-print books are often available at public libraries and bookstores. Reading material may also be downloaded from the Internet or accessed through CD-ROMs. The National Library Service for the Blind and Physically Handicapped (NLS) of the Library of Congress lends books and magazines in braille and on discs or audiocassettes and music scores in braille and large print, free of charge, to users with visual impairments in the United States.

Writing for pleasure (poetry, personal journals, letters to friends) is an activity that many students with visual impairments enjoy daily. Students may communicate with others in braille, print, on audiotape, or via E-mail. Computer technology makes it possible for students to communicate with people all over the world in a medium that is accessible to both parties. If a student wishes to keep a hard copy of the communication, a large-print or braille copy can be generated with specialized software and hardware (see Chapter 14). The teacher of students with visual impairments may join an Internet listserve to inquire whether specialists have students who are looking for pen pals. Other informal connections can be made at regional and national conferences.

Playing computer games and surfing the Net are popular activities for today's youths. With the necessary adapted software and hardware, they are easily accessible to computer users who are visually impaired. Many students with visual impairments enjoy researching topics of interest on the Internet, playing games on CD-ROM, and visiting Web sites and chat rooms. (See Chapter 14 for more information on technology.)

Like most other youths, students with visual impairments spend a lot of time listening to music on CDs and books on audiotape. CDs and audiocassettes may be labeled in large print or braille to give students quick and easy access to desired selections. The top 40 hits and popular artists are important topics of conversation among teenagers. Many of the best-selling books are commercially available on audiotape and may be purchased at local bookstores or borrowed from local libraries.

A few modifications are needed for a student who is blind who wishes to take music lessons after school. Some sheet music is available in braille, although special instruction in braille music is necessary to read it. Appropriate finger positioning may be demonstrated with hand-over-hand techniques. Some students may prefer to have a piece played for them several times so they can memorize it and play it by ear. (See Chapter 11 for a discussion of teaching music skills to students with visual impairments.)

Students with visual impairments may enjoy attending movies with their friends. Some theaters now provide audiodescription descriptive video services (DVS) for patrons with visual impairments; therefore, a student needs to telephone a local theater ahead of time to find out whether DVS is available. Aside from listening to and watching a movie, friends usually do something afterward, so "going to the movies" is an important social activity as well.

Gardening is often portrayed as a solitary recreation activity, even though gardening in a group (such as at a community garden) can be a great deal of fun and gives students a chance to learn about the life cycle of plants. A vast amount of information on gardening techniques is available on the Internet, including Web sites for some television gardening shows, to which students with visual impairments can gain access in their preferred reading mediums using specialized computer technology. Raised flower beds, guide ropes, and braille labels to mark rows of vegetables may assist gardeners who are visually impaired. With experience, gardeners learn to tell the difference between vegetables, flowers, and weeds and to identify herbs and other plants by breaking or crushing leaves to release their scents. When planting a vegetable garden, a gardener who is visually impaired should plant all seeds in a consistent manner (in vertical or horizontal rows) to make it easier to locate specific plants after the seeds have germinated. All pesticides and plant foods that are used in gardening should be labeled in an appropriate medium and stored in an organized manner.

SUMMARY

Recreation and leisure skills enrich one's life and offer opportunities for relaxation and social interactions outside school or work. These skills are part of the expanded core curriculum; therefore, the teacher of students with visual impairments has the ultimate responsibility for ensuring that students develop a wide range of recreation and leisure skills. By providing direct instruction in some activities and consulting with recreation specialists and other specialized instructors, students can participate in community recreation activities. The key is to expose students with visual impairments to a wide range of recreation and leisure skills from which they can choose those that match their particular interests.

ACTIVITIES

1. With a sighted partner serving as a guide, blindfold yourself and participate in one of the activities mentioned under non-competitive sports. Discuss your feelings about this experience, any problems you encountered, and concerns you have about a student who is blind participating in the same activity.

2. Modify a board game in such a way that it can be used by both students who are blind and those who have low vision.

3. Use paint, crayons, clay, or other materials to create a piece of artwork while using a blindfold or simulators (blindfolds or goggles that simulate different visual conditions). After the artwork has dried, exchange artwork with a partner and explore each other's artwork tactilely

while blindfolded or using the simulators. Discuss your impressions.

4. Think of a recreation or leisure-time activity that you enjoy. Analyze the activity on the basis of the following questions:

   ◆ What modifications would need to be made for a person with low vision and a person who is blind to participate in the activity?

   ◆ Would the amount of time that a person with a visual impairment needs to participate in the activity have to be modified?

   ◆ In addition to enjoyment, are there other benefits of this activity (social interactions, physical fitness)?

5. Keep a journal for one week in which you write down recreation and leisure-time activities in which you have participated. Consider the amount of time you spent on each activity and the variety of activities that you enjoyed. Were any of the people participating in these activities visually impaired? Could someone with a visual impairment participate in these activities, with or without adaptations?

6. Volunteer during a recreation activity at a local school or adult education program serving individuals with visual impairments. Note the modifications or adaptations that have been made, as well as the participants' level of involvement and enjoyment.

REFERENCES

Baxter, J. (1997). *Goalball: A great integration and inclusion game for sighted and non-sighted students.* Unpublished manuscript, Toronto: Toronto District School Board, Toronto, Canada.

Bina, M. J. (1986). Orienteering: Activities leading to skills development. *Journal of Visual Impairment & Blindness, 80,* 735–739.

Blakely, K., Lang, M. A., & Hart, R. (1991). *Getting in touch with play: Creating play environments for children with visual impairments.* New York: Lighthouse International.

Canadian Blind Sports Association. (1988). *Integrating the visually impaired student into physical education: A teacher's resource manual.* Ottawa: Canadian Blind Sports Association.

Connor, M. (1992). Low vision bicycling. *Journal of Visual Impairment & Blindness, 86,* 111–114.

Gleser, J. M., & Brown, P. (1986). Modified judo for visually handicapped people. *Journal of Visual Impairment & Blindness, 80,* 749–750.

Hatlen, P. H., & Curry, S. A. (1987). In support of specialized programs for blind and visually impaired children: The impact of vision loss on learning. *Journal of Visual Impairment & Blindness, 81,* 7–13.

Kelley, J. D., & Frieden, L. (Eds.). (1989). *Go for it: A book on sports and recreation for persons with disabilities.* Orlando, FL: Harcourt Brace Jovanovich.

Lieberman, L. J., & Cowart, J. F. (1996). *Games for people with sensory impairments: Strategies for including individuals of all ages.* Champaign, IL: Human Kinetics.

Loumiet, R., & Levack, N. (1993). *Independent living: A curriculum with adaptations for students with visual impairments.* Vol. 3: *Play and Leisure* (2nd ed.). Austin: Texas School for the Blind and Visually Impaired.

Ludwig, I., Luxton, L., & Attmore, M. (1988). *Creative recreation for blind and visually impaired adults.* New York: American Foundation for the Blind.

Lusher, R., & Lusher, B. (1987). *Alpine ski instruction for the visually disabled.* Mississauga: Ontario Ski Council and the Ministry of Tourism and Recreation.

PADI. (1988). *Open water diver manual.* Santa Ana, CA: Author.

Ponchillia, P. E. (1995). AccesSports: A model for adapting mainstream sports activities for individuals with visual impairments. *RE:view, 27,* 5–14.

Recreation Council on Disability in Nova Scotia. (1991). *Recreation for all.* Halifax: Author.

Stopka, C., Pomeranz, J., Siders, R., Dykes, M. K., & Goodman, A. (1999). Transitional skills for wellness. *Teaching Exceptional Children, 31*(3), 6–11.

Swallow, R. M., & Huebner, K. M. (1987). *How to thrive, not just survive: A guide to developing independent life skills for blind and visually impaired children and youths.* New York: American Foundation for the Blind.

Strategies for Teaching Recreation and Leisure Skills to Students with Visual Impairments and Additional Disabilities

Because the majority of students with visual impairments and additional disabilities may not be able to communicate their preferences, it may be possible to discern which recreation and leisure activities are motivating to them only after they are repeatedly exposed to myriad activities. When a student's vision is significantly impaired, parents and teachers may assume that some activities that are typically dependent on vision may not be enjoyable. When additional impairments accompany the vision loss, they may assume that the range of activities is further restricted. However, there are numerous benefits of active and frequent participation in recreation or leisure activities for these students:

◆ Any form of physical activity that is frequently engaged in improves respiratory, muscular, and cardiovascular activity, alertness and attention, sleep patterns, and emotional well-being. Activities that promote the mobility of joints and weight bearing minimizes the development of contractures and deformities and restrictions on the range of motion for students with significant postural deficits.

◆ Students who demonstrate some level of competence in leisure or recreation activities enjoyed by their families are more likely to be included in recreation outings. Family recreation activities not only promote family harmony, but provide an outlet for the stress that families of children with multiple disabilities often experience. *Exceptional Parent,* a monthly magazine for parents of children with disabilities, frequently publishes articles on leisure and recreation for individuals with disabilities and lists of vendors of recreation and leisure equipment and information on outings.

◆ Through participation in age-relevant recreation and leisure activities, students have contact with nondisabled peers and the opportunity to develop friendships and natural supports, share common interests, and have topics for conversations.

◆ The instructional opportunities that evolve from participation in recreation or leisure activities may be even more relevant for students with additional disabilities than for those with just visual impairments. In addition to learning to manage money, practicing travel skills, and acquiring social skills, participation in recreation and leisure activities can lead to the development and expansion of communication skills and greater independence. The exploration of leisure and recreation skills would be an excellent community-based instruction unit at the middle school and high school levels.

Students can engage in a multitude of recreation and leisure opportunities when their expectations are appropriate; modifications are made in their level of participation and in accessibility, environments, equipment, or rules; and the students, their families, and nondisabled children are given sufficient instructional support. Often, the primary intervention that is needed is a reconceptualization of how a game is played or of a student's role in the activity. The following are examples of the range of individ-

(continued on next page)

ual and team sports, individual and group activities, and games students with various levels of combined cognitive and communicative abilities, sensory impairments, and physical challenges can enjoy:

◆ Parents can involve their infants and toddlers in play groups with non-disabled infants and their parents, where they can assist the infants to engage in expected activities and both they and the infants can have opportunities to socialize. Mommy and Me and Gymboree programs also have excellent activities and equipment that encourage movements that facilitate strength and coordination and postural skills. Story time at a local library also offers exposure to other children and to language development. Participation in such group activities with the support of parents helps these infants and toddlers to accommodate to and integrate sensory information from multiple sources and eases the transition from the home to community settings.

◆ Students who have minimal to no light perception and have adapted well to sound may enjoy pressing buttons and pulling levers at a local arcade. Non-disabled children can enjoy the games just as much as the students by "facilitating" timing and the selection of buttons.

◆ Students can play games on Nintendo 64 or the Sony Playstation with nondisabled peers or siblings using dual controls. Students with severe cognitive impairments enjoy the noise of the games and activating the buttons and do not have to understand the "rules" or

guide the controls. Adaptive switches and joysticks are available for students with limited hand control.

◆ Students with dual sensory impairments may enjoy exploring the light-reflected toys and posters and glow-in-the-dark merchandise at novelty stores at a mall.

◆ Students may enjoy hands-on, interactive exhibits at children's museums or museums of science and natural history that provide intensive experiences with sound, illumination, and vibration and require minimal physical effort.

◆ For miniature golf, miniature beepers can be placed beside the ball to alert the student to the general direction in which to swing, or a friend can use hand-over-hand guidance to help the student to strike the ball. Even students in wheelchairs can enjoy miniature golf using child-size golf clubs.

◆ Many community bowling alleys have designated nights when the pins and surroundings are highlighted by ultraviolet (black) light, which makes focusing at a distance easier and tends to increase attention and motivation. Students with significant physical limitations may bowl by activating a switch that releases a lever holding the ball on a special frame. Students with weak grasps may find the bowling balls with recessed handles more manageable. Other students may enjoy placing the ball on the alley and simply rolling or pushing it, rather than picking it up and releasing it. Many alleys also have "bumpers" that can be activated to keep the balls from going into the gutters and

(continued on next page)

thus provide a greater opportunity for success.

◆ Students of all ages enjoy hanging out with their buddies at multimedia stores and large bookstores listening to the latest CDs at the stores' listening stations.

◆ Therapeutic horseback riding, often sponsored by Optimists or Kiwanis clubs, is available at a minimal cost to students with all types of disabilities. The movement of the horse stimulates pelvic mobility and leads to better balance, coordination, and postural control in addition to exposure to fresh air and sunshine. Typically, two volunteers walk or run on either side of the student, and a volunteer leads the horse.

◆ Specialized companies design and adapt bicycles and tricycles for students with all forms of disabilities. A student who needs exercise but cannot see to steer pedals behind a sighted person and holds on to a fixed handlebar. Other bikes are available that allow a student to ride in a seat in front of a sighted bicyclist.

◆ In addition to swimming, working out at the gym with friends is a great way both to develop fitness and to socialize. Students with the severest impairments can increase stamina and strength and maintain a range of motion on many of the machines, including elliptical walkers, treadmills, rowing machines, and trampolines. Although great caution must be exercised, when well supervised, both students who are ambulatory with assistance and those who are not

ambulatory enjoy the movement of trampolines and must actively work muscle groups to maintain their posture and balance.

◆ Special Olympics, Challenger Little League, and Unified Games are organized community-based activities that offer a wide variety of recreational benefits. Unified Games provide opportunities for students with disabilities to play alongside their nondisabled peers in intramural basketball and soccer games.

◆ Electronic games, especially those by Tiger electronics, can be enjoyed by students of all ability levels. Games, such as Henry, Bird Brain, and Star Wars, are memory games that require only a light touch to activate buttons that verbalize a variety of silly sounds, environmental noises, and phrases from the original *Star Wars* movie. Important social concepts, such as sharing and taking turns, are reinforced, and students can play the games without understanding the rules. Young children can enjoy board games and interactive games like Hungry Hippos, Hands Down, Bedbugs, Jinga, and Don't Wake Daddy, which require simple movements. Family members and friends can assist the students to take turns, and switches can be programmed to activate the components of games or to allow the students to indicate which moves they want to make.

M. BETH LANGLEY
Pinellas County Schools
St. Petersburg, FL

R E S O U R C E S

Suggested Resources for Teaching Recreation and Leisure Skills

Resource	Type	Source	Description
Braille playing cards, game equipment, and adapted toys	Play materials	LS&S Group National Federation of the Blind	Playing cards marked with braille, card holder, balls with beepers and bells, tactile ticktacktoe and checkers games, dominoes and chess, braille and large-print bingo cards, braille dice, and selected toys.
Creative Recreation for Blind and Visually Impaired Adults (Ludwig, Luxton, & Attmore, 1988)	Booklet	American Foundation for the Blind	A booklet on a variety of recreational activities; includes suggestions for family members and friends for adapting favorite leisure activities.
Getting in Touch with Play: Creating Play Environments for Children with Visual Impairments (Blakely, Lang, & Hart, 1991)	Book	Lighthouse International	A book about creating play environments for students with visual impairments. Demonstrates how outdoor play environments can be designed to provide stimulating activities through the manipulation of play elements, the organization of play spaces, and input from adults.
Go For It: A Book on Sports and Recreation for Persons with Disabilities (Kelley & Frieden, 1989)	Book	Harcourt Brace Jovanovich	A book about the many recreational opportunities available to persons with disabilities, from highly competitive athletic endeavors to casual games in neighborhood playgrounds, recreation centers, and sports clubs. Designed to motivate and stress possibilities, not limitations.

(continued on next page)

Suggested Resources *(Continued)*

Resource	Type	Source	Description
How to Thrive, Not Just Survive: A Guide to Developing Independent Life Skills for Blind and Visually Impaired Children and Youth (Swallow & Huebner, 1987)	Book	American Foundation for the Blind	A book that presents guidelines and strategies for helping visually impaired children develop, acquire, and apply skills that are necessary for independence in socialization, orientation and mobility, and leisure-time and recreational activities.
Independent Living: A Curriculum with Adaptations for Students with Visual Impairments: Volume 3 (Loumiet & Levack, 1993)	Handbook	Texas School for the Blind and Visually Impaired	The third of a three-volume set that addresses the nonacademic disability-specific needs of students with visual impairments. For many areas of play and leisure (such as social play, physical games and sports, music, and dance) the text presents goals and skills and a rich variety of useful resources.
The Official Scrabble Players Dictionary (braille edition)	Book	American Red Cross—Essex Chapter Braille Department	A dictionary designed specifically for the Scrabble player.

Contact information for each of the resources listed will be found in the Sources of Products, Materials, Equipment, and Services section at the back of this book.

CHAPTER 19

Career Education

Karen E. Wolffe

KEY POINTS

◆ Career education spans the years from preschool through high school and is crucial for achieving success in various areas of adult life, including employment.

◆ Much of the early exposure to jobs, work duties, and work ethics that sighted students obtain incidentally through visual observation is not available to students with visual impairments.

◆ Students who are blind or visually impaired need to have direct, active experiences with various jobs and responsibilities throughout their school careers.

◆ The teacher of students with visual impairments plays a direct role in ensuring that students gain the needed experiences during the school years to facilitate productive living and employment in adulthood.

The material in the section on Assessment is based, in large part, on Karen E. Wolffe, "Transition Planning and Employment Outcomes for Students Who Have Visual Impairments with Other Disabilities," in Educating Students Who Have Visual Impairments with Other Disabilities, *S. Z. Sacks and R. K. Silberman, Eds. (Baltimore, MD: Paul H. Brookes, 1998).*

VIGNETTE

On her way to the sixth-grade classroom, Ms. Harper paused at the preschool door. It seemed to be cleanup time. In the bustling group of 4 and 5 year olds, Ms. Harper had to search for a moment before she could spot Jeremy. Jeremy, who had light perception, was in the "manipulatives" area, kneeling on the floor beside a large plastic canister, completing an organized search on the floor around him for the set of small wooden blocks. As Ms. Harper watched, Jeremy made one last quick search and stood and picked up the canister. He carried the canister to the nearest set of low shelves, then trailed the edge of the upper shelf to the end. Just as he carefully placed the canister in the empty area on the second shelf, Damon, a lively sighted 4 year old, said, "Hey, you left two blocks under the chair!" Ms. Harper observed as Jeremy located the chair and the two blocks and quickly deposited them in their appropriate storage place.

Ms. Harper's primary purpose in coming to this school this day was to meet with Ms. Wallace, a sixth-grade teacher. Ms. Wallace was taking her class on a field trip to the local soft-drink bottling plant—a major employer in the community—the following week, and had asked Ms. Harper to accompany the class. Salvador Gomez, a student with low vision, might benefit from some individualized attention on this trip, Ms. Wallace had suggested. Ms. Harper had come to learn the final details of the plan and to let Ms. Wallace know that she had spoken by phone with the plant manager. The plant manager had offered to arrange for Salvador to have a close-up look at some of the equipment that was temporarily shut down because the working equipment was not safe to touch.

The plant manager had also given Ms. Harper the names of several employees who would talk with Salvador and the other students about their particular jobs. Even better, the manager said that the head of the shipping department, who was visually impaired, would be an excellent spokesperson for the entire group. "A really good role model," thought Ms. Harper. "Salvador may never work at the bottling plant or in a shipping department, but the more careers he knows about, the broader his horizons will become."

As she neared Salvador's classroom, Ms. Harper thought about Stacey, who had graduated from high school several years ago. At Ms. Harper's suggestion, Stacey had volunteered at the local YWCA during her junior year. At first, Stacey had worked in the office, but later, she had participated in basic child care activities with supervision. Today, Stacey was completing her degree in early childhood education. "It's *too* easy to overlook career education for students with visual impairments," mused Ms. Harper, "but without that volunteer experience, Stacey would probably never have known that such a career existed. How much richer her life will be now as a result!"

INTRODUCTION

The ideal education is not to teach the maximum, to maximize the results, but above all to learn to learn, to learn to develop, and to learn to continue to develop after leaving school (Piaget, 1976, p. 30).

Throughout this chapter, the term *career* is used in its broadest sense to mean the roles that one plays over the course of a lifetime—spouse, parent, worker, community activist, and so forth—in addition to being a performer of one's occupation. Although an important component of one's career is the work one performs, lives are multifaceted and include a variety of roles.

Career education begins during the preschool years and extends throughout children's school careers. During this time, children learn to be responsible and organized and to follow directions; develop solid academic skills, problem-solving skills, and work behaviors; and come to know what a multitude of workers do in the community. They also gain many other skills that provide the basis for a productive life and employment in adulthood. Sighted children learn a great deal about the world of work incidentally by observing what the adults in their lives do throughout the day. In addition, they observe what other, unknown adults are doing from the windows of their homes, and from their parents' cars, in the stores and homes they visit, and as they move through the community.

Children with visual impairments share the same need as sighted children to develop career education skills. However, since they are restricted in their ability to observe and learn incidentally about work and workers, they may miss many common work activities and workers' characteristics. If their parents and other adults do not describe what is going on in the environment, they may miss important cues about what is happening outside their immediate surroundings. Because children with severe visual impairments are usually unable to observe things beyond arm's reach, they are often unaware of the breadth of activities that are transpiring and of how adults' lives are shaped by their careers.

Some of the most mundane facts related to careers may be lost to children with visual impairments. For example, how would they know which workers wear uniforms, how those uniforms vary from season to season, and how the uniforms of men and women differ? How would they even know which clothes their mothers and fathers wear to work, to attend religious services, or to participate in other activities? How can these children learn what tools or supplies are associated with what jobs without seeing adult workers using them? And, how can they understand the physical, cognitive, and emotional demands of various workplaces without being able to watch workers in those environments? All these subtleties must be taught directly to children with visual impairments so they can make informed decisions about their future lives and work plans. Career education, starting as early as possible and taught through activities at home, in school, and in the community, is a viable way to ensure that students with visual impairments know what they need to know, develop healthy relationships, contribute to the community, and gain employment.

Sometimes, career education experiences may be infused into the general education curriculum and supported by input from teachers of students with visual impairments on how to make the activities meaningful. For example, a student with a visual impairment may be involved in a classroom project to set up a bake sale to raise money for a class trip. The specialist may help the student to devise systems to record the prices of items in the bake sale, collect money that is owed, and make the correct change. The student's systems may include using large-print or braille price tags, generating a braille or large-print list of common items and prices, using a bill identifier, learning how to fold bills so they can be identified and to determine the denomination of coins by touch, organizing like coins and bills so they are together and easily accessible, and keeping track of inventory and money with a large-print or speech-output calculator or an abacus.

At other times, students benefit from structured career education activities outside the general education program. For example, a teacher of students with visual impairments may take a student to a bank and orient him or her to the layout, the available services, and the workers who are present. Their visit may include a trip inside the vault, a hands-on demonstration of how coins are counted by machine, how deposits are handled at the counter and through the drive-up windows, and how ATMs operate; as well as an introduction to the different bank employees (tellers, receptionists, secretaries, financial managers, loan officers, and so forth). Wherever career education activities occur, the teacher of students with visual

impairments may discuss the pros and cons of such work responsibilities with the student and the availability of similar jobs in the community and tells the student about accessible resources so the student can further investigate these and other jobs.

This chapter presents an overview of the career development process and learning activities that promote the acquisition of vocational and functional life skills by students with visual impairments. Success following graduation hinges on the acquisition of these skills. This chapter details career education content and activities that teachers and other interested parties can use to structure learning in this critical area. Information is presented by approximate age group or grade level—preschool, elementary, middle school, and high school. An individual child's chronological age or actual grade level may not always correspond with the stages described, since children develop at different rates, but the sequence of the activities presented is appropriate.

ROLE OF THE TEACHER OF STUDENTS WITH VISUAL IMPAIRMENTS

The role of the teacher of students with visual impairments varies according to the students' needs. In some instances, the specialist simply supports career education activities that are integrated into the general education curriculum. In other instances, he or she plans and directs activities that enhance the students' understanding of the world of work and adult responsibilities outside the general education curriculum.

Regardless of how career education content is infused into the program for students with visual impairments, the teacher of students with visual impairments needs to indicate what career education competencies are being addressed in a student's Individualized Family Service Plan (IFSP), Individualized Transition Plan (ITP), or Individualized Education Program (IEP), under the Statement of Transition Services section. The specialist plays a key role in this process, since he or she has the knowledge and skills to address the needs of students with visual impairments. The teacher also plays an essential role in working with students with additional disabilities; strategies focusing on students with visual impairments and other disabilities and resources for teachers appear later in this chapter.

The IFSP is required for infants and toddlers who are eligible for services under provisions of the Individuals with Disabilities Education Act (IDEA). Transition planning is a mandated component of the IFSP to ensure that a child's movement from an early intervention program into an educational program is smooth (Patton & Dunn, 1998). Many of the skills necessary for a successful transition, such as the ability to follow directions and organizational skills, are critical career education skills and can be identified as such on the IFSP.

Planning for the transition from school to work is also mandated for all children with disabilities who receive services under IDEA and must be initiated by age 14. Some states require a separate ITP, whereas others allow the transition goals and objectives to be included in the IEP. Regardless of the form on which transition planning goals and objectives are identified, it is imperative that specific career education concerns be included for students with visual impairments. Throughout this chapter, appropriate career education goals and objectives are identified in the sidebars for consideration as possible IFSP, ITP, or IEP goals and objectives.

ASSESSMENT

To develop appropriate goals and objectives for IFSPs, ITPs, or IEPs, teachers of students with visual impairments need to assess the students with whom they are working. Although a number of formal psychoeducational assessment materials are available (for specific tests and testing procedures, see Barraga & Erin, 1992; Bradley-Johnson, 1994; and Lewis & Russo, 1998; see also Chapter 2), few career education assessment tools have been adapted for use with students who are visually impaired (McBroom, Seaman, Graves, & Freeman,

1988; Wolffe, 1998). The *Self-Directed Search* (Holland, 1994) is an inventory of career interests, abilities, and values available in both print and braille. Likewise, the *Comprehensive Vocational Evaluation System* (Dial, Mezger, Gray, Massey, Chan, & Hull, 1992) is available in alternative reading formats and, unlike the *Self-Directed Search*, it has been normed on individuals who are blind. Both these instruments are appropriate for high school students.

However, in addition to formalized tests and measures, a teacher of students with visual impairments can use ecological or naturalistic evaluation techniques to assess a student's acquisition of career education competencies by observing the student performing a range of activities that typify his or her daily activities. Observation sites may include the school (performing academic and other tasks in classrooms, traveling in the halls, eating in the cafeteria, playing on the playground or at athletic fields, waiting for the school bus, attending field trips, and so forth), the home (performing chores, preparing snacks or meals, eating with or without family members, engaging in leisure activities, and the like), and the workplace (performing work tasks, activity during breaks, getting to and from work, using adaptive equipment on the job, and so on), and in the community (shopping, doing various recreational activities, traveling, and the like). As much as possible, the teacher sees the student engaging in his or her daily routines, where the routines are performed and with whom they are performed (Wolffe, 1998).

An ecological assessment of career education skills and needs may follow this process:

♦ Review all the school and case records, notes of IEP or other team meetings, medical and therapy notes, information from the family, assessment information, and the like.

♦ Observe the student at school, at home, in the community, at work, during daily routines, during free time or on field trips, and so forth.

♦ Ask the personnel who provide services to

the student about the student's daily routines and strengths and weaknesses.

◆ Contact the student's parents or primary caregivers to ask about their goals, their goals for the student, and their perceptions of the student's strengths and weaknesses.

◆ Document everything you observe—where it took place, with whom, and under what circumstances.

A sample observation checklist that can be used to document observations is included in Appendix A to this chapter. Although it was designed to be used with middle school and high school students, it could easily be modified for use with elementary school students by substituting the word *classmates* for *coworkers*. The behaviors identified on the observation checklist are traditional work habits.

In addition to the specific behaviors listed on the observation checklist, a teacher of students with visual impairments or another evaluator may also want to consider the following when observing a student:

◆ Body language (posture, gait, mannerisms, gestures, and facial expressions);

◆ Personal grooming skills and dress (hygiene, hairstyle, care and age appropriateness of clothing, and appropriateness of clothing and grooming to the setting);

◆ Interaction with peers, family members, and authority figures (work supervisors, teachers, dormitory staff, cafeteria workers, administrative staff, and so forth);

◆ Mobility (in familiar and unfamiliar areas), including the use of mobility tools and low vision devices;

◆ Ability to manipulate materials and tools, including technology;

◆ Organizational skills and adaptive techniques; and

◆ Use of aids and appliances.

For an older, articulate student, an important component of an ecological evaluation is an in-depth interview. If a student is unable to participate in such an interview, the questions may be asked of a parent, guardian, or other adult who has known the student for a long time. Although the following list of questions is not meant to be comprehensive, it may provide guidance to an interviewer. Some, if not all, of the following questions may be used:

◆ Tell me a little bit about yourself and your family.

◆ Where do you plan to live after you leave school?

◆ What do you plan to do following high school?

◆ What kind of work do you want to do?

◆ How will you get a job?

◆ What skills have you learned in school?

◆ What skills do you still need to learn?

◆ What are your greatest strengths?

◆ What are your greatest weaknesses?

◆ Have you done volunteer work? If so, for whom? Doing what?

◆ Have you worked? If so, for whom? Doing what?

◆ What kinds of responsibilities do you have at home?

◆ What are your goals for this year? Five years from now?

◆ What help will you need to achieve your goals?

◆ What 5–10 adjectives describe you best?

◆ What classes do you prefer in school?

◆ What activities do you prefer outside school?

◆ What do you do for fun?

◆ Do you prefer to work alone or with others?

◆ Do you prefer to work indoors or outdoors?

◆ Do you like to work with people, data, or things?

◆ Can you describe your perfect job?

In addition to observing the student, the evaluator needs to conduct a series of interviews with the student's parents or caregivers, teachers and therapists, and any other significant people in the student's life. Consider asking concerned adults the following questions:

◆ What do you see as the student's strengths?

◆ What do you see as the student's weaknesses?

◆ What do you see the student doing after high school?

◆ Where do you see the student living after high school?

◆ What kinds of supports do you think the student will need to be successful after he or she leaves school?

INSTRUCTIONAL STRATEGIES

The career development of children with visual impairments mirrors that of children without disabilities and progresses in the following stages: career awareness, career exploration, career preparation, and career placement or assimilation (Brolin, 1995; Wolffe, 1996, 1999). Ideally, children begin the process of developing self-awareness, which is an integral part of career awareness, from birth. Dating from that time, a great deal of emphasis in preschool and elementary programs is on children's awareness of themselves and the world in which they live; career exploration usually begins late in elementary school or early in middle school; career preparation begins in earnest in middle school and intensifies in high school; and career placement typically occurs during high school and continues into adulthood. Students with visual impairments may move more slowly through the stages than do their sighted age-mates because of their inability to gather information from the environment incidentally through visual observation.

Career Education Activities in Preschool

The basic career education competencies that preschoolers need to acquire and possible IFSP goals and objectives are listed in Sidebar 19.1 and are discussed in this section (for additional goals, objectives, and activities, see Wolffe, 1999). Parents and teachers need to consider these competencies as they develop the activities in which they will engage preschoolers.

In preschool, children learn to be responsible for some of their basic care: feeding, toileting, dressing themselves, and so forth. As they learn these skills, they need to be given opportunities to practice them and to be expected to perform them. Parents and teachers have to step back and let children with visual impairments do things for themselves, as soon as possible, even if their initial efforts are less than perfect. In this way, children learn that they are capable of being independent and that others expect independence from them. Personal responsibility is one of the most important lessons that preschoolers can learn.

In preschool, children are expected to listen and follow directions from their parents, teachers, and others regarding play and other activities. Therefore, it is important to provide children with structured learning activities, such as arts and crafts projects in which they must follow directions to produce products. For example, making clay handprints or footprints gives children an opportunity to work in a medium that provides immediate tactile feedback and produces a concrete product, and games, such as pat-a-cake, ring-around-the-rosy, and London Bridge, teach children to work cooperatively with others and follow the rules of a game. (See Sidebar 19.2 for some age-appropriate projects and related leisure activities.) Parents and the teacher of students with visual impairments may need to teach young children who are visually impaired individually how to play these games that other children learn through observation. In addition, some games may need to be modified to make them more accessible to the children. For exam-

S I D E B A R   1 9 . 1

Career Education Competencies: Preschool

Career education competencies are presented in boldface type and are appropriate for inclusion in IFSPs as goals. Under each goal is a list of possible IFSP objectives.

LEARNING TO LISTEN

- The child orients toward the speaker.
- The child attends to the speaker.
- The child responds (smiles, laughs, coos) to the speaker.

LEARNING TO FOLLOW DIRECTIONS

- The child follows the teacher's movement (such as in the hand-over-hand manipulation of tools).
- The child follows one-word directions (like "sit" or "stand").
- The child follows more complex directions (for example, "Get your coat," "Get your backpack," or "Pick up your toys").

LEARNING TO BE RESPONSIBLE

- The child takes turns at games and waits in line at school.
- The child puts his or her clothes and supplies where they belong.
- The child follows class rules (such as no running, no hitting, and raise your hand to speak).

LEARNING BASIC ORGANIZATIONAL SKILLS

- The child uses a designated cubby to store school supplies and tools.

- The child uses tools, such as a backpack, to keep up with personal items.
- The child uses appropriate space like a lipped tray to store pieces of a project.

FANTASIZING ABOUT ADULT ROLES

- The child participates in creative dramatics (for instance, classroom or school plays).
- The child engages adults (parents, grandparents, friends, neighbors, and community workers) in conversations about their work.
- The child participates in make-believe/dress-up activities (such as playing school, hospital, fire station, or grocery store).

LEARNING TO PLAY

- The child engages in play with others (board games, playground games, and manipulatives like LEGOS or Lincoln Logs).
- The child plays alone (reads, puts together puzzles, watches television or videotapes, listens to music, and so forth).

Source: Adapted from K. E. Wolffe, Ed., *Skills for Success: A Career Education Handbook for Children and Adolescents with Visual Impairments* (New York: AFB Press, 1999).

ple, in the game of hide-and-seek, the person who is "it" may need to wear a bell so that a child who is blind can determine where "it" is.

Through leisure skills, playing board games (many of which are available in adapted forms or can be modified, as explained in Chapter 18) and

spending time on the playground, children learn to follow directions, to pay attention to the game pieces or equipment and the other players, and to determine the impact of their behaviors on other people. They come to understand some of the basics of turn taking, winning and losing gracefully,

Projects and Activities for Preschoolers that Focus on Manipulating Objects and Working with Others

- Make collages with brightly colored pictures or tactilely interesting materials.

- Make plaster of paris imprints of hands, feet, leaves, one's name, and so forth.

- Roll out sheets of modeling clay and cut out shapes with cookie cutters; make clay coils and snakes and cut them into beads, and the like.

- Use finger paints with bright colors (add texture like sand or glitter, too).

- Color with wire screen beneath the paper for tactile feedback.

- Make necklaces with different kinds of beads, pasta, dried berries, and so forth.

Beads with printed or brailled letters are popular and fun to make, as well.

- Make tile or mosaic trivets or trays.

- Make structures out of Popsicle sticks, Lincoln Logs, LEGOS, or similar materials.

- Participate in outdoor games and activities, such as London Bridge, ring-around-the-rosy, red rover, hide-and-seek, kick ball, T-ball, and so on.

- Play make-believe games, such as tea parties; school; house; driving the car, train, or bus; superheroes; and space travelers.

---

and competing with others. In learning to play sports, children also learn to follow directions, use their bodies to accomplish athletic feats, and work cooperatively with others and develop coordination, range of motion, and other physical abilities. Early childhood is about having fun while learning. Playing games and participating in athletics are venues for this type of learning. Playing with others and learning to play alone are both important goals of career education.

Teachers of students with visual impairments help students develop play activities through coactive involvement with them, literally moving through activities in tandem with the student and demonstrating how to manipulate toys and materials. Once the children understand how to use toys and play props, teachers can bring children together and encourage them to share and play with one another. When children are old enough to understand, the specialists help them learn techniques for engaging other children. For example, children who are blind need to learn to ask questions like, "Who's here? What are you doing? May I play?" to understand what other children are doing that may be of interest to them and join them appropriately.

As preschoolers interact with their parents, siblings, and caregivers, they learn to communicate and socialize, that is, to listen and to express themselves in effective ways, and hence must have opportunities to both speak and listen. At the dinner table, in the car, and during daily activities, it is important for adults to encourage open communication. From the beginning of their children's lives, most parents play communication games with their babies: "Where is the baby?" "Peek-a-boo!" "Where is Mommy or Daddy?" "What is this, where is that?" As children become more adept in verbalizing their wants and needs, parents and caregivers add social rule-building skills, "What is the magic word?" "How are you supposed to ask for ____?" "Say hello to ____," "Wave bye-bye," and so forth. They sing and read nursery rhymes and children's stories to their children. Children and adults alike enjoy these activities, and children learn in a meaningful way how people relate to one another and convey messages.

Parents and other caregivers can help children with visual impairments understand the nonverbal communication cues that the children miss and teach them how to communicate with their bodies. For instance, when preschoolers with visual impairments smile or frown, the adults in their lives can reinforce the correct facial expression with verbal reinforcement or help them understand the impact of a facial expression that is counter to what they are trying to express. Some body language, such as waving good-bye or hello, can be demonstrated or taught using hand-over-hand techniques. Subtle gestures like raising one's shoulders to indicate "I don't know" or raising both hands to shoulder height with palms upward to ask nonverbally, "What's going on?" (gestures without inherent meaning like good-bye or hello) require both demonstration and a verbal explanation. Once the child has been taught the movement or gesture, the instructional staff and family members can help to reinforce its use through positive feedback when the child demonstrates the gestures in social exchanges.

It is during preschool that children also learn many of the basic concepts that form the underpinning for the development of future academic and compensatory skills. Basic concepts like top, bottom, under, above, left, right, front, back, up, down, big, little, and so forth are critical building blocks for orientation and mobility, mathematics, science, and other academic areas that children will encounter throughout their lives, both in school and in the community. The teacher of students with visual impairments and parents can support the development of these skills by verbalizing for children where they are in relation to other known entities and things, where things in the environment are, what size something is in comparison to other things, and so forth.

In addition, it is during this period that children begin to develop basic organizational skills. They begin to organize their lives and to understand the organization of their homes, classrooms, and other places. They also understand how the placement of materials and possessions

helps or hinders retrieval at another time. Children with visual impairments need to be taught to organize their possessions so that they can minimize the time it takes to search for their things. The parents and specialist can help by labeling these possessions in a recognizable format (braille, large print, or pictorial labels, for instance). Furthermore, they can help the children learn to search for objects they want by providing auditory cues and hands-on demonstrations and then allowing the children to search. Active involvement in simple household chores helps children see how adults organize materials in the home. Suggestions for participation in simple household chores to help develop organizational techniques are included in Sidebar 19.3.

In the early years, most children enjoy fantasizing about adult roles—playing "dress-up" and establishing make-believe homes, stores, doctors' offices, schools, and other adult-like venues—and mimicking what they see and hear the adults in their lives doing. These activities actually help children gain awareness of the world of work and set the stage for expanded career awareness activities in elementary and secondary school.

These activities also provide opportunities for children and adults to communicate about career roles and for the adults to discuss what the props are and how the children can use them in their make-believe roles. For instance, when children are playing hospital, an adult could say, "Doesn't the doctor need a stethoscope?" or "I think the nurse needs a thermometer." Teachers of students with visual impairments and parents may want to provide different props and costumes to encourage this kind of fantasizing about jobs and adult roles. Simple braille or other tactile labels can make the props more readily identifiable to children without functional vision.

In summary, career education in preschool primarily involves helping children to develop good basic concepts about the world, good work behaviors, and basic self-help skills. Preschoolers with visual impairments need to be encouraged to explore their environment and to have opportunities to touch, listen, taste, see, and experience as much as possible. They need to participate to

---

SIDEBAR 19.3

Suggested Household Chores and Organizational Techniques for Preschoolers

- Select clothes to wear.

- Put dirty clothes in the clothes hamper.

- Load and unload clothes from the dryer.

- Help to fold clothes (small, flat items like washcloths first).

- Put dishes in the dishwasher, using silverware and unbreakable items first or using plastic plates, bowls, and glasses.

- Set the table, in line with simple

expectations at first, such as setting a spoon and bowl for cereal.

- Put toys in a toy chest or other designated storage space marked with the child's name printed or brailled and/or on a tactile or pictorial label.

- Put clothes in designated drawers.

- Put matching shoes together in the closet.

- Pick up and put away art supplies.

---

the maximum extent possible in the same activities as their sighted age-mates by playing indoors with toys and children and playing outdoors by themselves and with others. They need to experience life.

Career Education Activities in Elementary School

A list of career education competencies that elementary school students need to acquire is presented in Sidebar 19.4. (Many additional objectives and activities that are appropriate for elementary students with visual impairments are presented in Wolffe, 1999). Elementary school classes provide a foundation for the development of academic, social, and vocational skills. Teachers of students with visual impairments, parents, and other members of students' educational teams can encourage the development of these competencies and help children with visual impairments compete successfully throughout their academic and vocational careers by expecting them to perform the same quality and quantity of activities as their sighted age-mates.

In elementary school, children learn to follow more complex instructions than in preschool. To-

ward this end, they are encouraged to assume greater responsibilities at home and at school for chores and classroom assignments. Sidebar 19.5 provides some examples of household chores that may be expected from elementary school students with visual impairments.

The importance of assuming greater levels of responsibility with age cannot be overemphasized. Children with visual impairments often have things done for them and are then unable to perform routine personal and home management activities independently as adults. This dependence on others severely restricts the range of available career choices. Parents are the best teachers of domestic chores and household responsibilities because they are in the environment where these activities naturally occur; however, teachers of students with visual impairments or rehabilitation teachers may need to assist with adapted techniques for performing activities of daily living without vision. (See Chapter 16 for information about techniques for teaching activities of daily living.)

There is an increased emphasis on working individually in elementary school classes. Students receive classroom and homework assignments that they are expected to complete with a

Career Education Competencies: Elementary School

Career education competencies are presented in boldface type and are appropriate for inclusion in IEPs as goals. Under each goal is a list of possible IEP objectives.

LEARNING TO FOLLOW MORE COMPLEX INSTRUCTIONS

◆ The student follows oral or written directions to order materials from a variety of sources, such as the American Printing House for the Blind, National Library Service's regional library, and Recordings for the Blind and Dyslexic.

◆ The student follows oral or written directions to complete classroom assignments and homework.

◆ The student follows oral or written directions to complete correspondence (letters, cards, E-mail messages, and so forth).

LEARNING TO WORK INDIVIDUALLY AND IN A GROUP

◆ The student initiates class work without prompting from the teacher.

◆ The student works unassisted on classroom assignments, using adaptive tools and materials.

◆ The student actively participates in and contributes to classroom academic projects, such as group reports or group experiments.

◆ The student actively participates in class projects such as bake sales and car washes.

LEARNING TO RESPOND APPROPRIATELY TO ADULTS AND PEERS

◆ The student successfully engages peers in conversations.

◆ The student is actively engaged with peers during free time.

◆ The student understands the rules of interacting with adults (for example, raises his or her hand to be called on and does not speak out).

◆ The student exchanges pleasantries with adults (for instance, says "Hello" to a cafeteria worker before he or she places a lunch order and "Thank you" when he or she receives the order).

LEARNING TO BE RESPONSIBLE FOR ACTIONS

◆ The student puts his or her materials away in an appropriate location (classroom cupboard, backpack, closet, or locker).

◆ The student brings assistive devices to class in working order (charged audiotape recorders and electronic note takers, for instance).

◆ The student brings low vision devices (like eyeglasses, magnifiers, and telescopes) to class.

◆ The student demonstrates socially responsible behavior (such as covering his or her mouth when sneezing or coughing).

◆ The student tidies his or her work area at the completion of any project.

LEARNING TO ORGANIZE WORK-SCHOOL MATERIALS

◆ The student uses a backpack or similar tool to manage assistive devices and materials.

◆ The student uses three-ring binders or similar tools to organize class assignments and products.

(continued on next page)

◆ The student uses a calendar to keep up with assignments, projects, or tests.

◆ The student keeps his or her desk tidy and can retrieve materials when asked to do so.

ASSUMING RESPONSIBILITIES AT HOME AND AT SCHOOL

◆ The student helps with simple household chores (see the list of age-appropriate tasks in Sidebar 19.5).

◆ The student helps with simple school chores, such as picking up papers from other students, taking care of class pets or garden plots, and handing out art supplies.

◆ The student helps younger children at school with classroom assignments or homework.

IDENTIFYING DIFFERENT WORK ROLES AND ASSUMING THEM IN FANTASY AND PLAY

◆ The student acts out play roles as physician, lawyer, pilot, teacher, and so forth.

◆ The student talks about vocational dreams and aspirations (fantasizes about being a ballerina, football player, space explorer, and the like).

◆ The student participates in class or school plays that include different work-related roles with appropriate costumes and actions.

RECOGNIZING DIFFERENT COMMUNITY WORKERS

◆ The student can identify common community workers [police, firefighter, mail carrier, nurse, emergency medical service (EMS) worker, librarian, and so

forth] by describing services they perform.

◆ The student can identify whom to call on in the event of an emergency (hospital worker, doctor, police, firefighter, for instance).

◆ The student demonstrates an understanding of the functions performed, costumes worn, and types of experience necessary to engage in community service jobs.

UNDERSTANDING THE REWARDS OF WORK

◆ The student can identify the sum he or she can earn for specific tasks performed.

◆ The student demonstrates an understanding of how payment for work is affected by sloppy or inadequate performance.

◆ The student demonstrates an understanding of the consequences of nonperformance (the concept of no work equals no pay).

LEARNING TO SOLVE PROBLEMS

◆ The student attempts to find things before he or she asks for help.

◆ The student asks others how they have resolved problems and tries the ideas to see if they will work for him or her.

◆ The student tries different approaches to problem solving if the first attempt at solving a problem does not work.

DEVELOPING GOOD COMMUNICATION SKILLS

◆ The student attends to others when they are speaking, as demonstrated by

(continued on next page)

Career Education Competencies: Elementary School *(Continued)*

orienting toward the speaker, occasionally nodding his or her head, smiling or frowning at appropriate comments, doing nothing else when someone is speaking except taking notes and listening, and so forth.

- ◆ The student responds appropriately when addressed by answering questions accurately, sharing topic-related information in a conversation, waiting until the speaker has finished speaking before commenting, and the like.

- ◆ The student stays on topic in conver-

sations and does not change the focus to himself or herself, to some irrelevant detail, or to an unrelated topic.

DEVELOPING BASIC ACADEMIC SKILLS

- ◆ The student demonstrates grade-level reading skills using his or her preferred reading medium (braille, large print or audiotape).

- ◆ The student demonstrates grade-level writing skills.

- ◆ The student demonstrates grade-level calculation skills.

---

minimum of assistance, and their work is evaluated and compared to the work of other students in their classes. Although work performed in a group is typically directed by the teacher, the students are expected to work together interdependently and to contribute equally.

Teachers of students with visual impairments help by ensuring that their students have the compensatory skills, such as reading and writing with braille or low vision devices, that enable them to contribute meaningfully to group or individual classroom efforts. The specialists also facilitate

---

Suggested Household Chores and Organizational Techniques for Elementary School Students

SIDEBAR 19.5

- ◆ Sort clothes for the laundry.

- ◆ Measure and put soap into the clothes washer.

- ◆ Help to fold or hang clothes and put them away.

- ◆ Put soap and dishes in the dishwasher.

- ◆ Empty the dishwasher and put dishes away.

- ◆ Put away groceries.

- ◆ Take out the trash.

- ◆ Help prepare meals, using a microwave and stove.

- ◆ Set the table.

- ◆ Hang clothes in the proper closet after use.

- ◆ Pack clothes for camp or vacation trips.

- ◆ Pick up and put away school supplies and sports equipment.

- ◆ Help younger siblings.

- ◆ Label possessions and storage compartments.

these classroom processes by putting materials in accessible formats. If a student with a visual impairment is having difficulty keeping up with the demands of the classroom, the specialist performs a series of observations over time to determine what barriers may be preventing the student from participating fully.

In elementary school, students are expected to know and use organizational techniques to keep up with their school and extracurricular materials, such as retrieving assignments they have completed and taking notes or permission slips home to their parents. Therefore, it is important that students with visual impairments have backpacks and binders or similar tools to help them keep track of their materials. They need to be shown how to organize their materials in ways that they can and will use and to have systems for marking their possessions that are meaningful to them (using braille, large-print, or pictorial labels, for example).

Students are also expected to talk and act differently in the company of adults than they do with their peers and to understand the difference between strangers and familiar people. They will ultimately transfer their knowledge of these subtleties in levels of relating to others in the workplace when they recognize that conversations with one's boss tend to differ from conversations with one's coworkers. Teachers of students with visual impairments, parents, and others need to give students feedback on appropriate and inappropriate social interactions. Without visual cues, such as smiles or frowns, the students may have difficulty discerning when their interpersonal behaviors meet with approval or disapproval. Through the caring feedback of trusted adults and peers who can observe what works and does not work for them socially, students with visual impairments grow comfortable with social nuances.

During this period, students are learning to be responsible for their actions. They recognize that the amount of effort they put into projects is rewarded or punished with the grades they receive and that they are rewarded when they practice athletics or performing arts. They also recognize that how they behave with others positively influ-

ences friendships or can lead to social isolation. Children with visual impairments are at risk of having difficulty forming friendships, and the elementary years are a crucial time for them to learn how to interact appropriately with peers (Kekelis, Sacks, & Wolffe, 2000; MacCuspie, 1996; Sacks, Kekelis, & Gaylord-Ross, 1992).

Popular children usually understand how to join groups by observing what other children are doing and by contributing to these activities in meaningful ways. They understand that other children do not want to be intruded upon or bossed about. Children who learn how to be sensitive to their peers have an increased likelihood of making friends. They respond to the interests of others and in so doing complement the group's activity with their involvement. Finally, children who are socially adept understand how to avoid verbal and physical conflicts with their peers (Kekelis, Sacks, & Wolffe, 2000). Children with visual impairments must be taught to ask questions about what is going on in groups to determine if they would like to join the activities. They must learn to ask permission to join a group and not try to take over and force their ideas on others. Finally, they must be taught techniques for avoiding conflict; these skills can be taught through involvement in creative dramatics or role-playing activities; modeling and self-disclosure; and discussions with parents, teachers, and sighted students. (See Chapter 17 for information on strategies for developing social skills and Chapter 11 for strategies on teaching dramatics to students with visual impairments.)

Developing good communication skills is an integral component of elementary school education. Children refine their listening, speaking, reading, and writing abilities and learn to follow multistep instructions. Their parents may leave notes asking them to take care of certain chores and expect them to write thank-you notes to people who gave them gifts. Teachers put written assignments on the chalkboard or pass out worksheets describing what work needs to be performed, and students are expected to read these assignments and ask questions if they do not understand what they are to do.

Teachers of students with visual impairments can help their students develop good communication skills by modeling effective communication with others. They also help by talking with their students about how one relates differently to different kinds of people. One way to facilitate such a discussion is to have a student watch a television program or listen to a dramatic radio program and then analyze the communication styles evidenced by the various characters. Teachers of students with visual impairments can also encourage skill building in this area by leaving notes for students in their preferred reading medium about the tasks the students need to accomplish and asking students to write out "to do" lists for themselves.

During elementary school, students begin to identify different work roles and assume those roles in fantasy or play activities. They play out what they think they may want to do or become, such as a physician, nurse, teacher, parent, or musician. It is during elementary school that children usually have the opportunity to recognize and meet different community workers (for example, police, firefighters, physicians, teachers, bakers, bankers, and grocers).

By accompanying a student on field trips to explore community services and community workers, the teacher of students with visual impairments can describe what is going on in those environments that the student might have otherwise missed and encourage the student's active involvement. For example, rather than simply listening to a firefighter describe a typical day at the fire station while the sighted students look around at the tools of the trade, the student who is visually impaired would gain greater insight into what is involved in being a firefighter by walking through the station, tactilely exploring the various pieces of equipment and gear, sitting in the cab of the fire truck, walking around the fire truck, and exploring the equipment on the truck. The specialist needs to facilitate this exploration because the general education teacher and parent volunteers who are chaperoning the students may not have the time or specific motivation to do so.

As children mature, they come to understand the rewards of work. For example, they may receive an allowance that is contingent on their satisfactory performance of certain household chores, or their parents, other relatives, or neighbors may pay them for doing things like taking care of pets when they are on vacation or weeding the garden. They begin to handle money routinely: to pay for school lunches, field trips, extracurricular outings, and purchases in stores, for example. As they learn to handle money, their parents typically encourage them to save for special events or things that they want. This helps children to understand the value of money and to develop a work ethic.

When people value work and understand the importance of contributing to the community through work, they are said to have a work ethic. Children develop a work ethic when adults in their lives expect them to contribute at home, at school, and in the community. Children who perform chores at home or at school and help out at community events, such as food drives or beautification projects, are more likely to develop a strong work ethic than are children who do not do so. Encouraging active involvement in household and classroom chores, as well as participation in community efforts, is the best way to help students with visual impairments develop a work ethic.

Learning to solve problems is a significant component of the developmental process in elementary school. For many children, school is the first opportunity to confront problem situations without their parents. Teachers, paraprofessionals, and related service personnel need to let students with visual impairments attempt to solve problems before they intervene. Many people assume that children with visual impairments cannot do things independently that sighted children do routinely. For example, they may tell students where they have left their belongings, rather than let them think about where their things may be and check to see if they have remembered correctly.

Most children in elementary school are expected to bring to class the materials they need for taking notes or completing classroom assignments. This same standard can be applied to children with visual impairments. However, in many instances, students with visual impairments have such materials provided for them. Rather than anticipate the students' needs and supply them with paper, writing implements, audiotapes, and the like, teachers of students with visual impairments would do better to ask the students where their note-taking materials are or where they can obtain the materials. Problem solving is critical to success in life, and the basic skills are best learned early and reinforced over time. Students who learn to ask themselves, "What is the problem here, and what can I do about it?" are learning to solve problems and to assume personal responsibility, which builds self-esteem.

If children consistently have difficulty keeping up with their materials or finding supplies, the specialist may need to focus on organizational techniques or help them find available resources for obtaining specialty and generic organizational supplies. Students with visual impairments may benefit from a field trip to an office supply shop or a discount store that carries an array of school and organizational tools. They may also benefit from an orientation to the vendors of aids and appliances used by adults with visual impairments and instructional supplies to teachers and students. Students may have never had an opportunity to review the vendors' catalogs or sample their materials, and the teacher of students with visual impairments can make these materials available to them or request that vendors meet with students to demonstrate their products.

Finally, students develop their basic, foundation academic skills (reading, writing, and calculating) in the elementary grades. Parents and teachers of students with visual impairments can facilitate the development of reading skills by reading aloud to children and encouraging them to read to themselves and others. Providing books in braille or large-print and with enlarged or tactile pictures also reinforces reading. Likewise, weekly or monthly visits to a local library to check out materials that are recorded or available in other appropriate media stress the importance of reading and help children learn the value of libraries as a community resource. Community-based activities in which specialists and parents can engage students with visual impairments and reinforce their reading skills may include reading and ordering from a restaurant's menu (in some communities, restaurants have large-print or braille menus), locating and reading signs both for traveling in the community and for obtaining information (for example, from an ATM or in an elevator), going to a bus station or airport to obtain schedules or information about registering for a paratransit system (the students have to ask for the information in an alternative reading format), and so forth. (See Chapter 8 for more information on teaching reading skills.)

To be literate, children also need to acquire the fine motor skills necessary to write in print and then in cursive. This is an important life skill and one that students with visual impairments can usually develop if they are trained early in life. At a minimum, children without good functional vision need to be aware of how the letters of the alphabet are formed and to be given targeted instruction in manuscript, cursive, and signature writing. Children who are blind need to learn, at a minimum, to write their signatures. A signature is critical for signing checks, applications, and the sundry forms that one must process over the course of a lifetime. (See Chapter 8 for more information on teaching writing skills.)

Students who are nonprint readers and writers produce most written materials in braille or with the assistance of technology, such as electronic note takers and computers with speech and braille output or screen-enlargement programs. If they are not braille users, they may use audiotape recorders and have print papers transcribed from their tapes. (See Chapter 14 for more information on assistive technology). Regardless of the method used, students gain speed and accuracy by using the skills in daily life. Meaningful activities that can help reinforce writing skills may include keeping a diary or journal, writing thank-you notes and letters to friends and family members, filling out mail-order forms, writing stories to submit to the school newspaper or community-based newsletters (such as those of churchs, synagogues, temples, Girl Scouts, Boy

Scouts, recreational facilities, and so on), generating "to do" lists or shopping lists, and so forth.

Students in elementary school also need to learn numbers and basic mathematics skills (adding, subtracting, multiplying, and dividing). Students with severe low vision or who are blind are often taught these skills on an abacus. It is important that children understand basic calculations and number properties before they are introduced to talking calculators and other electronic devices for performing advanced calculations. Activities that can help reinforce mathematics skills may include helping at a community bake sale, selling Girl Scout cookies, taking orders for magazines or other school-sponsored fundraising efforts for extracurricular activities, and comparison shopping based on newspaper ads or telephone inquiries. (See Chapter 10 for more information on teaching mathematics skills.)

Specific career education objectives for students in elementary school center on making children aware of work. Students need to learn that energy expended to produce a product or provide a service is work. They need to understand what kinds of jobs the various members of their families perform. Both in school and at home, they need to be encouraged to develop and demonstrate good work habits (such as following instructions, assuming personal responsibility, being punctual, asking for assistance appropriately, attending to tasks, completing tasks, and cooperating).

In addition, these students develop basic work skills: sorting and matching by size, shape, texture, color, and so forth; putting things together and taking them apart; cutting, pasting, stapling, punching holes, and so on. Teachers of students with visual impairments can help them learn these skills by encouraging them to use basic tools like scissors, staplers, tape dispensers, and hole punches. When opportunities to work on these skills occur naturally, such as when conducting end-of-the-year inventories, the specialists can ask the students to help them sort, count, and package materials. If a specialist observes another student or an adult doing these things for the student with a visual impairment, he or she should take the individual aside and ask the person not to do so.

In general, the teacher of students with visual impairments needs to devote a great deal of time and energy to concepts that sighted students develop through incidental learning (for example, the differences between secular and religious holidays; representative activities performed in different seasons; temporal concepts; social rules and mores; clothing worn by different people at different times of the day; and jobs performed behind the scenes, such as a butcher working behind a Plexiglas barrier at a grocery store). Students need to know what kinds of clothes and jewelry other students in their schools are wearing and what movies and songs are popular. In short, they need sighted helpers who tell them about the things they see that may or may not seem important to them—everything from the color of the teacher's hair to the size of the kitchen tools in the school cafeteria.

When possible, teachers of students with visual impairments can help students acquire incidental information by explaining visual cues. For example, if a specialist sees that many sighted students are wearing red on Valentine's Day or green on St. Patrick's Day, he or she can explain to the student who is blind what the students are wearing and why the color is important for the particular holiday. When students are learning about different religions or cultures, the teacher of students with visual impairments can bring in artifacts that a student who is blind can explore tactilely to understand what the artifacts look like. If the items are not to scale, the specialist needs to inform the student of the difference between the object being explored and the counterpart that is larger or smaller. It is also important to engage the student in an activity that is representative of the concept being taught. For instance, if the class is reading about winter sports and the child lives in a warm climate where snow or ice does not occur naturally, it would be helpful to take the child to an ice-skating rink, so he or she can experience such a sport firsthand.

Students who are visually impaired need to work quickly and efficiently to finish required school tasks to set the stage for the demands of work after school. When a student with a visual impairment is unable to complete these tasks within a reasonable time, instructional personnel need to help him or her set short-term, achievable goals to build speed and quality over time. For example, a student with a visual impairment may start the school year able to complete only 5 mathematics problems in the time that the sighted students complete 25. The student can be encouraged to set an initial goal to complete 6 problems in that period, then 7, then 8, and so forth until he or she can complete 25 in the same amount of time as his or her peers. (See Chapter 5 for suggestions for accomplishing this.) Modified assignments that do not parallel the work expected of sighted classmates or provide for increases in complexity or quantity over time handicap students who are visually impaired, who will ultimately have to compete with sighted people for jobs as adults.

Career Education Activities in Middle School

When students move into middle school (grades 6, 7, and 8), the expectations of their teachers, related services personnel, and families change considerably. The career education competencies required of students in middle school are summarized in Sidebar 19.6 (for additional objectives and activities, see Wolffe, 1999).

Students in this age group are expected to be substantially more responsible for themselves and their things: to organize themselves to meet the increased demands on their time and to balance extracurricular and school activities with responsibilities at home and in the community organizations in which they participate. These kinds of activities are important for students with visual impairments as well. If sighted youngsters are baby-sitting for younger siblings and neighbors' children, so, too, should those who are visually impaired. Likewise, if their friends in the Scouts or religious youth groups are selling products and services or promoting the organizations in some other way, students with visual impairments need to do so as well.

Middle school is an excellent time for students with visual impairments to begin volunteer work,

which can be an important building block for future employment. Although middle school students are too young for paid employment—except informal work negotiated by family members and friends—they need to have opportunities to work. By contributing time and energy to others, students with visual impairments learn that they have talents and skills that are of interest to others. They also learn some of the rudimentary work habits that will be expected of them throughout their working lives: being on time and in attendance when expected, following a supervisor's directions, getting along with others by attending to coworkers' interests and needs, making one's own needs and interests known to others in a positive way, and so forth.

The teacher of students with visual impairments can facilitate volunteer activities by helping students prepare for work (refining work habits and skills, practicing orientation and mobility [O&M] skills, demonstrating organizational techniques, and so on). They can also support their students by helping them identify and locate prospective volunteer sites. For example, the specialist may suggest to a student who has strong reading skills that the residents of a local nursing home would probably enjoy having someone volunteer to read to them. Or for a student who expresses an interest in working with animals, the specialist and student might generate a list of nearby veterinary clinics or humane shelters at which the student might volunteer.

The teacher of students with visual impairments can help ensure that an upcoming volunteer experience will be positive by reviewing the following with the student:

◆ How the student will describe his or her visual impairment to a prospective employer;

◆ What skills the student has to offer an employer that are specific to the job desired;

◆ How the student will cope with an emergency situation;

◆ What work behaviors are expected of all employees (punctuality, attendance, hon-

Career Education Competencies: Middle School

Career education competencies are presented in boldface type and are appropriate for inclusion in IEPs as goals. Under each goal is a list of possible IEP objectives.

MEETING INCREASED DEMANDS FOR ORGANIZING TIME

- The student demonstrates the ability to organize school activities by arriving to classes on time with completed homework assignments.

- The student demonstrates the ability to organize school activities by participating in school clubs or groups.

- The student demonstrates the ability to organize school and extracurricular activities by participating in extra-curricular activities routinely and maintaining schoolwork.

MEETING INCREASED RESPONSIBILITIES AT HOME AND IN THE COMMUNITY

- The student demonstrates responsibility at home by completing assigned chores.

- The student demonstrates responsibility at home by performing volunteer and paid work for neighbors and family members.

- The student demonstrates responsibility at school through work for clubs, participation in a band, and the like.

- The student demonstrates responsibility in the community by volunteering.

MEETING INCREASED DEMANDS FOR SKILL DEVELOPMENT

- The student performs learned skills in academic areas independently.

- The student demonstrates greater speed in using skills at school (in a specific academic or other identified area, such as playing a musical instrument).

- The student demonstrates greater accuracy in using skills.

SHOWING A FULL UNDERSTANDING OF THE WORK PERFORMED BY ADULTS

- The student can identify the work performed by family members.

- The student can provide details (hours worked, major job duties, salaries, and qualifications) about the work performed by family members.

- The student can identify major community workers and their roles (police, firefighters, physicians, lawyers, social workers, teachers, and the like).

SHOWING A BEGINNING NOTION OF THE WORK HE OR SHE WANTS TO DO AS AN ADULT

- The student reads about the lives and work of famous Americans, including those with disabilities.

- The student writes book reports on materials read.

- The student reads about careers in general—what is available nationally, regionally, and locally.

- The student discusses careers of interest with teachers, parents, and other significant adults.

(continued on next page)

Career Education Competencies: Middle School *(Continued)*

◆ The student identifies specific jobs related to career interests and abilities.

INVESTIGATING IDENTIFIED AREAS OF INTEREST

◆ The student reads about specific careers of interest.

◆ The student conducts informational interviews with adults in the community who perform jobs that are of interest to him or her.

◆ The student participates in job-shadowing experiences.

---

esty, cooperation, following directions, and so forth);

◆ What behaviors could lead to trouble (talking back to an adult, not attending to details, dressing too casually or inappropriately, chewing gum or eating without permission, smoking, cursing, and other socially inappropriate behaviors); and

◆ What the organizational hierarchy is like at the facility where the student wants to volunteer.

Finally, the teacher of students with visual impairments can make herself or himself available to discuss with the student and prospective employer how someone without vision or with impaired vision could perform the job duties that will be assigned. The specialist can describe assistive devices or alternative techniques the student will use to perform the volunteer job and, if available, show photographs of the student performing similar tasks in other environments. Likewise, if the student has participated in similar activities that the specialist or other instructional staff observed, the specialist could incorporate that information into the discussion with the prospective employer.

Paid work for neighbors and family members can also help set the stage for future career decision making and successful work. (Examples of typical jobs for students in middle school are listed in Sidebar 19.7.) By working in their neighborhoods and homes, young people begin to de-

termine what they like and do not like about particular jobs or job responsibilities, which helps them decide what careers they would like to explore in greater detail and which they can rule out.

In addition to paid work experiences and formal volunteer experiences, youngsters in middle school can expand their involvement in clubs, band, athletics, youth groups, and other extracurricular activities. These activities also provide opportunities to explore careers and refine skills that may be viable for future employment or avocational pursuits and help youngsters develop social skills and network with peers with similar interests.

By the time students enter middle school, they should have a full understanding of the work performed by their family members and major community workers. To encourage ongoing learning in this area, teachers of students with visual impairments and parents may want to encourage students with visual impairments to read broadly about careers—autobiographies and biographies of famous people doing work in which they have indicated an interest and stories about adults who are visually impaired working in a variety of settings (see the Resources). It is imperative that middle school students begin to consider the kind of lives they want to lead and the work they want to do as adults.

The investigation of identified areas of interest can be fun and educational. Students should be encouraged to take notes when they read about careers or the lives of people they admire and to ask themselves what appeals to them about these

---

Suggested Paid Work Opportunities for Middle School Students

- Baby-sit at home and for neighbors.

- Do yardwork (such as edging; pulling weeds; planting seeds, bulbs, or plants; mowing; raking; bagging leaves; and shoveling snow) for relatives and neighbors.

- Wash and vacuum cars.

- Provide pet-sitting or pet-exercising services.

- Do household chores, such as washing and drying dishes; washing, drying, and folding clothes; ironing; sweeping; vacuuming; mopping; and cleaning out cupboards or garages.

- Provide companionship to an elderly or sick neighbor or relative.

- Take care of a pool (for example, by sweeping, bagging leaves, checking skimmer baskets, and adding chemicals as needed).

- Help prepare meals or shop for an ill or infirm person who is unable to leave his or her house.

---

people's lives and work and what else they would like to know about these career areas. If they capture these thoughts on paper, they can use them as a basis for researching areas of interest.

Once students have noted questions about certain jobs or career areas they would like to have answered, they can prepare for informational interviews to obtain answers to their questions. One way to do so is to observe teachers, counselors, and older students act out the information-interviewing process. Another way to practice is to perform mock interviews with adult service providers and peers or to role play interview situations that are similar to those they may encounter.

Job shadowing, in which students actually spend time with workers on their jobs, is another way for students to learn about jobs in the natural environment: the workplace. When students express interest in specific jobs, teachers of students with visual impairments can arrange for them to observe workers or have job-shadowing experiences. Students who are blind can be partnered with sighted students or adults to help them observe workers and work environments. Job shadowing takes observation to the next level by having a student spend days or weeks (whatever is appropriate for the student and worker) following a worker through his or her daily activities. In this way, the student gets an idea of what a job actually entails, how a typical worker functions, and the training that is required from an adult who is doing what the student wants ultimately to do.

A student who is blind or has low vision may be challenged by the visual demands of job shadowing. Thus, in addition to using a sighted partner, the student may want to develop a series of questions to pose to the worker he or she is assigned to observe, such as the following:

- What are your primary job duties?

- What do you like best and least about this job?

- Do you use any specialized tools or equipment to perform your job?

- Do you wear a uniform or any protective gear while on the job?

- If you complete an assignment, how do you know what to do next?

Questions such as these help students with visual impairments capture critical information that their sighted classmates are likely to notice through visual observation and can make them more independent during job shadowing.

As students advance in middle school, teachers present content that builds on skills developed in elementary school and expect that the students have mastered basic reading, writing, and mathematical skills and can independently apply what they have learned to complete new, more challenging assignments. In place of extensive teacher-directed activities, students are expected to keep up with their own assignments and materials and to perform in class with a minimum of intervention. They are expected to change classes and content areas throughout the day and keep up with new material by taking notes and reviewing them for tests or classroom assignments. Teachers of students with visual impairments can support these activities by ensuring that their students know about and use calendars and planners to keep up with assignments and test dates. In addition, they can ensure that students have acquired functional note-taking skills. Teachers of students with visual impairments need to be sure that their students can capture a lecturer's primary topic and key points that are relayed in a lecture. They need to check to be sure that students can retrieve their notes and interpret any cryptic notations, such as invented acronyms, abbreviations, stand alone names or dates, and the like. Finally, it behooves teachers to review students' notes periodically and give them feedback in reference to what points were in evidence on tests in comparison to their notes.

Career Education Activities in High School

The transition to high school is perhaps the greatest life transition that young people experience before they enter adult life. In high school, there are increased demands on their time, individual responsibility, and intellect as well as more classes and greater expectations in those classes for acquiring and using knowledge. Career education in high school focuses on melding academic content, social responsibilities, and occupational skills with life experiences to form a solid foundation for work in postsecondary training programs and/or jobs. The competencies that high school students with visual impairments must achieve are summarized in Sidebar 19.8 (see Wolffe and Johnson, 1997, for additional objectives and activities that are appropriate for high school students with visual impairments). These skills, coupled with those previously mastered, are essential to success in life.

Students are expected to enter high school with well-developed basic academic skills. They are expected to read and write at a level that is commensurate with that of typical adults in their communities, that is, at the ninth-grade level or better. They are expected to be able to perform all basic and many advanced mathematical procedures. They are also expected to demonstrate effective listening and speaking abilities—to listen to lectures, take notes, retain what they hear, and apply newly learned content in meaningful ways in their lives. Teachers expect them to be able to communicate what they have learned both in conversations and through such products as homework, written or oral reports, classroom projects, and tests.

Well-developed thinking skills are critical to success in life, and most students refine their thinking skills in high school. Students need to think creatively, solve problems, and make decisions without relying on others, yet still consider other people's needs and feelings. Employers expect high school graduates to learn the skills required to perform their jobs and to use reasoning skills to determine what is working well or not well for them in jobs and when to ask for help if things go wrong on the job (U.S. Department of Labor, 1991).

In addition, high school students must hone work behaviors or habits that are required to maintain and advance in jobs. They must be able to demonstrate responsibility; integrity; and a willingness to cooperate, follow directions, request assistance when needed, and so forth.

Self-esteem, the quality of feeling good about oneself, is ideally refined during the high school years. These are difficult years for young people (especially for those who are visually impaired) because their bodies are changing, their feelings

Career Education Competencies: High School

Career education competencies are presented in boldface type and are appropriate for inclusion in IEPs as goals. Under each goal is a list of possible IEP objectives.

SHOWING WELL-DEVELOPED ACADEMIC SKILLS

♦ The student demonstrates well-developed reading, writing, arithmetic, listening, and speaking skills by performing comparably to his or her sighted peers (define the classroom standards without adjusting the quantity or quality for the student's visual impairment).

♦ The student demonstrates well-developed reading, writing, arithmetic, listening, and speaking skills by performing at a level commensurate with the demands in the vocational area he or she intends to enter (define the occupational standard for entry-level workers in this area).

♦ The student consistently and satisfactorily completes classroom and homework assignments without assistance.

SHOWING WELL-DEVELOPED THINKING SKILLS

♦ When asked to think creatively, the student uses his or her imagination, connects known ideas in new ways, makes connections between seemingly unrelated ideas, and considers alternatives to known ideas.

♦ The student demonstrates the ability to set goals based on an analysis of the array of choices available to him or her.

♦ The student demonstrates the ability to recognize that a problem exists, defines the problem, identifies possible solutions, devises an action plan to resolve the problem, initiates the plan, evaluates its success, and revises the plan as needed.

♦ The student recognizes and uses his or her own learning style (visual, aural, tactile, kinesthetic), adapts to new situations and tools, and uses formal learning strategies (note taking and repeating new content aloud, for example).

♦ The student uses logic to draw conclusions from the content presented in the classroom and textbook.

SHOWING WELL-DEVELOPED WORK BEHAVIORS

♦ The student sets and meets self-defined standards for performance.

♦ The student pays attention to details.

♦ The student performs tasks even when the tasks are unpleasant or difficult.

♦ The student can describe his or her interests, abilities, values, and liabilities.

♦ The student is aware of the impression he or she makes on others.

♦ The student can describe his or her own needs and how to address them.

♦ The student works well with others.

♦ The student interacts with peers and adults appropriately.

♦ The student can be trusted with materials and tools.

PARTICIPATING IN WORK ACTIVITIES

♦ The student volunteers to help others.

♦ The student performs work tasks at home and at school.

♦ The student performs a job for pay in the community.

(continued on next page)

Career Education Competencies: High School *(Continued)*

PLANNING FOR LIFE BEYOND HIGH SCHOOL

◆ The student investigates postsecondary education or training options.

◆ The student develops a plan for post-secondary education or training related to his or her vocational interests, abilities, and values.

◆ The student develops a plan with short-

term, intermediate, and long-term goals for achieving satisfaction in life.

◆ The student identifies the supports he or she will need to move from high school into postsecondary environments (for example, housing, transportation, access to information, child care, personal care, home care, time management or money management, or assistance with leisure and recreational activities).

---

are in flux, and their families and adults in the community expect them to be or, at least, to act almost grown up. Without visual input, it is difficult to judge how one's body is changing in comparison to other people's and whether those changes are positive or negative. Parents, teachers of students with visual impairments, and other members of students' educational teams can give students feedback on their positive attributes and help them ascertain how to minimize any perceived flaws. In addition, it is imperative that students with visual impairments receive feedback on how their sighted peers are dressing and behaving so that they can make informed decisions about whether to emulate the sighted students or follow a different course. It is through this kind of open communication and sharing that adolescents with visual impairments establish and maintain high levels of self-esteem.

Participation in high school classes and extracurricular activities places considerable demands on students' social skills. High school students are expected to get along well with adults, peers, and younger students; to establish and maintain friendships and differentiate friends from acquaintances; and often to manage their first intimate relationships and cope with the intimacy of many of their peers.

Participation in work activities to demonstrate work skills and habits is strongly encouraged while students attend high school. There is evidence that

adolescents with disabilities who work while in high school are far more likely to be employed after graduation than are those who do not (Wehman, 1992). However, the results of the National Longitudinal Transition Study found that many students with visual impairments are attending school and *not* working both during and after high school. Rates of unemployment for high school graduates with visual impairments rival the rates for graduates with multiple disabilities, in spite of the former's academic achievements, which may be comparable to those of their sighted peers (Wagner, DíAmico, Marder, Newman, & Blackorby, 1992). Volunteerism or paid work in the community can provide much-needed experiential learning and documentation of the abilities of students with visual impairments outside their schools or homes.

Job opportunities for students with visual impairments are typical of those for sighted students with only a few exceptions, such as pizza delivery (for some popular options, see Sidebar 19.9). However, the most effective way to determine what job a student may want to consider is for the student and parent, teacher, or counselor to investigate what is available locally after a student has determined jobs of interest. Sidebar 19.10 presents a summary tip sheet that specialists may give to teenagers who are visually impaired to help them learn about jobs.

Once a student has identified the jobs that are of interest, he or she needs to conduct a discrep-

> ## Suggested Paid Work Opportunities for High School Students
>
>
> - Restaurants and cafeterias: prepare food, clean up, wash dishes, cook, or wait on tables.
>
> - Offices: answer phones and take messages or provide clerical assistance (typing, copying, shredding, and so forth).
>
> - Day care centers: assist teachers.
>
> - Nursing homes and summer camps: provide recreational assistance.
>
> - Libraries: read stories to children, provide information to patrons, teach Internet access, rewind videotapes and audio-tapes, check books in and out, put books away, straighten shelves; and pull braille or audiocassette books from the shelves and prepare them for mailing.
>
> - Retail stores: unpack and hang up clothes, dust and tidy shelves, provide information to customers, and assist in the human resources department.
>
> - Recreational facilities: play games with children, check sports equipment in and out, and coordinate activities.
>
> - Tutoring: teach lessons to younger students or peers, such as music, computer literacy, foreign languages, remedial academic skills.
>
> - Grocery stores: package food, bag groceries, sort inventory, and provide clerical support.

ancy analysis. The first step in this process is for the student to write a self-description, including his or her interests, abilities, values, and liabilities. (The teacher of students with visual impairments may want to facilitate this process by telling the student what he or she sees as the student's interests, abilities, values, and liabilities or by encouraging the student to obtain such feedback from family members and friends.) The next step is for the student to analyze jobs of interest by writing down the job titles, purposes, settings (locations and environments), major tasks, qualifications required, and any additional relevant information. Finally, the student compares his or her skills to the requirements of the jobs of interest to determine the similarities and differences. Differences are categorized as discrepancies, and the student is expected to determine which of the discrepancies are amenable to change or remediation or can be circumvented by using assistive technology (Wolffe, 1997).

Planning for life beyond high school necessitates the setting of short-term and long-term goals that focus on personal relationships, vocational and academic pursuits, and leisure activities. Students with visual impairments need to participate in structured activities that will help them develop their career-life plans. Teachers, counselors, parents, and other significant adults in their lives can facilitate goal setting by leading discussions in school rap sessions or in extracurricular groups, such as Scouts and religious youth groups. In the course of these discussions, it is important to consider how the students will negotiate with friends, relatives, and services providers for any supports they deem necessary to be successful in implementing their plans. For example, they may decide that they would like to live at home for a period after graduating to save money so they can afford their own apartments, or they may think that transportation assistance will be necessary for them to search for jobs or obtain training related to the kind of work they want to do.

The investigation of postsecondary training or work opportunities is best accomplished while still in high school. Many schools offer counseling

Tips for Teenagers: How to Learn More About Jobs

READINGS

Read *Jobs To Be Proud Of* (Kendrick, 1993), which describes, in the individual's own words, jobs performed by workers with visual impairments who do not have college degrees; *Career Perspectives* (Attmore, 1990), which describes, in the individual's own words, jobs performed by workers with visual impaiarments and college degrees; the Jobs That Matter Series, for example, *Teachers Who Are Blind or Visually Impaired* (Kendrick, 1998); *What Color Is Your Parachute?* (Bolles, 2000), a book for people without disabilities; and *Job Hunting Tips for the So-called Handicapped or People Who Have Disabilities* (Bolles & Brown, 2000), both of which discuss the career-search process and list many resources, including Internet sites; *Take Charge* (Rabby & Croft, 1989), which is a manual on job-seeking skills for people with visual impairments; and *Navigating the Rapids of Life,* which is the student manual in the *Transition Tote System* (Wolffe & Johnson, 1997). (See the Resources in this chapter for more information.) Also, read biographies and autobiographies of people who are blind or have low vision to help you understand how others before you have succeeded in life and the workplace.

INFORMATIONAL INTERVIEWS

Telephone and visit people in the community who are doing what you think you would like to do, including people with visual impairments who are doing similar jobs. Also contact consumer organizations, such as the American Council of the Blind and the National Federation of the Blind, and the AFB Careers and Technology Information Bank.

JOB SHADOWING

Spend time on the job with someone who is doing the kind of work in which you are interested to observe how the worker routinely spends his or her time and what tools the worker uses.

VOLUNTEERING

Help out without expectation of payment at a company where you would ultimately like to be a paid employee. Get to know the people who work there and learn as much as possible about the job you want to do in the future. Perform consistently well in your volunteer job and seek to increase your responsibilities over time.

WORKING

Work at home, at school, and in the community. Accept jobs in which you know you are interested and are able to do and those you are unsure of to determine what you like and do not like about them. Always do your best and meet your obligations to employers. Keep records of where you work and with whom for future reference. If you have a particularly good experience, ask your employer for a written recommendation or a note inviting prospective employers to telephone to verify your abilities.

and guidance to help students determine what they would like to do after high school and how to best prepare for the jobs they identify. Access to information (print materials and posted notices) may be more challenging for students with visual impairments, but with modern technology (particularly reading machines and access to the Internet) many of these difficulties can be alleviated.

By the time they graduate from high school, students will ideally have mastered these competencies and be able to apply them in their daily lives. The best way for teachers, parents, and employers to help students with visual impairments do so is to provide opportunities for them to work, to expect the same level of performance from them as from sighted students, to give them realistic feedback on their performance, and to encourage them to take on more and more responsibilities as they master their work tasks. (Instructional materials for teachers and related service providers are included in the Resources.)

VOCATIONAL EDUCATION ACTIVITIES IN HIGH SCHOOL

Vocational education is an educational process that focuses on training for specific occupations (such as the repair of small engines, cosmetology, cabinet making, furniture upholstery, office or clerical skills, and food services). Students are prepared to work in a particular vocational area and often apprentice or work part time in the trade or profession they are studying while they are still in high school. Vocational education classes are included as a component of a school's general education curriculum, but not all schools offer all vocational classes because of the highly specialized nature of the training and the demands of the local labor market. Some communities support magnet-like programs in which one high school is set aside as a vocational training center. Other communities offer two or three different vocational classes at each of the high schools in a school district.

Teachers of students with visual impairments can help their students actively participate in vocational education classes by serving as consultants to the vocational education teachers. As is true of general education teachers, vocational education teachers often do not understand how to modify the learning environment for students who are blind or have low vision. They are also unlikely to be aware of specialized tools, such as braille rulers and tape measures, beeping levels, talking scales, and electronic note-taking devices, that can help students with visual impairments work successfully in vocational classes. Teachers of students with visual impairments do not need to master the vocational skills being taught, but they should understand the nature of the content to decide how best to help integrate their students into the courses.

If a high school student with a visual impairment wants to participate in a vocational education course, he or she needs to meet with the instructor to ascertain what is required of the participants and whether any modifications to the learning environment are necessary. If the student and instructor are unable to determine what and how elements of the course work have to be modified for the student to participate fully, they may want to invite the teacher of students with visual impairments to join them in conference to discuss the situation. The specialist can help support the vocational instructor and the student by analyzing the demands of the classroom environment, determining the types of tools being used, whether there are any adapted tools that may facilitate the student's involvement, and what materials (such as guidebooks or manuals) need to be brailled, audiotaped, or enlarged. As much as possible, the student needs to be responsible for determining which modifications are necessary and for negotiating with the instructor.

Whether a student decides to pursue vocational education or needs ongoing exposure to career education content, these concerns need to be addressed in the student's IEP. Transisition planning is required by age 14, when most students enter high school, and the Individualized Transition Plan (ITP) is incorporated into the IEP. Transition planning focuses on the development of skills and gaining access to resources that will enable a student to be successful in the next environment beyond high school, whether the workplace, college, or a vocational training facility. The teacher of students with visual impairments can play an important role in the development of a student's ITP by actively participating with the team that develops the student's plan. Often, the specialist and the student are the best informed about the kinds of assistive technology and adapted equipment available to enable workers who are blind or visually impaired to perform their jobs. Therefore, a significant role for the specialist at the ITP meeting is that of resource person. In addition, the specialist and the student can work together to assess the student's strengths and weaknesses to estimate how well the student will be able to perform in a variety of future environments using the

Career Education Strengths/Problems Checklist (see Appendix B to this chapter) or a similar tool.

The major focus of career education at the high school level is for the student to do the bulk of the work in preparing for the responsibilities of adult life. The teacher of students with visual impairments is primarily a support person, who supplies feedback on the student's performance and offers leads when requested to do so. The exception is with students who have recently lost vision. In such cases, the specialist's responsibilities include direct instruction in compensatory skills and brainstorming with the students about the transferability of previously learned skills to new or revised career goals.

SUMMARY

Career education expands the core curriculum by introducing concepts that are essential for work and adult responsibilities. Children and youths with visual impairments need career education even more than do their sighted peers because of their inability to capture information about work and involvement in the community incidentally through vision. Therefore, parents, teachers of students with visual impairments, and other service providers are encouraged to keep career education competencies in mind as they work with students and to structure activities to facilitate the acquisition of these critical life skills.

ACTIVITIES

1. Choose an age range (preschool, elementary, middle school or junior high school, or high school) and write two or three career education activities or lessons designed to convey high expectations, promote the acquisition and use of compensatory skills, give students realistic feedback, develop appropriate social skills, and encourage opportunities for work.

2. Interview an adult with a visual impairment who is working successfully to determine the factors to which the worker attributes his or her success. What kinds of school-based or community-based activities did the worker participate in as a youngster that, in retrospect, he or she considers to have been the most helpful in relation to career education? What kinds of career education activities would he or she recommend for young people with visual impairments?

3. Interview an employer who has hired a worker with a visual impairment. What does the employer consider to be the worker's strengths and limitations? What kinds of accommodations did the employer make for the worker? What kinds of accommodations did the worker make? Why would the employer consider or not consider employing another person with a visual impairment?

4. Observe a work setting for about an hour. Using a recording sheet that is divided into two columns, record all the specific tasks that the workers carry out as part of their jobs in the first column and list any needed modifications or accommodations for persons who are blind or persons with low vision in the second column.

REFERENCES

Attmore, M. (1990). *Career perspectives: Interviews with blind and visually impaired professionals.* New York: American Foundation for the Blind.

Barraga, N. C., & Erin, J. N. (1992). *Visual handicaps and learning.* Austin, TX: Pro-Ed.

Bolles, R. N. (2000). *What color is your parachute? 2000: A practical manual for job-hunters and career changers* (30th anniversary ed.). Berkeley, CA: Ten Speed Press.

Bolles, R. N., & Brown, S. D. (2000). *Job-hunting tips for the so-called handicapped or people with disabilities: A supplement to What color is your parachute?* (rev. ed.). Berkeley, CA: Ten Speed Press.

Bradley-Johnson, S. (1994). *Psychoeducational assess-*

ment of students who are visually impaired or blind: *Infancy through high school* (2nd ed.). Austin, TX: PRO-ED.

Brolin, D. E. (1995). *Career education: A functional life skills approach* (3rd ed.). Englewood Cliffs, NJ: Merrill/Prentice Hall.

Dial, J., Mezger, C., Gray, S., Massey, T., Chan, F., & Hull, J. (1992). *The comprehensive vocational evaluation system.* Dallas, TX: McCarron-Dial Systems.

Employed ability: Blind persons on the job [Video]. (n.d.). New York: American Foundation for the Blind.

Erin, J. N., & Wolffe, K. E. (1999). *Transition issues related to students with visual disabilities.* Austin, TX: PRO-ED.

Everson, J. M. (1995). *Supporting young adults who are deaf-blind in their communities: A transition planning guide for service providers, families, and friends.* Baltimore, MD: Paul H. Brookes.

Holland, J. L. (1994). *Self-directed search.* Odessa, FL: Psychological Assessment Resources.

Kay, J. L., & Locke, L. (1996). *Career education teacher handbook.* Austin: Texas School for the Blind and Visually Impaired.

Kekelis, L. S., Sacks, S. Z., & Wolffe, K. E. (2000). *Focused on: Teaching social skills to visually impaired preschoolers.* New York: AFB Press (distributor).

Kendrick, D. (1993). *Jobs to be proud of: Profiles of workers who are blind or visually impaired.* New York: American Foundation for the Blind.

Kendrick, D. (1998). *Teachers who are blind or visually impaired.* New York: AFB Press.

Kendrick, D. (2000). *Business owners who are blind or visually impaired.* New York: AFB Press.

Lewis, S., & Russo, R. (1998). Educational assessment for students who have visual impairments with other disabilities. In S. Z. Sacks & R. K. Silberman (Eds.), *Educating students who have visual impairments with other disabilities* (pp. 39–71). Baltimore, MD: Paul H. Brookes.

McBroom, L. W. (1996). *Transition activity calendar for students with visual impairments.* Mississippi State, MS: Mississippi State University.

McBroom, L. W., Seaman, J., Graves, W. H., & Freeman, D. (1988). *Work assessment instruments for the vocational evaluation of people with visual disabilities.* Mississippi State: Mississippi State University.

MacCuspie, P. A. (1996). *Promoting acceptance of children with disabilities: From tolerance to inclusion.* Halifax, Nova Scotia: Atlantic Provinces Special Education Authority.

Navigating the rapids of life [Videotape]. (n.d.). Louisville, KY: American Printing House for the Blind.

Patton, J. R., & Dunn, C. (1998). *Transition from school to young adulthood.* Austin, TX: Pro-Ed.

Piaget, J. (1976). *The child and reality.* New York: Penguin Books.

Rabby, R., & Croft, D. (1989). *Take charge: A strategic guide for blind job seekers.* Boston: National Braille Press.

Sacks, S. Z., Kekelis, L. S., & Gaylord-Ross, R. J. (1992). *The development of social skills by blind and visually impaired students.* New York: American Foundation for the Blind.

Simpson, F., Huebner, K. M., & Roberts, F. K. (1986). *Transition from school to work: Programs in practice.* New York: American Foundation for the Blind.

U.S. Department of Labor, Secretary's Committee on Achieving Necessary Skills. (1991). *What work requires of schools.* Washington, DC: Author.

Wagner, M., DíAmico, R., Marder, C., Newman, L., & Blackorby, J. (1992). *What happens next? Trends in postschool outcomes of youth with disabilities.* Menlo Park, CA: SRI International.

Wehman, P. (1992). *Life beyond high school.* Baltimore, MD: Paul H. Brookes.

Wolffe, K. (1996). Career education for students with visual impairments. *RE:view, 28,* 89–93.

Wolffe, K. E. (1997). *Career counseling for people with disabilities.* Austin, TX: PRO-ED.

Wolffe, K. E. (1998). Transition planning and employment outcomes for students who have visual impairments with other disabilities. In S. Z. Sacks & R. K. Silberman (Eds.), *Educating students who have visual impairments with other disabilities* (pp. 339–368). Baltimore, MD: Paul H. Brookes.

Wolffe, K. E. (Ed.). (1999). *Skills for success: A career education handbook for children and adolescents with visual impairments.* New York: AFB Press.

Wolffe, K., & Johnson, D. (1997). *Transition tote system: Navigating the rapids of life.* Louisville, KY: American Printing House for the Blind.

Observation Checklist

Student: _____

Placement: _____

Date of observation: _____   Observer: _____

Observation time: _____   Location: _____

Task(s) performed/skill utilization:

_____

_____

_____

_____

_____

_____

_____

Work behaviors observed:	Yes	No	N/A
Punctual	____	____	____
Initiates work	____	____	____
Follows instructions	____	____	____
Attends to task	____	____	____
Attends to detail	____	____	____
Cooperates	____	____	____
Works consistently	____	____	____
Dresses appropriately	____	____	____
Solicits help, as needed	____	____	____
Problem-solves tasks	____	____	____
Interacts with coworkers	____	____	____
Follows work rules	____	____	____

(continued on next page)

Appendix A: Observation Checklist for Documenting Observations

Observation Checklist *(Continued)*

Work behaviors observed:	Yes	No	N/A
Attends to safety concerns	_____	_____	_____
Completes tasks	_____	_____	_____
Puts tools and materials away	_____	_____	_____

Comments: (List overall strengths and weaknesses. Make recommendations. Note the level of supervision required to perform assigned tasks. For example, can the student perform tasks independently when given oral, signed, or written instructions? Can the student perform with demonstrations or tactile cues? How often does the student require prompting to stay on task? Does the student respond to certain people in the work environment more favorably than to others? Note the accommodations necessary for the student to perform optimally.)

Source: Adapted from K. E. Wolffe, *Career Counseling for People with Disabilities* (Austin, TX: PRO-ED, 1997).

Career Education Strengths/Problems Checklist: High School

Name: _____ Date: _____

	YES	NO

Reading

I. How do you typically read?

	YES	NO
I can read regular print (unaided)	____	____
I can read regular print with low vision devices (type ____)	____	____
I can read large print (size ____)	____	____
I can read large print with low vision devices (type ____)	____	____
I can read braille (Grade 1 ____ Grade 2 ____)	____	____
I use audiocassette tapes for reading	____	____
I use Talking Books for reading	____	____
I use a computer with speech output for reading	____	____
I use a computer with braille output for reading	____	____
I use a computer with screen enlargement	____	____
I use a reader (paid or volunteer)	____	____
I use a reading machine (OCR)	____	____

Writing

II. How do you typically write?

	YES	NO
I write notes in regular print	____	____
I write notes in cursive script	____	____
I type notes	____	____
I use a slate and stylus to write notes in braille	____	____
I use a braillewriter to write notes in braille	____	____
I use a tape recorder for notes	____	____
I use a note taking device (type ____)	____	____
I use a computer	____	____

Speaking

III. How would you evaluate your speaking abilities?

	YES	NO
I speak English clearly	____	____
I speak a second language clearly (specify: _____)	____	____

(continued on next page)

Appendix B: Career Education Strengths/Problems Checklist: High School

Career Education Strengths/Problems Checklist *(Continued)*

Speaking *(continued)*

	YES	NO
People have trouble understanding my speech	_____	_____
I am comfortable speaking on the telephone	_____	_____
When I talk with a stranger, I am nervous	_____	_____
I am comfortable speaking in front of a group (class)	_____	_____
People say I talk too much	_____	_____
People say I don't talk enough (too quiet)	_____	_____
I never start conversations with strangers	_____	_____
I am comfortable asking for help	_____	_____

Transportation

IV. How do you usually go places?

	YES	NO
Family or friends drive me places	_____	_____
Someone helps me arrange transportation	_____	_____
I use school transportation	_____	_____
I use public transportation (buses, subway)	_____	_____
I use paratransit services (Special Transit)	_____	_____
I drive my car (motorcycle)	_____	_____
I ride my bicycle	_____	_____
I have a driver (paid)	_____	_____
I use private taxi companies	_____	_____
I walk with a white cane	_____	_____
I walk without a cane	_____	_____
I walk with a dog guide	_____	_____
I usually walk with a sighted guide	_____	_____
I use a sighted guide in new locations	_____	_____
I can easily get around in new locations	_____	_____
I get lost easily	_____	_____
I am afraid when I have to cross a street	_____	_____
I travel outside my hometown (by air, train)	_____	_____

(continued on next page)

Career Education Strengths/Problems Checklist *(Continued)*

	YES	NO
Daily Living Skills		
V. Do you have adequate daily living skills for independence?		
I perform chores at home	____	____
I do the following:		
Purchase my own clothes	____	____
Shop for groceries	____	____
Personal hygiene	____	____
Do laundry (wash/dry)	____	____
Iron my clothes	____	____
Bank (checking or savings)	____	____
Vacuum, dust room(s)	____	____
Wash/dry dishes	____	____
Take out the trash	____	____
I receive an allowance contingent on my performance	____	____
I receive an allowance that is not contingent on my performance	____	____
I keep a calendar	____	____
I make and keep appointments	____	____
I have money for incidentals at the end of the month	____	____
Sometimes I wonder if I can afford the things I need	____	____
I know the schedule for trash collection	____	____
I pay my bills on time	____	____
I know when holidays are coming up	____	____
I know how to plan a route in my neighborhood	____	____
I can read a map	____	____
I know pertinent bus/train schedules	____	____
I budget my money	____	____
When I shop, I take a shopping list	____	____
My room/apartment is well organized	____	____
I plan my meals in advance	____	____
I have trouble keeping my clothes clean	____	____
When I have an emergency, I know what to do	____	____
Other people say that my room/apartment is tidy	____	____
Other people say that I look well groomed	____	____
I have too many things to do	____	____

(continued on next page)

Career Education Strengths/Problems Checklist *(Continued)*

	YES	NO
Job Seeking		
VI. How do you find out about jobs and apply?		
I know what job I want	____	____
I know how to research jobs	____	____
I can find jobs I want	____	____
It is hard for me to know if a job is right for me	____	____
I have convinced someone to hire me	____	____
I use the telephone to find out about job openings	____	____
I have gone into businesses to pick up applications	____	____
I have completed applications without assistance	____	____
I have completed applications with a reader	____	____
I have completed applications with a friend or family member	____	____
I have a personal data sheet for filling out applications	____	____
I have a résumé	____	____
I can describe my disability to a prospective boss	____	____
I know what accommodations will be necessary to work	____	____
I need someone to help me find a job	____	____
It's hard for me to talk about things I do well	____	____
Job Maintenance		
VII. Can you keep a job?		
I have a job now	____	____
I have held a job for a year or more	____	____
I get along well with my coworkers (peers)	____	____
I have good attendance (in school and at work)	____	____
I am punctual	____	____
I make friends easily	____	____
I can't say no to people	____	____
I can usually speak up for myself	____	____
I go to the doctor often	____	____
I miss at least one day of school or work a month	____	____
I often feel lonely	____	____
I do not like to ask for help	____	____
I have applied for and received promotions	____	____

(continued on next page)

Career Education Strengths/Problems Checklist *(Continued)*

Job Maintenance *(continued)*

	YES	NO
I become upset if someone tells me I'm not working well	____	____
I have been fired from a job	____	____
I always try to do a good job	____	____
I have met some of my present friends at work	____	____

Leisure

VIII. What do you do for fun?

	YES	NO
I often watch television	____	____
I listen to the radio	____	____
I like to read a good book	____	____
I like to go out with friends	____	____
I like to go out by myself	____	____
I like to participate in athletics	____	____
I like to watch athletic events	____	____
I like to go to clubs	____	____
I like to dance	____	____
I like to sing	____	____
I like to go to the movies	____	____
I like to walk	____	____
I spend time on my hobbies	____	____
I get a lot of exercise	____	____
I often go out at night	____	____
I feel comfortable eating out	____	____
I volunteer in the community	____	____
It is difficult for me to go out and have a good time	____	____

Planning

IX. In the space below, please describe your plans for the future. What are your goals for this academic year? What are your goals for 5 years from now? What are your goals for 10 years from now?

Strategies for Teaching Career Education Skills to Students with Visual Impairments and Additional Disabilities

When a student with a visual impairment has other severe needs and challenges, his or her transition needs and outcomes should be addressed in the Statement of Transition Services section of the student's IEP at age 14. For students who are not considered able to participate in competitive employment, the choices and options for postschool services and activities may be extremely limited or nonexistent. When members of the student's educational team combine their knowledge about the student's strengths, preferences, and community resources, they may find creative and alternative solutions that lead to productive and rewarding vocational possibilities. The following are some suggestions:

◆ Students can begin to develop a work ethic by participating in school bake sales and community events, such as Earth Day, and recycling activities (see Chapter 17). They can participate in group sales activities for youth groups or athletic activities by selling candy using an augmentative system that has been programmed with anticipated responses (for example, "Will you support our baseball team?" "I have chocolate, chocolate with almonds, and vanilla; the cost is ___." "How many would you like?" "The money will be used to buy___"). Students gain personal social, money-management, and communication skills in addition to vocational experience from these activities.

◆ Students can learn to work cooperatively in an assembly-line fashion as they develop a small-goods company for the Economics Fair at their school. Simple low-cost projects, such as the Chocolate Spoon Factory (plastic spoons dipped in various types of chocolate, honey, and caramel for stirring coffee and tea) or the Multitalented Artists (gaining access to switches to activate a spin-art machine to produce a variety of T-shirts, cloth purses, and scarves), have a wide appeal. Students can activate a computer to print out a letter to request donations of funds for materials, use augmentative systems to list needed materials, extend tokens to use community transportation to purchase supplies, stamp the company name on the purchase order or receipt, and organize and classify items for production once they are back at the school. Students not only acquire cooperative work ethics, but gain feedback from social interaction and the pride of having made something others find valuable.

◆ By partially participating and using assistive devices, students can perform functional work-volunteer activities, such as being greeters, ushers, and accepters of donations at their houses of worship; helping with Meals on Wheels; cleaning cages and feeding animals at local animal shelters; and painting baseboards or cleaning windows during Habitat house-building sessions. Students can readily fulfill many volunteer opportunities that are advertised in local newspapers with minimal modifications.

◆ Vocational opportunities after high school need to include a variety of options, from volunteer positions to some aspect of competitive employment, if only on a

(continued on next page)

part-time basis. As soon as possible, a student and his or her family and other members of the educational team should meet to design and implement a Personal Futures Plan, in which the student's "dream" for work after high school is delineated, along with all the action plans and supports necessary to realize the dream. For example, the dream of one student may be to volunteer to turn on all the televisions, CD players, and radios in a department store. The necessary modifications may only be a peer to orient the student to the location of the appliances and the use of natural supports (employees) to help the student get to the bathroom and lunch area and to prompt the student intermittently to scoop his or her food during lunch.

Action plans may be to locate appropriate businesses, to perform a discrepancy analysis to determine the skills the student needs to acquire and essential support services that have to be provided, and to develop a contract with the designated business to ensure that all legal issues that need to be addressed are sufficiently covered.

◆ Students with additional disabilities need to acquire work-related daily living skills. Suggestions for modifications of tasks of daily living that are needed for success in a vocational setting are presented in Chapter 16.

M. BETH LANGLEY
Pinellas County Schools
St. Petersburg, FL

RESOURCES

Suggested Resources for Teaching Career Education

Resource	Type	Source	Description
Career Counseling for People with Disabilities: A Practical Guide to Finding Employment (Wolffe, 1997)	Book	PRO-ED	A text designed for use in rehabilitational counseling, educational pychology, and special education courses. People with disabilities and their families are encouraged to use this book to guide relevant career planning efforts.
Career Education Teacher Handbook (Kay & Locke, 1996)	Booklet	Texas School for the Blind and Visually Impaired	A booklet that describes the philosophy, policies, and procedures for the career education program at the school. Addresses guidelines for planning students' work experiences, vocational assessments, supported employment, work stipend programs, and more.
Career Perspectives: Interviews with Blind and Visually Impaired Professionals (Attmore, 1990)	Book	American Foundation for the Blind	Stories of how 20 people, blind or with low vision, decided on professional careers and achieved success in their careers.
Employed Ability: Blind Persons on the Job (n.d.)	Videotape	American Foundation for the Blind	People with visual impairments in a wide variety of occupations talk about career opportunities and their experiences in the workplace. Employers and coworkers speak openly about supervision and working alongside employees with visual impairments.

(continued on next page)

Suggested Resources *(Continued)*

Resource	Type	Source	Description
Jobs That Matter Series: *Teachers Who Are Blind or Visually Impaired* (Kendrick, 1998) and *Business Owners Who Are Blind or Visually Impaired* (Kendrick, 2000)	Books	AFB Press	A series of books designed to inspire young people who are visually impaired, their families, and the professionals who work with them about careers that are available.
Jobs to Be Proud Of: Profiles of Workers Who Are Blind or Visually Impaired (Kendrick, 1993)	Book	American Foundation for the Blind	A book about 12 people who are visually impaired that describes the jobs they do, why they chose the jobs, how their visual impairment impacts their jobs, and information about pay and benefits.
Navigating the Rapids of Life (n.d.)	Videotape	American Printing House for the Blind (APH)	A complementary product to APH's Transition Tote System; provides a wealth of information on successful employment for youths with visual impairments.
Skills for Success: A Career Education Handbook for Children and Adolescents with Visual Impairments (Wolffe, 1999)	Book	AFB Press	A book with practical ideas and activities for children and adolescents with visual impairments in career education. Activities focus on conveying high expectations, encouraging socialization, developing, compensatory skills, promoting opportunities to work, and providing realistic feedback.
Supporting Young Adults Who Are Deaf-Blind in Their Communities: A Transition Planning Guide for Service Providers, Families and Friends (Everson, 1995)	Book	Paul H. Brookes	A guide for service providers, family members, and friends in providing transition services to young adults who are deaf-blind. Expresses the unique needs of the deaf-blind population and integrates best practices into their transition services.
Take Charge: A Strategic Guide for Blind Job Seekers (Rabby & Croft, 1989)	Book	National Braille Press	A practical self-help guide that is based on the real-life experiences of job seekers who are blind. Proposes strategies for dealing with resistant employers.
Transition Activity Calendar for Students with Visual Impairments (McBroom, 1996)	Booklet	Mississippi State University	A booklet that lists the tasks students with visual impairments need to complete prior to exiting from high school in order to be ready to attend college.

(continued on next page)

Suggested Resources *(Continued)*

Resource	Type	Source	Description
Transition Issues Related to Students with Visual Disabilities (Erin & Wolffe, 1999)	Book	PRO-ED	A book that focuses on transition issues pertinent to students with visual disabilities. Issues addressed include functional academics, housing, transportation, employment, and leisure and recreation.
Transition Tote System: Navigating the Rapids of Life (Wolffe & Johnson, 1997)	Instructional materials	American Printing House for the Blind	A tool for preparing high school students (may be useful with some middle school students and some adults) who are visually impaired for the world of work. Encourages students to engage in hands-on experiences related to lessons. Five units: getting started, self-awareness, work exploration, job-seeking skills, job-keeping skills.
Transitions from School to Work: Programs in Practice (Simpson, Huebner, & Roberts, 1986)	Book	American Foundation for the Blind	A collection of information on a number of diverse programs and practices representing collaborative efforts that facilitate the transition of youths with disabilities into appropriate adult environments.

Contact information for each of the resources listed will be found in the Sources of Products, Materials, Equipment, and Services section at the back of this book.

Students with Visual Impairments and Additional Disabilities

Jane N. Erin

KEY POINTS

◆ Students with visual impairments and additional disabilities exhibit a wide range of individual characteristics and needs.

◆ A team of professionals and family members is needed to assess strengths and needs and to plan and implement an appropriate educational program for each student.

◆ The role of the teacher of students with visual impairments varies according to a student's needs, from being a provider of direct services for some students to serving as a consultant for others.

◆ Instruction is incorporated into daily, functional routines using appropriate prompts and reinforcements.

◆ Each student needs a long-term plan that realistically considers his or her individual strengths, needs, and life situation.

VIGNETTE

Sophie, aged 10, enjoys laughing with friends, eating ice cream, and swimming. Her severe cerebral palsy and mental retardation keep her from talking, but she communicates through smiles, laughter, voice sounds, body movements, and eye gazes. She is described as cortically visually impaired, but she often looks at objects or people. At other times, however, she stares forward and does not even blink when something moves toward her. Sophie's family has to feed her and change her diaper, and she will probably need this kind of assistance throughout her life. Sophie's mother believes it is important for Sophie to be pleasant and likable, since Sophie will always have to depend on others to help her.

Mark, aged 6, especially enjoys unusual sounds and machines that vibrate. He is blind as a result of retinopathy of prematurity, and some professionals have described him as autistic. Mark talks a lot, but much of his speech is echolalic (repetitive) or unrelated to what others have said to him. He likes his day to be well organized, and if something is unfamiliar, he sometimes screams and has a tantrum. Mark's parents hope that he will be able to read some braille someday, but their most important goal for Mark is to help him to accept changes in schedule more easily.

The favorite activity of Stanley, aged 15, is playing soccer with his friends. Stanley has low vision, a hearing impairment, and mild cerebral palsy as a result of his premature birth. Because of these conditions, he has to work harder to keep pace with the ball on the soccer field. However, he has learned to be a team player and knows when he can handle a play and when to let a teammate take over. Stanley earns average grades in school, using a hand magnifier to read regular textbooks, but since his handwriting is difficult to read, he uses a computer when possible. He is shy with girls, and his family hopes that the teacher of students with visual impairments can encourage him to be more outgoing.

INTRODUCTION

To an inexperienced teacher of students with visual impairments, instructing a student with a visual impairment and additional disabilities may seem like searching for a buried treasure without a map. All the factors that influence learning for a typical student are present; however, the effects of physical and mental impairments can make it difficult to determine a student's true abilities and interests. Scales of typical development are unreliable indicators of progress when a student has several disabilities, and even the most competent professional cannot predict exactly how a student will progress and develop.

The vignettes at the beginning of the chapter show the wide variations of effects that additional disabilities can have on a student who is visually impaired. For a student with such multiple disabilities, it is tempting to try to identify which disability is related to which of the individual's behaviors, but it may not be possible or useful to do so, since each disabling condition and each ability affect every other factor. For instructional purposes, it is far more important to identify what a student can do and how instruction can be shaped to expand his or her skills.

Although the effects of multiple disabilities vary, the following characteristics may be more common when a student has other disabilities along with a visual impairment:

Self-Focus. Because students may be unable to see or remember people or objects of interest, they may focus on themselves, relying on body play, voice sounds, and repetitive movements for entertainment. If they are able to speak, they may talk mostly about personal likes and may not pay attention to things that others say.

Emphasis on Routine. Because of limitations in memory and vision, students may rely on repetition and routines for learning and comfort. They may dislike unfamiliar situations and may not be interested in exploring new toys or materials because new objects are not predictable. For everyone, routines give a sense of control in a world that may seem full of random events, and these students are more comfortable when they can anticipate events.

Responses to Sensory Experiences. Many students who have neurological impairments and cannot see what is around them have unusual reactions to things they hear, see, touch, taste, or smell. In some cases, they withdraw from these experiences and appear defensive, as when a student refuses to touch finger paint or cries when he or she hears a washing machine. In other cases, they may enjoy or even crave sensations; eye poking and head banging are painful for most people, but some students with neurological difficulties seem to enjoy the feelings these behaviors produce.

Limited Incentive to Move. Because the combination of a visual impairment and impairments in memory and reasoning may result in difficulty understanding space and the environment, students may prefer to remain in one place, rather than move around and explore. They may not recall what objects are beyond their reach, and their curiosity may be limited to things that they can contact. The motivation to move and explore may be lessened because of reduced sensory input. Repetitive movements, such as swinging and rocking, may feel safer and more satisfying to these students than movements that lead them to an unknown place.

Although no generalities can be made about all students with visual impairments and additional disabilities, the foregoing characteristics should be considered when planning learning experiences. Teaching is most successful for these students when the steps for learning are gradual, when unfamiliar experiences are introduced in small increments, and when pleasant experiences are stronger than the unpleasant characteristics of an activity. With careful thought and planning, teachers of students with visual impairments can increase positive learning opportunities for these students, whose routes to learning are often atypical.

This chapter describes procedures for assessment and instruction that can reflect students' individual learning characteristics, but first discusses the role of the teacher of students with visual impairments in this process. It also addresses instructional issues and adaptations related to communication, orientation and mobility (O&M), and transition to adulthood.

ROLE OF THE TEACHER OF STUDENTS WITH VISUAL IMPAIRMENTS

The role of the teacher of students with visual impairments varies according to the needs of individual students. The specialist often serves as a consultant to the educational team, perhaps suggesting how a student can use touch, hearing, or vision more effectively or collecting data on a student's behavioral responses. When a student cannot express his or her wants and needs, it is essential for the specialist to communicate with other members of the student's educational team about what will facilitate learning. Team members need to establish a clear understanding of who is to be responsible for specific tasks, and the specialist may be responsible for implementing goals related to visual impairment during daily routines, such as toileting or feeding. Because the specialist's role and the composition of the team vary widely, it is vital for the team members to collaborate in planning.

It is also important that the teacher of students with visual impairments is aware of any specialized medical or physical difficulties a student may have. For example, many students with severe disabilities have seizures, some of which may be subtle and difficult to identify. Therefore, the specialist needs to know if certain behaviors precede the onset of a seizure, how to position a student during a seizure, and circumstances that warrant medical intervention. The primary teacher for these students is usually a special educator, often with a background in multiple disabilities. Although the teacher of students with visual impairments may not be the primary teacher, he or she must be aware of a student's medical needs and emergency procedures, including those related to tube feeding, the use of oxygen, the presence of a shunt, and medications prescribed for seizures or behavioral difficulties.

The teacher of students with visual impairments often plays an essential role in working with students with additional disabilities; resources for teachers appear later in this chapter.

ASSESSMENT

It is especially important to keep in mind that assessment is a process, not an event, when evaluating a student with a visual impairment and additional disabilities, because a one-dimensional approach will yield limited information that may not be representative of the student's abilities. The incorporation of observations, samples of behavior, measurement instruments, and documentation of behavior gives a clearer picture of a student's behaviors than does a reliance on any one technique. Furthermore, the types of assessment may vary, depending on the purpose of the process. The team may want to assess the student in such areas as gross or fine motor skills, daily living skills, communication or social skills. Assessments should reflect both the strengths and needs of a student. The approaches discussed in the following sections can yield useful information about a student's characteristics.

Types of Assessment

Standardized Instruments

Because students with visual impairments and additional disabilities show more individual variations than do those with only visual impairments, standardized instruments are of limited use. Scales that are based on observation and can be administered over time are probably the most useful. Few instruments are normed on these students, and most of these instruments are intended for students aged 8 or younger. (See the Resources later in this chapter for instruments that may be helpful to members of the educational team.)

Observational Approaches

Planned observations can yield a representative picture of a student's strengths and needs. To be most useful, however, observations should cover a variety of experiences, times, and settings. The purpose of an observation should be clearly defined before the session takes place, and the observation should be documented using anecdotal notes, quantitative data, or audio- or videotaped protocols.

When the student being observed is blind, the observer should make the student aware that he or she is being observed if a sighted student would be aware of the observer. It is unethical to withhold information about an observer's presence from a student who is blind because he or she cannot notice the observer. Even if the student seems unable to sense the presence of others, the observer should introduce himself or herself by a handshake or a touch on the hand. Arena assessments, videotaped protocols, and play-based assessments are three observational approaches that can be used to gather information about a student.

Arena Assessment. In an arena assessment, a group of observers, often with different specializations, watch as one or two people interact with the student. This type of assessment can provide a sample of common student behaviors, but should not be used if a student is uncomfortable or self-

conscious with others. Moreover, like other time-limited observations, it reflects responses on only one occasion and should be combined with other forms of assessment. In most cases, the results are described in a narrative report that includes sections written by each member of the student's educational team. These results often provide the foundation for more structured assessments of areas in which additional information is needed.

Videotaped Protocols. Videotaped protocols are a way of preserving observations, so members of the educational team can view the same behaviors. A selection of activities, including self-help skills, independent play, interactive play, work activities, gross motor activities, and other general categories, can provide a visual journal of a student's behaviors that can be used as a baseline with which future skills can be compared.

Play-Based Assessment. In a play-based assessment, a student is observed at play, interacting with materials and people that provide the opportunity for choice and initiative. Observations are recorded within categories of developmental skills identified in play-based assessment protocols. For example, Linder's (1990) play-based assessment includes an observational worksheet of 10 general areas of social-emotional skills: temperament; mastery motivation (including initiative, persistence, and task-directed behavior); social interaction with parents; interactions with parents while with a facilitator; characteristics of parent-child interaction; characteristics of facilitator-child interaction; characteristics of dramatic play; interaction with peers: dyad, humor, and conventions; and interactions with peers in a group. Each area includes three to six subareas under which an evaluator can record descriptions of a student's behaviors.

Ecological Assessment

The most representative information is usually gathered in an ecological assessment, which provides a structured way of observing a student's interaction with his or her environment. Since this type of assessment does not present a student with new tasks or test items that may be beyond his or her experiential repertoire, the team is more likely to learn about the student's abilities on the basis of established learning patterns. An ecological assessment includes the following steps:

Identifying Domains.   The team identifies the domains—general settings—in which the student's daily routine take place. For a young student, these domains may include the home, school, and community (such as a playground or supermarket). For an adolescent or young adult, work and leisure-time settings may also be included.

Identifying Activities.   The amount of time the student spends and the consistency of activities in each domain should be considered, and specific activities need to be delineated. For example, an infant probably spends most of the time at home and little time in the community, so more activities take place at home, and these activities will be considered priorities for learning.

All activities in which the student participates in each domain should be listed, regardless of the student's level of active participation. For instance, if a student is dressed by another person, he or she is still involved in that activity, and it will be a focus for later learning, even if the student is not now actively involved. A list of activities for Sherry, a 12-year-old girl who is deaf-blind, is presented in Sidebar 20.1. The assessment of a student's ability to perform an activity consists of four parts, described next.

1. *Identifying steps for a student without disabilities.* In the first part, the evaluator observes and lists the typical steps in the activity done by a student without disabilities (see Table 20.1). This list is used later to compare the typical steps in an activity with the way a student with a disability performs the activity.

2. *Identifying steps for the student with a disability.* In the second part, the evaluator first prompts the student with a disability to perform the activity. Then the evaluator lists the steps and documents the amount of assistance the student needs to do each step. If a student cannot do a

step, the evaluator performs it and continues to encourage the student through the routine, providing as little assistance as possible.

3. *Comparing the routines.* In the third part, the evaluator compares the steps done by the two students, noting the steps that the student with a

---

SIDEBAR 20.1

Sample Activity List for Sherry

HOME

- ◆ Eating meals
- ◆ Toileting
- ◆ Showering
- ◆ Watching television
- ◆ Preparing meals
- ◆ Playing video games
- ◆ Dressing and grooming
- ◆ Participating in bedtime routine (getting up and going to bed)

SCHOOL

- ◆ Eating lunch
- ◆ Toileting
- ◆ Attending classes

   Homeroom

   Mathematics

   Home economics

   Art

   Orientation and mobility

COMMUNITY

- ◆ Shopping
- ◆ Attending a house of worship
- ◆ Visiting neighbors
- ◆ Taking outdoor walks
- ◆ Swimming at a neighborhood pool

disability cannot perform independently. This comparison, called a *discrepancy analysis* or an *ecological inventory,* helps the evaluator to identify which steps need to be *adapted* and which steps need to be *taught* to the student with a disability. In the example in Table 20.1, Jessica is able to perform most steps in washing her hands independently. However, using the discrepancy analysis, the evaluator determined that Jessica needed assistance in locating the faucet, applying soap to her hands, and rubbing soap on her hands.

4. *Deciding whether to adapt or teach the steps that cannot be performed independently.* In the fourth part, the evaluator determines whether the steps that are necessary to the task but that the student cannot perform must be adapted or taught. Sometimes both adaptation and instruction are necessary. For Jessica (see Table 20.1), substitution of a pump bottle made it easier to teach her to put soap on her hands.

Selection of Skills to Be Taught

The most important result of an assessment is the selection of skills that are targeted for instruction. To select the skills, the family and the rest of the student's educational team establish priorities among the activities, taking the following factors into consideration:

How frequently is the activity performed? For example, dressing, which is done at least twice a day, is more frequent than singing a song at Sunday school once a week. An activity that is performed frequently is given a higher priority than one that is performed less frequently or only occasionally.

What activities do the family members want the child to perform? Toilet training may be an important priority for the family, so the child does not need to be taken to the bathroom or changed regularly. Thus, more time will be spent on this ac-

Table 20.1. Discrepancy Analysis for Jessica: Hand Washing

Steps for Persons Without Disabilities	Student's Peformance of Task	Skills Needed/ Adaptations
1. Walks to sink.	1. Walks to sink.	+
2. Visually locates faucet.	2. Turns head away and searches tactilely.	– T: Scan visually, verbal prompt
3. Grasps faucet handle.	3. Grasps faucet handle.	+
4. Pulls handle to turn on water.	4. Pulls handle to turn on water.	+
5. Rinses hands.	5. Rinses hands.	+
6. Grasps soap.	6. Searches tactilely for soap dish and drops soap.	– A: Use pump bottle T: Press pump and rub soap on hands, with reduced prompts
7. Rubs soap on hands.	7. Waits for others to rub soap on hands.	– T: Reduce prompts
8. Places soap on soap dish.	8. Drops soap in sink.	NA: Pump used
9. Rinses hands.	9. Rinses hands.	+
10. Turns off water.	10. Turns off water.	+
11. Locates towel visually.	11. Locates towel tactilely.	+
12. Dries hands.	12. Dries hands.	+

Note: + = skill is accomplished, – = skill requires adaptation (A) or teaching (T), and NA = not applicable.

tivity than on teaching the child to identify pictures of familiar objects. An activity that is a family priority should receive attention.

Is the activity functional? A functional activity (such as dressing, feeding, or bathing) is purposeful and usually needs to be performed for a student if she or he cannot do it independently. Functional activities are high priorities because they are necessary in adult life and their mastery leads to greater independence.

Will the activity make the student more competent in social situations? Because social interaction may be more difficult for some students with visual impairments and additional disabilities, activities that enhance social participation are high priorities. For example, the ability to participate in routines as part of a religious congregation or to entertain oneself appropriately while visiting someone else's home may be important activities to work on, so that a student will be given more opportunities to go places and interact with others. Not all high-priority activities should be functional routines at home and in school.

The process of conducting an ecological assessment and selecting skills to be taught gives the educational team the opportunity to observe the student and teach functional activities according to a variety of factors, including the student's ability. Nietupski and Hamre-Nietupski's (1987) detailed discussion of ecological assessment and instructional planning describes how to infuse skills that have been identified as requiring instruction into daily activities.

INSTRUCTIONAL PROCESSES

Although it is not possible to teach all of the activities in which a student engages at once, it does not mean that the student should be discouraged from participating in an activity, especially if it is part of the regular routine in the classroom or at home. In such a situation, the student should receive full or partial assistance for the steps that are not scheduled to be taught immediately and the parents or other caregivers continue to provide the student with information about the steps that

the student cannot yet perform. Once instruction in an activity begins, the student may be expected to do designated parts of the activity with less and less assistance, and new steps are presented when the student is able to accomplish the earlier steps.

Even with a student who has severe physical or cognitive disabilities, who always needs to have important elements of a routine done for him or her, *partial participation* should be encouraged. For example, if a student can flex one arm so it can be inserted in a sleeve or can pick up a toothbrush to initiate toothbrushing, he or she is involved in the task and has some control over it.

Planning for Instruction

Planning for instruction begins with identifying exactly what will be taught. This information comes directly from the discrepancy analysis, which identified the steps in a task that a student cannot do without assistance. The priorities for tasks to be taught are set according to the criteria described earlier.

In addition to the specific activity or steps in the activity, identified in a student's Individualized Education Program (IEP), the educational team has to consider the *skills* needed to perform the activity. A skill is a general behavior that can be used in many activities. For example, *visual scanning* is useful for many tasks: finding a lunch box, a door handle, and an empty seat. In identifying the skills that are important for a student, the educational team evaluates the usefulness of those skills in several activities. Because team members need to decide which skills should be taught, it makes sense for them to consider which skills are used in several activities and can be practiced in several contexts.

Adapting the Activity and Environment

After the educational team has identified the activities that are important for the student, the members consider whether adaptations—temporary or permanent—are needed to teach them.

Temporary adaptations are changes in positioning, materials, timing, lighting, or other factors that can assist the student in learning a new skill. For example, when a student with visual and physical disabilities is learning to drink and to scoop with a spoon, a brightly colored sticker on the student's cup can enhance its visibility and an adaptive plate with a raised edge can make scooping easier. Since it is inconvenient for the parents or other caregivers always to mark the student's cup or to take an adapted plate along when eating in different places, the goal is to reduce the need for and fade an external cue or a special piece of equipment as soon as the student has mastered the task.

Permanent adaptations are those that a student will always need to perform a task. For example, a student who is blind and can learn to read will always use braille because he or she does not have the vision necessary to read efficiently in print. A student with a physical disability will always use a wheelchair to move from place to place because he or she does not have the physical ability to walk.

When it is possible to complete a task efficiently without the use of an adaptation, the task should be taught that way. The use of individualized equipment and materials makes a student even more different, and low-tech solutions are always preferable to high-tech ones if they result in the same outcome. For example, a student who can read standard print comfortably by bringing his or her book closer should be encouraged to make this adaptation, rather than be given large-print books, which are more expensive and inconvenient, as well as less readily available.

The factors in the environment—primarily sensory (visual, auditory, and tactile) and physical features—that affect the accomplishment of tasks should also be considered when planning instruction. In a few activities, such as eating, taste and smell may also influence how a task is taught. The following characteristics should be considered in analyzing the teaching environment:

- Visual: lighting, color, contrast, visual clutter, visual movement, size of materials, and aesthetic responses (pleasant or unpleasant);

- Auditory: background sounds, audibility of sounds related to instruction, volume, pitch, and aesthetic responses (pleasant or unpleasant);

- Tactile: texture, temperature, pressure, intensity, and aesthetic responses (pleasant or unpleasant);

- Physical: position, duration of position, aesthetic responses (pleasant or unpleasant), proprioceptive input, and movement; and

- Gustatory and olfactory: variations in taste (sour, sweet, salty), odor, familiarity, and aesthetic responses (pleasant or unpleasant).

Many students with visual impairments and additional disabilities have atypical responses to information received through their senses. For example, a student with neurological difficulties may experience a texture that is a little rough but comfortable for most people as extremely rough and unpleasant. Therefore, for teaching a new activity or skill, the educational team needs to consider adaptations that will make the environment more comfortable.

Teaching Through Routines

For most students with visual impairments and additional disabilities, learning a new activity begins with experiencing it as a consistent part of their regular schedules. Before students are expected to perform steps in an activity, families and professionals should ensure that the students have routinely observed or participated in the activity. Routines are especially important for a student who is blind who cannot obtain information incidentally through observation. Thus, the student may not understand the intent of being placed on a toilet for the first time because he or she does not realize that others use a toilet to urinate and therefore may object to the unfamiliar process. Before the student is ready to be placed on the toilet, he or she should have the chance to associate the bathroom with toileting routines, perhaps by being shown how an older sibling sits on the toilet seat and hearing the sounds associated with toileting.

Two types of routines—functional and social—play a part in learning and must be a part of every student's process of development.

Functional Routines

Functional routines involve activities, such as dressing, eating, toileting, working for pay, and buying groceries, that are a regular part of one's life and are necessary to ensure physical survival and maintain health or social acceptability. They are performed regularly by most people in a community or culture.

Functional routines may not be pleasant for a student who does not understand the reason for these activities. For example, many students with mental retardation cannot understand abstract concepts, such as social acceptability or threats to safety, and hence may not be motivated to perform functional routines. Or a student who is blind may not want to put on shoes and may resist attempts to teach this skill because the soft carpeting feels better than shoes on his or her feet, even though wearing shoes is more socially appropriate when visiting others or going to a store. For this reason, functional tasks often need to be coordinated with some pleasant event or outcome. For example, a student who is allowed to listen to a favorite audiotaped song only when he or she participates in putting on shoes may be more willing to cooperate. Similarly, a student whose routine involves a chance to play ball with other students after he or she finishes brushing his or her teeth may participate more willingly in tooth brushing. Note that in the two examples, one pleasant event (reward) occurred immediately, and the other occurred after the routine was performed. The reason for the difference is that some students cannot remember what will happen after a task is over and hence need to have a reward while they are performing the task.

Many students with visual impairments and additional disabilities need to use adaptive devices, such as hearing aids or eyeglasses, to perform functional routines. Because they may not understand the purpose of these devices, they may find them unpleasant. Therefore, the teacher of students with visual impairments may need to work with a student's educational team to develop a plan to introduce a device gradually. For example, a student who dislikes wearing eyeglasses may begin wearing them for just half an hour twice a day while an adult looks at a picture book with him or her. When the student is able to accept the eyeglasses for this amount of time, then another activity can be chosen for which the student needs to wear them. The length of time for wearing the eyeglasses can be increased gradually. Often it is best to introduce a device during a preferred activity and then to use it for a less preferred one. It may also be helpful to have some students observe others wearing or using the device. The gradual introduction of the device during functional routines can allow the student to be more comfortable with using an adaptation that will make the environment more meaningful.

Social Routines

Social routines help students develop skills in communicating and interacting with other people and to view the presence of others as positive and enjoyable. Students with visual impairments and additional disabilities may not spontaneously enjoy or seek the company of others, especially if all their daily activities involve other people prompting them to do tasks that are not naturally motivating, such as self-care. Therefore, it is important that frequent routines, such as a morning song with the class, in which being with other people is a pleasant experience, are incorporated into their days.

Most people have regular social routines, such as watching or participating in sports, singing, playing cards, or having coffee with friends. These students can also enjoy regular social routines, but their routines must be brief and consistent. For a young student, a game of peek-a-boo, in which each partner takes a turn, is a common social routine. For a student who is just developing basic signals to communicate with other people, a social routine may include touching a friend to request more swinging, offering to shake hands in response to a greeting, or clapping to a song.

Routines are especially important because some students do not spontaneously develop attachments with others in the same way as do students without disabilities. Since the basis of communication is a relationship or desire for a relationship with others, a student will not communicate unless he or she perceives that there is value in interacting with people. For some students, a social routine may be as basic as learning to tolerate touching, being spoken to, and being moved. Later, it may evolve into turn taking, sharing materials, and requesting experiences. Building a relationship depends on the student associating people with positive sensations. Being rocked, fed, or entertained by music can help a student learn that contact with others is pleasant. As the student develops a greater understanding of the world, positive experiences become more complex and can be introduced and elaborated through the use of social routines.

A social routine, also called a "joint action routine," must have several elements to be an effective tool for learning. It must have a clear beginning and end and a role for each partner, and both partners must have the same understanding of its theme. Social routines are especially important for students who do not have an established language system, because they can provide the connection that will help these students understand that they can participate in and control interactions with other people and that such interactions can be pleasant.

Teaching an Activity or a Skill

After a routine has been identified as important, the educational team needs to decide how to teach it consistently, on the basis of the following considerations:

- ◆ *What expectations will be set?* Is it realistic to expect the student to work on all steps of

a routine that he or she has not mastered, or should only one step be addressed at a time? Will the student know what is expected by observing other people do the task, by listening to oral directions, or by placing his or her hands over the hands of someone who is performing the steps?

- ◆ *How will the student be prompted?* In most cases, the least intrusive prompt that will get a student to do a step in an activity should be chosen. Dote-Kwan (1995) presented the following hierarchy of prompts, listed from the least intrusive to the most intrusive (see also Table 20.2).

Natural cues are bits of information that are typically part of the activity. For example, a bell ringing signals that it is time to change classes, and a sign at a bank tells patrons where to stand while waiting for service. These cues are preferable to cues provided by another person because the student does not depend on someone else to accomplish the task.

Visual and tactile cues may be added to the materials of an activity to give a student extra information. The use of bright colors on eating utensils for a student with low vision or the arrangement of materials in a left-to-right sequence are examples of cues that can call attention to a task that needs to be performed.

Other cues, including gestural and oral cues, require the presence of another person. *Gestural cues,* such as pointing, provide general information about what to do or where something is located. If a student needs more specific information, *oral cues*—both *direct* ("Find the collar of the shirt") and *indirect* ("This looks like a delicious sandwich" to encourage a student to eat)—may be necessary. Students who have mental retardation or other cognitive difficulties may not understand that indirect oral cues are requesting a behavior. Thus, indirect verbal cues may not be appropriate for many students until their language and reasoning abilities have developed sufficiently.

Visual modeling can be used to prompt behaviors for students with low vision. For example,

Table 20.2. Hierarchy of Cues from the Least Intrusive to the Most Intrusive

Cue	Example
Natural cue	The end of dinner signals playtime.
Visual/tactile cue	Photos of toys are put on the shelf.
Gestural cue	The adult points toward a toy.
Direct verbal cue	The adult says, "Pick up the toy."
Indirect verbal cue	The adult says, "There are toys on the floor."
Visual modeling	The adult picks up the toy so the child will follow.
Physical prompt	The adult taps the child's hand.
Full physical guidance	The adult forms the child's hand around the toy and assists the child to lift it.

Source: Adapted from J. Dote-Kwan, "Instructional Strategies," in D. Chen and J. Dote-Kwan, Eds., *Starting Points: Instructional Practices for Young Students Whose Multiple Disabilities Include Visual Impairment* (Los Angeles: Blind Children's Center, 1995), pp. 43–56.

watching another student unwrap a sandwich can prompt a classmate to do the same thing. Sometimes a *physical prompt* is needed for a student to start the next step in an activity: a touch on the hand or placing a spoon into a student's hand can let him or her know what is expected next.

Full physical guidance, in which a person moves the student's hand or another body part, is the least desirable prompt. It should be used only when the student needs to experience the movement required to perform the skill. Physical guidance should never be used to force an unwilling student to do something he or she does not want to do. In this case, the problem is motivation, and external reinforcers, such as those suggested in the next section, should be considered.

Teaching for Generalization

When students with visual impairments have additional disabilities, especially those that affect learning and memory, they may have more difficulty accomplishing a familiar activity when features of the activity are changed. For example, students who can feed themselves at the lunch table

in school with their own dishes and utensils may not understand what is expected when they eat lunch at a friend's home. Or students who can help stock shelves in the school storeroom may need to relearn the task when they are asked to do it in a real store, where the shelves are arranged differently and the manager is unfamiliar.

The following are suggestions for teaching for generalization:

◆ Continue to teach and reinforce a skill even when the student has shown mastery of it.

◆ Seek opportunities for the student to generalize the skills. For example, a student who has learned to open the door of the classroom should also have the chance to open other doors at school, at stores, and at friends' homes.

◆ Change just one feature of the task to be generalized at a time; a new staff member, a different workplace, or a new time of day can be introduced when success has been attained after the changes have been made.

◆ Encourage the student to carry out a skill in all meaningful contexts. For some students, this means that the skill needs to be retaught in each new environment.

◆ Use individual instruction when necessary for a student who is easily distracted. However, some students with severe disabilities are able to learn new skills along with other students right from the beginning.

◆ Integrate skills that have been learned into tasks that are a part of the student's routine, so that they can be practiced regularly.

Building Motivation

The interests and motivations of a student with low vision and additional disabilities may vary from those of a nondisabled age-mate. However, the student can still enjoy many of the same experiences. For example, the student may like a lunch box because of the sparkly paint on it, and his or her nondisabled classmate may like it because of the cartoon characters pictured on it. For this reason, it is important to observe what materials and experiences a student prefers so they can be built into routines. When a teacher of students with visual impairments is getting to know a new student, he or she should keep an inventory of the student's preferred activities, materials, and friends that can be used to encourage the student to cooperate in nonpreferred activities and to create leisure-time options that will help the student make choices.

Students who are blind and have additional disabilities may not enjoy some of the reinforcers that are routinely used in typical classrooms. Receiving picture stickers, being patted on the back, winning a game, and even receiving oral praise may be meaningless or even unpleasant to a student who does not understand abstract concepts of approval and competition. Although the teacher of students with visual impairments should continue to use these typical rewards, the specialist may have to pair them with other rewards if he or she wants a student to learn a new task or participate in an activity that is not motivating. Sidebar 20.2 presents some examples of reinforcing materials and activities that are enjoyed by many students of various ages who are blind and have additional disabilities.

When selecting materials and experiences, the specialist needs to consider the student's chronological age. Even students who have particular sensory characteristics (such as an attraction to light or a preference for coarse textures) can en-

---

Examples of Reinforcing Materials and Activities for Students Who Are Blind and Have Additional Disabilities

SIDEBAR 20.2

PRESCHOOL- AND ELEMENTARY-AGE STUDENTS

◆ Sound toys or audiotapes of interesting sounds.

◆ Small, manipulative objects that can be kept in a pocket.

◆ Vibrating toys.

◆ Swinging, rocking, or bouncing.

◆ Tearing scrap paper of various textures.

◆ Playing with Play-Doh® or clay.

SECONDARY SCHOOL-AGE STUDENTS

◆ A dab of perfume or hand lotion.

◆ Dancing to music.

◆ Listening to audiotapes of music or of the voices of familiar people.

◆ Tape recording one's own voice.

◆ Cooking activities.

◆ Using appliances that vibrate or make noise (such as a blender, sweeper, and clothes washer).

joy these preferences through activities that are similar to those their nondisabled age-mates enjoy. Although it may be more difficult to find age-appropriate activities for older students who are developmentally young, team members should make an effort to do so to enhance the students' social acceptance by other students and adults.

It is often assumed that a student will learn to perform a task for social reinforcers, such as praise, a smile, or a hug. Although some students may do so, others students are not naturally motivated to please others, perhaps because their mental ability does not allow them to understand the meaning of words of praise or a smile or because differences in their brain actually make these experiences unpleasant.

Travis, a 12-year-old boy with autism and low vision, is an example of a child who found such experiences unpleasant. An observer noticed that each time the specialist praised Travis with an enthusiastic "Good boy!" and a pat on the shoulder when he recognized a picture, Travis drew back and flinched. After realizing that Travis found such encouragement unpleasant, the teacher of students with visual impairments began to praise him in a quiet voice and to allow him to use a brightly colored marker to draw with when he finished the activity. For Travis, this marker was more rewarding than the teacher's enthusiastic praise. However, the teacher continued to praise Travis quietly to help him associate words of praise with a pleasant experience.

When a student is not making progress in learning a new skill, it may be difficult to tell whether the reason is his or her inability to perform the skill or lack of motivation. If the student has performed the skill even once in another context, then the lack of motivation should be considered a possibility. If the task is unpleasant or the student has a limited memory span, the reinforcer should occur as soon as the student makes a response. After the student knows the steps of the routine and demonstrates enough memory to understand the idea of waiting, the reinforcer can be provided after the activity. For example, a student who is learning to help in dressing may enjoy hearing a few seconds of a favorite audiotape each time she or he does any step of dressing. Only after the student has mastered most of the steps and shows that she or he understands the entire activity can the reward be delayed until after the student is completely dressed.

Managing Challenging Behaviors

Like all students, those with visual impairments and additional disabilities may demonstrate a range of difficult behaviors at various times during their development. A few students may be noncompliant, verbally oppositional, or physically aggressive toward themselves and others. These behaviors may be responses to environmental factors, such as inconsistent expectations or the lack of appropriate models, or the result of brain impairments that result in poor impulse control, the need for a different level of stimulation, or the lack of understanding of the results of one's behaviors.

Identifying Behavioral Patterns. Intervention to manage an inappropriate behavior begins with identifying its pattern of occurrence, which may require careful observations of the behavior over several weeks. These observations can determine the times of the day the behavior occurs and other related factors, including the types of activities, adult supervision, and peer contacts, as well as where the activities take place. For example, Sam regularly hit his head when he was required to stop a preferred activity and begin a nonpreferred one, and Martha cursed at others and threw materials early in the afternoon when her classroom teacher took a lunch break and the afternoon classroom aide was beginning her shift. Recognizing patterns of inappropriate behaviors gives the educational team an opportunity to identify ways of preventing the inappropriate behaviors when they are most likely to occur. Mar and Cohen's (1998) list of conditions that suggest the need for therapeutic or other intervention is presented in Sidebar 20.3.

Preventing Challenging Behaviors. The prevention of challenging behaviors is one of the

---

Conditions that Suggest the Need for Intervention

◆ Behaviors that injure the student or others.

◆ Changes in the frequency or intensity of behavioral difficulties or emotional responses.

◆ New and unusual behaviors that persist and that interfere with functioning.

◆ Recent experiences that have created psychological stress.

◆ Behaviors that require disproportionate attention from the teacher.

◆ Frequent absences.

◆ Changes in physical appearance.

◆ Loss of interest in social interactions.

Source: Adapted from H. Mar & E. Cohen, "Educating Students with Visual Impairments Who Exhibit Emotional and Behavioral Problems," in S. Z. Sacks and R. K. Silberman, Eds., *Educating Students Who Have Visual Impairments and Other Disabilities* (Baltimore, MD: Paul H. Brookes, 1998), pp. 263–302.

SIDEBAR 20.3

---

most important aspects of intervention. Once a behavioral pattern has been documented, these questions can be considered to help determine preventive strategies:

◆ Was the student aware of expectations or routines when the behavior occurred?

◆ Was there a physical basis for the behavior (such as a decrease in the level of medication or an attempt to express discomfort, for example from a poorly fitting orthotic device)?

◆ Can the student express himself or herself in another way (for instance, by pushing away a task instead of hitting an adult)?

◆ Are all members of the educational team responding to the behavior in the same way?

◆ What is satisfying or rewarding to the student about continuing to behave this way?

The last question may be the most important, for a behavior that is frequently repeated must be serving some purpose. The student may be using the behavior to gain the attention of others, to meet a need for a greater level of physical stimula-

tion, or to avoid an unwanted activity or task. The answer to this question will help the team determine how the behavior can be prevented. For example, if the behavior is an attempt to gain attention, an effective strategy may be to provide attention when a student is behaving appropriately and withdraw attention when he or she is behaving inappropriately.

Identifying the causes of the behavior will help the team to plan ways of avoiding its occurrence in the future. Smith and Levack (1996) suggested the following strategies for making cooperation during a task more likely:

◆ Give the student a choice of tasks (for instance, "Do you want to wash your dish or wipe the table first?").

◆ Vary tasks to include some the student has already mastered.

◆ Pace the instruction (that is, provide short breaks and pause to let the student initiate a task before prompting).

◆ Include both partial and whole tasks.

◆ Reduce the difficulty of tasks.

◆ Adjust the level of prompting to reduce the amount of guidance.

- Make transitions simpler (for instance, associate a routine or object cue with a change).

- Provide structure.

- Redirect the student to a desired task rather than pay attention to an undesirable behavior.

Intervening When the Behavior Occurs. Although preventive measures may significantly reduce difficult behaviors, the educational team needs to devise a plan for dealing with difficult behaviors when they occur. Physical aggression toward self or others and temper tantrums require immediate attention by the staff, and a plan for responding to these behaviors should be in place.

When a student demonstrates signs of aggression, others should move away from, rather than close in on the student, which may result in increased anger. One adult should keep voice contact with the student, using a calm voice and brief, supporting phrases: "You can use your voice to tell us you are angry." Reasoning and lecturing are rarely effective when a student is extremely upset.

Physical restraint is the last resort. It should be used only when there is immediate physical danger to the student or others and the staff are well trained in restraint techniques. Physical restraint is never appropriate if a student is verbally abusive because it teaches the student that others are in control of his or her behavior and does not result in long-term changes in behavior. Rather, the staff should be trained in crisis prevention and the recognition of dangerous situations. Many students with visual impairments and additional disabilities have self-abusive behaviors, such as eye poking and head banging, that rarely pose an immediate danger. In such instances, the team should identify ways of redirecting the students and rewarding them when they are not abusive.

Some students who are blind have learned that they can use their voices to disrupt activities and take control of a situation, such as by swearing, shouting angrily at others, or talking excessively. When adults intervene by arguing, reasoning, or explaining, the students may feel rewarded by the extra attention. Therefore, verbal outbursts are best dealt with by a brief statement of consequences: "You are so angry that the rest of us cannot talk. The rest of us will go to the table to talk until you are talking in a calm voice." If the student does not cooperate after one restatement, then the consequence (e.g., the other students' leaving) should take place. *Time out* (moving the student away from an area) is effective only if the student wants to be with a group. If the student wants to be alone, this strategy can actually reinforce negative behavior and should not be used.

Ongoing behavioral difficulties require a consistent plan of behavioral intervention, so the team should include a behavior specialist who is well qualified in this area. This can be a special educator or a psychologist with preparation in behavior management. The teacher of students with visual impairments can work with the team to identify factors connected with a student's visual impairment that may influence the student's behavior, such as the inability to recognize cues that an activity is about to change.

COMMUNICATION

Most people consider speech to be their primary form of communication and thus may not be aware that the process of communicating is much broader than simply the form of expression, such as speech. Communication encompasses nonverbal messages, including gestures, facial expressions, and body language. Formal communication can take place only if a person has the mental capacity to understand concepts; to recall and apply symbols, such as words and pictures; and to understand the rules of a language system. When a student has a visual impairment and other disabilities, his or her capacity to communicate with others is affected by a variety of factors in addition to the visual impairment: mental abilities, physical abilities, opportunities for communication, and social and emotional characteristics.

Nonsymbolic Communication

Some students communicate using methods other than spoken words or manual signs. Students who cannot communicate through a language often have brain impairments that result in severe mental retardation. In some cases, they also have physical disabilities that limit their ability to express themselves through a specific form of language, such as speech.

When a student is a preschooler, it is not possible to predict whether he or she will develop language later. Creating an environment that has consistent routines and that allows the student to anticipate events and make choices will build a foundation for later communication, whether or not it includes language.

Infants in the early months communicate with others by noticing what happens when they produce a specific action. For example, when babies cry, their parents pick them up or give them something to eat. When they learn that something pleasant happens when they cry, they are more likely to cry again. Later, they figure out that crying in a different way, at a different place, or at a different time of day may make different things happen.

When a child is blind and has other severe disabilities, his or her ability to understand the connections between an action and a result may be delayed. Because of blindness, the child receives fewer cues about the results of the action; although the child may hear his or her parents' voices and footsteps, they do not provide a constant source of information in the way that visual information does. A child with a visual impairment and no other disabilities may learn to make the connection between his or her behavior and the result, on the basis of available information, but a child with neurological difficulties or mental retardation may not easily learn it. The child may require more repetitions of an experience to learn that he or she can make things happen, or he or she may not be able to make that connection at all.

To communicate actively, a student must first anticipate events and understand sequence. A student who responds to sounds or sights that ac-company regular routines may be ready to use forms of expressive communication. For example, a boy who bounces in his wheelchair when his cap is put on is communicating that he understands that he will be going outdoors, and a girl who goes to the table when she is given her placemat to carry shows that she knows that it is mealtime. Responding to these object signals represents the beginning of communication with others.

Once anticipation is established, the understanding that one's behavior has a result is the basis of active communication. Many students are not capable of connecting a symbol, such as a word or picture, with an idea, but they are able to initiate communication with others and to enjoy the satisfaction of an interaction or some other pleasant outcome. One such student is Joey, aged 15, who enjoys physical activities like rocking, swinging, and rolling on the floor. Even though his cerebral palsy and mental retardation have affected his ability to express specific ideas through words or other symbols, he can clearly let his family and friends know what he likes and dislikes. A student teacher who observed Joey in his classroom one morning noticed that he communicated in these ways:

- ◆ Laughing and bouncing to ask for more swinging,
- ◆ Turning his head away from the aide who was feeding him when he did not want any more applesauce,
- ◆ Lifting his arm and reaching toward a radio that he wanted to listen to,
- ◆ Making voice sounds when he wanted his clothing to be changed, and
- ◆ Turning his head and smiling to greet the teacher of students with visual impairments when she came into his classroom.

In all these instances, Joey used a movement or a sound with the expectation of a response. He had clearly learned that people would respond when he produced some behavior, and by moving or making a sound he demonstrated some control over his world.

For students like Joey who have visual impairments and additional disabilities, connecting behaviors with results can be especially challenging. They may not be as easily aware of the presence of others because they may not see them and therefore may not try to communicate unless others make their presence known. Sometimes it is helpful for others to touch such a student on the hand to indicate their availability for communication and to use a similar signal to indicate that they are leaving.

In addition, these students may not know what objects or events are in their environment, so they may not have a subject to communicate. Thus, their own bodies may become a primary source of play, and they may not attempt to explore their environment and hence may find it unnecessary to learn to communicate with others to obtain wanted objects or experiences.

Alternative and Augmentative Forms of Communication

Some students with visual impairments and additional disabilities may not be able to use speech to communicate because of physical limitations, hearing impairments, or neurological difficulties. Instead, they may learn to communicate using nonstandard forms that can be symbolic or nonsymbolic. Symbolic communication involves the use of a spoken word, object, picture symbol, or written code to express meaning. Nonsymbolic communication takes place through gestures, facial expressions, and voice sounds. Several forms of communication can be considered on the basis of two factors: level of abstraction and physical capabilities. Sidebar 20.4 describes forms of communication that may be considered for students who cannot use speech.

SIDEBAR 20.4

Forms of Communication

NONSYMBOLIC FORMS

Nonsymbolic forms of communication are used by students who do not understand or remember a relationship between a symbol (picture or word) and an idea. At first, forms, such as the following, may be unintentional, but later the students know that communication sends a message to others:

- Body movements (for example, turns head away from food that he or she does not like).

- Eye movements (for instance, looks toward a toy he or she wants).

- Vocalization (for example, laughs while swinging or rocking).

- Facial expression (for instance, smiles in response to a smile).

- Gestures (for example, points at something he or she wants).

- Objects (for instance, hands an adult a ball to request a ball game).

- Photographs of real objects (for example, hands an adult a photograph of a glass of milk to request milk).

SYMBOLIC/LINGUISTIC FORMS

The student uses a symbol that is unrelated to an idea to represent that idea, such as these:

- Sign language (use of representational signs from a standard system of signing).

- Picture communication (use of a communication board to make a request).

- Tactile symbols (use of nonrepresentational tactile symbols).

- Braille.

- Print.

- Speech.

Families and professionals often express concern about whether the use of another communication form, such as sign language, will discourage a student from learning to speak. In fact, the use of another symbolic system, such as sign language, pictures, or an augmentative speech device, often stimulates the development of spoken language in students who are physically able to produce speech.

Forms of Communication for Students with Low Vision

Students with low vision who need an alternative form of communication often use visual forms (like pictures or photographs) that have been adapted for enhanced visual access. The following adaptations may be considered for selected forms of communication.

Sign Language. A variety of forms of sign language are used to communicate without words, including American Sign Language, Signed English, and fingerspelling (Prickett, 1995). Students who receive information through signs produced by others can often distinguish signs more clearly if a high-contrast background (such as the clothing worn by the person doing the signing or the wall or environment behind the signer) is provided. Lighting can also affect the visibility of sign language. Clear, steady lighting from above and just in front of the signer creates the best visual effect. The signer should not stand in a backlighted situation, such as in front of a window.

The distance at which the sign is presented should be considered as well. Many students with reduced visual acuities see more clearly when a sign is presented within 4 feet. However, students with visual field losses, such as those resulting from retinitis pigmentosa (associated with Usher syndrome), may see best if the signer stands about 6 feet away so they can view the entire sign within the limited visual field. Therefore, it is important to try several distances to allow a student to indicate which is the best viewing distance.

Smith and Levack (1996) stated that space and rate should also be considered for a student with

low vision who is receiving information through signs. Some signs are large and cover a larger area, whereas the letters represented in fingerspelling are small and occupy a restricted space. According to Smith and Levack, the rapid rate of some fingerspelling can make the letters difficult for students with low vision to see and decode. Although teachers of students with visual impairments are not typically taught sign language, many learn basic or advanced skills as needed when their students use signs to communicate.

Picture Symbols. Some students use simple pictures or drawings as a way of giving or receiving information. Visual features of contrast, color, and positioning also have an effect on the visibility of picture symbols. High contrast between the background and foreground often improves visibility, although the preference for light against dark or dark against light varies from individual to individual. When possible, representative symbols should incorporate the colors of the original object to provide a cue to identification.

For students who are just beginning to understand the representative function of pictures, photographs of familiar objects are the most effective for communication. A photograph should picture the real object as the student knows it and should show the object against a high-contrast background with nothing else in the photograph. Initially, the photograph can be presented along with the object. After the student has made the association between the photograph and the object, the picture can be presented with the object out of sight; for example, a photograph of a ball can be placed on the lid of a box that contains a ball.

Some professionals believe that the first pictures to be used for communication should be those drawn by the student (Writer, 1987). For example, the student may be assisted to draw around a spoon and then to use the drawing to request a spoon. This method may work if the student has the physical ability to draw and if his or her memory span is sufficient to recall the experience of drawing the real object. In this case, the symbolization depends more on memory than on the visual similarity of the drawing to the object. For example, when it is time to go to the gym, a student can remember that he drew a picture of the red ball that he always plays with when he gets to the gym. When shown the picture of the ball, he will associate it with the gym and understand where he is going next. The student is more likely to make this association if he goes to the gym each day and sees the picture every time he goes there.

After a student understands the representative nature of photographs or personal drawings, he or she may be ready to begin using a standardized system of picture communication. Students may select from an array of pictures or hand pictures to others as a way to make choices, refuse or request objects or activities, recall past experiences, or indicate future plans. These pictures may be arranged on a permanent background to create a communication board to allow the student to make selections by touching or pointing. If picture communication will be a long-term method of expressive communication for a student with low vision, the arrangement, size, and complexity of the pictures should be considered in relation to the student's visual ability.

Teachers and families often assume that large pictures are more appropriate for students with visual impairments than are small pictures. However, most students do not require images larger than about 2 inches, and large pictures can actually inhibit the efficiency of a student with physical disabilities because they require additional head and body movements to view them, and students may not be able to scan an array as easily. Specialists can evaluate the smallest size needed by preparing several sets of pictures and assessing a student's ability to identify pictures of each size.

Communication for Students Who Are Blind

Students who are blind and do not use speech to communicate may be able to receive and express information through several other systems: sign language, tactile symbols, and augmentative speech devices.

Sign Language.   A student who is blind will learn sign language by exploring manual signs made by others. To ensure that a student understands the intent of the signs and does not just imitate them, it is essential that the signs are used in an appropriate context. It is also crucial for a student to be able to touch the hands of others who are signing, so he or she can become accustomed to how signs are formed and when the signs are used to refer to things. Unlike a student who can observe sign language or hear speech, a student who will notice it by touch has fewer opportunities for receptive input.

When a family member and the teacher of students with visual impairments begin to teach sign language to a student who is blind, they should make sure that the student is aware of the presence of others by touching the student's hand to indicate that they are present and by using another signal when they are about to leave. Otherwise, the student may attempt to sign without anyone being there to respond and may become discouraged when no response is received.

Tactile Symbols.   When a student cannot learn braille because of physical difficulties, such as cerebral palsy, or because of mental retardation, one option is to teach the use of tactile symbols for gathering information. These symbols can include concrete symbols that use an object or part of an object to represent an event, action, or experience (for example, the wheel from a roller skate to represent roller skating or a small piece of a blanket to represent bedtime). A tactile symbol can be given to a student who is learning basic representation through symbols before the activity or event that it represents begins, so the student can anticipate what will happen next.

For students who understand abstract symbols and relationships between ideas, more complex tactile symbol systems can be developed. One such system can include classes of words or ideas that share a common characteristic; for example, in the system used by the Texas School for the Blind and Visually Impaired, symbols for days of the week all have backgrounds made of cardboard ovals with a textured material (Hagood,

1997). Although these complex systems are not standardized and are typically developed for and used by only one student or a small group of students, they provide a way of preserving information for students who cannot use conventional reading systems. For example, a student may carry the symbol cards for items needed at a store in her pocket or fanny pack so she can remember which items to buy. Another student may create a list of daily activities with symbol cards so he can check the cards to see what activity will come next.

No matter what communication system is appropriate for an individual student, it is important to link the symbols with meaningful events and activities. Because a visual impairment often limits a student's access to the environment, the student may not understand topics for communication. To communicate, the student must understand the need for a partner and must have a message to convey. Without this motivation, the use of symbolic communication is simply a game that has no relation to real activities.

Communication and Socialization

Some students with visual impairments and additional disabilities do not develop or expand communication because they do not enjoy or understand the process of interacting with others. These students may learn enough signs or words to request wanted objects or events, such as eating, swinging, or playing with a favorite toy, but they may not seek out others or spontaneously communicate for the satisfaction of exchanging messages or getting a response from others.

For these students, it is especially important that there are times of the day when activity routines are established on the basis of their own preferences. To structure a day that includes only functional activities imposed by others may actually discourage a student from communicating because she or he will associate the presence of others with the requirement to perform some unwanted activity. Pairing a favorite activity with the presence of another person helps the student associate a preferred event with another person.

A calendar box is one way to help a student anticipate a routine and make choices among activities. Developed by Van Dijk (1967) for students who were deaf-blind, a calendar box is typically a long box with an open side that is divided into sections to represent regular events in the day. An object is placed in each section to represent a specific event, and the student learns to anticipate the sequence of events by looking at or touching the next item in the box. Sometimes items can be used to communicate with others, as when a student hands an object to another person to represent an activity.

Communication is also more likely if turn taking is built into a routine by pausing and waiting for the student to respond, so the student has an opportunity to produce as well as receive communication. If the communication partner talks constantly or guides the student's hands frequently, the student will not understand the interactive nature of communication and will be a passive partner who waits for the other person to initiate and continue the routine.

MOVEMENT, ORIENTATION, AND MOBILITY

When a student is not independently mobile or cannot communicate his or her needs and preferences, some professionals may assume that O&M instruction is not appropriate. However, students can acquire a variety of skills that can give them some control over their ability to remain oriented and control how they are moved by others. In many cases, students with visual impairments and additional disabilities can benefit from direct instruction by an O&M specialist. In addition, consultant services by an O&M specialist can assist the educational team in shaping instructional and environmental adaptations that will increase a student's independence. For students with visual impairments and additional disabilities, O&M may encompass the following factors:

◆ Control over how one is moved: If the student is verbal, can he or she express preferences about movement or describe what is comfortable for him or her? If nonverbal, can the student receive touch or visual signals that indicate that he or she will be moved, and can the student express preferences nonverbally?

◆ Anticipation and sequence: Can the student use visual, tactile, or auditory cues or landmarks to anticipate where he or she is going? Can the student give directions to others or express preferences about destinations?

◆ Generalization: Can the student apply a concept learned in one setting (such as stop at the corner) to another place at another time?

◆ Initiation: Can the student initiate a sequence of movements, or does she or he require a cue from an adult or a tactile cue to begin moving?

◆ Safety: Does the student understand ways to avoid accidents and falls? Does the student recognize that some things can be dangerous or result in pain? Does the student have a way of requesting assistance in situations that may be dangerous?

Because the interplay of memory, communication, physical ability to move, and sensory awareness influences a student's O&M skills, the educational team needs to decide how each member will participate in the development of skills. For example, the speech and language specialist and O&M specialist may decide together how to build communication into the route to the cafeteria, but the O&M specialist will teach the student the route.

Concept Development

Students who have learning difficulties and mental retardation may take a longer time to understand concepts related to their own bodies, movement through space, and their relationship to the world around them. Therefore, these students may require a more concrete, consistent presentation of concepts to understand and apply them.

Understanding a concept begins with the repeated occurrence of an experience at a predictable time or place. For a student who is visually impaired and has additional disabilities, this repetition must occur frequently in the same time or place before he or she begins to understand the consistent features. Only then can the concept begin to expand into other settings or at other times. For example, a student may associate food only with mealtimes and may be distressed or bewildered if unfamiliar food is offered at an unexpected time. It may be a long while before the student accepts different presentations of food.

It is often assumed that a student needs to understand certain concepts to be able to perform a motor skill or a complex sequence of movements. However, understanding a concept should not be confused with using language. For example, a student may have a sense of which side to turn on the way to the cafeteria even if he cannot identify his left hand, and he may learn to use listening skills to avoid trees and telephone poles even if he cannot identify or describe these obstacles. When a student has significant developmental disabilities, too much emphasis on readiness and prerequisites can obscure recognition of what skills will be truly functional. O&M instruction should focus on what the student can learn to do that will enhance the student's physical control over the world, even if that new learning is not rapidly generalized into other situations. For example, if a student learns to locate the bathroom in her dormitory independently, she can go there unassisted. This skill is convenient for her and her caregivers, even if she cannot use the same concepts to locate other rooms that are more difficult to find.

Functionality

The principles of discrepancy analysis, described earlier in this chapter, can also be applied in deciding what skills to teach in O&M. The student's immediate travel and movement needs should be high priorities. These skills may include those that will enable the student to make decisions regarding travel, initiate travel to a destination, and assume more control over the environment on the basis of the ability to understand and communicate concepts related to self and the environment.

For a student who has difficulty with learning and memory, it is important to teach skills in the real settings in which they occur and, when possible, at the appropriate time of day. For example, a student who is learning to travel to the school bus from the classroom is more likely to learn this skill if it is taught at the end of the day when the school bus is waiting at the curb, rather than late in the morning when the student must return to the classroom after practicing the route.

Every person's day includes a variety of opportunities to expand one's movement. Locating rooms at home, negotiating stairways and doorways, traveling to school or between classrooms, going to the lunchroom, locating objects in the classroom, and traveling in the community to stores or playgrounds all involve multiple skills that can be analyzed in terms of a student's abilities. For example, in one elementary school, all the students travel to the lunchroom before lunch. The students with disabilities each practice a different skill on that route:

- ◆ Sam, an 8 year old, walks to lunch using a walker and practices identifying the landmarks, keeping a straight line of travel, and giving directions aloud to a classmate. Soon he may be ready to travel to the lunchroom occasionally by himself to meet another classmate and help set the table before lunch.

- ◆ Sandra, also 8 years old, uses her wheelchair to travel to lunch and works on following directions that Sam gives her and on increasing her speed of travel.

- ◆ Kathryn, a 10 year old, travels in a wheelchair that is pushed by another person. She is learning that she can give a signal with her hand to tell the person when she wants to move. She now understands that they are going to the lunchroom when a place mat is placed on her lap.

Adaptations for Students with Physical Disabilities

Some students with physical disabilities, such as cerebral palsy or spina bifida, may not learn to walk. They often use wheelchairs or travel chairs (custom-made chairs for moving students with physical disabilities) as a means of mobility. These students should also be taught skills that will allow them to participate in decisions about moving and being moved.

Some students with severe disabilities may depend on others to position them comfortably during activities and to move them from place to place. For these students, it is particularly important that their teams include physical and/or occupational therapists. Appropriate positioning ensures that students have control over head and eye movements, so they can make the best use of their vision. For most students, a symmetrical and upright position is the most physically and socially comfortable. To maintain the best position, these students may need adapted seating, such as molded chairs, sandbags or pillows placed behind them, prone or supine standing support, or specially designed seating that will enable them to participate comfortably in activities. The physical and occupational therapists, teacher of students with visual impairments, and other members of the educational team need to work together to decide how to position a student for educational activities. The teacher of students with visual impairments can provide information on how each position affects the student's ability to use vision and other senses.

A variety of adaptations can assist the student who uses a wheelchair to remain oriented and to participate in travel routines. The following may be considered:

- ◆ An adapted cane with an extended length and grips for the student who will hold it from a sitting position;

- ◆ Sound-contact devices on a wheelchair, such as "curb-feelers" on automobile tires, to give a sound signal when contact is made with a wall or object; and

◆ Electronic travel aids to provide auditory and tactile feedback regarding obstacles.

Even students who cannot propel wheelchairs can have some control over their travel. The use of a signal to indicate when they want to be placed in or to be removed from their wheelchairs, a buzzer or sound device on the wheelchairs to signal stop, or the skills to describe directions and preferences in words are all ways that students can direct how and when others move them from place to place.

Students with visual impairments and additional disabilities often benefit from O&M instruction, and they should have the opportunity to control their own movement and travel. The satisfaction of initiating movement, locating wanted materials, selecting and moving to a destination, and carrying out a routine can be achieved more efficiently with attention to O&M skills.

PREPARATION FOR ADULT OPPORTUNITIES

In this society success in adulthood is often measured by such milestones as attending college; supporting oneself by holding a job; and living independently, alone or with others. For many students with visual impairments and additional disabilities, successful adult life may not include these milestones. The end of school may be marked by a certificate of graduation, not a diploma, and postsecondary education may be supported employment or other options. Many professionals who work with students with visual impairments have never met adults with visual and additional disabilities and thus sometimes set goals that imply that a student will be successful only if he or she makes the same progress at the same rate as students without disabilities. For these reasons, it is important for the educational team and the student's family to develop a realistic vision of what they believe a comfortable and satisfying adult life will be for the individual with visual and additional disabilities.

Case Study: Henry

Henry, a 25 year old who is blind and has moderate mental retardation, has just moved into a group home with three other young men. Each morning, he goes to a local pizza restaurant for several hours to help wrap silverware and prepare tables, for which he is paid $7 an hour. In the afternoon, Henry works around the house where he lives, gardens, or goes shopping with one of his roommates and a home supervisor. One afternoon a week, he attends an art group at the local association for people who are blind, and several evenings a week, runs on the track at the local community college with two sighted young men who became his friends after they volunteered at his group home through a college course. On weekends, he often visits his parents or his sister's family, who live about a half hour away in the next town.

Henry is usually outgoing and pleasant, but sometimes he talks too much about things that do not make sense to others. He likes his life in the group home, although he wishes he had more work in the daytime, and he would like to have a girlfriend. He recently met a young woman of around his age at the association for people who are blind, and the supervisor has promised to take him to visit her at the supervised apartment where she lives.

In many ways, Henry's life is similar to that of nondisabled people of the same age. He can take care of his personal needs and do many jobs around his home, and he is a pleasant and sociable individual. However, he needs to have someone nearby who can assist him with difficult or abstract skills. He cannot go beyond his immediate neighborhood without supervision because he cannot remember routes well enough to travel by himself and cannot choose alternatives if something unexpected happens. The important people in his life are his family, his friends with disabilities, the workers in his home, and some friends who began as volunteers; his social network is restricted by his disabilities. Henry can be considered a successful young adult, and it is likely that his education has contributed to his achievements.

Transition Planning

For individuals with visual impairments and additional disabilities like Henry, it is vital that planning for the transition to adulthood begin early. According to law, an Individualized Transition Plan (ITP) is required by age 14, and in many instances planning should begin even earlier. It is difficult for families to plan for the future when they do not know what the options are for individuals with multiple disabilities. The first steps in planning include encouraging the family to talk about their concerns and to ask questions and arranging contacts with other families if they wish. It is also important to provide opportunities for family members to visit optional living arrangements, such as group homes, and workplaces that include people with visual impairments and additional disabilities.

The futures planning process should consider living arrangements and occupational opportunities. When possible, the individual with multiple disabilities should participate in the planning process. Even if she or he cannot describe her or his own needs and wants, caregivers, family members, and friends should be sure to consider the individual's abilities and preferences in considering future options.

Romer and Romer (1995) described one version of a futures plan, known as a "lifestyle" plan—a four-step plan that includes initial considerations, a personal profile, the creation of a desirable vision of the future, and the development of strategies to enhance accomplishments. Planning meetings, which involve family members, friends, acquaintances, and professionals, emphasize the student's strengths and preferences. Through discussion, drawing, and writing, members of the group consider what a satisfying future might be for the student. The process emphasizes the student's social network and personal preferences and extends well beyond the skill-based planning that characterizes the development of educational plans.

Many people with visual impairments and additional disabilities need lifelong support in caring for their basic needs, and their families have to make plans to provide this support. Support may come from family members, paid attendants in the home, or caregivers in another living arrangement. Family members may also need to complete the legal process of assigning guardianship after the student reaches adulthood, depending on the law in their states. Guidance in managing these decisions can be provided by individuals with specialized expertise, often through an agency that serves people with developmental disabilities.

It is important that a member of the educational team, in some cases the teacher of students with visual impairments, knows how to contact the agency that can provide this kind of assistance with planning. As was mentioned earlier, it is also crucial to begin that planning in early adolescence, at the latest, because there are limited living options for people with severe disabilities, and hence the student may have to wait years for an appropriate placement. (See Everson, 1995, for additional information on the futures planning process for people with visual impairments and additional disabilities.)

Skills Needed for Adult Life

Self-Care Skills and Home Management

The ability to take care of one's personal needs and to assume responsibilities in one's home setting are essential skills. For people with visual impairments and additional disabilities, mastery of these skills begins early through perceptions of routines and their purposes.

Self-Care Skills.   Feeding oneself and taking care of one's own toileting, personal hygiene, and dressing are the most essential skill areas because they are required of everyone, every day. When a student is visually impaired and has additional disabilities, he or she may need arranged opportunities to notice that others perform these routines. The following suggestions might be helpful:

◆ Provide instruction in these skills at a time when and in the location where they are appropriate. Dressing should be done when a change of clothes is needed, and mealtimes should be regularly scheduled and consistent.

♦ Use the hand-under-hand technique (in which a student follows the movement of the teacher's hands) instead of the hand-over-hand technique (in which the teacher physically shapes a student's hand to the task). This allows the student to maintain control of his or her own movements rather than learn that the guidance of others is necessary for successful completion of a task.

♦ Encourage students to do at least part of the routine (partial participation) when it is not possible for them to learn the entire task.

♦ Set up a system that will allow students who are blind to anticipate when events are going to take place. For example, handing a student an object cue before the routine begins can result in greater participation and acceptance because the student knows what to expect.

Home Management Skills.   Home management skills enable an individual to be a member of a household and to perform tasks that will assist others, as well as the person who performs them. These skills include cleaning, doing laundry, vacuuming, preparing food, getting the mail, taking out the trash, and paying the bills. The curriculum, *Independent Living* (Loumiet & Levack, 1993), presents a comprehensive inventory of skills needed for home management and daily living.

An individual with a visual impairment and additional disabilities may be able to learn to perform home management routines with or without assistance. Some people may need to have a task adapted because of their visual or other disabilities, as follows:

♦ Adding color or visual contrast to materials,

♦ Providing a tangible location for storing of materials, or

♦ Teaching the individual a system for searching for materials or exploring a given area.

It can be difficult for some people with mental retardation to know when to perform a particular routine. When they are also blind, typical cueing systems like bulletin boards, work charts, and schedule books may not be useful and, therefore, alternative methods of keeping a schedule, including a tactile calendar or variation of a calendar box, an audiotaped schedule, or memorization of activities based on days of the week, may be necessary. When possible, a system should be devised to allow a person to initiate the task independently, rather than to rely on another person for a reminder.

Occupational Skills

Most people assume that adult life includes a job out of the home or a home-centered occupation such as caring for the home and raising children. For many people with visual impairments and additional disabilities, this is also an appropriate assumption. Specific assessments of strengths and abilities, arrangements of early work experiences, and reinforcement of the importance of work increase the likelihood that an individual will be gainfully employed or productively occupied as an adult.

To prepare young people for adult occupations:

♦ Expose students to the variety of jobs that are available to them.

♦ Expect students to carry out elements of a task that are appropriate.

♦ Allow students to take responsibility for such things as putting away work materials, learning to change tasks at the direction of others, initiating a conversation with others, and learning to persevere with an unpleasant task. These skills will help students become productive adults.

There are increasing work opportunities for people with multiple disabilities. Some individuals are employed in their communities with little or no adaptation; others require adaptations, and the Americans with Disabilities Act specifies that reasonable accommodations shall be made on the basis of an individual's ability. Other people need specialized training to learn work roles, often through *supported employment,* a model in which an individual is accompanied on the job by a job coach, who teaches and assists him or her to complete a task. In a supported-employment situation, the individual works in a job setting where others are not disabled.

Another modified work option is an *enclave,* in which a small group of people with disabilities do a particular job in a setting with others who are not disabled. For example, a group of people may travel in a van to do lawn care, house cleaning, or moving, each member assigned a different section of the task according to his or her strengths and abilities. Some people with visual impairments and additional disabilities prefer *sheltered employment,* in which they work only with others who are disabled to carry out a particular task. Although this form of employment separates those with disabilities from the general public, it provides a structured and safe environment. Sheltered employment is sometimes the choice of those with special health or transportation concerns, and it continues to provide opportunities for people who might otherwise not work at all.

Some people with visual and additional disabilities cannot work rapidly or efficiently enough to be competitively employed but still need to be occupied (such as by working part time or in volunteer tasks or engaging in recreational activities) to maintain their self-esteem, interact with others, and establish routines. Visiting with others, joining with a group to listen to music, helping put election materials in envelopes, creating artwork, and sorting recycling materials are examples of productive activities that they can participate in. Even if payment is not received for these activities, friends and caregivers can ensure that the activities are rewarding through praise, social benefits, and the development of skills.

Social and Communication Skills

Regardless of their functional abilities, people with visual impairments and additional disabilities will have more satisfying adult lives if they are able to interact positively with others. For them to do so, it is vital that they learn basic social and communication skills. Making eye contact, touching a caregiver with the hand to make a request, or smiling in response to another person's laughter may gain attention from others and increase a person's social participation.

In addition to social and communication skills, having a balanced social network as an adult requires planning. Some school-age students with severe disabilities have most of their interactions with others at school, but their social contacts with others as adults are often limited to other residents in the immediate living setting, paid caregivers, and their families.

It is important for the educational team to consider opportunities for interaction in the community beyond the living and work settings. These opportunities can include regular networks, such as religious groups or clubs, as well as occasional contacts, such as at concerts or plays, or interactions with service people, like a cashier at a grocery store.

When an individual is blind and has additional disabilities, socialization may require greater effort and information because the person may not see people who could be potential acquaintances. A friend or family member may need to initiate an interaction and describe to a new acquaintance how the individual with a disability communicates and why he or she does not make eye contact. Once established, these relationships can be rewarding because they expand social contacts and add new ways of communicating for all people who are involved.

When an individual with a visual impairment and additional disabilities is verbal, the teacher of students with visual impairments should work with the person to learn ways to introduce himself or herself and to respond to others' questions or concerns about his or her disability. Because others may treat the person like a child, encouraging appropriate assertiveness is an important skill to teach an older student.

Adults with visual impairments and additional disabilities have needs, wants, and goals that are similar to those of adults without disabilities. Early planning for home management, regular daily occupation, and social interaction will result in a smoother transition from school and, ultimately, in a more satisfying adult life.

SUMMARY

People with visual impairments and additional disabilities are as diverse as any cross section of the general population. The teacher of students with visual impairments may be one of many members of the educational team, for these students often require services from a variety of professionals. In many cases, the specialist will be a consultant who makes recommendations for adaptations in instructional programming, and in other cases, he or she will work collaboratively with another team member to teach a skill. Since the learning of students with visual impairments and additional disabilities is influenced by physical and health factors, temperament, and motivation, direct instruction by the teacher of students with visual impairments may not be the most useful approach.

In the successful education of these students, the following factors are key:

- Assessing abilities and specifically documenting progress;
- Incorporating the student's and family's preferences into the educational plan;
- Assessing vision, when appropriate, and arranging adaptations related to the student's visual needs;
- Establishing regular routines as the basis for learning;
- Presenting new skills in attainable steps at an appropriate pace for the student;
- Using appropriate prompts and motivators; and

- Creating a long-term plan in which the individual's capabilities and life situation are realistically considered.

Students with visual impairments and additional disabilities are entitled to and can benefit from IEPs that address their general abilities and their visual impairments. They may learn more slowly than students without disabilities, have difficulty gathering information through the senses, organize information differently, communicate using forms other than speech, and may perceive the world differently. However, the teacher of students with visual impairments who is beginning to work with these students needs to keep in mind that all have the capacity to learn and that the educational team's primary challenge is to discover how to unlock that ability.

ACTIVITIES

1. Make a list of the factors that influence the quality of life of adults with disabilities (such as transportation, occupation, recreational opportunities, and social experiences). Visit three adults with visual impairments and additional disabilities and talk with them and others in the setting about their home and daily routines. Make a chart that compares the living situations of each of these adults with respect to each of those factors and the quality of life it provides.

2. Locate a student with a visual impairment and additional disabilities who is demonstrating behavioral difficulties in school. Get permission to observe that student for at least five days in class and keep a record of the inappropriate behaviors. As part of the record, include the following:

    - A specific description of the behavior being observed;
    - A record of how often it occurs;
    - A description of what occurs right before the inappropriate behavior;

◆ If appropriate, a record of how long the behavior lasts; and

◆ A description of what happens when the student behaves inappropriately.

Look at the pattern of occurrence of the behavior and identify any patterns of precipitating events (what happens before the behavior) and consequences that cause it to continue or to stop. Write a summary of the findings and give this information to the student's classroom teacher and parents.

3. Create several pictures of a familiar object that have different levels of complexity, detail, and color. For example, one picture could be a photograph with a contrasting background, another could be simple outline, and another could be a detailed drawing with color. If possible, include a picture from a standard communications system, such as the Mayer Johnson *Picture Communications Symbols* (1981–2000). Obtain or make eyeglasses to simulate a low vision condition. Ask several friends or classmates who have not seen the pictures to observe and identify the pictures while they are wearing the simulators. Keep a record of which pictures are the easiest to identify and which are the most difficult. Think about how to use this information in developing a picture communication system for a student with low vision and additional disabilities.

4. Visit a classroom in which there is a student with a visual impairment and additional disabilities. Make a two-column list. In one column, include all the materials that the student uses every day, and in the other column, identify which materials have been adapted for the student and why. Think about whether these adaptations are permanent (will always be needed) or temporary (can be faded after the student has mastered the task).

5. Interview several parents of students with visual impairments and additional disabilities. Ask them about the kinds of services their children receive and how these services have changed as their children have grown older. Ask them to describe which professionals have been the most helpful to them in raising their children and why.

6. Use two assessments that are designed for young students to evaluate a young student with a visual impairment and additional disabilities and compare the kind of information you get from each instrument. Decide whether the assessments are useful in gathering information about a student with multiple disabilities.

REFERENCES

Alberto, P. A., & Troutman, A. C. (1999). *Applied behavior analysis* (5th ed.). Upper Saddle River, NJ: Merrill.

Chen, D. (1997). *What can baby see? Vision tests and intervention strategies for infants with multiple disabilities* [Video]. New York: AFB Press.

Chen, D., & Dote-Kwan, J. (Eds.). (1995). *Starting points: Instructional practices for young children whose multiple disabilities include visual impairment.* Los Angeles: Blind Children's Center.

Cushman, C., Heydt, K., Edwards, S., Clark, M. J., & Allon, M. (1992). *Perkins activity and resource guide: A handbook for teachers and parents of students with visual and multiple disabilities.* Watertown, MA: Howe Press of Perkins School for the Blind.

Dote-Kwan, J. (1995). Instructional strategies. In D. Chen, & J. Dote-Kwan (Eds.), *Starting points: Instructional practices for young students whose multiple disabilities include visual impairment* (pp. 43–56). Los Angeles: Blind Children's Center.

Dunst, C. (n.d.). *Family-focused intervention rating scales.* Morganton, NC: Family, Infant & Preschool Program.

Everson, J. M. (Ed.). (1995). *Supporting young adults who are deaf-blind in their communities: A transitional planning guide for service providers, families, and friends.* Baltimore, MD: Paul H. Brookes.

Hagood, L. (1997). *Communication: A guide for teaching students with visual and multiple impairments.* Austin: Texas School for the Blind and Visually Impaired.

Hatlen, P. (1996). *Core curriculum for blind and visually impaired students, including those with additional disabilities*. Austin: Texas School for the Blind and Visually Impaired. Available on-line: http://www.tsbvi.edu/education/corecurric.htm

Huebner, K. M., Joffee, E., Prickett, J. G., & Welch, T. R. (1995). *Hand in hand: Essentials of communication and orientation and mobility for your students who are deaf-blind*. New York: AFB Press.

Koenig, A. J., & Holbrook, M. C. (1995). *Learning Media Assessment of Students with Visual Impairments*. Austin: Texas School for the Blind and Visually Impaired.

Langley, M. B. (1999). *ISAVE: Individualized Systematic Assessment of Visual Efficiency*. Lexington, KY: American Printing House for the Blind.

Let's eat [Video]. (n.d.). Los Angeles: Blind Children's Center.

Linder, T. (1990). *Transdisciplinary play based assessment*. Baltimore, MD: Paul H. Brookes.

Loumiet, R., & Levack, N. (1993). *Independent living: A curriculum with adaptations for students with visual impairments*. Austin: Texas School for the Blind and Visually Impaired.

Mar, H., & Cohen, E. (1998). Educating students with visual impairments who exhibit emotional and behavioral problems. In S. Z. Sacks & R. K. Silberman (Eds.), *Educating students who have visual impairments and other disabilities* (pp. 263–302). Baltimore, MD: Paul H. Brookes.

Nietupski, J., & Hamre-Nietupski, S. (1987). An ecological approach to curriculum development. In L. Goetz, D. Guess, & K. Stremel-Campbell (Eds.), *Innovative program design for individuals with dual sensory impairments* (pp. 225–253). Baltimore, MD: Paul H. Brookes.

Picture Communication Symbols. Mayer-Johnson, Inc. Copyright 1981–2000.

Prickett, J. G. (1995). Manual and spoken communication. In M. H. Huebner, J. G. Prickett, T. R. Welch, & E. Joffee (Eds.), *Hand in hand: Essentials of communication and orientation and mobility for your students who are deaf-blind* (pp. 261–287). New York: AFB Press.

Romer, L., & Romer, M. (1995). Developing educational plans to support valued lifestyles. In N. Haring & L. Romer (Eds.), *Welcoming students who are deaf-blind into typical classrooms* (pp. 105–132). Baltimore, MD: Paul H. Brookes.

Sacks, S. Z., & Silberman, R. K. (1998). *Educating students who have visual impairments with other disabilities*. Baltimore, MD: Paul H. Brookes.

Sauerberger, D. (1993). *Independence without sight or sound: Suggestions for practitioners working with deaf-blind adults*. New York: American Foundation for the Blind.

Smith, A. J., & Cote, K. S. (1982). *Look at me: A resource manual for the development of residual vision in multiply impaired children*. Philadelphia: Pennsylvania College of Optometry Press.

Smith, M., & Levack, N. (1996). *Teaching students with visual and multiple impairments: A resource guide*. Austin: Texas School for the Blind and Visually Impaired.

Stenquist, G., & Robbins, N. (1978). *Curriculum for daily living*. Watertown, MA: Howe Press at Perkins School for the Blind.

Step-by-step guide to personal management for blind persons (2nd ed.). (1974). New York: American Foundation for the Blind.

Van Dijk, J. (1967). The non-verbal deaf-blind child and his world: His outgrowth toward the world of symbols. In *Proceedings of the Jaaverslag Instituut voor Doven, 1964–1967* (pp. 73–110). Sint Michielsgestel, The Netherlands: Instituut voor Doven.

Welch, T. R. (1995). *Hand in hand: It can be done!* [Video]. New York: AFB Press.

Writer, J. (1987). A movement-based activity approach to the education of students who are sensory impaired/multihandicapped. In L. Goetz, D. Guess, & K. Stremel-Campbell (Eds.), *Innovative program design for individuals with dual sensory impairments* (pp. 191–223). Baltimore, MD: Paul H. Brookes.

RESOURCES

Suggested Resources for Teaching Students with Additional Disabilities

Resource	Type	Source	Description
Applied Behavior Analysis (Alberto & Troutman, 1999)	Textbook	Merrill	A comprehensive, practical easy-to-read text on the principles and strategies for using applied behavior analysis for students with special needs.
Core Curriculum for Blind and Visually Impaired Students, Including Those with Additional Disabilities (Hatlen, 1996)	Article	Texas School for the Blind and Visually Impaired Available On-line: http://www.tsbvi.edu/ education/corecurric.htm	An in-depth discussion of the expanded core curriculum and its delivery. Includes information on students with visual impairments and additional disabilities.
Curriculum for Daily Living (Stenquist & Robbins, 1978)	Curriculum	Howe Press at Perkins School for the Blind	Written for use with deaf-blind students; designed for use by teachers, child care workers, houseparents, or others who are responsible for helping students develop daily living skills. Includes goals and objectives.
Educating Students Who Have Visual Impairments with Other Disabilities (Sacks & Silberman, 1998)	Book	Paul H. Brookes	A practical text that brings together experts from a broad range of disciplines to assist educators in developing exemplary methods and strategies to meet the unique educational needs of students with visual and other disabilities. Realistic vignettes, sample assessment and data forms, and examples of specialized curricula help the professional design instruction that is meaningful and generalizable. *(continued on next page)*

Suggested Resources *(Continued)*

Resource	Type	Source	Description
Family-Focused Intervention Rating Scales (Dunst, n.d.)	Assessment instrument	Family, Infant, & Preschool Program, Western Carolina Center	A family-focused interactive tool for an ecologically relevant and functional approach to assessment and intervention with families of severely disabled children.
Hand in Hand: Essentials of Communication and Orientation and Mobility for Your Students Who Are Deaf-Blind (Huebner, Joffee, Prickett, & Welch, 1995)	Book	AFB Press	A textbook on the development, education, and transition to adult life for students with deaf-blindness. Addresses orientation and mobility (O&M) skills and teaching strategies. Lists resources.
Hand in Hand: It Can Be Done (Welch, 1995)	Videotape	AFB Press	Part of a package created by the AFB Deaf-Blind Project; designed to develop resources for educators of children who have both visual and hearing impairments. Emphasis on communication and mobility skills that are crucial to independence.
Independence Without Sight or Sound: Suggestions for Practitioners Working with Deaf-Blind Adults (Sauerburger, 1993)	Book	American Foundation for the Blind	A book on methods and techniques for teaching deaf-blind people, as well as an integrated study of the needs of deaf-blind people. Presents numerous examples from actual experience and discussions of practical applications. Includes sections on O&M training, street crossings, and teaching O&M to people with limited language skills, communication with strangers and the public, and a survey of dog guide schools.
ISAVE: Individualized Systematic Assessment of Visual Efficiency (Langley, 1999)	Assessment instrument	American Printing House for the Blind	A functional vision assessment tool developed for use with both sighted and visually impaired infants, the developmentally young, and other difficult-to-test and learners who are severely physically impaired.
Learning Media Assessment of Students with Visual Impairments (Koenig & Holbrook, 1995)	Book	Texas School for the Blind and Visually Impaired	A Learning Media Assessment should be completed for all students with visual impairments, including those with additional disabilities. It includes a special section on working with students with multiple disabilities.

(continued on next page)

Suggested Resources *(Continued)*

Resource	Type	Source	Description
Let's Eat (n.d.)	Videotape	Blind Children's Center	Describes the process of learning to eat and self-feed, for children with multiple disabilities and visual impairments.
Look At Me: A Resource Manual for the Development of Residual Vision in Multiply Impaired Children (Smith & Cote, 1982)	Book	Pennsylvania College of Optometry Press	An evaluation of vision in children with multiple impairments; also presents teaching strategies to help these children achieve their optimum levels of visual functioning.
Perkins Activity and Resource Guide: A Handbook for Teachers and Parents of Students with Visual and Multiple Disabilities (Cushman, Heydt, Edwards, Clark, & Allon, 1992)	Book	Howe Press of Perkins School for the Blind	A reference book on activities and teaching strategies for those who work with students with visual impairments and additional disabilities.
Starting Points: Instructional Practices for Young Children Whose Multiple Disabilities Include Visual Impairment (Chen & Dote-Kwan, 1995)	Book	Blind Children's Center	A textbook addressing the knowledge and skills necessary for teaching young children with multiple disabilities, including visual impairments.
Step-by-Step Guide to Personal Management for Blind Persons (1974)	Book	American Foundation for the Blind	A book that presents instructional objectives related to the area of daily living skills including identification of the goal behavior, the conditions under which such a behavior will occur, and the criteria for acceptable performance. Includes step-by-step procedures for achieving each objective.
Supporting Young Adults Who Are Deaf-Blind in Their Communities: A Transitional Planning Guide for Service Providers, Families, and Friends (Everson, 1995)	Book	Paul H. Brookes	A book that guides service providers, family members, and friends in providing transition services to young adults who are deaf-blind. Expresses the unique needs of the deaf-blind population and integrates best practices into their transition services.
Teaching Students with Visual and Multiple Impairments: A Resource Guide (Smith & Levack, 1996)	Book	Texas School for the Blind and Visually Impaired	A resource guide for teachers of students with visual and additional impairments. Focuses on the population of those students who function within the range of mental retardation. Addresses best practices, assessment, instruction, transition, cortical visual impairment, biobehavior, infants and toddlers, deaf-blindness, and much more.

(continued on next page)

Suggested Resources *(Continued)*

Resource	Type	Source	Description
What Can Baby See? Vision Tests and Intervention Strategies for Infants with Multiple Disabilities (Chen, 1997)	Videotape	AFB Press	A video on common vision tests and methods used with infants and young children with multiple disabilities; helps identify visual impairments that require early intervention services. Also addresses early intervention and strategies for working with families.

Contact information for each of the resources listed will be found in the Sources of Products, Materials, Equipment, and Services section at the back of this book.

CHAPTER 21

Presenting Information to the General Public

M. Cay Holbrook, Jo Ellen Croft, and Christine Kline

KEY POINTS

- Teachers of students with visual impairments routinely make public presentations about visual impairments as a part of their advocacy efforts.

- Teachers who effectively communicate with general education teachers, students, parents, and civic groups have a positive effect on their students' social adjustment and academic and social success.

- A well-prepared demonstration of adaptive materials increases sighted classmates' acceptance of students with visual impairments.

- Presentations by the teacher of students with visual impairments help general education teachers fulfill their role as primary instructors in standard content areas and encourage parents to participate more fully in their children's education.

- Presentations to civic groups may encourage members to support programs and learn more about students with visual impairments.

VIGNETTE

A bit nervously, Regina Bradley secured the two boxes to her luggage carrier and strapped the braillewriter on top. One box held an assortment of braille books, slates, paper, abaci, braille rulers, and a talking calculator. The other held a slide projector, a tray of slides, and a videotape. A coworker, Dennis Taylor, had told her that the Lions Club would probably contribute to the purchase of the computer software she hoped to buy, *if* she would speak to them about her work. Regina was determined to be persuasive.

Regina was relieved to find Dennis waiting for her in the foyer. He led her to the nearly-empty meeting room, where he introduced her to the club leaders who were already present. Regina unpacked her materials and set up the slide projector. The television set and VCR she had requested were present, and she slid the videotape she had brought into the machine and made sure it was working. Finally, Regina sat down and reviewed her notes one more time.

What did she want this audience to hear? Regina knew that many people did not even realize that children who are blind were being educated in their local schools. First, she wanted to show them the slides of her students: reading, writing, calculating, typing, cooking, climbing and sliding, and traveling independently with their canes. Regina was convinced that these pictures would elicit more interest than her words, no matter how eloquent. Next, she wanted to demonstrate a few of the tools used in educating children with visual impairments. While discussing education, she would describe the amount of braille material that she was able to produce manually. The videotape was brief, just a few minutes that showed a teacher preparing a print worksheet on a computer and quickly producing copies in regular print, large print, and braille. This was what Regina hoped for: Her supervisor of special education had found room in the budget for a braille printer, but suggested that Regina might be able to locate funds for the necessary transcription software on her own. Regina was certainly going to do her best.

INTRODUCTION

The prospect of public speaking can send even the most experienced educator into a panic. However, communicating with the public about visual impairments is an important responsibility of teachers of students with visual impairments. Public misperceptions have resulted in negative interactions for much of history. Even today, many people do not understand the implications of visual impairments for the education, recreation, employment, and lifestyles of people who are blind or have low vision.

Therefore, it is important for teachers of students with visual impairments to overcome any fear they may have of public speaking and agree to speak about visual impairments to a variety of groups. To be most effective, they need to plan their presentations carefully. This chapter offers general suggestions for making public presentations and a guide for preparing and presenting information about visual impairments to the following groups:

◆ Students, both the classmates of a student who is visually impaired and students who

do not have a classmate who is visually impaired.

◆ Parents, as part of a special program or a regularly scheduled support-group activity and as a presentation to a meeting of a school's Parent-Teacher Association to educate the parents of all students in a school about the program for students with visual impairments.

◆ General education teachers and other professionals, at school- or district-level in-service workshops and students in introductory special education classes in teacher-preparation programs at local universities.

◆ Civic groups, such as Lions Clubs and Optimists Clubs, to raise members' awareness of visual impairments or to encourage financial or other types of support for the program for students with visual impairments in the local school district.

ROLE OF THE TEACHER OF STUDENTS WITH VISUAL IMPAIRMENTS

As a part of their advocacy efforts, teachers of students with visual impairments are responsible for providing comprehensive, honest information about visual impairments to help sighted classmates, teachers, parents, and members of the general public gain a realistic understanding of the strengths and challenges of students who are blind or have low vision. Teachers of students with visual impairments are responsible for the following:

◆ Seeking opportunities to provide information to sighted students, teachers, parents, and members of the general public;

◆ Planning, organizing, and implementing public-awareness programs to increase the public's understanding of visual impairments; and

◆ Responding to specific requests to present information to various groups.

PRINCIPLES OF PUBLIC SPEAKING

The following general tips and suggestions may help teachers provide effective presentations to groups:

◆ Read books about public speaking to gain helpful ideas about successful public presentations.

◆ Listen critically to others as they make speeches to understand the techniques that work and do not work.

◆ Have a clear understanding of what a particular group expects, including the amount of time available and the goals of the presentation.

◆ Prepare the presentation well in advance and practice in front of a mirror or before family members.

◆ Arrive at the location of the presentation early to become comfortable with the room and check on necessary equipment.

◆ Greet people as they enter the room and ask them for information about the group.

◆ Avoid reading the presentation. Write notes on 3-by-5-inch cards that can be glanced at throughout the talk.

◆ Be sensitive to the amount of time allotted for the presentation and keep to the schedule.

◆ Be prepared to answer questions, but feel free to say, "I don't know" and follow up with information later, if necessary.

◆ Ask for feedback from the group's contact person, but also evaluate how the presentation was received and the changes that need to be made for the next presentation.

Although each presentation is unique, several issues must be specifically addressed in planning any presentation on visual impairments. These issues are deciding which information to present to a group, choosing materials and activities, encouraging the group to participate, using humor to make a point, including students in a presentation, getting to know the participants, and speaking with a partner. This section addresses all these issues.

Deciding Which Information to Present

The type of information presented to different groups may be the same, but the amount of information may be different, depending on the group and the goals of the presentation. To decide which and how much information to include, teachers of students with visual impairments may find it helpful to do these things:

◆ Ask a contact person for the group to provide information about the group's goals or expectations for this presentation and the nature of the audience (for example, members of a fund-raising group, classmates of a student with a visual impairment, parent-members of an advocacy or self-help group).

◆ Think carefully about the goals. Is this presentation to be merely informational, or are there other motives?

◆ Plan the specific presentation on the basis of the group's goals and expectations, but have other information available in case additional questions are raised.

Four major categories of information are generally included in public presentations: medical information, information about how students with visual impairments read and write, including an explanation of braille, information about orientation and mobility, and information about technology. Although other types of information may be covered, depending on the goals of the presentation, these four categories are standard. Table 21.1 presents some basic guidelines relating to these major categories of information for inclusion in presentations to different groups.

Table 21.1. Information Useful in Public Presentations to Various Audiences

Issue	Sighted Students	General Education Teachers	Parents	Civic Groups
Medical information	Generally not appropriate. Be prepared to answer questions but do not provide extensive information about medical conditions.	Present information about medical issues as it relates to the functional use of vision in the classroom (such as the need for increased lighting and decreased glare).	Parents are generally interested in their children's specific medical conditions. If medical issues are a major focus of the presentation, consider bringing an ophthalmologist or optometrist to the presentation.	Some information about medical conditions, especially on common eye conditions or conditions that affect older people, will be of interest.
Information about braille	Give children lessons on the braille code, particularly on decoding words in uncontracted braille. Transcribe students' names into braille.	Give teachers more in-depth information about braille, including the uncontracted braille code and general information about braille contractions and teaching braille reading and writing.	Provide honest and positive information on braille, including the benefits of using braille as a literacy tool and the need to provide rich, varied literacy experiences at home.	Provide information on the braille code and samples of braille and explain how to read numbers on elevator displays, for example.
Information about orientation and mobility	Provide information on and a demonstration of sighted guide techniques to classmates of a student who is visually impaired. Children often ask about dog guides.	Give teachers information about safety issues around the school and how to encourage students to be independent while ensuring their safety. Teach appropriate sighted guide techniques and address the need for specialized training in orientation and mobility.	Provide a full overview of orientation and mobility techniques to help parents understand the need for independent travel and information on the specific techniques their children will use throughout life.	Discuss general orientation and mobility, including proper sighted guide techniques and the use of long canes and dog guides.
Technology	Students are most interested in the technology being used in their classroom.	Discuss how technology can encourage the inclusion of students with visual impairments in general education classrooms, so teachers understand how to work with a student who is blind or visually impaired.	Discuss how technology is currently being used and how it can be used in the future to help their children in school and employment. Give examples of successful adults who are visually impaired to help parents understand the importance of technology.	Demonstrate the use of a closed circuit television for enlarging print, talking calculators, and sophisticated devices that translate print to braille.

Choosing Materials and Activities

Using authentic materials and creative activities enhances the effectiveness of any presentation. Teachers of students with visual impairments usually have a large and rich reservoir of materials from which to choose, and the length of the program, the expectations of the participants, and the objectives of the presentation will dictate which materials are best suited to a particular program. The following general suggestions for choosing materials and activities may be helpful:

◆ Choose materials that visually, tactilely, or graphically illustrate the purpose of the presentation. For example, for a speech to a group of school administrators about the increased number of students in a particular school district, choose simple maps and charts that illustrate the areas of need.

◆ Place participants as close to the classroom situation as possible by bringing typical materials used by students who are visually impaired. Slick, high-tech materials are not essential. Teacher-made materials not only add warmth and a personal touch to a pre-sentation, but demonstrate some of the most clever and useful materials available. On the other hand, having a student demonstrate a new piece of technology may be an effective way to gain the participants' attention.

◆ Use videotapes and slides to keep the participants in touch with the students. Professional-quality films are not necessary. Films showing students using adaptive equipment, demonstrating skills in a variety of settings, working with professionals from other agencies, and having fun together are effective, as are those that depict interdisciplinary cooperation or a team approach.

◆ Keep handouts and other printed materials short. A one- or two-page sheet with general information about services provided to individuals of all ages with visual impair-ments in a local area is handy in almost any situation. Even though the presentation may focus on the education of children, participants often have questions about older people with visual impairments. This is a quick way to address a real concern without taking too much time from the topic at hand.

Encouraging the Group to Participate

Encouraging the group to participate in the presentation helps maintain interest and ensures greater involvement in the program for students with visual impairments. To encourage group participation, teachers may want to do the following:

◆ Set the tone for the presentation from the beginning. If the participants are going to have opportunities to interact throughout the presentation, begin the speech by encouraging them to talk. Otherwise, they may settle into the role of "listener" and may be reluctant to contribute when given the opportunity to do so.

◆ Use broad, inclusive questions in the introduction of the presentation. Open-ended questions allow the participants to become involved in setting the stage for the presentation.

◆ Ask the participants to introduce themselves. Consider asking them to describe any experiences they have had with people who are visually impaired or experiences they think were especially significant in their education. Such responses can then be referred to later in the presentation.

◆ Use interactive activities for small groups. If possible, organize participatory activities at tables and place instructions on a 3-by-5-inch card and a volunteer facilitator at each table. Make sure that interactive activities are fun and informative, rather than frustrating, humiliating, or overwhelming.

The key is to showcase how much can be accomplished through the development of skills, teamwork, and access to adaptive materials. If it is not possible to have small-group activities use in-person or video-taped demonstrations with large groups.

◆ Answer questions throughout the presentation. Sometimes the most basic questions are the ones that many participants have on their minds. Open and frank responses to questions often put people at ease to ask more questions. Although humor is an excellent tool for public speaking, it is best not to be humorous when answering questions because the use of humor may embarrass the persons who asked the questions.

Using Humor

All people enjoy listening to a presentation that makes them smile, but using humor in presentations can be tricky. Although self-deprecating humor is considered an asset in public speaking, students should always be depicted in the most capable, respectful, and advantageous light. Sarcasm and other forms of humor that are hurtful to others are never appropriate. Warm, funny stories are often the best way to show a school or students in a favorable light.

Including Students in a Presentation

If students are to be included in the presentation, it is advisable to go over the agenda with them beforehand. Even the most delightful, well-behaved students may behave unexpectedly when faced with a new audience. Watching students dissolve into giggles and horseplay while attempting to upstage one another completely disrupts a presentation and it can be disconcerting to both the participants and the speaker. The following suggestions may be helpful for involving a student in a presentation:

◆ Discuss appropriate behavior with the student before the presentation.

◆ Develop a system to indicate when it is time to complete the presentation, for example, a slight touch on the student's hand could indicate that there are two minutes left.

◆ Role-play the presentation with the student ahead of time.

◆ Make sure to talk with the student's parents and to obtain proper parental consent for the student's participation.

Getting to Know the Participants

Different groups listen to and expect different types of information. Whereas some are interested in the number and location of students, others simply want to know about the educational program for students who are visually impaired. The group's contact person can provide important information about the goals of the group so the presentation can be planned to meet those goals. To get a sense of the needs and interests of the group, it is best to arrive before the meeting to have time to speak briefly with the contact person, to determine how best to arrange the presentation materials, and to speak with the participants as they arrive.

Speaking with a Partner

Speaking with a partner often strengthens a presentation. Teachers of students with visual impairments who are nervous about speaking to the public find that working with a colleague may help relieve some of the strain. Even the most well-prepared teacher may worry that he or she will forget a crucial element of the presentation. It may put a speaker at ease to know that a partner will help cover the material and fill in the gaps. Some speakers find that working in pairs adds humor to the program, since the partners often play off each other's sense of humor.

Working with a partner may give balance to a teacher's speaking style. For the teacher who tends to speak fast and with an enthusiasm that occasionally takes on a strident tone, it may be beneficial to choose someone with a slower pace and a softer delivery. Teachers often find that choosing an orientation and mobility (O&M) specialist or a rehabilitation counselor for a speaking partner adds depth to their presentations. The important point is for a speaker to find someone with whom he or she feels comfortable. Partners who appreciate each other complement and bring out the best in each other's approach to public speaking.

SPEAKING TO STUDENTS

Misconceptions of blindness and low vision lead some people to have negative attitudes toward persons who are visually impaired. These attitudes may surface when a student who is visually impaired is placed in a general education classroom in a public school. Problems may occur not only for the student, but for the general education teacher and the sighted students in the classroom. If the general education teacher and students are properly educated about visual impairments, many of these problems may be reduced or eliminated (Scheffers, 1982).

Information on visual impairments may be given in a presentation or series of presentations at the beginning of the school year that focus on dispelling myths about visual impairments and creating an atmosphere that is conducive to the sighted students' acceptance of the student who is visually impaired in the classroom. When the general education teacher and students develop an appropriate awareness and understanding of visual impairments, they will adapt more easily to the inclusion of the student with a visual impairment.

In making a presentation to a class in which a student who is visually impaired is present, it is important to include information on the specific adaptations the student is using and to make sure that the presentation is designed and implemented to meet the student's unique needs. For instance, if the student's primary reading medium is braille, it is important to incorporate braille and blindfold activities into the presentation, and if the student has low vision, it is essential to include simulation activities and experiences with low vision devices. Sighted students are naturally inquisitive about the adaptive equipment and devices that the student who is visually impaired may use in the classroom. Addressing this curiosity helps create a more comfortable and accepting work environment for all the students.

To encourage the student who is visually impaired to participate in a presentation, it is important to include him or her as much as possible in every aspect of it—from the planning stage through the actual presentation—so he or she feels a part of the presentation and is comfortable with the topics that will be discussed. The degree to which the student participates in the actual presentation will depend on the student's age, strengths, and preferences. Students who are reluctant to participate should be encouraged, but not forced, to do so. Many students become more interested in participating when the plan begins to take shape. The student's parents and other family members should be told about the presentation and asked to participate, when appropriate. Their inclusion will enhance the presentation and may help the student feel more comfortable.

When planning a presentation in a classroom, it is important to take into account the students' ages, the size of the group, and the students' knowledge of visual impairments in deciding on the length of the presentation and how much information to include. For young students, it may be more effective to do a series of short presentations if time allows. In any case, determine the objectives of the presentation and plan accordingly. The following are some suggested strategies that may be incorporated into a classroom presentation:

Begin with a Questionnaire. A short questionnaire or a few questions asked orally will give an idea of the students' knowledge of people with visual impairments. Asking questions at the beginning may also encourage the students to participate and may stimulate discussion. After the activities and demonstrations are presented, return the original questionnaires to the students and discuss whether and how their attitudes and feelings have changed as a result of their experiences. The student who is visually impaired should participate in the final discussion and help answer questions to make the other students aware of appropriate interactions.

Read a Story or Show a Videotape.   Such activities are a good introduction to a presentation and stimulate the students' interest. There are many excellent books and videotapes on visual impairments for children of all ages (see the Resources at the end of this chapter for some examples).

Ask the Student Who Is Visually Impaired to Participate.   The student may describe his or her visual condition, discuss how to approach or interact with him or her in the cafeteria line or on the playground, and give suggestions on how and when to offer assistance. These suggestions will make the other students more comfortable. The student can also explain that people need to identify themselves orally during conversations and speak directly to him or her. If the student is reluctant to speak in front of the class, he or she may choose to make a personal videotape that can be shown to the class or, if the school has the technology, to the entire student body simultaneously. This strategy seems to be especially appealing to older students. Before the student makes the videotape, he or she may wish to consult the media specialist in the school for tips on how to produce it. In this situation, as in any in which a student is involved, it is critical to obtain the appropriate parental permissions.

Incorporate Blindfold Activities.   Appropriate activities for a blindfold experience may include identifying coins, practicing the sighted guide techniques, locating a dropped object, listening to a story being read aloud, or trying to follow a simulated class lecture. In any simulation activity, the teacher of students with visual impairments must make sure that there is appropriate assistance for the students who are blindfolded and explain to the students that their experiences vary greatly from those of a student who is visually impaired. Some professionals avoid blindfold activities because they think that a frightening or uncomfortable experience while blindfolded will have a negative impact on the attitudes of students who are sighted.

Have Students Practice the Sighted Guide Technique.   The teacher of students with visual impairments first demonstrates the technique to the class and then groups the students in pairs, with one student blindfolded and the other serving as a sighted guide. The students can then practice traveling around the classroom or later extend their travels to the immediate campus area. Students participating in blindfold experiences should be closely supervised throughout the activity. This is important to ensure the safety of the students and will allow the teacher to have more control over the learning experience. It may be effective to give the pairs an assignment, such as to drink from a water fountain or to wash hands. Afterward, the specialist can discuss with the class how a cane or dog guide helps persons who are visually impaired travel safely and independently.

Use Simulation Goggles.   Simulation goggles roughly duplicate various eye conditions. When they are used, each sighted student can be given an opportunity to perform tasks (such as copying information from the chalkboard, reading a short paragraph, locating a page in a book, doing a crossword puzzle or word-find activity, and locating a specific city on a map). The students can also try reading large-print books and using some low vision devices, such as inexpensive magnifiers, while wearing the goggles. During this activity, the teacher of students with visual impairments can tell the sighted students about the equipment that the student who is visually impaired is using in the classroom and discuss the many things students can see even though their vision is limited. If vision simulators are not readily available, they may be easily constructed at a reasonable expense (see Sidebar 21.1 for suggested materials and the procedure for making simulators).

Making Vision Simulators

MATERIALS NEEDED

Welding Cup Goggles

Buy welding cup goggles with interchangeable lenses from a local welding supply store.

Clear Plastic Lenses for the Goggles

Purchase at least 12 sets of lenses from the welding supply store. Interchange the lenses in the goggles to simulate a variety of eye conditions.

Materials to Simulate Eye Conditions

- White, clear, pink, or red nail polish;
- Waxed paper;
- Black construction paper; and
- Quick-drying glue.

PROCEDURE

Apply any of the materials listed to the clear plastic lenses to create approximations of different eye conditions. Polishes may be used to simulate reduced activity or hemorrhaging, waxed paper and plastic wrap for reduced acuity (one layer approximates 20/100; 2 layers, 20/200), and black construction paper for field restrictions or scotomas. Remove the glass lenses that come with the goggles and replace them with the simulated plastic lenses.

Have the Students Explore Braille Reading and Writing. Students of any age find the braille code fascinating and motivating. Start with braille alphabet sheets that identify each letter and the corresponding dot numbers and then incorporate braille activity sheets that involve decoding into the lesson (see Figure 21.1 for an example). Other activities may include a demonstration of and practice with the Perkins braillewriter and brailling each student's name. Students' names can be written in braille by the specialist or by the student who is visually impaired.

Collaborate with the General Education Teacher to Set Up a Braille Center. This center may include additional decoding sheets, braille bingo games, or braille flash cards. A classroom display of various types of braille materials would also be interesting. A braille bulletin board inside or outside the classroom is an informative display and may encourage students who are sighted to learn some of the braille code so that they can exchange simple notes with the braille reader in their class.

The teacher of students with visual impairments has a unique opportunity to be a bridge between the student who is visually impaired and his or her sighted classmates. Appropriate training and support encourage teamwork among students and foster a positive environment in the classroom. Education and communication are essential for appropriate social interactions and the ultimate success of a student who is visually impaired in a general education classroom.

Many teachers have developed excellent resources for their personal files to help in planning and implementing classroom presentations. One example that has been published is Scheffers (1982), who presented a series of flexible lesson plans to be used in general education classrooms that can be adapted for various age groups.

SPEAKING TO TEACHERS

As was mentioned earlier, teachers of students with visual impairments generally present information on visual impairments to general education teachers at faculty meetings, inservice sessions, and educational team meetings at school and to preservice teachers in university courses

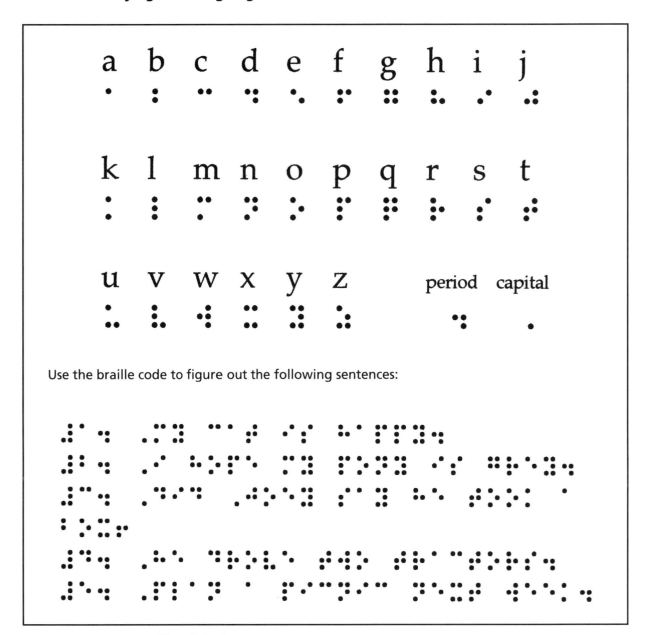

Figure 21.1. The Braille Alphabet

on general special education. Although the purposes of the presentations to these groups are different, the information presented is similar.

In contrast to the purposes of speaking to students or to members of civic groups, the primary purpose of a presentation to teachers is to provide information on appropriate adaptations and modifications and the teachers' responsibilities (mandated by the Individuals with Disabilities Education Act, IDEA) for educating students who are visually impaired. These presentations also set the stage for communication between general education teachers and the teacher of students with visual impairments. Both general education teachers and preservice teachers are likely to ask pointed questions about how to provide effective instruction to students who are visually impaired in an inclusive educational environment. The following are suggested topics to be included in these presentations.

Various Eye Conditions.   It is useful to describe a variety of eye conditions that students may have and that may result in individual functional difficulties in the classroom. The different modifications of classroom materials, activities, and environments that students with specific eye conditions may need can also be explained. For example, one student may require increased lighting and another may need decreased lighting. Presentations to regular education teachers should address the needs of the age groups of students in the teachers' classrooms. For instance, a presentation to preschool teachers should focus on the needs of preschool children who are visually impaired. Presentations to preservice teachers may include general suggestions that cross over age levels.

General Issues.   In presentations to preservice teachers, it is helpful to speak about general issues in the education of children who are visually impaired (e.g., the importance of specialized instruction for these students, the role of itinerant teachers, and procedures for obtaining accessible materials) and the need for qualified teachers of students who are visually impaired. A list of local resources can also be provided.

Specific Functional Concerns.   General education teachers may have basic questions about daily routines, such as movement to and from the cafeteria and bathroom, adaptations to and modifications of classroom activities, and communication of grades and feedback for assignments. Information about such matters is therefore generally welcome.

Role of the General Education Teacher.   The importance of communication with and the timely provision of materials in accessible formats to students with visual impairments needs to be stressed. The need for teachers to attend conferences and meetings pertaining to the students' educational needs is a topic of importance as well.

Literacy.   It is helpful to describe the braille code and how students use it to read and write. The importance of providing a rich literacy environment for students who are visually impaired should be emphasized and strategies for including braille in classrooms can be presented. Here are some strategies for introducing general education teachers to appropriate classroom adaptations and modifications:

- ◆ Have the participants practice using magnifiers to read a variety of materials (such as maps, dictionary and encyclopedia entries, problems in mathematics textbooks, and worksheets) in the different print sizes typically used in a classroom. Ask the participants to locate cities on a map, find words in a dictionary, or read a short paragraph in an encyclopedia using the magnifiers.

- ◆ Have the participants read signs with a telescope or monocular and practice the necessary tracking skills. For example, place a printed mock menu on a distant wall and ask the participants to use the monoculars to identify the prices of three items on the menu.

- ◆ Teach the participants to use an adapted tape recorder effectively. Include a short audiotaped passage from a textbook and an instruction card explaining the basic operations of the recorder. Ask the participants to answer three comprehension questions after they have listened to the selection.

- ◆ Introduce the braille code by providing each participant with an instruction card showing the braille alphabet and having each person braille one line using a braillewriter or a slate and stylus. Then pass the brailled sentences around so the participants can practice reading what the other participants have written.

SPEAKING TO PARENTS

Teachers of students with visual impairments often speak to groups of parents in programs presented to parent-support groups, at meetings for special camps, and in informational sessions. One major difference between these presentations and presentations to students and civic groups is that groups of parents typically have a great deal of knowledge about visual impairments. Therefore, it is especially important to find a group's goal or expectations for the presentation beforehand. Many parents have special interests that are based on the personal issues they are facing. In making presentations to parent groups, teachers of students who are visually impaired may want to do the following:

- ◆ Clearly state their qualifications, so the parents are well aware that the specialists are not physicians and cannot make medical recommendations. Specialists should also indicate how long they have been working with students who are visually impaired and their special areas of interest and acknowledge the expertise of parents in the group.

- ◆ Focus on what parents can do to foster their children's development (such as reading to their children and providing varied opportunities that help the children develop concepts). Stress the importance of parents' and other family members' involvement in the children's education and the need for consistent experiences in school and at home. Provide opportunities for parents to learn braille.

- ◆ Be positive and optimistic but realistic. In most groups, some parents have gathered a great deal of information on their own, others are in the process of doing so, and still others are just beginning to gather information. Because of this variety, teachers will need to respond honestly to parents' questions and concerns while encouraging them to continue exploring issues on their own.

- ◆ Allow plenty of time for questions after the presentation and give everyone who wants to a chance to speak. If a parent seems to have extensive questions, make arrangements to speak with him or her after the presentation. Speakers need to let parents know if they do not know the answer to a question and follow up with additional information, when possible.

- ◆ Give the parents a list of as many resources as possible that they can use to obtain further information.

SPEAKING TO CIVIC GROUPS

Civic groups or clubs generally function as service organizations and often help fund or raise money for special projects. Their support of educational programs has given many teachers of students with visual impairments opportunities to develop or purchase an array of specialized materials beyond the limit of their school budgets. By speaking to civic groups, specialists also establish an important link to their local communities, thus giving them and their students an opportunity to share their accomplishments, goals, and concerns and to help people in the community gain a greater awareness of the many challenges these students face in their local schools and about the schools' educational programs for these students.

Teachers of students with visual impairments can gain the interest and support of a civic group by attending its meetings once or twice a year. Most presentations to civic groups are part of larger group meetings and occur at the end of the meeting. Since they are often limited to 15 to 30 minutes, they need to be succinct and to focus on one or a few issues. Slides and video shows, demonstrations by students, and information on visual impairments are examples of appropriate ways to present information.

Establishing and maintaining contact with one or more members of a local civic group will strengthen the relationship between the teacher of students with visual impairments and the group and keep the specialist apprised of the group's interests and activities. Writing a thank-you note to a group after an engagement is essential for maintaining a relationship with the group. The following are some strategies that teachers of students with visual impairments can use for establishing relationships with and when speaking to civic groups:

- ◆ Give a brief progress report for the year or period since the last presentation. Present a slide show of the activities in which the students have been involved during that period. Be sure to feature books and materials that the civic group has funded.

- ◆ Go over plans for the future, projects to be considered, and goals to be achieved.

- ◆ Feature students in the engagement if possible and appropriate. Members of civic groups usually enjoy meeting students.

- ◆ Demonstrate the use of such mobility devices as telescopes and canes, as well as proper sighted guide and cane techniques, preferably with a student or students who are present.

- ◆ Have the students demonstrate technology or show videos of students using the devices. The students can explain how they use these devices in the classroom and how technological devices and other adaptive materials have improved their independence or strengthened their literacy skills. This approach promotes the students' understanding and appreciation of their achievements and improves their communication skills.

- ◆ For annual presentations, develop a yearly theme or topic (such as the Ever-Increasing Role of Technology in the Lives of Students with Visual Impairments, the Essential Role of General Education Classroom Teachers, or Mobility Issues for Active High School Students). Keep a card file of topics or themes, noting the date and the groups to which they are presented.

- ◆ If funding is to be considered, present a brief list of items, stating their prices and functions of technological devices or little-known items. If a local civic group donates a specific amount each year, it may not be necessary to include a written proposal; in such a case, it is a good idea to send a list of items to the club after they have been purchased.

- ◆ Write a thank-you note right after the engagement, expressing appreciation for the opportunity to share information with the group and for any support the group has provided.

- ◆ Inform the local school district of any funding proposals that the civic club is considering. School officials are more comfortable learning about funding for school items from teachers than from outside sources.

- ◆ In a funding proposal, state which items on a list of wanted items are priorities, so the civic group can choose items that are within its budget. A group is rarely able to fund an entire wish list.

- ◆ Invite members of the civic group to visit the school, so they can gain firsthand experience with the technological and adaptive devices and see adapted maps, graphs, and charts.

- ◆ Encourage students to get involved in the projects of civic or other community groups, either on their own or through the school's service groups, so they can learn that being givers is just as important as being receivers and the members of these groups can gain a fuller understanding of what the students can do.

EVALUATING THE PRESENTATION

After every speaking engagement, it is advisable to evaluate the presentation. One way to do so is to obtain feedback from the participants that can

Date: _____

	EXCELLENT	GOOD	AVERAGE	FAIR	POOR
Usefulness of the information	5	4	3	2	1
Preparedness of the speaker	5	4	3	2	1
Encouragment of participation	5	4	3	2	1
Manner of presentation	5	4	3	2	1
Organization of materials	5	4	3	2	1

The most useful aspect of the presentation was

Comments

What additional information would you like to have about blindness or low vision?

Figure 21.2. Sample Evaluation Form

be used to improve one's delivery and organization of speeches, develop new materials, and plan future representations.

Although presentations to the public are often not formally evaluated, some type of assessment should follow each speaking engagement. The following are some ideas for informally evaluating presentations:

◆ Write your own ideas in a spiral notebook immediately after each presentation (e.g., "Spend more time on uses of braille," or "Next time bring a slate and stylus").

◆ Record the presentation on a small audiotape recorder. Several days after the presentation, listen critically to the tape and make notes of necessary changes to content or format.

◆ Ask the group's contact person for constructive comments.

◆ Ask a colleague to attend the presentation and comment on the content, organization, and delivery of the material presented.

The use of a short evaluation form is appropriate for structured educational engagements. For example, when speaking to a group of teachers at a workshop or a group of principals or superintendents at a monthly meeting, ask the participants to complete a short evaluation form at the close of the program. Evaluation forms can be distributed either at the beginning of the program, along with other written material, or just after the closing remarks.

In an inservice training model developed by Morgan (1995), participants were given an evaluation form to assess the knowledge, preparedness, and the manner of speaker. A similar evaluation form is presented in Figure 21.2 for use in public speaking engagements.

SUMMARY

Providing information to the general public is an important responsibility of teachers of students with visual impairments. By providing honest, enthusiastic presentations, specialists can foster a fuller understanding by sighted students, general education teachers, parents, and members of community groups of the strengths and challenges of students who are visually impaired. Specialists who thoughtfully prepare and deliver these presentations will increase the public's awareness and acceptance of people with visual impairments.

ACTIVITIES

1. Plan and present a 20-minute speech to a civic group or class in a school about students who are visually impaired.

2. Create a slide or videotape show to be presented to civic groups about a special program for students who are visually impaired (such as a summer camp or recreational activity).

3. Create a series of handouts that could be used in public presentations to illustrate the braille code.

4. Survey local civic organizations about their requirements for presentations.

REFERENCES

Davidson, M. (1991). *Louis Braille: The boy who invented books for the blind.* New York: Scholastic.

Lundell, M. (1995). *A girl named Hellen Keller.* New York: Scholastic.

Monkhouse, B. (1991). *The complete speaker's handbook.* New York: Barnes & Noble Books.

Moore, E. (1996). *Buddy, the first seeing eye dog.* New York: Scholastic.

Morgan, E. (1995). *A national inservice training model for training early interventionists in a low incidence disabling condition: Visual impairment.* Logan: Project VIISA (Vision Impaired In-Service in America), Utah State University.

The new what do you do when you see a blind person? [Video]. 2000. New York: AFB Press.

Not without sight [Video]. (1975). New York: American Foundation for the Blind.

Oh, I see! [Video]. (1991). New York: American Foundation for the Blind.

Out of left field [Video]. (1984). New York: American Foundation for the Blind.

Scheffers, W. (1982). A special education introduction for normally sighted students. In S. Mangold (Ed.), *A teachers' guide to the special educational needs of blind and visually handicapped children.* (pp. 136–150). New York: American Foundation for the Blind.

The seven minute lesson [Video]. (1978). New York: American Foundation for the Blind.

Torres, I., & Corn, A. L. (1990). *When you have a visually handicapped child in your classroom: Suggestions for teachers.* New York: American Foundation for the Blind.

What do you do when you see a blind person? [Video]. (1971). New York: American Foundation for the Blind.

RESOURCES

Suggested Resources for Presenting Information

Resource	Type	Source	Description
Buddy, the First Seeing Eye Dog (Moore, 1996)	Children's book	Scholastic	A description of the early days of using guide dogs, intended for ages 7–9.
The Complete Speaker's Handbook (Monkhouse, 1991)	Book	Barnes & Noble Books	Simple suggestions for giving effective speeches.
A Girl Named Helen Keller (Lundell, 1995)	Children's book	Scholastic	An account of the life of Helen Keller. This book is a part of the Hello Reader! Series intended for ages 6–8.
Louis Braille: The Boy Who Invented Books for the Blind (Davidson, 1991)	Children's Book	Scholastic	An account of the life of Louis Braille and his invention of the braille code, intended for ages 7–10.
The New What Do You Do When You See a Blind Person? (2000)	Video	AFB Press	An updated version of the classic video that deals with misconceptions about people who are visually impaired.
Not Without Sight (1975)	Videotape (20 minutes)	American Foundation for the Blind	An overview that describes the major types of visual impairment and their causes and effects on vision, while camera simulations approximate what people with each impairment actually see.
Oh, I See! (1991)	Videotape (7 minutes)	American Foundation for the Blind	An explanation that shows what it means to have a visual impairment and how elementary and high school students with visual impairments function in school settings.

(continued on next page)

Suggested Resources *(Continued)*

Resource	Type	Source	Description
Out of Left Field: (1984)	Videotape (17 minutes)	American Foundation for the Blind	A resource that illustrates how children who are visually impaired are integrated with sighted children in a variety of recreational and athletic activities.
The Seven Minute Lesson (1978)	Videotape (7 minutes)	American Foundation for the Blind	A brief introduction to the basic techniques used when acting as a sighted guide for a person who is visually impaired.
A Special Education Introduction for Normally Sighted Students. In: S. Mangold (Ed.), *A Teachers Guide to the Special Educational Needs of Blind and Visually Handicapped Children.* (Scheffers, 1982)	Book Chapter	American Foundation for the Blind	A chapter that contains a comprehensive unit of lesson plans to teach students who are sighted about blindness.
What Do You Do When You See a Blind Person? (1971)	Videotape (14 minutes)	American Foundation for the Blind	Humorous treatments of the myths and misconceptions about people who are visually impaired.
When You Have a Visually Handicapped Child in Your Classroom: Suggestions for Teachers (Torres & Corn, 1990)	Pamphlet	American Foundation for the Blind	A listing of information of importance to general education teachers such as how to recognize symptoms of visual impairments, special devices that will be used in the classroom, and simple explanations of O&M.

Contact information for each of the resources listed will be found in the Sources of Products, Materials, Equipment, and Services section at the back of this book.

KEY READINGS

Alberto, P. A., & Troutman, A. C. (1998). *Applied behavior analysis for teachers* (5th ed.). Columbus, OH: Merrill.

Barraga, N., & Erin, J. (1992). *Visual handicaps and learning.* Austin, TX: PRO-ED.

Bishop, V. E. (1996). *Teaching visually impaired children* (2nd ed.). Springfield, IL: Charles C Thomas.

Blasch, B., Wiener, W., & Welsh, R. (Eds.). (1997). *Foundations of orientation and mobility* (2nd ed.). New York: AFB Press.

Bradley-Johnson, S. (1994). *Psychoeducational assessment of students who are visually impaired or blind* (2nd ed.). Austin, TX: PRO-ED.

Castellano, C., & Kosman, D. (1997). *The bridge to braille: Reading and school success for the young blind child.* Baltimore, MD: National Organization of Parents of Blind Children.

Corn, A. L., & Koenig, A. J. (Eds.) (1996). *Foundations of low vision: Clinical and functional perspectives.* New York: AFB Press.

Edman, P. K. (1992). *Tactile graphics.* New York: American Foundation for the Blind.

Harley, R. K., Truan, M. B., & Sanford, L. D. (1997). *Communication skills for visually impaired learners* (2nd ed.). Springfield, IL: Charles C Thomas.

Holbrook, M. C. (Ed.). (1996). *Children with visual impairments: A parents' guide.* Baltimore, MD: Woodbine House.

Hudson, L. J. (1997). *Classroom collaboration.* Watertown, MA: Perkins School for the Blind.

Kapperman, G., Heinze, A., & Sticken, J. (1997). *Strategies for developing mathematics skills in students who use braille.* Sycamore, IL: Research and Development Institute.

Olmstead, J. E. (1991). *Itinerant teaching: Tricks of the trade for teachers of blind and visually impaired students.* New York: American Foundation for the Blind.

Olson, M. R. (1981). *Guidelines and games for teaching efficient braille reading.* New York: American Foundation for the Blind.

Pogrund, R. L., Fazzi, D. L., & Lampert, J. S. (1992). *Early focus: Working with young blind and visually impaired children and their families.* New York: American Foundation for the Blind.

Sacks, S. Z., Kekelis, L. S., & Gaylord-Ross, R. J. (1992). *The development of social skills by blind and visually impaired students.* New York: American Foundation for the Blind.

Sacks, S. Z. & Silberman, R. K. (1998). *Educating students who have visual impairments with other disabilities.* Baltimore, MD: Paul H. Brookes Publishing Co.

Swallow, R. & Huebner, K. M. (1987). *How to thrive, not just survive.* New York: American Foundation for the Blind.

Swenson, A. M. (1999). *Beginning with braille: First-hand experiences with a balanced approach to literacy.* New York: AFB Press.

Willoughby, D. M., & Duffy, S. L. (1989). *Handbook for itinerant and resource teachers of blind and visually impaired students.* Baltimore, MD: National Federation of the Blind.

Wolffe, K. E. (Ed.) (1999). *Skills for success: A career education handbook for children and adolescents with visual impairments.* New York: AFB Press.

Wormsley, D. P., & D'Andrea, F. M. (Eds.) (1997). *Instructional strategies for braille literacy.* New York: AFB Press.

OSEP Policy Guidance on Educating Blind and Visually Impaired Students

November 3, 1995

To: Chief State School Officers

From: Judith E. Heumann
          Assistant Secretary
          Office of Special Education and
            Rehabilitative Services

          Thomas Hehir
          Director
          Officer of Special Education Programs

Subject: Policy Guidance on Educating Blind
          and Visually Impaired Students

INTRODUCTION

One of our highest priorities at the Office of Special Education and Rehabilitative Services (OSERS) is improving services for students with low incidence disabilities, particularly those with sensory deficits. On October 30, 1992, the Department published a Notice of Policy Guidance on Deaf Students Education Services[1] (Notice) to provide additional guidance to educators on the free appropriate public education (FAPE) requirements of Part B of the Individuals with Disabilities Education Act (Part B) and Section 504 of the Rehabil-

itation Act of 1973[2] as they relate to students who are deaf. In OSEP Memorandum 94-15, dated February 4, 1994, we clarified that the policy guidance in this Notice is equally applicable to all students with disabilities.

Nevertheless, it has come to our attention that services for some blind and visually impaired students are not appropriately addressing their unique educational and learning needs, particularly their needs for instruction in literacy, self-help skills, and orientation and mobility. We at OSERS are strongly committed to ensuring that our educational system takes the steps that are necessary to enable students who are blind or visually impaired to become productive and contributing citizens. Therefore, OSERS has determined that there is a need for additional guidance

---

[1]See 57 Fed. Reg. 49274 (Oct. 30, 1992).

[2]Section 504 of the Rehabilitation Act of 1973 (Section 504) prohibits discrimination on the basis of disability by recipients of Federal financial assistance. The

Department's regulations implementing Section 504, at 34 CFR Part 104, require recipients that operate public elementary and secondary education programs to provide appropriate educational services to disabled students. See 34 CFR §§104.33–104.36. Section 504 is enforced by the Department's Office for Civil Rights (OCR). The Americans with Disabilities Act of 1990 (ADA), Title II, prohibits discrimination on the basis of disability by State and local governments, whether or not they receive Federal funds; OCR enforces Title II of the ADA as it relates to public elementary and secondary educational institutions and public libraries, and interprets the requirements of Title II of the ADA as consistent with those of Section 504. OCR officials have reviewed this guidance and find it to be consistent with recipients' obligations to provide FAPE to blind and visually impaired students under Section 504 and Title II of the ADA.

on the FAPE requirements of Part B as they relate to blind and visually impaired students. This guidance will provide some background information on blind and visually impaired students and discussion of their unique needs, and will identify the steps that educators can take in meeting their responsibilities under Part B to blind and visually impaired students.

We hope that the attached guidance is helpful to you and educators in your State as you implement educational programs for blind and visually impaired students. If there are any questions, or if further information is needed, please contact the contact person listed above or Dr. JoLeta Reynolds in the Office of Special Education Programs at (202) 205-5507.

Attachment

cc: State Directors of Special Education
     RSA Regional Commissioners
     Regional Resource Centers
     Federal Resource Center
     Special Interest Groups
     Parent Training Centers
     Independent Living Centers
     Protection and Advocacy Agencies

BACKGROUND

The population of students who receive services under Part B because of blindness or visual impairment is extremely diverse. These students display both a wide range of vision difficulties and adaptations to vision loss. The diversity that characterizes the student population is true of the population of blind and visually impaired persons in general. So far as degree of vision loss is concerned, the student population includes persons who are totally blind or persons with minimal light perception, as well as persons with high levels of functional vision, though less than the norm. For some students, visual impairment is their only disability; while others have one or more additional disabilities that will affect, to varying degrees, their learning and growth.

Identifying other characteristics of this diverse population is far more complex. This is because adaptations to vision loss vary greatly and are shaped by individual differences in areas such as intellectual abilities and family supports. Degree of vision loss, therefore, does not give a full understanding of how that loss affects learning. Students with similar degrees of vision loss may function very differently. A significant visual deficit can pose formidable obstacles for some students and far less formidable obstacles for others. However, regardless of the degree of the student's vision loss or the student's ability to adapt to that loss, there is general agreement that blind and visually impaired students must acquire the skills necessary to function in settings in which the majority of people have vision sufficient to enable them to read and write by using regular print as well as to move about in their environment with ease.

To state the obvious, children begin at a very young age to imitate the actions of others, particularly by imitating what they see others doing. Typically, learning is based on this principle. The challenge for educators of blind and visually impaired students in schools is how to teach their students to learn skills that sighted children typically acquire through vision, including how to read, write, compose, and obtain access to information contained in printed materials. We recognize that blind and visually impaired students have used a variety of methods to learn to read and write. For example, for reading purposes, some students use braille exclusively; others use large print or regular print with or without low vision aids. Still others use a combination of methods, including braille, large print, and low vision aids while others have sufficient functional vision to use regular print, although with considerable difficulty. In order to receive an appropriate education under Part B, unless a student who is blind or visually impaired has other disabilities that would inhibit his or her ability to learn to read, we believe that instruction in reading must be provided for blind and visually impaired students in the medium that is appropriate for their individual abilities and needs to enable them to learn to read effectively.

One of the most serious concerns voiced by parents of blind children and their advocates, and by adults who are blind or visually impaired as well, is that the number of students receiving instruction in braille has decreased significantly over the past several decades. As a result, these individuals believe that braille instruction is not being provided to some students for whom it may be appropriate. Braille has been a very effective reading and writing medium for many blind and visually impaired persons. In fact, data from a recent study demonstrate that blind and visually impaired adults who know braille are more likely to be employed than those who do not, suggesting a strong correlation between knowledge of braille and a person's ability to obtain future employment. The American Foundation for the Blind's Careers and Technology Information Bank, which lists 1,000 different jobs held by blind and visually impaired people, indicates that 85 percent of those who use braille as their primary method of reading are employed.[3] Undoubtedly, there are numerous other benefits that individuals for whom braille instruction is appropriate would derive from knowledge of braille, particularly a heightened sense of self-esteem and self-worth that a student gains from the ability to read effectively.

Another significant concern voiced by parents of blind and visually impaired students and their advocates, as well as by many blind and visually impaired adults, is that these students are not receiving adequate instruction in orientation and mobility to address their individual needs. In some instances, it has been reported that these students do not even receive adequate evaluations of their needs for such instruction. The intent of Part B cannot be achieved fully if a blind or visually impaired student who needs instruction in orientation and mobility does not receive that instruction before completing his or her education.

I. Application of the Free Appropriate Public Education Requirements of Part B to Blind and Visually Impaired Students

Under Part B, each State and its public agencies must ensure that all children with specified disabilities have available to them a free appropriate public education (FAPE), and that the rights and protections of Part B are afforded to those students and their parents. FAPE includes, among other elements, special education and related services that are provided at no cost to parents under public supervision and direction, that meet State education standards and Part B requirements, that include preschool, elementary, or secondary school education in the State involved, and that are provided in conformity with an individualized education program (IEP).[4]

Before a student with a disability can receive special education and related services, a full and individual evaluation of the student's educational needs must be conducted in accordance with the requirements of 34 CFR §300.532.[5] Section 300.532 requires, among other factors, that the child be evaluated by a multidisciplinary team or group of persons, including at least one teacher or other specialist with knowledge in the area of suspected disability.[6] Thus, for blind or visually impaired students, an individual with knowledge of blindness and visual impairment would be an essential participant on this multidisciplinary team.

An assessment that meets the requirements of Part B must assess the child in all areas related to the suspected disability, including, if appropriate, "health, vision, hearing, social and emotional status, general intelligence, academic performance, communicative status, and motor abilities."[7] Assessments for blind and visually impaired students must evaluate the student in the areas listed above, as determined appropriate by the multidisciplinary team.

---

[3]Study of Issues and Strategies toward Improving Employment of Blind and Visually Impaired Persons in Illinois, American Foundation for the Blind (March 1991).

[4]20 U.S.C. §1412(2); 34 CFR §300.121; 20 U.S.C. §1401(a)(18) and 34 CFR §300.8.
[5]CFR §300.531.
[6]See 34 CFR §300.532(e).
[7]See 34 CFR §300.532(f).

For example, an assessment of academic performance would include an assessment of the student's ability to master the skills necessary for literacy, including reading, reading comprehension, composition, and computing. If appropriate, an assessment of vision would include the nature and extent of the student's visual impairment and its effect on the student's ability to learn to read, write, and the instructional method or methods that would be appropriate to enable the student to learn the above skills. For the teaching of reading and composition, these methods could include braille, large print or regular print with or without low vision optical devices, or a combination of braille and print. A range of devices that utilize computer-generated speech could be helpful tools in the instruction of children who are blind or visually impaired. Because of the importance for some blind and visually impaired students of mastering the skills necessary to acquire information, additional assessments may be necessary to determine whether the student should receive specific instruction in listening skills. Possible assessments that could be considered for this purpose could include assessments of hearing, general intelligence, or communicative status. The student's need for instruction in orientation and mobility and the appropriate method or methods for acquiring this skill could also be assessed. As with other educational decisions, the results of the student's assessments must be considered as the student's IEP[8] is developed, and the participants on the student's IEP team determine the specially designed instruction and related services to be provided to the student.

Under Part B, the public agency responsible for the student's education must initiate and conduct meetings to develop or review each student's IEP periodically, and if appropriate, revise its provisions. A meeting must be held for this purpose at least once a year.[9] Required participants at all IEP meetings include the child's teacher; an agency representative, who is qualified to provide or supervise the provision of special education; the parents, subject to certain limited exceptions; the child, if determined appropriate; and other individuals at the parent's or agency's discretion. If the IEP meeting occurs in connection with the child's initial placement in special education, the school district must ensure the participation of evaluation personnel, unless the child's teacher or public agency representative or some other person at the meeting is knowledgeable about the evaluation procedures used with the child and the results of those procedures.[10]

Each student's IEP must contain, among other components, a statement of annual goals including short-term objectives, the specific special education and related services to be provided to the student and the extent that the student will be able to participate in regular educational programs, and a statement of needed transition services under certain circumstances.[11] To ensure that blind and visually impaired students receive adequate instruction in the skills necessary to become literate, IEP teams must ensure that the instructional time that is allocated is appropriate for the required instruction or service.[12] For a student to become literate in braille, systematic and regular instruction from knowledgeable and trained personnel is essential. Likewise, for students with low vision, instruction in the utilization of remaining vision and in the effective use of low vision aids requires regular and intensive intervention from appropriately-trained personnel.

In all instances, IEP teams must consider how to address the needs of blind and visually impaired students for the skills necessary to achieve literacy. For students who are blind or for students with a minimal amount of residual vision, it is probable that braille will be the primary instructional method for teaching the student to learn to read. Therefore, for blind students and for students with a minimal amount of residual vision,

---

[8]The IEP is the written document that contains the statement for a disabled student of the program of specialized instruction and related services to be provided to a student. 34 CFR §§300.340–300.350.

[9]20 U.S.C. §1414(a)(5) and 34 CFR §300.343(d).

[10]34 CFR §300.344.

[11]34 CFR §300.346.

[12]Appendix C to 34 CFR Part 300 (question 51).

braille should be considered as the primary reading method, unless the student has a disability in addition to blindness that would make it difficult for the student to use his or her hands or would otherwise adversely affect the student's ability to learn to read. In developing IEPs for other students with low vision, IEP teams should not assume that instruction in braille would not be appropriate merely because the student has some useful vision. While IEP teams are not required to consider the need for braille instruction for every student with a visual impairment who is eligible for services under Part B, IEP teams may not fail to consider braille instruction for students for whom it may be appropriate. This consideration must occur despite factors such as shortages or unavailability of trained personnel to provide braille instruction, the ability of audiotapes and computers to provide blind and visually impaired persons with ready access to printed textbooks and materials, or the amount of time needed to provide a student with sufficient and regular instruction to attain proficiency in braille.

IEP teams also must select the method or methods for teaching blind and visually impaired students how to write and compose. Students whose appropriate reading medium is braille may benefit from using braille for these purposes. Alternatively, in addition to braille, they may benefit from using a personal computer with speech output for composition. Therefore, IEP teams must make individual determinations about the needs of blind and visually impaired students for instruction in writing and composition, and must include effective methods for teaching writing and composition in the IEPs of those students for whom instruction in this area is determined to be appropriate.

In addition to mastering the skills taught to all students, blind and visually impaired students must receive instruction in the skills necessary to acquire information, particularly because braille or large print documents frequently cannot be made accessible to them in a timely manner. The skills that could be taught to accomplish this include recordings that utilize compressed speech, personal computers with speech output, and optical scanners with speech output. As determined

appropriate, use of these devices and methods would be considered on an individual basis. In appropriate situations, one or more of these devices could be used to supplement braille instruction for students for whom braille is the primary reading medium, or to supplement print or large print for students using print as their primary reading medium. In rare instances, methods for acquiring information could be used in place of braille or print for students who, by reason of other disabilities, cannot be taught to read.

To ensure that IEPs for blind and visually impaired students address their specific needs effectively, the following unique needs should be considered as IEPs for these students are developed:

- Skills necessary to attain literacy in reading and writing, including appropriate instructional methods;
- Skills for acquiring information, including appropriate use of technological devices and services;
- Orientation and Mobility Instruction;
- Social Interaction Skills;
- Transition Services Needs;
- Recreation; and
- Career Education.

This list is not intended to be exhaustive. Participants on IEP teams could determine that it would be appropriate to consider an individual student's need for other skills, in addition to the skills listed above. Therefore, in making decisions about the educational programs for blind and visually impaired students, IEP teams must consider the full range of skills necessary to enable these students to learn effectively.

II. Least Restrictive Environment and Placement Requirements

Part B requires States to have procedures for assuring that, to the maximum extent appropriate, students with disabilities are educated with students who are not disabled, and that special classes, separate schooling, or other removal of students with disabilities from the regular educational environment occurs only when the nature or severity of the disability is such that education in regular classes with the use of supplementary aids and services cannot be achieved satisfactorily.[13] This requirement is known as the least restrictive environment (LRE) requirement.

Recognizing that the regular classroom may not be the LRE placement for every disabled student, the Part B regulations require public agencies to make available a continuum of alternative placements, or a range of placement options, to meet the needs of students with disabilities for special education and related services. The options on this continuum, which include regular classes, special classes, separate schools, and instruction in hospitals and institutions, must be made available to the extent necessary to implement the IEP of each disabled student.[14]

Part B requires that each child's placement must be based on his or her IEP.[15] Thus, it is the special education and related services set out in each student's IEP that constitute the basis for the placement decision. That is why placement determinations cannot be made before a student's IEP is developed. Rather, it is the special education and related services set out in the student's IEP that must constitute the basis for the placement decision. After the IEP of a blind or visually impaired student is developed, the placement determination must be made consistent with the special education and related services reflected in the student's IEP. In addition, the potential harmful effect of the placement on the visually impaired student or the quality of services he or she needs must be considered in determining the LRE.[16] The overriding rule in placement is that each student's place-

ment must be determined on an individual basis.[17] As in other situations, placements of blind and visually impaired students may not be based solely on factors such as category of disability, severity of disability, configuration of delivery system, availability of educational or related services, availability of space, or administrative convenience.

In addition to the Part B requirements applicable to placement in the LRE, Part B requires that each student's placement decision be made by a "group of persons, including persons knowledgeable about the child, the meaning of evaluation data, and placement options."[18] While Part B does not explicitly require the participation of the child's parent on this placement team, many States include parents in the group of persons that makes placement decisions. It also is important to emphasize that parents of blind and visually impaired students, through their participation on the student's IEP team, can play a critical role in ensuring that the student's unique needs are appropriately addressed. Public agencies and parent information centers should take steps to ensure that parents are fully informed about the instructional media that are available to address the unique needs arising from the student's visual impairment.

In implementing Part B's LRE requirements, in some instances, placement decisions are inappropriately made before IEPs that address a child's unique needs are developed. Determinations of appropriate special education and related services for blind and visually impaired students must be made through the IEP process, and must examine the development of skills necessary to address the effects of blindness or low vision on the student's ability to learn and to access the curriculum. Since Part B requires that each child's placement be based on his or her IEP, making placement decisions before a student's IEP is developed is a practice that violates Part B and could result in the denial of FAPE in the LRE.

Still in other instances, some students have been inappropriately placed in the regular classroom although it has been determined that their IEPs cannot be appropriately implemented in the

---

[13]20 U.S.C. §1412(5)(B); 34 CFR §300.550(b).

[14]See 34 CFR §§300.551 and 300.552(b).

[15]See 34 CFR §300.552(a)(2). That regulation requires that each child's placement is determined at least annually, is based on his or her IEP, and is in the school or facility as close as possible to the child's home. 34 CFR §300.552(a)(1)–(3). Further, unless a disabled student's IEP requires another arrangement, the student must be educated in the school or facility that he or she would attend if not disabled. 34 CFR §300.552(c).

[16]34 CFR §300.552(d).

---

[17]34 CFR §300.552 and Note 1.

[18]34 CFR §300.533(a)(3).

regular classroom even with the necessary supplementary aids and supports. In these situations, the nature of the student's disability and individual needs could make it appropriate for the student to be placed in a setting outside of the regular educational environment in order to ensure that the student's IEP is satisfactorily implemented. By contrast, there are other instances where some blind and visually impaired students have been inappropriately placed in settings other than the regular educational environment, even though their IEPs could have been implemented satisfactorily in the regular classroom with the provision of supplementary aids and services. As is true for all educational decisions under Part B, the above concerns about the misapplication of the LRE requirements underscore the importance of making individual placement determinations based on each student's unique abilities and needs.

In making placement determinations, it is essential that placement teams consider the full range of placement options for blind and visually impaired students. The following are some examples of placement options that could be considered:

- Placement in a regular classroom with needed support services provided in that classroom by an itinerant teacher or by a special teacher assigned to that school;

- Placement in the regular classroom with services outside the classroom by an itinerant teacher or by a special teacher assigned to that school;

- Placement in a self-contained classroom in a regular school; and

- Placement in a special school with residential option.

III. Procedural Safeguards

Part B also requires that public agencies afford parents a range of procedural safeguards. These include giving parents written notice a reasonable time before a public agency proposes to initiate, or change, the identification, evaluation, educa-

tional placement of the child, or the provision of a free appropriate public education to the child. This notice to parents must include a description of the action proposed, or refused, by the agency, an explanation of why the agency proposes, or refuses, to take the action, and a description of any options the agency considered and the reasons why those options were rejected.[19] The requirement to provide a description of any option considered includes a description of the types of placements that were actually considered, e.g., regular class placement with needed support services, regular classroom with pull-out services; and the reasons why these placement options were rejected. Providing this kind of information to parents will enable them to play a more knowledgeable and informed role in the education of their children. Part B affords parents and public educational agencies the right to initiate an impartial due process hearing on any matter regarding the identification, evaluation, or educational placement of the child, or the provision of a free appropriate public education to the child.[20]

Disagreements between parents and public agencies over issues such as the extent that braille instruction should be included in a student's IEP and the educational setting in which the child's IEP should be implemented are examples of some of the matters that can be the subject of a Part B due process hearing. Since many States procedures call for mediation before resorting to formal due process procedures, issues that can be the subject of a Part B due process hearing also can be addressed through mediation if the State has such a process, or through other alternative dispute resolution mechanisms. We strongly encourage alternative dispute resolution without a need to resort to due process and informing parents about such procedures. Public agencies also need to inform parents of blind and visually impaired students of their right to initiate a Part B due process hearing when agreement cannot be reached on important educational decisions.

---

[19]See 34 CFR §300.504(a) and 300.505(a)(2)–(4).
[20]See 20 U.S.C. §1415(b)(1)(E) and 34 CFR §300. 506(a).

APPENDIX B

The Core Curriculum for Blind and Visually Impaired Students, Including Those with Additional Disabilities

Philip Hatlen

Some years ago, a reporter asked a prominent blind woman, "What is it that blind people would want from society?" Her response was, "The opportunity to be equal and the right to be different."

Opportunities for equality grew tremendously in the 20th century, as Lowenfeld (1975) so graphically portrayed in *The Changing Status of the Blind: From Separation to Integration:*

> In the field of education then the move from separation to integration is evident. Educational provisions for blind children, the administration of these educational provisions, and teacher preparation, all moved from special or separated arrangements to integrated ones. This move has been consistently spearheaded and supported by legislation (p. 117).

Lowenfeld believed that the American creed (all of us are equal under the law) had resulted in educational integration for blind and visually impaired students. Integration with their sighted peers, which began for visually impaired students at the turn of the century, has provided these students with the opportunity to be equal. All of us—parents, consumers, and professionals—continue to promote equal opportunities for blind persons.

Source: RE:view *28(1),* [Spring 1996], 25–32. *Reprinted with permission of the Helen Dwight Reid Educational Foundation. Published by Heldref Publications, 1319 Eighteenth Street, NW, Washington, DC 20036-1802.* Copyright ©1996.

But how do we feel about, and how do we react to, "the right to be different?" What did this woman mean by two remarks that seem diametrically opposite? Perhaps she meant that print and Braille are equal, but very different; that the need for independent travel is similar for sighted and blind persons, but that blind people learn the skills very differently. Perhaps she was emphasizing that blind people should have the opportunity to learn the same knowledge and skills as sighted people, but that much of what sighted people learn incidentally and spontaneously blind people learn differently.

The integration (soon to be called *mainstreaming* and then *inclusion*) of blind students into regular classrooms in great numbers, beginning in the 1950s, brought with it the belief that adapted academic material was all that visually impaired students needed to be able to learn in the regular classroom. Few, if any, changes or additions were made to the curricula offered to these students. The efforts to include visually impaired students in regular classrooms sometimes attempted to provide "the opportunity to be equal" without recognizing the student's "right (and need) to be different."

Visually impaired students have succeeded in mastering the curriculum developed for sighted students. If the educational system provides students who have a necessary foundation of experiential learning with appropriate educational ma-

779

terials, and if there are excellent support services, including qualified and credentialed teachers of visually impaired students and orientation and mobility instructors, then the existing curriculum for sighted students will provide the visually impaired student the "opportunity to be equal."

However, "the right to be different" clearly implies that there is more to educating visually impaired students than providing them with curriculum identical to that of sighted students. This added curriculum that is specific to visually impaired students is well known, but has not been diligently implemented. Could it be that parents and professionals have no problem with the "opportunity to be equal" but have difficulty with "the right to be different?"

For many reasons, professionals in education for visually impaired learners have not easily accepted the concept that visually impaired students have educational needs that are in addition to the curriculum required for sighted students. Some are loathe to give up the belief that there is no difference between the educational needs of sighted students and visually impaired students. Others have difficulty accepting the idea that an expanded curriculum is the responsibility of educators; time or size of caseload, or both, make it impossible for others to add to their teaching responsibilities. Goal 8 of the National Agenda (see page 17) directly addresses this issue and will bring educators and parents together to ensure an appropriate education based on this expanded core curriculum for American young people who are blind and visually impaired, including those with additional disabilities.[1]

WHAT IS A CORE CURRICULUM?

Educators define core curriculum as the knowledge and skills, generally those related to aca-

demic subjects, a student should have learned by high school graduation. Each state in the United States establishes minimum standards for high school graduation, and this core curriculum becomes the foundation for almost all learning, from kindergarten through high school.

Educators of visually impaired students can use their expertise in curriculum adaptation to adapt any curriculum and make it readily available for visually impaired learners. If accessibility to learning materials is the only problem the visual impairment presents, then educating visually impaired students can be solved by adaptation of the existing core curriculum.

But most professionals firmly believe that visually impaired students need an *expanded* core curriculum that requires additional areas of learning. Experiences and concepts casually and incidentally learned by sighted students must be systematically and sequentially taught to the visually impaired student.

Professionals and parents have discussed the concept of a core curriculum for visually impaired learners for many years. It has had many names; the specialized curriculum, specialized needs, the unique curriculum, unique needs, nonacademic curriculum, the dual curriculum, and most recently, the disability-specific curriculum.

These terms sometimes distract from the important issue. Using the term core curriculum for blind and visually impaired students to define the basic educational needs for those young people conveys the same message as the original core curriculum. Words like *specialized, unique* and *disability-specific* are not needed and, indeed, may give an erroneous connotation to basic educational needs. Those terms imply two separate lists of educational needs for visually impaired students: one list that contains the elements of a traditional core curriculum; the second a list of *disability-specific* needs. Two lists might provide educators with options, such as a list of requirements and one of electives. There should be only one list—the required curriculum for visually impaired students.

The expanded core curriculum now being promoted is not new. Elements of it have been

---

[1] The term *including those with additional disabilities,* which appeared in the title, has not been repeated but should be assumed under the definition of *blind and visually impaired students.*

known for years. References to grooming skills date back to 1891. The need for social interaction skills appeared in the literature in 1929 and again in 1948. Between 1953 and 1975, more than two dozen books and articles were written about daily living skills and visually impaired students. Much more has been written about orientation and mobility and career education.

THE EXPANDED CORE CURRICULUM FOR BLIND AND VISUALLY IMPAIRED CHILDREN AND YOUTHS

The lists below incorporate the basic subject competencies now required by states and the competencies of the expanded core curriculum for visually impaired students. Some of the skills—compensatory or functional academic skills, including communication modes; orientation and mobility; social interaction skills, visual efficiency skills—are either not in the regular core curriculum or not in it with sufficient specificity to meet the needs of visually impaired students. Others—independent living skills, recreation and leisure skills, career education, and technology—although addressed in the regular core curriculum, are done so inadequately for the needs of visually impaired students.

Compensatory or Functional Academic Skills, Including Communication Modes

In this area, a distinction must be made between compensatory skills and functional skills. Compensatory skills are those that blind and visually impaired students need to access all areas of core curriculum. Mastery of compensatory skills will usually mean that the visually impaired student has access to learning in a manner equal to that of sighted peers. Functional skills refers to the skills that students with multiple disabilities learn that provide them with the opportunity to work, play, socialize, and take care of personal needs to the highest level possible.

These academic skills include learning experiences such as concept development, spatial understanding, study and organizational skills, speaking and listening skills, and the adaptations necessary for accessing all areas of the existing core curriculum. Communication needs will vary, depending on the degree of functional vision, the effects of additional disabilities, and the task to be done. Children may communicate through Braille, large print, print with the use of optical devices, regular print, tactile symbols, a calendar system, sign language, recorded materials, or combinations of these means. Whatever the choice of materials, each student with a visual impairment will need instruction from a teacher with professional preparation in each of the compensatory and

Existing Core Curriculum		Expanded Core Curriculum	
English language arts	Other languages to the extent possible	Compensatory academic skills, including communication modes	Orientation and mobility
Mathematics	Science		
Health	Physical education	Social interaction skills	Independent living skills
Social studies	History	Recreation and leisure skills	Career education
Economics	Business education	Use of assistive technology	Visual efficiency skills
Fine arts	Vocational education		

functional skills they need to master. These compensatory and functional needs of the visually impaired child are significant.

Orientation and Mobility

This is a vital area of learning, which requires delivery by teachers with specific preparation. It emphasizes the fundamental need and basic right of visually impaired people to travel as independently as possible, enjoying and learning to the greatest extent possible from the environment through which they are passing. Students will need to learn about themselves and the environment in which they move—from basic body image to independent travel in rural areas and busy cities.

Social Interaction Skills

Sighted children and adults have learned almost all their social skills by visually observing other people and behaving in socially appropriate ways based on that information. Blind and visually impaired individuals cannot learn skills of social interaction in this casual and incidental fashion. They learn then through careful, conscious, and sequential teaching. Instruction in these skills is such a fundamental need that it can often mean the difference between social isolation and a satisfying and fulfilling life as an adult.

Independent Living Skills

This area, often referred to as *daily living skills,* consists of all the tasks and functions people perform, according to their abilities, in order to live as independently as possible. These curricular needs are varied and include among others skills in personal hygiene, food preparation, money management, time monitoring, and organization. The existing core curriculum addresses some independent living skills, but they often are introduced as "splinter skills," appearing in learning material, disappearing, and then re-appearing. This approach will not adequately prepare blind and visu-

ally impaired students for adult life. Traditional classes in home economics and family life are not enough to meet the learning needs of most visually impaired students because they assume a basic level of knowledge, acquired incidentally through vision. As with the skills of social interaction, blind and visually impaired students cannot learn these skills without direct, sequential instruction by knowledgeable people.

Recreation and Leisure Skills

The existing core curriculum usually addresses the needs of sighted students for physical fitness through physical education in the form of team games and athletics. Many activities in physical education are excellent and appropriate for visually impaired students, but these students also need to develop recreational and leisure activities that they can enjoy throughout their lives. Sighted people usually select such activities by visually observing them and choosing those in which they wish to participate. Recreation and leisure skills must be deliberately planned and taught to blind and visually impaired students and should focus on the development of life-long skills.

Career Education

Many of the skills and knowledge offered to all students through vocational education will not be sufficient to prepare blind and visually impaired students for adult life. They will also need career education offered for them specifically because here, too, general instruction assumes a basic knowledge of the world of work based on prior visual experiences. Career education in an expanded core curriculum should begin in the earliest grades to give the visually impaired learner of all ages the opportunity to learn firsthand about the variety of work people do. It will give the student chances to explore strengths and interests in a systematic, well-planned manner. Unemployment and underemployment are leading problems facing visually impaired people in the United States, making this portion of the expanded core curriculum vital to students.

Technology

Technology is a tool to unlock learning and expand the horizons of students. It is not, in reality, a curriculum area, but it is added to the expanded core curriculum because of the special place it occupies in the education of blind and visually impaired students. Technology can be a great equalizer. For the Braille user, it will produce material in Braille for personal use and then in print for the teacher, classmates, and parents. Technology enables blind people to store and retrieve information and brings a library under the fingertips of the visually impaired person. It enhances communication and learning and expands the world of blind and visually impaired persons in many significant ways.

Visual Efficiency Skills

The visual acuity of children diagnosed as visually impaired varies greatly. With thorough, systematic training, most students with functional vision can learn to use their remaining vision better and more efficiently. Educational responsibility for performing a functional vision assessment, planning appropriate learning activities for effective visual use, and teaching students to use their functional vision effectively and efficiently falls to the professionally prepared teacher of visually impaired learners.

It is difficult to imagine that a congenitally blind or visually impaired person could be entirely at ease within the social, recreational, and vocational structure of the general community without mastering the elements of the expanded core curriculum. We know that unless congenitally blind and visually impaired students learn skills such as orientation and mobility, social interaction, and independent living they are at high risk for lonely, isolated, unproductive lives. For blind and visually impaired people, accomplishments and joys such as shopping, dining, attending and participating in recreational activities are a right, not a privilege. Responsibilities such as banking, taking care of health needs, and using public and private serv-

ices are a part of a full life for every one, including those who are blind or visually impaired. Adopting and implementing a core curriculum for blind and visually impaired students, including those with additional disabilities, will assure students of the opportunity to function well and completely in the general community.

This expanded core curriculum emphasizes the "right" of the visually impaired student "to be different." It is the heart of the responsibility of educators serving visually impaired students.

Children With Additional Disabilities

The components of the expanded core curriculum give educators the means to address the needs of visually impaired children with additional disabilities. The educational requirements of these children are often not met because their lack of vision is considered "minor," especially if the child has severe cognitive and physical disabilities. Appropriate professionals can further define each area in the expanded core curriculum to address the educational issues facing these children and assist parents and educators to fulfill their needs.

THE DELIVERY OF THE CORE CURRICULUM FOR BLIND AND VISUALLY IMPAIRED STUDENTS

For too many years, educators have behaved as though they were unaware of the unique and specialized needs of blind and visually impaired students. The outcome is a modern tragedy; too many products of our educational efforts live isolated, troubled lives. For too many years educators have known the content of the curricula that would equalize the education of blind and visually impaired learners by neutralizing the effects of visual impairments on incidental learning. And for too many years educators have found reasons not to implement the expanded core curriculum.

Once the profession of educators for visually impaired learners and parents of visually impaired students accept the necessity of the expanded core curriculum, how can they deliver the expanded core curriculum to visually impaired learners?

The additional learning experiences contained in the expanded core curriculum are not easy to implement. They will be difficult to complete in 12 years of education, especially for students who are high academic learners. They require time to teach, and the need for them does not diminish with age or competency. At this time, no single, simple method assures visually impaired students of accessing both traditional and expanded core curricula within the same length of time as their sighted peers. This remains a significant, but attainable challenge.

The professionally prepared teacher of visually impaired students must be responsible for assessment, instruction, and evaluation in unique and specialized curricular areas. This educator needs to teach the necessary skills and knowledge or to orchestrate their teaching by using other community resources.

The competencies in an expanded core curriculum require allocating educational time to teach them these skills. Programming that appropriately addresses all of the educational needs of the blind and visually impaired students must assume that most students will need sizable periods of time to master the competencies required in the expanded core curriculum. If the profession does not demand that this time be made available, it does a disservice to students with visual impairments and may disable them in their efforts to successfully make the transition from school to adulthood.

The expanded core curriculum must become the unifying issue among educators for visually impaired students. The profession must adopt it as the education that blind and visually impaired students need. Then the profession has the enormous task of carrying the curriculum message to parents, administrators, and the public at large. The message must transcend fiscal issues, conflicting philosophical and political positions, and the doubts and misgivings of educators and parents.

The spotlight must be on the individual child. The first step must be a thorough assessment of the child, covering every area of the expanded core curriculum. Using assessment results and invaluable information from parents, the child's IEP team must develop goals and objectives for that child, based on assessment. If assessment has truly covered every area of the expanded core curriculum, there probably will be goals and objectives for each area. The task of meeting, or orchestrating the meeting of, all goals and objectives will fall to the professional teacher for visually impaired children. Decisions must be made on placement, on priorities, and on frequency and duration of instruction. Care must be taken that the competencies contained in the expanded core curriculum receive equal attention with the academic competencies stressed in the existing curriculum.

A CALL TO ACTION FOR IMPLEMENTATION

The Advisory Council of the National Agenda calls all professionals and parents to action on this issue. Action requires three components.

- Familiarity—with the expanded core curriculum and the reasons why it is needed
- Acceptance—of the need to implement the expanded core curriculum
- Commitment—by educators and parents to change beliefs so that the expanded core curriculum will be implemented

Implementation means that our lives as professionals and parents will be dramatically changed; parents and professionals will become partners in preparing their children for a rich and fulfilling adult life. And, finally, implementation means that the blind and visually impaired students to whom we have committed our love, our hopes, and our talents and gifts for teaching will enjoy a full, exciting, and productive life.

APPENDIX C
The Role and Function of the Teacher of Students with Visual Handicaps

Susan Jay Spungin and Kay Alicyn Ferrell

Infants, children, and youth with visual handicaps receive special education and related services in a variety of settings that bring them into contact with a range of personnel. Perhaps the most important member of this team of professionals is the teacher of students with visual handicaps, whose specified training and experience often establish him or her as the individual best qualified to address the unique learning needs created by a visual handicap. Because of the variety of placement options available, however, there is often confusion about the role, function, and mandate of the teacher of students with visual handicaps.

It is the position of the Division for the Visually Handicapped that every infant, child, and youth with a visual handicap is entitled to the services of a teacher of students with visual handicaps, regardless of the severity of the disability or the presence of additional handicapping conditions. The nature of these services will depend on the individual needs of the student and will vary accordingly. In some cases, the teacher of students with visual handicaps will be the primary instructor of the infant, child, or youth with a visual handicap, while in other cases the teacher of students with visual handicaps will act as consultant to other teachers providing instruction. In *all* cases, it is the responsibility of the teacher of students with

Source: Council for Exceptional Children, Division on Visual Impairments Position Paper.

visual handicaps to carry out the following specialized activities:

I. *Assessment and Evaluation*

    A. Participate in the multidisciplinary assessment of infants, children, and youth with visual handicaps, assuming the primary responsibility to:

        1. Perform functional vision assessments.

        2. Obtain and interpret all ophthalmological, optometric, and functional vision reports and the implications thereof for educational and home environments, to families, classroom teachers, and other team members.

        3. Perform communications skills assessments in reading, writing, and listening.

        4. Recommend appropriate specialized evaluation as needed, such as low vision, orientation and mobility, physical therapy, occupational therapy, psychological, and adaptive physical education.

        5. Assist families to assess their own strengths and needs regarding their children's visual, academic, and functional development.

    B. Participate in the multidisciplinary team to develop Individualized Family Service

Plans (IFSPs), Individualized Education Programs (IEPs), and other similar documents for infants, children, and youth with visual handicaps, assuming the primary responsibility to:

1. Contribute to statements of present levels of performance by discussing how performance is affected by the visual handicap and by providing information on students' learning style, utilization of visual information, and other strengths unique to individual infants, children, and youth with visual handicaps.

2. Identify goals and objectives in specialized areas related to the visual needs of the student.

3. Identify instructional methods and materials for meeting goals and objectives.

4. Recommend appropriate service delivery options, including class placement, physical education, related services, specialized equipment, adaptations in testing procedures, and time frames for implementation.

C. Recommend as early as possible appropriate reading and writing media for the child with visual handicaps. Teachers of students with visual handicaps base such recommendations on the specific needs of individual students, as demonstrated by a thorough assessment that accounts for such factors as: reading distance, reading rates and accuracy, portability of reading skills, visual fatigue, and tactual sensitivity.

II. *Educational and Instructional Strategies: Learning Environment*

The teacher of students with visual handicaps usually acts as the primary mediator of the learning environment for children with visual handicaps and implements various strategies to facilitate students' assimilation into the classroom and school environment. In order to accomplish this, the teacher of students with visual handicaps takes steps to:

A. Assure that the student has all educational materials in the appropriate media.

B. Assure that the student is trained in the use of, and has available, all devices and technological apparatus necessary for learning.

C. Instruct the student in academic subjects and activities and developmental skills requiring adaptation and reinforcement as a direct result of the visual handicap.

D. Recommend seating and other environmental modifications that maximize students' utilization of visual information and facilitate movement of the student with visual handicaps within the class.

E. Assure that the teacher or other professional(s) providing direct instruction fully understands the unique needs of infants, children, and youth with visual handicaps.

F. Suggest modifications needed in assignments or testing procedures.

G. Collaborate with teachers and other professionals regarding various methods for including students with visual handicaps in routine learning experiences.

H. Act as a catalyst in developing understanding of visual loss by children without disabilities.

III. *Education and Instructional Strategies: Adapting the Curriculum*

Children with visual handicaps have the same curriculum needs as all children, but their visual handicap itself often imposes restrictions on their ability to access any curriculum presented in the usual method of learning and teaching. In order to assure access, the teacher of students with visual handicaps is responsible for providing direct instruction in the following areas:

A. Braille Reading and Writing—including braille readiness, braille reading instruction, and writing skills. These skills usually require introduction to the mechanical aspects of reading and writing, including spatial orientation to the page and use of the braille writer and slate and stylus, and include application and reinforcement of decoding, comprehension, and encoding strategies (introduced by the classroom teacher) to braille materials. The teacher of students with visual handicaps also provides instruction in braille mathematics, braille music, the computer braille code, and foreign language braille codes.

B. Visual Efficiency—For the student with low vision, the utilization of visual information underscores achievement in every skill area; academic, psycho-motor, self-help, vocational and social skills. The teacher of students with visual handicaps instructs infants, children, and youth in the utilization and interpretation of visual information under a variety of conditions.

C. Large Print and Optical Devices—The teacher of students with visual handicaps instructs with low vision in the utilization of reading aids (such as enlarged print, acetate sheets, reading stands, magnifiers, and telescopes) in order to participate independently in regular classroom activities.

D. Orientation and Mobility—Much of the orientation and mobility needs of students with visual handicaps are the responsibility of qualified orientation and mobility instructors. (In some cases, the teacher of students with visual handicaps is dually certified both as a teacher and an orientation and mobility instructor.) The responsibilities of, and the relationship between the teacher of students with visual handicaps and the orientation and mobility instructor must be clearly defined. It is possible that the teacher of students with visual handicaps will assume responsibility for assuring that students develop in sensory motor, gross, and fine motor domains, while the orientation and mobility specialist assumes responsibility for instruction in

environmental orientation and travel within the community. Children with visual handicaps must be taught to move in space and to be aware of the environment around them. They must learn to use tactual and auditory cues to identify their position in space and the relative position of other persons and objects around them.

E. Handwriting—or the student with low vision, certain aspects of both manuscript and cursive handwriting (e.g., size, configuration, place-keeping, review) are often the responsibility of the teacher of students with visual handicaps. The teacher of students with visual handicaps also teaches signature writing, and if appropriate, additional handwriting skills to students who are blind.

F. Typewriting—For most students with visual handicaps, typing may be the major means of communication between the child and his or her peers, family members, and teachers. Typing and keyboarding skills are carefully and thoroughly taught by the teacher of students with visual handicaps as soon as the student has sufficient fine motor skills.

G. Technology—The teacher of students with visual handicaps is responsible for collaborating with the teacher of computer technology to assist the student with visual handicaps in computer access through software and hardware applications that produce screen and print enhancements, speech access, and braille output.

H. Listening Skills—Instruction to develop listening skills is important to students with visual handicaps as a foundation for aural learning and reading, as well as for mobility clues, social conversation, and interpretation of a variety of auditory signals received from the environment. Listening becomes particularly important in the secondary grades, when print reading assignments become long and laborious. Students with visual handicaps begin to develop listening skills in infancy, and these skills are sequentially and deliberately expanded during the school years.

I. Study Skills—Skimming braille or large print materials, outlining in braille or large print, searching for significant information in recorded materials, and other note taking and report-writing skills are fundamental study skills which require instruction by the teacher of students with visual handicaps because of the unfamiliarity of the media to most classroom teachers.

J. Motor Development—The teacher of students with visual handicaps is knowledgeable about potential problem areas in motor development for infants, children, and youth with visual handicaps (such as body image, body in space concepts, visual motor coordination, abnormal reflex patterns, locomotion, rotation, weight transfer, gait, posture, etc.). The teacher of students with visual handicaps works collaboratively with early interventionists, physical education teachers, orientation and mobility specialists, and occupational or physical therapists to develop and enhance motor skills in infants, children and youth with visual handicaps.

K. Concept Development—The teacher of students with visual handicaps shares with other professionals the responsibility for the development of basic concepts, which is often at risk without vision to mediate and integrate other sensory information. Future learning is dependent upon the student's thorough understanding of basic spatial, environmental, social, and mathematical concepts.

L. Reasoning—The ability to reason, especially in the abstract, may require specific instruction from the teacher of students with visual handicaps. Students may need assistance in the development of decision-making skills, problem solving, and learning to live with occasional frustration and failure.

M. Tactual Skills—The development of tactual skills is not confined to the reading of braille. The teacher of students with visual handicaps provides instruction in tactual skills in a variety of environments and functional applications, assisting children with visual handicaps from infancy to use their fingers and hands well in order to explore, identify, discriminate, and appreciate all tangible materials in the environment.

N. Communication Development—Infants, children, and youth with visual handicaps may experience difficulties in language acquisition and application. Teachers of students with visual handicaps are knowledgeable about the ways in which a visual handicap can affect receptive and expressive communication and employ specific strategies to encourage use of functional, reality-based language. In addition, teachers of students with visual handicaps collaborate with other team members instructing students with multiple disabilities in the use of manual communication, communication boards, and other augmentative communication techniques. Visual handicaps impose restrictions on the use of these procedures, and the teacher of students with visual handicaps helps to devise alternative methods to make them accessible to infants, children, and youth with visual handicaps.

O. Activities of Daily Living—Through knowledge of the activities and techniques of daily living or personal management skills is needed to create independence so that students with visual handicaps may integrate more easily into their culture and society. Teachers of students with visual handicaps share responsibility with family members and other professionals for instruction in such areas as personal hygiene, eating habits, manners, dressing, grooming, verbal and nonverbal communication, and developing a positive self-image.

P. Physical Education—Teachers of students with visual handicaps assist physical education teachers in integrating the child with visual handicaps into the regular physical education curriculum by suggesting strategies for participation in team and individual sports. Visual handicaps often unnecessarily restrict movement and may result in poor physical fitness, unless systematic efforts are made to include children with visual handicaps in physical and recreational activities.

Q. Human sexuality—Teachers of students with visual handicaps, parents and others share the responsibility for gradual, sequential instruction in human sexuality for students with visual handicaps. Because programs in sex education for students without disabilities assume that much visual information has been previously attained, the student with visual handicaps may need a specific hands-on curriculum taught by appropriate, well-prepared professionals.

R. Career Education—Career education curricula that are developed for children without visual handicaps may need supplementary instruction from a teacher of students with visual handicaps. This instruction may include field trips into the community to explore work opportunities and job requirements, interviews with adults with visual handicaps about their various occupations, and assessment of individual abilities.

S. Vocational Counseling—Vocational counseling and transition to vocational opportunities are integral parts of programs designed for students with visual handicaps, and the teacher of students with visual handicaps, in conjunction with the vocational counselor or teacher, involves students with visual handicaps and their parents in the counseling process. The teacher of students with visual handicaps assists in the assessment of vocational strengths and weaknesses and facilitates students' participation in work-study, vocational training, and other appropriate experiences.

T. Leisure and Recreation—The teacher of students with visual handicaps, parents, and community agencies share a responsibility to expose the student to, and provide learning opportunities in, a wide variety of leisure time activities which have carryover value to adult life.

U. Transition—The teacher of students with visual handicaps assists in the smooth transition of infants, children, and youth with visual handicaps from one placement to another, by working with other team members, including parents, to identify appropriate options, preparing new teachers to accept the students with visual handicaps, and providing ongoing consultation. Such services regularly occur at the transition from early intervention to preschool programs, from preschool to school-age programs, and from secondary to adult services, but may also be necessary when a major change in placement occurs (e.g., from regular class to special class, or from residential school to regular class, placement,), or even in the regular grade level progression within the same educational facility.

IV. *Guidance and Counseling*

Teachers of students with visual handicaps provide guidance and counseling to infants, children, and youth with visual handicaps and their families to:

A. Interpret implications of visual impairment for overall development.

B. Facilitate understanding of society's attitudes concerning visual impairment and to assist students and families to formulate their responses to misconceptions, lowered expectations, and prejudice.

C. Explore similarities and differences in relation to all children.

D. Develop social awareness of self, others, and the community at large.

E. Encourage social interactions with peer groups.

F. Identify functional, academic, and vocational potential.

G. Encourage home involvement in program objectives.

H. Promote independence in infants, children, and youth with visual handicaps.

I. Plan for adult life by exploring options for college, technical or trade school, job coaching programs, industrial enclaves, and other post-secondary placements, as well as identifying independent living arrangements in the community.

J. Refer to other sources for additional guidance and counseling services.

V. *Administration and Supervision*

The teacher of students with visual handicaps, depending on the model(s) or service being utilized (residential school, special class, resource room, itinerant or teacher consultant) has a variety of administrative roles. In a large program, this may include supervision of other teachers of students with visual handicaps, in addition to working with Directors of Special Education, principals, regular classroom teachers, and other educational and related services personnel. Some of the most common activities in this area include:

A. Communication with Administrators— Teachers of students with visual handicaps keep administrators informed concerning:

1. Student information (e.g., visual status, grade level, prototype).

2. Program goals and activities.

3. Program evaluation.

4. Screening and referral procedures.

5. Relationships between the program for students with visual handicaps and regular and special education programs and support services.

6. Funding requirements for consultation, instruction, salaries, travel time, travel expenses, instructional materials, preparation time, conferences and benefits.

7. In-service needs for teachers and consultants of students with visual handicaps, as well as for other regular and special education personnel.

8. Staff scheduling requirements, including adequate time for planning, preparation, report writing, travel, direct instruction, team meetings, and staff conferences.

9. Physical facilities, including design and selection of classroom environments and office space, as well as adequate storage space for instructional materials and equipment.

10. Student scheduling, including preparation of a master schedule to be given to the supervisor and principal(s) of the building(s) in which the students are served.

11. Equipment needs, particularly in the area of technology, but also including materials production if necessary.

12. Availability of grants for curriculum expansion, including acquisition of materials and technological devices.

B. Record Keeping

1. Maintain records of student assessments, IEPs, IFSPs (and other planning documents), periodic reviews, progress reports, and signed parental release forms.

2. Maintain material and equipment requests.

3. Exchange information about students with visual handicaps with appropriate personnel, following school district or agency policies regarding confidentiality.

4. Maintain program-wide student cen-

sus information for purposes of annual count and eligibility for federal quota funds through the American Printing House for the Blind.

C. Casefinding and Student Referral Procedures

1. Act as a vision consultant for system-wide screening, materials, follow-up and recommendations.

2. Participate in school district's annual Child Find program.

3. Maintain a referral/communication system with nurses and other school staff.

VI. *School Community Relations*

School and community involvement requires the teacher of students with visual handicaps to be prepared to interpret the program to school personnel, boards of education, and other groups within the community. Activities include:

A. Acting as a liaison for the program for students with visual handicaps with:

1. Private and public agencies and schools, including those serving individuals with visual handicaps.

2. Other public and private resources within the community.

3. Parents and families (including extended family members).

4. Medical specialists and hospitals, particularly neonatal intensive care units.

5. Related services personnel.

6. Early interventionists.

7. Recreation resources.

8. Transition specialists.

9. Parent and advocacy groups.

10. Child study teams.

11. Volunteer groups.

B. Services Development

1. Coordinate ancillary groups and individuals, such as classroom aides, transcribers, recordists, readers for students with visual handicaps, counselors, orientation and mobility instructors, and rehabilitation teachers.

2. Assist in the initiation of new services as well as coordinating existing ones to bring the varied and necessary related services to the educational program.

3. Maintain on-going contact with parents to facilitate understanding of their child's abilities, progress, future goals, community resources, etc.

4. Attend professional meetings (in and out of the district) concerned with the education of students with visual handicaps.

5. Keep abreast of new developments in the education of infants, children and youth with visual handicaps.

6. Prepare grants for curriculum expansion and acquisition of materials and equipment.

The role of the teacher of students with visual handicaps is multifaceted and requires recognition by administrators that responsibilities and time commitments are unpredictable and may increase geometrically with each addition to the caseload. The amount of instruction and consultation required will vary according to individual student needs and will even vary for an individual student from one week to the next. Both administrators and teachers must approach their roles with flexibility and creativity in order to meet the dynamic, complex needs of infants, children, and youth with visual handicaps and their families within a rapidly changing service delivery system.

Expansion of the Role of the Teacher of Students with Visual Impairments: Providing for Students Who Also Have Severe/Multiple Disabilities

Rosanne K. Silberman and Sharon Sacks

All students with multiple disabilities including visual impairments are entitled to the services of a trained teacher of students with visual impairments. Students with multiple disabilities can be found in a variety of service delivery systems including residential school programs and special day classes in both public and private schools. In many cases, these students are served in a program with other children and youth with severe disabilities and are taught by a teacher who has generic training and certification. Therefore, it is essential for an itinerant teacher of students with visual impairments to provide consultant services to the classroom teacher and other transdisciplinary staff at the school as well as to provide direct services to the student with a visual impairment. Due to the increasing numbers of these students, educators of students with visual impairments should expand their roles, functions, and competencies. Many teachers are currently expected to serve children who have visual impairments in addition to a broad range of other disabilities including cerebral palsy, hearing impairment, mental retardation, and various neurological syndromes. Meeting the complex educational needs of these children and youth with visual impairments who also have severe/multiple disabilities

Source: Council for Exceptional Children, Division on Visual Impairments Position Paper.

in a wide variety of settings offers a unique challenge, which is the focus of this position paper.

It is the position of the DVI that all teachers of students with visual impairments have the competencies outlined in Spungin and Ferrell (in progress). These competencies include the areas of:

1. Assessment and Evaluation
2. Educational and Instructional Strategies: Learning Environment
3. Educational and Instructional Strategies: Adapting the Curriculum
4. Guidance and Counseling
5. Administration and Supervision
6. School Community Relations

Moreover, additional specific competencies now should be added to take into account the needs of students with visual impairments who also have severe/multiple disabilities.

In the first two competency areas identified above, Assessment and Evaluation and Educational and Instructional Strategies, it is the primary responsibility of the professionals in the field of education of students with visual impairments, especially teachers, to assess and enhance functional vision skills in all students with multiple disabilities regardless of the severity or multiplicity of impairments. Specifically, it is important that teachers of students with visual impairments demonstrate competence in Assessment and Instructional Strategies that include:

1. Knowledge of the common types of visual functioning difficulties in various populations with disabilities.
2. Knowledge of the effects of visual loss on the performance of functional vision tasks, e.g., feeding activities, vocational tasks, manual communication skills, and scanning of communication boards.
3. Ability to perform and interpret functional vision assessments for students with visual and multiple impairments.
4. Ability to design visual enhancement training in functional concepts, e.g., feeding, play time, vocational tasks, mobility.
5. Ability to communicate specific visual needs of students with visual and other multiple disabilities to other professionals serving this population.
6. Knowledge of effects of visual loss on movement patterns.
7. Knowledge of appropriate positioning and handling techniques for students with multiple disabilities that enhance efficient use of vision.
8. Knowledge of the effects of visual loss on language, social, and cognitive development.

While certain subject areas in which teachers of students with visual impairments should be trained are enumerated in the DVI position paper developed by Spungin and Ferrell (in press), the emphasis of these competencies is dramatically different when the focus is on education of students with visual and other multiple disabilities. These differences are particularly evident in the following areas:

1. Educational Assessment and Diagnosis.
2. Leisure and Recreation.

3. Human Sexuality.
4. Motor Development.
5. Cognitive Development.
6. Social Adjustment Skills.
7. Career and Vocational Education.

Areas of additional knowledge that all teachers need who serve students with visual impairments and other multiple disabilities include:

1. Early childhood development with specific emphasis on normal and abnormal motor, language, social, and cognitive development.
2. Informal assessment techniques: Ecological inventories, task analysis, discrepancy analysis, functional daily routines.
3. Augmentative communication systems.
4. Principles of behavior management.
5. Community-referenced curriculum.
6. Systematic instruction utilizing domain format: Self-management/home living, general community functioning, recreation/leisure, vocational.
7. Supported work models.
8. Transition programming to enhance adult living, employment and recreation/leisure options.

Students with visual impairments and other multiple disabilities are participating more frequently in diverse educational service deliver models and living successfully in various types of community facilities including their home, group homes, and residential schools. Therefore, additional relevant competencies needed by all teachers who serve students with visual impairments and other multiple disabilities are:

1. Types, advantages, and disadvantages of alternate service delivery models.
2. Organizational skills
   a. Time management
   b. Scheduling
   c. Use of space

3. Appropriate utilization of support personnel, e.g., teacher assistants, child care or residence workers.
4. Understanding and implementation of transdisciplinary team functioning.

Teachers of students with visual impairments should be able to function as an integral part of a transdisciplinary team in meeting the complex needs of students with visual impairments who also have severe/multiple disabilities. They will need to know and understand the roles and functions of the various disciplines including, but not limited to, medicine; education; social work; psychology; occupational, physical and speech therapies; and vocational rehabilitation. They must be knowledgeable in the terminologies utilized by each. Operating as part of such a team and offering direct and/or consultative services affords the teacher of students with visual impairments the opportunity to be both a teacher and a learner as he/she demonstrates his/her expertise and, in turn benefits from the knowledge and skills of the other team members from various fields, all on behalf of students with visual and other severe/multiple disabilities. The teacher of students with visual impairments and other team members need to acquire an understanding of the unique needs of this population which are directly attributable to their visual impairment. It also affords the teacher of students with visual impairments the opportunity to be an advocate for the student who also has multiple impairments and his/her family.

Also critical for a teacher is an understanding of the needs of families of students with visual impairments who have severe/multiple disabilities, as well as strategies for helping them to meet those needs. The ability to provide resources and information to families, to serve as an advocate for and with them, to establish counseling and support mechanisms, and to train them to assist in the development and implementation of their child's program are all facets of the teacher's role in a comprehensive family participation program.

Although not all qualified teachers of students with visual impairments will work with students with visual and other multiple impairments, those who do will need to have the additional competencies as described in this paper which would enable them to appropriately serve this population. Teacher preparation programs and inservice training options exist. These options could include the following:

1. Specialized graduate level training programs for teachers of students who are deaf-blind and/or teachers of children and youth with severe/multiple disabilities.
2. Courses designed to provide information and techniques for working with students with visual impairments and other severe/multiple disabilities.
3. Summer inservice workshops on various topics related to the student with visual and other severe/multiple disabilities, e.g., assessment, behavior management, alternative communication systems.
4. Utilization of consultants from the field of education of students with visual impairments and from other disciplines on a regular basis.
5. Provision of ongoing after-school topical workshops in areas such as vision assessment and enhancement, feeding, motor development, language development.
6. Opportunities for visitations to exemplary programs serving children and youth with visual impairments and other severe/multiple disabilities.
7. Utilization of available inservice training packages developed to train staff working with students with severe disabilities.
8. Training modules specifically designed to train teachers of students with visual impairments and other severe/multiple disabilities.

9. Encouragement for teachers of students with visual impairments to take additional courses in other disciplines.

Planning for the future offers exciting challenges and presents us with the need to change. The expansion of the roles, function, and competencies of the teacher of students with visual impairments will enable us to provide the best possible services to students with visual impairments who also have severe/multiple disabilities, and it will guarantee that our field will remain on the forefront of special education in the years to come.

REFERENCE

Spungin, S. J. & Ferrell, K. A. (In press.) *The role and function of the teacher of students with visual impairments.* Reston, VA: Division on Visual Impairment/Council for Exceptional Children.

Council for Exceptional Children (CEC) International Standards for Entry into Professional Practice

I. To be qualified to enter into practice as a special education teacher, an individual must possess no less than a bachelor's degree that encompasses the knowledge and skills consistent with the entry level into special education practice.

II. To be qualified to enter into practice as a special education teacher, an individual must possess the knowledge and skills set forth in the CEC Common Core of Knowledge and Skills Essential for Beginning Special Education Teachers.

III. To be qualified to enter into practice as a special education teacher, an individual must possess the knowledge and skills set forth in at least one of the CEC Specialized Knowledge and Skills Essential for Beginning Special Education Teachers.

IV. Each new professional in special education should receive a minimum of a 1-year mentorship during the first year of his or her professional special education practice in a new role. The mentor should be an experienced professional in the same or a similar role, who can provide expertise and support on a continuing basis.

V. Approval of individuals for professional practice in the field of special education should be for a limited period of time with periodic renewal.

VI. Each professional in the field of educating individuals with exceptionalities (e.g., teachers, supervisors, administrators, college/university faculty) should participate in a minimum of 25 clock hours each year of planned, preapproved, organized, and recognized professional development activities related to his or her field of professional practice. Such activities may include a combination of professional development units, continuing education units, college/university coursework, professional organization service (e.g., in CEC federations and chapters, divisions, subdivisions, and caucuses), professional workshops, special projects, or reading professional literature. Employing agencies should provide resources to enable each professional's continuing development.

Source: Council for Exceptional Children, www.cec.sped.org

CEC COMMON CORE OF KNOWLEDGE AND SKILLS ESSENTIAL FOR ALL BEGINNING SPECIAL EDUCATION TEACHERS

Preamble

The standards of the profession of special education are a formally codified set of beliefs. These belief statements represent the special educator's principles of appropriate ethical behavior and are based on several assumptions.

One assumption is that special education has within its heritage the perspectives of advocacy for persons with disabilities and of embracing individual differences. These differences include the traditional consideration of the nature and effect of exceptionalities. As the community of exceptional children, youth, and adults has become increasingly diverse, these perspectives have been broadened to include other characteristics that significantly influence their quality of life. To maintain their ability to successfully function as advocates for their multicultural clients, special educators must broaden their perspectives to ensure vigilant attention to the issues of diversity. Current demographic trends clearly indicate that:

◆ The numbers of children and youth from culturally and linguistically diverse backgrounds served in public schools are growing rapidly.

◆ Cultural and linguistic diversity is expected to continue as well as to increase.

◆ The number of professionals who are culturally and linguistically diverse entering the special education profession has been declining even as the numbers of students who are culturally and linguistically diverse are rising.

Given the pervasive nature of diversity, professional standards are needed that guide professional practice in ways that are relevant to the multicultural populations served in special education. Specifically, these standards reflect the premise that, to design effective interventions, special educators must understand the characteristics of their learners, including factors such as culture, language, gender, religion, and sexuality. This premise has been addressed in two ways. First, most statements are inclusive in nature; that is, they identify knowledge and skills essential to effectively serve all exceptional learners, including those from culturally and linguistically diverse

backgrounds. Second, selected items address the most critical aspects of diversity and are infused throughout the model.

Another assumption is that the sustained involvement of families and the larger community is fundamental to delivering high-quality educational services to individuals with exceptional learning needs. The knowledge and skills contained in this document should be interpreted broadly to include learners of all ages, beginning with infants and preschoolers and extending to young adults who are exiting the school program. Similarly, the term families should be interpreted broadly to include, as appropriate to given situations, biological mothers and fathers, adoptive parents, legal guardians, foster parents or primary caregivers, siblings, and extended family members. Finally, while not specifically stated, it is assumed that special educators may provide learning opportunities in a variety of learning environments, including the home, preschool, school, and community settings, as well as in both specialized and integrated environments.

This document focuses on the unique set of knowledge and skills needed to practice in special education, not on specific areas of exceptionality or age groupings, general education methods, or subject matter content. Special educators who practice in a specific area (or areas) of exceptionality or age grouping must possess the exceptionality-specific knowledge and skills adopted by CEC in addition to the Common Core. Also, it is assumed that a special educator who is required to teach specific subjects or content areas (such as science, social studies, foreign languages, vocational education) has additional preparation, practicum experiences, and expertise in those areas.

An additional assumption is that this Common Core of Knowledge and Skills will change over time. As with the adoption of the CEC Code of Ethics, time should be provided for continuing examination, debate, and further articulation of the knowledge and skills for entry-level special educators.

A final assumption of this Common Core of Knowledge and Skills is that the professional conduct of entry-level special educators is governed foremost by the CEC Code of Ethics. Special education professionals

- Are committed to developing the highest educational and quality of life potential of exceptional individuals.

- Promote and maintain a high level of competence and integrity in practicing their profession.

- Engage in professional activities that benefit exceptional individuals, their families, other colleagues, students or research subjects.

- Exercise objective professional judgment in the practice of their profession.

- Strive to advance their knowledge and skills regarding the education of exceptional individuals.

- Work within the standards and policies of their profession.

- Seek to uphold and improve, where necessary, the laws, regulations, and policies governing the delivery of special education and related services and the practice of their profession.

- Do not condone or participate in unethical or illegal acts, nor violate professional standards adopted by the Delegate Assembly of CEC.

It was through significant professional and personal commitment that the members of CEC crafted this product. In the process we learned not only about knowledge and skills but also about each other and developed a deep mutual respect. May those who use this Common Core of Knowledge and Skills experience that same mutual respect from all who serve children and their families.

KNOWLEDGE AND SKILLS STATEMENTS

CC: Common Core
1. Philosophical, Historical, and Legal Foundations of Special Education

Knowledge

K1 Models, theories, and philosophies that provide the basis for special education.

K2 Variations in beliefs, traditions, and values across cultures within society and the effect of the relationship among child, family, and schooling.

K3 Issues in definition and identification procedures for individuals with exceptional learning needs including individuals from culturally and/or linguistically diverse backgrounds.

K4 Assurances and due process rights related to assessment, eligibility, and placement.

K5 Rights and responsibilities of parents, students, teachers and other professionals, and schools as they relate to individuals with learning needs.

Skills

S1 Articulate personal philosophy of special education including its relationship to/with regular education.

S2 Conduct instructional and other professional activities consistent with the requirements of law, rules and regulations, and local district policies and procedures.

CC: Common Core
2. Characteristics of Learners

Knowledge

K1 Similarities and differences among the cognitive, physical, cultural, social, and emotional needs of individuals with and without exceptional learning needs.

K2 Differential characteristics of individuals with exceptionalities, including levels of severity and multiple exceptionalities.

K3 Characteristics of normal, delayed, and disordered communication patterns of individuals with exceptional learning needs.

K4 Effects an exceptional condition(s) may have on an individual's life.

K5 Characteristics and effects of the cultural and environmental milieu of the child and the family including cultural and linguistic diversity, socioeconomic level, abuse/neglect, and substance abuse.

K6 Effects of various medications on the educational, cognitive, physical, social, and emotional behavior of individuals with exceptionalities.

K7 Educational implications of characteristics of various exceptionalities.

Skills

S1 Access information on various cognitive, communication, physical, cultural, social, and emotional conditions of individuals with exceptional learning needs.

CC: Common Core
3. Assessment, Diagnosis, and Evaluation

Knowledge

K1 Basic terminology used in assessment.

K2 Ethical concerns related to assessment.

K3 Legal provisions, regulations, and guidelines regarding assessment of individuals.

K4 Typical procedures used for screening, prereferral, referral, and classification.

K5 Appropriate application and interpretation of scores, including grade score versus standard score, percentile ranks, age/grade equivalents, and stanines.

K6 Appropriate use and limitations of each type of assessment instrument.

K7 Incorporation of strategies that consider the influence of diversity on assessment, eligibility, programming, and placement of individuals with exceptional learning needs.

K8 The relationship between assessment and placement decisions.

K9 Methods for monitoring progress of individuals with exceptional learning needs.

Skills

S1 Collaborate with families and other professionals involved in the assessment of individuals with exceptional learning needs.

S2 Create and maintain records.

S3 Gather background information regarding academic, medical, and family history.

S4 Use various types of assessment procedures appropriately.

S5 Interpret information from formal and informal assessment instruments and procedures.

S6 Report assessment results to individuals with exceptional learning needs, parents, administrators, and other professionals using appropriate communication skills.

S7 Use performance data and information from teachers, other professionals, individuals with exceptionalities, and parents to make or suggest appropriate modification in learning environments.

S8 Develop individualized assessment strategies for instruction.

S9 Use assessment information in making instructional decisions and planning individual programs that result in appropriate placement and intervention for all individuals with exceptional learning needs, including those from culturally and/or linguistically diverse backgrounds.

S10 Evaluate the results of instruction.

S11 Evaluate supports needed for integration into various program placements.

CC: Common Core
4. Instructional Content and Practice

Knowledge

K1 Differing learning styles of individuals with exceptional learning needs and how to adapt teaching to these styles.

K2 Demands of various learning environments such as individualized instruction in general education classes.

K3 Curricula for the development of motor, cognitive, academic, social language, affective, and functional life skills for individuals with exceptional learning needs.

K4 Instructional and remedial methods, techniques, and curriculum materials.

K5 Techniques for modifying instructional methods and materials.

K6 Life skills instruction relevant to independent, community, and personal living and employment.

K7 Cultural perspectives influencing the relationship among families, schools, and communities as related to effective instruction for individuals with exceptional learning needs.

Skills

S1 Interpret and use assessment data for instructional planning.

S2 Develop and/or select instructional content, materials, resources, and strategies that respond to cultural, linguistic, and gender differences.

S3 Develop comprehensive, longitudinal individualized programs.

S4 Choose and use appropriate technologies to accomplish instructional objectives and to integrate them appropriately into the instructional process.

S5 Prepare appropriate lesson plans.

S6 Involve the individual and family in setting instructional goals and charting progress.

S7 Conduct and use task analysis.

S8 Select, adapt, and use instructional strategies and materials according to characteristics of the learner.

S9 Sequence, implement, and evaluate individual learning objectives.

S10 Integrate affective, social, and career/vocational skills with academic curricula.

S11 Use strategies for facilitating maintenance and generalization of skills across learning environments.

S12 Use instructional time properly.

S13 Teach individuals with exceptional learning needs to use thinking, problem-solving, and other cognitive strategies to meet their individual needs.

S14 Choose and implement instructional techniques and strategies that promote successful transition for individuals with exceptional learning needs.

S15 Establish and maintain rapport with learners.

S16 Use verbal and nonverbal communication techniques.

S17 Conduct self-evaluation of instruction.

CC: Common Core
5. Planning and Managing the Teaching and Learning Environment

Knowledge

K1 Basic classroom management theories, methods, and techniques for individuals with exceptional learning needs.

K2 Research-based best practices for effective management of teaching and learning.

K3 Ways in which technology can assist with planning and managing the teaching and learning environment.

Skills

S1 Create a safe, positive, and supportive learning environment in which diversities are valued.

S2 Use strategies and techniques for facilitating the functional integration of individuals with exceptional learning needs in various settings.

S3 Prepare and organize materials to implement daily lesson plans.

S4 Incorporate evaluation, planning, and management procedures that match learner needs with the instructional environment.

S5 Design a learning environment that encourages active participation by learners in a variety of individual and group learning activities.

S6 Design, structure, and manage daily routines, effectively including transition time, for students, other staff, and the instructional setting.

S7 Direct the activities of a classroom paraprofessional, aide, volunteer, or peer tutor.

S8 Create an environment that encourages self-advocacy and increased independence.

CC: Common Core
6. Managing Student Behavior and Social Interaction Skills

Knowledge

K1 Applicable laws, rules and regulations, and procedural safeguards regarding the planning and implementation of management of behaviors of individuals with exceptional learning needs.

K2 Ethical considerations inherent in classroom behavior management.

K3 Teacher attitudes and behaviors that positively or negatively influence behavior of individuals with exceptional learning needs.

K4 Social skills needed for educational and functional living environments and effective instruction in the development of social skills.

K5 Strategies for crisis prevention/intervention.

K6 Strategies for preparing individuals to live harmoniously and productively in a multiclass, multiethnic, multicultural, and multinational world.

Skills

S1 Demonstrate a variety of effective behavior management techniques appropriate to the needs of individuals with exceptional learning needs.

S2 Implement the least intensive intervention consistent with the needs of the individuals with exceptionalities.

S3 Modify the learning environment (schedule and physical arrangement) to manage inappropriate behaviors.

S4 Identify realistic expectations for personal and social behavior in various settings.

S5 Integrate social skills into the curriculum.

S6 Use effective teaching procedures in social skills instruction.

S7 Demonstrate procedures to increase the individual's self-awareness, self-control, self-reliance, and self-esteem.

S8 Prepare individuals with exceptional learning needs to exhibit self-enhancing behavior in response to societal attitudes and actions.

CC: Common Core
7. Communication and Collaborative Partnerships

Knowledge

K1 Factors that promote effective communication and collaboration with individuals, parents, and school and community personnel in a culturally responsive program.

K2 Typical concerns of parents of individuals with exceptional learning needs and appropriate strategies to help parents deal with these concerns.

K3 Development of individual student programs working in collaboration with team members.

K4 Roles of individuals with exceptionalities, parents, teachers, and other school and community personnel in planning an individualized program.

K5 Ethical practices for confidential communication to others about individuals with exceptional learning needs.

Skills

S1 Use collaborative strategies in working with individuals with exceptional learning needs, parents, and school and community personnel in various learning environments.

S2 Communicate and consult with individuals, parents, teachers, and other school and community personnel.

S3 Foster respectful and beneficial relationships between families and professionals.

S4 Encourage and assist families to become active participants in the educational team.

S5 Plan and conduct collaborative conferences with families or primary caregivers.

S6 Collaborate with regular classroom teachers and other school and community personnel in integrating individuals with exceptional learning needs into various learning environments.

S7 Communicate with regular teachers, administrators, and other school personnel about characteristics and needs of indi-

viduals with specific exceptional learning needs.

CC: Common Core
8. Professionalism and Ethical Practices

Knowledge

K1 Personal cultural biases and differences that affect one's teaching.

K2 Importance of the teacher serving as a model for individuals with exceptional learning needs.

Skills

S1 Demonstrate commitment to developing the highest educational and quality-of-life potential of individuals with exceptional learning needs.

S2 Demonstrate positive regard for the culture, religion, gender, and sexual orientation of individual students.

S3 Promote and maintain a high level of competence and integrity in the practice of the profession.

S4 Exercise objective professional judgment in the practice of the profession.

S5 Demonstrate proficiency in oral and written communication.

S6 Engage in professional activities that may benefit individuals with exceptional learning needs, their families, and/or colleagues.

S7 Comply with local, state, provincial, and federal monitoring and evaluation requirements.

S8 Use copyrighted educational materials in an ethical manner.

S9 Practice within the CEC Code of Ethics and other standards and policies of the profession.

Council for Exceptional Children (CEC) Knowledge and Skills for All Beginning Special Education Teachers of Students with Visual Impairments

KNOWLEDGE AND SKILLS STATEMENTS

VI: Visual Impairment
1. Philosophical, Historical, and Legal Foundations of Special Education

Knowledge

K1 Federal entitlements (e.g., American Printing House for the Blind Quota Funds) that relate to the provision of specialized equipment and materials for learners with visual impairments.

K2 Historical foundations for education of children with visual impairments, including the array of service options.

K3 Current educational definitions of students with visual disabilities, including identification criteria, labeling issues, and current incidence and prevalence figures.

Source: Reprinted, with permission, from What Every Special Educator Must Know: The International Standards for the Preparation and Licensure of Special Educators, 3rd ed. *(Reston, VA: The Council for Exceptional Children), pp. 75–80. ©1998 The Council for Exceptional Children.*

Skills

S1 Articulate the pros and cons of current issues and trends in special education visual impairment.

VI: Visual Impairment
2. Characteristics of Learners

Knowledge

K1 Normal development of the human visual system.

K2 Basic terminology related to the structure and function of the human visual system.

K3 Basic terminology related to diseases and disorders of the human visual system.

K4 Development of secondary senses (hearing, touch, taste, smell) when the primary sense is impaired.

K5 The effects of a visual impairment on early development (motor system, cognition, social/emotional interactions, self-help, language).

K6 The effects of a visual impairment on social behaviors and independence.

K7 The effects of a visual impairment on language and communication.

K8 The effects of a visual impairment on the individual's family and the reciprocal impact on the individual's self-esteem.

K9 Psychosocial aspects of a visual impairment.

K10 Effects of medications on the visual system.

K11 The impact of additional exceptionalities on students with visual impairments.

Skills

(None in addition to Common Core.)

VI: Visual Impairment
3. Assessment, Diagnosis, and Evaluation

Knowledge

K1 The impact of visual disorders on learning and experience.

K2 Specialized terminology used in assessing individuals with visual impairments, both as it relates to the visual system and in areas of importance.

K3 Ethical considerations and legal provisions, regulations, and guidelines (federal, state/provincial, and local) related to assessment of students with visual impairments (including the legal versus functional definitions of blindness and low vision).

K4 Specialized policies regarding referral and placement procedures for students with visual impairments.

K5 Procedures used for screening, prereferral, referral, and classifications of students with visual impairments, including vision screening methods, functional vision evaluation, and learning media assessment.

K6 Alternative assessment techniques for students who are blind or who have low vision.

K7 Appropriate interpretation and application of scores obtained as a result of assessing individuals with visual impairments.

K8 Relationships among assessment, IEP development, and placement as they affect vision-related services.

Skills

S1 Interpret eye reports and other vision-related diagnostic information.

S2 Use disability-specific assessment instruments appropriately (e.g., Blind Learning Aptitude Test, Tactile Test of Basic Concepts, Diagnostic Assessment Procedure).

S3 Adapt and use a variety of assessment procedures appropriately when evaluating individuals with visual impairments.

S4 Create and maintain disability-related records for students with visual impairments.

S5 Gather background information about academic, medical, and family history as it relates to the student's visual status for students with visual impairments.

S6 Develop individualized instructional strategies to enhance instruction for learners with visual impairments, including modifications of the environment, adaptations of materials, and disability-specific methodologies.

VI: Visual Impairment
4. Instructional Content and Practice

Knowledge

K1 Methods for the development of special auditory, tactual, and modified visual communication skills for students with visual impairments, including:

◆ Braille reading and writing.

◆ Handwriting for students with low vision and signature writing for students who are blind.

♦ Listening skills and compensatory auditory skills.

♦ Typing and keyboarding skills.

♦ The use of unique technology for individuals with visual impairments.

♦ The use of alternatives to nonverbal communication.

K2 Methods to acquire disability-unique academic skills, including:

♦ The use of an abacus.

♦ The use of a talking calculator.

♦ Tactile graphics (including maps, charts, tables, etc.).

♦ Adapted science equipment.

K3 Methods for the development of basic concepts needed by young students who do not learn visually.

K4 Methods for the development of visual efficiency, including instruction in the use of print adaptations, optical devices, and non-optical devices.

K5 Methods to develop alternative reasoning and decision-making skills in students with visual impairments.

K6 Methods to develop alternative organization and study skills for students with visual impairments.

K7 Methods to prepare students with visual impairments for structured precane orientation and mobility assessment and instruction.

K8 Methods to develop tactual perceptual skills for students who are or will be primarily tactual learners.

K9 Methods to teach human sexuality to students who have visual impairments, using tactile models that are anatomically accurate.

K10 Methods to develop adapted physical and recreation skills for individuals who have visual impairments.

K11 Methods to develop social and daily living skills that are normally learned or reinforced by visual means.

K12 Strategies for developing career awareness in and providing vocational counseling for students with visual impairments.

K13 Strategies for promoting self-advocacy in individuals with visual impairments.

K14 Functional life skills instruction relevant to independent, community, and personal living and employment for individuals with visual impairments including:

♦ Methods for accessing printed public information.

♦ Methods for accessing public transportation.

♦ Methods for accessing community resources.

♦ Methods for acquiring practical skills (e.g., keeping personal records, time management, personal banking, emergency procedures).

K15 Sources of specialized materials for students with visual impairments.

K16 Techniques for modifying instructional methods and materials for students with visual impairments, and assisting classroom teachers in implementing these modifications.

Skills

S1 Interpret and use unique assessment data for instructional planning with students with visual impairments.

S2 Choose and use appropriate technologies to accomplish instructional objectives for students with visual impairments, and integrate the technologies appropriately into the instructional process.

S3 Sequence, implement, and evaluate individual disability-related learning objectives for students with visual impairments.

S4 Use strategies for facilitating the maintenance and generalization of disability-related skills across learning environments for students with visual impairments.

S5 Teach students who have visual impairments to use thinking, problem-solving, and other cognitive strategies to meet their individual learning needs.

VI: Visual Impairment
5. Planning and Managing the Teaching and Learning Environment

Knowledge

K1 A variety of input and output enhancements to computer technology that address the specific access needs of students with visual impairments in a variety of environments.

K2 Model programs, including career-vocational and transition, that have been effective for students with visual impairments.

Skills

S1 Prepare modified special materials (e.g., in Braille, enlarged, outlined, highlighted) for students who have visual impairments.

S2 Obtain and organize special materials to implement instructional goals for learners with visual impairments.

S3 Design learning environments that are multisensory and that encourage active participation by learners with visual impairments in a variety of group and individual learning activities.

S4 Create a learning environment that encourages self-advocacy and independence for students with visual impairments.

S5 Transcribe, proofread, and interline grade

II Braille and Nemeth Code Braille materials.

S6 Use Braillewriter, slate and stylus, and computer technology to produce Braille materials.

VI: Visual Impairment
6. Managing Student Behavior and Social Interaction Skills

Knowledge

K1 Teacher attitudes and behaviors that affect the behaviors of students with visual impairments.

Skills

S1 Prepare students with progressive eye conditions to achieve a positive transition to alternative skills.

S2 Prepare students who have visual impairments to access information and services from the community at large.

S3 Prepare students who have visual impairments to respond to societal attitudes and actions with positive behavior, self-advocacy, and a sense of humor.

VI: Visual Impairment
7. Communication and Collaborative Partnerships

Knowledge

K1 Strategies for assisting parents and other professionals in planning appropriate transitions for students who have visual impairments.

K2 Sources of unique services, networks, and organizations for students with visual impairments.

K3 Roles of paraprofessionals who work directly with students who have visual impairments (e.g., sighted readers, transcribers, aides) or who provide special materials to them.

K4 Need for role models who have visual impairments, and who are successful.

Skills

S1 Help parents and other professionals to understand the impact of a visual impairment on learning and experience.

S2 Report disability-related results of evaluations to students who have visual impairments, their parents and administrators and other professionals in clear, concise, "laymen's" terms.

S3 Manage and direct the activities of paraprofessionals or peer tutors who work with students who have visual impairments.

VI: Visual Impairment
8. Professionalism and Ethical Practices

Knowledge

K1 Consumer and professional organizations, publications, and journals relevant to the field of visual impairment.

Skills

S1 Belong to and participate in the activities of professional organizations in the field of visual impairment.

GLOSSARY

Abacus A device used for performing mathematical computations by sliding beads along rods.

Academic literacy skills The basic reading and writing skills taught in a conventional literacy medium (print or braille) during the elementary and middle school years. *See also* Emergent literacy skills; Functional literacy skills; Literacy skills

Acquired Immune Deficiency Syndrome *See* AIDS

Activities of daily living (ADLs) The routine activities that an individual must be able to perform to live independently.

Adaptation The modification of instructional materials to the needs of students who are visually impaired. *See also* Auditory adaptations; Tactile adaptations; Visual adaptations

Adaptive physical education teacher An educator who has been specially trained to work with children who need individualized instruction to improve motor skill development.

Adaptive technology *See* Assistive technology

Adventitious blindness Loss or impairment of vision that occurs after birth, usually as a result of an accident or disease. *See also* Congenital visual impairment

Affective communication A social skill that enables individuals to communicate nonverbally, that is, through actions, gestures, visual expression, and body language.

AIDS (Acquired Immune Deficiency Syndrome) A chronic disease of the immune system that is caused by infection with the human immune deficiency virus. As a result of a compromised immune system, individuals with AIDS may develop eye conditions leading to visual impairment, such as cytomegalovirus retinitis, the most frequent opportunistic intraocular infection among individuals with AIDS.

Americans with Disabilities Act (ADA) of 1990 An act granting civil rights to individuals with disabilities. The ADA prohibits discrimination against individuals with disabilities in the areas of public accommodations, employment, transportation, state and local government services, and telecommunications. It is the most far-reaching civil rights legislation ever enacted in the history of disability policy in the United States.

Applied behavior analysis A systematic approach to learning that incorporates the principles of behavior modification and structured reinforcement to change a desired behavior.

Arena assessment A form of observation in

which a group of observers, often with different specialties, observe one or two people interacting with a student.

Arts Education Assessment Framework A method of evaluating a students knowledge in the arts within personal, social, cultural, and historical contexts as well as in the areas of aesthetics, form, and structure.

Assessment In education, the process through which present needs and skill levels of the student are determined.

Assistive technology Equipment used to help individuals compensate for the loss of vision or a visual impairment such as speech, braille, and large-print devices that enable a person who is visually impaired to use a personal computer and software programs.

Assistive technology assessment A method of determining the most appropriate technological tools for current and future education tasks.

Assistive technology specialist A professional who assists the student in identifying which assistive devices most effectively meet a specific need. Auditory adaptations Modifications of classroom materials into a format that can be heard.

Aural reading The gathering of information from audiotaped materials and books.

Blindness The inability to see; the absence or severe reduction of vision. *See also* Adventitious visual impairment; Congenital visual impairment

Bold-line writing guide A handwriting guide for students with low vision that utilizes highly visible lines to give some measure of visual guidance for writing.

Braille A system of raised dots that enables blind persons to read and write.

Braille literacy A student's proficiency in using braille to accomplish reading and writing tasks.

Braille printer A computer printer that embosses braille by using software to convert from print to grade 2 braille.

Braillewriter A machine used for embossing braille.

Career education skills The ability to function in the work environment by interacting with others, having appropriate O&M skills, and managing the tasks of daily living.

Case manager An individual designated by a team to assume primary responsibility for compiling all information relevant to educational program planning for a student.

Certification A formalization indication or approval attesting to the fact that indicates that an individual is recognized as meeting all the criteria necessary for practice within a profession.

Chaining An instructional strategy used to teach sequential tasks by teaching each task one at a time in sequential order.

Checklists Lists of skills of increasing difficulty or related to a set of objectives that are used to monitor student progress.

Child find system A legal mandate of the IDEA that requires each state to have a plan to locate and evaluate all children (including infants and toddlers) with disabilities and referring them for service.

Clinical low vision assessment Evaluation to determine whether an individual with low vision can benefit from optical devices, nonoptical devices, or adaptive techniques to enhance visual function.

Clinical low vision specialist An ophthalmologist or optometrist who specializes in low vision care.

Closed-circuit television (CCTV) An optical device, which electronically enlarges print, pictures, and objects, that consists of a camera, lenses, and a monitor.

Clues Bits of temporary sensory information that can be used in orientation and mobility to tell where one is or the direction in which one wants to go.

Code of ethics A standard, typically consisting of guidelines, intended to ensure that those who have entered a profession have the appropriate preparation and that they practice in accordance with acceptable and respected principles.

Cognitive abilities Functions involving those operations of the mind by which students become aware of objects or thought or perception, including understanding and reasoning. *See also* Intellectual ability

Color vision The ability to discriminate different hues and saturations of colors.

Communication notebooks Records of events at school and home made by teachers, parents, and students.

Compensatory education The knowledge and skills that make it possible for the student with a visual impairment to achieve educational objectives at a rate and level similar to that of his or her sighted classmates.

Comprehensive assessment An evaluation of all the skills that are specifically related to the student's visual impairment, including the functional vision assessment, the learning media assessment, braille reading and writing, potential for using assistive technology, and the use of other aids, academic achievement, and so forth.

Comprehensive Vocational Evaluation System (CVES) A system developed specifically for individuals with visual impairments. It is a norm-referenced test battery that assesses intelligence,

academic achievement, motor skills, tactile skills, adaptive behavior, work behavior, and emotionality.

Concept development The development of mental ideas of things, which is one of the building blocks for independence and an essential element in orientation and mobility training.

Concurrent validity A type of criterion-related validity that compares a student's performance on two or more tests within a short period. If the student performs similarly on both tests, the accuracy of the results is considered more reliable. *See also* Criterion-related validity; Validity

Congenital visual impairment Loss or impairment of vision that is present at birth. *See also* Adventitious visual impairment

Content validity A determination of how clearly the items sampled on the test represent the content that the test purports to measure. *See also* Validity

Contrast sensitivity The ability to detect differences in grayness and background.

Core curriculum The general education curriculum that all students are expected to master, including language arts, science, mathematics, and social studies.

Criterion-referenced tests Formal or informal instruments that compare the student's performance to the overall mastery of the skill being evaluated. They are judged against a predetermined level of mastery that is often expressed as a percentage.

Criterion-related validity A determination of how accurately a test measures what it purports to measure by comparing the scores with other criteria that are considered indicators of the same trait or skill as that being measured. *See also* Concurrent validity; Predictive validity; Validity

Curriculum-based assessment An evaluation of a student's progress by reviewing comparing skills with the content of the student's curriculum.

Developmental assessment An evaluation of motor and personal-social skills. In the case of students who are blind or visually impaired, the evaluator must take into account the extent to which such development in preschool children depends on the extent of useful vision.

Developmentally delayed Functioning at a level below expectancy for one's chronological age.

Diagnostic teaching The analysis of learning difficulties during lessons, and targeted instruction to minimize or eliminate the difficulties identified.

Disability A condition that exists when, in a particular setting, an individual cannot independently perform a specific set of functional activities. Distance education Academic or other learning programs to accommodate students by offering instruction off campus, such as at satellite locations or over the Internet.

Echolocation The use of reflected sound (including ambient sound) to detect the presence of objects, such as walls, buildings, doors, and openings.

Ecological assessment A structured way of observing a student's interaction with his or her environment.

Education for All Handicapped Children Act (PL 94-142) Federal legislation enacted in 1975 that guarantees free appropriate public education in the least restrictive environment, with special education, related services, and Individualized Education Programs mandated for each child needing special services. Now known as the Individuals with Disabilities Education Act (IDEA), it is the most significant legislation on behalf of students with disabilities.

Electronic magnification systems Machines that produce enlarged images, including closed-circuit televisions, computer systems, and low vision enhancement devices.

Emergent literacy skills The earliest attempts by young children to bring meaning to reading and writing. *See also* Academic literacy skills; Functional literacy skills; Literacy skills

Environmental assessment An analysis of the student's school environment.

Environmental modifications Changes in the environment to maximize the use of vision.

Event records A record that focuses on specific targeted behaviors, such as reading, working, and talking, as they occur within an observational period. *See also* Observational methods

Expanded core curriculum A curriculum that covers the unique, disability-specific skills, such as independent living skill and orientation and mobility skills, that students with visual impairments need to live independently and productively.

Experiential learning An approach to teaching in which the environment is arranged to motivate children to explore, investigate, ponder, and question so they can construct knowledge for themselves.

Field expansion systems A variety of optical devices for individuals with reduced visual fields, including prism lenses, mirror magnifiers, and reverse telescopes.

Field of vision *See* Visual field

Formal tests Evaluations that require careful adherence to directions for their administration and scoring, may have time limits, and result in a numerical or quantitative score that is compared to the scores of a particular group. *See also* Informal tests; Norm-referenced tests; Standardized tests

Functional blindness Condition in which some useful vision may or may not be present but in which the individual uses tactile and auditory channels most effectively for learning.

Functional literacy skills The application of literacy skills and the use of a variety of literacy tools (such as listening and technology) to accomplish daily tasks in the home, school, community, and work settings. *See also* Academic literacy skills; Emergent literacy skills; Functional literacy skills; Literacy skills

Functional vision The ability to use vision in planning and performing a task.

Functional vision assessment An assessment of an individual's use of vision in a variety of tasks and settings, including measures of near and distance vision; visual fields; eye movements; and responses to specific environmental characteristics, such as light and color. The assessment report includes recommendations for instructional procedures, modifications or adaptations, and additional tests.

General education teacher An instructor in an inclusive environment who is not especially trained to modify instruction for students with visual impairments. *See also* Teacher of students with visual impairments

Glare An annoying sensation produced by too much light in the visual field that can cause both discomfort and a reduction in visual acuity.

Group tests Evaluations designed to be administered to more than one individual at a time. *See also* Individual tests

Inclusion A philosophy that promotes the placement of a student with a disability in a general education classroom for all or part of the school day; often used interchangeably with "mainstreaming."

Independent living skills Skills for performing daily tasks and managing personal needs, such as those for self-care, planning and cooking meals, maintaining a sanitary living environment, traveling independently, budgeting one's expenses, and functioning as independently as possible in the home and in the community.

Individualized Education Program (IEP) A written plan of instruction by a transdisciplinary educational term, which includes a student's present levels of educational performance, annual goals, short-term objectives, specific services needed, duration of services, evaluation, and related information. Under the Individuals with Disabilities Education Act (IDEA), each student receiving special services must have such a plan.

Individualized Family Service Plan (IFSP) A plan for the coordination of early intervention services for infants and toddlers with disabilities, similar to the Individualized Education Program (IEP) that is required for all school-age children with disabilities. A requirement of the Individuals with Disabilities Education Act (IDEA).

Individualized Transition Plan (ITP) A plan that focuses on the development of skills and gaining access to resources that will enable a student to be successful in a future environment, whether it be further education, the workplace, or a vocational training facility. Sometimes the ITP is incorporated into the IEP. See also Individualized Education Program

Individuals with Disabilities Education Act (IDEA) (P.L. 101.476) The 1990 amendments to the Education for All Handicapped Children Act(P.L. 94.142), the federal legislation that safeguards a free, appropriate public education for all eligible children with disabilities in the United States.

Individual tests Evaluations administered on a one-to-one basis. See also Group tests

Informal tests Evaluations that allow flexibility in the manner in which they are administered (as compared with formal tests) and have no time limit. *See also* Criterion-referenced tests; Formal tests; Portfolios

Integration The placement of children with impairments in regular classrooms with children who are not disabled.

Intellectual ability assessment A measurement that can include more than 100 different elements related to intelligence. Therefore, different assessment tools measure measure different abilities and/or behaviors depending on that tests definition of intelligence. *See also* Cognitive abilities

Interdisciplinary team Professionals from various disciplines who conduct and share the results of assessments and jointly plan instructional programs. *See also* Multidisciplinary team; Transdisciplinary team

Intervention strategies Plans for instructional interventions for students with visual impairments and disabilities that follow the changing needs of the individual.

Interviews and questionnaires Assessment technique based on open-ended questions asked orally and recorded by the examiner or presented in written format and recorded by the respondent.

Itinerant teacher An instructor who moves from place to place (e.g., from home to home, school to hospital, or school to school) to provide instruction and support to students with special needs.

Landmarks Objects in homes or classrooms that are easily identified, permanent, and unique to their particular setting.

Language-experience approach A method of instruction that uses the child's actual experiences as the basis for written stories that are then used to teach reading.

Large print Print that is larger (14-18 points) than that commonly found in magazines, newspapers, and books (6-12 points).

Learned helplessness A form of depression that occurs when an individual learns to become depend on others for support and assistance, usually because few expectations on placed on him or her to achieve.

Learned optimism An outlook based on positive thinking that occurs when an individual thinks positively about events in his or her life based on life experiences.

Learning media The range of visual, auditory, and tactile materials, tools, and equipment used for learning.

Learning media assessment An examination of the child's use of sensory information, need for general learning media, and specific literary media.

Least-restrictive environment (LRE) Placement of a child with a disability in a classroom environment that is adapted only to the extent necessary to maximize learning.

Legal blindness Visual impairment in which distance visual acuity is 20/200 or less in the better eye after best correction with conventional lenses or visual field restriction is 20 degrees or less.

Lifestyle plan A four-step plan that includes initial considerations, a personal profile, the creation of a desirable vision of the future, and the development of strategies to enhance accomplishments.

Listening skills The ability to hear specific sounds, to understand the main idea and specific facts presented by lecturers and readers, and to recall auditory information and critically interpret the material.

Literacy The ability to read and write.

Literacy medium or media The form(s) of the printed word (print and/or braille) that an individual uses to read and write.

Literacy skills The ability to use reading, writing, and other literacy tools to gather and understand important information and to convey information to themselves or others. *See also* Academic literacy skills; Emergent literacy skills; Functional literacy skills

Locus of control A phenomenon that allows an individual to take responsibility for his or her actions and activities and to take advantage of opportunities to achieve a greater sense of independence.

Long-range goals The measure of performance to be obtained by the end of the educational program.

Low vision A visual impairment after correction, but with the potential for use of available vision, with or without optical or nonoptical compensatory visual strategies, devices, and environmental modification, to plan and perform daily tasks.

Low vision device A type of optical or nonoptical device used to enhance the visual capability of persons with visual impairments. Low vision devices range from bold-line felt-tip markers to magnifiers and telescopes.

Magnifier A device used to increase the size of an image through the use of lenses or lens systems; a magnifier may be used at any distance from the eye (e.g., stand type, handheld, or spectacle mounted).

Mainstreaming The placement of a student with a disability in a general education classroom with children who are not disabled for all or part of the school day; often used interchangeable with "inclusion."

Mathematics skills The abilities needed to understand, interpret, and apply numerical concepts in practical and abstract situations. Includes an understanding of such concepts as conservation, seriation, quantity concepts, word problems, measurements, graphs, algebra, and geometry, and the use of calculating tools, tactile displays, and the Nemeth Code.

Mathematical skills assessment Evaluation of mathematical skills using formal and informal assessment tools.

Mechanical skills The abilities necessary for efficient braille reading, including finger dexterity and wrist flexibility, hand movement skills and finger positions, light finger touch, and tactile perception and discrimination skills.

Mental math The ability to calculate mentally with efficiency and without the use of such instruments as the calculator, abacus, and braillewriter.

Mobility The act or ability to move from one's present position to one's desired position in another part of the environment. See also Orientation

Mobility skills The skills used by a person to travel in different directions to move from one location to another.

Modeling A form of instruction in which the teacher provides a model or demonstration of the task or skill for the student to use as a guide in attempting to perform the task or skill.

Motility The coordinated movement of the eyes in conditions in which irregular eye movements occur.

Motor skills *See* Orientation and Mobility

Multidisciplinary team A team made up of professionals from different disciplines who work independently to conduct assessments of a student, write and implement separate plans, and evaluate the student's progress within the parameters of their own disciplines.

Multiple disabilities Two or more concomitant disabilities (physical, mental, or emotional) that have a direct effect on the ability to learn.

Multisensory learning approaches A learning strategy that encourages students to use all their senses in exploring and learning and results in a rich learning experience.

Narrative records Anecdotal and running records of a student's activities that are significant in terms of the student's ability to learn. *See also* Observational methods

Nemeth code A braille code system designed for use in science and mathematics.

Nonoptical adaptations Devices or techniques, such as lamps, filters, bold-lined paper, and writing guides, that alter the visual environment by adjusting the space, illumination, color contrast, or other physical features of the environment.

Nonparallel instruction Teaching braille skills at some point after students have acquired basic print literacy skills. *See also* Parallel instruction

Nonstandardized tests Informal assessment tools that do not have rigid procedures for administration and do not provide norms for comparison or interpretation. *See also* Standardized tests

Nonsymbolic communication Methods of communication, such as laughing, bouncing, limb movement, and vocal sounds, that do not involve spoken words or manual signs. *See also* Symbolic communication

Norm-referenced tests Tests in which the student's results are compared to that of a larger group on which the test was standardized. *See also* Standardized tests

Number sense An intuitive ability to attach meaning to numbers and number relationships; to understand the magnitude of numbers as well as the relativity of measuring numbers; and to use logical reasoning for estimation.

Observational method Watching and recording behaviors to help understand the student through anecdotal records, running records, and event records. *See also* Career education skills; Event records; Narrative records; Occupational skills

Occupational therapist A professional who focuses on maximizing an individuals potential for age appropriate functional behaviors, particularly in daily living activities, through purposeful activities.

Ophthalmologist A physician who specializes in the medical and surgical care of the eyes and is qualified to prescribe ocular medications and to perform surgery on the eyes. May also perform refractive and low vision work, including eye examinations and other vision services.

Optical character recognition (OCR) A system used to convert printed material into computer files so it can be produced in a form (such as braille or voice output) that is useful for people with sensory losses, using a scanner interfaced with a computer.

Optical device Any system of lenses that enhances visual function.

Optometrist A health care provider who specializes in refractive errors, prescribes eyeglasses or contact lenses, and diagnoses and manages conditions of the eye as regulated by state laws. May also perform low vision examinations.

Orientation The knowledge of one's distance and direction relative to things observed or remembered in one's surroundings and the ability to keep track of these spatial relationships as they change during locomotion. *See also* Clues; Landmarks; Mobility

Orientation and mobility (O&M) The field dealing with systematic techniques by which persons who are blind or visually impaired orient themselves to their environments and move about independently. *See also* Mobility; Orientation

Orientation and mobility (O&M) assistants Paraeducators who are trained and certified to practice specified skills under the direction of orientation and mobility instructors.

Orientation and mobility (O&M) specialist A professional who specializes in teaching travel skills to persons who are visual impaired, including the use of canes, dog guides, sophisticated electronic traveling aids, as well as the sighted guide technique.

Paraeducator An individual who works under the direction and supervision of a qualified educator and who typically does not hold a teaching certificate or license. Typical duties include preparing adapted materials in braille, large-type, and other accessible media; assisting a student with practicing skills that were taught previously by the teacher of students with visual impairments or other qualified educator; and assisting in the classroom and school as directed.

Parallel instruction Teaching braille and print currently and with the same level of intensity. See also Nonparallel instruction

Partial sight A term formerly often used to indicate visual acuity of 20/70 to 20/200 but also used to describe visual impairment in which usable vision is present.

Performance tests Evaluations in which students actually carry out activities to demonstrate their abilities. See also Verbal tests

Peripheral vision The perception of objects, motion, or color outside the direct line of vision or by other than the central retina.

Personnel preparation programs Programs that offer college and university courses to prepare specialized teachers to educate students with visual impairments.

Physical education teacher *See* Adaptive physical education teacher

Play-based assessment A method of evaluation in which a student is observed at play, interacting with materials and people in situations that provide opportunities for choice and initiative.

Portfolios Collections of the results of various assessments and samples of the student's work that are used to evaluate and provide a complete overview of the student's progress.

Predictive validity A type of criterion-related validity that refers to a test's ability to predict a student's success in a related area at a later time. *See also* Criterion-related validity; Validity

Print literacy A student's proficiency in using print media, with or without adaptations, to accomplish reading and writing tasks.

Prism lenses Special triangle-shaped lenses that are incorporated into regular eyeglasses, to redirect the rays of light entering the eye, resulting in a realignment of the eyes or, in some cases, a shifting of image to permit binocular vision.

Prompting An instructional procedure in which the teacher provides the student with minimal assistance so that the student can complete a task that he or she has not yet completely mastered.

Psychological assessment A professional determination of whether an individual possess the emotional stability to handle stresses associated with performing a particular job or learning a particular skill.

Questionnaires See Interviews and questionnaires

Reading efficiency The speed at which an individual reads with comprehension.

Recreational/leisure skills Abilities, which are part of the expanded core curriculum, that enable the student with visual impairments to participate in recreational activities. The student should be exposed to a variety of activities, receive direct instruction in these activities or prerequisite skills, consult with recreation specialists, and link these activities with his or her academic curriculum.

Refreshable braille display An electronic device that connects to a computer by a cable and translates information displayed on the computer screen into braille in the form of electronically driven plastic pins that pop up to form braille characters.

Reliability The consistency with which a student's performance on a test is repeated over multiple administrations over time.

Resource room A service delivery option designed to support students with visual impairments who are enrolled in a general education classroom by providing specialized instruction and support from a qualified teacher who is housed on site.

Scanner A device that uses a moving electronic beam to convert visual images, such as printed text or graphic images, into an electronic format that can be transmitted or converted into other formats.

Self-concept The collection of thoughts and feelings one has about oneself.

Self-efficacy A person's judgments of his or her capability to organize and execute courses of action required to attain designated types of performances.

Self-esteem The affective dimensions of one's self-concept.

Sensory channels The senses through which the student acquires information.

Shaping An instructional procedure in which a teacher permits a student to move gradually toward mastering a task by accepting and reinforcing student behavior at each successive approximation of the task.

Shared reading A whole-language strategy in which the teacher and child read together in a risk-free environment with no predetermined expectations.

Short-term objectives Specified measurable outcomes along the way to achieving a long-range goal.

Sight The capacity of the visual system to receive originating or reflected light from objects.

Signature writing The ability of a student who is visually impaired to develop a basic level of print-writing so that he or she has a legal signature.

Sign language A system of communication that uses manual signs instead of words.

Slate and stylus A portable device for writing braille by hand consisting of the slate (a metal template with a series of braille cells) and the stylus (the implement used to press braille dots into the paper).

Snellen chart The traditional eye chart whose top line consists of the letter E and which is used in routine eye examinations.

Social competence The ability to demonstrate a repertoire of behaviors and actions that promise positive relationships.

Social skills assessment An evaluation, usually informal, of the student's ability to interact with others. Skills in this area may include taking turns, paying attention to others, initiating conversations, and understanding and using common age-appropriate expressions and behaviors.

Social studies and science skills assessment An evaluation of the student's mastery of compensatory skills necessary to achieve educational objectives in social studies and science at a rate and level commensurate with sighted peers.

Sound localization skills The ability of the student to use sounds to pinpoint the location of objects.

Specialized assessments An evaluation of the student's efficiency in using sensory information and the implications for instructional programming as determined by the functional vision assessment, the learning media assessment, and the assistive technology assessment.

Specialized instruction The teaching of the student with a visual impairment by emphasizing concrete experiences, learning by doing, and unifying experiences to overcome the limitations imposed by the visual impairment.

Speech and language therapist A professional trained to evaluate and improve the student's ability to understand what another person is conveying to them and to express what they want.

Standardized tests Formal instruments that have been standardized with regard to the manner in which they are administered and the population to which they relate and have already been administered to large groups of individuals with similar backgrounds to establish the noms against which other results will be compared. *See also* Nonstandardized tests; Norm-referenced tests

Symbolic communication A method of communication that involves the use of a spoken word, object, picture symbol, or written code. *See also* Nonsymbolic communication

Tactile Related to or experienced through the sense of touch.

Tactile adaptations Modifications of classroom materials mainly by the transcription of text, handouts, tests, and other written materials into braille.

Tactile skills The ability to explore objects systematically so that student's can observe all the features of an object by using their available senses.

Tactile symbols A form of communication, often used when a student cannot learn braille because of physical difficulties, that uses concrete and abstract symbols to teach students to gather information.

Talking book program A free national library program administered by the National Library Service for the Blind and Physically Handicapped (NLS) of the Library of Congress for persons with visual and physical limitations, in which books and magazines are produced in braille and on recorded discs and cassettes and are distributed to a cooperative network of regional libraries that circulate them to eligible borrowers; the program also lends the devices on which the recordings are played.

Teacher of students with visual impairments A specially trained and certified teacher who is qualified to teach special skills to students with visual impairments.

Technology device *See* Assistive technology

Telescopic device A lens system that makes small objects appear closer and larger.

Tracking The ability of the eyes to follow a moving object; also, the skill used to follow a line of type or braille across and to locate the next line.

Transdisciplinary team A team made up of professionals from different disciplines who cooperate and collaborate during initial assessment and planning phases of designing a student's educational program and offer ongoing support and input. Implementation of the program is carried out by one or a few team members who are designated as primarily responsible for providing direct care or services.

Transition IEP A program, written for a student age 14 and older, that addresses the need for transition services in the areas of employment, education and training, leisure and recreation, and living arrangements and details the proposed activities to achieve desired outcomes, establishes time lines for reaching these goals, and assigns responsibility for providing support to the agencies and individuals responsible for following through on each activity.

Validity A determination of how accurately a test measures what it purports to measure. *See also* Concurrent validity; Construct validity; Content validity; Criterion-related validity; Predictive validity

Verbal tests Evaluations that rely on verbal presentations of questions, problems , or directions and require verbal responses from the student. *See also* Performance tests

Videotaped protocols A method of preserving observations to members of the educational team that provides a visual journal of a student's behaviors that can be used as a baseline for assessing future skills.

Vision The ability to interpret what is seen.

Vision screening Initial assessment of a student's visual acuity and general observation of his or her eyes to determine the need for referral to an eye care specialist or other specialists.

Visual acuity test An assessment of detailed central vision; infants are tested by ascertaining pupillary responses to light and, later, light fixation reflexes; subsequent assessments include the standard Snellen Chart and other charts.

Visual adaptations Modifications of educational materials by enlargement, increased clarity and contrast, increased illumination, decreased glare, and decreased visual clutter so that a student with low vision is more successful in using his or her vision to complete a task.

Visual capacity An individual's potential to develop visual efficiency.

Visual disability A disability that causes a real or perceived disadvantage in performing specific tasks.

Visual efficiency The degree to which specific visual tasks can be performed with ease, comfort, and minimum time, contingent on personal and environmental variables; the extent to which available vision is used effectively.

Visual environmental awareness The extent to which children and adults with low vision are aware of objects in their environment.

Visual field The area that can be seen when looking straight ahead, measured in degrees from the fixation point.

Visual functions The abilities of the visual system, such as visual acuity, visual field, color discrimination, dark adaptation, and contrast sensitivity, as measured by performance on standardized tests of sight.

Visual impairment Any degree of vision loss that affects an individual's ability to perform the tasks of daily life, caused by a visual system that is not working properly or not formed correctly.

Visual memory The retention of mental imagery of environments or objects in one's environment gained through original visual input.

Vocational rehabilitation A system of services that evaluates personal, work, and work-related traits, designed to result in optimal placement in employment.

R E S O U R C E S

A wide variety of organizations and groups provide information, assistance, materials, and equipment to benefit students who are visually impaired, their families, and the professionals who work with them. The listings that follow attempt to provide a representative sampling of the resources that are available and relate to the education of students who are visually impaired; a more complete listing can be found in the AFB Directory of Services for Blind and Visually Impaired Persons in the United States and Canada, *published by the American Foundation for the Blind.*

The following section on national and governmental organizations presents sources of further information and referral. Readers should bear in mind that elements such as names and addresses, specific product and publication information, and information related to the Internet constantly change and may need later verification.

American Association of the Deaf-Blind
814 Thayer Avenue, Suite 302
Silver Spring, MD 20910
(301) 588-6545 (TTY/TDD)
Fax: (301) 588-8705
Promotes better opportunities and services for people who are deaf-blind and strives to ensure that a comprehensive, coordinated system of services is accessible to all deaf-blind people, enabling them to achieve their maximum potential through increased independence, productivity, and integration into the community.

American Council of the Blind
1155 15th Street, N.W., Suite 720
Washington, D.C. 20005
(202) 467-5081 or (800) 424-8666
Fax: (202) 467-5085
E-mail: ncrabb@access.digex.net
http://www.acb.org
Strives to improve the well-being of all blind and visually impaired people, through state, regional, and special-interest affiliates by: serving as a representative national organization of blind people; elevating the social, economic, and cultural levels of blind people; improving educational and rehabilitation facilities and opportunities; cooperating with the public and private institutions and organizations concerned with blind services; encouraging and assisting all blind persons to develop their abilities; and conducting a public education program to promote greater understanding of blindness and the capabilities of people who are blind. Provides information and referral on all aspects of blindness, scholarship assistance to blind and visually impaired post-secondary students, public education and awareness training, support to consumer advocates and legal assistance on matters relating to blindness, leadership and legislative training, consultation to

industry regarding employment of blind and visually impaired individuals, and governmental monitoring, consultation, and advocacy. Publishes *The Braille Forum.*

American Foundation for the Blind
11 Penn Plaza, Suite 300
New York, NY 10001
(212) 502-7600 or (800) 232-5463
Fax: (212) 502-7777
E-mail: afbinfo@afb.net
http://www.afb.org

Provides services to and acts as an information clearinghouse for people who are blind or visually impaired and their families, professionals, organizations, schools, and corporations through legislative advocacy, program initiatives, and publications. Conducts research and mounts program initiatives to promote the inclusion of and improve services to people who are blind or visually impaired, including the National Literacy Program and the National Technology Program; advocates for services and legislation; maintains the M. C. Migel Library and Information Center and the Helen Keller Archives and a toll-free information line; provides information and referral services; operates the National Technology Center and the Careers and Technology Information Bank; produces videos and publishes books, pamphlets, the *Directory of Services for Blind and Visually Impaired Persons in the United States and Canada,* the *Journal of Visual Impairment & Blindness,* and *AccessWorld.* Maintains the following offices throughout the country in addition to the headquarters' office:

AFB Midwest
401 N. Michigan Avenue, Suite 308
Chicago, IL 60611
(312) 245-9961
Fax: (312) 245-9965
E-mail: chicago@afb.net

AFB Southeast
National Literacy Program
100 Peachtree Street, Suite 620
Atlanta, GA 30303

(404) 525-2303
Fax: (404) 659-6957
E-mail: atlanta@afb.net

AFB Southwest
260 Treadway Plaza
Exchange Park
Dallas, TX 75235
(214) 352-7222
Fax: (214) 352-3214
E-mail: afbdallas@afb.net

AFB West
111 Pine Street, Suite 725
San Francisco, CA 94111
(415) 392-4845
Fax: (415) 392-0383
E-mail: sanfran@afb.net

Governmental Relations
820 First Street, N.E., Suite 400
Washington, D.C. 20000
(202) 408-0200
Fax: (202) 289-7880
E-mail: afbgov@afb.net

American Printing House for the Blind
P.O. Box 6085
Louisville, KY 40206-0085
(502) 895-2405 or (800) 223-1839
Fax: (502) 895-1509
E-mail: info@aph.org
http://www.aph.org

Produces a variety of books and learning materials in braille and other media; manufactures computer-access equipment, software, and special education and reading devices for persons who are visually impaired; maintains an educational research and development program and reference-catalog databases providing information about textbooks and other materials produced in accessible media.

Association for Education and Rehabilitation of the Blind and Visually Impaired (AER)
4600 Duke Street, Suite 430
Alexandria, VA 22304
(703) 823-9690
Fax: (703) 823-9695
E-mail: aer@aerbvi.org
http://www.aerbvi.org
Promotes all phases of education and work for people of all ages who are blind or visually impaired, strives to expand their opportunities to take a contributory place in society, and disseminates information. Serves as the primary professional organization for teachers, counselors, orientation and mobility specialists, and other professionals in the field of blindness and low vision and is organized into a variety of special divisions. Publishes *RE:view* and *AER Report.*

Council for Exceptional Children
Division on Visual Impairments
1920 Association Drive
Reston, VA 22091-1589
(703) 620-3660 or (800) 328-0272
TDD: (703) 620-3660
Fax: (703) 264-9494
http://www.cec.sped.org
Acts as a professional organization for educators and other individuals serving children with disabilities and children who are gifted and is organized into a variety of specialized divisions. Primary activities include: advocating for appropriate government policies; setting professional standards; providing continuing professional development; and helping professionals obtain conditions and resources necessary for effective professional practice. Publishes numerous related materials, journals, and newsletters.

DB-LINK
National Information Clearinghouse on Children Who Are Deaf-Blind
c/o Teaching Research Division of Western Oregon State College
345 North Monmouth Avenue
Monmouth, OR 97361
(800) 438-9376

TDD: (800) 854-7013
Fax: (503) 838-8776
E-mail: dblink@tr.wou.edu
http://www.tr.wou.edu/dblink/index.htm
Serves as an information clearinghouse that identifies, coordinates, and disseminates information concerning children and young adults who are deaf-blind. Maintains a resource database. A collaborative effort between Helen Keller National Center for Deaf-Blind Youths and Adults, Perkins School for the Blind, and Teaching Research.

Hadley School for the Blind
700 Elm Street
Winnetka, IL 60093-0299
(847) 446-8111 or (800) 323-4238
Fax: (847) 446-9916
E-mail: Info@Hadley-School.org
http://www.hadley-school.org
Provides accredited distance education programs that allows students to study at home with free correspondence course materials. Courses are offered to parents of blind children, professionals working with people who are blind or visually impaired, high school students preparing for college, and adults who have become blind.

Helen Keller National Center for Deaf-Blind Youths and Adults
111 Middle Neck Road
Sands Point, NY 11050
(516) 944-8900
TDD: (516) 944-8637
Fax: (516) 944-7302
Provides short-term rehabilitation services, comprehensive vocational and personal adjustment training, job preparation and placement, and diagnostic services to people who are deaf-blind through its national center and 10 regional offices. Provides technical assistance and training to those who work with deaf-blind people. Publishes *Nat-Cent News.* Sponsors the National Family Association for the Deaf-Blind [(800) 255-0411, ext. 275].

**National Association for Parents
of Children with Visual Impairments**
P.O. Box 317
Watertown, MA 02272-0317
(800) 562-6265 or (617) 972-7441
Fax: (617) 972-7444
http://www.spedex.com/NAPVI/index.htm
Provides leadership, support, and training to assist parents and families of children and young adults with visual impairments. Operates a national clearinghouse for information, education, and referral; initiates outreach programs and networking; and advocates for the educational needs and well-being of children who are blind or visually impaired. Publishes a newsletter, *Awareness.*

National Association for Visually Handicapped
22 West 21st Street, 6th Floor
New York, NY 10010
(212) 889-3141
Fax: (212) 727-2951
Provides information and services to people with low vision, their families, and professionals. Offers a catalog of low vision devices and large-print publications.

National Braille Association
3 Townline Circle
Rochester, NY 14623
(716) 427-8260
Fax: (716) 427-0263
Assists in the development of skills and techniques required for the production of reading materials for individuals who are print handicapped through seminars, workshops, consultation, and publications on the production of braille, tape recording, tactile graphics, and computer assisted transcription. Provides braille textbooks and materials at reduced cost to students and professionals. Publishes the *NBA Bulletin.*

National Federation of the Blind
1800 Johnson Street
Baltimore, MD 21230
(410) 659-9314
Fax: (410) 685-5653
http://www.nfb.org

Strives to improve social and economic conditions of blind persons and to integrate people who are blind or visually impaired as equal members of society. Evaluates and assists in establishing programs and provides public education and scholarships. Interest groups include the National Organization of Parents of Blind Children and the Committee on the Concerns of the Deaf-Blind. Publishes *The Braille Monitor* and *Future Reflections,* a magazine for parents.

**National Information Center for Children
and Youth with Disabilities**
P.O. Box 1492
Washington, D.C. 20013-1492
(202) 884-8200
TDD: (800) 695-0285
Fax: (202) 844-8441
Serves as a national clearinghouse for information about children and youngsters with disabilities. Provides information and referral to national, state, and local resources. Disseminates numerous free publications.

**National Library Service for the Blind
and Physically Handicapped**
Library of Congress
1291 Taylor Street, N.W.
Washington, D.C. 20542
(202) 707-5100 or (800) 424-8567
Fax: (202) 707-0712
Conducts a national program to distribute free reading materials of a general nature to individuals who are blind or who have physical disabilities. Provides reference information on all aspects of blindness and other physical disabilities that affect reading. Conducts national correspondence courses to train sighted persons as braille transcribers and blind persons as braille proofreaders.

**National Technical Assistance Consortium
for Children and Young Adults Who Are
Deaf-Blind**
c/o Teaching Research Division of Western Oregon State College
345 North Monmouth Avenue
Monmouth, OR 97361

(503) 838-8391
Fax: (503) 838-8150

and

Helen Keller National Center (see Helen Keller National Center for Deaf-Blind Youths and Adults)
Voice & TTY: (516) 944-8900, ext. 307
Fax: (516) 944-8751
E-mail: ntac@wou.edu
http://www.tr.wou.edu/ntac/ntac.htm
Provides technical assistance, including training, information, and support, to families and agencies serving children and young adults who are deaf-blind through state and multistate projects for children who are deaf-blind. NTAC assists in the development and maintenance of comprehensive services for families, early intervention programs, educational programs, and adult services to meet the unique needs of children and young adults who are deaf-blind. The primary mission of NTAC is to assist states in improving the quality of services for individuals (birth to age 28) who are deaf-blind, and to increase the numbers of children, young adults, their families, and their service providers who will benefit from these services. NTAC is a consortium of Teaching Research and the Helen Keller National Center for Deaf-Blind Youths and Adults.

Office of Special Education Programs
U.S. Department of Education
400 Maryland Avenue, S.W.
Washington, D.C. 20202
(202) 205-5507
http://www.ed.gov/offices/OSERS/OSEP/
index.html
Administers the Individuals with Disabilities Education Act and related programs for the free appropriate public education of children and youth with disabilities from birth through age 21, including research and demonstration projects, support to states and local school districts for the education of disabled children, and special programs, such as centers and services for children who are deaf-blind.

Prevent Blindness America
500 East Remington Road
Schaumburg, IL 60173
(847) 843-2020 or (800) 221-3004
(800) 331-2020 PBA Center for Sight
Fax: (847) 843-8458
E-mail: preventblindness@compuserve.com
http://www.prevent-blindness.org
Conducts a program of public and professional education, research, and industrial and community services to prevent blindness. Services include public education concerning vision conservation, vision screenings in schools, promotion of industrial eye safety, and efforts to improve environmental conditions affecting eye health in schools and colleges. Collects data on the nature and extent of causes of blindness and defective vision. Maintains the PBA Fight for Sight research division and the PBA Center for Sight information line.

Recording for the Blind and Dyslexic
20 Roszel Road
Princeton, NJ 08540
(609) 452-0606 or (800) 221-4792
Fax: (609) 987-8116
E-mail: info@rfbd.org
www.rfbd.org
Provides recorded and computerized textbooks, library services, and other educational resources to people who cannot read standard print because of visual, physical, or specific learning disabilities. Maintains a lending library of recorded books and acts as a recording service for additional titles.

The Association for Persons with Severe Handicaps (TASH)
29 West Susquehanna Avenue
Suite 210
Baltimore, MD 21204
(410) 828-8274
Fax: (410) 828-6706
E-mail: nweiss@tash.org
http://www.tash.org
Promotes full inclusion and participation of persons with disabilities in all aspects of life through local chapters. Publishes a monthly newsletter, quarterly journal, and other publications.

SOURCES OF PRODUCTS, MATERIALS, EQUIPMENT, AND SERVICES

The following section provides the contact information for all the sources of products, materials, equipment, and services mentioned in each chapter and listed in the chapter's Suggested Resources sections throughout this volume.

Ableware
661 Route 23 South
Wayne, NJ 07470
(973) 628-7600
Fax: (201) 305-0841
E-mail: custservice@maccak.com
www.maddak.com

**Active Living Alliance for Canadians
with a Disability**
720 Belfast Road, Suite 104, Ottawa, Ontario,
K1G 0Z5
(613) 244-0052 or (800) 771-0663
Fax: (613) 244-4857
E-mail: info@ala.ca
www.ala.ca

AdaptAbility
75 Mill Street
P. O. Box 515
Colchester, CT 06415-0515
(800) 228-9941
Fax: (800) 566-6678
E-mail: service@snswwide.com
www.snswwide.com

AFB Press (American Foundation for the Blind)
Customer Service
P.O. Box 1020
Sewickley, PA 15143-1020
(800) 232-3044
Fax: (412) 741-0609
www.afb.org

Allyn & Bacon
160 Gould Street
Needham Heights, MA 02194

American Action Fund for Blind Children and Adults
18440 Oxnard Street
Tarzana, CA 91356
(818) 343-2022

American Alliance for Health, Physical Education, Recreation and Dance
1900 Association Drive
Reston, VA 20191
(703) 476-3400 or (800) 213-7193
E-mail: webmaster@aahperd.org

American Association of Diabetes Educators
100 West Monroe
Chicago, IL 60602
(312) 424-2426
Fax: (312) 424-2427
E-mail: aade@aadenet.org
www.aadenet.org

American Guidance Service
Publishers' Building
Circle Pines, MN 55014-1796
(612) 786-4343
www.agsnet.com

American Printing House for the Blind
P.O. Box 6085
Louisville, KY 40206-0085
(502) 895-2405 or (800) 223-1839
Fax: (502) 899-2274
E-mail: info@aph.org
www.aph.org

American Red Cross—Essex Chapter
Braille Department
106 Washington Street
P. O. Box 838
East Orange, NJ 07019

American Thermoform Corporation
2311 Travers Avenue
City of Commerce, CA 90040
(800) 331-3676
Fax: (323) 728-8877
www.atcbrleqp.com

Ann Morris Enterprises
551 Hosner Mountain Road
Stormville, NY 12582
(800) 454-3175
Fax: (845) 226-2793
E-mail: annmor@netcom.com
www.annmorris.com

Art Education for the Blind
160 Mercer Street
New York, NY 10012
(213) 334-3700
E-mail: toku@idt.net

Associates for World Action in Rehabilitation Education
P. O. Box 96
Mohegan Lake, NY 10547
(914) 528-0567
Fax: (914) 528-3945

E-mail: AWAREUSA@awareusa.org
www.awareusa.org

Association for Education and Rehabilitation of the Blind and Visually Impaired
4600 Duke Street, Suite 430
P.O. Box 22397
Alexandria, VA 22304
(703) 823-9690
Fax: (703) 823-9695
E-mail: aer@aerbvi.org

Atlantic Provinces Special Education Authority
5940 South Street
Halifax, Nova Scotia, Canada
(902) 424-8500
Fax: (902) 424-0543
www.apsea.com

Axis Dance Company
5337 College Avenue
Suite 630
Oakland, CA 94618
(510) 287-5792
www.axisdance.org

Barnes & Noble Books
120 Fifth Avenue
New York, NY 10011
(212) 633-3300
Fax: (212) 727-3300

Bishop, Virginia
4312 Duval Street, #206
Austin, TX 788751

Blazie Education Services
See **Blazie Engineering.**

Blazie Engineering
105 East Jarrettsville Road
Forest Hills, MD 21050
(410) 893-9333
Fax: (410) 836-5040
E-mail: support@blazie.com
www.blazie.com

Blind Children's Center
4120 Marathon Street
Los Angeles, CA 90029
(213) 664-2153
Fax: (213) 665-3828
E-mail: info@blindcntr.org
www.blindcntr.org/bcc

Blind Children's Fund
4740 Okemos Road
Okemos, MI 48864-1673
(517) 347-1357
Fax: (517) 347-1459
E-mail: blindchfnd@aol.com
www.blindchildrensfund.org

Braille Authority of North America (BANA)
P. O. Box 6085
Louisville, KY 40206
(502) 895-2405
Fax: (502) 899-2274

Braille Planet
408 South Baldwin Street
Madison, WI 53703
(800) 347-9594
Fax: (608) 257-4143
E-mail: davidh@brailleplanet.org

Brookline Books
P.O. Box 381047
Cambridge, MA 02238-1047
(800) 666-2665
www.brooklinebooks.com

Canadian Blind Sports Association
1600 James Naismith Drive
Gloucester, Ontario, Canada
K1B 5N4
(613) 748-5609
Fax: (613) 748-5899

Carolina Biological Supply Company
2700 York Road
Burlington, NC 27215
(800) 334-5551

Carolyn's
P. O. Box 14577
Bradenton, FL 34280-4577
(800) 648-2266
Fax: (941) 739-5503
E-mail: magnify@bhip.infi.net

Center on Disabilities
California State University, Northridge
18111 Nordhoff Street
Northridge, CA 91330-8340
(818) 677-2578 (voice/TTY)
Fax: (818) 677-4929
www.csun.edu/cod/

Charles C Thomas, Publisher
2600 South First Street
Springfield, IL 62704
(800) 258-8980
www.ccthomas.com

Charles E. Tuttle Company
Airport Industrial Park
364 Innovation Drive
North Clarendon, VT 05759-9436
(800) 526-2778
www.tuttle-periplus.com

CIL Publications and Audiobooks
500 Greenwich Street, Third Floor
New York, NY 10013
(888) 245-8333
Fax: (212) 219-4078
E-mail: cilpubs@visionsvcb.org
www.cilpubs.com

Closing the Gap
P. O. Box 68
Henderson, MN 56044
(507) 248-3294
Fax: (507) 248-3810
www.closingthegap.com

Consultants for Visually Impaired
P. O. Box 8594
Hermitage, TN 37076
(615) 885-0764

Curriculum Associates
153 Rangeway Road
North Billerica, MA 01862
(800) 225-0248
Fax: (800) 366-1158
www.cahomeschool.com

Descriptive Video Service
DVS Home Video Customer Service
P. O. Box 55742
Indianapolis, IN 46205
(317) 579-0439
www.wgbh.org/dvs/

Duxbury Systems
270 Littleton Road, Unit 6
Westford, MA 01886-3523
(978) 692-3000
Fax: (978) 692-7912
E-mail: info@duxsys.com
www.duxburysystems.com

Dykema, Dorothy
604 N. Allen
Carbondale, IL 62901

Exceptional Teaching Aids
20102 Woodbine Avenue
Castro Valley, CA 94546
(800) 549-6999
Fax: (510) 582-5911
E-mail: exteaching@aol.com
www.exceptionalteaching.com

Family, Infant, and Preschool Program
Western Carolina Center
300 Enola Road
Morganton, NC 28655
(828) 438-6457
www.fipp.org

Frey Scientific
100 Paragon Parkway
Mansfield, OH 44903
(888) 252-1417
www.junebox.com/frey/

Grant Wood Area Education Agency
4401 Sixth Street SW
Cedar Rapids, IA 52404
(319) 399-6700

Hadley School for the Blind
700 Elm Street
P. O. Box 299
Winnetka, IL 60093-0299
(800) 323-4238
Fax: (847) 446-9916
E-mail: Hadley@theramp.net or Info@Hadley-School.org
www.hadleyschool.org

Harcourt
6277 Sea Harbor Drive
Orlando, FL 32887
(407) 345-2000 or (800) 225-5425
www.harcourt.com

Hawthorne Educational Services
800 Gray Oak Drive
Columbia, MO 65201

Howe Press of Perkins School for the Blind
175 North Beacon Street
Watertown, MA 02172
(617) 924-3490
Fax: (617) 926-2027

HumanWare
6245 King Road
Loomis, CA 95650
(800) 722-3393
Fax: (916) 652-7296
E-mail: info@humanware.com
www.humanware.com

Independent Living Aids
27 East Mall
Plainview, NY 11803
(800) 537-2118
Fax: (516) 752-3135
www.independentliving.com

Iowa State University Media Resources Center
Ames, IO 50011
(515) 294-8022

Jackson County Education Service District
101 North Grape Street
Medford, OR 97501
(503) 776-8550

Jackson Service Center
See **Jackson County Education Service District.**

Journal of Visual Impairment & Blindness
See **AFB Press.**

Lawrence Hall of Science Center for Multisensory Learning
University of California
1 Centennial Drive
Berkeley, CA 94720-5200
(510) 642-8941
www.lhs.berkeley.edu

Library of Congress
See **National Library Service for the Blind and Physically Handicapped.**

Lighthouse Enterprises Consumer Products Division
111 East 59th Street
New York, NY 10022
(800) 829-0500
Fax: (718) 786-5620
E-mail: thestore@lighthouse.org
www.lighthouse.org

Lighthouse International
111 East 59th Street
New York, NY 10022
(800) 829-0500
E-mail: info@lighthouse.org
www.lighthouse.org

Living Skills Center for the Visually Handicapped
2430 Road 20, B112
San Pablo, CA 94806

(510) 234-4984
Fax: (510) 234-4986
E-mail: skillscn@flash.net
www.livingskillscenter.locality.com

LS&S Group
P. O. Box 673
Northbrook, IL 60065
(800) 468-4789 or TTY (800) 317-8583
Fax: (847) 498-1482
E-mail: lssgroup@aol.com
www.lssgroup.com

MAVIS (Mathematics Accessible to Visually Impaired Students)
New Mexico State University
Math Department, MSC 3MB
P. O. Box 30001
Las Cruces, NM 88003
(505) 646-2664
Fax: (505) 646-1064
www.nmsu.edu/~mavis

Maxi-Aids
42 Executive Boulevard
P. O. Box 3209
Farmingdale, NY 11735
(800) 522-6294 or (631) 752-0521
Fax: (631) 752-0689
www.maxiaids.com

McCallum, B. J.
1296 Mariposa Avenue
San Jose, CA 95126

McGraw-Hill
1221 Avenue of the Americas
New York, NY 10020
(212) 512-4100 or (800) 352-3566
Fax: (212) 512-4105
E-mail: bookstore@mcgraw-hill.com

Merrill Education
Columbus, OH
(800) 974-7700
www.merrilleducation.com

Minnesota Educational Services
Office of Special Education
Capitol Square Building
550 Cedar Street
St. Paul, MN 55101-2273
(612) 483-4442
Fax: (612) 483-0234

Mississippi State University
P. O. Box 5325
Mississippi State, MS 39762
www.msstate.edu

National Arts and Disability Center
UCLA University Affiliated Program
300 UCLA Medical Plaza, Suite 3330
Los Angeles, CA 90095-6967
(310) 794-1141
www.npi.ucla.edu/

National Association for Parents of Children with Visual Impairments
P. O. Box 317
Watertown, MA 02471-0317
(617) 972-7441 or (800) 562-6265

National Braille Association
3 Townline Circle
Rochester, NY 14623
(716) 427-0263

National Braille Press
88 St. Stephen Street
Boston, MA 02115
(617) 266-6160
Fax: (617) 437-0456
E-mail: orders@nbp.org
www.nbp.org

National Dance Association
1900 Association Drive
Reston, VA 20191
(703) 476-3436
E-mail: nda@aahperd.org
www.aahperd.org/nda/nda-contact.html

National Federation of the Blind
1800 Johnson Street
Baltimore, MD 21230
(410) 659-9314
www.nfb.org

National Library Service for the Blind and Physically Handicapped
Library of Congress
1291 Taylor Street, N.W.
Washington, DC 20542
(202) 707-5100 or (800) 424-8567
Fax: (202) 707-0712
lcweb.loc.gov/nls/nls

National Organization of Parents of Blind Children
See **National Federation of the Blind.**

OPUS Technologies
13333 Thunderhead Street
San Diego, CA 92129-2329
(619) 538-9401

Oregon School for the Blind
700 Church Street SE
Salem, OR 97301
(503) 378-3820

Parent Consultants
P. O. Box 12114
Ogden, UT 84412

Paul H. Brookes Publishing Co.
P. O. Box 10642
Baltimore, MD 21285-0624
(800) 638-3775
Fax: (410) 337-8539
E-mail: custserv.@brookespublishing.com
www.pbrookes.com

Pennsylvania College of Optometry Press
8360 Old York Road
Elkins Park, PA 19027
(215) 780-1361

Perkins School for the Blind
See **Howe Press of Perkins School for the Blind.**

PRO-ED, Inc.
8700 Shoal Creek Blvd.
Austin, TX 78757
(800) 897-3202 or (512) 541-3245
Fax: (512) 451-8545
www.proedinc.com

Program Development Associates
P. O. Box 2038
Syracuse, NY 13220
(800) 543-2119
Fax: (315) 452-0710
E-mail: pda@pdassoc.com
www.pdassoc.com

Psychological Corporation
555 Academic Court
San Antonio, TX 78204
(800) 211-8378
Fax: (800) 232-1223
E-mail: customer_care@harcourt.com
www.psychcorp.com

Region IV Educational Service Center
Special Education Department
7145 West Tidwell
Houston, TX 77092-2096
(713) 744-6364
Fax: (713) 744-8133

Repro-Tronics
75 Carver Avenue
Westwook, NH 07675
(800) 948-8453
www.repro-tronics.com

Re:view
See **Association for Education and Rehabilitation of the Blind and Visually Impaired (AER).**

Rocklage, L.
P. O. Box 971022
Ypsilanti, MI 48197

Royal National Institute for the Blind Scientific Research Unit
224 Great Portland Street
London W1N 6AA, United Kingdom
Fax: 44 171 388 7747
www.rnib.org.uk

Sammons, Preston
P. O. Box 5071
Bolingbrook, IL 60440-5071
(800) 323-5547
Fax: (800) 547-4333

Santa Clara County Schools
See **McCallum, B. J.**

Scholastic Inc.
555 Broadway
New York, NY 10012
(212) 343-6100
Fax: (212) 343-6930

Science Products for the Blind
P. O. Box 888
Southeastern, PA 19399
(800) 888-7400
Fax: (215) 296-0488

Seedlings Braille Books for Children
P. O. Box 51924
Livonia, MI 48151-5924
(800) 777-8552
Fax: (734) 427-8552
E-mail: seedlink@aol.com
www.seedlings.org

Tack-Tiles
Los Olvidados Ltd.
P. O. Box 475
Plaistow, NH 03865
(603) 382-1904

TAEVIS Online
1149 South Campus Court-E
Purdue University
W. Lafayette, IN 47907-1149
(765) 495-2856
www.taevisonline.purdue.edu

Texas School for the Blind and Visually Impaired
1100 West 45th Street
Austin, TX 78756-3495
(512) 454-8631 or (512) 206-9224
Fax: (512) 206-9452
www.tsbvi.edu

They Shall Have Music
604 North Allyn
Carbondale, IL 62901

Trace Center, University of Wisconsin
S-151 Waisman Center
1500 Highland Avenue
Madison, WI 53705
(608) 262-6966
Fax: (608) 262-8848
www.trace.wisc.edu

Very Special Arts
1300 Connecticut Avenue, NW
Suite 700
Washington, DC 20036
(202) 628-2800
Fax: (202) 737-0725
www.vsarts.org

Vision Associates
7512 Dr. Phillips Boulevard
Orlando, FL 32819
(407) 352-1200
Fax: (407) 352-5632
E-mail: vassociates@sprintmail.com

Visually Impaired Preschool Services
1229 Garvin Place
Louisville, KY 40203
(502) 636-3207
Fax: (502) 636-0024

VTECH
101 East Palatine Road
Wheeling, IL 60090-6500
(800) 521-2010
Fax: (847) 215-8613
E-mail: vtechkids@vtechkids.com
www.vtechkids.com

Woodbine House
6510 Bells Mill Road
Bethesda, MD 208817
(800) 843-7323

WEB SITES

www.accessexpressed.net/index.htm
Access Expressed Network!, an interactive website created by Very Special Arts Massachusetts with help of *General Interactive Inc.* to provide people with disabilities access to information about the many arts and entertainment opportunities that exist across the country.

www.artsedge.kennedy-center.org
Arts Edge, a website established under a cooperative agreement between the John F. Kennedy Center for the Performing Arts and the National Endowment for the Arts (with additional support from the U.S. Department of Education).

www.artsednet.getty.edu
Website of the Getty Education Institute for the Arts.

www.Artswire.org/artswire/ad/index.html/
Website of Arts Wire, a communications network for the arts community.

www.converto.org
Converto-Braille, Groupe Galarneau Group, Inc., distributors of Concert-O-Braille, a program designed to facilitate braille transcription of music scores.

www.cstp.umkc.edu/personal/bhugh/braillem.
html
Website of Braille M, designed for discussing and learning about all aspects of the braille music code.

www.ed.gov/offices/OSERS/IDEA
U.S. Department of Education information site on PL 105-17, the 1997 amendments to IDEA.

www.isc.rit.edu
Website of the Rochester Institute of Technology and Equal Access to Software and Information for Persons with Disabilities (EASI).

www.sag.com/disabilityfaqa.html
Website of the Screen Actors Guild.

www.snow.utoronto.ca/index.html
Website of the Special Needs Opportunity Window.

www.tsbvi.edu
Texas School for the Blind and Visually Impaired's website.

www.taevisonline.purdue.edu
Online source for large-print or tactile graphics in biology, chemistry, physics, and mathematics at the secondary school level.

INDEX